Economic Analysis
for Lawyers

Economic Analysis for Lawyers

THIRD EDITION

Henry N. Butler
GEORGE MASON UNIVERSITY FOUNDATION PROFESSOR OF LAW AND
EXECUTIVE DIRECTOR, LAW & ECONOMICS CENTER,
GEORGE MASON UNIVERSITY SCHOOL OF LAW

Christopher R. Drahozal
JOHN M. ROUNDS PROFESSOR OF LAW,
UNIVERSITY OF KANSAS SCHOOL OF LAW

Joanna Shepherd
PROFESSOR OF LAW,
EMORY UNIVERSITY SCHOOL OF LAW

CAROLINA ACADEMIC PRESS
Durham, North Carolina

ISBN: 978-1-59460-997-8
LCCN: 2014943567

Carolina Academic Press
700 Kent Street
Durham, NC 27701
Telephone (919) 489-7486
Fax (919) 493-5668
www.cap-press.com

2016 Printing
Printed in the United States of America

Contents

Table of Cases

Preface to the Third Edition

This is a microeconomics book that relies on numerous examples from the law and public policy to illustrate practical economic concepts in action. As explained in the prior prefaces, the first three chapters are foundational and should be taught first. The basic narrative is to explain how ideal markets operate, the consequences of interfering with market price adjustments, a consideration of "market failures" as a justification for government intervention in markets, and then the harsh reality that government interventions are often as imperfect as the markets they aspire to correct.

After the first three chapters, subsequent chapters can be taught in whatever order works best. In essence, chapters IV through X are free standing. This third edition includes two new chapters—Chapter VII on Crime and Punishment and Chapter VIII on Labor Markets. These chapters were added in response to suggestions by many of the hundreds of judges who have attended the Economics Institute for Judges offered by the Law & Economics Center at George Mason University School of Law.

We acknowledge the valuable suggestions of professors who adopted the second edition. In particular, Bruce Johnsen and James Cooper have provided detailed suggestions and Cooper helped revise Chapter IX on Market Structure and Antitrust. Several research assistants helped update examples and cases. The George Mason team consisted of Nate Harris, Matt Wheatley, Mark Weiss, Allen Gibby, Sam Banks, Maurio Fiore, Christopher Mufarriage, Jason Greaves, Mark Ericson, and Taylor Hoverman. The Emory team consisted of Robin Caskey, Steve Ferketic, Kasia Hebda, Sarah O'Donohue, Caitlin Pardue, Luka Stanic, and Dimitri Dzagnidze.

Henry N. Butler
Arlington, Virginia

Christopher R. Drahozal
Lawrence, Kansas

Joanna Shepherd
Atlanta, Georgia

Preface to the Second Edition

This second edition continues to reflect our belief in the value of the building block approach to teaching economics to lawyers and law students, and in the usefulness of cases as a supplement to that approach. Our use of the first edition in class, and the feedback from our students, has reinforced those beliefs. Our goal in preparing this second edition has been to reorganize and streamline the materials in response to comments from professors, law students, and judges, while staying true to the pedagogical approach of the first edition.

The first three chapters remain the core materials and should be covered first. Those chapters cover much of the same ground as in the first edition, but with a somewhat different organization. Chapter 1 introduces the economics approach, examining such topics as the economist's assumptions about human and firm behavior and the fundamental concepts of opportunity cost and property rights. Among the new material in the chapter is a note summarizing some of the recent scholarship on behavioral law and economics. Chapter 2 develops the basic supply-and-demand model in a variety of market and legal settings. Chapter 3 examines the economics of government regulation (and government failure—i.e., public choice economics), and includes a new section on the economics of the court system.

The remaining chapters may be covered in whatever order the instructor prefers. As with the first edition, the organization is by economic concept rather than by substantive legal area. Chapter 4 discusses externalities and legal responses to externalities. Chapter 5 combines two chapters from the first edition (on the economics of information and on organizational economics) into a single chapter dealing with information costs and transaction costs. The remaining three chapters have been updated but largely follow the same structure as their counterparts in the first edition. Chapter 6 discusses risk, Chapter 7 deals with competition and monopoly, and Chapter 8 addresses valuation issues.

By design, this edition is substantially shorter than the first edition. We have accomplished this both by excluding some topics covered in the first edition, and by a careful editing of the cases to focus on the key aspects (both legal and factual) of the case. The result, we hope, is that reading assignments will be of a more manageable size but without any significant loss of substance. There remains ample material for a one semester course in law and economics.

Thanks to our families for their support and patience with us during this revision. In addition, we very much appreciate the research assistance of Eric Hatchett, Matt Koenigsdorf, and Sean McGivern, and financial support from the University of Kansas School of Law.

Henry N. Butler
Orange, California

Christopher R. Drahozal
Lawrence, Kansas

Preface to the First Edition

This casebook is designed to help law students and lawyers learn the principles of microeconomics. A quick review of the table of contents reveals that economics concepts provide the organizational structure of the book. Instead of organizing around substantive areas of the law, it follows the building block approach used in most successful principles of economics textbooks. This proven approach to teaching economics differs from other law-and-economics casebooks that tend to focus on applications of economics to legal issues rather than teaching economics. After fifteen years of teaching economics — often to law students, law school professors, lawyers, and judges — I am convinced of the pedagogical advantages of this approach. For the many law professors who share this view and have been forced to supplement principles of economics textbooks with cases, I believe that this casebook offers a more convenient and coherent alternative.

My involvement with this casebook started as an effort to revise the first edition of *Quantitative Methods for Lawyers* by Professor Steven M. Crafton and Margaret F. Brinig of George Mason University School of Law. Their ambitious effort to create a casebook introduction to economics, finance, accounting, statistics, and econometrics has met with considerable success as judged by adoptions at numerous leading law schools. Nevertheless, my interest in these materials quickly turned to concentrating on a more traditional approach to teaching economics. The result is a very different type of casebook than Crafton and Brinig's initial effort. Keith Sipe, the publisher of Carolina Academic Press, has encouraged me to incorporate some materials from the first edition of *Quantitative Methods for Lawyers* and I have done so in numerous areas of this casebook. It is our hope that many of the materials presented here will be incorporated in the second edition of *Quantitative Methods for Lawyers* by Crafton and Butler. The materials remain a "work in progress." I encourage you to send your comments, criticisms, and suggestions for improvements of subsequent editions.

This casebook is not intended to be an encyclopedic treatise on either the principles of economics or the economic analysis of law. Some topics typically covered in a principles textbook are not found here; similarly, numerous legal issues susceptible to economic analysis are not covered. Nevertheless, there is plenty of material for a typical one-semester course. I encourage you to work through the first five chapters and then choose chapters according to your interests. Figures are available in PowerPoint. Many of the edited cases presented here are longer than one would expect if they were excerpted in a specialized casebook on their particular area of the law. The pedagogical reason for this is that I was concerned that first or second year law students needed to have more information about the particular substantive law (especially in some regulatory cases) in order to understand the economic issues. I have attempted to ease this pain by minimizing and shortening many case citations in the cases presented.

Numerous individuals have helped me complete this book. I am especially grateful to two individuals. Geoffrey Lysaught, a J.D./Ph.D. in finance student at the University of Kansas, has been involved in every aspect of the project. He was especially helpful on the finance and risk issues covered in Chapters IV, IX, and XI. Christopher Drahozal, a colleague in the School of Law, provided detailed comments and suggestions on the entire manuscript. Geoff and Chris, thank you! I also acknowledge the valuable contributions of research assistants Gary Eastman, Matt Hoy, and Alok Srivastava. The Smith Richardson Foundation provided essential financial support at the start of this project.

I have used earlier drafts of these materials in my Law and Economics classes as well as in the *Economics Institutes for State Judges* offered by the University of Kansas Law and Organizational Economics Center (LOEC). Comments from law students, professors in the *Economics Institutes for State Judges* (Barry Baysinger, Keith Chauvin, and Maurice Joy of Kansas; Terry L. Anderson of PERC and the Hoover Institution; and W. Kip Viscusi of Harvard Law School), and judges have improved the final product. I would like to offer my thanks to three judges—Victor T. Barrera of California, Richard T. Jessen of Minnesota, and Donald S. Owens of Michigan—who took great pride in their ability to spot typos. Accordingly, any remaining typos are their responsibility.

Finally, I wish to express my sincerest gratitude and appreciation to Cathy Lysaught and Missy Amlong at the LOEC for their loyal and tireless assistance. They "hung in there" during the long and tedious process of compiling these materials.

Henry N. Butler
Lawrence, Kansas

Economic Analysis
for Lawyers

Chapter I

The Economics Perspective: Incentives Matter

Economics is an analytical discipline and a practical science. Its aim is to provide a set of tools to understand, analyze, and, sometimes, solve problems. Just as a physicist must take into account the effects of gravity, so too must a lawyer understand the effects of economic forces. In a very real sense, economic forces are the gravity of the social world—often invisible, but omnipresent. As imposing as this view of economics may sound, this casebook presupposes no prior exposure to economics—it concentrates on the few foundational concepts and analytical tools necessary for the lawyer to take advantage of the economics perspective.

Economics is the study of the rational behavior of individuals when choices are limited or constrained in relation to human desires. This broad definition should serve to dispel two common myths about economics. First, economics is not simply about money—it is about how incentives influence behavior. In fact, the crucial point of economics is that **incentives matter**. Second, economics is concerned with more than just economy-wide, macroeconomic phenomena such as inflation, unemployment, trade deficits, and business cycles. It also includes microeconomics, which uses individual decision-makers and individual markets as the basic units of analysis. In this casebook, the principles of microeconomics are introduced by analyzing the impact of changes in various legal rules on the behavior of economic actors.[1] Changes in laws and regulations affect incentives, and incentives matter!

Where the Buses Run on Time

Austan Goolsbee

Slate.com (March 16, 2006)

On a summer afternoon, the drive home from the University of Chicago to the north side of the city must be one of the most beautiful commutes in the world. On the left on Lake Shore Drive you pass Grant Park, some of the world's first skyscrapers, and the Sears Tower. On the right is the intense blue of Lake Michigan. But for all the beauty,

---

1. Microeconomics is also referred to as price theory. It is important to note that there is much more agreement among economists about certain principles of microeconomic theory than there is about macroeconomic theory and policy. See Dan Fuller & Doris Geide-Stevenson, *Consensus Among Economists: Revisited*, 34 Journal of Economic Education 369 (2003) (reporting results of survey of economists).

the traffic can be hell. So, if you drive the route every day, you learn the shortcuts. You know that if it backs up from the Buckingham Fountain all the way to McCormick Place, you're better off taking the surface streets and getting back onto Lake Shore Drive a few miles north.

A lot of buses, however, wait in the traffic jams. I have always wondered about that: Why don't the bus drivers use the shortcuts? Surely they know about them — they drive the same route every day, and they probably avoid the traffic when they drive their own cars. Buses don't stop on Lake Shore Drive, so they wouldn't strand anyone by detouring around the congestion. And when buses get delayed in heavy traffic, it wreaks havoc on the scheduled service. Instead of arriving once every 10 minutes, three buses come in at the same time after half an hour. That sort of bunching is the least efficient way to run a public transportation system. So, why not take the surface streets if that would keep the schedule properly spaced and on time?

You might think at first that the problem is that the drivers aren't paid enough to strategize. But Chicago bus drivers are the seventh-highest paid in the nation; full-timers earned more than $23 an hour, according to a November 2004 survey. The problem may have to do not with how much they are paid, but how they are paid. At least, that's the implication of a new study of Chilean bus drivers by Ryan Johnson and David Reiley of the University of Arizona and Juan Carlos Muñoz of Pontificia Universidad Católica de Chile.

Companies in Chile pay bus drivers one of two ways: either by the hour or by the passenger. Paying by the passenger leads to significantly shorter delays. Give them incentives, and drivers start acting like regular people do. They take shortcuts when the traffic is bad. They take shorter meal breaks and bathroom breaks. They want to get on the road and pick up more passengers as quickly as they can. In short, their productivity increases.

They also create new markets. At the bus stops in Chile, people known as sapos (frogs) literally hop on and off the buses that arrive, gathering information on how many people are traveling and telling the driver how many people were on the previous bus and how many minutes ago it sat at the station. Drivers pay the sapos for the information because it helps them improve their performance.

Not everything about incentive pay is perfect, of course. When bus drivers start moving from place to place more quickly, they get in more accidents (just like the rest of us). Some passengers also complain that the rides make them nauseated because the drivers stomp on the gas as soon as the last passenger gets on the bus. Yet when given the choice, people overwhelmingly choose the bus companies that get them where they're going on time. More than 95 percent of the routes in Santiago use incentive pay.

Perhaps we should have known that incentive pay could increase bus driver productivity. After all, the taxis in Chicago take the shortcuts on Lake Shore Drive to avoid the traffic that buses just sit in. Since taxi drivers earn money for every trip they make, they want to get you home as quickly as possible so they can pick up somebody else.

* * *

———

This chapter introduces the economics perspective by describing several fundamental concepts and assumptions. In Section A, economists' assumptions about human behavior and firm behavior as well as the key concepts of scarcity, opportunity costs, and marginal analysis are developed. In Section B, the importance of private property rights to a functioning market economy is explored. Section C contrasts the ex ante (forward-looking) perspective of economics with the ex post (backward-looking) perspective typical of legal analysis. Section D presents game theory as an explanation for much economic behavior. Finally, Section E compares positive economic analysis, which describes the world as it is, with normative economic analysis, which describes the world as it should be.

A. Economic Behavior

The concept of scarcity is fundamental to the study of economics. **Scarcity** means that our behavior is constrained because we live in a world of limited resources and unlimited desires. Scarcity is thus a relative concept in that it indicates we cannot satisfy every desire. The fact that there is an "abundance" of a particular resource does not mean that there is not scarcity; it simply means that at current prices everyone who wants to control a certain amount of that resource can do so by paying the market price. Scarcity implies that individuals, families, governments, businesses, and other economic actors must make choices or trade-offs among competing uses of limited resources.

Economic actors are assumed to maximize their well-being subject to constraints. In this section, assumptions about what guides decision making by individuals and firms are developed.

1. Opportunity Costs, Economic Choices, and the Margin

There are only twenty-four hours in a day, and any decision to engage in one activity entails a decision to forego some other activity. People must choose how to spend their time, and choice requires a sacrifice. This sacrifice illustrates the fundamental economic concept of **opportunity cost**. In general, the opportunity cost of using a resource in a particular manner is defined as the value of the next best alternative use of that resource. For example, your time—a valuable resource—can be used in several different ways: sleeping, studying, partying, vacationing, exercising, working, eating, watching television, and so forth. The opportunity cost to you of reading this material is the next best alternative use of your time. Similarly, the opportunity cost of working as a lawyer is the next best alternative career you may have chosen.

The classic phrase that illustrates the concept of opportunity cost is "There ain't no such thing as a free lunch," or "TANSTAAFL." Someone else may pay for your lunch, but you gave up some other activity in order to go to lunch. Another way to think of the concept of opportunity cost is to recognize that "whenever you have a choice, there is a cost."

Choices or trade-offs, however, are rarely between extremes. For example, individuals are rarely faced with the choice between a twelve-course feast or going hungry; more often, individuals confront choices of a smaller magnitude—say, between steak and hamburger. Economists assert that economic actors make choices "at the margin," where the **margin** refers to the impact of a small change in one variable on another variable. For example, if the price (cost) of a product increases relative to the prices of other products, then people "at the margin" will substitute the now lower cost product for the higher cost product. Raise the price of Toyotas and some people will buy fewer Toyotas and more (say) Nissans. Raise the price of heating oil, and even people who "need" it will substitute other products (e.g., sweaters and blankets) to keep warm. In general, the margin refers to the difference in cost, benefit, or some other measure (e.g., profit, revenue, etc.) between the existing situation and a proposed change.

Suppose, for example, that you attempt to purchase a bag of pretzels by inserting fifty cents into a vending machine and pushing the appropriate buttons. Your actions demonstrate that your expected marginal benefit from the bag of pretzels is greater than fifty cents. Unfortunately, you failed to notice (prior to selecting the pretzels) that the next slot for a pretzel bag was empty, and you did not receive anything for your fifty cents. You are very confident that a bag of pretzels will be dispensed if you pay another fifty cents. Your friend says you are crazy to pay $1.00 for a bag of pretzels, but you reply that on the margin the next bag costs fifty cents and that the marginal benefit to you of a bag of pretzels is still more than fifty cents. You buy the pretzels, but your friend gives you a hard time for paying so much. You then explain to him that the first fifty cents was in the past, and there was nothing that could be done about it. The first fifty cents was a **sunk cost**, and sunk costs do not affect your future decisions because you make decisions on the margin.

The basic marginal analysis decision-making rule is that *if the marginal benefit of an activity is greater than the marginal cost of that activity, then do it!* It is important to appreciate the individual basis of decision making because many costs and benefits are subjective in the sense that they differ from individual to individual. Thus, an observer is often left to infer relative costs and benefits from observed behavior. All economic analysis is concerned with consequences "at the margin." Thus, one would expect that a change in a legal rule that affects a cost or benefit — that is, affects incentives — will have measurable (at least in principle) effects at the margin.

2. Assumptions About Human Behavior

Economists employ certain abstractions and assumptions to help predict the behavioral consequences of changes in the constraints faced by individuals, businesses, and other economic actors. One of the most important assumptions is that individuals behave rationally — that is, they seek to maximize their "self-interest." The self-interest assumption does not mean that individuals are cold, harsh calculators; rather it means that their behavior is consistent with a model of rational choice. Self-interest also does not imply that individuals are necessarily selfish; rational decision makers may benefit — that is, receive satisfaction — from making others happy. The significance of the self-interest assumption is that it allows economists to anticipate changes in individual behavior in response to changes in economic variables. These variables include activities that are not explicitly within a market activity, such as marriage, crime, and driving. The rational maximizer responds to changes in incentives in a predictable manner.

The Nature of Man*

Michael C. Jensen and William H. Meckling
7 Journal of Applied Corporate Finance 4–19 (Summer 1994)

* * *

The usefulness of any model of human nature depends on its ability to explain a wide range of social phenomena; the test of such a model is the degree to which it is consistent

---

* We use the word "man" here in its use as a non-gender-specific reference to human beings. We have attempted to make the language less gender-specific because the models being discussed describe

with observed human behavior. A model that explains behavior only in one small geographical area, or only for a short period in history, or only for people engaged in certain pursuits is not very useful. For this reason we must use a limited number of general traits to characterize human behavior. Greater detail limits the explanatory ability of a model because individual people differ so greatly. We want a set of characteristics that captures the essence of human nature, but no more.

While this may sound abstract and complex, it is neither. Each of us has in mind and uses models of human nature every day. We all understand, for example, that people are willing to make trade-offs among things that they want. Our spouses, partners, children, friends, business associates, or perfect strangers can be induced to make substitutions of all kinds. We offer to go out to dinner Saturday night instead of the concert tonight. We offer to substitute a bicycle for a stereo as a birthday gift. We allow an employee to go home early today if the time is made up next week.

If our model specified that individuals were never willing to substitute some amount of a good for some amounts of other goods, it would quickly run aground on inconsistent evidence. It could not explain much of the human behavior we observe. While it may sound silly to characterize individuals as unwilling to make substitutions, that view of human behavior is not far from models that are widely accepted and used by many social scientists (for example, Maslow's hierarchy of human needs and sociologists' models portraying individuals as cultural role players or social victims).

* * *

RESOURCEFUL, EVALUATIVE, MAXIMIZING MODEL: REMM

... While the term is new, the concept is not. REMM is the product of over 200 years of research and debate in economics, the other social sciences, and philosophy. As a result, REMM is now defined in very precise terms, but we offer here only a bare-bones summary of the concept. Many specifics can be added to enrich its descriptive content without sacrificing the basic foundation provided here.

Postulate I. Every individual cares; he or she is an evaluator.

(a) The individual cares about almost everything: knowledge, independence, the plight of others, the environment, honor, interpersonal relationships, status, peer approval, group norms, culture, wealth, rules of conduct, the weather, music, art, and so on.

(b) REMM is always willing to make trade-offs and substitutions. Each individual is always willing to give up some sufficiently small amount of any particular good (oranges, water, air, housing, honesty, or safety) for some sufficiently large quantity of other goods. Furthermore, valuation is relative in the sense that the value of a unit of any particular good decreases as the individual enjoys more of it relative to other goods.

(c) Individual preferences are transitive—that is, if A is preferred to B, and B is preferred to C, then A is preferred to C.

* * *

Postulate II. Each individual's wants are unlimited.

(a) If we designate those things that REMM values positively as "goods," then he or she prefers more goods to less. Goods can be anything from art objects to ethical norms.

---

the behavior of both sexes. We have been unable to find a genderless term for use in the title which has the same desired impact.

(b) REMM cannot be satiated. He or she always wants more of some things, be they material goods such as art, sculpture, castles, and pyramids; or intangible goods such as solitude, companionship, honesty, respect, love, fame, and immortality.

Postulate III. Each individual is a maximizer.

He or she acts so as to enjoy the highest level of value possible. Individuals are always constrained in satisfying their wants. Wealth, time, and the laws of nature are all important constraints that affect the opportunities available to any individual. Individuals are also constrained by the limits of their own knowledge about various goods and opportunities; and their choices of goods or courses of action will reflect the costs of acquiring the knowledge or information necessary to evaluate those choices.

The notion of an opportunity set provides the limit on the level of value attainable by any individual. The opportunity set is usually regarded as something that is given and external to the individual. Economists tend to represent it as a wealth or income constraint and a set of prices at which the individual can buy goods. But the notion of an individual's opportunity set can be generalized to include the set of activities he or she can perform during a 24-hour day or in a lifetime.

Postulate IV. The individual is resourceful.

Individuals are creative. They are able to conceive of changes in their environment, foresee the consequences thereof, and respond by creating new opportunities.

Although an individual's opportunity set is limited at any instant in time by his or her knowledge and the state of the world, that limitation is not immutable. Human beings are not only capable of learning about new opportunities, they also engage in resourceful, creative activities that expand their opportunities in various ways.

The kind of highly mechanical behavior posited by economists—that is, assigning probabilities and expected values to various actions and choosing the action with the highest expected value—is formally consistent with the evaluating, maximizing model defined in Postulates I through III. But such behavior falls short of the human capabilities posited by REMM; it says nothing about the individual's ingenuity and creativity.

REMMs AT WORK

One way of capturing the notion of resourcefulness is to think about the effects of newly imposed constraints on human behavior. These constraints might be new operating policies in a corporation or new laws imposed by governments. No matter how much experience we have with the response of people to changes in their environment, we tend to overestimate the impact of a new law or policy intended to constrain human behavior. Moreover, the constraint or law will almost always generate behavior which was never imagined by its sponsors. Why? Because of the sponsors' failure to recognize the creativity of REMMs. REMMs' response to a new constraint is to begin searching for substitutes for what is now constrained, a search that is not restricted to existing alternatives. REMMs will invent alternatives that did not previously exist.

An excellent illustration of how humans function as REMMs is the popular response to the 1974 federal imposition of a 55-mile-per-hour speed limit in all states under penalty of loss of federal transportation and highway moneys. The primary reason offered for this law was the conservation of gasoline and diesel fuel (for simplicity, we ignore the benefits associated with the smaller number of accidents that occur at slower speeds).

The major cost associated with slower driving is lost time. At a maximum speed of 55 mph instead of 70 mph, trips take longer. Those who argue that lost time is not important must recognize that an hour of time consumed is just as irreplaceable as — and generally more valuable than — the gallon of gasoline consumed. On these grounds, the law created inefficiencies, and the behavior of drivers is consistent with that conclusion.... People responded in REMM-like fashion to this newly imposed constraint in a number of ways. One was to reduce their automobile, bus, and truck travel, and, in some cases, to shift to travel by other means such as airplanes and trains. Another response was to defy the law by driving at speeds exceeding the 55 mph maximum. Violating the speed limit, of course, exposes offenders to potential costs in the form of fines, higher insurance rates, and possible loss of driver's licenses. This, in turn, provides incentives for REMMs to search out ways to reduce such costs. The result has been an entire new industry, and the rapid growth of an already existing one. Citizen's Band radios (CBs), which had been used primarily by truckers, suddenly became widely used by passenger car drivers and almost all truckers.... CB radios have been largely replaced by radar detectors that warn drivers of the presence of police radar. These devices have become so common that police have taken countermeasures, such as investing in more expensive and sophisticated radar units that are less susceptible to detection. Manufacturers of radar detectors retaliated by manufacturing increasingly sophisticated units.

The message is clear: people who drive value their time at more than [the savings in fuel costs from the lower speed limit]. When the 55 mph maximum speed limit was imposed, few would have predicted the ensuing chain of events. One seemingly modest constraint on REMMs has created a new electronic industry designed to avoid the constraint. And such behavior shows itself again and again in a variety of contexts — for example, in taxpayers' continuous search for, and discovery of, "loopholes" in income tax laws; the development of so-called clubs with private liquor stock in areas where serving liquor at public bars is prohibited; the ability of General Dynamics' CEO George Anders and his management team, when put under a lucrative incentive compensation plan tied to share-holder value, to quadruple the market value of the company even as the defense industry was facing sharp cutbacks; and the growth in the number of hotel courtesy cars and gypsy cabs in cities where taxi-cab licensing results in monopoly fares.

These examples are typical of behavior consistent with the REMM model, but not, as we shall see, with other models that prevail in the social sciences. The failure of the other models is important because the individual stands in relation to organizations as the atom is to mass. From small groups to entire societies, organizations are composed of individuals. If we are to have a science of such organizations, it will have to be founded on building blocks that capture as simply as possible the most important traits of humans. Although clearly not a complete description of human behavior, REMM is the model of human behavior that best meets this criterion.[2]

* * *

---

2. REMM is not meant to describe the behavior of any particular individual. To do so requires more complete specification of the preferences, values, emotions, and talents of each person. Moreover, individuals respond very differently to factors such as stress, tension, and fear, and, in so doing, often violate the predictions of the REMM model. For purposes of organizational and public policy, many of these violations of REMM "cancel out" in the aggregate across large groups of people and over time — but by no means all. For a discussion of a Pain Avoidance Model (PAM) that complements REMM by accommodating systematically non-rational behavior, see Michael C. Jensen, "Economics, Organizations, and Non-Rational Behavior," *Economic Inquiry* (1995).

Notes and Questions

1. The Self-Interest Assumption and the Critics' "Straw Man": Economics is often criticized based on the mistaken impression that economists assume that economic decision-makers are only interested in money. To the contrary, economists recognize that individuals gain utility from any variety of activities and any number of sources—not just money. People enjoy looking at art, obtain satisfaction from their jobs over and above the salaries they earn, and feel good when helping others. Clearly, properly understood, the self-interest assumption does not mean that individuals are cold, "Dickensian" Scrooges, totally selfish and uncaring in their choices.

2. Transitive Preferences: An important assumption about economic behavior is that economic actors' preferences are transitive (that is, if A is preferred to B, and B is preferred to C, then A is preferred to C), at least over short periods of time. Suppose a woman goes into a restaurant and is informed that the only three entrees are chicken, lobster, and steak. She orders chicken, but the waiter returns and tells her that they are out of chicken. She replies, "I'll settle for the lobster." However, the waiter returns again and says, "I made a mistake, it turns out that we do have chicken after all. Would you prefer chicken instead of lobster?" To which she replies: "No, I'd like the steak." Such behavior violates the transitive preferences assumption.

3. Uncertainty and Risk Aversion: Individuals often make decisions when they are not certain of the outcome. Such uncertainty introduces risk into the decision making process. Economists assume that most individuals are **risk averse**. When given a choice between a certain value, say $1,000, and an uncertain outcome of a coin toss—heads you win $2,000, and tails you get $0—a risk averse individual will prefer the certain amount even if the expected payoff from the coin toss is also $1,000. [The expected value of the coin toss is the weighted average of the possible payoffs. So, in this example, the expected value is (.5 x $2,000) + (.5 x $0) = $1,000.00.] The concept of risk aversion is the basis for many important insights in economics, finance, and law. Chapter VI, "Risk," explores this important assumption about economic decision making in great detail.

4. Beware of Unintended Consequences: Many laws and regulations are intended to correct perceived problems with the market allocation of goods and services. It is important in designing laws and regulations to consider how rational economic actors are likely to respond to new constraints on their behavior. Consider, for example, the Superfund requirement that contaminated soil at toxic waste sites be sterilized. This requirement means that companies looking for new industrial sites steer away from Superfund sites for fear of being held liable for cleaning up someone else's pollution (the Superfund law calls for joint and several liability of anyone who has ever owned the site). As a result, companies tend to locate in areas where the soil is not contaminated, and we end up with two dirty lots instead of one. "Brownfield" is the name that has been given to this unintended but totally predictable result.

5. Bounded Rationality: The assumption that individuals are rational maximizers is, of course, an oversimplification. We don't always seek to maximize our utility, and we all certainly have our irrational moments. But that is the idea of a model—it is a simplified version of reality that generates predictions about behavior. The validity of a model is determined by the accuracy of its predictions—on which the economic model does extremely well. The fact that individuals sometimes act irrationally merely adds noise to the model, so long as the irrational behavior is essentially random. But if the irrationality is systematic, such that individuals consistently behave in a particular (non-rational) way, it may be possible to develop a model that generates better predictions about behavior.

Footnote 5 to the Jensen and Meckling article describes one attempted model of non-rational behavior, what Jensen calls the Pain Avoidance Model. The growing field of behavioral law and economics is a broader attempt to identify such systematic irrationalities, which may result in predictions that differ from the more traditional law-and-economics model. Cass Sunstein provides some highlights:

> The idea of bounded rationality includes several different points. The first involves the kind of cognitive errors that can come from biases in judgment and from efforts to economize on decision costs ("heuristics"). Biases fall in various categories; they include hindsight bias, optimistic bias, and extremeness aversion. Efforts to economize on decision costs are responsible for *rules of thumb*, or heuristics. Rules of thumb—as in the process of deciding on appropriate numbers (for many things, including real estate prices or pain-and-suffering awards) by choosing an "anchor" and then making adjustments—reduce the costs of making decisions, but they may not be fully rational....
>
> A second form of bounded rationality comes from *framing effects*. People's reaction to a choice may depend on how it is described; hence identical, but differently worded, problems can elicit quite different responses. Consider clients deciding whether to settle or to go to trial. If they are told that, of 100 litigants, 90 who go to trial win, they may be far more likely to go to trial than if they are told that of 100 litigants, 10 who go to trial lose....
>
> Some aspects of bounded rationality are modeled by *prospect theory*, which is intended as a more accurate description of behavior than expected utility theory. For purposes of law, the first key feature of prospect theory, departing from expected utility theory, is that people are *loss averse*, that is, they dislike losses more than they like corresponding gains.... The second key finding is that people care a great deal about *certainty* (thus people would prefer a reduction of risk from 0.1 to 0.0 to a reduction of 0.3 to 0.1).... An important implication is that people are risk seeking for losses (they would choose an 80% chance to lose $4,000 over a certain loss of $3,000) and risk averse for gains (they would prefer a certain gain of $3,000 over an 80% chance to gain $4,500).

Cass R. Sunstein, *Behavioral Law and Economics: A Progress Report*, 1 American Law & Economics Review 115, 123–24 (1999).

Most of the research to date on behavioral law and economics is based on experiments, which obviously raises questions about how well the experimental results transfer to the real world. Judge Richard Posner identifies an important limitation of experimental research:

> Selection effects suggest that the experimental and real-world environments will differ systematically. The experimental subjects are chosen more or less randomly; but people are not randomly sorted to jobs and other activities. People who cannot calculate probabilities will either avoid gambling, if they know their cognitive weakness, or, if they do not, will soon be wiped out and thus be forced to discontinue gambling. People who are unusually "fair" will avoid (or, again, be forced out of) roughhouse activities—including highly competitive businesses, trial lawyering, and the academic rat race. Hyperbolic discounters will avoid the financial services industry. These selection effects will not work perfectly, but they are likely to drive a big wedge between experimental and real-world consequences of irrationality.

Richard A. Posner, *Rational Choice, Behavioral Economics, and the Law*, 50 Stanford Law Review 1551, 1570–71 (1998). In essence, Posner's argument is that markets will correct for much of the non-rational behavior that individuals may exhibit, even if it is systematic rather than random. As a result, the traditional law-and-economics model is far from being supplanted.

3. Assumptions about Firm Behavior

A corollary of the self-interest assumption for individual behavior is the assumption that business firms attempt to maximize economic profit. Economic profit is defined as the total revenues received from selling a product or service *minus* the total costs of producing the product or service, including the opportunity costs.

Matsushita Elec. Indus. Co. v. Zenith Radio Corp.

Supreme Court of the United States
475 U.S. 574 (1986)

POWELL, J.

* * *

Petitioners, defendants below, are 21 corporations that manufacture or sell "consumer electronic products" (CEPs) — for the most part, television sets. Petitioners include both Japanese manufacturers of CEPs and American firms, controlled by Japanese parents, that sell the Japanese-manufactured products. Respondents, plaintiffs below, are Zenith Radio Corporation (Zenith) and National Union Electric Corporation (NUE). Zenith is an American firm that manufactures and sells television sets. NUE is the corporate successor to Emerson Radio Company, an American firm that manufactured and sold television sets until 1970, when it withdrew from the market after sustaining substantial losses. Zenith and NUE began this lawsuit in 1974, claiming that petitioners had illegally conspired to drive American firms from the American CEP market. According to respondents, the gist of this conspiracy was a "'scheme to raise, fix and maintain artificially *high* prices for television receivers sold by [petitioners] in Japan and, at the same time, to fix and maintain *low* prices for television receivers exported to and sold in the United States.'" These "low prices" were allegedly at levels that produced substantial losses for petitioners....

* * *

... The thrust of respondents' argument is that petitioners used their monopoly profits from the Japanese market to fund a concerted campaign to price predatorily and thereby drive respondents and other American manufacturers of CEPs out of business. Once successful, according to respondents, petitioners would cartelize the American CEP market, restricting output and raising prices above the level that fair competition would produce. The resulting monopoly profits, respondents contend, would more than compensate petitioners for the losses they incurred through years of pricing below market level.

* * *

... According to petitioners, the alleged conspiracy is one that is economically irrational and practically infeasible. Consequently, petitioners contend, they had no motive to engage in the alleged predatory pricing conspiracy; indeed, they had a strong motive not to conspire in the manner respondents allege. Petitioners argue that, in light of the absence of any apparent motive and the ambiguous nature of the evidence of conspiracy, no trier of fact reasonably could find that the conspiracy with which petitioners are charged actually existed. This argument requires us to consider the nature of the alleged conspiracy and the practical obstacles to its implementation.

IV

A

A predatory pricing conspiracy is by nature speculative. Any agreement to price below the competitive level requires the conspirators to forgo profits that free competition would offer them. The forgone profits may be considered an investment in the future. For the investment to be rational, the conspirators must have a reasonable expectation of recovering, in the form of later monopoly profits, more than the losses suffered. As then-Professor Bork, discussing predatory pricing by a single firm, explained:

> "Any realistic theory of predation recognizes that the predator as well as his victims will incur losses during the fighting, but such a theory supposes it may be a rational calculation for the predator to view the losses as an investment in future monopoly profits (where rivals are to be killed) or in future undisturbed profits (where rivals are to be disciplined). The future flow of profits, appropriately discounted, must then exceed the present size of the losses." R. Bork, The Antitrust Paradox 145 (1978).

As this explanation shows, the success of such schemes is inherently uncertain: the short-run loss is definite, but the long-run gain depends on successfully neutralizing the competition. Moreover, it is not enough simply to achieve monopoly power, as monopoly pricing may breed quick entry by new competitors eager to share in the excess profits. The success of any predatory scheme depends on *maintaining* monopoly power for long enough both to recoup the predator's losses and to harvest some additional gain. Absent some assurance that the hoped-for monopoly will materialize, *and* that it can be sustained for a significant period of time, "[the] predator must make a substantial investment with no assurance that it will pay off." For this reason, there is a consensus among commentators that predatory pricing schemes are rarely tried, and even more rarely successful.

These observations apply even to predatory pricing by a *single firm* seeking monopoly power. In this case, respondents allege that a large number of firms have conspired over a period of many years to charge below-market prices in order to stifle competition. Such a conspiracy is incalculably more difficult to execute than an analogous plan undertaken by a single predator. The conspirators must allocate the losses to be sustained during the conspiracy's operation, and must also allocate any gains to be realized from its success. Precisely because success is speculative and depends on a willingness to endure losses for an indefinite period, each conspirator has a strong incentive to cheat, letting its partners suffer the losses necessary to destroy the competition while sharing in any gains if the conspiracy succeeds. The necessary allocation is therefore difficult to accomplish. Yet if conspirators cheat to any substantial extent, the conspiracy must fail, because its success depends on depressing the market price for *all* buyers of CEPs. If there are too few goods at the artificially low price to satisfy demand, the would-be victims of the conspiracy can continue to sell at the "real" market price, and the conspirators suffer losses to little purpose.

Finally, if predatory pricing conspiracies are generally unlikely to occur, they are especially so where, as here, the prospects of attaining monopoly power seem slight. In order to recoup their losses, petitioners must obtain enough market power to set higher than competitive prices, and then must sustain those prices long enough to earn in excess profits what they earlier gave up in below-cost prices. Two decades after their conspiracy is alleged to have commenced, petitioners appear to be far from achieving this goal: the two largest shares of the retail market in television sets are held by RCA and respondent Zenith, not by any of petitioners. Moreover, those shares, which together approximate 40% of sales, did not decline appreciably during the 1970's. Petitioners' collective share rose rapidly during this period, from one-fifth or less of the relevant markets to close to 50%. Neither the District Court nor the Court of Appeals found, however, that petitioners' share presently allows them to charge monopoly prices; to the contrary, respondents contend that the conspiracy is ongoing—that petitioners are still artificially *depressing* the market price in order to drive Zenith out of the market. The data in the record strongly suggest that goal is yet far distant.[3]

The alleged conspiracy's failure to achieve its ends in the two decades of its asserted operation is strong evidence that the conspiracy does not in fact exist. Since the losses in such a conspiracy accrue before the gains, they must be "repaid" with interest. And because the alleged losses have accrued over the course of two decades, the conspirators could well require a correspondingly long time to recoup. Maintaining supra competitive prices in turn depends on the continued cooperation of the conspirators, on the inability of other would-be competitors to enter the market, and (not incidentally) on the conspirators' ability to escape antitrust liability for their *minimum* price-fixing cartel. Each of these factors weighs more heavily as the time needed to recoup losses grows. If the losses have been substantial—as would likely be necessary in order to drive out the competition— petitioners would most likely have to sustain their cartel for years simply to break even.

Nor does the possibility that petitioners have obtained supra competitive profits in the Japanese market change this calculation. Whether or not petitioners have the means to sustain substantial losses in this country over a long period of time, they have no motive to sustain such losses absent some strong likelihood that the alleged conspiracy in this country will eventually pay off. The courts below found no evidence of any such success, and—as indicated above—the facts actually are to the contrary: RCA and Zenith, not any of the petitioners, continue to hold the largest share of the American retail market in color television sets. More important, there is nothing to suggest any relationship between petitioners' profits in Japan and the amount petitioners could expect to gain from a conspiracy to monopolize the American market. In the absence of any such evidence, the possible existence of supra competitive profits in Japan simply cannot overcome the economic obstacles to the ultimate success of this alleged predatory conspiracy.

* * *

... [P]etitioners had no motive to enter into the alleged conspiracy. To the contrary, as presumably rational businesses, petitioners had every incentive not to engage in the conduct with which they are charged, for its likely effect would be to generate losses for petitioners with no corresponding gains....

---

3. Respondents offer no reason to suppose that entry into the relevant market is especially difficult, yet without barriers to entry it would presumably be impossible to maintain supra competitive prices for an extended time. Judge Easterbrook, commenting on this case in a law review article, offers the following sensible assessment:

> ... There are no barriers to entry into electronics, as the proliferation of computer and audio firms shows. The competition would come from resurgent United States firms, from other foreign firms (Korea and many other nations make TV sets), and from defendants themselves. In order to recoup, the Japanese firms would need to suppress competition among themselves. On plaintiffs' theory, the cartel would need to last at least thirty years, far longer than any in history, even when cartels were not illegal. None should be sanguine about the prospects of such a cartel, given each firm's incentive to shave price and expand its share of sales. The predation recoupment story therefore does not make sense, and we are left with the more plausible inference that the Japanese firms did not sell below cost in the first place. They were just engaged in hard competition.

Easterbrook, *The Limits of Antitrust*, 63 Texas L. Rev. 1, 26–27 (1984) (footnotes omitted).

* * *

... [T]he absence of any plausible motive to engage in the conduct charged is highly relevant to whether a "genuine issue for trial" exists within the meaning of Rule 56(e). Lack of motive bears on the range of permissible conclusions that might be drawn from ambiguous evidence: if petitioners had no rational economic motive to conspire, and if their conduct is consistent with other, equally plausible explanations, the conduct does not give rise to an inference of conspiracy.... Here, the conduct in question consists largely of (i) pricing at levels that succeeded in taking business away from respondents, and (ii) arrangements that may have limited petitioners' ability to compete with each other (and thus kept prices from going even lower). This conduct suggests either that petitioners behaved competitively, or that petitioners conspired to *raise* prices. Neither possibility is consistent with an agreement among 21 companies to price below market levels. Moreover, the predatory pricing scheme that this conduct is said to prove is one that makes no practical sense: it calls for petitioners to destroy companies larger and better established than themselves, a goal that remains far distant more than two decades after the conspiracy's birth. Even had they succeeded in obtaining their monopoly, there is nothing in the record to suggest that they could recover the losses they would need to sustain along the way. In sum, in light of the absence of any rational motive to conspire, neither petitioners' pricing practices, nor their conduct in the Japanese market, nor their agreements respecting prices and distribution in the American market, suffice to create a "genuine issue for trial."

* * *

The decision of the Court of Appeals is reversed, and the case is remanded for further proceedings consistent with this opinion.

It is so ordered.

Notes and Questions

1. Rationality and Profit Maximization: The Court assumes the Japanese firms behaved rationally by selecting profit maximizing strategies. The plaintiffs' theory, in contrast, required irrational behavior by the Japanese manufacturers. Thus, the Court rejected the plaintiffs' theory as being inconsistent with standard assumptions about economic behavior.

2. Managerial Incentives: The Court implicitly assumes that profit maximization is the goal of the firm, but firms are managed by individuals whose incentives may not always be aligned with this goal. Managers may be more interested in increasing their salary or the size of the firm than in maximizing profits. This divergence between managers' incentives and the firm's profit maximization goal is an example of the **principal-agent problem**. Managers, who are agents of the firm's owners (the principals), do not always act in their principals' best interest. For corporations with publicly traded shares and dispersed shareholders, the principal-agent problem is often characterized as the result of a "separation of ownership and control."

3. Profits and Cartel Agreements: The Court recognizes that each Japanese firm, as a profit maximizer, would have incentives to cheat on the cartel agreement both before and after any success in dominating the market. Again, the assumption of profit maximizing behavior strained the credibility of the plaintiffs' theory.

4. Opportunity Cost of Profits Earned in Japan: The plaintiffs argue that the profits earned in Japan and then, allegedly, used to subsidize losses in the United States, are somehow not as valuable as other profits—herein lies the incentive to accept the present lost profits in hope of greater future profits from exploiting American consumers. But that cross-subsidization argument ignores the fundamental economic concept of opportunity cost. Profits are profits, regardless of their source. In deciding what to do with those profits—whether to use them to finance continued losses in the American market or to put them to some other use—the Japanese manufacturers necessarily will consider the next best alternative use of those profits, i.e., the opportunity cost. Conversely, the losses the manufacturers suffered in the American market are not lessened in any way by the fact that they were making profits in Japan. As a result, that the manufacturers are making large profits in Japan does not make it any more rational for them to incur ongoing losses in a predatory pricing scheme in the United States than if they had to look to other sources of financing to cover their American losses.

5. Costs of Production and Economic Profit: Profit is defined as total revenue minus total costs. Economists use the phrase **costs of production** in a way that reflects the concept of opportunity cost. In order for a firm to undertake a productive activity, it must attract inputs (resources or factors of production) from other alternative uses. The firm attracts inputs by paying the owners of the inputs at least the value of their services in their next best alternative use—opportunity cost. Costs of production (firm outlays) are the payments made to the owners of resources to assure the availability of those resources for use in the firm's production process. In discussing the costs of production, economists and many courts are careful to recognize both the **explicit costs** recorded in the firm's books and the **implicit costs** that reflect the value of resources used in production by the firm for which no explicit payments are made. When a firm does not make an explicit payment for the use of resources it owns, then the implicit cost is the income that those resources could have commanded in some alternative use. A consideration of explicit and implicit costs reveals the total opportunity cost of the production process.

Consider, for example, a small "Mom & Pop" tavern organized as a sole proprietorship and located on a busy corner of an area undergoing a commercial "boom." "Mom & Pop" own the building in which the tavern is located. Their explicit costs of operation include the payments for inventory, advertising, legal and accounting services, and labor. Each of these payments involves an explicit contractual outlay that is recorded as a cost in the firm's books. On the other hand, "Mom & Pop" may leave out some important implicit costs of production. For example, "Mom & Pop" may not record on the firm books a salary for their own services. Or, they may enter a salary below what they could earn while working for another firm. The opportunity cost of working for themselves is an implicit cost—a real economic cost—that should be relevant in their decision making process. Another implicit cost that may be left out of "Mom & Pop's" accounting records is the opportunity cost of using their building. If "Mom & Pop" did not occupy the building, it could be rented to another business or sold (with the proceeds invested in another income earning asset). The failure to include the implicit cost of using the building means that the firm is ignoring an important opportunity cost: the **opportunity cost of capital**—the value of the payments that they could receive from the next best alternative investment of the capital tied up in the firm. The opportunity cost of capital is typically assumed to be the market rate of return on an asset of similar risk, and is an implicit cost of production.

Including implicit costs as well as explicit costs in the cost calculation lets one determine **economic profit**—the difference between total revenue and total cost of production. In contrast, the **accounting profit** found on a firm's income statement is the amount by which total revenue exceeds total explicit costs. Obviously, if accounting costs do not account for implicit costs, then accounting profit may overstate actual (economic) profit. In other words, positive accounting profit does not necessarily imply that positive economic profit is being earned. To the contrary, a positive accounting profit can be consistent with an economic loss.

A final, related point about a firm's cost of production concerns the accounting convention of relying on **historical costs**, i.e., payments that were incurred in the past. Historical cost means that the accounting value of an asset—such as inventory or a building—is determined by the price that the firm paid for the asset. This is the exact opposite of the perspective inherent in the concept of opportunity cost. Opportunity cost is forward-looking—it involves a decision today to commit resources to one use as opposed to another use. Thus, in a real sense, opportunity cost is the value of "the road not taken." Decisions by economic actors rely on predictions about the future, not on past events. Past outlays (unless they affect prospective costs) are not costs because they exert no influence on current decisions.

Consider, for example, the market value today of a commercial building purchased in 1995 for $1,000,000. If the market price of the building has fallen to $500,000, should the owner refuse to sell at that price simply because its current **book value** (historical cost minus accumulated depreciation) is $800,000? Alternatively, if the owner of the building tried to use it as collateral for a bank loan, would the banker use historical value or current market value as an indicator of its value as collateral? The prudent banker will look at the market value.

6. Economic Survival of the Fittest: What if businesses did not seek to maximize profits, but instead made business decisions for no apparent reason and changed their strategies entirely at random? Wouldn't the most successful businesses still be those that (however randomly) chose strategies that were the most profitable? And wouldn't businesses that chose unprofitable strategies lose money and eventually go out of business? Thus, even if businesses do not consciously follow a profit maximization strategy, the results of marketplace competition will look much as if they did—the economic fittest will survive. This process is often referred to as **Economic Darwinism**. James Brickley, Clifford Smith, and Jerold Zimmerman apply this perspective to competition among firms: "The collapse of Enron, Charles Darwin might have noted, is an example of how competition tends to weed out the less fit. As described in *The Origin of Species*, natural history illustrates the principle of 'survival of the fittest.' In industry, we see Economic Darwinism in operation as competition weeds out ill-designed organizations that fail to adapt. Competition in the market provides strong pressures for efficient decisions. Competition among firms dictates that only those firms with low costs will survive. If firms adopt inefficient, high-cost policies, competition will place strong pressures on these firms to either adapt or close." James Brickley et al., Managerial Economics and Organizational Architecture 7 (3rd ed. 2004).

B. Property Rights and Exchange in a Free Market Economy

The fundamental problem faced by any economic system is the allocation of society's scarce resources among the unlimited desires of the individuals who make up that society. A **capitalistic market economy**, which is the basis of the American economic system, attempts to solve this social problem by tapping the individual's self-interest in a manner that encourages him or her to put resources to their most highly valued use. Scarce re-sources—i.e., resources that have an opportunity cost—are combined by individuals or firms to produce economic goods and services which are desired by other economic actors. In the American economic system, economic goods and services are allocated primarily through the market system. The willingness and ability of individuals to trade-off the al-ternative uses of the resources at their command determine who receives the goods and services.

A **property right** is a socially enforced right to determine and control the use of an economic good. A property right is private when it is assigned to a specific person. Property rights are alienable in that they can be transferred (sold or given) to other individuals. The ownership of private property rights is the foundation of a free market economy. Owners of land and other resources have the legal rights to decide how to use these resources and frequently trade their rights to other individuals. They are free to start new businesses and to close existing businesses. In contrast, in centrally planned economies, property tends to be owned by the state; government officials decide how to use these re-sources. In a system of private property, the individual (as opposed to the government) holds the right to control property. The individual receives the benefit and must pay the costs associated with the use of the property. In a capitalist society, the law protects property rights. Without some guarantee that property rights will be protected, there would be little incentive to accumulate capital stock and, therefore, to grow economically. Without state guarantees of rights to property, individuals would have to protect their own property at a high personal cost.

The economics of property rights has received a great deal of attention with the de-velopment of law and economics. A simple example of ownership of a pasture is used to illustrate some of the important insights. If Sarah owns a pasture, she can forbid others from grazing their cattle on it—and, importantly, there is no need for her to negotiate an agreement for exclusive use.

1. An Overview of the Efficient Property Rights System

Legal protection of property rights is important because it creates incentives to use resources efficiently. A truly efficient system of property rights requires three attributes: (1) universality—every resource is owned; (2) exclusivity—the owner of property may exclude all others from using it; and (3) transferability—it is costless for possessors of property rights to exchange their rights. A property rights system with these attributes, when combined with a free market economy, will generate the efficient allocation of resources. The legal system and property law, however, do not always fulfill these criteria.

In general, the granting of property rights confers two types of economic benefits, static and dynamic. Static refers to the impact of the property right on behavior during one particular time period—for example, one year or one growing season. The static benefit is illustrated by considering alternative assignments of property rights to a natural, uncultivated pasture. If the property rights are attenuated—that is, not exclusive or fully enforceable—so that Sarah can't exclude others from using her pasture (or cannot secure compensation when others use the pasture without her permission), then the property will not be used in a value maximizing manner because some (or, perhaps, all) users of the pasture will ignore the costs they impose on other users in deciding how much to let their cattle graze in the pasture. The use of the pasture by the trespassers imposes a cost on Sarah, and also biases the use of the pasture towards overgrazing. The overgrazing results in reduced total weight for cattle because the owners of the cattle allow their cattle to expend more energy in finding enough to eat than they would expend if each cattle owner had to pay the full cost of the grass, which is the case when the cattle owner has exclusive use of his own pasture. The attenuated property rights—even in the static situation—result in an outcome that is clearly not optimal. However, granting enforceable property rights to Sarah will result in the static benefit of preventing overgrazing.

The dynamic benefit of a property right is the incentive to invest in the creation or improvement of some resource over time. For example, if Sarah is guaranteed exclusive rights to the pasture in both period 1 and period 2, then she has the incentive to invest resources (for example, through fertilization and careful management to avoid overgrazing) in period 1. She can then reap the benefits of the investment in period 2. Sarah would be unwilling to make such an investment if she were not able to exclude other potential users of the pasture in period 2. Similarly, a business firm is less likely to invest resources on the research and development of a new product if competing firms that have not borne that expense can duplicate it without having to compensate the original firm. As a result, when property rights are not enforceable, the initial investment is less likely to occur or, if it is forthcoming, it is likely to be smaller than with enforceable property rights. Thus, attenuated (poorly defined) property rights prevent the achievement of the optimal outcome in the dynamic setting as well as the static setting.

The transferability of property rights facilitates the maximization of the static and dynamic benefits of well-defined property rights. In the preceding example, one would expect the cattle owners to attempt to capture the static and dynamic benefits of private property by negotiating a set of exclusive use property rights among themselves, provided their numbers are small enough for negotiation to occur (that is, provided that transaction costs are less than the gains from the transaction).

Costless transfer of property rights assures that the property rights are allocated to the highest valued uses. For example, if Sarah (the owner of the pasture) is a relatively unproductive rancher, then she should be able to increase her wealth by selling the pasture to a more productive rancher at a price that reflects some portion of the increased value of the pasture in the hands of the more productive rancher.

The allocation and use of property rights is affected by **transaction costs**—the costs of acquiring information about alternative uses and of negotiating and enforcing contracts. In general, if the potential benefits of a transaction are greater than the costs of reaching and enforcing a bargain, then a voluntary, mutually-beneficial exchange will result in the property rights being controlled by the parties that value them the most. Private property rights tend to be more carefully defined, more fully allocated, and better enforced when transaction costs are relatively low or benefits of defining rights are relatively high, other things being equal.

2. Enforcement of Property Rights

An important distinction in the economic analysis of property rights concerns the type of legal rule that protects the rights. A **property rule** is a legal rule that protects a property right through the absolute right to exclude others, such as with an injunction. In the preceding example, Sarah's property right is protected by a property rule—she has the absolute right to exclude others from her property. Of course, she is allowed to reach voluntary agreements that allow others to use the property in return for some type of compensation.

Another way to protect Sarah's property right is with a **liability rule** under which Sarah has the right to collect damages from anyone who uses the pasture without her permission. Whereas a property rule requires that bargaining occur before others use the property, a liability rule allows the other party to use the property and then pay damages. Property rules require voluntary exchanges, while liability rules result in forced exchanges. Thus, liability rules are the domain of tort law, since it is impossible to negotiate a tort prior to its occurrence. For example, a driver that might cause a tortious car accident could not possibly negotiate with every other potential driver before getting in his car. Much of the economic analysis of law has been concerned with identifying situations where one rule is more appropriate than the other.

Property Rules, Liability Rules, and Inalienability: One View of the Cathedral

Guido Calabresi & A. Douglas Melamed
85 Harvard Law Review 1089, 1092–93, 1105–06 (1972)

Only rarely are Property and Torts approached from a unified perspective. Recent writings by lawyers concerned with economics and by economists concerned with law suggest, however, that an attempt at integrating the various legal relationships treated by these subjects would be useful both for the beginning student and the sophisticated scholar. By articulating a concept of "entitlements" which are protected by property, liability, or inalienability rules, we present one framework for such an approach....

* * *

An entitlement is protected by a property rule to the extent that someone who wishes to remove the entitlement from its holder must buy it from him in a voluntary transaction in which the value of the entitlement is agreed upon by the seller....

Whenever someone may destroy the entitlement if he is willing to pay an objectively determined value for it, the entitlement is protected by a liability rule. This value may be what it is thought the original holder of the entitlement would have sold it for. But the holder's complaint that he would have demanded more will not avail him once the objectively determined value is set.

* * *

An entitlement is inalienable to the extent that its transfer is not permitted between a willing buyer and a willing seller....

It should be clear that most entitlements to most goods are mixed. Taney's house may be protected by a property rule in situations in which Marshall wishes to purchase it, by a liability rule where the government decides to take it by eminent domain, and by a rule of inalienability in situations where Taney is drunk or incompetent....

* * *

Whenever society chooses an initial entitlement it must also determine whether to protect the entitlement by property rules, by liability rules, or by rules of inalienability. In our framework, much of what is generally called private property can be viewed as an entitlement protected by a property rule. No one can take the entitlement to private property from the holder unless the holder sells it willingly and at the price at which he subjectively values the property. Yet a nuisance with sufficient public utility to avoid an injunction has, in effect, the right to take property with compensation. In such a circumstance the entitlement to the property is protected only by what we call a liability rule: an external, objective standard of value used to facilitate the transfer of the entitlement from the holder to the nuisance. Finally, in some instances we will not allow the sale of the property at all, that is, we will occasionally make the entitlement inalienable.

* * *

Notes and Questions

1. Entitlements: Property and Liability Rules: Property rules are premised on an actual exchange between a willing seller and a buyer—in other words, a party whose property interest is protected by a property rule can refuse to sell unless the price is right. Liability rules, by contrast, are premised on a hypothetical, rather than actual, exchange. As a result, isn't all property taken subject to a liability rule undervalued because by definition there is no willing seller? That is, doesn't the person with the property before the taking value it more highly than the price set for the right under the liability rule? What public policy justifications can you think of for creating such a rule?

2. Entitlements and Inalienability: What incentive does inalienability have on creating wealth? Is alienability only paternalistic in scope or is there another purpose behind the doctrine?

3. Why the Distinction?: Why is there this distinction between property and liability rules and inalienability? Is it merely semantics? Or are there different policy reasons that affect the implementation and enforcement of these doctrines?

3. Poorly Defined Property Rights

Some resources, like air and water, are not privately owned. Because of the common ownership of these resources, no one has adequate legal rights to protect against their use. Thus, economic actors are able to use such resources without paying for them. For example, pollution occurs because manufacturers are able to avoid paying the cost of the damage to the air. Such externalities would not occur, or at least people would have to pay for them (that is, internalize them), if the three attributes of an efficient property rights system were satisfied.

Common ownership means that the property rights to a resource are nonexistent or poorly defined. As a result, anyone may use or consume the resource. Common ownership often destroys the static and dynamic benefits of private ownership. The fundamental economic disadvantage of common ownership is the absence of any incentive to invest in the productivity of the common property. Rather, each person with access to the resource has an incentive to exploit it and neglect the effects of his or her actions on the resource's productivity.

The Tragedy of the Commons

Garrett Hardin

162 Science 1243, 1244–45 (1968)

The tragedy of the commons develops this way. Picture a pasture open to all. It is to be expected that each herdsman will try to keep as many cattle as possible on the commons.... At this point, the inherent logic of the commons remorselessly generates tragedy.

As a rational being, each herdsman seeks to maximize his gains. Explicitly or implicitly, more or less consciously, he asks, "What is the utility to me of adding one more animal to my herd?" This utility has one negative and one positive component.

1. The positive component is a function of the increment of one animal. Since the herdsman receives all the proceeds from the sale of the additional animal, the positive utility is nearly +1.

2. The negative component is a function of the additional overgrazing created by one animal. Since, however, the effects of overgrazing are shared by all the herdsmen, the negative utility for any particular decision-making herdsman is only a fraction of -1.

Adding together the component partial utilities, the rational herdsman concludes that the only sensible course for him is to add another animal to his herd. And another; and another.... But this is the conclusion reached by each and every rational herdsman sharing a commons. Therein is the tragedy. Each man is locked into a system that compels him to increase his herd without limit—in a world that is limited. Ruin is the destination toward which all men rush, each pursuing his own best interest in a society that believes in the freedom of the commons. Freedom in a commons brings ruin to all.

* * *

Notes and Questions

1. Tragedy Everywhere: The Tragedy of the Commons has been used for hundreds of years (at least since Reverend C.L. Dodgson—a.k.a. Lewis Carroll—first introduced collective action analysis) to explain why mankind cannot achieve total economic prosperity. That is, rational self-interested people have limits as to how far they can progress without controls and laws to shape the overall economy. What laws and reforms are centered around this argument?

2. Congress, Businesses, and Law Schools: The U.S. Congress is arguably the most expensive example of a tragedy of the commons. Because of the pressure to get reelected, Senators and Representatives try to pass legislation to benefit their constituents, without regard to the whole country. Vote trading and logrolling result in numerous pork barrel projects that would not pass if evaluated on an individual basis. Other economic organizations—such as businesses and law schools—are not exempt from this tragedy either. Can you think of examples where one person has rationally pursued his or her self-interest only to hurt, directly or otherwise, the common interests?

The following case illustrates how the Tragedy of the Commons impacts oil and gas extraction.

Wronski v. Sun Oil Co.

Michigan Court of Appeals
279 N.W.2d 564 (1979)

HOLBROOK, J.

[Plaintiffs own several tracts of land comprising 200 acres within the Columbus 3 oil pool. Defendant Sun Oil has drilled several wells on nearby property. The Supervisor of Wells, Michigan Department of Natural Resources, issued an order, under the authority of the Michigan oil and gas conservation act, establishing 20-acre well drilling units for the Columbus 3 pool; this order limits the number of wells that may be drilled to one well for each designated 20-acre tract within the boundaries of this oil field. The Supervisor also issued an order which limited production from each well within the field to a maximum of 75 barrels of oil per day. Plaintiffs contend that Sun Oil illegally overproduced oil from three wells and that such oil was drained from beneath the plaintiffs' tracts. The trial court found that Sun Oil had intentionally and unlawfully produced 150,000 barrels of oil, and that 50,000 barrels had been drained from beneath plaintiffs' property. The court awarded compensatory and exemplary damages to the plaintiffs. Sun Oil appealed.]

* * *

Oil and gas, unlike other minerals, do not remain constantly in place in the ground, but may migrate across property lines. Because of this migratory tendency the rule of capture evolved. This rule provides:

> The owner of a tract of land acquires title to the oil and gas which he produces from wells drilled thereon, though it may be proved that part of such oil or gas migrated from adjoining lands. Under this rule, *absent some state regulation of drilling practices*, a landowner ... is not liable to adjacent landowners whose lands are drained as a result of such operations.... The remedy of the injured landowner under such circumstances has generally been said to be that of self-help "go and do likewise."

This rule of capture was a harsh rule that could work to deprive an owner of oil and gas underneath his land. To mitigate the harshness of this rule and to protect the landowners' property rights in the oil and gas beneath his land, the "fair share" principle emerged[:]

* * *

> Within reasonable limits, each operator should have an opportunity equal to that afforded other operators to recover the equivalent of the amount of recoverable oil (and gas) underlying his property. The aim should be to prevent reasonably avoidable drainage of oil and gas across property lines that is not offset by counter drainage.

This fair-share rule does not do away with the rule of capture, but rather acts to place limits on its proper application.

* * *

Michigan recognizes the fair-share principle and its subsequent modifications of the rule of capture.... This right to have a reasonable opportunity to produce one's just and equitable share of oil in a pool is the common-law right that the trial court found Sun Oil violated. [I]f it can be said that Sun Oil's overproduction deprived plaintiffs of the opportunity to claim and take the oil under their respective properties, then Sun Oil will be liable for a conversion.

Production in the Columbus 3 field was restricted to 75 barrels of oil per well per day. Compulsory pooling was also in effect, limiting the number of oil wells to one per twenty acres, and specifying their location. The purpose behind proration is that the order itself, if obeyed, will protect landowners from drainage and allow each to produce their fair share. A violation of the proration order, especially a secret violation, allows the violator to take more than his fair share and leaves the other landowners unable to protect their rights unless they also violate the proration order. We therefore hold that any violation of a proration order constitutes conversion of oil from the pool, and subjects the violator to liability to all the owners of interests in the pool for conversion of the illegally-obtained oil. The trial court found that Sun Oil produced 150,000 barrels of oil from the Columbus 3 pool in contravention of the order of the Supervisor of Wells, and that 50,000 barrels of this oil had been drained from the lands of plaintiffs, which the trial court identified as a violation of the plaintiffs' common-law rights. The finding that Sun Oil is liable to plaintiffs for the conversion of 50,000 barrels of oil is affirmed.

Notes and Questions

1. Fishing: The **Tragedy of the Commons** argument applies to both renewable resources, such as fish, and nonrenewable resources, such as oil. Consider the example of fishing in international waters. In international waters, anyone may acquire exclusive ownership of fish by catching them, and no one has rights to the fish until they are caught. This system causes each fisherman to ignore the effect of the well-known biological law that the current stock of a species of fish determines its reproductive life. Thus, the fish harvested today reduce today's stock and thereby affect the size of tomorrow's stock and tomorrow's harvesting costs and revenues. However, overfishing results because no single fisherman has an incentive to act on this bioeconomic relationship. If all fishermen would cooperate to restrain themselves today, tomorrow's stock would be larger and future harvesting cheaper and more profitable. However, under competitive conditions, each individual knows that if he or she abstains now, rivals will not abstain and much of the effect of one individual's abstention will be lost. Further, the reduction in future costs would accrue to everyone, not just to the abstainer. Hence, each person has little reason to abstain since the major effect is to lower others' future costs at the immediate present cost to the abstainer.

2. Three Solutions to Overfishing: *(1) A Single Owner:* Individual ownership removes this dilemma. If only one person is fishing, he or she need not worry that rivals will not abstain. (Of course, groups such as tribes of indigenous people can also be sole owners, but the group must be able to control the behavior of its members with respect to the resource.) *(2) Contracting Among Multiple Owners:* When there is more than one owner, all parties involved could negotiate an agreement to abstain and all would benefit. The fact that such agreements are not usually successful in negotiations is due to the cost of dealing with all current and potential people who will fish and the difficulty in ensuring that all abstain as agreed. *(3) Government Regulation:* A third method of dealing with the Tragedy of the Commons in international fishing is government regulation. Such regulation usually sets an annual catch quota. To allocate the quota, regulators rely on restrictions on fishing technology or simply close the season when the quota is taken. Both means create difficult enforcement problems and potential economic waste. If the season is closed when the quota is taken, for example, excess profits are dissipated in competition among fishermen to buy bigger, faster boats and thus get a larger share of the quota. The season progressively shrinks, and resources stand idle for much of the year or are devoted to inferior employment.

3. Environmental Protection and Federalism: A leading rationale for federal domination of environmental regulation is to prevent states from competing for economic growth opportunities by lowering their environmental standards in a so-called "race to the bottom." The notion is that all states compete for economic growth by lowering environmental standards below the level they would select if they acted collectively at the national level. What is individually rational for each state is collectively irrational at the national level. Professor Richard Stewart describes the implication of this dynamic in concise terms:

> ... Given the mobility of industry and commerce, any individual state or community may rationally decline unilaterally to adopt high environment standards that entail

substantial costs for industry and obstacles to economic development for fear that the resulting environmental gains will be more than offset by movement of capital to other areas with lower standards. If each locality reasons in the same way, all will adopt lower standards of environmental quality than they would prefer if there were some binding mechanism that enabled them simultaneously to enact higher standards, thus eliminating the threatened loss of industry or development.

Richard B. Stewart, *Pyramids of Sacrifice? Problems of Federalism in Mandating State Implementation of National Environmental Policy*, 86 Yale Law Journal 1196, 1212 (1977). Thus, according to this logic, federal regulation is necessary to correct a political market failure at the state level. For thorough documentation of the influence of this argument, as well as a devastating critique, see Richard L. Revesz, *Rehabilitating Interstate Competition: Rethinking the "Race-to-the-Bottom" Rationale for Federal Environmental Regulation*, 67 New York University Law Review 1210, 1233–44 (1992).

4. Tragedy of the Anticommons: Whereas the Tragedy of the Commons describes situations in which multiple owners of property are unable to exclude each other, resulting in overuse of the property, the Tragedy of the Anticommons refers to situations in which multiple owners of property are able to exclude each other, resulting in underuse of the property. Michael Heller explains:

> Socialist rule stifled markets and often left store shelves bare. One promise of the transition "from Marx to markets" was that new entrepreneurs would acquire the stores, create businesses, and fill the shelves. However, after several years of reform, storefronts often remained empty, while flimsy metal kiosks, stocked full of goods, mushroomed up on Moscow streets. Why did new merchants not come in from the cold?
>
> * * *
>
> [E]ven if the initial endowment of property rights were clearly defined, corruption held in check, and the rule of law respected, storefronts would remain empty because of the way governments are creating property rights. Transition regimes have often failed to endow any individual with a bundle of rights that represents full ownership of storefronts or other scarce resources. Instead, those regimes have ratified the expectations of powerful socialist-era stakeholders by making them rights-holders in the new economy. Rights were made alienable in the hope that new owners would trade them to more productive users. In a typical Moscow storefront, one owner may be endowed initially with the right to sell, another to receive sale revenue, and still others to lease, receive lease revenue, occupy, and determine use. Each owner can block the others from using the space as a storefront. No one can set up shop without collecting the consent of all of the other owners.
>
> Empty Moscow storefronts are a stark example of anticommons property, a type of property regime that may result when initial endowments are created as disaggregated rights rather than as coherent bundles of rights in scarce resources. More generally, one can understand anticommons property as the mirror image of commons property.
>
> * * *

Michael A. Heller, *The Tragedy of the Anticommons: Property in the Transition from Marx to Markets*, 111 Harvard Law Review 621, 622-23 (1988).

How might our existing patent system be vulnerable to creating a Tragedy of the Anticommons?

4. Public Goods

A public good is a good where one individual's consumption of the good does not reduce or exclude the ability of other individuals to consume the good. A pure public good is both nonrival and nonexcludable. A good is nonrival when the quantity available for other people does not diminish when one consumes it. A good is nonexcludable if it is prohibitively costly to provide the good only to people who pay for it while preventing or excluding other people from obtaining it. The classic example of a public good is national defense. Once provided to one person, national defense is available to all on a noncompeting or nonrivalrous basis. It is difficult or impossible to exclude anyone from the use of the national defense public good, and its enjoyment by one person does not prevent its use by another.

In contrast, a private good is consumed exclusively by the person who owns it. If you eat an apple, one less apple remains for other people. If you watch a television show, however, your action does not reduce the number of viewers who can watch the show on their own televisions.

Public goods present a unique economic problem because firms have little incentive to produce them. Few buyers willingly pay for nonexcludable goods because they can get them free. The problem facing producers of public goods is that **free riding** behavior makes it difficult to discover the true preferences of consumers of a public good. Individuals will not reveal their true preferences for public goods because it is not in their self interest to do so. For example, your neighborhood might try to organize a crime watch group. Many neighbors might not contribute but would still appreciate any protection provided, thus concealing group preferences for the service. On the other hand, some who do contribute voluntarily might be totally disinterested in the service. Free riding makes it difficult to determine the true level of demand for the public good. The free rider problem holds the equilibrium quantity of public goods below the economically efficient quantity.

If everyone free rides and no one contributes to the production of public goods, then everyone will be worse off as a result. Although each individual would like some provision of public goods, none will be produced. Herein lies the rationale for government provision of public goods. The government has the power of coercion and taxation, and it can force consumers to contribute to the production of public goods. Citizens cannot refuse to pay taxes; they are forced to contribute to the cost of the public sector output.

Government provision of public goods has two main drawbacks. First, the government lacks information about the amount of money that various people are willing to pay for any particular public good. This creates two more problems. The government cannot calculate the economically efficient level of a public good, and accordingly it may tax some people more (and others less) than they are willing to pay for the public good. The counterargument to this objection is that the government may get closer to the economically efficient level of the public good than would emerge in the free market. The second main drawback of government provision of public goods is that the actual government program will reflect political pressures to benefit special interests rather than the provision of true public goods. That is, the political determination of what is a "public good" may stray from the economic definition of a public good. The role of defense contractors in lobbying for weapons systems illustrates the private benefits associated with the political definition of "public goods."

5. Externalities, Property Rights, and the Coase Theorem

If producing firms incur all of the costs associated with the production of their product, they are well situated to balance the marginal costs and marginal benefits of their actions. However, in many instances, some of the costs of producing a product "spill over" and injure third parties that are not part of the production process. The total cost to society in terms of resources consumed is the sum of the private costs paid by the producer and the external costs that must be borne by third parties. If the legal system does not require the producer to compensate third parties, then the producer will be able to operate at a cost of production that does not fully reflect the cost in terms of society's resources. Thus, the consequences of self-interested behavior may not always be in the best interest of society.

Externalities exist when the actions of one party affect the utility or production possibilities of another party outside the exchange relationship. Externalities can prevent a free market from being efficient. If a firm emits pollution into the air, it can adversely affect the welfare of its surrounding neighbors. If the firm does not bear these costs, it is likely to select an inefficient level of pollution (that is, to overpollute). In choosing how much to invest in pollution control equipment, the firm will consider only its own private costs and benefits. A socially-efficient investment would also consider the costs and benefits imposed on the neighbors. Externalities are covered in detail in Chapter IV.

Prior to 1960, most economists thought that externalities would surely prevent a free market from producing an efficient allocation of resources. Government intervention seemed to be needed to enhance efficiency. For example, the traditional recommendation would have been to tax firms based on their levels of pollution. Given this tax, firms would have incentives to reduce pollution in order to reduce their taxes.

In 1960, Nobel Laureate Ronald Coase presented a convincing argument that free-market exchange is much more powerful in producing efficient results than many economists had thought. As long as property rights can be traded, there is an incentive to rearrange these rights to enhance economic efficiency. The often-recommended government intervention might be unnecessary and, in many cases, undesirable. Suppose that a firm has the legal right to pollute as much as it wants. The neighbors can always offer to pay the firm to reduce its pollution level. Thus, the firm faces a cost for polluting (if the firm pollutes, there is an opportunity cost of not receiving compensation from its neighbors). The firm will pollute only if the pollution generating activity is more valuable to the firm than the costs it imposes on its neighbors.

Consider a factory belching smoke over a nearby community. Figure I-1 illustrates the analysis. Firm output per unit of time is given along the horizontal axis. The marginal benefits to the firm of producing this output are given in dollar terms on the vertical axis. For the sake of this analysis, marginal benefits (MB) can be thought of as the net profits of producing additional units of output. The MB schedule, therefore, declines with increases in output because the rate of return on additional production generally declines. The marginal cost (MC) curve represents the externality caused by the firm's production. It is also given in dollar terms along the vertical axis. The MC measures the additional costs created at each output level by additional smoke. (Assuming that the amount of smoke the firm produces is directly related to its rate of output, more production will cause more smoke.) The MC curve rises as output increases.

If the homeowners in the surrounding neighborhood own the right to clean air, and assuming that bargaining costs nothing, the factory will be able to purchase the right to pollute up to output Q, where MB = MC. For rates of output up to Q, the MB > MC—

Figure I-1. The Coase Theorem

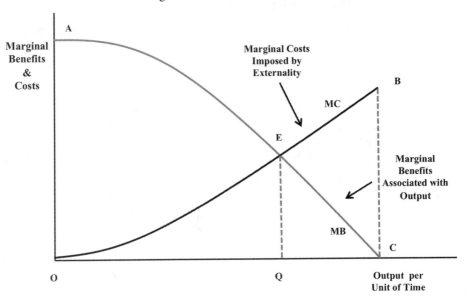

the firm's profits on those units are greater than the additional pollution costs borne by the neighborhood. This means that the firm would be willing to buy and the neighborhood willing to sell the right of using the air to produce those units. The total benefit of producing output Q is indicated by AEQO. Since the total cost of the externality caused by this output is represented by the area under the MC curve, OEQ, a bargain can be struck between the firm and the neighborhood to produce Q by agreeing on how to divide the surplus benefit, AEO. Beyond Q, MC > MB. A bargain to produce these units cannot be reached between the firm and the neighborhood because the firm would not be willing to bid enough to obtain the right to produce those units. So Q, where MB = MC, is the equilibrium outcome when the neighborhood is given the transferable right to use the air.

Suppose that a judge decided to award the firm the right to use the air as it chooses. The same analysis indicates that the neighborhood would pay the firm to produce less output. For up to Q units of output, MB > MC, which means that the neighborhood will not offer a large enough sum of money to induce the firm to reduce its output and its smoke. Beyond Q, the situation has changed. The firm would be willing to accept an offer of money to reduce its output. Beyond Q, the smoke causes EBCQ in damage to the neighborhood and the benefits to the firm for this output are only ECQ. The neighborhood is therefore willing to make it worthwhile to the firm to reduce pollution to the point where MB = MC at Q.

This is a powerful result. No matter who has the legal right to use the air, the amount of pollution is the same. When the firm must pay to pollute, it produces Q. When the firm has the unfettered right to pollute, it produces Q. In a world where bargaining costs nothing, the assignment of legal liability does not matter. A certain equilibrium level of output and its resulting level of pollution will exist regardless of whether firms or consumers own the air. The insight that the same property rights assignment will emerge regardless of the initial assignment of ownership rights, when the costs of negotiation are nonexistent or trivial, is referred to as the **Coase Theorem.**

Miller v. Schoene

Supreme Court of the United States
276 U.S. 272 (1928)

Mr. Justice STONE delivered the opinion of the Court.

Acting under the Cedar Rust Act of Virginia, Acts Va. 1914, c. 36, as amended by Acts Va. 1920, c. 260, defendant in error, the state entomologist, ordered the plaintiffs in error to cut down a large number of ornamental red cedar trees growing on their property, as a means of preventing the communication of a rust or plant disease with which they were infected to the apple orchards in the vicinity. The plaintiffs in error appealed from the order to the circuit court of Shenandoah county which, after a hearing and a consideration of evidence, affirmed the order and allowed to plaintiffs in error $100 to cover the expense of removal of the cedars. Neither the judgment of the court nor the statute as interpreted allows compensation for the value of the standing cedars or the decrease in the market value of the realty caused by their destruction whether considered as ornamental trees or otherwise. But they save to plaintiffs in error the privilege of using the trees when felled.

* * *

As shown by the evidence and as recognized in other cases involving the validity of this statute, cedar rust is an infectious plant disease in the form of a fungoid organism which is destructive of the fruit and foliage of the apple, but without effect on the value of the cedar. Its life cycle has two phases which are passed alternately as a growth on red cedar and on apple trees. It is communicated by spores from one to the other over a radius of at least two miles. It appears not to be communicable between trees of the same species, but only from one species to the other, and other plants seem not to be appreciably affected by it. The only practicable method of controlling the disease and protecting apple trees from its ravages is the destruction of all red cedar trees, subject to the infection, located within two miles of apple orchards.

The red cedar, aside from its ornamental use, has occasional use and value as lumber. It is indigenous to Virginia, is not cultivated or dealt in commercially on any substantial scale, and its value throughout the state is shown to be small as compared with that of the apple orchards of the state. Apple growing is one of the principal agricultural pursuits in Virginia. The apple is used there and exported in large quantities. Many millions of dollars are invested in the orchards, which furnish employment for a large portion of the population, and have induced the development of attendant railroad and cold storage facilities.

On the evidence we may accept the conclusion of the Supreme Court of Appeals that the state was under the necessity of making a choice between the preservation of one class of property and that of the other wherever both existed in dangerous proximity. It would have been none the less a choice if, instead of enacting the present statute, the state, by doing nothing, had permitted serious injury to the apple orchards within its borders to go on unchecked. When forced to such a choice the state does not exceed its constitutional powers by deciding upon the destruction of one class of property in order to save another which, in the judgment of the legislature, is of greater value to the public. It will not do to say that the case is merely one of a conflict of two private interests and that the misfortune of apple growers may not be shifted to cedar owners by ordering the destruction of their property; for it is obvious that there may be, and that here there is, a preponderant public concern in the preservation of the one interest over the other.

* * *

Fontainebleau Hotel Corp. v. Forty-Five Twenty-Five, Inc.

District Court of Appeal of Florida
114 So. 2d 357 (1959)

PER CURIAM.

This is an interlocutory appeal from an order temporarily enjoining the appellants from continuing with the construction of a fourteen-story addition to the Fontainebleau Hotel, owned and operated by the appellants. Appellee, plaintiff below, owns the Eden Roc Hotel, which was constructed in 1955, about a year after the Fontainebleau, and adjoins the Fontainebleau on the north. Both are luxury hotels, facing the Atlantic Ocean. The proposed addition to the Fontainebleau is being constructed twenty feet from its north property line, 130 feet from the mean high water mark of the Atlantic Ocean, and 76 feet 8 inches from the ocean bulkhead line. The 14-story tower will extend 160 feet above grade in height and is 416 feet long from east to west. During the winter months, from around two o'clock in the afternoon for the remainder of the day, the shadow of the addition will extend over the cabana, swimming pool, and sunbathing areas of the Eden Roc, which are located in the southern portion of its property.

In this action, plaintiff-appellee sought to enjoin the defendants-appellants from proceeding with the construction of the addition to the Fontainebleau (it appears to have been roughly eight stories high at the time suit was filed), alleging that the construction would interfere with the light and air on the beach in front of the Eden Roc and cast a shadow of such size as to render the beach wholly unfitted for the use and enjoyment of its guests, to the irreparable injury of the plaintiff.... It was also alleged that the construction would interfere with the easements of light and air enjoyed by plaintiff and its predecessors in title for more than twenty years....

The chancellor heard considerable testimony on the issues made by the complaint and the answer and, as noted, entered a temporary injunction restraining the defendants from continuing with the construction of the addition. His reason for so doing was stated by him, in a memorandum opinion, as follows:

> "In granting the temporary injunction in this case the Court wishes to make several things very clear. The ruling is not based on any alleged presumptive title nor prescriptive right of the plaintiff to light and air nor is it based on any deed restrictions nor recorded plats in the title of the plaintiff nor of the defendant nor of any plat of record. It is not based on any zoning ordinance nor on any provision of the building code of the City of Miami Beach nor on the decision of any court, nisi prius or appellate. It is based solely on the proposition that no one has a right to use his property to the injury of another. In this case it is clear from the evidence that the proposed use by the Fontainebleau will materially damage the Eden Roc...."

This is indeed a novel application of the maxim *sic utere tuo ut alienum non laedas*. This maxim does not mean that one must never use his own property in such a way as to do any injury to his neighbor. It means only that one must use his property so as not to injure the lawful *rights* of another. [U]nder this maxim, ..."it is well settled that a property owner may put his own property to any reasonable and lawful use, so long as he does not thereby deprive the adjoining landowner of any right of enjoyment of his property which is recognized and protected by law, and so long as his use is not such a one as the law will pronounce a nuisance."

No American decision has been cited, and independent research has revealed none, in which it has been held that—in the absence of some contractual or statutory obligation—a landowner has a legal right to the free flow of light and air across the adjoining land of his neighbor. Even at common law, the landowner had no legal right, in the absence of an easement or uninterrupted use and enjoyment for a period of 20 years, to unobstructed light and air from the adjoining land....

There being, then, no legal right to the free flow of light and air from the adjoining land, it is universally held that where a structure serves a useful and beneficial purpose, it does not give rise to a cause of action, either for damages or for an injunction under the maxim *sic utere tuo ut alienum non laedas*, even though it causes injury to another by cutting off the light and air and interfering with the view that would otherwise be available over adjoining land in its natural state, regardless of the fact that the structure may have been erected partly for spite....

We see no reason for departing from this universal rule. If, as contended on behalf of plaintiff, public policy demands that a landowner in the Miami Beach area refrain from constructing buildings on his premises that will cast a shadow on the adjoining premises, an amendment of its comprehensive planning and zoning ordinance, applicable to the public as a whole, is the means by which such purpose should be achieved. (No opinion is expressed here as to the validity of such an ordinance, if one should be enacted pursuant to the requirements of law. Cf. City of Miami Beach v. State ex rel. Fontainebleau Hotel Corp., Fla.App.1959, 108 So.2d 614, 619; certiorari denied, Fla.1959, 111 So.2d 437.) But to change the universal rule—and the custom followed in this state since its inception— that adjoining landowners have an equal right under the law to build to the line of their respective tracts and to such a height as is desired by them (in absence, of course, of building restrictions or regulations) amounts, in our opinion, to judicial legislation....

The record affirmatively shows that no statutory basis for the right sought to be enforced by plaintiff exists. The so-called Shadow Ordinance enacted by the City of Miami Beach at plaintiff's behest was held invalid in City of Miami Beach v. State ex rel. Fontainebleau Hotel Corp., supra. It also affirmatively appears that there is no possible basis for holding that plaintiff has an easement for light and air, either express or implied, across defendants' property, nor any prescriptive right thereto....

* * *

Since it affirmatively appears that the plaintiff has not established a cause of action against the defendants by reason of the structure here in question, the order granting a temporary injunction should be and it is hereby reversed with directions to dismiss the complaint.

Reversed with directions.

Notes and Questions

1. The Coase Theorem: Coase's analysis suggests that free-market economies will tend to produce an efficient resource allocation whenever property rights are clearly assigned and the transaction costs of exchanging them are sufficiently low. When these conditions are met, efficiency will occur regardless of the initial distribution of property rights.

For example, in *Miller v. Schoene*, the apple grower would assess the probable damage to his crop and be willing to pay up to that amount to eliminate the damage. Similarly, the cedar grower would assess the additional value of his standing trees over their cut value, and be willing to accept any greater amount to cut them down. Thus, regardless of the initial distribution of property rights, if the apple growers' damage was greater than the cedar growers' additional value of standing trees, and, again, assuming costless transactions, the apple grower would compensate the cedar grower to cut down his trees. For additional discussion of *Miller v. Schoene*, see James M. Buchanan, *Politics, Property, and the Law: An Alternative Interpretation of* Miller et al. v. Schoene, 15 Journal of Law & Economics 439, 443 (1972).

Moreover, according to the Coase Theorem, government intervention in the form of pollution guidelines, tax penalties, and the like cannot improve upon a settlement negotiated by those parties who are directly involved in the externality problem. The Coase Theorem, which is discussed in more detail in Chapter IV on Externalities, was first published in 1960. Ronald H. Coase, *The Problem of Social Cost*, 3 Journal of Law & Economics 1–44 (1960), is the most cited economics article for the period since its publication. Other economists, not Coase himself, named his insight The Coase Theorem.

2. Let the Bargaining Begin: In order for the Coasian bargaining to begin, property rights must be clearly assigned and alienable. Suppose that there was no legal system to enforce property rights and contracts dealing with property rights. Neighbors would be reluctant to pay a firm not to pollute because, after accepting the payment, the firm could renege on its promise to reduce pollution and the neighbors would have no legal recourse. Obviously, one would be surprised to see market solutions to externality problems under such conditions. In one sense, the *Fontainebleau* case is merely about clarifying the initial assignment of rights. Once it is clear that the Fontainebleau has the right to build, there is opportunity for the Eden Roc to purchase that right from it. On the other hand, suppose the plaintiff had won the lawsuit and the court issued a permanent injunction against building the addition. Does the initial assignment of property rights affect the ultimate allocation?

3. Caveat: Transaction Costs: Coase recognized that, in order for the free market to solve the problem of externalities, transaction costs—which include search and information costs, bargaining and decision costs, and policing and enforcement costs—must be low. High transaction costs can prevent a preferred, wealth enhancing exchange from occurring. In our pollution example, the firm might be willing to limit its pollution for a payment that is far less than the collective damage imposed on the neighbors, but the costs of bargaining with the firm combined with the costs of reaching agreement on how the neighbors split the payment can prevent the mutually beneficial agreement from being reached. Generally, the costs of reaching an agreement increase with the number of bargainers. In our example, the likelihood of reaching an efficient agreement is highest if the firm only has to bargain with one neighbor who owns all the surrounding property. One exception, however, is when two parties are locked into dealing with each other, rather than being able to seek out another party with whom to deal (the problem of "bilateral monopoly"). Were the transaction costs low in *Fontainebleau*?

4. Caveat: Wealth Effects: The Coase Theorem concerns the allocation of resources; it also has important implications for the distribution of resources (wealth). For example, the initial allocation of legal rights means that the initial holder of the rights will be able to continue a given activity without having to pay or will have to be paid to stop engaging in the activity, instead of vice versa. The opportunity cost of refusing to sell one's initial allocation of property rights is determined by how much others are willing to pay. If the others do not have the wealth to purchase the rights, then transactions will not occur. Moreover, some parties might find it easier to refuse to accept offers to buy their rights than to garner the resources to buy the rights if they are initially allocated to the other party.

5. Politics and the Assignment of Property Rights: The Coase Theorem demonstrates how voluntary exchange can solve conflicts over the use of property. The plaintiff in *Fontainebleau* attempted to avoid the bargaining process by using the political process to engineer the passage of the Shadow Ordinance. Evidently, the plaintiff believed that it was cheaper to use the power of the state to coerce the defendant into not building the addition than to pay for the right. The plaintiff then attempted a novel legal theory to avoid having to pay the Fontainebleau not to expand.

C. Legal Analysis and the Art of Economics

An important distinction between traditional legal analysis of cases and the economic analysis of law is found in the overall perspectives of legal versus economic analysis. Legal analysis tends to adopt an *ex post* perspective while economic analysis adopts an *ex ante* perspective. An *ex post* **perspective** means that one makes a decision today on the basis of yesterday's activity. By the time a case reaches a courtroom, the events that have precipitated the litigation have occurred. In other words, the court is faced with apportioning gains (or losses) among the parties to the suit, with the total gain (or loss) having been fixed by the prior events. Traditional legal analysis tends to focus on the distribution of wealth in a static setting. Yet, any decision by the court that modifies or creates a legal rule will affect the decisions of future parties. In contrast, an *ex ante* **perspective** means that one considers the consequences of today's decisions on tomorrow's activity. Instead of after-the-fact static analysis of the distributional consequences of a ruling, the *ex ante* perspective considers the dynamic consequences of today's decision on future economic actors who are not parties to the present dispute.

The *ex ante* perspective is merely a reflection of economic principles:

> The art of economics consists in looking not merely at the immediate but also at the longer effects of any act or policy; it consists in tracing the consequences of that policy not merely for one group but for all groups.[4]

Economics is forward looking. For example, the concept of opportunity cost tells us that the cost of engaging in any activity is the value of the next best alternative activity that could have been undertaken. That is, opportunity cost is determined by making the decision to do one activity in the future at the expense of some alternative future activity. Also, economics says that incentives matter — alternative legal rules will have an impact on future behavior.

Eldred v. Ashcroft

Supreme Court of the United States
537 U.S. 186 (2003)

JUSTICE GINSBURG delivered the opinion of the Court.

This case concerns the authority the Constitution assigns to Congress to prescribe the duration of copyrights. The Copyright and Patent Clause of the Constitution, Art. I, § 8, cl. 8, provides as to copyrights: "Congress shall have Power ... to promote the Progress of Science ... by securing [to Authors] for limited Times ... the exclusive Right to their ...

---

4. Henry Hazlitt, Economics in One Lesson 5 (1947).

Writings." In 1998, in the measure here under inspection, Congress enlarged the duration of copyrights by 20 years. Copyright Term Extension Act (CTEA), Pub. L. 105-298, § 102(b) and (d). As in the case of prior extensions, principally in 1831, 1909, and 1976, Congress provided for application of the enlarged terms to existing and future copyrights alike.

Petitioners are individuals and businesses whose products or services build on copyrighted works that have gone into the public domain. They seek a determination that the CTEA fails constitutional review under ... the Copyright Clause's "limited Times" prescription.... Under the 1976 Copyright Act, copyright protection generally lasted from the work's creation until 50 years after the author's death. Under the CTEA, most copyrights now run from creation until 70 years after the author's death. Petitioners do not challenge the "life-plus-70-years" time span itself.... Congress went awry, petitioners maintain, not with respect to newly created works, but in enlarging the term for published works with existing copyrights....

In accord with the District Court and the Court of Appeals, we reject petitioners' challenges to the CTEA. In that 1998 legislation, as in all previous copyright term extensions, Congress placed existing and future copyrights in parity. In prescribing that alignment, we hold, Congress acted within its authority and did not transgress constitutional limitations.

* * *

We address first the determination of the courts below that Congress has authority under the Copyright Clause to extend the terms of existing copyrights. Text, history, and precedent, we conclude, confirm that the Copyright Clause empowers Congress to prescribe "limited Times" for copyright protection and to secure the same level and duration of protection for all copyright holders, present and future.

* * *

Congress' consistent historical practice of applying newly enacted copyright terms to future and existing copyrights reflects a judgment stated concisely by Representative Huntington at the time of the 1831 Act: "Justice, policy, and equity alike forbid" that an "author who had sold his [work] a week ago, be placed in a worse situation than the author who should sell his work the day after the passing of [the] act." The CTEA follows this historical practice by keeping the duration provisions of the 1976 Act largely in place and simply adding 20 years to each of them. Guided by text, history, and precedent, we cannot agree with petitioners' submission that extending the duration of existing copyrights is categorically beyond Congress' authority under the Copyright Clause.

Satisfied that the CTEA complies with the "limited Times" prescription, we turn now to whether it is a rational exercise of the legislative authority conferred by the Copyright Clause. On that point, we defer substantially to Congress.

The CTEA reflects judgments of a kind Congress typically makes, judgments we cannot dismiss as outside the Legislature's domain. As respondent describes, a key factor in the CTEA's passage was a 1993 European Union (EU) directive instructing EU members to establish a copyright term of life plus 70 years. Consistent with the Berne Convention, the EU directed its members to deny this longer term to the works of any non-EU country whose laws did not secure the same extended term. By extending the baseline United States copyright term to life plus 70 years, Congress sought to ensure that American authors would receive the same copyright protection in Europe as their European counterparts. The CTEA may also provide greater incentive for American and other authors to create and disseminate their work in the United States.

In addition to international concerns, Congress passed the CTEA in light of demographic, economic, and technological changes,[5] and rationally credited projections that longer terms would encourage copyright holders to invest in the restoration and public distribution of their works.[6]

* * *

As we read the Framers' instruction, the Copyright Clause empowers Congress to determine the intellectual property regimes that, overall, in that body's judgment, will serve the ends of the Clause. Beneath the facade of their inventive constitutional interpretation, petitioners forcefully urge that Congress pursued very bad policy in prescribing the CTEA's long terms. The wisdom of Congress' action, however, is not within our province to second guess. Satisfied that the legislation before us remains inside the domain the Constitution assigns to the First Branch, we affirm the judgment of the Court of Appeals.

It is so ordered.

JUSTICE STEVENS, dissenting

* * *

… [R]espondent relies on concerns of equity to justify the retroactive extension. If Congress concludes that a longer period of exclusivity is necessary in order to provide an adequate incentive to authors to produce new works, respondent seems to believe that simple fairness requires that the same lengthened period be provided to authors whose works have already been completed and copyrighted. This is a classic non sequitur. The reason for increasing the inducement to create something new simply does not apply to an already-created work. To the contrary, the equity argument actually provides strong support for petitioners. Members of the public were entitled to rely on a promised access to copyrighted or patented works at the expiration of the terms specified when the exclusive privileges were granted. On the other hand, authors will receive the full benefit of the exclusive terms that were promised as an inducement to their creativity, and have no equitable claim to increased compensation for doing nothing more.

---

5. Members of Congress expressed the view that, as a result of increases in human longevity and in parents' average age when their children are born, the pre-CTEA term did not adequately secure "the right to profit from licensing one's work during one's lifetime and to take pride and comfort in knowing that one's children — and perhaps their children — might also benefit from one's posthumous popularity." Also cited was "the failure of the U.S. copyright term to keep pace with the substantially increased commercial life of copyrighted works resulting from the rapid growth in communications media."

6. JUSTICE BREYER urges that the economic incentives accompanying copyright term extension are too insignificant to "move" any author with a "rational economic perspective." Calibrating rational economic incentives, however, like "fashioning … new rules [in light of] new technology," is a task primarily for Congress, not the courts. Congress heard testimony from a number of prominent artists; each expressed the belief that the copyright system's assurance of fair compensation for themselves and their heirs was an incentive to create. We would not take Congress to task for crediting this evidence which, as JUSTICE BREYER acknowledges, reflects general "propositions about the value of incentives" that are "undeniably true."

Congress also heard testimony from Register of Copyrights Marybeth Peters and others regarding the economic incentives created by the CTEA. According to the Register, extending the copyright for existing works "could … provide additional income that would finance the production and distribution of new works." "Authors would not be able to continue to create," the Register explained, "unless they earned income on their finished works. The public benefits not only from an author's original work but also from his or her further creations. Although this truism may be illustrated in many ways, one of the best examples is Noah Webster[,] who supported his entire family from the earnings on his speller and grammar during the twenty years he took to complete his dictionary."

* * *

JUSTICE BREYER, dissenting.

* * *

This statute, like virtually every copyright statute, imposes upon the public certain expression-related costs in the form of (1) royalties that may be higher than necessary to evoke creation of the relevant work, and (2) a requirement that one seeking to reproduce a copyrighted work must obtain the copyright holder's permission. The first of these costs translates into higher prices that will potentially restrict a work's dissemination. The second means search costs that themselves may prevent reproduction even where the author has no objection....

* * *

What copyright-related benefits might justify the statute's extension of copyright protection? First, no one could reasonably conclude that copyright's traditional economic rationale applies here. The extension will not act as an economic spur encouraging authors to create new works. No potential author can reasonably believe that he has more than a tiny chance of writing a classic that will survive commercially long enough for the copyright extension to matter. After all, if, after 55 to 75 years, only 2% of all copyrights retain commercial value, the percentage surviving after 75 years or more (a typical pre-extension copyright term) — must be far smaller. And any remaining monetary incentive is diminished dramatically by the fact that the relevant royalties will not arrive until 75 years or more into the future, when, not the author, but distant heirs, or shareholders in a successor corporation, will receive them. Using assumptions about the time value of money provided us by a group of economists (including five Nobel prize winners), Brief for George A. Akerlof et al. as *Amici Curiae* 5–7, it seems fair to say that, for example, a 1% likelihood of earning $100 annually for 20 years, starting *75 years into the future*, is worth less than seven cents today.

What potential Shakespeare, Wharton, or Hemingway would be moved by such a sum? What monetarily motivated Melville would not realize that he could do better for his grandchildren by putting a few dollars into an interest-bearing bank account? The Court itself finds no evidence to the contrary. It refers to testimony before Congress (1) that the copyright system's incentives encourage creation, and (2) (referring to Noah Webster) that income earned from one work can help support an artist who " 'continues to create.' " But the first of these amounts to no more than a set of undeniably true propositions about the value of incentives *in general*. And the applicability of the second to *this* Act is mysterious. How will extension help today's Noah Webster create new works 50 years after his death? Or is that hypothetical Webster supposed to support himself with the extension's present discounted value, *i.e.*, a few pennies? Or (to change the metaphor) is the argument that Dumas *fils* would have written more books had Dumas *pere*'s Three Musketeers earned more royalties?

Regardless, even if this cited testimony were meant more specifically to tell Congress that somehow, somewhere, some potential author might be moved by the thought of great-grandchildren receiving copyright royalties a century hence, so might some potential author also be moved by the thought of royalties being paid for two centuries, five centuries, 1,000 years, "til the End of Time." And from a rational economic perspective the time difference among these periods *makes no real difference*. The present extension will produce a copyright period of protection that, even under conservative assumptions, is worth more than *99.8%* of protection *in perpetuity* (more than *99.99%* for a songwriter like Irving Berlin and a song like Alexander's Ragtime Band). The lack of a practically meaningful distinction from an author's *ex ante* perspective between (a) the statute's extended terms and (b) an infinite term makes this latest extension difficult to square with the Constitution's insistence on "limited Times."

* * *

In any event, the incentive-related numbers are far too small for Congress to have concluded rationally, even with respect to new works, that the extension's economic-incentive effect could justify the serious expression-related harms earlier described. And, of course, in respect to works already created—the source of many of the harms previously described—*the statute creates no economic incentive at all.*

Second, the Court relies heavily for justification upon international uniformity of terms. Although it can be helpful to look to international norms and legal experience in understanding American law, in this case the justification based upon foreign rules is surprisingly weak.

* * *

Finally, the Court mentions as possible justifications "demographic, economic, and technological changes"—by which the Court apparently means the facts that today people communicate with the help of modern technology, live longer, and have children at a later age. The first fact seems to argue not for, but instead against, extension. The second fact seems already corrected for by the 1976 Act's life-plus-50 term, which automatically grows with lifespans. And the third fact—that adults are having children later in life—is a makeweight at best, providing no explanation of why the 1976 Act's term of 50 years after an author's death—a longer term than was available to authors themselves for most of our Nation's history—is an insufficient potential bequest. The weakness of these final rationales simply underscores the conclusion that emerges from consideration of earlier attempts at justification: There is no legitimate, serious copyright-related justification for this statute.

* * *

This analysis leads inexorably to the conclusion that the statute cannot be understood rationally to advance a constitutionally legitimate interest. The statute falls outside the scope of legislative power that the Copyright Clause, read in light of the First Amendment, grants to Congress. I would hold the statute unconstitutional. I respectfully dissent.

Notes and Questions

1. Ex Post v. Ex Ante Analysis: Now-Judge (then-law professor) Frank Easterbrook explains the distinction between *ex post* and *ex ante* analysis from an economic perspective, with specific application to intellectual property cases:

> The nature of litigation invites judges to treat the parties' circumstances as fixed and to apportion gains and losses.... [For example,] [o]nce a firm possesses a patent and tries to extract royalties, it may seem wise to restrict the devices available to that end; the royalties lead to less use of the invention and consequent social loss, while restricting the collection of royalties has no visible social costs....
>
> When judges take the positions of the parties as given, however, they forfeit any opportunity to create gains through the formulation of the legal rule. The principles laid down today will influence whether similar parties *will be* in similar situations tomorrow. Indeed, judges who look at cases merely as occasions for the fair apportionment of gains and losses almost invariably ensure that there

will be fewer gains and more losses tomorrow.... [Thus,] [w]hen a court restricts the patent holder's ability to collect royalties, it reduces the rewards anticipated from patents and thus the incentive for other people to invent.

* * *

... Judges who see economic transactions as zero-sum games are likely to favor "fair" divisions of the gains and losses. If the stakes are established in advance and will not be altered by courts, why should judges harshly require one party to bear the whole loss or allow another to take the gain? Yet if legal rules can create larger gains (or larger losses), the claim from fairness becomes weaker. The judge will pay less attention to today's unfortunates and more attention to the affects of rules.

* * *

The first line of inquiry, then is whether the Justices take an ex ante or an ex post perspective in analyzing issues. Which they take will depend, in part, on the extent to which they appreciate how the economic system creates new gains and losses; those who lack this appreciation will favor "fair" treatment of the parties.

Frank H. Easterbrook, *The Supreme Court, 1983 Term: Foreword: The Court and the Economic System*, 98 Harvard Law Review 4, 10–12 (1984). In other words, the perspective the court adopts, either *ex ante* or *ex post* or some combination, will change incentives and behavior at the margin.

2. Why Protect Intellectual Property Rights?: The standard economic case for protecting intellectual property rights, such as the copyright protection given to creative works at issue in *Eldred*, takes very much an *ex ante* perspective: to provide a greater incentive for authors to write, musicians to compose, and artists to paint by restricting the ability of others to copy those works without permission (and possible royalty payment to the creator). Mark Lemley describes this "traditional economic justification for intellectual property" as follows:

> Ideas are public goods: they can be copied freely and used by anyone who is aware of them without depriving others of their use. But ideas also take time and money to create. Because ideas are so easy to spread and so hard to control, only with difficulty may creators recoup their investment in creating the idea. As a result, absent intellectual property protection, most would prefer to copy rather than create ideas, and inefficiently few ideas would be created.

Mark A. Lemley, *Ex Ante versus Ex Post Justifications for Intellectual Property*, 71 University of Chicago Law Review 129, 129 (2004); see also William M. Landes & Richard A. Posner, The Economic Structure of Intellectual Property Law 11–36 (2003) (comparing the economics of property rights generally with the economics of intellectual property rights). Thus, an important justification for the Copyright Term Extension Act (CTEA), which extended the term of copyright protection by twenty years, was that it would "provide greater incentive for American and other authors to create and disseminate their work in the United States." Conversely, an *ex post* perspective on intellectual property rights would, as Judge Easterbrook indicated, focus on the "fairness" of the distribution of royalties, without regard to any incentive effects.

3. How Much Greater of an Incentive?: The majority and dissent disagreed in *Eldred* over how much of an additional incentive (i.e., incentive at the margin) the additional twenty years of protection would provide. Because those additional years are added to the end of the previous term (the creator's lifetime plus fifty years), we need to adjust the potential value of any additional royalties for how long it will be before the creator receives them. That adjustment is made by calculating the present value of the additional royalties. As we will see throughout these materials, present value is a fundamental concept underlying value. The present value of an asset (or anything) is a single number that captures the future stream of benefits or costs of an activity, adjusted for the fact that a benefit received later is worth less than the same benefit received sooner. This adjustment is calculated by discounting the stream by the appropriate interest rate. The process is explained in more detail in Chapter X, but the economists' brief in *Eldred* does the calculations for us, demonstrating that the marginal benefit today of the future royalties is exceedingly small. As Justice Breyer's dissent states: "for example, a 1% likelihood of earning $100 annually for 20 years, starting *75 years into the future*, is worth less than seven cents today."

4. Ex Post Analysis: Dividing Up the Pie: However, the CTEA extended the copyright term not only for newly created works, but also for existing works. Justice Breyer plainly is correct that the additional royalties cannot increase the incentive for creating existing works because those works already have been created! So what justification is there for extending the copyright term for existing works? Here the government in defending the statute fell back on considerations of fairness, arguing that fairness required existing copyright holders to be treated the same as creators of new works. But what about fairness to those who wanted to use the existing works without having to incur the costs of negotiating permission agreements or paying royalties? In enacting the CTEA, Congress basically redivided the pie between existing copyright holders and potential users of works in the public domain. Indeed, one of the strongest supporters of the CTEA was the Disney Corporation, whose copyright on Mickey Mouse was soon to expire. Hence, the CTEA is sometimes called the "Mickey Mouse Law" (pun intended, no doubt). In Chapter III we will discuss further how interest groups lobby for laws that provide them with special benefits and protections, an activity economists call "rent seeking."

5. Law and Economics and Justice: Sometimes law and economics is criticized for not taking into account the "justice" element of a case or controversy. How does the ex ante perspective help us understand ex post "justice"?

D. Game Theory

Many economic decisions are made in a setting of imperfect information where one decision maker knows that the actions of other decision makers will impact the outcome of his or her decision. This interdependence requires decision makers to develop a strategy for dealing with the imperfect information. Game theory is the area of economics that has developed to deal with mutual interdependence and imperfect information. Recent developments in game theory have provided many insights for the economic analysis of law.

Game theory analyzes the behavior of "players" in conflict situations governed by rules. As one might expect, the expected outcome—or **dominant strategy**—of the games is determined by the stakes under alternative rules. The relevance of this area of economics to law is obvious, as law is often concerned with conflict within a set of rules. Game theory helps predict how the strategies of players change and how the expected outcomes vary as the players are faced with alternative rules.

The most basic model of game theory is the Prisoners' Dilemma. The Prisoners' Dilemma is best introduced through a hypothetical story. Adam and Baker work together in the accounting office of a major New York bank. They are best friends. One day an auditor shows up and, after a thorough audit of the bank's accounts, determines that $1 million has been embezzled. Upon further investigation, all available circumstantial evidence indicates that only Adam or Baker could have committed the crime. However, there is no evidence—such as conspicuous consumption of automobiles, vacations, and so forth—to indicate which one committed the crime. In fact, the police suspect that they were in it together. Remember, they are (were?) best friends. Both Adam and Baker are charged with embezzlement. The police are confident that they can convict both defendants on the available evidence, but securing a confession of a conspiracy from one of the defendants would save the police a lot of time and effort. Both Adam and Baker claim to be innocent.

Immediately following their arrests, Adam and Baker are held in separate cells in the City Jail. They are totally shut off from one another—communication of any type is impossible. The City Prosecutor, who does not want to go through a long trial, makes the following offer to Adam: (I) If you refuse to testify, and if Baker continues to maintain his silence, you will be convicted of criminally negligent bookkeeping (a new crime created in the wake of the Enron and WorldCom debacles of 2001 and 2002) and sentenced to 3 years in prison; (II) If you agree to testify against Baker, and if Baker continues to maintain his silence, then the charges against you will be dropped; (III) If you refuse to testify, and if Baker testifies against you, then you will go to jail for 15 years; (IV) If both you and Baker testify against each other, then you will both go to jail for 10 years. Finally, the City Prosecutor says that his assistant is simultaneously making the exact same offer to Baker.

The Prisoners' Dilemma is evident when Adam's choices are presented in matrix form. The payoffs to Adam under alternative strategies are represented in Figure I-2 (a). Cells I-IV indicate the rules of the game as set forth by the City Prosecutor. Baker's behavior, which is totally exogenous (beyond Adam's control), is represented by the column on the left side of the matrix. Adam's strategy is represented by the row at the top of the matrix. The four cells represent the four possible outcomes of Adam's dilemma. In the formal language of game theory, the four cells are referred to as the "choice space" or "opportunity set." Consideration of the matrix reveals that the testify strategy **dominates** the silence strategy. No matter what strategy Baker chooses, Adam is better off having chosen to testify. But this is not the end of the story.

Recall that at the same time that the City Prosecutor is making his pitch to Adam, his assistant is making the exact same offer to Baker. Baker's opportunity set is presented in Figure I-2 (b). Clearly, the testify strategy also dominates for Baker—it always results in the lowest jail sentence.

The Prisoners' Dilemma is revealed when the symmetrical payoff functions are combined in a single matrix. In Figure I-2 (c), the payoffs to Adam are indicated by the right-hand numbers in each cell. The payoffs to Baker are indicated by the left-hand numbers. Since the prosecutors' rules make it individually rational for each party to adopt the testify strategy, the **solution** to this game is predicted to be Cell IV. In economic models, such a predictable solution is referred to as an equilibrium. The true nature of the Prisoners' Dilemma is revealed by the observation that Cell IV contains the largest total number of years in prison. Adam and Baker would both be better off if they could make an enforceable contract under which both agree to remain silent. Cell I appears very attractive relative to ending up in Cell IV.

Figure I-2. Prisoner's Dilemma

Figure (a) - Adam's Payoff

	Adam Stays Quiet	Adam Talks
Baker Stays Quiet	I -3	II 0
Baker Talks	III -15	IV -10

Figure (b) - Baker's Payoff

	Adam Stays Quiet	Adam Talks
Baker Stays Quiet	I -3	II -15
Baker Talks	III 0	IV -10

Figure (c) - Combined Payoffs (Adam, Baker)

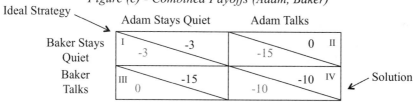

Ideal Strategy

	Adam Stays Quiet	Adam Talks
Baker Stays Quiet	I -3 / -3	II -15 / 0
Baker Talks	III 0 / -15	IV -10 / -10

Solution

Page v. United States

United States Court of Appeals for the Seventh Circuit

884 F.2d 300 (1989)

Easterbrook, J.

Students of strategy and bargaining cut their teeth on the game of Prisoners' Dilemma. Two prisoners, unable to confer with one another, must decide whether to take the prosecutor's offer: confess, inculpate the other, and serve a year in jail, or keep silent and serve five years. If the prisoners could make a (binding) bargain with each other, they would keep silent and both would go free. But they can't communicate, and each fears that the other will talk. So both confess. Studying Prisoners' Dilemma has led to many insights about strategic interactions. See Thomas C. Schelling, *The Strategy of Conflict* 53–80, 119–61 (1960; 1980 rev.); Robert Axelrod, *The Evolution of Cooperation* (1984). Eldon Page did not have the leisure to study the game before he had to play it.

Page and Maurice Falls were charged with armed bank robbery. On the day set for Page's trial, the prosecutor appeared with Falls in tow. Falls had signed an agreement promising, in exchange for a lower sentence, to plead guilty and testify against Page. After the judge accepted Falls' plea, Page caved in and pleaded guilty too. Back in jail, Falls and Page were able at last to coordinate. Each presently asked leave to withdraw his plea. Too late, the judge said. Both were sentenced and appealed. We affirmed in an unpublished order.

Page tried again, filing a petition under 28 U.S.C. § 2255 and arguing that trial counsel rendered ineffective assistance in letting him plead guilty. This was brought up short by the fact that Page had not argued on his original appeal that trial counsel was constitutionally inadequate. Because Page had fresh counsel for the appeal, the omission forfeits the point unless Page could establish "cause" for and "prejudice" from the neglect. See *Wainwright v. Sykes*, 433 U.S. 72 (1977). Ineffective assistance of counsel is "cause," so Page maintains that his appellate counsel was ineffective in failing to challenge the effectiveness of trial counsel. Page also points to other aspects of appellate counsel's performance that he finds deficient. Fearing infinite regress, the district judge brushed aside all questions concerning appellate counsel and went straight to the foundation of the claim, holding that Page's trial counsel had supplied effective assistance and denying the petition for relief.

The first question facing us on Page's appeal is whether ineffective assistance of counsel may be raised at all, and if so in which court. The United States Attorney insists that the attack on appellate counsel comes too late. It, too, was surrendered because not raised on appeal. Such an argument is better suited to the works of Ionesco and Beckett than to the Federal Reporter. How could appellate counsel attack his own competence? Although this is not logically impossible (counsel could say, for example, that although he knew he ought to challenge trial counsel he had not had the time to prepare a brief on the subject), it is so implausible that we cannot demand it of counsel. Few of us have insight into our shortcomings; fewer still have the nerve to flaunt our own failings. Just as trial counsel need not attack his competence during trial, appellate counsel need not protest his inadequacies. That may be left to the next step in the process without fear of forfeiture.

"Where" is slightly more difficult than "whether." Two courts of appeals have held that the defendant's exclusive recourse is a motion asking the court of appeals to recall its mandate on the ground of counsel's inadequacy. *Feldman v. Henman*, 815 F.2d 1318, 1321–22 (9th Cir. 1987); *United States v. Winterhalder*, 724 F.2d 109, 111 (10th Cir. 1983). They reason that because district judges must obey the mandate of the court of appeals, and may not issue orders compelling appellate courts to do anything (such as hear the appeal anew, a common remedy for deficient appellate counsel), the claim must come to the court of appeals in the first instance. Other courts of appeals have allowed defendants to start in the district courts. E.g., *Mack v. Smith*, 659 F.2d 23, 25–26 (5th Cir. 1981); *United States v. DeFalco*, 644 F.2d 132, 137 (3d Cir. 1979). We join this latter group.

Section 2255 authorizes collateral attacks on criminal judgments. It also specifies the forum: "the court which imposed the [contested] sentence." That statutory designation prevails even though relief may call for revision of a judgment that has been affirmed by the court of appeals. Review of existing judgments simply defines a "collateral" attack. If the court of appeals has actually considered and rejected a claim of ineffective assistance of counsel on appeal, that decision binds the district court unless there has been an intervening change of law. But if the issue has never been presented on appeal, it is open in the district court as any other question would be under § 2255.

Relief does not require the district court to issue orders to the court of appeals. District courts may grant relief. Ineffective assistance may justify vacating and reentering the judgment of conviction, allowing a fresh appeal. It may also justify a new trial on occasion. Counsel is ineffective only if performance below the norms of the profession causes prejudice. *Strickland v. Washington*, 466 U.S. 668, 687 (1984). Prejudice means a "reasonable probability that, but for counsel's unprofessional errors, the result of the [appeal] would have been different," *id.* at 694. Showing a "reasonable probability" but not certainty supports a new judgment and a new appeal (so that we may decide whether the outcome *actually* would have been different). If the showing goes further and establishes to the district court's satisfaction that reversal would have been a sure thing, this must mean that the district judge has become convinced that there was a fatal error in the trial. *That* error—which may be reached once the ineffective assistance clears away the bar of

Wainwright v. Sykes—requires a new trial or other remedy adequate to rectify the wrong. So whether the remedy turns out to be a new appeal or a new trial, the district judge need not issue an order binding on this court. No rule of law forbids district courts to entertain proceedings that call into question the adequacy of counsel's performance on appeal. Because district courts are the best forums to conduct any inquiries into counsel's strategic decisions that may prove necessary, we conclude that Page properly filed this petition in the district court rather than our court.

Having got this far, however, Page is stymied. For appellate counsel need not raise all possible claims of error. One of the principal functions of appellate counsel is winnowing the potential claims so that the court may focus on those with the best prospects. Defendants need dedicated, skillful appellate counsel, not routineers who present every non-frivolous claim. (Recall the saw: "He needed a lawyer, and all he had was a member of the bar.") Page has not argued that his appellate counsel failed to advocate his cause skillfully on the initial appeal. He has argued, instead, that counsel left out an issue he deems meritorious. The district court responded by deciding that trial counsel had furnished effective assistance, as if the claim of ineffective appellate counsel were equivalent to proof.

The threshold question is not whether trial counsel was inadequate but whether trial counsel was so *obviously* inadequate that appellate counsel had to present that question to render adequate assistance. Counsel could be constitutionally deficient in omitting a dead-bang winner even while zealously pressing other strong (but unsuccessful) claims. Page falls well short of making such a showing, however. Counsel advised Page to get the best deal he could after Falls turned against him. Page is not the first and will not be the last to feel the sting of Prisoners' Dilemma, and the Constitution does not demand that counsel escape a predicament that game theorists consider inescapable in one-shot performances. The district judge found that Page's lawyer prepared conscientiously for trial, made appropriate motions, and would have gone forward had Page stood on his former plea of innocence. Page insists that trial counsel lied when informing him that Falls would testify against him; as the district court observed, this is what Falls had promised to do in the written plea agreement. We need not agree with the district court's conclusion that trial counsel was adequate to see that appellate counsel could have made a reasoned decision to pursue other arguments instead. Page's remaining claims—that appellate counsel did not consult "meaningfully" with him in preparing the appeal, that counsel's briefs were vague, that counsel did not file a petition for rehearing after losing—are insufficient to call into question the adequacy of the representation.

AFFIRMED.

Notes and Questions

1. Rational Self-Interest: Given the rules of the Prisoners' Dilemma game, neither party would make a different choice even if they could talk before they made their plea. In their meeting, they could say that they would cooperate with each other and not confess, however, a rational self-interested person would nonetheless confess. Also, even if each person *knew* what the other would do, they would still choose to confess on each other. Many students find it difficult to understand why individuals like Adam and Baker are *always* better off by confessing. The most common mistake is inadvertently to change the rules of the game. For instance, many people use sanctions (like the Mafia) to change outcomes or they use personal feelings to change the game. Many people say that they would rather cooperate and feel "good" about themselves. However, subject to the caveat in the next note, it is always better to confess against the other person than spend a few extra years in prison.

2. Solving the Prisoners' Dilemma: It has been suggested that one of the reasons the Mafia — or organized crime, in general — has been successful is that the threat of **sanctions** (that is, execution) for testifying against another member has enabled them to avoid Cell IV. What happens in this scenario is that the Mafia changes the payoffs of the game. A few more years in prison is preferable to a lesser sentence where you are killed. The federal witness protection program is intended to counteract the threat of revenge.

3. The Prosecutor's Incentives: The rules of the game determine the outcome, and the prosecutor makes the rules. A final point about the nature of game theory is revealed by a consideration of the prosecutor's strategy in the earlier story. Suppose the prosecutor is paid based on how many years of prison sentences he produces annually. Alternatively, suppose the prosecutor is paid based on the number of years times the number of individuals convicted. What is the prosecutor's optimal strategy under either set of rules?

4. Game Theory and the Law: Game theory has many applications to the economic analysis of law. As suggested by the basic Prisoners' Dilemma model, it raises questions about the procedural rules that apply to codefendants being represented by the same lawyer. Other applicable areas include cartel theory and antitrust law, bankruptcy and voidable preferential transfers, bank runs and deposit insurance, constitutional economics and social choice theory, apparently coercive contract terms, and the regulation of two-tier tender offers.

5. Advertising Wars: The Prisoners' Dilemma model helps explain behavior observed in the business world. Promotions by large fast-food chains are a prime example. McDonalds and Burger King participate in these promotions which raise production costs (prizes, promotional fees, etc.) to try and steal away the competitor's customers. As shown by Figure I-3, McDonalds would be better off to have the promotion, because no matter what Burger King does, McDonalds realizes more profits (and Burger King has less profits). Of course, Burger King applies the same logic and both franchises offer promotional contests. The dilemma for Burger King and McDonalds is that their joint profits could be maximized if they could coordinate and stay in Cell I. Unfortunately for the firms, they are not allowed to communicate about these contests because it would probably be a violation of the antitrust laws. The best action for each firm acting alone is Cell IV.

6. Game Theory in Law School: Many law school exams are graded on a curve and the professor is required to give grades so that a specific average, such as a B+, is attained.

Figure I-3. McDonald's & Burger King Prisoner's Dilemma

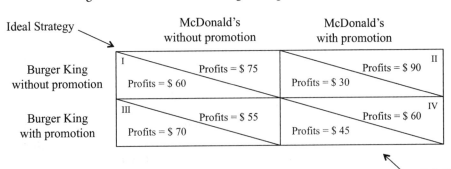

How does the Prisoners' Dilemma model explain the amount of effort law students devote toward studying for such an exam?

7. One-Shot versus Multiple Series Games: One of the major arguments against the Prisoners' Dilemma game is that it is only played one time. That is, if the actors could play multiple times they would realize the dilemma of the game and move from Cell IV to Cell I. These tacit collusive solutions — outcomes without specific, formal agreement — exist where, over an indefinite period of time, firms recognize their own interests will be served when they cooperate and maximize both firms' profits. However, in a multiple series game, where there is a definite ending point, there is a major incentive to cheat on the last round. That is, each firm cooperates until the last round, then they cheat. However, since each firm knows the other will cheat in the last round they cheat in the round before, and this logic works itself backward until the first round of the game. This is known as backward induction.

E. Positive versus Normative Economic Analysis

Economists have traditionally distinguished between positive and normative analysis. **Positive economic analysis** seeks to describe the world as it is, not as one thinks it should be, and thus is (theoretically) "value free." It seeks to explore the "natural" economic forces that constrain economic behavior. For example, positive economics look to the consequences of a change in a legal rule. Thus, positive economic analysis looks to the future in an effort to compare the consequences of alternative incentive structures. In some instances, the positive economist will identify one arrangement as more **efficient** (within the context of the model) than another, but the positive economist will not say that efficiency is necessarily the best outcome.

Normative analysis, in contrast, makes value judgments when it describes the world as it "ought to be." There is nothing inherently wrong with making normative statements about alternative economic arrangements; much of our Western philosophical tradition from Plato and Aristotle to Pope John Paul II (see, e.g., Centesimus Annus) is concerned with such issues. However, according to the dominant epistemology, there is no scientific way to show whether so-called normative statements are correct. Normative statements cannot be empirically tested. They cannot be falsified.

1. Positive Economic Analysis and Scientific Methodology

Positive economic analysis employs the scientific method — it uses logic to develop **hypotheses**, and tests these hypotheses against empirical evidence. The major advantage of engaging in positive analysis is that you will be able, at least theoretically, to identify the testable implications — in terms of benefits and costs — of implementing alternative institutional arrangements. That is, positive economic analysis provides a method to identify the trade-offs inherent in many policy decisions. As a result, positive economics helps inform the normative decision-making process.

However, as discussed by Nobel Laureate Milton Friedman, the conclusions of positive economics are rarely dispositive on policy issues: "Laymen and experts alike are inevitably tempted to shape positive conclusions to fit strongly held normative preconceptions and to reject positive conclusions if their normative implications — or what are said to be their normative implications — are unpalatable." Milton Friedman, Essays in Positive Economics 2 (1953). Moreover, even agreement about the conclusions of positive economics does not necessarily yield agreement about policy decisions: "Two individuals may agree on the consequences of a particular piece of legislation. One may regard them as desirable on balance and so favor the legislation; the other, as undesirable and so oppose the legislation." Id.

Because of the complexity of markets, economists use numerous abstract models, such as supply and demand (the subject of Chapter II), to develop social science theories about real world behavior. Theory may help us to **understand** and to explain **why**; it helps to develop a broad framework that can be applied to a large number of phenomena. A theory cannot be merely descriptive and dependent upon personalities, like history, but must develop a framework that survives over time. In the jargon of logic, theory deals in **universals.**

Additionally, a theory does not have to be realistic in order to be useful. Obviously, in order to have broad applicability, a theory must simplify and abstract from reality. In one important sense, a theory can be viewed as an instrument, whose value is not how well it conforms with complex reality, but rather in how well it predicts the results of certain events. The supply and demand model, for example, has proven to be very useful in predicting the price and quantity consequences of various stocks on almost every conceivable type of market, even when the market does not exhibit all the characteristics (assumptions) of the model. Thus, it is clear that in one important sense — **prediction** — a theory does not have to be realistic in order to be useful.

Economists employ a rigorous **scientific methodology** in investigating economic phenomena. Standard data collection and testing procedures must be followed in order for conclusions to be accepted as valid. Economists are often called upon to testify in lawsuits. In order for an economist's testimony to be admitted as evidence, the economist must adhere to scientific standards. As illustrated by the following case, the question of appropriate scientific methodology has taken on added significance in recent years.

In re Aluminum Phosphide Antitrust Litigation

United States District Court for the District of Kansas

893 F. Supp. 1497 (1995)

Kathryn H. Vratil, United States District Judge

This price-fixing case comes before the Court on *Defendants' Joint Motion in Limine to Exclude Dr. Richard C. Hoyt's Testimony and Expert Report From this Case*, filed May 5, 1995. Class action plaintiffs claim that defendants engaged in an illegal price-fixing conspiracy under the Sherman Act, 15 U.S.C. § 1, and — more specifically — that defendants conspired to fix the case price of aluminum phosphide pellets and tablets in the United States from January 1, 1988, through December 31, 1992. Plaintiffs seek damages on behalf of all entities (except those owned by defendants) which purchased such products during that period. Movants seek to preclude certain portions of the testimony and report of plaintiffs' economic expert, Dr. Richard C. Hoyt, under Federal Rules of Evidence 104(a), 403, 702, and 703.

On May 16, 1995, the Court held an evidentiary hearing on defendants' motion and heard the testimony of both Dr. Hoyt and defendants' economic expert, Dr. John J. Siegfried. Having considered the evidence adduced at that hearing, along with the expert reports of both Dr. Hoyt and Dr. Siegfried, the Court finds that defendants' motion should be and hereby is sustained in the respects and for the reasons set forth below.

A. Factual Background

Aluminum phosphide is a fumigant used to control insects in the storage of raw agricultural commodities and other food and non-food products. Aluminum phosphide reacts with moisture in the air and releases phosphine gas, which is toxic to insects. In the United States, aluminum phosphide is primarily sold in pellets and tablets....

* * *

In the late summer and early fall of 1991, the United States Department of Justice issued subpoenas with respect to an ongoing investigation of criminal price-fixing in the aluminum phosphide industry. On November 1, 1993, that investigation resulted in criminal indictments against [a number of companies in the industry. Defendants here are companies that pleaded guilty or *nolo contendere* to criminal price fixing charges.]

B. Findings of Fact

* * *

Once causation of damages has been established, the amount of damages may be determined by a just and reasonable estimate, as long as the jury verdict is not the product of speculation or guesswork.

Plaintiffs propose to supply this evidence through the expert testimony of Richard C. Hoyt, Ph.D., president of Analytics, Inc., an economics and statistical consulting firm in Excelsior, Minnesota. Dr. Hoyt has a doctorate in Agriculture and Applied Economics. He held teaching positions at the William Mitchell College of Law in St. Paul, Minnesota from 1977 to 1978, and the College of St. Thomas in St. Paul, Minnesota from 1978 to 1979. Since that time, Dr. Hoyt has devoted his full-time attention to forensic ends: a "partial list" of his experience as an expert witness includes 121 cases (42 antitrust cases, 15 contract cases, 21 discrimination cases, 29 injury/death cases, two patent cases, 10 stockholder suits, and two toxic waste cases).... Dr. Hoyt is an expert for hire.

Before and After Model

Dr. Hoyt proposes to testify to the fact and amount of damages caused by defendants' alleged conspiracy. Dr. Hoyt's opinion, according to his report dated March 27, 1995, is as follows: ... [T]he fact and the extent of defendants' supra competitive pricing can be measured by a "before and after" model which "generally compares defendants' prices in two distinct time periods (conspiratorial and normative) and calculates the degree to which prices were raised and/or maintained at artificially high levels." All parties agree that the "before and after" model is well accepted within the field of economics, and that it may be properly applied to determine the fact and the amount of damages in this case. The dispute is whether Dr. Hoyt indeed applied the "before and after" model, or whether his purported application is so fundamentally flawed as to render his conclusions inadmissible under *Daubert v. Merrell Dow Pharmaceuticals, Inc.*, U.S., 113 S. Ct. 2786 (1993).... As noted, the "before and after" model requires that actual prices during the conspiracy period be compared to estimated competitive prices that would have prevailed during that period, absent the conspiracy. The model therefore required Dr. Hoyt to determine estimated prices that would have prevailed during the conspiracy period, based on prices that prevailed during the normative or non-conspiratorial period....

In this case, Dr. Hoyt made the following findings and opinions concerning the estimated competitive prices that would have prevailed in the absence of a conspiracy:

(1) Estimated competitive prices for the conspiracy period (January 1, 1988 through December 31, 1992) are the prices which prevailed during the normative

period (the ten consecutive months from January 1 through October 31, 1993); and (2) The sole cause of the actual price differences between the conspiracy period and the normative period was the conspiracy itself.

The two prongs of Dr. Hoyt's analysis are critical to plaintiffs' case and they are discussed, in detail, below.

Selection of January 1 to October 31, 1993 as the Normative Period

Plaintiffs' price-fixing claim is set against a stage of generally declining prices after 1980.... [P]rior to 1980, the aluminum phosphide industry was dominated by a legal patent. After the patent expired, new competitors entered the market. Prices fell steadily as the advantage of the original patent monopoly eroded and four new competitors ... gained market share. The overall decline in the selling price of aluminum phosphide progressed steadily and continuously from 1980 through October, 1993 — except for a noticeable spike during roughly two quarters of 1990, coinciding with the admitted price-fixing episode by [several of the defendants].

* * *

Dr. Hoyt's opinion is that absent a conspiracy, the prices which prevailed during the first ten months of 1993 — the normative period — would have prevailed throughout each of the five preceding years, from January 1, 1988 through December 31, 1992.

* * *

Upon analysis, Dr. Hoyt's opinion is flawed in several obvious respects which render his conclusions irrelevant and inadmissible in this case:

First, Dr. Hoyt's opinion ignores the before component of the "before and after" model. Dr. Hoyt concedes that if pre-conspiracy data is available, the preferred scientific approach is to consult the data both before and after the conspiracy period. Under that approach, the economist has statistical bookends and may *interpolate* an estimated price line for any given conspiracy period instead of extrapolating an estimated price line from a single point in time. Although Dr. Hoyt had price information for all defendants for 1986 and 1987, his opinion does not address in any way the pre-conspiracy period. Therefore, Dr. Hoyt cannot account for the fact that prices before the alleged conspiracy are so substantially higher than the purportedly normal prices after the conspiracy.

* * *

Dr. Hoyt's methodology in selecting a normative period is not sound. Scientific learning in the field of economics offers no defensible reason why a prudent economist would select January 1 through October 31, 1993 as the normative period in this case. Recognized methodology for distinguishing the alleged violation period from the alleged non-violation period requires analysis of price patterns and statistical tests, including a "dummy variable approach," to determine whether for any proposed violation period the price was systematically higher than it would otherwise have been.[7] Because Dr. Hoyt failed to perform this and other relevant analysis, his choice of a normative period is not consistent with accepted economic practice. To use Dr. Siegfried words, "the way he selected the benchmark is [not] consistent with the way an economist would do it."

---

7. Dr. Siegfried applied the dummy variable approach to Dr. Hoyt's purported normative period, with surprising results. For two of the four companies on which Dr. Siegfried performed the dummy variable analysis, the statistical indicator method revealed that defendants' prices were actually *lower* than what would have been expected during the conspiracy period, January, 1988 through December, 1992. As a result, Dr. Siegfried concluded that Dr. Hoyt's benchmark period had "no basis."

Cause of Price Differences between the Conspiracy Period and the Normative Period

... In applying the "before and after" model of damages, it is fundamentally necessary to explain the pattern of forces outside the violation period using factors that might have changed (*i.e.*, supply, demand, and differences in competition) to predict the prices during the conspiratorial period. In this context, as in most economic problems, failure to keep "other things equal" is one of the known "pitfalls ... in the path of the serious economist." This case presents two potential normative periods, a "before" period and an "after" period that have distinctly different price levels. One therefore must identify the reasons for the disparate price levels. According to Dr. Siegfried, the field of economics supplies a statistical methodology for making this determination on a scientific basis, and the generally accepted means of predicting the prices that would have prevailed absent the conspiracy is regression analysis. At a minimum, regression analysis addresses supply and demand factors by looking at price trends over time. A prudent economist must account for these differences and would perform a minimum regression analysis if utilizing the "before and after" model.

Dr. Hoyt did not perform a regression analysis to address such obvious points as (1) why normative prices before the alleged conspiracy so greatly exceeded allegedly normative prices after the alleged conspiracy; or (2) the effect of supply, demand, competition or other factors that might impact price levels during both normative periods. Instead, Dr. Hoyt opined that any price increase between 1993 and the conspiracy period was caused solely by the alleged conspiracy. He took a simple weighted average of the actual prices for ten months during 1993 and assumed that price should have prevailed at all prior points in history. In doing so, Dr. Hoyt ignored price trends inside and outside the 1993 period, violating a fundamental rule of application for the "before and after" model. According to Dr. Siegfried, Dr. Hoyt's calculations did not take into account the effect of four factors: (1) a precipitous decline in demand for aluminum phosphide pellets and tablets, with downward pressure on prices, after 1988; (2) increased competition, with downward pressure on prices, because of new entrants into the market; (3) marked re-alignment in position between 1990 and 1993, as newcomers to the market ... captured the majority of the pellets and tablets market, leaving the existing sellers to defend the residual market by reducing prices; and (4) the fact that the aluminum phosphide market is an oligopolistic market, characterized by interdependent pricing, in which no independent seller believes that its actions will be ignored by the other sellers....

* * *

C. Conclusions of Law

* * *

In *Daubert*, the United States Supreme Court held that Rule 702, in conjunction with Rule 104(a), requires the trial judge to act as gatekeeper to ensure that scientific expert testimony is both reliable and relevant. The court found that the term "scientific knowledge" establishes a standard of evidentiary reliability. The court noted that the adjective "scientific" implies a "grounding in the methods and procedures of science," and the word "knowledge" means more than subjective belief or unsupported speculation and applies to any body of known facts or ideas inferred from such facts or accepted as truths on good grounds. The court concluded that in order to qualify as scientific knowledge, proposed expert testimony must be supported by appropriate validation, *i.e.*, good grounds based on what is known.... Plaintiffs argue that Daubert applies only to "hard" physical sciences which may be tested by scientific method, not social sciences such as economics. *Daubert* indeed enumerates four non-exclusive non-dispositive factors which the Court may consider: (1) whether the scientific theory or technique can be (and has been) tested; (2) whether the theory or technique has been subjected to peer review and publication; (3) known or potential rate of error; and (4) general acceptance in the scientific community. While each of these factors may not be relevant in determining the reliability of expert testimony on non-scientific or social science subjects, the Court has no doubt that *Daubert* requires it to act as a gatekeeper, to determine whether Dr. Hoyt's testimony and report are reliable and relevant under Rule 702. To the extent that *Daubert* factors are relevant to its determination, the Court considers them along with any other relevant factors.

* * *

Here ... plaintiffs call upon Dr. Hoyt not to supply specialized knowledge, but to plug evidentiary holes in plaintiffs' case, to speculate, and to surmise. One does not need an expert economist to do what Dr. Hoyt proposes to do. A non-expert, using Dr. Hoyt's criteria, could pick as an equally valid normative period any arbitrary time period, of any length, occurring at any time after the date of the admitted conspiracy. Dr. Hoyt's analysis is driven by a desire to enhance the measure of plaintiffs' damages, even at the expense of well-accepted scientific principles and methodology. Nothing in Dr. Hoyt's analysis makes the data for his so-called "normative" period more relevant than the data for any other pre- or post-conspiracy period, and the record yields no factual basis for any hypothesis that will support his calculations and opinion. Similarly, a non-expert could *assume* that price-fixing accounts for all differences in price between the conspiratorial period and the normative period. To the extent that Dr. Hoyt purports to cast that assumption as an affirmative declaration based upon scientific reason and analysis, however, the Court must reject it. Dr. Hoyt's conclusions are scientifically unsound and irrelevant under *Daubert*.

* * *

Notes and Questions

1. The Hired Gun: Dr. Hoyt's application of the "before and after" model was a poorly disguised attempt to increase the damages owed to the plaintiffs. Damages are supposed to be the difference between the actual price paid by the plaintiffs and the hypothetical price they would have paid "but for" the conspiracy. Obviously, the plaintiffs want to show that prices would have been much lower "but for" the conspiracy. In fact, the actual "before" prices were higher than the actual "after" prices. Not surprisingly, Dr. Hoyt opted for the lower "after" price, but Judge Vratil was not favorably impressed by the rigor of his analysis.

2. Ceteris paribus: Dr. Siegfried explained that Dr. Hoyt's approach was overly simplistic and did not take advantage of the standard economic techniques for investigating explanations for price changes. Market prices are determined by the interaction of supply and demand. The basic supply and demand model assumes that all forces that could impact market prices are held constant. This *ceteris paribus* assumption—*ceteris paribus* is the Latin phrase for "all other things held constant"—allows for the isolation and analysis of important variables. Unfortunately for Dr. Hoyt, the real world is more complicated—with numerous events impacting market prices at any given time. Economists have developed and applied statistical techniques to study the simultaneous impact of numerous changes on market prices. Thus, Judge Vratil simply held Dr. Hoyt to the professional standards of economists, as articulated by Dr. Siegfried.

3. Econometrics and Multiple Regression Analysis: Econometrics is the use of statistics to study and test economic phenomena. Multiple regression analysis is a statistical process for making precise and quantitative estimates of the effects of different factors on some variable of interest. For example, the variable of interest in the present case is the market price of aluminum phosphide. Data about factors that would be expected to impact on market price—that is, the factors affecting market demand and supply—could be collected for the periods before, during, and after the conspiracy. For example, demand could be affected by the crop size at a particular time of the year; supply could be affected by a change in the cost of a major input into the aluminum phosphide production process, or by an increase in the number of competitors supplying the compound to the market. In effect, multiple regression analysis attempts to isolate the impact of one variable on the price of aluminum phosphide by holding everything else constant (the *ceteris paribus* assumption). In other words, multiple regression analysis is a statistically controlled experiment designed to estimate the impact of the conspiracy on market prices.

4. New Entrants: The entrance of new competitors (after the expiration of the patent) is one possible explanation for the decline in prices. Dr. Hoyt made no effort to isolate the impact of the new entrants. This type of incomplete economic analysis has been attacked in other cases. For example, Judge Posner has lamented the failure of an expert to segregate the effect of the entrance of a new competitor in the market from the effect of unlawful acts:

> For years we have been saying, without much visible effect, that people who want damages have to prove them, using methodologies that need not be intellectually sophisticated but must not insult the intelligence. *Post hoc ergo propter hoc* will not do; nor the enduing of simplistic extrapolation and childish arithmetic with the appearance of authority by hiring a professor to mouth damages theories that make a joke of the concept of expert knowledge. The expert should have tried to separate the damages that resulted from the lawful entry of a powerful competitor ... from the damages that resulted from particular forms of misconduct allegedly committed by that competitor.... No such effort was made.

Schiller & Schmidt, Inc. v. Nordisco Corp., 969 F.2d 410, 415–16 (7th Cir. 1992).

5. Scientific Methodology: "Scientific methodology today is based on generating hypotheses and testing them to see if they can be falsified; indeed, this methodology is what distinguishes science from other fields of human inquiry." Daubert v. Merrell Dow Pharmaceuticals, Inc., 509 U.S. 579, 593 (1993). Economic theory could have been used to generate hypotheses about the impact of the conspiracy on market prices, and econometric techniques could have been used to reject or accept the hypotheses. Dr. Hoyt failed to produce a report that took declining demand and new entrants in the market into account. Thus, Judge Vratil held that Dr. Hoyt's testimony was "economically unreliable" and therefore inadmissible at trial. The court concluded that Dr. Hoyt's testing procedures were not sufficient for his conclusions to be valid. Should experts be allowed to testify at trial to explain their testing procedures and assumptions or should they have to prove beforehand that their procedures are valid?

2. Efficiency and Other Normative Goals

Appreciation of the distinction between positive and normative analysis can help to clarify disputes about trade-offs between efficiency and other goals, such as equity.

Efficiency has many different meanings. Most non-economists are concerned with what economists call **productive efficiency**—are goods and services being produced at the lowest cost of production? If the answer is no, then we are wasting resources. Although productive efficiency is an important concept, most economists' discussions of efficiency are concerned with **allocative efficiency**—are resources being allocated to their highest value use?

The traditional definition of allocative efficiency deals with whether a change in the allocation of some relevant economic resource creates more benefits than it does costs. If no possible changes in economic arrangements which result in greater benefits than costs can be identified, then it can be said that the wealth of society is maximized. However, the crucial question is whose costs and benefits are to be compared (and, maybe more critical for public policy considerations, how one measures "costs" and "benefits"). Of the two most commonly used formulations of the traditional definition, one takes a very individualistic approach, while the other takes a broader, more collective view.

The **Pareto efficiency** criterion is based on the belief that the individual is the best judge of his own welfare: a Pareto efficient allocation of resources (a particular state of the world) is one in which the welfare of any one member of society cannot be improved without reducing the welfare of any other member of society. If a change in the allocation of resources would result in greater benefit to one party than cost to another party, then one would expect to see a voluntary transaction take place to capture the gain—assuming the gain is greater than the costs of engaging in the transaction. If such a transaction takes place, it is considered to be **Pareto superior**—both parties are better off (or at least no worse off). Thus, the criterion of Pareto efficiency prevents external observers from assessing a change in policy by comparing the gain in welfare of one individual to the loss in welfare of another. The Pareto criterion would require the losing party to be compensated so that he is at least as well off as before the change occurred. Thus, in order to satisfy the Pareto criterion, there must be unanimity among the parties affected by any transaction. Any trade between consenting parties is considered Pareto superior, ex ante, since both parties believe they will be better off. An allocation in which all voluntary exchanges have taken place is Pareto efficient.

Another definition of efficiency is based on the **Kaldor-Hicks efficiency** criterion. A change is Kaldor-Hicks superior if those who gain from the change—for example, parties who gain from a tax change or from a change in a liability or property rule—could theoretically compensate those that have been harmed by the change and still have a net gain overall. The Kaldor-Hicks rule, which is often referred to as **cost-benefit analysis**, can be viewed as a quasi-Pareto rule—the gainers could compensate the losers, but they are **not** required to do so. Thus, in order to satisfy this cost-benefit efficiency standard, the harmed party does not actually have to be compensated for the harm that resulted from the policy change. The result is that changes in legal rules that meet the cost-benefit standard may involve non-compensated harms for some individuals. For example, the building of a new irrigation project may bring about benefits to farmers of $100 million at the cost to taxpayers of $75 million. This would be considered a Kaldor-Hicks superior move even though those who receive the benefits are not required to compensate the taxpayers.

The Kaldor-Hicks criterion is thought by planners to be a more practical basis for evaluating alternative public policies than the Pareto rule for the simple reason that the Pareto standard has severe informational requirements. Since it is virtually impossible to identify or measure all of the impacts of a change in legal rules, much of the impact being subjective and thus immeasurable, when most public policy analysts speak of efficiency, they mean Kaldor-Hicks efficiency. In general, when all potential changes that satisfy the criteria of Kaldor-Hicks efficiency are realized, then it is argued that resources are being allocated to their most highly valued uses. No one change can increase net benefits. Often, economic analyses of public policies are concerned with identifying the conditions under which changes that have net benefits can be achieved.

The term **equity** refers to the distribution of income or wealth among individuals. Both equity and efficiency are politically accepted as goals of public policies on various issues. In contrast to the allocative concerns of efficiency, equity is concerned with the "division of the pie," rather than "maximizing the size of the pie." Another way of stating the relationship between equity and efficiency is that equity addresses distributional issues, and efficiency addresses allocational issues. The discussion of Kaldor-Hicks efficiency illustrates some distributional considerations that may be involved in the analysis of changes in legal rules.

In many instances, equity and efficiency goals appear to be incompatible. The pursuit of either goal often involves costs in terms of reduced ability to pursue the other goal. The most straightforward example concerns a policy designed to impose an equitable distribution of income, where equitable is defined as equal. If everyone is entitled to the same income, the overall wealth of society will surely decline because there is no monetary reward for superior performance. The potential conflict between equity and efficiency arises in many areas of law and economics.

Positive economic analysis allows for the presentation of economic costs and benefits of alternative public policies; it does not require the analyst to impose his or her own value judgments. Understanding what is optimal from the perspective of allocative efficiency does not necessarily make it the "best" policy. In many areas, our political process has exhibited a willingness to sacrifice efficiency in order to further other social policies. The use of economic analysis can identify the magnitude of the allocative costs of a given policy before the trade-off is made.

Chapter II

Markets and the Price System

A fundamental tool of economic analysis is the supply-and-demand model of price and quantity determination. The supply-and-demand model can be used to analyze many real-world events. In a free market, consumers' demands for products and producers' ability to supply the products interact to determine a market price and quantity. Consumers and businesses make numerous decisions on the basis of the information contained within the market price. This interaction between buyers and sellers in the market has been formalized by economists in the Laws of Supply and Demand.

Both "Laws" state empirically verified relationships between the price and quantity of a good. The law of demand states that there is an inverse relationship between price and the quantity of goods that consumers are willing and able to purchase. As price rises, the quantity demanded decreases; as price falls, the quantity demanded increases. The law of supply states that there is a positive relationship between price and the quantity that producers are willing and able to supply. As price rises, the quantity supplied increases; as price falls, the quantity supplied decreases. When market prices change, producers and consumers simultaneously adjust their production and consumption decisions until the quantity supplied equals the quantity demanded. Many powerful insights into the effects of various changes in market conditions can be made by applying this abstract analysis to complicated situations.

Section A introduces the law of demand in more detail, while Section B discusses the law of supply. Section C examines the meaning of market price and quantity in a dynamic market setting. It also explores the idea of individual preferences relative to market prices and considers the ways in which the subjective valuations of individuals may be protected. In Section D, the gains from trade (consumer surplus and producer surplus) as well as the limits of mutually beneficial exchange are analyzed. Section E considers changes in demand and supply — that is, the impact of changes in non-price variables on market price and quantity. In Section F, the effects of artificial controls on market prices are demonstrated. In Section G, the supply-and-demand model is used to analyze the responsiveness of both consumers and suppliers to price changes. Finally, the role of prices in coordinating economic activity in a market system is examined in Section H.

A. The Law of Demand

The **law of demand** states that, other things being equal, an inverse relationship exists between price and quantity demanded. Thus, the **quantity demanded** of a good or service—the amount that buyers are willing and able to purchase—increases as the price of the good or service declines. In general, this holds for individuals (as explained by the theory of consumer choice) and markets (where market demand is an aggregation of individual demand).

1. Consumer Choice

The assumptions regarding individual behavior introduced in Chapter I—that consumers are resourceful, evaluative maximizers—are consistent with the law of demand. Why is it that an individual is willing to purchase more of a particular good or service as price decreases? One answer to this question can be found in the theory of consumer choice and the law of diminishing marginal utility.

Individuals desire to consume goods and services because they perceive a benefit in doing so. Economists define the benefit that individuals derive from consumption activities as **utility**. In relation to our understanding of human behavior developed in Chapter I, we can say that REMMs seek to maximize their utility. However, the ability of individuals to consume those goods and services that provide them with the greatest amount of utility faces an important constraint—individuals must choose those items that provide the highest level of utility attainable within their given **income constraint**. How does the consumer decide to allocate scarce income resources among the goods and services that provide the most utility? An economic proposition that helps guide this analysis is the law of diminishing marginal utility.

The **law of diminishing marginal utility** states that as greater quantities of any good or service are consumed, the utility derived from each additional (or marginal) unit consumed will decrease—holding all else constant. For example, consider your desire for pizza when you go to lunch. At first, you are very hungry and the satisfaction derived from the first piece of pizza consumed is very high. As additional pieces are consumed, however, the utility derived from each additional piece declines. In other words, the second piece does not provide as much satisfaction as the first, and the thought of eating a tenth piece may make you sick. In trying to maximize **total utility**, an individual consumer will consider the **marginal utility** of purchasing each additional unit of any good or service. To the extent that an individual consumer has more than one item that can be consumed next, a rational individual will choose to spend their next dollar on the item which offers the highest marginal utility per dollar spent. A consumer's total utility is maximized when the utility derived from the last dollar spent on each item is equal. Intuitively, this makes sense. If the utility derived from the last dollar spent on each item is equal, then the consumer would have no rational reason to adjust his or her consumption pattern. When no alterations to the consumption pattern can make the consumer better off within given income constraints, then total utility has been maximized. This utility maximizing situation is known as **consumer equilibrium**.

Consider the relationship between the law of diminishing marginal utility and the law of demand. What happens to an individual in consumer equilibrium if the price of good x changes? If the price of good x decreases, then the per dollar cost of a marginal unit of utility derived from x becomes relatively less expensive, thus upsetting the consumer equilibrium. In other words, the marginal utility per dollar spent on x increases as the price of x falls relative to other goods or services. Thus, as the price of a good decreases relative to the prices of other goods, consumers tend to buy more of the lower priced good. This tendency is known as the **substitution effect**. A decrease in the price of good x, holding income and the prices of other goods constant, will also increase the real purchasing power of the consumer. This **income effect** allows the consumer to purchase more goods and services overall. In sum, a change in the quantity demanded is composed of a substitution effect and an income effect, both of which are rational responses formulated under the law of diminishing marginal utility.

2. Market Demand

In addition to the individual consumer choice and law of diminishing marginal utility explanations of individual demand, economists are interested in understanding the consumption behavior of a large set of individuals—**market demand**. Market demand is simply the aggregation of each individual consumer's demand. Regardless of the level of analysis, both individual and market demand reflect the same basic properties—an inverse relationship between price and quantity demanded.

In discussing the law of demand, the only variables are the price and the quantity demanded. All other things that might have an effect on the price or quantity demanded— such as income, tastes and preferences, laws and regulations, and the prices of other goods—are held constant. This "holding constant" assumption is what economists mean when they say *ceteris paribus*. The assumption *ceteris paribus* is used in order to clarify and isolate the relationship between price and quantity demanded in the determination of market price.

For most analytical purposes, demand curves can be drawn to illustrate the inverse relationship between price and quantity demanded. A **market demand curve** represents the quantities of a good or service that consumers are willing and able to purchase at different prices. Figure II-1 demonstrates how the demand curve D_1 reflects the law of

Figure II-1. The Law of Demand

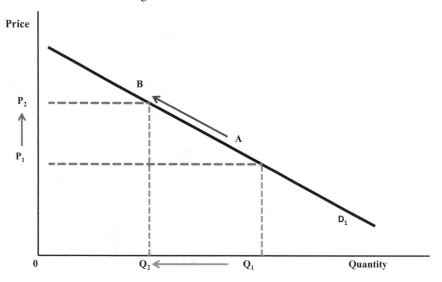

demand. It is important to understand that a change in price causes a movement along a stationary demand curve—that is, a change in price causes a change in quantity demanded. For example, an increase in price from P_1 to P_2 causes a decrease in quantity demanded from Q_1 to Q_2—a movement from point A to point B along the demand curve. A change in price does not cause a change in the position of the curve.

B. The Law of Supply

The supply side of any market represents the willingness of individuals controlling certain resources to transfer those resources to other parties for a price. Obviously, a supplier will not be willing to part with its goods unless the compensation received is greater than the value of the goods in the supplier's control. In other words, in order for a good to be supplied, the good's value in exchange (price) must exceed its value in use (opportunity cost).

The **law of supply** states that, other things being equal, there is a positive relationship between price and the quantity supplied. Thus, owners of resources are willing and able to sell greater quantities of a good or service as the price of that good or service rises. The law of supply can be explained in two related ways—one is based on demand theory and opportunity cost; the other is based on the technical characteristics of the costs of production. As with the law of demand, our analysis of the incentives to supply goods and services begins with the *individual's* supply curve. Then, we will consider the *market* supply curve, which is simply the aggregation of all individual supply curves in the market.

1. The Opportunity Costs of Supply

The positive relationship underlying the law of supply is merely a reflection of the law of demand, as illustrated by the following almost true story. Imagine a beautiful, deserted, Caribbean island. John Marshall is dropped off by a dinghy from a cruise ship. He is by himself, looking forward to a day of relaxation on the beach. Fortunately, John has lugged along a cooler containing twenty-four cans of ice-cold beer and an abundant quantity of ice. John asserts that beer and salt water are complementary goods—their use together increases their value. After a short swim, John is ready to drink and the perceived marginal benefit from that first can of beer is extremely high. We can imagine that the marginal benefit John derives from consuming the beer would look something like Figure II-2. For convenience, we use price as a proxy for utility and John's marginal benefit curve becomes a demand curve.

The marginal benefit from the first beer is extremely high as John has been planning this day on the island for years. But as he continues to drink the perceived marginal benefit from each additional beer consumed decreases—remember the law of diminishing marginal utility.

Now imagine that a clone of John is dropped off by a dinghy from another cruise ship. It's Mohn Jarshall! John says, "Hey Mohn!" These two are the same in every way, including their preference for beer consumption. However, there is one difference between John and Mohn—the only thing that Mohn has with him is cash (remember that all John has is beer). Mohn is incredibly thirsty, and he is very disappointed when he realizes that there are no thatched roof tiki bars on the island. Normally, John would have just given Mohn a beer, but John really wanted to be alone. However, John might be willing to sell some beer to Mohn. Consider the process of exchange that might develop.

Figure II-2. John's Demand for Beer

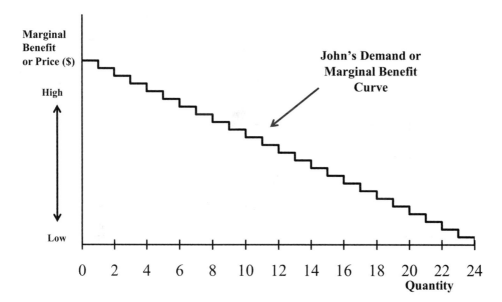

The threshold question is which of his twenty-four beers will John sell first? Obviously, he will part with the one worth the least to him. The twenty-fourth beer that John could consume will be the one that he chooses to sell first, because it has the lowest perceived benefit. Mohn wants to buy this twenty-fourth beer because he really wants a beer. Mohn's marginal utility from his first beer is sure to be very high—in fact, as we know, it is the same as John's marginal utility from his first beer. Moreover, Mohn's marginal utility of his first beer is greater than John's marginal utility of his twenty-fourth beer. Obviously, Mohn and John can make each other better off by exchanging dollars for beer. We cannot determine the exact price at which the exchange would take place. Nonetheless, a large amount of gains from trade exist at the twenty-fourth beer and an exchange will occur.

What if Mohn wants to buy a second beer? Or a third? Figure II-3 demonstrates that the process of exchange will continue in the same manner as above. John will be willing to sell the unit that represents the lowest perceived benefit—opportunity cost—to him at that point in time. Thus, John will supply his 23rd and 22nd beers, respectively. Every additional unit sold will follow this same pattern—as Mohn buys more beer from John, he will move up John's demand curve. Thus, John's supply curve is the mirror image of his demand curve. Equilibrium will occur at 12 units under the assumption that their preferences are the same.

How many beers will John sell? The answer to this supply question is found in a surprising place—John's demand curve. To see this graphically, simply consider the mirror image of Figure II-3. By taking the mirror image of the demand curve, as in Figure II-4, it should become clear that John's supply curve is simply a reflection of his demand curve. Thus, the law of supply is merely a reflection of the law of demand.

It is important to observe that both John and Mohn were made better off by the process of exchange that developed on the island. John was better off because he valued cash more highly than beers 13 to 24 and Mohn was better off because he valued those same 12 beers more highly than the cash he paid to John. The physical property of the beer

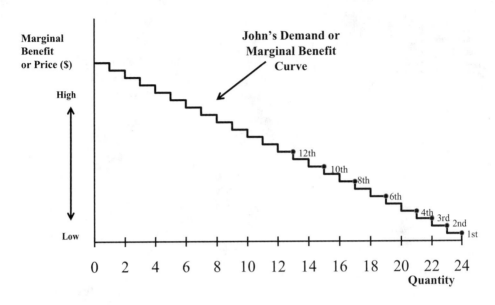

Figure II-3. Which Beer Would John Sell First?

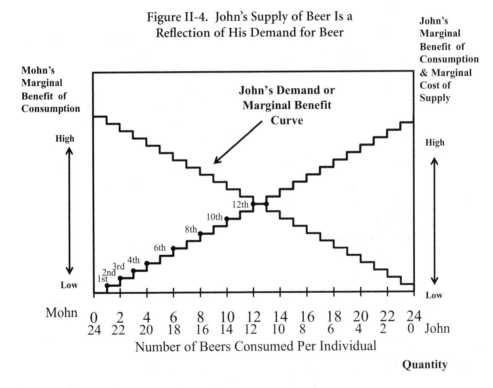

Figure II-4. John's Supply of Beer Is a Reflection of His Demand for Beer

was the same in Mohn's possession as in John's. Likewise, the absolute dollar value of the cash Mohn paid is the same in both Mohn and John's possession. However, a process of exchange arose because of a difference in the subjective value that each of these individuals placed upon the twenty-fourth beer and the first dollar paid. In other words, John and Mohn *disagreed* about the value of those 12 beers — the beer that John values the least, Mohn values the most; and the dollar that Mohn values the least, John values the most. Moreover, note that no coercive force compelled John to exchange with Mohn; no overriding humanitarian goal drove John to share his beer. Instead, because of a difference in the subjective value that each of these individuals placed upon a particular set of beers, a process of mutually beneficial exchange arose in which both parties were made better off by following their own self-interest.

2. Supply and Costs of Production

The Mohn Jarshall example considers the exchange of goods already in existence. However, the law of supply also deals with the incentives to produce goods and services. Remember that the law of supply states that firms are *willing* and *able* to supply more of any good or service as price increases. When relative price increases, it is a signal that more of a particular good or service is desired in the market place. If the market price of any good or service increases relative to the rest of the market, firms have an incentive to shift factors of production into the relatively higher priced good or service because they can capture some of that price increase in the form of increased profits. In this way, price acts as a signal to existing and potential suppliers about the relative rewards for producing various goods. This process helps to explain why producers are *willing* to move factors of production to their highest valued use.

Higher prices also increase the *ability* of firms to supply more of any good or service. Because of scarcity, as the output of any particular good or service increases, resources are drawn away from the production of other goods and services. The increased demand for these various factors of production causes the price of these inputs to rise. Thus, for each additional unit of output, the marginal costs rise. In order for firms to increase output, price must increase so that the firm can afford to purchase additional factors of production away from alternative uses. **Factors of production** may be placed into several different classifications. **Natural resources** include land, air, and water. **Human resources** consist of labor and entrepreneurship. **Capital resources** are machinery and buildings. Remember that economics deals with the allocation of resources in the face of varying levels of scarcity. Because of scarcity, our choices regarding resource usage always involve opportunity costs. The factors of production mentioned above are scarce resources and thus, determining their appropriate allocation is important. As noted above, the law of supply plays both a signaling and incentive role in the allocation process. A more detailed analysis of the costs of production is presented in Chapter IX.

Like the law of demand, the law of supply can also be depicted in a graph. A **supply curve** shows the quantities of any good or service that a firm is willing and able to supply at any given price at a particular point in time, *ceteris paribus*. As was the case with the law of demand, the *ceteris paribus* qualification is invoked in order to clarify and isolate the relationship between price and quantity supplied. In Figure II-5, the positively-sloped supply curve S_1 represents the direct relationship between price and quantity supplied. For example, as price increases from P_1 to P_2, the quantity supplied increases from Q_1 to Q_2 — a movement from point A to point B along the supply curve.

An important element in combining factors of production and supplying finished goods to the market is the entrepreneur. An appreciation of entrepreneurship provides many valuable insights into economic behavior. An **entrepreneur** is an individual who believes that he or she sees profit opportunities that others do not. These profit opportunities

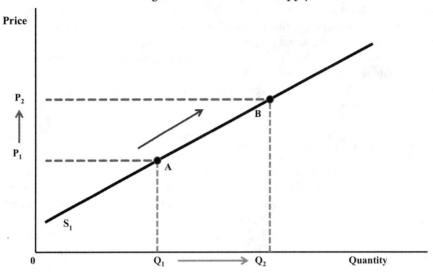

Figure II-5. The Law of Supply

come from combining scarce resources in a new way. In other words, the entrepreneur believes he can obtain a profit because the market has not fully reflected the price of resources in a new, unanticipated, higher valued use. By taking the initiative to combine scarce resources in a new way, the entrepreneur assumes a risk. The primary risk borne by the entrepreneur is that the market will not value this new combination of scarce resources higher than the cost of acquiring them. Beyond identifying new ways to combine scarce resources and organizing the production of this new combination, entrepreneurs also inform other market participants of the availability of the new good or service. A successful entrepreneur is rewarded by earning an economic profit.

C. Equilibrium: Market Price and Quantity

A market exists when the continuous interactions of buyers and sellers force price toward the level where quantity demanded equals quantity supplied. When the quantity demanded is equal to the quantity supplied, the market is said to be in **equilibrium**. The price that prevails at equilibrium is called the **market price**. Thus, the market process forces prices to adjust until the plans of buyers and sellers coincide. This spontaneous coordination occurs because of the voluntary interaction of resourceful, evaluative, maximizing individuals.

The interaction of supply and demand can be illustrated by combining supply and demand curves on a single graph, as in Figure II-6. If the price is P_2, then the quantity supplied, Q_2, is greater than the quantity demanded, Q_0. This excess supply is called a **surplus** and is indicated by the quantity Q_0 to Q_2. The excess of quantity supplied over quantity demanded means that suppliers will have to lower their prices in order to sell their goods. The lower price will encourage additional consumption — that is, cause the quantity demanded to increase — and discourage production — that is, cause the quantity supplied to decrease. As a result of the change in price, the quantity demanded converges

Figure II-6. Equilibrium: Market Price & Quantity

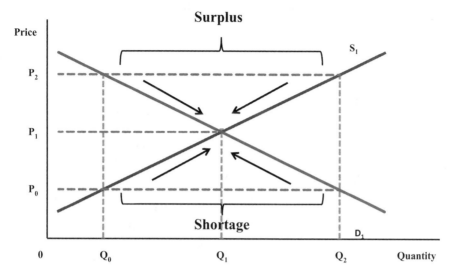

towards the quantity supplied. When quantity demanded equals quantity supplied, the market clears. The equilibrium or market clearing price in Figure II-6 is P_1, where quantity demanded equals the quantity supplied.

If the price is below P_1, then the quantity demanded is greater than the quantity supplied. This excess demand is known as a **shortage**. Through a similar adjustment process, the excess demand will cause the market price to rise, which in turn discourages consumption and encourages additional production. The price adjusts to correct a temporary disequilibrium in the market.

1. Market Price and Quantity

In the theoretical supply-and-demand model, market price and quantity are determined by the intersection of supply and demand. In reality, dynamic markets often make it difficult to determine market prices because different sellers might be selling the same product at different prices because they have different opinions about where the market price is headed. The competitive process rewards the sellers and buyers who are best at interpreting market conditions. The following case illustrates that manufacturers and their retailers sometimes underestimate demand and are surprised by the market price for their products.

Sedmak v. Charlie's Chevrolet, Inc.

Missouri Court of Appeals
622 S.W. 2d 694 (1981)

Satz, J.

In their petition, plaintiffs, Dr. and Mrs. Sedmak (Sedmaks), alleged they entered into a contract with defendant, Charlie's Chevrolet, Inc. (Charlie's), to purchase a Corvette automobile for approximately $15,000. The Corvette was one of a limited number manufactured to commemorate the selection of the Corvette as the Pace Car for the Indianapolis

500. Charlie's breached the contract, the Sedmaks alleged, when, after the automobile was delivered, an agent for Charlie's told the Sedmaks they could not purchase the automobile for $15,000 but would have to bid on it.

The trial court found the parties entered into an oral contract and also found the contract was excepted from the Statute of Frauds. The court then ordered Charlie's to make the automobile "available for delivery" to the Sedmaks.

Charlie's raises three points on appeal: (1) the existence of an oral contract is not supported by the credible evidence; (2) if an oral contract exists, it is unenforceable because of the Statute of Frauds; and (3) specific performance is an improper remedy because the Sedmaks did not show their legal remedies were inadequate.

... [T]he record reflects the Sedmaks to be automobile enthusiasts, who, at the time of trial, owned six Corvettes. In July, 1977, "Vette Vues," a Corvette fancier's magazine to which Dr. Sedmak subscribed, published an article announcing Chevrolet's tentative plans to manufacture a limited edition of the Corvette. The limited edition of approximately 6,000 automobiles was to commemorate the selection of the Corvette as the Indianapolis 500 Pace Car. The Sedmaks were interested in acquiring one of these Pace Cars to add to their Corvette collection. In November, 1977, the Sedmaks asked Tom Kells, sales manager at Charlie's Chevrolet, about the availability of the Pace Car. Mr. Kells said he did not have any information on the car but would find out about it. Kells also said if Charlie's were to receive a Pace Car, the Sedmaks could purchase it.

On January 9, 1978, Dr. Sedmak telephoned Kells to ask him if a Pace Car could be ordered. Kells indicated that he would require a deposit on the car, so Mrs. Sedmak went to Charlie's and gave Kells a check for $500. She was given a receipt for that amount bearing the names of Kells and Charlie's Chevrolet, Inc. At that time, Kells had a pre-order form listing both standard equipment and options available on the Pace Car. Prior to tendering the deposit, Mrs. Sedmak asked Kells if she and Dr. Sedmak were "definitely going to be the owners." Kells replied, "yes." After the deposit had been paid, Mrs. Sedmak stated if the car was going to be theirs, her husband wanted some changes made to the stock model. She asked Kells to order the car equipped with an L82 engine, four speed standard transmission and AM/FM radio with tape deck. Kells said that he would try to arrange with the manufacturer for these changes. Kells was able to make the changes, and, when the car arrived, it was equipped as the Sedmaks had requested.

Kells informed Mrs. Sedmak that the price of the Pace Car would be the manufacturer's retail price, approximately $15,000. The dollar figure could not be quoted more precisely because Kells was not sure what the ordered changes would cost, nor was he sure what the "appearance package" — decals, a special paint job — would cost. Kells also told Mrs. Sedmak that, after the changes had been made, a "contract" — a retail dealer's order form — would be mailed to them. However, no form or written contract was mailed to the Sedmaks by Charlie's.

On January 25, 1978, the Sedmaks visited Charlie's to take delivery on another Corvette. At that time, the Sedmaks asked Kells whether he knew anything further about the arrival date of the Pace Car. Kells replied he had no further information but he would let the Sedmaks know when the car arrived. Kells also requested that Charlie's be allowed to keep the car in their showroom for promotional purposes until after the Indianapolis 500 Race. The Sedmaks agreed to this arrangement.

On April 3, 1978, the Sedmaks were notified by Kells that the Pace Car had arrived. Kells told the Sedmaks they could not purchase the car for the manufacturer's retail price because demand for the car had inflated its value beyond the suggested price. Kells also told the Sedmaks they could bid on the car. The Sedmaks did not submit a bid. They filed this suit for specific performance.

[The court held that the contract was enforceable, and then turned to the specific performance issue.]

* * *

Finally, Charlie's contends the Sedmaks failed to show they were entitled to specific performance of the contract. We disagree. Although it has been stated that the determination whether to order specific performance lies within the discretion of the trial court, this discretion is, in fact, quite narrow. When the relevant equitable principles have been met and the contract is fair and plain, "specific performance goes as a matter of right." Here, the trial court ordered specific performance because it concluded the Sedmaks "have no adequate remedy at law for the reason that they cannot go upon the open market and purchase an automobile of this kind with the same mileage, condition, ownership and appearance as the automobile involved in this case, except, if at all, with considerable expense, trouble, loss, great delay and inconvenience." Contrary to defendant's complaint, this is a correct expression of the relevant law and it is supported by the evidence.

Under the [Uniform Commercial] Code, the court may decree specific performance as a buyer's remedy for breach of contract to sell goods "where the goods are unique or in other proper circumstances." [§ 2-716(1).] The general term "in other proper circumstances" expresses the drafters' intent to "further a more liberal attitude than some courts have shown in connection with the specific performance of contracts of sale." [§ 2-716] Comment 1. This Comment was not directed to the courts of this state, for long before the Code, we, in Missouri, took a practical approach in determining whether specific performance would lie for the breach of contract for the sale of goods and did not limit this relief only to the sale of "unique" goods....

The Pace Car ... was not unique in the traditional legal sense. It was not an heirloom or, arguably, not one of a kind. However, its "mileage, condition, ownership and appearance" did make it difficult, if not impossible, to obtain its replication without considerable expense, delay and inconvenience. Admittedly, 6,000 Pace Cars were produced by Chevrolet. However, as the record reflects, this is limited production. In addition, only one of these cars was available to each dealer, and only a limited number of these were equipped with the specific options ordered by plaintiffs. Charlie's had not received a car like the Pace Car in the previous two years. The sticker price for the car was $14,284.21. Yet Charlie's received offers from individuals in Hawaii and Florida to buy the Pace Car for $24,000 and $28,000 respectively. As sensibly inferred by the trial court, the location and size of these offers demonstrated this limited edition was in short supply and great demand. We agree with the trial court. This case was a "proper circumstance" for ordering specific performance.

Judgment affirmed.

Notes and Questions

1. Knowledge of Market Conditions: The dealership refused to sell the car at the manufacturer's suggested retail price because "demand for the car had inflated its value beyond the suggested price." In other words, because quantity demanded exceeded quantity supplied, a market shortage existed at the manufacturer's suggested price. A market shortage places upward pressure on price, discourages consumption, and encourages additional production. In this case, however, the Corvette Pace Car was to be a special edition and therefore its supply was fixed. Because supply was fixed, the market price ended up higher than the manufacturer's suggested retail price. If the Chevrolet manufacturer had known the strength of demand for Corvette Pace Cars, it might have responded by increasing the suggested retail price or increasing the quantity supplied. Alternatively, the "shortage" may have been created as a marketing strategy to generate interest in the Corvette model — not just the Pace Car.

2. Least-Cost Avoider of Changing Market Conditions: In *Sedmak*, an interesting question arises that is salient throughout the study of the law: who should bear the costs or benefits of a change in market conditions? When answering this question, it is important to understand the ex ante concerns discussed in Chapter I. For instance, if sellers of special edition Corvettes are allowed to refuse to sell at previously agreed-to prices, how will this change prospective buyers' incentives to make bids on future Corvettes? Another way of framing the question is to ask who is the least-cost risk avoider? Who, at the margin, will economize more efficiently on new information so that value and resource allocation will be maximized?

3. Who Draws These Graphs Anyway?: How did Charlie's Chevrolet know that the market price was significantly higher than the manufacturer's suggested retail price? Did Mr. Kells think through the supply and demand model? Did he draw a supply and demand graph? In practice, most consumers and businesses do not draw graphs to illustrate what is happening in the market. Consumers and businesses, at the margin, respond to changes in their individual circumstances. If a business notices that its inventory of a particular good has fallen below its usual level, then the business may rationally respond by raising the price of the good while at the same time ordering more of the good from the producer. Such spontaneous price adjustments bring order to the market.

4. Assumptions about the Supply and Demand Model: Relative Prices, Constant Quality, and Flows: Price theory is concerned with how prices are determined and how they affect peoples' behavior. Microeconomic theory suggests that individuals respond to changes in relative prices. Responding to **relative prices** means that an individual's behavior is guided by the price of a product stated in terms of what other goods could be purchased for the same amount of money — the opportunity cost of a product. Consumers respond to changes in the prices of goods relative to one another, rather than the absolute dollar price of something. Consider, for example, a period of inflation during which the price of all goods and services increases by 10%. In other words, the absolute dollar price of all goods and services increases by the same percentage amount. Therefore, the ratio of the price of one good in terms of another would not change. What effect would this have on an individual's purchasing decisions? Under the assumption that personal income also increases by 10%, individuals are not expected to alter their purchasing decisions. This result stems from the fact that there has been no change in the relative price of goods and services. Thus, individuals are not expected to alter their purchasing decisions if the opportunity cost of purchasing a product has not changed.

In addition to focusing on relative prices, a distinction must be drawn between the money price and the full price of a product or service. Stating the obvious, the **money price** is the actual dollar amount required by the seller to consummate the exchange. The **full price** includes the money price plus the opportunity costs of a particular purchase. For example, consider the cost of getting the oil changed in your car. Suppose that the auto mechanic charges $30 for an oil change. Does $30 adequately represent the cost of having your oil changed? What about the time you spend driving to the auto garage, sitting in the waiting room, waiting in line to pay, and driving home? You could have done something else with your time — your next best alternative or opportunity cost. These are real costs and must always be considered in any economic analysis. Thus, the supply-and-demand model is concerned with the full price of any good or service. Any time that the term price is used in economic analysis, it is assumed to be the full price.

Microeconomic analysis typically relies on the simplifying assumption that the *quality* of a particular economic good or service is held constant. For example, in a discussion involving the market price and quantity for shoes, it is assumed that there is no difference in the quality of any particular pair of shoes relative to others, regardless of its source. "Price" should be understood to mean the relative price of a quantity of any particular unit without regard to the quality. Unless otherwise indicated, economic analysis is conducted as if all units are identical and, therefore, of **constant quality**.

Finally, microeconomic theory is interested in the flow of goods and services. A **flow** is a quantity received, used, or spent at a particular rate over a specified time period. In contrast, a **stock** is a quantity of something that exists at a moment in time. Price theory is concerned with the relative price of constant quality units received, used, or spent over a given time period. For example, microeconomists might analyze the quantity of shoes sold per year at a given relative price. They are not particularly concerned with the total quantity of shoes in existence on a given date.

5. Why Specific Performance? The Market for Substitutes: Specific performance is valuable when there is not a well-developed market for substitute goods. If there is a well-developed market for substitutes, then either the buyer or seller could purchase a replacement product for roughly the same price, and there is no need to require the seller to do anything other than pay compensatory damages for the breach of contract. Was there a well-developed market for substitute Corvette Pace Cars? Could the Sedmaks have gone out and purchased a different Corvette Pace Car for the manufacturer's suggested retail price?

6. Tiger Woods, Alex Rodriguez, Maria Sharapova, LeBron James, and Many Professional Athletes: Why do professional athletes get paid so much when their "value" to society is not as great as, say, an elementary school teacher? Is this simply supply and demand? How is value reflected in the market?

7. Cost-Price Illusion: It is often difficult to determine why market prices have changed. In many instances, the retailer of a particular product will blame price increases on the higher prices charged by the retailer's suppliers (which represent the retailer's costs). However, the important issue in determining why the retailer's prices changed is to identify why the supplier's prices were raised. For example, an increase in the demand for computer processing chips would, other things equal, cause the price of such chips to increase. Consumers might notice this price increase when they go to purchase a new computer. In other words, the increased cost of processing chips would be reflected in higher prices for computers. When consumers ask the computer maker about the higher prices for computers, the computer maker may simply respond by noting that the cost of computer processing chips has gone up. This answer focuses on the cost of production—the supply side of the market—and ignores the fact that the price increase was a result of increased demand. In general, one should be skeptical of explanations for price increases that concentrate on only one side of the market—the cost-price illusion.

2. Market Prices and Subjective Value

Market prices represent an objective measure of the value of the products or services exchanged in a particular market. Market prices often do not reveal much information about individuals' personal subjective valuations of the products or services. Recall that mutually beneficial exchange occurs so long as the buyer values the product more than the seller. A market price can be viewed as determining the division of the gains from trade. The subjective valuations of the marginal buyers and sellers — that is, the last transaction to occur — are close to each other and determine the market price. At the margin, the gains from trade are small. The inframarginal subjective valuations are not revealed by market prices. All that is learned from the market price is that the buyers valued the product more than market price and the sellers valued it less than the market price.

Families often value their home substantially more than the market price — that is, their subjective value is greater than the market's objective valuation. Their subjective value is revealed by their decision to not sell their home at the market price. Figure II-7 represents a market for existing, constant-quality, single-family homes sold in a year. The supply curve reflects the number of homeowners who are willing to sell their homes at the different prices. The homes are already built, thus, the supply curve reflects different valuations by individuals, not the cost of building a new home. The number of transactions that actually occur in this market is represented by Q*. Actual buyers of homes, represented by the transactions that actually occur — those to the left of Q* — value their homes more than the market price, as indicated by the shaded area to the left of Q*. Thus, transactions move the homes from a lower to a higher valued use. Potential suppliers of homes to the right of the market clearing quantity, Q*, value their homes more than the market price as indicated by the shaded area to the right of Q*. The existence of subjective value is revealed by market behavior — however, the precise amount is inherently subjective and cannot be objectively determined by simply observing market behavior.

In many instances, our legal system has great difficulty in dealing with subjective value because, well, it is subjective. Consider two examples. First, although the Takings Clause of the Fifth Amendment requires "just compensation" for governmental takings of private property for public use, the Supreme Court has interpreted "just compensation" to mean market value. See, e.g., United States v. Miller, 317 U.S. 369, 374 (1943). Some homeowners who have their homes taken for a public purpose are not compensated for their lost

Figure II-7. Market for Existing Single-Family Homes

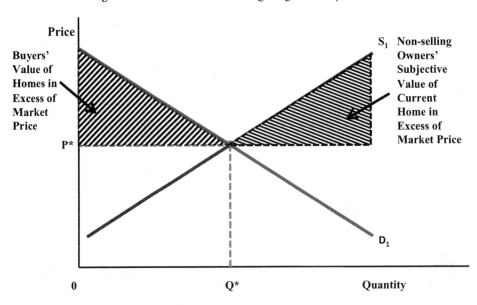

subjective value. In Figure II-7, this is represented by homeowners to the right of Q^* on supply curve S_1. Second, most property insurance contracts do not cover lost subjective value because of concerns that compensation for such losses would encourage the insured party to overstate their subjective value and then not exercise appropriate care in protecting the property because loss of the property would result in a windfall for the insured. ("Items that are overinsured tend to catch on fire or disappear.") The latter behavior is referred to as a **moral hazard**.

In other instances, however, a contract could provide for the recognition of subjective value. Freedom of contract is a fundamental principle of the common law. As long as the parties to the contract have legal capacity and the performance of the contract does not violate public policy, the general rule is that parties may structure their contractual relations in any manner they desire, and the courts will enforce the terms of their contract. One advantage of this principle is that it allows individuals to protect assets that are more valuable to them personally than they are valued in the market. In general, freedom of contract allows the idiosyncratic, subjective preferences of individuals to be protected — but not always.

Peevyhouse v. Garland Coal & Mining Co.

Supreme Court of Oklahoma

382 P.2d 109 (1962)

JACKSON, J.

In the trial court, plaintiffs Willie and Lucille Peevyhouse sued the defendant, Garland Coal and Mining Company, for damages for breach of contract. Judgment was for plaintiffs in an amount considerably less than was sued for. Plaintiffs appeal and defendant cross-appeals.

In the briefs on appeal, the parties present their arguments and contentions under several propositions; however, they all stem from the basic question of whether the trial court properly instructed the jury on the measure of damages.

Briefly stated, the facts are as follows: plaintiffs owned a farm containing coal deposits, and in November, 1954, leased the premises to defendant for a period of five years for coal mining purposes. A "strip-mining" operation was contemplated in which the coal would be taken from pits on the surface of the ground, instead of from underground mine shafts. In addition to the usual covenants found in a coal mining lease, defendant specifically agreed to perform certain restorative and remedial work at the end of the lease period. It is unnecessary to set out the details of the work to be done, other than to say that it would involve the moving of many thousands of cubic yards of dirt, at a cost estimated by expert witnesses at about $29,000. However, plaintiffs sued for only $25,000.

During the trial, it was stipulated that all covenants and agreements in the lease contract had been fully carried out by both parties, except the remedial work mentioned above; defendant conceded that this work had not been done.

Plaintiffs introduced expert testimony as to the amount and nature of the work to be done, and its estimated cost. Over plaintiffs' objections, defendant thereafter introduced expert testimony as to the "diminution in value" of plaintiffs' farm resulting from the failure of defendant to render performance as agreed in the contract — that is, the difference between the present value of the farm, and what its value would have been if defendant had done what it agreed to do.

At the conclusion of the trial, the court instructed the jury that it must return a verdict for plaintiffs, and left the amount of damages for jury determination. On the measure of damages, the court instructed the jury that it might consider the cost of performance of the work defendant agreed to do, "together with all of the evidence offered on behalf of either party."

It thus appears that the jury was at liberty to consider the "diminution in value" of plaintiffs' farm as well as the cost of "repair work" in determining the amount of damages.

It returned a verdict for plaintiffs for $5000 — only a fraction of the "cost of performance," *but more than the total value of the farm even after the remedial work is done.*

On appeal, the issue is sharply drawn. Plaintiffs contend that the true measure of damages in this case is what it will cost plaintiffs to obtain performance of the work that was not done because of defendant's default. Defendant argues that the measure of damages is the cost of performance "limited, however, to the total difference in the market value before and after the work was performed."

* * *

... [T]he authorities are not in agreement as to the factors to be considered in determining whether the cost of performance rule or the value rule should be applied. The American Law Institute's Restatement of the Law, Contracts, Volume 1, Sections 346(1)(a)(i) and (ii) submits the proposition that the cost of performance is the proper measure of damages "if this is possible and does not involve *unreasonable economic waste*"; and that the diminution in value caused by the breach is the proper measure "if construction and completion in accordance with the contract would involve *unreasonable economic waste*." (Emphasis supplied). In an explanatory comment immediately following the text, the Restatement makes it clear that the "economic waste" referred to consists of the destruction of a substantially completed building or other structure. Of course no such destruction is involved in the case now before us.

On the other hand, in McCormick, Damages, Section 168, it is said with regard to building and construction contracts that "... in cases where the defect is one that can be repaired or cured without *undue expense*" the cost of performance is the proper measure of damages, but where "... the defect in material or construction is one that cannot be remedied without *an expenditure for reconstruction disproportionate to the end to be attained*" (emphasis supplied) the value rule should be followed. The same idea was expressed in Jacob & Youngs, Inc. v. Kent, 230 N.Y. 239, as follows:

> "The owner is entitled to the money which will permit him to complete, unless the cost of completion is grossly and unfairly out of proportion to the good to be attained. When that is true, the measure is the difference in value."

It thus appears that the prime consideration in the Restatement was "economic waste"; and that the prime consideration in McCormick, Damages, and in Jacob & Youngs, Inc. v. Kent, supra, was the relationship between the expense involved and the "end to be attained" — in other words, the "relative economic benefit."

* * *

We therefore hold that where, in a coal mining lease, lessee agrees to perform certain remedial work on the premises concerned at the end of the lease period, and thereafter the contract is fully performed by both parties except that the remedial work is not done, the measure of damages in an action by lessor against lessee for damages for breach of contract is ordinarily the reasonable cost of performance of the work; however, where the contract provision breached was merely incidental to the main purpose in view, and where the economic benefit which would result to lessor by full performance of the work is grossly disproportionate to the cost of performance, the damages which lessor may recover are limited to the diminution in value resulting to the premises because of the non-performance.

* * *

Under the most liberal view of the evidence herein, the diminution in value resulting to the premises because of non-performance of the remedial work was $300.00. After a careful search of the record, we have found no evidence of a higher figure, and plaintiffs do not argue in their briefs that a greater diminution in value was sustained. It thus appears that the judgment was clearly excessive, and that the amount for which judgment should have been rendered is definitely and satisfactorily shown by the record....

We are of the opinion that the judgment of the trial court for plaintiffs should be, and it is hereby, modified and reduced to the sum of $300.00, and as so modified it is affirmed.

IRWIN, J. (dissenting).

* * *

Although the contract speaks for itself, there were several negotiations between the plaintiffs and defendant before the contract was executed. Defendant admitted in the trial of the action, that plaintiffs insisted that the above provisions be included in the contract and that they would not agree to the coal mining lease unless the above provisions were included.

In consideration for the lease contract, plaintiffs were to receive a certain amount as royalty for the coal produced and marketed and in addition thereto their land was to be restored as provided in the contract.

Defendant received as consideration for the contract, its proportionate share of the coal produced and marketed and in addition thereto, the *right to use* plaintiffs' land in the furtherance of its mining operations.

The cost for performing the contract in question could have been reasonably approximated when the contract was negotiated and executed and there are no conditions now existing which could not have been reasonably anticipated by the parties. Therefore, defendant had knowledge, when it prevailed upon the plaintiffs to execute the lease, that the cost of performance might be disproportionate to the value or benefits received by plaintiff for the performance.

Defendant has received its benefits under the contract and now urges, in substance, that plaintiffs' measure of damages for its failure to perform should be the economic value of performance to the plaintiffs and not the cost of performance.

If a peculiar set of facts should exist where the above rule should be applied as the proper measure of damages, (and in my judgment those facts do not exist in the instant case) before such rule should be applied, consideration should be given to the benefits received or contracted for by the party who asserts the application of the rule.

Defendant did not have the right to mine plaintiffs' coal or to use plaintiffs' property for its mining operations without the consent of plaintiffs. Defendant had knowledge of the benefits that it would receive under the contract and the approximate cost of performing the contract. With this knowledge, it must be presumed that defendant thought that it would be to its economic advantage to enter into the contract with plaintiffs and that it would reap benefits from the contract, or it would have not entered into the contract.

Therefore, if the value of the performance of a contract should be considered in determining the measure of damages for breach of a contract, the value of the benefits received under the contract by a party who breaches a contract should also be considered. However, in my judgment, to give consideration to either in the instant action, completely rescinds and holds for naught the solemnity of the contract before us and makes an entirely new contract for the parties....

I therefore respectfully dissent to the opinion promulgated by a majority of my associates.

* * *

Notes and Questions

1. Bargaining for Subjective Value: The court seems to treat the plaintiffs' claimed damages as unreasonable in light of the very large expenditure necessary to restore the property relative to the very small increase in market value. For example, the court accepts the defendant's contention that "damages should be limited to [diminution in value] because that is all that plaintiffs have lost." An alternative interpretation is that the plaintiffs accepted a lower royalty rate in order to get the defendant to agree to restore the land. Under this view, the plaintiffs have already paid for the restoration. Why would the plaintiffs be willing to pay so much for work that has an objective market value of only $300? Perhaps the plaintiffs' actions revealed that their subjective valuation of the restoration is at least $29,000. In this case, should the remedy be cost of completion ($29,000) or diminution in value ($300)? What happened to freedom of contract?

2. Efficient Breach: If contingencies occur that make it unprofitable for a promisor to perform as promised, the promisor may refuse to perform the contract and pay damages to the non-breaching party. If damages are measured properly, then the non-breaching party is as well-off as he would have been if the contract had been performed, and the breaching party is better off because he bought his way out of an unprofitable situation by paying damages. This scenario would seem to satisfy the criteria for Pareto efficiency: one party is made better off without harming another party. For this reason, this situation is often referred to as one of "efficient breach." Is the preceding case an example of an efficient breach? What contingencies occurred to make performance unprofitable? Were damages measured properly?

3. Bargaining During Performance: Assume that the plaintiffs initially valued restoration at $29,000 and that the terms of the contract reflected the cost to the defendant of restoration. Also, assume that there is no doubt that the court will award damages based on cost of completion. Now, assume that the plaintiffs have a change of heart and no longer value the restoration more than its impact on market value ($300). Because the plaintiffs still have the right to a remedy that will cost the defendant $29,000, there is a clear opportunity for gain through settlement at an amount somewhere between $300 and $29,000. Obviously, the plaintiffs would prefer to collect $29,000 in cash from the defendant, but the defendant can thwart that opportunity by spending (or threatening to spend) the $29,000 restoring the land—thereby providing the plaintiffs with only the $300 increase in market value. Does the potential for this type of strategic bargaining provide an argument for the doctrine of economic waste?

4. There Is More Than One Way to Skin a Cat: The plaintiffs' desire for restoration could be realized through a clause requiring specific performance or a clause requiring damages to be measured by the cost of completion. However, uncertainty over judicial enforcement of a cost-of-completion clause — that is, the possibility that the court will order diminution in value damages instead of cost of completion — means that contracting parties will often prefer a clause with specific performance as a remedy. The particular legal rule governing these types of transactions does not affect the ultimate allocation of resources because the parties can contract around the rules, provided transaction costs are low. If the remedies of cost of completion and specific performance are not available (because of judicial concerns about "economic waste"), the landowners can still receive the desired result by charging a higher royalty rate to reflect the cost of restoration and then using the additional funds to hire an additional contractor to do the restoration. Is it "efficient" to require the landowners to go through this two-step process?

D. Gains From Trade: Consumer Surplus and Producer Surplus

Individuals and firms engage in exchange when the benefits of doing so are greater than the costs. This means that for any particular transaction, both the buyer and the seller perceive the exchange as being in their best interest. In other words, voluntary transactions are mutually beneficial exchanges — observed market transactions are win-win situations. Economists call the buyer's winnings a consumer surplus and the seller's winnings a producer surplus. **Consumer surplus** is the difference between the maximum amount a buyer would have been willing to pay for a good or service and the actual purchase price that she paid. **Producer surplus** is the difference between the minimum amount a supplier would have been willing to sell a particular quantity of some good or service for and its actual selling price. Together, consumer and producer surplus represent the total **gains from trade**.

The idea of consumer and producer surplus can best be illustrated graphically. Figure II-8 represents a market for cheeseburgers that is in equilibrium at P* = $3.00 and Q* = 5. The demand curve represents the quantity of cheeseburgers that individuals are willing and able to purchase at a particular price. In our example, some individuals are willing to pay $4.00 for one cheeseburger — indicated by point A. Despite the fact that some individuals are willing to consume one cheeseburger for four dollars, the equilibrium market price is $3.00. This means that some consumers are willing to pay $4.00, but only have to pay $3.00. The difference between their individual valuation and the purchase price ($4.00 – $3.00 = $1.00) represents consumer surplus. In fact, the entire area under the demand curve and to the left of Q* represents the consumer utility derived from the cheeseburgers actually purchased. The area under the demand curve, to the left of Q* and above the market price P* ($3.00), represents the total consumer surplus in this market.

A similar reasoning process applies for producer surplus. The supply curve represents the quantity of a given good or service that suppliers are willing and able to supply at a particular price. Thus, in our cheeseburger market, some suppliers are apparently willing and able to sell one cheeseburger for $2.00 — indicated by point B. Despite this, all cheeseburgers sell at the market price of $3.00. The difference between the minimum amount the seller is willing to accept and the market price represents producer surplus. Graphically, producer surplus is equal to the area above the supply curve, to the left of the equilibrium quantity Q* and below the market price P* ($3.00).

The sum of consumer surplus and producer surplus represents the gains available from trade. All gains from trade are realized at the market clearing price and quantity.

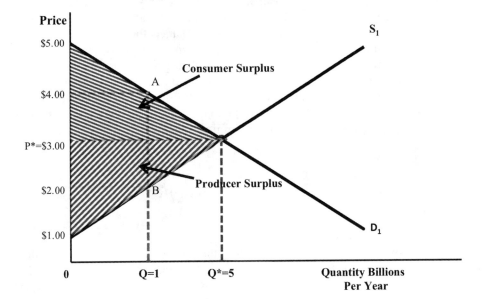

Figure II-8. Gains from Trade: Consumer Surplus & Producer Surplus

That is, when the market is in equilibrium, the sum of consumer and producer surplus is maximized.

1. Mutually Beneficial Exchange

A key point in understanding the operation of markets is to appreciate the significance of the observation that market exchanges are voluntary. Individuals engage in transactions because they expect to receive more than they give up. An exchange results in reciprocal net benefits. In very real terms, mutually beneficial exchange increases the wealth of both parties. For example, assume that Taylor is willing to sell her car for $10,000 and Andy is willing to pay $12,000 for it. If Taylor sells the car to Andy for $11,000, then both Taylor and Andy are $1,000 better off than before the transaction. The $2,000 in gains from trade represents the increase in wealth created by the transaction. This simple mutually beneficial exchange illustrates how wealth is created simply by transferring the same physical good from one individual to another. Mutually beneficial exchanges not only create wealth (and, for many individuals, happiness), but they also allocate resources to their most highly valued use — e.g., the car is worth more to Andy than to Taylor. Moreover, when all possible mutually beneficial exchanges are realized, then resources are allocated to their most highly valued uses and society's wealth is maximized. In sum, voluntary exchange means that wealth is created.

In the preceding example, the gains from trade arose from differences in preferences. The buyer and seller simply placed different values on the item of trade. Another important source of gains from trade is that the seller may be able to produce the item at a lower cost than the buyer and thus may have a **comparative advantage** in its production. Even if a lawyer is able to type faster than her secretary (that is, the lawyer has an absolute advantage over her secretary), it still makes sense for the secretary to handle the typing because the opportunity cost of the lawyer's time is probably much higher than the secretary's foregone opportunity. Thus, the secretary has a comparative advantage over the lawyer in the sense that she can produce typed pages more cheaply than the lawyer. (Or as economist Gregory Mankiw puts it, New England Patriot's quarterback Tom Brady should not mow his own lawn, even if his athletic skills make him an incredibly fast lawn mower, because Brady has much more valuable alternative uses of his time than the employee of the local lawn service does.)

In advanced economies, individuals specialize in producing goods and services where they have a comparative advantage and make trades to acquire other goods. Specialization greatly enhances the standard of living in a society. It also enhances the productivity of economic organizations, such as law firms. Moreover, specialization often lowers the opportunity cost of production. The concept of comparative advantage also teaches us that following the maxim "if you want it done right, do it yourself" can be very expensive.

Despite the simplicity of the comparative advantage argument, we often see laws and regulations that ignore this principle. Consider, for example, the many tariffs and quotas placed on goods traded internationally. The law of comparative advantage is often used to explain the benefits of international trade. Resources are used most effectively when they are moved to their most highly valued use. By definition, this means putting resources in their lowest marginal opportunity cost use relative to other resources available for production. Countries that ignore this logic by enacting tariffs and quotas will become overly self-sufficient and therefore waste resources. The more mutually beneficial transactions that a society undertakes, the more wealth it creates. International trade is based on mutually beneficial exchange. Tariffs and quotas increase the costs of international trade and, thus, decrease the quantity of mutually beneficial transactions and deter wealth creating transactions.

2. Individual Self-Interest, Free Markets, and Social Welfare: The Invisible Hand

An important economic principle about market allocation of resources is that resources tend to flow towards their most highly valued uses if voluntary exchange is permitted. For example, producers of digital cameras and computers compete with each other for skilled labor and materials to produce their final products. The reason some entrepreneurs are willing to pay more for particular resources is that they think that the final output produced by the combination of resources will be worth more to consumers than any other product that could be produced from those same resources. This activity causes the value of resources ("costs") to be determined by the prices consumers are willing to pay for final products.

The process of voluntary exchange facilitates the allocation of resources to those uses in which the value to consumers, as measured by their willingness and ability to pay, is highest. This allocation of resources has traditionally been considered to be efficient. This point was best made in 1776 by Adam Smith, the father of economic analysis of the free-market system.

An Inquiry into the Nature and Causes of the Wealth of Nations

Adam Smith
(1776; reprint, Edwin Cannan, ed.,
New York: Modern Library, 1937, p. 423)

[E]very individual necessarily labours to render the annual revenue of the society as great as he can. He generally, indeed, neither intends to promote the public interest, nor knows how much he is promoting it. By preferring the support of domestic to that of foreign industry, he intends only his own security; and by directing that industry in such a manner as its produce may be of the greatest value, he intends only his own gain, and he is in this, as in many other cases, led by an invisible hand to promote an end which was in no part of his intention. Nor is it always the worse for the society that it was no part of it. By pursuing his own interest he frequently promotes that of the society more effectually than when he really intends to promote it. I have never known much good done by those who affected to trade for the public good. It is an affectation, indeed, not very common among merchants, and very few words need to be employed in dissuading them from it.

What is the species of domestic industry which his capital can employ, and of which the produce is likely to be of the greatest value, every individual, it is evident, can, in his local situation, judge much better than any statesman or lawgiver can do for him. The statesman, who should attempt to direct private people in what manner they ought to employ their capitals, would not only load himself with a most unnecessary attention, but assume an authority which could safely be trusted, not only to no single person, but to no council or senate whatever, and which would nowhere be so dangerous as in the hands of a man who had folly and presumption enough to fancy himself fit to exercise it.

———————

As the following essay illustrates, this "invisible hand" coordinates the actions of millions of people from around the world into a productive whole without any overarching plan. F. A. Hayek called such unplanned but harmonious coordination "spontaneous order."

I, Pencil: My Family Tree as Told to Leonard E. Read

Leonard E. Read (Dec. 1958)

I am a lead pencil—the ordinary wooden pencil familiar to all boys and girls and adults who can read and write.

* * *

I have a profound lesson to teach. And I can teach this lesson better than can an automobile or an airplane or a mechanical dishwasher because—well, because I am seemingly so simple.

Simple? Yet, *not a single person on the face of this earth knows how to make me.* This sounds fantastic, doesn't it? Especially when it is realized that there are about one and one-half billion of my kind produced in the U.S.A. each year.

Pick me up and look me over. What do you see? Not much meets the eye—there's some wood, lacquer, the printed labeling, graphite lead, a bit of metal, and an eraser.

* * *

My family tree begins with what in fact is a tree, a cedar of straight grain that grows in Northern California and Oregon. Now contemplate all the saws and trucks and rope and the countless other gear used in harvesting and carting the cedar logs to the railroad siding. Think of all the persons and the numberless skills that went into their fabrication: the mining of ore, the making of steel and its refinement into saws, axes, motors; the growing of hemp and bringing it through all the stages to heavy and strong rope; the logging camps with their beds and mess halls, the cookery and the raising of all the foods. Why, untold thousands of persons had a hand in every cup of coffee the loggers drink!

The logs are shipped to a mill in San Leandro, California. Can you imagine the individuals who make flat cars and rails and railroad engines and who construct and install the communication systems incidental thereto? These legions are among my antecedents.

Consider the millwork in San Leandro. The cedar logs are cut into small, pencil-length slats less than one-fourth of an inch in thickness. These are kiln dried and then tinted for the same reason women put rouge on their faces. People prefer that I look pretty, not a pallid white. The slats are waxed and kiln dried again. How many skills went into the making of the tint and the kilns, into supplying the heat, the light and power, the belts, motors, and all the other things a mill requires? Sweepers in the mill among my ancestors? Yes, and included are the men who poured the concrete for the dam of a Pacific Gas & Electric Company hydroplant which supplies the mill's power!

Don't overlook the ancestors present and distant who have a hand in transporting sixty carloads of slats across the nation.

Once in the pencil factory—$4,000,000 in machinery and building, all capital accumulated by thrifty and saving parents of mine—each slat is given eight grooves by a complex machine, after which another machine lays leads in every other slat, applies glue, and places another slat atop—a lead sandwich, so to speak. Seven brothers and I are mechanically carved from this "wood-clinched" sandwich.

My "lead" itself—it contains no lead at all—is complex. The graphite is mined in Ceylon. Consider these miners and those who make their many tools and the makers of the paper sacks in which the graphite is shipped and those who make the string that ties the sacks and those who put them aboard ships and those who make the ships. Even the lighthouse keepers along the way assisted in my birth—and the harbor pilots.

The graphite is mixed with clay from Mississippi in which ammonium hydroxide is used in the refining process. Then wetting agents are added such as sulfonated tallow—animal fats chemically reacted with sulfuric acid. After passing through numerous machines, the mixture finally appears as endless extrusions—as from a sausage grinder—cut to size, dried, and baked for several hours at 1,850 degrees Fahrenheit. To increase their strength and smoothness the leads are then treated with a hot mixture which includes candelilla wax from Mexico, paraffin wax, and hydrogenated natural fats.

My cedar receives six coats of lacquer. Do you know all the ingredients of lacquer? Who would think that the growers of castor beans and the refiners of castor oil are a part of it? They are. Why, even the processes by which the lacquer is made a beautiful yellow involve the skills of more persons than one can enumerate!

Observe the labeling. That's a film formed by applying heat to carbon black mixed with resins. How do you make resins and what, pray, is carbon black?

My bit of metal—the ferrule—is brass. Think of all the persons who mine zinc and copper and those who have the skills to make shiny sheet brass from these products of nature. Those black rings on my ferrule are black nickel. What is black nickel and how is it applied? The complete story of why the center of my ferrule has no black nickel on it would take pages to explain.

Then there's my crowning glory, inelegantly referred to in the trade as "the plug," the part man uses to erase the errors he makes with me. An ingredient called "factice" is what does the erasing. It is a rubber-like product made by reacting rape-seed oil from the Dutch East Indies with sulfur chloride. Rubber, contrary to the common notion, is only for binding purposes. Then, too, there are numerous vulcanizing and accelerating agents. The pumice comes from Italy; and the pigment which gives "the plug" its color is cadmium sulfide.

* * *

Does anyone wish to challenge my earlier assertion that no single person on the face of this earth knows how to make me?

Actually, millions of human beings have had a hand in my creation, no one of whom even knows more than a very few of the others. Now, you may say that I go too far in relating the picker of a coffee berry in far off Brazil and food growers elsewhere to my creation; that this is an extreme position. I shall stand by my claim. There isn't a single person in all these millions, including the president of the pencil company, who contributes more than a tiny, infinitesimal bit of know-how. From the standpoint of know-how the only difference between the miner of graphite in Ceylon and the logger in Oregon is in the *type* of know-how. Neither the miner nor the logger can be dispensed with, any more than can the chemist at the factory or the worker in the oil field—paraffin being a by-product of petroleum.

Here is an astounding fact: Neither the worker in the oil field nor the chemist nor the digger of graphite or clay nor any who mans or makes the ships or trains or trucks nor the one who runs the machine that does the knurling on my bit of metal nor the president of the company performs his singular task because he wants me. Each one wants me less, perhaps, than does a child in the first grade. Indeed, there are some among this vast multitude who never saw a pencil nor would they know how to use one. Their motivation is other than me. Perhaps it is something like this: Each of these millions sees that he can thus exchange his tiny know-how for the goods and services he needs or wants. I may or may not be among these items.

* * *

There is a fact still more astounding: the absence of a master mind, of anyone dictating or forcibly directing these countless actions which bring me into being. No trace of such a person can be found. Instead, we find the Invisible Hand at work. This is the mystery to which I earlier referred.

* * *

I, Pencil, am a complex combination of miracles: a tree, zinc, copper, graphite, and so on. But to these miracles which manifest themselves in Nature an even more extraordinary miracle has been added: the configuration of creative human energies— millions of tiny know-hows configurating naturally and spontaneously in response to human necessity and desire and *in the absence of any human master-minding!*

* * *

Notes and Questions

1. Individual Wealth Maximization and Social Welfare: According to Smith, a baker does not bake bread because he or she is benevolent or has the interests of society at heart.

The baker bakes bread to earn a profit, and it is this self-interest, or "invisible hand," that causes the baker to do something for others. As a result, consumers are freed from the task of baking their own bread and can use their time in a more efficient manner. Although Smith's reasoning (as well as his insightful critique of government intervention) has been refined considerably by economists over the years, his basic logic is still the cornerstone for the free market. Whether or not one agrees with the proposition that "wealth maximization" should be the goal of public policy, it has been demonstrated empirically that in an entrepreneurial competitive economy, the constant reallocation of resources by entrepreneurs to higher valued uses does maximize the "size of the economic pie."

2. Individual Judgment: One advantage of the market system is that individuals decide for themselves what is best for them and can pursue those activities that increase their own well-being. They are motivated by self-interest to get the highest price for their resources. These resources will be purchased by those (of the many competing users) who have the highest valued use, because it is those users who are willing to pay the highest price. The well-being of society is enhanced by each individual acting in this way, because each of society's resources is used in the most efficient manner possible to produce goods and services for which individuals are willing to pay. Society is protected against an inefficient use of resources because it costs users, in terms of lost profits, to use resources inefficiently.

3. Dynamic Market Adjustment Process: Another advantage of the market system is that it constantly adjusts to changes in consumers' tastes and desires because producers have a profit incentive to seek out information concerning what consumers want. The profit incentive also leads producers to develop and implement new technology which allows them to produce at a lower cost, and saves society's limited resources.

4. Spontaneous Order and Market Coordination: Another advantage of the market system is the low cost manner through which it coordinates economic activity. As Leonard Read's classic essay illustrates, no one individual in the world knows everything about how to make something as simple as a pencil. Yet millions of them are produced every year. The market system provides incentives and rewards for individuals to engage in all of the activities necessary to produce pencils in the most efficient manner possible, and it also punishes those who fail.

5. Decentralized Decision-Making: Another advantage of the market system is that decision-making is decentralized. If a large number of people wanted the government to change one of its policies, it could take years for Congress to do so after much debate and consumption of resources. However, if a large number of people wanted a new product produced or even a different color of a current product, you can be sure that the self-interest of some producer would guide the producer to do so. Resources in the market system are allocated according to decisions made by millions of individuals and producers. Millions of households decide how their budgets will be spent according to their preferences, and thousands of businesses compete not only to give consumers what they desire, but to do so by the most efficient means possible, so they can offer such goods and services at lower prices than their competitors. While mistakes are often made by decision-makers, their impact is overwhelmed by the correct decisions made by the vast majority of others. This decentralized system should be strongly contrasted with the economic systems that existed in formerly Communist countries that relied on a centralized authority to allocate resources. When those with concentrated economic decision-making power made mistakes, their impact was felt throughout the entire economy, and there was no self-correcting mechanism to eliminate the mistakes. In a market economy, mistakes are eliminated through the demise of unprofitable enterprises.

3. Unequal Bargaining Power and the Limits of Mutually Beneficial Exchange

Economic analysis focuses on the voluntary, consensual, and reciprocal aspects of exchange. *Ex ante*, individuals would not agree to a contract unless it were in their interest to do so. In some instances, individuals agree to contracts that do not appear to be good deals from the perspective of a reasonable external observer. It is often alleged that such *ex ante* unfair contracts are the result of unequal bargaining power and that the courts should reform the contracts or specific terms of the contract. In the next two sub-sections, two categories of contracts that are often attacked as alleged manifestations of unequal bargaining power are examined: unconscionable contracts for consumer goods and opportunistic modifications to contracts during performance.

a. Unconscionability

Section 2-302 of the Uniform Commercial Code allows the courts to choose not to enforce "unconscionable" contracts. In general, an unconscionable contract may be said to be one that is so grossly unfair that it shocks the conscience of the court. This provision is designed to prevent oppression and unfair surprise. Thus, it is a form of consumer protection legislation. The principle is most frequently applied in retail sales to individuals who cannot read or do not understand the terms of a contract. The following case illustrates the type of situation where courts will refuse to enforce a contract because it is unconscionable.

Williams v. Walker Thomas Furniture Co.

District of Columbia Court of Appeals
198 A.2d 914 (1964)

QUINN, J.

Appellant, a person of limited education separated from her husband, is maintaining herself and her seven children by means of public assistance. During the period 1957–1962 she had a continuous course of dealings with appellee from which she purchased many household articles on the installment plan. These included sheets, curtains, rugs, chairs, a chest of drawers, beds, mattresses, a washing machine, and a stereo set. In 1963 appellee filed a complaint in replevin for possession of all the items purchased by appellant, alleging that her payments were in default and that it retained title to the goods according to the sales contracts. By the writ of replevin appellee obtained a bed, chest of drawers, washing machine, and the stereo set. After hearing testimony and examining the contracts, the trial court entered judgment for appellee.

Appellant's principal contentions on appeal are (1) there was a lack of meeting of the minds, and (2) the contracts were against public policy.

Appellant signed fourteen contracts in all. They were approximately six inches in length and each contained a long paragraph in extremely fine print. One of the sentences in this paragraph provided that payments, after the first purchase, were to be prorated on all purchases then outstanding. Mathematically, this had the effect of keeping a balance due on all items until the time balance was completely eliminated. It meant that title to the first purchase, remained in appellee until the fourteenth purchase, made some five years later, was fully paid.

At trial appellant testified that she understood the agreements to mean that when payments on the running account were sufficient to balance the amount due on an individual item, the item became hers. She testified that most of the purchases were made at her home; that the contracts were signed in blank; that she did not read the instruments; and that she was not provided with a copy. She admitted, however, that she did not ask anyone to read or explain the contracts to her.

* * *

A careful review of the record shows that appellant's assent was not obtained "by fraud or even misrepresentation falling short of fraud." This is not a case of mutual misunderstanding but a unilateral mistake. Under these circumstances, appellant's first contention is without merit.

Appellant's second argument presents a more serious question. The record reveals that prior to the last purchase appellant had reduced the balance in her account to $164. The last purchase, a stereo set, raised the balance due to $678. Significantly, at the time of this and the preceding purchases, appellee was aware of appellant's financial position. The reverse side of the stereo contract listed the name of appellant's social worker and her $218 monthly stipend from the government. Nevertheless, with full knowledge that appellant had to feed, clothe and support both herself and seven children on this amount, appellee sold her a $514 stereo set.

We cannot condemn too strongly appellee's conduct. It raises serious questions of sharp practice and irresponsible business dealings. A review of the legislation in the District of Columbia affecting retail sales and the pertinent decisions of the highest court in this jurisdiction disclose, however, no ground upon which this court can declare the contracts in question contrary to public policy. We note that were the Maryland Retail Installment Sales Act, Art. 83 §§ 128–153, or its equivalent, in force in the District of Columbia, we could grant appellant appropriate relief. We think Congress should consider corrective legislation to protect the public from such exploitive contracts as were utilized in the case at bar.

Affirmed.

Williams v. Walker Thomas Furniture Co. II

United States Court of Appeals for the District of Columbia Circuit
350 F.2d 445 (1965)

J. SKELLY WRIGHT, J.

* * *

Appellants' principal contention, rejected by both the trial and the appellate courts below, is that these contracts, or at least some of them, are unconscionable and, hence, not enforceable....

* * *

We do not agree that the court lacked the power to refuse enforcement to contracts found to be unconscionable. In other jurisdictions, it has been held as a matter of common law that unconscionable contracts are not enforceable.... Since we have never adopted or rejected such a rule, the question here presented is actually one of first impression.

Congress has recently enacted the Uniform Commercial Code, which specifically provides that the court may refuse to enforce a contract which it finds to be unconscionable at the time it was made. The enactment of this section, which occurred subsequent to the contracts here in suit, does not mean that the common law of the District of Columbia was otherwise at the time of enactment, nor does it preclude the court from adopting a similar rule in the exercise of its powers to develop the common law for the District of Columbia. In fact, in view of the absence of prior authority on the point, we consider the congressional adoption of § 2-302 persuasive authority for following the rationale of the cases from which the section is explicitly derived. Accordingly, we hold that where the element of unconscionability is present at the time a contract is made, the contract should not be enforced.

Unconscionability has generally been recognized to include an absence of meaningful choice on the part of one of the parties together with contract terms which are unreasonably favorable to the other party. Whether a meaningful choice is present in a particular case can only be determined by consideration of all the circumstances surrounding the transaction. In many cases the meaningfulness of the choice is negated by a gross inequality of bargaining power. The manner in which the contract was entered is also relevant to this consideration. Did each party to the contract, considering his obvious education or lack of it, have a reasonable opportunity to understand the terms of the contract, or were the important terms hidden in a maze of fine print and minimized by deceptive sales practices? Ordinarily, one who signs an agreement without full knowledge of its terms might be held to assume the risk that he has entered a one-sided bargain. But when a party of little bargaining power, and hence little real choice, signs a commercially unreasonable contract with little or no knowledge of its terms, it is hardly likely that his consent, or even an objective manifestation of his consent, was ever given to all the terms. In such a case the usual rule that the terms of the agreement are not to be questioned should be abandoned and the court should consider whether the terms of the contract are so unfair that enforcement should be withheld.

In determining reasonableness or fairness, the primary concern must be with the terms of the contract considered in light of the circumstances existing when the contract was made. The test is not simple, nor can it be mechanically applied. The terms are to be considered "in the light of the general commercial background and the commercial needs of the particular trade or case." Corbin suggests the test as being whether the terms are "so extreme as to appear unconscionable according to the mores and business practices of the time and place." We think this formulation correctly states the test to be applied in those cases where no meaningful choice was exercised upon entering the contract.

Because the trial court and the appellate court did not feel that enforcement could be refused, no findings were made on the possible unconscionability of the contracts in these cases. Since the record is not sufficient for our deciding the issue as a matter of law, the cases must be remanded to the trial court for further proceedings.

So ordered.

DANAHER, J. (dissenting):

The District of Columbia Court of Appeals obviously was as unhappy about the situation here presented as any of us can possibly be. Its opinion in the *Williams* case ... concludes: "We think Congress should consider corrective legislation to protect the public from such exploitive contracts as were utilized in the case at bar."

My view is thus summed up by an able court which made no finding that there had actually been sharp practice. Rather the appellant seems to have known precisely where she stood.

There are many aspects of public policy here involved. What is a luxury to some may seem an outright necessity to others. Is public oversight to be required of the expenditures of relief funds? A washing machine, e.g., in the hands of a relief client might become a fruitful source of income. Many relief clients may well need credit, and certain business establishments will take long chances on the sale of items, expecting their pricing policies will afford a degree of protection commensurate with the risk. Perhaps a remedy when necessary will be found within the provisions of the "Loan Shark" law, D.C. Code §§ 26-601 *et seq.* (1961).

I mention such matters only to emphasize the desirability of a cautious approach to any such problem, particularly since the law for so long has allowed parties such great latitude in making their own contracts. I dare say there must annually be thousands upon thousands of installment credit transactions in this jurisdiction, and one can only speculate as to the effect the decision in these cases will have.

I join the District of Columbia Court of Appeals in its disposition of the issues.

Notes and Questions

1. Bargaining Power and Freedom of Choice: No one forced Williams to purchase the household goods. Indeed, some of the goods do not appear to be necessities. The court says Williams had "no meaningful choice." Williams had the freedom to choose not to purchase the products, but it is not clear that she had the opportunity to purchase the same items from a different seller. What does the court mean? Can you think of a plausible economic justification for the court's position?

2. Ex Ante Versus Ex Post Analysis of Terms: Assume the terms were fully and clearly explained to Williams and that she still accepted the contract. Would it still be unconscionable? Does the doctrine of unconscionability have any economic meaning?

3. Ex Post Versus Ex Ante Analysis of Cases: Are decisions like *Williams* good for consumers or bad for consumers? If the case had come out the other way, would it have been a "pro-business" decision? Professor Richard Epstein addresses the question, while commenting on criticisms of U.S. Supreme Court decisions as "pro-business":

> ... [I]t is always critical to distinguish between the ex ante and ex post effects of decisions. Under the ex post perspective, the question of who wins is asked after the dice have been rolled; here, commentators find it easy to classify outcomes as pro- or anti-business.
>
> But that judgment is much more difficult to make when these cases are reexamined from the ex ante perspective, where the question is to figure out the overall social gains and losses that are likely to flow from the choice of any particular rule before any particular dispute arises. The stumbling block in the analysis is that any decision that benefits particular consumers, say, in the ex post state of the world, may well harm consumers as a broader class in the ex ante state of the world.
>
> To see why this is possible, recall that much litigation benefits only a small fraction of consumers as a whole and that the costs of the decision must be absorbed into the overall costs for the firm to stay in business. In the ex ante state of the world, it is often difficult for business to know which consumers will be in a position to sue and which will not. Accordingly, the increase in costs will be passed back, at least in part, to consumers who do not benefit from the favorable outcome in a particular case. Why favor litigious consumers over others?

Richard A. Epstein, *The Myth of a Pro-Business SCOTUS*, Defining Ideas: A Hoover Institution Journal (July 9, 2013).

4. Effect of Unconscionability on Availability of Credit: Williams is just one of many cases in which low-income households have used the doctrine of unconscionability to get the courts to rewrite their contracts. In many of the cases, the prices are very high because state usury laws—price ceilings on interest rates—prevent the sellers from charging an interest rate that reflects the true risk of lending to very low-income households. That is, the higher prices are really a way to get around the interest rate ceilings. For example, in *Jones v. Star Credit Corp., infra* the plaintiffs were welfare recipients. They purchased a freezer which had a fair market value of approximately $300. They signed a sales contract agreeing to pay $1,439.69 for the freezer which included $900 for the purchase price with an additional amount for credit charges, credit life insurance, and so forth. The plaintiffs sued to reform the contract after paying $619.88 on the grounds that it was unconscionable under § 2-302 of the U.C.C. The court held that the contract was unconscionable as a matter of law. With respect to the interest rate charged on the installment sales contract, the court said:

> There is no question about the necessity and even the desirability of installment sales and the extension of credit. Indeed, there are many, including welfare recipients, who would be deprived of even the most basic conveniences without the use of these devices. Similarly, the retail merchant selling on installment or extending credit is expected to establish a pricing factor which will afford a degree of protection commensurate with the risk of selling to those who might be default prone. However, neither of these accepted premises can clothe the sale of the freezer with respectability.

> Having already paid more than $600 toward the purchase of this $300 freezer unit, it is apparent that the defendant had already been amply compensated. In accordance with the statute, the application of the payment provision should be limited to amounts already paid by the plaintiffs and the contract be reformed and amended by changing the payments called for therein to equal the amount of payment actually so paid by the plaintiffs.

If the courts do not allow merchants to "establish a pricing factor which will afford a degree of protection commensurate with the risk of selling to those who might be default prone," what do you think will happen to the availability of credit for the "default prone"? In the second paragraph, the court suggests that this "default prone" plaintiff had paid her fair share, but this analysis ignores the possibility that other "default prone" debtors may have defaulted before they paid even $100. In effect, the "default prone" debtors who pay off their debts are bearing the cost of the merchant's granting credit to similarly-situated debtors. Of course, ex ante, the merchant can't tell who is going to pay and who is going to default. If the merchant could tell, then some would get credit and some would not, and those who got it would get it at a lower interest rate. So, the bottom line is, will the availability of credit to welfare recipients increase or decrease as a result of decisions like *Jones* and *Williams*? Given the choice between being able to purchase a freezer on credit or having to go without a freezer, what choice do you think the Joneses would have taken?

5. Adhesion Contracts: Consider the facts of *Henningsen v. Bloomfield Motors*, 161 A.2d 69 (N.J. 1960). Plaintiffs Claus and Helen Henningsen purchased a Plymouth from the defendant, Bloomfield Motors. Mr. Henningsen signed a preprinted purchase order which contained various provisions setting out the rights and liabilities of each party to the contract. One of the provisions limited the liability of the manufacturer, Chrysler, and the dealer, defendant Bloomfield Motors, to a 90-day warranty on "each new motor vehicle ... chassis or parts manufactured by it to be free from defects in material or workmanship under normal use and service," with the remedy limited to repair or replacement of defective parts. Any other warranties, express or implied, made by any party, were expressly disavowed. Ten days and 468 miles after the purchase, the steering mechanism failed, causing Mrs. Henningsen to crash into a brick wall, totaling the car and seriously injuring her. Plaintiffs sued for breach of express and implied warranties, and negligence. Defendants relied on the signed purchase order as a defense to the allegations.

> It seems obvious in this instance that the motive was to avoid the warranty obligations which are normally incidental to such sales. The language gave little and withdrew much. In return for the delusive remedy of replacement of defective parts at the factory, the buyer is said to have accepted the exclusion of the maker's liability for personal injuries arising from the breach of the warranty, and to have agreed to the elimination of any other express or implied warranty. An instinctively felt sense of justice cries out against such a sharp bargain. But does the doctrine that a person is bound by his signed agreement, in the absence of fraud, stand in the way of any relief?

* * *

> The warranty before us is a standardized form designed for mass use. It is imposed upon the automobile consumer. He takes it or leaves it, and he must take it to buy an automobile. No bargaining is engaged in with respect to it. In fact, the dealer through whom it comes to the buyer is without authority to alter it; his function is ministerial—simply to deliver it. The form warranty is not only standard with Chrysler but, as mentioned above, it is the uniform warranty of the American Automobile Manufacturers Association. Members of the Association are: General Motors, Inc., Ford, Chrysler, Studebaker-Packard, American Motors, (Rambler), Willis Motors, Checker Motors Corp., and International Harvester Company. Of these companies, the "Big Three" (General Motors, Ford, and Chrysler) represent 93.5% of the passenger-car production for 1958 and the independents 6.5%. And for the same year the "Big Three" had 86.72% of the total passenger vehicle registrations.

> The gross inequality of bargaining position occupied by the consumer in the automobile industry is thus apparent. There is no competition among the car makers in the area of the express warranty. Where can the buyer go to negotiate for better protection? Such control and limitation of his remedies are inimical to the public welfare and, at the very least, call for great care by the courts to avoid injustice through application of strict common-law principles of freedom of contract....

> ... The status of the automobile industry is unique. Manufacturers are few in number and strong in bargaining position. In the matter of warranties on the sale of their products, the Automotive Manufacturers Association has enabled them to present a united front. From the standpoint of the purchaser, there can be no arms length negotiating on the subject. Because his capacity for bargaining is so grossly unequal, the inexorable conclusion which follows is that he is not permitted to bargain at all. He must take or leave the automobile on the warranty terms dictated by the maker. He cannot turn to a competitor for better security.

Id. at 85, 87, 94. How does the doctrine of adhesion contracts affect the relative bargaining positions of the parties to a contract? Is the doctrine only applicable when parties have grossly disparate bargaining power? Isn't the court doing exactly what the free market would do anyway? In the oligopoly-type situation, as described here, wouldn't it be profitable for a car manufacturer to have a contract which states that the manufacturers are liable for everything (at a price premium, of course)? Here, in effect, the court imposes the same contract terms on all manufacturers and all consumers by allowing some consumers to sue and recover. In sum, everyone pays for the ability to recover when their car fails instead of just those who would be willing to pay the premium. Is freedom of contract the solution? Modern warranties generally run for three years or 36,000 miles, and sometimes even longer. Domestic automobile manufacturers no longer enjoy the dominant position they held in 1958. (What does this tell you about the dynamic process of markets, in particular the market for automobiles?) How would a modern court analyze a situation similar to that in *Henningsen* with these additional facts? What cost do modern consumers face as a result of increased warranty coverage and length? Should consumers be allowed to waive liability claims against manufacturers in exchange for a lower price? See also the discussion of warranties and information asymmetries in Chapter V.

b. Modification and the Pre-Existing Duty Rule

Occasionally contingencies occur that make performance by one party a losing deal. Assume D is the party disadvantaged by the contingency, and A is the other party. After the contingency occurs, D is faced with three possible choices: (1) D can perform as promised and lose money; (2) D can breach the contract and pay damages (so-called efficient breach); or (3) D and A can renegotiate the terms of the contract in a way that makes them both better off than they would be under option (2). In general, each contracting party has incentives to engage in good faith modification if the total cost of performance can be minimized through cooperation. The courts will enforce modifications if they are supported by consideration.

Alaska Packers' Association v. Domenico

United States Court of Appeals for the Ninth Circuit

117 F. 99 (1902)

ROSS, J.

* * *

The evidence shows without conflict that on March 26, 1900, at the city and county of San Francisco, the libelants entered into a written contract with the appellant, whereby they agreed to go from San Francisco to Pyramid Harbor, Alaska, and return, on board such vessel as might be designated by the appellant, and to work for the appellant during the fishing season of 1900, at Pyramid Harbor, as sailors and fishermen, agreeing to do "regular ship's duty, both up and down, discharging and loading; and to do any other work whatsoever when requested to do so by the captain or agent of the Alaska Packers' Association." By the terms of this agreement, the appellant was to pay each of the libelants $50 for the season, and two cents for each red salmon in the catching of which he took part.... Under [this contract], the libelants sailed on board the Two Brothers for Pyramid Harbor, where the appellant had about $150,000 invested in a salmon cannery. The libelants arrived there early in April of the year mentioned, and began to unload the vessel and fit up the cannery. A few days thereafter, to wit, May 19th, they stopped work in a body, and demanded of the company's superintendent there in charge $100 for services in operating the vessel to and from Pyramid Harbor, instead of the sums stipulated for in and by the contracts; stating that unless they were paid this additional wage they would stop work entirely, and return to San Francisco. The evidence showed, and the court below found, that it was impossible for the appellant to get other men to take the places of the libelants, the place being remote, the season short and just opening; so that, after endeavoring for several days without success to induce the libelants to proceed with their work in accordance with their contracts, the company's superintendent, on the 22d day of May, so far yielded to their demands as to instruct his clerk to copy the contracts executed in San Francisco, including the words "Alaska Packers' Association" at the end, substituting, for the $50 ... payments ... the sum of $100, which document, so prepared, was signed by the libelants before a shipping commissioner whom they had requested to be brought from Northeast Point; the superintendent, however, testifying that he at the time told the libelants that he was without authority to enter into any such contract, or to in any way alter the contracts made between them and the company in San Francisco. Upon the return of the libelants to San Francisco at the close of the fishing season, they demanded pay in accordance with the terms of the alleged contract of May 22d, when the company denied its validity, and refused to pay other than as provided for by the contracts of March 26th....

* * *

The real questions in the case as brought here are questions of law, and, in the view that we take of the case, it will be necessary to consider but one of those. Assuming that the appellant's superintendent at Pyramid Harbor was authorized to make the alleged contract of May 22d, and that he executed it on behalf of the appellant, was it supported by a sufficient consideration? From the foregoing statement of the case, it will have been seen that the libelants agreed in writing, for certain stated compensation, to render their services to the appellant in remote waters where the season for conducting fishing operations is extremely short, and in which enterprise the appellant had a large amount of money invested; and, after having entered upon the discharge of their contract, and at a time when it was impossible for the appellant to secure other men in their places, the libelants, without any valid cause, absolutely refused to continue the services they were under contract to perform unless the appellant would consent to pay them more money. Consent to such a demand, under such circumstances, if given, was, in our opinion, without consideration, for the reason that it was based solely upon the libelants' agreement to render the exact services, and none other, that they were already under contract to render....

* * *

It results from the views above expressed that the judgment must be reversed, and the cause remanded, with directions to the court below to enter judgment for the respondent, with costs. It is so ordered.

Notes and Questions

1. Cost Minimization or Opportunism?: A cost-minimization modification would take place after a contingency made it uneconomical for one party to perform, and this modification of the terms could make both parties better off. The key in *Alaska Packers* is that there was no triggering contingency. The workers merely noticed that the cannery owners were in a very vulnerable position—the workers could appropriate all of the cannery's expected net cash flow for that summer because it was too late for the cannery to hire replacement workers for the season—and engaged in an opportunistic modification of the contract. In other words, nothing had changed since the signing of the original contract, there was no incentive for joint cost minimization, and the workers gave nothing to the cannery which would contribute to cost minimization — in fact, all the workers did was increase the cannery's costs.

2. Modification as Extortion: Richard Posner has addressed opportunistic contract modification in the following terms:

> In economic terms, the making of a contract may confer on the seller a monopoly vis-à-vis the buyer which the seller can exploit by threatening to terminate the contract unless the buyer agrees to pay a higher price than originally agreed upon.... This raises the question ... whether extortion can be given a meaningful definition in the modification setting. To answer this question, it is helpful to distinguish three situations in which modification might be sought:
>
> 1. Nothing has changed since the contract was made, but the promisor, realizing that the remedies for breach of contract would not fully compensate the promisee, gives the promisee the unhappy choice of either paying the promisor more to complete the contract or pursuing his legal remedies.
>
> 2. Something has changed since the contract signing: the promisee has given up alternative sources of supply or otherwise increased his dependence on the promisor. If modification is permitted the promisor can extract a monopoly rent from the promisee.
>
> 3. Something has changed since the contract signing: an unexpected event which ... prevents the (willing) promisor from completing the promised performance without a modification of the contract.
>
> The third case is the clearest for allowing modification. The inability of a willing promisor to complete performance removes the factor of strategic behavior that is present is cases one and two.... The first case might also seem one where modification should be allowed, ... the legal obligation is to perform or pay damages. If the promisee wants more — wants in effect specific performance — he must pay extra for it. That is all that *seems* to be involved in the first case but if we pause to ask why the promisee in the first case would ever agree to pay extra, we shall see that the first case is in reality a version of the second, the monopoly case. If the promisee in the first case has equally good alternative sources of supply, or at least no worse than he had when he made the original contract, he will have no incentive to pay a premium above the contract price for the promisor to perform as agreed; he will allow the promisor to breach and turn elsewhere. He will pay the premium only if his dependence on the promisor has increased since the signing of the contract, i.e., only if the contract gave the promisor a monopoly position vis-à-vis the promisee.

Richard A. Posner, *Gratuitous Promises in Economics and Law,* 6 Journal of Legal Studies 411, 422–23 (1977). How does *Alaska Packers* fit into this analysis? For further discussion of such opportunistic contract modifications, see Chapter V.

3. U.C.C. §2-209: The Uniform Commercial Code modifies the common law pre-existing duty rule to provide for contract enforcement so long as the modification is made in good faith. Charles J. Goetz and Robert E. Scott offer the following insights on the relative merits of the common law and U.C.C. rules:

> Contract rules policing contractual modification are another response to the heightened risk of extortion in specialized environments. For example, the common-law preexisting duty rule can be usefully contrasted with the more permissive regulation of contractual modification under the Uniform Commercial

Code. The preexisting duty rule denies enforcement of a renegotiation or contractual modification where an obligor agrees merely to do that which he is already contractually obligated to do. The rule is primarily designed to reduce the incidence of extortionate modification in construction, employment, and other specialized contractual relationships.

The preexisting duty rule, however, often fails accurately to mirror the underlying bad faith behavior. First, the rule discourages cost-reducing negotiations in addition to threats. Moreover, the obligor satisfies the rule by assuming *any* additional obligations whether or not the "additional" duties are themselves part of the strategic maneuver. The Code abandoned this ill-fitting rule of thumb and instead applies a general good faith standard.... Because this standard is substantially more difficult to enforce, however, the Code may not deter extortionate renegotiation as effectively as did the common law. Nonetheless, if parties generally execute contracts for the sale of goods in the context of a well-developed market for substitutes, the costs saved through legitimate renegotiations will exceed the increased enforcement costs of policing bad faith modification....

Courts also express concern with bad faith extortion through the rules restraining economic duress. Such cases arise when the obligor has *performed* the modified contract, but the "injured party" seeks restitution of the value of his performance because economic duress forced his agreement to modified terms. The market for substitutes is the key variable in economic duress cases. Because a market for substitutes will effectively control a defendant's behavior with no need for legal rules, a prima facie claim of economic duress thus requires a plaintiff to show a specialized environment.

It is difficult to police such bad faith behavior, however, because the distinction between legitimate requests for renegotiation and bad faith threats lies entirely in the honesty of a party's assertion that a readjustment contingency made *performance* less attractive than quasi-performance (breach with damages).

Goetz & Scott, *The Mitigation Principle: Toward a General Theory of Contractual Obligation,* 69 Virginia Law Review 967, 1007 n.106 (1983).

E. Changes in Demand and Supply

The discussion of the supply-and-demand model has focused on the manner in which price and quantity interact when everything else is held constant. The supply-and-demand model can also be used to investigate the impact of changes in non-price variables on market price and quantity. Those variables are the items which were held constant in the previous analysis. Understanding the dynamics of price change in response to market conditions enables one to think about the determination of market prices as a spontaneous and dynamic process. This section examines the impact on market price and quantity of changes in demand and supply.

1. Changes in Demand

Changes in non-price determinants of market demand—the other things that are normally held constant—can cause shifts in the entire demand curve. Only variables other

Figure II-9. Changes in Demand

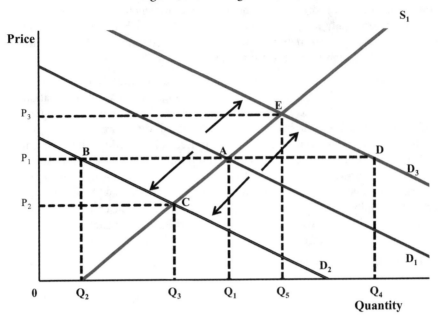

than price can shift the position of the demand curve, and the shift can go left or right depending on the nature of the change. A shift to the left is called a **decrease in demand**, which indicates that consumers are no longer willing to purchase the same quantity at the initial price. The shift from D_1 to D_2 in Figure II-9 represents a decrease in demand. Note that the decrease in demand means that quantity demanded at P_1 has declined from Q_1 to Q_2—indicated by points A and B. As a result of the decrease in demand, the market is in disequilibrium—the quantity supplied, Q_1, is greater than quantity demanded, Q_2. Equilibrium is restored when the market clearing price declines from P_1 to P_2 and the equilibrium quantity declines from Q_1 to Q_3—indicated by point C.

An **increase in demand** is indicated by a shift to the right—for example, from D_1 to D_3 in Figure II-9. The increase in demand tells us that consumers are willing to purchase more at the same price than they were willing to purchase before the shift. Note that the increase in demand means that the quantity demanded at P_1 has increased from Q_1 to Q_4—indicated by points A and D. As a result, the equilibrium price moves from P_1 to P_3 and the equilibrium quantity increases from Q_1 to Q_5—indicated by point E.

The types of non-price developments that can cause shifts in demand include changes in (1) income, (2) prices of related goods, (3) expectations about the future prices or availability of the good, (4) tastes and preferences, (5) population, and (6) laws and regulations.

A change in income can affect both individual and firm demand for a particular good or service. Economists have categorized the effects of changes in income on demand for goods and services into two categories. **Normal goods** are those goods and services for which demand increases (decreases) as income increases (decreases). Consider for example, the demand for medical services. As income increases, most individuals will consult their doctors more often. In contrast, **inferior goods** are those goods and services for which an increase (decrease) in income causes a decrease (increase) in demand. An example of an inferior good is public transportation. As their income increases, most individuals stop riding the city bus.

The demand for a particular good or service is affected by the prices of related goods. This relationship can take one of two forms—substitutes or complements. **Substitute goods** are goods that can replace the utility provided by another good. Butter and margarine are straightforward examples of substitutes. **Complementary goods** are goods used in conjunction with one another. Examples include bread and butter, tennis rackets and tennis balls, airplanes and airports, or, in the case of Mohn Jarshall, beer and salt water. Substitute and complementary goods are identified and distinguished in terms of how the change in the price of one commodity affects the demand for the other commodity. If there is a positive relationship between the changes, the goods are substitutes. If the relationship is negative, they are complements. For example, if an increase in the price of butter causes an increase in the demand for margarine (a shift to the right for the demand of margarine), the goods are said to be substitutes. The same increase in the price of butter could also decrease the demand for bread (shift to the left), which would indicate that bread and butter are complementary products.

Changes in expectations about future prices or the availability of goods in the future often have immediate effects on the demand for goods. For example, if the price of personal computers is expected to decline substantially within a few months, then some potential customers may alter their plans and decide to wait for the price decrease. Of course, if enough customers decide to wait, then the decline in market demand may cause the price to fall sooner than expected. Similarly, expectations of an impending "shortage" often create a real shortage in the short run as demand increases before merchants have a chance to raise prices.

It is clear that the demand for products is determined by the tastes and preferences of consumers. However, economists do not have a quantitative method for determining or predicting consumers' tastes and preferences. For example, the demand for hula hoops virtually disappeared—that is, the demand shifted to the left as consumers lost interest in the product—and then reappeared. Why consumers lose interest in any particular good has not yet been systematically quantified. Economists do study the economics of advertising and information. Advertising does have an impact on tastes and preferences of consumers, but the effect is often very difficult to quantify.

Similarly, laws and regulations can affect consumer demand by altering consumer preferences. For example, several states are currently considering laws that would require food manufacturers to label foods containing genetically modified ingredients. Consumer demand for genetically modified foods would likely decrease after the law change. The addition of the label might persuade consumers that they should be concerned about genetically modified foods, even if they were indifferent about these foods prior to the law change.

Finally, the population of a given market can obviously affect demand for a product as well. If the population of New York City suddenly doubled, there would clearly be more demand for housing in the city.

2. Changes in Supply

The supply curve shifts positions in response to changes in non-price variables in much the same manner as the demand curve. An increase in supply is represented by a shift of the supply curve to the right. An **increase in supply** indicates that suppliers are willing

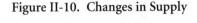

Figure II-10. Changes in Supply

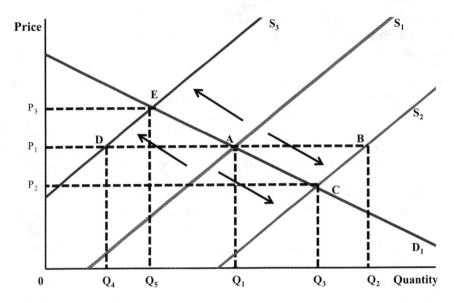

to sell a greater quantity at the initial price than they were previously. For example, in Figure II-10, a shift from S_1 to S_2 demonstrates an increase in supply. Note that the increase in supply means that the quantity supplied at P_1 has increased from Q_1 to Q_2—indicated by points A and B. The interaction of the increased supply with the demand curve indicates that the equilibrium price declines to P_2 while the equilibrium quantity increases to Q_3—indicated by point C. Thus, an increase in supply with no corresponding change in demand results in a decrease in market price and an increase in quantity. A **decrease in supply** means that the supply curve shifts to the left—for example, from S_1 to S_3. Such a shift indicates that suppliers are now only willing to supply Q_4 at P_1—indicated by point D. Hence, the market is in disequilibrium—the quantity demanded, Q_1 is greater than the quantity supplied, Q_4. Assuming no change in demand, a decrease in supply causes the new equilibrium quantity to decrease from Q_1 to Q_5, while the market price increases from P_1 to P_3—indicated by point E.

Changes in the supply curve can be caused by changes in the prices of inputs, improvements in technology, or certain international trade restrictions. For example, an increase in the costs of inputs causes the supply curve to shift to the left. However, improvements in technology lower the costs of production, thereby causing the supply curve to shift to the right. International trade restrictions—such as tariffs or quotas—reduce the number of suppliers to domestic markets. Such a reduction is a shift to the left of the supply curve—causing an increase in the market price and a decrease in quantity available.

Competitive Enterprise Institute v.
National Highway Traffic Safety Admin.

United States Court of Appeals for the District of Columbia Circuit
956 F.2d 321 (1992)

Williams, J.

Choice means giving something up. In deciding whether to relax the previously established "corporate average fuel economy" ("CAFE") standard for model year 1990, the National Highway Traffic Safety Administration ("NHTSA") confronted a record suggesting that refusal to do so would exact some penalty in auto safety. Rather than affirmatively choosing extra energy savings over extra safety, however, NHTSA obscured the safety problem, and thus its need to choose. Because NHTSA failed to reason through to its decision ... we remand the case for further consideration.

* * *

The Energy Policy and Conservation Act, Pub.L. No. 94-163, 89 Stat. 871, requires every major car maker to keep the average fuel economy of its fleet, in each model year, at or above a prescribed level. The Act holds manufacturers to a standard of 27.5 miles per gallon for model year 1985 and each model year thereafter, but authorizes NHTSA to modify the standard, up or down. Where the agency chooses to modify, it must set the replacement standard at the "maximum feasible average fuel economy level." In determining "feasibility," NHTSA has always taken passenger safety into account, and the agency maintains that safety concerns are relevant to whether the agency should adopt one CAFE standard over another.

In August 1988, at the behest of various parties, including several major car makers and petitioner Competitive Enterprise Institute ("CEI"), NHTSA initiated a rulemaking proceeding on whether to reduce the CAFE standards for model years 1989 and 1990. The agency quickly lowered the standard for model year 1989 to 26.5 mpg, but it continued to hear public comment on whether to reduce the 1990 standard as well. Then, in May 1989, NHTSA terminated its proceedings on that issue and left the statutory standard in place.

While the agency rejected a variety of attacks on that standard, we are concerned with only one of the defeated arguments: the contention that the standard will force car makers to produce smaller, less safe cars, thus making it more difficult and expensive for consumers to buy larger, safer cars. We find that the agency has not coherently addressed this concern.

* * *

We must remand this case to NHTSA if the agency has not adequately explained why one of the following is false: (1) adopting a 27.5 standard (as opposed to a lower standard) will have some constraining effect on car makers; (2) car makers will, as one consequence of the standard, decrease the average size of their cars below what it would have been absent the standard; (3) this decrease will make it more difficult for consumers to drive large cars; and (4) all other things being equal, a large car is safer than a small car. The agency actually admits the truth of the fourth proposition, and we can find no passage in the record where the agency has coherently explained the falsehood of any of the others.

Constraining Automakers.

As the agency conceded at oral argument, the 27.5 mpg standard obviously affects car makers' behavior—if not in model year 1990, at least in subsequent years. Under the statute, if a car maker exceeds the applicable CAFE standard in one year, it earns credits that it may use to offset CAFE deficiencies over the next three years. See 15 U.S.C. § 2002(l). At the very least, keeping the 1990 standard at 27.5 mpg reduces the number of carry over credits that GM can use to blunt the effect of the CAFE standards for model years 1991–93.... In fact, NHTSA recently declared that it would be unlawful for it to set "CAFE standards deliberately low enough to be—nonconstraining.'" It seems obvious, then, that the 27.5 mpg standard is constraining in one way or another.

Automakers' Likely Choice to Downsize.

Second, the agency insisted at oral argument that even if the 27.5 standard constrains the behavior of car makers, it will not lead to smaller cars. Yet nowhere has the agency actually justified this claim or even purported to make such a finding....

* * *

The historical fact is, however, that car makers respond to CAFE standards by reducing the size of their fleets. NHTSA itself has explicitly acknowledged as much in the past, and we ourselves have insisted that "the evidence shows that manufacturers are likely to respond to lower CAFE standards by continuing or expanding production of larger, heavier vehicles." Even in the decision below the agency acknowledged this link, explaining that "Chrysler's CAFE has been higher than that of GM or Ford in recent years primarily because it does not compete, or compete as heavily, in all the market segments in which GM and Ford sell cars, particularly the large car market."

The agency now tries to obscure this reality by pointing out that "the average fuel economy of the new car fleet has improved steadily from 26.6 mpg in model year 1982 to 28.2 mpg in model year 1987, while the average weight of a new car increased two pounds during the same period." This argument misses the point. The appropriate comparison, which NHTSA must but did not address, is between the world with more stringent CAFE standards and the world with less stringent standards. The fact that weight has remained constant over time despite mileage improvements shows the effect of technological improvements, to be sure, but in no way undermines the natural inference that weight is lower than it would be absent CAFE regulation. Here we can be quite sure that it is lower, since, as NHTSA observed in this decision, economic recovery and declining gasoline prices sharply raised consumer demand for large cars over the relevant period. If consumers demanded substantially bigger cars, car makers—absent regulation—would have produced substantially bigger cars, not cars that remained, on average, within two pounds of the cars made when consumers favored smaller cars. Moreover, NHTSA has given us no reason to think that whatever technological innovations permitted automakers to meet CAFE requirements while keeping weight constant did not also cost consumers more, again pricing some consumers out of the market for new large cars.

Effect on Consumer Access to Large Cars.

NHTSA also argues that even if the 27.5 mpg standard will deplete the supply of large GM or Ford cars, a consumer looking for a big car "will buy a large car from another manufacturer, or will buy a minivan, or will keep his or her older, large car.... [A]ny one of those alternative consumer outcomes is far more likely than the possibility that the consumer will buy a smaller car than he or she wanted to buy." Nothing in the record suggests that any of these will give consumers large-car safety at the prices that would have prevailed if NHTSA had made a less stringent choice.

The reference to buying large cars from "another manufacturer" is somewhat in the spirit of Marie Antoinette's suggestion to "let them eat cake." By NHTSA's own hypothesis, the "other manufacturers" are Chrysler, which has essentially removed itself from the large car market, and foreign manufacturers, which are subject to CAFE standards on their U.S. sales.... To the limited extent that foreign firms produce truly large cars at all, they are expensive ones....

In suggesting minivans (which are exempt from the 27.5 standard), the agency disingenuously obscures their dangers by citing safety figures only for vans in general. As NHTSA itself has amply documented, however, minivans are considerably less safe than vans generally, with a fatality rate per registered vehicle about 25–33% higher than that of large cars. Finally, NHTSA's notion that the consumer should "keep his or her older, large car" ignores both its own finding that new cars "appear to experience fewer accidents per mile traveled," and the plight of consumers seeking to buy a large car for the first time.

Impact on Safety.

By making it harder for consumers to buy large cars, the 27.5 mpg standard will increase traffic fatalities if, as a general matter, small cars are less safe than big ones. They are, as NHTSA itself acknowledges. The agency explains:

> Occupants of the smaller cars generally are at greater risk because: (a) the occupant's survival space is generally less in small cars (survival space, in simple terms, means enough room for the occupant to be held by the vehicle's occupant restraint system without being smashed into injurious surfaces, and enough room to prevent being crushed or hit by a collapsing surface); (b) smaller and lighter vehicles generally have less physical structure available to absorb and manage crash energy and forces; and (c) in most collisions between vehicles of different weight, the forces imposed on occupants of lighter cars are proportionately greater than the forces felt by occupants of heavier vehicles.

NHTSA, *Small Car Safety in the 1980's* at 64 (1980).[1]

The agency tries to skirt the obvious conclusion with two specious arguments. First, it essentially argues that the 27.5 mpg standard will have no effect on the availability of large cars (i.e., will accomplish nothing at all). This, we have seen, is simply untrue. Second, the agency observes that new cars now come with a variety of mandatory and optional safety features (airbags, anti-lock brakes, etc.) that will presumably compensate for a decline in size.

There are two things wrong with this latter argument. First, so far as we can tell, the agency nowhere claims that these safety innovations fully or even mostly compensate for the safety dangers associated with downsizing. More critically, as in the relation between fuel economy and downsizing, the relevant inquiry is whether stringent CAFE standards reduce auto safety below what it would be absent such standards. That new safety devices may be coming on the market is all well and good, but it is immaterial to our inquiry unless the implementation of those devices somehow depends on or is caused by more stringent CAFE standards; no one even hints at such a link. Whatever extra safety devices may contribute to either type, small cars remain more dangerous than large ones, *all other things being equal.*

---

1. One might argue that the third factor indicates that if all cars were small, there would be fewer traffic fatalities. Any such inference appears quite doubtful. Cars can hit a variety of objects, including trucks, trees, and other cars; fatalities in car-to-car crashes do not account for even a majority of passenger-car occupant fatalities. Moreover, while the record is not clear on the matter, it appears that the chance of fatality in crashes involving two big cars is substantially lower than the chance of fatality in crashes involving two small ones.

* * *

Nothing in the record or in NHTSA's analysis appears to undermine the inference that the 27.5 mpg standard kills people, although, as we observed before, we cannot rule out the possibility that NHTSA might support a contrary finding. Assuming it cannot, the number of people sacrificed is uncertain. Forced to confront the issue, the agency might arrive at an estimate lower than that of two independent analysts who came up with an annual death rate running into the thousands (for the cars produced in any *one* model year). See Robert W. Crandall & John D. Graham, T*he Effect of Fuel Economy Standards on Automobile Safety*, 32 J.L. & Econ. 97 (April 1989). Yet the actual number is irrelevant for our purposes. Even if the 27.5 mpg standard for model year 1990 kills "only" several dozen people a year, NHTSA must exercise its discretion; that means conducting a serious analysis of the data and deciding whether the associated fuel savings are worth the lives lost.

When the government regulates in a way that prices many of its citizens out of access to large-car safety, it owes them reasonable candor. If it provides that, the affected citizens at least know that the government has faced up to the meaning of its choice. The requirement of reasoned decision making ensures this result and prevents officials from cowering behind bureaucratic mumbo-jumbo. Accordingly, we order NHTSA to reconsider the matter and provide a genuine explanation for whatever choice it ultimately makes.

So ordered.

Notes and Questions

1. Gasoline Prices and the Demand for Big Cars: The court, citing the NHTSA ruling, observes that "economic recovery and declining gasoline prices sharply raised consumer demand for large cars over the relevant period." The negative relationship between gasoline prices and consumer demand for large cars indicates that these two goods are complements.

2. First Order Effects: Impacts on Supply and Demand: Economics can be used to predict the effects of changes in constraints such as price, income, and regulations. CAFE requirements constrain manufacturers' choices regarding the possible combinations of fuel efficiency and safety in new cars. Thus, when the CAFE standard is changed, manufacturers must attempt to maximize profits subject to the new constraint. Let us assume that automobile manufacturers respond to the new constraint by shifting the productive capacity of their factories from large cars to small cars, because new technology is either too expensive or not currently available. Remember, however, that this substitution is at the margin. In other words, the manufacturers do not stop making large cars. The impact of these marginal changes on the markets for large and small cars can be seen by using supply and demand diagrams. Consider Figure II-11, which provides a diagrammatic representation of the large and small car markets prior to the imposition of higher CAFE standards. Note that before the standard is increased, the large car market is in equilibrium at price P_1 and quantity Q_1 and the small car market is in equilibrium at price P_2 and quantity Q_2. In order to increase the average fuel efficiency of their fleets, economic theory predicts that car manufacturers will respond by changing their production mix. That is, they shift their productive capacity from large cars to small, more fuel efficient, cars. This action is represented by an increase in supply for the small car market—a shift from S_1 to S_2—and a decrease in supply for large cars—a shift from S_3 to S_4. The effect of this action is to increase the quantity of small cars available—a move from Q_2 to Q_3—while

Figure II-11.

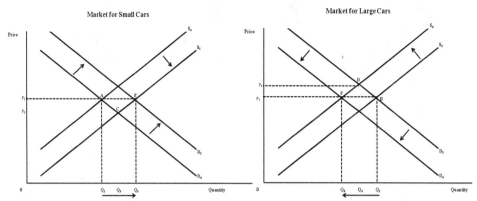

simultaneously decreasing the number of large cars available—a move from Q_1 to Q_4. Moreover, as the supply of small cars increases, the equilibrium price for small cars will fall to P_3 at Q_3. In the large car market, the decrease in supply leads to an increase in market price to P_4 at Q_4.

3. Second Order Effects: Impacts on Supply and Demand: The increase in the price of large cars and the decrease in the price of small cars, described as first order effects in note 2, will have an additional (or second order) effect on the market for cars. Among the other things that are usually held constant, the price of substitutes impacts the demand for products. The first order effects increase the price of large cars relative to small cars and decrease the price of small cars relative to large cars. These changes in relative prices should impact the demand for large and small cars. Specifically, we would expect a decrease in the demand for large cars and an increase in demand for small cars. In Figure II-11, this can be seen as an increase in demand from D_1 to D_2 in the small car market and a decrease in demand from D_3 to D_4 in the large car market. Both the first and second order effects cause the quantity of small cars to increase and the quantity of large cars to decrease. What is the ultimate impact on price?

4. Supply, Demand, and Changes in Technology: Assume that in order to meet the demand for large cars and also conform with more stringent CAFE standards, automakers could add a new fuel efficient technology to each new large car. This new technology can be added at a marginal cost of $5,000. With this added marginal cost, what would happen to the supply of large cars? An increase in the marginal cost of production causes the supply curve to shift to the left, indicating a decrease in supply. The effect of this change in supply is to decrease the quantity of large cars available and to increase the price of large cars. The end result is that fewer large cars are purchased and more small cars are purchased. Thus, regardless of whether manufacturers respond by changing the mix of small and large cars they produce (as in notes 2 and 3) or by adding new fuel efficient technology to new large cars, the effect in the new car market is an increase in the quantity of small cars and a decrease in the quantity of large cars. In other words, no matter how you want to look at it, the net effect of an increase in the CAFE standards is reduced automobile safety as small cars are substituted for large cars.

5. The Market for Used Cars: In general, older cars are less fuel efficient and emit more pollution than newer cars. Studies indicate that about 80% of automobile emission pollution is caused by about 20% of cars. An alternative to forgoing the purchase of a new large car would be to hold on to your old large car or purchase a large used car. This seems to circumvent the intent of the Energy Policy and Conservation Act. Given that people are rational maximizers, it seems that the likely effects of more stringent CAFE standards are an increase in sales of small cars — resulting in a loss in safety — and a longer life for large old cars — resulting in higher gas consumption and pollution. A common source of error in economic policy analysis is to ignore the secondary effects of any action.

6. Judge Williams and the Margin: "The appropriate comparison, which NHTSA must but did not address, is between the world with more stringent CAFE standards and the world with less stringent standards." Marginal analysis concerns the costs and benefits caused by a change in the law, regulation or some other constraint.

7. Manufacturers' Opportunity Costs: If manufacturers could comply with a 27.5 standard, why should they be concerned about the increase from 26.5 to 27.5? Remember, whenever there is a choice, there is a cost.

8. Consumers Substitute at the Margin: The increase in the price of large cars and the decrease in the price of small cars would lead some consumers to purchase small cars instead of large cars. Some consumers will shift to smaller cars and, in doing so, knowingly increase their risk of being killed in an automobile accident. For these marginal consumers, their "marginal cost" of the additional risk is less than the marginal benefit due to savings from buying a cheaper, smaller, more fuel efficient, and riskier car. People often claim that life is priceless, but consumers' behavior often indicates that they are willing to trade off the increased risk of being killed in order save money on the purchase of an automobile.

9. Infra-Marginal Consumers: Some consumers are not at the margin. For example, an increase in the relative price of a bigger car may not affect an individual's decision to purchase a big car. Such consumers are said to be **infra-marginal;** that is, the higher price for bigger cars does not affect their decision. This could be a reflection of their attitude toward the risk associated with getting killed in an automobile accident or it could be a reflection of their strong preference for bigger cars. Can you think of products where a price change would not affect your behavior?

F. Price Controls

In general, the interaction of supply and demand results in a market clearing price where the quantity demanded equals the quantity supplied. Occasionally, however, artificial (non-market) restraints on the ability of the market price to adjust to disequilibria between the quantity demanded and quantity supplied are imposed. The most common types of **price controls** are price ceilings and price floors.

1. Price Ceilings

A **price ceiling** is a restraint on the maximum price that may be charged for a particular good or service. In order to have an impact on market behavior, the price ceiling must be set below the market clearing price. The impact of a price ceiling is demonstrated in Figure II-12, where P^* and Q^* represent the market clearing price and quantity. P_C represents the price ceiling. At P_C, the quantity demanded, Q_D, is greater than the quantity supplied, Q_S. When the quantity demanded is greater than the quantity supplied, a

Figure II-12. Price Controls: A Price Ceiling

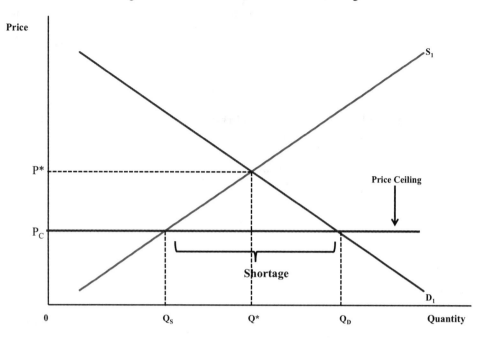

shortage or excess demand exists. However, the price control prevents the market from adjusting to correct this disequilibrium.

In general, as illustrated by the next two cases, the existence of a shortage usually results in the allocation of supply through less efficient means such as waiting in line, bribes, or the requirement that the buyer also purchase other goods from the seller.

M. Kraus & Bros., Inc. v. United States

Supreme Court of the United States
327 U.S. 614 (1945)

Justice Murphy announced the conclusion and judgment of the Court.

The problem here is whether the petitioner corporation was properly convicted of a crime under the Emergency Price Control Act of 1942.

The petitioner is engaged in the wholesale meat and poultry business in New York City. Poultry is a commodity subject to the provisions of Revised Maximum Price Regulation No. 269, promulgated by the Price Administrator pursuant to §2(a) of the Emergency Price Control Act of 1942....

The theory of the Government is that [during Thanksgiving in November, 1943] the petitioner was guilty of an evasion of the price limitations set forth in this particular regulation if it required the purchase of chicken feet and skin as a necessary condition to obtaining the primary commodity, the poultry. This practice is commonly known as a "combination sale" or a "tying agreement." It is argued that the petitioner thereby received for the poultry the ceiling price plus the price of the secondary commodities, the chicken parts.

* * *

The jury acquitted petitioner's president but convicted the petitioner on nine counts. Petitioner was fined $2,500 on each count, a total of $22,500. The conviction was affirmed by the court below.... In our opinion, however, the conviction must be set aside.

* * *

The Price Administrator, pursuant to § 2(a) [of the Emergency Price Control Act of 1942], issued Revised Maximum Price Regulation No. 269 on December 18, 1942, which regulation was in effect at the time the poultry sales in question were made. § 1429.5 of this regulation ... is entitled "Evasion" and reads as follows: "Price limitations set forth in this Revised Maximum Price Regulation No. 269 shall not be evaded whether by direct or indirect methods, in connection with any offer, solicitation, agreement, sale, delivery, purchase or receipt of, or relating to, the commodities prices of which are herein regulated, alone or in conjunction with any other commodity, or by way of commission, service, transportation, or other charge, or discount, premium, or other privilege or other trade understanding or otherwise."

* * *

Th[e] delegation to the Price Administrator of the power to provide in detail against circumvention and evasion, as to which Congress has imposed criminal sanctions, creates a grave responsibility. In a very literal sense the liberties and fortunes of others may depend upon his definitions and specifications regarding evasion. Hence to these provisions must be applied the same strict rule of construction that is applied to statutes defining criminal action. In other words, the Administrator's provisions must be explicit and unambiguous in order to sustain a criminal prosecution; they must adequately inform those who are subject to their terms what conduct will be considered evasive so as to bring the criminal penalties of the Act into operation.

* * *

In light of these principles we are unable to sustain this conviction of the petitioner based upon § 1429.5 of Revised Maximum Price Regulation No. 269. For purposes of this case we must assume that the Administrator legally could include tying agreements and combination sales involving the sale of valuable secondary commodities at their market value among the prohibited evasion devices.... The only issue bearing upon the regulation which is open in this criminal proceeding is whether the Administrator did in fact clearly and unmistakably prohibit tying agreements of this nature by virtue of the language he used in § 1429.5. That issue we answer in the negative.

Section 1429.5, so far as here pertinent, provides that price limitations shall not be evaded by any method, direct or indirect, whether in connection with any offer or sale of a price-regulated commodity alone "or in conjunction with any other commodity," or by way of any trade understanding "or otherwise." No specific mention is made of tying agreements or combination sales.

* * *

The language of § 1429.5 is appropriate to and consistent with a desire on the Administrator's part to prohibit only those tying agreements involving tied-in commodities that are worthless or that are sold at artificial prices. The Administrator may have thought that other tied-in sales did not constitute a sufficient threat to the price economy of the nation to warrant their outlawry, or that they were such an established trade custom that they should be recognized. But we are told that he had no such thought, that prohibition of all tying agreements is essential to prevent profiteering, and that this blanket prohibition is the only policy consistent with the purposes of the Act. All of this may well be true. But these are administrative judgments with which the courts have no concern in a criminal proceeding. We must look solely to the language actually used in § 1429.5. And when we do we are unable to say that the Administrator has made his position in this respect self-evident from the language used.

* * *

The case must therefore be remanded for a new trial, allowing full opportunity for the introduction of evidence as to the value of the chicken parts and charging the jury in accordance with the proper interpretation of § 1429.5.

It is so ordered.

* * *

Black, J. dissenting.

We were at war in 1943. Scarcity of food had become an acute problem throughout the nation. To keep the public from being gouged the government had set ceiling prices.... When Thanksgiving Day approached there were not enough turkeys to supply the demand of the many American families who wanted to celebrate in customary style.

... This meat shortage was felt acutely during the Thanksgiving season, when petitioner instead of his usual 100 to 150 cars of turkeys received only one car. When the retail butchers and poultry market proprietors came clamoring for their share of the small supply (which the defendant rationed among them) they found that along with the turkeys which they wanted so badly petitioner gave and charged them for large amounts of chicken feet, skins and gizzards which they had not asked for at all and which for the most part they had never before sold as separate items. While the butchers paid in addition to the ceiling price charged for the turkeys the price charged for the chicken skins and feet, they did so only because they understood that unless they bought these unwanted items they could get no turkeys. Only one of the butchers sold all the chicken skins to his customers. He explained that he operated his store in a poor neighborhood where the food shortage had become so acute that people were willing to buy anything they could get. As to the rest of the butchers, some simply dumped the chicken skins and feet while others, after diligent efforts, sold a few pounds then gave the rest away either to their customers, or to charitable institutions. Certainly these particular butchers forced to buy these unwanted items for the first time were not the regular retail outlet for disjointed chicken feet and peeled chicken skins, if there ever was such an outlet on a voluntary basis. It is clear therefore that as a result of petitioner's forcing his customers to buy the feet and skins along with the turkeys, the retailers' cost price of the turkeys was in effect increased beyond the ceiling.

In my opinion petitioner's practice in forcing the butchers to buy unwanted chicken feet in order to get wanted turkeys amounted to a direct violation of the Price Control Act. It certainly was no less a violation of the Administrator's regulation against evasion. In promulgating this regulation the Administrator could not possibly foresee every ingenious scheme or artifice the business mind might contrive to shroud violations of the Price Control Act. The regulation does not specifically describe all manner of evasive device. The term "tying agreement" nowhere appears in it and a discussion of such agreements is irrelevant. We need not decide whether what a petitioner did would have violated every possible hypothetical regulation the Administrator might have promulgated. The regulation here involved prohibits every evasion of the Price Control Act....

* * *

When food is scarce and people are hungry it is a violation, both of the letter and spirit of the Price Control Laws, to require consumers or retail stores where they make their purchases, to buy things that they neither need nor want as a condition to obtaining articles which they must have. I dissent from the Court's disposition in this case.

Notes and Questions

1. The Value of Chicken Feet and Skin: In this case, the Court does not say anything regarding the merits of price control laws. Rather, the Court finds the regulation regarding evasion of the price control law to be defective. The defect identified by the Court is that the section lacks clarity regarding the types of behavior that would be regarded as evasive. Specifically, the regulatory language was consistent with a prohibition against tie-in sales involving only worthless commodities — it is possible that the chickens' feet and skin had a market value equal to the difference between the total price paid to petitioner and the market value of the turkey. Whether the chickens' feet and skin was a worthless commodity is a decision left to the finder of fact upon remand.

2. Punishing the Nature of Man?: The Court applies a "strict rule of construction" in defining the evasion provision. This is done because the price fixing regulation was enforced with criminal penalties. Why does the Court use a higher standard of interpretation when criminal penalties are involved? What implicit assumption regarding human behavior is the Court using to justify this standard?

3. Price Gouging or a Change in Demand?: We often hear political and social commentators accuse the business world of engaging in price gouging. It is supposed that price gouging occurs when the seller recognizes that supply will be short in the future and raises present prices in order capture a windfall. Does this allegation make any sense? What do you think happened to the demand for plywood after hurricane Katrina hit Louisiana and Mississippi during the 2005 hurricane season? Based on the tremendous amount of damage to housing, it is likely that the demand for plywood increased. As suppliers of plywood in Louisiana and Mississippi recognized that they did not have enough plywood in stock, we would expect profit maximizing individuals in the rest of the country to begin sending plywood to Louisiana and Mississippi. Thus, the price of plywood would be expected to increase in Louisiana and Mississippi and the remainder of the country due to the increase in demand for this commodity. In general, one should be very skeptical of accusations of price gouging.

4. Using the Market to Solve the Hurricane Problem: From the previous note, we know that as a result of the hurricanes, the demand for plywood in Louisiana and Mississippi increased causing the price of plywood across the country to rise. Consider the effect that a price increase would have on consumer behavior. Suppose Walt Williams, who lives in Virginia, is thinking about building his dog a house. As the price of plywood increases, Walt decides that it is getting too expensive to build a dog house and that his dog can just sleep in the rain. However, the people who have lost their homes in Louisiana and Mississippi value this same plywood very highly — they are pleased with Walt's decision. In fact, social welfare is maximized by having the people in Louisiana and Mississippi use the plywood to rebuild their homes, as opposed to Walt building a dog house. Was any law passed by Congress to get this result? Did the President need to issue an executive order commanding that plywood not be used to build dog houses? Was the fact that the hardware store in Walt's neighborhood raised its price for plywood — because people were willing to pay more in Louisiana and Mississippi — generally helpful or harmful to society? Did Walt forgo the use of wood because he is a humanitarian and felt sorry for the homeless people in Louisiana and Mississippi? The answer to all of these questions is that the market works—it quickly and anonymously allocates resources to those who desire them the most. In times of natural disasters, so-called "price gouging" encourages suppliers to provide important goods, such as plywood, water, gasoline, etc., to the necessary markets.

5. Using Price Controls to Solve the Hurricane Problem: What would have happened in the hurricanes example if Congress had enacted an Emergency Plywood Price Control Act? Assume that the price control imposes a market price equal to the historical price level for plywood. What effect does this have on consumer behavior? What does Walt now think about building his dog a house? Because the price of plywood is now at its historical level, Walt decides to build a dog house. Thus, less plywood is available to rebuild homes in Louisiana and Mississippi—quantity demanded exceeds quantity supplied. In other words, we have a shortage in the plywood market. Prices kept artificially low discourage the extra effort among suppliers to bring important goods to market during times of natural disasters. Is the result achieved using the market or price controls more beneficial to society in general?

6. Laws Against Scarcity?: Justice Black observes that scarcity of food had become a nationwide problem and that "[t]o keep the public from being gouged"—that is, facing higher prices—"the government had set ceiling prices." Moreover, "[w]hen Thanksgiving Day approached there were not enough turkeys to supply the demand of many American families who wanted to celebrate in the customary style." It should be obvious by this point that Justice Black is misguided in his assessment that the public is being gouged—see note 3. However, what do you think about his statement regarding the supply of turkey? Justice Black observes that there will not be enough turkeys for many Americans to celebrate Thanksgiving in the "customary style." What is the point of this observation? The facts of the case seem to indicate that the same quantity of turkey will be available no matter what the method of distribution. That is, even if a price control were imposed and there was no evasion, people would still have to stand in a line in hopes of getting one of the few available turkeys. In fact, the same number of people who got a turkey with the evasion present will get one without it. The flip side of this is that, no matter what, the same number of Americans will be able to celebrate Thanksgiving in the "customary way."

Perhaps Justice Black is concerned with the "fairness" of the distribution method. The likely alternative if all evasion could be stopped would be a long line forming in front of the store. Is this the best use of our time and resources? Consider two possible results of full enforcement of price control laws. First, everyone takes off work to get in line, days ahead of time, in order to get a turkey. Would this have been a good result? Remember that during this time period, labor was in great demand—the opportunity cost of not working was high. Second, a more likely story is that people would not have taken off work because they could not afford to sacrifice that income for a turkey. Thus, only those families generating enough income to allow some family members not to work outside of the home, would be able to stand in the line to buy turkey. Was this the desired result? Even here we have an efficiency loss, because these individuals are no longer working at home if they are standing in line. If the market had been allowed to work (i.e., no price controls), families with greater incomes probably would have purchased the turkeys. The fact that turkeys would have sold for a higher price and would have been allocated to those who valued turkey the highest is further supported by a third possibility. Even if turkeys were somehow allocated in a random manner at the price controlled level, an incentive exists for a black market to develop. That is, individuals who get a turkey for the controlled price will turn around and sell it to someone else for a higher price—presumably, the market price. This analysis seems to indicate that through some way or another, turkeys will be allocated to those individuals willing to pay the *market* price. Then why opt for the less efficient distribution method?

7. Anti-Price Gouging Laws and the Black Market: Just as the price-ceiling discussed in the previous note would likely result in a black market for turkeys, there are numerous examples of black markets developing after governments enact anti-price gouging laws. For example, after Hurricane Sandy restricted gasoline supply in New Jersey in November of 2012, anti-price gouging laws were supposed to keep pump prices low. However, black markets immediately appeared: Twitter posted tweets offering to pay much higher prices than retailers could legally charge; on-line ads offered gasoline for $15 or $25 per gallon, and other ads even proposed a variety of personal services, instead of a cash payment, in exchange for gasoline.

8. The Chicken Skin Entrepreneur?: It is a fact of the case that not only is turkey scarce, but food in general is scarce. According to the testimony of one of the butchers, he was able to sell the chicken skin to his customers. That is, people who were not able to afford turkey or find other food now had food available to purchase. Thus, we can assume that to many consumers these skin and feet were worth something. In fact, those butchers who threw the skin away wasted a resource that some consumers value. Moreover, for Justice Black to assume that these commodities have a zero value adopts a static view of the market process. In other words, perhaps when turkey is widely available, chicken skin has zero value, but when turkey and food in general are more difficult to obtain, chicken skin is valuable to those who are hungry. When an individual sees a new use for a resource that is valued more highly than its opportunity cost, that individual is called an entrepreneur and is rewarded with economic profits. Why is the petitioner not seen in this light? Why is the petitioner not rewarded for his entrepreneurial behavior?

The next case, *Jones v. Star Credit Corp.,* involves the sale of a freezer for four times its retail value to a welfare recipient. At the time of sale, the state of New York had imposed usury laws which put a limit on the maximum interest rate that creditors could charge — a limit on the maximum price that can be charged for a loan. How would you expect the market to allocate credit under a usury, price ceiling scenario? While reading the case, consider how Star Credit Corp. attempts to circumvent the usury law. Furthermore, is this an efficient way to allocate credit?

Jones v. Star Credit Corp.

Supreme Court of New York
298 N.Y.S.2d 264 (1969)

Sol Wachtler, J.

On August 31, 1965 the plaintiffs, who are welfare recipients, agreed to purchase a home freezer unit for $900 as the result of a visit from a salesman representing Your Shop At Home Service, Inc. With the addition of the time credit charges, credit life insurance, credit property insurance, and sales tax, the purchase price totaled $1,234.80. Thus far the plaintiffs have paid $619.88 toward their purchase. The defendant claims that with various added credit charges paid for an extension of time there is a balance of $819.81 still due from the plaintiffs. The uncontroverted proof at the trial established that the freezer unit, when purchased, had a maximum retail value of approximately $300. The question is whether this transaction and the resulting contract could be considered unconscionable within the meaning of Section 2-302 of the Uniform Commercial Code....

There was a time when the shield of "caveat emptor" would protect the most unscrupulous in the marketplace—a time when the law, in granting parties unbridled latitude to make their own contracts, allowed exploitive and callous practices which shocked the conscience of both legislative bodies and the courts.

The effort to eliminate these practices has continued to pose a difficult problem. On the one hand it is necessary to recognize the importance of preserving the integrity of agreements and the fundamental right of parties to deal, trade, bargain, and contract. On the other hand there is the concern for the uneducated and often illiterate individual who is the victim of gross inequality of bargaining power, usually the poorest members of the community.

Concern for the protection of these consumers against overreaching by the small but hardy breed of merchants who would prey on them is not novel. The dangers of inequality of bargaining power were vaguely recognized in the early English common law when Lord Hardwicke wrote of a fraud, which "may be apparent from the intrinsic nature and subject of the bargain itself; such as no man in his senses and not under delusion would make." ...

The law is beginning to fight back against those who once took advantage of the poor and illiterate without risk of either exposure or interference. From the common law doctrine of intrinsic fraud we have, over the years, developed common and statutory law which tells not only the buyer but also the seller to beware. This body of laws recognizes the importance of a free enterprise system but at the same time will provide the legal armor to protect and safeguard the prospective victim from the harshness of an unconscionable contract.

* * *

Fraud, in the instant case, is not present; nor is it necessary under the statute. The question which presents itself is whether or not, under the circumstances of this case, the sale of a freezer unit having a retail value of $300 for $900 ($1,439.69 including credit charges and $18 sales tax) is unconscionable as a matter of law. The court believes it is.

Concededly, deciding the issue is substantially easier than explaining it. No doubt, the mathematical disparity between $300, which presumably includes a reasonable profit margin, and $900, which is exorbitant on its face, carries the greatest weight. Credit charges alone exceed by more than $100 the retail value of the freezer. These alone, may be sufficient to sustain the decision. Yet, a caveat is warranted lest we reduce the import of Section 2-302 solely to a mathematical ratio formula. It may, at times, be that; yet it may also be much more. The very limited financial resources of the purchaser, known to the sellers at the time of the sale, is entitled to weight in the balance. Indeed, the value disparity itself leads inevitably to the felt conclusion that knowing advantage was taken of the plaintiffs. In addition, the meaningfulness of choice essential to the making of a contract can be negated by a gross inequality of bargaining power. (Williams v. Walker-Thomas Furniture Co.)

There is no question about the necessity and even the desirability of installment sales and the extension of credit. Indeed, there are many, including welfare recipients, who would be deprived of even the most basic conveniences without the use of these devices. Similarly, the retail merchant selling on installment or extending credit is expected to establish a pricing factor which will afford a degree of protection commensurate with the risk of selling to those who might be default prone. However, neither of these accepted premises can clothe the sale of this freezer with respectability.

* * *

Having already paid more than $600 toward the purchase of this $300 freezer unit, it is apparent that the defendant has already been amply compensated. In accordance with the statute, the application of the payment provision should be limited to amounts already paid by the plaintiffs and the contract be reformed and amended by changing the payments called for therein to equal the amount of payment actually so paid by the plaintiffs.

Notes and Questions

1. Usury Laws: A Form of Price Control: A limit on the maximum interest rate that a lender can charge is called a usury law. To be effective, the maximum interest rate must be set at a level below the current market interest rate. A usury law is therefore simply a form of price ceiling—an interest rate is simply the price paid for financing. When the maximum legal rate is below the market rate, the quantity of credit demanded will exceed the quantity of credit supplied. However, because of the legal constraint, interest rates will not be allowed to adjust upward in order to eliminate the shortage. Thus, it appears as if a shortage will continue to exist. However, this is not the end of the story. Creditors and borrowers have an incentive to get around usury laws. In other words, loans will be allocated by a non-interest rate mechanism.

2. Interest Rates: In general, an interest rate has three components contributing to its sum. First, a portion of the interest rate reflects the opportunity cost of the principal in some other use. Second, an addition is made to reflect the expectation of inflation. Third, a premium is added to any interest rate based upon the risk of default. The riskier the investment, the higher the rate. This formulation of the interest rate suggests that a systematic bias will develop under usury laws. Namely, high risk individuals will not be able to obtain loans. The question then becomes: are these high risk individuals better off paying high interest rates for credit or not having the option of credit at all?

3. Circumventing Usury Laws: Some firms that extend credit to high risk individuals as a regular part of their business have found ways to circumvent usury laws. Consider the local appliance store that wishes to make a sale on credit to a high risk individual but cannot charge the market interest rate. Instead of forgoing the sale, store owners have developed resourceful methods for maximizing profits. For example, assume that the market price for the new appliance is $500. The customer, however, is considered to be a high risk for default. Thus, an interest rate in excess of the legal limit would be required to consummate the sale. One way around this is for the seller to charge the buyer a price in excess of the market price for the appliance. For example, the appliance store may charge $750 for the appliance despite its market price of $500. The seller has parted with a $500 appliance, but is charging interest on the principal of $750. Monthly payments to the store owner will include an amount based on the principal and interest on this fictional credit extension. The payments on the fictional credit of $250, paid back over the course of the loan at the legal interest rate, will be sufficient to compensate the store owner as if he had charged the high risk interest rate on the true market price of $500. By raising the price, and therefore the original principal, above the market price, the seller is compensated for the risk below market interest rate. The calculation of such numbers is covered in Chapter X, Principles of Valuation.

2. Price Floors

A **price floor** is a price control that prevents the sale of a product below a certain minimum level. A price floor must be set greater than the market clearing price in order

Figure II-13. Price Floor

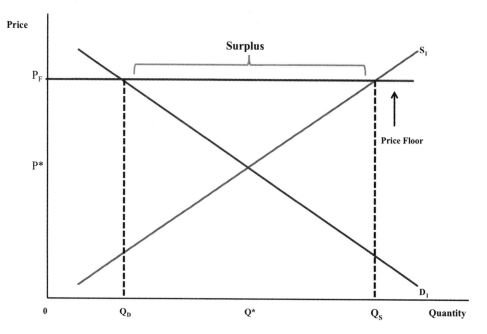

to have an impact on market behavior. In Figure II-13, the equilibrium price and quantity are indicated by P* and Q*, respectively. The price floor, P_F, causes quantity supplied, Q_S, to be greater than quantity demanded, Q_D. This disequilibrium condition is referred to as a **surplus** or **excess supply**. In order to sell their goods and services when the market is constrained by a price floor, the sellers must offer non-price incentives, such as better services, "free" gifts, and rebates.

A familiar example of a price floor is the minimum wage law enacted by the federal government, which is discussed in more detail in Chapter VIII. The intent of the minimum wage law is to provide workers with a "fair wage" for their work and to reduce the incidence of poverty. Using the supply and demand model, we can quickly determine whether minimum wage laws work and whether they have unintended consequences.

In order for the minimum wage to have an impact, it must be set at a rate above the market wage for those employees who are the intended beneficiaries of the law. In Figure II-14, the market wage is represented by W* and the mandated minimum wage is denoted by W_{MIN}. As we observed above, the result of mandating a price floor is to cause quantity supplied to exceed quantity demanded. At the higher wage, the quantity demanded decreases to Q_1 and the quantity supplied increases to Q_2. The excess supply, equal to $Q_2 - Q_1$, is a surplus of labor. However, because of the minimum wage law, price and quantity cannot adjust back to the market equilibrium. Under an effective minimum wage—that is, a minimum wage above the market clearing wage—some individuals keep their jobs and increase their earnings, some individuals lose their jobs, and some individuals enter the job market seeking the now higher wage.

Think about the result of minimum wage laws: the quantity of available jobs has decreased but those who do have jobs are paid a higher "fair wage." Moreover, the remaining jobs are allocated in a highly competitive process to those with the best potential or skill.

Figure II-14. Minimum Wage Law's Effect on the Labor Market

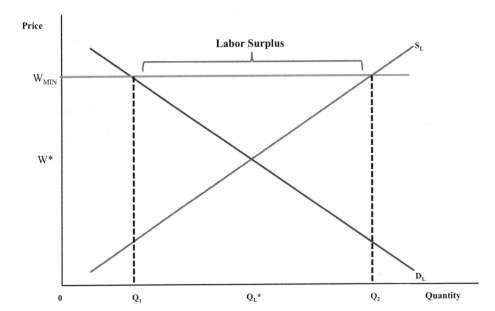

Those who cannot find jobs in the labor market are those with lower education or little work experience. Such laws seem to perpetuate the poverty of some while increasing the wages of others. Was this the intended consequence?

In July 2013, Wal-Mart announced that it would abandon plans to build three new stores in Washington, D.C., if the D.C. Council approved a proposal to require non-unionized "big box" stores to pay a "living wage" — $12.50 an hour, a 50 percent premium over the D.C. minimum wage. Is this an illustration of the predicted economic effects of a price floor or simply strategic bargaining by Wal-Mart?

3. The Quality of Products and Services in a Price-Controlled Market

An additional implication of price controls is interesting and relevant to understanding the competitive market process. We have assumed in the foregoing discussion that the quality of goods and services produced remains the same after price controls are established. However, this is generally not the case. Consider a price control example from the area of property law.

Rent controls are a form of price ceiling. Often the justification for such laws is the protection of low income individuals. Nonetheless, the long run effect of rent control seems to harm low income individuals the most. For example, one effect of rent control is the decay of the buildings. This is understandable because landlords' maintenance costs often exceed their rental income. Furthermore, what incentive for improvements exists when rental income is fixed? A second negative effect is the disincentive rent controls create for building new rental property. As populations grow, the demand for rental space begins to exceed supply. However, because of rent control there is little incentive to build new rental property. Thus, it is not unusual to find families living in very cramped quarters. Rent controls also create the incentive for a black market to develop. Those who were lucky enough to be renting property at the controlled rate make a profit by subletting at very high prices. The market clears, but only with the help of illegal transactions.

Price ceilings such as rent control can also lead to discrimination. In a free market, prices adjust to eliminate shortages so that the buyers willing to pay the market price are typically able to purchase the good. However, shortages induced by price ceilings require suppliers to choose among the many buyers that are willing to purchase a good. According to Armen Alchian:

> [I]f the government imposes rent controls that keep the rent below the free-market level, the price the landlord pays to discriminate falls, possibly to zero. The rent control does not magically reduce the demand for apartments. Instead, it reduces every potential tenant's ability to compete by offering more money. The landlord, now unable to receive the full money price, will discriminate in favor of tenants whose personal characteristics — such as age, sex, ethnicity, and religion — he favors. Now the black woman seeking an apartment cannot offset the disadvantage of her skin color by offering to pay a higher rent.
>
> Competition for apartments is not eliminated by rent controls. What changes is the "coinage" of competition. The restriction on private property rights reduces competition based on monetary exchanges for goods and services and increases competition based on personal characteristics. More generally, weakening private property rights increases the role of personal characteristics in inducing sellers to discriminate among competing buyers and buyers to discriminate among sellers.

Armen A. Alchian, *Property Rights*, in The Concise Encyclopedia of Economics (2008).

G. Elasticity: The Responsiveness of Supply and Demand to a Price Change

The supply and demand framework is helpful in analyzing many real-world problems. Thus far, we have established the simple proposition that the quantity supplied or demanded will be responsive to changes in the market price. This proposition leads us to a second line of analysis — *how responsive* are quantity demanded and supplied to changes in price? Will a small change in price lead to a large change in the quantity demanded or only a relatively small change? Economists use the concept of elasticity to measure the relative responsiveness of the quantity demanded or supplied to changes in price. In general, **elasticity** is a measure of the relative responsiveness of a dependent variable to a change in an independent variable. As such, many different types of elasticity can be measured. In this section, we are only concerned with price elasticity. **Price elasticity** is a measure of the relative responsiveness of the quantity demanded or supplied to changes in price.

1. Elasticity of Demand

Elasticity of demand is a measure of consumer responsiveness to price changes. Specifically, the elasticity of demand is the percent change in quantity demanded divided by the percent change in price.[2] The elasticity of demand is often indicated by the demand

---

2. In actual calculation, the demand elasticity coefficient will always be negative, because of the law of demand. If price goes up, quantity demanded for a good or service goes down, and vice versa.

elasticity coefficient E_d—a numerical representation of the ratio of the percent change in quantity over the percent change in price.

Elasticity of Demand = % Change in Quantity Demanded ÷ % Change in Price

Elastic demand describes a situation in which the percent change in quantity demanded is greater than the percent change in price—thus, the demand elasticity coefficient is greater than 1. Elastic demand means buyers are very responsive to price changes. As the demand elasticity coefficient increases above 1, demand becomes more elastic. In contrast, **inelastic demand** describes a situation in which buyers are not very responsive to changes in price—the percent change in quantity demanded is less than the percent change in price. In this situation, the demand elasticity coefficient is less than 1. As the coefficient moves away from 1 and becomes infinitely closer to 0, demand is said to become more inelastic. **Unit elasticity of demand** is a situation in which the percent change in quantity demanded is the same as the percent change in price. Thus, the demand elasticity coefficient is equal to 1.

Figure II-15 illustrates the relationship between price and quantity demanded for the different categories of elasticity. Each panel shows the effect of a 25% price increase on the quantity demanded. Thus, the shifting of price along the vertical axis is the same in all three panels. In terms of impact on the quantity demanded, each of the panels shows a different horizontal shift. The varying results for quantity demanded are a result of differently sloped demand curves. In panel (a), quantity demanded falls by 10% which is less than the 25% change in price. Thus, panel (a) provides an example of an inelastic demand curve. Notice that inelastic demand curves have a relatively steeper slope—a slope with an absolute value greater than one. Price and quantity both change by 25% in panel (b) indicating the presence of unit elasticity. Demand curves exhibiting unit elasticity have a slope with an absolute value equal to one. Quantity demanded falls by 35% in panel (c) which exceeds the 25% change in price. The demand curve in panel (c) is therefore elastic as demonstrated by its relatively flat slope—a slope with an absolute value less than one.

Two extreme forms of the demand curve are helpful in analyzing many economic problems. Figure II-16(a) shows a demand curve that is totally elastic. When the demand curve is **totally elastic**, the quantity demanded is completely responsive to price changes—a small increase in price will cause the quantity demanded to disappear. Thus, the demand elasticity coefficient equals infinity. A totally elastic demand curve would occur in a perfectly competitive market. However, perfectly competitive markets are rare. Figure II-16(b) shows a demand curve that is **totally inelastic**—quantity demanded is unresponsive to changes in price. A totally inelastic demand curve has a demand elasticity coefficient of zero. It is often suggested that a heroin addict's demand for heroin is totally inelastic.

For ease of exposition, demand curves are usually drawn as straight lines. The elasticity of demand for such linear demand curves contains portions that are elastic, unit elastic, and inelastic. Thus, the elasticity coefficient will vary along demand curves. For example, consider the market demand for pizza graphed in Figure II-17. The slope of the curve is constant throughout, as indicated by the fact that the increase in quantity demanded in response to a price decrease of $1 is the same for every $1 price interval. Another way

---

For purposes of our exposition, this point is irrelevant to the interpretation of elasticity. We will accordingly eliminate the use of a negative sign before the demand elasticity coefficient.

Figure II-15. Elasticities of Demand

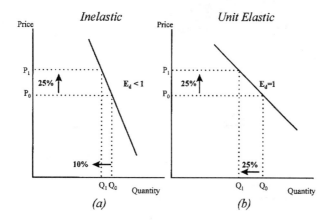

(a)

(b)

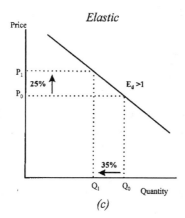

(c)

Figure II-16. Totally Elastic & Inelastic Demand Curves

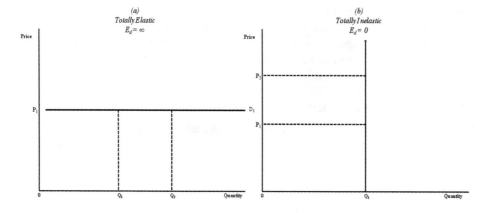

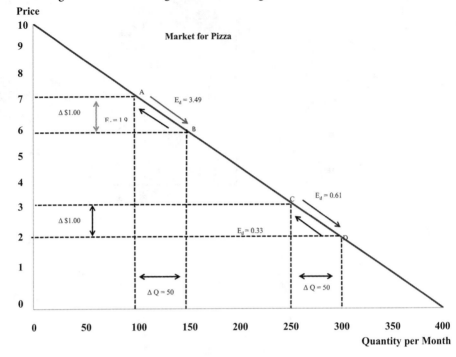

Figure II-17. Differing Elasticities along a Market Demand Curve

of stating this is to observe that a decline in price from $7 to $6 results in the same increase in the quantity demanded as does a decline from $3 to $2. Despite this, the elasticity of demand is greater at the higher prices. The move from A to B represents a 50% increase in quantity demanded and a 14.29% decrease in price—and this translates into an elasticity of demand of 3.49. Note that the move from B to A indicates elasticity of 1.9. The difference between the calculations illustrates that the relevant percentages change depending on the direction of the change in price. A $1 decline resulting in a move from C to D yields a relatively inelastic demand of 0.61—a 20% increase in quantity and a 33% decrease in price.

Two conclusions can be drawn from the analysis in Figure II-17. First, it does not make sense to refer to the demand for a particular good or service as being elastic or inelastic unless that reference is qualified by a price range. This is due to the fact that the elasticity of goods and services can change as prices change. Second, consumers are generally more responsive to price changes at higher prices than lower prices. Notice that the portion of the demand curve associated with higher prices is elastic and the portion associated with lower prices is inelastic. In Figure II-18, the point at which the curve goes from being elastic to inelastic is where there is unitary elasticity of demand.

The demand elasticity concept can also be utilized to analyze the effect of price changes on total revenue or total expenditures. First, it is necessary to point out that the terms total revenue and total expenditures describe two perspectives for the same money. **Total revenue** is the product of price times quantity. Total revenue represents the total amount of money that the supplier receives from the buyer. It is intuitive that a dollar spent by the consumer is the same dollar that the seller considers to be revenue. Thus, **total expenditures** can also be defined as the product of price and quantity. Total expenditures represent the total amount of money that the buyer gives to the supplier.

Figure II-18. Elasticity & Higher Prices

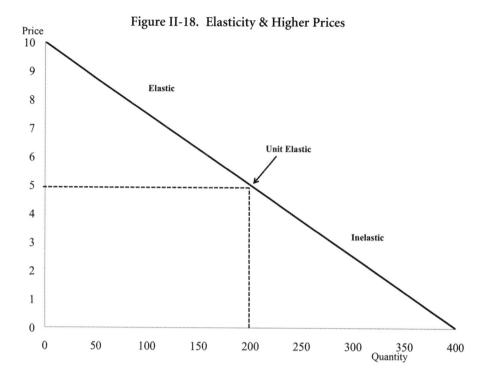

What happens to total revenue (total expenditures) when price decreases? According to the law of demand, if the price falls, the quantity demanded increases. The lower price means that revenue (expenditures) per unit decreases, which tends to decrease total revenue (total expenditures). However, the greater quantity demanded means that the number of units sold increases, and this tends to increase total revenue (total expenditures). The overall change in total revenue (total expenditures) resulting from a lower price is the net result of these opposite effects. When demand is elastic, the percentage increase in quantity demanded exceeds the percentage decrease in price, so a price decrease will increase total revenue (total expenditures). When demand is unit elastic, the percentage increase in quantity demanded is just equal to the percentage decrease in price, so a price decrease will not change total revenue (total expenditures). Finally, when demand is inelastic, the percentage increase in quantity demanded is less than the percentage decrease in price, so a price decrease will decrease total revenue (total expenditures). These relationships are illustrated in Figure II-19. Thus, the general rule is that if price and total revenue (total expenditures) move in the same direction, then demand is inelastic; if price and total revenue (total expenditures) move in opposite directions, then demand is elastic.

There are three major determinants of the elasticity of demand. First, and most important, the number, availability, and price of substitutes indicates the ability of buyers to purchase other products in response to a price increase. Second, in general, the size and importance of the product in the consumer's budget determines whether or to what extent the consumer will respond to a price change—the larger and more important the product to the budget, the more likely consumers will respond to a change in price. Third, the time period involved in the adjustment to a price change will affect the elasticity of demand. The effect of time will be discussed in more detail in a later section.

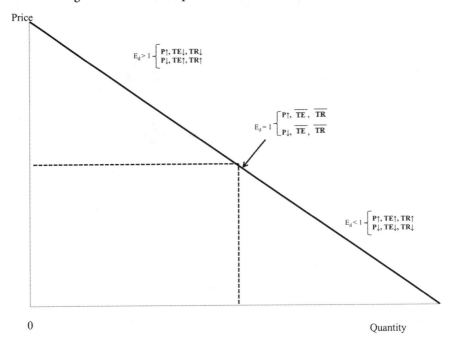

Figure II-19. Total Expenditures/Total Revenues & Demand

The law of demand states that, other things being equal, an inverse relationship exists between price and quantity demanded. The law of demand is an undefeated proposition in economics. Nonetheless, in analyzing individuals' demand curves for a product, we may occasionally be presented with a situation that appears not to support the law of demand. Consider the impact of a $0.25 increase in the price of a Big Mac. It is undoubtedly true that some individuals will not reduce their consumption of Big Macs in the face of the price increase, but that does not refute or even contradict the law of demand. Although some individuals do not react to the price increase, others will reduce their consumption. The individuals who reduce their consumption are referred to as the **marginal consumers**—the economic actors who are the first to respond to a change in relative prices. Another way to describe the marginal consumers is to say that their elasticity of demand for Big Macs is greater than the elasticity of the consumers who did not change their quantity demanded in the face of a price increase.

2. Elasticity of Supply

Elasticity of supply is a measure of producer responsiveness to changes in the market price for goods or services. Specifically, the elasticity of supply is the percent change in quantity supplied divided by the percent change in price. Thus, an elasticity of supply coefficient can be calculated for any type of supply curve.

Elasticity of Supply = % Change in Quantity Supplied ÷ % Change in Price

Elastic supply describes a situation in which the percent change in quantity supplied is greater than the percent change in price—the supply elasticity coefficient is greater than 1. Elastic supply means that suppliers are very responsive to price changes. The larger the supply elasticity coefficient is above 1, the more elastic supply is said to be. In contrast, **inelastic supply** describes a situation in which suppliers are not very responsive to changes in price—the percent change in quantity supplied is less than the percentage change in price. In this situation, the supply elasticity coefficient is less than 1. As the coefficient moves away from 1 and becomes closer to 0, supply is said to be more inelastic.

As was the case with demand elasticity, study of the totally elastic and totally inelastic supply curves is helpful in analyzing many types of economic problems. **Totally elastic supply** is represented graphically by a horizontal supply curve—as in Figure II-20. At any price below P producers will supply a quantity of zero. As the price moves from just below P to P producers will supply an unlimited amount to the market—a totally elastic supply curve has an elasticity coefficient of infinity. In this case, the quantity actually supplied to the market depends upon the demand curve. At the other extreme is the case of the totally inelastic supply curve. **Totally inelastic supply** curves are vertical and represent a zero percentage change in the quantity supplied regardless of the percentage change in price. Figure II-20 shows the relationship between price and quantity supplied for the totally inelastic supply curve. Total inelasticity reflects a market with completely unresponsive suppliers and results in a supply elasticity coefficient of zero.

The responsiveness of the quantity supplied to an increase in price will depend on the supplier's willingness and ability to transfer resources to the production of that good. If it is perceived to be economically costly to transfer resources from other uses, then it will take a large price increase to obtain a given quantity increase, and supply will be relatively inelastic. On the other hand, if resources can be transferred at a relatively low economic cost, a smaller price increase will suffice to bring about a given increase in quantity, and supply will be relatively elastic.

Figure II-20. Totally Elastic & Inelastic Supply Curves

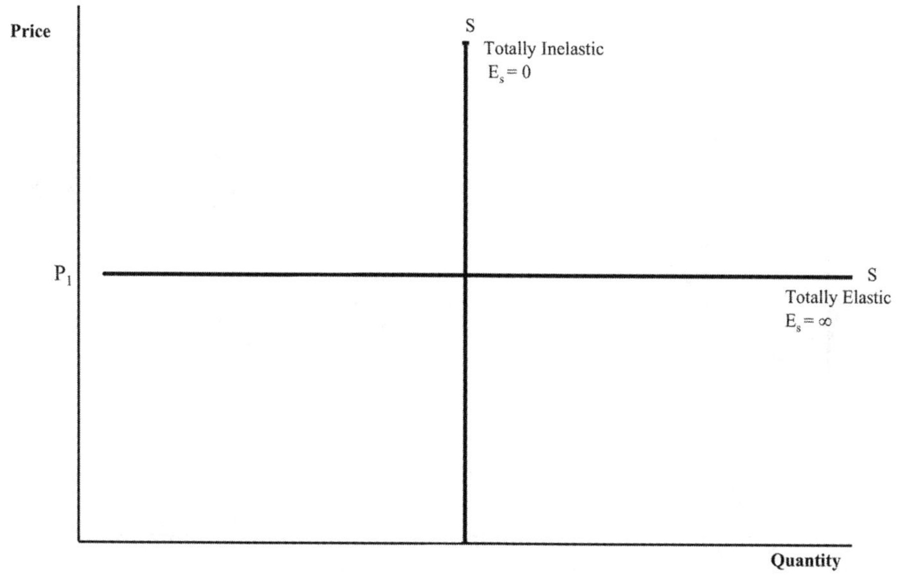

3. Time and Elasticity

Both supply and demand elasticity are affected by the time period allowed for adjustment. The more time that suppliers have to adjust to the price change, the more elastic supply will be. Likewise, elasticity of demand increases the longer consumers have to react to any given price change. To analyze the responsiveness of supply and demand over a period of time, economists have divided the time of adjustment into three periods: the market period, the short run, and the long run. The following example, in the supply elasticity context, demonstrates the effect of time on elasticity.

Assume that Congress passes, and the President signs, legislation that imposes sweeping new regulatory requirements on business. In order to comply with the regulations, businesses demand additional legal services. In Figure II-21, we show this as an increase in demand from D_1 to D_2. However, in the market period, the supply curve for legal services is perfectly inelastic—represented by S_1. Because resources cannot be shifted to new uses instantaneously, the supply of legal services is fixed. Thus, in the market period, supply is fixed in the face of increasing demand resulting in an increase in price from P_1 to P_2—indicated by movement from point A to point B. Individuals providing legal services will notice that the price that can be charged has increased. The new higher price creates the incentive to shift resources into the provision of legal services. In the short run, lawyers will shift currently available resources into the provision of legal services. This may include spending more time at work and less time in leisure activities or more time on regulatory law than divorce law. The effect of this short run supply response is illustrated by S_2 and P_3—indicated by movement from point B to point C.

If an economic profit is still being earned after all currently available resources have been moved into the provision of regulatory legal services, then an incentive exists to make further changes. In the long run, all possible adjustments can be made and resources that were not available in the short run can now be shifted into the provision of regulatory legal services. For example, law firms that were previously unsure of the permanency of the change will

Figure II-21. Time & Elasticity of Supply

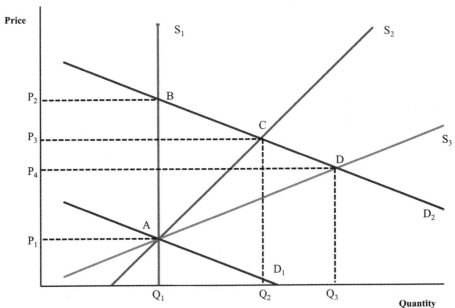

now begin to provide regulatory legal services, persons with law degrees who are not practicing will take the bar, and college graduates seeking the higher incomes of lawyers relative to other professions will apply and graduate from law schools. The effect of these long run adjustments will be to shift the long run supply curve to S_3 and increase the quantity supplied to Q_3—indicated by movement from point C to point D. Note that the effect of all of these responses is to increase the number of lawyers and reduce price towards the old level. Will price fall back to P_1? This depends upon factors specific to the industry. The main point to remember is that the elasticity of supply will tend to increase over time.

The same type of analysis applies to demand elasticity. As a general rule, the more time that both producers and consumers have to respond to a change in market price, the more elastic supply and demand will be.

4. Tax Incidence

A major source of revenue for governments is the excise tax. An **excise tax** is a per unit tax on the sale of a particular item. Well known examples of excise taxes are those levied on the sale of cigarettes, tires, and gasoline. Confusion often arises as to who pays an excise tax. Because the seller sends a check to the government, many people believe that the seller bears the burden of an excise tax. However, sellers might be capable of passing the burden of an excise tax on to consumers through increased prices. A study of **tax incidence** reveals whether consumers or sellers bear the burden of a particular tax. Analyzing tax incidence uses the supply and demand elasticity concepts introduced in the previous sections. A simple example will help explain the tax incidence concept.

Consider a $2.00 tax levied on every automobile tire sold. The tire tax is paid to the government by the tire manufacturer. Figure II-22 shows the supply and demand for tires prior to the $2.00 excise tax—represented by D_1 and S_1. Prior to the tax, the market was in equilibrium at 50 million tires produced for a price of $50.00 per tire—indicated by

Figure II-22. Elasticity & Tax Incidence: The Original Case

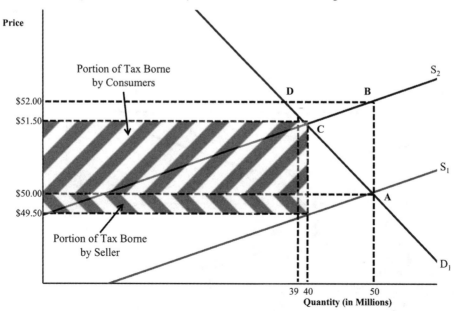

point A. What is the effect on market price and quantity of imposing a $2.00 per tire tax? Remember that the supply curve represents the amount that sellers are willing and able to supply at each price. Once the tax is imposed, suppliers' per unit costs will be $2.00 higher at each quantity level. Thus, the result of the excise tax is to shift the supply curve to the left—to S_2. The vertical distance between S_1 and S_2 is equal to the excise tax amount of $2.00. From Figure II-22 it is easy to see that one effect of the tax is to reduce the total quantity of tires sold. This is because the demand for tires is not totally inelastic. Despite the fact that the supply curve shifts to reflect the excise tax, the demand curve does not move because nothing has happened to change the demand for tires—only the quantity demanded will be affected.

As a result of the tax, sellers would be willing to supply the old equilibrium quantity of 50 million tires at a price of $52.00—indicated by point B. However, because the demand for tires is not totally inelastic, consumers are not willing to purchase 50 million tires at $52.00. At $52.00, consumers are only willing to purchase 39 million tires— indicated by point D. Therefore, at $52.00, a market surplus would develop putting downward pressure on price and quantity supplied. After the imposition of the tax we can see that the market moves to a new equilibrium price of $51.50 and quantity of 40 million—indicated by point C. The shaded area represents the tax revenue collected, which is equal to the quantity of tires sold multiplied by the $2.00 tax rate. In our example, the total tax revenue equals 40,000,000 × $2.00 = $80,000,000. Note that the old equilibrium price line indicates how both the seller and purchaser are affected by the excise tax. Prior to the tax, the equilibrium price was $50.00. The new equilibrium price is $51.50, so consumers must now pay $1.50 more for a tire. Thus, consumers bear 75% of the new $2.00 tax as indicated by the shaded area above the original equilibrium price. Although the price increases by $1.50, sellers must send $2.00 to the government for every tire sold. The remaining $0.50 must come from the seller. Thus, at a market price of $51.50, the sales price net of taxes is $49.50. This is $0.50 below the old equilibrium price of $50.00. The sellers' burden is reflected diagrammatically as the shaded portion below the old equilibrium price—the seller bears 25% of the tax burden.

Tax incidence changes with changes in the elasticity of demand. If demand is highly elastic, sellers tend to bear more of the burden. Figure II-23 shows the original tire market in equilibrium at 50 million tires for $50.00 per tire—indicated by point A. The only

Figure II-23. Elasticity & Tax Incidence: The Case of Greater Demand Elasticity

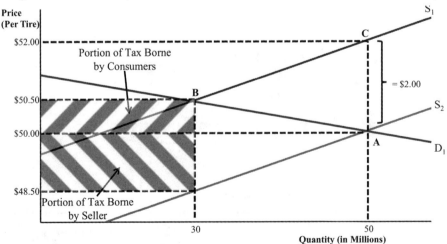

difference between this and the previous example is that the slope of the demand curve is flatter, representing more elastic demand. As in the previous example, a $2.00 tax is levied per tire causing the supply curve to shift to the left by an amount equal to $2.00 for each possible quantity. In this example, the new equilibrium price is only $50.50—indicated by point B. This is $0.50 above the old equilibrium price and thus consumers bear 25% of the $2.00 tax burden. The seller must still send $2.00 to the government and can only force the consumer to pay for $0.50 of the tax. Thus, the seller must deduct $1.50 from the old $50.00 selling price, meaning that the sales price net of taxes is $48.50. This means the seller now bears 75% of the tax burden.

A comparison of the examples in Figures II-22 and II-23 indicates that relatively elastic demand means that consumers bear less of the burden of an excise tax. Sellers cannot pass on as much of the tax when demand is relatively elastic. However, when demand is relatively inelastic, consumers bear more of the tax in the form of higher prices. In addition, note that when demand was more elastic, the total quantity demanded by the market fell by a greater amount than when demand was relatively inelastic. As a result, an excise tax is a more effective revenue source when the demand for the taxed good is relatively inelastic.

The elasticity of supply plays a similar role in the tax incidence question. In all instances, the supply curve shifts to the left by an amount equal to the per unit tax. However, the slope of the supply curve—its relative elasticity—will play a role in whether consumers or suppliers bear the tax burden. In general, the more elastic supply, the more a tax is passed on to consumers in the form of higher prices. The flip side of this is that the more inelastic supply, the more the tax burden is borne by the supplier.

In general, an excise tax increases the price that consumers must pay and decreases the price that sellers receive. Obviously, this is a cost to the particular individuals who engage in buying and selling the taxed good or service. It is a cost for these individuals because it represents a loss in their respective consumer or producer surpluses. This loss is demonstrated in Figure II-24, which shows the effect of an excise tax on tires. The area above the equilibrium market price and below the demand curve represents consumer surplus, and the area under the equilibrium market price and above the supply curve is

Figure II-24. Deadweight Loss or Excess Burden Due to a Government Excise Tax

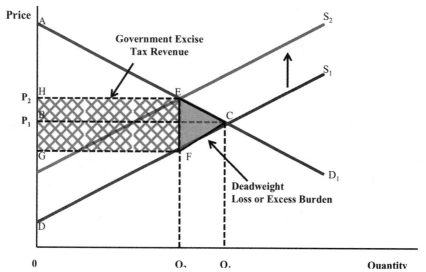

producer surplus. Prior to the tax, consumer surplus was equal to the area ABC, and producer surplus was equal to the area BCD. After the imposition of the tax, the supply curve shifts to the left—indicated by movement from S_1 to S_2—and market price moves from P_1 to P_2. The vertical distance between S_1 and S_2 is equal to the amount of the excise tax. Notice that as a result of the tax, consumer and producer surplus has been reduced by the area HECFG.

The entire reduction in consumer and producer surplus due to the excise tax should not be viewed as a loss borne by society. Remember that the government gains tax revenue in an amount equal to the area HEFG. The government revenue is spent either by purchasing goods and services directly or by giving the money to other citizens (e.g., welfare payments) for them to spend on goods and services. If the benefit to consumers and producers of government spending is equal to the area HEFG, then the remaining area of lost consumer and producer surplus is equal to ECF. This is the real cost of the tax. This area represents a reduction in the total output of the economy due to the tax that can *never* be regained. This loss, represented by the area ECF, is known as the **deadweight loss** of the tax or the **excess burden** of the tax.

H. The Role of Prices

An important attribute of the market allocation is that it reduces the amount of information consumers need to know in order to make rational decisions—that is, consumers do not need to know why relative prices change in order for the price system to work. In this regard, the allocation role of the decentralized price system may be viewed as a huge informational network through which the relative scarcity of different goods and services is transmitted by price changes. For example, a prolonged drought in the Midwest will decrease the supply of wheat available for making bread. However, this will not result in a shortage of bread. The decreased supply of wheat will result in the price of wheat being bid up, and part of that price increase will be passed on to consumers in the form of higher prices for bread and other bakery products. As a result of the higher price, some farms will not purchase grain for their livestock and some consumers will not purchase as much bread. There will not be a shortage of bread. The market clears, but more importantly, it allocates the scarce resources to their highest valued uses in a very low cost manner.

The Use of Knowledge in Society

Friedrich von Hayek

35 American Economic Review 519–30 (1945)

The peculiar character of the problem of a rational economic order is determined precisely by the fact that the knowledge of the circumstances of which we must make use never exists in concentrated or integrated form but solely as the dispersed bits of incomplete and frequently contradictory knowledge which all the separate individuals possess. The economic problem of society is thus not merely a problem of how to allocate "given resources." ... It is rather a problem of how to secure the best use of resources known to any of the members of society, for ends whose relative importance only these individuals know.... [I]t is a problem of the utilization of knowledge which is not given to anyone in its totality.

* * *

But a little reflection will show that there is beyond question a body of knowledge of the particular circumstances of time and place. It is with respect to this that practically every individual has some advantage over all others because he possesses unique information of which beneficial use might be made, but of which use can be made only if the decisions depending on it are left to him or are made with his active co-operation.

* * *

If we can agree that the economic problem of society is mainly one of rapid adaptation to changes in the particular circumstances of time and place, it would seem to follow that the ultimate decisions must be left to the people who are familiar with these circumstances, who know directly of the relevant changes and of the resources immediately available to meet them.... We must solve it by some form of decentralization. But this answers only part of our problem. We need decentralization because only thus can we insure that the knowledge of the particular circumstances of time and place will be promptly used. But the "man on the spot" cannot decide solely on the basis of his limited but intimate knowledge of the facts of his immediate surroundings. There still remains the problem of communicating to him such further information as he needs to fit his decisions into the whole pattern of changes of the larger economic system.

* * *

There is hardly anything that happens anywhere in the world that *might* not have an effect on the decision he ought to make. But he need not know of these events as such, nor of *all* their effects.... All that is significant for him is how *much more or less* difficult to procure they have become compared with other things with which he is also concerned, or how much more or less urgently wanted are the alternative things he produces or uses. It is always a question of the relative importance of the particular things with which he is concerned, and the cases which alter their relative importance are of no interest to him beyond the effect on those concrete things of his own environment.

It is in this connection that what I have called the "economic calculus" (or the Pure Logic of Choice) helps us, at least by analogy, to see how this problem can be solved, and in fact is being solved, by the price system....

* * *

The whole acts as one market, not because any of its members surveys the whole field, but because their limited individual fields of vision sufficiently overlap so that through many intermediaries the relevant information is communicated to all....

... The most significant fact about this system is the economy of knowledge with which it operates, or how little the individual participants need to know in order to be able to take the right action. In abbreviated form, by a kind of symbol, only the most essential information is passed on and passed on only to those concerned.

* * *

But those who clamor for "conscious direction"—and who cannot believe that anything which has evolved without design (and even without our understanding it) should solve problems which we should not be able to solve consciously should remember this: The problem is precisely how to extend the span of our utilization of resources beyond the span of the control of any one mind; and, therefore, how to dispense with the need of conscious control and how to provide inducements which will make the individuals do the desirable things without anyone having to tell them what to do.

* * *

As Alfred Whitehead has said in another connection ..."Civilizations advance by extending the number of important operations which we can perform without thinking about them."

Notes and Questions

1. Who Can Do Better Than the Market?: The discussion of the laws of supply and demand suggests several important societal roles for prices and the market process. The market price simultaneously fulfills at least two roles in solving the economic problem of limited resources and unlimited desires. First, price rations the supply of goods among consumers. Second, price provides an incentive to suppliers to produce the goods and services that society desires most. The efficiency of the market system as a means of allocating resources to their most highly valued uses is unparalleled. Interference with the functioning of the market, through policies such as price controls, carries a substantial cost in terms of reduced allocative efficiency.

2. Competition and Market Coordination: The American economic system is characterized by freely competitive markets. Competition tends to keep prices of goods and services at a reasonable level, usually the costs of production plus a reasonable profit for the sellers. When the number of buyers and sellers is large, no individual buyer or seller can affect the market price of a product or service. No single buyer purchases enough to affect market price, and no single seller can acquire enough power to alter the market for his or her gain. Crucial to the effects of large numbers is the condition that firms be free to enter and leave markets in response to profit opportunities or actual losses. New firms entering particular lines of business, bankruptcies, and business failures are expected consequences of a competitive system. Competition requires that entry and exit into business be free and unregulated. Businesses must be free to fail. Coordinating the billions of individual decisions involved in competition is an interconnected system of prices for inputs and outputs that is so complex that no individual or computer can fully comprehend it. Thus, an economy driven by central planning can *never* match the results of competitive economic markets. In other words, the wealth maximizing results of mutually beneficial exchange will not occur under central planning.

3. Experimental Data: In reviewing the results of a wide array of economic experiments on asset markets, Professor Shyam Sunder wrote the following:

> The Hayekian hypothesis about the importance of the informational role of prices in markets has received consistent support. Dissemination of information, from informed to the uninformed, and aggregation of individual traders' diverse bits of information through the market process alone have been shown to be concrete, verifiable phenomena, bringing abstract theory into empirical domain.

J.H. Kagel & A.E. Roth, Handbook of Experimental Economics (1995).

4. Orange Juice and Election: As one implication of the informational role of prices, various studies suggest that market predictions of events may be more accurate than predictions by experts. For example, one study concluded that changes in the market price of orange juice futures (contracts to buy and sell orange juice at some future date) better predicted the weather in Florida than did the National Weather Service. The same seems to be true for election results. Since 1988, the University of Iowa has run the Iowa Electronic Markets, in which individuals can buy and sell shares that pay off depending on who wins the United States presidential (and other) elections. Researchers have found that, on average, the price of shares in the election market more accurately predicted the percentage of popular vote received by the winner than did pre-election polls. A number of private wagering services now maintain betting markets on any number of events—ranging from future terrorist attacks to the identity of the new Pope.

5. Predictive Markets and the National Defense: Several years ago, the U.S. Defense Department began developing what eventually became known as the Policy Analysis Market—a market for shares on various political events, including the possibility of future terrorist attacks. The goal explicitly was to tap into the informational function of prices for national defense purposes. Once the program became publicly known, however, a loud outcry followed, with politicians and others objecting to the idea of betting on terrorism (as well as possible "insider" trading by terrorists). Then-Senator Hilary Rodham Clinton, for example, described the Policy Analysis Market as "a market in death and destruction, and not in keeping with our values," while Senator Tom Daschle complained that "this program could provide an incentive actually to commit acts of terrorism." The project was cancelled on July 29, 2003.

Chapter III

The Legislative Process and the Courts

Free enterprise, the freedom to pursue one's economic self-interest, is an intrinsic part of the capitalist system. Men and women are free to choose their own line of work with few or no governmental restraints or subsidies, and businesses and entrepreneurs are free to combine any resources at their command to produce products and services for profit. Workers and consumers are free to produce, purchase, and exchange any good or service, provided that their activity does not infringe on others' rights. Of course, individuals are not free of the constraints of limited resources and unlimited wants. Moreover, some actions are also constrained by the rule of law.

American capitalism as an economic system is based on the principle of *laissez-faire* (from the French, meaning, roughly, "to let do"). **Laissez-faire** has come to mean minimum government interference and regulation in private and economic lives. In a pure **laissez-faire economy**, government has a role limited to setting the rules—a system of law establishing and defining contract and property rights, ensuring national defense, and providing certain public goods that the private sector cannot and would not provide. Public goods are goods and services, such as roads, canals, and national defense, that are not always generated by market transactions.

In reality, the role of government in modern American capitalism is greatly expanded from merely setting the rules and providing public goods. No society has ever conformed to the laissez-faire ideal. In particular, in addition to government efforts to provide public assistance and to attempt to stabilize the economy, government intervention is often the response to widely recognized failures of the free market system. Section A describes various market failures that are often used to justify government regulation. Section B provides an introduction to public choice economics: a theory of why government bodies—in particular, legislatures and administrative agencies—may fail to achieve their putative goals. Finally, Section C looks at the economics of the court system. It discusses public choice theory as applied to the courts, as well as offers an economic perspective on why parties file suit and settle (or do not settle) cases, court procedures such as discovery and class actions, and the growing use of arbitration as an alternative to the public courts.

A. Normative Grounds for Government Intervention

Under some fairly well-defined circumstances, economists recognize that the market fails to produce the allocative efficiencies predicted by economic theory. A **market failure** is a situation where the private market fails to produce the optimal level of a particular good. Widely recognized market failures are information problems (market prices cannot reflect risks unless those risks are known), externalities (positive or negative third-party effects that are not considered in private decision making), monopoly (dominance of a product market by a single firm), and public goods (goods for which it is very costly to exclude consumption by individuals who are not willing to pay for the good). These market failures are discussed in greater detail later in this section.

Market failures are often viewed as justifications for government intervention in a market. If the normative goal of government policy is to improve economic efficiency, then government intervention to correct market failures can be justified as the pursuit of that goal. In order to achieve improved economic efficiency, the marginal cost of the intervention must not exceed that marginal benefit derived from correcting the market failure. The government can respond to market failures in a number of ways. One approach is for the government not to do anything at all. Such an approach could be a reflection of an ideological position that absolute freedom in the market place is more important than government intervention in the name of efficiency. This approach may also reflect a belief that the cost of the cure can be greater than the cost of the disease. A second approach, and one that occupies the opposite end of the continuum of possible responses, is for the government to take over the market or industry and try to do a more efficient job. An intermediate approach calls for the government to intervene in the market as a regulator of certain limited activities of otherwise competitive firms. Regulation can range from requiring certain types of warnings on package labels, to tax incentives, to total control over prices.

1. Market Failures

The four most widely accepted economic justifications for government intervention in the free market are information problems, externalities, monopoly, and public goods.

a. Information Problems

In the economist's purely competitive market, all economic actors are assumed to have perfect knowledge of all information relevant to making a decision. Under those conditions, the consumer's decision to purchase an "unsafe" product—for example, a product for which normal use results in a serious injury to one percent of the users over the useful life of the product—is simply a decision on the part of the consumer to bear the risk. Of course, the producer bears part of the risk in the form of a lower price. Thus, the market makes adjustments to account for risk properly. Similar examples of market adjustment under perfect information about relevant risks can be developed for the sale of risky securities and employment at unsafe workplaces. The fact that the market takes the risk into account means that the market is functioning properly—that is, according to theory.

In the real world, however, the market may fail to make adjustments because one of the parties to a transaction—typically the worker or consumer—does not have the information that is necessary to make an informed choice about the risk bearing that the individual is about to undertake. The failure of the market to assimilate all relevant information is referred to as an **information problem**. This is not to say that informed choices regarding risk are not commonly made in the real world. For example, a worker's decision to go to work for a company is based on many considerations, including hours, wages, retirement benefits, health insurance, job security, and working conditions (including safety and the overall environment). It is conceivable that a worker would accept a very risky job if the wages were high enough to compensate for the risk of getting killed. (The workers who hang girders in skyscrapers willingly accept the risk because either they prefer the risk, or they are compensated for it, or both.) On the other hand, in many industrial workplaces there is a possibility of coming into contact with dangerous chemicals that appear harmless, but may nevertheless have serious long-term effects. If the employer knows of the problem and conceals it from employees, the employer benefits through lower operating costs — including lower wages that do not reflect the risk of the job. And, workers are harmed monetarily by lower wages and physically by the increased risk of illness. Thus, under some circumstances, government intervention in the form of safety inspections, research, and worker's compensation may be justified on efficiency grounds. In some instances, even the employer will not know that the chemical is dangerous. Accordingly, the risk is not known. Obviously, neither the market nor government regulators can adjust to unknown risks.

Several major federal regulatory schemes, including securities, consumer protection, and worker safety, are designed to correct the information problems in the market. The primary philosophy of the federal securities laws, which govern the issuance and trading of corporate stock and bonds, is the disclosure of information about the soundness of financial instruments. Even if the information disclosed reveals that the instrument is very risky, the company is allowed to sell the instrument because the investor is assumed to have based his or her decision to incur the risk on the truthful information made available under the regulation. Product-safety and worker-safety legislation addresses some of the information issues raised in the preceding paragraphs. Consumer-protection legislation regarding deceptive trade practices and debtor-creditor relations may be viewed as government solutions to problems that can arise when one party to a transaction has an informational advantage. Here, the primary regulatory response is to require the disclosure of information in an understandable manner. The economics of risk is discussed in more detail in Chapter VI.

b. Externalities

The operation of the invisible-hand mechanism envisioned by Adam Smith was based in part on the assumption that producing firms incur all of the costs associated with the production of their product. The industrialization and urbanization of society have made individuals' actions much more interdependent than in Smith's time. In many instances, some of the costs of producing a product "spill over" and injure third parties that are not part of the production process. The total cost to society in terms of resources consumed is the sum of the private costs paid by the producer and the external costs — **externalities** — that are borne by the third party. If the legal system does not provide for compensation to the third parties, then the producer will be able to operate at a cost of production that does not fully reflect the cost in terms of society's resources. Thus, the presence of externalities suggests that the social consequences of self-interested behavior may not always be in the interest of "society."

Pollution is the most obvious example of an externality. The traditional manner in which the law has dealt with externalities is through tort law. **Tort law** enables property owners to bring lawsuits whenever their private-property rights are infringed upon in a manner inconsistent with their use of the property. However, tort law is generally inadequate to handle the problems associated with externalities such as industrial pollution, because of the inability to define enforceable property rights in clean air and clean water. Moreover, the large number of individuals who may claim a right to clean air are not able to negotiate with the polluter because of the enormous transaction costs. Affected third parties often do not have the incentive or the legal right to bring suit. As a result, in some instances, tort law may be inadequate to force polluters to bear the full cost of their activities. In the absence of regulation, polluters will generally produce a greater output (of both goods and pollution) than would have been forthcoming in a competitive market with zero transaction costs and well-defined property rights. This overallocation of resources to the production of a product is considered a misallocation from society's perspective.

The misallocation of resources that results from the inability of the market to define or enforce property rights in "free" goods like air and water provides a theoretical justification for government intervention in the market. The federal government's response to externalities is reflected in a number of environmental protection statutes, which are the basis of several cases in this casebook. More generally, externalities are the subject of Chapter IV.

c. *Monopoly*

The competitive market system is the primary regulator of the behavior of businesses. Rivalry generated in the pursuit of profits forces firms to produce at maximum efficiency. Competition among firms prevents the realization of excessive private economic power. As with any general rule, however, there are exceptions. For several different reasons, an individual firm (or group of competing firms acting as one firm) may occasionally dominate a particular market—that is, become a **monopoly.** For example, DeBeers dominates the world diamond trade because it controls the primary source of new diamonds.

Monopoly power may lead to a misallocation of resources that justifies government intervention in the market. A monopoly restricts the production of its product, resulting in buyers bidding up the product's price until it becomes so high that some buyers decide to stop bidding (that is, they drop out of the market). The consumers who end up purchasing the product at the higher price have done so voluntarily and thus have indicated that the exchange is mutually beneficial. The economic problem with a monopoly is that the potential gains from the mutually beneficial exchanges that would have occurred at the competitive market price, but which do not occur at the higher monopoly price, are not realized. Those potential gains from trade are lost forever. The consumers who dropped out of the market for the monopolized product will be able to spend their money elsewhere. However, because they would have preferred to purchase the monopolized good at the competitive price, these consumers are worse off than they would have been in a competitive market. In summary, the misallocation of resources that results from a monopoly is related to the restriction of output, which suggests that resources are underallocated to the monopolized market. Moreover, the pursuit of monopoly power through government restrictions—an activity referred to as **rent seeking**—wastes resources because some resources are devoted to using the political power of the state to coerce the redistribution of resources. Obviously, rent seeking is very different than the mutually beneficial exchange that characterizes voluntary market transactions—as developed in Section B below. The analysis of monopoly as a market failure is developed in more detail in Chapter IX.

The misallocation of resources attributed to monopoly is another theoretical justification for government intervention into the market. The federal antitrust laws are the government's response to this market failure. It is important to realize, however, that the antitrust laws present business with a perplexing paradox. On the one hand, becoming the biggest and the best at the particular business is the goal of almost all firms; on the other hand, the antitrust laws do not look favorably upon firms that have grown to dominate their industry. Thus, it has been suggested that the antitrust laws inhibit firms from maximizing their economic potential. However, this inherent conflict is not generally much of a problem. Antitrust cases are presented and analyzed throughout this book.

d. Public Goods

A public good is a good where consumption by one individual does not prevent its consumption by other individuals. This means that when a supplier provides a public good to one person, he or she supplies the good to all. In contrast, a **private good** is one that, when consumed by one individual, cannot be consumed by other individuals. An example of a private good is a cheeseburger; once I eat that cheeseburger, no one else can consume it. Individuals have an incentive to hide their preferences or demands for public goods. They cannot be excluded from consuming public goods produced by others, so why should they volunteer to pay for those goods? For individuals, such **free riding** behavior is rational.

The classic example of a public good is national defense. National defense must protect all individuals in the country; it is physically impossible to protect some people and leave others unprotected. Everyone agrees that national defense is needed. But will everyone, as individuals, supply it, or will everyone rely on someone else to do it? Rational, self-interested people would like to enjoy the benefits of national defense, while letting everyone else pay for it. Because national defense is a public good, if someone else defends the country, you are defended for free. You can be a free rider. The problem is that everyone has an incentive to be a free rider, but if everyone is a free rider, then there won't be any national defense. In such cases, the government can step in to require that everyone pay part of the cost of national defense to make sure that no one is a free rider.

2. Distributional Issues

Some individuals do not fare very well under the market system, while others prosper. Lawyers, law professors, the federal government, the president, and Congress devote much time, rhetoric, and effort to the equity of income distribution (or, as the case may be, income redistribution). Whether the proposal is imposing new gasoline taxes, extending dairy price supports, or decreasing corporate income taxes, the equity of such an action is sure to be debated. In following these debates, it becomes clear that there is much genuine disagreement over what constitutes a fair distribution of income. Opponents of higher gasoline taxes will argue that higher taxes on gasoline are unfair to poor Americans who must use their cars to commute to work; in turn, advocates of higher gasoline taxes will argue that it is only fair for car users to be taxed, since they cause many of the pollution problems in urban areas. Members of the farm lobby will argue for price supports on milk to increase the incomes of poor dairy farmers; consumer groups will oppose the measure on the grounds that it unfairly transfers income away from milk consumers.

Some economists also may have strong personal views concerning the equity of various income distributions. However, economists recognize that their views are subjective value judgments. In spite of his or her personal subjective views, most economists recognize that positive economic analysis cannot generate testable hypotheses concerning the optimal distribution of income in society. Because of their training in scientific methodology, most economists (as economists) are agnostic with regards to such questions.

Instead of evaluating the fairness of various income distributions, economists tend to focus on other aspects of redistribution proposals. In particular, they pay much attention to the efficiency consequences of various proposals to redistribute income. Although it is tempting to imagine that programs such as tax reform simply transfer income from those who need it less to those who need it more without any adverse side effects, redistribution never works so simply. Inevitably, some individuals will incur costs to avoid paying higher taxes, while others will adjust their circumstances to qualify for new subsidies. Due to such activity, it almost always ends up costing some groups in society more than a dollar for each dollar that is transferred to other groups. Economists, therefore, are aware that any program to redistribute income involves a trade-off between equity and efficiency. And, as discussed above, economists are ill-equipped to evaluate the correctness of such a trade-off.

B. Public Choice Economics

Most of economics is concerned with private choices. Numerous analytical tools, such as the supply-and-demand model and marginal analysis, have been developed to help economists understand how markets work. Public choice economics applies the methodology of economics to political decision making. In other words, it applies generally accepted principles of rational economic behavior to decisions made by politicians, bureaucrats, and interest groups.

The basic assumption of public choice economics is that political decision makers behave just like consumers and businesses—they attempt to maximize their own self-interest. For example, the politician is viewed as responding to incentives in the same utility maximizing manner when making legislative and executive decisions as he or she does when shopping for groceries, housing, or an automobile. This is hardly a startling revelation for long-time observers and participants in the Washington public policy arena, but it is important to take these incentives into consideration when analyzing laws, regulations, and other new political institutions. In this view, interest groups, lobbyists, politicians, bureaucrats, and even public policy analysts have one thing in common— they all are entrepreneurs. They are constantly looking to exploit opportunities for gain within the political system. As a consequence, much government regulation fails to achieve its putative goals.

This section illustrates the public choice perspective by considering the incentives of two groups involved in the development of public policies—politicians and bureaucrats. Government policy making is far removed from the anonymous decision making that characterizes market transactions. Although markets appear to be chaotic, they guide resources to their highest value uses when allowed to work. In contrast, government is personal and political, and it is a serious mistake to talk about "the government" or "the federal and state governments" as if they are benevolent despots. When "the government" guides the allocation of resources, every decision becomes a political decision. Moreover, it is naive to view government decision makers as merely benign agents of the people, carrying out the people's will.

The public choice perspective on legislation suggests that interest groups compete against one another for the passage of favorable legislation. In this view, legislation is the result of a rent-seeking process in which legislation is "sold" by legislators and "bought" by the highest bidders. Special-interest legislation provides relatively large benefits (rents) to a relatively small, but well-organized group, at the expense of a much larger number of unorganized voters—taxpayers and consumers. A large amount of empirical research provides support for interest-group explanations for the emergence of economic regulations that apply to specific industries. Interest groups demand—and all levels of government supply—protective regulation, monopoly, and other special privileges. The political activity of interest groups seeking special favors from legislators and other government decision makers is referred to as **rent seeking,** where the excessive (monopoly) profits earned by interest groups as a result of their political activity are referred to as rents. Recently, this approach to legislative activity has incorporated a more entrepreneurial role for legislators.

Money for Nothing: Politicians, Rent Extraction, and Political Extortion
Fred S. McChesney (1997) pp. 20–23, 41–42

... [T]he basic economic model of regulation ... remains one of rent creation. Rent creation is the standard perspective undoubtedly because ... the economic model of regulation ... [is] ... one of *exchange....* Politicians and their beneficiaries conclude a bargain that, like the typical contract, makes them both better off. Newly created rents are exchanged for votes and money; the multiparty auction allocates rents across groups. To the understandable confusion of lawyers, economists frequently use the word "bribe" to describe the "consideration" (the lawyers' term) paid over—quite legally—to politicians in return for regulatory favors.

It is not surprising that, perhaps instinctively, economists would turn to models of contract (exchange) to model regulation. Economics is often described as the study of the allocation of scarce resources among competing ends.... The principal mechanism by which scarce goods and services are allocated in market-based economies is exchange. Thus, economists have been interested in exchange since the development of economic science as a distinct discipline. Adam Smith began *The Wealth of Nations* (1776) with a description of people's "propensity to truck, barter and exchange one thing for another."

But analysis of regulation via a contract-based model entails three conceptual problems. First, the essence of contract is Pareto superiority: contracting parties are better off, and no one is worse off. That is obviously not true in the regulatory setting, where the benefits to producers (to some extent shared with politicians) come at the expense of consumers.[1] ...

Second, consider that the "contract" between regulator-supplier and regulated beneficiary is not an ordinary legal contract. Payment is made in order to make the private party better off, and in the process the politician gains as well. But were the politician to take the money and then refuse to create the rents, the aggrieved private party would have no legal recourse. The law effectively does not prohibit an agreement involving money in exchange for political favors (although ... it does regulate it). But the law does not enforce it, either.

The rent-creation contract is not illegal, but extralegal. The parties to the regulatory contract therefore must find their own, self-help ways to ensure that the promised performance is rendered on both sides. In this sense, rent creation is no different from any number of private exchanges made every day, in which individuals rely on one another's good faith and the desirability of continued relations, not the courts, for enforcement of the agreement.

Describing regulation as essentially a contract between politicians and regulated beneficiaries entails a third conceptual question: might other sorts of relationships also exist

---

1. Indeed, since the losses to consumers must be greater than the gains to producers, the regulatory contract is not even Kaldor-Hicks superior, which is the same as saying that regulation, unlike private contracts, is on net wealth-reducing.

between the two groups? In the real world, voluntary contracts do not make up the complete set of human interactions.... People are thrown together involuntarily—on one side at least, if not both—in settings involving torts, even crimes, such as theft.

Obviously, these interactions do not leave both sides better off. But to the criminal (thief), the fact that his victims suffer while he gains is of scant importance. His only concern is whether he gains more through the involuntary exchange (theft) than he could by any voluntary exchange.[2]

In short, bribery (contract) is not the only form of interaction observed in the world. "In the general case, the individual will observe two ways to persuade: by a threat and by a bribe." In the course of the ordinary day, an individual will typically combine bribes to some people (for example, his spouse) with threats to others (for example, his children) in order to induce the behavior that is desired or expected. Other people do the same with him: his boss probably relies on a combination of carrots and sticks.

Why would politicians not use the same dual strategy in their dealings with people? Certainly, private beneficiaries may pay bribes (legal or illegal) to politicians for regulatory largesse. But instead of or in addition to accepting bribes, might not politicians also take, or extort, from private parties?

A politician has alternative ways to interact with private parties. He may seek votes or money from producers and offer rents from consumers in exchange, as in the orthodox economic theory of regulation-as-bribery. But a politician may also make his demands on private parties, not by promising benefits, but by threatening to impose costs—a form of political extortion or blackmail. If the expected cost of the act threatened exceeds the value of what private parties must give up to avoid legislative action, they rationally will surrender the tribute demanded of them. With constant marginal utility of wealth, a private citizen will be just as willing to pay legislators to have rents of $1 million created as she will to avoid imposition of $1 million in losses. With declining marginal utility of income, the citizen will pay more to avoid the losses than she will to obtain the gains.

Once the politician is seen as an independent actor in the regulatory process, his objective function cannot be treated as single-valued. He will maximize total returns to himself by equating at the margin the returns from votes, contributions, bribes, power, and other sources of personal gain or utility. All these, in turn, are positive functions not only of private benefits he confers but also of private costs he agrees not to impose.

The political strategy of cost forbearance can assume several forms. Perhaps most obvious is the threat to deregulate an industry previously cartelized. Expected political rents created by earlier regulation are quickly capitalized into firm share prices. If politicians later breach their contract and vote unexpectedly to deregulate, the shareholders suffer a wealth loss. Rather than suffer the costs of deregulation, shareholders will pay politicians a sum, up to the amount of wealth loss threatened, to have them refrain from deregulating. And in fact one routinely observes payments to politicians to protect previously enacted cartel measures. Dairy interests pay handsomely for continuation of congressional milk-price supports; physician and dentist political action committees (PACs) contribute large sums for continuation of self-regulation....

---

2. ... Of course, an agreement to make payments to avoid imposition of harm could be called a contract, in the same sense that responding to the choice "Your money or your life," offered by one wielding a gun, could be deemed a gift. Both popularly and legally, however, such a transaction—whatever option is chosen—"is still regarded as a robbery even though the participation of the victim was necessary to its completion, for the victim is compelled to choose between two alternatives, both of which are his as of right."

Subsequent payments to avoid postcontractual opportunism by politicians are to be distinguished from contractual payments to enhance rent longevity *ex ante*. Both politicians and rent recipients gain when the durability of regulation can be increased, that is, when legislators are held to longer contracts. But new arrivals on both sides succeed to the interests of the original contracting parties. A legislator not party to the original bargain has less incentive to abide by the political rent-creation deal struck by his predecessors unless he too is compensated. Guaranteed rent durability is thus impossible. Among owners of firms, subsequent purchasers of shares with expected rents capitalized into their prices are vulnerable to extraction of previously created rents on the part of opportunistic politicians. Payments to political newcomers to secure performance of previously negotiated contracts earn no rents. Rather, they protect against windfall losses that new legislators could impose otherwise.

* * *

The rent-extraction model ... is essentially a model of extortion by politicians. They are paid not to legislate — money for nothing. The model extends the economic theory of regulation to include the gains available to politician-maximizers from alleviating costs threatened or actually imposed on private actors by legislators themselves and by specialized bureaucratic agencies. Status as a legislator confers a property right not only to create political rents but also to impose costs that would destroy private rents. In order to protect these returns, private owners have an incentive to strike bargains with legislators, as long as the side payments to politicians are lower than the losses expected from the law threatened.

Their ability to impose costs enables politicians to demand payments not to do so. As with rent creation, the process of rent extraction in the short run might seem to involve only transfers — from capital owners to politicians, rather than from consumers to producers. But the long-run implications are the more important ones. The transfers required to protect returns to private investments create disincentives to invest in valuable specific capital in the first place. Even when politicians eventually eschew intervention, the mere threat and the payments required to remove it must distort private investment decisions.

The model of rent extraction set out here in no way undermines the orthodox model of rent-creating regulation; rather, it supplements the rent-creation model by recognizing alternative sources of political gains.[3] Indeed, [Nobel Laureate George] Stigler's original article foreshadowed a complementary rent-extraction model: "The state — the machinery and power of the state — is a potential resource or threat to every industry in the society. With its power to prohibit or compel, to take or give money, the state can and does selectively help or hurt a vast number of industries.... Regulation may be actively sought by an industry, or it may be thrust upon it." Conditions that make political rent creation relatively unattractive to politicians make private rent extraction more attractive. The relative attraction of rent extraction has also increased as constitutional protection of private rights has diminished.

True, credibility issues, problems of political opportunism, and perhaps other imperfections in private-capital protection may create disincentives for capital owners to buy off legislators — just as opportunism and political-rent protection may discourage

---

3. To return to the bribery/extortion analogy, one who solicits bribes from some people to increase their welfare is hardly precluded thereby from demanding payment from other people not to decrease theirs.

payments for rent creation. Yet rent creation is an ongoing, frequently observed phenomenon of modern politics. The complementary question thus is posed: do private actors in fact pay significant sums to induce government *not* to act?

* * *

If so, one cost of government regulation has been missed. Heretofore, the economic model has identified several different costs of government regulation: deadweight consumer loss, resources expended as private parties seek rents, costs of compliance with regulation.... To these should be added the costs of protecting private capital, even when politicians ultimately are persuaded not to regulate....

Notes and Questions

1. Regulation—Public Interest v. Private Interest: The history of economic regulation shows that industry-specific regulatory agencies tend to lose sight of their public interest mission over time. That is, although an agency may be created to control a particular industry, experience reveals that most regulatory agencies eventually adopt the perspective of the industries they regulate. This is referred to as **regulatory capture.** Thus, eventually, the regulated industry frequently benefits from the regulation.

This observation has led some students of the regulatory process to suggest that one should look to the beneficiaries of the regulation in attempting to identify the parties that demanded and procured the regulation. For example, the Interstate Commerce Commission was created to control price discrimination by railroads. Some customers complained that price cuts were helping large shippers at the expense of small shippers. However, the primary effect of price discrimination was the destruction of the railroads' cartel which tried to raise prices above competitive levels. The railroads were competing for the large customers through price cuts and rebates, and the cartel was crumbling as a result. This socially beneficial competition was eliminated by the government's imposition of fixed rates which effectively enforced the cartel. Consumers, who presumably represented the "public interest," did not benefit from the regulation. Instead the benefits flowed to the railroads through the higher prices that resulted from the elimination of competition. In fact, some scholars have argued that the railroads engineered (pun intended) the creation of the ICC.

It is not unusual for administrative agencies to act in the interest of the regulated industry rather than in the so-called public interest. One explanation that has often been given is that the selection of board or commission members is biased toward choosing individuals from the industry. This is likened to hiring the fox to guard the henhouse. On the other hand, the hiring of industry insiders may be necessary because they may be the only available individuals with the special knowledge of the industry that is required to make a meaningful contribution to the agency. Such knowledge is rarely found in "outsiders." Further, it is not clear that selecting board and commission members from outside the industry would change the result. As outsiders become aware of the special problems facing an industry, they are likely to become sympathetic and supportive of the industry.

There are other reasons why regulated industries will tend to have relatively more impact on regulations than representatives of the public interest. The regulated industry has the greatest interest in the rules and regulations to be promulgated by the agency. Thus, in administrative hearings on proposed rule-makings, their perspective is likely to be better articulated than that of the public interest. This bias is not surprising, because individual citizens do not have the incentive to voice their positions on public policy issues due to free-rider problems. Thus, there is an underrepresentation of dispersed citizens' interests in the political process in general and the administrative process in particular. The economics of regulation has revealed numerous instances when public-interest sounding regulations in the name of public safety and health have turned out to be well-disguised restrictions on competition. This is especially true in fields where licenses and board certifications are required.

Economists and legal commentators often treat the adoption and implementation of public policies as if the individuals who make up "the government" selflessly act in the public interest. However, experience teaches us that self-interested government decision makers often do not make decisions that are in the public interest.

Public Choice scholarship also assumes that the public interest is more difficult to ascertain than the normal political science scholarship assumes. Government is not assumed to be an "it" but a "they" that is made up of individual actors who have preferences, just like any other economic actor.

2. Incentives of Regulators: The economic theory of regulation emphasizes the competition among interest groups to influence legislators and bureaucrats. The theory gives rise to various predictions about the likely outcomes of this competition—i.e., about which interest groups are more likely to succeed in obtaining favorable regulations. Andrew P. Morriss, Bruce Yandle, and Andrew Dorchak summarize some of the central predictions, which they describe as "principles that characterize agency incentives":

- "All else being equal, in a competitive struggle among interest groups seeking political favors, the winning group will be one that is relatively small in size, so that the political benefits are concentrated and the cost of achieving agreement is low."

- "All else being equal, the political process will prefer regulatory outcomes that spread the costs of regulations over a large and diverse population to outcomes that concentrate costs on smaller, more homogenous populations."

- "All else being equal, the winning interest group will be the one that has the lowest cost of organizing and communicating with politicians."

- "Politicians and all other participants in the political process, including members of the bureaucracy, seek to minimize their own costs when acting on behalf of interest groups or the general public."

- "Politicians must signal their performance to interest groups that support them by taking actions that reflect the symbolic preferences of the interest group, that deliver real benefits to the group, or that impose real costs on other groups to the advantage of the interest group."

- "The unorganized general public is rationally ignorant about the details of specialized legislation or regulation designed by politicians and regulators to favor particular groups."

- "Interest groups prefer long-term, uninterrupted political benefits to short-term arrangements."

- "Regulations typically have differential effects on regulated entities."

Andrew P. Morriss et al., *Choosing How to Regulate*, 29 Harvard Environmental Law Review 179, 223–28 (2005) (italics omitted). As you read the other cases in this chapter (and in this casebook), think about how well these principles explain the government regulations involved. How well does the economic theory explain what regulations get adopted?

3. Rationally-Ignorant Voters: One of the principles noted by Morriss et al. is that politicians are able to cater to special interests because they are not closely monitored by voters. Interestingly, the self-interest that is so important in the market system leads to ignorance in the political system. Recall that every activity involves an opportunity cost. The time a voter spends becoming knowledgeable about the candidates requires the voter to forego some other valuable use of that time. Hence, rational voters would require that they gain some benefit from the use of such time. Clearly, there is some benefit to each voter if the best candidate wins an election. However, the only time a single vote in an election has any value is when it is the tie breaking vote. With millions of voters, the chance of any one voter casting the tie breaking vote is minuscule. The expected benefit of casting an informed vote is therefore virtually zero. Faced with a comparison of the marginal cost of informing oneself about the candidates and the marginal benefit of doing so, it is little wonder that voters are simply advancing their self-interest by spending their time where it will have the greatest impact on their well-being. Thus, many voters are **rationally ignorant** of politicians and public policies. They take a free ride, and legislators are able to pass legislation that does not come close to anyone's understanding of the public interest. Moreover, by cloaking interest-group legislation in public-interest rhetoric, politicians make it even more costly to monitor their behavior.

4. Baptists and Bootleggers: Can you think of an example where two different special interest groups would favor the same piece of legislation for different reasons? Sometimes the legislative process makes for strange bedfellows. For example, two different groups supported state laws requiring liquor stores to be closed on Sundays. Baptists found such legislation to be favorable for religious reasons, while bootleggers found their covert trade to be much more profitable when liquor was not legally available. Thus, the bootleggers and Baptists joined forces in the fight for Sunday closing laws. More generally, this "Baptists and Bootleggers" theory suggests that regulations are more likely to be enacted when supported by those who favor it for moral reasons (e.g., the Baptists) and by those who benefit economically (e.g., the bootleggers). Can you think of other examples?

5. The Welfare Costs of Rent Seeking and Rent Extraction: Rent seeking is harmful to society because it results in two types of social costs. First, the political creation of monopoly harms society in the same way as any other monopoly—through the restriction of output and misallocation of resources. Second, the potential for government-conferred rents leads interest groups to use resources to capture those rents through the political process. Such rent-seeking expenditures attempt to transfer wealth from one group to another. This use of scarce resources represents a social loss, because the resources could have been used for productive purposes instead of merely dividing up the economic pie. See, for example, Gordon Tullock, *The Welfare Costs of Tariffs, Monopoly, and Theft*, 32 Western Economic Journal 5 (1967); Richard A. Posner, *The Social Costs of Monopoly and Regulation*, 83 Journal of Political Economy 807 (1975). See also the graphical analysis in Chapter IX.

6. Public Policy Analysts and the Search for Market Failures: Many economists, public policy analysts, and legal commentators scrutinize markets looking for market imperfections which provide justification for some form of government intervention. It is generally and implicitly assumed by such investigators that the government policy that emerges will be faithfully executed by legislators and bureaucrats. Public choice economists, in contrast, are specialists at identifying government failures—instances where the incentive structures facing legislators and regulators make it almost impossible for a government policy to meet its stated objectives. Indeed, many economists believe that the government has the incentive to over-regulate because decision makers do not fully consider all of the costs and benefits of market intervention. When this occurs, the government is more likely to cause a negative externality than reduce one. See, for example, Leland Yeager, *Is There a Bias Toward Overregulation,* in Is the Market a Test of Truth and Beauty?: Essays in Political Economy 321–348 (Leland B. Yeager, ed., 1983).

City of Columbia v. Omni Outdoor Advertising, Inc.

Supreme Court of the United States
499 U.S. 365 (1991)

JUSTICE SCALIA delivered the opinion of the Court.

This case requires us to clarify the application of the Sherman Act to municipal governments and to the citizens who seek action from them.

I

Petitioner Columbia Outdoor Advertising, Inc. (COA), a South Carolina corporation, entered the billboard business in the city of Columbia, South Carolina (also a petitioner here), in the 1940's. By 1981 it controlled more than 95% of what has been conceded to be the relevant market. COA was a local business owned by a family with deep roots in the community, and enjoyed close relations with the city's political leaders. The mayor and other members of the city council were personal friends of COA's majority owner, and the company and its officers occasionally contributed funds and free billboard space to their campaigns. According to respondent Omni Outdoor Advertising, Inc., these beneficences were part of a "longstanding" "secret anticompetitive agreement" whereby "the City and COA would each use their [*sic*] respective power and resources to protect ... COA's monopoly position," in return for which "City Council members received advantages made possible by COA's monopoly."

In 1981, Omni, a Georgia corporation, began erecting billboards in and around the city. COA responded to this competition in several ways. First, it redoubled its own billboard construction efforts and modernized its existing stock. Second—according to Omni—it took a number of anticompetitive private actions, such as offering artificially low rates, spreading untrue and malicious rumors about Omni, and attempting to induce Omni's customers to break their contracts. Finally (and this is what gives rise to the issue we address today), COA executives met with city officials to seek the enactment of zoning ordinances that would restrict billboard construction. COA was not alone in urging this course; concerned about the city's recent explosion of billboards, a number of citizens, including writers of articles and editorials in local newspapers, advocated restrictions.

In the spring of 1982, the city council passed an ordinance requiring the council's approval for every billboard constructed in downtown Columbia. This was later amended to impose a 180-day moratorium on the construction of billboards throughout the city, except as specifically authorized by the council. A state court invalidated this ordinance on the ground that its conferral of unconstrained discretion upon the city council violated both the South Carolina and Federal Constitutions. The city then requested the State's regional planning authority to conduct a comprehensive analysis of the local billboard situation as a basis for developing a final, constitutionally valid, ordinance. In September 1982, after a series of public hearings and numerous meetings involving city officials, Omni, and COA (in all of which, according to Omni, positions contrary to COA's were not genuinely considered), the city council passed a new ordinance restricting the size, location, and spacing of billboards. These restrictions, particularly those on spacing, obviously benefited COA, which already had its billboards in place; they severely hindered Omni's ability to compete.

In November 1982, Omni filed suit against COA and the city in Federal District Court, charging that they had violated §§ 1 and 2 of the Sherman Act, as well as South Carolina's Unfair Trade Practices Act. Omni contended, in particular, that the city's billboard ordinances were the result of an anticompetitive conspiracy between city officials and COA that stripped both parties of any immunity they might otherwise enjoy from the federal antitrust laws. In January 1986, after more than two weeks of trial, a jury returned general verdicts against the city and COA on both the federal and state claims. It awarded damages, before trebling, of $600,000 on the § 1 Sherman Act claim, and $400,000 on the § 2 claim. The jury also answered two special interrogatories, finding specifically that the city and COA had conspired both to restrain trade and to monopolize the market. Petitioners moved for judgment notwithstanding the verdict, contending among other things that their activities were outside the scope of the federal antitrust laws. In November 1988, the District Court granted the motion.

A divided panel of the United States Court of Appeals for the Fourth Circuit reversed the judgment of the District Court and reinstated the jury verdict on all counts. We granted certiorari.

II

In the landmark case of *Parker* v. *Brown*, 317 U.S. 341 (1943), we rejected the contention that a program restricting the marketing of privately produced raisins, adopted pursuant to California's Agricultural Prorate Act, violated the Sherman Act. Relying on principles of federalism and state sovereignty, we held that the Sherman Act did not apply to anticompetitive restraints imposed by the States "as an act of government."

* * *

It suffices for the present to conclude that here no more is needed to establish, for *Parker* purposes, the city's authority to regulate than its unquestioned zoning power over the size, location, and spacing of billboards.

Besides authority to regulate, however, the *Parker* defense also requires authority to suppress competition—more specifically, "clear articulation of a state policy to authorize anticompetitive conduct" by the municipality in connection with its regulation. We have rejected the contention that this requirement can be met only if the delegating statute explicitly permits the displacement of competition. It is enough, we have held, if suppression of competition is the "foreseeable result" of what the statute authorizes. That condition is amply met here. The very purpose of zoning regulation is to displace unfettered business freedom in a manner that regularly has the effect of preventing normal acts of competition, particularly on the part of new entrants. A municipal ordinance restricting the size, location, and spacing of billboards (surely a common form of zoning) necessarily protects existing billboards against some competition from newcomers.

The Court of Appeals was therefore correct in its conclusion that the city's restriction of billboard construction was prima facie entitled to *Parker* immunity. The Court of Appeals upheld the jury verdict, however, by invoking a "conspiracy" exception to *Parker* that has been recognized by several Courts of Appeals....

There is no such conspiracy exception. The rationale of *Parker* was that, in light of our national commitment to federalism, the general language of the Sherman Act should not be interpreted to prohibit anticompetitive actions by the States in their governmental capacities as sovereign regulators....

* * *

For these reasons, we reaffirm our rejection of any interpretation of the Sherman Act that would allow plaintiffs to look behind the actions of state sovereigns to base their claims on "perceived conspiracies to restrain trade." We reiterate that, with the possible market participant exception, *any* action that qualifies as state action is "*ipso facto* ... exempt from the operation of the antitrust laws." This does not mean, of course, that the States may exempt *private* action from the scope of the Sherman Act; we in no way qualify the well-established principle that "a state does not give immunity to those who violate the Sherman Act by authorizing them to violate it, or by declaring that their action is lawful."

III

While *Parker* recognized the States' freedom to engage in anticompetitive regulation, it did not purport to immunize from antitrust liability the private parties who urge them to engage in anticompetitive regulation. However, it is obviously peculiar in a democracy, and perhaps in derogation of the constitutional right "to petition the Government for a redress of grievances," U.S. Const., Amdt. 1, to establish a category of lawful state action that citizens are not permitted to urge. Thus, beginning with *Eastern Railroad Presidents Conference* v. *Noerr Motor Freight, Inc.,* [365 U.S. 127 (1961),] we have developed a corollary to *Parker*: The federal antitrust laws also do not regulate the conduct of private individuals in seeking anticompetitive action from the government. This doctrine, like *Parker*, rests ultimately upon a recognition that the antitrust laws, "tailored as they are for the business world, are not at all appropriate for application in the political arena." That a private party's political motives are selfish is irrelevant: "*Noerr* shields from the Sherman Act a concerted effort to influence public officials regardless of intent or purpose."

Noerr recognized, however, what has come to be known as the "sham" exception to its rule: "There may be situations in which a publicity campaign, ostensibly directed toward influencing governmental action, is a mere sham to cover what is actually nothing more than an attempt to interfere directly with the business relationships of a competitor and the application of the Sherman Act would be justified." The Court of Appeals concluded that the jury in this case could have found that COA's activities on behalf of the restrictive billboard ordinances fell within this exception. In our view that was error.

The "sham" exception to *Noerr* encompasses situations in which persons use the governmental *process*—as opposed to the *outcome* of that process—as an anticompetitive weapon. A classic example is the filing of frivolous objections to the license application of a competitor, with no expectation of achieving denial of the license but simply in order to impose expense and delay. A "sham" situation involves a defendant whose activities are "not genuinely aimed at procuring favorable government action" at all, not one "who 'genuinely seeks to achieve his governmental result, but does so *through improper means*.'"

Neither of the Court of Appeals' theories for application of the "sham" exception to the facts of the present case is sound. The court reasoned, first, that the jury could have concluded that COA's interaction with city officials "'was actually nothing more than an attempt to interfere directly with the business relations [*sic*] of a competitor.'" This analysis relies upon language from *Noerr*, but ignores the import of the critical word "directly." Although COA indisputably set out to disrupt Omni's business relationships, it sought to do so not through the very process of lobbying, or of causing the city council to consider zoning measures, but rather through the ultimate *product* of that lobbying and consideration, viz., the zoning ordinances. The Court of Appeals' second theory was that the jury could have found "that COA's purposes were to delay Omni's entry into the market and even to deny it a meaningful access to the appropriate city administrative and legislative fora." But the purpose of delaying a competitor's entry into the market does not render lobbying activity a "sham," unless (as no evidence suggested was true here) the delay is sought to be achieved only by the lobbying process itself, and not by the governmental action that the lobbying seeks....

Omni urges that if, as we have concluded, the "sham" exception is inapplicable, we should use this case to recognize another exception to *Noerr* immunity—a "conspiracy" exception, which would apply when government officials conspire with a private party to employ government action as a means of stifling competition. We have left open the possibility of such an exception, as have a number of Courts of Appeals....

Giving full consideration to this matter for the first time, we conclude that a "conspiracy" exception to *Noerr* must be rejected. We need not describe our reasons at length, since they are largely the same as those set forth in Part II above for rejecting a "conspiracy" exception to *Parker*. As we have described, *Parker* and *Noerr* are complementary expressions of the principle that the antitrust laws regulate business, not politics; the former decision protects the States' acts of governing, and the latter the citizens' participation in government. Insofar as the identification of an immunity-destroying "conspiracy" is concerned, *Parker* and *Noerr* generally present two faces of the same coin. The *Noerr*-invalidating conspiracy alleged here is just the *Parker*-invalidating conspiracy viewed from the standpoint of the private-sector participants rather than the governmental participants. The same factors which, as we have described above, make it impracticable or beyond the purpose of the antitrust laws to identify and invalidate lawmaking that has been infected by selfishly motivated agreement with private interests likewise make it impracticable or beyond that scope to identify and invalidate lobbying that has produced selfishly motivated agreement with public officials....

IV

Under *Parker* and *Noerr*, therefore, both the city and COA are entitled to immunity from the federal antitrust laws for their activities relating to enactment of the ordinances....

* * *

... The judgment of the Court of Appeals is reversed, and the case is remanded for further proceedings consistent with this opinion.

It is so ordered.

Notes and Questions

1. American Federalism: The United States Constitution is based on the principle of federalism. Federalism conceives of governmental power that is split between a central governing body and state governments. In the United States, the federal government's scope of activity is limited by the powers granted in the Constitution. All other powers are reserved to the states. In *City of Columbia v. Omni Outdoor Advertising*, the Court clarifies the limits of the Sherman Act. The justification for these limits is federalism.

2. **Parker** *State Action Immunity v. Perfect Competition:* In the 1943 Supreme Court case of *Parker v. Brown*, 317 U.S. 341 (1943), the Court held that state officials and private economic entities who act pursuant to "state action" are provided antitrust immunity. Thus, states could adopt laws that stifled local competition. The *Parker* decision was based on the notion of federalism. In effect, the *Parker* state action immunity represents a willingness to sacrifice some of the benefits of competition in the name of federalism. How significant is this trade-off? From an economic perspective, was *Parker* the correct decision?

3. The Right to Seek Rents?: The Court observes that "with *Eastern Railroad Presidents Conference v. Noerr Motor Freight, Inc.* we have developed a corollary to *Parker*: the federal antitrust laws also do not regulate the conduct of private individuals in seeking anticompetitive action from the government." The right to seek anticompetitive action seems to be a prima facie example of rent seeking. Is the Court condoning rent seeking by its decision in *Noerr* and the application of *Noerr* to the facts in *Omni*? Alternatively, is the Court merely deferring to other laws in the protection of the policy making process? Clearly, some rent-seeking behavior like bribing public officials will be disciplined by other laws. However, conduct such as lobbying appears to be an acceptable form of rent seeking. Is there an optimal level of rent seeking? Is rent seeking ever good?

4. More Rent-Seeking Behavior: Clearly, the billboard ordinances benefited COA. In fact, these ordinances helped to solidify COA's monopoly position. As a monopolist, COA will be able to set output and price at a level that creates monopoly profits, but will COA actually see any of these profits? A careful reading of the facts reveals how important these monopoly profits are to COA. The Court's summary of the facts indicates that COA contributed money to the campaign funds of local officials and donated billboard space. When Omni attempted to enter the market in 1981, one of COA's counter measures was to develop and support billboard ordinances. After a year of meeting with city officials, ordinances were finally enacted to protect COA's monopoly. In addition, the Supreme Court opinion came in 1992, ten years after Omni's attempted entry. At any time during the past ten years, COA could have settled or come to some other agreement with Omni. Instead, it obviously saw the benefits of a victory in the Supreme Court after ten years of litigation expense to be worth the cost. In sum, this case is a clear example of rent-seeking behavior by a monopolist. It is likely that much of the monopolist's profits were devoured by its attempt to protect those profits. The resources used in rent seeking could have been consumed instead in productive industries.

5. Rationally-Ignorant Voters: Why don't the voters of Columbia seem to care about the dominant position granted to COA in the billboard market? How does the fact that COA gives free space to political candidates figure into this analysis? Does the fact that voters are rationally ignorant detract from the Court's reliance on federalism in deciding this case? It would certainly seem like companies who advertised via billboard would have an incentive to organize and fight legislation limiting their choices. Why doesn't this happen? What incentives exist for two different special interest groups seeking two separate pieces of favorable legislation from the same government?

6. Federalism v. Rent Seeking: The Court uses both *Parker* and *Noerr* to draw a line between the actions of COA and the City of Columbia, and actions that fall within the scope of the Sherman Act. *Parker* is based upon the notion that the federal government shall not interfere with those decisions which belong to the states—federalism. States can therefore enact policies that limit intrastate competition. *Noerr* allows citizens to encourage the states to use the powers that they have been granted under the state action exemption of *Parker*. Thus, citizens can ask the states to make policy that limits intrastate competition. Does the combination of these two decisions clear the way for rent-seeking behavior regarding state policy? It appears as if the Court is willing to allow some amount of rent-seeking behavior at the state level in order to protect federalism and self-determination. Is this trade-off wise? How about in the long-run?

7. Constitutional Constraints on Rent Seeking?: The United States Courts of Appeals are split on whether the Due Process and Equal Protection Clauses of the U.S. Constitution provide a basis for invalidating state laws that protect business from competition. In *Craigmiles v. Giles*, 312 F.3d 220 (6th Cir. 2002), the Sixth Circuit struck down a Tennessee law forbidding the sale of caskets other than by a state-licensed funeral director. According to the court, the law "was nothing more than an attempt to prevent economic competition," *id.* at 225, which "[c]ourts have repeatedly recognized … is not a legitimate governmental purpose," *id.* at 224. The court of appeals' opinion concluded:

> Judicial invalidation of economic regulation under the Fourteenth Amendment has been rare in the modern era. Our decision today is not a return to *Lochner*, by which this court would elevate its economic theory over that of legislative bodies. *See Lochner v. New York*, 198 U.S. 45 (1905). No sophisticated economic analysis is required to see the pretextual nature of the state's proffered explanations for the 1972 amendment. We are not imposing our view of a well-functioning market on the people of Tennessee. Instead, we invalidate only the General Assembly's naked attempt to raise a fortress protecting the monopoly rents that funeral directors extract from consumers. This measure to privilege certain businessmen over others at the expense of consumers is not animated by a legitimate governmental purpose and cannot survive even rational basis review.

Id. at 229; *see also* St. Joseph Abbey v. Castille, 712 F.3d 215, 227 (5th Cir. 2013) (same). By comparison, the Tenth Circuit in *Power v. Harris*, 379 F.3d 1208 (10th Cir. 2004), upheld a similar Oklahoma statute against constitutional challenge. According to the court, "the Supreme Court has consistently held that protecting or favoring one particular intrastate industry, absent a specific federal constitutional or statutory violation, is a legitimate state interest." *Id.* at 1220. It held:

> Because we find that intra-state economic protectionism, absent a violation of a specific federal statutory or constitutional provision, is a legitimate state interest, we have little difficulty determining that the [Oklahoma statute] satisfies rational-basis review…. [T]he [Act] need only be rationally related to the legitimate state interest of intrastate industry protection. There can be no serious dispute that the [Act] is "very well tailored" to protecting the intrastate funeral-home industry. As such, "our inquiry is at an end."

Id. at 1222–23. The court of appeals distinguished the cases relied on by the court in *Craigmiles* as being based on interstate rather than intrastate protectionism. *Id.* at 1219. Should that matter?

West Lynn Creamery, Inc. v. Healy

Supreme Court of the United States
512 U.S. 186 (1994)

JUSTICE STEVENS delivered the opinion of the Court.

A Massachusetts pricing order imposes an assessment on all fluid milk sold by dealers to Massachusetts retailers. About two-thirds of that milk is produced out of State. The entire assessment, however, is distributed to Massachusetts dairy farmers. The question presented is whether the pricing order unconstitutionally discriminates against interstate commerce. We hold that it does.

I

Petitioner West Lynn Creamery, Inc., is a milk dealer licensed to do business in Massachusetts. It purchases raw milk, which it processes, packages, and sells to wholesalers, retailers, and other milk dealers. About 97% of the raw milk it purchases is produced by out-of-state farmers. Petitioner LeComte's Dairy, Inc., is also a licensed Massachusetts milk dealer. It purchases all of its milk from West Lynn and distributes it to retail outlets in Massachusetts.

Since 1937, the Agricultural Marketing Agreement Act, 7 U.S.C. § 601 *et seq.*, has authorized the Secretary of Agriculture to regulate the minimum prices paid to producers of raw milk by issuing marketing orders for particular geographic areas. While the Federal Government sets minimum prices based on local conditions, those prices have not been so high as to prevent substantial competition among producers in different States. In the 1980's and early 1990's, Massachusetts dairy farmers began to lose market share to lower cost producers in neighboring States. In response, the Governor of Massachusetts appointed a Special Commission to study the dairy industry. The commission found that many producers had sold their dairy farms during the past decade and that if prices paid to farmers for their milk were not significantly increased, a majority of the remaining farmers in Massachusetts would be "forced out of business within the year." On January 28, 1992, relying on the commission's report, the Commissioner of the Massachusetts Department of Food and Agriculture (respondent) declared a State of Emergency. In his declaration he noted that the average federal blend price had declined from $14.67 per hundred pounds (cwt) of raw milk in 1990 to $12.64/cwt in 1991, while costs of production for Massachusetts farmers had risen to an estimated average of $15.50/cwt. He concluded:

> "Regionally, the industry is in serious trouble and ultimately, a federal solution will be required. In the meantime, we must act on the state level to preserve our local industry, maintain reasonable minimum prices for the dairy farmers, thereby ensure a continuous and adequate supply of fresh milk for our market, and protect the public health."

Promptly after his declaration of emergency, respondent issued the pricing order that is challenged in this proceeding.

The order requires every "dealer" in Massachusetts to make a monthly "premium payment" into the "Massachusetts Dairy Equalization Fund." The amount of those payments is computed in two steps. First, the monthly "order premium" is determined by subtracting the federal blend price for that month from $15 and dividing the difference by three; thus if the federal price is $12/cwt, the order premium is $1/cwt. Second, the premium is multiplied by the amount (in pounds) of the dealer's Class I sales in Massachusetts. Each month the fund is distributed to Massachusetts producers. Each Massachusetts producer receives a share of the total fund equal to his proportionate contribution to the State's total production of raw milk.

Petitioners West Lynn and LeComte's complied with the pricing order for two months, paying almost $200,000 into the Massachusetts Dairy Equalization Fund. Starting in July 1992, however, petitioners refused to make the premium payments, and respondent commenced license revocation proceedings. Petitioners then filed an action in state court seeking an injunction against enforcement of the order on the ground that it violated the Commerce Clause of the Federal Constitution. The state court denied relief and respondent conditionally revoked their licenses.

The parties agreed to an expedited appellate procedure, and the Supreme Judicial Court of Massachusetts transferred the cases to its own docket. It affirmed, because it concluded that "the pricing order does not discriminate on its face, is evenhanded in its application, and only incidentally burdens interstate commerce." ... We granted certiorari, and now reverse.

II

The Commerce Clause vests Congress with ample power to enact legislation providing for the regulation of prices paid to farmers for their products. An affirmative exercise of that power led to the promulgation of the federal order setting minimum milk prices. The Commerce Clause also limits the power of the Commonwealth of Massachusetts to adopt regulations that discriminate against interstate commerce. "This 'negative' aspect of the Commerce Clause prohibits economic protectionism—that is, regulatory measures designed to benefit in-state economic interests by burdening out-of-state competitors.... Thus, state statutes that clearly discriminate against interstate commerce are routinely struck down ... unless the discrimination is demonstrably justified by a valid factor unrelated to economic protectionism...."

The paradigmatic example of a law discriminating against interstate commerce is the protective tariff or customs duty, which taxes goods imported from other States, but does not tax similar products produced in State. A tariff is an attractive measure because it simultaneously raises revenue and benefits local producers by burdening their out-of-state competitors. Nevertheless, it violates the principle of the unitary national market by handicapping out-of-state competitors, thus artificially encouraging in-state production even when the same goods could be produced at lower cost in other States.

Because of their distorting effects on the geography of production, tariffs have long been recognized as violative of the Commerce Clause. In fact, tariffs against the products of other States are so patently unconstitutional that our cases reveal not a single attempt by any State to enact one. Instead, the cases are filled with state laws that aspire to reap some of the benefits of tariffs by other means....

Under these cases, Massachusetts' pricing order is clearly unconstitutional. Its avowed purpose and its undisputed effect are to enable higher cost Massachusetts dairy farmers to compete with lower cost dairy farmers in other States. The "premium payments" are effectively a tax which makes milk produced out of State more expensive. Although the tax also applies to milk produced in Massachusetts, its effect on Massachusetts producers is entirely (indeed more than) offset by the subsidy provided exclusively to Massachusetts dairy farmers. Like an ordinary tariff, the tax is thus effectively imposed only on out-of-state products. The pricing order thus allows Massachusetts dairy farmers who produce at higher cost to sell at or below the price charged by lower cost out-of-state producers.[4] If there were no federal minimum prices for milk, out-of-state producers might still be able to retain their market share by lowering their prices. Nevertheless, out-of-staters' ability to remain competitive by lowering their prices would not immunize a discriminatory

---

4. A numerical example may make this effect clearer. Suppose the federal minimum price is $12/cwt, that out-of-state producers can sell milk profitably at that price, but that in-state producers need a price of $15/cwt in order to break even. Under the pricing order, the tax or "order premium" will be $1/cwt (one-third the difference between the $15/cwt target price and the $12/cwt federal minimum price). Assuming the tax generates sufficient funds (which will be the case as long as two-thirds of the milk is produced out of State, which appears to be the case), the Massachusetts farmers will receive a subsidy of $3/cwt. This subsidy will allow them to lower their prices from $15/cwt to $12/cwt while still breaking even. Selling at $12/cwt, Massachusetts dairy farmers will now be able to compete with out-of-state producers. The net effect of the tax and subsidy, like that of a tariff, is to raise the after-tax price paid by the dealers. If exactly two-thirds of the milk sold in Massachusetts is produced out of State, net prices will rise by $1/cwt. If out-of-state farmers produce more than two-thirds of the raw milk, the Dairy Equalization Fund will have a surplus, which will be refunded to the milk dealers. This refund will mitigate the price increase, although it will have no effect on the ability of the program to enable higher cost Massachusetts dairy farmers to compete with lower cost out-of-staters.

measure. In this case, because the Federal Government sets minimum prices, out-of-state producers may not even have the option of reducing prices in order to retain market share. The Massachusetts pricing order thus will almost certainly "cause local goods to constitute a larger share, and goods with an out-of-state source to constitute a smaller share, of the total sales in the market." In fact, this effect was the motive behind the promulgation of the pricing order. This effect renders the program unconstitutional, because it, like a tariff, "neutraliz[es] advantages belonging to the place of origin."

* * *

III

* * *

Respondent's principal argument is that, because "the milk order achieves its goals through lawful means," the order as a whole is constitutional. He argues that the payments to Massachusetts dairy farmers from the Dairy Equalization Fund are valid, because subsidies are constitutional exercises of state power, and that the order premium which provides money for the fund is valid, because it is a nondiscriminatory tax. Therefore the pricing order is constitutional, because it is merely the combination of two independently lawful regulations. In effect, respondent argues, if the State may impose a valid tax on dealers, it is free to use the proceeds of the tax as it chooses; and if it may independently subsidize its farmers, it is free to finance the subsidy by means of any legitimate tax.

Even granting respondent's assertion that both components of the pricing order would be constitutional standing alone, the pricing order nevertheless must fall. A pure subsidy funded out of general revenue ordinarily imposes no burden on interstate commerce, but merely assists local business. The pricing order in this case, however, is funded principally from taxes on the sale of milk produced in other States. By so funding the subsidy, respondent not only assists local farmers, but burdens interstate commerce. The pricing order thus violates the cardinal principle that a State may not "benefit in-state economic interests by burdening out-of-state competitors."

More fundamentally, respondent errs in assuming that the constitutionality of the pricing order follows logically from the constitutionality of its component parts. By conjoining a tax and a subsidy, Massachusetts has created a program more dangerous to interstate commerce than either part alone. Nondiscriminatory measures, like the evenhanded tax at issue here, are generally upheld, in spite of any adverse effects on interstate commerce, in part because "[t]he existence of major in-state interests adversely affected ... is a powerful safeguard against legislative abuse." However, when a nondiscriminatory tax is coupled with a subsidy to one of the groups hurt by the tax, a State's political processes can no longer be relied upon to prevent legislative abuse, because one of the in-state interests which would otherwise lobby against the tax has been mollified by the subsidy. So, in this case, one would ordinarily have expected at least three groups to lobby against the order premium, which, as a tax, raises the price (and hence lowers demand) for milk: dairy farmers, milk dealers, and consumers. But because the tax was coupled with a subsidy, one of the most powerful of these groups, Massachusetts dairy farmers, instead of exerting their influence against the tax, were in fact its primary supporters.

* * *

Finally, respondent argues that any incidental burden on interstate commerce "is outweighed by the 'local benefits' of preserving the Massachusetts dairy industry." In a closely related argument, respondent urges that "the purpose of the order, to save an industry from collapse, is not protectionist." If we were to accept these arguments, we would make a virtue of the vice that the rule against discrimination condemns. Preservation of local industry by protecting it from the rigors of interstate competition is the hallmark of the economic protectionism that the Commerce Clause prohibits....

In [another] case, also involving the welfare of Massachusetts dairy farmers,[5] Justice Jackson described the same overriding interest in the free flow of commerce across state lines:

> "Our system, fostered by the Commerce Clause, is that every farmer and every craftsman shall be encouraged to produce by the certainty that he will have free access to every market in the Nation, that no home embargoes will withhold his exports, and no foreign state will by customs duties or regulations exclude them. Likewise, every consumer may look to the free competition from every producing area in the Nation to protect him from exploitation by any. Such was the vision of the Founders; such has been the doctrine of this Court which has given it reality." *H. P. Hood & Sons, Inc. v. Du Mond*, 336 U.S. 525, 539 (1949).

The judgment of the Supreme Judicial Court of Massachusetts is reversed.

It is so ordered.

Notes and Questions

1. Constitutional Constraints on Rent Seeking? Interstate v. Intrastate Protectionism: The Supreme Court in *Healy* states that "tariffs against the products of other States are so patently unconstitutional that our cases reveal not a single attempt by any State to enact one," and then proceeds to invalidate the combined milk tax-subsidy at issue in the case as indistinguishable from a tariff. Why is it so clear that interstate protectionism is unconstitutional, but much less clear whether the same is true for intrastate protectionism (see note 7 following *Omni Advertising*)? As a matter of constitutional law, the reason is that it is well-established that "the very purpose of the Commerce Clause was to create an area of free trade among the several States." Wyoming v. Oklahoma, 502 U.S. 432, 470 (1992). The same cannot be said of the Due Process and Equal Protection Clauses. Is there any economic justification for the distinction?

2. The Economics of Free Trade: Most economists agree that barriers to free trade are undesirable. Indeed, a survey of economists has found a "strong" consensus that "[t]ariffs and import quotas usually reduce the general welfare of society." Dan Fuller & Doris Geide-Stevenson, *Consensus Among Economists: Revisited*, 34 Journal of Economic Education 369, 372 (2003). As discussed in Chapter II, even if one country (or state) has an absolute advantage in producing two goods, the country (or state) is still better off specializing in production of one of the goods and trading for the other (the so-called Theory of Comparative Advantage). Trade barriers like tariffs interfere with such beneficial exchanges.

3. Public Choice and Tariffs: The beneficiaries of interstate tariffs are clear: in-state producers avoid competition from lower cost out-of-state producers and so are able to charge higher prices. Out-of-state producers lose markets for their goods (although if the state is a price-taker in the interstate market it will not be able to affect the interstate market price). The real losers from tariffs are in-state consumers, who pay higher prices

---

5. A surprisingly large number of our Commerce Clause cases arose out of attempts to protect local dairy farmers. The reasons for the political effectiveness of milk producers are explored in G. Miller, The Industrial Organization of Political Production: A Case Study, 149 J. Institutional & Theoretical Economics 769 (1993).

for goods than they otherwise would. Revenue from a tariff goes to the state treasury. In *Healy*, the tax revenue did not go to the state treasury but instead to in-state producers as a subsidy. Note the role that public choice analysis plays in the *Healy* Court's opinion. The Court indicated that ordinarily in-state producers would be one of the interest groups opposing a tax on milk—the higher price would reduce demand for milk. But in *Healy*, "because the tax was coupled with a subsidy, one of the most powerful of these groups, Massachusetts dairy farmers, instead of exerting their influence against the tax, were in fact its primary supporters."

4. Why Milk?: In footnote 22 (footnote 5 in this excerpt), the Court in *Healy* notes that "[a] surprisingly large number of our Commerce Clause cases arose out of attempts to protect local dairy farmers." Why might that be so? Is it really so surprising that local milk producers would have more pull with state governments than out-of-state milk producers or consumers?

5. Economics and Appellate Advocacy: Healy is a good illustration of the potential, but too often untapped, value of economic analysis for advocates. The legal issue in *Healy* was whether the Massachusetts milk tax-subsidy combination was more like an unconstitutional tariff or more like a constitutionally permitted subsidy. In international economics, it is well accepted that a tariff is a subsidy "financed in a very particular way—solely by a tax on consumers of that particular product." W.M Corden, Trade Policy and Economic Welfare 45 (1972). From the perspective of international economics, then, *Healy* is an easy (and correctly decided) case. But strikingly, none of the parties to *Healy* discussed or even cited the international economics literature in its Supreme Court brief, despite its obvious relevance.

C. The Economics of the Court System

Legislatures and administrative agencies obviously are not the only branches of government that make legal rules. Courts do so as well. The rest of this chapter examines the economics of the court system in more detail. First, it looks at public choice theory as applied to the courts. Second, it examines the incentives of parties to sue and settle court cases. Third, the chapter analyzes court procedures from an economic perspective, focusing on discovery and class actions. Finally, fourth, it discusses the use of private alternatives to the public courts.

1. Public Choice and the Courts

We have discussed possible government failures in the legislative and administrative processes identified by public choice theory. Interest groups lobby legislators and bureaucrats to obtain favorable government regulation and to avoid unfavorable government regulation. How does the theory apply to the court system? Institutionally, courts differ in important ways from the legislative and administrative processes. Judges (with the exception of some appellate courts) do not set their own agendas. Instead, they take the cases brought to them by the parties. As a result of the adversarial process, judges generally hear both sides of an issue (although undoubtedly with differing degrees of effectiveness) before deciding a case.

Moreover, the judiciary is more insulated from the political process than any other branch of government and, as a result, judges seem less vulnerable than legislators and bureaucrats to the influence of interest group politics. Therefore, scholars of both law and economics and public choice theory have traditionally had a strong preference for more active judicial involvement in law-making. These scholars have maintained that although the law created by legislatures is often inefficient, the common law system has generally led to efficient laws. However, despite the general preference for litigation over legislation, the judiciary is also susceptible to inappropriate rent-seeking. The courts simply represent another opportunity for interest groups to shape the law.

Republican Party of Minnesota v. White
United States Court of Appeals for the Eighth Circuit
416 F.3d 738 (2005) (en banc)

BEAM, Circuit Judge.

* * *

I. BACKGROUND

Canon 5A(1) and 5B(1) [of the Minnesota Code of Judicial Conduct], the partisan-activities clause, and B(2), the solicitation clause, rein in the political speech and association of judicial candidates in Minnesota. The partisan-activities clause states, in relevant part:

> Except as authorized in Section 5B(1), a judge or a candidate for election to judicial office shall not:
>
> (a) identify themselves as members of a political organization, except as necessary to vote in an election;....
>
> (d) attend political gatherings; or seek, accept or use endorsements from a political organization.

Section 5B(1)(a) provides that "[a] judge or a candidate for election to judicial office may ... speak to gatherings, *other than political organization gatherings*, on his or her own behalf." (emphasis added). The solicitation clause states,

> A candidate shall not personally solicit or accept campaign contributions or personally solicit publicly stated support. A candidate may, however, establish committees to conduct campaigns for the candidate through media advertisements, brochures, mailings, candidate forums and other means not prohibited by law.... Such committees are not prohibited from soliciting and accepting campaign contributions and public support from lawyers, but shall not seek, accept or use political organization endorsements. Such committees shall not disclose to the candidate the identity of campaign contributors nor shall the committee disclose to the candidate the identity of those who were solicited for contribution or stated public support and refused such solicitation....

The facts of this case demonstrate the extent to which these provisions chill, even kill, political speech and associational rights. In his 1996 bid for a seat as an associate justice of the Minnesota Supreme Court, appellant Gregory Wersal (and others working on his behalf) identified himself as a member of the Republican Party of Minnesota, attended and spoke at the party's gatherings, sought the endorsement of the party, and personally solicited campaign contributions. In response to Wersal's appearance at and speech to a Republican Party gathering, a complaint was filed with the Minnesota Lawyers Professional Responsibility Board, alleging that Wersal's actions violated Canon 5A(1)(d). Although the Minnesota Office of Lawyers Professional Responsibility (OLPR) ultimately dismissed the complaint, the complaint accomplished its chilling effect. Wersal, fearful that other complaints might jeopardize his opportunity to practice law, withdrew from the race.

Wersal made a second bid for a seat on the Minnesota Supreme Court in 1998. In 1997 and 1998, Wersal asked the OLPR for advisory opinions regarding the solicitation and partisan-activities clauses. The OLPR's response was mixed, stating it would not issue an opinion regarding personal solicitation, in light of proposed amendments to the Canon and the fact that there were no judicial elections scheduled that particular year. It also stated that it would enforce the partisan-activities clause. Wersal then initiated this litigation....

II. DISCUSSION

A. Judicial Selection in Minnesota

Minnesota has chosen to elect the judges of its courts. Minn. Const. art. 6, § 7.... Some thirty-three states employ some form of contested election for their trial courts of general jurisdiction, their appellate courts, or both. As federal judges, we confess some bias in favor of a system for the appointment of judges. Indeed, there is much to be said for appointing judges instead of electing them, perhaps the chief reason being the avoidance of potential conflict between the selection process and core constitutional protections. In promoting the newly drafted United States Constitution, Hamilton argued in Federalist No. 78 that if the people were to choose judges through either an election or a process whereby electors chosen by the people would select them, the judges would harbor "too great a disposition to consult popularity to justify a reliance that nothing would be consulted but the Constitution and the laws." Arguably, concerns about judicial independence and partisan influence, posited by Minnesota as grounds for regulating judicial election speech, are generated, fundamentally, not by the exercise of political speech or association, but by concerns surrounding the uninhibited, robust and wide-open processes often involved in the election of judges in the first place. As Justice O'Connor noted in her ... concurrence [in Republican Party of Minnesota v. White, 536 U.S. 765 (2002)], "the very practice of electing judges undermines [an] interest" in an actual and perceived impartial judiciary.

Yet, there is obvious merit in a state's deciding to elect its judges, especially those judges who serve on its appellate courts. It is a common notion that while the legislative and executive branches under our system of separated powers make and enforce public policy, it is the unique role of the judicial branch to *interpret*, and be quite apart from making that policy.

But the reality is that "the policymaking nature of appellate courts is clear." Michael R. Dimino, Pay No Attention To That Man Behind the Robe: Judicial Elections, The First Amendment, and Judges as Politicians, 21 Yale L. & Pol'y Rev. 301, 364 (2003); Stephen J. Ware, Money, Politics and Judicial Decisions: A Case Study of Arbitration Law in Alabama, 30 Cap. U. L. Rev. 583, 594 (2002) ("[It is a] myth that courts are apolitical and do not make policy. The Legal Realists exploded that myth and showed that judges do make policy. This is especially true of judges on states' highest courts."). Courts must often fill gaps created by legislation. And in particular, by virtue of what state appellate courts are called upon to do in the scheme of state government, they find themselves as a matter of course in a position to establish policy for the state and her citizens. "At the [state] appellate level, common-law functions such as the adoption of a comparative fault standard, or the determination of a forced spousal share of intestate property distribution, require a judiciary that is sensitive to the views of state citizens." The courts' policy-making power is, of course, ever subject to the power of the legislature to enact statutes that override such policy. But that in no way diminishes the reality that courts are involved in the policy process to an extent that makes election of judges a reasonable alternative to appointment.

Without question, Minnesota may choose (and has repeatedly chosen) to elect its appellate judges. The very nature of its sovereignty within our federal system guarantees that.... If Minnesota sees fit to elect its judges, which it does, it must do so using a process that passes constitutional muster.

B. The First Amendment and Political Speech

Within this context, Minnesota has enacted Canon 5 in an effort to regulate judicial elections. In *White*, the Court held the announce clause of Canon 5, which prohibits judicial candidates from stating their views on disputed legal issues, unconstitutional. It falls to us now to determine whether the partisan-activities and solicitation clauses of Canon 5 are acceptable under the First Amendment.

* * *

It cannot be disputed that Canon 5's restrictions on party identification, speech to political organizations, and solicitation of campaign funds directly limit judicial candidates' political speech. Its restrictions on attending political gatherings and seeking, accepting, or using a political organization's endorsement clearly limit a judicial candidate's right to associate with a group in the electorate that shares common political beliefs and aims.

* * *

D. Minnesota's Purported Compelling State Interest

... Minnesota ... argue[s] that judicial independence, as applied to the issues in this case, springs from the need for impartial judges. Apparently, the idea is that a judge must be independent of and free from outside influences in order to remain impartial and to be so perceived....

One possible meaning of "impartiality" is a "lack of preconception in favor of or against a particular *legal view*." Quickly discounting this uncommon use of the word, the Court [in *White*] said it could not be a compelling interest for a judge to "lack ... predisposition regarding the relevant legal issues in a case" because such a requirement "has never been thought a necessary component of equal justice." ... We follow the Court's direction and likewise dismiss the idea that this meaning of impartiality could be a compelling state interest.

A second possible meaning is a "lack of bias for or against either *party* to [a] proceeding." Calling this the traditional understanding of "impartiality" and the meaning used by Minnesota and amici in their due process arguments, the Court explained that this notion "guarantees a party that the judge who hears his case will apply the law to him in the same way he applies it to any other party." The Court implied, and we find it to be substantially evident, that *this* meaning of impartiality describes a state interest that is compelling....

Being convinced that protecting litigants from biased judges is a compelling state interest, we turn to the "narrow tailoring" examination of the partisan-activities clause under this particular meaning of judicial impartiality....

* * *

1. Unbiased Judges and the Narrow Tailoring of the Partisan-Activities Clause

In one sense, the underlying rationale for the partisan-activities clause — that *associating with a particular group* will destroy a judge's impartiality — differs only in form from that which purportedly supports the announce clause—that *expressing one's self on particular issues* will destroy a judge's impartiality.... Indeed, Minnesota argues that a party label is nothing more than shorthand for the views a judicial candidate holds.... Thus, the Supreme Court's analysis of the announce clause under this meaning of "impartiality," to wit judicial bias, is squarely applicable to the partisan-activities clause.

> To be sure, when a case arises that turns on a legal issue on which the judge (as a candidate) had taken a particular stand, [be that through *announcing* or *aligning with* particular views,] the party taking the opposite stand is likely to lose. But not because of any bias against that party, or favoritism toward the other party. *Any* party taking that position is just as likely to lose. The judge is applying the law (as he sees it) evenhandedly.

* * *

Political parties are, of course, potential litigants, as they are in this case.... Yet even then, any credible claim of bias would have to flow from something more than the bare fact that the judge had associated with that political party. That is because the associational activities restricted by Canon 5 are, as we have pointed out, part-and-parcel of a candidate's speech for or against particular *issues* embraced by the political party. And such restrictions, we have also said, do not serve the due process rights of *parties*. In the case of a political party involved in a redistricting dispute, for example, the fact that the matter comes before a judge who is associated with the Republican or Democratic Party would not implicate concerns of bias for or against that party unless the judge were in some way involved in the case beyond simply having an "R" or "D," or "DFL" (denoting Minnesota's Democratic-Farmer-Labor Party) after his or her name. Thus, the partisan-activities clause does not advance an interest in impartiality toward litigants in a case where, without more, it is a like-minded political party which is one of the litigants.

And in those political cases where a judge is more personally involved, such as where the redistricting case is a dispute about how to draw that judge's district, and even in those cases discussed above that merely involve a political party as a litigant, recusal is the least restrictive means of accomplishing the state's interest in impartiality articulated as a lack of bias for or against parties to the case. Through recusal, the same concerns of bias or the appearance of bias that Minnesota seeks to alleviate through the partisan-activities clause are thoroughly addressed without "burning the house to roast the pig." ...

Therefore, the partisan-activities clause is barely tailored at all to serve any interest in unbiased judges, and, at least, is not the least-restrictive means of doing so. Accordingly, it is not narrowly tailored to any such interest and fails under strict scrutiny.

2. Impartiality Understood as "Openmindedness," and the Partisan-Activities Clause

The third possible meaning of "impartiality" articulated by the Supreme Court in *White*, and the one around which its analysis of the announce clause revolved, was "described as openmindedness." The Court explained,

> This quality in a judge demands, not that he have no preconceptions on legal issues, but that he be willing to consider views that oppose his preconceptions, and remain open to persuasion, when the issues arise in a pending case. This sort of impartiality seeks to guarantee each litigant, not an *equal* chance to win the legal points in the case, but at least *some* chance of doing so.

* * *

We conclude that the partisan-activities clause is ..."woefully underinclusive" ... [and] that the underinclusiveness of the partisan-activities clause causes it to fail strict scrutiny.

a. Underinclusiveness Belies Purported Purpose

Underinclusiveness in a regulation may reveal that motives entirely inconsistent with the stated interest actually lie behind its enactment....

The same is true of the partisan-activities clause.... A regulation requiring a candidate to sweep under the rug his overt association with a political party for a few months during a judicial campaign, after a lifetime of commitment to that party, is similarly underinclusive in the purported pursuit of an interest in judicial openmindedness. The few months a candidate is ostensibly purged of his association with a political party can hardly be expected to suddenly open the mind of a candidate who has engaged in years of prior political activity. And, history indicates it will be rare that a judicial candidate for a seat on the Minnesota Supreme Court will not have had some prior, substantive, political association....

As for the appearance of impartiality, the partisan-activities clause seems even less tailored than the announce clause to an interest in openmindedness. While partisan activity may be an indirect indicator of potential views on issues, an affirmative enunciation of views during an election campaign more directly communicates a candidate's beliefs. If, as the Supreme Court has declared, a candidate may *speak* about her views on disputed issues, what appearance of "impartiality" is protected by keeping a candidate from simply *associating* with a party that espouses the same or similar positions on the subjects about which she has spoken? ... Given this "woeful underinclusiveness" of the partisan-activities clause, it is apparent that advancing judicial openmindedness is not the purpose that "lies behind the prohibition at issue here."[6]

b. Underinclusiveness Betrays "Compelling" Claim

While it is not necessary for us to reach the question of whether judicial openmindedness as defined in *White* is sufficiently compelling to abridge core First Amendment rights, we note that the underinclusiveness of Canon 5's partisan activities clause clearly establishes that the answer would be no.... A clear indicator of the compelling nature of an interest is whether the state has bothered to enact a regulation that guards the interest from all significant threats.... Minnesota worries that a judicial candidate's consorting with a political party will damage that individual's impartiality or appearance of impartiality as a judge, apparently because she is seen as aligning herself with that party's policies or procedural goals. But that would be no less so when a judge as a judicial candidate aligns herself with the constitutional, legislative, public policy and procedural beliefs of

---

6. Rather, the fruits of Canon 5 appear to bear witness to its remarkably pro-incumbent character.

In 2004, of the three Minnesota Supreme Court seats up for election, only one was contested.... In the race that was contested, the incumbent enjoyed a nearly thirty-two percent margin in contributions from outside, non-loan sources. The data from the Minnesota Court of Appeals is even more striking. Of the five Court of Appeals seats up for election, only two were contested. In those two races, the incumbents were able to collect a combined total of $104,172.21 in contributions against a combined challengers' total of just $4,546.46 — nearly twenty-three times as much.

In 2000, Supreme Court incumbents raised a combined $505,120.66. Only two of the challengers raised enough money to trigger disclosure. Their combined total was $23,582.67.

Notably, donations from lawyers and law firm-related political funds account for a substantial portion of incumbents' re-election war chests. In one 2004 Court of Appeals race, such contributions accounted for over forty-three percent of the incumbent's total campaign funds. In the 2004 Supreme Court race, they made up over half of the incumbent's funds.

organizations such as the National Rifle Association (NRA), the National Organization for Women (NOW), the Christian Coalition, the NAACP, the AFL-CIO, or any number of other political interest groups.... Indeed, associating with an interest group, which by design is usually more narrowly focused on particular issues, conveys a much stronger message of alignment with particular political views and outcomes. A judicial candidate's stand, for example, on the importance of the right to keep and bear arms may not be obvious from her choice of political party. But, there can be little doubt about her views if she is a member of or endorsed by the NRA. Yet Canon 5 is completely devoid of any restriction on a judicial candidate attending or speaking to a gathering of an interest group; identifying herself as a member of an interest group; or seeking, accepting, or using an endorsement from an interest group. As a result, the partisan-activities clause unavoidably leaves appreciable damage to the supposedly vital interest of judicial open-mindedness unprohibited, and thus Minnesota's argument that it protects an interest of the highest order fails.

* * *

3. The Solicitation Clause

We now turn to an analysis of portions of the solicitation clause. The solicitation clause bars judicial candidates from personally soliciting individuals or even large gatherings for campaign contributions.... Restricting speech based on its subject matter triggers the same strict scrutiny as does restricting core political speech....

* * *

Since strict scrutiny is clearly invoked, the solicitation clause must also be narrowly tailored to serve a compelling state interest. Minnesota asserts that keeping judicial candidates from personally soliciting campaign funds serves its interest in an impartial judiciary by preventing any undue influence flowing from financial support. We must determine whether the regulation actually advances an interest in non-biased or open-minded judges.[7]

a. Unbiased Judges and the Narrow Tailoring of the Solicitation Clause

... Canon 5 provides specifically that all contributions are to be made to the candidate's *committee*, and the committee "shall not" disclose to the candidate those who either contributed or rebuffed a solicitation.... An actual or mechanical reproduction of a candidate's signature on a contribution letter will not magically endow him or her with a power to divine, first, to whom that letter was sent, and second, whether that person contributed to the campaign or balked at the request. In the same vein, a candidate would be even less able to trace the source of funds contributed in response to a request transmitted to large assemblies of voters. So, the solicitation clause's proscriptions against a candidate

---

7. The dissent cites polls from other states that show concern on the part of those surveyed that lawyers' and plaintiffs' campaign contributions to judicial candidates influence the decisions of judges. The dissent asserts that political parties embody similar threats of "outside influence" on the judiciary. But these poll numbers provide clear evidence that the perception of influence is of a far different kind, one that is not regulated by Canon 5.

While Canon 5 severs judicial candidates from like-minded voters during an election, it expressly allows lawyers, law firms and other interest groups to donate money to their campaigns. In the 2004 Minnesota Supreme Court election, approximately thirty-two percent of all campaign contributions came from law firm political funds and lawyers. And in the only contested race, over ninety-seven percent of such contributions went to the incumbent. We need not speculate about the impact these lawyer contributions have on the appearance of the judiciary's integrity—the poll numbers noted by the dissent leave little question.

personally signing a solicitation letter or making a blanket solicitation to a large group, does not advance any interest in impartiality articulated as a lack of bias for or against a party to a case.

b. Open-minded Judges and the Narrow Tailoring of the Solicitation Clause

We next consider whether the solicitation clause as applied by Minnesota serves an interest in impartiality articulated as "openmindedness." ... Given that Canon 5 prevents a candidate from knowing the identity of contributors or even non-contributors, to believe so would be a "challenge to the credulous." Thus, Minnesota's solicitation clause seems barely tailored to in any way affect the openmindedness of a judge. Accordingly, the solicitation clause, as applied by Minnesota, cannot pass strict scrutiny when applied to a state interest in impartiality articulated as openmindedness.

III. CONCLUSION

... [W]e hold that [the partisan-activities and solicitation clauses] ... do not survive strict scrutiny and thus violate the First Amendment. We therefore reverse the district court, and remand with instructions to enter summary judgment for Appellants.

JOHN R. GIBSON, Circuit Judge, with whom McMILLIAN and MURPHY, Circuit Judges, join, dissenting.

* * *

... [T]he Minnesota Supreme Court has recently reconsidered the provisions of Canon 5 at issue here, held hearings, and received public comment. It is a matter of interest that the parties in this case, in briefing and argument, made no mention of this development. As the canon was reconsidered, amended in part and reiterated in part while this case was pending on rehearing, failure to consider the effect of these developments may well cause this Court's opinion to be moot from its inception.

* * *

The Advisory Committee appointed by the Minnesota Supreme Court to study the issue concluded that there was a threat to the state's interest that required regulation of partisanship in judicial campaigns.... While we do not have access to the evidence before the Committee, widely available and publicized evidence substantiates the fear that the majority of the public believes that partisanship does influence the decisions of state courts. For instance, a poll conducted in 1999 showed that 81% of the respondents agreed that "politics influences court decisions." The Advisory Committee recommended deleting the party identification and the attend and speak clauses on narrow tailoring grounds. After receiving the Committee report and conducting a hearing and receiving public comment, the Minnesota Supreme Court decided to retain all three partisan activities clauses.

The Advisory Committee unanimously recommended against changing the ban on the judicial candidate's personal solicitation of campaign contributions. Again, widely available poll numbers support the Committee's conclusion that solicitation of campaign contributions carries with it a significant threat to the state's interest in freedom from external coercion of judges. For example, "a recent Wisconsin poll found that more than three-quarters of those surveyed believe that campaign contributions from lawyers and plaintiffs in high-profile cases influence the decisions of these judges in court," and a study in Texas "found that 83 percent of the public and 79 percent of lawyers believe that campaign contributions have a significant influence on a judge's decision." ... [A] poll from Texas showed that 48% of state appellate and trial judges surveyed believed that campaign contributions had a fairly significant or very significant degree of influence over judicial decisionmaking. A Pennsylvania survey of registered voters showed that 95% of those surveyed believed that judges' decisions were influenced by large contributions to their election campaigns at least some of the time. This is the kind of evidence that would substantiate the threat to judicial open-mindedness (and the appearance of it) from partisan obligations and from judicial campaign fund-raising.

* * *

There can be no question that the interests at stake here are compelling. There are questions of fact—first, as to whether the threat to those interests posed by partisan involvement in judicial elections and personal solicitation of contributions are severe enough to warrant the measures taken by the Minnesota Supreme Court and second, as to whether the particular remedy chosen was truly selected for the asserted reason. I would remand to the district court for trial of these factual questions in light of new evidence of the Minnesota Supreme Court's most recent deliberations on the subject....

Notes and Questions

1. Public Choice and Elected Judges: Application of public choice theory to elected judges seems relatively straightforward (at least more straightforward than applying it to unelected judges, as discussed below). The incentives of elected judges are expected to be similar to the incentives of legislators—judges decide cases so as to maximize the likelihood they will be reelected. Indeed, several judges have admitted that reelection concerns may influence their judicial rulings. For example, former California Supreme Court Justice Otto M. Kaus commented: "To this day, I don't know to what extent I was subliminally motivated by the thing you could not forget—that it might do you some good politically to vote one way or the other."

Numerous empirical studies have found a relationship between elections and judicial decision making. Some studies have found that judges cast more politically popular votes as their reelection approaches and electoral pressures intensify. See, for example, Melinda Gann Hall, *Electoral Politics and Strategic Voting in State Supreme Courts*, 54 Journal of Politics 427 (1992); Gregory A. Huber & Sanford C. Gordon, *Accountability and Coercion: Is Justice Blind when It Runs for Office?*, 48 American Journal of Political Science 247 (2004). Other studies have found a stronger relationship between electoral pressure and judicial decision making for judges elected on partisan ballots. For example, Alex Tabarrok and Eric Helland find that partisan-elected judges are more likely to redistribute wealth in tort cases from out-of-state businesses to in-state plaintiffs, who also are voters. Alexander Tabarrok & Eric Helland, *Court Politics: The Political Economy of Tort Awards*, 42 Journal of Law and Economics 157 (1999).

Are there any ways in which elected judges differ from legislators (other than the obvious one of deciding cases rather than enacting legislation)? As lawyers involved with the court system, are judges subject to ethical duties or professionalism norms that might constrain their behavior? Are lawyer-legislators subject to similar constraints?

2. Who Benefits?: The surveys cited by the dissent find that many people (and many judges) are concerned about the effect of elections on the incentives of judges. On the other hand, the court rejects such concerns, largely on the ground that the Minnesota restrictions on judicial campaigns at issue in the case are likely to have little effect on public confidence in the courts. If that is so, then why have those restrictions at all? Keep in mind that the campaign restrictions were not enacted by the legislature, but were adopted by the Minnesota Supreme Court. In footnote 9 of the *White* opinion (footnote 6 in this excerpt), the court of appeals observes that "the fruits of Canon 5 appear to bear witness to its remarkably pro-incumbent character." Why might incumbent judges favor those sorts of restrictions?

3. Follow the Money—Campaign Contributions and Judicial Elections: Since the 1980s, judicial elections have grown increasingly competitive and expensive. Throughout the 1990s, only $83.3 million was contributed to state supreme court candidates; in contrast, candidates raised $206.9 million between 2000–2009. Because a substantial campaign war chest is imperative to winning elections, judges seeking reelection have the incentive to issue judicial decisions that will help them to attract much-needed campaign contributions. Numerous empirical studies find that judges tend to favor campaign contributors in their decisions. For example, Shepherd has found that contributions from various interest groups are associated with increases in the probability that state supreme court judges will vote for the litigants whom those interest groups favor. Joanna M. Shepherd, *Money, Politics, and Impartial Justice*, 58 Duke Law Journal 623 (2009). For an extreme example, see Caperton v. A.T. Massey Coal Co., 556 U.S. 868, 873 (2009) (holding that failure of a state Supreme Court justice to recuse himself violated due process when the board chairman and principal officer of the corporate defendant in the case had made $3 million in campaign contributions in support of the justice's election, "more than the total amount spent by all other … supporters [of the justice] and three times the amount spent by [the justice's] own committee").

4. Lawyers and Judicial Elections: Lawyers are one of the interest groups that contribute substantial amounts to judicial election campaigns. As stated in footnote 15 of the *White* opinion (footnote 7 in this excerpt), lawyers and law firms made thirty-two percent of all contributions during the 2004 elections for Minnesota Supreme Court justices. Footnote 9 (footnote 6 in this excerpt) indicates that the percentage of contributions from lawyers was even higher in other judicial elections in the state. In other words, lawyers are yet another interest group seeking favorable rules and rulings. What sorts of legal rules might lawyers favor?

Most interest groups contribute both direct expenditures to candidates' campaigns and independent expenditures for TV and other advertising (that do not go directly to candidates). However, lawyers' contributions are almost exclusively direct campaign contributions. Why would lawyers prefer giving money directly to judges' campaigns instead of spending money independently on advertising?

5. Judges Seeking Reappointment: In many states, judges must be reappointed by the governor or legislature instead of reelected by voters. Like judges seeking reelection, judges seeking reappointment also have incentives to vote strategically. For example, judges facing reappointment by the governor or legislature may feel pressure to vote in ways that favor the executive or legislative branches. The power over judicial reappointment held by the governor or legislature offers the political branches of government direct opportunities to sanction judges for unpopular rulings. Judges who consistently vote against the interests of the other branches of government may hurt their chances for reappointment. Indeed, empirical studies have found evidence suggesting that, in the types of cases in which state governments have a stake, the decision making of judges seeking reappointment is influenced by reappointment concerns. See, for example, Paul Brace, Melinda Gann Hall, & Laura Langer, *Judicial Choice and the Politics of Abortion: Institutions, Context, and the Autonomy of Courts*, 62 Albany Law Review 1265 (1999); Joanna Shepherd, *Are Appointed Judges Strategic Too?*, 58 Duke Law Journal 1589 (2009).

6. The Incentives of Judges with Permanent Tenure: The majority of American state-court judges serve without permanent tenure and must be retained—either by voters, legislatures, or the governor—on a regular basis. In fact, only in a handful of states—Rhode Island, Massachusetts, New Hampshire, and some judges in Kansas—do judges enjoy permanent appointments. U.S. federal judges are similarly granted permanent tenure.

Applying public choice analysis to judges with permanent tenure is more difficult. As Judge Richard Posner has written:

> At the heart of economic analysis of law is a mystery that is also an embarrassment: how to explain judicial behavior in economic terms, when almost the whole thrust of the rules governing the compensation and other terms and conditions of judicial employment is to divorce judicial action from incentives—to take away the carrots and sticks, the different benefits and costs associated with different behaviors, that determine human action in an economic model.

Richard A. Posner, *What Do Judges and Justices Maximize? (The Same Thing Everybody Else Does)*, 3 Supreme Court Economic Review 1, 2 (1993). Various elements of a judicial utility function (i.e., what judges and justices seek to maximize) have been suggested, including the enjoyment of making decisions (or, as Judge Posner puts it, the "pure utility of voting"); prestige and respect from being a judge; the prospects for promotion to a higher court; being averse to reversal; and leisure time. These different elements of the judicial utility function obviously have different implications for judicial behavior, and some have argued that only a "meager harvest" of insights is likely to result from such models. *See* Richard A. Epstein, *The Independence of Judges: The Uses and Limitations of Public Choice Theory*, 1990 BYU Law Review 827.

In at least some contexts, however, judges behave very much as predicted by economic models of rationality. For example, federal judges have tried for years to regulate the process by which judges hire law clerks, delaying hiring until late in the second year or early in the third year of law school. The incentives for judges to comply with rules that delay hiring have been compared to the incentives of competitors that form a cartel to raise prices (indeed, both can be analyzed as forms of the "Prisoners Dilemma" game described in Chapter I). Even if the judges are collectively better off by agreeing to delay hiring, individually each judge has an incentive to hire before the deadline to gain the best available law clerks. The result of such "cheating on the cartel" is that the agreement to delay breaks down altogether—exactly the result economic theory predicts.

7. Interest Groups in the Courts: Interest groups participate in court cases in a variety of capacities, the most direct of which is as a party to the case. In addition, particularly before appellate courts, interest groups may file amicus briefs, containing arguments different from or in addition to those made by the parties. It is unclear how effective such filings are in influencing decisions on the merits of the case, but there is evidence of a positive relationship between the filing of amicus briefs and the likelihood a court will grant discretionary review in a case. *E.g.*, Kevin T. McGuire, The Supreme Court Bar: Legal Elites in the Washington Community 182 (1993) (finding U.S. Supreme Court more likely to grant certiorari in cases with one or more amici supporting the cert petition).

8. Evolution of the Common Law: A well-known theory in law and economics is that the common law, whether consciously or unconsciously, progresses towards efficiency. In the first article applying an evolutionary model to the common law, Rubin argued that because inefficient rules impose a loss on one party that is greater than the gain to the other, litigation becomes more likely when rules are inefficient, and so inefficient rules are subject to greater selection pressure, and more likely to be overturned. Paul H. Rubin, *Why is the Common Law Efficient?*, 6 Journal of Legal Studies 51 (1977).

There have since been countless extensions and modifications of this evolutionary approach. Law and economics scholars have also advanced important counterarguments. In one of the most influential criticisms of evolutionary models, Hirshleifer showed that the law could evolve to favor whichever party could most easily organize and mobilize resources for litigation to overturn unfavorable precedents, even if efficient. Hence, just as with the legislative process, interest groups can push the development of the common law in social welfare-reducing directions. Jack Hirshleifer, *Evolutionary Models in Economics and Law*, in Research in Law and Economics (P. Rubin and R. Zerbe eds., 1982).

According to Professor Todd Zywicki, both of these views are partly correct:

> From its inception, an animating insight of the economic analysis of law has been the observation that the common law process appears to have a strong tendency to produce efficiency-enhancing legal rules. But many recent commentators have also concluded that recent decades have seen an evolution away from this traditional principle, as the common law appears to increasingly reflect interest-group pressures that have attenuated this traditional evolutionary tendency toward efficiency.

Todd J. Zywicki, *The Rise and Fall of Efficiency in the Common Law: A Supply-Side Analysis*, 97 Northwestern University Law Review 1551, 1551 (2003). Zywicki argues that the "fall of efficiency in the common law" is due to changes in what he calls "supply side" characteristics of the legal process, such as stronger adherence to the doctrine of precedent and less competition among courts, as well as doctrinal changes, such as less respect for the freedom of contract and less reliance on custom in deciding cases. *Id.* at 1554.

2. Suit and Settlement

The previous section dealt with the broader institutional question of how public choice theory applies to the courts. The section takes on a narrower topic, looking at why parties litigate a particular case. Very few legal disputes go to trial. In fact, about 95% of cases settle or are resolved on dispositive motions. The decision whether to file a lawsuit is merely a variant of the general economic rule of decision: if the marginal benefits of filing suit exceed the marginal costs of filing suit, then sue!

Economists typically analyze parties' litigation decisions using what is known as the expected value model. Under the model, litigants assign an expected value for possible case outcomes based on each outcome's likelihood and payout. The model includes all of the twists and turns the case may take, the probability the litigant will prevail at each of the necessary steps of the case, and the likely recovery if the litigant does prevail. By combining these factors, each outcome is assigned a number weighted according to its likelihood and potential payout. Between two outcomes with equal payouts, the outcome more likely to occur is weighted more heavily than the outcome less likely to occur in the expected value calculation. For a more detailed explanation of how to calculate expected values, see Chapter VI on Risk.

Assume, for example, that Julia is deciding whether to file suit after being injured in a car accident. Julia consults with her lawyers, who plan to demand a jury trial but believe that the defendant will likely file a motion to dismiss the case for failure to state a claim. Julia's lawyers estimate that if the case makes it to the jury, Julia has a 50% chance of recovering $10,000 and a 50% chance of recovering nothing. In addition, the lawyers estimate that the defendant has a 10% chance of prevailing on the motion to dismiss. If the case makes it to the jury, Julia's expected recovery is $5,000, calculated in the equation (0.5 * $10,000) + (0.5 * $0). In the equation, the first 0.5 represents the 50% chance of recovery and the second 0.5 represents the likelihood of no recovery. $10,000 is the payout that is conditioned upon the 50% chance of recovery. $0 is the payout conditioned on the 50% possibility that Julia will receive nothing. Those numbers are added together to calculate the expected recovery if the case gets to a jury.

Next, the expected recovery given that the case will make it to a jury must be tempered to reflect the 10% probability that the defendant's motion to dismiss will prove successful, Julia has a 90% chance of getting the case to the jury, so Julia's expected recovery if she files suit is $4,500 (0.9 * $5,000). This is calculated by multiplying the 0.9, or 90% chance the case survives the motion to dismiss, by the expected recovery if the case makes it to a jury. So long as her expected costs of litigating the case, also calculated using the expected value model, are less than $4,500, Julia should sue. In other words, after subtracting the potential expected cost of litigation given various potential outcomes of the case, if the expected value of pursuing litigation is greater than zero, Julia should sue because she has the chance to become better off.

In practice, many attorneys make these sorts of judgments intuitively, but not always.

Kohls v. Duthie

Court of Chancery of Delaware
765 A.2d 1274 (2000)

LAMB, Vice Chancellor

I. INTRODUCTION

This is an application for a preliminary injunction against a management buy-out transaction being sponsored by a third-party venture capital fund....

Plaintiffs argue that the disclosures made in connection with the proposed transaction are deficient and that elements of the valuation work performed on behalf of the Special Committee are materially in error....

* * *

II. FACTUAL BACKGROUND

* * *

A. Kenetech's Liquidity Crisis

Kenetech Corporation ("Kenetech") is a small publicly traded company, operating largely in the electric utility market....

In the mid-1990s, Kenetech faced a serious liquidity crisis when its largest wholly-owned subsidiary, Kenetech Windpower, Inc. ("KWI"), was forced to file for bankruptcy protection. In response, Kenetech began selling assets and reducing its staff size.

B. Kenetech's Search for Strategic Alternatives

[Although] Kenetech ... weathered its serious liquidity crisis, it did so only by selling most of its operating assets and firing most of its employees. Because of its small equity capitalization and lack of access to financial markets, Kenetech publicly announced in March 1999 its intention to explore strategic alternatives, including going private or seeking a merger or acquisition partners....

C. The Derivative Litigation

In October 1997, Mark Lerdal, president and chief executive officer of Kenetech, was approached by Mark Laskow of The Hillman Company ("Hillman"), the owner of nearly a third of Kenetech's common shares. Laskow told Lerdal that Hillman planned to sell its shares by year-end in order to take a tax loss in 1997. Laskow asked Lerdal if he knew of anyone who might be willing to pay a meaningful amount for the stock. Laskow also told Lerdal that Hillman would, as a last resort, sell its shares at a nominal price and asked if Lerdal might be interested in purchasing them. Lerdal said he would be. The record also reflects that, either in this initial conversation or at a later time, Lerdal and Laskow discussed whether Kenetech could buy the shares and, apparently, agreed that it could not due to its several financial defaults and its apparent capital impairment....

* * *

Laskow called Lerdal again around December 15, 1997 and told him that Hillman had not found a buyer for its shares. He offered to sell Lerdal the stock for either $1,000 or $5,000. Naturally, Lerdal chose to pay $1,000 for the 12.8 million shares, and the transaction closed December 29, 1997.

This transaction forms the core basis of plaintiffs' claim that Lerdal usurped a corporate opportunity. The complaint alleges that the timing of this purchase by Lerdal renders the transaction suspect. Allegedly, Lerdal knew that [Kenetech would soon be able to pay off all of its debts and regain profitability.] It is also alleged that the other apparent obstacles to Kenetech repurchasing its own shares could have been overcome.

The derivative action was filed on February 3, 2000 and seeks the cancelation of Lerdal's shares. The complaint alleges that, at the time of filing, the shares acquired by Lerdal for $1,000 were worth over $8.2 million. In the context of the current transaction, in which $1.04 is being offered for each share of Kenetech common stock, Lerdal's shares are worth even more.

D. The ValueAct Merger Proposal

In June 2000, Jeffrey Ubben of the venture capital fund, ValueAct Capital Partners, L.P., approached Lerdal with the possibility of taking Kenetech private. Ubben was personally familiar with Lerdal and with Kenetech's search for strategic alternatives.

1. Creation of the Special Committee

Lerdal reported Ubben's contact at a special board meeting held on June 21, 2000. The board decided to pursue the possibility of a ValueAct transaction and, by June 29, a confidentiality agreement was reached between ValueAct and Kenetech. Shortly thereafter, Ubben raised with Lerdal the possibility that Lerdal should take an equity position in the purchaser by contributing his Kenetech shares. Lerdal informed the Kenetech board of this development at a July 5 meeting of the directors. Lerdal then withdrew from the meeting and the remaining directors decided to create a Special Committee for the purpose of evaluating any offers from ValueAct. The resolution creating the committee delegated to it broad powers to control the negotiation of a transaction, including the power to "say no."...

* * *

The Special Committee met on July 5, 2000, immediately after its creation, and next met on August 17 for the purpose of hiring the Wilmington, Delaware law firm of Potter, Anderson & Corroon, L.L.P. ("Potter"). The committee also discussed the need to hire a financial advisor and discussed several possible candidates....

2. Negotiations with ValueAct

On August 23, ValueAct made an offer priced at $ 0.95 per share to close before December 31, 2000....

On August 24, the Special Committee retained Houlihan, Lokey, Howard & Zukin Financial Advisors, Inc. to assist in evaluating the ValueAct proposal and negotiating a transaction....

The Special Committee and ValueAct engaged in extensive negotiations over price and other terms of the proposed transaction. After considering a range of alternatives and a presentation by Houlihan, Lokey that described a preliminary range of fairness of $0.93 to $1.27 per share, the Special Committee made a counter-offer priced at $1.17.

* * *

The Special Committee met on October 24 and 25 to review the final agreements.... During the course of these meetings, Houlihan, Lokey made its final presentation, explained that it had narrowed its range of fairness to $0.96 to $1.13, and delivered its formal opinion that the consideration offered in the transaction was fair to the Kenetech stockholders other than Lerdal from a financial point of view. At the conclusion of its meetings, the Special Committee voted unanimously to approve the transaction and to recommend it to the full board of Kenetech. On October 25, the full board, with Lerdal abstaining, approved the merger agreement after receiving advice from the Special Committee, Houlihan, Lokey, and Potter.

Of particular interest on this motion for preliminary injunction is Houlihan, Lokey's $0.01 per share valuation of the derivative claim, formally presented to the Special Committee on October 25, 2000. Houlihan, Lokey based its valuation of that claim on Potter's assessment of the probable outcomes of the litigation. Houlihan, Lokey also estimated the costs associated with the various outcomes and the likely net result to the corporation. It then created a "decision tree" that yielded the expected value. Plaintiffs have criticized Houlihan, Lokey's work for any number of reasons but have not submitted any evidence of their own valuing the litigation. I will discuss plaintiffs' criticisms of Houlihan, Lokey's work later in this opinion.

* * *

III. Legal Analysis

* * *

C. Adequacy of the Disclosures

When proposing a transaction to stockholders for their consideration and approval, directors have a fiduciary obligation to provide full and fair disclosure of all material information within their control. As a general rule, information is considered material if a reasonable investor would have viewed it as altering the total mix of information available. Plaintiffs maintain that defendants have not provided shareholders with adequate disclosure by both omitting facts and misleading shareholders regarding several aspects of the proposed transaction with ValueAct.

After the complaint attacking the proposed transaction was filed, the defendants published extensive supplemental disclosures ("Supplemental Disclosures"), no doubt intended to moot all of plaintiffs' disclosure claims. The Supplemental Disclosures describe the allegations of the second amended complaint, and contain additional detailed information on a number of topics addressed at the scheduling conference on the instant motion. Most significantly, these address issues relating to Houlihan, Lokey's valuation work, including its valuation of the derivative claim....

* * *

The materials sent to stockholders tell them that Houlihan, Lokey valued the derivative action at $0.01 per share. Plaintiffs object both because they take issue with Houlihan, Lokey's methodologies and conclusions and because they say the disclosure materials do not adequately explain what Houlihan, Lokey did.

In his November 22, 2000 deposition, James R. Waldo, Jr., a senior vice president of Houlihan, Lokey who performed the valuation, explained his methodology for valuing the derivative action. He arrived at his conclusion by employing a "decision tree" methodology that allowed him to calculate the expected value of the litigation by taking into account all of the factors he deemed relevant to the calculation, including the likelihood of success on the merits, attorney's fees and other costs, taxes, probability that the suit would be maintained, probability of success, and probability that the cancellation of shares or equivalent damages would be awarded if successful.[8] In preparing the valuation, Houlihan, Lokey relied on the expert advice of Potter in assessing the probabilities of events occurring. Substantially the same information is found in the Supplemental Disclosures and is adequate disclosure of what Houlihan, Lokey did.

On its merits, the Houlihan, Lokey valuation of the derivative claim appears to be the product of a logical methodology, and plaintiffs provide no alternative to it. They cavil about details of Houlihan, Lokey's work but, on the whole, their objections do not suggest a material deficiency in the result.

* * *

In light of the full disclosures made by the corporation, ... I see no reason to see why shareholders should not be the final authority on whether this ... transaction takes place.

IV. CONCLUSION

For all of the foregoing reasons, the motion for preliminary injunction will be denied. IT IS SO ORDERED.

Notes and Questions

1. Decision Trees and Valuing Claims: A way that economists map out the potential outcomes and payouts in litigation is through the creation of decision trees. Decision trees represent strategic choices or alternate outcomes graphically (in a tree shape). Each branch of a decision tree represents a potential decision, made by at least one party to the litigation—including the court—and indicates likely outcomes based on each decision. In the example of Julia's unfortunate car accident, her lawyer would calculate the likelihood and payout from each potential outcome and map it in a decision tree, like the one below.

---

8. Houlihan, Lokey's analysis is as follows: canceling the shares would be worth $0.4781 per share to the remaining shareholders. With a 25 percent attorney's fee awarded and a corporate tax of 40 percent, this yields an extra $0.2152 per share. Discounting this by a 25 percent chance of success (as suggested by Potter), and a 35 to 40 percent chance that the suit would be maintained by plaintiffs, and factoring the costs associated with the litigation, the valuation of the derivative action comes to $0.0172 to $0.0151 per share.

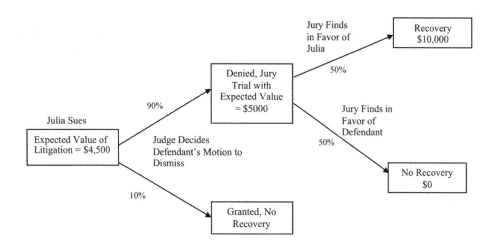

The process of mapping the potential outcomes of a case is a helpful exercise for lawyers to understand how the case will likely play out. It may serve to inform the lawyer of the range of settlement values that are acceptable at each stage of the case and ultimately may demonstrate whether to sue in the first place. *See also* Saunders v. C.I.R., 136 T.C. 406, 418 (U.S. Tax Ct. 2011) (discussing use of decision trees to value claims for tax purposes: "there are recognized methods of valuing choses in action by assuming various outcomes, assigning probabilities to those outcomes, and quantifying the results").

The facts of *Kohls* are complex, but the most interesting part of the case is the discussion of the value of the shareholders' derivative claim. Footnote 29 (footnote 8 in this excerpt) describes how Houlihan, Lokey came up with the expected value of the claim. The potential recovery from the lawsuit was valued at $0.4781 per share of stock. Of that amount, 25% would go to the plaintiff's attorney under a contingent fee contract, and 40% of the remainder would go to taxes. Subtracting those values from the potential recovery would leave the corporation with a net of $0.2152 per share. As estimated by the corporation's lawyers, there was "a 35 to 40 percent chance that the suit would be maintained by plaintiffs" (reflecting perhaps the director demand requirement), and only a 25 percent chance of plaintiffs winning if the case proceeded to judgment. Houlihan, Lokey estimated that subtracting an unspecified amount of litigation costs left the case with a positive expected value of $0.0151 to $0.0172 (1.5 to 1.7 cents) per share. That is, a (barely) positive expected value.

2. The Plaintiff's Decision Whether to Sue: Under the expected value model, the plaintiff will sue so long as the claim has a positive expected value — in other words, so long as **the expected benefits of suing exceed the expected costs.** In *Kohls* — not considering the complications from the fact that the case involved a shareholder derivative suit — because the claim has a positive expected value, the model predicts that the plaintiffs would file suit.

3. Negative Expected Value Claims: Of course, if the claim has a negative expected value, the model predicts that the claimant will not sue: the expected benefits from suing are less than the expected costs. That a claim has a negative expected value does not necessarily mean that it is frivolous; it may be a meritorious claim, but one that simply is too expensive to pursue. Although as a general matter one would not expect plaintiffs to file negative expected value suits, under some circumstances it may be rational to do so. For example, an attorney may be able to develop a reputation for filing negative expected value suits. Rather than incur the litigation costs in such a case, the defendant may go ahead and settle the claim. Other circumstances in which a plaintiff might file a negative expected value claim include when the parties possess differing amounts of information about the claim or when the claimant and defendant incur their litigation costs at different times. Why would a plaintiff file a claim in those situations?

4. A Real Options Alternative: Although the expected value model is the economic approach most commonly used to study civil litigation, it is based on a highly unrealistic assumption. As Bradford Cornell explains:

> In deciding whether to sue or whether to settle, the litigants consider the costs and benefits under the assumption that they must either settle promptly or go to trial. There are no intermediate decisions to be made along the way. Under these conditions, the discounted cash flow model can be used to analyze litigation investments.

Bradford Cornell, *The Incentive to Sue: An Option-Pricing Approach*, 19 Journal of Legal Studies 173, 173 (1990). In actual litigation, of course, plaintiffs have a number of intermediate points at which they can decide simply to drop their claim (and save the remaining costs of litigating the case) rather than continuing to trial. At each of these intermediate points, the plaintiff has an option to continue with the case (like an option to buy stock or renew a lease) that it can exercise by incurring its costs of litigation. Cornell describes the implications of this "real options approach" as follows:

> These options make a lawsuit a more valuable investment than it would be if the plaintiff had to choose initially between trying the case and not filing suit....
>
> Because the value of an option grows when the variance of the underlying random variable rises, increasing uncertainty regarding court awards will make a lawsuit a more attractive investment. For this reason, the granting of a few huge awards can greatly increase the incentive to sue by making litigation options more valuable. Suits will be filed even when the probability of winning such an award is so small that the discounted cash flow expected value is negative because the plaintiff has the option to drop the case at the optimal moment.

Id. at 174, 182–83.

Although it generates interesting predictions, the real options model is much more complex than the expected value model. Despite its unrealistic assumptions, the expected value model has proven helpful in understanding the economics of many aspects of the litigation process, and continues to be used in law-and-economics scholarship today.

5. The Economics of Settlement: A settlement agreement is a contract like any other contract for the sale of goods or services. Consider the following example from everyday life. Jim owns a bicycle and Harry wants to buy it. When will the sale happen? The sale will happen when Harry is willing to pay a price that Jim is willing to accept. This will only occur if Harry values the bicycle more than Jim does. For example, if Harry values the bicycle at $200 he is willing to pay any price up to $200 for it. If Jim values the bicycle at $150 he is willing to accept anything more than $150 to sell it. Therefore, a sale is possible at any price between $150 and $200. However, no sale is possible if Jim values the bicycle at $250, since Harry is only willing to pay up to $200.

The same principles apply to settlement. In a settlement, however, it is not the bicycle for sale; it is the plaintiff's right to sue. The plaintiff owns a legal right to sue the defendant, and a settlement involves the plaintiff selling his right to the defendant. Once the plaintiff has filed suit, the defendant must do its own valuation of the expected value of the claim and determine how to proceed. Because both parties will incur litigation costs to proceed with the case, it may be in their mutual interest to settle the case and save those costs. Indeed, since the vast majority of cases do settle before trial, the parties presumably have very strong incentives to settle rather than try the case.

According to the expected value model, the parties will have an incentive to settle under the following circumstances:

> The necessary condition for settlement is that the plaintiff's minimum offer — the least amount he will take in settlement of his claim — be smaller than the defendant's maximum offer. This is not a sufficient condition: the parties may find it impossible to agree upon a mutually satisfactory settlement price. But we shall assume that settlement negotiations are rarely unsuccessful for this reason and therefore that litigation occurs only when the plaintiff's minimum offer is greater than the defendant's maximum offer. The plaintiff's minimum offer is the expected value of the litigation to him plus his settlement costs, the expected value of the litigation being the present value of the judgment to him if he wins, multiplied by the probability (as he estimates it) of his winning, minus the present value of his litigation expenses. The defendant's maximum offer is the expected cost of the litigation to him and consists of his litigation expenses, plus the cost of an adverse judgment multiplied the probability as he estimates it of the plaintiff's winning (which is equal to one minus the probability of *his* winning), minus his settlement costs.[9]

Richard A. Posner, *An Economic Approach to Legal Procedure and Judicial Administration*, 2 Journal of Legal Studies 399, 417–18 (1973). If the parties have identical estimates of the likelihood that the plaintiff will win and the amount of the plaintiff's damages, the plaintiff's expected value of the case will be the same as the defendant's expected loss from the case: the plaintiff expects to win what the defendant expects to lose. In such a case, the parties have an incentive to settle: they will save the costs of litigating the case and reach a conclusion that both parties expect. The settlement range in the case (the difference between the defendant's maximum offer and the plaintiff's minimum offer) clearly is positive and will equal the sum of both parties' expected litigation expenses.

The parties have an incentive to settle so long as their settlement range is positive. They may not be able to agree on a settlement amount due to various bargaining failures (each party trying to get too big a piece of the settlement pie), but they have an incentive to do so. However, in some cases there is no settlement range. If, for example, both parties are very optimistic about their chance of winning, the plaintiff may estimate a high expected value for the case while the defendant may estimate a low expected loss. Even taking into account both parties' litigation costs, the settlement range may be negative: the parties have no incentive to settle the case.

For example, suppose that Andy sues a hotel for negligence after slipping on a sidewalk after a snowstorm. The lawyers for the hotel are considering whether to settle. Assume that Andy's likelihood of success is 60% and that he expects a trial award of $50,000 in damages if he prevails. Also assume that each side will spend $10,000 in litigation costs if the case goes through trial. Can Andy and the hotel settle this lawsuit? If so, what is the settlement range?

---

9. If a party is either risk averse or risk preferring rather than risk neutral the expected utility of litigation may be smaller or larger than its expected value. We assume risk neutrality except where otherwise indicated, but the analysis could easily be modified to take account of the existence of nonneutral attitudes toward risk....

Andy will demand a settlement that makes him at least as well off as going to trial. Using the expected value model to compute Andy's expected gain from trial, first multiply the probability of winning by the expected award (0.6 * $50,000) and then subtract the cost of litigation ($10,000) to get Andy's minimum settlement value, or the lowest point at which he should be willing to accept a settlement offer. Here it is $20,000.

Next, find the hotel's maximum amount for which it will settle rather than try the case. To compute the hotel's expect loss from trial, multiply its probability of losing by the amount of damages it will pay (0.6 * $50,000) and then add the hotel's litigation costs ($10,000). Therefore, the hotel should be willing to settle for any amount less than or equal to $40,000.

The settlement range is $20,000 to $40,000 — Andy is willing to accept a settlement as low as $20,000, and the hotel willing to offer as much as $40,000 for a settlement. The two parties should be able to settle, but the exact result will depend on the bargaining power of each side.

6. Settlement and Case Selection Bias: The economic analysis of settlement has given rise to "one of the fundamental results in the law and economic analysis of civil procedure," what is known as "case selection bias." Geoffrey P. Miller, *The Legal-Economic Analysis of Comparative Civil Procedure*, 45 American Journal of Comparative Law 905, 914 (1997). The insight, first developed by George L. Priest and Benjamin Klein in their article *The Selection of Disputes for Litigation*, 13 Journal of Legal Studies 1 (1984), predicts that systematic differences among courts (such as differences among the judges' ideological viewpoints) or laws (such as differences among state laws) will have little or no impact on how often plaintiffs win at trial because of selection effects. The model explains that, because trying a case is costly, both potential litigants would prefer to settle to avoid trial costs and, if they are risk averse, uncertainty. The potential litigants form rational estimates of likely trial outcomes, and settle the simpler, more predictable cases to avoid a costly trial. Thus, the only cases that go to trial are those for which the outcome cannot be easily predicted and in which the parties' expectations diverge. Because the cases with predictable outcomes are settled, the model anticipates that plaintiffs should win approximately 50 percent of the remaining unpredictable cases that go to trial.

For example, assume that state law requires the plaintiff to prove negligence to recover in tort, and that under the negligence rule plaintiffs win 50 percent of the cases that go to trial. The state supreme court, overruling its prior precedent, adopts a rule of strict liability, holding defendants liable in tort even if the defendant wasn't negligent. Surprisingly, plaintiffs continue to win 50 percent of the cases that go to trial. Does that mean that a strict liability rule is no better for plaintiffs than a negligence rule? Certainly not. Although the change in the legal rule did not affect plaintiffs' success rate at trial, it almost certainly affected the terms of the settlements that parties entered into before trial. The only cases that made it to trial under either legal rule were the tough cases — those in which, for example, both sides thought they had a good chance of success, like the mutual optimism scenario described above. However, the tough cases under a strict liability rule are different from the tough cases under a negligence rule — indeed, they are probably cases that were clear losers under a negligence rule and would never even have made it to trial. Different assumptions about the characteristics of cases can result in different predictions about the expected rate at which plaintiffs and defendants win at trial. But the important insight of case selection bias nonetheless holds: that it can be very difficult to draw conclusions from empirical observations of trial outcomes; the legal rules may have their effects outside of court rather than inside.

7. Markets in Claims: A still small but rapidly growing industry consists of firms that provide funding for legal claims:

[I]n recent years, a new breed of third-party litigation financing has evolved in the United States. Large litigation finance corporations now exist that provide capital in exchange for a share of a corporate plaintiff's eventual recovery.... [T]he new litigation finance corporations routinely loan several million dollars in exchange for shares of recoveries that can be in the billion dollar range. Currently, six corporations invest in commercial lawsuits in the United States. However, only two publicly traded corporations exist primarily to invest in American commercial litigation: Juridica Investments and Burford Capital. Both of these corporations manage investment funds of well over $100 million. Of the remaining four corporations, three are private companies that provide little information about their investments — ARCA Capital, Calunius Capital, and Juris Capital — and the other, IMF Ltd., is publicly traded but invests primarily in litigation outside of the United States. A handful of other corporations, investment banks, and hedge funds have recently formed litigation funding divisions to buy interests in commercial lawsuits.

Joanna M. Shepherd, *Ideal Versus Reality in Third-Party Litigation Financing*, 8 Journal of Law, Economics & Policy 593, 594 (2012). Before deciding whether to invest in a claim, the firms must value the claim and contract with the party asserting the claim. Many legal uncertainties remain, and the practice has been criticized:

> Third-party litigation financing has substantial support from practitioners and legal scholars. The basis of their support is that third-party financing of litigation can reduce barriers to justice that result when risk-averse, financially constrained plaintiffs are pitted against risk-neutral, well-financed defendants. By relieving a risk-averse plaintiff of much of the litigation risk, third-party financing can offset a risk-neutral defendant's bargaining advantage and level the playing field in negotiations. This would improve plaintiffs' compensation and promote more accurate deterrence.

> However, the goal of third-party investors is not to improve access to justice for financially constrained or risk-averse plaintiffs. Instead, third-party investors aspire only to maximize the returns from their investments in litigation. Moreover, the cases with the largest potential return are often the cases where the existing substantive law advantages, rather than disadvantages, the plaintiffs. As a result, many of the cases financed by third-party investors are the opposite of the types of cases where financing could improve access to justice for vulnerable plaintiffs. Thus, the reality of third-party financiers' investment strategy directly conflicts with the theoretical ideal of third-party financing.

Id. at 594–95. Is third-party litigation funding another step toward markets in legal claims? Would such a markets be a good thing?

3. The Economics of Court Procedures

Economists have analyzed a wide range of court procedures. This section discusses only two — but two of the most visible and controversial — discovery and class actions.

a. Discovery

Discovery — whether document production, depositions, or interrogatories — is an important characteristic of American litigation. Under modern discovery practice, as the Supreme Court stated in *Hickman v. Taylor*, "no longer can the time-honored cry of 'fishing expedition' serve to preclude a party from inquiring into the facts underlying his opponent's case." 329 U.S. 495, 507 (1947). Discovery benefits the parties and the court system by promoting more accurate outcomes: it enables decisions to be made on the basis of more complete information and reduces the chance for one party to surprise the other at trial. Society also benefits by realizing deterrence gains from greater outcome accuracy and reduced process costs with a higher settlement rate. But discovery has costs as well, as is obvious to anyone who has responded to a document request or attended a deposition (or, worse yet, been deposed!). Discovery also imposes administrative costs when discovery disputes must be resolved judicially, and parties can potentially use discovery for purposes other than legitimate fact-finding. Some forms of discovery are more costly than others; new technologies have only increased the potential costs.

Hagemeyer North America, Inc. v. Gateway Data Sciences Corp.

United States District Court for the Eastern District of Wisconsin
222 F.R.D. 594 (2004)

DECISION AND ORDER

This matter comes before the Court on a motion to compel discovery. The plaintiff, Hagemeyer North America, Inc. n/k/a Hagemeyer N.A. Holdings, Inc. ("Hagemeyer") seeks to compel production of e-mails, financial statements, employee billing statements, computer backup tapes, and other documents from the defendant, Gateway Data Sciences, also known as Brownshire Holdings, Inc. ("Gateway").

* * *

II. DISCUSSION

* * *

... Hagemeyer asked Gateway to search all of its backup tapes for e-mails containing certain search terms. Gateway refused, citing the undue burden and expense involved in restoring the documents and then searching them. Hagemeyer also offered to search the tapes at its own expense, but Gateway refused. Hagemeyer now moves to compel Gateway to restore and search the backup tapes. Gateway argues that Hagemeyer should defray the costs of restoration because they are too burdensome. There are, therefore, "competing hardships" that the Court must balance: Gateway's — for having to search the tapes at great expense — and Hagemeyer's — for being deprived of potentially useful information.

A party may discover "any matter, not privileged, that is relevant to the claim or defense of any party...." Fed. R. Civ. P. 26(b)(1). The Court may limit discovery, however, if it finds that the discovery request is more easily obtained from another source, including information already collected; that the requesting party has had sufficient opportunity to obtain discovery; or that the request is unduly burdensome or expensive. Fed. R. Civ. P. 26(b)(2). Rule 26(b)(2)(iii) provides five factors to help the Court determine whether the burden or expense of a discovery request is proportional to the needs of the case:

> The frequency or extent of use of ... discovery ... shall be limited by the court if it determines that:

* * *

(iii) the burden or expense of the proposed discovery outweighs its likely benefit, taking into account [(A)] the needs of the case, [(B)] the amount in controversy, [(C)] the parties' resources, [(D)] the importance of the issues at stake in the litigation, and [(E)] the importance of the proposed discovery in resolving the issues.

There is a presumption that "the responding party must bear the expense of complying with discovery requests...." However, when the request violates the Rule 26(b)(2) proportionality test, the Court may "condition[] discovery on the requesting party's payment of the costs of discovery." The party opposing discovery must show good cause for its refusal and, thus, bears the burden of proof.

1. The Unique Burden of Producing Backup Tapes

Gateway raises the issue of cost shifting by stating that restoring and searching the backup tapes would be "extremely time-consuming and expensive." ...

Backup tapes record a "snapshot" of the contents of the computer system at the moment the backup is run. *See McPeek v. Ashcroft*, 202 F.R.D. 31, 32 (D.D.C. 2001) ("*McPeek I*"). "The data on a backup tape are not organized for retrieval of individual documents or files, but for wholesale, emergency uploading onto a computer system." In case the system "crashes," and all the information created since the previous backup is lost, the contents of the tape can be loaded onto the system, restoring the lost information. *See Zubulake v. U.B.S. Warburg LLC*, 217 F.R.D. 309, 314 (S.D.N.Y. 2003) ("*Zubulake I*"). Since crashes presumably occur infrequently, backup tapes need not be as convenient to access as, say, a CD-ROM. At the same time, backup tapes must have the capacity to store large amounts of information since they are relied upon to replace all the information contained on a computer system after a crash. It is understandable, then, that backup tapes sacrifice accessibility for storage capacity, since to have both would be impractical and costly. Indeed, one court has revealed a correlation between the inaccessibility of backup tapes and the cost of searching them.

One of the reasons for the high cost of searching backup tapes is that they store more information than most other storage media. To illustrate, a CD-ROM's storage capacity is 650 megabytes, the equivalent of 325,000 typewritten pages; computer networks create backup data measured in terabytes—1,000,000 megabytes—which is the equivalent of 500 billion typewritten pages.

Additionally, backup tapes require more time and labor to search than other media because of the way data is organized on them; "tape drives ... are sequential-access devices, which means that to read any particular block of data, you need to read all the preceding blocks." This type of organization is a main reason that each backup tape may take anywhere from several minutes to five days to restore. Adding to the difficulty, each must be restored separately onto a hard drive in order to be searched.

Accordingly, the cost to review the backup tapes can be hundreds of thousands of dollars depending on the number of tapes that are to be searched.

2. Different Approaches to Cost-Shifting

A number of district courts have recognized the unique burden of producing documents stored on backup tapes and, by invoking Rule 26(c) to fashion orders to protect parties from undue burden or expense, have conditioned production on payment by the requesting party. *See, e.g., Zubulake I*, 217 F.R.D. 309; *Rowe Entm't, Inc. v. William Morris Agency, Inc.*, 205 F.R.D. 421 (S.D.N.Y. 2002); *McPeek v. Ashcroft*, 202 F.R.D. 31 (D.D.C. 2001). Although the power to shift the costs of discovery is discretionary, these courts have identified four approaches to help them determine when cost-shifting is proper. The Court of Appeals for this circuit has not addressed this issue.

a. Cost-Benefit Analysis

Cost-benefit analysis is a strict cost-based approach that requires the most primitive cost-shifting analysis: the requesting party always bears the burden of producing computer-generated data. Cost-benefit analysis is based, as its title suggests, on economic principles, most importantly "that an individual will pay what he assumes is a fair value for that which he seeks." Proponents of this approach argue that since the costs of responding to requests for electronic discovery are higher than those for other types of discovery, it is especially fertile territory for abuse. In short, it is in the requesting party's best interest to demand more discovery than it needs in order to increase the responding party's costs of litigation. If the requesting party bears the costs of producing electronically stored documents, it will only request what it needs for the case.

The Court rejects this approach for two reasons: first, it fails to accommodate documents stored on electronic media that are cheaper to produce than paper-based documents and, second, it ignores the presumption that the requesting party pays the costs of production.

b. The Marginal Utility Approach

The marginal utility approach, like the cost-benefit analysis which it rejects, is based on economic principles: "the more likely it is that the backup tape contains information that is relevant to a claim or defense, the fairer it is that the [responding party] search at its own expense." The court in *McPeek I*, which originated the marginal utility approach, delayed deciding whether to shift the costs of restoration until it knew the likely costs and benefits. To that end, the court ordered the responding party to search a sample of the backup tapes and to produce any responsive e-mails from that sample, keeping record of its monetary cost. Besides making the cost-shifting analysis fact-based, the marginal utility approach adheres closely to the Rule 26(b)(2) proportionality test.

c. The Rowe Test

The test that was used by the court in *Rowe* balanced eight factors:

(1) the specificity of the discovery requests;

(2) the likelihood of discovering critical information;

(3) the availability of such information from other sources;

(4) the purposes for which the responding party maintains the requested data;

(5) the relative benefit to the parties of obtaining the information;

(6) the total cost associated with production;

(7) the relative ability of each party to control costs and its incentive to do so; and

(8) the resources available to each party.

Although for a time the *Rowe* test was "the gold standard," it has a few shortcomings. First, the *Rowe* test omits two factors specified in Rule 26(b)(2)(iii) of the Federal Rules of Civil Procedure: (1) the amount in controversy and (2) the importance of the issues at stake in the litigation. Second, the fourth factor, i.e., the purposes for retaining the data, has no direct impact on the accessibility of computerized information and is, therefore, nonessential to determining the likely costs of production. Finally, the approach is flawed because "courts have given equal weight to all of the factors, when certain factors should predominate."

d. The Zubulake *Factors*

The court in *Zubulake I,* after identifying the defects in the *Rowe* test, created a new seven-factor test. The *Zubulake* test takes into consideration:

(1) The extent to which the request is specifically tailored to discover relevant information;

(2) The availability of such information from other sources;

(3) The total cost of production, compared to the amount in controversy;

(4) The total cost of production, compared to the resources available to each party;

(5) The relative ability of each party to control costs and its incentive to do so;

(6) The importance of the issues at stake in the litigation; and

(7) The relative benefits to the parties of obtaining the information.

The *Zubulake* factors improved the *Rowe* test because, unlike the *Rowe* test, the *Zubulake* factors are weighed in descending order of importance, not equally. Thus, the first two factors, which mirror the marginal utility test found in *McPeek I,* are the most important. Furthermore, the court in *Zubulake I,* like the *McPeek I* court, ordered the responding party to produce responsive documents from a sample of backup tapes. Therefore, the court was able to base its cost-shifting analysis on facts rather than speculation.

3. Conclusion

In short, *Zubulake* brought the cost-shifting analysis closer to the Rule 26(b)(2) proportionality test by adding two of the factors that *Rowe* had omitted and made the analysis dependent on the facts of the case. For these reasons, the Court is persuaded by the reasoning in *Zubulake* and will adopt the seven-factor *Zubulake* test.

Rule 26(c) of the Federal Rules of Civil Procedure gives the Court broad discretion to create any order that would spare a party undue burden or expense, including orders shifting the costs of production. However, the Court should only issue such an order when a request truly threatens to subject the responding party to undue burden or expense. Therefore, the Court will follow the reasoning of *McPeek* and *Zubulake* and require Gateway to restore a sample of backup tapes and require the parties to make additional submissions addressing whether the burden or expense of satisfying the entire request is proportionate to the likely benefit. The Court will then further address the search of Gateway's backup tapes....

* * *

Notes and Questions

1. Is Discovery Necessary? The assumption underlying the discovery rules is that without legal compulsion, a party will not turn evidence over to the other side. That seems intuitively obvious, but there are at least some circumstances in which parties might voluntarily produce evidence even if not required to do so by the discovery rules. For example, a plaintiff might reveal evidence favorable to its case to the defendant (or vice versa) to try and persuade the defendant to settle sooner or on better terms. Indeed, the plaintiff might produce even unfavorable evidence, if he or she believes that the defendant views the plaintiff's evidence as worse (i.e., more favorable to the defendant) than it actually is. On the other hand, the value of surprise at trial cuts against disclosure in both types of cases. Certainly a party has little reason to disclose evidence that is unfavorable to it and that the opposing party is unlikely to find out about otherwise. It is this sort of evidence that, at a minimum, the discovery process may make available to the other side—the marginal benefit of the discovery rules, as it were.

2. Discovery and Settlement: How does discovery affect the likelihood that a case will settle? As with many economic questions, the answer is that "it depends." Recall from the discussion above that a case is unlikely to settle when both parties are optimistic about their chances of success; if so, the settlement range may be small or nonexistent. Discovery may promote settlement in such a situation when it requires one party to disclose evidence favorable to its case; that evidence may reduce the optimism of the other side and expand the settlement range (or create one if one does not exist previously). But as Judge Posner writes: "if discovery may reduce mutual optimism by inducing the communication of information that causes a party to reduce his estimate of his chances of prevailing, so may it reduce mutual pessimism, and hence increase the likelihood of litigation, by generating information about the opponent's case that causes a party to become more optimistic." Richard A. Posner, *An Economic Approach to Legal Procedure and Judicial Administration*, 2 Journal of Legal Studies 399, 423 (1973). In both cases, the greater the costs of discovery, the greater the incentive to settle to avoid those costs.

3. Discovery Abuse: Much has been written about abuses of the discovery process, with one party making burdensome discovery requests to impose substantial costs on the other. In cases like *Hagemeyer*, the burdens of producing the requested material can be substantial: searches through back-up computer tapes for possibly responsive electronic documents or e-mail messages. A 2012 RAND Institute study of e-discovery costs found total expenditures in a sample of cases ranging "from a seemingly modest $17,000 (in an intellectual property matter) to $27 million (in a product-liability case), with a median value of $1.8 million." *See* RAND Institute for Civil Justice, Where the Money Goes: Understanding Litigant Expenditures for Producing Electronic Discovery 17 (2012).

The court in *Hagemeyer* describes a number of competing approaches other courts have considered in determining who should bear the cost of such burdensome discovery. The default, as noted by the court, is for the party responding to the request to bear the costs. The court describes a number of tests for identifying cases in which the costs will be shifted to the requesting party. Two of the tests are explicitly economic in their formulation. The first, which the opinion calls "cost-benefit analysis," imposes the cost of producing back-up tapes on the requesting party. The second, which the opinion calls the "marginal-utility approach," balances the likely benefits of the search against its costs, and imposes the costs on the requesting party unless the benefits of the search are sufficiently high relative to the costs. How are these different approaches to cost allocation likely to affect the parties' behavior? Is the Coase Theorem relevant?

b. Class Actions

Another common (and often controversial) procedural device is the class action, whereby individual claims are aggregated into a single lawsuit pursued on behalf of the class by a representative plaintiff or plaintiffs. Class actions have a number of potential benefits. They may permit plaintiffs to achieve economies of scale in litigating their case and thus reduce litigation costs. For claims too small to be worth pursuing on an individual basis, aggregating the claims into a class action may be the only way to make the suit economical to bring (although other means, such as fee-shifting statutes, may give plaintiffs the incentive to sue even for small claims). Without such small-claims class actions, defendants might well escape liability altogether for actions that cause small harms to many victims. But class actions have potential costs as well.

In re Bridgestone/Firestone, Inc.

United States Court of Appeals for the Seventh Circuit
288 F.3d 1012 (2002)

Easterbrook, *Circuit Judge.*

Firestone tires on Ford Explorer SUVs experienced an abnormally high failure rate during the late 1990s. In August 2000, while the National Highway Transportation Safety Administration was investigating, Firestone recalled and replaced some of those tires. Ford and Firestone replaced additional tires during 2001. Many suits have been filed as a result of injuries and deaths related to the tire failures. Other suits were filed by persons who own (or owned) Ford Explorers or Firestone tires that have so far performed properly; these persons seek compensation for the risk of failure, which may be reflected in diminished resale value of the vehicles and perhaps in mental stress. The Judicial Panel on Multidistrict Litigation transferred suits filed in, or removed to, federal court to the Southern District of Indiana for consolidated pretrial proceedings under 28 U.S.C. § 1407(a). Once these have been completed, the cases must be returned to the originating districts for decision on the merits. In an effort to prevent retransfer, counsel representing many of the plaintiffs filed a new consolidated suit in Indianapolis and asked the judge to certify it as a nationwide class action, which would make all other suits redundant. The district court obliged and certified two nationwide classes.... More than 60 million tires and 3 million vehicles fit [within the classes].

No class action is proper unless all litigants are governed by the same legal rules. Otherwise the class cannot satisfy the commonality and superiority requirements of Fed. R. Civ. P. 23(a), (b)(3). Yet state laws about theories such as those presented by our plaintiffs differ, and such differences have led us to hold that other warranty, fraud, or products-liability suits may not proceed as nationwide classes. The district judge, well aware of this principle, recognized that uniform law would be essential to class certification. Because plaintiffs' claims rest on state law, the choice-of-law rules come from the state in which the federal court sits. The district judge concluded that Indiana law points to the headquarters of the defendants, because that is where the products are designed and the important decisions about disclosures and sales are made. Ford and Firestone engaged in conduct that was uniform across the nation, which the district court took to imply the appropriateness of uniform law. This ruling means that all claims by the Explorer class will be resolved under Michigan law and all claims by the tire class will be resolved under Tennessee law....

Both Ford and Firestone petitioned for interlocutory review under Fed. R. Civ. P. 23(f). We granted these requests because ... the suit is exceedingly unlikely to be tried. Aggregating millions of claims on account of multiple products manufactured and sold across more than ten years makes the case so unwieldy, and the stakes so large, that settlement becomes almost inevitable—and at a price that reflects the risk of a catastrophic judgment as much as, if not more than, the actual merit of the claims. Permitting appellate review before class certification can precipitate such a settlement is a principal function of Rule 23(f). Another function is permitting appellate review of important legal issues that otherwise might prove elusive. The district court's conclusion that one state's law would apply to claims by consumers throughout the country—not just those in Indiana, but also those in California, New Jersey, and Mississippi—is a novelty, and, if followed, would be of considerable import to other suits. Our review of this choice-of-law question is plenary, so we start there.

* * *

... If recovery for breach of warranty or consumer fraud is possible, the injury is decidedly where the *consumer* is located, rather than where the seller maintains its headquarters. A contract for the sale of a car in Indiana is governed by Indiana law unless it contains a choice-of-law clause, and plaintiffs do not want to enforce any choice-of-law clause.... It follows that Indiana's choice-of-law rule selects the 50 states and multiple territories where the buyers live, and not the place of the sellers' headquarters, for these suits.

* * *

Because these claims must be adjudicated under the law of so many jurisdictions, a single nationwide class is not manageable. Lest we soon see a Rule 23(f) petition to review the certification of 50 state classes, we add that this litigation is not manageable as a class action even on a statewide basis. About 20% of the Ford Explorers were shipped without Firestone tires. The Firestone tires supplied with the majority of the vehicles were recalled at different times; they may well have differed in their propensity to fail, and this would require sub-subclassing among those owners of Ford Explorers with Firestone tires. Some of the vehicles were resold and others have not been; the resales may have reflected different discounts that could require vehicle-specific litigation. Plaintiffs contend that many of the failures occurred because Ford and Firestone advised the owners to underinflate their tires, leading them to overheat. Other factors also affect heating; the failure rate (and hence the discount) may have been higher in Arizona than in Alaska. Of those vehicles that have not yet been resold, some will be resold in the future (by which time the tire replacements may have alleviated or eliminated any discount) and some never will be resold. Owners who wring the last possible mile out of their vehicles receive everything they paid for and have claims that differ from owners who sold their Explorers to the second-hand market during the height of the publicity in 2000. Some owners drove their SUVs off the road over rugged terrain, while others never used the "sport" or "utility" features; these differences also affect resale prices.

Firestone's tires likewise exhibit variability; that's why fewer than half of those included in the tire class were recalled.... There are other differences too, but the ones we have mentioned preclude any finding "that the questions of law or fact common to the members of the class predominate over any questions affecting only individual members, and that a class action is superior to other available methods for the fair and efficient adjudication of the controversy." Fed. R. Civ. P. 23(b)(3). Regulation by the NHTSA, coupled with tort litigation by persons suffering physical injury, is far superior to a suit by millions of *uninjured* buyers for dealing with consumer products that are said to be failure-prone.

The district judge did not doubt that differences within the class would lead to difficulties in managing the litigation. But the judge thought it better to cope with these differences than to scatter the suits to the winds and require hundreds of judges to resolve thousands of claims under 50 or more bodies of law. Efficiency is a vital goal in any legal system — but the vision of "efficiency" underlying this class certification is the model of the central planner. Plaintiffs share the premise of the ALI's *Complex Litigation Project* (1993), which devotes more than 700 pages to an analysis of means to consolidate litigation as quickly as possible, by which the authors mean, before multiple trials break out. The authors take as given the benefits of that step. Yet the benefits are elusive. The central planning model—one case, one court, one set of rules, one settlement price for all involved—suppresses information that is vital to accurate resolution. What is the law of Michigan, or Arkansas, or Guam, as applied to this problem? Judges and lawyers will have to guess, because the central planning model keeps the litigation far away from state courts. (Ford asked us to certify legal questions to the Supreme Court of Michigan, to ensure that genuine state law was applied if Michigan's law were to govern the whole country; the plaintiffs stoutly resisted that proposal.) And if the law were clear, how would the facts (and thus the damages per plaintiff) be ascertained? One suit is an all-or-none affair, with high risk even if the parties supply all the information at their disposal. Getting things right the first time would be an accident. Similarly Gosplan or another central planner *may* hit on the price of wheat, but that would be serendipity. Markets instead use diversified decisionmaking to supply and evaluate information. Thousands of traders affect prices by their purchases and sales over the course of a crop year. This method looks "inefficient" from the planner's perspective, but it produces more information, more accurate prices, and a vibrant, growing economy. See Thomas Sowell, *Knowledge and Decisions* (1980). When courts think of efficiency, they should think of market models rather than central-planning models.

Our decision in *Rhone-Poulenc Rorer* made this point, and it is worth reiterating: only "a decentralized process of multiple trials, involving different juries, and different standards of liability, in different jurisdictions" (51 F.3d at 1299) will yield the information needed for accurate evaluation of mass tort claims. Once a series of decisions or settlements has produced an accurate evaluation of a subset of the claims (say, 1995 Explorers in Arizona equipped with a particular tire specification) the others in that subset can be settled or resolved at an established price.

No matter what one makes of the decentralized approach as an original matter, it is hard to adopt the central-planner model without violence not only to Rule 23 but also to principles of federalism. Differences across states may be costly for courts and litigants alike, but they are a fundamental aspect of our federal republic and must not be overridden in a quest to clear the queue in court. Tempting as it is to alter doctrine in order to facilitate class treatment, judges must resist so that all parties' legal rights may be respected.

The motion to certify questions of law to the Supreme Court of Michigan is denied as unnecessary in light of this opinion. The district court's order certifying two nationwide classes is reversed.

Notes and Questions

1. Class Actions and Settlement: The court of appeals states that class actions are "exceedingly unlikely to be tried" because "aggregating millions of claims on account of multiple products manufactured and sold across more than ten years makes the case so unwieldy, and the stakes so large, that settlement becomes almost inevitable." Given our discussion earlier of the economics of suit and settlement, that isn't surprising. The high litigation costs of class actions create a large settlement range, which, all else being equal, makes settlement more likely.

2. "Blackmail Settlements"?: The court is concerned about more than merely the likelihood of settlement. It asserts that settlement is likely to take place "at a price that reflects the risk of a catastrophic judgment as much as, if not more than, the actual merit of the claims." In other words, given the potential for huge liability, risk averse defendants will likely settle rather than litigate even what they see as a meritless claim. Judge Posner made this point in his well-known opinion in *Rhone-Poulenc*:

> Suppose that 5,000 of the potential class members are not yet barred by the statute of limitations. And suppose the named plaintiffs ... win the class portion of this case to the extent of establishing the defendants' liability under either of the two negligence theories. It is true that this would only be prima facie liability, that the defendants would have various defenses. But they could not be confident

that the defenses would prevail. They might, therefore, easily be facing $25 billion in potential liability (conceivably more), and with it bankruptcy. They may not wish to roll these dice. That is putting it mildly. They will be under intense pressure to settle.... Judge Friendly, who was not given to hyperbole, called settlements induced by a small probability of an immense judgment in a class action "blackmail settlements." Henry J. Friendly, *Federal Jurisdiction: A General View* 120 (1973).

In re Rhone-Poulenc Rorer, Inc., 51 F.3d 1293, 1298 (7th Cir. 1995).

Not all scholars are persuaded, however. Professors Bruce Hay and David Rosenberg note that plaintiffs, too, face an "all-or-nothing gamble" in a class action, which "exerts pressure on risk-averse class counsel and class members to settle for less than the value of the class claim." Bruce Hay & David Rosenberg, *"Sweetheart" and "Blackmail" Settlements in Class Actions: Reality and Remedy*, 75 Notre Dame Law Review 1377, 1403 (2000). Moreover, plaintiffs—but not defendants—face the same problem in the litigation of an individual case: "trial is an all-or-nothing event for the plaintiff; a loss may be catastrophic. But it is not an all-or-nothing event for the defendant firm; a loss means paying only one plaintiff." *Id.* at 1404 n.53. How are these differing dynamics likely to affect settlement negotiations?

3. Back to the USSR? Class Actions and the "Central Planning Model": A related cost of class actions identified by the court is the cost of errors: if a class action goes to trial and the judge or jury makes a mistake, that mistake affects every claim. If each case is litigated separately, a mistake affects primarily that one case, subject to application of the doctrines of res judicata and collateral estoppel. (Of course, if the class action gets it right, then all parties are subject to the single, correct result.) Judge Easterbrook argues that "the vision of 'efficiency' underlying this class certification is the model of the central planner"—bringing up visions of the former Soviet Union at its worst—while comparing individually litigated cases to sellers in a market. According to Judge Easterbrook, "when courts think of efficiency, they should think of market models rather than central-planning models." Is the comparison an apt one? Like markets, multiple proceedings provide information that is unavailable in a single case. But is there competition among courts the same way there is among sellers in a market? Is there reason to think the results in a series of cases will tend to converge to a single outcome? If so, are the benefits worth the costs?

Lane v. Facebook, Inc.

United States Court of Appeals for the Ninth Circuit
696 F.3d 811 (2012)

Hug, Circuit Judge:

The question presented is whether the district court abused its discretion in approving the parties' $9.5 million settlement agreement as "fair, reasonable, and adequate," either because a Facebook employee sits on the board of the organization distributing cy pres funds or because the settlement amount was too low. We hold that it did not.

I

Facebook is an online social network where members develop personalized web profiles to interact and share information with other members....

In November of 2007, Facebook launched a new program called "Beacon." ... The program operated by updating a member's personal profile to reflect certain actions the member had taken on websites belonging to companies that had contracted with Facebook to participate in the Beacon program. Thus, for example, if a member rented a movie through the participating website Blockbuster.com, Blockbuster would transmit information about the rental to Facebook, and Facebook in turn would broadcast that information to everyone in the member's online network by publishing to his or her personal profile.

Although Facebook initially designed the Beacon program to give members opportunities to prevent the broadcast of any private information, it never required members' affirmative consent. As a result, many members complained that Beacon was causing publication of otherwise private information about their outside web activities to their personal profiles without their knowledge or approval. Facebook responded to these complaints (and accompanying negative media coverage) first by releasing a privacy control intended to allow its members to opt out of the Beacon program fully, and then ultimately by discontinuing operation of the program altogether.

Unsatisfied with these responses, a group of nineteen plaintiffs filed a putative class action in federal district court against Facebook and a number of other entities that operated websites participating in the Beacon program. The class-action complaint alleged that the defendants had violated various state and federal privacy statutes.... The plaintiffs sought damages and a variety of equitable remedies for the alleged privacy violations.

* * *

[A]fter two mediation sessions and several months of negotiations, Facebook and the plaintiffs arrived at a settlement agreement. In September of 2009, plaintiff Sean Lane submitted the parties' finalized settlement agreement to the district court for preliminary approval.

The terms of the settlement agreement provided that Facebook would permanently terminate the Beacon program and pay a total of $9.5 million in exchange for a release of all the plaintiffs' class claims. Of the $9.5 million pay-out, approximately $3 million would be used to pay attorneys' fees, administrative costs, and incentive payments to the class representatives. Facebook would use the remaining $6.5 million or so in settlement funds to set up a new charity organization called the Digital Trust Foundation ("DTF"). The stated purpose of DTF would be to "fund and sponsor programs designed to educate users, regulators[,] and enterprises regarding critical issues relating to protection of identity and personal information online through user control, and the protection of users from online threats." The parties' respective counsel arrived at the decision to distribute settlement funds through a new grant-making organization, rather than simply give the funds to an existing organization, at the suggestion of the private mediator overseeing their negotiations. Neither Facebook's nor the plaintiffs' class counsel was comfortable with selecting in advance any particular non-profit or non-profits to receive the entirety of the settlement fund, so they acceded to the mediator's suggestion that Facebook set up a new entity whose sole purpose was to designate fund recipients consistent with DTF's mission to promote the interests of online privacy and security.

According to DTF's Articles of Incorporation, DTF would be run by a three-member board of directors. [One of] [t]he initial three directors [was] ... Timothy Sparapani, Facebook's Director of Public Policy and former counsel for the American Civil Liberties Union. The Articles of Incorporation further provided that all of DTF's funding decisions had to be supported by at least two members of the three-member board of directors but that the plan for succession of directors required unanimous approval. Finally, the Articles of Incorporation provided that DTF would be strictly a grant-making organization and could not engage in lobbying or litigation.

The settlement agreement also provided for the creation of a Board of Legal Advisors within DTF, which would consist of counsel for both the plaintiff class and Facebook. The purpose of the Board of Legal Advisors would be to advise and monitor DTF to ensure that it acted consistently with its mission as articulated in the settlement agreement.

* * *

Following a final settlement approval hearing in which the district court heard from both the parties and Objectors, the district court entered an order certifying the settlement class and approving the class settlement....

Objectors now appeal, contending that the district court abused its discretion in approving the parties' settlement. We have jurisdiction pursuant to 28 U.S.C. § 1291, and we affirm.

II

A district court's approval of a class-action settlement must be accompanied by a finding that the settlement is "fair, reasonable, and adequate." Fed.R.Civ.P. 23(e). Appellate review of the district court's fairness determination is "extremely limited," and we will set aside that determination only upon a "strong showing that the district court's decision was a clear abuse of discretion."

* * *

The settlement in this case provides for a cy pres remedy. A cy pres remedy, sometimes called "fluid recovery," is a settlement structure wherein class members receive an indirect benefit (usually through defendant donations to a third party) rather than a direct monetary payment. As we recently recognized, the "cy pres doctrine allows a court to distribute unclaimed or non-distributable portions of a class action settlement fund to the 'next best' class of beneficiaries." For purposes of the cy pres doctrine, a class-action settlement fund is "non-distributable" when "the proof of individual claims would be burdensome or distribution of damages costly." The district court's review of a class-action settlement that calls for a cy pres remedy is not substantively different from that of any other class-action settlement except that the court should not find the settlement fair, adequate, and reasonable unless the cy pres remedy "account[s] for the nature of the plaintiffs' lawsuit, the objectives of the underlying statutes, and the interests of the silent class members...."

III

Objectors challenge the district court's conclusion that the settlement in this case was "fair, reasonable, and adequate" within the meaning of Rule 23(e)....

* * *

Objectors' first and strongest objection to the settlement goes to the structure of DTF, the organization that would distribute cy pres funds under the settlement agreement. Objectors contend that the presence of Tim Sparapani, Facebook's Director of Public Policy, on DTF's board of directors creates an unacceptable conflict of interest that will prevent DTF from acting in the interests of the class.

* * *

We find no substance in Objectors' claim that the presence of a Facebook employee on DTF's board of directors categorically precludes DTF from serving as the entity that will distribute cy pres funds.... Here, in exchange for its promise to pay the plaintiff class approximately $9.5 million, Facebook insisted on preserving its role in the process of selecting the organizations that would receive a share of that substantial settlement fund by providing that one of its representatives would sit on DTF's initial board of directors, and the plaintiffs readily agreed to this condition. That Facebook retained and will use its say in how cy pres funds will be distributed so as to ensure that the funds will not be used in a way that harms Facebook is the unremarkable result of the parties' give-and-take negotiations, and the district court properly declined to undermine those negotiations by second-guessing the parties' decision as part of its fairness review over the settlement agreement.

* * *

Objectors' second argument on appeal is that the district court did not sufficiently evaluate the plaintiffs' claims and compare the value of those claims with the class's $9.5 million recovery in the settlement agreement. Objectors contend that the value of the plaintiffs' claims was in fact greater than the $9.5 million the plaintiffs settled for, in large part because some unidentified number of the class members may have a claim under the Video Privacy Protection Act ("VPPA"). The VPPA prohibits any "video tape service provider" from disclosing "personally identifiable information" about one of its consumers, and it provides for liquidated damages in the amount of $2,500 for violation of its provisions. 18 U.S.C. §§ 2710(b) and 2710(c)(2)....

* * *

The record here convincingly establishes that the district court accounted for the potential value of the VPPA claims of some class members, and the district court's review of the circumstances surrounding the settlement was sufficiently comprehensive to ensure that class representatives and their counsel did not throw absent class members under the proverbial bus to secure a disproportionate benefit for themselves. That review was accordingly compliant with this circuit's requirement that the district court apply heightened review to a class-action settlement reached before formal certification. This is particularly manifest in that the district court's detailed approval order included the specific factual finding that the settlement agreement "was only achieved after intense and protracted arm's-length negotiations conducted in good faith and free from collusion." Objectors have not made any showing, let alone a "strong" one, that this or any of the district court's other findings was erroneous or amounted to a "clear abuse of discretion."

* * *

AFFIRMED.

Kleinfeld, Senior Circuit Judge, dissenting:

I respectfully dissent. This settlement perverts the class action into a device for depriving victims of remedies for wrongs, while enriching both the wrongdoers and the lawyers purporting to represent the class.

* * *

The class action rule was designed to facilitate lawsuits where individuals' or small groups' judgments would not add up to enough money to justify hiring lawyers, but judgments for large numbers of similarly situated victims of misconduct would....

This procedural device has obvious attendant risks, because class counsel's "clients" are not clients at all in the traditional sense; they do not hire the lawyer, they do not agree on a fee with him, and they do not control whether he settles their case. They are in no position to prevent class counsel from pursuing his own interests at their expense. The named plaintiffs, those who actually have some chance of directing their lawyers, typically get amounts of cash without much relation to their individual damages, so their incentives align more with class counsel than with their fellow class members.

Defendant and class counsel, in any class action, have incentives to collude in an agreement to bar victims' claims for little or no compensation to the victims, in exchange for a big enough attorneys' fee to induce betrayal of the interests of the purported "clients." The defendant's agreement not to oppose some amount for the fee creates the same incentive as a payment to a prizefighter to throw a fight. A real client may refuse a settlement that is bad for him but benefits his lawyer, but a large class of unknown individuals lacks the knowledge or authority to say no. It is hard to imagine a real client saying to his lawyer, "I have no objection to the defendant paying you a lot of money in exchange for agreement to seek nothing for me." "The absence of individual clients controlling the litigation for their own benefit creates opportunities for collusive arrangements in which defendants can pay the attorneys for the plaintiff class enough money to induce them to settle the class action for too little benefit to the class (or too much benefit to the attorneys, if the claim is weak but the risks to the defendants high)."

Rule 23 protects against these risks much as the courts have traditionally protected against similar risks when attorneys represent children, estates of deceased persons, and unknown persons, by requiring judicial approval of settlements. Approval and review, though, are a weak substitute for real clients, because judges know little about the case beyond what the lawyers tell them. That works much better when the lawyers are on different sides than when they are on the same side. Judges also may face an incentive problem, where a heavy docket cannot easily withstand the additional weight of a huge lawsuit that does not settle. Objectors provide a critically valuable service of providing knowledge from a different point of view, but one that is too often not used effectively. Our review process is supposed to assure that settlement of a class action, despite the risk of perverse incentives, is "fair, reasonable, and adequate" and that notice is given "in a reasonable manner" so that those bound by the settlement have an opportunity to be heard.

In this case, the process has failed. The attorneys for the class have obtained a judgment for millions of dollars in fees. The defendant, Facebook, has obtained a judgment that bars claims by millions of people victimized by its conduct.... The victims, on the other hand, have obtained nothing. Under the settlement, Facebook even preserved the right to do the same thing to them again.

* * *

Strikingly, the settlement here goes even further than coupon settlements, where class members get only discounts if they buy again from the defendant claimed to have wronged them before, while their purported lawyers get huge amounts of money. Here the Facebook users get nothing at all, not even coupons. Every nickel of the remainder of the $9,500,000 after class counsel's cut, administrative costs, and incentive payments to the named plaintiffs, goes not to the victims, but to an entity partially controlled by Facebook and class counsel. The new entity, dressed to look good in old law French with its "cy pres" award and "non-profit" status, can spend the money to "educate" people about privacy on the internet, perhaps via some instructional videos on how to use all the privacy features available in Facebook.

* * *

The majority approves ratification of a class action settlement in which class members get no compensation at all. They do not get one cent. They do not get even an injunction against Facebook doing exactly the same thing to them again. Their purported lawyers get millions of dollars. Facebook gets a bar against any claims any of them might make for breach of their privacy rights. The most we could say for the cy pres award is that in exchange for giving up any claims they may have, the exposed Facebook users get the satisfaction of contributing to a charity to be funded by Facebook, partially controlled by Facebook, and advised by a legal team consisting of Facebook's counsel and their own purported counsel whom they did not hire and have never met.

Facebook deprived its users of their privacy. And now they are deprived of a remedy.

Notes and Questions

1. Agency Costs and Class Actions: In class actions involving small claims, no plaintiff has enough at stake to monitor the lawyers handling the case. Even in class actions involving larger claims, individual claimants have an incentive to free ride on the monitoring efforts of others, potentially resulting in deficient monitoring. As a result, class actions tend to be run by what Professor John Coffee has called "entrepreneurial lawyers" who sometimes may put their own interests ahead of the interests of their clients. John J. Coffee, Jr., *The Regulation of Entrepreneurial Litigation: Balancing Fairness and Efficiency in a Large Class Action*, 54 University of Chicago Law Review 877, 882 (1987).

2. "Sweetheart Settlements": One manifestation of the agency cost problems facing class actions is a concern that the defendant and the plaintiff's lawyers will cut a deal that benefits themselves at the expense of the class, a so-called "sweetheart settlement." The potential divergence of interests between attorneys and clients—particularly when it comes to settlement—is of course not limited to class actions (see Chapter V); as Judge Henry Friendly put it, "a juicy bird in the hand is worth more than the vision of a much larger one in the bush." *Alleghany Corp. v. Kirby*, 333 F.2d 327, 347 (2d Cir. 1964). The problem is particularly pronounced in the class action setting, however, precisely because of the lack of incentives for clients to monitor their lawyer. Stated bluntly, the fear is that lawyers will sell out their putative clients, agreeing to settle cases on terms that provide significant benefits to the attorneys (in the form of fees) but little or no benefit to the clients. The requirement of court approval for class action settlements is designed to prevent such shenanigans, but does not always seem to succeed.

Class action settlements in which consumers get a coupon towards a future purchase of the defendant's product are often cited as examples. The value of the settlement to each class member is minuscule, while the defendant is released from all liability and the plaintiffs' attorneys receive millions of dollars in fees. Indeed, some class action settlements, while resulting in sizable fees for the attorneys, may actually make the plaintiff class worse off. *See, e.g.*, Kamilewicz v. Bank of Boston, 92 F.3d 506, 508 (7th Cir. 1996) (identifying one class member who later tried unsuccessfully to attack the settlement collaterally) who recovered $2.19 on his claim but had to pay $91.33 in attorneys' fees). Several provisions of the Class Action Fairness Act of 2005, 119 Stat. 4 (2005), seek to remedy these types of problems—by restricting the award of attorneys' fees in coupon settlements and by requiring greater court supervision of the settlement itself. But the dissenting judge in the *Facebook* case certainly does not see the problem as resolved.

3. So Which Is It, Sweetheart Settlements or Blackmail Settlements?: One criticism of settlements in class actions is that defendants pay too much to settle the case (i.e., blackmail settlements). Another criticism is that defendants pay too little, at least to the plaintiff class (i.e., sweetheart settlements). Are these criticisms consistent? Can both apply to the same case? Do they apply to different kinds of cases? Or does one undercut the other?

4. Other Procedural Issues: For a good introduction to the economics of civil procedure, as well as more detailed discussions of these and other procedural rules and doctrines, see Robert G. Bone, Civil Procedure: The Economics of Civil Procedure (2003).

4. Arbitration

Not all dispute resolution takes place in the courts. Very much the contrary—for example, private adjudication (that is, arbitration) is the predominant means of resolving international commercial disputes, and in recent years has become an increasingly common means of resolving domestic commercial disputes, including employment and consumer disputes. In arbitration, the parties hire a private judge (an arbitrator) to make a binding decision that resolves their dispute. Both federal law and the law of virtually all states make arbitration agreements and arbitration awards enforceable for most types of contracts.

The most common way for a dispute to end up in arbitration is for the parties to agree to arbitrate before a dispute arises—i.e., to enter into pre-dispute arbitration agreement. For consumers and employees, the arbitration clause typically is included in a standard form contract prepared by the business or employer. Challenges to the enforceability of arbitration agreements by consumers and employees often rely on the doctrine of unconscionability; much of what was said about the doctrine in Chapter II applies here as well.

Carbajal v. H&R Block Tax Services, Inc.
United States Court of Appeals for the Seventh Circuit
372 F.3d 903 (2004)

EASTERBROOK, *Circuit Judge.*

In 1999 H&R Block prepared Roy Carbajal's 1998 federal tax return. Its calculations showed that Carbajal could expect a refund of $5,001. Carbajal applied for what Block calls a "rapid refund," a transaction that couples a loan with the assignment of the refund as security for repayment. The documents underlying this refund-anticipation loan provide that the lender also may use the money to retire any earlier year's loan (a balance due could exist if the actual refund was less than anticipated and the taxpayer did not return the excess), and that any dispute between the parties will be arbitrated. After Carbajal signed on the dotted line, he received about $1,800 in cash; the balance was used to pay off an earlier loan that a lender in Block's program contended was outstanding. Carbajal filed this suit under the Fair Debt Collection Practices Act, plus other federal and state laws, contending that he had been snookered. Block and the other defendants asked the district court to refer the dispute to arbitration.

[The district judge] dismissed [the suit] in reliance on the arbitration clause. An outright dismissal in favor of arbitration is a "final decision," see *Green Tree Financial Corp. v. Randolph*, 531 U.S. 79, 148 (2000), entitling Carbajal to appeal under 28 U.S.C. § 1291.

Paragraph 6 of the refund-anticipation loan (RAL) agreement [included an arbitration clause, under which Carbajal "agree[d] that any claim or dispute (whether in contract, tort or otherwise) in any way relating to the Agreements or such similar agreements for prior years involving the same parties or relating to the relationships of such parties, including the validity or enforceability of this arbitration provision or any part thereof (collectively the "Claim"), shall be resolved, upon the election of either party, by binding arbitration pursuant to this arbitration provision and the Code of Procedure of the National Arbitration Forum...."]

It would be hard to draft a broader clause. This covers all claims "relating to" the 1999 loan plus all disputes "relating to" any earlier tax year and any preceding refund-anticipation loan. It also covers any dispute about "the validity or enforceability of this arbitration provision or any part thereof"—a clause evidently tailored to come within the rule that people may agree to arbitrate whether a given dispute is arbitrable. If so, this litigation is pointless. Even if we indulge the district court's assumption that the court determines arbitrability, Carbajal still must arbitrate.

* * *

Is enforcement of this clause unconscionable? How could it be? Arbitration is just a forum; people may choose freely which forum will resolve their dispute. This is so when the agreement concerns venue within a judicial system, see *Carnival Cruise Lines, Inc. v. Shute*, 499 U.S. 585 (1991), and equally so when the agreement specifies a non-judicial forum.

The whole deal, including ¶ 6, was offered on a take-it-or leave-it basis, which leads Carbajal to call it a "contract of adhesion," but few consumer contracts are negotiated one clause at a time. Forms reduce transactions costs and benefit consumers because, in competition, reductions in the cost of doing business show up as lower prices (here, a slightly lower rate of interest on the loan). The forum selection clause in *Carnival Cruise Lines* was printed on the back of a ticket, and the Court nonetheless enforced it—just as the terms of limited warranties and many other provisions not negotiated separately are enforced routinely....

Section 2 of the Federal Arbitration Act says that an agreement to arbitrate "shall be valid, irrevocable, and enforceable, save upon such grounds as exist at law or in equity for the revocation of any contract." Thus arbitration specified in a form contract must be treated just like any other clause of the form. Unless Delaware (whose law applies) would refuse to enforce limited warranties, clauses curtailing the time available to file suit, and the like, then this arbitration clause must be enforced. Carbajal does not offer any reason to think that Delaware generally refuses to enforce details on the back of an auto-rental contract or equivalent form; thus this agreement to arbitrate is valid. The cry of "unconscionable!" just repackages the tired assertion that arbitration should be disparaged as second-class adjudication. It is precisely to still such cries that the Federal Arbitration Act equates arbitration with other contractual terms. People are free to opt for bargain-basement adjudication—or, for that matter, bargain-basement tax preparation services; air carriers that pack passengers like sardines but charge less; and black-and-white television. In competition, prices adjust and both sides gain. "Nothing but the best" may be the motto of a particular consumer but is not something the legal system foists on all consumers.

As for the contention that portions of this clause are incompatible with federal law—because, say, they require the parties to bear their own costs, while the FDCPA entitles prevailing litigants to recover attorneys' fees—there are two problems. First, the arbitrator rather than the court determines the validity of these ancillary provisions. Second, no general doctrine of federal law prevents people from waiving statutory rights (whether substantive or procedural) in exchange for other things they value more, such as lower prices or reduced disputation. Whether any particular federal statute overrides the parties' autonomy and makes a given entitlement non-waivable is a question for the arbitrator.

AFFIRMED

Notes and Questions

1. Opting Out of the Legal System: By agreeing to arbitrate their disputes, parties opt out of the public legal system—except to the extent one of the parties relies on the public courts to enforce the arbitration agreement or the arbitrator's award. Why do parties choose private adjudication over the public courts? The answer, of course, depends on the type of contract involved. For international contracts, two reasons commonly given for the widespread use of arbitration clauses are that arbitration provides a neutral forum (rather than having the case proceed in the national courts of one of the parties) and that arbitration awards are more readily enforceable than court judgments. For consumer and employment contracts, reasons commonly cited include having an arbitrator rather than a judge or jury deciding the case, the ability to tailor the process (such as by limiting the discovery available), the greater degree of confidentiality in arbitration than in court, the lack of class actions in arbitration (albeit with some exceptions), and so forth. Do those reasons benefit both parties to the arbitration agreement or just the business or employer? Under what circumstances might consumers and employees benefit from arbitration?

2. The Incentives of Arbitrators: As noted above, an important difference between arbitration and the courts is who makes the decisions, an arbitrator or a judge or jury. Because they are dependent on being selected by the parties to serve, arbitrators have very different incentives in deciding cases than do judges or juries. Judges get paid the same regardless of how many cases they decide or the quality of their decisions. While the parties can select the court in which the case will proceed, they have very limited ability to select the judge. Juries get paid virtually nothing and are selected essentially randomly. By contrast, the parties select the arbitrator or arbitrators, who get paid only when selected and only for the work they do on the case. Thus, arbitrators have a much greater incentive to decide cases in ways that benefit the parties ex ante. In some cases, however, arbitral incentives may be counterproductive, such as when the outcome of the arbitration affects some third party who is not a party to the contract (e.g., a child in the case of a family law dispute). In such cases, judges rather than arbitrators may be the preferred decision maker.

3. Baptists, Bootleggers, and Arbitration Law: Recall the earlier description of the "Baptist and Bootlegger" theory of regulation: that regulations are most likely to be enacted when supported by some groups on policy or moral grounds and by other groups who benefit economically from the regulation. How does the theory apply to legislation that would limit or preclude pre-dispute arbitration clauses in consumer and employment contracts? Groups that favor the laws include consumer and employee groups (the Baptists who support the laws on policy grounds) and plaintiffs' lawyers (the Bootleggers who would benefit economically from the laws by having more cases remain in court). Interestingly, the first federal law enacted to restrict arbitration bars pre-dispute arbitration clauses in motor vehicle franchise agreements, that is, contracts between car manufacturers and car dealers. One does not usually think of car dealers as a group that needs protection from unfair contract terms, certainly not as compared to other groups, such as individual car buyers. Yet no law precludes car dealers from including arbitration clauses in contracts with their customers, and increasingly car dealers are doing so.

Chapter IV

Externalities

Economic analysis often begins with the assumption that economic actors bear all the costs and receive all the benefits of their decisions. However, in many instances, an economic actor's decisions can influence the well-being of third parties, and the economic actor neither pays nor receives compensation for influencing the third parties' well-being. These third party effects are called externalities. Externalities can occur when the costs of producing or consuming a product "spill over" and injure third parties that are not associated with the economic actor's decision process. Similarly, externalities can occur when some of the benefits of producing or consuming a product "spill over" and benefit third parties. The existence of externalities means that an allocation of resources that creates an efficient supply and demand equilibrium between producers and consumers does not always account for societal costs or benefits. Self-interested behavior may not always be in the best interest of society because the self-interested economic actor will not take into account the costs or benefits his behavior imposes on others. In this sense, externalities are a form of market failure because they cause markets to allocate resources inefficiently. As a form of market failure, externalities are an often-stated justification for government intervention in the market system. Much of the public policy discussion of externalities concerns negative externalities — primarily pollution.

Externalities exist because of poorly defined property rights. For example, if no one owns the air, then no property owner can use the legal system to force the polluter to stop polluting. This chapter thus builds on the discussion of property rights and the Coase Theorem in Chapter I. Section A provides a more technical definition of externalities and their welfare effects. Section B considers a variety of ways in which externalities can be addressed — including establishing property rights, corrective taxes, and government regulation. Finally, Section C uses the tools of public choice economics to critique the (often implicit) assumption that imperfect governments can correct imperfect markets, and concludes by reconsidering market-based approaches.

A. Externalities

Economics is the study of how economic actors allocate scarce resources. Sometimes the scarce resource is not capital but a natural resource such as clean air and water. Just as economics can help determine the optimal amount of widgets produced, economics can help determine the socially optimal amount of clean air and water. Economics addresses the incentives and tradeoffs associated with polluting the air and water, conserving or destroying natural resources, and conducting economic activities that affect ecological systems and could eradicate entire species. Consider an example where a widget producer also produces pollution in the widget production process. To determine the socially optimal amount of widgets and pollution produced, one must consider the total cost to society, which is the sum of the producer's widget production costs and the pollution costs borne by third parties. If the legal system does not require the producer to compensate the third parties for the pollution costs, then the producer will operate at a cost of production that does not fully reflect the social costs of the resources consumed. Without incorporating the social costs into the widget producer's decision process, the widget producer will produce widgets and pollution beyond the socially optimal level. Some of the producer's costs are then *external* to its production decisions. Pollution and similar problems occur when the pollution producers do not bear all of the costs of their actions. Without a property right in clean air, society cannot hold the widget producer liable for infringing upon that property right. The legal incentive system — the assignment of property rights — or lack thereof, allows polluters to impose polluted air or water on the rest of society. The producer will produce until the marginal benefit of production is equal to the marginal cost of production. When producers do not bear the total costs of production, they have the incentive to overuse or destroy natural resources. Incentives matter!

Analysis of these problems begins by making a careful distinction between the private costs and social costs, as well as the private benefits and social benefits, of human actions. The **private cost** of producing a good is the cost paid by the firm that produces and sells it. Sometimes producing a good creates costs for other people as well, such as when a producer's factory causes air pollution that harms people who live in the factory's vicinity. Therefore, the total cost of producing a good should include the value of the harm that the pollution creates for society. The social cost of pollution is measured by the amount of money the people affected by the pollution would be willing to pay to eliminate the harm — the value they place on clean air. Consumption of some products may also impose costs on other people, such as when driving a car pollutes the air. The **social cost** of producing a good is the total private cost plus the total third party cost from producing various quantities of the good.

Private costs and social costs differ whenever production or use of a good influences the well-being of people who do not buy or sell it. When a factory pollutes the air, the social costs of the good produced include the harm to other people from that pollution. Similarly, the social cost of driving a car includes the pollution harm imposed on third parties.

Economic behavior may also yield private and social benefits. The difference between private benefits and social benefits is distinguished in the same way as private and social costs. The **private benefit** of consuming a good is its benefit to those who buy and consume the good, while the **social benefit** is the total benefit that results from the private beneficiary's purchase and consumption of the good. For example, the private actor benefits from education with increased wages. The social benefit includes a more informed electorate and, subsequently, an improved government and community. If a scientist discovers a better medicine to treat a disease, her gains are realized when she sells the medicine for a profit. The gains to people who use the medicine are also private benefits. The social benefits include these private benefits plus third party gains, which are realized when the scientist's discovery facilitates new ideas that help scientists working on other problems. Third party gains may also be realized when health care costs are reduced.

An externality occurs when the private costs or benefits of a good differ from its social costs or benefits. A **negative externality** occurs when the social cost exceeds the private cost, resulting in producers producing more than the socially optimal level. A **positive externality** occurs when the social benefit exceeds the private benefit, resulting in producers producing less than the socially optimal level.

1. Negative Externalities

A common example of a negative externality is a factory's emission of smoke as a byproduct of production. If the factory is able to avoid responsibility for the consequences of its smoke, such as the expenses for painting soot-covered buildings nearby or laundering dirty clothes, the output of the factory will be higher than the socially optimal level. This occurs because when a producer decides to produce an additional unit, the producer considers only the marginal benefit and marginal cost associated with producing that unit. If the producer's marginal benefit of production exceeds its marginal cost of production, it will produce the additional unit. Although the additional unit's social costs exceed its social benefit, the producer will produce the additional unit anyway. The producer will produce additional units, without regard to the social costs and benefits, unless the producer's production function mirrors society's production function. If the factory were held responsible for the damage done by its smoke, its costs would rise, its product would become more expensive, and it would produce less because the factory's production function would resemble society's production function.

Any economic entity, including firms, government agencies, and individuals, can create a negative externality. Examples of negative externalities include exhaust emissions of automobiles, a neighbor's excessively loud stereo, low flying jet airplanes landing at an airport, drunk drivers, the contamination of underground water by toxic chemical dumps, poor health practices that raise others people's chances of contracting contagious diseases, and travelling with rambunctious children on airplanes.

Figure IV-1 shows a basic demand and supply graph with a negative externality. The graph shows the demand for a product, its marginal private cost (MPC), and its marginal social cost (MSC). The marginal private cost of producing a good is the increase in total private cost from producing one more unit. The negative externality is the marginal cost to third parties from producing that same additional unit. The marginal social cost of producing a good is the increase in the total social cost from producing one more unit.

The marginal social cost (MSC) curve lies above the marginal private cost (MPC) curve. The cost of the negative externality (E) is the vertical difference between MSC and MPC, so that $E = MSC - MPC$. Note that marginal social benefit (MSB) equals marginal private benefit (MPB) because it is assumed that there are no positive externalities associated with consumption or production. The private, market-determined level of production is Q_M, where $MPC = MPB$. The socially optimal level of production is Q^*, where $MSC = MSB$. Any quantity produced above Q^* is economically inefficient because the MSC of production is greater than the MSB. In Figure IV-1, there is an overproduction of the product as indicated by the difference between the market equilibrium at Q_M and the social optimum at Q^*.

As previously discussed, the market failure associated with negative externalities occurs when individuals' decisions are based on private rather than social cost. When production decisions are based on private costs and benefits, production could be either above or below the optimum level. The market failure caused by a negative externality is shown

Figure IV-1. Equilibrium with a Negative Externality

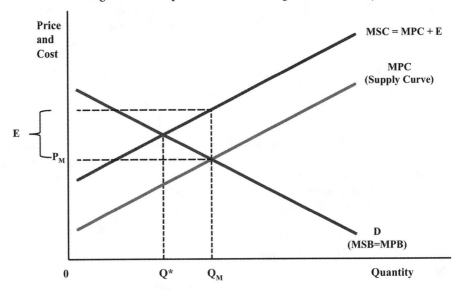

as a **deadweight social loss** in Figure IV-2. The shaded area indicates that the marginal social cost of producing units Q^* to Q_M is greater than the marginal social benefit. Notice that consumers would buy the economically efficient quantity of the product if its price were P^*; but the equilibrium price, P_M, is less than P^*, so firms produce and people buy more than the economically efficient quantity. This divergence between the market outcome and the optimal outcome is often used as justification for government intervention in the form of taxation or regulation.

Figure IV-2. Equilibrium & Economic Inefficiency with a Negative Externality

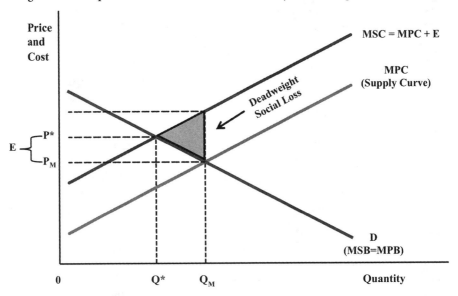

Also, notice in Figure IV-2 that the economically efficient quantity (Q^*) of the good is positive, not zero. Applying this analysis to pollution, we find that it would not be economically efficient to eliminate pollution entirely because it would require doing without the product. Some pollution would result even if firms were to produce the economically efficient quantity of the product. Thus, the economically efficient level of the pollution is not zero. Rather, the economically efficient level of pollution occurs when the marginal benefit of producing it equals the marginal cost of producing it.

Orchard View Farms, Inc. v. Martin Marietta Aluminum, Inc.

United States District Court for the District of Oregon
500 F. Supp. 984 (1980)

Barns, Chief Judge:

HISTORY OF THIS CASE

This diversity case is before the court on remand from the Ninth Circuit Court of Appeals for a retrial on the issue of punitive damages.

On March 31, 1971, Orchard View Farms, Inc. (Orchard View) filed this trespass action, seeking compensatory and punitive damages for injuries to its orchards between March 31, 1965 and the filing date. These injuries were alleged to have been caused by fluoride emitted from the aluminum reduction plant operated by Martin Marietta Aluminum, Inc. (the company or Martin Marietta). In April and May, 1973, the case was tried to a jury, which awarded Orchard View $103,655 compensatory damages and $250,000 punitive damages. The company appealed this judgment on numerous grounds.

The Ninth Circuit affirmed the award of compensatory damages but reversed and remanded the punitive damages award because in various rulings at the trial I erroneously admitted evidence of certain events that had occurred before the 1965–71 claim period, events which had been insufficiently linked by the evidence to the company's conduct and policies during the claim period.

* * *

FACTUAL BACKGROUND

Martin Marietta Aluminum, Inc., is a California corporation that owns and operates aluminum reduction plants, including plants located in The Dalles, Oregon, and Goldendale, Washington....

Orchard View Farms, Inc., is an Oregon corporation. It operates three orchards with a combined total acreage of approximately five hundred acres. The orchards are located between 2.5 and 5 miles from the aluminum plant....

This case is one of an ever-increasing number filed against ... Martin Marietta, by orchardists who charged that fluorides emitted from the plant have damaged their crops. The first such suit was filed in May, 1961. It was finally closed in 1966 when the court approved a consent decree providing for arbitration of the growers' claims and dismissal of the related actions filed in state court during the interim. Since February, 1977, thirteen actions have been filed in the United States District Court. These suits seek compensatory and punitive damages for injury allegedly inflicted by emissions from the plant during the years 1971 through 1977.

OPINION

* * *

I. OREGON LAW OF PUNITIVE DAMAGES.

The Oregon Supreme Court has provided specific guidance on punitive damage liability in the context of industrial air pollution....

* * *

[For example,] the court in *Harrell v. Travelers Indemnity Company*, 279 Or. 199, 567 P.2d 1013 (1977), noted:

> One whose business involves the operation of a plant which emits smoke, fumes or "particulates" may also have ... liability for punitive damages, even in the absence of any "wanton" or "fraudulent" conduct, upon the ground that he has "intentionally" permitted fumes, smoke or particles to be released and blown by the wind upon another's property, for the reason that "[t]he intentional disregard of the interest of another is the legal equivalent of legal malice and justifies punitive damages for trespass."

Additional guidance, though of less precedential value, is provided by *Reynolds Metals Company v. Lampert*, 316 F.2d 272 (9th Cir. 1963). The District of Oregon trial judge had withdrawn the issue of punitive damages liability from the jury. The Ninth Circuit reversed and remanded.

* * *

> To justify an award of punitive damages, it is not necessary that the act have been done maliciously or with bad motive. Where it has become apparent, as it has here, that compensatory damages alone, while they might compensate the injured party, will not deter the actor from committing similar trespasses in the future, there is ample justification for an award of punitive damages.... Accordingly, the issue of punitive damages should have been submitted to the jury.

* * *

This guidance provided by the Oregon Supreme Court and the Ninth Circuit Court of Appeals, though specific to the context of industrial air pollution, does not define with precision the circumstances justifying the imposition of punitive damage liability. A broad synthesis of these opinions provides the conclusion that punitive damage awards may be imposed for business activities, harmful to others, carried out in disregard of the corporation's societal obligations. In brief, the issue is whether the defendant has damaged the property of plaintiff by conduct evidencing an "I don't give a damn" attitude. For a case as complex as this, however, it is important to describe in some greater detail the societal obligations of business enterprises.

II. SOCIETAL OBLIGATIONS OF BUSINESS ENTERPRISES.

In essence, any business is socially obliged to carry on an enterprise that is a net benefit, or at least not a net loss, to society....

In a world where all costs of production were borne by the enterprise, determining whether a firm produced a net benefit, or at least not a net detriment, to society would be as simple as examining the company's balance sheet of income and expenses. In the real world the task is more complex, because enterprises can sometimes shift a portion of their costs of production onto others. In the case of an industrial plant emitting pollution, those harmed by the emissions are, in effect, involuntarily bearing some of the firm's production costs.

Our society has not demanded that such externalized costs of production be completely eliminated. Instead, we tolerate externalities such as pollution as long as the enterprise remains productive: that is, producing greater value than the total of its internalized and externalized costs of production. A business that does not achieve net productivity is harmful to society, detracting from the standard of living it is designed to enhance. Because firms can sometimes impose a portion of their production costs upon others, the mere fact that a company continues to operate at a profit is not in itself conclusive evidence that it produces a net benefit to society.

Our system of law attempts to ensure that businesses are, on balance, socially beneficial by requiring that each enterprise bear its total production costs, as accurately as those costs can be ascertained. A fundamental means to this end is the institution of tort liability, which requires that persons harmed by business or other activity be compensated by the perpetrator of the damage. In the context of pollution, however, the tort system does not always operate smoothly to impose liability for compensatory damages. Among the difficulties encountered are: (1) that the harm may be gradual or otherwise difficult to perceive; (2) that the cause of the harm may be difficult to trace to the pollution and from the pollution to its source; and (3) that the harm may be inflicted in small amounts upon a large number of people, none of whom individually suffer sufficient damage to warrant the time and expense of legal action and whose organization into a plaintiff class is hindered by what has come to be known as the tragedy of the commons.[1]

Because of these impediments to smooth operation of the tort system and to ensuring that each enterprise bears its own costs of production, the law imposes upon businesses a societal obligation not to obstruct legal procedures designed to provide compensation to persons harmed by externalized costs of production. Enterprises must cooperate with their neighbors in ascertaining the nature, severity and scope of the harm and in arranging to prevent the damage or to neutralize it through some form of compensation.

A breach of societal obligations justifies the imposition of punitive damages to deter uncooperative behavior that impedes the legal system from ensuring that enterprises produce a net benefit to society.

III. EVALUATION OF THE DEFENDANT'S CONDUCT IN LIGHT OF ITS SOCIETAL OBLIGATIONS.

Although the company did not fail to carry out its societal obligations in every respect, I have concluded that the overall conduct of the business with respect to ascertaining the harm from the plant's emissions, efficiently controlling the harmful emissions and arranging to compensate for the remaining harm constitutes breach of societal responsibility sufficient to justify the imposition of punitive damages.

A. Ascertaining the Harm from Plant Emissions.

A business enterprise has a societal obligation to determine whether its emissions will result in harm to others. Because the damage from pollution can be difficult to perceive due to its subtle or incremental nature, and because it can be difficult to trace to its cause, the obligation of the enterprise extends not only to observation of property in the surrounding region but also to initiation and completion of unbiased scientific studies

---

1. Organizing a plaintiff class is hindered by the fact that the benefit of a successful lawsuit against the polluter for compensation is not limited to the plaintiffs. Persons damaged by the pollution but not contributing to the legal action also benefit due to the collateral estoppel effects of the initial lawsuit in subsequent actions and because the first plaintiff or group of plaintiffs has already done the work of organizing some relevant evidence and locating experts willing to testify. Thus, each person damaged by the pollution has an economic incentive to let someone else bring the first lawsuit and then to take a "free ride" or at least a discount excursion to obtaining his own compensation.

designed to detect the potential adverse effects of the substances emitted. I find that the company failed to fulfill this obligation before or during the 1965–71 claim period by taking less than full cognizance of the damage inflicted upon the orchards and by generally shirking its responsibility to undertake competent scientific inquiry into the adverse effects of its emissions.

* * *

B. Efficiently Controlling the Harmful Emissions.

During the claim period the company had a societal obligation to adopt and maintain reasonable pollution control measures, at least those capable of reducing the harm at a cost less than the damage caused by the emissions. Failure to adhere to such a course would result in a net detriment to society. An efficient program of pollution control also requires at least occasional monitoring of emissions as a check on the effectiveness of the control strategy.

* * *

Although the company's social obligation extends to the implementation of only those pollution control measures that efficiently reduce the damage to others, an award of punitive damages does not require the plaintiff to provide detailed analyses of alternative emission control strategies and their costs. Instead, the plaintiff need only show, by a preponderance of the evidence, the existence of pollution reduction measures that could have been adopted and reasonably might have been expected to efficiently decrease the plant's emissions. It then becomes the burden of the company, with its superior access to scientific, technological, engineering, economic and management expertise, to show, by a preponderance of the evidence, that the measures proposed by the plaintiff were not available before or during the claim period or would not have resulted in efficient emission control.

My examination of the evidence leads me to conclude that the company failed to implement reasonably efficient and economical pollution control measures that could have reduced the fluoride emissions from the plant during the 1965–71 claim period.

* * *

4. Mitigation Measures.

It is possible that the adverse effects of emissions from the plant might have been reduced by a strategy of mitigation, including the installation of tall stacks to propel the fluorides through the occasional atmospheric inversion layer and the spraying of susceptible fruit with a calcium chloride solution.

* * *

The company did not fulfill its societal obligation to adopt and maintain reasonable, efficient pollution control measures.... [U]se of tall or high-velocity stacks might have prevented the occasional concentration of emissions beneath the atmospheric inversion layer. The company's sponsorship of calcium chloride spraying of peach trees was laudable but not sufficient to overcome the preponderance of evidence showing that the company faltered in carrying out its social responsibility to control its harmful emissions.

C. Arranging to Compensate for the Remaining Harm.

As the court in determining the propriety of a punitive damage award may consider evidence of harm by the defendant's conduct to persons other than the plaintiff, so should the court take note of the defendant's efforts to neutralize that harm by voluntary payment of compensation, even though this compensation did not extend to the damage for which the jury in this case made a compensatory award.

In 1961 the company agreed to compensate peach and apricot growers in the vicinity of the plant for soft suture damage to their peaches and for apricot leaf necrosis believed to inhibit tree growth ... [T]he company paid out about $100,000 in settlements during the 1961–66 period.

On November 3, 1966, the United States District Court entered a consent decree settling the claims of 15 orchardists filed against the company in federal court and providing for the dismissal of 17 other cases then pending in the Oregon state courts....

* * *

Paragraph 10 of the decree provided for a three-member claim arbitration panel, one member selected by the company, one by the orchardists and the third member by the other two, to settle claims....

On February 11, 1971, the claim arbitration panel awarded the 15 orchardist plaintiffs a total of $942,305 for damage to their crops and trees during the 1960–69 period. On February 19, 1972, the panel awarded $120,900 to five orchardists for damage during 1970 and 1971. The orchardists then terminated the arbitration agreement, and no further voluntary settlements have been reached.

The company's agreement to recognize that the plant's emissions were damaging the orchards and to compensate the orchardists for the damage under an arbitration arrangement is to be complimented, and future such agreements to be encouraged. Such conduct is strong evidence that the company was attempting to fulfill its societal obligations by accounting for the damage its operations were causing to its neighbors. Though laudable, this conduct does not entirely shield the company from punitive damages liability, for it came about after some eight years of the plant's operation and after the company was faced with numerous lawsuits claiming damages....

* * *

If the company during the 1965–71 claim period had cooperated fully in ascertaining the harm from the plant's emissions and in effecting some combination of efficient emission control combined with compensation for the remaining harm, I would rule against the plaintiff's request for punitive damages. The company's participation in the arbitration system is certainly indicative of corporate social responsibility but is insufficient to overcome its failure in the other two respects.

IV. AWARD OF PUNITIVE DAMAGES.

I am satisfied by the evidence in this case that an award of punitive damages is appropriate for the earlier portion of the claim period. It is difficult to put a precise date on the watershed of the company's conduct showing a sufficient compliance with societal obligation so as to rule out punitive damages. In this regard, I rely heavily upon the testimony of Barney McPhillips, who may almost be regarded as the father of Oregon's pollution control progress. While his testimony was generalized, and did not contain any particular dates, nonetheless it furnishes more than adequate support for a finding that midway through the 1965–71 claim period a change occurred in both the attitude of the company and its efforts to carry out pollution control measures so as to behave like a good neighbor. One cannot look at a single event alone, since the attitude of society (both private and governmental) was in a state of substantial change. And as society's attitude changed, as was evidenced by the movement toward a more careful attention to the earth around us and the necessity of its preservation, so also did society's laws and regulations, and with that the response of its components — both of the antagonists here, aluminum company and orchardist. I conclude, therefore, that a punitive damage award is available for the claim years 1965 through 1968. If the claim years here were only 1969–71, I would not award punitive damages. By this time — the late 60s and early 70s — on the record in this case, it cannot be said that the company was in sufficient disregard of its societal obligations so as to be liable for punitive damages....

Because the company did not cooperate in ascertaining the nature, severity and scope of the harm inflicted upon the plaintiff by the plant's emissions or in arranging to prevent this damage or to neutralize it through voluntary compensation arrangements, the company is liable to the plaintiff for an award of punitive damages.

Previous judicial opinions provide little guidance as to the proper amount of such an award. Courts often state that such an award should be sufficient to deter continuation or repetition of the offending conduct. In this case the offending conduct was the company's refusal either to implement economically efficient emission control measures or voluntarily to compensate the plaintiff for the damage caused by the plant's emissions. Thus, punitive damages should be awarded in an amount that will deter this and other companies from attempting to impose a portion of their costs of production upon their neighbors by compelling those damaged by the emissions to resort to the uncertainties of the legal process in order to obtain compensation.

Under the circumstances here, I believe an appropriate and measured award for punitive damages is $200,000 for the claim period here through the year 1968, but none thereafter.

The foregoing constitutes findings of fact and conclusions of law, pursuant to Rule 52, Fed.R.Civ.P.

Notes and Questions

1. Punitive Damages: Property Rule Versus Liability Rule?: The court quoted the *Reynolds Metals* case in which the Ninth Circuit stated: "To justify an award of punitive damages, it is not necessary that the act have been done maliciously or with bad motive. Where it has become apparent, as it has here, that compensatory damages alone, while they might compensate the injured party, will not deter the actor from committing similar trespasses in the future, there is ample justification for an award of punitive damages." A liability rule would allow the trespasser to pollute at will so long as the trespasser paid compensation to the injured property owner. Obviously, the court was not satisfied with that result. Would the court accept a property rule that required bargaining prior to the pollution? Or, would the court still be concerned that other property owners were not protected?

2. Externalities and Efficiency: The court noted "we tolerate externalities such as pollution as long as the enterprise remains productive: that is, producing a greater value than the total of its internalized and externalized costs of production." Does this perspective require compensation of the injured party? Recall the discussion of Kaldor-Hicks and Pareto Efficiency in Chapter I. Under Kaldor-Hicks Efficiency, all that is necessary is for the polluter to be able to compensate injured parties and still realize a net gain. Pareto Efficiency requires actual compensation of injured parties.

3. Class Actions and Incentives: Do you agree with the court's analysis of class actions? Are there any entrepreneurs who have the incentive to solve the free rider problem? If so, does the court's logic justify the imposition of punitive damages when a business fails to meet its "societal obligation not to obstruct legal procedures designed to provide compensation to persons harmed by externalized costs of production"?

4. Bargaining and the Coase Theorem: Does the creation of societal obligations and the possibility of punitive damages increase or decrease the likelihood of Coasian bargaining? Has the court merely increased the bargaining position of landowners? Or, has it increased the transaction costs of a negotiated solution? Going forward, what actions would you expect the parties to take?

2. Positive Externalities

Positive externalities exist when the social benefits of engaging in an activity are greater than the private benefits to the individual or individuals engaging in that activity. Classic examples of positive externalities include inoculation against contagious disease, home renovations that increase neighbors' property values, and the pollination of fruit trees by a beekeeper's bees. For example, in the case of inoculation against contagious disease, when a patient purchases and takes a vaccination against polio, he receives the private benefit of reduced risk of contracting polio, and society receives a benefit because it is less likely that others will contract polio from the patient or anyone else. The nature of the positive externality is illustrated further by recognition that if everyone except Hank were inoculated, then there would be no need for Hank to be inoculated.

Positive externalities, by definition, occur when the marginal social benefit is greater than the marginal private benefit of the activity. In general, the presence of positive externalities means that the activity producing the positive externality occurs at a rate below the socially optimal level—where marginal social benefit equals marginal social cost. As previously discussed, individuals in a market economy make decisions based on comparisons of their marginal private benefits and marginal private costs. The market failure associated with positive externalities is that individuals' decisions are based on private rather than social benefits. When there is a positive externality, production decisions based on private costs and benefits result in production below the optimum level.

The market failure of positive externalities is shown in Figure IV-3. Marginal private benefits (MPB) are less than marginal social benefits (MSB). The positive externality (E)

Figure IV-3. Equilibrium & Inefficiency with a Positive Externality

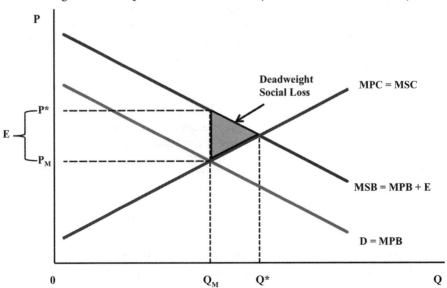

is the difference between the marginal private benefits and the marginal social benefits, so that E = MSB − MPB. Marginal private costs (MPC) equal marginal social costs (MSC), which means negative externalities are not present. The private market solution is at Q_M, where MPB = MPC. The optimal level of production is at Q^*, where MSC = MSB. Thus, the market failure is illustrated by the suboptimal level of production, $Q^* - Q_M$. For units of output between Q^* and Q_M, the marginal benefit to society is greater than the marginal cost to society, but those transactions do not occur in the private market. The deadweight social loss as a result of the positive externality is indicated by the shaded area.

In some instances, individuals have incentives to capture, or *internalize*, the positive externalities created by their activities. For example, a beekeeper benefits the owner of a nearby apple orchard when the beekeeper's bees increase the pollination of the apple trees, which increases the orchard's productivity. The beekeeper's bees fly into the orchard and pollinate the apple blossoms, making the orchard more productive. If the beekeeper were to reap the consequences of the increased value of the orchard, the yield on his investment in bees would rise and he would raise more bees. But, under these circumstances, his bees' social services are provided free. The beekeeper can internalize, or capture, the excess benefits by purchasing the orchard. After internalizing the benefit, the beekeeper will raise more bees and his newly acquired apple orchard will be more productive than before. Instead of purchasing the orchard, the beekeeper and the orchard owner could bargain over the excess benefit. To enhance the bees' contribution to the orchard's productivity, the orchard owner could contract with the beekeeper to supply more bees. Alternatively, the orchard owner could raise his own bees. As long as the beekeeper's marginal costs of raising additional bees are less than the value the bees contribute to the orchard owner, it will be possible for both parties to reach an agreement that will leave each better off. Such private contracting effectively internalizes, and subsequently eliminates, the apple/bee externality. Instead of private contracting, the government could intervene and mandate the beekeeper raise more bees to benefit the apple orchard owner. When would such government intervention make sense? When would government intervention not make sense?

A more dramatic example of the internalization of positive externalities is the development of Disney World in central Florida. The Disney Corporation knew that the building of Disney World would greatly increase the value of the land surrounding the actual site of Disney World. Instead of simply giving this benefit to the surrounding landowners, Disney secretly purchased much more land than was needed for its own development before announcing its development plans to the public. As a result, Disney captured a large portion—but clearly not all—of the positive externalities associated with its development of Disney World.

In other instances, individuals may not have the incentive or ability to capture the positive externalities associated with their activities. This, of course, is the definition of a market failure. In order to solve the market failure, government intervention may be necessary in order to get producers to produce the optimal level of output. The possible forms of government intervention are discussed below.

B. Dealing with Externalities

The world is full of trivial externalities, in the sense that the situation is not worth the effort to do anything about it. Your neighbor's messy yard may disturb your sense of propriety, so you may be willing to pay her $50 a year to clean up the mess—but her price to clean it up is $600 a year. The messy yard is a nuisance, but not enough of a nuisance to cause sufficient demand to get the yard cleaned up. On principle, the best thing to do with an irrelevant externality is to leave it alone because it costs more than it is worth to correct the problem. By comparison, a relevant externality creates sufficient demand, on the part of those affected by it, to change the situation. Suppose that your neighbor is willing to clean up her messy yard for $10, and you are willing to pay your neighbor as much as $50 to clean up her yard. In this case, you value the clean yard more than your neighbor values the effort to clean up her yard. If you pay your neighbor some amount between $10 and $50 both you and your neighbor will be better off. You can make an effective offer to correct the externality and reach a deal with your neighbor. With relevant externalities, it is worthwhile to correct the situation because the parties are better off as a result of the transaction.

When market incentives and private contractual arrangements result in output that is greater than or less than the social optimum, the externality is said to have created a market failure. In an economy with an ideal government that has perfect information and is interested in promoting the general welfare through increased economic efficiency, the government would attempt to correct the market failure attributable to externalities. To do so, the government would promote the production of goods that create positive externalities and discourage the production of goods that create negative externalities. In order for government intervention to make economic sense, the marginal benefit of the intervention must exceed its marginal cost. Given that the costs of government intervention will always be positive, it is obvious that some externalities are so small or trivial that they are not worth correcting through government intervention.

Further consider that the above analysis assumes the government has perfect information with regard to which economic activities create which type of externalities. Not only does the cost of government intervention need to be less than the marginal benefit of the intervention, but also the cost of the intervention coupled with the information costs must not exceed the marginal benefit of intervention.

Economic theory suggests that the correction of non-trivial externalities can be approached in a number of different ways. In general, these can be categorized as defining property rights and allowing bargaining, taxing negative externalities and subsidizing positive externalities, or establishing regulatory controls.

1. The Assignment and Enforcement of Property Rights

The existence of externalities is not, by itself, justification for government intervention to correct the externality. In some instances, private contractual arrangements can make public intervention unnecessary. This was illustrated for positive externalities in the bee example where it was possible for the orchard owner to contract with the beekeeper for an increase in the number of bees. Externality problems generally persist because of the presence of some element of common ownership or nonownership. However, the beekeeper's and the apple grower's ownership rights are clearly established and easily transferable. In such a situation, it will be in the interests of both parties to reach an agreement that places resources in their most highly valued uses. In the case of a polluting factory, does the factory have the right to use the air as it pleases or do the people in the surrounding community have the right to clean air? Air use rights are indefinite and non-transferable. It is generally impossible for people to buy and sell rights to use the air. In this case, there is no reason to suspect that the pursuit of individual interests will promote the use of air in the most highly valued manner. Since nonownership is a source of market failure, the creation of ownership is a means of correcting market failure. Under some circumstances, the establishment of ownership rights is a potential means of eliminating problems associated with externalities.

a. Bargaining and the Coase Theorem

If property rights are well-defined and if transaction costs are low, negative externalities can be internalized through bargaining and contracting. Assume that Ken owns all of the land surrounding a polluting factory and that he does not own any rights to have clean air (indeed, no one owns those rights). This means, in effect, that the factory has the right to pollute the air. Assume that the pollution is very localized and affects only Ken's property. Since all of the external costs of the pollution are borne by Ken, it is reasonable to assume that he is in a position to bargain with the factory about the amount of pollution emitted by the factory. For example, if the pollution reduces the value of Ken's land by $1,000, then Ken would be willing to pay up to $1,000 to reduce the pollution. If the factory can reduce the pollution at a cost less than $1,000, say $800, then the factory will benefit from contracting with Ken for the reduction in pollution emissions. The contract price will be somewhere between $1,000 and $800. If the factory cannot reduce the pollution at Ken's price, then it will continue to pollute. Note, however, that the imposition of the negative externality in the latter case is not free: the factory forfeits a potential payment of up to $1,000 when it decides to pollute. In economic terms, Ken's willingness to pay represents an opportunity cost to the factory.

An interesting and important insight about the contractual solution to externalities is that the solution is not altered even if Ken has a legally enforceable property right to smoke-free air. Once again, if the pollution can be abated at a cost of less than $1,000, then the factory will not pollute. If pollution abatement will cost more than $1,000, then the factory will offer Ken enough money to induce Ken to agree to allow the factory to emit the smoke (at least $1,000). With this new set of property rights, the opportunity cost to Ken of breathing clean air is whatever the factory is willing to pay to pollute.

As discussed in Chapter I, the insight that the same property rights assignment will emerge regardless of the initial assignment of ownership rights, when the costs of negotiation are nonexistent or trivial, is referred to as the **Coase Theorem.** Moreover, Coase pointed out that the same degree of pollution will occur even if the neighbors have the legal right to stop the firm from emitting any pollution, rather than the firm having the legal right to pollute as much as it wants. In this case, the firm can pay the neighbors for the right to pollute. Regardless of whether the firm or the neighbors have the initial right, the gains from trade are exhausted when the marginal benefit to the firm of polluting is equal to the marginal cost that is imposed on the neighbors.

Prah v. Maretti

Supreme Court of Wisconsin
321 N.W.2d 182 (1982)

Abrahamson, Justice.

This appeal from a judgment of the circuit court for Waukesha county ... was certified to this court by the court of appeals as presenting an issue of first impression, namely, whether an owner of a solar-heated residence states a claim upon which relief can be granted when he asserts that his neighbor's proposed construction of a residence (which conforms to existing deed restrictions and local ordinances) interferes with his access to an unobstructed path for sunlight across the neighbor's property. This case thus involves a conflict between one landowner (Glenn Prah, the plaintiff) interested in unobstructed access to sunlight across adjoining property as a natural source of energy and an adjoining landowner (Richard D. Maretti, the defendant) interested in the development of his land.

The circuit court concluded that the plaintiff presented no claim upon which relief could be granted and granted summary judgment for the defendant. We reverse the judgment of the circuit court and remand the cause to the circuit court for further proceedings.

I.

According to the complaint, the plaintiff is the owner of a residence which was constructed during the years 1978–1979. The complaint alleges that the residence has a solar system which includes collectors on the roof to supply energy for heat and hot water and that after the plaintiff built his solar-heated house, the defendant purchased the lot adjacent to and immediately to the south of the plaintiff's lot and commenced planning construction of a home. The complaint further states that when the plaintiff learned of defendant's plans to build the house he advised the defendant that if the house were built at the proposed location, defendant's house would substantially and adversely affect the integrity of plaintiff's solar system and could cause plaintiff other damage. Nevertheless, the defendant began construction. The complaint further alleges that the plaintiff is entitled to "unrestricted use of the sun and its solar power" and demands judgment for injunctive relief and damages.

After filing his complaint, the plaintiff moved for a temporary injunction to restrain and enjoin construction by the defendant. In ruling on that motion the circuit court heard testimony, received affidavits and viewed the site.

The record made on the motion reveals the following additional facts: Plaintiff's home was the first residence built in the subdivision, and although plaintiff did not build his house in the center of the lot it was built in accordance with applicable restrictions. Plaintiff advised defendant that if the defendant's home were built at the proposed site it would cause a shadowing effect on the solar collectors which would reduce the efficiency of the system and possibly damage the system. To avoid these adverse effects, plaintiff requested defendant to locate his home an additional several feet away from the plaintiff's lot line, the exact number being disputed. Plaintiff and defendant failed to reach an agreement on the location of defendant's home before defendant started construction. The Architectural Control Committee of the subdivision and the Planning Commission of the City of Muskego approved the defendant's plans for his home, including its location on the lot. After such approval, the defendant apparently changed the grade of the property without prior notice to the Architectural Control Committee. The problem with defendant's proposed construction, as far as the plaintiff's interests are concerned, arises from a combination of the grade and the distance of defendant's home from the defendant's lot line.

The circuit court denied plaintiff's motion for injunctive relief, declared it would entertain a motion for summary judgment and thereafter entered judgment in favor of the defendant.

* * *

The plaintiff presents three legal theories to support his claim that the defendant's continued construction of a home justifies granting him relief: (1) the construction constitutes a common law private nuisance; (2) the construction is prohibited by sec.

844.01, Stats. 1979–80; and (3) the construction interferes with the solar easement plaintiff acquired under the doctrine of prior appropriation.[2]

* * *

We consider first whether the complaint states a claim for relief based on common law private nuisance. This state has long recognized that an owner of land does not have an absolute or unlimited right to use the land in a way which injures the rights of others. The rights of neighboring landowners are relative; the uses by one must not unreasonably impair the uses or enjoyment of the other. When one landowner's use of his or her property unreasonably interferes with another's enjoyment of his or her property, that use is said to be a private nuisance.

The private nuisance doctrine has traditionally been employed in this state to balance the conflicting rights of landowners, and this court has recently adopted the analysis of private nuisance set forth in the Restatement (Second) of Torts. The Restatement defines private nuisance as "a nontrespassory invasion of another's interest in the private use and enjoyment of land." Restatement (Second) of Torts sec. 821D (1977). The phrase "interest in the private use and enjoyment of land" as used in sec. 821D is broadly defined to include any disturbance of the enjoyment of property....

Although the defendant's obstruction of the plaintiff's access to sunlight appears to fall within the Restatement's broad concept of a private nuisance as a nontrespassory invasion of another's interest in the private use and enjoyment of land, the defendant asserts that he has a right to develop his property in compliance with statutes, ordinances and private covenants without regard to the effect of such development upon the plaintiff's access to sunlight. In essence, the defendant is asking this court to hold that the private nuisance doctrine is not applicable in the instant case and that his right to develop his land is a right which is per se superior to his neighbor's interest in access to sunlight. This position is expressed in the maxim "cujus est solum, ejus est usque ad coelum et ad infernos," that is, the owner of land owns up to the sky and down to the center of the earth. The rights of the surface owner are, however, not unlimited.

* * *

Many jurisdictions in this country have protected a landowner from malicious obstruction of access to light (the spite fence cases) under the common law private nuisance doctrine. If an activity is motivated by malice it lacks utility and the harm it causes others outweighs any social values. This court was reluctant to protect a landowner's interest in sunlight even against a spite fence, only to be overruled by the legislature. Shortly after this court upheld a landowner's right to erect a useless and unsightly sixteen-foot spite fence four feet from his neighbor's windows, the legislature enacted a law specifically defining a spite fence as an actionable private nuisance. Thus a landowner's interest in sunlight has been protected in this country by common law private nuisance law at least in the narrow context of the modern American rule invalidating spite fences.

This court's reluctance in the nineteenth and early part of the twentieth century to provide broader protection for a landowner's access to sunlight was premised on three policy considerations. First, the right of landowners to use their property as they wished, as long as they did not cause physical damage to a neighbor, was jealously guarded.

---

2. Under the doctrine of prior appropriation the first user to appropriate the resource has the right of continued use to the exclusion of others.

The doctrine of prior appropriation has been used by several western states to allocate water, and by the New Mexico legislature to allocate solar access, secs. 47-3-1 to 47-3-5, N.M. Stats. 1978.

Second, sunlight was valued only for aesthetic enjoyment or as illumination. Since artificial light could be used for illumination, loss of sunlight was at most a personal annoyance which was given little, if any, weight by society.

Third, society had a significant interest in not restricting or impeding land development. This court repeatedly emphasized that in the growth period of the nineteenth and early twentieth centuries change is to be expected and is essential to property and that recognition of a right to sunlight would hinder property development....

... These three policies are no longer fully accepted or applicable. They reflect factual circumstances and social priorities that are now obsolete.

First, society has increasingly regulated the use of land by the landowner for the general welfare.

Second, access to sunlight has taken on a new significance in recent years. In this case the plaintiff seeks to protect access to sunlight, not for aesthetic reasons or as a source of illumination but as a source of energy. Access to sunlight as an energy source is of significance both to the landowner who invests in solar collectors and to a society which has an interest in developing alternative sources of energy.

Third, the policy of favoring unhindered private development in an expanding economy is no longer in harmony with the realities of our society. The need for easy and rapid development is not as great today as it once was, while our perception of the value of sunlight as a source of energy has increased significantly.

Courts should not implement obsolete policies that have lost their vigor over the course of the years. The law of private nuisance is better suited to resolve landowners' disputes about property development in the 1980's than is a rigid rule which does not recognize a landowner's interest in access to sunlight.... We read *State* v. *Deetz*, 66 Wis. 2d 1, 224 N.W.2d 407 (1974), as an endorsement of the application of common law nuisance to situations involving the conflicting interests of landowners and as rejecting *per se* exclusions to the nuisance law reasonable use doctrine.

* * *

We recognized in *Deetz* that common law rules adapt to changing social values and conditions.

* * *

Yet the defendant would have us ignore the flexible private nuisance law as a means of resolving the dispute between the landowners in this case and would have us adopt an approach, already abandoned in *Deetz*, of favoring the unrestricted development of land and of applying a rigid and inflexible rule protecting his right to build on his land and disregarding any interest of the plaintiff in the use and enjoyment of his land. This we refuse to do.[3]

---

3. Defendant's position that a landowner's interest in access to sunlight across adjoining land is not "legally enforceable" and is therefore excluded per se from private nuisance law was adopted in *Fontainebleau Hotel Corp.* v. *Forty-five Twenty-five, Inc.*, 114 So. 2d 257 (Fla. Ct. App. 1959), *cert. den.* 117 So. 2d 842 (Fla. 1960). The Florida district court of appeals permitted construction of a building which cast a shadow on a neighboring hotel's swimming pool. The court asserted that nuisance law protects only those interests "which [are] recognized and protected by law," and that there is no legally recognized or protected right to access to sunlight. A property owner does not, said the Florida court, in the absence of a contract or statute, acquire a presumptive or implied right to the free flow of light and air across adjoining land. The Florida court then concluded that a lawful structure which causes injury to another by cutting off light and air—whether or not erected partly for spite—does not give rise to a cause of action for damages or for an injunction.

Private nuisance law, the law traditionally used to adjudicate conflicts between private landowners, has the flexibility to protect both a landowner's right of access to sunlight and another landowner's right to develop land. Private nuisance law is better suited to regulate access to sunlight in modern society and is more in harmony with legislative policy and the prior decisions of this court than is an inflexible doctrine of non-recognition of any interest in access to sunlight across adjoining land.

We therefore hold that private nuisance law, that is, the reasonable use doctrine as set forth in the Restatement, is applicable to the instant case. Recognition of a nuisance claim for unreasonable obstruction of access to sunlight will not prevent land development or unduly hinder the use of adjoining land. It will promote the reasonable use and enjoyment of land in a manner suitable to the 1980's. That obstruction of access to light might be found to constitute a nuisance in certain circumstances does not mean that it will be or must be found to constitute a nuisance under all circumstances. The result in each case depends on whether the conduct complained of is unreasonable.

Accordingly we hold that the plaintiff in this case has stated a claim under which relief can be granted. Nonetheless we do not determine whether the plaintiff in this case is entitled to relief. In order to be entitled to relief the plaintiff must prove the elements required to establish actionable nuisance, and the conduct of the defendant herein must be judged by the reasonable use doctrine.

* * *

Because the plaintiff has stated a claim of common law private nuisance upon which relief can be granted, the judgment of the circuit court must be reversed. We need not, and do not, reach the question of whether the complaint states a claim under sec. 844.01, Stats. 1979–80, or under the doctrine of prior appropriation.

For the reasons set forth, we reverse the judgment of the circuit court dismissing the complaint and remand the matter to circuit court for further proceedings not inconsistent with this opinion.

* * *

William G. Callow, J. (dissenting)

* * *

The majority arrives at its conclusion that the common law private nuisance doctrine is applicable by analogizing this situation with the spite fence cases which protect a landowner from *malicious* obstruction of access to light.... Clearly, the spite fence cases, as their name implies, require malice which is not claimed in this case.

The majority then concludes that this court's past reluctance to extend protection to a landowner's access to sunlight beyond the spite fence cases is based on obsolete policies which have lost their vigor over the course of the years. The three obsolete policies cited by the majority are: (1) Right of landowners to use their property as they desire as long as no physical damage is done to a neighbor; (2) In the past, sunlight was valued only

---

We do not find the reasoning of *Fontainebleau* persuasive. The court leaped from rejecting an easement by prescription (the doctrine of ancient lights) and an easement by implication to the conclusion that there is no right to protection from obstruction of access to sunlight. The court's statement that a landowner has no right to light should be the conclusion, not its initial premise. The court did not explain why an owner's interest in unobstructed light should not be protected or in what manner an owner's interest in unobstructed sunlight differs from an owner's interest in being free from obtrusive noises or smells or differs from an owner's interest in unobstructed use of water. The recognition of a *per se* exception to private nuisance law may invite unreasonable behavior.

for aesthetic value, not a source of energy; and (3) Society has a significant interest in not impeding land development. The majority has failed to convince me that these policies are obsolete.

It is a fundamental principle of law that a "landowner owns at least as much of the space above the ground as he can occupy or use in connection with the land." ... I firmly believe that a landowner's right to use his property within the limits of ordinances, statutes, and restrictions of record where such use is necessary to serve his legitimate needs is a fundamental precept of a free society which this court should strive to uphold.

* * *

I know of no cases repudiating policies favoring the right of a landowner to use his property as he lawfully desires or which declare such policies are "no longer fully accepted or applicable" in this context.[4] The right of a property owner to lawful enjoyment of his property should be vigorously protected, particularly in those cases where the adjacent property owner could have insulated himself from the alleged problem by acquiring the land as defense to the potential problem or by provident use of his own property.

* * *

Regarding the third policy the majority apparently believes is obsolete (that society has a significant interest in not restricting land development), it cites *State* v. *Deetz*, 66 Wis. 2d 1, 224 N.W.2d 407 (1974). I concede the law may be tending to recognize the value of aesthetics over increased volume development and that an individual may not use his land in such a way as to harm the *public*. The instant case, however, deals with a private benefit.... While the majority's policy arguments may be directed to a cause of action for public nuisance, we are presented with a private nuisance case which I believe is distinguishable in this regard.[5]

I would submit that any policy decisions in this area are best left for the legislature. "What is 'desirable' or 'advisable' or 'ought to be' is a question of policy, not a question of fact. What is 'necessary' or what is 'in the best interest' is not a fact and its determination by the judiciary is an exercise of legislative power when each involves political considerations." I would concur with these observations of the trial judge: "While temptation lingers for the court to declare by judicial fiat what is right and what should be done, under the facts in this case, such action under our form of constitutional government where the three branches each have their defined jurisdiction and power, would be an intrusion of judicial egoism over legislative passivity."

The legislature has recently acted in this area. Chapter 354, Laws of 1981 (effective May 7, 1982), was enacted to provide the underlying legislation enabling local governments

---

4. Perhaps one reason courts have been hesitant to recognize a cause of action for solar blockage is that such a suit would normally only occur between two abutting landowners, and it is hoped that neighbors will compromise and reach agreement between themselves. This has, undoubtedly, been done in a large percentage of cases. To now recognize a cause of action for solar blockage may thwart a policy of compromise between neighbors.

5. I am amused at the majority's contention that what constitutes a nuisance today would have been accepted without question in earlier times. This calls to mind the fact that, in early days of travel by horses, the first automobiles were considered nuisances. Later, when automobile travel became developed, the horse became the nuisance. This makes me wonder if we are examining the proper nuisance in the case before us. In other words, could it be said that the solar energy user is creating the nuisance when others must conform their homes to accommodate his use? I note that solar panel glare may temporarily blind automobile drivers, reflect into adjacent buildings causing excessive heat, and otherwise irritate neighbors. Certainly in these instances the solar heating system constitutes the nuisance.

to enact ordinances establishing procedures for guaranteeing access to sunlight. This court's intrusion into an area where legislative action is being taken is unwarranted, and it may undermine a legislative scheme for orderly development not yet fully operational.

* * *

In order for a nuisance to be actionable in the instant case, the defendant's conduct must be "intentional and unreasonable." It is impossible for me to accept the majority's conclusion that Mr. Maretti, in lawfully seeking to construct his home, may be intentionally and unreasonably interfering with the plaintiff's access to sunlight. In addressing the "unreasonableness" component of the actor's conduct, it is important to note that "[t]here is liability for a nuisance only to those to whom it causes significant harm, of a kind that would be suffered by a normal person in the community or by property in normal condition and used for a normal purpose." Restatement (Second) of Torts sec. 821F (1979). The comments to the Restatement further reveal that "[if] normal persons in that locality would not be substantially annoyed or disturbed by the situation, then the invasion is not a significant one, even though the idiosyncracies of the particular plaintiff may make it unendurable to him."

I conclude that plaintiff's solar heating system is an unusually sensitive use. In other words, the defendant's proposed construction of his home, under ordinary circumstances, would not interfere with the use and enjoyment of the usual person's property. "The plaintiff cannot, by devoting his own land to an unusually sensitive use, such as a drive-in motion picture theater easily affected by light, make a nuisance out of conduct of the adjoining defendant which would otherwise be harmless."

* * *

I further believe that the majority's conclusion that a cause of action exists in this case thwarts the very foundation of property law. Property law encompasses a system of filing and notice in a place for public records to provide prospective purchasers with any limitations on their use of the property. Such a notice is not alleged by the plaintiff. Only as a result of the majority's decision did Mr. Maretti discover that a legitimate action exists which would require him to defend the design and location of his home against a nuisance suit, notwithstanding the fact that he located and began to build his house within the applicable building, municipal, and deed restrictions.

* * *

... I do not believe that an adjacent lot owner should be obliged to experience the substantial economic loss resulting from the lot being rendered unbuildable by the contour of the land as it relates to the location and design of the adjoining home using solar collectors.[6]

* * *

Because I do not believe that the facts of the present case give rise to a cause of action for private nuisance, I dissent.

---

6. Mr. Prah could have avoided this litigation by building his own home in the center of his lot instead of only ten feet from the Maretti lot line and/or by purchasing the adjoining lot for his own protection. Mr. Maretti has already moved the proposed location of his home over an additional ten feet to accommodate Mr. Prah's solar collector, and he testified that moving the home any further would interfere with his view of the lake on which the property faces.

Notes and Questions

1. Opportunity Costs, Bargaining, and the Coase Theorem: Whenever you have a choice, there is a cost. Review subsection B.5 in Chapter I, "Externalities, Property Rights, and the Coase Theorem." Pay particular attention to the graphical analysis as well as the *Notes and Questions* after *Fontainebleau.*

2. A Benchmark for Analysis of Internalization of Externalities: The Coase Theorem provides a benchmark for analyzing externality problems. It shows what would have happened in a world of zero bargaining and transaction costs. Many real world externality problems can be analyzed with the Coase Theorem. The Coase Theorem implies that the market is more important than the law under some circumstances. Every conflict does not require a judicial or regulatory solution. There are, however, numerous caveats to this analysis, which are discussed in Chapter I and the remainder of this Chapter.

3. Technological Changes and the Evolution of Property Rights: Private property rights can provide a powerful way to internalize externalities. However, costs of acquiring and enforcing property rights in some resources may be high. For example, it is harder to find and enforce property rights in the air because the wind blows and the air moves. How could anyone know whose air it is, whose air is whose? This drawback makes private property rights nearly impossible in some cases while technology provides a solution to the problem in other cases. For example, when grazing lands in the American West became crowded in the mid-nineteenth century, people found it difficult to keep their cattle separate and it became hard to enforce property rights in cattle. Fences might have helped, but wood to make fences was too expensive. The solution emerged from two new ideas, branding cattle and barbed wire fencing, which was cheaper than wood.

4. Transaction Costs: In addition to the distributional considerations involved in selecting a particular legal rule, the transaction costs—that is, the costs of negotiating and enforcing agreements—of allocating property rights in response to particular legal rules can play an important role in evaluating whether a particular legal rule is efficient. This is the topic of the following subsection.

b. Transaction Costs

In many instances involving negative externalities, the private solutions to externalities envisioned by Coase are of little practical importance because transaction costs make it impossible to reach agreement among all affected parties. In the pollution example, it would be impossible to negotiate a private agreement if thousands of property owners lived within the geographic area affected by the smoke. Coase clearly recognized that transaction costs were an important part of his analysis. High transaction costs could prevent private exchanges from taking place, thus making judicial and regulatory solutions more likely. The importance of transaction costs is illustrated by the following hypothetical.

Assume that smoke from a factory causes $75 of damage to the laundry hung outdoors by 5 nearby residents. If no corrective action is taken, the damages (the negative externalities) imposed on the neighbors equal $375 ($75 x 5). There are several ways to solve this externality. One possible solution is for a smoke screen to be installed at the factory. This would cost $150, or $30 per resident. Another alternative is that electric dryers could be purchased for $50 each by the residents. Or each resident could move, let's say at $100, for a total cost of $500. Finally, the factory could move for $500. Given this set of facts, the efficient solution in terms of cost minimization is the smoke screen, because it only costs $150.

The residents are mad about the smoke. What happens? The first step in this analysis is to determine the entitlement. Who has the right to what and why? This is usually a political decision. The second step in the analysis is to determine the rule to protect the entitlement, either a property rule or a liability rule. There are four possible combinations of entitlements and rules:

Rule #1—the factory has the right to pollute. Under this property rule, the factory could sell its right to pollute.

Rule #2—the factory has the right to pollute, but residents have the right to clean air and are entitled to damages. This is called a liability rule, because the residents do not have to consent to the factory's decision to impose costs on them. Under this liability rule, the residents' rights are limited to the receipt of compensation in the form of damages.

Rule #3—the residents are entitled to an injunction forbidding pollution. Under this property rule in favor of the residents, the residents may get the injunction or they can sell the right to impose the injunction.

Rule #4—the residents are entitled to an injunction, but must pay compensatory damages to the factory (e.g., if the residents force the factory to move). This is a liability rule where damages are imposed on the factory.

The impact of alternate rules can be analyzed by comparison of the results under two conditions—zero transaction costs and positive transaction costs. The efficient solution in Table IV-1 is indicated by the asterisk (*). With zero transaction costs, the smokescreen

Table IV-1. Impact of Transaction Costs on Allocation of Property Rights

(A) Zero Transaction Costs	(B) Positive Transaction Costs
Rule 1- Factory has right to pollute. (Property Rule)	
Residents have 4 choices:	
1) be injured for $375	1) $375
* 2) *buy smokscreens for $150*	2) $150 + $300 (TC) = $450
3) buy dryers for $250	* 3) *$250*
4) move $500	4) $500
Rule 2- Factory has right to pollute, but residents have right to clean air and are entitled to damages. (Liability Rule)	
Factory has 4 choices:	
1) pay damages of $375	1) $375
* 2) *install smokescreens for $150*	* 2) *$150*
3) buy dryers for $250	3) $250
4) shut down for $500	4) $500
Rule 3- Residents are entitled to an injunction forbidding pollution. (Property Rule)	
Factory has 4 choices:	
1) pay damages of $375	1) $375
* 2) *install smokescreens for $150*	* 2) *$150*
3) buy dryers for $250	3) $250
4) shut down $500	4) $500
Rule 4- Residents are entitled to an injunction, but must pay compensatory damages to the factory. (Liability Rule for Damages imposed on the factory)	
Residents have 5 choices:	
1) be injured for $375	1) $375
* 2) *buy smokescreens for $150*	2) $150 + $300 (TC) = $450
3) buy dryers for $250	* 3) *$250*
4) move $500	4) $500
5) get injunction & pay $500	5) $500 + $300 (TC) = $800

is installed for $150 under all four rules as indicated in column A. This is the efficient solution. The addition of positive transaction costs impacts the allocation of rights. Assume it costs each resident $60 to get together to negotiate with the factory or to agree on collective action. In column B, we see that the outcome changes under the different rules due to the transaction costs. Rules 2 and 3 still result in the factory installing the smokescreen. The factory does not need to engage in any collective decision making with itself. Rules 1 and 4 have different outcomes because the transaction costs (labeled TC in the table) make the buying of dryers more attractive relative to the collective action and negotiation associated with people agreeing to pay for the smokescreen and then having the factory install it. Thus, the Coase Theorem suggests that when transaction costs are high, it is important for property rights to be allocated to the party that values them most highly. The transaction costs prevent the property right from freely going to the highest value user. Who determines the highest value user? If information costs are high, can the government or a judge correctly determine which user is the highest value user? Keep these questions in mind when reading the following case.

Boomer v. Atlantic Cement Co.

Court of Appeals of New York
257 N.E.2d 870 (1970)

Bergan, J.

Defendant operates a large cement plant near Albany. These are actions for injunction and damages by neighboring land owners alleging injury to property from dirt, smoke and vibration emanating from the plant. A nuisance has been found after trial, temporary damages have been allowed; but an injunction has been denied.

The public concern with air pollution arising from many sources in industry and in transportation is currently accorded ever wider recognition accompanied by a growing sense of responsibility in State and Federal Governments to control it. Cement plants are obvious sources of air pollution in the neighborhoods where they operate.

But there is now before the court private litigation in which individual property owners have sought specific relief from a single plant operation. The threshold question raised by the division of view on this appeal is whether the court should resolve the litigation between the parties now before it as equitably as seems possible; or whether, seeking promotion of the general public welfare, it should channel private litigation into broad public objectives.

A court performs its essential function when it decides the rights of parties before it. Its decision of private controversies may sometimes greatly affect public issues. Large questions of law are often resolved by the manner in which private litigation is decided. But this is normally an incident to the court's main function to settle controversy. It is a rare exercise of judicial power to use a decision in private litigation as a purposeful mechanism to achieve direct public objectives greatly beyond the rights and interests before the court.

Effective control of air pollution is a problem presently far from solution even with the full public and financial powers of government. In large measure adequate technical procedures are yet to be developed and some that appear possible may be economically impracticable.

It seems apparent that the amelioration of air pollution will depend on technical research in great depth; on a carefully balanced consideration of the economic impact of close regulation; and of the actual effect on public health. It is likely to require massive public expenditure and to demand more than any local community can accomplish and to depend on regional and interstate controls.

A court should not try to do this on its own as a by-product of private litigation and it seems manifest that the judicial establishment is neither equipped in the limited nature of any judgment it can pronounce nor prepared to lay down and implement an effective policy for the elimination of air pollution. This is an area beyond the circumference of one private lawsuit. It is a direct responsibility for government and should not thus be undertaken as an incident to solving a dispute between property owners and a single cement plant — one of many — in the Hudson River valley.

The cement making operations of defendant have been found by the court at Special Term to have damaged the nearby properties of plaintiffs in these two actions. That court, as it has been noted, accordingly found defendant maintained a nuisance and this has been affirmed at the Appellate Division. The total damage to plaintiffs' properties is, however, relatively small in comparison with the value of defendant's operation and with the consequences of the injunction which plaintiffs seek.

The ground for the denial of injunction, notwithstanding the finding both that there is a nuisance and that plaintiffs have been damaged substantially, is the large disparity in economic consequences of the nuisance and of the injunction. This theory cannot, however, be sustained without overruling a doctrine which has been consistently reaffirmed in several leading cases in this court and which has never been disavowed here, namely that where a nuisance has been found and where there has been any substantial damage shown by the party complaining an injunction will be granted.

The rule in New York has been that such a nuisance will be enjoined although marked disparity be shown in economic consequence between the effect of the injunction and the effect of the nuisance.

* * *

Although the court at Special Term and the Appellate Division held that injunction should be denied, it was found that plaintiffs had been damaged in various specific amounts up to the time of the trial and damages to the respective plaintiffs were awarded for those amounts. The effect of this was, injunction having been denied, plaintiffs could maintain successive actions at law for damages thereafter as further damage was incurred.

The court at Special Term also found the amount of permanent damage attributable to each plaintiff, for the guidance of the parties in the event both sides stipulated to the payment and acceptance of such permanent damage as a settlement of all the controversies among the parties. The total of permanent damages to all plaintiffs thus found was $185,000. This basis of adjustment has not resulted in any stipulation by the parties.

This result at Special Term and at the Appellate Division is a departure from a rule that has become settled; but to follow the rule literally in these cases would be to close down the plant at once. This court is fully agreed to avoid that immediately drastic remedy; the difference in view is how best to avoid it.[7]

One alternative is to grant the injunction but postpone its effect to a specified future date to give opportunity for technical advances to permit defendant to eliminate the nuisance; another is to grant the injunction conditioned on the payment of permanent

---

7. Respondent's investment in the plant is in excess of $45,000,000. There are over 300 people employed there.

damages to plaintiffs which would compensate them for the total economic loss to their property present and future caused by defendant's operations. For reasons which will be developed the court chooses the latter alternative.

If the injunction were to be granted unless within a short period—e.g., 18 months—the nuisance be abated by improved methods, there would be no assurance that any significant technical improvement would occur.

The parties could settle this private litigation at any time if defendant paid enough money and the imminent threat of closing the plant would build up the pressure on defendant. If there were no improved techniques found, there would inevitably be applications to the court at Special Term for extensions of time to perform on showing of good faith efforts to find such techniques.

Moreover, techniques to eliminate dust and other annoying by-products of cement making are unlikely to be developed by any research the defendant can undertake within any short period, but will depend on the total resources of the cement industry nationwide and throughout the world. The problem is universal wherever cement is made.

For obvious reasons the rate of the research is beyond control of defendant. If at the end of 18 months the whole industry has not found a technical solution a court would be hard put to close down this one cement plant if due regard be given to equitable principles.

On the other hand, to grant the injunction unless defendant pays plaintiffs such permanent damages as may be fixed by the court seems to do justice between the contending parties. All of the attributions of economic loss to the properties on which plaintiffs' complaints are based will have been redressed.

The nuisance complained of by these plaintiffs may have other public or private consequences, but these particular parties are the only ones who have sought remedies and the judgment proposed will fully redress them. The limitation of relief granted is a limitation only within the four corners of these actions and does not foreclose public health or other public agencies from seeking proper relief in a proper court.

It seems reasonable to think that the risk of being required to pay permanent damages to injured property owners by cement plant owners would itself be a reasonable effective spur to research for improved techniques to minimize nuisance.

The power of the court to condition on equitable grounds the continuance of an injunction on the payment of permanent damages seems undoubted.

The damage base here suggested is consistent with the general rule in those nuisance cases where damages are allowed. "Where a nuisance is of such a permanent and unabatable character that a single recovery can be had, including the whole damage past and future resulting therefrom, there can be but one recovery." It has been said that permanent damages are allowed where the loss recoverable would obviously be small as compared with the cost of removal of the nuisance.

* * *

Thus it seems fair to both sides to grant permanent damages to plaintiffs which will terminate this private litigation. The theory of damage is the "servitude on land" of plaintiffs imposed by defendant's nuisance.

The judgment, by allowance of permanent damages imposing a servitude on land, which is the basis of the actions, would preclude future recovery by plaintiffs or their grantees.

This should be placed beyond debate by a provision of the judgment that the payment by defendant and the acceptance by plaintiffs of permanent damages found by the court shall be in compensation for a servitude on the land.

Although the Trial Term has found permanent damages as a possible basis of settlement of the litigation, on remission the court should be entirely free to re-examine this subject. It may again find the permanent damage already found; or make new findings.

The orders should be reversed, without costs, and the cases remitted to Supreme Court, Albany County to grant an injunction which shall be vacated upon payment by defendant of such amounts of permanent damage to the respective plaintiffs as shall for this purpose be determined by the court.

Jasen, J. (dissenting)

I agree with the majority that a reversal is required here, but I do not subscribe to the newly enunciated doctrine of assessment of permanent damages, in lieu of an injunction, where substantial property rights have been impaired by the creation of a nuisance.

It has long been the rule in this State, as the majority acknowledges, that a nuisance which results in substantial continuing damage to neighbors must be enjoined. To now change the rule to permit the cement company to continue polluting the air indefinitely upon the payment of permanent damages is, in my opinion, compounding the magnitude of a very serious problem in our State and Nation today.

* * *

The harmful nature and widespread occurrence of air pollution have been extensively documented. Congressional hearings have revealed that air pollution causes substantial property damage, as well as being a contributing factor to a rising incidence of lung cancer, emphysema, bronchitis and asthma.

The specific problem faced here is known as particulate contamination because of the fine dust particles emanating from defendant's cement plant. The particular type of nuisance is not new, having appeared in many cases for at least the past 60 years. It is interesting to note that cement production has recently been identified as a significant source of particulate contamination in the Hudson Valley. This type of pollution, wherein very small particles escape and stay in the atmosphere, has been denominated as the type of air pollution which produces the greatest hazard to human health. We have thus a nuisance which not only is damaging to the plaintiffs, but also is decidedly harmful to the general public.

I see grave dangers in overruling our long-established rule of granting an injunction where a nuisance results in substantial continuing damage. In permitting the injunction to become inoperative upon the payment of permanent damages, the majority is, in effect, licensing a continuing wrong. It is the same as saying to the cement company, you may continue to do harm to your neighbors so long as you pay a fee for it. Furthermore, once such permanent damages are assessed and paid, the incentive to alleviate the wrong would be eliminated, thereby continuing air pollution of an area without abatement.

It is true that some courts have sanctioned the remedy here proposed by the majority in a number of cases, but none of the authorities relied upon by the majority are analogous to the situation before us. In those cases, the courts, in denying an injunction and awarding money damages, grounded their decision on a showing that the use to which the property was intended to be put was primarily for the public benefit. Here, on the other hand, it is clearly established that the cement company is creating a continuing air pollution nuisance primarily for its own private interest with no public benefit.

This kind of inverse condemnation may not be invoked by a private person or corporation for private gain or advantage. Inverse condemnation should only be permitted when the public is primarily served in the taking or impairment of property. The promotion of the interests of the polluting cement company has, in my opinion, no public use or benefit.

Nor is it constitutionally permissible to impose servitude on land, without consent of the owner, by payment of permanent damages where the continuing impairment of the land is for a private use. This is made clear by the State Constitution (art. I, §7, subd. [a]) which provides that "[p]rivate property shall not be taken for *public use* without just compensation" (emphasis added). It is, of course, significant that the section makes no mention of taking for a private use.

In sum, then, by constitutional mandate as well as by judicial pronouncement, the permanent impairment of private property for private purposes is not authorized in the absence of clearly demonstrated public benefit and use.

I would enjoin the defendant cement company from continuing the discharge of dust particles upon its neighbors' properties unless, within 18 months, the cement company abated this nuisance.

It is not my intention to cause the removal of the cement plant from the Albany area, but to recognize the urgency of the problem stemming from this stationary source of air pollution, and to allow the company a specified period of time to develop a means to alleviate this nuisance.

I am aware that the trial court found that the most modern dust control devices available have been installed in defendant's plant, but, I submit, this does not mean that *better* and more effective dust control devices could not be developed within the time allowed to abate the pollution.

Moreover, I believe it is incumbent upon the defendant to develop such devices, since the cement company, at the time the plant commenced production (1962), was well aware of the plaintiffs' presence in the area, as well as the probable consequences of its contemplated operation. Yet, it still chose to build and operate the plant at this site.

In a day when there is a growing concern for clean air, highly developed industry should not expect acquiescence by the courts, but should, instead, plan its operations to eliminate contamination of our air and damage to its neighbors.

Accordingly, the orders of the Appellate Division, insofar as they denied the injunction, should be reversed, and the actions remitted to Supreme Court, Albany County to grant an injunction to take effect 18 months hence, unless the nuisance is abated by improved techniques prior to said date.

Notes and Questions

1. The Assignment of Property Rights: Who has the entitlement? How was it protected? Which "rule" (from the example preceding the case) is adopted by the court? Is the rule efficient? In what sense? What is the relevance of the firm's investment? What is meant by permanent damages?

2. Bargaining and the Coase Theorem: Did high transaction costs prevent bargaining to resolve the incompatible uses of property? Or, was the absence of clearly defined property rights the reason for the lawsuit?

3. The Normative Coase Theorem: The preceding analysis leads to the development of what is referred to as the Normative Coase Theorem: if efficiency is the goal, the preferred legal rule is the rule that minimizes the effects of transactions costs. If the law is able to reduce transaction costs, then voluntary exchange will be more likely to lead to efficiency. In other words, the law should "lubricate" bargaining by reducing the impediments to bargaining (transaction costs).

4. Property Rule or Liability Rule?: When an externality has arisen, the court should choose between a liability rule and a property rule on the basis of the parties' ability to cooperate in resolving the dispute. When transactions costs are low, either a property rule (injunction) or liability rule (damages) will result in efficiency because the parties can bargain to reach the efficient outcome. However, an injunction is cheaper for a court to implement because it must only clarify the property right. Damages, on the other hand, are more difficult and costly for a court to implement because it must assess the monetary value of damage that was done. Moreover, the court's incorrect assessment of damages could lead to inefficient outcomes even in low transaction cost settings. Consider an example: a factory causes $375 worth of damage because of the smoke it emits, and the problem can be avoided by either the factory installing a smoke screen for $150 or the residents purchasing electric dryers for $500. The efficient outcome is clearly for the factory to install the smoke screen. However, what if the court incorrectly assesses damages of $100? This would result in the factory choosing to emit smoke and pay the $100 instead of choosing the efficient solution for $150. Thus, when transaction costs are low, a property rule is the preferred damage rule because it avoids both the court's cost of computing damage and the possibility of an inefficient outcome.

What about high transaction cost situations? As previously explained, in these situations it is important for property rights to be allocated to the party that values them most highly (and would end up with them if transactions costs were low and the efficient solution was reached). In high transaction cost settings, liability rules (damages) improve the chances of reaching the efficient outcome because they give injurers the choice between imposing the harm and paying damages or ceasing the harm to avoid damages. Consider the previous example with different values: a factory causes $375 worth of damage because of the smoke it emits, and the problem can be avoided by either the factory installing a smoke screen for $450 or the residents purchasing electric dryers for $500. A liability rule will result in the efficient outcome (factory pays $375 in damages) but a property rule will not (the injunction requires the factory to install the smoke screen for $450). What if, instead, the smoke screen cost $200? Now the property rule will result in the efficient outcome ($200 smoke screen). The liability rule will also result in the efficient outcome because the rule gives the factory the choice between imposing the harm and paying $375 in damages or installing the smoke screen for $200 to avoid damages. Thus, when transaction costs are high so that bargaining will not ensure efficiency, a liability rule is the preferred rule because it gives the injurer the choice between paying damages or ceasing the harm. In contrast, a property rule requires the injurer to cease the harm.

When these standards are applied in practice, the preferred remedy depends in large part on how many parties must participate in the settlement. The larger the number of parties, the more preferable the liability rule with damages because transaction costs are likely high. The fewer the parties, the more preferable the property rule of injunctive relief because transaction costs are likely low. In general, a property rule works best for private wrongs, a liability rule better for public wrongs. In many instances the public wrongs are dealt with through land use planning, environmental regulations, or public nuisance laws.

5. Property Rule or Liability Rule in Patent Infringement Cases: Patent infringement cases often involve only a few parties: the patent holder and the alleged infringer. Injunctive relief has traditionally been the remedy in these cases. However, in eBay Inc v. MercExchange, L.L.C., 547 U.S. 388 (2006), the U.S. Supreme Court determined that eBay had infringed MercExchange's patent and awarded damages. Justice Kennedy stated in his concurring opinion that "[i]n cases now arising trial courts should bear in mind that in many instances the nature of the patent being enforced and the economic function of the patent holder present considerations quite unlike earlier cases." Why, in the current environment with so-called "patent trolls" holding many patents and the growing number of vague business method patents, might a liability rule be preferable to a property rule even though there are only a few parties involved?

6. Trivial Externalities: Generally, when transaction costs are high, government intervention to correct the market failure associated with negative externalities may be justified on efficiency grounds. It is important to recognize, however, that the combination of small externalities and nontrivial costs of government intervention suggests that many externalities are not worth correcting. For example, the playing of loud music at a public park may impose external costs on people who went to the park to enjoy its peace and quiet, but the costs of governmental intervention to silence the portable stereos—BOOM BOXES—might be much greater than the benefits to the other parties.

Spur Industries, Inc. v. Del E. Webb Development Co.

Supreme Court of Arizona
494 P.2d 700 (1972)

Cameron, J.

From a judgment permanently enjoining the defendant, Spur Industries, Inc., from operating a cattle feedlot near the plaintiff Del E. Webb Development Company's Sun City, Spur appeals. Webb cross-appeals. Although numerous issues are raised, we feel that it is necessary to answer only two questions. They are:

1. Where the operation of a business, such as a cattle feedlot is lawful in the first instance, but becomes a nuisance by reason of a nearby residential area, may the feedlot operation be enjoined in an action brought by the developer of the residential area?

2. Assuming that the nuisance may be enjoined, may the developer of a completely new town or urban area in a previously agricultural area be required to indemnify the operator of the feedlot who must move or cease operation because of the presence of the residential area created by the developer?

The facts necessary for a determination of this matter on appeal are as follows. The area in question is located in Maricopa County, Arizona, some 14 to 15 miles west of the urban area of Phoenix, on the Phoenix–Wickenburg Highway, also known as Grand Avenue. About two miles south of Grand Avenue is Olive Avenue which runs east and west. 111th Avenue runs north and south as does the Agua Fria River immediately to the west....

Farming started in this area about 1911. In 1929, with the completion of the Carl Pleasant Dam, gravity flow water became available to the property located to the west of the Agua Fria River, though land to the east remained dependent upon well water for irrigation. By 1950, the only urban areas in the vicinity were the agriculturally related communities of Peoria, El Mirage, and Surprise located along Grand Avenue. Along 111th Avenue, approximately one mile south of Grand Avenue and 1 1/2 miles north of Olive

Avenue, the community of Youngtown was commenced in 1954. Youngtown is a retirement community appealing primarily to senior citizens.

In 1956, Spur's predecessors in interest, H. Marion Welborn and the Northside Hay Mill and Trading Company, developed feed-lots, about 1/2 mile south of Olive Avenue, in an area between the confluence of the usually dry Agua Fria and New Rivers. The area is well suited for cattle feeding and in 1959, there were 25 cattle feeding pens or dairy operations within a 7 mile radius of the location developed by Spur's predecessors. In April and May of 1959, the Northside Hay Mill was feeding between 6,000 and 7,000 head of cattle and Welborn approximately 1,500 head on a combined area of 35 acres.

In May of 1959, Del Webb began to plan the development of an urban area to be known as Sun City. For this purpose, the Marinette and the Santa Fe Ranches, some 20,000 acres of farmland, were purchased for $15,000,000 or $750.00 per acre. This price was considerably less than the price of land located near the urban area of Phoenix, and along with the success of Youngtown was a factor influencing the decision to purchase the property in question.

By September 1959, Del Webb had started construction of a golf course south of Grand Avenue and Spur's predecessors had started to level ground for more feedlot area. In 1960, Spur purchased the property in question and began a rebuilding and expansion program extending both to the north and south of the original facilities. By 1962, Spur's expansion program was completed and had expanded from approximately 35 acres to 114 acres.

Accompanied by an extensive advertising campaign, homes were first offered by Del Webb in January 1960 and the first unit to be completed was south of Grand Avenue and approximately 2 1/2 miles north of Spur. By 2 May 1960, there were 450 to 500 houses completed or under construction. At this time, Del Webb did not consider odors from the Spur feed pens a problem and Del Webb continued to develop in a southerly direction, until sales resistance became so great that the parcels were difficult if not impossible to sell....

* * *

By December 1967, Del Webb's property had extended south to Olive Avenue and Spur was within 500 feet of Olive Avenue to the north. Del Webb filed its original complaint alleging that in excess of 1,300 lots in the southwest portion were unfit for development for sale as residential lots because of the operation of the Spur feedlot.

Del Webb's suit complained that the Spur feeding operation was a public nuisance because of the flies and the odor which were drifting or being blown by the prevailing south to north wind over the southern portion of Sun City. At the time of the suit, Spur was feeding between 20,000 and 30,000 head of cattle, and the facts amply support the finding of the trial court that the feed pens had become a nuisance to the people who resided in the southern part of Del Webb's development. The testimony indicated that cattle in a commercial feedlot will produce 35 to 40 pounds of wet manure per day, per head, or over a million pounds of wet manure per day for 30,000 head of cattle, and that despite the admittedly good feedlot management and good housekeeping practices by Spur, the resulting odor and flies produced an annoying if not unhealthy situation as far as the senior citizens of southern Sun City were concerned. There is no doubt that some of the citizens of Sun City were unable to enjoy the outdoor living which Del Webb had advertised and that Del Webb was faced with sales resistance from prospective purchasers as well as strong and persistent complaints from the people who had purchased homes in that area.

Trial was commenced before the court.... Findings of fact and conclusions of law were requested and given. The case was vigorously contested, including special actions in this court on some of the matters. In one of the special actions before this court, Spur agreed to, and did, shut down its operation without prejudice to a determination of the matter on appeal. On appeal the many questions raised were extensively briefed.

It is noted, however, that neither the citizens of Sun City nor Youngtown are represented in this lawsuit and the suit is solely between Del E. Webb Development Company and Spur Industries, Inc.

MAY SPUR BE ENJOINED?

The difference between a private nuisance and a public nuisance is generally one of degree. A private nuisance is one affecting a single individual or a definite small number of persons in the enjoyment of private rights not common to the public, while a public nuisance is one affecting the rights enjoyed by citizens as a city or neighborhood. To constitute a public nuisance, the nuisance must affect a considerable number of people or an entire community or neighborhood.

Where the injury is slight, the remedy for minor inconveniences lies in an action for damages rather than in one for an injunction. Moreover, some courts have held, in the "balancing of conveniences" cases, that damages may be the sole remedy. See Boomer v. Atlantic Cement Co., 257 N.E.2d 870 (1970).

Thus, it would appear from the admittedly incomplete record as developed in the trial court, that, at most, residents of Youngtown would be entitled to damages rather than injunctive relief.

We have no difficulty, however, in agreeing with the conclusion of the trial court that Spur's operation was an enjoinable public nuisance as far as the people in the southern portion of Del Webb's Sun City were concerned.

* * *

It is clear that as to the citizens of Sun City, the operation of Spur's feedlot was both a public and a private nuisance. They could have successfully maintained an action to abate the nuisance. Del Webb, having shown a special injury in the loss of sales, had a standing to bring suit to enjoin the nuisance. The judgment of the trial court permanently enjoining the operation of the feedlot is affirmed.

MUST DEL WEBB INDEMNIFY SPUR?

A suit to enjoin a nuisance sounds in equity and the courts have long recognized a special responsibility to the public when acting as a court of equity....

* * *

In addition to protecting the public interest, however, courts of equity are concerned with protecting the operator of a lawfully, albeit noxious, business from the result of a knowing and willful encroachment by others near his business.

In the so-called "coming to the nuisance" cases, the courts have held that the residential landowner may not have relief if he knowingly came into a neighborhood reserved for industrial or agricultural endeavors and has been damaged thereby:

> "Plaintiffs chose to live in an area uncontrolled by zoning laws or restrictive covenants and remote from urban development. In such an area plaintiffs cannot complain that legitimate agricultural pursuits are being carried on in the vicinity, nor can plaintiffs, having chosen to build in an agricultural area, complain that the agricultural pursuits carried on in the area depreciate the value of their homes. The area being *primarily agricultural*, any opinion reflecting the value of such

property must take this factor into account. The standards affecting the value of residence property in an urban setting, subject to zoning controls and controlled planning techniques, cannot be the standards by which agricultural properties are judged.

"People employed in a city who build their homes in suburban areas of the county beyond the limits of a city and zoning regulations do so for a reason. Some do so to avoid the high taxation rate imposed by cities, or to avoid special assessments for street, sewer and water projects. They usually build on improved or hard surface highways, which have been built either at state or county expense and thereby avoid special assessments for these improvements. It may be that they desire to get away from the congestion of traffic, smoke, noise, foul air and the many other annoyances of city life. But with all these advantages in going beyond the area which is zoned and restricted to protect them in their homes, they must be prepared to take the disadvantages."

* * *

Were Webb the only party injured, we would feel justified in holding that the doctrine of "coming to the nuisance" would have been a bar to the relief asked by Webb, and, on the other hand, had Spur located the feedlot near the outskirts of a city and had the city grown toward the feedlot, Spur would have to suffer the cost of abating the nuisance as to those people locating within the growth pattern of the expanding city....

We agree, however, with the Massachusetts court that:

"The law of nuisance affords no rigid rule to be applied in all instances. It is elastic. It undertakes to require only that which is fair and reasonable under all the circumstances. In a commonwealth like this, which depends for its material prosperity so largely on the continued growth and enlargement of manufacturing of diverse varieties, 'extreme rights' cannot be enforced ..." Stevens v. Rockport Granite Co., 216 Mass. 486, 488, 104 N.E. 371, 373 (1914).

There was no indication in the instant case at the time Spur and its predecessors located in western Maricopa County that a new city would spring up, full-blown, alongside the feeding operation and that the developer of that city would ask the court to order Spur to move because of the new city. Spur is required to move not because of any wrongdoing on the part of Spur, but because of a proper and legitimate regard of the courts for the rights and interests of the public.

Del Webb, on the other hand, is entitled to the relief prayed for (a permanent injunction), not because Webb is blameless, but because of the damage to the people who have been encouraged to purchase homes in Sun City. It does not equitably or legally follow, however, that Webb, being entitled to the injunction, is then free of any liability to Spur if Webb has in fact been the cause of the damage Spur has sustained. It does not seem harsh to require a developer, who has taken advantage of the lesser land values in a rural area as well as the availability of large tracts of land on which to build and develop a new town or city in the area, to indemnify those who are forced to leave as a result.

Having brought people to the nuisance to the foreseeable detriment of Spur, Webb must indemnify Spur for a reasonable amount of the cost of moving or shutting down. It should be noted that this relief to Spur is limited to a case wherein a developer has, with foreseeability, brought into a previously agricultural or industrial area the population which makes necessary the granting of an injunction against a lawful business and for which the business has no adequate relief.

It is therefore the decision of this court that the matter be remanded to the trial court for a hearing upon the damages sustained by the defendant Spur as a reasonable and direct result of the granting of the permanent injunction. Since the result of the appeal may appear novel and both sides have obtained a measure of relief, it is ordered that each side will bear its own costs.

Affirmed in part, reversed in part, and remanded for further proceedings consistent with this opinion.

Notes and Questions

1. The Assignment of Property Rights: Who has the entitlement? How was it protected? Which "rule" (from the example preceding the *Boomer* case) is adopted by the court? Is the rule efficient? In what sense?

2. Reciprocal Causation: Who "caused" the injury?

3. Bargaining and the Coase Theorem: Did high transaction costs prevent bargaining to resolve the incompatible uses of property? Or, was the absence of clearly defined property rights the reason for the lawsuit?

2. Corrective Taxes and Subsidies

One government strategy for dealing with externalities is to encourage decision makers to internalize the externalities by taxing the production of negative externality goods and subsidizing the production of positive externality goods. When the government taxes firms that produce negative externality goods, the goal is to set the per unit tax so that the producer's marginal private costs of production plus the tax equals the marginal social cost of production. The strategy was developed by English economist A.C. Pigou and is known as a Pigouvian Tax.

The impact of an excise tax on the sale of a product that involves negative externalities is shown in Figure IV-4. The tax is assumed to be paid by the producer, so it is treated

Figure IV-4. Tax on Pollution

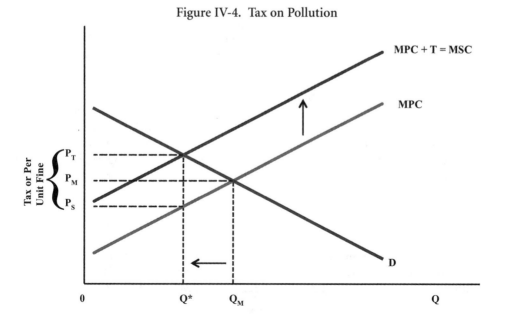

as an addition to the marginal private costs of production (MPC). That is, the optimal tax should be equal to the difference between the MPC and MSC, so that MPC + T = MSC. The competitive firm would equate MSC to price (MPC + T = MSC = P) and the externality would be internalized in the firm's output decision. That is, the firm will produce the output where MSC = P, which is the correct output from society's point of view. The tax causes the market to clear at Q^*, the optimal level of production. The new market price is at P_T, which indicates that the market price did not increase by the full amount of the tax. That is, the burden of the tax is shared by both the producers who receive a lower after-tax price ($P_S = P_T - T$) and consumers who pay P_T instead of P_M. Prior to the imposition of the corrective tax, consumers as well as producers benefited from the producers' ability to shift some costs to third parties. Also notice in Figure IV-4 that the slope of the demand curve determines the relative burdens on the producer and consumer. Why is it important to understand who bears the burdens of a government imposed tax?

Taxation is a form of indirect regulation. Thus, taxing a firm that pollutes forces the firm to act as if it were taking all social costs of its activities into account, thereby resulting in an optimum level of output. Remember, the socially optimal level of pollution is not zero because at some point, clean air costs more than it is valued by society.

The government can impose the correct tax in Figure IV-4 only if it has sufficient information to calculate the marginal external cost imposed on third parties, so that it can set the appropriate level of the tax and then adjust the tax rate when the marginal cost to third parties changes. Such information is necessarily subjective (since some people are more sensitive to some externalities than others) and, consequently, is revealed through the political process.

In some situations, taxing the production of negative externality goods may prevent efficient outcomes altogether. Consider the negative externality created by low-flying airplanes near airports. The government could tax the airlines so that they take steps to reduce the amount of airline noise by making planes quieter or requiring steeper descents so that fewer airport neighbors are affected. However, what if the cheapest way to eliminate the airplane noise externality is for the airport neighbors to soundproof their homes? If the government imposes a tax on airlines, and transactions costs are high enough to prevent bargaining between airlines and airport neighbors, the efficient outcome will never be reached. Even though the airport neighbors could most efficiently prevent the problem, they will have no incentive to do so if the tax induces airlines to reduce the noise. Thus, when the government does not know who can solve the externality at lowest cost, imposing a tax may prevent efficient outcomes.

Similarly, a **subsidy** is a government cash grant or tax break to producers of certain goods. The government might grant subsidies when economic behavior creates positive externalities. The goal of the subsidy is for the producing firm to internalize the benefits of its production. Such internalization will, like in the case of the Pigouvian tax, change the price and quantity equilibrium to the understood socially optimal price and quantity equilibrium. Examples of goods subsidized because they produce positive externalities include vaccinations and schools. The optimal subsidy is equal to the size of the positive externality—the difference between the marginal private benefits and the marginal social benefits of consuming the good. Instead of paying the subsidy to the consumers, which would increase the marginal private benefit of consumption, a subsidy is typically paid to the producers. The impact of a per unit subsidy is illustrated in Figure IV-5. The subsidy reduces the marginal private cost of production from MPC to MPC_S. As a result, the

Figure IV-5. Positive Externality & Per Unit Subsidy

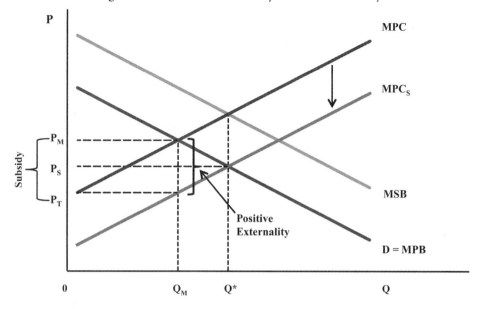

market output increases to Q^*, where $MPC_S = MPB$. The price falls to P_S, indicating that the producers pass on some of the subsidy to consumers.

3. Government Regulation

Another government strategy for dealing with externalities is direct regulation of the behavior of firms. An example of this type of response to market failure is local land-use zoning laws, which, for instance, prohibit the opening of a 24-hour convenience store in certain residential areas. Another example is the current federal regulation of industrial pollution. The primary federal response to pollution has been to place limits on the amount that firms can legally discharge.

The efficiency goal of the government regulation is to require industry output to be the economically efficient level at the quantity where the marginal private benefit equals marginal social costs. In the 1970s, the federal government sought to control pollution through direct regulation of polluters. Environmental regulation traditionally has consisted of detailed rules about the technology that firms must adopt to control pollution. Firms in identified industries must install special pollution control equipment as a condition of being able to stay in the industry. This is a practical way to control pollution. Each firm must clean up its emissions in the prescribed manner. Note that direct regulation does not allow firms to choose the most efficient means of staying below the allowable level of pollution, nor are firms allowed to choose to pollute (and pay compensatory damages), or to not pollute, or to select among different types of pollution control technology. They must follow the detailed rules set by the government. Eliminating producers' choices increases the information cost burden placed on the government. The more the government undertakes to regulate, the more difficult it becomes for the government to determine the appropriate amount of pollution, which firms can pollute, how firms can pollute, how firms must abate their pollution, etc. When the government assumes control of these variables, the risk of deadweight loss and reduced consumer welfare increases.

The experience of over thirty years of intensive federal regulation of environmental risks has demonstrated some severe drawbacks of centralized environmental policy. The "command and control" regulatory strategy that has dominated environmental policy has been strongly criticized on a variety of grounds: that it has failed to set intelligent priorities; squandered resources devoted to environmental quality; discouraged environmentally superior technologies; and imposed unnecessary penalties on innovation and investment. As one critic concludes:

> Our current environmental regulatory system was an understandable response to a perceived need for immediate controls to prevent a pollution crisis. But the system has grown to the point where it amounts to nothing less than a massive effort at Soviet-style central planning of the economy to achieve environmental goals. It strangles investment and innovation. It encourages costly and divisive litigation and delay. It unduly limits private initiative and choice. The centralized command system is simply unacceptable as a long-term environmental protection strategy for a large and diverse nation committed to the market and decentralized ordering.

Richard B. Stewart, *Controlling Environmental Risks Through Economic Incentives*, 13 Columbia Journal of Environmental Law 153, 154 (1988).

a. Direct Regulation Versus Corrective Taxes

Regulation can be effective from an efficiency perspective, however, only if the government also has reliable, up-to-date information about the economically efficient quantity and it can impose that quantity on firms in an efficient manner—and remember, information is costly. On the other hand, taxes can provide better incentives than regulations. For example, suppose that the government wants to limit the total amount of pollution from an industry. If it does so through regulation, a firm that discovers a new method of reducing pollution may have no incentive to adopt that method. However, if the government limits pollution by taxing it, the firm may be able to reduce its taxes and raise its profits by adopting the new method. The firm thus has the incentive to innovate cleaner production mechanisms. Also, taxes can provide firms with more effective incentives to use new lower cost methods of reducing pollution than can regulations. Some economists argue that corrective taxes have a second potential benefit over regulations designed to internalize externalities. They generate revenue for the government, theoretically allowing reductions in other taxes. If the government were to receive $100 billion from taxes on pollution, it could reduce income taxes by that amount, lowering the deadweight social losses from both the income taxes and pollution.

b. Selling Rights to Pollute

A straightforward alternative to corrective taxes and direct regulation is to establish a market for externality rights, such as the right to pollute. Under this approach, the government sets an allowable level of pollution and sells the right to pollute. In theory, this market works like any other market. Those who value the pollution rights must, however, buy and hold them. Firms will make decisions about whether it is less costly to install pollution control equipment or to buy pollution rights. Unlike direct regulation, the government does not tell the industry how to clean up the air. Instead, it sets the allowable level of pollution and lets firms decide how to control their pollution. This solution shifts some of the information cost burden from the government to the polluting firms. This market-like approach to pollution control has the virtue of insuring that the acceptable level of pollution is reached at the lowest possible cost.

In fact, the 1990 Amendments to the Clean Air Act allowed the federal government to set up a program of marketable emission permits for smoke stack emissions of public utilities. Under this program, utilities are allowed to trade pollution rights. Environmental policy analysts argued that the market for pollution rights would give utilities the incentives to lower the cost of their pollution control efforts. The results of this program are encouraging, as suggested by the following excerpt:

> By far the best known emissions trading program arises under Title IV of the 1990 Clean Air Act Amendments, which implemented an emissions cap and allowance trading program for emissions of sulfur dioxide (SO_2). Under the program (the SO_2 emissions trading program), total nationwide emissions of SO_2 emitted from power plants were capped, and allowances to emit that sum total were distributed among the largest and dirtiest power plants. Each allowance entitles the holder to emit one ton of SO_2 and can be used to emit, banked for future use, or sold to a willing buyer. The EPA, which administers the program, imposes very few restrictions upon trading. Enforcement is accomplished by a requirement that continuous emissions monitors be installed in all smokestacks to record and report the quantity of SO_2 actually emitted. Penalties for exceeding the amount of emissions are quite severe—$2,000 per excess ton—when compared with prices for allowances themselves, which have ranged between a low of $65 per ton in 1996 to a high of $326 in 1992. This differential has enabled firms to buy a margin of error in order to avoid a costly penalty. Other emissions trading programs are in place, most of them modeled after the SO_2 emissions trading program.

* * *

> Foremost among the advantages of [such] efficiency-based programs is the potential to achieve greater economic efficiency through trading. In decentralized trading programs, efficiency is achieved when allowances to pollute ... gravitate towards those that can make the highest and best use of the allowance. Gains from trading pollution allowances result because facilities with higher marginal abatement costs will place a higher value on having an allowance than facilities with lower marginal abatement costs and will pay the latter for their allowances. The overall societal result is that the reduction in emissions imposed by the emissions cap will be accomplished at the lowest overall cost. A second reason that decentralized trading programs lead to economic efficiency is that polluting firms may be able to choose from a greater variety of compliance strategies than they would have under traditional fairness-based schemes. This flexibility necessarily lowers compliance costs.

> The empirical evidence on whether gains from trading have occurred is clearly positive. Lower-than-expected allowance prices suggest unanticipated cost savings that would not have been identified under more rigid fairness-based programs. Early predictions of SO_2 emissions allowances put the value of allowances in the $300–$400 per ton range, but as it turned out, prices dipped to as low as $65 per ton in 1996, before rebounding to $180 in August, 2003. Under another program, established by a special statutorily-mandated Northeastern regional entity, the Ozone Transport Commission, an NOx emissions trading program was established to deal with the region's chronic and severe ozone problem. The emissions trading program was overlaid on top of the Title IV traditional fairness-based regulation, as well as other NOx regulations. Allowance prices debuted in 1999 at approximately $2000 per ton,

but have since dropped to $750 per ton, suggesting substantial compliance cost savings in that program as well.

Cost savings have been confirmed on a larger scale as well. Analysis by researchers at Resources for the Future has found trading opportunities under the SO_2 emissions trading program worth as much as $250 million. Denny Ellerman has estimated the cost savings of trading to have been $358 million per year from 1995–1999 (Phase I of the Acid Rain Program), and as much as $2.3 *billion* per year for 2000–2007 (Phase II & banking). And because of consolidation in the electricity generation industry, it seems likely that what were once trading opportunities between different firms have now become opportunities to realize savings through intra-firm adjustments.

Decentralized trading programs are also likely to be more economically efficient in that the flexibility afforded to firms enables them to coordinate compliance strategies with each other. The trading of emissions permits is not only a form of least-cost compliance, but also a way of coordinating *who* will pollute. And because emissions allowances can be "banked" for future use, they also allow polluting firms to allocate *when* they will pollute....

Economic theory thus seems to have been for the most part vindicated by decentralized trading programs thus far....

Shi-Ling Hsu, *Fairness Versus Efficiency in Environmental Law*, 31 Ecology Law Quarterly 303, 365–66, 377–79 (2004).

Difficulties can arise in such a permit marketing scheme, however. Indeed, someone must determine the optimal level of pollution under a pollution tax, direct regulation, or pollution permit market. The relevant knowledge in this case is economic rather than technical. The government's interest is not in describing the damage done by varying degrees of air pollution, rather it is in determining the values individuals and our society attach to the different degrees of damage. Again, such knowledge is extremely costly. After all, if firms had perfect information would they internalize the external costs through bargaining? What puts the government in a better situation to determine information than the firms? Moreover, both the tax scheme and pollution rights scheme, in a manner very similar to direct regulation, must be monitored and enforced by the government. With such actions, tax evasion and pollution without permit will be serious problems.

C. Market Failures and Government Failures

In Chapter III, public choice economics was introduced as a theory of government failure. Political institutions often prevent economic regulations from achieving their theoretical goals. Accordingly, it is naive to expect imperfect markets to be replaced by perfect government regulations and perfect government regulators. In the following essay, Professor Terry Anderson challenges much of the conventional wisdom about governmental efforts to correct externalities.

Markets and the Environment: Friends or Foes?

Terry L. Anderson

55 Case Western Reserve Law Review 81 (2004)[*]

If you take a course in environmental economics, you are likely to be dazzled with fancy graphs using isoquants, budget constraints, and even social welfare functions. From these fancy tools, F. Bator went so far as to determine a "bliss point," suggesting that these tools could take society to its maximum level of well-being. I still have the book from which these graphs were taken and I can still remember distinctly sitting through this lecture and just thinking, can you believe it? I am going to learn how to take society to its bliss point!

This type of analysis illustrates the way economists often approach problems, namely using marginal analysis to maximize some value subject to opportunity cost constraints. From this analysis follows one of the main tenets of economics: if the marginal benefits are greater than the marginal cost, do it. We economists think this marginal analysis is a pretty powerful way of thinking about the world. In determining how clean the air should be, we need to know what the additional benefits of clean air are, what the additional costs of clean air are, and as long as the additional benefits exceed the additional cost then clean it up. If you want to know whether to save an endangered species, the answer is the same: if the marginal benefits exceed the marginal costs, save it.

Let us apply this to the issue of wolf reintroduction into Yellowstone National Park. A few years ago, during the Clinton administration, Bruce Babbitt, then Secretary of the Interior, released a few Canadian timber wolves in Yellowstone with the idea that wolves were an important missing link in the ecosystem. If you asked an economist about whether we should do this and, if so, how many wolves should be released, the answer would depend on marginal benefits and marginal costs. If the marginal benefits of wolf reintroduction exceed the marginal costs, reintroduce them. However, nobody asked economists that question and, in fact, with most environmental issues, nobody ever asks the economists. Indeed courts have even said the laws do not allow decision makers to look at the costs and benefits. If the law says clean it up, cleanup must occur regardless of costs. The simple fact is that the notion of marginal benefits and marginal costs and hence, the notion of efficiency, is not something on which most people focus. As my colleague, Rick Stroup, put it after working at the Department of Interior, "efficiency has no constituency."

But this does not necessarily mean that interested parties do not focus on the benefits and costs they face. Rather, the benefits and costs on which they focus depend on the hat they wear. Consider the view from under a cowboy hat. People with livestock thought that we had already reached the optimal number of wolves — zero — by putting a bounty on wolves and shooting them. From this view, why would you spend millions of dollars to undertake reintroduction?

Now consider the view from under the hunter's hat. From here the benefits and costs are a little bit tougher to determine, because the wolf may be a potential huntable species, in which case more wolves could provide benefits to hunters, or it could be a predator on big game animals such as elk, thus shifting the wolf to the cost side of the equation. Given that the politics make it unlikely that wolves are ... going to be hunted in the near future and that the rapid growth in the wolf population has taken a heavy toll on elk

---

[*] Copyright © 2004 by Case Western Reserve Law Review. Reprinted with permission.

numbers in and around Yellowstone, it is not surprising that hunters are increasingly concluding that the marginal costs of another wolf exceed the marginal benefits.

What about the people who wear the "Smokey the Bear" hat and manage Yellowstone? How do they perceive the benefits and costs? If you know anything about budgets for parks, you know that one of the driving factors in park budgets is visitors. And with wolves being reintroduced into Yellowstone, the number of visitors, especially in the winter, has increased. Furthermore, park managers now have larger budgets for doing research on wolves. And, believing that their mission is to maintain the Yellowstone ecosystem, they believe that wolf reintroduction restored the park to "a full complement of vertebrates." Therefore, for national park managers, the marginal benefits of wolf reintroduction are greater than the marginal costs.

And how do environmentalists perceive the benefits and costs? In the same way that ranchers see the costs as virtually infinite and the benefits as trivial, environmentalists see the benefits as virtually infinite and the costs as trivial. From this perspective, wolves should be allowed to increase with the only limit on wolf numbers coming from the size of the prey populations.

Not surprisingly the views from this array of hats has generated what author Hank Fischer called "wolf wars." Public policy regarding wolves has been acrimonious to say the least, and unfortunately such acrimony permeates environmental policy creating a gridlock at the federal level.

My purpose here is to suggest that there is an alternative to political environmentalism and that is free market environmentalism. To develop this concept, I begin by describing environmental policy since the 1970s and ask how well the political approach has worked. I then explain how and why free market environmentalism would be a better alternative.

POLITICAL ENVIRONMENTALISM

Consider some examples of how we have approached environmental policy since the early 1970s. When national forest lands were set aside in the early 1900s, the concern was that commercial logging would lead to a timber famine that could only be prevented by having public management of national forests for timber production and later some other multiple uses such as grazing and recreation. President Teddy Roosevelt got Gifford Pinchot, who knew a great deal about managing forests from his experiences in Germany, to fashion the U.S. Forest Service as an agency that would sustain timber production. For decades, there was not much controversy about how national forests should be managed. Maximum sustainable yield was the guiding principle and management was done mostly at the local level where forest rangers knew about growing conditions.

Over time, however, national forest management has gotten more controversial because there are many more voices coming from under many different hats other than those wearing hard hats and carrying chain saws. Take, for example, the issue of diseased and insect infested trees. Sustainable timber management would harvest these trees, but environmental interests would let nature take her course, letting the trees die and decay or burn.

From these latter demands came the Wilderness Act of 1964, which sailed through Congress with virtually no opposition. With no lands totally closed to commodity production and motorized vehicles, wilderness advocates called for wilderness designation of areas where people would "leave only footprints and take only pictures." At the time the Act passed, advocates called for 20 million acres, but since then we have set aside 120 million acres as official wilderness lands, and under President Clinton's roadless rule, added another 58 million acres that were not to be roaded.

It should come as no surprise that further wilderness designation is controversial. For people who want commodity production, roads for access, or trails for off-road-vehicles, the marginal costs of another acre of wilderness exceed the marginal benefits, and vice versa for wilderness advocates. When a wilderness bill was introduced in the Senate calling for an additional 3 million acres of wilderness in Montana, the incumbent senator from Montana lost his seat in his reelection bid mainly because he supported this bill.

And wilderness designation is not the only controversial part of forest management. Controversy abounds regarding whether the Forest Service is doing its job in terms of maintaining the quality of those forests. Wildfires dominate the news each summer in many western states with residents pointing fingers at the U.S. Forest Service for mismanagement. Recreational crowding is another problem. Hunters complain of too many people hunting on public lands, campers complain of insufficient camp spaces, and hikers complain of competition from mountain bikes, horses, and off-road-vehicles.

If all the acrimony over use were not enough, the budgetary losses raise many hackles and generate calls for an end to subsidies. Most of the fiscal focus is on losses generated by commodity production. For example, between 1994 and 1996, timber production on federal lands lost approximately $290 million per year and grazing lost $66 million per year.

* * *

Clearly, commodity production on federal lands does lose money, but consider the biggest money loser of all, recreation. Those of us who backpack, fish, hunt, camp, and picnic are the biggest pigs at the public land trough. For the years 1994 through 1996, recreation on federal lands lost $355 million per year. Our demands for trails, roads, campgrounds, signs, rescues—and the list goes on and on—cost money. And for the most part we pay nothing for our public land use. Given that we are getting something of great value for free, this is a real subsidy.

Let me turn to another example of political environmentalism, the Endangered Species Act. When the act was passed, the bald eagle was the poster child for passage. Here was the national bird going extinct, and no one was going to ask an economist to do a benefit cost analysis of whether it was worth saving. The Endangered Species Act, like the Wilderness Act, sailed through Congress and passed with people saying we have to stop destroying species. The act specifically prohibits "taking" a species. It was clear that this meant you could not deliberately kill an endangered species, but it was not clear whether you could eliminate habitat. Suppose, for example, I cut down trees that could provide habitat for the red-cockaded woodpecker, an endangered species that lives in the southeastern United States. Suppose that you know your neighbor cut down some pine trees that had woodpeckers living in them and was fined by the U.S. Fish and Wildlife Service. Now ask yourself this question: if woodpeckers have not moved onto your property but are close by, would you cut your trees sooner to eliminate the prospect of regulation under the ESA? Researchers examined this question empirically and found that, *ceteris paribus,* the average harvest on properties with no red-cockaded woodpeckers in a 25 mile radius was approximately 70 years; with 25 colonies in a 25 mile radius, the average age dropped to less than 40 years; and with over 400 colonies in a 25 mile radius, the average dropped to less than 20 years.

Water provides another prime example of the problems with political environmentalism. Starting in 1902 with passage of the Reclamation Act, the national government began building dams and water delivery systems. No thought was given to impacts on free-flowing rivers and salmon populations. The purpose of the Act was to "make the desert bloom like a rose" through subsidies to irrigators.

Consider the fiscal implications of these subsidies. After the federal government had spent a good deal of money building dams in the Uinta mountains of Utah, but had not completed the delivery system for the Central Utah Project, Orrin Hatch, the senator from Utah, asked the Senate to appropriate funds to complete the Project. Bill Bradley, the senator from New Jersey, called for the Congressional Budget Office to do a benefit-cost analysis. The CBO found that the marginal cost of delivering an acre foot of water (one foot of water covering one acre of land or approximately 325,000 gallons) to the farmers was about $300. When that water was put on the crops, mostly alfalfa, it was going to be worth less than $30 in added output. The farmers, however, would pay less than eight dollars for that water that would be worth $30 to them. Despite this analysis, the project went forward. This is not about efficiency; it is about politics. In fact, if you look at all the big federal projects in the West, you will be hard pressed to find one that passes benefit-cost muster and this does not include environmental costs.

Turning to pollution issues, Congress was quick to pass the Clean Air Act and the Clean Water Act in the early 1970s. Those acts cleared Congress with images of burning rivers and children not able to play outside. To be sure, air and water quality have improved, but no consideration is given to costs and benefits. And in some cases, environmental quality may have gotten worse.

Take the case of the Clean Air Act amendments of 1977. These amendments required that coal-fired power plants install scrubbers on their smoke stacks to reduce sulfur emissions. Bruce Ackerman and W.T. Hasler have explained that we could have had cleaner air by burning low sulfur western coal, but that eastern coal interests lobbied for scrubbers that were more costly and more polluting. Once scrubbers were required, dirtier eastern coal, which was cheaper, became the preferred fuel. The air is dirtier and electricity is more expensive thanks to political environmentalism.

FREE MARKET ENVIRONMENTALISM

The alternative I propose is free market environmentalism. For the most part, markets have been seen as the cause of environmental problems, not the solution. But free market environmentalism can be summarized in two points. The first, and the one that I think is increasingly understood, is that wealth makes a difference to environmentalism. Those of us with full stomachs, good clothes to wear, transportation, housing, medical care, education, and so on demand and get a cleaner environment. As Aaron Wildavsky, the late political scientist from Berkeley, liked to put it, "wealthier is healthier." The second point is quite simply, incentives matter. Or as a Montana rancher puts it, "if it pays, it stays."

Data increasingly support the first point. Economists have estimated the correlation between income and environmental quality and have consistently found that, although there may be an initial degradation of the environment as economic growth occurs, environmental quality eventually increases with income. For many environmental measures, the turning point is between a GDP of $4000 and $8000 per capita. For others, such as wilderness designation or net-carbon reductions, the turning point is much higher, but it still occurs. In his book, *The Skeptical Environmentalist,* Bjorn Lomborg plots GDP per capita by country against an index of environmental indicators. His data again support the point that rich countries such as the United States, Canada, or Japan have much cleaner environments than countries such as Ethiopia or Zimbabwe. Couple these data with the fact that market-based economies with property rights and a rule of law are more likely to have economic growth, and the case for free market environmentalism begins to take shape.

The second point is supported by numerous case studies. For example, in the East and the South, private landowners manage for land values other than just timber, and they do so at a profit. The International Paper Company's wildlife and recreation program is a prime example. International Paper employs specialists to oversee wildlife and recreation on its lands, including the 16,000-acre Southlands Experiment Forest located near Bainbridge, Georgia. At Southlands, researchers develop forest management practices that enhance wildlife populations as well as profits. White-tailed deer, turkeys, rabbits, bobwhite quail, mourning dove, and other species are beginning to reap the benefits of these new management techniques. Habitat is improved by controlled burning, buffer zones along streams, and tree-cutting practices that leave wildlife cover and plenty of forage.

According to company officials, investing in wildlife research and habitat production makes sound business sense. On its 1.2-million-acre mid-South region, which includes parts of Texas, Louisiana, and Arkansas, profits from hunting, hiking, fishing, and camping are an impressive 25 percent of total profits. By far the biggest revenue generator is the multiyear hunting lease. In early 1994, approximately 2,100 clubs paid from $2 to $5 per acre to lease company land for hunting. Between 1977 and 1998, recreational revenue rose from $300,000 to $5.5 million.

These returns from hunting leases paid dividends for wildlife as well as for the company. Populations of deer, turkey, fox, quail, and duck are up substantially since the program began. In addition, company biologists carry out an assortment of projects to help non-game species, from putting up bluebird boxes to protecting heron rookeries. Even though non-game species have no explicit market, hunters, campers, anglers, and hikers are willing to pay more for a diversified experience.

Return to the wolf example for more free market environmentalism at work. The growing list of entrepreneurial pragmatists in the environmental movement includes Hank Fischer, the former Northern Rockies director of Defenders of Wildlife. Having fought in the "wolf wars," Hank searched for a better alternative and came up with an insurance-like strategy to protect both wolves and ranchers. Wolves are viewed by ranchers in the same way that environmentalists view pollution; wolves reintroduced into Yellowstone National Park spill out of its borders and harm ranchers when they kill an occasional cow or sheep. To deal with this pollution problem, Defenders of Wildlife established its privately funded wolf compensation fund and offered to pay the ranchers for livestock losses due to wolf predation. Between its inception in 1987 and April 2000, the fund paid compensation totaling $109,476.77 to 111 ranchers in the area surrounding Yellowstone National Park, central Idaho, and northwestern Montana.

Clearly this insurance-type scheme is not perfect because it does not pay the rancher for the time spent proving that the animal was killed by wolves or for the cost of actually purchasing a replacement animal. According to Margaret Soulen Hinson, a sheep rancher in Idaho who was paid from the fund for sheep lost to wolves, "we would rather have no losses than compensation."

But given the highly emotional climate surrounding wolf reintroduction, imperfection is not surprising. And because ranchers' historic means of excluding wolves was to kill them, a system that compensates for the conflicting use of habitat—ranchers wanting land for grazing and environmentalists wanting it for wolves—moves wolf policy in the direction of negotiated settlements. Even Margaret Hinson recognizes that "it does make you more tolerant to participate in this program."

To further improve the program, Defenders of Wildlife established another fund to reward ranchers for allowing wolves to live on their private property. Hank Fischer recognized that the compensation program, at best, made ranchers neutral toward wolves; that is to say, with compensation, ranchers are not being asked to bear the full cost. By offering a reward to any rancher who has a wolf raise a litter of pups on private property, Defenders is trying to change the incentives. In the spring of 1994, a rancher near Augusta, Montana, collected a $5,000 reward from Defenders for having three wolf pups successfully raised on his property. The rancher told his cowboys to leave the wolves alone following advice from state and federal biologists about how to minimize human disturbance. By offering a reward to a rancher who allows the raising of wolves on his land, Defenders may be able to turn the liability of providing a public good into an asset.

To illustrate how free market environmentalism can work for pollution, consider the Tar-Pamlico area of North Carolina. In 1983, a serious fish kill occurred in Tar Pamlico Sound as a result of oxygen depletion caused by nutrients, mainly phosphates and nitrates. This happened despite the fact that The U.S. Environmental Protection Agency (EPA) and state authorities had set water quality discharge standards. All of the 26 regulated dischargers were in compliance with the standards. To improve water quality in the sound through tighter standards for point dischargers, the EPA estimated the cost to be from $860 to $7,861. The cost of reaching the nutrient goal by having farmers reduce their effluent ranged from $67 to $119 per pound. To move in the direction of lowering the costs, the Tar-Pamlico River Basin Association was formed in 1989. Recognizing that command and control was likely to make dischargers face the higher cost estimate, they suggested that its members help defray the cost to farmers of reducing their discharge. By doing it this way, instead of spending as much as $100 million to protect water quality, the cost was only around $10 million.

My final example is the CAMPFIRE program (the Communal Areas Management Programme for Indigenous Resources) in southern Africa. Entrepreneurs who understand the problems of wildlife management in southern Africa are working with the local communities and national governments to change the incentives faced by indigenous people on the communal lands. Between 60 and 80 percent of Africa's people live in rural areas, and the overwhelming majority of them barely scrape by with subsistence farming and ranching. The lands they use are communally owned, and the soils are often poor for growing crops or forage for cattle. These same lands that are marginal for agriculture, however, can provide excellent wildlife habitat. The problem is that sustainable wildlife populations have not meant sustainable human populations.

CAMPFIRE is an entrepreneurial approach to rural development based on the principle that the benefits from wildlife must go to those who pay the financial and social costs of coexisting with wild animals. The CAMPFIRE concept devolves the responsibility of managing wildlife to local communities that can profit from it.

The Nyaminyami District Council, with a human population of 35,000 and communal lands totaling 363,000 hectares, offers a prime example of how CAMPFIRE can work. In 1989, its inaugural years, Nyaminyami's CAMPFIRE project generated $108,800 from safari hunting and another $18,800 from culling to keep local wildlife populations under control. With the major capital costs of $80,773 covered by funds donated by conservation groups, the district had $6,400 to distribute among the twelve separate communities after paying operating and administrative costs and allocating 12 percent for capital investment and reserves. If these amounts seem small, realize that the average income per household was less than $100 per year in 1989.

* * *

CONCLUSION

These examples are not the result of environmentalists suddenly discovering the wisdom of Adam Smith in *The Wealth of Nations,* but are simply a matter of pragmatic people who probably do not know anything about economics, who probably do not know a lot about law, but who do know that, if you can get the incentives right, you are more likely to save some of the things that you want. Aldo Leopold, the author of the *Sand County Almanac,* clearly understood the importance of incentives when he said "Conservation will ultimately boil down to rewarding the private landowner who conserves the public interest."

This is not to say that there is no role for government and regulation. Regulations have helped improve the environment in some cases, but for the most part we have picked the low fruit from the tree. With the high fruit, i.e., high cost, left, we must find alternatives. If we wish to continue to improve the environment, ultimately we are going to have to turn the environment into an asset; make it something that people, who are the stewards, are rewarded for producing. As Leigh Perkins, owner of the Orvis Company and long-time conservationist, said in his biography, "as we move into this next century, the environmental movement will have to rely more and more on market solutions if we wish to conserve our precious natural resources." If we can do this, we can get more stewardship and environmental improvements with less acrimony.

Notes and Questions

1. Externalities and Residual Claims: Externalities exist because of poorly defined property rights, high transaction costs, or some combination of the two. What are the reasons for the externalities in the examples described by Anderson? In this regard, government ownership of natural resources looks a lot like poorly defined property rights — everyone owns the national forests, so no one owns them. This inherently makes the transaction costs too high for a private solution. So the government would appear to be the best solution to the problem. However, because government managers are not residual claimants, they do not have the incentive to maximize the value of the forest. Absent some objective way to measure their performance, government policies are particularly susceptible to political meddling.

2. Interest Groups and Environmental Protection: According to Anderson, what interest groups were involved in the controversy over whether to reintroduce wolves into Yellowstone National Park? Which interest groups were most successful? Is your conclusion consistent with the characteristics of successful interest groups described in Chapter III? What about the various "government failures" of environmental regulation cited by Anderson?

3. Market Failure Versus Government Failure: This chapter started by describing pollution as a classic example of an externality, a form of market failure often used to justify government regulation. It ends by discussing possible market solutions to government failure in the environmental arena. If "free market environmentalism" is such a good thing, why didn't the market preempt the need for government regulation in the first place? Are market-based solutions a substitute for, or a complement to, government regulation? What about property rights? Are we better able to assign and enforce property rights than we used to be? Or do we simply have a better appreciation of their importance?

Chapter V

Information Costs and Transaction Costs

In the theoretically ideal market, all mutually beneficial transactions occur and all gains from trade are realized because economists assume that markets operate without cost. For example, the assumption of zero information costs means that all potentially mutually beneficial transactions are identified by market participants. Similarly, the assumption of zero transaction costs means that no potential transactions are defeated by the cost of negotiating and enforcing contracts. Obviously, this is not an accurate depiction of the real world where there is a lot of friction that prevents the realization of all potential gains from trade. This chapter considers how market participants function when confronted with information costs and transaction costs.

Information is necessary to the proper functioning of any market. However, information is scarce and costly to obtain. Individuals invest in information until the expected marginal benefits of collecting additional information equal the marginal costs of collecting additional information. This suggests that, in many instances, individuals will act without complete information; that is, rational individuals will act when uncertain about the results of their action. The positive costs of information mean that individuals often gamble on their decision making.

In many instances, either the costs of collecting information or the costs of acting without complete information are trivial. This is especially true for frequently purchased products, such as individual food products in the grocery store. On the other hand, the technical characteristics of many goods and services make it very difficult (i.e., costly) for purchasers to gather the amount of information necessary to make satisfactory choices. For example, most purchasers do not possess the technical expertise to evaluate the quality of automobiles, washing machines, televisions, doctors, lawyers, and so forth. Because mistakes in the purchasing of such goods and services can be very expensive, consumers gather information from numerous sources, including sales staff, *Consumer Reports*, as well as friends and relatives. Moreover, sellers attempt to convey information to consumers by developing reputations for providing the level of quality that the consumer desires.

Transaction costs are the out-of-pocket and opportunity costs of negotiating, drafting, and enforcing contracts. Transaction costs can frustrate potential mutually beneficial market transactions—i.e., contracts—and cause firms to take the transaction away from the market by moving the gains from trade inside the firm. Contract law is a system of rules for enforcing promises. It demonstrates the extent to which our society allows people to make promises or commitments that are legally binding, and the legal consequences of failure by one party to perform as promised. Transaction costs—primarily negotiation and enforcement costs—increase the costs of exchange and thus decrease the number of mutually beneficial exchanges. Contract law reduces transaction costs by imposing external rules that create rights and duties for each party to the exchange and provides remedies in the event that the duties are breached. Instantaneous exchanges, such as the purchase of a Diet Coke from a street vendor, occur without any assistance from contract law. Thus, contract law is most important in situations where the negotiations are not immediately followed by simultaneous performances on both sides of the transaction.

Of course, voluntary, mutually beneficial exchanges also take place in the absence of contract law. Continued dealing with the same parties reduces negotiation costs and increases the likelihood that a contract will be performed in good faith. One may seek to reduce transaction costs by limiting his or her trading partners to only those who have a reputation for honesty and fair dealing. In a sense, therefore, the market controls dishonest and unfair behavior by reducing the demand for the goods and services provided by dishonest and unfair traders. That is, market adjustments act as an enforcement mechanism against dishonest and unfair practices.

Contract law reduces transaction costs in a number of ways. First, contract law enforces contract terms by imposing costs—typically in the form of a court ordering the payment of damages—on parties who breach their promises. For example, contract law enforces an agreed upon allocation of risk after the occurrence of a contingency that may make performance appear unattractive to one of the parties. Second, the common law of contracts provides a number of standard form, off-the-rack, contractual provisions that specify the basic details and fill gaps in negotiated contracts. Unless contradicted by the explicit terms of a contract, the common law rules are an implied part of all contracts. This reduces transaction costs by allowing contracting parties to form enforceable contracts without having to specify every standard of performance and without having to negotiate the allocation of risk associated with every conceivable contingency. All executory contracts face the risk of disruption due to totally unanticipated contingencies—circumstances with which the contract cannot deal because the contracting parties don't know what might occur—and contract law provides the basic rules to deal with various contingencies. Third, contract law discourages careless contracting by penalizing behavior which induces other parties to act in reliance on the first party's actions or representations. In effect, this saves transaction costs by allowing contracting parties to rely on the other party's actions without having to worry about what information the other party really means to convey.

Contract law produces the greatest reduction in transaction costs if the off-the-rack contract rules supplied by contract law mimic the agreements for which most contracting parties would bargain if negotiation costs were zero. For example, if every contracting party would agree that payment should be in U.S. dollars, it is clear that negotiation costs can be reduced by making such a term an implicit part of every contract. This bargaining principle provides an analytical framework for analyzing the rules of contract law, as well as other substantive areas of law such as corporation law and bankruptcy.

In applying the bargaining principle, it is essential to recognize that **freedom of contract** is an overriding philosophy of contract law. The contracting parties are almost always able to contract around the off-the-rack rules when they decide that it is in their interest to do so. Conceptually, if the benefits of altering the standard form rules are greater than the transaction costs of contracting, then the parties are made better off through modification of the standard contract rules. The philosophy of freedom of contract also explains why the common law of contracts is likely to be efficient in the sense that it comes close to satisfying the bargaining principle. Inefficient contract rules will not be used because contracting parties will contract around them until the courts recognize that the old default rules should be abandoned due to disuse.

Section A presents an overview of market and contractual responses to asymmetric information. Section B introduces agent-principal contracting and the economics of monitoring performance. Section C goes into greater detail about the costs of using markets to coordinate economic activity and the contractual arrangements that have evolved to control transaction costs. Finally, Section D applies the agency perspective to the issue of corporate governance and examines how market forces resolve some of the conflicts between managers and shareholders in large, publicly held corporations.

A. Asymmetric Information and Market Responses

Consumers frequently do not know how quality varies across brands of products or services. There is asymmetric information: one party (usually the seller) to a transaction knows a material fact (the quality of the good or service) that the other party (usually the buyer) does not know. At first glance, the phenomenon of asymmetric information appears to present sellers with the opportunity to exploit buyers. However, further analysis reveals that asymmetric information can be a major problem for the seller.

1. The Market for "Lemons"

The used car market is a nice vehicle (pun intended) for illustrating this point. Assume that Paige wants to sell her 2012 Ford Mustang GT. Paige has perfect information about the quality of her car—she is the original owner of the car; she has been a careful, non-abusive driver; she has followed all routine maintenance procedures; the car has not required any major repairs; and in sum, she knows that the car is in great condition. However, it is well known that (1) some Mustang GTs have had serious problems requiring numerous major repairs; and (2) many owners of Mustang GTs drive them hard and fast. Unfortunately for both Paige and the potential buyers of 2012 Ford Mustang GTs, it is very difficult for potential buyers to distinguish between Paige's "cream puff" and the "lemons" lurking in the market. At best, potential buyers know the probability of getting a good car.

If buyers cannot distinguish between good and bad used cars, all used 2012 Mustang GTs sell for the same price (assuming they have the same mileage). As a result, bad cars are overvalued and good cars are undervalued. But this is not the end of the analysis. Because Paige knows that she has a good car, she is not going to sell it at a market price that undervalues her car. Moreover, the owners of bad cars are encouraged to sell their cars because the market overvalues bad cars. This phenomenon is referred to as **adverse selection**: the only sellers who select to participate in the market are the ones who benefit from the asymmetric information. As more bad cars are offered for sale and fewer good cars are offered, the market price is forced downward to reflect the increasing probability that any given buyer will end up with a lemon. The bad cars drive out the good cars, and there is no market for good used cars. The lemons sour the market.

Obviously, the "lemons market" phenomenon has the potential to destroy markets whenever there is asymmetric information. Both sellers and buyers, who see potential mutually-beneficial exchanges frustrated, have incentives to solve the lemons problem.

Paige, for example, could show her maintenance records (and even her driving record) to potential buyers. However, many buyers will remain suspicious of the quality of her information. Used car dealers attempt to solve the lemons problem by offering warranties on "certified pre-owned cars." Numerous alternative mechanisms for solving problems associated with asymmetric information are discussed in this section.

2. Adverse Selection and Insurance Contracts

The "lemons market" phenomenon poses a particularly challenging problem in insurance markets because the parties wishing to purchase insurance often know much more about their own particular circumstances than it is possible for insurers to know. For example, individuals who apply for health insurance know their own health record and tendency towards risky behavior and may be able to conceal important information from insurers. The asymmetric information can lead to adverse selection in the insurance pool, as high risk individuals find insurance to be a good deal for themselves but low risk individuals decide to forego insurance coverage. Thus, the selection of people who purchase insurance is not a normal, random sample of the population, but rather includes some people with private information about their personal situations that increases the likelihood they will receive a higher than average level of benefit under the insurance policy. For example, high risk patients (e.g., cancer-prone, drug users, etc.) apply to insurance companies while young healthy persons do not. As more high risk individuals purchase insurance, higher payouts by insurance companies will force them to raise rates which, in turn, makes the insurance less attractive to low risk individuals. Insurance companies, of course, are well aware of this potential and devote a great deal of effort to avoiding adverse selection. For example, life insurance companies and health insurance companies attempt to control the riskiness of their insurance pools by requiring applicants to answer detailed questions, like whether they enjoy extreme sports, on the application form and to undergo medical examinations. Insurance companies set limits on pre-existing conditions, through either limited coverage or higher premiums for the additional risk. Chapter VI on risk includes a detailed discussion of the economics of insurance.

3. Reputational Bonds and Other Market Mechanisms for Disclosing Information About Quality

Consumers are understandably concerned about the quality of the products and services that they purchase in the market. This concern presents a problem for sellers of high-quality products and services because some consumers are not going to pay for quality unless they are assured that they will receive it. Many sellers respond to this problem by offering warranties, guarantees, and follow-up services. Sellers also invest in developing a reputation for high quality products and services. A reputation is an important asset of a seller but it is also very fragile because it can be quickly destroyed by the seller failing to live up to the expectations generated by the reputation. Imagine the damage done to the reputation of Ikea in 2013 when horsemeat was found in the retailers' Swedish meatballs and wiener sausages. Indeed, because the reputational asset can be destroyed by the firm's own behavior, it is very similar to a performance bond. Thus, a forfeitable reputational bond assures consumers that they will get what they bargained for. This is just one of many examples of how firms attempt to solve information problems in the market.

The Role of Market Forces in Assuring Contractual Performance

Benjamin Klein & Keith Leffler

89 Journal of Political Economy 615 (1981)

I. Introduction

An implicit assumption of the economic paradigm of market exchange is the presence of a government to define property rights and enforce contracts. An important element of the legal-philosophical tradition upon which the economic model is built is that without some third-party enforcer to sanction stealing and reneging, market exchange would be impossible. But economists also have long considered "reputations" and brand names to be private devices which provide incentives that assure contract performance in the absence of any third-party enforcer. This private-contract enforcement mechanism relies upon the value to the firm of repeat sales to satisfied customers as a means of preventing non-performance. . . .

This paper examines the nongovernmental repeat-purchase contract-enforcement mechanism. To isolate this force, we assume throughout our analysis that contracts are not enforceable by the government or any other third party. Transactors are assumed to rely solely on the threat of termination of the business relationship for enforcement of contractual promises.[1] This assumption is most realistic for contractual terms concerning difficult-to-measure product characteristics such as the "taste" of a hamburger. However, even when the aspects of a contract are less complicated ... and performance more easily measurable by a third party such as a judge, specification, litigation, and other contract-enforcement costs may be substantial. Therefore, explicit guarantees to replace or repair defective goods (warranties) are not costless ways to assure contract performance. Market arrangements, such as the value of lost repeat purchases, which motivate transactors to honor their promises may be the cheapest method of guaranteeing the guarantee. . . . [O]ur approach is general in the sense that the value of future exchanges can motivate fulfillment of all types of contractual promises. . . .

In Section II, the conditions are outlined under which firms will either honor their commitments to supply a high level of quality or choose to supply a quality lower than promised. In order to emphasize the ability of markets to guarantee quality in the absence of any government enforcement mechanism, a simple model is presented which assumes that consumers costlessly communicate among one another. Therefore, if a firm cheats and supplies to any individual a quality of product less than contracted for, all consumers in the market learn this and all future sales are lost. A major result of our analysis is that even such perfect interconsumer communication conditions are not sufficient to assure high quality supply. Cheating will be prevented and high quality products will be supplied only if firms are earning a continual stream of rental income that will be lost if low quality output is deceptively produced. The present discounted value of this rental stream must be greater than the one-time wealth increase obtained from low quality production.

This condition for the "notorious firm" repeat-purchase mechanism to assure high quality supply is not generally fulfilled by the usual free-entry, perfectly competitive

---

1. This assumption is consistent with the pioneering work of Macaulay (1963), where reliance on formal contracts and the threat of explicit legal sanctions was found to be an extremely rare element of interfirm relationships. Macaulay provides some sketchy evidence that business firms prevent non-fulfillment of contracts by the use of effective nonlegal sanctions consisting primarily of the loss of future business. This "relational" nature of contracts has been recently emphasized by Macneil (1974). . . .

equilibrium conditions of price equal to marginal and average cost. It becomes necessary to distinguish between production costs that are "sunk" firm-specific assets and those production costs that are salvageable (i.e., recoverable) in uses outside the firm. Our analysis implies that firms will not cheat on promises to sell high quality output only if [the] price is sufficiently above salvageable production costs. [That is, the price of the product must be sufficiently high to assure profits above those that can be recovered by liquidating the assets to assure high quality.] While the perfectly competitive price may imply such a margin above salvageable costs, this will not necessarily be the case. The fundamental theoretical result of this paper is that market prices above the competitive price and the presence of nonsalvageable capital are means of enforcing quality promises.

In Section III our theoretical model (of quality-guaranteeing price premiums above salvageable costs) is extended to examine how the capital value of these price-premium payments can be dissipated in a free-entry equilibrium. The quality-guaranteeing nature of nonsalvageable, firm-specific capital investments is developed. Alternative techniques of minimizing the cost to consumers of obtaining a high quality product are investigated. We also explore market responses to consumer uncertainty about quality-assuring premium levels. Advertising and other production and distribution investments in "conspicuous" assets are examined as competitive responses to simultaneous quality and production-cost uncertainties. Finally, a summary of the analysis and some concluding remarks are presented in Section IV.

II. Price Premiums and Quality Assurance

* * *

Intuitively, the quality-assuring price treats the potential value of not producing minimum quality as an explicit opportunity cost to the firm of higher quality production. Hence the quality-assuring price must not only compensate the firm for the increased average production costs incurred when quality above that detectable prior to purchase is produced, but must also yield a normal rate of return on the foregone gains from exploiting consumer ignorance. This price "premium" stream can be thought of as "protection money" paid by consumers to induce high quality contract performance. Although the present discounted value of this stream equals the value of the short-run gain the firm can obtain by cheating, consumers are not indifferent between paying the "premium" over time or permitting the firm to cheat. The price "premium" is a payment for high quality [rather than spending time and energy determining quality before purchase]. The relevant consumer choice is between demanding minimum quality output at a perfectly competitive (costless information) price or paying a competitive price "premium," which is both necessary and sufficient, for higher quality output.

* * *

III. Competitive Market Equilibrium: Firm-specific Capital Investments

Our analysis has focused on the case where costless information (perfectly competitive) prices do not imply sufficient firm-specific rents to motivate high quality production. A price premium was therefore necessary to induce high quality supply ....

A. Brand Name Capital Investments

Competition to dissipate the economic profits ... involves *firm-specific capital* expenditures. This firm-specific capital competition motivates firms to purchase assets with (nonsalvageable) costs equal to the capital value of the premium rental stream earned when high quality is supplied at the quality-assuring price.... Such firm-specific capital costs could, for example, take the form of sunk investments in the design of a firm logo or an expensive sign promoting the firm's name. Expenditures on these highly firm-specific assets are then said to represent brand name (or selling) capital investments.

* * *

If the firm decides to cheat it will experience a capital loss equal to its anticipated future profit stream.... That is, the market value of the competitive firm's brand name capital is equal to the value of total specific or "sunk" selling costs made by the firm which, in turn, equals the present value of the anticipated premium stream from high quality output....

What assures high quality supply is the capital loss ... of future business if low quality is produced. Since the imputed value of the firm's brand name capital is determined by the firm's expected quasi rents on future sales, this capital loss from supplying quality lower than promised is represented by the depreciation of this firm-specific asset. [As direct profits are gained from lower quality goods they are offset by indirect losses in the form of lost reputation.] The expenditures on brand name capital assets are therefore similar to collateral that the firm loses if it supplies output of less than anticipated quality and in equilibrium the premium stream provides only a normal rate of return on this collateral asset.

* * *

C. Consumer Cost Uncertainty: A Role for Advertising

The discussion to this point has assumed complete consumer knowledge of firms' costs of producing alternative quality outputs and knowledge of the extent to which any capital production costs or brand name capital selling costs are salvageable. This knowledge is necessary and sufficient to accurately calculate both the quality-guaranteeing premium and price. However, consumers are generally uncertain about cost conditions and therefore do not know the minimum quality-guaranteeing price with perfect accuracy. In fact, consumers cannot even make perfect anticipated quality rankings across firms on the basis of price. That one firm has a higher price than another may indicate a larger price premium or, alternatively, more inefficient production. In this section, we examine how the more realistic assumption of consumer cost uncertainty influences market responses to prepurchase quality uncertainty.

We have shown that increases in the price premium over average recoverable cost generally increase the relative returns from production of promised (high) quality rather than deceptive minimum (low) quality. The existence of a high price premium also makes expenditures on brand name capital investments economically feasible. The magnitude of brand name capital investments in turn indicates the magnitude of the price premium. When a consumer is uncertain about the cost of producing a particular high quality level of output and therefore the required quality-assuring premium, information about the actual level of the price premium will provide information about the probability of receiving high quality. If consumers are risk averse, this uncertainty about receiving anticipated high or deceptively low quality output will increase the premium that will be paid. The premium will include both a (presumably unbiased) estimate of the quality-assuring premium and an extra payment to reduce the risk of being deceived.

... Implicit information about the sufficiency of price as a guarantee can be supplied by "conspicuous" specific asset expenditures. Luxurious storefronts and ornate displays or signs may be supplied by a firm even if yielding no direct consumer service flows. Such firm-specific assets inform consumers of the magnitude of sunk capital costs ... and hence the opportunity cost to the firm if it cheats. Both the informational services and the direct utility producing services of assets are now relevant considerations for a firm in deciding upon the most valuable form the brand name capital investment should take.

The value of information about the magnitude of a firm's specific or "sunk" capital cost, and therefore the magnitude of the price premium, is one return from advertising. Indeed, the role of premiums as quality guarantors provides foundation for Nelson's (1974) argument that advertising, by definition, supplies valuable information to consumers—namely, information that the firm is advertising. A sufficient investment in advertising implies that a firm will not engage in short-run quality deception since the advertising indicates a nonsalvageable cost gap between price and production costs. [T]hat is, the existence of a price premium. This argument essentially reverses Nelson's logic. It is not that it pays a firm with a "best buy" to advertise more, but rather that advertising implies the supply of "best buys," or more correctly, the supply of promised high quality products. Advertising does not directly "signal" the presence of a "best buy," but "signals" the presence of firm-specific selling costs and therefore the magnitude of the price premium. We would therefore expect, ceteris paribus, a positive correlation not between advertising intensity and "best buys," as Nelson claims, but between advertising intensity and the extent of quality that is costly to determine prepurchase.

Conspicuous sunk costs such as advertising are, like all sunk costs, irrelevant in determining future firm behavior regarding output quality. However, consumers know that such sunk costs can be profitable only if the future quasi rents are large. In particular, ... a price premium on future sales sufficient to prevent cheating is estimated to exist....

Our theory also suggests why endorsements by celebrities and other seemingly "noninformative" advertising such as elaborate (obviously costly to produce) commercials, sponsorships of telethons, athletic events, and charities are valuable to consumers. In addition to drawing attention to the product, such advertising indicates the presence of a large sunk "selling" cost and the existence of a price premium. And because the crucial variable is the consumers' estimate of the stock of advertising capital (and not the flow), it also explains why firms advertise that they have advertised in the past (e.g., "as seen on 'The Tonight Show'"). Rather than serving a direct certifying function (e.g., as recommended by *Good Housekeeping* magazine), information about past advertising informs consumers about the magnitude of the total brand name capital investment.

Firms may also provide valuable information by publicizing the large fees paid to celebrities for commercials. Information about large endorsement fees would be closely guarded if the purpose were to simulate an "unsolicited endorsement" of the product's particular quality characteristics rather than to indicate the existence of a price premium. Viewed in this context, it is obviously unnecessary for the celebrity to actually use the particular brand advertised. This is contrary to a recent FTC ruling (see Federal Trade Commission 1980).

This analysis of advertising implies that consumers necessarily receive something when they pay a higher price for an advertised brand. An expensive name brand aspirin, for example, is likely to be better than unadvertised aspirin because it is expensive. The advertising of the name brand product indicates the presence of a current and future price premium. This premium on future sales is the firm's brand name capital which will be lost if the firm supplies lower than anticipated quality. Therefore, firms selling more highly advertised, higher priced products will necessarily take more precautions in production.[2]

---

2. The greater is the cost to consumers of obtaining deceptively low quality, the greater will be the demand for quality assurance. The very low market share of "generic" children's aspirin (1 percent) vis-à-vis generic's share of the regular aspirin market (7 percent) is consistent with this implication.

* * *

IV. Conclusion

… We have analyzed the generally unrecognized importance of increased market prices and nonsalvageable capital as possible methods of making quality promises credible. We obviously do not want to claim that consumers "know" this theory in the sense that they can verbalize it but only that they behave in such a way as if they recognize the forces at work. They may, for example, know from past experience that when a particular type of investment is present such as advertising they are much less likely to be deceived. Therefore, survivorship of crude decision rules over time may produce consumer behavior very similar to what would be predicted by this model without the existence of explicit "knowledge" of the forces we have examined.

Our analysis implies that consumers can successfully use price as an indicator of quality. We are not referring to the phenomenon of an ignorant consumer free riding on the information contained in the market price paid by other more informed buyers but rather to the fact that consumer knowledge of a gap between firm price and salvageable costs, that is, the knowledge of the existence of a price premium, supplies quality assurance. …

* * *

We do not wish to suggest that use of implicit (price premium-specific investment) contracts is always the cheapest way to assure quality supply. When quality characteristics can be specified cheaply and measured by a third party, and hence contract enforcement costs are anticipated to be low, explicit contractual solutions with governmentally enforced penalties (including warranties) may be a less costly solution. When explicit contract costs are high and the extent of short-run profit from deceptively low quality supply and hence the quality-assuring price premium is also high, governmental specification and enforcement of minimum quality standards may be an alternative method of reducing the costs of assuring the supply of high quality products.

* * *

… More generally, however, all market transactions, including those "within" the firm such as employer-employee agreements, consist of a combination of the two basic forms of contractual arrangements. Some elements of performance will be specified and enforced by third-party sanctions and other elements enforced without invoking the power of some outside party to the transaction but merely by the threat of termination of the transactional relationship.

* * *

Notes and Questions

1. A Price Premium for Being a Hostage: The Klein-Leffler analysis claims that price premiums are quality guaranteeing because the present value of the price premiums is a return on a firm-specific, non-salvageable investment. If the firm does not produce the promised quality, it will lose the price premium and go out of business. The firm-specific investment will be lost. The firm effectively holds itself hostage by promising to "fall on the sword" if it does not perform as promised. Consumers are convinced of the value of

---

Many individuals who claim "all aspirin is alike" apparently pay the extra price for their children where the costs of lower quality are greater and therefore quality assurance is considered more important.

the guarantee. Try to come up with examples of these types of investments. Start, perhaps, by looking at law firms.

2. Reputation as a Bonding Mechanism: Individuals or businesses invest in developing their reputation for good-faith performance, high-quality workmanship, etc. These investments take time and cost money, and they are very valuable assets. If a business develops a good reputation, it can purchase supplies on more favorable terms and charge higher prices to customers. However, if the business then starts acting in a manner inconsistent with the reputation, the business reputation is forfeited. In other words, reputation is a forfeitable performance bond—if the business fails to perform as promised, it is penalized in the market. The potential penalty not only gives firms the incentive to perform, it also saves transaction costs by allowing contracting parties to rely on less formal contractual arrangements when dealing with a more reputable firm.

3. Advertising as "Collateral": Klein and Leffler state that a celebrity does not have to use the product to show the existence of a price premium. If that is the case, do companies need celebrities at all or will other large public expenditures also show their dedication to high quality?

4. Is Advertising "Good" or "Bad" for Consumers?: **Advertising** is defined as any communication that businesses offer customers in an effort to increase demand for their products. No subject in the economics of market structure—industrial-organization economics—has been debated as intensively as advertising. Some economists consider advertising to be wasteful or "self-canceling," while others consider it to be evidence of the presence of vigorous competition. One of the primary sources of debate among economists has been over the information content of advertising. Critics of advertising argue that most ads are tasteless, wasteful assaults on consumers' senses and that it creates illusory differences between products that are actually very close substitutes for one another. In this view, advertising is not productive because it merely allocates demand among competing firms producing goods that are fundamentally alike. On the other hand, defenders of advertising argue that it offers real information about products and their characteristics (including their prices). The provision of such information lowers the consumers' cost of searching for goods, and permits consumers to make a rational choice among competing goods. Moreover, the Klein-Leffler excerpt argues that the very fact that a firm is advertising (that is, investing in a firm-specific non-salvageable asset) conveys important information to consumers. Regardless of one's position on the value of nonfraudulent information, almost all economists would accept the proposition that false advertising is socially wasteful. In fact, all of the questionable criticisms of nonfraudulent advertising are valid criticisms of false advertising. False advertising is not only socially wasteful, but it also harms consumers by inducing them to purchase goods and services that they might otherwise not purchase. Moreover, it harms competing producers who lose potential customers to the fraudulent advertiser.

5. Search Costs and the Economics of Advertising: As discussed in Chapter IX, in the perfect competition model, firms are price takers. If one firm raises its price above the equilibrium price, it loses all of its customers. In most markets, however, buyers have limited information. When a store raises its price, many buyers may not realize that the product is cheaper elsewhere, so the store may lose only some of its customers. Similarly, when a store reduces its price, many people may continue to buy from higher-priced competitors because the consumers have not learned about the price cut. Firms face downward-sloping demand curves when buyers have limited information about prices. A buyer with limited information may search for the best price. This search for a lower price or better products has costs (of time, travel, phone calls, and so forth). Search costs are the time and money costs of obtaining information about prices and products. The optimal amount of search occurs when the expected marginal benefit of searching (the expected benefit of trying one more store) equals its expected marginal cost. Because of search costs, it is perfectly rational for people to pay a high price when they are reasonably sure that a lower price is available. In most instances, people do not know which stores charge high prices. They must learn from experience and from other sources, such as talking with friends about the expected benefits of searching and paying attention to advertising.

6. The Distribution of Prices: Some buyers know more about prices than others. Tourists, for example, have less information than local residents about which stores charge higher prices. Moreover, it may be costly for tourists to acquire that information. For that reason, tourists are more likely to buy products at high-priced stores. When some customers have better information than others, a distribution of prices can exist even in very competitive markets. Informed consumers go to low-priced stores. Some uninformed consumers go to the low-priced stores by chance, but others buy from high-priced stores because they do not know that other stores offer lower prices.

7. Better Information Reduces Prices: As consumers acquire better information about prices, they pay lower prices on average. With better information, more buyers go to low-priced stores and fewer to high-priced stores, which in turn gives high-priced stores the incentive to reduce their prices. Better information can reduce prices even if all consumers are not equally informed because the information improves their own estimates about which stores charge lower prices.

8. Search Costs Versus Advertising Costs: Evaluate the following statement: "If it were not cheaper for sellers to provide the information in lieu of having consumers search for it, some sellers would cease to advertise and would lower their prices by more than the cost to consumers of getting the information. Non-advertising sellers could then drive out of the market those sellers who continued to advertise. This, of course, has not happened."

B. Monitoring Contractual Performance: Agent-Principal Contracting

Specialization and comparative advantage mean that individuals often find it desirable to hire someone to engage in activities on their behalf. In the jargon of the law-and-economics literature, a **principal** hires an **agent** to do something on his or her behalf. People hire a general contractor to build their house, a real estate agent to sell their house, and a stock broker to buy and sell stocks for them. Shareholders hire managers (officers and directors) to run their corporations. Citizens elect legislators to represent their interests. Professors hire publishing companies to publish their books, and so forth.

These principal-agent contracts are usually executory in the sense that performance takes place some period of time after the agency relationship is created. In order to make sure that the agent does what he has agreed to do, the principal must monitor the agent's performance. This monitoring involves at least three types of costs. First, the principal incurs information costs because information about the agent's performance is scarce and costly to obtain. Second, there are opportunity costs because the principal must spend some time monitoring the agent. Third, the principal often lacks the specialized knowledge to determine whether the agent is in fact doing what he promised to do. In addition to these monitoring costs, there are **agency costs**, which are the costs associated with the agent's ability not to act in the principal's best interest. Agency costs include the costs to the principal of the agent not acting as promised plus the costs incurred by the principal to prevent the agent from deviating from the promised action. Like all economic decisions, the principal has the incentive to monitor his or her agent's behavior up to the point where the marginal cost of additional monitoring is equal to the expected marginal benefit from ensuring that the agent behaves according to their agreement. The existence of positive monitoring costs means that the principal will make a rational decision not to attempt to monitor all of the agent's actions.

Positive monitoring costs also means that the agent knows that there is a range of activity in which the agent can shirk, or not perform as promised, with little concern about repercussions. Moreover, this incentive to shirk is often exacerbated by the existence of more immediate incentive conflicts between the best interests of the principal and the best interests of the agent. **Agent-principal conflicts** arise when the agent's incentives are not aligned with the principal's interests. Specifically, when the agent acting on behalf of the principal bears costs that the principal does not bear, or when the agent receives benefits that the principal does not receive, the divergence between costs and benefits is likely to drive a wedge between what is best for the agent and what is best for the principal.

Attorney-client relationships are fraught with potential agent-principal conflicts. Consider the situation of a personal injury lawyer working under a contingent fee. Assume that the client, Charles, has retained the lawyer, Sue, to represent him in a case involving the alleged wrongful death of his wife. Sue is to receive 33.33% of any amount recovered through settlement, trial, or appeal. Sue is an experienced litigator, and she has determined that their chances for success depend on the amount of time and effort that Sue (and her team of associates, clerks, and paralegals) devotes to the case. The defendant's insurance company is pushing for a negotiated settlement prior to trial. The settlement offer is tempting for Sue because one-third of the proposed offer is a guaranteed fee for the firm—it is the proverbial "bird in the hand"—while a potentially larger recovery is speculative and will require much more work by her team. Nevertheless, Sue believes that the additional effort by her team will increase both the dollar amount of future settlement offers and the potential amount awarded after the trial. On the other hand, Sue's continued prosecution of the case involves considerable opportunity cost— her practice is booming and continued work on Charles's case takes her away from other profitable opportunities. Charles is interested only in maximizing his expected value of recovery.

The potential agent-principal conflict can be demonstrated diagrammatically. In Figure V-1(a), expected value of recovery (EVR) is shown on the vertical axis and Sue's effort (a proxy for the effort of her litigation team) on the horizontal axis. The EVR curve begins at level S because the settlement amount (S) can be recovered without any additional effort. The EVR curve then increases at an increasing rate, but eventually increases at an decreasing rate as the law of diminishing marginal returns sets in, and ultimately begins to decline at E_C. Charles would prefer, and probably expects, Sue to use effort level E_C. However, Sue's incentives are different because she must bear the marginal costs of additional effort by her team. In order to demonstrate this, we need to transform the EVR curve (which depicts *total* EVR) into a marginal curve, MEVR, which is shown in Figure V-1(b).

Now, consider Sue's decision. Assume, for convenience, that Sue's team has constant marginal costs, or MC_S, in Figure V-1(b). On the margin, Sue expects to recover one-third of Charles' MEVR. In Figure V-1(b), this is shown as $MEVR_S$. Sue will continue

Figure V-1(a). Agent-Principal Conflict

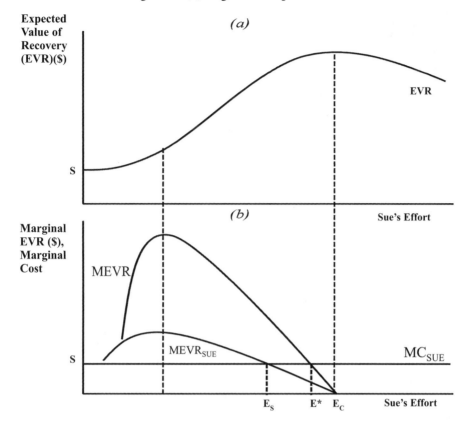

devoting effort to this case up to the effort level where her marginal expected value of recovery, $MEVR_S$, is equal to her marginal cost, MC_S. Note that the level of effort that maximizes Sue's EVR is E_S.

The agent-principal conflict is clear. Charles wants Sue to work up to E_C, while Sue wants to work up to E_S. Sue's marginal cost drives a wedge between what is best for her principal and what is best for her team.

At one level of analysis, principal-agent conflicts are simply contracting problems. Informed parties can recognize the potential for conflict and write detailed contracts that specify the precise terms of the principal-agent relationship. For example, Charles could include a clause in his agreement with Sue that requires Sue to act as if her marginal costs were zero. Alternatively, Charles and Sue could negotiate a cost sharing arrangement such that one-third of the MC is paid by Sue and two-thirds is paid by Charles. Arrangements such as these move both parties to E^*, where the combined MEVR equals their combined MC. However, negotiating, writing, and enforcing those contracts is a costly endeavor. For example, consider the difficulty of negotiating a contract that allocates a portion of the law firm's overhead costs to this specific case. Because of those transaction costs, not all agency costs will be addressed in the contract.

At another level of analysis, agent-principal conflicts are resolved because the anticipated shirking affects the contract price and, thus, agents have incentives to take steps that convince principals that they will not shirk. Agents who develop a reputation of "going the extra mile" for their principals will likely be more highly valued in the market.

Manufacturers of some types of goods likewise face agency costs when they attempt to distribute their output through separately owned distribution networks. The basic problem is the best interests of the distributors and retailers who handle the manufacturer's goods will not always coincide with the manufacturer's best interests. This conflict of interest presents opportunities for dealers to take opportunistic "free rides" to the detriment of manufacturers.

Whenever the demand for a particular product is positively related to the amount of point-of-sale and post-sale services provided, there exists the possibility of transaction failures caused by free riding. An automobile dealership illustrates the provision of these types of services. The typical dealership provides an elaborate showroom, a trained sales force, large amounts of local advertising, a substantial inventory, and a parts department. Of course, these services are costly for dealers to provide. A dealer (dealer X), therefore, would incur these costs only if there was a reasonable expectation of a larger market share and higher profits. The potential for opportunistic behavior will take the form of dealers "free riding" on the service efforts of other dealers. In other words, dealers will not have the incentive to provide the necessary services when they know that the demand for the product has been increased by the service efforts of other dealers of the same brand.

Consider what would happen if another dealer (dealer Y) selling the same brand, but not providing services, opens a dealership across the street from dealer X. As a result, some of the benefits of X's provision of services will flow to Y, and X's expected return on services will not be realized. Since Y does not provide point-of-sale and post-sale services, his lower costs will enable him to charge a lower price for automobiles. The rational consumer will take advantage of X's showroom services and then cross the street and purchase his car from Y. Clearly, Y is taking a "free ride" on X's provision of services.

A transaction failure, an overall degeneration in the provision of services, is caused by this intrabrand free-riding behavior. Since X does not capture the benefits of providing services, he will not do so. This reduction in the provision of point-of-sale services, a transaction failure, reduces sales and thus reduces the manufacturer's profits. Consumers are also harmed because they are denied access to valuable services for which they would have been willing to pay. See Leegin Creative Leather Prods., Inc. v. PSKS, Inc., 551 U.S. 877 (2007), *infra*, Chapter IX, and accompanying Notes and Questions.

C. Opportunism: Market and Contractual Solutions

Opportunism has been defined as "self-interest seeking with guile." *See* Oliver E. Williamson, *Transaction-Cost Economics: The Governance of Contractual Relations*, 22 Journal of Law & Economics 233, 234 n.3 (1979). In more technical terms, opportunism occurs when one party to a transaction recognizes that the other party cannot economically retaliate against post-contractual manipulation of the terms of trade, and then engages in such manipulation in order to effectuate an unexpected transfer of wealth from the other party to himself.

Two examples illustrate the basic phenomenon of opportunistic behavior. First, consider a plaintiff's attorney in a private antitrust action. The plaintiff and the attorney have negotiated a contingent fee contract in which the attorney's fee will equal one-tenth of the total damages award in the case. Suppose the attorney, who has become intimately involved in the case and cannot be replaced on short notice, has presented a very effective case so that prior to final arguments all observers agree that the plaintiff will win the case and recover a substantial treble damages award. However, immediately prior to final arguments, the attorney tells the plaintiff he will intentionally lose the case unless the plaintiff agrees to increase his fee to twenty-five percent. Ignoring for the moment the ethical issues and the legal enforceability of the increase, the plaintiff must meet the attorney's opportunistic demand or lose the case.

As a second example, suppose individual A owns a vacant lot and individual B wishes to build a house. A could lease the lot to B for a short time and B could build on the lot, but after the lease expires, A will be able to engage in opportunism by raising the rent to reflect the costs to B of moving the house to another lot. Instead of submitting himself voluntarily to the possibility of such behavior, B, a rational individual, may choose to avoid the exchange altogether. Another solution to this problem would be for B to purchase the building lot. Conceptually, this would be a form of vertical integration. *See* Benjamin Klein et al., *Vertical Integration, Appropriable Rents, and the Competitive Contracting Process*, 21 Journal of Law & Economics 297, 299 (1978) (emphasizing that vertical integration is a means of economizing on costs and avoiding risks of appropriation of quasi-rents in specialized assets by opportunistic individuals). The costs imposed on one trading party by the opportunistic behavior of the other trading party are important components of transaction costs.

Potential victims of opportunism are protected through several types of activities. Other than avoiding the transaction altogether, the following five methods of eliminating or reducing the risk of becoming victims should be emphasized:

1. *Vertical Integration:* It may be possible to avoid the risk of opportunism through vertical integration. In the above examples, the use of an in-house attorney and the purchase of the building lot would avoid the possibility of opportunism.

2. *Price Adjustment:* The potential victim may adjust the initial price to deter the occurrence of the opportunism. For example, if the attorney's initial fee in the first example had been twenty instead of ten percent, then the attorney's opportunistic threat would have been less credible because the attorney would have had more to lose, now a potential twenty percent instead of ten, had he "thrown" the case.

3. *Brand Name:* Adverse market adjustments may prevent a substantial portion of myopic opportunism. The future value of the attorney's services, for example, will surely diminish as a result of his opportunistic fee manipulation. A lawyer, like a manufacturer, has an economic incentive to establish and maintain a good reputation, a lawyer's "brand name."

4. *Implicit Contracts:* Although potential victims may have signed relatively simple contracts, they can rely on implicit contract terms based on legal principles that do not allow for the enforcement of certain types of post-contractual modifications. For example, the attorney's opportunistic modification may not be enforceable under the pre-existing duty rule.

5. *Explicit Contracts:* The parties can agree to and write a complete, fully specified contingent contract and rely on the courts to enforce the agreement. For example, the landowner and the homeowner could specify contractually how the future rent is to be determined upon expiration of the initial lease.

These methods will not act as a complete deterrent to opportunism in all circumstances. After all, contracting parties will invest in controlling opportunism only up to the point where the expected marginal benefit is equal to the marginal cost—but they can substantially reduce the risks associated with many transactions.

1. Firm-Specific Investments and the Appropriation of Quasi-Rents

Transaction failures in procurement and production resulting from opportunistic behavior are most likely to occur when firms become specialized with respect to each other. A major reason firms invest in assets that are specialized when compared to the assets of other firms is to gain the technological advantages of coordinated or joint production processes. The cost savings generated from the improvement in productive efficiency are called "appropriable quasi-rents." These "quasi-rents" represent wealth that is potentially appropriable by an opportunistic party.

One form of opportunism involves the post-contractual manipulation of transfer prices by a supplier and a manufacturer who have become specialized to each other. Consider the example of steel production. The fabrication of steel products requires the shaping of molten steel. If fabrication facilities are located near the point where steel ingots are cast, production efficiency is improved by the reduced cost of transporting and reheating ingots. However, obtaining these technical efficiencies does not require joint ownership of the steel ingots facilities, only physical proximity. Yet ingot casting and fabrication facilities are often commonly owned and vertically integrated because, in the absence of integration, opportunism between separate ingot casting and steel fabrication firms would preclude technical efficiency.

This proposition is easily demonstrated. Imagine that an ingot producer builds an ingot casting plant that is physically integrated with a steel fabricating facility owned by another firm. These separately owned facilities are designed to work together; each is highly specialized to the other. As a result, there are no other ingot facilities that can supply cast steel to the fabricator as cheaply as the caster, and no other fabrication plant that can make steel products from the ingot producer's castings as cheaply as the specialized fabricator. Under these circumstances, opportunistic price manipulation can occur with respect to the transfer price for ingot. If the transfer price of the ingot is greater than the going market price of cold delivered ingot (of comparable quality) plus the costs associated with reheating it, the purchaser can threaten to go to the outside supply source unless the ingot casting plant lowers its price. The price could be forced below the market price plus the cost of reheating, but the ingot caster need not take less than market price of cold ingot. Thus a bargaining range exists that, depending upon circumstances, can leave one of the firms with a much lower than expected rate of return on the investment. More importantly, this uncertainty about the division of the technical cost savings and the rate of return on investment can have an adverse impact on investment behavior.

In the steel example, it was assumed that the ingot and fabrication plants were already built in close physical proximity. The most important transaction failure occurs, however, when the *prospect* of opportunism leads a firm not to become as specialized. Although individuals may agree in advance to split the cost savings, each knows that the other may renege *once the plants are built*. Once this occurs, the next best alternative is poor. Thus, each firm becomes subject to opportunistic behavior if it leaves the eventual outcome solely to market-mediated exchange. Opportunistic appropriation of quasi-rents, however, rarely interferes with a market-mediated exchange, because firms have developed nonmarket or market-suppressing solutions in response to potential transaction failures. In this regard, the transaction costs that would have led to transaction failures are replaced by negotiation and search costs.

Lake River Corp. v. Carborundum Co.

United States Court of Appeals for the Seventh Circuit
769 F.2d 1284 (1985)

POSNER, Circuit Judge.

This diversity suit between Lake River Corporation and Carborundum Company requires us to consider questions of Illinois commercial law, and in particular to explore the fuzzy line between penalty clauses and liquidated-damages clauses.

Carborundum manufactures "Ferro Carbo," an abrasive powder used in making steel. To serve its midwestern customers better, Carborundum made a contract with Lake River by which the latter agreed to provide distribution services in its warehouse in Illinois. Lake River would receive Ferro Carbo in bulk from Carborundum, "bag" it, and ship the bagged product to Carborundum's customers. The Ferro Carbo would remain Carborundum's property until delivered to the customers.

Carborundum insisted that Lake River install a new bagging system to handle the contract. In order to be sure of being able to recover the cost of the new system ($89,000) and make a profit of 20 percent of the contract price, Lake River insisted on the following minimum-quantity guarantee:

> In consideration of the special equipment [i.e., the new bagging system] to be acquired and furnished by LAKE-RIVER for handling the product, CARBORUN-DUM shall, during the initial three-year term of this Agreement, ship to LAKE-RIVER for bagging a minimum quantity of [22,500 tons]. If, at the end of the three-year term, this minimum quantity shall not have been shipped, LAKE-RIVER shall invoice CARBORUNDUM at the then prevailing rates for the difference between the quantity bagged and the minimum guaranteed.

If Carborundum had shipped the full minimum quantity that it guaranteed, it would have owed Lake River roughly $533,000 under the contract.

After the contract was signed in 1979, the demand for domestic steel, and with it the demand for Ferro Carbo, plummeted, and Carborundum failed to ship the guaranteed amount. When the contract expired late in 1982, Carborundum had shipped only 12,000 of the 22,500 tons it had guaranteed. Lake River had bagged the 12,000 tons and had billed Carborundum for this bagging, and Carborundum had paid, but by virtue of the formula in the minimum-guarantee clause Carborundum still owed Lake River $241,000 — the contract price of $533,000 if the full amount of Ferro Carbo had been shipped, minus what Carborundum had paid for the bagging of the quantity it had shipped.

When Lake River demanded payment of this amount, Carborundum refused, on the ground that the formula imposed a penalty. At the time, Lake River had in its warehouse 500 tons of bagged Ferro Carbo, having a market value of $269,000, which it refused to release unless Carborundum paid the $241,000 due under the formula. Lake River did offer to sell the bagged product and place the proceeds in escrow until its dispute with Carborundum over the enforceability of the formula was resolved, but Carborundum rejected the offer and trucked in bagged Ferro Carbo from the East to serve its customers in Illinois, at an additional cost of $31,000.

Lake River brought this suit for $241,000, which it claims as liquidated damages. Carborundum counterclaimed for the value of the bagged Ferro Carbo when Lake River impounded it and the additional cost of serving the customers affected by the impounding. The theory of the counterclaim is that the impounding was a conversion, and not as Lake River contends the assertion of a lien. The district judge, after a bench trial, gave judgment for both parties. Carborundum ended up roughly $42,000 to the good: $269,000 + $31,000 – $241,000 – $17,000, the last figure representing prejudgment interest on Lake River's damages. (We have rounded off all dollar figures to the nearest thousand.) Both parties have appealed.

The only issue that is not one of damages is whether Lake River had a valid lien on the bagged Ferro Carbo that it refused to ship to Carborundum's customers—that, indeed, it holds in its warehouse to this day. Although Ferro Carbo does not deteriorate with age, the domestic steel industry remains in the doldrums and the product is worth less than it was in 1982 when Lake River first withheld it. If Lake River did not have a valid lien on the product, then it converted it, and must pay Carborundum the $269,000 that the Ferro Carbo was worth back then.

* * *

[The court held that Lake River's asserted lien was not a lien.]

The hardest issue in the case is whether the formula in the minimum-guarantee clause imposes a penalty for breach of contract or is merely an effort to liquidate damages. Deep as the hostility to penalty clauses runs in the common law, we still might be inclined to question, if we thought ourselves free to do so, whether a modern court should refuse to enforce a penalty clause where the signator is a substantial corporation, well able to avoid improvident commitments. Penalty clauses provide an earnest of performance. The clause here enhanced Carborundum's credibility in promising to ship the minimum amount guaranteed by showing that it was willing to pay the full contract price even if it failed to ship anything. On the other side it can be pointed out that by raising the cost of a breach of contract to the contract breaker, a penalty clause increases the risk to his other creditors; increases (what is the same thing and more, because bankruptcy imposes "deadweight" social costs) the risk of bankruptcy; and could amplify the business cycle by increasing the number of bankruptcies in bad times, which is when contracts are most likely to be broken. But since little effort is made to prevent businessmen from assuming risks, these reasons are no better than makeweights.

A better argument is that a penalty clause may discourage efficient as well as inefficient breaches of contract. Suppose a breach would cost the promisee $12,000 in actual damages but would yield the promisor $20,000 in additional profits. Then there would be a net social gain from breach. After being fully compensated for his loss the promisee would be no worse off than if the contract had been performed, while the promisor would be better off by $8,000. But now suppose the contract contains a penalty clause under which the promisor if he breaks his promise must pay the promisee $25,000. The promisor will be discouraged from breaking the contract, since $25,000, the penalty, is greater than $20,000, the profits of the breach; and a transaction that would have increased value will be forgone.

On this view, since compensatory damages should be sufficient to deter inefficient breaches (that is, breaches that cost the victim more than the gain to the contract breaker), penal damages could have no effect other than to deter some efficient breaches. But this overlooks the earlier point that the willingness to agree to a penalty clause is a way of making the promisor and his promise credible and may therefore be essential to inducing some value-maximizing contracts to be made. It also overlooks the more important point that the parties (always assuming they are fully competent) will, in deciding whether to include a penalty clause in their contract, weigh the gains against the costs—costs that include the possibility of discouraging an efficient breach somewhere down the road—and will include the clause only if the benefits exceed those costs as well as all other costs.

On this view the refusal to enforce penalty clauses is (at best) paternalistic—and it seems odd that courts should display parental solicitude for large corporations. But however this may be, we must be on guard to avoid importing our own ideas of sound public policy into an area where our proper judicial role is more than usually deferential. The responsibility for making innovations in the common law of Illinois rests with the courts of Illinois, and not with the federal courts in Illinois. And like every other state, Illinois, untroubled by academic skepticism of the wisdom of refusing to enforce penalty clauses against sophisticated promisors, see, e.g., Goetz & Scott, *Liquidated Damages, Penalties and the Just Compensation Principle*, 77 Colum. L. Rev. 554 (1977), continues steadfastly to insist on the distinction between penalties and liquidated damages. To be valid under Illinois law a liquidation of damages must be a reasonable estimate at the time of contracting of the likely damages from breach, and the need for estimation at that time must be shown by reference to the likely difficulty of measuring the actual damages from a breach of contract after the breach occurs. If damages would be easy to determine then, or if the estimate greatly exceeds a reasonable upper estimate of what the damages are likely to be, it is a penalty.

The distinction between a penalty and liquidated damages is not an easy one to draw in practice but we are required to draw it and can give only limited weight to the district court's determination....

Mindful that Illinois courts resolve doubtful cases in favor of classification as a penalty, we conclude that the damage formula in this case is a penalty and not a liquidation of damages, because it is designed always to assure Lake River more than its actual damages. The formula—full contract price minus the amount already invoiced to Carborundum— is invariant to the gravity of the breach. When a contract specifies a single sum in damages for any and all breaches even though it is apparent that all are not of the same gravity, the specification is not a reasonable effort to estimate damages; and when in addition the fixed sum greatly exceeds the actual damages likely to be inflicted by a minor breach, its character as a penalty becomes unmistakable. This case is within the gravitational field of these principles even though the minimum-guarantee clause does not fix a single sum as damages.

Suppose to begin with that the breach occurs the day after Lake River buys its new bagging system for $89,000 and before Carborundum ships any Ferro Carbo. Carborundum would owe Lake River $533,000. Since Lake River would have incurred at that point a total cost of only $89,000, its net gain from the breach would be $444,000. This is more than four times the profit of $107,000 (20 percent of the contract price of $533,000) that Lake River expected to make from the contract if it had been performed: a huge windfall.

Next suppose (as actually happened here) that breach occurs when 55 percent of the Ferro Carbo has been shipped. Lake River would already have received $293,000 from Carborundum. To see what its costs then would have been (as estimated at the time of contracting), first subtract Lake River's anticipated profit on the contract of $107,000 from the total contract price of $533,000. The difference—Lake River's total cost of per-formance—is $426,000. Of this, $89,000 is the cost of the new bagging system, a fixed cost. The rest ($426,000 – $89,000 = $337,000) presumably consists of variable costs that are roughly proportional to the amount of Ferro Carbo bagged; there is no indication of any other fixed costs. Assume, therefore, that if Lake River bagged 55 percent of the con-tractually agreed quantity, it incurred in doing so 55 percent of its variable costs, or $185,000. When this is added to the cost of the new bagging system, assumed for the moment to be worthless except in connection with the contract, the total cost of performance to Lake River is $274,000. Hence a breach that occurred after 55 percent of contractual performance was complete would be expected to yield Lake River a modest profit of $19,000 ($293,000 – $274,000). But now add the "liquidated damages" of $241,000 that Lake River claims, and the result is a total gain from the breach of $260,000, which is almost two and a half times the profit that Lake River expected to gain if there was no breach. And this ignores any use value or salvage value of the new bagging system, which is the property of Lake River—though admittedly it also ignores the time value of money; Lake River paid $89,000 for that system before receiving any revenue from the contract.

To complete the picture, assume that the breach had not occurred till performance was 90 percent complete. Then the "liquidated damages" clause would not be so one-sided, but it would be one-sided. Carborundum would have paid $480,000 for bagging. Against this, Lake River would have incurred its fixed cost of $89,000 plus 90 percent of its variable costs of $337,000 or $303,000. Its total costs would thus be $392,000, and its net profit $88,000. But on top of this it would be entitled to "liquidated damages" of $53,000, for a total profit of $141,000—more than 30 percent more that its expected profit of $107,000 if there was no breach.

The reason for these results is that most of the costs to Lake River of performing the contract are saved if the contract is broken, and this saving is not reflected in the damage formula. As a result, at whatever point in the life of the contract a breach occurs, the damage formula gives Lake River more than its lost profits form the breach—dramatically more if the breach occurs at the beginning of the contract; tapering off at the end, it is true. Still, over the interval between the beginning of Lake River's performance and nearly the end, the clause could be expected to generate profits ranging from 400 percent of the expected contract profits to 130 percent of those profits. And this is on the assumption that the bagging system has no value apart from the contract. If it were worth only $20,000 to Lake River, the range would be 434 percent to 150 percent.

* * *

... [I]t is apparent from the face of the contract that the damages provided for by the "liquidated damages" clause are grossly disproportionate to any probable loss and penalize some breaches much more heavily than others regardless of relative cost....

* * *

The fact that the damage formula is invalid does not deprive Lake River of a remedy. The parties did not contract explicitly with reference to the measure of damages if the agreed-on damage formula was invalidated, but all this means is that the victim of the breach is entitled to his common law damages. In this case that would be the unpaid contract price of $241,000 minus the costs that Lake River saved by not having to complete the contract (the variable costs on the other 45 percent of the Ferro Carbo that it never had to bag). The case must be remanded to the district judge to fix these damages.

* * *

The judgment of the district court is affirmed in part and reversed in part, and the case is returned to that court to redetermine both parties' damages in accordance with the principles in this opinion. The parties may present additional evidence on remand, and shall bear their own costs in this court.

Notes and Questions

1. Firm-Specific Investment, Forfeitable Reputational Bonds and Penalty Clauses: Firm-specific investment, reputation, brand name, advertising, etc., all play important roles in ensuring contractual performance. Consider the negotiations between Lake River and

Carborundum. Carborundum induced Lake River to make a contract-specific investment in the bagging system. (Obviously, the system could be used to bag other products, but its most valuable use to Lake River and, indeed, the reason for the investment, was to bag Ferro Carbo.) Apparently, Carborundum did not have any other distributors of Ferro Carbo and, therefore, probably did not have a well-developed reputation for good faith dealing with distributors. In economic terms, Carborundum did not have a forfeitable reputational bond to ensure its performance after Lake River made the investment and, thus, Lake River would not have been willing to make the contract-specific investment unless Carborundum could bond its performance. In this regard, a penalty stipulated damages clause is a substitute for a reputational bond because both carry substantial penalties for nonperformance. Thus, because Carborundum could not bond its performance with a well-developed (yet forfeitable) reputational bond, it convinced Lake River to make the investment by offering a penalty clause. A major difference between the reputational bond and the penalty clause is that the reputational bond penalty is not paid to the promisee and, thus, there is no incentive to induce breach. Does this analysis suggest that penalty clauses such as the one in Lake River should be evaluated in terms of their overall economic context — for example, should the absence of a reputational bond be taken into account?

2. Unenforceable Penalty Clauses: Efficiency or Paternalism?: The distinction between enforceable and unenforceable penalty clauses is interesting from a policy perspective. A stipulated damage clause that amounts to a penalty may merely reflect the promisee's very strong desire to have the project finished on schedule. Moreover, it seems unreasonable to suspect that the inclusion of a penalty clause does not impact other terms in the contract, including the negotiation of the completion date and the total value of the contract. Thus, the refusal of the common law courts to enforce penalty clauses appears to be based on some type of paternalistic notion. On the other hand, it has been suggested that the distinction between penalty clauses and reasonable damage clauses is justified on efficiency grounds because penalty clauses create perverse incentives for the beneficiary of the clauses to induce the breach of the contract in order to collect the penalty. Consider the following analysis:

> An important cost of stipulated damage clauses ... results from activities that may induce breach and from activities to prevent breach inducement, both of which waste scarce resources. Consider, for example, a contract to build a bridge with a stipulated damage clause of $500 for each day of delay beyond a specified completion date chosen to correspond with the first day that the purchaser expects to use the bridge. If the clause is carefully drafted, the $500 will closely approximate the expected damage to the purchaser from the actual delay. Suppose, however, that during construction (or, for that matter, even at the time of the initial contract) the cost of delay to the purchaser becomes zero because the bridge could not be used until much later than originally planned. Since the producer's breach would now actually improve the purchaser's position, the purchaser has an incentive to undertake activities to cause delay as long as the additional expected revenues from creating delay ($500 multiplied by the number of days of delay) exceed the additional costs.... [E]ven if all stipulated damage clauses are enforced, the incentive to induce breach would exist only when the potential breach-inducer knows that actual damages will be less than the stipulated amount. This may occur either at the time of initial contracting or, more likely, at some time during performance when circumstances change, affecting the likely amount of damages upon breach.

When the incentive for breach inducement is present, a further cost could be incurred since the producer might devote time and resources to detect and prevent possible breach-inducing activities. This may entail additional personnel to acquire information about the purchaser or to monitor activities of the purchaser.

Resources spent both on breach-inducing activities and on detecting and preventing breach inducement are wasteful. They do not produce any real good or service that the contracting parties value, nor do they move resources to production of goods or services whose value is greater than to the contracting parties. Accordingly, the value of *all* resources expended in inducement is wasted and increases the costs of forming, completing, and monitoring the contract. Such expenditures, like those employed to defraud others, are merely necessary inputs in obtaining the benefits from induced breach and, again, like real resources spent to defraud, contribute to overall costs without producing real products. If these costs could be avoided while retaining the desirable outcomes of stipulated damage clauses (and without incurring any new costs), contracting parties as a group, and hence society, would gain.

Besides incentive, the potential breach-inducer needs opportunity before he will induce breach. Since detected inducement would result in nonenforcement of the clause, thereby removing the incentive to waste resources, breach inducement will present special difficulties only when the courts are unable to detect it easily. The opportunity to induce breach does arise, however, in situations where inducement is exceedingly costly to detect, particularly where the producer's performance depends at least in part upon the purchaser's cooperation and assistance. For example, a party may intentionally withhold useful information for a critical period of time, yet still comply with the contract. Thus, in our bridge hypothetical, the purchaser may withhold certain information whose existence or source is not known to the producer, such as information about difficult construction conditions. Further, if the contract calls for close cooperation with respect to the building specifications, the purchaser may delay (or become unexpectedly "fussy") in providing assistance necessary to complete construction on time. It may also be possible to supply information or resources that are clearly inferior but within the limits of the contract. Purchasing parties may even provide misleading or erroneous data, such as on the condition of the river bed soil in the bridge case....

Although the policy underlying the distinction has baffled the legal community, for hundreds of years courts have categorized stipulated damage clauses as either liquidated damages or penalties. Finding the previous explanations of this distinction to be unsatisfactory, we have asked whether economic efficiency could justify nonenforcement of stipulated damages in certain situations, and, if so, whether the justification could explain the results, if not the reasoning, of the reported decisions. The answer to both questions supports an economic distinction between liquidated damages and penalties. Through a broad, poorly articulated reasonableness test, the courts appear to have attained efficient results....

Kenneth W. Clarkson et al., *Liquidated Damages v. Penalties: Sense or Nonsense?*, 1978 Wisconsin Law Review 351, 368–372, 378. Do the facts in *Lake River* suggest that the breach was induced by Lake River? The court clearly demonstrates the incentive for Lake River to breach, but did Lake River have the opportunity to induce breach? Given that the court recognized the penal nature of the stipulated damages clause, isn't it reasonable to assume that the contracting parties recognized this as well and took it into account in their initial negotiations over price and other terms?

3. Opportunistic Renegotiation and Appropriable Quasi-Rents: Exchanges between individuals or firms often require that the parties invest in an asset that is transaction specific. That is, the value of the asset in question is clearly maximized when used for the specific purpose called for in the transaction. These types of assets are highly specialized, meaning that the asset's value in its current use far exceeds its next best alternative. Thus, an attempt to switch specialized assets from one use to another can involve substantial costs to the owner. In a sense, parties who invest in specialized assets are "locked into" the deal and part of the investment can be appropriated by the other contracting party. The notion of "appropriable quasi-rents" has been developed as follows:

> Assume an asset is owned by one individual and rented to another individual. The quasi-rent value of the asset is the excess of its value over its salvage value, that is, its value in its next best *use* to another renter. The potentially appropriable specialized portion of the quasi-rent is that portion, if any, in excess of its value to the second highest-valuing *user*.

Benjamin Klein et al., *Vertical Integration, Appropriable Rents, and the Competitive Contracting Process*, 21 Journal of Law & Economics 297, 298 (1978) (emphasis in original.). When parties are required to bring a specialized asset to the exchange, each has an incentive to take advantage of the other party—the so called **"hold-up" problem.** The buyer can refuse to accept unless the price is reduced and the seller can refuse to deliver unless the price is increased. The buyer will be able to extort a price discount equal to the difference between the agreed upon price and the value of the specialized asset in its next best use. Likewise, the seller can extort a price increase equal to the difference between the agreed upon price and the cost to the buyer of finding a new supplier. This difference, which is the asset owners' quasi-rent, can be opportunistically appropriated. Individuals who bring specialized assets to a transaction desire protection from others' opportunistic behavior. That is, the owners of specialized assets will seek out devices to protect their quasi-rents from being appropriated or "held-up." Klein, Crawford, and Alchian give a numerical example of the determination of the opportunistic post-contractual bargaining range:

> Imagine a printing press owned and operated by party A. Publisher B buys printing services from party A by leasing his press at a contracted rate of $5,500 per day. The amortized fixed cost of the printing press is $4,000 per day and it has a current salvageable value if moved elsewhere of $1,000 (daily rental equivalent). Operating costs are $1,500 and are paid by the printing-press owner, who prints final printed pages for the publisher. Assume also that a second publisher C is willing to offer at most $3,500 for daily services. The current quasi rent on the installed machine is $3,000 ($5,500 − $1,500 − $1,000), the revenue minus operating costs minus salvageable value. However, the daily quasi rent from publisher B relative to use of the machine for publisher C is only $2,000 ($5,500 − $3,500). At $5,500 revenue daily from publisher B the press owner would break even on his investment. If the publisher were then able to cut his offer for the press from $5,500 down to almost $3,500, he would still have the press service available to him. He would be appropriating $2,000 of the quasi rent from the press owner. The $2,000 difference between his prior agreed-to-daily rental of $5,500 and the next best revenue available to the press once the machine is purchased and installed is less than the quasi rent and therefore is potentially appropriable. If no second party were available at the present site,

the entire quasi rent would be subject to threat of appropriation by an unscrupulous or opportunistic publisher.

Klein et al., *supra*, at 298–99.

4. Deterrence of Efficient Breaches: The court summarizes one economic view of penalty clauses as follows: "[S]ince compensatory damages should be sufficient to deter inefficient breaches (that is, breaches that cost the victim more than the gain to the contract breaker), penal damages could have no effect other than to deter some efficient breaches." Does the potential forfeiture of a reputational bond deter efficient breaches, that is, does it lead to "inefficient performance"?

2. Franchising

Manufacturers, restaurant franchisors, nationwide tax preparation services, and many other providers of goods and services often rely on a system of wholesale distributors and retailers to move their goods and services to consumers. A wide variety of distribution systems are used. Obviously, grocery stores, department stores, and discount stores carry many different competing brands of goods. At the other end of the continuum is the franchisee that represents only one brand, say McDonald's.

Consider the possibilities for opportunism in a successful franchised motel chain. The franchisor's trademark—which is the franchisor's most important asset—signals to consumers a specific standard of quality, service, and rates. Individual franchisees must undertake expenditures if they wish to maintain these attributes. The possibility for opportunistic behavior arises because customers base their decision to stay at franchised motels on their experiences with other motels in the chain. This gives an individual franchisee the incentive to engage in free-riding by shirking on expenditures on quality because he will continue to attract customers who, based on their experience with other motels in the chain, expect to receive, and are willing to pay for, the higher quality. The free-riding franchisee benefits by the entire amount of his savings on expenditures and bears only a portion of the costs, which is shared by the franchisor and the other franchisees through the decreased value of the trademark. Consumers, of course, are also injured.

Similarly, the franchisor has opportunities to engage in opportunistic behavior because the franchisee is required to make transaction-specific investments, including payment of an initial franchise fee, which are potentially appropriable by the franchisor. For example, McDonald's franchisees must make considerable McDonald's-specific investments in the building, equipment, and training. These investments, which are of little value if not used in a McDonald's franchise, make the franchisee vulnerable to extortion by the franchisor. Moreover, franchisors often include a clause allowing for unilateral "at will" termination of the franchise arrangement. The "at will" clause might enable the franchisor to engage in opportunistic behavior by terminating a franchisee without cause, thereby appropriating the franchise fee and purchasing the franchise rights at a distress price. Thus, the typical franchise contract appears to be "unfair" to the franchisees. However, it is important to remember that the franchise relationship is founded on a mutually beneficial exchange. With these economic concepts in mind, evaluate the relative economic positions of the contracting parties in the following case.

Corenswet, Inc. v. Amana Refrigeration, Inc.

United States Court of Appeals for the Fifth Circuit
594 F.2d 129 (1979)

Wisdom, J.

* * *

I.

The primary facts are not disputed.

The plaintiff, Corenswet, Inc., is an independent wholesale distributor of appliances, dishware, and similar products. Since 1969 Corenswet has been the exclusive distributor of Amana refrigerators, freezers, room air conditioners, and other merchandise in southern Louisiana. Amana is a Delaware corporation domiciled in Iowa. Under the Amana system, products manufactured by Amana are sold to wholesale distributors such as Corenswet and to Amana's factory wholesale branches. The independent distributors and the factory branches then resell the merchandise to retail dealers who, in turn, sell to the public. The first distributorship agreement executed between Amana and Corenswet was of indefinite duration, but terminable by either party at any time "with or without cause" on ten days' notice to the other party. According to the record, the agreement was modified twice, in 1971 and again in July 1975, before the institution of this lawsuit. The 1975 agreement modified the termination provision to allow termination by either party "at any time for any reason" on ten days' notice.

As is so often the case with franchise and distributorship relationships, the termination clause in the standard form contract was of little interest or concern to the parties so long as things were going well between them. At the hearing before the district court, Corenswet introduced testimony that it understood, in the early 1970's, that the relationship would be a lasting one, a relationship that would continue so long as Corenswet performed satisfactorily. According to Corenswet, it developed an organization for wholesale distribution of Amana merchandise: it hired a manager and salesmen for the line, as well as specially trained repairmen. Corenswet also expanded its physical plant. In all, Corenswet contended, it invested over $1.5 million over the period of 1969 to 1976 in developing the market for Amana products in the southern Louisiana area. The parties stipulated in district court that the annual sales of Amana products in the distributorship area increased from $200,000 in 1969 to over $2.5 million in 1976. The number of retail outlets selling Amana products in the area increased from six in 1969 to seventy-two in 1976. Corenswet, in short, developed an important new market for Amana products. And Amana became as important to Corenswet as Corenswet became to Amana: sales of Amana products as a percentage of Corenswet's total sales of all products swelled from six percent in 1969 to nearly twenty-six percent in 1976. Over the seven and one-half-year period, Amana representatives repeatedly praised Corenswet for its performance.

At the 1976 mid-year meeting of Amana distributors, however, George Foerstner, Amana's president, informed Corenswet that Amana would soon terminate its relationship with Corenswet because Corenswet was underfinanced. The parties agree that in early 1976 Corenswet had exceeded its credit limit with Amana, and that Amana at that time indicated that it might have to take a security interest in Corenswet's Amana inventory. According to a January communication from Amana, however, the "problem" was viewed by Amana as "a good kind of problem," reflecting, as it did, the growth of Corenswet's sales and hence purchases of Amana products. It is Corenswet's contention that the problem was not a serious one. Amana executives, the record reflects, assured

Corenswet at the 1976 mid-year meeting that "satisfactory arrangements would be made" and that, Foerstner's statement notwithstanding, Corenswet would retain its distributorship.

There followed a complicated sequence of negotiations concerning Amana's security for credit extended. Amana sought a security interest in Corenswet's Amana inventory, to which Corenswet agreed. Amana asked also that Corenswet obtain more working capital from its parent corporation, Select Brands, Inc., as well as a bank letter of credit or line of credit. There is ample evidence in the record that Corenswet responded adequately to each Amana request, but that Amana persisted in changing its requirements as quickly as Corenswet could respond to its requests. In September, 1976, Corenswet met in New Orleans with Amana's representative, George Tolbert. Sam Corenswet, the company's president, informed Tolbert that Corenswet was ready and able to meet Amana's latest request: a $500,000 bank letter of credit. Tolbert relayed the information to Foerstner. Within a week Corenswet received a letter, prepared by Tolbert at Foerstner's direction, notifying Corenswet of its decision to terminate the distributorship because Corenswet was "unable to provide us with what we felt to be the minimum guarantees and/or security to sustain a continuing pattern of growth with Amana."

In October 1976, Corenswet filed suit for damages and injunctive relief in state court alleging that Amana had breached the distributorship agreement by terminating it arbitrarily. The reasons given by Amana for the termination, it contended, were pretextual. The state court issued a temporary restraining order barring termination. The TRO was retained in force after Amana removed the case to federal district court.

The district court conducted a three-day hearing on Corenswet's prayer for a preliminary injunction. The court concluded that Amana had indeed acted arbitrarily in deciding to terminate Corenswet. The record reflects that in early 1976, well before the mid-year distributor meeting, Amana began negotiating with another New Orleans concern, George H. Lehleitner & Co., about transferring its area distributorship to Lehleitner. The beginning of Amana's alleged concern over Corenswet's finances corresponded neatly with its Lehleitner negotiations. There was ample evidence in the record, moreover, to support the district court's conclusion that the real factor motivating Foerstner's decision was animosity towards Fred Schoenfeld, the president of Corenswet's parent corporation, Select Brands, Inc. That animosity dated back to 1972, when Schoenfeld's action in protesting to Raytheon Corporation, Amana's parent, aborted Amana's attempt to transfer the distributorship from Corenswet to Corenswet's then Amana sales manager.

The district court ruled that the arbitrary termination was a breach of the distributorship agreement. The court rejected Amana's argument that the termination clause, which permitted either party to terminate the contract "for any reason," permitted termination for any reason be that reason good, bad, or indifferent. Although unwilling to accept Corenswet's position that the term "for any reason" imported a good or just cause limitation, the court ruled that the term means "for some reason, not for no reason ... for something that appeals to the reason, to the mind, to the judgment, not for something that is arbitrary, capricious or wanton." In the alternative, the court ruled that the U.C.C.'s "good faith" principle forbids the bad faith termination of exclusive distributorships and found Amana's actions to have been in bad faith. The court issued the preliminary injunction prohibiting Amana from terminating or attempting to terminate the relationship in November 1976.

In late 1977, Corenswet filed a declaratory judgment action in response to Amana's request that Corenswet sign the new standard form distributorship agreement.... In

September of 1977, Amana filed a motion requesting the court to modify or vacate the preliminary injunction to permit Amana to terminate the distributorship. Amana urged that Corenswet's refusal to execute the new distributorship agreement was sufficient cause or reason under the existing agreement and the injunction to justify termination of Corenswet's distributorship. The court denied Amana's motion, but amended the injunction to require Corenswet to execute the agreement within five days or suffer termination of the agreement, and to place restrictions on Amana's rights to refuse to renew the one-year term of the new agreement. The modification of the injunction, entered in November 1977, forbade Amana to refuse to renew the distributorship term "without reason" and enjoined Amana to accord Corenswet equal treatment with Amana's other distributors.

II.

* * *

Amana asserts that the district court erred in construing the contract's termination clause to prohibit unilateral termination of the distributorship except for some "reason" that appeals to the mind. The contractual language "for any reason," it argues, was intended to remove all limitations upon the exercise of the termination power. Because the district court looked to extrinsic evidence in construing the contract its interpretation is, under Iowa law, treated as a factual one. Amana, therefore, has the burden of persuading us that the court's interpretation was clearly erroneous.

* * *

The starting point ... is the express terms of the agreement. Under the contract, Amana was free to terminate the relationship "at any time and for any reason." The district court did not expressly rely on record evidence concerning the parties' understanding or the common understanding of the term "any reason" in concluding that the term means "something that appeals to the reason, to the mind." In the common understanding, it seems to us, the phrase "for any reason" means "for any reason that the actor deems sufficient." The phrase, that is, is ordinarily used not to limit a power, but to free it from implied limitations of "cause." That this is the intendment of the phrase becomes all the more clear when it is read in conjunction with the immediately preceding phrase "at any time." That phrase plainly frees the termination power from limitations as to timing. The exact parallelism of the two phrases reinforces the interpretation of the "any reason" language as negating any limitations whatsoever....

* * *

... Amana never conceded that it needed a justification, in the sense of a reason grounded in Corenswet's conduct, for ending the relationship. Even if it is assumed that Amana needed "some reason" to terminate the contract, that reason is supplied by its evident desire to give the New Orleans distributorship to the Lehleitner company, just as we think that Corenswet would, under the contract, be entitled to terminate the relationship by reason, to take an example, of its wish to handle Kelvinator, rather than Amana, products.

* * *

We take Corenswet to be arguing that the contractual language must be interpreted in light of Amana's historical treatment of Corenswet and its other distributors.... In this case, however, no reasonable construction can reconcile the contract's express terms with the interpretation Corenswet seeks to glean from the conduct of the parties. The conflict could not be more complete: Amana's past conduct, with regard both to Corenswet and to its other distributors, may have created a reasonable expectation that Amana would not terminate a distributor arbitrarily, yet the contract expressly gives Amana the right to do so. We can find no justification, except in cases of conduct of the sort giving rise to promissory estoppel, for holding that a contractually reserved power, however distasteful, may be lost through nonuse. The express contract term cannot be construed as Corenswet would constitute it, and it therefore controls over any allegedly conflicting usage or course of dealing.

The district court's alternative rationale was that arbitrary termination of a distributorship agreement contravenes the Code's general obligation of good faith dealing....

* * *

The parties have not cited and we have not found Iowa cases on the issue decided under the Uniform Commercial Code. The Iowa case law on this question is pre-Code and follows the common law rule, which is essentially [that "[w]here the contract provides for successive performance but is indefinite in duration it is valid for a reasonable time but unless otherwise agreed may be terminated at any time by either party."]

* * *

... When a contract contains a provision expressly sanctioning termination without cause there is no room for implying a term that bars such a termination. In the face of such a term there can be, at best, an expectation that a party will decline to exercise his rights.

As a tool for policing distributorship terminations, moreover, the good faith test is erratic at best. It has been observed that the good faith approach "is analytically unsound because there is no necessary correlation between bad motives and unfair terminations.... The terminated dealer seeks relief against the harsh effects of termination which may be unfairly placed on him, not against the manufacturer's ill will." The better approach ... is to test the disputed contract clause for unconscionability.... The question these cases present is whether public policy forbids enforcement of a contract clause permitting unilateral termination without cause. Since a termination without cause will almost always be characterizable as a "bad faith" termination, focus on the terminating party's state of mind will always result in the invalidation of unrestricted termination clauses. We seriously doubt, however, that public policy frowns on any and all contract clauses permitting termination without cause. Such clauses can have the salutary effect of permitting parties to end a soured relationship without consequent litigation. Indeed when, as here, the power of unilateral termination without cause is granted to both parties, the clause gives the distributor an easy way to cut the knot should he be presented with an opportunity to secure a better distributorship from another manufacturer. What public policy does abhor is economic overreaching, the use of superior bargaining power to secure grossly unfair advantage. That is the precise focus of the Code's unconscionability doctrine; it is not at all the concern of the Code's good faith performance provision. It is the office of the unconscionability concept, and not of the good faith concept, to strike down "unfair" contract terms.

We conclude that, under the better view, the Code does not *ipso facto* bar unilateral arbitrary terminations of distributorship agreements....

Corenswet's rights with respect to termination extend only to a right to notice.... But any claim that Corenswet might have based on inadequate notice would not entitle Corenswet to injunctive relief....

The district court's decisions are REVERSED, and the preliminary injunction is VACATED.

Transaction Cost Determinants of "Unfair" Contractual Arrangements

Benjamin Klein

70 American Economic Review Papers & Proceedings
356, 356–62 (1980)

Terms such as "unfair" are foreign to the economic model of voluntary exchange which implies anticipated gains to all transactors. However, much recent statutory, regulatory and antitrust activity has run counter to this economic paradigm of the efficiency properties of "freedom of contract." The growth of "dealer day in court" legislation, FTC franchise regulations, favorable judicial consideration of "unequal bargaining power," and unconscionability arguments, are some examples of the recent legal propensity to "protect" transactors. This is done by declaring unenforceable or illegal particular contractual provisions that, although voluntarily agreed upon in the face of significant competition, appear to be one-sided or unfair. Presentation of the standard abstract economic analysis of the mutual gains from voluntary exchange is unlikely to be an effective counterweight to this recent legal movement without an explicit attempt to provide a positive rationale for the presence of the particular unfair contractual term. This paper considers some transaction costs that might explain the voluntary adoption of contractual provisions such as termination at will and long-term exclusive dealing clauses that have been under legal attack.

I. The "Hold-up" Problem

... Given the presence of incomplete contractual arrangements, wealth-maximizing transactors have the ability and often the incentive to renege on the transaction by holding up the other party, in the sense of taking advantage of unspecified or unenforceable elements of the contractual relationship. Such behavior is, by definition, unanticipated and not a long-run equilibrium phenomenon. Oliver Williamson has identified and discussed this phenomenon of "opportunistic behavior," and my recent paper with Robert Crawford and Armen Alchian attempted to make operational some of the conditions under which this holdup potential is likely to be large. In addition to contract costs, and therefore the incompleteness of the explicit contract, we emphasized the presence of appropriable quasi-rents due to highly firm-specific investments. After a firm invests in an asset with a low-salvage value and a quasi-rent stream highly dependent upon some other asset, the owner of the other asset has the potential to hold up by appropriating the quasi-rent stream. For example, one would not build a house on land rented for a short term. After the rental agreement expires, the landowner could raise the rental price to reflect the costs of moving the house to another lot....

II. Contractual Solutions

Since the magnitude of the potential holdup may be anticipated, the party to be cheated can merely decrease the initial price he will pay by the amount of the appropriable quasi-rents. For example, if an employer knows that an employee will cheat a certain amount each period, it will be reflected in the employee's wage. Contracts can be usefully thought to refer to anticipated rather than stated performance. Therefore the employee's behavior should not even be considered "cheating." A secretary, for example, may miss work one day a week on average. If secretary time is highly substitutable, the employer can cut the secretary's weekly wage 20 percent, hire 20 percent more secretaries, and be indifferent. The secretary, on the other hand, presumably values the leisure more than the additional income and therefore is better off. Rather than cheating, we have a voluntarily determined, utility-maximizing contractual relationship.

In many cases, however, letting the party cheat and discounting his wage will not be an economical solution because the gain to the cheater and therefore his acceptable compensating wage discount is less than the cost to the firm from the cheating behavior. For example, it is easy to imagine many cases where a shirking manager will impose costs on the firm much greater than his personal gains. Therefore the stockholders cannot be made indifferent to this behavior by cutting his salary and hiring more lazy managers. The general point is that there may not be perfect substitutability between quantity and quality of particular services. Hence, even if one knew that an unspecified element of quality would be reduced by a certain amount in attempting the holdup, an ex ante compensatory discount in the quoted price of the promised high-quality service to the cost of providing the anticipated lower-quality supply would not make the demander of the service indifferent. Individuals would be willing to expend real resources to set up contractual arrangements to prevent such opportunism and assure high-quality supply.

The question then becomes how much of the holdup problem can be avoided by an explicit government-enforced contract, and how much remains to be handled by an implicit self-enforcing contract. This latter type of contract is one where opportunistic behavior is prevented by the threat of termination of the business relationship rather than by the threat of litigation. A transactor will not cheat if the expected present discounted value of quasi-rents he is earning from a relationship is greater than the immediate holdup wealth gain. The capital loss that can be imposed on the potential cheater by the withdrawal of expected future business is then sufficient to deter cheating.... [O]ne way in which the future-promised rewards necessary to prevent cheating can be arranged is by the payment of a sufficiently high-price "premium." This premium stream can usefully be thought of as "protection money" paid to assure noncheating behavior. The magnitude of this price premium will be related to the potential holdup, this is, to the extent of contractual incompleteness and the degree of specific capital present. In equilibrium, the present discounted value of the price-premium stream will be exactly equal to the appropriable quasi-rents, making the potential cheater indifferent between cheating and not. But the individual paying the premium will be in a preferable position as long as the differential consumer's surplus from high-quality (noncheating) supply is greater that the premium.

One method by which this equilibrium quasi-rent stream can be achieved without the existence of positive firm profits is by having the potential cheater put up a forfeitable-at-will collateral bond equal to the discounted value of the premium stream. Alternatively, the potential cheater may make a highly firm-specific productive investment which will have only a low-salvage value if he cheats and loses future business. The gap between price and salvageable capital costs is analytically equivalent to a premium stream with the nonsalvageable asset analytically equivalent to a forfeitable collateral bond.

III. "Unfair" Contractual Terms

Most actual contractual arrangements consist of a combination of explicit and implicit enforcement mechanisms. Some elements of performance will be specified and enforced by third-party sanctions. The residual elements of performance will be enforced without invoking the power of some outside party to the transaction but merely by the threat of termination of the transactional relationship. The details of any particular contract will consist of forms of these general elements chosen to minimize transaction costs (for example, hiring lawyers to discover contingencies and draft explicit terms, paying quality-assurance premiums, and investing in nonsalvageable "brand name" assets) and may imply the existence of what appear to be unfair contract terms.

Consider, for example, the initial capital requirements and termination provisions common in most franchise contractual arrangements. These apparently one-sided terms may be crucial elements of minimum-cost quality-policing arrangements. Given the difficulty of explicitly specifying and enforcing contractually every element of quality to be supplied by a franchisee, there is an incentive for an individual opportunistic franchisee to cheat the franchisor by supplying a lower quality of product than contracted for. Because the franchisee uses a common trademark, this behavior depreciates the reputation and hence the future profit stream of the franchisor.

The franchisor knows, given his direct policing and monitoring expenditures, the expected profit that a franchisee can obtain by cheating. For example, given the number of inspectors hired, he knows the expected time to detect a cheater. Given the costs of low-quality inputs, he knows the expected extra short-run cheating profit that can be earned. Therefore the franchisor may require an initial lump sum payment from the franchisee equal to this estimated short-run gain from cheating. This is equivalent to a collateral bond forfeitable at the will of the franchisor. The franchisee will earn a normal rate of return on that bond if he does not cheat, but it will be forfeited if he does cheat and is terminated.

* * *

It is important to recognize that franchise termination, if it is to assure quality compliance on the part of franchisees, must be unfair in the sense that the capital cost imposed on the franchisee that will optimally prevent cheating must be larger than the gain to the franchisee from cheating. Given that less than infinite resources are spent by the franchisor to monitor quality, there is some probability that franchisee cheating will go undetected. Therefore, termination must become equivalent to a criminal-type sanction. Rather than the usually analyzed case of costlessly detected and policed contract breach, where the remedy of making the breaching party pay the cost of the damages of his specific breach makes economic sense, the sanction here must be large enough to make the expected net gain from cheating equal to zero. The transacting parties contractually agree upon a penalty-type sanction for breach as a means of economizing on direct policing costs. Because contract enforcement costs (including litigation costs which generally are not collectable by the innocent party in the United States) are not zero, this analysis provides a rationale against the common-law prohibition of penalty clauses.

The obvious concern with such seemingly unfair contractual arrangements is the possibility that the franchisor may engage in opportunistic behavior by terminating a franchisee without cause, claiming the franchise fee and purchasing the initial franchisee's investment at a distress price. Such behavior may be prevented by the depreciation of the franchisor's brand name and therefore decreased future demand by potential franchisees to join the arrangement. However, this protective mechanism is limited by the relative importance of new franchise sales compared to the continuing franchising operation, that is, by the "maturity" of the franchise chain.

More importantly, what limits reverse cheating by franchisors is the possible increased cost of operating the chain through an employee operation compared to a franchise operation when such cheating is communicated among franchisees. As long as the implicit collateral bond put up by the franchisee is less than the present discounted value of this cost difference, franchisor cheating will be deterred. Although explicit bonds and price premium payments cannot simultaneously be made by both the franchisee and the franchisor, the discounted value of the cost difference has the effect of a collateral bond put up by the franchisor to assure his noncheating behavior. This explains why the franchisor does not increase the initial franchise fee to an arbitrarily high level and correspondingly decrease its direct policing expenditures and the probability of detecting franchisee cheating. While such offsetting changes could continue to optimally deter franchisee cheating and save the real resource cost of direct policing, the profit from and hence the incentive for reverse franchisor cheating would become too great for the arrangement to be stable.

Franchisees voluntarily signing these agreements obviously understand the termination-at-will clause separate from the legal consequences of that term to mean unopportunistic franchisor termination. But this does not imply that the court should judge each termination on these unwritten but understood contract terms and attempt to determine if franchisor cheating has occurred. Franchisees also must recognize that by signing these agreements they are relying on the implicit market-enforcement mechanism outlined above, and not the court, to prevent franchisor cheating. It is costly to use the court to regulate these terminations because elements of performance are difficult to contractually specify and to measure. In addition, litigation is costly and time consuming, during which time the brand name of the franchisor can be depreciated further. If these costs were not large and the court could cheaply and quickly determine when franchisor cheating had occurred, the competitive process regarding the establishment of contract terms would lead transactors to settle on explicit governmentally enforceable contracts rather than rely on this implicit market-enforcement mechanism.

The potential error here is, after recognizing the importance of transaction costs and the incomplete "relational" nature of most real-world contracts, to rely too strongly on the government as a regulator of unspecified terms. While it is important for economic theory to handle significant contract costs and incomplete explicit contractual arrangements, such complexity does not imply a broad role for government. Rather, all that is implied is a role for brand names and the corresponding implicit market-enforcement mechanism I have outlined.

IV. Unequal Bargaining Power

An argument made against contract provisions such as termination-at-will clauses is that they appear to favor one party at the expense of another. Hence it is alleged that the terms of the agreement must have been reached under conditions of "unequal bargaining power" and therefore should be invalid. However, a further implication of the above analysis is that when both parties can cheat, explicit contractual restraints are often placed on the smaller, less well-established party (the franchisee), while an implicit brand-name contract-enforcement mechanism is relied on to prevent cheating by the larger, more well-established party (the franchisor).

If information regarding quality of product supplied by a large firm is communicated among many small buyers who do not all purchase simultaneously, the potential holdup relative to, say, annual sales is reduced substantially compared to the case where each buyer purchased from a separate independent small firm. There are likely to be economies of scale in the supply of a business brand name, because in effect the large firm's total brand-name capital is put on the line with each individual sale. This implies a lower cost of using the implicit contract mechanism, that is, a lower-price premium necessary to assure non-breach, for a large firm compared to a small firm. Therefore one side of the contract will be relatively more incomplete.

For example, in a recent English case using the doctrine of inequality of bargaining power to bar contract enforcement, an individual songwriter signed a long-term (ten-year) exclusive service contract with a music publisher for an agreed royalty percentage.

Since it would be extremely costly to write a complete explicit contract for the supply of publishing services (including advertising and other promotion activities, whose effects are felt over time and are difficult to measure), after a songwriter becomes established he has an incentive to take advantage of any initial investment made by a publishing firm and shift to another publisher. Rather than rely on the brand name of the songwriter or require him to make a specific investment which can serve as collateral, the exclusive service contract prevents this cheating from occurring.

The major cost of such explicit long-term contractual arrangements is the rigidity that is created by the necessity of setting a price or a price formula ex ante. In this song publishing case, the royalty formula may turn out ex post to imply too low a price to the songwriter (if, say, his cooperative promotional input is greater than originally anticipated). If the publisher is concerned about his reputation, these royalty terms will be renegotiated, a common occurrence in continuing business relationships.

If an individual songwriter is a small part of a large publisher's total sales, and if the value of an individual songwriter's ability generally depreciates rapidly or does not persist at peak levels so that signing up new songwriters is an important element of a publisher's continuing business, then cheating an individual songwriter or even all songwriters currently under contract by refusing to renegotiate royalty rates will imply a large capital cost to the publisher. When this behavior is communicated to other actual or potential composers, the publisher's reputation will depreciate and future business will be lost. An individual songwriter, on the other hand, does not generally have large, diversified long-term business concerns and therefore cannot be penalized in that way. It is therefore obvious, independent of any appeal to disparity of bargaining power, why the smaller party would be willing to be bound by an explicit long-term contract while the larger party is bound only implicitly and renegotiates terms that turn out ex post to be truly divergent from ex ante, but unspecified, anticipations.

However, the possibility of reverse publisher cheating is real. If, for example, the songwriter unexpectedly becomes such a great success that current sales by this one customer represents a large share of the present discounted value of total publisher sales, the implicit contract enforcement mechanism may not work. Individuals knowingly trade off these costs of explicit and implicit-enforcement mechanisms in settling upon transaction cost-minimizing contract terms. Although it would be too costly in a stochastic world to attempt to set up an arrangement where no cheating occurs, it is naive to think that courts can cheaply intervene to discover and "fix up" the few cases of opportunistic behavior that will occur. In any event, my analysis makes it clear that one cannot merely look at the agreed-upon, seemingly "unfair" terms to determine if opportunism is occurring....

Notes and Questions

1. The Termination Clause: Klein offers several explanations for why it is mutually beneficial for franchisors and franchisees to have termination clauses included in the franchise agreement. Do those explanations apply to the inclusion of the clause in the Amana contract?

2. Market Protection Against Arbitrary Termination: Franchisors are in the business of selling franchises at the highest price obtainable, with the price being determined by the value of the trademark and the franchisor's reputation for dealing fairly with franchisees. A franchisor, in effect, depreciates the value of the trademark when he opportunistically or arbitrarily terminates a franchisee. Managerial talent is limited, competition among franchisors is intense, and the market for franchises offers potential franchisees a large number of opportunities. Even if all franchisors were offering the same expected net cash flow, the best franchisees would not pay as much for franchises from franchisors that have a reputation for mistreating their franchisees.

3. Managerial Discretion, Personal Preferences, and Agency Costs: In *Corenswet,* was Amana's termination of Corenswet in Amana's best interest or was it a personal vendetta by George Foerstner, the president of Amana? Amana publicly stated that Corenswet was underfinanced and, thus, should not be allowed to continue as a dealer of Amana products. However, behind the scenes, there was strong evidence of a personal feud between the two company presidents. Amana's president desired to terminate Corenswet and replace it with George H. Lehleitner & Co. Would you expect word of the personal feud to have a negative impact on Amana's ability to attract other dealers? If so, can you determine whether Foerstner was a good agent for Raytheon, Amana's parent?

4. Relative Bargaining Power of Franchisors and Franchisees: Corenswet's Experience: Footnote 12 of the *Corenswet* opinion offers some insights into the relative bargaining power of franchisees and franchisors:

> To prevail on a theory of unconscionability Corenswet would have to demonstrate (1) that it had no "meaningful choice" but to deal with Amana and accept the contract as offered, and (2) that the termination clause was "unreasonably favorable" to Amana. *Williams v. Walker-Thomas Furniture Co.,* 1965, 121 U.S. App. D.C. 315, 319, 350 F.2d 445, 449. The record evidence relevant to these questions is scanty. Sam Corenswet testified that Amana in 1969 aggressively sought Corenswet as a distributor and that he only reluctantly decided to commit his company to Amana. Another Corenswet witness, at one point in his testimony, said of the 1975 amended contract that, in view of Corenswet's heavy investment in the Amana line, "we had to take it." The court interrupted that testimony and expressed its view that it was irrelevant to the hearing issues. There was no other evidence regarding the parties' relative bargaining power at the time the relationship began, nor any evidence as to the relative usefulness of the termination clause to the two sides.

Corenswet, 594 F.2d at 139. Ex ante Corenswet was courted, but after Corenswet made Amana-specific investments it was vulnerable to opportunistic amendment of the contract. In light of the analysis of the preceding note and the Klein excerpt, one should be hesitant to evaluate individual clauses or individual actions without considering the totality of the circumstances. For example, was the 1975 amendment a substantial change in the contract or was it merely a formal statement of the "off-the-rack" implied terms?

5. Franchisees as "Victims": The United States Supreme Court, in granting relief to "victims" of the alleged superior bargaining power of franchisors, has exhibited a sympathetic policy to franchisees. Consider, for example the Court's treatment of the Midas Muffler franchise contract. In *Perma Life Mufflers, Inc. v. International Parts Corp.,* 392 U.S. 134 (1968), a group of franchise dealers operating Midas Muffler shops charged that Midas, its parent International Parts, and two other subsidiaries unlawfully conspired to restrain competition under section 1 of the Sherman Act and section 3 of the Clayton Act. The dealers had accepted contracts to sell Midas mufflers at prices fixed by Midas and agreed to not deal with any of Midas's competitors. In considering these franchise agreements, the Supreme Court noted: "Petitioners (the dealers) apparently accepted many of these restraints solely because their acquiescence was necessary to obtain an otherwise attractive business opportunity." *Id.* at 139. The franchised dealers, who clearly wished to take the benefits of the bargain without the burdens, alleged that Midas and its parent had conspired against them, forcing them to accept the onerous terms of the franchise agreements. The Court apparently viewed the dealers as victims of a superior economic force that had bound them to an unfair and ill-advised bargain. The oppressed dealers, according to the Supreme Court, were entitled to relief under the antitrust laws, which, in effect, allowed the federal courts to rewrite their contracts for them. The Supreme Court's willingness to rewrite contracts because of their apparently "unfair" terms reflects the inability of the Court to understand the importance of transaction costs and the relational nature of franchising arrangements. For example, in order to deter franchisee shirking and intrabrand free riding, both of which depreciate the franchisor's brand name, the franchisor insists on a swift and stiff penalty embodied in the termination-at-will clause for cheating franchisees that are caught. The apparent fear of the Supreme Court is that franchisors will not act in "good faith" and will abuse the "unfair" provisions. Although the Court fears that the franchisors may behave opportunistically, it ignores the market forces that deter such opportunistic behavior.

6. Consumers and Employees as "Victims"?: Even more commonly than franchisees, courts (and legislatures) treat consumers and employees as victims (or at least potential victims) of unfair contract terms in so-called "contracts of adhesion." To what extent does Klein's argument apply to consumers and employees as well as to franchisees?

7. Opportunism and Wasted Resources: Parties who recognize the possibility of being subjected to opportunistic behavior will invest real resources in attempting to avoid manipulation. On the other hand, parties who recognize the potential to act opportunistically will invest real resources in perpetrating opportunism. These joint expenditures of resources are socially wasteful, in that real resources are not invested for the purpose of creating wealth but solely for the purpose of transferring wealth. Unlike a mutually beneficial exchange, which is a positive sum game, opportunism is a negative sum game. The threat of opportunism, moreover, increases the transaction costs of exchange, which in turn reduces the volume of mutually beneficial exchanges. The net result of this allocation of real resources, for the purpose of opportunistically transferring wealth, is a reduction in the wealth of society and, *a fortiori,* consumer wealth.

8. Other Uncompensated Wealth Transfers and Wasted Resources: Opportunistic behavior wastes resources. One activity that results in an analogous waste of resources is theft. Theft involves more than the transfer of wealth from one party to another. It also involves the investment of time and other resources by thieves in managing the transfer, as well as the investment of resources by potential victims in avoidance of the transfer. In the absence of theft, these resources would be invested in other, presumably more productive, uses. *See* Gary S. Becker, *Crime and Punishment: An Economic Approach,* 76 Journal of Political Economy 169, 209 (1968) (optimal legislative policies to combat illegal behavior are part of an optimal allocation of resources); Gordon Tullock, *The Welfare Costs of Tariffs, Monopolies, and Theft,* 5 Western Economic Journal 224, 231 (1967) ("A successful bank robbery will inspire potential thieves to greater efforts, lead to the installation of improved protective equipment in other banks, and perhaps result in the hiring of additional policemen."). See the more detailed discussion in Chapter VIII.

9. Long-Term, Incomplete, and Relational Contracts: As previously discussed, the common law of contracts provides a number of standard form, off-the-rack contractual provisions that specify the basic details and fill gaps in negotiated contracts. Unless contradicted by the explicit terms of a contract, the common law rules are an implied part of all contracts. This reduces transaction costs by allowing contracting parties to form enforceable contracts without having to specify every standard of performance and without having to negotiate the allocation of risk associated with every conceivable contingency. All executory contracts face the risk of disruption due to unanticipated or remote contingencies—circumstances the contract is ill-suited to resolve because the contracting parties do not know all that might occur, or circumstances not worth dealing with because there is only a small probability that they will arise.

Occasionally, however, the bargaining situation becomes too complicated and otherwise mutually beneficial transactions fail to occur. In those situations, one alternative is for the parties to integrate into a single entity, which substitutes firm coordination for market coordination. Another alternative to transaction failure is for the inter-firm activity to be coordinated by a relational contract. The nature of a relational contract is found in its contrast with the traditional contingent contract:

> A contract is relational to the extent that the parties are incapable of reducing important terms of the arrangement to well-defined obligations. Such definitive obligations may be impractical because of inability to identify uncertain future conditions or because of inability to characterize complex adaptations adequately even when the contingencies themselves can be identified in advance.

Charles J. Goetz & Robert E. Scott, *Principles of Relational Contracts*, 67 Virginia Law Review 1089, 1091 (1981). The goal of relational contract law is the maintenance of the relationship in the face of conflict that would usually result in termination under traditional contract law approaches. Founded in mutually beneficial exchange, the relational approach abandons the strict reliance on discrete contracts and focuses on the relationship itself. In a sense, the relationship takes on the properties of "a minisociety with a vast array of norms beyond the norms centered on the exchange and its immediate processes." Ian R. Macneil, *Contracts: Adjustment of Long-Term Economic Relations Under Classical, Neoclassical, and Relational Contract Law*, 72 Northwestern Law Review 854, 901 (1978). The exchange is no longer dominant; that is, the original contractual agreement is no longer considered the only source of party-initiated adjustment processes when the relationship is in trouble. Instead, "[t]he reference point is the entire relation as it had developed to the time of the change in question (and in many instances as it has developed since the change). This may or may not include an 'original agreement;' and if it does, may or may not result in great deference being given to it." *Id.* at 890. Thus, a relational contract system attempts to save contractual relationships that are in trouble by going beyond the four corners of the original contract and looking to "the overall context of the whole relation." *Id.* A significant advantage of relational contracting is that it not only provides for the sharing of risks but also a possible reduction of risk. This reduction is possible because the long-term nature of relational contracts reduces the incentives of contracting parties to engage in the types of opportunistic behavior that lead to transaction failures in discrete market transactions.

D. Corporate Governance

In the modern corporation, the key contract is between the owners of the corporation, i.e., the shareholders, and the managers (agents) hired to run the firm. Under this particular contract, a shareholder invests capital in the corporation in return for a residual claim to the net cashflows that result from differences between inflows of cash and promised payments to the other contractual parties which comprise the firm. Shareholders bear the residual risk inherent in the ownership of resources *specific* to the corporation and thus will *demand* the right to **control** the organization. In other words, while a corporation is a nexus of contracts among its customers, managers, suppliers of materials, etc., the corporation vests control in the constituency that bears the residual risk of the organization.

Corporate law puts no restrictions on those who can own residual claims and thus makes it possible for other contractual participants to avoid bearing any of the residual risks. Hence, the fact that anyone can own a residual claim allows specialization in risk-bearing by those investors who choose to do so. In addition, unrestricted stock ownership distributes the residual risk of the firm among many individuals. Individuals can reduce the cost of bearing such risks by holding a diversified portfolio of investments. Because the firm only has to pay investors to bear undiversifiable risk, it will be able to raise capital at a lower cost.

A major intellectual theme in the study of the modern corporation is the "**separation of ownership and control**" thesis, which Adolf A. Berle and Gardiner C. Means first popularized in their famous 1932 book *The Modern Corporation and Private Property*. The basic notion is that dispersed owners of the modern corporation do not have the incentive to control corporate management—directors and officers—and that managers often act in their own interests rather than in the stockholders' interests. Over the years, the Berle and Means thesis has provided the basis for many calls for more stringent legal controls on managerial behavior. This area of corporate policy is called "corporate governance," which refers to the manner in which the relations between the parties to the corporate contract are restrained by government regulation or private ordering.

1. Shareholder Voting and Rationally Ignorant Shareholders

The Berle and Means thesis is quite simple: managers have gained control of modern corporations and have effectively disenfranchised the owners/voters, i.e., the shareholders. With this control, managers have been able to follow their own agendas to the detriment of shareholders. In other words, managers have been able to maximize their own utility by not maximizing the profits of the corporation. This, of course, is a classic agency problem where the manager-agents are not acting in the best interests of their shareholder-principals. Since management does not generally "own" the corporation, managers receive little or no benefit as a result of an increase in monetary profits that ultimately belongs to the residual claimants, i.e., the common shareholders. Moreover, Berle and Means argued that existing corporate law did not provide sufficient mechanisms for owners to control the management. More specifically, Berle and Means argued that there were few contested elections for boards of directors because the management controlled the proxy mechanism and was therefore able to rig the process. As a result of the Berle and Means thesis, political pressures developed (especially during the New Deal) to increase what is referred to as **corporate democracy**. This is not surprising since the Berle and Means model is a political rather than an economic model of the corporation. One political result of the Berle and Means thesis was sections of federal securities laws that increased access by shareholders to the proxy mechanism. Much to the consternation of those who politically adopted the Berle and Means thesis, however, shareholders showed little interest in these statutory rights.

The Berle and Means critique of the publicly traded corporation was based in part on the assumption that shareholders wanted direct control over managers. However, simple economics suggests that shareholders' specialization in bearing the residual risk of the firm does not mean that they have the incentive to actively monitor their agents. In fact, Berle and Means characterize shareholders as **rationally ignorant** because of the large costs associated with staying informed about the corporation's internal affairs and the very small expected benefits to the individual shareholder of being informed.

Moreover, even after bearing the costs of informing themselves, the shareholders are unlikely to be able to influence the corporation's policies and in any event they must share the benefits of intervention if they are successful. Given the divergence of costs and benefits, small shareholders find it rational to **free ride** on other shareholders' monitoring activity:

> Of all those standing in relation to the large corporation, the shareholder is least subject to its power. Through the mechanism of the security markets, his relation to the corporation is rendered highly abstract and formal, quite limited in scope, and readily reducible to monetary terms. The market affords him a way of breaking this relation that is simple and effective. He can sell his stock, and remove himself, qua shareholder, at least from the power of the corporation.
>
> Shareholder democracy, so-called, is misconceived because the shareholders are not the governed of the corporation whose consent must be sought. If they are, it is only in the most limited sense. Their interests are protected if financial information is made available, fraud and overreaching are prevented, and a market is maintained in which their share may be sold. *A priori*, there is no reason for them to have any voice, direct or representational, in the catalogue of corporate decisions ... on prices, wages, and investment. They are no more affected than nonshareholding neighbors by these decisions.... [T]hey deserve the voiceless position in which the modern development left them.

Abram Chayes, *The Modern Corporation and the Rule of Law*, in The Corporation in Modern Society 25, 40–41 (Edward S. Mason ed. 1960). If a shareholder does not like what is happening to his or her shares, then that shareholder can exit, i.e., can sell his or her shares. Hence, given the cost and benefits of such ignorance, it is rational for most shareholders to be ignorant of most corporate matters, thus ignoring the "proxy" control mechanism.

Limited liability clearly facilitates this specialization by shareholders because it allows shareholders to be "rationally ignorant" of managerial practices. Because their risk is limited to their initial investment, shareholders do not waste their time trying to monitor managerial behavior. Thus, limited liability allows investors to be passive with respect to the internal affairs of companies and to concentrate on the externally observable traits like profits and rate of return on investment.

2. Agency Costs and Owner/Manager Conflicts

In general, agency theory suggests that unity of ownership and control is not a necessary condition of efficient performance of a firm. This perspective stresses the voluntary, contractual nature of the corporation. A first step in understanding this market-oriented approach is to recognize that it is based in part on the assumption that the shareholders' primary interest is in the maximization of the value of their investments, and that the contractual relations among participants in the firm must convince shareholders that managers will not abuse the shareholders' interests. A corporation's managers, which are defined to include its officers and directors, are agents of the shareholders. In this view, the so-called separation of ownership and control in the large corporation is an agency relationship, which exists because the benefits of the relationship exceed the agency costs associated with it. That is, the agency relationship exists because both the principal and the agent share in the benefits of the relationship.

At this point, it is helpful to be more precise in the identification of conflicts between managers and shareholders in the corporate firm:

1. *Effort*: A primary concern of agency theory and the separation of ownership and control literature is whether entrenched managers have the incentives to maximize their efforts in pursuing the maximum rate of return for shareholders.

2. *Horizon*: This conflict refers to the issue of how to encourage a manager to act in the shareholders' interests as the manager approaches retirement or prepares to leave the firm for other opportunities.

3. *Risk Aversion*: Entrenched managers have an incentive to avoid bankruptcy at all costs, but shareholders with diversified portfolios are risk neutral with respect to individual securities in their portfolios. In the absence of corrective governance mechanisms, managers' interests will be more closely aligned with those of bondholders than shareholders.

4. *Underleveraged*: Within a certain range the tax savings from debt and increased leverage can increase a firm's profit. Risk averse managers may not like the increased risk associated with increased leverage and debt service demands, but, once again, shareholders could prefer the undertaking of such risk because they specialize in bearing such risks.

5. *Dividend Payout Problem*: Risk averse managers may prefer to reinvest their firm's profits in the firm rather than distribute them to shareholders even though the shareholders could put them to a more productive use.

This list of conflicts between managers and shareholders is not exhaustive, but it serves as a reference for discussing the roles of different corporate governance mechanisms that control corporate agency costs.

Agency theory and transaction cost economics attempt to explain the development of institutional arrangements that convince shareholders voluntarily to allow managers to control their resources. The resources devoted to controlling agency costs are properly identified as agency costs. Thus, agency costs include not only the direct costs associated with agents acting in their own interest at the expense of shareholders, but also the costs of controlling managerial agents through legal or market governance arrangements. Nonetheless, recognizing that the parties to the contract will bear the agency costs implicit in the arrangement is crucial to understanding the agency problem. Thus, agents have the incentive to attempt to minimize agency costs by writing contracts that provide monitoring and bonding activities to the point where the marginal costs of such activities equals the marginal gain of reducing agency costs. According to the contractual theory discussed below, managers select the least costly manner of controlling agency costs. The use of corporate governance mechanisms merely reveals that the costs of monitoring are justified by reducing the costs of an agent's deviation from the behavior that would occur if the agent and principal were one.

3. The Contractual Theory of the Corporation

The fundamental insight of the Berle and Means theory—that shareholders should be concerned about delegating control over their financial capital to corporate managers—provides the cornerstone of the contractual theory of the corporation. This section offers a summary of the governance mechanisms and powerful market forces that encourage managers to act in shareholders' interests. Taken together, the identification of these market forces and the understanding of their interaction represent the contractual theory of the corporation. The corporation is based on voluntary contracts, and the realities of the corporate agency relationship dictate that the corporation's managers select the contractual terms that are then offered to potential investors. In order to raise capital at the lowest possible price, managers must offer contract terms—including evidence of the existence of intra-firm incentive structures—that convince investors that agency costs will be minimized.

a. The Market for Corporate Control

If managers control the corporation, then it seems reasonable for shareholders to be concerned that manager-created intra-firm corporate governance devices, such as managerial incentive contracts, may not always be effective in controlling managerial agency costs. An alternative control mechanism, beyond the direct control of entrenched managers, is found in the stock market. The stock market discipline of managers is manifest in the threat of tender offers, takeovers, or other forms of changes in corporate control whenever entrenched managers adopt strategies and behavior that fail to maximize the value of the corporation's shares. The so-called market for corporate control provides an *external* monitoring mechanism that forces managers to be concerned about their shareholders. Prior to this theoretical development by Henry G. Manne (see Manne, *Mergers and the Market for Corporate Control*, 73 Journal of Political Economy 110 (1965)), commentators on the modern corporation were at a total loss when it came to explaining how corporate managers could be constrained to act in their shareholders' interests. Because the market for corporate control plays the preeminent role in the other governance mechanisms in the contractual theory of the corporation, it warrants further discussion.

A viable market for corporate control requires freely transferable voting shares so that dissatisfied shareholders can sell their shares rather than attempt to control agency problems through internal control mechanisms. The result of this exit process is that the shares of poorly managed firms trade at a discount below the price that could be attained with better and more loyal managers. This creates the possibility of large capital gains from purchasing shares and replacing incompetent or shirking managers with a new group of more efficient managers.

The identification of firms trading below their potential value due to management problems, however, is very costly. Prospective bidders monitor the performance of managerial teams by comparing a corporation's potential market value with its value under current management. In this regard, management inefficiency must be understood to include not only the failure to minimize costs and maximize profits through current operations, but also failures to distribute excess cash flow, take advantage of acquisitions and restructuring opportunities, and communicate to the stock market the health and prospects of the company. If a firm is not performing up to its financial potential under current and expected market conditions, regardless of the reason, then it is an attractive target for a change in corporate control. According to the theory, the acquiring firm purchases the stock of the target company, replaces the inefficient managers with efficient managers, and then reaps a large profit as the stock price rises to reflect the increased earning potential under the more efficient managerial team. The market for corporate control operates through many different forms of control transactions. Of course, the most dramatic is the takeover via a hostile tender offer. In addition, friendly mergers, negotiated tender offers, sales of control by large shareholders, and proxy contests are mechanisms for changing control of corporations and replacing inefficient managers with more efficient ones. In basic terms, the firm's assets are worth more in the hands of the new managers. In many instances, the source of the premium for the replacement of managers is the reduction of agency costs. But a more general view of the role of the market for corporate control is that it is the *threat* of takeover, not the actual occurrence of a takeover, which serves to align managers' interests with shareholders' interests.

Notes on the Market for Corporate Control

1. Takeovers, Managers, and the Williams Act: Tender offers are regulated by the Williams Act, which was an amendment to the Securities Exchange Act of 1934. A tender offeror is required to file a Schedule 13D, which in effect mandates complete disclosure of the tender offeror's background, sources of financing, and plans for the corporation if the tender offer is successful. The stated purpose of this regulation was to establish "an even playing field." However, while that may be the "intent" of the Act, unintended (or, perhaps, intended) consequences of the Williams Act quickly surfaced. Incumbent managers surely benefited from the reduced threat of hostile takeovers.

2. Empirical Evidence: The role of the market for corporate control in the governance of the modern corporation is not based on some mystical or ideological belief in the power of market forces, but rather it is supported by numerous empirical studies. *See* Michael C. Jensen & Richard S. Ruback, *The Market for Corporate Control: The Scientific Evidence*, 11 Journal of Financial Economics 5 (1983); Gregg A. Jarrell et al., *The Market for Corporate Control: The Empirical Evidence Since 1980*, 2 Journal of Economic Perspectives 49 (1988); *see also* Frank H. Easterbrook, *Managers' Discretion and Investors' Welfare: Theories and Evidence*, 9 Delaware Journal of Corporate Law 540 (1984). The role of the stock market in controlling managerial discretion was one of the first important applications of economics to corporation law and facilitated the development of the contractual theory of the corporation.

3. Managerial Responses to Tender Offers: One of the most heated debates in corporate law during the 1980's involved the question of the proper role of incumbent managers of a target corporation when presented with a tender offer for control. The incumbent managers, who are faced with the prospect of losing their jobs if the takeover is successful, may have an incentive to try to defeat the takeover even if it appears to be in the shareholders' best interests. Shareholders encounter a dilemma in deciding whether managerial defensive tactics are in their best interests. If a firm is a target, the shareholders benefit if the managers' defensive activities result in a higher price as long as their activities do not actually defeat the tender offer. If the defensive tactics defeat the tender offer, shareholders are clearly worse off—the managers have, in effect, denied them the opportunity to sell their shares at a higher price. But all of this reflects an ex post analysis of the proper managerial response once a takeover has been initiated; an economic perspective adopts an ex ante view of the proper managerial response when the shareholders are not certain that their corporation will become a target. *See* Frank H. Easterbrook & Daniel R. Fischel, *The Proper Role of a Target's Management in Responding to a Tender Offer*, 94 Harvard Law Review 1161, 1177 (1981). In actuality, most firms are never takeover targets (although all are potential targets and thus must respond to the threat of tender offers). The threat effect of a takeover often means that firms will not be attractive targets—the managers are already being forced to act in the shareholders' best interests. Establishing ex ante a rule allowing managers to defend against takeover increases the costs of (and reduces the effectiveness of) the market for corporate control as a monitoring mechanism and thus merely increases the problems associated with the separation of ownership and control. That is, raising the defensive tactics provides managers with more room to act in their own interest without being totally concerned about shareholder-welfare. It has been argued that, given a choice, shareholders as a group would be better off ex ante under a system that forces all managers to act in the shareholders' best interests at all times as opposed to a system that occasionally results in high stakes takeover battles. This reasoning has led to calls for mandating the role of the market for corporate control in all corporations by legally restricting the ability of managers to defend against takeover bids.

4. Stakeholders: Some commentators, especially those who are concerned about adverse employment effects or harm to some communities, argue that corporate managers should consider more than just shareholders' interests in deciding whether to attempt to defeat a hostile tender offer. In effect, these commentators characterize shareholders as just one of the many constituencies, sometimes referred to as stakeholders, of the company. The contractual theory of the corporation suggests that those commentators misunderstand the role of shareholders. Shareholders are not equal to these other constituencies because they bear the residual risk inherent in the ownership of resources *specific* to the corporation and thus will *demand* the right to control the organization. In other words, while a corporation is a nexus of contracts among its customers, managers, suppliers of materials, etc., the corporate contract vests control in the constituency that bears the residual risk of the organization.

5. The Glue: Exclusive reliance on the market for corporate control to solve all of the potential conflicts of interest associated with the separation of ownership and control is neither justified nor necessary. Managerial discretion is constrained by other market and legal mechanisms. For example, in some large corporations, agency costs are reduced by the corporation being owned by shareholders who hold a large percentage of outstanding stock and therefore have the incentive to monitor managerial behavior closely. Nevertheless, the market for corporate control provides a last resort mechanism for correcting excessive managerial discretion and, as a direct consequence, reduces the likelihood that shareholders will be harmed by their agents. The market for corporate control provides the glue that holds together the nexus of contracts.

b. Product Market Competition

Product market competition forces managers to attempt to maximize the profits of the corporation. Failure to maximize profits in competitive markets often means the failure of the firm, which may be as costly for the managers as it is for the shareholders. Because of firm-specific investments in their own human capital and the likelihood of compensation in the form of stock or stock options, managers typically have a larger percentage of their total wealth tied up in the firm they work for relative to the percentage of the typical diversified shareholder. Thus, managers of firms that do not have market power have a strong incentive to act in the shareholders' interests. Moreover, if a firm does have market power, the market will have already capitalized the higher expected profits into the corporation's stock price so a failure to maximize profits will result in a below-average return on the shareholders' investments, thus making the firm an attractive takeover target.

c. Capital Market Competition and Capital Structure

Most corporations use a mixture of debt and equity financing. In a path-breaking 1958 article, Franco Modigliani and Merton Miller showed that, under a set of specified assumptions including absence of transaction and information costs, the capital structure of a firm—that is, its debt to equity mix—was irrelevant to the total value of the firm. *See* Franco Modigliani & Merton H. Miller, *The Cost of Capital, Corporation Finance, and the Theory of Investment*, 48 American Economic Review 261 (1958); *see also* Merton H. Miller, *The Modigliani Miller Propositions After Thirty Years*, 2 Journal of Economic

Perspectives 99 (1988). This raises the issue of why different capital structures are observed across firms. The contractual theory of the corporation demonstrates its analytical strength by answering the Modigliani and Miller riddle. In a landmark article, Michael Jensen and William Meckling used agency problems and monitoring of managers to identify the relevance of capital structure to the value of a firm. *See* Michael C. Jensen & William H. Meckling, *Theory of the Firm: Managerial Behavior, Agency Costs, and Ownership Structure*, 3 Journal of Financial Economics 305 (1976). An all-equity structure gives substantial discretion to managers to use corporate assets for their own benefit, subject only to the vague proscriptions of fiduciary duties. However, managers have an incentive to minimize their combined costs of debt and equity capital because failure to do so would make them vulnerable to takeover. In order to raise equity capital at the lowest possible cost, a corporation's managers must convince potential shareholders that agency costs will be minimal. Bondholders also must address conflict of interest problems. For example, a debt-heavy structure induces those who hold equity and managers who are responsive to their interests to make highly risky investments that may produce great benefits to the equity holders if they succeed and losses to the debt holders if they fail. Bondholders contain and monitor these agency costs by using contracts that expressly limit the discretion of management to act against their interests. Under the Jensen-Meckling view, different capital structures may be responses to different types of agency costs. There is no one optimal capital structure for all corporations.

d. Corporate Performance and Executive Compensation

Managerial salaries and other forms of compensation are often linked to how well the firm is performing. Managers monitor each other's performances and reward achievements with bonuses and salary adjustments as a form of "ex post settling up" that substantially alleviates incentive problems. Also, if managers enjoy especially favorable salaries or other terms of employment, they may be disciplined by the prospect of being fired. A high salary—that is, higher than a manager's opportunity cost or next best paying job—can be thought of as "two-edged sword." On the one hand, the high salary can be viewed as evidence that the manager's compensation is not being effectively monitored by the board; on the other hand, the manager may be extremely motivated to work hard to keep a position when she knows she is overpaid. Managers' proclivities towards shirking can be reduced even further by the use of stock options, restricted stock, and bonus plans which alter a manager's time horizon for her managerial decisions so as to ensure that she acts in accordance with the long-term interests of her principals. As managers approach retirement, defined benefit pension plans under which benefits are linked to the last period's salary resolve some of the horizon problems. Stock options in retirement packages can also serve to alleviate horizon problems.

In general, corporate compensation packages appear to be structured in a manner to solve most of the conflicts between managers and shareholders. Analytically, corporate compensation packages can include three components: (1) unconditional compensation, such as salary and pension and insurance benefits; (2) compensation conditioned on stock market-based performance, such as stock options, restricted stock, and bonuses; and (3) compensation conditioned on accounting-based performance, such as profit sharing. Stock market-based performance measures are beyond managers' direct control or manipulation because stock prices reflect all available information, including the discounted value of long-term consequences of short-term actions, regarding the value of a firm. On the other hand, accounting-based performance measures are subject to manipulation by senior executives through, for example, decisions to maximize short-term accounting profits at the expense of greater long-term profits, which are beyond managers' employment terms. Thus, accounting-based performance measures are a potential source of agency costs, and most senior executives' compensation contracts do not include a component based on accounting performance.

Kamin v. American Express Co.

Supreme Court of New York
383 N.Y.S.2d 807 (1976)

Edward J. Greenfield, Judge

In this stockholders' derivative action, the individual defendants, who are the directors of the American Express Company, move for an order dismissing the complaint for failure to state a cause of action ... and alternatively, for summary judgment....

The complaint is brought derivatively by two minority stockholders of the American Express Company, asking for a declaration that a certain dividend in kind is a waste of corporate assets, directing the defendants not to proceed with the distribution, or, in the alternative, for monetary damages. The motion to dismiss the complaint requires the court to presuppose the truth of the allegations. It is the defendants' contention that, conceding everything in the complaint, no viable cause of action is made out.

After establishing the identity of the parties, the complaint alleges that in 1972 American Express acquired for investment 1,954,418 shares of common stock of Donaldson, Lufken and Jenrette, Inc. (hereafter DLJ), a publicly traded corporation, at a cost of $29,900,000. It is further alleged that the current market value of those shares is approximately $4,000,000. On July 28, 1975, it is alleged, the board of directors of American Express declared a special dividend to all stockholders of record pursuant to which the shares of DLJ would be distributed in kind. Plaintiffs contend further that if American Express were to sell the DLJ shares on the market, it would sustain a capital loss of $25,000,000 which could be offset against taxable capital gains on other investments. Such a sale, they allege, would result in tax savings to the company of approximately $8,000,000, which would not be available in the case of the distribution of DLJ shares to stockholders. It is alleged that on October 8, 1975 and October 16, 1975, plaintiffs demanded that the directors rescind the previously declared dividend in DLJ shares and take steps to preserve the capital loss which would result from selling the shares. This demand was rejected by the board of directors on October 17, 1975.

It is apparent that all the previously-mentioned allegations of the complaint go to the question of the exercise by the board of directors of business judgment in deciding how to deal with the DLJ shares. The crucial allegation which must be scrutinized to determine the legal sufficiency of the complaint is paragraph 19, which alleges: "19. All of the defendant Directors engaged in or acquiesced in or negligently permitted the declaration and payment of the Dividend in violation of the fiduciary duty owed by them to Amex to care for and preserve Amex's assets in the same manner as a man of average prudence would care for his own property."

* * *

Examination of the complaint reveals that there is no claim of fraud or self-dealing, and no contention that there was any bad faith or oppressive conduct....

... [T]he question of whether or not a dividend is to be declared or a distribution of some kind should be made is exclusively a matter of business judgment for the board of directors. "Courts will not interfere with such discretion unless it be first made to appear that the directors have acted or are about to act in bad faith and for a dishonest purpose. It is for the directors to say, acting in good faith of course, when and to what extent dividends shall be declared. The statute confers upon the directors this power, and the minority stockholders are not in a position to question this right, so long as the directors are acting in good faith." *Liebman v Auto Strop Co.*, 241 NY 427, 433–434.

Thus, a complaint must be dismissed if all that is presented is a decision to pay dividends rather than pursuing some other course of conduct. A complaint which alleges merely that some course of action other than that pursued by the board of directors would have been more advantageous gives rise to no cognizable cause of action. Courts have more than enough to do in adjudicating legal rights and devising remedies for wrongs. The directors' room rather than the courtroom is the appropriate forum for thrashing out purely business questions which will have an impact on profits, market prices, competitive situations, or tax advantages. As stated by Cardozo, J., when sitting at Special Term, the substitution of someone else's business judgment for that of the directors "'is no business for any court to follow.'" (*Holmes v Saint Joseph Lead Co.*, 84 Misc 278, 283, quoting from *Gamble v Queens County Water Co.*, 123 NY 91, 99.)

It is not enough to allege, as plaintiffs do here, that the directors made an imprudent decision, which did not capitalize on the possibility of using a potential capital loss to offset capital gains. More than imprudence or mistaken judgment must be shown. "Questions of policy of management, expediency of contracts or action, adequacy of consideration, lawful appropriation of corporate funds to advance corporate interests, are left solely to their honest and unselfish decision, for their powers therein are without limitation and free from restraint, and the exercise of them for the common and general interests of the corporation may not be questioned, although the results show that what they did was unwise or inexpedient." *Pollitz v Wabash R.R. Co.*, 207 NY 113, 124.

* * *

Nor does this appear to be a case in which a potentially valid cause of action is inartfully stated. The defendants have moved alternatively for summary judgment and have submitted affidavits…, and plaintiffs likewise have submitted papers enlarging upon the allegations of the complaint. The affidavits of the defendants and the exhibits annexed thereto demonstrate that the objections raised by the plaintiffs to the proposed dividend action were carefully considered and unanimously rejected by the board at a special meeting called precisely for that purpose at the plaintiffs' request. The minutes of the special meeting indicate that the defendants were fully aware that a sale rather than a distribution of the DLJ shares might result in the realization of a substantial income tax saving. Nevertheless, they concluded that there were countervailing considerations primarily with respect to the adverse effect such a sale, realizing a loss of $25,000,000, would have on the net income figures in the American Express financial statement. Such a reduction of net income would have a serious effect on the market value of the publicly traded American Express stock. This was not a situation in which the defendant directors totally overlooked facts called to their attention. They gave them consideration, and attempted to view the total picture in arriving at their decision. While plaintiffs contend that according to their accounting consultants the loss on the DLJ stock would still have to be charged against current earnings even if the stock were distributed, the defendants' accounting experts assert that the loss would be a charge against earnings only in the event of a sale, whereas in the event of distribution of the stock as a dividend, the proper accounting treatment would be to charge the loss only against surplus. While the chief accountant for the SEC raised some question as to the appropriate accounting treatment of this transaction, there was no basis for any action to be taken by the SEC with respect to the American Express financial statement.

The only hint of self-interest which is raised, not in the complaint but in the papers on the motion, is that 4 of the 20 directors were officers and employees of American Express and members of its executive incentive compensation plan. Hence, it is suggested, by virtue of the action taken earnings may have been overstated and their compensation affected thereby. Such a claim is highly speculative and standing alone can hardly be regarded as sufficient to support an inference of self-dealing. There is no claim or showing that the four company directors dominated and controlled the 16 outside members of the board. Certainly, every action taken by the board has some impact on earnings and may therefore affect the compensation of those whose earnings are keyed to profits. That does not disqualify the inside directors, nor does it put every policy adopted by the board in question. All directors have an obligation, using sound business judgment, to maximize income for the benefit of all persons having a stake in the welfare of the corporate entity. What we have here as revealed both by the complaint and by the affidavits and exhibits, is that a disagreement exists between two minority stockholders and a unanimous board of directors as to the best way to handle a loss already incurred on an investment. The directors are entitled to exercise their honest business judgment on the information before them, and to act within their corporate powers. That they may be mistaken, that other courses of action might have differing consequences, or that their action might benefit some shareholders more than others present no basis for the superimposition of judicial judgment, so long as it appears that the directors have been acting in good faith. The question of to what extent a dividend shall be declared and the manner in which it shall be paid is ordinarily subject only to the qualification that the dividend be paid out of surplus (Business Corporation Law, § 510, subd [b]). The court will not interfere unless a clear case is made out of fraud, oppression, arbitrary action, or breach of trust.

Courts should not shrink from the responsibility of dismissing complaints or granting summary judgment when no legal wrongdoing is set forth. ...

In this case it clearly appears that the plaintiffs have failed as a matter of law to make out an actionable claim. Accordingly, the motion by the defendants for summary judgment and dismissal of the complaint is granted.

Notes and Questions

1. Market Evaluation of American Express's Investment in DLJ: In terms of stock market valuation of the business, American Express made a poor business decision by not taking the substantial capital loss and resulting tax savings. The large accounting loss would have been anticipated by investors who, after all, could observe what had happened to the market value of American Express's investment in DLJ. That is, prior to the board's decision, AMEX's market price already reflected the anticipated losses (and tax savings) from the decline in DLJ stock. By not taking the large capital loss, the expected future cash flows to American Express declined because they now had to pay higher taxes. The stock market price should have fallen in response to this unexpected change.

2. Accounting-Based Compensation. Accounting is an art that involves many subjective, discretionary decisions that can impact the reported financial position of a company. Accounting data can be manipulated by senior managers. In *Kamin*, the senior managers wanted to avoid showing an accounting loss from the DLJ investment. Consider how the executives' incentives structures affected this transaction. Four members of the Board of Directors apparently were compensated according to the accounting profits of the firm. In most basic terms, accounting profit is the residual after subtracting expenditures from revenues. Shareholders are interested in maximizing the value of their shares, but accounting profits do not always relate directly to stock price. In this case, the directors avoided recognizing the loss on the DLJ investment and thus made profits appear larger than they would have if they had followed the traditional route of selling the shares and distributing the proceeds to the shareholders. This unusual result occurred because the compensation of the directors was linked to accounting profits instead of stock market price. They could not take the large capital loss without substantially affecting their bonuses, so they came up with a novel way to avoid taking the loss. However, this creative decision to directly distribute the stock to the shareholders cost American Express and its shareholders the tax benefits of the anticipated accounting loss. This move clearly was not in the best interests of shareholders — it cost them in the form of higher than anticipated taxes. The incentive structure was the problem.

3. The Business Judgment Rule: Judicial interpretations of the fiduciary duty of due care protect managers from second-guessing informed business decisions. See the discussion in this section, *infra*.

4. Typical Compensation Arrangements: Accounting-based profit-sharing arrangements are often used for middle and lower-level employees who are generally not in a position to manipulate accounting data. However, for top-level executives, compensation is usually linked to stock price. The stock market is an external monitor of firm performance and is difficult to fool with using accounting shenanigans. With the proper compensation system in place, manipulation does not occur and shareholders are better off. However, if the incentives are wrong and if directors do not diligently monitor the executives who have the ability to manipulate accounting numbers, then disaster can strike. The meltdowns of Enron, WorldCom, and Arthur Andersen in 2001 are examples of how bad things can get when incentives are misaligned, and board monitoring is non-existent.

e. Markets for Managers

Corporate managers recognize that they can improve the performance of the firm by reducing agency costs. Managers compete with one another to attain the top positions in their companies, and most promotion decisions are made on the basis of an individual's productivity. Shareholders benefit as managers attempt to climb the corporate ladder by improving their productivity and impressing their superiors. Moreover, top-level managers often increase their salaries by jumping to other firms (or at least threatening to do so). Thus, competition for managerial services, both inside and outside the corporation, encourages managers to act in shareholders' best interests.

f. The Board of Directors

At the heart of Berle and Means' attack on the large publicly traded corporation is the board of directors' acquiescence to the decisions of the management. In this perspective, the board is assumed to reflect the same agency problems as managers. Recent developments in the economics of corporate hierarchy have helped to clarify the board's role as a monitor of managerial decisions. This analysis takes the separation of ownership (residual risk bearing) and control (decision management) analysis one step further and looks at the specialization of functions by agents who control the firm. One branch of this analysis has concentrated on the complementary roles of managers and directors.

The role for the board of directors is to establish an effective decision monitoring structure. The control of the corporation by agents is separated according to function whereby decision management (the initiation and implementation of strategic plans) is entrusted to senior managers and decision control (the ratification and monitoring of the strategy formulation and implementation process) is the domain of the board of directors. That is, the management control functions are delegated to the board by the residual claimants, and the board then delegates most decision management functions and many decision control functions to internal agents. However, the board retains ultimate control over the internal agents—including the right to ratify and monitor major policy initiatives and to hire, fire, and set the compensation of top level decision managers. Agency problems are reduced by tying compensation to these specialized activities. Thus, unlike the Berle and Means perspective, which views directors as pawns in the managers' hands, the role of the directors is important to the control of agency costs and, hence, the long-term survival of the firm. However, when directors behave the way Berle and Means describe, disasters such as Enron and WorldCom are more likely.

g. Ownership Structure

Ownership structure often plays an important role in the governance of corporations. In contrast to the convention of viewing the governance role of residual claimants as that of being "rationally ignorant" of the firm's internal affairs and exiting the firm upon dissatisfaction, owners of large blocks of shares may have so much of their wealth tied up in a firm that they cannot afford to ignore the governance of the corporation. Monitoring, or the possibility of monitoring, by large shareholders alters managerial behavior and reduces agency costs. Thus, ownership structure is another of the many corporate governance mechanisms that can be utilized in controlling agency costs. Of course, in many corporations, the ownership structure is so diffuse that shareholders are truly rationally ignorant, making the other governance mechanisms relatively more important.

In the last few decades however, the rise of hedge funds has led to an increase of shareholder activism. Marcel Kahan and Edward Rock argue that unlike large institutional investors, which have the ownership stakes to impact managers' decision making but also the diversification that makes control unnecessary and uneconomical, hedge funds typically have similar ownership stakes and a focused investment strategy that makes active fund management economical. *See* Marcel Kahan & Edward B. Rock, *Hedge Funds in Corporate Governance and Corporate Control*, 155 University of Pennsylvania Law Review 1021 (2007). Investors pay hedge fund managers to actively manage their money in search of uncorrelated and superior returns in the market. One way hedge fund managers achieve those results is by concentrating funds on a smaller number of companies than traditional institutional investors. This allows them to monitor their portfolio companies' managers more closely. Institutional investors are willing to follow the hedge funds' lead, giving them enough votes to hold management more accountable than under the traditional Berle and Means model.

h. Corporate Law and Fiduciary Duties

Emphasis on the interaction of market forces under the contractual theory of the corporation has led some scholars to argue that markets will lead managers to adopt optimal governance structures and that corporate law is irrelevant. However, market mechanisms may be inadequate to deal with last-period, or one-time, divergences when the agent rationally concludes that the benefits of the one-time use of discretion is worth whatever penalties may be forthcoming in the employment market for the agent's services. In this regard, the corporate law of fiduciary duties serves as a legal constraint on managerial opportunism.

Moreover, because markets do not operate without cost, it appears that corporate law plays a productive role in the contractual theory of the corporation by providing a standard form contract that reduces the transaction and negotiating costs of reaching and adhering to optimal contracts. In fact, some commentators have argued that it is appropriate to view corporation law as a standard form contract. Through the law of fiduciary duties, which proscribes theft and specifies standards of care and loyalty, corporate law serves as a substitute for costly, fully contingent contracts. The directors and the officers occupy a **fiduciary relationship** with the corporation and its shareholders. As fiduciaries, the directors and officers have a duty to act with the highest standard of good faith when acting on behalf of the corporation and its shareholders. The primary enforcement mechanism is to hold directors and officers liable for the losses to the corporation that result from their failure to fulfill their fiduciary duties.

Jordan v. Duff and Phelps, Inc.

United States Court of Appeals for the Seventh Circuit
815 F.2d 429 (1987)

EASTERBROOK, Circuit Judge.

Flamm v. Eberstadt, 814 F.2d 1169 (7th Cir.1987), holds that a corporation need not disclose, to investors trading in the stock market, ongoing negotiations for a merger. A public corporation may keep silent until the firms reach agreement in principle on the price and structure of the deal. Things are otherwise for closely held corporations. *Michaels v. Michaels*, 767 F.2d 1185, 1194–97 (7th Cir.1985), holds that a closely held firm must disclose material information to investors from whom it purchases stock, and that a decision to seek another firm with which to merge may be the sort of material information that must be disclosed to the investor selling his shares, even though the firm has not reached agreement in principle on the price and structure of a deal.

The treatment of public and private corporations is different because of the potential effects of disclosure. Often negotiations must be conducted in secrecy to increase their prospects of success. The prospect of disclosure to the public, and therefore to potential rival bidders, may reduce the willingness of some firms to enter negotiations and lead others to cut back on the best price they will offer. Investors are entitled to the benefits of secrecy during the negotiations; a law designed to prevent frauds on investors tolerates silence that yields benefits for investors as a group. *Flamm* also points out that negotiating firms need to know when they must disclose. Uncertainty may lead to premature disclosures that investors would like to avoid. A close corporation may disclose to an investor without alerting the public at large, however, so that disclosure does not injure investors as a whole. Moreover, a rule that the close corporation (or its managers) must disclose in the course of negotiating to purchase stock supplies a timing rule on which the firm may rely. It need disclose the existence of the decision to sell (and the status of negotiations) only to the person whose stock is to be acquired. The face-to-face negotiations allow the investor to elicit the information he requires, while permitting the firm to extract promises of confidentiality that safeguard the negotiations.

This case contains two wrinkles. First, it involves the acquisition of a closely held corporation by a public corporation. Second, the investor in the closely held corporation was an employee, and he was offered shares to cement his loyalty to the firm; yet he quit (and was compelled by a shareholders' agreement to sell his shares) for reasons unrelated to the value of the stock. The parties hotly contest the effects of these facts.

* * *

Duff and Phelps, Inc., evaluates the risk and worth of firms and their securities. It sells credit ratings, investment research, and financial consulting services to both the firms under scrutiny and potential investors in them. Jordan started work at Duff & Phelps in May 1977 and was viewed as a successful securities analyst. In 1981 the firm offered Jordan the opportunity to buy some stock. By November 1983 Jordan had purchased 188 of the 20,100 shares outstanding. He was making installment payments on another 62 shares. Forty people other than Jordan held stock in Duff & Phelps.

Jordan purchased his stock at its "book value" (the accounting net worth of Duff & Phelps, divided by the number of shares outstanding). Before selling him any stock, Duff & Phelps required Jordan to sign a "Stock Restriction and Purchase Agreement" (the Agreement). This provided in part:

> Upon the termination of any employment with the Corporation … for any reason, including resignation, discharge, death, disability or retirement, the individual whose employment is terminated or his estate shall sell to the Corporation, and the Corporation shall buy, all Shares of the Corporation then owned by such individual or his estate. The price to be paid for such Shares shall be equal to the adjusted book value (as hereinafter defined) of the Shares on the December 31 which coincides with, or immediately precedes, the date of termination of such individual's employment.

* * *

While Jordan was accumulating stock, Hansen, the chairman of the board, was exploring the possibility of selling the firm. Between May and August 1983 Hansen and Francis Jeffries, another officer of Duff & Phelps, negotiated with Security Pacific Corp., a bank holding company. The negotiators reached agreement on a merger, in which Duff & Phelps would be valued at $50 million, but a higher official within Security Pacific vetoed the deal on August 11, 1983. As of that date, Duff & Phelps had no irons in the fire.

Jordan, however, was conducting a search of his own — for a new job. Jordan's family lived near Chicago, the headquarters of Duff & Phelps, and Jordan's wife did not get along with Jordan's mother. The strain between the two occasionally left his wife in tears. He asked Duff & Phelps about the possibility of a transfer to the firm's only branch office, in Cleveland, but the firm did not need Jordan's services there. Concluding that it was time to choose between his job and his wife, Jordan chose his wife and started looking for employment far away from Chicago. His search took him to Houston, where Underwood Neuhaus & Co., a broker-dealer in securities, offered him a job at a salary ($110,000 per year) substantially greater than his compensation ($67,000) at Duff & Phelps. Jordan took the offer on the spot during an interview in Houston, but Underwood would have allowed Jordan to withdraw this oral acceptance.

On November 16, 1983, Jordan told Hansen that he was going to resign and accept employment with Underwood. Jordan did not ask Hansen about potential mergers; Hansen did not volunteer anything. Jordan delivered a letter of resignation, which Duff & Phelps accepted the same day. By mutual agreement, Jordan worked the rest of the year for Duff & Phelps even though his loyalties had shifted. He did this so that he could receive the book value of the stock as of December 31, 1983 — for under the Agreement a departure in November would have meant valuation as of December 31, 1982. Jordan delivered his certificates on December 30, 1983, and the firm mailed him a check for $23,225, the book value (at $123.54 per share) of the 188 shares of stock. Jordan surrendered, as worthless under the circumstances, the right to buy the remaining 62 shares.

Before Jordan cashed the check, however, he was startled by the announcement on January 10, 1984, of a merger between Duff & Phelps and a subsidiary of Security Pacific. Under the terms of the merger Duff & Phelps would be valued at $50 million. If Jordan had been an employee on January 10, had quickly paid for the other 62 shares, and the merger had closed that day, he would have received $452,000 in cash and the opportunity to obtain as much as $194,000 more in "earn out" (a percentage of Duff & Phelps's profits to be paid to the former investors—an arrangement that keeps the employees' interest in the firm keen and reduces the buyer's risk if profits fall short). Jordan refused to cash the check and demanded his stock back; Duff & Phelps told him to get lost. He filed this suit in March 1984, asking for damages measured by the value his stock would have had under the terms of the acquisition.

* * *

All of this supposes that Duff & Phelps had a duty to disclose anything to Jordan. Most people are free to buy and sell stock on the basis of valuable private knowledge without informing their trading partners. Strangers transact in markets all the time using private information that might be called "material" and, unless one has a duty to disclose, both may keep their counsel. The ability to make profits from the possession of information is the principal spur to create the information, which the parties and the market as a whole may find valuable. The absence of a duty to disclose may not justify a lie about a material fact, but Duff & Phelps did not lie to Jordan. It simply remained silent when Jordan quit and tendered the stock, and it offered the payment required by the Agreement. Duff & Phelps maintains that it was entitled to be silent … even though it could not have lied in response to the questions Jordan should (in retrospect) have asked but did not.

This argument is unavailing on the facts as we know them. The "duty" in question is the fiduciary duty of corporate law. Close corporations buying their own stock, like knowledgeable insiders of closely held firms buying from outsiders, have a fiduciary duty to disclose material facts....

Because the fiduciary duty is a standby or off-the-rack guess about what parties would agree to if they dickered about the subject explicitly, parties may contract with greater specificity for other arrangements.... The obligation to break silence is itself based on state law, and so may be redefined to the extent state law permits. But we need not decide how far contracts can redefine obligations to disclose. Jordan was an employee at will; he signed no contract.

The stock was designed to bind Duff & Phelps's employees loyally to the firm. The buy-sell agreement tied ownership to employment. Understandably Duff & Phelps did not want a viper in its nest, a disgruntled employee remaining only in the hope of appreciation of his stock. So there could have been reason to divorce the employment decision from the value of the stock. Perhaps it would have been rational for each employee to agree with Duff & Phelps to look to salary alone in deciding whether to stay. A contractual agreement that the firm had no duty to disclose would have uncoupled the investment decision from the employment decision, leaving whoever was in the firm on the day of a merger to receive a surprise appreciation. Some might lose by leaving early; some might reap a windfall by buying just before the announcement; all might think it wise to have as little as possible said in the interim.

Yet an explicit agreement to make all employment decisions in ignorance of the value of the stock might not have been in the interests of the firm or its employees. Duff & Phelps was trying to purchase loyalty by offering stock to its principal employees. The package of compensation contained salary and the prospect of appreciation of the stock. Perhaps it paid a lower salary than, say, Underwood Neuhaus & Co., because its package contained a higher component of gain from anticipated appreciation in the stock. It is therefore unwarranted to say that the implicit understanding between Jordan and Duff & Phelps should be treated as if it had such a no-duty clause; we are not confident that this is the clause firms and their employees regularly would prefer. Duff & Phelps has not identified any firm that adopted such a clause explicitly, and the absence of explicit clauses counsels caution in creating implicit exceptions to the general fiduciary duty.

* * *

The closest Duff & Phelps came is the provision in the Agreement fixing the price of the stock at book value. Yet although the Agreement fixed the price to be paid those who quit, it did not establish the terms on which anyone would leave....

* * *

Our dissenting colleague concludes that all of this is beside the point because Hansen could have said, on receiving Jordan's letter on November 16: "In a few weeks we will pull off a merger that would have made your stock 20 times more valuable. It's a shame you so foolishly resigned. But even if you hadn't resigned, we would have fired you, the better to engross the profits of the merger for ourselves. So long, sucker." This would have been permissible, under our colleague's interpretation, because Jordan was an employee at will and therefore could have been fired at any time, even the day before the merger, for any reason—including the desire to deprive Jordan of a share of the profits. The ability to fire Jordan enabled the firm to "call" his shares, at book value, on whim. On this view, it is foolish to say that Duff & Phelps had a duty to disclose, because disclosure would have been no use to Jordan.... Perhaps Duff & Phelps does not want to establish a reputation for shoddy dealing; as our dissenting brother observes, a firm's desire to preserve its reputation is a powerful inducement to treat its contractual partners well. To attribute to a litigant an argument that it will take every possible advantage is to assume that the party wishes to dissipate its reputation, and the assumption is unwarranted.

More than that, a person's status as an employee "at will" does not imply that the employer may discharge him for every reason. Illinois, where Jordan was employed, has placed some limits on the discharge of at-will employees.... The silence of the parties may make it necessary to imply other terms—those we are confident the parties would have bargained for if they had signed a written agreement. One term implied in every written contract and therefore, we suppose, every unwritten one, is that neither party will try to take opportunistic advantage of the other. "[T]he fundamental function of contract law (and recognized as such at least since Hobbes's day) is to deter people from behaving opportunistically toward their contracting parties, in order to encourage the optimal timing of economic activity and to make costly self-protective measures unnecessary." Richard A. Posner, *Economic Analysis of Law* 81 (3d ed. 1986)....

Employment creates occasions for opportunism. A firm may fire an employee the day before his pension vests, or a salesman the day before a large commission becomes payable. Cases of this sort may present difficult questions about the reasons for the decision (was it opportunism, or was it a decline in the employee's performance?). The difficulties of separating opportunistic conduct from honest differences of opinion about an employee's performance on the job may lead firms and their employees to transact on terms that keep such disputes out of court—which employment at will usually does. But no one ... doubts that an *avowedly* opportunistic discharge is a breach of contract, although the employment is at-will.... An employer may be thoughtless, nasty, and mistaken. Avowedly opportunistic conduct has been treated differently, however.

The stock component in Jordan's package induced him to stick around and work well. Such an inducement is effective only if the employee reaps the rewards of success as well as the penalties of failure. We do not suppose for a second that if Jordan had not resigned on November 16, the firm could have fired him on January 9 with a little note saying: "Dear Mr. Jordan: There will be a lucrative merger tomorrow. You have been a wonderful employee, but in order to keep the proceeds of the merger for ourselves, we are letting you go, effective this instant. Here is the $23,000 for your shares." Had the firm fired Jordan for this stated reason, it would have broken an implied pledge to avoid opportunistic conduct....

The timing of the sale and the materiality of the information Duff & Phelps withheld on November 16 are for the jury to determine....

* * *

REVERSED AND REMANDED.

* * *

POSNER, Circuit Judge, dissenting.

* * *

Jordan's deal with Duff and Phelps required him to surrender his stock at book value if he left the company. It didn't matter whether he quit or was fired, retired or died; the agreement is explicit on these matters. My brethren hypothesize "implicit parts of the relations between Duff & Phelps and its employees." But those relations are totally defined by (1) the absence of an employment contract, which made Jordan an employee at will; (2) the shareholder agreement, which has no "implicit parts" that bear on Duff and Phelps' duty to Jordan, and explicitly ties his rights as a shareholder to his status as an employee at will; (3) a provision in the stock purchase agreement between Jordan and Duff and Phelps (signed at the same time as the shareholder agreement) that "nothing herein contained shall confer on the Employee any right to be continued in the employment of the Corporation." There is no occasion to speculate about "the implicit understanding" between Jordan and Duff and Phelps. The parties left nothing to the judicial imagination. The effect of the shareholder and stock purchase agreements (which for simplicity I shall treat as a single "stockholder agreement"), against a background of employment at will, was to strip Jordan of any contractual protection against what happened to him, and indeed against worse that might have happened to him. Duff and Phelps points out that it would not have had to let Jordan withdraw his resignation had he gotten wind of the negotiations with Security Pacific and wanted to withdraw it. On November 14 Hansen could have said to Jordan, "I accept your resignation effective today; we hope to sell Duff and Phelps for $50 million but have no desire to see you participate in the resulting bonanza. You will receive the paltry book value of your shares as of December 31, 1982." The "nothing herein contained" provision in the stockholder agreement shows that this tactic is permitted. Equally, on November 14, at the board meeting before Hansen knew that Jordan wanted to quit, the board could have decided to fire Jordan in order to increase the value of the deal with Security Pacific to the remaining shareholders.

These possibilities eliminate any inference that the stockholder agreement obligated Duff and Phelps to inform Jordan about the company's prospects. Under the agreement, if Duff and Phelps didn't want to give him the benefit of the information all it had to do to escape any possible liability was to give him the information and then fire him....

* * *

Was Jordan a fool to have become a shareholder of Duff and Phelps on such disadvantageous terms as I believe he agreed to? (If so, that might be a reason for doubting whether those were the real terms.) He was not. Few business executives in this country have contractual entitlements to earnings, bonuses, or even retention of their jobs. They would rather take their chances on their employer's good will and interest in reputation, and on their own bargaining power and value to the firm, than pay for contract rights that are difficult and costly to enforce. If Jordan had had greater rights as a shareholder he would have had a lower salary; when he went to work for a new employer in Houston and received no stock rights he got a higher salary.

I go further: Jordan was protected by Duff and Phelps' own self-interest from being exploited. The principal asset of a service company such as Duff and Phelps is good will. It is a product largely of its employees' efforts and skills. If Jordan were a particularly valuable employee, so that the firm would be worth less without him, Hansen, desiring as he did to sell the firm for the highest possible price, would have told him about the prospects for selling the company. If Jordan was not a particularly valuable employee — if his departure would not reduce the value of the firm — there was no reason why he should participate in the profits from the sale of the firm, unless perhaps he had once been a particularly valuable employee but had ceased to be so. That possibility might, but did not, lead him to negotiate for an employment contract, or for stock rights that would outlast his employment. By the type of agreement that he made with Duff and Phelps, Jordan gambled that he was and would continue to be such a good employee that he would be encouraged to stay long enough to profit from the firm's growth. The relationship that the parties created aligned their respective self-interests better than the legal protections that the court devises today.

My brethren are well aware that Duff and Phelps faced market constraints against exploiting its employee shareholders, but seem to believe that this implies that the company also assumed contractual duties. Businessmen, however, are less enthusiastic about contractual duties than lawyers are, see Macauley, *Non-Contractual Relations in Business: A Preliminary Study,* 28 Am. Sociological Rev. 55, 64 (1963), so it is incorrect to infer from the existence of market constraints against exploitation that the parties also imposed a contractual duty against exploitation. Contractual obligation is a source of uncertainty and cost, and is therefore an expensive way of backstopping market forces. That is why employment at will is such a common form of employment relationship. It is strange to infer that firms invariably assume a legal obligation not to do what is not in their self-interest to do, and stranger to suppose — in the face of an explicit disclaimer — that by "allow[ing] employees to time their departures to obtain the maximum advantage from their stock," Duff and Phelps obligated itself to allow them to do this.

* * *

The majority's view that "the silence of the parties" is an invitation to judges to "imply other terms — those we [judges] are confident the parties would have bargained for if they had signed a written agreement" is doubly gratuitous. The parties did not want their relationship dragged into court and there made over by judges. And the parties were not silent. The stockholder agreement provides that Jordan's rights under it do not give him any employment tenure.... There was no "implied pledge to avoid opportunistic conduct" any more than there were "implicit parts of the relations" giving rise to contractual obligations....

And if Duff and Phelps had fired Jordan (or refused to let him withdraw his resignation), this would not necessarily have been opportunistic. One might equally well say (in the spirit of Villada) that by trying to stick around merely to participate in an unexpectedly lucrative sale of Duff and Phelps, Jordan would have been the opportunist. The majority says that "understandably Duff & Phelps did not want a viper in its nest, a disgruntled employee remaining only in the hope of appreciation of his stock." I call that "viper" an opportunist.

* * *

Notes and Questions

1. Easterbrook versus Posner: Which of the judges—both law-and-economics scholars—gets the better of the argument?

2. Contract and Incorporation: Although considerable historical and economic evidence indicates that the corporation is founded in private contract, legal recognition of the corporation is gained through the granting of a charter from a state. In essence, the state's corporation law specifies the terms of the contract, including the property rights of the parties to the contract—the shareholders, directors, and officers. Most corporation laws are enabling statutes in the sense that they reflect the philosophy of freedom of contract that has guided corporation law since the first truly modern general incorporation laws were passed in the late nineteenth century. Most, if not all, of the terms can be altered by a specific provision in the articles or bylaws. The state law specifies the terms of the contract in the absence of a specific provision amending the laws. By defining rights, the articles of incorporation perform a function analogous to that of a private constitution. Firms may alter some aspects of the corporation law applicable to them by amending the corporation's articles of incorporation or bylaws to suit their particular needs.

3. Duty of Care, the Business Judgment Rule, and Shareholders' Interests: Directors are supposed to direct the management of the corporation's affairs. Failure to do so may result in liability for the resulting losses. A major problem in this area of corporation law, however, is deciding when a director has failed to fulfill the obligations of the position. In general, the courts are hesitant to second-guess managerial decisions that turn out to be mistaken. In most cases, courts give managers the benefit of the doubt and relieve them of liability through application of the **business judgment rule**. This rule protects decisions made by an honest, unbiased judgment, and it also benefits shareholders. A major policy reason in support of the business judgment rule is that holding directors liable in situations where hindsight reveals that they made a mistake would make it difficult to attract top-quality individuals to serve on boards of directors. In recognition of the adverse impact of holding directors and officers liable when they acted in good faith, several states' corporation laws authorize corporations to indemnify (reimburse) directors for liability payments or for expenses incurred in defending against unwarranted suits.

While it is often stated that corporate directors and officers will be liable for negligence in carrying out their corporate duties, such a statement is misleading. Whereas an automobile driver who makes a mistake in judgment as to speed or distance and injures a pedestrian will likely be called upon to respond in damages, a corporate officer who makes a mistake in judgment as to economic conditions, consumer tastes, or production line efficiency will rarely, if ever, be found liable for the damages suffered by the corporation. Whatever the terminology, the fact is that liability is rarely imposed upon corporate directors or officers simply for bad judgment, and this reluctance to impose liability for unsuccessful business decisions has been doctrinally labeled the business judgment rule. Although the rule has suffered under academic criticism, it is not without rational basis.

First, shareholders to a very real degree voluntarily undertake the risk of bad business judgment. Investors do not need to buy stock, for investment markets offer an array of opportunities less vulnerable to mistakes in judgment by corporate officers. Nor do investors need to buy stock in particular corporations. In the exercise of genuine free choice, the quality of a firm's management is often decisive and information is available from professional advisors. Since shareholders can and do select among investments partly on the basis of management, the business judgment rule merely recognizes that shareholders assume the risk of bad business decisions.

Second, courts recognize that after-the-fact litigation is an imperfect device to evaluate corporate business decisions. The circumstances surrounding a corporate decision are not easily reconstructed in a courtroom years later, since business imperatives often call for quick decisions, inevitably based on less than perfect information. The entrepreneur's function is to encounter risks and to confront uncertainty. A decision that was well-reasoned at the time it was made may seem a wild hunch when viewed years later against a background of perfect knowledge.

Third, because potential profit often corresponds to the potential risk, it is very much in the interest of shareholders that the law not create incentives for overly cautious corporate decisions. Some opportunities offer great profits at the risk of very substantial losses, while the alternatives offer less risk of loss but also less potential profit. Shareholders can reduce the volatility of risk by diversifying their holdings. In the case of the diversified shareholder, the seemingly more risky alternatives may well be the best choice since great losses in some stocks will over time be offset by even greater gains in others. With mutual funds and similar forms of diversified investment, courts need not bend over backwards to give special protection to shareholders who refuse to reduce the volatility of risk by not diversifying. A rule which penalizes the choice of seemingly riskier alternatives thus may not be in the interest of shareholders generally.

Whatever its merit, however, the business judgment rule extends only as far as the reasons which justify its existence. Thus, it does not apply in cases in which, e.g., the corporate decision lacks a business purpose, is tainted by a conflict of interest, is so egregious as to amount to a no-win decision, or results from an obvious and prolonged failure to exercise oversight or supervision. Other examples may occur. Joy v. North, 692 F.2d 880, 885–86 (7th Cir. 1982).

4. The Evolution of Business Organizations: Much of the economic literature on the governance of the modern corporation reflects an evolutionary view of the development and use of certain governance mechanisms. This view is clearly reflected in the following statement: "Absent fiat, the form of organization that survives in an activity is the one that delivers the product demanded by customers at the lowest price while covering costs." Eugene F. Fama & Michael C. Jensen, *Separation of Ownership and Control*, 26 Journal of Law & Economics 301, 301 (1983). The modern corporation appears to be passing the test of time.

i. Corporate Federalism

The relationship between shareholders and managers is governed by two sources of law. Federal securities laws, which are primarily concerned with securities transactions, set forth detailed procedures for shareholder votes. Otherwise, state corporation law governs the internal affairs of corporations. Importantly, corporations (or, more correctly, corporations' managers) can incorporate under the laws of any state, regardless of the location of the corporate headquarters. To the extent that there are differences in corporate laws across states, corporate law is one of the governance mechanisms that *can be* selected by the contracting parties to minimize corporate agency costs. States, however, don't always offer laws that appear to be in shareholders' best interests. See, e.g., Amanda Acquisition Corp. v. Universal Foods Corp., 877 F.2d 496 (7th Cir. 1989).

Questions on Corporate Federalism

1. Race for the Bottom: The competition among the states — which is often referred to as a race for the bottom — has been criticized because it allegedly lowers the standards of managerial accountability to shareholders. Justice Louis Brandeis provided an early articulation of the negative effects of jurisdictional competition in the interstate market for charters: "Companies were early formed to provide charters for corporations in states where the cost was lowest and the laws least restrictive. The states joined in advertising their ware. The race was not one of diligence but of laxity." *Liggett Co. v. Lee,* 288 U.S. 517, 256 (1933) (Brandeis, J., dissenting). In the modern debate on corporate governance, the attack on competition among the states is based on the following syllogism: states gain from chartering corporations; managers prefer fewer restraints on their accountability to shareholders; managers effectively control the selection of the chartering states; therefore, states compete through lowering (to the bottom) the legal fiduciary standards of managerial performance and accountability to shareholders. Assuming, for the sake of argument, that the competition does result in a lowering of standards of managerial conduct, the appropriate policy response still depends on how important fiduciary standards are to controlling managerial behavior. Conflicting policy recommendations may be the result of different conceptions of the corporation.

2. Race for the Top: Judge Ralph Winter has questioned the logic of the "race to the bottom" analysis:

> (1) If Delaware permits corporate management to profit at the expense of share-holders and other states do not, then earnings of Delaware corporations must be less than earnings of comparable corporations chartered in other states and shares in the Delaware corporations must trade at lower prices. (2) Corporations with lower earnings will be at a disadvantage in raising debt or equity capital. (3) Corporations at a disadvantage in the capital market will be at a disadvantage in the product market and their share price will decline, thereby creating a threat of takeover which may replace management. To avoid this result, corporations must seek out legal systems more attractive to capital. (4) States seeking corporate charters will thus try to provide legal systems which optimize the shareholder-corporation relationship.

Ralph K. Winter, Jr., *State Law, Shareholder Protection, and the Theory of the Corporation,* 6 Journal of Legal Studies, 251, 256 (1977).

j. Corporate Federalization

While traditionally corporate law is the domain of state law, the federal government has followed the general trend of hastily passing corporate governance legislation in the wake of major economic downturns. For example, the Securities and Exchange Acts of 1933 and 1934 were a product of the 1929 stock-market crash and Great Depression. More recently, two major federal laws passed in the wake of the last two downturns have vastly expanded the federal government's role in regulating corporate governance—the Sarbanes-Oxley Act of 2002 and the Dodd-Frank Wall Street Reform and Consumer Protection Act of 2010. John C. Coffee, Jr., *The Political Economy of Dodd-Frank: Why Financial Reform Tends to Be Frustrated and Systemic Risk Perpetuated*, 97 Cornell L. Rev. 1019, 1020 (2012).

Notes and Questions on Corporate Federalization

1. Sarbanes-Oxley and the End of Jurisdictional Competition in Corporation Law?: In late 2001 and early 2002, following a stock-market bubble and recession, American stock markets were further hit with reports of several massive financial accounting frauds. The collapse and bankruptcy of Enron in December 2001 was the most spectacular. Numerous corporations were reporting accounting irregularities and restating their financial reports. Although Congress held hearings in the spring of 2002, it appeared that significant legislative intervention was unlikely. However, when WorldCom declared bankruptcy in the summer of 2002, Congress responded by passing the Sarbanes-Oxley Act of 2002 (SOX). For a history of the passage of SOX, see Roberta Romano, *The Sarbanes-Oxley Act and the Making of Quack Corporate Governance*, 114 Yale Law Journal 1521 (2005).

Prior to SOX, the states were the primary source of the law of corporate governance. In general, this remains true today. Delaware, of course, is the leader in the competition among the states for corporate chartering. Jurisdictional competition is a dynamic process that penalizes mistakes and forces state law to evolve to meet the changing needs of businesses or to become extinct. This competition has served us well since 1875 when New Jersey passed the first truly modern general incorporation law. Yet, SOX effectively nationalized several substantive areas of corporate law—and, in the process, struck a major blow against our long established system of creating corporate law—without serious in-depth analysis of the value or the consequences of the changes. For example, SOX imposed four changes in substantive corporate law—(1) independent audit committees; (2) provision of non-audit services; (3) executive loans; and (4) executive certification of financial statements. The weight of academic evidence strongly suggests that these changes do not provide any benefits to shareholders. Will they do harm? Yes, if they impose costs without providing offsetting benefits. From a structural perspective, SOX's intrusion into internal corporate affairs is problematic. Competition among the states provides a mechanism for corporations to move away from inefficient legal regimes, whereas nationalization of corporation law takes away the self-correcting forces generated by competition. Of course, competition continues—it just becomes competition between nations. In this international competition, SOX hurts the competitiveness of all American businesses instead of the few located in a wayward state. International competition might ultimately save American corporations from SOX—because, to the extent SOX penalizes American businesses, there will be political pressure to correct the mistakes in Washington.

Agency theory provides a useful framework for thinking about the role of SOX in protecting shareholder value from managerial malfeasance. A good starting point is to remember that the optimal amount of corporate malfeasance is not zero because the cost of eliminating all malfeasance is greater than the benefit it would provide. In the extreme, we can stop all malfeasance only by outlawing the corporation. But given that the optimal amount of malfeasance is not zero, how do we determine the optimal amount? One approach is to put it in the context of risk—specifically, risk bearing by shareholders. Shareholders are the residual risk bearers in the corporation; they don't get paid until all other claimants are satisfied. Shareholders are assumed to own a diversified portfolio of stocks. Shareholders diversify many different risks—including the risks of managerial ineptness, managerial entrenchment, accounting fraud, malfeasance, lawsuits, and so forth. Prior to SOX, the corporate governance system relied on a combination of ex ante incentives and ex post penalties to control managerial behavior while at the same time allowing managers to take reasonable business risks on behalf of shareholders. Such reasonable business risks would include strategic decisions—markets to enter, mergers and acquisitions, research and development, and so forth—as well as organizational control issues—such as how much to invest in internal controls and in monitoring employee performance. In general, these business decisions were protected by the business judgment rule, which reflected a public policy of allowing managers to take reasonably informed risks without fear of second-guessing by litigious shareholders with 20-20 hindsight. Corporation law implicitly recognizes that shareholders want directors and executives to take calculated risks—as long as the expected benefits are greater than the expected costs—of all different kinds. In a diversified portfolio, some stocks will perform poorly because of risk taking and some will exceed expectations. Shareholders voluntarily take on these diversified risks in order to achieve a superior combination of risk and return than they could achieve by concentrating their portfolio. To some extent, the investor protection mandates of SOX treat shareholders as if they have concentrated portfolios. Shareholders, however, do not want this type of protection because they can diversify the risk. Forcing directors and managers to be overly concerned about malfeasance builds in underperformance in the sense that it requires managers to devote resources to reducing risks when it is not justified by rational cost-benefit analysis.

2. The Great Recession and the Dodd-Frank Act of 2010: True to form after the massive financial crisis and recession of 2007–2009, Congress, empowered by interest group and populist outrage at large financial institutions, passed another omnibus financial and corporate regulation bill called the Dodd-Frank Wall Street Reform and Consumer Protection Act in 2010. Although the legislation's main purpose is to end "too big to fail" banks that are systemically risky to the economy, it includes many corporate governance provisions that apply to all corporations. These corporate governance provisions shift more corporate regulation and monitoring from the states, primarily Delaware, to the federal government and its agencies.

The Dodd-Frank Act aims to change two major aspects of corporate governance. The Act first aims to reduce "excessive" executive compensation. Over the preceding three decades boards of directors, attempting to align management and shareholder interests, have increased the use of stock and other pay-for-performance compensation plans. Many commentators including Harvard Law School's Lucian Bebchuk argue these compensation plans incentivized management to take too much risk in search of short term gains in the form of stock price increases. Secondly, the Act aims to increase proxy access to give active shareholders more influence in choosing the board of directors. The inclusion of the proxy access provisions have little connection to the immediate problems associated with the crisis but made their way into the bill nonetheless.

Stephen Bainbridge argues that the changes to corporate governance are a mixture of therapeutic disclosures and potentially distorting one-size-fits-all rules. The drafters of the Dodd-Frank Act designed the disclosure rules specifically to "shame" corporations into reducing executive compensation, but it is expensive for businesses to implement the disclosures because the data required to comply is complex and difficult to analyze.

The rules include a provision to penalize executives for failed investments ex post. The provision will likely meet the aim of reducing the amount of risk executives take, but it necessarily includes risks the shareholders *want* the executives to take. Market forces continue to cap the upside of an investment, but now the down side has potentially greater negative value for the managers beyond that of the shareholders. Thus, managers will now be *even more* risk averse than the shareholders. However, other provisions in the act like say-on-pay and increased proxy access may overpower provisions reducing managers' propensity to take risks on behalf of shareholders. Although the stated purpose of including the governance provisions in the Act was to increase management risk aversion, these provisions, if they work as designed, are likely to further align shareholder and management risk taking goals. The ultimate problem with trying to reduce systemic risk through corporate governance, like the Dodd-Frank Act attempts to do, is the fundamental mis-alignment of goals between shareholders and society. Shareholders want managers to be less risk averse, but society wants managers—specifically bank managers—to be more risk averse. Thus the changes made by the Dodd-Frank Act may have the exact opposite consequences as the drafters intended and may facilitate rather than prevent another crisis. Stephen M. Bainbridge, *Dodd-Frank: Quack Federal Corporate Governance Round II*, 95 Minn. L. Rev. 1779 (2011).

3. Post-Post-Crisis Equilibrium: The post-crisis legislative reaction is not the end of the story. John Coffee, Jr. notes that after the crisis subsides, the main stage shifts back to the states and courts where manager and investor interest groups are more effective. He argues the provisions that are better stay around and the provisions that do the most damage are slowly repealed or overruled by the courts. The most recent example is the repeal of SOX section 404 as part of the Dodd-Frank Act. After the passage of SOX, it became clear that section 404 was expansive, unpopular, and ineffective. Courts and administrative agencies chipped away at the section before Congress finally repealed it in 2010. John C. Coffee, Jr., *The Political Economy of Dodd-Frank: Why Financial Reform Tends to Be Frustrated and Systemic Risk Perpetuated*, 97 Cornell Law Review 1019, 1020 (2012).

Chapter VI

Risk

Life, by its very nature, is risky. Most people do not like risk, yet reducing risk is expensive. Individuals, businesses, and governments must make tradeoffs between the costs of living in a risky world and the costs of reducing that risk. Everyone through their behavior indicates that they are willing to take on certain risks in their lives. The fact that people ride in automobiles, as opposed to riding in tanks or armored vehicles which are much safer, indicates that individuals make tradeoffs between the cost and comfort of an automobile and a safer mode of travel. In general, individuals engage in risk avoidance activities up to the point where the marginal benefit of the reduced risk is equal to the marginal cost of reducing the risk. The fact that people do not spend the resources to make their life risk free suggests that life itself is not priceless.

This chapter covers several ways individuals and society attempt to deal with risk. After a review of the economics of uncertainty and risk in Section A, the next two sections consider essentially private, market-based ways of dealing with risk. Section B covers the demand for and supply of insurance. Section C is an overview of the manner in which market prices for products, services, and jobs adjust to reflect the associated risk. Section D analyzes how tort law deals with accidents and injuries that result from a non-contractual, non-negotiated relationship. Finally, Section E presents an overview and critique of federal risk regulation.

A. Economics of Uncertainty and Risk

Individuals and firms must make decisions when they are not certain of the outcome. However, they often have some idea of the range of possible outcomes. This section explains how the size of the range of possible outcomes has an impact on decision making. The first subsection introduces basic concepts from probability theory which are then used to calculate some descriptive statistics—expected value and variance—regarding the range of possible outcomes for a decision. The next subsection describes the assumption that individuals are risk averse and explores some implications of that assumption.

1. Basic Probability Theory

Some theoretical economic models—for example, the perfect competition model in Chapter VII—rely on the assumption that individuals have perfect information regarding the outcome of any particular decision. Such decisions have **certain outcomes**. A more realistic assumption is that individuals contemplate a variety of potential outcomes and assign relative likelihoods to their actual occurrence. In such cases, the decisions have **uncertain outcomes**. When decision makers have information regarding possible outcomes and their relative likelihoods, the tools of probability theory can be used to analyze economic decisions.

A **probability** is a number between 0 and 1, inclusive, that expresses the likelihood that some specific event will occur. Some probabilities can be estimated through a process of experimentation. For example, we would expect that the probability of getting "tails" as a result of flipping a fair coin is 0.5 (which is equal to 1/2 or 50%). When probabilities can be established in this fashion, they are **objective probabilities**. In other cases, probabilities are estimated on the basis of a subjective "best guess" or one's prior experiences. When a particular individual's opinion enters the estimation, she is using a **subjective probability**.

It will often be useful to identify situations in which two probabilistic events are independent of each other. Events are **independent** when the probabilistic outcome of one decision does not affect the probabilistic outcome of a second decision. For example, while driving through Missouri on a cross-country road trip, Jerry decides to purchase a state lottery ticket. This decision over the use of funds has an uncertain outcome to which probabilities can be assigned. After purchasing the Missouri state lottery ticket, Jerry continues his trip across the country. While in Kansas, Jerry decides to purchase a lottery ticket for that state's lottery. However, by purchasing a lottery ticket in Kansas, Jerry has not changed the probability that he will win the lottery in Missouri. Thus, the probabilities for winning either lottery are independent of each other. Note that this is different than estimating the probability that Jerry would win both lotteries. The probability of two independent events both occurring is simply the product of the probabilities. Thus, if Jerry had a 25% chance of winning the Missouri lottery and a 25% chance of winning the Kansas lottery, then his chance of winning both lotteries would be 25% x 25% = 6.25%.

For purposes of analysis, assume that outcomes and probabilities are both **complete** and **mutually exclusive**. Completeness suggests that while the decision maker does not know the specific outcome of any decision, she is aware of all potential outcomes. Mutual exclusivity indicates that the result of a particular decision will be x or y, not x and y. These two assumptions allow the use of the notion of an expected value in analyzing uncertain decisions.

2. Expected Value and Variance

Given a set of objective or subjective probabilities and all possible outcomes, the expected outcome of an uncertain decision can be calculated. The **expected value** of an uncertain decision is the product of outcomes and their probabilities summed across all possible outcomes:

$$E(x) = P_1(x_1) + P_2(x_2) + \ldots + P_n(x_n)$$

where $E(x)$ is the expected value of x, P_i is the probability of any outcome i, and x_i is the actual value of outcome i. Each P_i must be between 0 and 1, inclusive; and the sum of all P_is must equal 1. This sum provides the likely value of potential outcomes, where only one of the outcomes will occur.

Consider the following example. Suppose that you are representing a widower in a wrongful death suit. The case has just gone to the jury, and the defendants offer to settle for $1,000,000. In deciding whether to accept this offer, you must consider the amount of damages you expect to collect by waiting to hear from the jury. Based upon your experience as an attorney and the willingness of the defendant to settle at this point in the litigation, you feel quite confident that the plaintiff will be awarded a substantial judgment. Moreover, because the trial is complete, your costs in terms of time and resources are the same whether you settle or wait for the jury. You feel that there is a 30% chance that the jury will award $750,000, a 50% chance that the jury will award $1,000,000, and a 20% chance that the jury will award $2,000,000. Thus, the expected value of the jury award is:

$$E(x) = 0.3(\$750,000) + 0.5(\$1,000,000) + 0.2(\$2,000,000) = \$1,125,000$$

By your calculation, the expected result of the jury award exceeds the settlement offer by $125,000. In other words, based upon your experience, you believe that the jury award will probably be greater than the settlement offer. Is there any question about what to do?

The decision about whether to accept the settlement offer could be guided by the following simple decision rule: When faced with uncertain outcomes, choose that decision with the highest expected value. However, such a decision rule often does not comport with the way people actually make decisions. While the expected jury award is $1,125,000, there is a 30% chance that the award will be $750,000 — $250,000 less than the settlement offer. Are you willing to advise your client to take this risk? Moreover, are there any professional responsibility implications for advising your client to take this risk? On the other hand, there is a 20% chance that the jury will award $2,000,000, which exceeds the settlement value by $1,000,000. There is the possibility of doubling your client's money by taking the risk.

The analysis in the preceding paragraph suggests that there might be some level of variability in the results that would discourage some individuals from choosing the option with the highest expected value. Greater variability implies that there is less certainty regarding the potential outcome, and thus more risk involved in the decision. Consider the same example, only this time, you feel that there is a 40% chance that the jury will find in favor of the defendant and award $0, a 50% chance that the jury will award $1,000,000, and a 10% chance that the jury will award $5,250,000. Using the same formula as above, the expected value is still the same, even though there plainly is greater variability in outcomes.

$$E(x) = 0.4(\$0) + 0.5(\$1,000,000) + 0.1(\$6,250,000) = \$1,125,000$$

To the extent that individuals are concerned about the riskiness of decisions, they are interested in some measure of the variability of outcomes for any particular decision.

Variability, or risk, is quantified by a measure of the average dispersion of actual results around the expected value, which is known as the **variance**. Variance is equal to the weighted average of squared deviations from the expected value:

$$\sigma^2 = P_1(x_1 - E(x))^2 + P_2(x_2 - E(x))^2 + \ldots + P_n(x_n - E(x))^2$$

where σ^2 is the variance, P_i the probability of the outcome i, x_i is the actual result for outcome i, and E(x) is the expected value as calculated above. Thus, for the jury award contemplated earlier, the variance is:

$$\sigma^2 = 0.3(\$750,000 - \$1,125,000)^2 + 0.5(\$1,000,000 - \$1,125,000)^2 +$$
$$0.2(\$2,000,000 - \$1,125,000)^2$$
$$= \$203,125,000,000$$

Because of the squared terms in the variance calculation, the answer is not in the same units as the inputs — in this case, dollars. As a result, it is sometimes difficult to interpret the meaning of the variance calculation. This difficulty can be resolved by using standard deviation. **Standard deviation** is also a measure of the dispersion around expected values, and it is measured in the same units as the original inputs. Standard deviation is simply the square root of the variance. For the jury award example, the standard deviation of possible awards is:

$$\sigma = \$450,694$$

The variance and standard deviation for the greater variability example above are:

$$\sigma^2 = \$3,014,062,500,000$$
$$\sigma = \$1,736,106$$

The decision as to whether a dispersion or variability of $450,694 is too risky is a matter of individual preference. The key to analyzing decisions under uncertainty is to recognize the fundamental economic tradeoff involved in these decisions. Specifically, how willing is a particular individual to sacrifice some amount of expected value for a reduction in risk? Ultimately, the decision regarding whether to take the certain settlement or the uncertain jury award depends upon the decision maker's subjective attitude toward risk.

3. Expected Utility and Risk Preference

Most people do not like risk and thus might be willing to sacrifice some amount of expected money value for a reduction in risk. People tend to prefer certain outcomes to uncertain outcomes, even if the expected value of the uncertain outcome is greater than that of the certain outcome. In other words, sometimes individuals get more utility — the benefit or satisfaction from a choice or course of action — from reducing risk than maximizing expected money outcomes. When faced with uncertainty, individuals attempt to maximize expected utility, not expected value.

Figure VI-1 presents a utility function for a hypothetical individual. Money value is marked along the horizontal axis and utility on the vertical axis — for this example, utility is a function of money value. Notice that the utility function, U, increases at a decreasing rate. This suggests that an individual with this type of utility function exhibits **diminishing marginal utility of money value.**

Consider an individual who starts off with $5,000. Such an individual has a utility of 300 utils — an imaginary measurement of utility. If this individual's money holdings were increased by $1,000, her utility would increase to 350 utils — an increase of 50 utils. On the other hand, if $1,000 were taken away from this individual, her utility would decline to 200 utils — a loss of 100 utils. Thus, this individual's utility is affected more by losses than by gains: the loss of $1,000 would decrease utility by a larger amount than utility increases when the individual gains $1,000. This indicates that the individual exhibits diminishing marginal utility of money. Moreover, the individual's utility associated with a certain amount of $5,000 is 300 utils. However, if she was involved in a lottery with a 50% chance of winning $4,000 and a 50% chance of winning $6,000, her expected utility would be only 275 utils (E(U)=0.5(200) + 0.5(350)) even though the expected value of the lottery

Figure VI-1. Utility Curve Exhibiting Diminishing Marginal Utility of Money Value

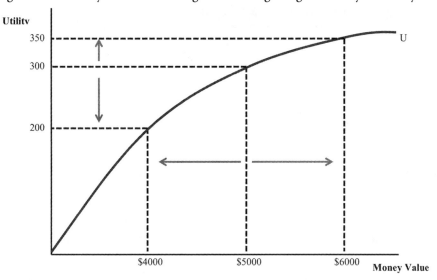

winnings was the same $5,000. We can conclude from this analysis that the individual is **risk averse**. Risk averse individuals prefer certain outcomes over uncertain outcomes that have the same expected value and exhibit diminishing marginal utility of money.

Figure VI-2 presents the dynamics of decision making under uncertainty for the risk averse individual. The uncertain decision faced by this individual has an expected value of $10,000. However, there is a 50% chance that the payoff from this uncertain decision

Figure VI-2. Decision Making under Uncertainty for Risk Averse Individuals

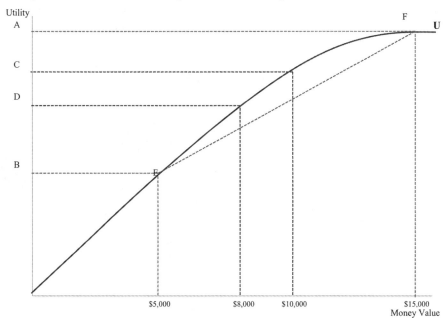

will be $15,000 and a 50% chance of a $5,000 payoff. The utility curve indicates how this individual regards uncertain decisions. Notice that a certain $15,000 payoff provides the individual with utility corresponding to level A. A certain $5,000 payoff provides utility that corresponds to level B. Furthermore, the utility from a certain $10,000 payoff provides utility up to level C. However, the uncertain decision does not provide $10,000 with certainty. In fact, although $10,000 is the expected value, it will not occur. When the expected value is some combination of $5,000 and $15,000, the expected utility from the payoff can be determined by using the dotted line segment from E to F. The expected utility associated with an expected value of $10,000 corresponds to level D—found by moving directly to the left from the dotted line segment until intersecting with the utility curve. The expected utility from an expected value of $10,000—level D—is less than the utility associated with a certain $10,000 payoff—level C. In general, greater concavity in the utility function—the more the marginal utility of money value diminishes—suggests that individuals are more risk averse and less willing to accept uncertain outcomes.

Figure VI-2 also demonstrates that risk averse individuals might be willing to sacrifice some amount of money value for reduced risk. Notice that a certain $8,000 payoff provides the same utility as the expected uncertain $10,000 payoff. The $8,000 payoff is known as the **certainty equivalent** of the expected uncertain $10,000 payoff. The certainty equivalent of an uncertain amount is the sum of money which, if received with certainty will yield the same utility as the uncertain amount. Thus, a risk averse individual might be willing to sacrifice an amount equal to $2,000 ($10,000 – $8,000) to avoid having to take the uncertain outcome. This $2,000 payment is known as a **risk premium**. The risk premium is the maximum amount a person is prepared to pay to avoid an uncertain outcome. For example, this amount would correspond to how much an individual is willing to pay for fire insurance and avoid the risk of losing the entire value of her home if it burns down. This topic will be addressed in greater detail in the section on insurance.

Risk aversion describes the preferences revealed by much of the normal behavior observed everyday. Yet, this does not mean that all individuals are risk averse. Some individuals are **risk neutral**—they appear to be indifferent toward risk. Moreover, some individuals seem to actively seek risky situations. Such individuals are known as **risk seekers**. Both risk neutral and risk seeking behavior can be incorporated into expected utility analysis.

Figure VI-3 presents expected utility analysis for the risk neutral individual. Notice that, unlike the utility curve of the risk averse individual, which exhibits diminishing marginal utility of money, the utility curve of the risk neutral individual increases at a constant rate. This suggests that an increase in money holdings would have the same marginal effect on utility as an equal loss in money holdings. Consider the relationship between the utility for a certain payoff of $10,000 and an uncertain expected payout of $10,000. The straight utility function indicates that the utility of the certain outcome is the same as the utility for the uncertain outcome. Thus, risk neutral individuals are indifferent between certain and uncertain outcomes—their decisions are guided only by expected value. To these individuals, there is no difference between a $1 million bet and a $1 bet so long as the expected value is the same. When risk neutral individuals maximize their expected value, they are also maximizing their expected utility.

Figure VI-4 presents the expected utility analysis for a risk-seeking individual. Notice that the utility curve increases at an increasing rate, exhibiting increasing marginal utility of money. This suggests that an increase in money holdings would have a greater marginal effect on utility than would an equal loss in money holdings. Consider the relationship between the utility for a certain payoff of $10,000 and an uncertain expected payout of

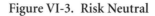

Figure VI-3. Risk Neutral

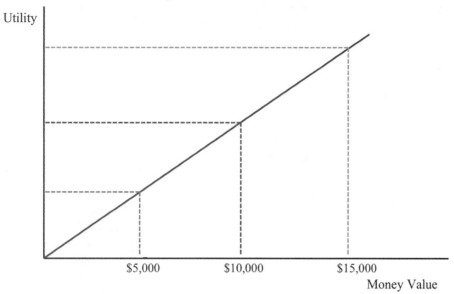

$10,000. Because of the upward sloping nature of the utility function, the utility of the certain outcome (u_A) is less than the utility for the uncertain outcome (u_B). Risk seekers prefer uncertain outcomes to certain outcomes.

A final possibility is suggested by what is called "prospect theory"—a theory developed by behavioral psychologists Daniel Kahneman and Amos Tversky (recall the discussion

Figure VI-4. Risk Seeker

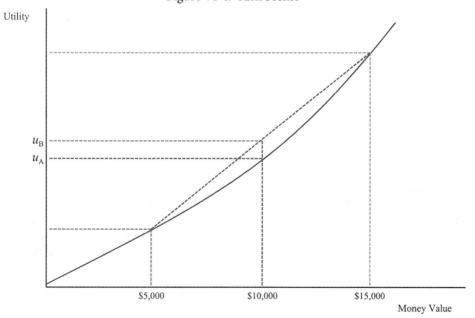

of behavioral law and economics in Part A.2 of Chapter I). As explained by Professor Chris Guthrie, one of the central components of prospect theory is that

> … people evaluate decision options relative to some reference point, generally the status quo. When choosing between options that appear to be gains relative to that reference point, people tend to make risk-averse choices; when choosing between options that appear to be losses, people tend to make risk-seeking choices. For example, people will generally choose a definite $1,000 prize over a 50% chance at receiving a $2,000 prize but will opt to face a 50% chance at having to pay a $2,000 fine over having to pay a definite $1,000 fine. This result is inconsistent with rational choice theory, which generally assumes either risk neutrality or risk aversion in the face of both gains and losses.

Chris Guthrie, *Prospect Theory, Risk Preference, and the Law*, 97 Northwestern University Law Review 1115, 1118–19 (2003). In other words, prospect theory holds that people's risk preferences vary. For events that occur with moderate or high probability, most people are risk averse when facing the prospect of a gain, but are risk seeking when facing a loss. However, for events that occur with low probability, the reverse is true: most people are risk seeking with gains (they play the lottery) and risk averse with losses (they buy insurance).

How might the predictions from prospect theory be used to explain the unwillingness of plaintiffs (who face the prospect of a gain) and defendants (who face the prospect of a loss) to settle cases with a positive settlement range?

B. Insurance

People are generally risk averse concerning risks that potentially affect a significant proportion of their wealth. An important behavioral implication of such risk aversion is that these individuals are willing to sacrifice certain amounts of money (up to their risk premium) in order to avoid the prospect of large losses. An example of this is the decision to purchase insurance. People who purchase health insurance, automobile insurance, disability insurance, or homeowners insurance give up a certain relatively small sum of money in order to avoid an uncertain, yet potentially larger, loss. This section considers the demand and supply of insurance, as well as some of the problems facing insurance providers.

1. Demand for Insurance

The demand for insurance is derived from individuals' risk preferences. Perhaps the best way to see this is to consider an everyday example. Suppose an individual owns a home that is worth $100,000. If there is a one percent chance that the home will be destroyed by fire in the next year, the expected loss from the fire is $1,000. If an individual does not purchase insurance, one of two things will happen: the house will survive the year unscathed and there will be no loss; or, the house will be destroyed by fire and there will be a $100,000 loss. Thus, the expected loss for the year is $1,000, although the individual will never be exactly $1,000 dollars worse off. The individual will either lose nothing or lose $100,000. Intuitively, the variance across possible outcomes is wide. A risk averse individual might be willing to pay, let's say, up to $2,000 for insurance to guarantee that the house is replaced in the event that it is destroyed. The individual's position for the year then is $98,000—$100,000 minus the $2,000 insurance premium—with certainty as opposed to an uncertain $99,000—$100,000 minus the expected loss of $1,000. As a result of purchasing insurance, there is only one possible outcome—$98,000—and the variance of possible outcomes is zero. In this case, insurance reduces the individual's financial risk to zero.

2. Supply of Insurance

Insurance companies are in a much different situation than the individual homeowner. Insurance companies are in the business of pooling the risk of a large number of homeowners. A statistical phenomenon known as the "law of large numbers" allows insurance companies to pool the risks of a large number of homeowners. The law of large numbers holds that as the pool size increases, unpredictable events become more predictable. For example, an insurance company can estimate with near certainty the number of homes that will be destroyed by fire. If all homes have a one percent chance of being destroyed by fire in the next year, and the insurance company has written policies for 1,000 homes, then the expected number of homes to burn in any year is one percent times 1,000 = 10. Assuming an average loss of $100,000 per home, the insurance company would expect to pay out $1,000,000 per year for 10 houses burning down. Due to the law of large numbers, the variance of the insurance company's estimates approaches certainty as more homes are added to the risk pool. Moreover, as the number of insured homes increases, the insurance company becomes indifferent to the risk or loss; it deals purely with the monetary calculations.

However, each individual homeowner is still faced with the large potential variance in the results between losing $0 or $100,000. The expected claim per policy for the insurance company is $1,000—that is, the $1,000,000 the insurer expects to pay out divided by the 1,000 homes insured. Earlier, it was assumed that homeowners are willing to pay up to $2,000 per insurance policy. The difference between the price the consumer is willing to pay and the cost to the insurance company of providing the insurance creates an opportunity for an insurance market to emerge.

Insurance companies also have administrative costs associated with the selling and pricing of policies, servicing policy holders, and adjusting claims. Successful insurance companies must price their policies so they cover their expected losses and their administrative costs. Moreover, insurance companies that do a better job of investing their cash reserves (before they have to pay out the claims owed to policyholders) receive a larger return and are able to offer lower prices. To the extent that the insurance market is competitive, prices are pushed below the $2,000 per policy that consumers are willing to pay towards a price that reflects the cost of operating in the industry.

Controlling the cost of operation is an important challenge for all insurance companies. Every insurer must deal with two basic problems—adverse selection and moral hazard.

a. Adverse Selection

Adverse selection is a precontractual problem that derives from the fact that potential insured parties know much more about their own risk than does the potential insurer. This information is asymmetric, meaning it is difficult for the insurer to determine the risk characteristics of the potential insured. As a result of this asymmetric information, people who are risky (that is, pose a greater than average risk) are more likely to attempt to purchase insurance than are people who have a below average risk. This adverse selection can lead to a "lemons market"—a concept that was introduced in Chapter V—a phenomenon that has the potential to destroy markets whenever there is asymmetric information.

Insurance companies attempt to deal with adverse selection by providing exclusions for coverage dealing with preexisting conditions, looking for various statistical phenomena that are likely to result in higher claims from various groups, checking out applicants' backgrounds, and a variety of other devices that are designed to avoid ending up with a pool of lemons. Sometimes risky insureds might be allowed into the pool, but they will have to pay higher rates. Typical examples of ways to deal with this type of adverse selection include charging higher homeowners and health insurance rates for people who smoke, higher automobile insurance rates for males under age 25, and so forth.

Hall v. Continental Casualty Co.

United States District Court for the Western District of Wisconsin
207 F. Supp. 2d 903 (2002)

BARBARA B. CRABB, District Judge.

In this civil action for monetary relief, plaintiff Valerie K. Hall contends that defendant Continental Casualty Company breached its long-term disability insurance policy by denying her claim for long-term disability benefits on the ground that plaintiff's lung cancer is a pre-existing condition excluded from coverage. Plaintiff also alleges that defendant denied her claim for benefits in bad faith....

* * *

OPINION

A. Breach of Contract

It is common for health and long-term disability insurance policies to exclude the treatment of pre-existing conditions from coverage. Although the definition of "pre-existing condition" can vary, the policy reasons for enforcing pre-existing condition exclusions are uniform. First, losses stemming from pre-existing conditions are not fortuitous. In the case of a true pre-existing condition, the insured knows that she will be incurring losses because of the condition. Second, losses stemming from pre-existing conditions have the potential of undermining the insurer's risk pool. If an insured does not disclose to the insurer that she has a pre-existing condition when applying for coverage, the insurer cannot calculate its potential liability accurately. Finally, such losses create problems of adverse selection. An insured who has been diagnosed with a condition could apply for insurance without revealing the condition, costing the insurer more than it had anticipated.

Although these policy concerns are economically sound, extending pre-existing condition exclusions too far has a deleterious effect on the insured. If undergoing a standard diagnostic test before the effective date of a policy could be considered receiving treatment for a pre-existing condition, individuals could be discouraged from seeking preventive medical care. If an insurer can point to pre-coverage symptoms that turn out to be consistent with a condition diagnosed after coverage becomes effective, any prior symptoms not inconsistent with the ultimate diagnosis could become a ground for denying benefits. Ermenc v. American Family Mutual Ins. Co., 221 Wis. 2d 478, 484, 585 N.W.2d 679, 682 (Ct. App. 1998). Similarly, if an insurer can point to the fact that doctors suspected a condition before an effective date because of certain risk factors, such as a history of smoking, the definition of pre-existing condition would become so broad as to make the term meaningless. For example, it is likely that any doctor would suspect cancer as a possible cause of respiratory problems in a heavy smoker. It would be absurd to find this suspicion sufficient to deny coverage of all subsequent treatment on the ground that cancer is a pre-existing condition. Because "insurance contracts should be given a reasonable interpretation and not one that leads to an absurd result," these policy concerns demand that pre-existing condition exclusions not be read too broadly.

Under the terms of plaintiff's policy in this case, a pre-existing condition is "a condition for which medical treatment or advice was rendered, prescribed or recommended within three months prior to [the insured's] effective date of insurance." The central issue is whether plaintiff's lung cancer constitutes a pre-existing condition under plaintiff's policy, which both parties agree became effective on September 1, 1999....

... In *Ermenc*, the leading Wisconsin case on the coverage of pre-existing condition exclusions, the Wisconsin Court of Appeals held that the insured's cancer was not a pre-existing condition despite pre-existing symptoms. Although defendant tries to distinguish *Ermenc*, I find the reasoning dispositive.

* * *

The facts of this case are similar to those in *Ermenc*. Before the effective date of her policy, plaintiff went to the emergency room complaining of chest pain, shortness of breath and numbness in her left arm and was diagnosed as having pneumonia, tachycardia and asthma. X-rays taken that day revealed a spot on her lung that could have resulted from several conditions, including pneumonia or cancer. The radiologist who interpreted the x-ray recommended a follow-up x-ray to determine whether the spot was caused by pneumonia. If not, further testing would be necessary to determine the cause of the spot and to rule out cancer. After the effective date of plaintiff's insurance policy, plaintiff's primary physician ordered follow-up x-rays and tests that led to a diagnosis of lung cancer.

The only material difference between the facts in this case and those in *Ermenc* is that here, plaintiff's doctors suspected cancer before the effective date. Defendant relies heavily on this fact, asserting that the fact that Ermenc's doctors did not suspect cancer led the court to conclude that they did not give her advice about cancer or treat her for it. However, in neither case did the doctors make a diagnosis of cancer before the effective date. In plaintiff's case, the doctors narrowed the possible diagnoses to a handful of conditions, one of which was cancer; they did not order the follow-up x-rays solely to rule out the possibility of cancer. Moreover, the facts suggest that even if the emergency room doctors had not suspected cancer, they would have ordered the same sequence of x-rays in order to track plaintiff's pneumonia. Because plaintiff had been a smoker for many years, she had a high risk factor for lung cancer, making it an obvious condition to suspect. As in *Ermenc*, plaintiff's symptoms that manifested before the effective date were non-specific and could have been caused by a variety of conditions. Defendant has not shown that plaintiff was treated for lung cancer both before and after the effective date of plaintiff's policy, or that she was given advice about cancer before the effective date. Taking all facts in the light most favorable to the non-moving party, I conclude that defendant has failed to establish that plaintiff's cancer was a condition for which "medical treatment or advice was rendered, prescribed or recommended" in the three months before the policy took effect.

Policy considerations reinforce the conclusion that plaintiff did not receive treatment or advice for cancer before the effective date of her policy. None of the concerns that weigh in favor of enforcing pre-existing condition clauses come into play. Neither plaintiff nor her doctors knew that she had cancer before the effective date of her policy; she did not discover that she had cancer and then purchase a long-term disability policy from defendant. Although the cost of providing long-term disability insurance to plaintiff may cost defendant more than it had anticipated, this circumstance is not through any fault of plaintiff. It falls instead to the insurer and its risk pool.

In contrast, policy considerations that weigh in favor of protecting the insured do come into play. When plaintiff underwent a chest x-ray at the emergency room and when the emergency room doctors recommended a follow-up x-ray, they were following standard diagnostic procedures, which should not be discouraged. Although the doctors suspected that the spot on plaintiff's lung could result from cancer, this suspicion was based, in part, on plaintiff's history as a smoker, which put her at greater risk for lung cancer. Individuals should not be denied coverage because they carry risk factors that make them more prone to certain health conditions that, in turn, make a doctor more suspicious of these ailments. Instead, insurers should (and do) consider such risk factors when computing insurance premiums.

* * *

B. Bad Faith Denial

To prevail on a claim for bad faith, an insured must establish that (1) there was no reasonable basis for denying the claim under an objective standard and (2) the insurer acted with knowledge or reckless disregard for the lack of a reasonable basis.... When an insured's claim is "fairly debatable" either in fact or law, an insurer cannot be said to have denied the claim in bad faith.... [B]ecause I find that the law addressing pre-existing condition clauses is "fairly debatable," defendant's denial of coverage cannot be characterized as a bad faith denial.

Although the undisputed facts are insufficient to establish that defendant investigated plaintiff's claim reasonably, this lack of evidence is not fatal to defendant's argument. On the basis of the undisputed facts surrounding plaintiff's medical treatment as applied to case law, it is "fairly debatable" whether plaintiff's lung cancer constituted a pre-existing condition. Although I am not convinced by the factual distinctions that defendant tries to draw between the facts of this case and those in *Ermenc*, there is room to argue that the two cases are distinguishable. In addition, the survey of federal and state court cases that the parties undertook demonstrates that other jurisdictions have reached different conclusions on the basis of arguably similar facts. Because there is an arguable basis for distinguishing *Ermenc* and other jurisdictions have found pre-existing condition clauses to apply in relatively similar circumstances, I conclude that plaintiff's claim for coverage was "fairly debatable," precluding a finding that defendant denied coverage in bad faith. Defendant's motion for summary judgment as to this claim will be granted.

* * *

Notes and Questions

1. Adverse Selection: The selection of people who purchase insurance is not a normal, random sample of the population, but rather includes some people with private information about their personal situations that makes it likely they will receive a higher than average level of benefit under the insurance policy. For example, high-risk patients (e.g., cancer-prone, drug users, etc.) apply to insurance companies, while young healthy persons do not. Insurance deals with this adverse selection problem in a variety of ways. The most obvious is to require the disclosure of information on the long application forms with boiler-plate provisions to try and keep out risky patients. Insurance companies set limits on pre-existing conditions, through either limited coverage or higher premiums for the additional risk.

2. Regulation by the Court: Isn't the court saying that whenever there is a discrepancy between the insurance company and the consumer, the consumer gets the benefit of the doubt if he or she acted in good faith? If so, isn't the court simply regulating the market? Companies will increase premiums on all consumers to pay for those consumers who "slip through the cracks." Thus, we all pay for this ability to receive the benefit of the doubt.

3. Adverse Selection and the Affordable Care Act: The existence of adverse selection in the market for health insurance was one of the justifications for the "individual mandate" of the Patient Protection and Affordable Care Act of 2010, which requires individuals to buy a certain minimum amount of health insurance coverage or face a penalty. The Supreme Court described the issue in its decision upholding the Affordable Care Act as follows:

> The Government's first argument is that the individual mandate is a valid exercise of Congress's power under the Commerce Clause and the Necessary and Proper Clause. According to the Government, the health care market is characterized by a significant cost-shifting problem. Everyone will eventually need health care at a time and to an extent they cannot predict, but if they do not have insurance, they often will not be able to pay for it. Because state and federal laws nonetheless require hospitals to provide a certain degree of care to individuals without regard to their ability to pay, see, e.g., 42 U. S. C. §1395dd; Fla. Stat. Ann. §395.1041, hospitals end up receiving compensation for only a portion of the services they provide. To recoup the losses, hospitals pass on the cost to insurers through higher rates, and insurers, in turn, pass on the cost to policy holders in the form of higher premiums. Congress estimated that the cost of uncompensated care raises family health insurance premiums, on average, by over $1,000 per year.

> In the Affordable Care Act, Congress addressed the problem of those who cannot obtain insurance coverage because of preexisting conditions or other health issues. It did so through the Act's "guaranteed-issue" and "community-rating" provisions. These provisions together prohibit insurance companies from denying coverage to those with such conditions or charging unhealthy individuals higher premiums than healthy individuals.

> The guaranteed-issue and community-rating reforms do not, however, address the issue of healthy individuals who choose not to purchase insurance to cover potential health care needs. In fact, the reforms sharply exacerbate that problem, by providing an incentive for individuals to delay purchasing health insurance until they become sick, relying on the promise of guaranteed and affordable coverage. The reforms also threaten to impose massive new costs on insurers, who are required to accept unhealthy individuals but prohibited from charging them rates necessary to pay for their coverage. This will lead insurers to significantly increase premiums on everyone.

> The individual mandate was Congress's solution to these problems. By requiring that individuals purchase health insurance, the mandate prevents cost-shifting by those who would otherwise go without it. In addition, the mandate forces into the insurance risk pool more healthy individuals, whose premiums on average will be higher than their health care expenses. This allows insurers to subsidize

the costs of covering the unhealthy individuals the reforms require them to accept. The Government claims that Congress has power under the Commerce and Necessary and Proper Clauses to enact this solution.

National Federation of Independent Business v. Sebelius, 132 S. Ct. 2566, 2585 (2012).

b. Moral Hazard

Moral hazard is the problem that arises when the insured's behavior changes after purchasing insurance, so that the probability of loss or size of loss increases. Moral hazard is a post-contractual problem concerned with insured parties changing their behavior once they have become insured. Insured individuals change their behavior because the risk has now been shifted to the insurer. Thus, the insured no longer have the same incentive to take risk-reducing precautions. The changes in behavior can range from an individual deciding to take up skydiving shortly after purchasing a life insurance policy to exercising less care with respect to preventing a car or other personal property from being stolen when it is protected by insurance.

Insurance companies must recognize these moral hazard incentives and develop methods to deal with them. Insurance companies deal with the moral hazard problem by a combination of deductibles and copayments. Deductibles are the amount that must be paid by the insured party prior to any payment by the insurer; insured parties essentially "self-insure" up to the amount of the deductible. Once the deductible is met, the insurer pays the rest. By requiring the insured to pay a portion of any loss, deductibles give the insured an incentive to avoid the loss, and thus reduce the moral hazard problem. Copayments are payments by the insured of a proportion of any loss; the insurer pays the remaining share. Copayments similarly deter moral hazard by forcing insured parties to pay for at least a portion of the consequences of their risky behavior.

Atwater Creamery Co. v. Western National Mutual Insurance Co.

Supreme Court of Minnesota
366 N.W.2d 271 (1985)

WAHL, Justice.

Atwater Creamery Company (Atwater) sought a declaratory judgment against its insurer, Western National Mutual Insurance Company (Western), seeking coverage for losses sustained during a burglary of the creamery's storage building.... The Kandiyohi County District Court ... dismissed the jury for lack of disputed issues of fact and ordered judgment in favor of the insurer, concluding that the burglary insurance policy in effect defined burglary so as to exclude coverage of this burglary. We ... reverse as to the policy coverage.

Atwater does business as a creamery and as a supplier of farm chemicals in Atwater, Minnesota. It was insured during the time in question against burglary, up to a ceiling of $20,000, by Western under Mercantile Open Stock Burglary Policy SC10-1010-12, which contained an "evidence of forcible entry" requirement in its definition of burglary. The creamery had recovered small amounts under this policy for two separate burglaries prior to the events in this case.

Atwater built a separate facility, called the Soil Center, a few blocks away from its main plant in 1975 for the purpose of storing and selling chemicals. The Soil Center is a large rectangular building with two regular doors along the north side and two large, sliding doors, one each on the east and west sides. There are no other entrances or exits to or from the building itself. One of the doors on the north side leads into the office in the northwest corner of the building. It is secured by a regular deadbolt lock, opened with a key. There is no access into the main portion of the building from the office. Persons entering the main area must use the other door on the north side, which is secured by a padlock after hours. The large sliding doors on the east and west are secured by large hasps on each side of each door which are held tight by turnbuckles that must be loosened before the doors can be opened.

Inside the main area of the building, along the north wall, is a large storage bin with three separate doors, each of which is secured by a padlock. Between the storage bin and the office is an "alleyway," entered through the large sliding doors, which runs east and west the length of the building. Trucks are stored in the alleyway when not in use.

Sometime between 9:30 p.m., Saturday, April 9, and 6 a.m., Monday, April 11, 1977, one or more persons made unauthorized entry into the building, took chemicals worth $15,587.40, apparently loading them on the truck that had been parked inside and driving away after loosening the turnbuckles on the east door and closing it. The truck was later found parked near the town dump, with the key still in the ignition.

Larry Poe, the plant manager at the Soil Center, had left at 9:30 p.m. on Saturday, after making sure everything was properly secured. On Monday morning, the north side doors were locked securely, but two of the three doors to the storage bin were ajar. Their padlocks were gone and never found. The turnbuckles had been loosened on the east sliding door so that it could be easily opened or closed.

An investigation by the local police, the Kandiyohi County Sheriff's Department, and the Minnesota Bureau of Criminal Investigation determined that no Atwater Creamery employees, past or present, were involved in the burglary. Suspicion settled on persons wholly unconnected with the creamery or even with the local area, but no one has been apprehended or charged with the crime.

Atwater filed a claim with Western under the burglary policy. Western denied coverage because there were no visible marks of physical damage to the exterior at the point of entrance or to the interior at the point of exit, as required by the definition of burglary in the policy. The creamery then brought suit against Western for the $15,587.40 loss, $7,500 in other directly related business losses and costs, disbursements and reasonable attorney fees.

Charles H. Strehlow, the owner of the Strehlow Insurance Agency in Willmar, Minnesota, and Western's agent, testified that he is certain he mentioned the evidence-of-forcible-entry requirement to Poe and members of the Atwater Board of Directors but was unable to say when the discussion occurred. Poe and the board members examined do not remember any such discussion. None of the board members had read the policy, which is kept in the safe at the main plant, and Poe had not read it in its entirety. He stated that he started to read it but gave up because he could not understand it.

The issue[] on appeal [is] ... whether the reasonable expectations of the insured as to coverage govern to defeat the literal language of the policy....

* * *

The definition of burglary in this policy is one used generally in burglary insurance. Courts have construed it in different ways. It has been held ambiguous and construed in favor of coverage in the absence of visible marks of forceable entry or exit. We reject this analysis because we view the definition in the policy as clear and precise. It is not ambiguous.

In determining the intent of the parties to the insurance contract, courts have looked to the purpose of the visible-marks-of-forcible-entry requirement. These purposes are two: to protect insurance companies from fraud by way of "inside jobs" and to encourage insureds to reasonably secure the premises. As long as the theft involved clearly neither an inside job nor the result of a lack of secured premises, some courts have simply held that the definition does not apply.

In the instant case, there is no dispute as to whether Atwater is attempting to defraud Western or whether the Soil Center was properly secured. The trial court found that the premises were secured before the robbery and that the law enforcement investigators had determined that it was not an "inside job." To enforce the burglary definition literally against the creamery will in no way effectuate either purpose behind the restrictive definition. We are uncomfortable, however, with this analysis given the right of an insurer to limit the risk against which it will indemnify insureds.

At least three state courts have held that the definition merely provides for one form of evidence which may be used to prove a burglary and that, consequently, other evidence of a burglary will suffice to provide coverage. The Nebraska Supreme Court recently rejected this argument[, holding] ... that the definition is not a rule of evidence but is a limit on liability, is unambiguous and is applied literally to the facts of the case at hand. We, too, reject this view of the definition as merely a form of evidence. The policy attempts to comprehensively define burglaries that are covered by it. In essence, this approach ignores the policy definition altogether and substitutes the court's or the statute's definition of burglary. This we decline to do, either via the conformity clause or by calling the policy definition merely one form of evidence of a burglary.

Some courts and commentators have recognized that the burglary definition at issue in this case constitutes a rather hidden exclusion from coverage. Exclusions in insurance contracts are read narrowly against the insurer. Running through the many court opinions refusing to literally enforce this burglary definition is the concept that the definition is surprisingly restrictive, that no one purchasing something called burglary insurance would expect coverage to exclude skilled burglaries that leave no visible marks of forcible entry or exit. Professor Robert E. Keeton, in analyzing these and other insurance cases where the results often do not follow from the rules stated, found there to be two general principles underlying many decisions. These principles are the reasonable expectations of the insured and the unconscionability of the clause itself or as applied to the facts of a specific case....

The doctrine of protecting the reasonable expectations of the insured is closely related to the doctrine of contracts of adhesion. Where there is unequal bargaining power between the parties so that one party controls all of the terms and offers the contract on a take-it-or-leave-it basis, the contract will be strictly construed against the party who drafted it. Most courts recognize the great disparity in bargaining power between insurance companies and those who seek insurance. Further, they recognize that, in the majority of cases, a lay person lacks the necessary skills to read and understand insurance policies, which are typically long, set out in very small type and written from a legalistic or insurance expert's perspective. Finally, courts recognize that people purchase insurance relying on others, the agent or company, to provide a policy that meets their needs. The result of the lack of insurance expertise on the part of insureds and the recognized marketing techniques of insurance companies is that "[t]he objectively reasonable expectations of applicants and intended beneficiaries regarding the terms of insurance contracts will be honored even though painstaking study of the policy provisions would have negated those expectations."

The traditional approach to construction of insurance contracts is to require some kind of ambiguity in the policy before applying the doctrine of reasonable expectations. Several courts, however, have adopted Keeton's view that ambiguity ought not be a condition precedent to the application of the reasonable-expectations doctrine.

As of 1980, approximately ten states had adopted the newer rule of reasonable expectations regardless of ambiguity. Other states, such as Missouri and North Dakota, have joined the ten since then. Most courts recognize that insureds seldom see the policy until the premium is paid, and even if they try to read it, they do not comprehend it. Few courts require insureds to have minutely examined the policy before relying on the terms they expect it to have and for which they have paid.

The burglary definition is a classic example of a policy provision that should be, and has been, interpreted according to the reasonable expectations of the insured....

Atwater had a burglary policy with Western for more than 30 years. The creamery relied on Charles Strehlow to procure for it insurance suitable for its needs. There is some factual dispute as to whether Strehlow ever told Poe about the "exclusion," as Strehlow called it. Even if he had said that there was a visible-marks-of-forcible-entry requirement, Poe could reasonably have thought that it meant that there must be clear evidence of a burglary. There are, of course, fidelity bonds which cover employee theft. The creamery had such a policy covering director and manager theft. The fidelity company, however, does not undertake to insure against the risk of third-party burglaries. A business that requests and purchases burglary insurance reasonably is seeking coverage for loss from third-party burglaries whether a break-in is accomplished by an inept burglar or by a highly skilled burglar. Two other burglaries had occurred at the Soil Center, for which Atwater had received insurance proceeds under the policy. Poe and the board of the creamery could reasonably have expected the burglary policy to cover this burglary where the police, as well as the trial court, found that it was an "outside job."

The reasonable-expectations doctrine gives the court a standard by which to construe insurance contracts without having to rely on arbitrary rules which do not reflect real-life situations and without having to bend and stretch those rules to do justice in individual cases. As Professor Keeton points out, ambiguity in the language of the contract is not irrelevant under this standard but becomes a factor in determining the reasonable expectations of the insured, along with such factors as whether the insured was told of important, but obscure, conditions or exclusions and whether the particular provision in the contract at issue is an item known by the public generally. The doctrine does not automatically remove from the insured a responsibility to read the policy. It does, however, recognize that in certain instances, such as where major exclusions are hidden in the definitions section, the insured should be held only to reasonable knowledge of the literal terms and conditions. The insured may show what actual expectations he or she had, but the factfinder should determine whether those expectations were reasonable under the circumstances.

* * *

In our view, the reasonable-expectations doctrine does not automatically mandate either pro-insurer or pro-insured results. It does place a burden on insurance companies to communicate coverage and exclusions of policies accurately and clearly. It does require that expectations of coverage by the insured be reasonable under the circumstances. Neither of those requirements seems overly burdensome. Properly used, the doctrine will result in coverage in some cases and in no coverage in others.

We hold that where the technical definition of burglary in a burglary insurance policy is, in effect, an exclusion from coverage, it will not be interpreted so as to defeat the reasonable expectations of the purchaser of the policy. Under the facts and circumstances of this case, Atwater reasonably expected that its burglary insurance policy with Western would cover the burglary that occurred. Our holding requires reversal as to policy coverage.

Notes and Questions

1. Why the Physical Damage Requirement?: There are two stated reasons for the physical damage requirement. First, insurance companies are trying to protect themselves from "inside jobs" by giving insured employers incentives to monitor their employees' fidelity. Clearly, the employers are in a better position to assess the risk of employee infidelity. Second, the requirement gives the insured company the incentive to invest in security precautions up to the point that any burglar must leave some physical trace of entry. Thus, the insurance company, by providing this "loophole," helps to align the insured's incentives to invest in the company's security.

2. Dealing with Moral Hazard: Insurance companies recognize the presence of moral hazard incentives and attempt to develop methods to deal with them. Clearly, Western's physical damage requirement attempts to address such issues. Given the outcome in *Atwater*, how might Western now go about protecting itself from moral hazard incentives? The court suggests that insurance companies now have a burden to communicate coverage and exclusions accurately and clearly. How would an insurance company prove that it did so? Would the insurance company face further incentive problems in collecting such evidence? One possibility is to have the insured place her initials on the contract next to the exclusions as the insurer explains them. Would such a practice help insurers to avoid the reasonable-expectations doctrine? Wouldn't the difficulty of obtaining proof of accurate and clear communication result in higher premiums, therefore excluding some from insurance altogether?

3. Getting What You Paid For: The general policy of construing exclusions narrowly makes it more difficult for insurance companies to protect against moral hazard incentives. In effect, such a policy expands the insurers' risk exposure. Atwater paid premiums that were related to Western's expected risk exposure. Who bears the cost when Western is forced to pay on a risk not contemplated by the insurance contract? Did Atwater get more than it paid for? Economic efficiency would seem to suggest that the least cost avoider of risk should bear the cost. Does the court's result achieve this end?

c. Insurer's Duty to Settle

The insurance market, like any other voluntary market, is founded on mutually beneficial exchange. The claims payment process, as indicated by the prior cases in this section, can often result in conflicts between the insured and the insurer. Potential conflicts arise when a plaintiff is attempting to negotiate a settlement with an insured defendant and the defendant's insurance company. Consider the incentives faced by the insured and insurer in the following case.

Mowry v. Badger State Mutual Casualty Co.

Supreme Court of Wisconsin
385 N.W.2d 171 (1986)

CECI, J.

This is a review of the circuit court's decision and judgment against Badger State Mutual Casualty Company (Badger State) in the amount of $159,000. In a decision filed on May

23, 1984, the circuit court for Waukesha county, Robert T. McGraw, circuit judge, held that Badger State breached its contract and committed bad faith in refusing to defend its insured and in refusing to settle the third-party claim of victim Bradley Mowry within the liability limits of an insurance policy. We reverse the judgment of the circuit court.

* * *

The issue is whether the circuit court erred in holding that Badger State breached its contract with its insured and committed the tort of bad faith in refusing to defend its insured and in refusing to negotiate a settlement within policy limits when Badger State had sought a separate trial on the issue of coverage....

The historical facts of this case are undisputed. On May 3, 1975, Bradley Mowry, then age 19, was injured in an automobile accident and suffered serious bodily injury, including the amputation of part of one foot. He was a passenger in an automobile driven by Steven McCarthy. The vehicle left a roadway and collided with a bridge abutment. McCarthy's parents were insured by Badger State and had policy limits of $15,000 for damages to any one person and medical coverage up to $1,000.

Upon being notified of the accident, Badger State began to investigate the circumstances surrounding the accident. The claims manager for Badger State, John Graeber, concluded after reading the police report and interviewing all of the automobile's occupants that the case was one of probable liability on McCarthy's part. He also determined that the case would probably involve damages to Mowry in excess of the $16,000 policy limits.

Badger State's investigations indicated to it, however, that a question of policy coverage existed. The question revolved around the ownership of the vehicle which McCarthy was driving at the time of the accident. The insurer believed that it was unclear whether McCarthy or his parents were the true owners of the automobile involved in the accident. Its investigation disclosed that the car was titled in McCarthy's mother's name, but that McCarthy had paid for the car with his own money, did not need permission to drive the car, and had told several people at the scene of the accident that he owned the vehicle and that it was uninsured. Given these circumstances, Graeber concluded that the issue of ownership was debatable and that a serious question of coverage had arisen.

In March, 1976, ten months after the accident, Mowry filed suit against McCarthy, McCarthy's parents, Badger State, and an insurance agent....

On September 13, 1977, Mowry issued a formal demand of settlement for the full amount of the liability insurance coverage, $15,000. Badger State's attorney, Kurt Frauen, responded that Badger State had denied coverage under the policy, but that he would inform Badger State of the offer. Badger State did not accept the offer.

At a pretrial conference on September 26, 1977, Attorney Frauen requested that Mowry's counsel and other parties present agree to a bifurcated trial in which a determination on coverage would precede any trial on the issue of liability. In relating the events of the pretrial conference to Badger State, Attorney Frauen wrote, "Everyone seemed to feel that if the coverage issue were resolved, the rest of the case would not have to be tried." Mowry's counsel reiterated Mowry's offer of settlement on September 26, 1977, but Badger State again refused to accept it.

A subsequent stipulation and order set April 4, 1979, as the commencement date for the trial on the issue of coverage; the issues of liability and damages were to be held in abeyance until the resolution of the coverage issue. On March 12, 1979, approximately three weeks before the coverage trial, Mowry once more demanded that Badger State pay the limits of McCarthy's liability insurance policy plus $1,000 under the medical payments coverage; he set a March 23, 1979, deadline for its acceptance. Badger State's counsel, in correspondence to Mowry's counsel, stated that he felt the settlement demand was contrary to the stipulation and order separating the coverage issue from the liability and damages issues: "The court has in fact bifurcated the trial ... to resolve the coverage dispute before proceeding with the plaintiff's case." Mowry's counsel responded that he believed that stipulating to a bifurcation of issues "should not in any way be construed as barring plaintiff from attempting to negotiate settlement of his entire claim."

Badger State refused Mowry's March 12 settlement offer. On April 4, 1979, the coverage issue was tried before a jury. The jury returned a verdict the next day which found that McCarthy's parents owned the vehicle in question at the time of the accident. Coverage was thereby afforded Steven McCarthy under the policy.

On April 6, 1979, Badger State offered the limits on its liability policy and medical payments coverage. On January 10, 1980, Badger State's counsel informed McCarthy that it would assume McCarthy's defense in the action. Following negotiations between counsel for Mowry and Badger State, the parties entered into a stipulation of judgment in October, 1980, thereby rendering a trial on the liability and damages issues unnecessary. The judgment was in favor of Mowry and against Badger State for $16,000 and against Steven McCarthy for $175,000. The stipulation further called for McCarthy to assign to Mowry any and all causes of action which McCarthy might have against Badger State, in satisfaction of Mowry's judgment against McCarthy. Following that stipulation and entry of judgment, Mowry, suing under McCarthy's assignment of rights, brought the present action against Badger State for bad faith and breach of contract.

The circuit court, in holding that Badger State breached its contract in refusing to defend and that it committed bad faith in refusing to negotiate a settlement, was indignant that an insurer would delay settlement negotiations until the coverage issue has been judicially determined, particularly when liability and excess damages are undisputed. The court felt that Badger State's posture of not negotiating a settlement until the determination of the coverage issue placed all the risk of an excess judgment on the insured. It found that an insurance company who refuses to defend and refuses to negotiate may not protect itself from a claim for damages in excess of policy limits by tendering the policy limits only upon losing the coverage issue of a bifurcated trial.... Judge McGraw stated that the proper rule should be "'when an offer of settlement within the policy limits has been made and ignored, a good faith refusal to defend is not a valid defense to a claim in excess of the policy limits.... '" The court then awarded Mowry damages in the amount of $159,000, representing the stipulated amount of liquidated damages for which Badger State would be liable in any action brought by Mowry as assignee against Badger State.

Badger State appealed. The court of appeals, in its certification memorandum, framed the issue to be whether an insurance carrier "should be held liable for damages in excess of its policy coverage where its belief that there was no coverage led it to reject" an earlier offer of settlement within the policy limits. The court noted that this particular scenario presents an unaddressed area of insurance law in this state.

* * *

We note the competing interests on each side of this case. When an insurer is certain of its insured's liability for an accident and where damages to the victim exceed policy limits, the insurer would normally be responsible for indemnifying its insured to the extent of its policy limits. The insurer, however, experiences a conflict of interests whenever an offer of settlement within policy limits is received where a legitimate question of coverage under the policy also exists. The insurer will be reluctant to settle within policy limits if there is a likelihood that coverage does not exist. On the other hand, an insurer's failure to settle a victim's claim within policy limits may subject an insured to a judgment in excess of his policy limits. This case presents a good example of these conflicting interests.

BAD FAITH CLAIM

An insurer owes a general duty to its insured to settle or compromise a claim made against the insured. This duty does not arise out of an express contractual provision; rather, it is implied from the terms of the contract which give the insurer the absolute control of the defense of the action against the insured.

The insurer has the right to exercise its own judgment in determining whether a claim should be settled or contested. But "exercise of this right should be accompanied by considerations of good faith." In order to be made in good faith, a decision not to settle a claim must be based on a thorough evaluation of the underlying circumstances of the claim and on informed interaction with the insured. This gives rise to several obligations on the part of the insurer. First, the insurer must exercise reasonable diligence in ascertaining facts upon which a good-faith decision to settle or not settle must be based. Second, where a likelihood of liability in excess of policy limits exists, the insurer must so inform the insured so that the insured might properly protect himself. Third, the insurer must keep the insured timely abreast of any settlement offers received from the victim and of the progress of settlement negotiations.... Mowry argues that the insurer's mistaken decision about the nonexistence of coverage should render Badger State liable for the excess judgment entered against the insured. He does not assert that Badger State breached any of the three traditional obligations arising out of the general duty to settle. Rather, he asserts that Badger State acted in bad faith in deciding to disclaim coverage where it was convinced that no real issue as to liability or damages existed. Moreover, he argues that Badger State's liability for damages caused by its refusal to settle an excess liability claim is not excused by a good-faith failure to defend.

* * *

Mowry also cites *Comunale v. Traders & General Ins. Co.*, 50 Cal. 2d 654, 328 P.2d 198 (1958)....

The *Comunale rule*, in effect, renders an insurer strictly liable for any decision not to settle within policy limits, whether or not made in good faith, when a subsequent judgment against the insured exceeds policy limits....

Although we acknowledge the apparent goal of the California approach—to protect the insured from liability for an excess judgment by placing the risk of an erroneous decision not to settle on an insurer—we decline to accept that strict approach for this jurisdiction. Such a policy is unduly oppressive on insurance companies and would force them to settle claims where coverage may be dubious. The California approach is particularly unseemly in a jurisdiction such as our own, where an insurer may seek judicial determination of coverage issues prior to litigating liability and damages issues. The California approach is unrealistic if only to the extent that an insurer's belief that an insurance policy does or does not provide coverage must necessarily "affect a decision as to whether the settlement offer in question is a reasonable one."

* * *

We hold that the circuit court erred in finding in this case that Badger State committed bad faith by refusing to settle and negotiate a settlement within policy limits. A finding of bad faith must not be measured solely against a backdrop that coverage was ultimately found to exist under the policy. Bad faith should be found in this case only if there was no fairly debatable coverage question. However, the circuit court, sitting without a jury, did not use this standard to reach its bad faith conclusion. The court concluded that Badger State's posture of waiting to defend the action and to negotiate a settlement until the coverage issue was determined itself constituted bad faith. Because the circuit court did not rely on appropriate and applicable law in making its bad faith determination, its holding is an abuse of discretion and, as such, is erroneous.

The upshot of the trial court's holding would be to require the insurer to accept an offer within policy limits even where a fairly debatable coverage question exists. We have, however, rejected the California approach, which would make an insurer strictly liable for an offer of settlement within policy limits.

Although this court might otherwise remand a matter to the circuit court for further consideration where the appropriate law has not been applied, we choose to decide the bad faith issue as a matter of law.

* * *

We hold that Badger State did not act in bad faith in initially denying coverage to McCarthy. The record establishes a reasonable basis for Badger State's denial of coverage. Although the vehicle was registered in Mildred McCarthy's name, other items within the record suggest Steven McCarthy's ownership of the vehicle. Eugene McCarthy, Steven's father, stated that Steven paid for the car with money from Steven's own checking account, but that Eugene also "gave him some money." McCarthy apparently had approached his father about the idea of "buy[ing] the car" from a third party. Steven, according to the elder McCarthy, paid $150 for the car, but Mildred McCarthy's name appeared on the title. McCarthy never had to ask his father or mother for permission to use the car. Eugene McCarthy suggested that his son obtain insurance on the vehicle. In a statement made to a Badger State representative, McCarthy claimed that his mother owned the car on the date of the accident but that he had paid for it. One of the vehicle's occupants on the date of the accident stated that McCarthy said at the accident scene that he owned the car and that it was uninsured.

Although the record itself does not conclusively establish that the vehicle in question was covered under the elder McCarthy's insurance policy (that task was undertaken and resolved by the jury in the coverage trial), the record sufficiently establishes that Badger State was presented with a fairly debatable coverage issue. There is no absence of a reasonable basis for Badger State's denial of coverage. The record gives no indication that Badger State failed to properly investigate the claim, or that important facts were recklessly ignored and disregarded. Badger State did not commit bad faith in failing to settle Mowry's claim within policy limits even though McCarthy's liability for the accident was probable and damages were concededly in excess of policy limits. The question of coverage under the policy was fairly debatable.

Badger State could have protected both its interests and its insured's interests by settling under a reservation of rights agreement, Mowry and the circuit court assert. The record reflects that Badger State's counsel and its claims manager considered such an option, but ultimately decided to pursue the bifurcation procedure. A reservation of rights agreement would result in a settlement of the injured's claims, while preserving the insurer's right to litigate the coverage issue. The insured benefits from this procedure because it is protected from excess judgment. Badger State argues, however, that the reservation of rights procedure will rarely result in the insurer's recouping the payments it made to the victim from the insured where coverage is found not to exist under the policy, because the insured may be judgment-proof.

An insurer is always at liberty to seek a reservation of its rights in settling a claim. But Badger State's failure to seek such a reservation in this case does not, by itself, constitute bad faith. Badger State merely sought a statutory mechanism to bifurcate the coverage issue from the liability and damages issues. To require an insurer to enter into a reservation of rights agreement in addition to proceeding within a separation framework would run contrary to the bifurcation allowed by [statute]. Even though Badger State's determination that coverage did not exist was wrong, its mistake does not mean that it acted in bad faith in refusing to settle if the issue of coverage was fairly debatable....

Mowry argues that it is inherently unfair for McCarthy to be liable for a judgment in excess of policy limits when the judgment could have been wholly avoided had Badger State settled within policy limits when it had the opportunity to do so. But to require an insurer to settle any claim within policy limits where the insured's liability and the victim's damages in excess of policy limits are relatively certain, without consideration as to whether coverage exists, may result in extortionate lawsuits against the insurer.... The bad faith standard ... strikes an acceptable balance between the insurer's and insured's competing interests concerning settlement offers within policy limits where liability and damages in excess of policy limits are apparent.

* * *

Because the trial court held that Badger State committed bad faith in refusing to negotiate or settle a claim within its policy limits and did not apply the fairly debatable standard to the coverage question, the trial court erred as a matter of law. We hold that when a coverage issue is fairly debatable, an insurer will not have acted in bad faith in refusing to settle within policy limits, even when the insured's liability for the incident is undisputed and when the victim's damages appear to exceed policy limits. Because no determination was made that the coverage issue was fairly debatable, the circuit court abused its discretion in holding that Badger State acted in bad faith and in holding it liable for McCarthy's excess judgment.

* * *

Notes and Questions

1. Specifying the Conflict of Interest: Mowry presents a clear conflict of interest between the insured and the insurer. The parties face a situation in which the insured's liability is near certain and there is a high probability that damages will be in excess of insurance coverage. Thus, the insured has a strong incentive to take any settlement offer that is within the coverage limits. However, to the extent that there is an issue regarding coverage, the insurer's incentives deviate from those of the insured. Specifically, if the insurer pays the settlement and later wins on the coverage issue, the chance of recovering the amount paid in settlement from the insured is remote. Therefore, the insurer prefers to decide the coverage issue first. In short, the issue in *Mowry* is who bears the risk that, by refusing settlement, damages in excess of the policy limits will be awarded. Do the concepts of freedom of contract and Coasian bargaining have any implications for your analysis of this conflict of interest?

2. Strict Liability Duty to Settle: Under a strict liability rule, the insurer always bears the risk of an excess judgment. Insurers could exercise reservation rights, but the value of such rights is diminished by the low probability of ex post collection. The court observes that such a rule provides an incentive for "extortionate" lawsuits. Why does the court state that the rule provides that incentive? How is this so? Moreover, notice that a strict liability rule constrains the ability of an insurer to negotiate a settlement. In other words, the victim can offer to settle at the maximum required under the policy with a large degree of confidence that the offer will be accepted. Why is this so? How does a strict liability rule impact the cost of providing insurance? From a public policy perspective, why should cost matter?

3. Good Faith Duty to Settle: Under a good faith rule, the insurer can shift the risk of an excess judgment on to the insured. Does this prevent "extortionate" lawsuits and provide a greater degree of flexibility in negotiating settlements? Does a good faith rule place the risk of an excess judgment on the party who ex ante was the least cost avoider? How does a good faith rule impact the cost of providing insurance? From a public policy perspective is this a better result than under a strict liability rule?

3. Self-Insurance

Rather than purchasing insurance, some individuals decide to bear the risk themselves. That is, they self insure. Self-insurance creates incentives to do a number of different things. First, individuals can invest resources to minimize the probability of an uncertain event occurring. Examples of this would be an individual clearing the brush away from the area surrounding their house to minimize the likelihood that their house will burn down in the event of a brush fire. Second, self-insurance also creates incentives to invest in security precautions to minimize the monetary loss in the event the contingency actually occurs. Thus, individuals could install a sprinkler system, fire alarms, and smoke detectors with telephone links to the local fire station to minimize the monetary loss in the event that their dwelling catches on fire. Third, self-insurance gives individuals the incentive to set aside reserve funds to cover possible losses. Many large companies self insure their employees' health insurance. The companies often hire a third-party administrator to administer the self-insurance process within the company in order to save on transactions costs and to take advantage of the administrator's expertise.

C. Risk and Market Prices

Markets help individuals and firms deal with uncertainty and risk by adjusting and discounting the market price to reflect the risk. This is clearly seen in the case of financial products where riskier stocks receive a higher return than less risky stocks. Similarly, unsafe products or services are often sold at a discount. For example, many people (perhaps mistakenly) believe that some of the discount airlines are not as safe as the major airlines and, thus, they are not willing to fly on the discount airlines even though the price is lower. One way to characterize the market adjustment process here is that the low fare airlines must reduce fares to get people to take on the perceived increased risk associated with flying on those airplanes. In general, the market demand curve shifts back to the left as consumers react adversely to labeling of a product as "unsafe." The result is that unsafe products (that is, products individuals perceive to be riskier than other products) sell at a discounted price relative to the price of safer products.

1. Financial Products

Financial products offer perhaps the clearest evidence of market adjustment to risk. Investors typically require higher expected returns as compensation for bearing greater risks. Consider two alternative investments, A and B. A and B have the same expected annual return for each of the next ten years and thus have the same net present value. However, A offers a risk-free rate of return, and B has considerable variance in the possible cash flow in each year. In order to induce investors to purchase asset B, it must be sold at a discounted price relative to A. By forcing the purchase price of B down, the return on that investment increases. Therefore, the market forces a higher expected return for the riskier investment.

The Rights of Creditors of Affiliated Corporations

Richard A. Posner

43 U. Chi. L. Rev. 499, 501–03 (1976)

Mr. A. Smith wants to borrow $1 million to invest in a mining venture together with $2 million of his own money. He wants the loan for only a year since by the end of the year it will be apparent whether the venture has succeeded; if it has, he would then want to obtain longer-term financing. Since Smith is a man of means, if he gives his personal note to the lender the latter would regard a one-year loan of $1 million as riskless and would offer Smith the riskless short-term interest rate, say six percent. But Smith is reluctant to stake more than $2 million on the outcome of the mining venture. He proposes to the lender a different arrangement, whereby the lender will agree to look for repayment of the loan exclusively to the assets of the mining venture, if any exist, a year hence. Under this arrangement, Smith will be able to limit his liability to his investment in the venture.

The lender estimates that there is an 80 percent probability that the venture will be sufficiently successful to enable repayment of the loan and interest on the due date, and a 20 percent probability that the venture will fail so badly that there will be insufficient assets to repay even a part of the loan.[1] On these assumptions the solution to the lender's problem is purely mechanical; he must calculate the amount, payable at the end of a year, that when multiplied by 80 percent (the probability that payment will in fact be made) will equal $1,060,000, the repayment he would have received at the end of the year had he made the riskless loan. That amount is $1,325,000.[2] Accordingly, the lender will charge Smith 32.5 percent interest for the loan if Smith's obligation to repay is limited to the assets of the venture. At this rate of interest the lender is indifferent as between the riskless and the risky loan.

This example illustrates the fundamental point that the interest rate on a loan is payment not only for renting capital but also for the risk that the borrower will fail to return it. It may be wondered why the borrower might want to shift a part of the risk of business failure to the lender, given that he must compensate him for bearing added risk. There are two reasons why the lender might be the superior risk bearer. First, the lender may be in a better position than the borrower to appraise the risk. Compare the positions of the individual shareholder in a publicly held corporation and the banks that lend the corporation its working capital. It may be easier and hence cheaper for the bank to appraise the risk of a default and the resulting liability than it would be for the shareholder, who may know little or nothing about the business in which he has invested. Second, the borrower may be risk averse and the lender less so (or risk neutral, or even risk preferring).[3]

---

1. Plus the additional assumption that the lender is "risk neutral." This term is explained in note [3] infra.

2. Calculated by solving .8x = $1,060,000 for x.

3. An individual is risk averse if he prefers the certain equivalent of an expected value to the expectation—the certainty of receiving $1 to a 10 percent chance of receiving $10. A risk preferrer

Thus, unlimited liability would discourage investment in business ventures by individuals who wanted to make small, passive investments in such ventures. It would also discourage even substantial entrepreneurial investments by risk-averse individuals—and most individuals are risk averse.

A borrower could in principle negotiate with the lender for an express limited-liability provision. The more usual course, however, is to incorporate and have the corporation borrow the money. The basic principle of corporation law is that the shareholders of a corporation are not personally liable for the corporation's debts unless they agree to assume such liability. Corporate borrowing therefore automatically limits the borrower's liability to his investment in the corporation. The fact that the law permits Smith to limit his liability by conducting his mining venture in the corporate form does not imply, however, that the law is somehow tilted against creditors or enables venturers to externalize the risks of business failure.... Although incorporation permits Smith to shift a part of the risk of failure to the lender, there is no externality; the lender is fully compensated by the higher interest rate that the corporation must pay by virtue of enjoying limited liability. Moreover, the lender is free to insist as a condition of making the loan that Smith guarantee the debts of the corporation personally or that he consent to including in the loan agreement other provisions that will limit the lender's risk—though any reduction in the risk will reduce the interest rate the lender can charge since a portion of that rate is, as we have seen, compensation to the lender for agreeing to bear a part of the risk of the venture.

There is an instructive parallel here to a fundamental principle of bankruptcy law: the discharge of the bankrupt from his debts. This principle, which was originally developed for the protection of business rather than individual bankrupts, enables the venturer to limit his risk of loss to his current assets; he is not forced to hazard his entire earning capacity on the venture. Incorporation performs the same function of encouraging investment by enabling the risk averse to limit their risk of loss to their investment.

Far from externalizing the risks of business ventures, the principle of limited liability in corporation law facilitates a form of transaction advantageous to both investors and creditors; in its absence the supply of investment and the demand for credit might be much smaller than they are....

2. Products and Services: Risk Allocation and Contract Law

Prices for products and services adjust to reflect the risk associated with the transaction. In essence, freedom of contract allows parties to allocate risk according to which party is willing to accept the risk in light of the price adjustment. This subsection considers various areas where contracts allocate risk.

a. Assumption of Risk

Individuals often engage in activities that involve the risk of injury. As a defense to a negligence claim, the doctrine of assumption of the risk prohibits recovery for injuries

---

would have the opposite preference, and a risk-neutral individual would be indifferent. A corporation is less likely to be risk averse than an individual because the shareholders of the corporation can offset any risks incurred by that corporation by holding a diversified portfolio of securities. Moreover, a large lender can eliminate or greatly reduce the risk of loss on a particular loan by holding a diversified portfolio of loans. On both counts it seems likely that individual investors would often be more averse to bearing unlimited personal liability for the failure of an enterprise in which they had invested than lenders would be to bearing the risk of that failure to the extent of their loan to the enterprise.

that an individual receives when he voluntarily exposes himself to a known and appreciated danger. Four elements are required to establish an assumption of the risk defense. The plaintiff must: (1) have knowledge of facts which constitute a dangerous condition, (2) know that the condition is dangerous, (3) appreciate the nature or extent of the danger, and (4) voluntarily expose himself to the danger. Although in some cases, a written contract expressly provides for an assumption of the risk, the aforementioned elements make it clear that an implied assumption of the risk is comparable to an implied contractual agreement.

Suppose, for example, that two electric drills available in a hardware store are priced at $20 and $50. It is explicitly stated on the package of the lower priced drill that it is not safe for use in drilling through concrete. A purchaser of the lower priced drill who plans to drill through concrete does so because the added protection of the more expensive drill is not worth the added cost. Thus, the purchaser assumes the risk of injury that may occur when drilling through concrete. Under contract law and tort law, the purchaser may not be able to recover damages from the manufacturer because voluntarily bearing the risk of injury often serves as a bar to recovery. However, a person can only assume known and appreciated risks. An example often given is a spectator at a baseball game assumes a certain amount of risk that he or she will be injured if hit by a baseball. A spectator probably assumes the risk of being hit by a baseball in areas that are not protected by screens because most can appreciate the risk they are taking. However, spectators do not assume the risk that a ball will penetrate a protective screen and cause them harm since it is difficult to assess the risk of such an event.

Avram Wisna v. New York University

Supreme Court of New York
Docket No. 114439/2005 (Jan. 23, 2008)

CAROL R. EDMEAD, Judge.

* * *

The following facts are not in dispute. During the spring of 2004, plaintiff Avram Wisnia was a matriculated student at NYU, completing his junior year. He resided at an NYU residence hall, Third Avenue North, that is located at 75 Third Avenue, New York, New York (the Premises). During his junior year, plaintiff was elected as a Secretary of the Third Avenue North Student Counsel (TASC), a student-run organization responsible for, among other things, planning and overseeing dormitory events. As part of its spring activities, TASC organized a "Beach Bash Event" to take place in the courtyard of the Premises on May 1, 2004. The activities on that day included: a DJ, a "moon-bounce," jell-o wrestling in a kiddie pool, volleyball, water guns, and water balloons. Plaintiff took part in planning the Beach Bash. He was responsible for advertising the event to other students living in the residence hall and he was in charge of supplying food for the event.

On May 1, 2004, plaintiff alleges that he took a trip to the store to purchase snacks for the day's events. Upon his return to the Premises, several of his friends from TASC beckoned him to investigate the quality of the jell-o in the kiddie pool. Plaintiff placed the items he purchased from the store on a nearby table and proceeded to walk over to look at the pool. When he arrived at the pool, two members of TASC, Alex and Carmen, grabbed plaintiff and pushed him into the kiddie pool. Plaintiff climbed out of the pool, removed his cell phone and wallet from his pocket, walked over to Carmen and started grappling with the young man. At that time, they were in close proximity to the kiddie pool. After several seconds of horse-play, both men landed in the kiddie pool after being pushed in by another member of TASC. It is during this second fall that plaintiff allegedly sustained an injury to his hip.

The entire incident was captured on video by a DJ hired to video record the event. As a result, plaintiff commenced this lawsuit asserting a cause of action for negligence, asserting damages in the amount of one million dollars.

* * *

Assumption of the risk

Despite plaintiff's argument to the contrary, it is difficult to imagine a more compelling set of facts for the application of the doctrine of primary assumption of risk. That doctrine provides that a voluntary participant in a sporting or recreational activity "consents to those commonly appreciated risks which are inherent in and arise out of the nature of the sport [or recreational activity] generally and flow from such participation." Contrary to defendant's contention, individuals are not restricted to playing organized sports for this doctrine to apply. The doctrine also applies to various types of unorganized sports as well as many forms of recreational activity.

A plaintiff who voluntarily participates in a recreational activity is deemed to consent to the apparent or reasonably foreseeable consequences of that activity. This includes those risks associated with the construction of the playing surface and any open and obvious condition on it. Moreover, it is not necessary to the application of the doctrine that the injured plaintiff may have foreseen the exact manner in which the injury occurred, so long as he or she is aware of the potential for injury from the mechanism from which the injury results. Therefore, "if the risks of the activity are fully comprehended or perfectly obvious, the plaintiff has consented to them and the defendant has performed its duty."

In his examination before trial, plaintiff testified that he took part in planning the events of the Beach Bash, which included a DJ, moon-bounce, jell-o wrestling in a kiddie pool, waterguns, water-balloons, and volleyball. In said testimony, plaintiff acknowledged that he was aware of the existence of, and the dangerous nature of, conducting a jell-o wrestling match in a kiddie pool on the concrete surface of the courtyard. In fact, it was plaintiff who suggested placing gym mats underneath the pool to provide added safety.

However, plaintiff argues that he did not voluntarily enter into the kiddie pool, and thus should not be deemed to have assumed the risk for his injuries. This Court is not persuaded by plaintiff's argument. Plaintiff voluntarily entered the Premises to take part in the activities that were planned on that day. Those activities included a jell-o-wrestling match. The record also reveals that, after the first roughhousing incident that landed plaintiff into the kiddie pool, plaintiff climbed out of the pool, took his cell phone and wallet out of his pocket, placed them on a table, approached Carmen (who was standing in front of the kiddie pool), grappled with him and they were subsequently pushed into the pool a second time. Plaintiff testified that it was this second incident that caused his injuries. Thus, it is clear from plaintiff's testimony that he voluntarily engaged in grappling, wrestling, and rough play on the concrete surface in front of the pool. Although plaintiff may not have foreseen the exact manner in which his injury occurred, he was aware of the potential for injury when he decided to grapple with another student in front of a kiddie pool on a concrete surface. Under these facts, plaintiff fully comprehended the risk of the activity in which he was engaged and assumed the risk of the injuries which he sustained.

Notes and Questions

1. Risk Preferences and Assumption of Risk: In general, it is costly for a defendant to satisfy a duty of care owed to a plaintiff. Often, the costs of providing the level of care indicated by tort are passed on to consumers in the form of higher prices, entrance fees, rates, etc. However, some consumers might be willing to release the potential tortfeasor from its duty in order to obtain a lower price. The assumption of risk doctrine allows parties to contract to bear a risk when they have a comparative advantage in risk bearing. That is, the assumption of risk doctrine facilitates voluntary, mutually beneficial exchange.

2. Least Cost Avoiders and Assumption of Risk: Economic efficiency is enhanced if risk is reduced in the least costly manner. In the absence of the assumption of risk doctrine, defendants bear the cost of reducing risk regardless of whether they have a comparative advantage. In some instances, the party to whom a duty is owed may be able to insure against the occurrence of particular risks more cheaply than the defendant. Such parties would find it in their economic self-interest to relieve the defendant of its duty of care by express agreement.

b. The Bargaining Principle and Least-Cost Risk Avoider

As discussed in Chapter V, contract law reduces transaction costs when it supplies default terms for contracts that are the terms for which most contracting parties would bargain if negotiation were costless. This **bargaining principle** provides a framework for analyzing numerous contract law rules, as well as rules in other substantive areas of law such as bankruptcy and corporate law. Although it is not clear what terms most bargaining parties would negotiate for in the absence of negotiation costs, economics can derive some general principles from assumptions about behavior and mutually beneficial exchange. Most economic actors are risk averse—they are willing to pay (or accept a lower price) in order to increase certainty. Moreover, because negotiating parties wish to maximize the total gain from the exchange, they will allocate risk to the lowest-cost risk avoider (i.e., the party with the comparative advantage at avoiding or bearing risk) if transaction costs are zero. This analysis has implications for how courts should interpret contracts when an unforeseeable contingency occurs—courts should allocate risk according to how the contracting parties would have allocated the risk themselves if they had known of the risk at the time of contracting. This determination requires analysis of the relative risk-bearing abilities of the contracting parties. In general, the party with the comparative advantage at bearing a particular risk—the so-called least-cost risk avoider—will be required to bear the risk.

c. The Allocation of Risk—Impracticability and Mistake

The ex ante expected mutual benefits of a contract may change as a result of the occurrence of some unforeseen contingency, sometimes causing the contract to appear unfair ex post. Commercial impracticability and mistake (mutual or unilateral) are the defenses under which a court might excuse a promisor from performance under such changed circumstances. Impracticability and mistake cases can be distinguished as follows: Impracticability deals with a performance made burdensome by an exogenous event (such as a dramatic, unprecedented increase in prices caused by some unpredictable event beyond the control of the contracting parties). Mistake, on the other hand, deals with the materialization of an endogenous risk (such as the parties' realization that the subject of the contract is of a different make or model of automobile than they had thought). As with any potential excuse from performance, courts must be careful to make sure an opportunistic promisor does not use the excuse to take advantage of the changed circumstances.

Eastern Air Lines, Inc. v. Gulf Oil Corp.

United States District Court for the Southern District of Florida
415 F. Supp. 429 (1975)

JAMES LAWRENCE KING, District Judge.

Eastern Air Lines, Inc., hereafter Eastern, and Gulf Oil Corporation, hereafter Gulf, have enjoyed a mutually advantageous business relationship involving the sale and purchase of aviation fuel for several decades.

This controversy involves the threatened disruption of that historic relationship and the attempt, by Eastern, to enforce the most recent contract between the parties. On March 8, 1974, the correspondence and telex communications between the corporate entities culminated in a demand by Gulf that Eastern must meet its demand for a price increase or Gulf would shut off Eastern's supply of jet fuel within fifteen days.

Eastern responded by filing its complaint with this court, alleging that Gulf had breached its contract and requesting preliminary and permanent mandatory injunctions requiring Gulf to perform the contract in accordance with its terms. By agreement of the parties, a preliminary injunction preserving the status quo was entered on March 20, 1974, requiring Gulf to perform its contract and directing Eastern to pay in accordance with the contract terms, pending final disposition of the case.

Gulf answered Eastern's complaint, alleging that the contract was not a binding requirements contract, was void for want of mutuality, and, furthermore, was "commercially impracticable" within the meaning of Uniform Commercial Code § 2-615.

[After determining that the requirements contract was enforceable and that Eastern had not breached it, the court addressed the § 2-615 issue.]

In short, for U.C.C. § 2-615 to apply there must be a failure of a pre-supposed condition, which was an underlying assumption of the contract, which failure was unforeseeable, and the risk of which was not specifically allocated to the complaining party. The burden of proving each element of claimed commercial impracticability is on the party claiming excuse.

The modern U.C.C. § 2-615 doctrine of commercial impracticability has its roots in the common law doctrine of frustration or impossibility and finds its most recognized illustrations in the so-called "Suez Cases," arising out of the various closings of the Suez Canal and the consequent increases in shipping costs around the Cape of Good Hope. Those cases offered little encouragement to those who would wield the sword of commercial impracticability. As a leading British case arising out of the 1957 Suez closure declared, the unforeseen cost increase that would excuse performance "must be more than merely onerous or expensive. It must be positively unjust to hold the parties bound." Ocean Tramp Tankers v. V/O Sovfracht (The Eugenia), 2 Q.B. 226, 239 (1964)....

Other recent American cases similarly strictly construe the doctrine of commercial impracticability. For example, one case found no U.C.C. defense, even though costs had doubled over the contract price, the court stating, "It may have been unprofitable for defendant to have supplied the pickers, but the evidence does not establish that it was impossible. A mere showing of unprofitability, without more, will not excuse the performance of a contract."

Recently, the Seventh Circuit has stated: "The fact that performance has become economically burdensome or unattractive is not sufficient for performance to be excused." We will not allow a party to a contract to escape a bad bargain merely because it is burdensome." "[The] buyer has a right to rely on the party to the contract to supply him with goods regardless of what happens to the market price. That is the purpose for which such contracts are made...." ...

[The court held that Gulf had not shown the hardship required for performance to be commercially impracticable.]

But even if Gulf had established great hardship under U.C.C. § 2-615, which it has not, Gulf would not prevail because the events associated with the so-called energy crises were reasonably foreseeable at the time the contract was executed. If a contingency is foreseeable, it and its consequences are taken outside the scope of U.C.C. § 2-615, because the party disadvantaged by fruition of the contingency might have protected himself in his contract.

* * *

The record is replete with evidence as to the volatility of the Middle East situation, the arbitrary power of host governments to control the foreign oil market, and repeated interruptions and interference with the normal commercial trade in crude oil. Even without the extensive evidence present in the record, the court would be justified in taking judicial notice of the fact that oil has been used as a political weapon with increasing success by the oil-producing nations for many years, and Gulf was well aware of and assumed the risk that the OPEC nations would do exactly what they have done.

IV. REMEDY

Having found and concluded that the contract is a valid one, should be enforced, and that no defenses have been established against it, there remains for consideration the proper remedy.... Gulf presently supplies Eastern with 100,000,000 gallons of fuel annually or 10 percent of Eastern's total requirements. If Gulf ceases to supply this fuel, the result will be chaos and irreparable damage.... It has previously been found and concluded that Eastern is entitled to Gulf's fuel at the prices agreed upon in the contract. In the circumstances, a decree of specific performance becomes the ordinary and natural relief rather than the extraordinary one. The parties are before the court, the issues are squarely framed, they have been clearly resolved in Eastern's favor, and it would be a vain, useless and potentially harmful exercise to declare that Eastern has a valid contract, but leave the parties to their own devices. Accordingly, the preliminary injunction heretofore entered is made a permanent injunction and the order of this court herein. * * *

Notes and Questions

1. Ex Ante and Ex Post Fairness: Reciprocal benefit is the basis of contractual interaction. Each party agrees to the contract terms in anticipation of benefiting from the other's performance. The fairness of contract terms can be evaluated from two perspectives. An ex ante perspective views the terms at the time of agreement, *before* unknown or unanticipated contingencies occur. Ex ante fairness reflects the mutually beneficial aspect of contractual exchange—if both parties agreed to and understood the terms, then the contract is fair. Ex post fairness means evaluating the contract after the agreement and after the occurrence of contingencies. Some of the most interesting problems in contract law deal with the question of when courts should not enforce contract terms agreed to ex ante because of the occurrence of events ex post. Recognition of the important roles of contract law in enforcing contract terms and allocating risk ex ante reveals the potential problems of ex post judicial reconstruction of contracts. Moreover, the fairness or unfairness of particular contract terms should not be judged in isolation, but should be evaluated in light of all aspects of the bargaining process.

2. Least-Cost Risk Avoider: As a starting point for the analysis of the efficiency of contractual risk allocation, it must be recognized that some parties in the economy possess a comparative advantage at minimizing the costs associated with risk. Such parties are referred to as the "least-cost avoider of risk." Good examples of such people are grain dealers, who buy and sell contracts for the future delivery of grain. In essence, grain dealers minimize risk by engaging in numerous buy and sell contracts so an unexpected fluctuation—either up or down—in the market price of grain is not disastrous to them. Moreover, the grain dealers specialize in understanding the grain market and are able to hedge their risks on the basis of their specialized information. On the other hand, the individual farmer does not have the expertise to engage in the pooling of risks on his or her own, but may lock into a guaranteed price long before the market price at harvest is determined. The farmer clearly benefits from not exposing his or her entire income stream to a last minute fluctuation in the market price of grain. Put another way, the grain dealer specializes in maintaining a diversified portfolio while the individual farmer has a non-diversified portfolio. The grain dealer sells insurance (i.e., lower risk) to the risk-averse farmer. Understanding and appreciation of the risk allocation role of contracts leads to richer analyses of various doctrines of contract law. In general, legal rules that enforce contracts when the risk is borne by the least-cost avoider of risk are efficient.

3. Cost Minimization and Least-Cost Risk Avoider: At the time of contracting, the parties have a mutual interest in reducing the costs associated with the contract as much as possible. If the parties consider the potential risks that might thwart performance or make performance impractical, they would place the risk on the party best able to deal with it—that is, the party with the comparative advantage in buying insurance or foreseeing or taking appropriate precautions to reduce the costs of the risk. In general, in the absence of a specific agreement, contract law imposes the risk on the party that seems to have the comparative advantage in bearing risk. Indeed, this is how similarly situated parties would be expected to allocate risks if required to bargain explicitly in advance. By assigning risks of nonperformance to the party who can best control the performance, contract law encourages parties to consider risk when negotiating a contract.

Wilkin v. 1st Source Bank

Court of Appeals of Indiana, Third District
548 N.E.2d 170 (1990)

HOFFMAN, J.

Respondents-appellants Terrence G. Wilkin and Antoinette H. Wilkin (the Wilkins) appeal from the judgment of the St. Joseph Probate Court in favor of petitioner-appellee 1st Source Bank (Bank). The Bank, as personal representative of the estate of Olga Mestrovic, had filed a petition to determine title to eight drawings and a plaster sculpture owned by Olga Mestrovic at the time of her death but in the possession of the Wilkins at the time the petition was filed. The probate court determined that the drawings and sculpture were the property of the estate, and the court ordered the Wilkins to return the items to the Bank.

At the request of the Bank, the probate court entered findings of fact and conclusions of law. Neither party disputes the validity of the findings of fact. Accordingly, this Court will accept the findings as true. The findings of fact may be summarized as follows.

Olga Mestrovic died on August 31, 1984. Her last will and testament was admitted to probate on September 6, 1984, and the Bank was appointed personal representative of the estate.

At the time of her death, Olga Mestrovic was the owner of a large number of works of art created by her husband, Ivan Mestrovic, an internationally-known sculptor and artist.[4] By the terms of Olga's will, all the works of art created by her husband and not specifically devised were to be sold and the proceeds distributed to members of the Mestrovic family.

Also included in the estate of Olga Mestrovic was certain real property. In March of 1985, the Bank entered into an agreement to sell the real estate to the Wilkins. The agreement of purchase and sale made no mention of any works of art, although it did provide for the sale of such personal property as the stove, refrigerator, dishwasher, drapes, curtains, sconces and French doors in the attic.

Immediately after closing on the real estate, the Wilkins complained that the premises were left in a cluttered condition and would require substantial cleaning effort. The Bank, through its trust officer, proposed two options: the Bank could retain a rubbish removal service to clean the property or the Wilkins could clean the premises and keep any items of personal property they wanted. The Wilkins opted to clean the property themselves. At the time arrangements were made concerning the cluttered condition of the real property, neither the Bank nor the Wilkins suspected that any works of art remained on the premises.

During their clean-up efforts, the Wilkins found eight drawings apparently created by Ivan Mestrovic. They also found a plaster sculpture of the figure of Christ with three small children. The Wilkins claimed ownership of the works of art, based upon their agreement with the Bank that if they cleaned the real property then they could keep such personal property as they desired.

The probate court ruled that there was no agreement for the purchase, sale or other disposition of the eight drawings and plaster sculpture. According to the lower court, there was no meeting of the minds, because neither party knew of the existence of the works of art.

On appeal, the Wilkins contend that the court's conclusions of law were erroneous....

Mutual assent is a prerequisite to the creation of a contract. Where both parties share a common assumption about a vital fact upon which they based their bargain, and that assumption is false, the transaction may be avoided if because of the mistake a quite different exchange of values occurs from the exchange of values contemplated by the parties. There is no contract, because the minds of the parties have in fact never met.

The necessity of mutual assent, or "meeting of the minds," is illustrated in the classic case of *Sherwood v. Walker* (1887), 66 Mich. 568, 33 N.W. 919. The owners of a blooded cow indicated to the purchaser that the cow was barren. The purchaser also appeared to believe that the cow was barren. Consequently, a bargain was made to sell at a price per pound at which the cow would have brought, approximately $80.00. Before delivery, it was discovered that the cow was with calf and that she was, therefore, worth from $750.00 to $1,000.00. The court ruled that the transaction was voidable:

---

4. Ivan Mestrovic lived from 1883 to 1962. A Yugoslavian sculptor, Mestrovic became internationally known and spent his final working years in the United States. He taught at Syracuse University and at the University of Notre Dame. Much of his instruction as well as his own creative work involved religious themes.

Mestrovic is represented in the United States in the Brooklyn Museum, Art institute of Chicago, Colgate University, Syracuse University, Syracuse Museum of Fine Arts and University of Notre Dame; in England, in the Leeds Art Gallery, Birmingham Museum of Art, Victoria and Albert Museum and Tate Gallery; and in various collections in Canada, Spain, Belgium and Italy. A great number of churches in various parts of the world own his works.

"The mistake was not of the mere quality of the animal, but went to the very nature of the thing. A barren cow is substantially a different creature than a breeding one. There is as much difference between them … as there is between an ox and a cow.…"

Like the parties in *Sherwood*, the parties in the instant case shared a common presupposition as to the existence of certain facts which proved false. The Bank and the Wilkins considered the real estate which the Wilkins had purchased to be cluttered with items of personal property variously characterized as "junk," "stuff" or "trash." Neither party suspected that works of art created by Ivan Mestrovic remained on the premises.

As in *Sherwood*, one party experienced an unexpected, unbargained-for gain while the other party experienced an unexpected, unbargained-for loss. Because the Bank and the Wilkins did not know that the eight drawings and the plaster sculpture were included in the items of personalty that cluttered the real property, the discovery of those works of art by the Wilkins was unexpected. The resultant gain to the Wilkins and loss to the Bank were not contemplated by the parties when the Bank agreed that the Wilkins could clean the premises and keep such personal property as they wished.

The following commentary on *Sherwood* is equally applicable to the case at bar:

"Here the buyer sought to retain a gain that was produced, not by a subsequent change in circumstances, nor by the favorable resolution of known uncertainties when the contract was made, but by the presence of facts quite different from those on which the parties based their bargain."

Palmer, Mistake and Unjust Enrichment 16–17 (1962). The probate court properly concluded that there was no agreement for the purchase, sale or other disposition of the eight drawings and plaster sculpture, because there was no meeting of the minds.

The judgment of the St. Joseph Probate Court is affirmed.

Notes and Questions

1. Mistake or Ex Ante Risk Allocation?: The defense of mistake applies to situations where there was a genuine misunderstanding of the facts at the time the contract was made, not where some contingency occurred after the contract was made. Therefore, the fundamental issue is not risk allocation, but rather whether the parties actually agreed. Subsequent legal research on the facts of *Sherwood v. Walker* has revealed that, at the time of contract, both parties recognized that there was some probability that the cow, Rose 2d of Aberlone, was not barren. If this is correct, then didn't the contract terms reflect the probability that Rose 2d could become pregnant? That is, didn't the parties agree to shift the risk? If so, then why should the contract be set aside and the seller allowed to keep the gain that resulted from the occurrence of the highly unlikely contingency? Moreover, since the seller was in a better position to calculate the probability of the contingency occurring, doesn't the decision in the case represent an unwarranted windfall for him?

2. Mistake, Fraud, Disclosure, and Regulation: The producer or seller typically has an informational advantage over the buyer. A market-oriented response to concerns that sellers will use their informational advantage to abuse purchasers is that the market will eventually punish a seller for such indiscretions. See the discussion of reputational sanctions in Chapter V. While generally effective, the process of market adjustment is inadequate to address the harm caused by the first occurrence of fraud, deception, or accident due to unsafe design. For example, an individual who has been permanently maimed by an unsafe product takes little pleasure in knowing that the market will adjust to prevent the future sale of the company's unsafe products. Thus, the market adjustment process is supplemented by common law rules and statutory regulations. Indeed, government intervention is often justified when informational asymmetries are such that consumers, investors, and workers are exposed to risks of which they are unaware. Such government intervention can take the form of disclosure regulation (e.g., federal securities regulation) or direct regulation of acceptable risks (e.g., the Occupational Safety and Health Administration's workplace regulations, or the Food and Drug Administration's drug approval process). Market adjustments to different types of risk are discussed in the following section.

3. Compensating Wage Differentials and Market Levels of Safety

The theory of compensating wage differentials can provide many insights into how the market place deals with risk and perceptions of risk. In order to isolate the impact of risk of injury on the job, it is necessary to assume that the compensating wage differentials for every other dimension of the job have already been established. To obtain a complete understanding of the job selection process and its outcomes, it is necessary, as always, to consider both the employer and the employee sides of a market.

Life is full of tradeoffs. Workers are often willing to trade the risk of injury for the receipt of higher wages. The worker who is offered a job for $10.00 per hour in a business firm in which four percent of the work force is injured each year would achieve a certain level of utility from that job. If the risk of injury increased to five percent holding the other job characteristics constant, then the job would have to pay a higher wage to produce the same level of utility. In this regard, compensating wage differentials provide an ex ante compensation related to injury risk. People, of course, differ in their aversion to the risk of being injured. Those who are very sensitive to risk require large wage increases for any increase in risk, while those who are less sensitive require smaller wage increases to hold utility constant.

Workers can also be compensated to keep utility constant by ex post payments for damages. Workers' compensation insurance provides for ex post payments, but these payments are typically incomplete. There is no way to compensate a worker for his or her own death, and workers' compensation does not cover the psychic costs of disfigurement due to permanent impairment. Moreover, the lost income associated with temporary impairments is not fully replaced by workers' compensation because not all injury-related losses are completely compensated ex post. The advantage of ex post compensation comes from the difficulty of estimating some risks. The combination of ex ante compensating wage differentials and ex post damage payments holds worker utility constant in the face of increased risk.

Employers face a wage risk tradeoff of their own. In general, competitive forces on the employers' side of the market tend to cause low risk to be associated with low wages and high risk to be associated with higher wages, holding other things constant. This conclusion follows from three assumptions. First, it is presumably costly to reduce the risk of injury to employees. Safety equipment must be placed on machines, production time must be sacrificed for training sessions, protective clothing and other safety gear must be furnished to workers, and so forth. Second, competitive pressures force many firms to operate at zero economic profits—that is, at a point at which all costs are covered and the rate of return on capital is about what it is for similar investments. Third, all of the job characteristics are already determined. The consequence of these assumptions is that if a firm undertakes a program to reduce the risk of injury, it must reduce wages to remain competitive—the more a competitive firm spends on safety, the less it can spend on other things. Although this analysis could focus on the tradeoff between safety and other working conditions, it focuses on wage tradeoffs because wages are easy to measure and form the largest component of compensation.

From the employer's perspective, there are diminishing marginal returns to safety expenditures. The first expenditure of the firm to reduce risk will have a relatively high return because the firm will clearly choose to attack the most obvious and cheaply eliminated hazard. Thus, at first, the risk and accompanying cost reductions are relatively large and the firm need not reduce wages very much to keep profits constant. At some point, additional expenditures by the firm to reduce risk have diminishing returns because all of the easy ways to solve safety problems have been used. Thus, expanding the safety effort beyond this point results in large wage reductions because further increases in safety are very costly. Furthermore, employers differ in the ease with which they can reduce hazards. In firms where injuries are costly to reduce, large wage reductions are required to keep profits constant when a safety program is implemented.

The market matches employers and employees based on, among other things, their wage-risk preference tradeoffs. Of course, not all firms are the same, and those with a comparative advantage at risk reduction have a comparative advantage at attracting relatively more risk averse workers. Similarly, not all workers are the same, and those who are relatively less risk averse will seek out firms that pay a risk premium because of their comparative disadvantage in reducing risk.

Figure VI-5 illustrates the market determination of workplace safety. The range of possible safety levels, from zero safety to no risk, is on the horizontal axis. The marginal costs to the employer of providing additional units of safety increase as the workplace becomes safer. The marginal benefits to workers of "consuming" additional units of

Figure VI-5. Market Determination of Workplace Safety

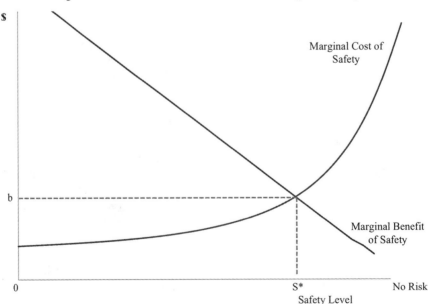

workplace safety decline as the level of risk approaches zero. The price that workers are willing to pay for increased safety by accepting a lower wage declines as risk declines. Employers respond to workers' preferences for safety by providing additional units of safety up to the level where the marginal benefit is equal to the marginal cost. In Figure VI-5, the market determined level of workplace safety is S*. Note that this level is to the left of the no-risk level of safety. At S*, the employer spends the shaded area on workplace safety. The employer does not incur the additional expenditures beyond S* because it costs more to provide the additional safety than the employees are willing to pay by accepting lower wages.

4. Information, Risk, and Price Adjustments

In order for the market to adjust to reflect risky products or risky jobs, it is necessary for the buyers in the marketplace to have information regarding the risk they are undertaking. If the risk is not readily observable and is not known to other people in the marketplace, the market price will not reflect the risk. In some instances, the manufacturers of the product may be aware of a risk of which they have not informed consumers. Certainly, many products liability cases have involved allegations of this type of situation. Asymmetric information is often reduced through regulations requiring warning labels to be placed on various products to alert consumers of the risks they are undertaking. The federal government uses a combination of disclosure regulation and explicit risk reduction regulation to deal with various kinds of risk. In general, disclosure regulation covers many financial and other economic risks, while direct regulation covers many health and safety risks.

D. Tort Law

The law of torts provides a set of legal rules that allows parties injured as the result of the actions of others to collect damages under certain well-defined circumstances. Bearing the costs of injurious acts provides an incentive to potentially liable parties to alter their behavior to reduce the risk of injury. For instance, many state courts have held grocery store owners liable to customers mugged in unlit parking lots. Impliedly, courts are saying that it is cheaper for stores to light their parking lots to prevent muggings than for customers to hire security guards or provide some other form of personal security. Several often-stated economic goals of tort law are reviewed in this section.

1. Behavior Modification and Minimizing the Costs of Accidents

The economic analysis of tort law begins with the assumption that alternative tort liability rules affect the behavior of individuals and firms in predictable ways. The problem addressed by alternative tort liability rules is how to induce both the potential tortfeasor and the potential victim to exercise an appropriate level of care. One way to characterize economic analysis of tort law is that it is primarily concerned with preventing accidents. However, within this view, it is clear that not all accidents are worth preventing. Thus, the economic perspective on tort law has concentrated on developing rules that minimize the total cost associated with accidents, where the total cost is defined as the sum of the cost of prevention and the actual cost of the accidents that occur. When the expected costs of an accident are greater than the cost of accident avoidance, then an efficient legal rule would be one that imposes liability on the party who could have avoided the accident at the lowest possible cost.

The behavior modification goal of tort law is most evident in the comparison of incentives to invest in accident avoidance activities under alternative liability rules. The starting point is an analysis of the duties owed by a reasonable person under a negligence liability standard. Four elements are traditionally required in a cause of action for negligence: (1) a duty to protect the plaintiff against unreasonable risks, (2) a failure to perform the duty, (3) actual loss or damage to the plaintiff, and (4) a reasonably close connection between defendant's conduct and the plaintiff's injury—also known as causation. All four of the elements are important because a cause of action usually fails if any one of the elements is lacking. However, the second element has received a great deal of attention due to Judge Learned Hand's famous economic formulation of the reasonable person standard.

United States v. Carroll Towing Co.

United States Court of Appeals for the Second Circuit
159 F.2d 169 (1947)

L. HAND, Circuit Judge.

These appeals concern the sinking of the barge, "Anna C," on January 4, 1944, off Pier 51, North River. The Conners Marine Co., Inc., was the owner of the barge, which the Pennsylvania Railroad Company had chartered; the Grace Line, Inc., was the charterer of the tug, "Carroll," of which the Carroll Towing Co., Inc., was the owner. The decree in the limitation proceeding held the Carroll Company liable to the United States for the loss of the barge's cargo of flour, and to the Pennsylvania Railroad Company, for expenses in salvaging the cargo and barge; and it held the Carroll Company also liable to the Conners Company for one half the damage to the barge; these liabilities being all subject to limitation. The decree in the libel suit held the Grace Line primarily liable for the other half of the damage to the barge, and for any part of the first half, not recovered against the Carroll Company because of limitation of liability; it also held the Pennsylvania Railroad secondarily liable for the same amount that the Grace Line was liable. The Carroll Company and the Pennsylvania Railroad Company have filed assignments of error.

The facts, as the judge found them, were as follows. On June 20, 1943, the Conners Company chartered the barge, "Anna C." to the Pennsylvania Railroad Company at a stated hire per diem, by a charter of the kind usual in the Harbor, which included the services of a bargee, apparently limited to the hours 8 A.M. to 4 P.M. On January 2, 1944, the barge, which had lifted the cargo of flour, was made fast off the end of Pier 58 on the Manhattan side of the North River, whence she was later shifted to Pier 52. At some time not disclosed, five other barges were moored outside her, extending into the river; her lines to the pier were not then strengthened. At the end of the next pier north (called the Public Pier), lay four barges; and a line had been made fast from the outermost of these to the fourth barge of the tier hanging to Pier 52. The purpose of this line is not entirely apparent, and in any event it obstructed entrance into the slip between the two piers of barges. The Grace Line, which had chartered the tug, "Carroll," sent her down to the locus in quo to "drill" out one of the barges which lay at the end of the Public Pier; and in order to do so it was necessary to throw off the line between the two tiers. On board the "Carroll" at the time were not only her master, but a "harbormaster" employed by the Grace Line. Before throwing off the line between the two tiers, the "Carroll" nosed up against the outer barge of the tier lying off Pier 52, ran a line from her own stem to the middle bit of that barge, and kept working her engines "slow ahead" against the ebb tide which was making at that time. The captain of the "Carroll" put a deckhand and the "harbormaster" on the barges, told them to throw off the line which barred the entrance to the slip; but, before doing so, to make sure that the tier on Pier 52 was safely moored, as there was a strong northerly wind blowing down the river. The "harbormaster" and the deckhand went aboard the barges and readjusted all the fasts to their satisfaction, including those from the "Anna C." to the pier.

After doing so, they threw off the line between the two tiers and again boarded the "Carroll," which backed away from the outside barge, preparatory to "drilling" out the barge she was after in the tier off the Public Pier. She had only got about seventy-five feet away when the tier off Pier 52 broke adrift because the fasts from the "Anna C," either rendered, or carried away. The tide and wind carried down the six barges, still holding together, until the "Anna C" fetched up against a tanker, lying on the north side of the pier below—Pier 51—whose propeller broke a hole in her at or near her bottom. Shortly thereafter: i.e., at about 2:15 P.M., she careened, dumped her cargo of flour and sank. The tug, "Grace," owned by the Grace Line, and the "Carroll," came to the help of the flotilla after it broke loose; and, as both had syphon pumps on board, they could have kept the "Anna C" afloat, had they learned of her condition; but the bargee had left her on the evening before, and nobody was on board to observe that she was leaking. The Grace Line wishes to exonerate itself from all liability because the "harbormaster" was not authorized to pass on the sufficiency of the fasts of the "Anna C" which held the tier to Pier 52; the Carroll Company wishes to charge the Grace Line with the entire liability because the "harbormaster" was given an over-all authority. Both wish to charge the "Anna C" with a share of all her damages, or at least with so much as resulted from her sinking. The Pennsylvania Railroad Company also wishes to hold the barge liable. The Conners Company wishes the decrees to be affirmed.

* * *

We cannot ... excuse the Conners Company for the bargee's failure to care for the barge, and we think that this prevents full recovery. First as to the facts. As we have said, the deckhand and the "harbormaster" jointly undertook to pass upon the "Anna C's" fasts to the pier; and even though we assume that the bargee was responsible for his fasts after the other barges were added outside, there is not the slightest ground for saying that the deckhand and the "harbormaster" would have paid any attention to any protest which he might have made, had he been there. We do not therefore attribute it as in any degree a fault of the "Anna C" that the flotilla broke adrift. Hence she may recover in full against the Carroll Company and the Grace Line for any injury she suffered from the contact with the tanker's propeller, which we shall speak of as the "collision damages." On the other hand, if the bargee had been on board, and had done his duty to his employer, he would have gone below at once, examined the injury, and called for help from the "Carroll" and the Grace Line tug. Moreover, it is clear that these tugs could have kept the barge afloat, until they had safely beached her, and saved her cargo. This would have avoided what we shall call the "sinking damages." Thus, if it was a failure in the Conner Company's proper care of its own barge, for the bargee to be absent, the company can recover only one third of the "sinking" damages from the Carroll Company and one third from the Grace Line. For this reason the question arises whether a barge owner is slack in the care of his barge if the bargee is absent.

* * *

... [T]here is no general rule to determine when the absence of a bargee or other attendant will make the owner of the barge liable for injuries to other vessels if she breaks away from her moorings. However, in any cases where he would be so liable for injuries to others obviously he must reduce his damages proportionately, if the injury is to his own barge. It becomes apparent why there can be no such general rule, when we consider the grounds for such a liability. Since there are occasions when every vessel will break from her moorings, and since, if she does, she becomes a menace to those about her; the owner's duty, as in other similar situations, to provide against resulting injuries is a function of three variables: (1) The probability that she will break away; (2) the gravity of the resulting injury, if she does; (3) the burden of adequate precautions. Possibly it serves to bring this notion into relief to state it in algebraic terms: if the probability be called P; the injury, L; and the burden, B; liability depends upon whether B is less than L multiplied by P: i.e., whether B less than PL. Applied to the situation at bar, the likelihood that a barge will break from her fasts and the damage she will do, vary with the place and time; for example, if a storm threatens, the danger is greater; so it is, if she is in a crowded harbor where moored barges are constantly being shifted about. On the other hand, the barge must not be the bargee's prison, even though he lives aboard; he must go ashore at times. We need not say whether, even in such crowded waters as New York Harbor a bargee must be aboard at night at all; it may be that the custom is otherwise ... ; and that, if so, the situation is one where custom should control. We leave that question open; but we hold that it is not in all cases a sufficient answer to a bargee's absence without excuse, during working hours, that he has properly made fast his barge to a pier, when he leaves her. In the case at bar the bargee left at five o'clock in the afternoon of January 3rd, and the flotilla broke away at about two o'clock in the afternoon of the following day, twenty-one hours afterwards. The bargee had been away all the time, and we hold that his fabricated story was affirmative evidence that he had no excuse for his absence. At the locus in quo—especially during the short January days and in the full tide of war activity—barges were being constantly 'drilled' in and out. Certainly it was not beyond reasonable expectation that, with the inevitable haste and bustle, the work might not be done with adequate care. In such circumstances we hold—and it is all that we do hold— that it was a fair requirement that the Conners Company should have a bargee aboard (unless he had some excuse for his absence), during the working hours of daylight.

* * *

Notes and Questions

1. The Hand Formula: Judge Hand's negligence formula is really just a cost-benefit analysis. Under the famous BPL formulation, B is the cost of undertaking a particular precautionary measure. P is the probability that an accident will occur if a particular precautionary measure is not taken. L is the loss that will result if the accident occurs. Thus, P x L is the benefit of undertaking a particular precautionary measure because it is the weighted loss of the accident that is avoided by the precautionary measure. If B < PL, the benefit exceeds the cost and the reasonable person would have taken the precautionary measure. If they did not take this precaution, then they should be held negligent. If B > PL, the cost exceeds the benefit and the reasonable person would not have taken the precautionary measure to avoid the accident and, thus, would not be held liable for negligence if the injury occurred. What assumptions regarding risk preferences does the Hand Formula make?

2. Hand Formula Example: Suppose that the sunken barge in U.S. v Carroll Towing and its cargo are worth $100,000. Assume that the probability that the barge would break loose if the bargee is not present is 0.0005. Paying the bargee to stay on the barge will cost the barge owner $25. If the barge owner does not incur this $25 expense, is his behavior negligent under the Hand rule?

3. Ex ante Analysis: Because the economic model is based on behavior modification and liability rules are supposed to be a guide to behavior, the BPL test should be applied to conditions existing before the accident—at the time the potential tortfeasor was making the decision about how much to invest in accident avoidance. Thus, ex ante, the BPL formulation provides a guideline for avoiding negligence through investment in accident avoidance. Obviously, the type of activity will dictate the degree of care that is required. Under the Hand Formula, a dangerous activity which has a high probability of causing very serious injuries to many people would require great expenditures in order to avoid a judgment of negligence. On the other hand, if the activity is "safe"—that is, the probability of an accident is very low and the expected injuries are minor—then the expenditures required to avoid a judgment of negligence would be small. Under the Hand Formula, it is not negligence if an injury occurs for which the cost of preventing the injury exceeds the *expected* benefits derived from such expenditures. For example, preventing *all* injuries from flying baseballs in a stadium would be prohibitively expensive, and the likelihood and severity of injury in certain areas of the stands may be quite low. Therefore, failure to protect fans in the right field stands, where the risk of being hit by a baseball is low, may not be negligent. Failure to protect fans behind home plate, however, where the risk of injury is great, may be negligent.

4. Least Cost Avoider of Accidents: The behavioral modification or deterrence view of tort law generates a public policy prescription based on economic efficiency. If the goal of tort law is to minimize the total cost of accidents, then the "least cost avoider" should be held liable. Of course, this broad public policy view raises important questions about who was the least cost avoider. Alternative liability rules, such as negligence, contributory negligence, comparative negligence, and strict liability, can be viewed as placing the risk on the parties who are the least cost risk avoiders under different circumstances. In practice, the identification of the "least-cost avoider" is not always obvious. According to Professor (now-judge) Guido Calabresi, one of the leading commentators on tort law, a number of guidelines can be used to identify the party who should bear the loss of accident. According to Calabresi, the person who should bear the loss of accident should be the party who can: (1) better evaluate the risk involved; (2) better evaluate the accident-proneness of potential parties on the other side; (3) cause prices to reflect this knowledge; (4) insure most cheaply against liability; and/or (5) more likely avoid having the loss shifted in a way that reduces the incentive to avoid the loss. Guido Calabresi, *Faults, Accidents, and the Wonderful World of Blum and Kalven*, 75 Yale Law Journal 216 (1965). Can you determine from Calabresi's criteria what he views as the purpose (or purposes) of tort law?

5. Marginal Analysis: Recall from Chapter I that our basic decision rule for individuals, firms, or government regulators is that it is optimal to engage in an activity up to the point where the marginal benefit equals the marginal cost. In this regard, a more precise statement of the Hand Formula should be based on marginal costs and marginal benefits from investing in care. This can be illustrated diagrammatically as shown in Figure VI-6. The horizontal axis indicates units of care in terms of risk avoidance activity. The B curve starts low at low units of care and rises rapidly taking on an upward sloping shape because it is assumed that the cost of reducing accidents or reducing the damages associated with accidents goes up as the likelihood of accidents or the cost of accidents is reduced—that is, on the margin, the cost of further reductions in risk increase as the units of care increase. The PL curve is downward sloping based on the notion that as more units of

Figure VI-6. The Hand Formula

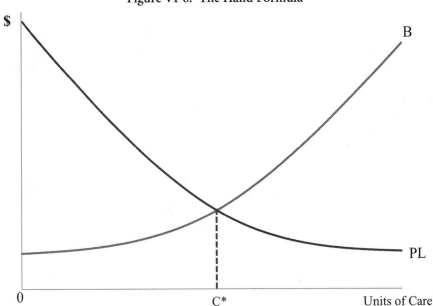

care are incurred, either P will be reduced because of a lower probability of accidents or L will be reduced in the sense that the damage that will be caused when more units of care are invested is likely to be less. B can be thought of as a marginal cost curve which increases with the number of units of care. The PL curve is a marginal benefit curve which suggests that the marginal benefit of additional units of care declines as more and more units of care are used. The marginal benefit and marginal cost of investing in care are equal at C* units of care. That is the efficient standard of care. Any additional investments in care mean that the marginal cost is greater than the marginal benefit, so that the investments are not cost effective. Fewer investments in care indicate that the reduced marginal benefit from reducing care is greater than the marginal costs that are saved from reducing the care, so that making the investments would be cost effective. Under this marginal formulation of the Hand Formula, an individual should be held negligent if they failed to invest C* units of care. That is, to the left of C*, B < PL and they should be held liable under the Hand negligence standard. Firms or individuals who invest more than C* are operating in the range where B > PL, and they should not be held liable under the negligence standard. Thus, the negligence standard of care is expected to induce the efficient amount of accident avoidance expenditures.

6. Strict Liability and Deterrence Effects: An important insight derived from this model of accident avoidance is that if the liability rule is changed from negligence to strict liability—where the tortfeasor pays even if not at fault—then the injurer will theoretically invest the same amount in accident avoidance as under the negligence rule where negligence is determined by the Hand Formula. This is because up until the C* level of care the expected cost to the injurer associated with accidents is greater than the expected cost of risk avoidance (B). Because of those expectations, the benefit of avoiding accidents is greater than the cost of accidents up to the level C*. Beyond that level, the cost of avoiding accidents is greater than the expected payout to injured parties. Thus, the injurer will decide not to make investments beyond C* even though the injurer realizes that he or she will have to pay damages in the event an accident occurs. Thus, rather than focusing on deterrence and behavior modification, the strict liability standard appears to some extent to be driven by distributional considerations.

7. Strict Liability and Victims' Incentives: In many situations, both potential tortfeasors and potential victims can take precautionary measures to avoid accidents. Although both a strict liability rule and a negligence rule should induce tortfeasors to invest the same amount in accident avoidance, the liability rules produce differing incentives for victims. Under a rule of strict liability, potential victims have little incentive to take precautionary measures because they are compensated for any accidents (assuming the courts award damages that fully compensate victims for their losses). Under a rule of negligence, on the other hand, tortfeasors meeting the legal standard of care will not be found liable and victims will bear the loss resulting from accidents. Thus, under a negligence rule, victims have incentives to take cost-effective precautions to reduce the risk of accidents that they would receive no compensation for if tortfeasors were found not liable. As a result, in situations where both potential torfeasors and potential victims can take precautions to reduce the risk of accidents, negligence rules give both parties the incentive to do so.

Can you offer an economic justification for why the owner of a dog is liable for the harm it causes due to his negligence (at least initially), but the owner of a tiger is strictly liable for any harm that it causes?

8. Defenses to Negligence: Because the economic perspective on tort law concentrates on minimizing the total costs associated with accidents, the Hand Formula should also be applied to the behavior of potential victims. The defenses to negligence rely in part on a similar analysis of the cost of avoiding the injury and the expected loss from the injury. A potential defendant did not exercise reasonable care if the injury could have been avoided at a cost that is lower than the expected cost of the injury. A similar analysis can be applied to the plaintiff's decision making. A plaintiff did not exercise reasonable care if she failed to take precautions that cost less than the expected cost of the injury.

9. Contributory and Comparative Negligence: Contributory and comparative negligence are defenses to negligence when the plaintiff is at least partially responsible for his or her injury. The defense of **contributory negligence** is the failure of the plaintiff—the injured party—to exercise reasonable care that contributes to the injury. Traditionally, contributory negligence would completely bar recovery for injuries. Most states have now adopted the doctrine of **comparative negligence**, which allows a proration of the damages resulting from the combined negligence of the parties. If a plaintiff's injuries amount to $100,000, and they are 40% the result of plaintiff's negligence and 60% the result of defendant's negligence, then the plaintiff's recovery would be limited to only $60,000. Compared to a simple negligence rule with no defenses, do either contributory negligence or comparative negligence defenses change potential victims' incentives to take precautionary measures to avoid accidents? Do they change potential tortfeasors' incentives? The answer is much more complicated than it seems. See, for example, Oren Bar-Gill & Omri Ben-Shahar, *The Uneasy Case for Comparative Negligence*, 5 American Law and Economics Review 433 (2003).

What about an accident between a Kia and a Ferrari? Assuming both drivers are equally negligent, is it fair to expect the Kia driver to be responsible for 50% of the damages to the Ferrari? In a system of strict contributory negligence, both drivers would be responsible for the damages to their own cars, because their own negligence would prevent recovery in tort. Does comparative negligence lead to the externalization of costs associated with owning expensive cars? Do the rich benefit more from comparative negligence? *See* Michael

Krauss, *In Defense of Contributory Negligence*, PointofLaw.com (Oct. 31, 2008), http://www.pointoflaw.com/archives/2008/10/in-defense-of-c.php.

10. Negligence Versus Strict Liability, and Activity Levels: Professor Steven Shavell has added some additional elements to the basic BPL model of negligence liability:

> By definition, under the negligence rule all that an injurer needs to do to avoid the possibility of liability is to make sure to exercise due care if he engages in his activity. Consequently, he will not be motivated to consider the effect on accident losses of his choice of whether to engage in his activity or, more generally, of the level at which to engage in his activity; he will choose his level of activity in accordance only with the personal benefits so derived. But surely any increase in his level of activity will typically raise expected accident losses (holding constant the level of care). Thus he will be led to choose too high a level of activity; the negligence rule is not "efficient."
>
> Consider by way of illustration the problem of pedestrian-automobile accidents (and, ... let us imagine the behavior of pedestrians to be fixed). Suppose that drivers of automobiles find it in their interest to adhere to the standard of due care but that the possibility of accidents is not thereby eliminated. Then, in deciding how much to drive, they will contemplate only the enjoyment they get from doing so. Because (as they exercise due care) they will not be liable for harms suffered by pedestrians, drivers will not take into account that going more miles will mean a higher expected number of accidents. Hence, they will do too much driving; an individual will, for example, decide to go for a drive on a mere whim despite the imposition of a positive expected cost to pedestrians.
>
> However, under a rule of strict liability, the situation is different. Because an injurer must pay for losses whenever he is involved in an accident, he will be induced to consider the effect on accident losses of both his level of care and his activity level. His decisions will therefore be efficient. Because drivers will be liable for losses sustained by pedestrians, they will decide not only to exercise due care in driving, but also to drive only when the utility gained from it outweighs expected liability payments to pedestrians.

Steven Shavell, *Strict Liability versus Negligence*, 9 Journal of Legal Studies 1, 2–3 (1980). In effect, a strict liability standard forces the manufacturer to be an insurer of unavoidable risks. Thus, according to Shavell, a strict liability standard forces the manufacturer to contemplate the level of unavoidable risk that results from its activity. Why, even in this case, is the manufacturer assumed to be the least cost avoider? Does Shavell's "externality argument" simply obscure the issue of economic efficiency?

11. Court Errors: Suppose a particular court systematically imposes excessive damages (greater than the actual harm resulting from accidents). What will this do to potential tortfeasors' incentives to take precautionary measures to avoid accidents under a rule of strict liability or a rule of negligence? What if the errors are random (they are not systematically too high or too low)?

Suppose instead that the court systematically sets the legal standard of care above the efficient level of care (C^* in Figure VI-6). What will this do to potential tortfeasors' incentives to take precautionary measures to avoid accidents under a rule of negligence? What if the errors are random (they are not systematically above or below the efficient level of care)?

12. Behavior Modification and Compensation: The pure behavioral modification perspective on tort law suggests that compensation of the accident victim is irrelevant. The important point is that the potential tortfeasor expects to pay damages if held liable and, thus, responds to the incentives created by the liability rule. Damages can be paid to anyone—the victim, the state, the authors of this casebook—because it is assumed that the potential recipient of the damages does not affect the potential tortfeasor's incentives. After all, distributional considerations are routinely ignored when the tortfeasor is not liable in the sense that the victim isn't compensated for the injury suffered. This is not to suggest, however, that deterrence should be the exclusive goal of tort law.

2. Loss Spreading and Insurance

Another economic approach to tort law is to consider it as a form of insurance. Recall that risk averse individuals buy insurance to reduce the downside risk associated with many of life's activities. In the absence of tort liability, tort victims would be forced to bear large losses. Tort rules can be used to compensate unlucky victims. According to this view, the party who is in the best position to spread the loss of the injury should be held liable. With respect to injuries resulting from products, for example, it is argued that the manufacturer is often in the best position to cover the costs of compensation because a portion of the expected accident costs is reflected in the price of the product. All consumers, not just the unlucky few who happen to be injured by the product, bear some of the costs. All purchasers of a product pay a slightly higher price that, in effect, buys them an insurance policy for compensation in the event of injury while using the product.

Greenman v. Yuba Power Products, Inc.

Supreme Court of California

377 P.2d 897 (1963)

TRAYNOR, J.

Plaintiff brought this action for damages against the retailer and the manufacturer of a Shopsmith, a combination power tool that could be used as a saw, drill, and wood lathe. He saw a Shopsmith demonstrated by the retailer and studied a brochure prepared by the manufacturer. He decided he wanted a Shopsmith for his home workshop, and his wife bought and gave him one for Christmas in 1955. In 1957 he bought the necessary attachments to use the Shopsmith as a lathe for turning a large piece of wood he wished to make into a chalice. After he had worked on the piece of wood several times without difficulty, it suddenly flew out of the machine and struck him on the forehead, inflicting serious injuries. About 10 1/2 months later, he gave the retailer and the manufacturer written notice of claimed breaches of warranties and filed a complaint against them alleging such breaches and negligence.

After a trial before a jury, the court ruled that there was no evidence that the retailer was negligent or had breached any express warranty and that the manufacturer was not liable for the breach of any implied warranty. Accordingly, it submitted to the jury only the cause of action alleging breach of implied warranties against the retailer and the causes of action alleging negligence and breach of express warranties against the manufacturer. The jury returned a verdict for the retailer against plaintiff and for plaintiff against the manufacturer in the amount of $65,000. The trial court denied the manufacturer's motion for a new trial and entered judgment on the verdict. The manufacturer and plaintiff appeal. Plaintiff seeks a reversal of the part of the judgment in favor of the retailer, however, only in the event that the part of the judgment against the manufacturer is reversed.

Plaintiff introduced substantial evidence that his injuries were caused by defective design and construction of the Shopsmith. His expert witnesses testified that inadequate set screws were used to hold parts of the machine together so that normal vibration caused the tailstock of the lathe to move away from the piece of wood being turned permitting it to fly out of the lathe. They also testified that there were other more positive ways of fastening the parts of the machine together, the use of which would have prevented the accident. The jury could therefore reasonably have concluded that the manufacturer negligently constructed the Shopsmith. The jury could also reasonably have concluded that statements in the manufacturer's brochure were untrue, that they constituted express warranties, and that plaintiff's injuries were caused by their breach.

The manufacturer contends, however, that plaintiff did not give it notice of breach of warranty within a reasonable time and that therefore his cause of action for breach of warranty is barred by section 1769 of the Civil Code....

* * *

The notice requirement of section 1769, however, is not an appropriate one for the court to adopt in actions by injured consumers against manufacturers with whom they have not dealt. "As between the immediate parties to the sale [the notice requirement] is a sound commercial rule, designed to protect the seller against unduly delayed claims for damages. As applied to personal injuries, and notice to a remote seller, it becomes a booby-trap for the unwary. The injured consumer is seldom 'steeped in the business practice which justifies the rule,' and at least until he has had legal advice it will not occur to him to give notice to one with whom he has had no dealings."... We conclude, therefore, that even if plaintiff did not give timely notice of breach of warranty to the manufacturer, his cause of action based on the representations contained in the brochure was not barred.

Moreover, to impose strict liability on the manufacturer under the circumstances of this case, it was not necessary for plaintiff to establish an express warranty. A manufacturer is strictly liable in tort when an article he places on the market, knowing that it is to be used without inspection for defects, proves to have a defect that causes injury to a human being. Recognized first in the case of unwholesome food products, such liability has now been extended to a variety of other products that create as great or greater hazards if defective.

Although in these cases strict liability has usually been based on the theory of an express or implied warranty running from the manufacturer to the plaintiff, the abandonment of the requirement of a contract between them, the recognition that the liability is not assumed by agreement but imposed by law, and the refusal to permit the manufacturer to define the scope of its own responsibility for defective products make clear that the liability is not one governed by the law of contract warranties but by the law of strict liability in tort. Accordingly, rules defining and governing warranties that were developed to meet the needs of commercial transactions cannot properly be invoked to govern the manufacturer's liability to those injured by its defective products unless those rules also serve the purposes for which such liability is imposed.

We need not recanvass the reasons for imposing strict liability on the manufacturer. They have been fully articulated in [our prior cases]. The purpose of such liability is to insure that the costs of injuries resulting from defective products are borne by the manufacturers that put such products on the market rather than by the injured persons who are powerless to protect themselves. Sales warranties serve this purpose fitfully at best. In the present case, for example, plaintiff was able to plead and prove an express warranty only because he read and relied on the representations of the Shopsmith's ruggedness contained in the manufacturer's brochure. Implicit in the machine's presence on the market, however, was a representation that it would safely do the jobs for which it was built. Under these circumstances, it should not be controlling whether plaintiff selected the machine because of the statements in the brochure, or because of the machine's own appearance of excellence that belied the defect lurking beneath the surface, or because he merely assumed that it would safely do the jobs it was built to do. It should not be controlling whether the details of the sales from manufacturer to retailer and from retailer to plaintiff's wife were such that one or more of the implied warranties of the sales act arose. "The remedies of injured consumers ought not to be made to depend upon the intricacies of the law of sales." To establish the manufacturer's liability it was sufficient that plaintiff proved that he was injured while using the Shopsmith in a way it was intended to be used as a result of a defect in design and manufacture of which plaintiff was not aware that made the Shopsmith unsafe for its intended use.

* * *

The judgment is affirmed.

Notes and Questions

1. Overlap of Deterrence and Loss Spreading Goals: It is often argued that the manufacturer's superior ability to spread the loss can be consistent with the goal of minimizing the costs of accidents, as Justice Traynor wrote in *Escola v. Coca Cola Bottling Co.,* 150 P.2d 436 (1944):

> ... In my opinion it should now be recognized that a manufacturer incurs an absolute liability when an article that he has placed on the market, knowing that it is to be used without inspection, proves to have a defect that causes injury to human beings.... Even if there is no negligence, ... public policy demands that responsibility be fixed wherever it will most effectively reduce the hazards to life and health inherent in defective products that reach the market. It is evident that the manufacturer can anticipate some hazards and guard against the recurrence of others, as the public cannot. Those who suffer injury from defective products are unprepared to meet its consequences. The cost of an injury and the loss of time or health may be an overwhelming misfortune to the person injured, and a needless one, for the risk of injury can be insured by the manufacturer and distributed among the public as a cost of doing business. It is to the public interest to discourage the marketing of products having defects that are a menace to the public. If such products nevertheless find their way into the market it is to the public interest to place the responsibility for whatever injury they may cause upon the manufacturer, who, even if he is not negligent in the manufacture of the product, is responsible for its reaching the market. However intermittently such injuries may occur and however haphazardly they may strike, the risk of their occurrence is a constant risk and a general one. Against such a risk there should be general and constant protection and the manufacturer is best situated to afford such protection.

Id. at 453 (Traynor, J., concurring). This view, in effect, turns a manufacturer into an insurer. Justice Traynor appears to be assuming that manufacturers can insure against non-negligent risk more cheaply than consumers. Is there any justification for this assumption?

2. The Limits of Risk Aversion and Loss Spreading: Although loss spreading is a widely accepted goal of tort law, some judges do recognize that there must be limits to how many injuries can be compensated under such a theory. In *Shepard v. Superior Court*, 76 Cal. App. 3d 16 (1977), a dissenting judge argued against allowing recovery for the plaintiffs' alleged physical injuries resulting from the emotional shock of watching their daughter being killed in an automobile accident:

> ... To start with, it is noted that the avowed purpose of imposing strict liability upon the manufacturer is twofold: (1) loss-distribution or risk-spreading and (2) injury-reduction by enhanced safety. The first rationale, risk-spreading, holds the manufacturer liable for injuries resulting from the use of his product because he is in the best position to distribute the loss either by insurance or by increasing the price of his product.... The second rationale, the theory of injury reduction, holds the manufacturer liable because he is in the best position to discover and correct the dangerous aspects of his products before any injury occurs. Again, the manufacturer may pass on to the consumer the increased product costs by incorporating them in the purchase price of the merchandise.
>
> Although since its inception the courts have generally tended to broaden the scope of products liability, there are few cases, if any, which have embarked on a thorough and delicate analysis to explore whether the above stated policy goals are indeed promoted by the ever-expanding scope of enterprise liability. It is time for such an examination.
>
> The basic facts of economy teach us that the fashionable trend of a wholesale extension of strict liability proves to be counterproductive in many instances by hampering and arresting, rather than promoting, the policy objectives underpinning the doctrine.... While some portion of the ever growing safety and insurance cost may pass directly to the consumer by way of a higher dollar price, the remainder will take the form of decreased quality not affecting safety and decreased profits. The decreased profits affect the manufacturers first (among them mainly the large segment of small businessmen with limited or marginal capital who have to shoulder the strict enterprise liability side by side with the huge corporations), then society as a whole. The motion and realistic operation of economic forces have been graphically described by one observer as follows: "*Decreased profits, however, do not stop with the manufacturer.* He distributes them to the shareholders of his corporation, just as he distributes increased prices to the consumers of his product. Moreover, decreased profits do not stop with the shareholders. *Rather, in more or less attenuated form, they pass on to other, broader classes.* The major distribution of decreased profits occurs when shareholders switch their investment to other, more profitable enterprises. When this happens, the liability-bearing manufacturer's enterprise loses its ability to attract investment capital resulting in decreased industrial activity. *This decreased activity results in losses to several categories. First, the consumer will feel the loss because the manufacturer's ability to produce a better, safer product will diminish. Second, reduced industrial activity will affect labor. Severely diminished profits may force the manufacturer out of business. Even less drastic reductions, however, could reduce the number of new jobs. Finally, reduced economic activity will affect the entire society, in a more or less attenuated form, through lower tax revenues, lower wages, and lower profits for distribution.*" (Alden D. Holford, The Limits of Strict Liability for Product Design and Manufacture (1973) 52 Tex.L.Rev. 81, 87, emphasis added.)

Paying heed to economic realities rather than our own fancy, the courts as a matter of judicial policy must stop the further extension of the strict liability of entrepreneurs, at least to areas where, as here, the determination of damages is speculative and conjectural rather than real and definable. In doing so, we are in line with established law which holds that the manufacturer is not an insurer of the product and that the strict liability of entrepreneurs may not be equated with absolute, limitless liability. As has been emphasized time and time again, in determining the parameters of enterprise liability we must draw a proper balance between the need for adequate recovery and the survival of viable enterprises. The guiding principles to achieve these goals are judicial temperance, evenhandedness and, first and foremost, fairness to all.

Id. at 26–31. This opinion clearly recognizes the presence of opportunity costs in a loss spreading theory of strict liability. Should courts consider such costs in their application of liability rules? Does Justice Traynor consider such costs in *Greenman*?

The Current Insurance Crisis and Modern Tort Law

George Priest

96 Yale Law Journal 1521 (1987)

This paper is an effort to understand the source of the crisis in insurance that has recently disrupted product and service markets in the United States. From press accounts, the crisis seemed to peak in the early months of 1986, when reports became common of extraordinary changes in commercial casualty insurance markets. Insurers had increased premiums drastically for an unusual set of products, such as vaccines, general aircraft, and sports equipment, and for an equally diverse set of services, such as obstetrics, ski lifts, and commercial trucking. In still other cases—intrauterine devices, wine tasting, and day care—insurers had refused to offer coverage at any premium, forcing these products and services to be withdrawn from the market.

* * *

This paper argues that the characteristic of contemporary tort law most crucial to understanding the current crisis is the judicial compulsion of greater and greater levels of provider third-party insurance for victims. The progressive shift to third-party corporate insurance coverage, since its beginnings in the mid-1960's, has systematically undermined insurance markets.

* * *

This explanation of the crisis uncovers what I believe to be a tragic paradox of our modern civil liability regime. The expansion of liability since the mid-1960's has been chiefly motivated by the concern of our courts to provide insurance to victims who have suffered personal injury. The most fundamental of the conceptual foundations of our modern law is that the expansion of tort liability will lead to the provision of insurance along with the sale of the product or service itself, with a portion of the insurance premium passed along in the product or service price. Expanded tort liability, thus, is a method of providing insurance to individuals, especially the poor, who have not purchased or cannot purchase insurance themselves. This insurance rationale suffuses our modern civil law, and must be acknowledged as one of the great humanitarian expressions of our time.

The paradox exposed by my theory is that the expansion of tort liability has had exactly the opposite effect. The insurance crisis demonstrates graphically that continued expansion of tort liability on insurance grounds leads to a reduction in total insurance coverage available to the society, rather than to an increase. The theory also shows that the parties most drastically affected by expanded liability and by the current insurance crisis are the low-income and poor, exactly the parties that courts had hoped most to aid.

* * *

II. MODERN TORT LAW AND ITS ECONOMIC EFFECTS

Since the early 1960's, courts have steadily expanded tort liability for injuries suffered in the context of product and service use. These changes in the law result from the acceptance of a coherent and powerful theory that justifies the use of tort law to compensate injured parties, a theory its founders called "enterprise liability." According to the theory, expanded provider liability serves three important functions: to establish incentives for injury prevention; to provide insurance for injuries that cannot be prevented; and to modulate levels of activity by internalizing costs, including injury costs.

The second feature of the theory—the importance of providing insurance for unpreventable losses—is most crucial for understanding our current insurance crisis. According to enterprise liability theory, expanded legal liability does more than achieve optimal control of accident and activity rates. Expanded tort liability improves social welfare, in addition, because it provides a form of compensation insurance to consumers. A provider, especially a corporate provider, is in a substantially better position than a consumer to obtain insurance for product- or service-related losses, because a provider can either self-insure or can enter one insurance contract covering all consumers—in comparison to the thousands of insurance contracts the set of consumers would need—and can easily pass the proportionate insurance premium along in the product or service price. Most importantly, to tie insurance to the sale of the product or service will provide insurance coverage to consumers who might not otherwise obtain first-party coverage, in particular the poor or low-income among the consuming population.

The insurance rationale was central to the first judicial adoption of enterprise liability theory, by the California Supreme Court in Greenman v. Yuba Power Products, in 1963. The approach was rapidly extended across the various state jurisdictions, first in the products liability field and, later, in other areas of tort law. Briefly, however, enterprise liability theory has justified both restrictions in available legal defenses and expansion of substantive liability standards.

* * *

The economic effects of steadily increasing provider liability … are quite simple in structure. A liability rule can compel providers of products and services to make investments that reduce the accident rate up to the level of optimal (cost-effective) investments. After providers have invested optimally in prevention, however, any further assignment of liability affects only the provision of insurance. More extensive provider liability will generate more extensive provider insurance and nothing more.

The expansion of liability under modern tort law has obviously increased the provision of provider insurance. Any standard beyond a bare cost-benefit test (often identified with negligence) will provide an insurance effect. Courts, of course, have extended liability far beyond the simple cost-benefit standard. Thus, modern tort law compels a very substantial level of provider insurance.

More precisely, modern tort law has broadly shifted the insurance obligation from first-party insurance to third-party or self-insurance by providers. Even a bare-bones cost-benefit standard has insurance consequences: Such a standard creates an obligation of potential victims to obtain market insurance or to self-insure for unpreventable losses. Modern tort law has shifted that obligation to providers, requiring providers either to obtain third-party market insurance or to self-insure for the losses suffered by consumers of their products or services. The expansion of tort liability since the mid-1960's has expanded the range of contexts in which provider insurance must be offered. Courts understand this point perfectly. Much of the modern extension of tort liability has been expressly justified by the salutary insurance consequences that are supposed to result. Thus it is a paradox that the modern regime somehow has led to the reduction of insurance availability.

* * *

III. HOW INSURANCE OPERATES

* * *

Tort law, of course, provides insurance through a third-party mechanism: the insurer pays money to the victim through the medium of the product or service provider who purchases the insurance policy. Although third-party institutional arrangements are somewhat more complex than first-party arrangements, the determinants of the insurance function are the same.

In third-party insurance, there are two sets of risk pools. Consumers of products or services comprise one set of risk pools. To consumers, the insurance policy and the premium are tied to the sale of the product. It is advantageous to define risk pools narrowly for consumers in third-party contexts for exactly the same reasons that it is advantageous to define risk pools narrowly in typical first-party insurance contexts. Defining consumer risk pools narrowly increases product sales, because the premium added to the price of the product more closely approximates the consumer's expected loss.

Manufacturers, for example, will attempt to segregate consumers into risk pools by product design and by advertising and marketing techniques. A chain-saw manufacturer, for example, may design one model appropriate for industrial use and a second model appropriate for occasional gathering of firewood. Of course, such design differences may also be related to different consumer preferences for product features — in this example, features related to safety. But the point is that, if the demand for chain saw injury insurance coverage differs between the professional and the weekender, both consumers and the manufacturer will gain if the manufacturer can design products that differentiate the two markets. In this example, market differentiation would reduce one very broad risk pool into two more narrow risk pools. Narrowing the pools allows the manufacturer to charge different insurance premiums to the two markets and to increase product sales.

Similarly, the accident insurance premium added to the price of an airline ticket from the United States to Europe will be greater on, say, the Concorde than on low-budget or charter lines. The risk of an accident among the various airlines may be the same, but the accident payout risks brought into the pool by passengers on the Concorde are likely to be much greater than the risks brought by charter passengers, if only because of their greater expected future income. The third-party insurance premium must be adjusted in response. In this respect, the qualitative differences between the Concorde and the charters in terms of accident insurance are no different than qualitative differences in meals, time of transit, or other amenities. Indeed, much of the attraction of the charters derives exactly from the ability of these firms to narrow the pool of consumers of their product. Those passengers who travel on low-fare flights are those who prefer or are willing to tolerate lower levels of amenities in return for a lower ticket price.

The second set of risk pools within third-party insurance contexts includes the service and product providers themselves. Providers of products and services purchase market insurance for the same purposes as any first-party insured: to equalize monetary returns over time in the face of some probabilistic chance of loss. Providers will choose market insurance if its costs are lower than the costs of alternatives.

The costs a provider faces by deciding not to purchase insurance depend upon diversification within the provider firm or the provider's ability to diversify risk by other means. As suggested above, marketing different models of a product is a form of diversification, if the risks of loss attending sales of the respective models are uncorrelated. Of course, organization in the conglomerate form or investing retained earnings in diversified assets are other ways in which providers can self-insure.

Insurance companies, however, can (and do) compete for the custom of providers by trying to define narrow risk pools that make market insurance more attractive than self-insurance alternatives. Insurers attempt to aggregate within a pool a set of providers whose risks are uncorrelated, and will set individual premiums for the firms according to the risk each brings to the pool. The insurer's diversification of risk, again, can be achieved either by aggregating a very disparate pool, by holding other assets whose riskiness is un-correlated, or by reinsuring—hiring another insurer to provide meta-diversification.

These simple insurance principles seem very general, but they provide an explanation for the insurance crisis we are currently observing. The next Section attempts to apply these principles to the changes in tort law discussed in Section II, in order to predict the effects of modern law on insurance availability.

IV. HOW CONTEMPORARY TORT LAW AFFECTS INSURANCE MARKETS

… [T]he expansion of corporate liability has progressively undermined the insurance function by increasing the variance (coefficient of variation) of existing insurance risk pools.… [I]ncreasing the variance of a risk pool endangers the pool because it increases the likelihood that the pool will unravel as low-risk members drop out, either by self-insuring or by ceasing to engage in the potentially injury-related activity. This Section … shows that contemporary tort law has restricted rather than expanded insurance availability. The parties that have been most adversely affected are the low-income and poor who, in terms of tort recoveries, are the low-risk members of the consuming population.

* * *

I believe that there are very clear insurance reasons why the shift towards third-party coverage has undermined the commercial casualty insurance industry, generating the crisis. In comparison to first-party insurance, third-party tort law insurance provides coverage in excessive amounts, in a manner that substantially restricts risk segregation, and at costs that far exceed the costs of first-party insurance. For both consumer and provider risk pools, these differences will increase the correlation of risks within existing pools and, as a consequence, increase the extent of adverse selection, leading to the breakdown of the pools.

* * *

Provider tort law insurance coverage differs substantially from first-party insurance coverage. One of the objectives of the tort system is to create incentives for appropriate investments in preventing injury. To obtain optimal incentives for injury prevention, a party that has violated a legal standard must pay full losses to the victim, including both pecuniary and non-pecuniary losses.

The award of both pecuniary and non-pecuniary losses, however, is inappropriate for providing optimal insurance for unpreventable losses. The effort to extend insurance coverage through modern tort law represents a confusion of incentive objectives with insurance objectives. Third-party insurance payments administered through the tort system differ from first-party insurance payments in two ways. First, … no first-party insurance market provides coverage of non-pecuniary losses. Non-pecuniary losses do not affect the marginal value of wealth across states of the world. In addition, moral hazard and adverse selection problems make coverage of these losses exceedingly costly. Losses representing pain and suffering or other emotional effects of an injury, therefore, are never insured in first-party markets because it is not worthwhile for consumers to pay the premiums necessary to support coverage of them.

Secondly, deductibles and co-insurance are features of every first-party insurance contract. Third-party insurance through the tort system, in contrast, never incorporates deductibles or co-insurance to control victim moral hazard. Yet victim moral hazard is as serious a problem in a third-party context as in a first-party context. Preferences for extra visits to a doctor, prolonged hospitalization, or more advanced forms of medical treatment do not diminish because the source of the injury is a third-party defendant.

These two differences mean that, for the same injury, first-party insurance coverage—which corresponds to what consumers are willing to purchase—is substantially different in magnitude than the third-party insurance coverage provided through tort law.

* * *

The shift from first-party to third-party insurance sources, thus, will prompt greater expenditures for advanced medical care, as well as more extended and elaborate hospitalization and subsequent care. For example, holding severity of injury constant, the frequency of claims for twenty-four hour nursing care is likely to be substantially higher under third-party tort law insurance than under first-party insurance.

* * *

Some might regard the additional level of insurance coverage provided by tort law to be beneficial to consumers because it affords them greater compensation for the injuries they suffer. But this view misunderstands the consumer interest in insurance. Of course, after an injury has been suffered, the victim would prefer a greater to a lesser award. But the ex ante interest of the victim is an award tied to the victim's pecuniary losses, not an award greater than these losses. Where the victim is the product or service purchaser, the victim must pay for the insurance in advance. To compel insurance greater than the amount demanded by the purchaser reduces, rather than increases, his or her welfare. To illustrate: if my $100,000 home burns down, I of course would be happier if my insurer gave me $234,000 rather than the $100,000 of coverage I purchased. But, I would object strongly if I were compelled in advance of the fire to purchase $234,000 coverage since I could replace the home in its entirety for an amount in the range of $100,000. A similar concern for optimal insurance extends to contexts involving pure third-party injuries—for example, when bystanders are harmed by the product or service use of others. In modern society, all of us are at once product and service purchasers and bystanders of products and services used by others. Again, in terms solely of insurance, each of us ex ante prefers that the optimal level of insurance be provided by tort law, the level that optimizes insurance coverage subject to insurance costs.

The provision of insurance coverage through tort law in amounts greater than consumers would willingly purchase has additional effects that implicate the recent crisis. An increase of 64% to 134% in the level of insurance coverage under tort law will not operate as a scalar, but will increase consumer risk pool variance and will lead to the unraveling of consumer risk pools.

The increase in the level of insurance coverage from the shift to the third-party tort mechanism is not likely to be uniform over all cases. The empirical observation that pain and suffering awards constitute 47% of total damages is an average figure. Pain and suffering and other non-pecuniary amounts comprise a much higher proportion of large damage judgments. For this reason, risk pool variance is likely to be greater under third-party tort insurance than under first-party insurance.

More importantly, segregating risks into narrow risk pools is substantially more difficult in third-party than in first-party insurance contexts. First-party insurers, by using insurance applications, can distinguish insureds by age, income, occupation, the level of coverage desired, and other personal characteristics related to levels of risk brought to the insurance pool. Moreover, the administration of first-party insurance allows the insurer to distinguish insureds by past loss experience. The collection of these data allows a first-party insurer to define risk pools of very narrow scope, increasing the likelihood that low-risk individuals will find insurance attractive. Narrow risk differentiation maximizes the availability of insurance.

Very little information about individual risks, however, is available to third-party insurers. A product manufacturer, for example, may design and market a product with reference to characteristics of discrete sets of average consumers. But the manufacturer must sell the product on equivalent terms to all who wish to buy it, and cannot distinguish among consumers with respect to the insurance policy provided in the product price.

Some products, of course, will attract relatively homogeneous sets of consumers. A very wide range of products, however, are accessible to and are purchased by consumers of different income levels. Studies of consumers of individual products show that, for virtually all products, the income levels and personal characteristics of consumers of the product differ widely.

The difficulty of segregating risk pools in third-party contexts means that third-party tort insurance pools are likely to be substantially broader than first-party pools even without the effects, described above, of levels of coverage. Compare, for example, the risks of non-preventable injuries from auto use. The first-party insurer can create separate driver pools for teenagers and other age groups; it can segregate insureds by levels of driving, total mileage, distance from home to office, and car type; and it can rate the policies by accident experience and by moving violations within previous time periods. It can allow the insured to choose whether to purchase medical expense and disability coverage in the auto policy or to rely on separate medical and disability policy coverage set according to the deductible the insured prefers and according to the insured's income level. Each of these techniques helps keep premiums low for the low-risk drivers of the consuming population—those who drive little, are very skilled or careful, or generate small claims because of low expected income losses.

In contrast, the auto manufacturer—that must buy third-party liability insurance for all those injured in its cars and pass on the premiums in vehicle prices—can implement none of these distinctions. Some auto models may be more or less attractive to commuters, to teenagers, or to the very wealthy, but, except for these crude distinctions, the auto manufacturer must provide insurance to all who buy the model, high-risk and low-risk alike. Consequently, the variance in the insurance pool is vastly greater in the third-party context, and the premium is commensurately higher—even if the same level of coverage is offered. Of course, given the greater amount of coverage provided under a third-party policy, the variance and the premium are higher yet.

One of the most seriously deleterious effects of lumping consumers into undifferentiated third-party risk pools is glaringly inconsistent with the judicial objective of aiding the poor. That is the regressive redistributional effect of third-party insurance. The largest items of damages in most third-party personal injury contexts, especially those involving permanent disability, are lost income and pain and suffering, which are highly correlated with individuals' expected future income streams. As a consequence, these damage elements constitute the largest component of the third-party insurance premium tied to the sale of any product or service.

The third-party premium is set with reference to average expected loss. Thus, the high correlation of total awards with income means that premiums reflect the average income of the population of consumers. The implication of charging each consumer a premium related to average income is that consumers with high incomes are charged a premium lower than their expected loss, and consumers with low incomes are charged a premium higher than their expected loss. Third-party insurance thus requires low-income consumers to subsidize high-income consumers.

* * *

As a consequence, the disadvantages of third-party insurance coverage are substantial. Courts justified third-party insurance coverage based on how easy it seemed to be for manufacturers or service providers to aggregate risks by adding an insurance premium to the price of the product or service. Whatever comparative advantage providers enjoy in risk aggregation, however, is overwhelmed by the disadvantages of excessive coverage, the inability to segregate risks in third-party contexts, and regressive distributive effects.

How do the differences between first-party and third-party tort insurance mechanisms affect the behavior of consumers? The shift towards greater corporate-provided tort law insurance will lead low-risk consumers to reduce consumption of products whose prices incorporate high tort insurance premiums. For low-risk consumers, especially low-income consumers, the tort law insurance premium tied to the product or service price may be much greater than the benefit the insurance provides. As a consequence, though the effect may be subtle, these consumers will drop out of the market.

* * *

Notes and Questions

1. The Enterprise Liability Paradox: Enterprise liability is motivated by a desire to provide insurance to victims of non-negligent accidents. At its base, the theory supposes that expanded tort liability will lead to the provision of insurance along with the sale of the product or service itself. Manufacturing and service providers will pass on as much of the liability insurance premium through price as is possible, given demand elasticity. According to the theory, the poor are especially benefitted by expanded liability because they could not otherwise afford to purchase insurance for such loses. But Professor Priest suggests that this ever-expanding liability has had a paradoxical effect. That is, enterprise liability theory has led to a reduction in the total insurance coverage available to society, rather than an increase. Particularly harmed by enterprise liability under Priest's analysis are the poor. Do you find Professor Priest's analysis persuasive? If so, what type of action should be taken to correct this judicially imposed problem?

2. Variance in Risk Pools: At the heart of Professor Priest's analysis is the fact that enterprise liability has led to an increase in risk pool variance. In general, an individual is willing to purchase insurance if the premium paid reflects the expected damages. When insurers are able to segregate risk pools, they are able to take full advantage of the law of large numbers—they can predict with certainty the total losses which any risk pool will incur. In other words, segregating risk pools and taking advantage of the law of large numbers allows insurers to substantially reduce the variance of expected losses. In turn, this reduced variance allows insurers to set premiums at a level that reflects the expected damages of risk pool members. Anything that would cause variance to increase results in the premium charged being less reflective the expected damages of some risk pool members. For high-risk members of the pool this is a subsidy. Low-risk members find that the premium is too high in comparison to expected damages. Therefore, low-risk members drop out of the risk pool. Within this line of reasoning, Professor Priest identifies two factors that have contributed to an insurance crisis. First are damages for non-pecuniary losses and the corresponding adverse selection and moral hazard problems associated with such damages. Second are the greater difficulties in risk pool segregation due to the third-party context. Can you think of other factors that contribute to risk pool variance? Does enterprise liability have any impacts that reduce risk pool variance? Are there any mitigating factors that justify a continuation of enterprise liability theory?

3. Ending the Vicious Circle: Following the reasoning of Professor Priest's analysis leads one into a vicious circle. As low-risk insureds drop out of the risk pool, premiums increase. The increased premiums cause further dropouts and so on. How does this vicious circle resolve itself? Professor Priest provides examples of several services that were forced out of the market due to enterprise liability theory. Is this result acceptable? Justifiable? What do such results portend for the future of American business?

4. Ultrahazardous Activities, Personal Injury, and Risk Spreading: Is the argument for imposition of enterprise liability more powerful when applied to ultrahazardous activities? In *Richman v. Charter Arms Corp.*, 571 F. Supp. 192 (E.D. La. 1983), a murder victim's mother brought a wrongful death action against a manufacturer of the handgun used in the killing, seeking to recover on strict liability theories of an unreasonably dangerous product and ultrahazardous activity. In refusing to grant summary judgment for the manufacturer on the ultrahazardous activity claim, the court said:

> The defendant maintains that, if liability is imposed in this case, no company that markets handguns for sale to the general public will be able in the future to obtain insurance. The result, according to the defendant, will be catastrophic for handgun manufacturers: all such companies will be forced either to alter their marketing practices radically or to go out of business. This argument has a ring of plausibility to it. At the same time, however, it is highly speculative.

> * * *

> Perhaps the most significant fact the defendant ignores is that increased insurance costs can be passed on to consumers in the form of higher prices for handguns. The people who benefit most from marketing practices like the defendant's are handgun manufacturers and handgun purchasers. Innocent victims rarely, if ever, are beneficiaries. Consequently, it hardly seems unfair to require manufacturers and purchasers, rather than innocent victims, to pay for the risks those practices entail. Furthermore, economic efficiency seems to require the same result. In an important article on ultrahazardous activities and risk allocation, Professor Clarence Morris makes just this point. Morris, "Hazardous Enterprises and Risk Bearing Capacity," 61 Yale L.J. 1172 (1952). In his view, "the avowed goal of the absolute liability approach is allocation of loss to the party better equipped to pass it on to the public: the superior risk bearer." Id. at 1176. Professor Morris discusses a variety of examples to show that the defendant is not always the superior risk bearer in an ultrahazardous activity case. Here is what he says, however, about bodily injury and risk-bearing capacity:

The financial burden of disabling personal injury overwhelms most people. While many can bear the cost of minor injury, prolonged infirmity and extended medical expense often exceed the financial competence of common men. Unless [common man] happens to be rich or covered by one of the more generous workman's compensations plans, he will probably bear the risk less easily than Enterpriser. The preponderant likelihood is that Enterpriser is the better risk bearer of the two. Id. at 1177.

... Thus, both fairness and economic efficiency suggest that the community would be better off if the defendant's marketing practices were classified as ultrahazardous.

Id. at 202–204. How does this analysis square with that of Professor Priest? The Fifth Circuit reversed the district court's decision on appeal, holding that "[t]he marketing of handguns to the general public falls far beyond the boundaries of the Louisiana doctrine of ultrahazardous activities." Perkins v. F.I.E. Corp., 762 F.2d 1250, 1268 (5th Cir. 1985). The court explained that "a ruling that the marketing of handguns constitutes an ultrahazardous activity 'would in practice drive manufacturers out of business' and 'would produce a handgun ban by judicial fiat.'" *Id.* at 1268–69.

5. Other Goals of Tort Law: Appeasement: Appeasement as a goal of tort law means that the purpose of the law is to limit the negative impact of the infliction of injury to the event of the injury itself. Tort law provides a way to right the wrong without the injured party retaliating through some destructive means. That is, the victim's vengeance is bought off by imposing tort liability on the wrongdoer. The victim is appeased in two ways: receipt of compensation and knowledge of the fact that the transgressor is punished by being required to pay.

6. Other Goals of Tort Law: Justice and Liability: The law of torts is sometimes viewed as the expression of a moral principle—one who by his fault has caused damage to another ought to make compensation as a matter of justice. There are two views in support of this position—and either variant is simply a different way of saying the same thing. First, the principle of ethical retribution places emphasis upon the fact that the payment of compensation is harmful to the offender, and that justice requires that the offender suffer the harm. Second, the principle of ethical compensation looks at the same situation form the point of view of the victim. It emphasizes the fact that the payment of compensation is a benefit to the victim of the wrong, and declares that justice requires that the victim should receive this compensation. Regardless of the perspective one chooses, the policy implications are the same.

3. Allocative Efficiency

The risk of injury associated with products or services is sometimes characterized as an externality imposed on third parties. In this view, tort law increases allocative efficiency by forcing the internalization of externalities. However, to the extent the risk of injury is known by the injured party, the market price should reflect the risk so that there is no externality. Nevertheless, under some circumstances, there might be questions about the ability of the market price to reflect the risk.

Doe v. Miles Laboratories, Inc.

United States District Court for the District of Maryland
675 F. Supp. 1466 (1987)

RAMSEY, District Judge.

A plague inflicts society and this Court is called upon to adjudicate the extent to which the effects will be visited upon its victims. The facts are tragic. In the autumn of 1983, plaintiff Jane Doe, who a week previous had given birth, sought emergency medical treatment for vaginal bleeding. During the course of treatment, the attending physician ordered the administration of 500 units of "Konyne," a blood-coagulation-factor concentrate produced by Cutter Laboratories, a division of Miles. Treatment appeared successful and plaintiff eventually was discharged.

Over the course of the months to follow, plaintiff suffered from a succession of ailments, ultimately being diagnosed as infected by the HTLV-III virus, and as having Acquired Immuno-Deficiency Syndrome-Related Complex (ARC), a predecessor of AIDS. On July 6, 1986, plaintiffs Jane and John Doe filed suit, alleging claims for strict liability in tort, for breach of warranties, and for loss of consortium. Later plaintiffs amended the complaint to include negligence counts, and for punitive damages. Defendant Miles, following other procedural actions, filed this motion for summary judgment on plaintiffs' counts for breach of warranties, for strict liability in tort, and for strict liability in tort—failure to warn; and further seeks summary judgment on the counts for loss of consortium and punitive damages to the extent they are derivative of the first three.

* * *

Products Liability Law

Defective products cause accidents that result in both economic losses and injuries either to persons or property. Allowing victims to recover for such losses was long a controversial issue. Indeed, the common law has followed a confusing and torturous path in perceiving and remedying the situation.

* * *

Once liability in negligence became established, the concept of strict products liability gained favor as an alternative theory of recovery for injuries from defective products. It is commonly stated that there are three reasons for holding manufacturers and dealers strictly liable for personal or property injury caused by defective products. First, innocent victims should not be forced to bear the costs of accidents, which still occurs far too often, for even a negligence action may impose an evidentiary burden impossible to meet. Second, that strict liability promotes accident prevention, for the manufacturers are in a better position to ascertain and control the risks associated with their products. Third, that manufacturers are in a better position than victims to bear the costs, for they can distribute the losses across the many who purchase the product, whereas an individual victim, unless he or she is exceptionally well-to-do or heavily insured, will be driven into bankruptcy or into social welfare programs.

Implicit in the above justification for strict products liability, though perhaps not clearly articulated, is a fourth argument, namely that strict products liability can promote the efficient allocation of resources. Society has chosen to allow market forces to set the price for goods and thus to determine their availability and distribution. In some respects the market is very efficient. The price purchasers pay invariably reflects direct costs such as raw products, capital investment, labor, plus a reasonable rate of return. However, in other respects the market is not efficient. Prices often do not reflect indirect costs. These hidden costs can include the effects of pollution or the expenses of accidents, and are what economists refer to as "externalities."

When the price of an item does not reflect both its direct costs and its externalities, the price will be lower than its actual cost. This lower price will stimulate an inefficient allocation of resources, for persons will be encouraged to buy more of the product than they might if they were paying its true price. Society thus may increase the consumption of the very goods that create pollution, and thus have indirect cleanup costs, or that are defective, and thus have indirect accident costs. Strict products liability shifts the cost back to manufacturers, who will then reprice the goods to reflect their actual costs. Strict products liability therefore affords society a mechanism for a rational allocation of resources.[5] Absent it, the costs of externalities are thrust upon victims or upon society through its governmental welfare programs. In essence, without it there is a subsidy given to the polluting or defective product.

* * *

Whatever the theory of recovery, whether negligence or strict liability, it is now clear that the test in products liability is the same. A plaintiff must show 1) the existence of a defect; 2) the attribution of the defect to the seller; and 3) a causal relation between the defect and the injury.

* * *

STRICT LIABILITY IN TORT

Defendant argues ... for an exemption from strict liability in tort for blood or blood products....

* * *

Do policy considerations warrant exempting blood and blood products from strict products liability in tort? Defendant argues that the "unavoidably unsafe products" exemption provided to § 402A by Comment *k* applies to it. Comment *k* reads:

> There are some products which, in the present state of human knowledge, are quite incapable of being made safe for their intended and ordinary use. These are especially common in the field of drugs. An example is the vaccine for the Pasteur treatment of rabies, which not uncommonly leads to very serious and even permanently injurious consequences when it is injected. Since the disease itself invariably results in a dreadful death, both the marketing and the use of the vaccine are fully justified, notwithstanding the unavoidably high degree of risk which they involve. Such a product, properly prepared and accompanied by proper directions and warnings, is not defective, nor is it *unreasonably* dangerous. The same is true of many other vaccines, drugs and the like, many of which for

---

5. The argument is often made that strict products liability has the potential to bankrupt manufacturers. Such an argument misses the salutory economic role strict products liability plays. Understood properly, it can be seen that strict liability promotes a rational market place. Society cannot make rational decisions concerning the allocation of resources unless the price reflects the true costs. When the price rises greatly, reflecting the fact the product produces either substantial direct costs or creates widespread externalities, it is rational to discourage or even abandon consumption of that product. Strict products liability thus allows the marketplace to make better informed decisions.

that very reason cannot legally be sold except to physicians, or under the prescription of a physician.... The seller of such products, again with the qualification that they are properly prepared and marketed, and proper warning is given where the situation calls for it, is not to be held to strict liability for unfortunate consequences attending to their use, merely because he has undertaken to supply the public with an apparently useful and desirable product, attended with a known but apparently reasonable danger.

Maryland courts have never expressly adopted Comment *k*. Several decisions in this federal district court, though, have relied on Comment *k*, holding that Maryland courts would adopt it if an appropriate case were before them. Those cases, however, involved prescription medications and did not address whether blood, especially blood infected with disease, fell within Comment *k*'s exemption.

This Court is not prepared to find that HTLV-III carrying blood presents a "reasonable danger" as Comment *k* requires. It is estimated that up to 95% of severe hemophiliacs test positive for exposure to the HTLV-III virus. The nearly complete exposure by the group most in need of coagulant-factors and the inevitably fatal nature of the disease for those who actually develop it are stark facts. The fact the virus was indetectible prior to 1985 is not a mitigating factor. The best view is to consider blood containing indetectible diseases to be a defective product and therefore that strict liability is applicable.

It is argued that providers of blood and blood products are promoting the general welfare by making possible improved health. It is argued that it is a fundamental social policy of the State of Maryland to promote the supply of blood and blood products. And it is argued that to allow strict products liability, which given the wide exposure to AIDS due to transfusions could create potentially substantial liability, would so raise costs of production that the supply of blood could be choked off.

The arguments are unpersuasive.... Those who choose to operate in the economic marketplace play by the rules applicable to all.

The arguments in favor of strict products liability apply as persuasively to blood and blood products as they do to any other product. First, there is no reason why victims of defective blood should bear the costs where victims of other defective products do not. Second, strict liability would provide the incentive to promote all possible accident prevention, for it is a rational business decision to keep costs down. Third, the producers are in a better position to spread the costs than are individual consumers. Finally, it makes for a more efficient allocation of social resources when the price of a transfusion of blood or blood products reflects its true costs.

Entrepreneurs by their nature are risk taking individuals. To the extent they need an incentive to engage in socially beneficial activities, the law already provides it in the form of a corporate shield on personal liability. To do as defendant argues, and exempt blood from strict liability would be to subsidize the product by forcing either victims or government through its social welfare programs to bear accident costs. In the absence of a clear expression on the part of the legislature of an intent to subsidize a particular product, it is not this Court's role to create the subsidy indirectly by carving out a Judge made exemption to strict products liability.

Accordingly, the Court will deny defendant's motion for summary judgment on plaintiffs' claim for strict products liability.

*   *   *

Notes and Questions

1. Strict Liability and Externalities: Markets characterized by zero transaction costs, perfect information, and risk-neutral participants are able to obtain the optimal level of accident prevention even in the absence of any liability standard. If information regarding risk is not perfectly communicated, then there is an economic justification for a strict liability standard. In general, however, a strict liability standard does not result in a greater level of accident prevention relative to a negligence standard. Thus, strict liability serves only to allocate responsibility for insuring against non-negligent accidents. Certainly, the presence of non-negligent accidents represents a cost that society would like to avoid. Economic efficiency suggests that such costs be borne by the party who can most cost effectively insure against non-negligent accidents. The court clearly assumes that Miles Laboratories can most cost effectively insure against such risks. Is there any justification for this conclusion? If someone other than Miles could provide the most cost-effective insurance, is it fair to say that such defendants receive a "subsidy" from the victims or government?

2. Externalities, Property Rights, and Coase Theorem: In general, externalities arise because of poorly defined or unenforceable property rights. What property rights were in question in *Miles Laboratories*? Did the supposed externalities arise because of poorly defined property rights, an inability to enforce such rights, or some other reason? What implications does the Coase Theorem have for this problem? Does strict liability allow the Coase Theorem to operate? Do you agree with the court's belief that its interpretation of strict liability supports a rational marketplace? In a sense, doesn't the court's externality approach really just obscure much of the efficiency analysis of alternative liability rules?

4. Tort Damages and Incentives

Losing tort defendants are generally subject to the rule that they must make their victims whole by paying sufficient damages to put plaintiffs in the same positions as before the tortious act. The possibility of being ordered to pay damages provides an economic incentive that alters the behavior of potential tortfeasors. Damages affect the PL portion of the Hand Formula, thereby shifting C* and the optimal amount of prevention.

a. Compensatory Damages

Most of the damages awarded in individual tort cases are intended to make the plaintiff whole again, at least financially. Such **compensatory damages** usually consist of three major types of loss: (1) past and future medical expenses, (2) past and future economic loss, and (3) past and future pain and suffering.

b. Punitive Damages

Punitive damages are damages designed to punish individual defendants and to deter potential tortfeasors. The typical cases in which punitive damages could be awarded are intentional torts and negligence cases where the defendant's conduct fell to a level of "gross negligence" or "willful and wanton" disregard for the plaintiff's safety. The deterrence model of tort law suggests that punitive damages should also be awarded in cases where claims are unlikely to be brought against a culpable defendant (or damages are difficult to measure). That is, the basic economic justification for punitive damages is in offsetting the low probability of ultimate liability (due to low probabilities of detection, enforcement, or liability). *See* A. Mitchell Polinsky & Steven Shavell, *Punitive Damages: An Economic Analysis*, 111 Harvard Law Review 869, 890 (1998).

The deterrence model considers the potential tortfeasor's expected marginal benefits and marginal costs of the contemplated activity, where the expected costs are the probability of harm multiplied by the likely amount of harm (P x L). However, a complete analysis requires consideration of the likelihood that the injured parties will be able to recover — that is, the expected cost to the potential tortfeasor must be discounted by the likelihood that the tortfeasor will be detected and successfully sued. In fraud cases, for example, defendants typically seek not only to conceal their wrongdoing, but also to make it difficult to determine who committed the wrongdoing, so that the victim does not even discover the fraud or who victimized them. Awarding compensatory damages only in the cases in which the fraud is discovered will result in under-deterrence of the defendant's wrongful conduct. Punitive damages could therefore be awarded in an amount equal to the damages caused by the defendant to victims who are unlikely to sue. A second economic case for punitive damages is when the conduct being sanctioned has no redeeming societal value — e.g., the utility a thug receives from beating people up. Punitive damages awards for intentional torts would fit into this category. In cases of intentional torts, like fraud or assault, there is often overlap between the deterrent and punitive goals of criminal punishment and punitive damages. *See* Jeffery W. Grass, *The Penal Dimensions of Punitive Damages*, 12 Hastings Constitutional Law Quarterly 241 (1985) (arguing that punitive damages serve the same purpose as criminal law but fail to provide the constitutional protections provided in criminal courts). Whether this is a good thing or a bad thing, it does potentially relieve pressure on the criminal justice system.

Mathias v. Accor Economy Lodging, Inc.

United States Court of Appeals for the Seventh Circuit

347 F.3d 672 (2003)

POSNER, *Circuit Judge.*

The plaintiffs brought this diversity suit governed by Illinois law against affiliated entities (which the parties treat as a single entity, as shall we) that own and operate the "Motel 6" chain of hotels and motels. One of these hotels (now a "Red Roof Inn," though still owned by the defendant) is in downtown Chicago. The plaintiffs, a brother and sister, were guests there and were bitten by bedbugs, which are making a comeback in the U.S. as a consequence of more conservative use of pesticides. The plaintiffs claim that in allowing guests to be attacked by bedbugs in a motel that charges upwards of $100 a day for a room and would not like to be mistaken for a flophouse, the defendant was guilty of "willful and wanton conduct" and thus under Illinois law is liable for punitive as well as compensatory damages. The jury agreed and awarded each plaintiff $186,000 in punitive damages though only $5,000 in compensatory damages. The defendant appeals, complaining primarily about the punitive-damages award....

The defendant argues that at worst it is guilty of simple negligence, and if this is right the plaintiffs were not entitled by Illinois law to any award of punitive damages. It also complains that the award was excessive — indeed that any award in excess of $20,000 to each plaintiff would deprive the defendant of its property without due process of law. The first complaint has no possible merit, as the evidence of gross negligence, indeed of recklessness in the strong sense of an unjustifiable failure to avoid a *known* risk was amply shown. In 1998, EcoLab, the extermination service that the motel used, discovered bedbugs in several rooms in the motel and recommended that it be hired to spray every room, for which it would charge the motel only $500; the motel refused. The next year, bedbugs were again discovered in a room but EcoLab was asked to spray just that room. The motel tried to negotiate "a building sweep [by EcoLab] free of charge," but, not surprisingly, the negotiation failed. By the spring of 2000, the motel's manager "started noticing that there were refunds being given by my desk clerks and reports coming back from the guests that there were ticks in the rooms and bugs in the rooms that were biting." She looked in some of the rooms and discovered bedbugs. The defendant asks us to disregard her testimony as that of a disgruntled ex-employee, but of course her credibility was for the jury, not the defendant, to determine.

Further incidents of guests being bitten by insects and demanding and receiving refunds led the manager to recommend to her superior in the company that the motel be closed while every room was sprayed, but this was refused. This superior, a district manager, was a management-level employee of the defendant, and his knowledge of the risk and failure to take effective steps either to eliminate it or to warn the motel's guests are imputed to his employer for purposes of determining whether the employer should be liable for punitive damages. The employer's liability for compensatory damages is of course automatic on the basis of the principle of respondeat superior, since the district manager was acting within the scope of his employment.

The infestation continued and began to reach farcical proportions, as when a guest, after complaining of having been bitten repeatedly by insects while asleep in his room in the hotel was moved to another room only to discover insects there; and within 18 minutes of being moved to a third room he discovered insects in that room as well and had to be moved still again. (Odd that at that point he didn't flee the motel.) By July, the motel's management was acknowledging to EcoLab that there was a "major problem with bed bugs" and that all that was being done about it was "chasing them from room to room." Desk clerks were instructed to call the "bedbugs" "ticks," apparently on the theory that customers would be less alarmed, though in fact ticks are more dangerous than bedbugs because they spread Lyme Disease and Rocky Mountain Spotted Fever. Rooms that the motel had placed on "Do not rent, bugs in room" status nevertheless were rented.

It was in November that the plaintiffs checked into the motel. They were given Room 504, even though the motel had classified the room as "DO NOT RENT UNTIL TREATED," and it had not been treated. Indeed, that night 190 of the hotel's 191 rooms were occupied, even though a number of them had been placed on the same don't-rent status as Room 504. . . .

Although bedbug bites are not as serious as the bites of some other insects, they are painful and unsightly. Motel 6 could not have rented any rooms at the prices it charged had it informed guests that the risk of being bitten by bedbugs was appreciable. Its failure either to warn guests or to take effective measures to eliminate the bedbugs amounted to fraud and probably to battery as well. . . . There was, in short, sufficient evidence of "willful and wanton conduct" within the meaning that the Illinois courts assign to the term to permit an award of punitive damages in this case.

But in what amount? In arguing that $20,000 was the maximum amount of punitive damages that a jury could constitutionally have awarded each plaintiff, the defendant points to the U.S. Supreme Court's recent statement that "few awards [of punitive damages] exceeding a single-digit ratio between punitive and compensatory damages, to a significant degree, will satisfy due process." *State Farm Mutual Automobile Ins. Co. v. Campbell*, 538 U.S. 408 (2003). The Court went on to suggest that "four times the amount of compensatory damages might be close to the line of constitutional impropriety." *Id*. Hence the defendant's proposed ceiling in this case of $20,000, four times the compensatory damages awarded to each plaintiff. The ratio of punitive to compensatory damages determined by the jury was, in contrast, 37.2 to 1.

The Supreme Court did not, however, lay down a 4-to-1 or single-digit-ratio rule — it said merely that "there is a presumption against an award that has a 145-to-1 ratio" — and it would be unreasonable to do so. We must consider why punitive damages are awarded and why the Court has decided that due process requires that such awards be limited. The second question is easier to answer than the first. The term "punitive damages" implies punishment, and a standard principle of penal theory is that "the punishment should fit the crime" in the sense of being proportional to the wrongfulness of the defendant's action, though the principle is modified when the probability of detection is very low (a familiar example is the heavy fines for littering) or the crime is potentially lucrative (as in the case of trafficking in illegal drugs). Hence, with these qualifications, which in fact will figure in our analysis of this case, punitive damages should be proportional to the wrongfulness of the defendant's actions.

Another penal precept is that a defendant should have reasonable notice of the sanction for unlawful acts, so that he can make a rational determination of how to act; and so there have to be reasonably clear standards for determining the amount of punitive damages for particular wrongs.

And a third precept, the core of the Aristotelian notion of corrective justice, and more broadly of the principle of the rule of law, is that sanctions should be based on the wrong done rather than on the status of the defendant; a person is punished for what he does, not for who he is, even if the who is a huge corporation.

What follows from these principles, however, is that punitive damages should be ad-measured by standards or rules rather than in a completely ad hoc manner, and this does not tell us what the maximum ratio of punitive to compensatory damages should be in a particular case. To determine that, we have to consider why punitive damages are awarded in the first place.

England's common law courts first confirmed their authority to award punitive damages in the eighteenth century, at a time when the institutional structure of criminal law enforcement was primitive and it made sense to leave certain minor crimes to be dealt with by the civil law. And still today one function of punitive-damages awards is to relieve the pressures on an overloaded system of criminal justice by providing a civil alternative to criminal prosecution of minor crimes. An example is deliberately spitting in a person's face, a criminal assault but because minor readily deterrable by the levying of what amounts to a civil fine through a suit for damages for the tort of battery. Compensatory damages would not do the trick in such a case, and this for three reasons: because they are difficult to determine in the case of acts that inflict largely dignatory harms; because in the spitting case they would be too slight to give the victim an incentive to sue, and he might decide instead to respond with violence — and an age-old purpose of the law of torts is to provide a substitute for violent retaliation against wrongful injury — and because to limit the plaintiff to compensatory damages would enable the defendant to commit the offensive act with impunity provided that he was willing to pay, and again there would be a danger that his act would incite a breach of the peace by his victim.

When punitive damages are sought for billion-dollar oil spills and other huge economic injuries, the considerations that we have just canvassed fade. As the Court emphasized in *Campbell*, the fact that the plaintiffs in that case had been awarded very substantial compensatory damages — $1 million for a dispute over insurance coverage — greatly reduced the need for giving them a huge award of punitive damages ($145 million) as well in order to provide an effective remedy. Our case is closer to the spitting case. The defendant's behavior was outrageous but the compensable harm done was slight and at the same time difficult to quantify because a large element of it was emotional. And the defendant may well have profited from its misconduct because by concealing the infestation it was able to keep renting rooms. Refunds were frequent but may have cost less than the cost of closing the hotel for a thorough fumigation. The hotel's attempt to pass off the bedbugs as ticks, which some guests might ignorantly have thought less unhealthful, may have postponed the instituting of litigation to rectify the hotel's misconduct. The award of punitive damages in this case thus serves the additional purpose of limiting the defendant's ability to profit from its fraud by escaping detection and (private) prosecution. If a tortfeasor is "caught" only half the time he commits torts, then when he is caught he should be punished twice as heavily in order to make up for the times he gets away.

Finally, if the total stakes in the case were capped at $50,000 (2 x [$ 5,000 + $20,000]), the plaintiffs might well have had difficulty financing this lawsuit. It is here that the defendant's aggregate net worth of $1.6 billion becomes relevant. A defendant's wealth is not a sufficient basis for awarding punitive damages. That would be discriminatory and would violate the rule of law, as we explained earlier, by making punishment depend on status rather than conduct. Where wealth in the sense of resources enters is in enabling the defendant to mount an extremely aggressive defense against suits such as this and by doing so to make litigating against it very costly, which in turn may make it difficult for the plaintiffs to find a lawyer willing to handle their case, involving as it does only modest stakes, for the usual 33–40 percent contingent fee.

In other words, the defendant is investing in developing a reputation intended to deter plaintiffs. It is difficult otherwise to explain the great stubborness with which it has defended this case, making a host of frivolous evidentiary arguments despite the very modest stakes even when the punitive damages awarded by the jury are included.

As a detail (the parties having made nothing of the point), we note that "net worth" is not the correct measure of a corporation's resources. It is an accounting artifact that reflects the allocation of ownership between equity and debt claimants. A firm financed largely by equity investors has a large "net worth" (= the value of the equity claims), while the identical firm financed largely by debt may have only a small net worth because accountants treat debt as a liability.

All things considered, we cannot say that the award of punitive damages was excessive, albeit the precise number chosen by the jury was arbitrary. It is probably not a coincidence that $5,000 + $186,000 = $191,000/191 = $1,000: i.e., $1,000 per room in the hotel. But as there are no punitive-damages guidelines, corresponding to the federal and state sentencing guidelines, it is inevitable that the specific amount of punitive damages awarded whether by a judge or by a jury will be arbitrary. (Which is perhaps why the plaintiffs' lawyer did not suggest a number to the jury.) The judicial function is to police a range, not a point.

But it would have been helpful had the parties presented evidence concerning the regulatory or criminal penalties to which the defendant exposed itself by deliberately exposing its customers to a substantial risk of being bitten by bedbugs. That is an inquiry recommended by the Supreme Court. See *State Farm Mutual Automobile Ins. Co. v. Campbell*, 123 S. Ct. at 1520, 1526. But we do not think its omission invalidates the award. We can take judicial notice that deliberate exposure of hotel guests to the health risks created by insect infestations exposes the hotel's owner to sanctions under Illinois and Chicago law that in the aggregate are comparable in severity to that of the punitive damage award in this case.

"A person who causes bodily harm to or endangers the bodily safety of an individual by any means, commits reckless conduct if he performs recklessly the acts which cause the harm or endanger safety, whether they otherwise are lawful or unlawful." 720 ILCS 5/12-5(a). This is a misdemeanor, punishable by up to a year's imprisonment or a fine of $2,500, or both. 720 ILCS 5/12-5(b); 730 ILCS 5/5-8-3(a)(1), 5/5-9-1(a)(2). Of course a corporation cannot be sent to prison, and $2,500 is obviously much less than the $186,000 awarded to each plaintiff in this case as punitive damages. But this is just the beginning. For, what is much more important, a Chicago hotel that permits unsanitary conditions to exist is subject to revocation of its license, without which it cannot operate. Chi. Munic. Code §§ 4-4-280, 4-208-020, 050, 060, 110. We are sure that the defendant would prefer to pay the punitive damages assessed in this case than to lose its license.

AFFIRMED.

Notes and Questions

1. Aren't They Designed to Punish?: Punitive damages are designed to punish the firm that commits a malicious tort. However, the punitive damages should "bear some reasonable proportion to the actual damages." Why? Doesn't this view of punitive damages skew the entire purpose behind them? That is, punitive damages are designed to punish the tortious firm rather than have *anything* to do with the victim. In essence, this view of the application of punitive damages gives potential tortfeasors the incentive to act grossly negligent or maliciously as long as the damages caused by the defective product are lower than the profit earned from the sale of the product. Is a better view the one taken by the jury? They essentially strip the firm of all profit created by this unsafe design. Is this the correct approach? What are the problems with this application of punitive damages?

2. Punitive Damages and Optimal Levels of Deterrence: Recall the discussion earlier of the Hand Formula and the economics of negligence versus strict liability standards. Both standards, when applied properly from an economic perspective, result in defendants (and plaintiffs) taking the optimal level of precautions—the level of precaution where the marginal cost of the precaution equals the marginal benefit. But what if a judge or jury can impose punitive damages in addition to compensatory damages? One would expect the defendant to take more precautions, even though the marginal benefit of those precautions to society might be less than the marginal cost. The availability of punitive damages thus may lead to over-deterrence—defendants taking wasteful precautions or ceasing production of a useful product altogether. The concern with over-deterrence is even more pronounced when punitive damage awards are unpredictable; however, there is a great deal of scholarly debate about the unpredictability of punitive damages and its impact. *See, e.g.,* Neil Vidmar and Mirya Holman, *The Frequency, Predictability, and Proportionality of Jury Awards of Punitive Damages in State Courts in 2005: A New Audit,* 43 Suffolk University Law Review 855 (2010); Theodore Eisenberg et al., *Juries, Judges and Punitive Damages: An Empirical Study,* 87 Cornell Law Review 743 (2002); A. Mitchell Polinsky, *Are Punitive Damages Really Insignificant, Predictable, and Rational? A Comment on Eisenberg et al.,* 26 Journal of Legal Studies 663 (1997).

3. Intentional Torts, Unintentional Torts, and Statistics: An intentional tort involves a deliberate action that results in an injury. For example, a company commits an intentional tort when it knowingly makes false statements about the quality of a competitor's products. A negligent tort is an unintentional tort that arises from the failure to use reasonable care toward one to whom a duty is owed, which results in injury. Unintentional torts occur in a variety of business settings—ranging from slip-and-fall accidents in a showroom, to defectively designed products. For many types of business behavior, distinguishing between intentional and unintentional torts is not obvious. For example, a hand tool manufacturer that sells millions of power saws per year knows for a statistical fact—because of the large numbers involved—that a certain number of consumers per year will be injured by the saws. But such injuries are typically analyzed as unintentional torts—the manufacturer did not intend to injure any particular individual. Therefore, the distinction appears to be based, in part, on whether the wrongdoer knows the identity of the injured party prior to the occurrence of the tort. From an economic perspective, however, the cases plainly are distinguishable: in the false statement case, we are far less worried about over-deterrence than we are in the hand tool case. Unlike the making of false statements, the sale of hand tools, even when they are statistically certain to cause injury, has positive social value.

4. Juries and the Hand Formula: The Hand Formula not only provides a framework for determining liability, it also provides guidance to individuals and businesses about what risk level is acceptable to society. In essence, the Hand Formula suggests that businesses should go through the type of cost-benefit analysis that the tool manufacturer could have applied in the preceding note—for example, the tool manufacturer could have compared the cost of making the product safer with the expected value of injuries avoided. This may sound good in theory. And, without a doubt, businesses routinely engage in such calculations—indeed, as a society we want these tradeoffs to be considered. However, juries are not very understanding of such cold, hard calculations, and they tend punish business for making the tradeoffs. Experimental evidence indicates that juries punish defendants who have carefully weighed costs and benefits. See Cass R. Sunstein et al., Punitive Damages: How Juries Decide (2002), finding that mock juries tended to agree in their moral judgments about the defendant's conduct, yet rendered erratic and unpredictable dollar awards. The study found that the process of jury deliberation produced a striking "severity shift" toward ever-higher awards, and that jurors tended to ignore instructions from the judges; showed "hindsight bias," believing that what happened should have been foreseen; and penalized corporations that had based their decisions on careful cost-benefit analyses. Although judges made many of the same errors, they performed better in some areas, suggesting that judges (or other specialists) may be better equipped than juries to decide punitive damages.

5. Tort Reform, Caps on Punitive Damages, and Insurance: The tort reform movement has championed several reforms in recent years. Some type of cap on punitive damages is almost always part of legislative reform packages. Is a cap on punitive damages a "silver bullet" to solve problems with products liability and tort litigation? Professor George Priest suggests that punitive damages are just part of the problem and, thus, caps on punitive damages cannot solve the problem:

> ... [V]arious tort reform statutes have been supported by a coalition of business and insurance interests, chiefly on the simple ground that modern tort liability is excessive and unfair. Observers have not generally appreciated, however, that each of these reform provisions will affect insurance markets in a similar way: they reduce the variance in insurance risk pools. Obviously, caps on non-economic and punitive damages reduce the range of potential liability outcomes. Similarly, abrogation of the doctrine of joint and several liability in favor of strict comparative fault reduces the risk that any one of a group of joint defendants will ultimately be required to satisfy the entire judgment. Deducting first-party insurance benefits from tort judgments will also reduce risk pool variance. More generally, of course, altering liability standards to make recovery more difficult for plaintiffs will

diminish expected liability. To the extent that variance in risk pools is reduced, third-party tort law insurance becomes more supportable.

These reforms, while helpful, constitute only partial contributions toward solution of the problems caused by modern tort law. The provision of insurance through tort law has undermined insurance markets. In my view, these markets will not be fully restored until these insurance issues are dealt with more systematically. The insurance function must be excised from tort law altogether. None of the recent statutory reforms achieves that effect.

* * *

... [L]imitations on punitive damages may reduce risk pool variance to some extent. In my view, however, it is appropriate not only to restrain, but to prohibit, punitive damage awards in product liability and other tort contexts. Punitive damage awards can be justified only where there is some likelihood (1) that normal damage measures cannot measure loss accurately—such as in defamation cases; (2) where there is substantial difficulty in detecting the existence of the injury—such as in fraud or, perhaps, some antitrust actions; or (3) where other incentives are needed to stimulate litigation. For cases in which manufacturers or other providers have deliberately misrepresented product safety or effectiveness ... punitive damages should be awarded on grounds of the fraudulent behavior itself, not on grounds of the defective character of the product. There is no further need to award punitive damages in typical products and service liability contexts. In this respect, a legislative maximum on punitive damage awards or limitations on the conditions under which punitive awards may be made, constitutes only a partial solution.

The source of the insurability crisis is not the level of damages alone. Rather, the diffuse and indiscriminate expansion of substantive tort liability has led to the unraveling of insurance markets in an increasing number of contexts. This unraveling can be arrested only if substantive standards of liability are redefined to focus exclusively on the accident reduction goal. In my view, modern tort law provides inadequate controls on the accident rate and simultaneously creates a tort law insurance regime that disrupts insurance markets and harms the poor. The objectives of tort law reform are uncontroversial: to reduce the accident rate and to provide a more coherent and comprehensive regime of compensation insurance. These objectives cannot be achieved by tinkering with damage measures and by limited changes in liability standards for particularly sympathetic sets of defendants, such as governmental entities, dramshops or non-profit organizations. Instead, modern tort law must be reformed systematically: by a complete redefinition of liability standards to better achieve accident reduction and insurance.

George Priest, *The Current Insurance Crisis and Modern Tort Law*, 96 Yale Law Journal 1521, 1587–90 (1987).

c. *The Collateral Source Rule*

The collateral source rule applies to situations where the victim receives compensation for his damages from a source independent of the tortfeasor. Under this rule, the payments received from the independent source are not deducted from the award the victim would otherwise receive from the tortfeasor. Therefore, the tortfeasor is not able to benefit from the victim's foresight in purchasing insurance. From an economic perspective, the collateral source rule raises two primary issues. First, what impact does the collateral source rule have on deterrence? Second, does the collateral source rule allow the victim a double recovery?

Helfend v. Southern California Rapid Transit District

Supreme Court of California

465 P.2d 61 (1970)

TOBRINER, Acting Chief Justice

* * *

1. The facts.

Shortly before noon on July 19, 1965, plaintiff drove his car in central Los Angeles east on Third Street approaching Grandview. At this point Third Street has six lanes, four for traffic and one parking lane on each side of the thoroughfare. While traveling in the second lane from the curb, plaintiff observed an automobile driven by Glen A. Raney, Jr., stopping in his lane and preparing to back into a parking space. Plaintiff put out his left arm to signal the traffic behind him that he intended to stop; he then brought his vehicle to a halt so that the other driver could park.

At about this time Kenneth A. Mitchell, a bus driver for the Southern California Rapid Transit District, pulled out of a bus stop at the curb of Third Street and headed in the same direction as plaintiff. Approaching plaintiff's and Raney's cars which were stopped in the second lane from the curb, Mitchell pulled out into the lane closest to the center of the street in order to pass. The right rear of the bus sideswiped plaintiff's vehicle, knocking off the rearview mirror and crushing plaintiff's arm, which had been hanging down at the side of his car in the stopping signal position.... Plaintiff acquired some permanent discomfort but no permanent disability from the injuries sustained in the accident....

Plaintiff filed a tort action against the Southern California Rapid Transit District, a public entity, and Mitchell, an employee of the transit district. At trial plaintiff claimed slightly more than $2,700 in special damages, including $921 in doctor's bills, a $336.99 hospital bill, and about $45 for medicines. Defendant requested permission to show that about 80 percent of the plaintiff's hospital bill had been paid by plaintiff's Blue Cross insurance carrier and that some of his other medical expenses may have been paid by other insurance....

After the jury verdict in favor of plaintiff in the sum of $16,300, defendants appealed, raising only two contentions: (1) The trial court committed prejudicial error in refusing to allow the introduction of evidence to the effect that a portion of the plaintiff's medical bills had been paid from a collateral source. (2) The trial court erred in denying defendant the opportunity to determine if plaintiff had been compensated from more than one collateral source for damages sustained in the accident.

We must decide whether the collateral source rule applies to tort actions involving public entities and public employees in which the plaintiff has received benefits from his medical insurance coverage.

2. The collateral source rule.

The Supreme Court of California has long adhered to the doctrine that if an injured party receives some compensation for his injuries from a source wholly independent of the tortfeasor, such payment should not be deducted from the damages which the plaintiff would otherwise collect from the tortfeasor. As recently as August 1968 we unanimously reaffirmed our adherence to this doctrine, which is known as the "collateral source rule."

Although the collateral source rule remains generally accepted in the United States, nevertheless many other jurisdictions have restricted or repealed it. In this country most commentators have criticized the rule and called for its early demise....

The collateral source rule as applied here embodies the venerable concept that a person who has invested years of insurance premiums to assure his medical care should receive the benefits of his thrift. The tortfeasor should not garner the benefits of his victim's providence.

The collateral source rule expresses a policy judgment in favor of encouraging citizens to purchase and maintain insurance for personal injuries and for other eventualities. Courts consider insurance a form of investment, the benefits of which become payable without respect to any other possible source of funds. If we were to permit a tortfeasor to mitigate damages with payments from plaintiff's insurance, plaintiff would be in a position inferior to that of having bought no insurance, because his payment of premiums would have earned no benefit. Defendant should not be able to avoid payment of full compensation for the injury inflicted merely because the victim has had the foresight to provide himself with insurance.

Some commentators object that the above approach to the collateral source rule provides plaintiff with a "double recovery," rewards him for the injury, and defeats the principle that damages should compensate the victim but not punish the tortfeasor. We agree with Professor Fleming's observation, however, that "double recovery is justified only in the face of some exceptional, supervening reason, as in the case of accident or life insurance, where it is felt unjust that the tortfeasor should take advantage of the thrift and prescience of the victim in having paid the premiums." (Fleming, Introduction to the Law of Torts (1967) p. 131.) ...

Furthermore, insurance policies increasingly provide for either subrogation or refund or benefits upon a tort recovery, and such refund is indeed called for in the present case. (See Fleming, The Collateral Source Rule and Loss Allocation in Tort Law, *supra*, 54 Cal.L.Rev. 1478, 1479.) Hence, the plaintiff receives no double recovery; the collateral source rule simply serves as a means of by-passing the antiquated doctrine of non-assignment of tortious actions and permits a proper transfer of risk from the plaintiff's insurer to the tortfeasor by way of the victim's tort recovery. The double shift from the tortfeasor to the victim and then from the victim to his insurance carrier can normally occur with little cost in that the insurance carrier is often intimately involved in the initial litigation and quite automatically receives its part of the tort settlement or verdict.

Even in case in which the contract or the law precludes subrogation or refund of benefits, or in situations in which the collateral source waives such subrogation or refund, the rule performs entirely necessary functions in the computation of damages. For example, the cost of medical care often provides both attorneys and juries in tort cases with an important measure for assessing the plaintiff's general damages. To permit the defendant to tell the jury that the plaintiff has been recompensed by a collateral source for his medical costs might irretrievably upset the complex, delicate, and somewhat indefinable calculations which result in the normal jury verdict.

We also note that generally the jury is not informed that plaintiff's attorney will receive a large portion of the plaintiff's recovery in contingent fees or that personal injury damages are not taxable to the plaintiff and are normally deductible by the defendant. Hence, the plaintiff rarely actually receives full compensation for his injuries as computed by the jury. The collateral source rule partially serves to compensate for the attorney's share and does not actually render 'double recovery' for the plaintiff. Indeed, many jurisdictions that have abolished or limited the collateral source rule have also established a means for assessing the plaintiff's costs for counsel directly against the defendant rather than imposing the contingent fee system. In sum, the plaintiff's recovery for his medical expenses from both the tortfeasor and his medical insurance program will not usually give him "double recovery," but partially provides a somewhat closer approximation to full compensation for his injuries.

If we consider the collateral source rule as applied here in the context of the entire American approach to the law of torts and damages, we find that the rule presently performs a number of legitimate and even indispensable functions. Without a thorough revolution in the American approach to torts and the consequent damages, the rule at least with respect to medical insurance benefits has become so integrated within our present system that its precipitous judicial nullification would work hardship. In this case the collateral source rule lies between two systems for the compensation of accident victims: the traditional tort recovery based on fault and the increasingly prevalent coverage based on non-fault insurance. Neither system possesses such universality of coverage or completeness of compensation that we can easily dispense with the collateral source rule's approach to meshing the two systems. The reforms which many academicians propose cannot easily be achieved through piecemeal common law development; the proposed changes, if desirable, would be more effectively accomplished through legislative reform. In any case, we cannot believe that the judicial repeal of the collateral source rule, as applied in the present case, would be the place to begin the needed changes.

* * *

Notes and Questions

1. The Collateral Source Rule and Deterrence: From a deterrence perspective, the collateral source rule reaches the right conclusion. Consider a defendant's incentives if allowed to set up the plaintiff's insurance coverage as a defense to his own responsibility in damages. Suppose that the expected harm from the accident equals $500 and that this harm can be avoided by the defendant at a cost of $400. The defendant's failure to incur these costs results in a finding of negligence under the Hand Formula. However, if the plaintiff's receipt of $500 from the insurance company relieves the defendant of his damages, he no longer has an incentive to avoid this liability. Thus, potential tortfeasors tend to underinvest in accident prevention in the absence of the collateral source rule. Does this analysis require the potential tortfeasors to know whether their potential victims have purchased insurance?

2. Insurance Rates, Accident Avoidance Costs, and the Collateral Source Rule: Some potential tortfeasors may make investments in accident avoidance because of concern that accidents will cause their insurance rates to increase even if the collateral source rule did not preclude payment of the claim. How does this point affect the analysis in note 1?

3. Insurance Markets, Risk Pools, and the Collateral Source Rule: Abolition of the collateral source rule could improve the functioning of insurance markets because, as suggested by Professor Priest: "Deducting first-party insurance benefits from tort judgments will also reduce risk pool variance." Evaluate this argument.

4. The Collateral Source Rule and Double Recovery: The collateral source rule is not a free lunch for insured victims because insurance rates will adjust to reflect whether the insurance company must cover the victim's expenses. The premiums that an insured pays are a reflection of the rights that the coverage purchases. Consider two different insurance contracts. First, an insurance company could offer a contract that obligated it to pay damages upon the injury of the insured as a result of a third party's negligence without providing the insurer with rights to sue the negligent third party. In short, under this contract, the insurer is stuck with the loss. However, the insurer will charge the insured a higher premium for this contract. Second, consider a contract that contains a term that assigns the legal rights of the insured to the insurer once the insured has been paid under the policy. Under this contract, the insurer has greater protection against bearing the loss and as a result will charge the insured a smaller premium. From this analysis, it is easy to see that when a victim is able to recover from both the insurance company and the defendant, the victim has paid for this so-called "double recovery" through higher insurance premiums. Therefore, it does not represent a windfall to the victim. However, are all insured parties better off with or without the collateral source rule?

5. Fortuitous Benefits and the Collateral Source Rule: What if, through the negligence of someone else, you are forced to change your plans, and in doing so meet the love of your life? Presumably, the benefit of marriage and a blissful life with your newfound love outweigh the damages done to you by the tortfeasor. However, the collateral source rule does not contemplate fortuitous benefits any more than it does collateral benefits. *See* Michael I. Krauss & Jeremy Kidd, *Collateral Source and Tort's Soul*, 48 University of Louisville Law Review 1, 33–35 (2009). Should you still be able to recover damages even though, in hindsight, you are happy to have incurred the loss and would gladly do so again?

E. Risk Regulation

The earlier discussion of compensating wage differentials demonstrated that the market determined level of workplace safety is below a no-risk level of safety. At some point, workers, consumers, and investors voluntarily accept risk. However, in an increasing number of situations, politicians and government regulators have decided that the risk associated with particular products, services, or activities is unacceptably high and thus should be subjected to regulation. A large portion of the federal regulatory structure deals with health and safety regulations. Examples of agencies responsible for such regulation include the Occupational Safety and Health Administration (OSHA), the Environmental Protection Agency (EPA), the Consumer Product Safety Commission (CPSC), and the National Highway Traffic Safety Administration (NHTSA). Over the last thirty years, government risk regulation has become a big business. The purpose of this section is to provide an economic perspective on risk regulation.

1. Cost-Benefit Analysis

Many regulators and the legislative mandates from which they operate contemplate risk-free levels of safety. However, because risk reduction is costly and involves tradeoffs, risk-free standards are not feasible. The practical impact of regulators pursuing risk-free standards is that cost considerations are often ignored. Rational economic decision making requires that government risk regulations be subjected to some type of cost-benefit analysis. In considering additional levels of risk reduction, the relevant economic analysis occurs at the margin. The marginal cost of reducing the risk associated with various activities increases as more risk is eliminated. Conversely, the marginal benefits of reduced risk decline as greater amounts of risk are eliminated. The optimal risk level occurs at the point where the marginal benefits of risk reduction equal the marginal costs. Beyond this point, risk reduction can occur only if allocative efficiency is sacrificed.

UAW v. Occupational Safety & Health Administration

United States Court of Appeals for the District of Columbia Circuit
938 F.2d 1310 (1991)

STEPHEN F. WILLIAMS, Circuit Judge:

Representatives of labor and industry challenge a regulation of the Occupational Safety and Health Administration, "Control of Hazardous Energy Sources (Lockout/Tagout)," 54 *Fed.Reg.* 36,644 (1989). The regulation deals not with the effects of such subtle phenomena as electrical energy fields but with those of ordinary industrial equipment that may suddenly move and cut or crush or otherwise injure a worker. "Lockout" and "tagout" are two procedures designed to reduce these injuries. Lockout is the placement of a lock on an "energy isolating device", such as a circuit breaker, so that equipment cannot start up until the lock is removed. Tagout is the similar placement of a plastic tag to alert employees that the tagged equipment "may not be operated" until the tag is removed. Although OSHA had previously issued specific standards governing especially dangerous equipment, the present rule extends lockout/tagout to virtually all equipment in almost all industries. It generally requires employers to use lockout procedures during servicing and maintenance, unless the employer can show that tagout will provide the same level of safety.

* * *

... [T]he National Association of Manufacturers [contends] that Congress has given so little guidance for rules issued under §6(b) [of the Occupational Safety and Health Act] but *not* covered by §6(b)(5) that as to such rules the Act invalidly delegates legislative authority. Although we reject that claim, we find that the interpretation offered by the Secretary is, in light of nondelegation principles, so broad as to be unreasonable. We note, however, the existence of at least one interpretation that is reasonable and consistent with the nondelegation doctrine.

* * *

I

[The court first rejected petitioner UAW's contention that §6(b)(5) provided the statutory criteria for the lockout rule.]

II

The removal of §6(b)(5) as a direct constraint on OSHA regulation outside the area of toxics gives point to the NAM's claim of an excessive delegation of legislative power. The only evident source of constraints remaining is §3(8). It defines an "occupational safety and health standard" as a standard which requires conditions, or the adoption or use of one or more practices, means, methods, operations, or processes, reasonably necessary or appropriate to provide safe or healthful employment and places of employment." Though the language is exceedingly vague, the *Benzene* plurality found it the source of a threshold requirement of "significant risk," without which OSHA was not to act under §6(b) at all. It justified this narrowing construction with the argument (among others) that otherwise "the statute would make such a 'sweeping delegation of legislative power' that it might be unconstitutional under the Court's reasoning in *A.L.A. Schechter Poultry Corp. v. United States*, 295 U.S. 495 (1935)....

The *Benzene* construction was, of course, a manifestation of the Court's current general practice of applying the nondelegation doctrine mainly in the form of "giving narrow constructions to statutory delegations that might otherwise be thought to be unconstitutional." ... In effect we require a clear statement by Congress that it intended to test the constitutional waters.

We thus turn to possible constructions.

A

One can imagine broader constructions than the one proposed by OSHA, but not easily....

* * *

It is true that price and wage controls blanketing the entire economy have been sustained under quite vague legislative directions. But in view of the inevitable tensions in such controls between such purposes as price stabilization on the one hand and the need for adjustments on ground of changes in cost and other market conditions on the other, an insistence on greater clarity from Congress would deny it any power to impose price controls at all. Not so here. Congress can readily articulate some principle by which the beneficent health and safety effects of workplace regulation are to be traded off against the adverse welfare effects. "Policy direction is all that was ever required, and policy direction is what is lacking in much contemporary legislation." John Hart Ely, Democracy and Distrust 133 (1980). OSHA's reading of the Act finds no such direction.

We note that OSHA's claimed discretion is procedurally confined. The agency sets "standards," which would normally apply across an industry, or to a category of machines, or to some other reasonably broad category. Thus, even under its view OSHA would normally not be free to single out the Jones Company for standards embodying strict feasibility while letting the Smith Company off on ones reflecting some different principle. But even the use of general standards leaves opportunities for dangerous favoritism. The cost of compliance with a standard will vary among firms in an industry, so the power to vary the stringency of the standard is the power to decide which firms will live and which will die. At the simplest level, for example, compliance may involve economies of scale, so that a tough standard will erase small, marginal firms and leave the field to a small group of larger ones. Compare Ann P. Bartel & Lacy Glenn Thomas, "Direct and Indirect Effects of Regulation: A New Look at OSHA's Impact," 28 J.L. & Econ. 1, 23–25 (1985).

OSHA's proposed analysis would give the executive branch untrammelled power to dictate the vitality and even survival of whatever segments of American business it might choose. Although in *Benzene* the Court focused perhaps more on the severity of the power claimed by OSHA than on its variability, the plurality's point is apt here: "In the absence of a clear mandate in the Act, it is unreasonable to assume that Congress intended to give the Secretary the unprecedented power over American industry that would result from the Government's view...." 448 U.S. at 645. At least if reasonable alternative readings can be found, OSHA's must be rejected as unreasonable.

B

The NAM argues (as a fallback to its nondelegation claim) that Congress's use of "reasonably necessary or appropriate" in § 3(8) contemplates "cost-benefit" analysis. Under this interpretation, in imposing standards under §6(b) but outside the realm of toxics, OSHA may adopt a safety standard if its benefits outweigh its costs, and not otherwise.

Cost-benefit analysis is certainly consistent with the language of §3(8). "Reasonableness" has long been associated with the balancing of costs and benefits. The "reasonable" person of tort fame is one who takes a precaution if the gravity of the injuries averted, adjusted for their probability, exceeds the precaution's burden. United States v. Carroll Towing Co., 159 F.2d 169, 173 (2d Cir.1947).

And while the legislative history is almost blank on the subject, it suggests concern with market failures, and properly conducted cost-benefit analysis should yield a solution approximating that of a market undistorted by market failures.[6] Application of cost-benefit analysis to safety standards also gives effect to Congress's distinction between slow-acting hazards and others, with its "particular concern for health hazards of 'unprecedented complexity' that had resulted from chemicals whose toxic effects 'are only now being discovered.'"

Moreover, courts have often taken the word "reasonable" in a statute to require that burdens be justified by the resulting benefits....

* * *

The union argues that prior cases preclude a cost-benefit interpretation here. They do not. The Supreme Court has expressly reserved the question. In *Cotton Dust*, upholding the Secretary's understanding that the "feasib[ility]" criterion of §6(b)(5) was not a cost-benefit standard, the Court observed that "[w]hen Congress has intended that an agency engage in cost-benefit analysis, it has clearly indicated such intent on the face of the statute." 452 U.S. at 510. But it cited approvingly *Forester* and *Aqua Slide 'N' Dive* (which find "unreasonable risk" to incorporate cost-benefit balancing), id. at 510–11 n. 30, and went on explicitly to leave open the question of §3(8)'s meaning apart from toxics regulation: "This is not to say that §3(8) might not require the balancing of costs and benefits for standards promulgated under provisions other than §6(b)(5) of the Act." Id. at 513 n. 32.

* * *

As there appear to be many confusions about cost-benefit analysis, it may be important to make clear what we are not saying when we identify it as a reasonable interpretation of §3(8) as applied outside the §6(b)(5) realm. Cost-benefit analysis requires identifying values for lost years of human life and for suffering and other losses from non-fatal injuries. Nothing we say here should be taken as confining the discretion of OSHA to choose among reasonable evaluation methods. While critics of cost-benefit analysis argue that any such valuation is impossible, that is so only in the sense that pin-point figures are necessarily arbitrary, so that the decisionmaker is effectively limited to considering some range of values. In fact, we make implicit life and safety valuations each day when we decide, for example, whether to travel by train or car, the former being more costly (at least if several family members are traveling together) but safer per passenger-mile. Where

---

6. Indeed, the Regulatory Impact Analysis of the Lockout/Tagout rule assessed it precisely on that basis, identifying worker lack of information and immobility as the relevant sources of market failure. Compare generally W. Kip Viscusi, Risk by Choice (1983), and especially *id.* at 44 (finding the safety incentives created by observed job-risk premiums nearly 3000 times stronger than those created by OSHA fines), and *id.* at 77 (finding systemic preference for jobs whose risks are not readily understood). As OSHA never adopted the Regulatory Impact Analysis as its own reasoning, we cannot treat the rule as an application of cost-benefit analysis; accordingly we do not review the Regulatory Impact Analysis to determine whether it would satisfy that standard.

government makes decisions for others, it may reasonably be expected to make the trade-offs somewhat more explicitly than individuals choosing for themselves. The difficulty of securing agreement even on a range of values hardly justifies making decisions on the basis of a pretense that resources are not scarce. In any event, OSHA has an existing obligation under Executive Order No. 12,291, 46 Fed.Reg. 13,193 (1981), to complete a cost-benefit analysis for each major rulemaking, so use of such a standard not only is doable in the qualified sense of which we have spoken but can be done without additional regulatory resources.

Thus, cost-benefit analysis entails only a systematic weighing of pros and cons, or what Benjamin Franklin referred to as a "moral or prudential algebra." Writing to a friend who was perplexed by a difficult decision, he explained his own approach:

> When those difficult cases occur, they are difficult, chiefly because while we have them under consideration, all the reasons pro and con are not present to the mind at the same time.... To get over this, my way is to divide half a sheet of paper by a line into two columns; writing over the one Pro, and over the other Con. Then, during three or four days consideration, I put down under the different heads short hints of the different motives, that at different times occur to me, for or against the measure. When I have thus got them all together in one view, I endeavor to estimate their respective weights.... And, though the weight of reasons cannot be taken with the precision of algebraic quantities, yet when each is thus considered, separately and comparatively, and the whole lies before me, I think I can judge better, and am less liable to make a rash step, and in fact I have found great advantage from this kind of equation, in what may be called moral or prudential algebra.

Reprinted in Edward M. Gramlich, Benefit-Cost Analysis of Government Programs 1–2 (1981).

As we accept the NAM's contention that § 3(8)'s "reasonably necessary or appropriate" criterion can reasonably be read as requiring cost-benefit analysis, we must reject its non-delegation claim.

We hold only that cost-benefit is a permissible interpretation of § 3(8). Given the ambiguity inherent in that section, there may be other interpretations that conform to nondelegation principles. Accordingly we remand to OSHA, noting that its treatment of some of the parties' other claims, discussed below, will likely turn on its decision. We note, however, that Executive Order No. 12,291 may bear on OSHA's authority to promulgate a safety standard whose benefits fail to outweigh its costs. Section 2 of that order provides:

> In promulgating new regulations ... all agencies, *to the extent permitted by law, shall* adhere to the following requirements....
>
> (b) *Regulatory action shall not be undertaken unless the potential benefits to society for the regulation outweigh the potential costs to society;*
>
> (c) Regulatory objectives shall be chosen to maximize the net benefits to society....

46 Fed.Reg. 13,193 (1981) (emphasis added).

* * *

Accordingly, in light of the NAM's nondelegation claim we reject OSHA's view that under § 3(8) it may impose any restriction it chooses so long as it is "feasible," but we also reject the NAM's nondelegation claim in light of our view that § 3(8) may reasonably be read as providing for cost-benefit analysis.

* * *

Accordingly, we remand the case to OSHA for further consideration in light of this opinion.

So ordered.

STEPHEN F. WILLIAMS, Circuit Judge, concurring:

I write separately to address the UAW's apparent assumption that application of the significant risk/feasibility analysis associated with §6(b)(5) is necessarily more protective of health and safety than a cost-benefit criterion. This is not self-evidently true.

First, if OSHA applies cost-benefit analysis, then more risks seem likely to qualify as "significant" within the meaning of *Benzene*; many risks that may seem insignificant if their discovery triggers regulatory burdens limited only by feasibility, as under §6(b)(5), may be significant if the consequence is cost-justified corrective measures.

Second, even where the application of cost-benefit analysis would result in less stringent regulation, the reduced stringency is not necessarily adverse to health or safety. More regulation means some combination of reduced value of firms, higher product prices, fewer jobs in the regulated industry, and lower cash wages. All the latter three stretch workers' budgets tighter (as does the first to the extent that the firms' stock is held in workers' pension trusts). And larger incomes enable people to lead safer lives. One study finds a 1 percent increase in income associated with a mortality reduction of about 0.05 percent. Jack Hadley & Anthony Osei, "Does Income Affect Mortality?," 20 Medical Care 901, 913 (September 1982). Another suggests that each $7.5 million of costs generated by regulation may, under certain assumptions, induce one fatality. Ralph L. Keeney, "Mortality Risks Induced by Economic Expenditures," 10 Risk Analysis 147, 155 (1990) (relying on E.M. Kitagawa & P.M. Hauser, *Differential Mortality in the United States of America: A Study of Socioeconomic Epidemiology*(1973)). Larger incomes can produce health by enlarging a person's access to better diet, preventive medical care, safer cars, greater leisure, etc. See Aaron Wildavsky, *Searching for Safety* 59–71 (1988).

Of course, other causal relations may be at work too. Healthier people may be able to earn higher income, and characteristics and advantages that facilitate high earnings (e.g., work ethic, education) may also lead to better health. Compare C.P. Wen, et al., "Anatomy of the Healthy Worker Effect: A Critical Review," 25 J. of Occupation Medicine 283 (1983). Nonetheless, higher income can secure better health, and there is no basis for a casual assumption that more stringent regulation will always save lives.

It follows that while officials involved in health or safety regulation may naturally be hesitant to set any kind of numerical value on human life, undue squeamishness may be deadly. Incremental safety regulation reduces incomes and thus may exact a cost in human lives. For example, if analysis showed that "an individual life was lost for every $12 million taken from individuals [as a result of the regulation], this would be a guide to a reasonable value tradeoff for many programs designed to save lives." Keeney, "Mortality Risks Induced by Economic Expenditures," 10 Risk Analysis at 158. Such a figure could serve as a ceiling for value-of-life calculated by other means, since regulation causing greater expenditures per life expected to be saved would, everything else being equal, result in a net loss of life.

Notes and Questions

1. Marginal Cost-Marginal Benefit Analysis: Cost-benefit analysis, when performed properly, should be an analysis of marginal costs and marginal benefits. Reliance on average costs and average benefits can lead to mistakes. Consider, for example, the En-

Table VI-1. Cost per Life Saved for Arsenic Regulation

Stringency	Standard Level (mg/m3)	Average Cost per Life Saved	Marginal Cost per Life Saved
Loose	0.10	$1.25 million	$1.25 million
Medium	0.05	$2.95 million	$11.5 million
Tight	0.004	$5.63 million	$68.1 million

vironmental Protection Agency's regulation of acceptable levels of exposure to arsenic.[7] Table VI-1 shows the average and marginal costs per life saved by moving from relatively loose to strict standards. Assume the regulators are using $7.5 million per life saved as the marginal benefit. (Note that average benefit is equal to marginal benefit because the marginal benefit is constant.). Comparison of average cost per life saved to the value of the life saved indicates that the strict standard should be adopted. However, the comparison of marginal cost per life saved indicates that it would be very wasteful to require the strict standard. The loose standard would be optimal. If policy decisions were guided by the average cost per life saved (which was substantially below the standard value of life measurements used in risk management), an economically inefficient level of regulation would result.

2. Risk Assessment and Risk Management: When analyzing cases that involve cost-benefit analysis, it is helpful to set the framework for the analysis by considering the areas of risk assessment and risk management. These important parts of the regulatory system are described by Judge (now Justice) Stephen Breyer in his influential book, *Breaking the Vicious Cycle: Toward Effective Risk Regulation*:

> The [regulatory] system has two basic parts, a technical part, called "risk assessment," designed to measure the risk associated with the substance, and a more policy-oriented part, called "risk management," which decides what to do about it.
>
> Risk assessment can itself be divided into four activities: (a) *Identifying the potential* hazard, say benzene in respect to cancer: Is it benzene in any context, or just benzene used in industry, or undiluted benzene, or certain solutions of benzene in certain places? (b) *Drawing a dose/response curve:* How does the risk of harm vary with the person's exposure to that substance? The question is critically important, for, as Paracelsus pointed out over four hundred years ago, "the dose alone determines the poison." Drinking a bottle of pure iodine is deadly; placing a drop of diluted iodine on a cut is helpful. Regulators will try to use statistical studies of, say, cancer in humans (epidemiological studies), or experiments with high substance-doses given to animals, to estimate the potential effects of human exposure to low substance-doses over varying periods of time. (c) *Estimating the amount of human exposure:* How many persons in a particular workforce, or in a particular region, or in the public generally, will be exposed to different doses of the substance, and for how long? Suppose exposure to a solution of five parts per million every day for twenty years will be likely to cause five extra deaths per year per million persons. Exposing the entire population may mean 1,250 extra deaths; exposing a hundred thousand persons may mean

---

7. This example is from W. Kip Viscusi et al., Economics of Regulation and Antitrust 667–68 (2d ed. 1995).

one extra death every two years. And even in the latter case, if only two persons are exposed to the substance, so that each runs a 50 percent risk of death, there may be a regulatory problem. (d) *Categorizing the result:* Is the substance, in fact, a carcinogen? A strong carcinogen or a weak carcinogen? Based upon the dose/response and exposure findings, how should the risk assessment describe (or categorize) the hazard? In carrying out these activities, particularly in making dose/response and exposure estimates, regulators often find that they simply lack critically important scientific or empirical data: they do not know how many Americans inhale how much benzene at gasoline stations; they do not know the extent to which the biology of a rat or mouse resembles, or differs from, that of a human being. In such instances, they will often make a "default assumption"—a formalized guess—designed to fill the gap and to permit the regulator to continue the analysis.

Risk management determines what the regulator should do about the risks that the assessment reveals. Ideally, the risk manager will consider what will be likely in fact to occur should he choose each of several regulatory potions. On the one hand, to what extent will the regulation actually diminish the specific risk at issue? On the other hand, to what extent will regulation itself produce *different* risks? (Will childproof aspirin bottle tops save children, or will they lead many parents, unable to open the top easily, simply to leave the top off? Will saccharin users, denied saccharin, switch to sugar, gain weight, and die of heart attacks?) To what extent will the regulation deprive users of benefits the substance now brings? To what extent will it impose added costs? The manager also must consider practical problems, such as the difficulty of enforcing a regulation or the political reaction that its promulgation might bring. Ultimately, in light of the identified risks, the risks associated with alternatives, the effect on benefits, the costs, and the practicalities, the risk managing regulator will reach a decision.

Stephen G. Breyer, Breaking the Vicious Cycle: Toward Effective Risk Regulation 9–10 (1993).

3. Cost-Benefit Analysis, Compensating Wage Differentials, and Voluntary Risk Taking: A safety or health standard is socially desirable only if the value workers place on risk reduction is commensurate with the cost of complying with the standard. The value workers place on risk reduction can be estimated, in theory at least, from knowledge of compensating wage differentials. However, even if compensating wage differentials were accurately calculated from observations in a market characterized by both widespread information and choice, there are still objections to their use in assessing the benefits of OSHA standards. First, compensating wage differentials reflect the preferences of only those directly involved in the contractual relationship between the employer and employee. It is frequently argued that members of society who are not directly affected by the risk reduction program might be willing to pay something for the benefits that accrue to those who are directly affected. Presumably, this willingness to pay is strongest for family members, relatives, and close friends and weakest for strangers. However, even strangers would have some interest in reducing injury and disease if they were to be taxed in order to subsidize the medical treatment of those who are injured or become ill. Thus, it is argued the benefits of OSHA standards extend beyond the direct beneficiaries to other external parties whose willingness to pay should also be counted. The second argument against using only the apparent willingness of workers to pay for risk reduction as a measure of its benefit is that workers may not really know what's best for themselves in the long run. Society frequently prohibits, or at least tries to prohibit, people from indulging in activities that are dangerous to their welfare. Laws against the use of narcotics and gambling are two examples. Some argue that OSHA standards limiting exposure to dangerous substances or situations fall under the category of preventing workers from doing harm to themselves by being lured into dangerous work. Therefore, it is argued, to ask how much they value risk reduction is irrelevant. The conflict between those who claim that workers know what is best for themselves and those who claim they do not, can only be resolved on philosophical grounds. A final argument is that workers often lack negotiating power in the labor market. Say, for example, that you are an uneducated coal miner in a small mining community with high unemployment and few other economic opportunities. Your boss decides that she does not want to pay for gas masks anymore and that she is cutting your pay by five percent. Do you have any recourse?

4. Worker Safety, Compensating Wage Differentials, and the Best Interests of Workers: In 1970, Congress passed the Occupational Safety and Health Act which directed the U.S. Department of Labor to issue and enforce safety and health standards for all private employers. The stated goal of the Act was to ensure the "highest degree of health and safety protection for the employee." Despite the ideal that employees should face the minimum possible risk in the work place, implementing this ideal as social policy is not necessarily in the best interest of workers. Some workers are more willing than others to perform risky jobs, and they are usually rewarded with a compensating wage differential. When the government mandates the reduction of risk in a market where workers are compensated for the risk they take, it penalizes workers who are not terribly sensitive to risk and appreciate the higher wages associated with higher risk. The critical issue, of course, is whether workers have the knowledge and choice necessary to generate compensating wage differentials. Many people believe that workers are uninformed, unable to comprehend different risk levels, or immobile and thus that most do not choose risky jobs voluntarily. If this belief were true, government regulations could make workers better off. Indeed, while the evidence of a positive relationship between wage and risk of death should challenge the notion that information and mobility are generally insufficient to create compensating differentials, there are specific areas in which problems obviously exist. For example, the introduction each year of new workplace chemicals whose effects on humans may be unknown for two or more decades, owing to long gestation of most cancers and lung diseases, clearly presents substantial information problems to affected labor market participants. To say that worker utility can be increased by government regulation does not then imply that it will be increased. The outcome depends on how well the unregulated market functions and how careful the government is in setting its standards for risk reduction.

5. OSHA's Feasibility Standard: OSHA proposes the use of a feasibility test in setting regulatory standards. Regulatory stringency under such a test can be characterized as requiring only that technology-based standards be affordable (i.e., capable of being done). Clearly then, a feasibility test does not contemplate a balancing of the marginal costs and marginal benefits. Rather, under a feasibility standard, OSHA simply looks for a "kink" in the marginal cost curve. That is, at what point does it become prohibitively costly to raise the standard. Such a kink may of course occur past the point at which marginal benefits equal marginal costs. What justification can OSHA offer for a feasibility test? Does Judge Williams' concurring opinion adequately address such arguments? The Supreme Court's *Cotton Dust* opinion allows OSHA to use a feasibility standard in the regulation of toxics. What justification allows the feasibility standard to exist in the case of workplace toxics?

6. The Impact of Risk Regulation: Questions regarding the effectiveness of the current regulatory system don't stop after applying a cost-benefit test to stringency levels. In order to justify the existence of regulatory agencies, the regulations should have the desired impact on market behavior:

> Firms will choose to make the necessary investments in health and safety if the OSHA enforcement policy in conjunction with market incentives for safety makes it in the firm's financial self-interest to do so. More specifically, a firm will comply with an OSHA regulation if

$$\begin{array}{c} \text{Expected cost} \\ \text{of compliance} \end{array} < \begin{array}{c} \text{Probability} \\ \text{inspection} \end{array} \times \begin{array}{c} \text{Expected no.} \\ \text{of violations} \\ \text{per inspection} \end{array} \times \begin{array}{c} \text{Average} \\ \text{penalty per} \\ \text{violation} \end{array}$$

> As discussed, the three links in establishing these incentives—inspections, violations, and penalties—are all relatively weak. A firm has less than one chance in 200 of being inspected in any given year. If inspected, it expects to be found guilty of less than two violations of the standards, and for each violation the average penalty is under $60. Overall, the financial cost per worker is just over fifty cents. A useful comparison is that market forces through compensating differentials in combination with workers' compensation premiums imposed costs in excess of $800 per worker for the same period. Quite simply, OSHA's enforcement effort is too modest to create truly effective financial incentives for safety.

W. Kip Viscusi et al., Economics of Regulation and Antitrust 816 (2d ed. 1995). A simple way of stating this is that firms will not comply with regulations if the cost of compliance is lower than the expected cost of getting caught. Based on this information what justification is there for the continued existence of OSHA? Does the market have a comparative advantage in allocating the types of risk that OSHA is attempting to regulate? It appears that in regard to both stringency and enforcement, regulatory agencies like OSHA have ignored the reality of the market.

7. Wealthier Is Healthier: Judge Stephen Williams, in his concurring opinion, cautions that the costs of health and safety regulations might actually result in more lives lost than saved. This counter-intuitive result flows from the empirical evidence that shows strong correlations between average national income levels and measures of national health, such as life expectancy and infant mortality. Wealthier is healthier. Moreover, regulations—even those that are supposed to reduce risk—that do not pass a cost-benefit analysis can reduce wealth and, thus, reduce health. Jobs are lost and wealth is destroyed when regulations force businesses to make inefficient expenditures. Similarly, new product innovation is suppressed whenever government overregulates the development, distribution, and use of products with life-saving potential. Risk experts Richard J. Zeckhauser and W. Kip Viscusi argue that "overreaction to very small risks impedes the kind of technological progress that has historically brought dramatic improvements in both health and material well-being." Richard J. Zeckhauser &W. Kip Viscusi, *Risk Within Reason*, 248 Science 559 (1990). Does the court give adequate attention to such facts? What incentives would drive OSHA to ignore such facts?

8. Marginal Analysis and Heterogeneity: Use of marginal analysis suggests something about the manner in which regulatory standards should be applied across different industries or firms. Consider the case of a regulation that would be applied across several different industries. According to the regulator, the marginal benefit per unit of safety is the same across all industries. However, it is unlikely that firms in each of these different industries face the same marginal cost curves. Therefore, across industries, the level of safety at which marginal benefits equal marginal costs will be different. Suppose that the regulating agency sets safety standards based on a representative firm. If a single standard is imposed regardless of industry, then the regulating agency loses the opportunity for further risk reduction. If a firm has lower marginal costs than contemplated by the regulation, then it would be efficient for this firm to be required to have a higher safety standard. Thus, a single standard misses inexpensive opportunities to reduce risk. On the other hand, if a firm has higher marginal costs than supposed by the regulation, then the single standard will result in economic inefficiency. This results in lower incomes and therefore sacrificed safety. By using marginal analysis, regulatory agencies would be able to maximize the risk-reducing benefits of their regulations across industries and across firms.

2. Measuring Risk: All Risks Are Relative

Absolute levels of risk provide very little relevant information in the absence of some relative comparison. For example, suppose that living five years at the boundary of a nuclear power plant site increased one's annual death risk by one chance in one million. Should you be concerned? Should there be additional regulation? Now consider the fact that the risk of traveling six minutes by canoe will also increase your annual death risk one chance in one million. Both of these risks have the same impact on annual death rates. However, many individuals might be outraged if tax dollars were being spent to eliminate the risk of being killed during a six minute canoe trip. By considering a risk that sounds intimidating relative to risks that individuals freely undertake daily, it becomes much easier to achieve a conceptual understanding of risk measures. Gaining a conceptual measure of risk is important because regulatory agencies often attempt to regulate risks that are very small relative to the types of risks that individuals expose themselves to in their everyday lives. Furthermore, gaining an appreciation for the relative impacts of different risk reduction proposals helps in analyzing the efficacy of regulatory performance.

Corrosion Proof Fittings v. Environmental Protection Agency
United States Court of Appeals for the Fifth Circuit
947 F.2d 1201 (1991)

JERRY E. SMITH, Circuit Judge:

The Environmental Protection Agency (EPA) issued a final rule under section 6 of the Toxic Substances Control Act (TSCA) to prohibit the future manufacture, importation, processing, and distribution of asbestos in almost all products. Petitioners claim that ... the rule was not promulgated on the basis of substantial evidence.... Because the EPA failed to muster substantial evidence to support its rule, we remand this matter to the EPA for further consideration in light of this opinion.

I. Facts and Procedural History.

Asbestos is a naturally occurring fibrous material that resists fire and most solvents. Its major uses include heat-resistant insulators, cements, building materials, fireproof gloves and clothing, and motor vehicle brake linings. Asbestos is a toxic material, and occupational exposure to asbestos dust can result in mesothelioma, asbestosis, and lung cancer.

The EPA began these proceedings in 1979, when it issued an Advanced Notice of Proposed Rulemaking announcing its intent to explore the use of TSCA "to reduce the risk to human health posed by exposure to asbestos." ...

An EPA-appointed panel reviewed over one hundred studies of asbestos and conducted several public meetings. Based upon its studies and the public comments, the EPA concluded that asbestos is a potential carcinogen at all levels of exposure, regardless of the type of asbestos or the size of the fiber. The EPA concluded in 1986 that exposure to asbestos "poses an unreasonable risk to human health" and thus proposed at least four regulatory options for prohibiting or restricting the use of asbestos, including a mixed ban and phase-out of asbestos over ten years; a two-stage ban of asbestos, depending upon product usage; a three-stage ban on all asbestos products leading to a total ban in ten years; and labeling of all products containing asbestos.

Over the next two years, the EPA updated its data, received further comments, and allowed cross-examination on the updated documents. In 1989, the EPA issued a final rule prohibiting the manufacture, importation, processing, and distribution in commerce of most asbestos-containing products. Finding that asbestos constituted an unreasonable risk to health and the environment, the EPA promulgated a staged ban of most commercial uses of asbestos. The EPA estimates that this rule will save either 202 or 148 lives, depending upon whether the benefits are discounted, at a cost of approximately $450–800 million, depending upon the price of substitutes.

* * *

IV. The Language of TSCA.

* * *

B. The EPA's Burden Under TSCA

* * *

We conclude that the EPA has presented insufficient evidence to justify its asbestos ban. We base this conclusion upon two grounds: the failure of the EPA to consider all necessary evidence and its failure to give adequate weight to statutory language requiring it to promulgate the least burdensome, reasonable regulation required to protect the environment adequately. Because the EPA failed to address these concerns, and because the EPA is required to articulate a "reasoned basis" for its rules, we are compelled to return the regulation to the agency for reconsideration.

1. Least Burdensome and Reasonable.

TSCA requires that the EPA use the least burdensome regulation to achieve its goal of minimum reasonable risk. This statutory requirement can create problems in evaluating just what is a "reasonable risk." Congress's rejection of a no-risk policy, however, also means that in certain cases, the least burdensome yet still adequate solution may entail somewhat more risk than would other, known regulations that are far more burdensome on the industry and the economy. The very language of TSCA requires that the EPA, once it has determined what an acceptable level of non-zero risk is, choose the least burdensome method of reaching that level.

In this case, the EPA banned, for all practical purposes, all present and future uses of asbestos—a position the petitioners characterize as the "death penalty alternative," as this is the most burdensome of all possible alternatives listed as open to the EPA under TSCA....

By choosing the harshest remedy given to it under TSCA, the EPA assigned to itself the toughest burden in satisfying TSCA's requirement that its alternative be the least burdensome of all those offered to it. Since, both by definition and by the terms of TSCA, the complete ban of manufacturing is the most burdensome alternative—for even stringent regulation at least allows a manufacturer the chance to invest and meet the new, higher standard—the EPA's regulation cannot stand if there is any other regulation that would achieve an acceptable level of risk as mandated by TSCA.

* * *

Much of the EPA's analysis is correct, and the EPA's basic decision to use TSCA as a comprehensive statute designed to fight a multi-industry problem was a proper one that we uphold today on review. What concerns us, however, is the manner in which the EPA conducted some of its analysis. TSCA requires the EPA to consider, along with the effects of toxic substances on human health and the environment, "the benefits of such substance[s] or mixture[s] for various uses and the availability of substitutes for such uses," as well as "the reasonably ascertainable economic consequences of the rule, after consideration for the effect on the national economy, small business, technological innovation, the environment, and public health."

The EPA presented two comparisons in the record: a world with no further regulation under TSCA, and a world in which no manufacture of asbestos takes place. The EPA rejected calculating how many lives a less burdensome regulation would save, and at what cost. Furthermore the EPA, when calculating the benefits of its ban, explicitly refused to compare it to an improved workplace in which currently available control technology is utilized. This decision artificially inflated the purported benefits of the rule by using a baseline comparison substantially lower than what currently available technology could yield.

Under TSCA, the EPA was required to evaluate, rather than ignore, less burdensome regulatory alternatives. TSCA imposes a least-to-most-burdensome hierarchy. In order to impose a regulation at the top of the hierarchy—a total ban of asbestos—the EPA must show not only that its proposed action reduces the risk of the product to an adequate level, but also that the actions Congress identified as less burdensome also would not do the job. The failure of the EPA to do this constitutes a failure to meet its burden of showing that its actions not only reduce the risk but do so in the Congressionally-mandated least burdensome fashion.

Thus it was not enough for the EPA to show, as it did in this case, that banning some asbestos products might reduce the harm that could occur from the use of these products. If that were the standard, it would be no standard at all, for few indeed are the products that are so safe that a complete ban of them would not make the world still safer.

This comparison of two static worlds is insufficient to satisfy the dictates of TSCA. While the EPA may have shown that a world with a complete ban of asbestos might be preferable to one in which there is only the current amount of regulation, the EPA has failed to show that there is not some intermediate state of regulation that would be superior to both the currently-regulated and the completely-banned world. Without showing that asbestos regulation would be ineffective, the EPA cannot discharge its TSCA burden of showing that its regulation is the least burdensome available to it.

Upon an initial showing of product danger, the proper course for the EPA to follow is to consider each regulatory option, beginning with the least burdensome, and the costs and benefits of regulation under each option. The EPA cannot simply skip several rungs, as it did in this case, for in doing so, it may skip a less-burdensome alternative mandated by TSCA. Here, although the EPA mentions the problems posed by intermediate levels of regulation, it takes no steps to calculate the costs and benefits of these intermediate levels. Without doing this it is impossible, both for the EPA and for this court on review, to know that none of these alternatives was less burdensome than the ban in fact chosen by the agency.

The EPA's offhand rejection of these intermediate regulatory steps is "not the stuff of which substantial evidence is made." While it is true that the EPA considered five different ban options, these differed solely with respect to their effective dates. The EPA did not calculate the risk levels for intermediate levels of regulation, as it believed that there was no asbestos exposure level for which the risk of injury or death was zero. Reducing risk to zero, however, was not the task that Congress set for the EPA in enacting TSCA. The EPA thus has failed "cogently [to] explain why it has exercised its discretion in a given manner," by failing to explore in more than a cursory way the less burdensome alternatives to a total ban.

2. The EPA's Calculations.

Furthermore, we are concerned about some of the methodology employed by the EPA in making various of the calculations that it did perform. In order to aid the EPA's reconsideration of this and other cases, we present our concerns here.

First, we note that there was some dispute in the record regarding the appropriateness of discounting the perceived benefits of the EPA's rule. In choosing between the calculated costs and benefits, the EPA presented variations in which it discounted only the costs, and counter-variations in which it discounted both the costs and the benefits, measured in both monetary and human injury terms. As between these two variations, we choose to evaluate the EPA's work using its discounted benefits calculations.

Although various commentators dispute whether it ever is appropriate to discount benefits when they are measured in human lives, we note that it would skew the results to discount only costs without according similar treatment to the benefits side of the equation. Adopting the position of the commentators who advocate not discounting benefits would force the EPA similarly not to calculate costs in present discounted real terms, making comparisons difficult. Furthermore, in evaluating situations in which different options incur costs at varying time intervals, the EPA would not be able to take into account that soon-to-be-incurred costs are more harmful than postponable costs. Because the EPA must discount costs to perform its evaluations properly, the EPA also should discount benefits to preserve an apples-to-apples comparison, even if this entails discounting benefits of a non-monetary nature.

When the EPA does discount costs or benefits, however, it cannot choose an unreasonable time upon which to base its discount calculation. Instead of using the time of injury as the appropriate time from which to discount, as one might expect, the EPA instead used the time of exposure.

The difficulties inherent in the EPA's approach can be illustrated by an example. Suppose two workers will be exposed to asbestos in 1995, with worker X subjected to a tiny amount of asbestos that will have no adverse health effects, and worker Y exposed to massive amounts of asbestos that quickly will lead to an asbestos-related disease. Under the EPA's approach, which takes into account only the time of exposure rather than the time at which any injury manifests itself, both examples would be treated the same. The EPA's approach implicitly assumes that the day on which the risk of injury occurs is the same day the injury actually occurs. Such an approach might be proper when the exposure and injury are one and the same, such as when a person is exposed to an immediately fatal poison, but is inappropriate for discounting toxins in which exposure often is followed by a substantial lag time before manifestation of injuries.

* * *

Under the EPA's calculations, a twenty-year-old worker entering employment today still would be at risk from workplace dangers for more than thirty years after the EPA's analysis period had ended. The true benefits of regulating asbestos under such calculations remain unknown. The EPA cannot choose to leave these benefits high and then use the high unknown benefits as a major factor justifying EPA action.

* * *

3. Reasonable Basis.

* * *

Most problematical to us is the EPA's ban of products for which no substitutes presently are available. In these cases, the EPA bears a tough burden indeed to show that under TSCA a ban is the least burdensome alternative, as TSCA explicitly instructs the EPA to consider "the benefits of such substance or mixture for various uses and the availability of substitutes for such uses." These words are particularly appropriate where the EPA actually has decided to ban a product, rather than simply restrict its use, for it is in these cases that the lack of an adequate substitute is most troubling under TSCA.

As the EPA itself states, "[w]hen no information is available for a product indicating that cost-effective substitutes exist, the estimated cost of a product ban is very high." Because of this, the EPA did not ban certain uses of asbestos, such as its use in rocket engines and battery separators. The EPA, however, in several other instances, ignores its own arguments and attempts to justify its ban by stating that the ban itself will cause the development of low-cost, adequate substitute products.

As a general matter, we agree with the EPA that a product ban can lead to great innovation, and it is true that an agency under TSCA, as under other regulatory statutes, "is empowered to issue safety standards which require improvements in existing technology or which require the development of new technology." As even the EPA acknowledges, however, when no adequate substitutes currently exist, the EPA cannot fail to consider this lack when formulating its own guidelines. Under TSCA, therefore, the EPA must present a stronger case to justify the ban, as opposed to regulation, of products with no substitutes.

* * *

This presents two problems. First, TSCA instructs the EPA to consider the relative merits of its ban, as compared to the economic effects of its actions. The EPA cannot make this calculation if it fails to consider the effects that alternate substitutes will pose after a ban.

Second, the EPA cannot say with any assurance that its regulation will increase workplace safety when it refuses to evaluate the harm that will result from the increased use of substitute products. While the EPA may be correct in its conclusion that the alternate materials pose less risk than asbestos, we cannot say with any more assurance than that flowing from an educated guess that this conclusion is true.

Considering that many of the substitutes that the EPA itself concedes will be used in the place of asbestos have known carcinogenic effects, the EPA not only cannot assure this court that it has taken the least burdensome alternative, but cannot even prove that its regulations will increase workplace safety. Eager to douse the dangers of asbestos, the agency inadvertently actually may increase the risk of injury Americans face. The EPA's explicit failure to consider the toxicity of likely substitutes thus deprives its order of a reasonable basis.

* * *

In short, a death is a death, whether occasioned by asbestos or by a toxic substitute product, and the EPA's decision not to evaluate the toxicity of known carcinogenic substitutes is not a reasonable action under TSCA. Once an interested party brings forth credible evidence suggesting the toxicity of the probable or only alternatives to a substance, the EPA must consider the comparative toxic costs of each. Its failure to do so in this case thus deprived its regulation of a reasonable basis, at least in regard to those products as to which petitioners introduced credible evidence of the dangers of the likely substitutes.

4. Unreasonable Risk of Injury.

The final requirement the EPA must satisfy before engaging in any TSCA rulemaking is that it only take steps designed to prevent "unreasonable" risks. In evaluating what is "unreasonable," the EPA is required to consider the costs of any proposed actions and to "carry out this chapter in a reasonable and prudent manner [after considering] the environmental, economic, and social impact of any action."

As the District of Columbia Circuit stated when evaluating similar language governing the Federal Hazardous Substances Act, "[t]he requirement that the risk be 'unreasonable' necessarily involves a balancing test like that familiar in tort law: The regulation may issue if the severity of the injury that may result from the product, factored by the likelihood of the injury, offsets the harm the regulation itself imposes upon manufacturers and consumers." Forester v. CPSC, 559 F.2d 774, 789 (D.C.Cir.1977)....

That the EPA must balance the costs of its regulations against their benefits further is reinforced by the requirement that it seek the least burdensome regulation. While Congress did not dictate that the EPA engage in an exhaustive, full-scale cost-benefit analysis, it did require the EPA to consider both sides of the regulatory equation, and it rejected the notion that the EPA should pursue the reduction of workplace risk at any cost....

Even taking all of the EPA's figures as true, and evaluating them in the light most favorable to the agency's decision (non-discounted benefits, discounted costs, analogous exposure estimates included), the agency's analysis results in figures as high as $74 million per life saved. For example, the EPA states that its ban of asbestos pipe will save three lives over the next thirteen years, at a cost of $128–227 million ($43–76 million per life saved), depending upon the price of substitutes; that its ban of asbestos shingles will cost $23–34 million to save 0.32 statistical lives ($72–106 million per life saved); that its ban of asbestos coatings will cost $46–181 million to save 3.33 lives ($14–54 million per life saved); and that its ban of asbestos paper products will save 0.60 lives at a cost of $4–5 million ($7–8 million per life saved). Were the analogous exposure estimates not included, the cancer risks from substitutes such as ductile iron pipe factored in, and the benefits of the ban appropriately discounted from the time of the manifestation of an injury rather than the time of exposure, the costs would shift even more sharply against the EPA's position.

While we do not sit as a regulatory agency that must make the difficult decision as to what an appropriate expenditure is to prevent someone from incurring the risk of an asbestos-related death, we do note that the EPA, in its zeal to ban any and all asbestos products, basically ignored the cost side of the TSCA equation. The EPA would have this court believe that Congress, when it enacted its requirement that the EPA consider the economic impacts of its regulations, thought that spending $200–300 million to save approximately seven lives (approximately $30–40 million per life) over thirteen years is reasonable.

* * *

The EPA's willingness to argue that spending $23.7 million to save less than one-third of a life reveals that its economic review of its regulations, as required by TSCA, was meaningless. As the petitioners' brief and our review of EPA caselaw reveals, such high costs are rarely, if ever, used to support a safety regulation. If we were to allow such cavalier treatment of the EPA's duty to consider the economic effects of its decisions, we would have to excise entire sections and phrases from the language of TSCA. Because we are judges, not surgeons, we decline to do so.[8]

* * *

VI. Conclusion.

In summary, of most concern to us is that the EPA has failed to implement the dictates of TSCA and the prior decisions of this and other courts that, before it imposes a ban on a product, it first evaluate and then reject the less burdensome alternatives laid out for it by Congress. While the EPA spent much time and care crafting its asbestos regulation, its explicit failure to consider the alternatives required of it by Congress deprived its final rule of the reasonable basis it needed to survive judicial scrutiny.

* * *

Finally, the EPA failed to provide a reasonable basis for the purported benefits of its proposed rule by refusing to evaluate the toxicity of likely substitute products that will be used to replace asbestos goods. While the EPA does not have the duty under TSCA of affirmatively seeking out and testing all possible substitutes, when an interested party comes forward with credible evidence that the planned substitutes present a significant, or even greater, toxic risk than the substance in question, the agency must make a formal finding on the record that its proposed action still is both reasonable and warranted under TSCA.

We regret that this matter must continue to take up the valuable time of the agency, parties and, undoubtedly, future courts. The requirements of TSCA, however, are plain, and the EPA cannot deviate from them to reach its desired result. We therefore GRANT the petition for review, VACATE the EPA's proposed regulation, and REMAND to the EPA for further proceedings in light of this opinion.

Notes and Questions

1. All Risk Is Relative: Much of the court's opinion discusses the relative risk of asbestos alternatives. In many instances, there was evidence that suggested that the risk of substitute products outweighed the risk of asbestos. By ignoring the relative risks of different products, the EPA's rulemaking might have resulted in a net increase in lost lives. Why does the EPA choose to ignore such tradeoffs? Why isn't the EPA more concerned with regulating these substitute products?

The use of this kind of analysis was initially embraced by the EPA in a 1987 study entitled *Unfinished Business: A Comparative Assessment of Environmental Problems.* The study relied on an emerging technique known as **comparative risk analysis** (CRA). CRA is an economic tool used to quantitatively assess, compare, and rank different environmental and health risks. The study looked at over thirty health concerns and ranked them in terms of various risks including cancer, non-cancer, ecological, and welfare risks. A fol-

---

8. As the petitioners point out, the EPA regularly rejects, as unjustified, regulations that would save more lives at less cost. For example, over the next 13 years, we can expect more than a dozen deaths from ingested toothpicks—a death toll more than twice what the EPA predicts will flow from the quarter-billion-dollar bans of asbestos pipe, shingles, and roof coatings. See L. Budnick, Toothpick-Related Injuries in the United States, 1979 Through 1982, 252 J. Am. Med. Ass'n, Aug. 10, 1984, at 796 (study showing that toothpick-related deaths average approximately one per year).

low-up study by an EPA subcommittee published in 1990 entitled *Reducing Risk* found fault with many of the methods used in the original study but concluded that:

> The Subcommittee developed a strong consensus that the relative risk assessment process is a good mechanism to formulate public policy from a scientific base of data and mechanistic processes. We recommend that the Agency institutionalize this approach on a regular basis, and provide the trained personnel and scientific data-bases needed to establish a scientific credibility for the process.

The use of this method remains controversial, and the academic community has split over the correct methods and utility of this approach. Do you think this is a good way to allocate scarce social resources to address health and safety risks? Could this method be usefully applied to other areas of public policy? Should other government agencies adopt the use of comparative risk analysis? Should private individuals?

2. Cost-Benefit Analysis and Discounting: In some cases, the benefits that may result from regulatory efforts are not realized until many years into the future. For example, environmental regulations often contemplate current expenditures for delayed benefits. In order to determine the relevant costs and benefits of such regulations, regulators must discount future benefits and costs to present values. The basic economic approach is that immediate benefits are more valuable than benefits in the future because of the likelihood of changing circumstances and the uncertainty of success. On numerous occasions, the EPA has argued that future benefits should not be discounted. But by not discounting, the benefits of EPA regulations appear to be much larger than they otherwise would be.

3. Establishing an Unreasonable Risk: The Toxic Substances Control Act (TSCA) contemplates that "unreasonable" risks will be regulated. In interpreting this statutory language, courts often refer to the reasonableness standard used in tort law. That is, if the severity of injury multiplied by the probability of injury is greater than the costs of regulation, then an unreasonable risk is presumed to exist. Even under an interpretation of the evidence most favorable to the EPA, the court has doubts as to the need for any regulation. Do you agree with the court's conclusion in this regard? The court often gave dollar values for the cost of lives saved under the EPA regulation. What value was the court placing on the expected benefit of a life saved, and how do you think the court determined the value of a life to begin with? After considering the numerous methodological and procedural errors made by the EPA is it clear that an unreasonable risk exists? Was the EPA simply sloppy in quantifying the riskiness of asbestos? What other incentives might the EPA face which would cause it to make the type of errors discussed by the court?

4. The Least Burdensome Regulation: Once an unreasonable risk has been identified, the TSCA requires that the least burdensome approach to regulation be taken. The EPA provides information regarding the benefits and costs of essentially a complete ban on asbestos. The court's primary concern in this regard is that it does not have information as to whether a complete ban or some other level of regulation provides the largest net benefit. In other words, the court interprets the TSCA as requiring the most bang for the regulatory buck. Can you explain this standard in terms of marginal analysis? Is this an appropriate guide by which risk regulation should be approached?

Note that the court vacates the decision and remands the case back to the EPA for further proceedings. Seeing as the court was clearly skeptical of the EPA's analysis and found many of its conclusions lacking in support, is this the best remedy? What guarantees are there that the EPA will do a more thorough job the second time around? Is the only safeguard that the EPA can again be sued if the future form of this regulation continues to be insufficient?

5. Irrationality and Uncertainty: Empirical studies suggest that many individuals have difficulty conceptualizing probabilities. As a result, individuals tend to overestimate the risks of low probability events and underestimate the risks of high probability events. This result has a variety of implications for risk regulation. First, it suggests that even if market participants were supplied with full information, the optimal level of risk might not prevail. However, in the case of small probabilities such results would suggest the presence of overregulation. Second, to the extent that policy makers are responsive to public perceptions of risk, government regulation will not be optimal. Furthermore, studies suggest that individuals tend to overestimate the risks of events which are frequently reported on the news. Thus, even though the chance of being killed in a car wreck is substantially higher than death from AIDS, public perception often places the relative likelihoods of these two risks much closer together.

Consider an example. Steven Levitt, an economist at the University of Chicago, wrote an article noting that many parents may be hesitant to allow their children to play at the house of a friend whose parents own guns, but that they are rarely concerned with the presence of a pool. This assessment ignores the relative risks of those two factors. Levitt writes that:

> What's more dangerous: a swimming pool or a gun? When it comes to children, there is no comparison: a swimming pool is 100 times more deadly.

> In 1997 alone (the last year for which data are available), 742 children under the age of 10 drowned in the United States last year alone. Approximately 550 of those drownings—about 75 percent of the total—occurred in residential swimming pools. According to the most recent statistics, there are about six million residential pools, meaning that one young child drowns annually for every 11,000 pools.

> About 175 children under the age of 10 died in 1998 as a result of guns. About two-thirds of those deaths were homicides. There are an estimated 200 million guns in the United States. Doing the math, there is roughly one child killed by guns for every one million guns.

> Thus, on average, if you both own a gun and have a swimming pool in the backyard, the swimming pool is about 100 times more likely to kill a child than the gun is.

> Don't get me wrong. My goal is not to promote guns, but rather, to focus parents on an even greater threat to their children. People are well aware of the danger of guns and, by and large, gun owners take the appropriate steps to keep guns away from children. Public attitudes towards pools, however, are much more cavalier because people simply do not know the facts.

Steven D. Levitt, *Pools More Dangerous Than Guns*, Chicago Sun-Times, July 28, 2001.

3. Risk versus Risk

Well-intentioned risk regulations often have the unintended consequence of increasing other types of risk. For example, empirical studies indicate that regulations requiring safety belts in cars changed drivers' attitudes towards speeding. In short, when safely buckled into their cars, many drivers felt that it was less risky to speed. The unintended consequence was to increase the risk to pedestrians and motorcyclists of being hit by a car. Thus, the safety belt regulation, while potentially saving the lives of those driving cars, inadvertently increased the risk to other groups of people being killed.

Perhaps the most basic error made by risk regulators in this regard is to forget that risk outcomes are a function of both the characteristics of the product or service in question and individual behavior. As a consequence, regulators often ignore the predictable rational economic responses of resourceful individuals. Recall the REMM model from Chapter I. Suppose that government regulators believed that requiring child resistant caps on cleaning products would reduce the risk of child poisoning from 1 in 100,000 children to 1 in 200,000 children per year. Before adopting this regulation, however, the agency should engage in **risk tradeoff analysis** (RTA). RTA forces regulators to go through the process of thinking about how reducing one form of risk impacts human behavior and consequently the presence of other types of risk — risk versus risk. For example, the child resistant cap regulation proposed above may have an impact on parents' perceptions of the marginal benefits of precautionary measures that they took to avoid child poisonings prior to the adoption of the regulation. For instance, because of the child safety caps, parents might be less diligent about placing cleaning products on high shelves, and some children might be poisoned because they have easier access to the cleaning products. Thus, the RTA suggests that some portion of the benefits derived from child safety caps might be offset by a reduction in individual care. The difficulty from the regulators' perspective is to quantify these risk tradeoffs in order to determine the net risk impact.

Competitive Enterprise Institute v. NHTSA

United States Court of Appeals for the District of Columbia Circuit
956 F.2d 321 (1992)
and accompanying Notes and Questions
Read *supra*, Chapter II

4. Risk Regulation Priorities

Risk reduction is costly. Every decision to reduce a particular risk therefore entails opportunity costs — the opportunity to reduce some other form of risk. Thus, decisions need to be made regarding which risks will be attacked through regulation. The analysis in preceding subsections suggests several guidelines that should be kept in mind when setting these priorities. First, risk reduction at a point where marginal costs are greater than marginal benefits not only increases risk by reducing the size of the economic pie, but also takes resources away from cost-effective risk reduction efforts. Second, risk-tradeoff analysis suggests that regulations with the largest net reduction in risk per dollar spent should be pursued first. In other words, regulations that save lives at lower costs should take priority over those that save lives at higher costs. An empirical study by Dr. Tammy Tengs suggests that the current regulatory approach ignores these factors:

> Results indicate that we incur opportunity costs of approximately $31.1 billion, 60,200 premature deaths, or 636,000 years of life lost every year in order to maintain our present pattern of investment in these 185 life-saving interventions. At our current level of resource consumption, we could double the survival benefits of our expenditures. Alternatively, we could retain our present level of risk reduction and, in addition, save billions of dollars.

Tammy O. Tengs, *Optimizing Societal Investments in the Prevention of Premature Death*, doctoral dissertation, Harvard School of Public Health 2 (June 1994).

In the context of determining the appropriate priorities for risk regulation, it is important to recognize that regulation does not operate within a vacuum. Specifically, both the market and the legal system have an impact on prevailing safety levels. Thus, the prioritization question should not be limited to the cost effectiveness of different regulations, but rather should include the relative cost effectiveness of all sources of risk reduction. For example, empirical evidence on compensating wage differentials suggests that workers are generally capable of identifying on the job safety hazards, such as working with dangerous machinery. On the other hand, workers have a more difficult time identifying health hazards, such as the carcinogenic risk due to on the job toxins. Despite these facts, OSHA has focused its emphasis primarily on regulating safety hazards.

5. Political Economy of Health and Safety Regulation

Cost-benefit analysis suggests that many risk regulations are too strict, yet government regulators continue to promulgate such regulations. Rather than assuming that the regulators are either ignorant, evil, or both, it might be helpful to consider the political incentives of those responsible for the oversight of the regulatory process. In general, risk regulators' incentives push them to adopt regulations that ignore the efficient determination of optimal risk levels. Three specific sources of these perverse incentives should be noted.

First, the literature on the economics of bureaucracy suggests that bureaucrats are motivated to maximize the size of their budget. In this regard, risk regulators have an incentive to increase the size and budget of their agency by using command and control methods of regulation rather than encourage the most efficient means for risk reduction. Often times, regulators attempt to reduce risk by imposing a particular set of technological requirements on an industry. This provides the regulatory agency with a large degree of control over how risk reduction is achieved. The agency needs a larger budget in order to control activity.

Second, both politicians and regulators tend to be risk averse because negative news impacts their personal interest more than positive news. Consider the case of a new drug that is expected to save 1,000 lives within its first year. Unfortunately, 100 individuals are expected to die because of adverse side effects. Politicians and bureaucrats reasonably expect that the 100 killed will be bigger news than the 1,000 saved. When budgets and re-election are a function of political popularity, very few individuals will want to be known as the regulator or politician who allowed a new drug to go on the market that killed 100 people. Understandably, bureaucrats and politicians have an incentive to seek higher than optimal levels of risk reduction in order to maintain their jobs or their political status. Furthermore, to the extent that politicians respond to voter preferences and voters overestimate the risk of low probability events and underestimate the risk of higher probability events, an inefficient level of risk regulation is likely to result.

Finally, risk regulators and politicians often ignore the costs that they impose on others. The cost-benefit analysis of risk regulations clearly indicates that many areas are being regulated too intensively. More intelligent priority setting—that is, reallocation of risk reducing resources from one area to another—seems to be called for. However, it's important to recognize that the cost-benefit analysis compares the private cost of one industry with the benefits to society. If a particular industry is granted regulatory relief, the money saved by that industry is not available to regulators to use more wisely in regulating other industries—the savings belong to the first industry. Thus, regulators have little to gain by reducing regulation to the optimal level.

Chapter VII

The Economics of Crime and Punishment

A. The Economics of Criminal Behavior

Beginning with the work of economist and Nobel laureate Gary Becker in 1968, economists have invaded the field of criminology, using their all-embracing model of individual rational behavior. Assuming that individual preferences are constant, the model can be used to predict how changes in the probability and severity of sanctions and in various socio-economic factors may affect the amount of crime. Even if individuals who violate certain laws differ systematically from those who abide by the same laws, the former, like the latter, do respond to incentives (i.e., to sanctions and economic conditions). Indeed, numerous empirical studies confirm the predictions of the economic theory.

This chapter summarizes the literature on the economic analysis of the criminal law. First, it discusses the positive theory of criminal behavior and reviews the empirical evidence in support of the theory. Then, it explains the normative theory of how public law enforcement should be designed to minimize the social costs of crime. Finally, it reviews recent trends in crime rates and the explanations for the dramatic decrease in crime over the last few decades.

1. The Rational Choice Model

Although the economic theory of criminal behavior had its modern genesis in the work of Gary Becker, several of Becker's ideas were foreshadowed by earlier writers — Cesare Beccaria in 1767 and Jeremy Bentham in 1789. These early scholars, though not economists, developed several concepts that would later be associated with the economic theory of criminal behavior: "the profit of the crime is the force which urges man to delinquency: the pain of the punishment is the force employed to restrain him from it. If the first of these forces be the greater, the crime will be committed; if the second, the crime will not be committed." Jeremy Bentham, An Introduction to the Principles of Morals and Legislation (1907 [1789], p. 399).

However, from the beginning of the 20th century interest in their point of view dwindled as a plethora of other theories were developed. Fortunately, the main idea of Bentham was revitalized and modernized in Becker's path-breaking article, "Crime and Punishment," where he suggests that "a useful theory of criminal behavior can dispense with special theories of anomie, psychological inadequacies, or inheritance of special traits and simply extend the economist's usual analysis of choice." Gary Becker, *Crime and Punishment: An Economic Approach*, 76 Journal of Political Economy 169, 170 (1968). In Becker's model, a criminal act is preferred and chosen if the expected benefits from committing a crime exceed the expected costs, including the costs of any foregone legal alternatives. The economic theory of crime is regarded as a special case of the general theory of rational behavior under uncertainty.

Crime and Punishment: An Economic Approach

Gary Becker

76 The Journal of Political Economy 169, 176–177 (1968)

* * *

1. The Supply of Offenses

Theories about the determinants of the number of offenses differ greatly, from emphasis on skull types and biological inheritance to family up-bringing and disenchantment with society. Practically all the diverse theories agree, however, that when other variables are held constant, an increase in a person's probability of conviction or punishment if convicted would generally decrease, perhaps substantially, perhaps negligibly, the number of offenses he commits. In addition, a common generalization by persons with judicial experience is that a change in the probability has a greater effect on the number of offenses than a change in the punishment, although, as far as I can tell, none of the prominent theories shed any light on this relation.

The approach taken here follows the economists' usual analysis of choice and assumes that a person commits an offense if the expected utility to him exceeds the utility he could get by using his time and other resources at other activities. Some persons become "criminals," therefore, not because their basic motivation differs from that of other persons, but because their benefits and costs differ. I cannot pause to discuss the many general implications of this approach, except to remark that criminal behavior becomes part of a much more general theory and does not require ad hoc concepts of differential association, anomie, and the like, nor does it assume perfect knowledge, lightening-fast calculation, or any of the other caricatures of economic theory.

This approach implies that there is a function relating the number of offenses by any person to his probability of conviction, to his punishment if convicted, and to other variables, such as the income available to him in legal and other illegal activities, the frequency of nuisance arrests, and his willingness to commit an illegal act.

* * *

2. The Benefits and Costs from Crime

Thus, the economic model of criminal behavior assumes that the decision to commit a crime is the result of a cost-benefit analysis that individuals undertake either consciously or subconsciously. The gains and losses included in the economic model are usually meant to represent all kinds of benefits and costs that have an effect on the people's decisions. People are assumed to allocate time to criminal activity until marginal benefits equal marginal costs. For some people marginal benefits of crime are probably always lower than marginal costs of crime; the economic model would predict that these people will never commit crimes. For others, the marginal benefits often exceed the marginal costs;

we would expect these people to specialize in crime. For most of us, the marginal costs usually exceed the marginal benefits. However, every once in a while the marginal costs seem particularly low or the marginal benefits seem particularly high, and we commit a crime. For example, we may be driving on a stretch of country road where police seem unlikely (low marginal cost of speeding) or we are driving a Ferrari (high marginal benefit of speeding) so we decide to speed.

The kinds of gains obtained from a criminal act vary, depending on the type of crime and the individual criminal. Some are monetary, such as the gains obtained from theft, robbery, insurance fraud, killing a rival drug dealer, etc. Others are psychic, such as the thrill of danger, peer approval, retribution, sense of accomplishment, or "pure" satisfaction of wants (rape). Obviously, the psychic benefits from crime will be different for different people: young men tend to enjoy the thrill of danger more than older women and gang members tend to get more peer approval than church-goers when they commit a crime. Incarcerated criminals may also gain human capital in committing future crimes if they learn techniques from other criminals or meet future potential crime partners while imprisoned.

The costs of crime also depend on the crime and individual. The costs can include direct material costs, psychic costs, opportunity costs, and expected punishment costs. The material costs include the cost of supplies purchased to commit crimes (equipment, guns, vehicles, face masks). Psychic costs include any guilt, anxiety, fear, dislike of risk, or other emotions associated with committing crime. The opportunity cost of crime consists of the net benefit of the legal activity forgone while planning, performing and concealing the criminal act. The lower an individual's level of income, the lower is his or her opportunity cost of engaging in illegal activity. The amount a person can earn in the legal sector may depend on factors such as age, sex, race, education, training, region, rate of unemployment, and IQ. People that are only able to earn a low wage will have a low opportunity cost of crime, as they are not giving up substantial legal income.

The expected punishment costs include the cost of all formal and informal sanctions, as well as the pecuniary costs arising from litigation (lost income and lawyers' fees). When the formal sanction is a fine, the punishment cost is the amount of the fine. When the formal sanction is a prison term, the punishment cost incorporates the cost to the criminal of going to prison: the lost income, the monetary equivalent of the loss of liberty, the monetary equivalent of whatever harms come to the individual while in prison, etc. The costs of the informal sanctions result from the social stigma that accompanies arrest, conviction, and imprisonment. These sanctions can include the reactions of employers, family, and friends and the reduced legitimate income a criminal will earn once he has a criminal record. These expected punishment costs must be weighted by the probability that the individual will be arrested, convicted, and imprisoned. An individual facing a 50 percent chance of receiving a 10-year prison sentence has higher expected punishment costs that an individual facing a 5 percent chance of the same prison sentence. The probability of punishment will be different for different people. Some are cleverer than others at concealing the offense and eluding the police. There are also differences in the abilities of defending oneself in court, or in engaging good lawyers. Morriss Hoffman, Paul H. Rubin, and Joanna Shepherd, *An Empirical Study of Public Defender Effectiveness: Self-Selection by the 'Marginally Indigent,'* 3 Ohio State Journal of Criminal Law 223 (2005). To estimate the expected penalty that a particular individual faces, we multiply all costs of punishment by the probability of receiving those punishments.

a. The Stigma of Criminal Activity

The stigma from criminal activity can be social (inability to find a spouse) or economic (inability to find a job with a criminal record). Several scholars have attempted to measure the economic stigma. Lott finds a short-run income reduction of 39 percent after a bank embezzlement conviction and a 41 percent reduction after a bank larceny conviction. John Lott, *Do We Punish High-Income Criminals Too Heavily?*, 30 Economic Inquiry 583 (1992). Grogger finds that an arrest record can explain about two-thirds of the black-white youth employment differential in his sample. Jeffrey Grogger, *Arrests, Persistent Youth Joblessness, and Black-White Employment Differentials*, 74 Review of Economics and Statistics 100 (1992). However, in another study, he finds only a short-lived effect of arrest records on youth earnings. Jeffrey Grogger, *The Effect of Arrest on the Employment and Earnings of Young Men*, 90 Quarterly Journal of Economics 51 (1995). Is it possible for the stigma from criminal activity to be negative? That is, in what circumstances might a criminal history improve earning potential?

b. The Criminal's Discount Rate

The rate at which individuals discount the future also affects the expected benefits and costs from criminal activity. The gains from crime often occur immediately, whereas punishment is something that might come in the future, and be stretched over a long period of time. An individual with a high discount rate will therefore tend to commit more crime because he weighs the present (and the gains from criminal activity) much more heavily than the future (and the potential costs from criminal activity). How will an individual's risk preferences affect the expected benefits and costs of criminal activity?

c. The Economic Theory of Recidivism

Recidivism, or repeat criminal behavior, is sometimes explained by erratic behavior, a lack of self-control, or evidence that the deterrence model doesn't work. However, a high rate of recidivism is consistent with the model of rational choice. Serving time in jail may reduce legal opportunities so that the opportunity cost of future criminal activity is lower. Additionally, convicts may acquire human capital in illegal activities—prison is an excellent place to "network" with other criminals and learn the skills of the trade. Thus, if it was rational to commit a crime in the first place, for many criminals the incentives will only be stronger after having served a prison sentence.

In contrast, a prior conviction or imprisonment might increase some criminals' evaluations of how probable or severe sanctions might be. For these criminals, the expected costs of additional crime may be higher than the expected costs accompanying their initial crime and they will tend not to recidivate.

d. Economics versus Criminology

How does the economic approach to criminal activity differ from the criminology approach? The criminological literature is essentially composed of three branches. One branch focuses on the biological factors contributing to crime, such as brain abnormalities or hormonal imbalances. The economic approach doesn't deny that biological factors matter, it just assumes that these factors explain the baseline level of crime that exists regardless of the incentives created by other costs and benefits of criminal activity. The second branch of the criminological literature asserts that people turn to crime when they are prevented from reaching their goals through legal means. This assertion is consistent with the economic model that predicts that people with limited legal opportunities may turn to crime. However, the economic approach, in contrast to the criminological approach, predicts that individuals weigh the relative costs and benefits of crime and legal activities, and only engage in crime if it is relatively more attractive. The third branch of the criminological literature is concerned with the social interactions through which criminal behavior is learned or culturally transmitted. This approach is also consistent with the economic model that maintains that community influences and cultural factors can influence various costs and benefits of crime: an individual committing a crime may feel less of a stigma (a cost of crime) or even gain approval (a benefit) depending on how others in his social circle view criminal activity; an individual may feel more or less internal guilt (a cost) depending on their religion or community; individuals may learn smarter criminal tactics when they associate with other criminals. Thus, the economic model of crime, for the most part, encompasses many of the criminological explanations for crime. The difference between the two approaches is mainly one of emphasis. For further reading, see Steven D. Levitt & Thomas J. Miles, *Empirical Study of Criminal Punishment*, in Handbook of Law and Economics 455 (A. Mitchell Polinsky & Steven Shavell eds., 2007)

e. Are Criminals Really Rational?

The economic approach posits that everyone (except, perhaps, individuals with severe mental disabilities) responds, to some degree, to changes in the expected costs and benefits of criminal activity. Several authors have discussed whether people have sufficient information about the environment and about outcomes of actions to make rational choices. Becker and others maintain that even if choices are based on subjective beliefs that are wrong, the choices are meaningful from a subjective point of view, and behavior can be explained and understood on this basis. Moreover, even if people are not exactly accurate in their estimation of the expected benefits or costs of criminal activity, an obvious increase in an expected cost of crime or decrease in an expected benefit of crime should still influence (albeit imperfectly) the incentives to commit crime.

As Economy Dips, Arrests for Shoplifting Soar

Ian Urbina and Sean D. Hamill
New York Times (December 22, 2008)

* * *

As the economy has weakened, shoplifting has increased, and retail security experts say the problem has grown worse this holiday season. Shoplifters are taking everything from compact discs and baby formula to gift cards and designer clothing.

Police departments across the country say that shoplifting arrests are 10 percent to 20 percent higher this year than last. The problem is probably even greater than arrest records indicate since shoplifters are often banned from stores rather than arrested.

Much of the increase has come from first-time offenders ... making rash decisions in a pinch, the authorities say. But the ease with which stolen goods can be sold on the Internet has meant a bigger role for organized crime rings, which also engage in receipt fraud, fake price tagging and gift card schemes, the police and security experts say.

And as temptation has grown for potential thieves, so too has stores' vulnerability.

"More people are desperate economically, retailers are operating with leaner staffs and police forces are cutting back or being told to deprioritize shoplifting calls," said Paul Jones, the vice president of asset protection for the Retail Industry Leaders Association.

* * *

Compounding the problem, stores are more reluctant to stop suspicious customers because they fear scaring away much-needed business. And retailers are increasingly trying to save money by hiring seasonal workers who, security experts say, are themselves more likely to commit fraud or theft and are less practiced at catching shoplifters than full-time employees are.

More than $35 million in merchandise is stolen each day nationwide, and about one in 11 people in America have shoplifted, according to the nonprofit National Association for Shoplifting Prevention.

"We used to see more repeat offenders doing it because of drug addiction," said Samyah Jubran, an assistant district attorney in Knoxville who for 13 years has handled the bulk of the shoplifting cases there. "But many of these new offenders may be doing it because of the economic situation. Maybe they're hurting at home, and they're taking a risk they may not take otherwise."

Much of the stolen merchandise is sold online.

* * *

Security experts say retail theft is also being facilitated by Web sites that sell fake receipts that thieves can use to obtain cash refunds for stolen merchandise.

* * *

Local law enforcement and retailers have been trying new tactics to battle shoplifting and other forms of retail crime.

In Savannah, Ga., a local convenience store chain has linked its video surveillance to a police station so officers can help monitor the store for shoplifting and other crimes. In Louisiana, the police have been requiring shoplifters, even first-time offenders, to post $1,000 bail or stay in jail until their court date. On Staten Island, malls have started posting the mug shots of repeat shoplifters on video screens.

* * *

Shoplifters also seem to be getting bolder, according to industry surveys.

Thieves often put stolen items in bags lined with aluminum foil to avoid detection by the storefront alarms. Others work in teams, with a decoy who tries to look suspicious to draw out undercover security agents and attract the attention of security cameras, the police said.

"We're definitely seeing more sprinters," said an undercover security guard at Macy's near Oakland, Calif., referring to shoplifters who make a run for the door.

The guard said that most large department stores instructed guards not to chase shoplifters more than 100 feet outside the store, because research showed that confrontations tended to become more serious beyond that point.

The holidays are a particularly popular time for pilfering.

About 20 percent of annual retail sales occur in November and December, and even with precautions, the increased customer traffic makes it tougher to track thieves. Moreover, cashiers are rushed by long lines, making them less vigilant about checking for stolen credit cards.

Mr. [Richard R.] Johnson, who was arrested last month, said that after being laid off from his $20-an-hour job at a trailer factory a year ago, he took a job for $6.55 an hour at McDonald's. Six months later, he was laid off and has not been able to find a job since.

He and his two small children rely on his wife's minimum-wage job at Wal-Mart, groceries from a food bank and help from his mother, he said.

"I just know things are going to get a lot rougher," said Mr. Johnson, who is awaiting trial. He added that no matter how tough it became, he had no intention of shoplifting again.

Mr. Johnson said he was shocked that the store had decided to prosecute him for stealing such a small amount [a $4.99 bottle of sleep medication]. A manager at Martin's Supermarket said the store had a policy of prosecuting all shoplifting.

Retail security experts, however, say that people like Mr. Johnson do not pose the biggest threat to stores. People like Tommy Joe Tidwell do.

Mr. Tidwell, 35, pleaded guilty last month to running a shoplifting ring out of Dayton, Ohio, that netted more than $1 million, according to court papers.

After Mr. Tidwell would print fraudulent UPC bar code labels on his home computer, he and several conspirators would place them on items at Wal-Mart and other stores, then buy the merchandise for a fraction of the real price. They would resell the goods on the Internet, according to court papers.

Joe LaRocca, vice president of loss prevention for the National Retail Federation, said that as the holidays approached, retail security workers were keeping a close eye on receipt fraud.

But to entice shoppers, three times as many stores as last year have loosened their return policies, extending the return period and being more lenient with shoppers who lack receipts, according to the federation.

"Retailers are trying to find a balance," Mr. LaRocca said. "They want to provide good customer service at a time when it's crucial for customers to be able to shop comfortably or to return unwanted or duplicate gifts.

"But they also want to prevent criminals from taking advantage of them."

Notes and Questions

1. Costs and Benefits: In the article, what are the various expected costs and benefits that are affecting incentives to commit crime?

2. A Numerical Example: Two robbers, Jeff and Steve, are contemplating committing separate armed robberies. Jeff and Steve both believe that there is a 75% chance that they will be able to steal $400,000 if they rob the stores. However, to commit the robbery, each will have to buy a $100 gun. Jeff believes that the probability he will be caught and convicted is 10%. If Jeff is caught and convicted, he will serve 4 years in prison. During that 4 years, he will miss out on earning $400,000 in legitimate income and he will miss being with his friends and family which is worth $1,600,000 to him. Moreover, a first-time criminal conviction will reduce Jeff's future earning potential after he gets out of prison. The present value of the decrease in his future earnings is $1,000,000. Because Steve has a known history of armed robbery, he believes that the probability that he will be caught and convicted is 25%. If Steve is caught and convicted, he will serve 10 years in prison (because he is a repeat offender). During that 10 years, he will miss out on earning $400,000 in legitimate income and he will miss being with his friends and family which is worth $1,000,000 to him. Since he is a repeat offender, the additional conviction will not worsen his future job prospects. In fact, prison may improve his future job prospects because he will be able to network with other criminals. Steve thinks that he will make more money with his new criminal friends after the 10 years in prison than he would have made if he hadn't gone to prison. The present value of the additional income is $300,000. Who will rob the store?

B. Empirical Studies of the Economic Model of Crime

Predictions from the economic model of crime have been tested in a great number of empirical studies. However, these empirical studies face several challenges. First, although the economic model of crime is based on individual rational choice, the data available to empirical researchers is based on levels of aggregation ranging from countries and states down to municipalities and campuses. Thus, the empirical results can tell us only about general deterrence — the effects on people in general — rather than the effects on an individual's decision making.

Second, it is extremely difficult to identify causal relationships in empirical studies of crime. For example, in testing the relationship between imprisonment and crime, one may find a positive relationship (imprisonment and crime increase together or decrease together). Based on these results, some scholars may conclude that prison increases crime, when in fact, the positive relationship may be attributable to higher crime rates producing more potential prisoners.

Controlling for the factors that lead to high crime could solve the problem, but it is impossible to quantify and control for every factor, so omitted variable bias can be a problem. More recent empirical studies have devised clever ways to tease out causal relationships, for example by taking advantage of exogenous changes in imprisonment levels, such as court-ordered prison releases, that could not be caused by crime. Steven D. Levitt, *The Effect of Prison Population Size on Crime Rates: Evidence from Prison Overcrowding Litigation*, 111 Quarterly Journal of Economics 319 (1996).

The third challenge is the difficulty in distinguishing incapacitation and deterrence. The economic model of crime assumes that increases in imprisonment increase the expected costs of crime and deter some individuals from committing crimes. However, an empirical finding that increases in imprisonment are associated with decreases in crime might not be evidence of deterrence. Crime could also decrease because more criminals are behind bars due to the increased imprisonment. Although the end result is the same, the rational choice model assumes that individuals can be deterred from committing crime. Thus, if the entire decrease in crime was caused by incapacitating criminals, this would not confirm the predictions of the economic model of crime.

There are various other challenges that involve the correct variables to control for in empirical analyses, the particular methodology to employ, and other sophisticated empirical questions. Nevertheless, the awareness of the methodological problems and easier access to various statistical methods has gradually led to more sophisticated empirical studies that address several of these challenges.

Cognizant of these empirical challenges, law and economics scholars have studied the relationship between crime and various costs and benefits of criminal activity. Summarizing the entire empirical literature, which consists of thousands of articles, is beyond the scope of this chapter, but below we discuss the general consensus or important articles studying the effects of different variables.

1. Police

The majority of empirical studies find that policing levels have a large negative relationship with crime—i.e., more police mean less crime. *See, e.g.*, Rafael Di Tella & Ernesto Schargrodsky, *Do Police Reduce Crime? Estimates Using the Allocation of Police Forces After a Terrorist Attack*, 94 American Economic Review 115 (2004); Hope Corman & Naci Mocan, *A Time-Series Analysis of Crime and Drug Use in New York City*, 90 American Economic Review 584 (2000); Steven D Levitt, *Using Electoral Cycles in Police Hiring to Estimate the Effect of Police on Crime*, 87 American Economic Review 270 (1997).

2. Imprisonment

Most studies find that imprisonment also has a negative effect on crime rates. Some of this effect is due to deterrence and some is due to incapacitation. *See, e.g.*, Steven D. Levitt, *Why Do Increased Arrest Rates Appear to Reduce Crime: Deterrence, Incapacitation, or Measurement Error?*, 36 Economic Inquiry 353 (1998); Daniel Kessler & Steven D. Levitt, *Using Sentence Enhancements to Distinguish Between Deterrence and Incapacitation*, 42 Journal of Law and Economics 343 (1999). Severe prison conditions also have a deterrent effect. Lawrence Katz, et al., *Prison Conditions, Capital Punishment, and Deterrence*, 5 American Law and Economics Review 318 (2003).

3. Capital Punishment

The effect of capital punishment continues to be hotly debated. The majority of empirical papers find a deterrent effect of capital punishment. *See, e.g.*, Hashem Dezhbakhsh & Paul Rubin, *From the 'Econometrics of Capital Punishment' to the 'Capital Punishment' of Econometrics: On the Use and Abuse of Sensitivity Analysis*, 43 Applied Economics 3655 (2011); Hashem Dezhbakhsh, et al., *Does Capital Punishment Have a Deterrent Effect? New Evidence from Postmoratorium Panel Data*, 5 American Law and Economics Review 344 (2003); Naci H. Mocan & R. Kaj Gittings, *Getting Off Death Row: Commuted Sentences and the Deterrent Effect of Capital Punishment*, 46 Journal of Law and Economics 453 (2003). Some studies have found that the deterrent effect exists only in some states. Joanna Shepherd, *Deterrence versus Brutalization: Capital Punishment's Differing Impacts Among States*, 104 Michigan Law Review 203 (2005). Others argue that the deterrence finding is extremely sensitive to methodological choices in the empirical analysis. John J. Donohue III & Justin Wolfers, *Uses and Abuses of Empirical Evidence in the Death Penalty Debate*, 58 Stanford Law Review 791 (2006).

There is a tendency to conflate findings regarding capital punishment with general issues of deterrence. In the contemporary U.S. capital punishment is rare and unpredictable. It could be that the rarity of this punishment reduces or even eliminates any deterrent effect. It is also possible that its rarity means that statistical methods are unable to detect a deterrent effect even if one exists. Nonetheless, even if we cannot detect a deterrent effect of capital punishment, this does not mean that more normal punishments such as jail time do not deter.

4. Gun Laws

The effect of gun laws on crime is also hotly debated. Some studies have found evidence that laws allowing citizens to carry concealed handguns decrease crime; presumably the possibility of encountering a victim with a gun deters potential criminals from committing crime in the first place. John R. Lott Jr., More Guns, Less Crime (2010); John R. Lott Jr. & David B. Mustard, Crime, *Deterrence, and Right-to-Carry Concealed Handguns*, 26 Journal of Legal Studies 1 (1997). In contrast, other studies find that gun laws do not decrease crime. Ian Ayres, & John J. Donohue III, *Shooting Down the "More Guns, Less Crime" Hypothesis*, 55 Stanford Law Review 1193 (2003); Hashem Dezhbakhsh & Paul H. Rubin, *Lives Saved or Lives Lost: The Effect of Concealed Handgun Laws on Crime*, 88 American Economic Review 468 (1988).

5. Income

No systematic relationship appears between various measures of income and crime. Indeed, several studies find that high legitimate wages (an opportunity cost of crime) are associated with low crime rates. Stephen Machin & Costas Meghir, *Crime and Economic Incentives*, 39 Journal of Human Resources 958 (2004); C. Cornwell & W. N. Trumbull, *Estimating the Economic Model of Crime with Panel Data*, 76 Review of Economics and Statistics 360 (1994). On the other hand, some studies find that higher pecuniary benefits to crime (a benefit of crime) are associated with increases in crime. Edward L. Glaeser & Bruce Sacerdote, *Why is There More Crime in Cities?*, 107 Journal of Political Economy 225 (1999). This ambiguity in results is likely due to the fact that the income measures used represent benefits not only of legal activities, but also of illegal ones: higher legal incomes tend to make work more attractive than crime, but to the extent that higher legal income in a region produces a greater number of more profitable targets for crime, crime also becomes more attractive. If these mechanisms are at work simultaneously, and their relative strength is not universally constant, it is not surprising that the results of various studies differ.

6. Income Inequality

A large income differential may indicate that crime is a comparatively rewarding activity for the very-low-income group that may find a lot to steal from the very rich. Nevertheless, empirical studies also find no systematic relationship between income inequality and crime. Several studies find that greater income inequality does lead to increases in crime. P. Fajnzylber, D. Lederman, & N. Loayza, *Inequality and Violent Crime*, 45 Journal of Law and Economics 1 (2002). In contrast, others find no statistically significant relationship between income inequality and crime. E. Neumayer, *Inequality and Violent Crime: Evidence from Data on Robbery and Violent Theft*, 42 Journal of Peace Research 101 (2005).

7. Unemployment

Unemployment is a measure of the lack of legal income opportunities; the unemployed have lower opportunity costs of crime as they are not giving up legitimate employment. The majority of studies find that higher rates of unemployment correlate with higher levels of crime. E. Gould, B. Weinberg & D. Mustard, *Crime Rates and Local Labor Market Opportunities in the United States: 1979–1995*, 84 Review of Economics and Statistics 45 (2002); S. Raphael & R. Winter-Ebmer, *Identifying the Effect of Unemployment on Crime*, 44 Journal of Law and Economics 259 (2001). For a review of studies, see R.B. Freeman, *The Labor Market*, in Crime 171 (J. Q. Wilson and J. Petersilia, eds; 1995).

Notes and Questions

1. Explaining the Statistics: Use the economic model of crime to explain the statistical relationships we see between crime and other variables: for example, education or various demographic variables such as age, gender, and race.

2. Private Enforcement: Should the state encourage ex ante observable precautions (bars on windows, alarm system signs, barking dogs) or non-ex ante observable precautions (better door locks, video cameras, booby traps, guns)?

3. It's the Law: In Kennesaw, GA, there is an ordinance requiring all homeowners to keep a gun in their home. How might this fact increase your security? How might this fact decrease your security?

C. The Economics of Law Enforcement

The economic theory of public law enforcement is based on a specific perception of justice as efficiency. Under this perception, the purpose of public law enforcement is to maximize social welfare, where social welfare is the benefits that individuals obtain from crime minus the costs of committing crime, the costs of harm to victims, and the costs of enforcement. The government can maximize the social welfare function through three policy instruments: the probability of capture and punishment, the length of prison terms, and the level of fines. In setting these policy instruments at their ideal levels, the economic model assumes that criminals behave rationally and weigh the costs and benefits of criminal activity before turning to crime.

Deterrence is the goal in the traditional economic model of public law enforcement. The optimal amount of deterrence occurs at the point where the marginal social cost of additional deterrence equals the marginal social benefit. Thus, under the traditional definition, efficient deterrence balances the marginal costs of enforcement and the reduction in illegal gains to criminals against the marginal benefit of enforcement, which is the reduction in harm that results from enforcement. Thus, deterrence is inefficient if the marginal gains to criminals plus marginal enforcement costs exceed the marginal harm to victims.

However, many researchers have questioned whether the gains to criminals should be considered. See, e.g. George J. Stigler, *The Optimum Enforcement of Laws*, 78 Journal of Political Economy 526 (1970); Steven Shavell, *Criminal Law and the Optimal Use of Non-monetary Sanctions as a Deterrent*, 85 Columbia Law Review 1232 (1985). If we ignored these gains, optimal deterrence would occur at the point where the marginal enforcement costs equal the marginal enforcement benefits (which is the marginal harm to victims). With fewer costs of deterrence to consider (i.e., ignoring the reduction in criminal gains that results from deterrence), the optimal level of deterrence increases.

United States v. United States Gypsum Co.

Supreme Court of the United States
438 U.S. 422 (1978)

MR. CHIEF JUSTICE BURGER delivered the opinion of the Court.

* * *

This case presents the following questions: (a) whether intent is an element of a criminal antitrust offense....

* * *

I

Gypsum board, a laminated type of wallboard composed of paper, vinyl, or other specially treated coverings over a gypsum core, has in the last 30 years substantially replaced wet plaster as the primary component of interior walls and ceilings in residential and commercial construction. The product is essentially fungible; differences in price, credit terms, and delivery services largely dictate the purchasers' choice between competing suppliers. Overall demand, however, is governed by the level of construction activity, and is only marginally affected by price fluctuations.

The gypsum board industry is highly concentrated, with the number of producers ranging from 9 to 15 in the period 1960–1973. The eight largest companies accounted for some 94% of the national sales, with the seven "single-plant producers" accounting for the remaining 6%. Most of the major producers and a large number of the single-plant producers are members of the Gypsum Association, which, since 1930, has served as a trade association of gypsum board manufacturers.

* * *

Beginning in 1966, the Justice Department, as well as the Federal Trade Commission, became involved in investigations into possible antitrust violations in the gypsum board industry. In 1971, a grand jury was empaneled and the investigation continued for an additional 28 months. In late 1973, an indictment was filed in the United States District Court for the Western District of Pennsylvania charging six major manufacturers and various of their corporate officials with violations of § 1 of the Sherman Act, 15 U.S.C. § 1.

The indictment charged that the defendants had engaged in a combination and conspiracy "[b]eginning sometime prior to 1960 and continuing thereafter at least until sometime in 1973," in restraint of interstate trade and commerce in the manufacture and sale of gypsum board. The alleged combination and conspiracy consisted of:

> "[A] continuing agreement understanding and concert of action among the defendants and coconspirators to (a) raise, fix, maintain and stabilize the prices of gypsum board; (b) fix, maintain and stabilize the terms and conditions of sale thereof; and (c) adopt and maintain uniform methods of packaging and handling such gypsum board."

* * *

The focus of the Government's price-fixing case at trial was interseller price verification — that is, the practice allegedly followed by the gypsum board manufacturers of telephoning a competing producer to determine the price currently being offered on gypsum board to a specific customer. The Government contended that these price exchanges were part of an agreement among the defendants, had the effect of stabilizing prices and policing agreed-upon price increases, and were undertaken on a frequent basis until sometime in 1973.

Defendants disputed both the scope and duration of the verification activities, and further maintained that those exchanges of price information which did occur were for the purposes of complying with the Robinson-Patman Act and preventing customer fraud. These purposes, in defendants' view, brought the disputed communications among competitors within a "controlling circumstance" exception to Sherman Act liability—at the extreme, precluding, as a matter of law, consideration of verification by the jury in determining defendants' guilt on the price-fixing charge, and, at the minimum, making the defendants' purposes in engaging in such communications a threshold factual question.

The instructions on the verification issue given by the trial judge provided that, if the exchanges of price information were deemed by the jury to have been undertaken "in a good faith effort to comply with the Robinson-Patman Act," verification, standing alone, would not be sufficient to establish an illegal price-fixing agreement. The paragraphs immediately following, however, provided that the purpose was essentially irrelevant if the jury found that the effect of verification was to raise, fix, maintain, or stabilize prices. The instructions on verification closed with the observation:

> "The law presumes that a person intends the necessary and natural consequences of his acts. Therefore, if the effect of the exchanges of pricing information was to raise, fix, maintain, and stabilize prices, then the parties to them are presumed, as a matter of law, to have intended that result."

The aspects of the charge dealing with the Government's burden in linking a particular defendant to the conspiracy, and the kinds of evidence the jury could properly consider in determining if one or more of the alleged conspirators had withdrawn from or abandoned the conspiracy were also a subject of some dispute between the judge and defense counsel. On the former, the disagreement was essentially over the proper specificity of the charge. Defendants requested a charge directing the jury to determine "what kind of agreement or understanding, if any, existed as to each defendant" before any could be found to be a member of the conspiracy. The trial judge was unwilling to give this precise instruction, and instead emphasized at several points in the charge the jury's obligation to consider the evidence regarding the involvement of each defendant individually, and to find, as a precondition to liability, that each defendant was a knowing participant in the alleged conspiracy.

* * *

[T]he jury returned guilty verdicts against each of the defendants.

* * *

II

We turn first to consider the jury instructions regarding the elements of the price-fixing offense charged in the indictment. Although the trial judge's instructions on the price-fixing issue are not without ambiguity, it seems reasonably clear that he regarded an effect on prices as the crucial element of the charged offense. The jury was instructed that, if it found interseller verification had the effect of raising, fixing, maintaining, or stabilizing the price of gypsum board, then such verification could be considered as evidence of an agreement to so affect prices. They were further charged, and it is this point which gives rise to our present concern, that, "if the effect of the exchanges of pricing information was to raise, fix, maintain, and stabilize prices, then the parties to them are presumed, as a matter of law, to have intended that result."

The Government characterizes this charge as entirely consistent with "this Court's longstanding rule that an agreement among sellers to exchange information on current offering prices violates Section 1 of the Sherman Act if it has either the purpose or the effect of stabilizing prices."

In this view, the trial court's instructions would not be erroneous, even if interpreted, as they were by the Court of Appeals, to direct the jury to convict if it found that verification had an effect on prices, regardless of the purpose of the respondents. The Court of Appeals rejected the Government's "effects alone" test, holding instead that, in certain limited circumstances, a purpose of complying with the Robinson-Patman Act would constitute a controlling circumstance excusing Sherman Act liability, and hence an instruction allowing the jury to ignore purpose could not be sustained.

We agree with the Court of Appeals that an effect on prices, without more, will not support a criminal conviction under the Sherman Act, but we do not base that conclusion on the existence of any conflict between the requirements of the Robinson-Patman and the Sherman Acts. Rather, we hold that a defendant's state of mind or intent is an element of a criminal antitrust offense which must be established by evidence and inferences drawn therefrom, and cannot be taken from the trier of fact through reliance on a legal presumption of wrongful intent from proof of an effect on prices. Since the challenged instruction, as we read it, had this prohibited effect, it is disapproved. We are unwilling to construe the Sherman Act as mandating a regime of strict liability criminal offenses.

A

We start with the familiar proposition that "[t]he existence of a mens rea is the rule of, rather than the exception to, the principles of Anglo-American criminal jurisprudence." In a much-cited passage in Morissette v. United States, Mr. Justice Jackson, speaking for the Court, observed:

> "The contention that an injury can amount to a crime only when inflicted by intention is no provincial or transient notion. It is as universal and persistent in mature systems of law as belief in freedom of the human will and a consequent ability and duty of the normal individual to choose between good and evil. A relation between some mental element and punishment for a harmful act is almost as instinctive as the child's familiar exculpatory 'But I didn't mean to,' and has afforded the rational basis for a tardy and unfinished substitution of deterrence and reformation in place of retaliation and vengeance as the motivation for public prosecution. Unqualified acceptance of this doctrine by English common law in the Eighteenth Century was indicated by Blackstone's sweeping statement that, to constitute any crime, there must first be a 'vicious will.'"

Although Blackstone's requisite "vicious will" has been replaced by more sophisticated and less colorful characterizations of the mental state required to support criminality, intent generally remains an indispensable element of a criminal offense. This is as true in a sophisticated criminal antitrust case as in one involving any other criminal offense.

This Court, in keeping with the common law tradition and with the general injunction that "ambiguity concerning the ambit of criminal statutes should be resolved in favor of lenity," has on a number of occasions read a state-of-mind component into an offense even when the statutory definition did not in terms so provide. Indeed, the holding in Morissette can be fairly read as establishing, at least with regard to crimes having their origin in the common law, an interpretative presumption that mens rea is required. "[M]ere omission … of intent [in the statute] will not be construed as eliminating that element from the crimes denounced"; instead Congress will be presumed to have legislated against the background of our traditional legal concepts which render intent a critical factor, and "absence of contrary direction [will] be taken as satisfaction with widely accepted definitions, not as a departure from them."

While strict liability offenses are not unknown to the criminal law, and do not invariably offend constitutional requirements, the limited circumstances in which Congress has created and this Court has recognized such offenses, attest to their generally disfavored status. Certainly far more than the simple omission of the appropriate phrase from the statutory definition is necessary to justify dispensing with an intent requirement. In the context of the Sherman Act, this generally inhospitable attitude to non-mens rea offenses is reinforced by an array of considerations arguing against treating antitrust violations as strict liability crimes.

B

The Sherman Act, unlike most traditional criminal statutes, does not, in clear and categorical terms, precisely identify the conduct which it proscribes. Both civil remedies and criminal sanctions are authorized with regard to the same generalized definitions of the conduct proscribed—restraints of trade or commerce and illegal monopolization—without reference to or mention of intent or state of mind. Nor has judicial elaboration of the Act always yielded the clear and definitive rules of conduct which the statute omits; instead open-ended and fact-specific standards like the "rule of reason" have been applied to broad classes of conduct falling within the purview of the Act's general provisions. Simply put, the Act has not been interpreted as if it were primarily a criminal statute; it has been construed to have a "generality and adaptability comparable to that found to be desirable in constitutional provisions."

Although, in Nash v. United States, the Court held that the indeterminacy of the Sherman Act's standards did not constitute a fatal constitutional objection to their criminal enforcement, nevertheless, this factor has been deemed particularly relevant by those charged with enforcing the Act in accommodating its criminal and remedial sanctions. The 1955 Report of the Attorney General's National Committee to Study the Antitrust Laws concluded that the criminal provisions of the Act should be reserved for those circumstances where the law was relatively clear and the conduct egregious:

> "The Sherman Act, inevitably perhaps, is couched in language broad and general. Modern business patterns, moreover, are so complex that market effects of proposed conduct are only imprecisely predictable. Thus, it may be difficult for today's businessman to tell in advance whether projected actions will run afoul of the Sherman Act's criminal strictures. With this hazard in mind, we believe that criminal process should be used only where the law is clear and the facts reveal a flagrant offense and plain intent unreasonably to restrain trade."

The Antitrust Division of the Justice Department took a similar, though slightly more moderate, position in its enforcement guidelines issued contemporaneously with the 1955 Report of the Attorney General's Committee:

> "In general, the following types of offenses are prosecuted criminally: (1) price-fixing; (2) other violations of the Sherman Act where there is proof of a specific intent to restrain trade or to monopolize; (3) a less easily defined category of cases which might generally be described as involving proof of use of predatory practices (boycotts for example) to accomplish the objective of the combination or conspiracy; (4) the fact that a defendant has previously been convicted of or adjudged to have been, violating the antitrust laws may warrant indictment for

a second offense.... The Division feels free to seek an indictment in any case where a prospective defendant has knowledge that practices similar to those in which he is engaging have been held to be in violation of the Sherman Act in a prior civil suit against other persons."

While not dispositive of the question now before us, the recommendations of the Attorney General's Committee and the guidelines promulgated by the Justice Department highlight the same basic concerns which are manifested in our general requirement of mens rea in criminal statutes and suggest that these concerns are at least equally salient in the antitrust context.

Close attention to the type of conduct regulated by the Sherman Act buttresses this conclusion. With certain exceptions for conduct regarded as per se illegal because of its unquestionably anticompetitive effects, the behavior proscribed by the Act is often difficult to distinguish from the gray zone of socially acceptable and economically justifiable business conduct. Indeed, the type of conduct charged in the indictment in this case—the exchange of price information among competitors—is illustrative in this regard. The imposition of criminal liability on a corporate official, or for that matter on a corporation directly, for engaging in such conduct which only after the fact is determined to violate the statute because of anticompetitive effects, without inquiring into the intent with which it was undertaken, holds out the distinct possibility of overdeterrence; salutary and procompetitive conduct lying close to the borderline of impermissible conduct might be shunned by businessmen who chose to be excessively cautious in the face of uncertainty regarding possible exposure to criminal punishment for even a good faith error of judgment. Further, the use of criminal sanctions in such circumstances would be difficult to square with the generally accepted functions of the criminal law. The criminal sanctions would be used not to punish conscious and calculated wrongdoing at odds with statutory proscriptions, but instead simply to regulate business practices regardless of the intent with which they were undertaken. While, in certain cases, we have imputed a regulatory purpose to Congress in choosing to employ criminal sanctions, the availability of a range of nonpenal alternatives to the criminal sanctions of the Sherman Act negates the imputation of any such purpose to Congress in the instant context.

For these reasons, we conclude that the criminal offenses defined by the Sherman Act should be construed as including intent as an element.

* * *

Notes and Questions

1. Overdeterrence: In *U.S. Gypsum*, the Supreme Court recognizes the possibility of criminal sanctions overdeterring certain behaviors. What type of behavior is the court concerned with overdeterring?

2. Corporate Criminal Liability: The economic model of law enforcement assumes that efficient penalties can achieve optimal deterrence. When the issue is corporate criminal liability, several questions arise. Are criminal penalties even necessary to achieve adequate deterrence or are civil penalties sufficient? Should penalties be imposed on the corporation itself, or on its principals or agents? See, e.g. Vikramaditya S. Khanna, *Corporate Criminal Liability: What Purpose Does it Serve?*, 109 Harvard Law Review 1477 (1996); Jennifer Arlen, *The Potentially Perverse Effects of Corporate Criminal Liability*, 23 Journal of Legal Studies 832 (1994).

3. Efficient murders: Do we want as much crime prevention as possible? Is the efficient number of murders zero?

4. Getting Tough on Crime: Explain why "getting tough" on crime might cause a shift to more dangerous crimes and give examples.

1. Certainty versus Severity

Law enforcement can influence various policy instruments to achieve the optimal level of deterrence: the probability of punishment, the length of prison terms, and the level of fines. The probability of punishment depends on policing levels, arrest rates, conviction rates, imprisonment rates, funding for law enforcement, funding for courts and prosecutors, etc. In the economic model of law enforcement, the probability of punishment is often referred to as the *certainty* of punishment. In contrast, the length of prison terms and level of fines, which law enforcement can also influence, are referred to as the *severity* of punishment.

In deciding to commit a crime, a criminal's expected penalty is the product of the certainty of punishment and the severity of punishment. Table VII-1 shows several combinations of certainty and severity (presented as either a fine or the cost of imprisonment) that produce identical expected penalties (recall the discussion of expected value in Chapter VI).

If potential offenders are risk neutral and have no wealth constraints, all of the combinations of probability and severity should produce identical levels of deterrence. However, more severe sanctions are cheaper for society to implement. Increasing a monetary fine imposes almost no additional collection costs; rather, it generates additional revenue for society. Thus, a low probability/high fine combination will achieve the same deterrence as a high probability/low fine combination, but at much lower cost to society.

In contrast to fines, increasing the severity of imprisonment imposes significant costs on society that include the costs of running a prison (estimates suggest that it costs $40,000 a year to house a prisoner), the productivity costs of removing a criminal from society (assuming he provided some positive benefits to his community), and any psychic or stigma costs the criminal experiences while imprisoned. Despite these significant costs associated with imprisonment, it may still be relatively cheaper to increase the severity of imprisonment than to increase the probability of sanctions. Although the longer prison sentences increase enforcement costs, fewer individuals are imprisoned, which decreases enforcement costs and offsets some of the increase from longer sentences.

Thus, regardless of the form of sanction, in the basic economic model of law enforcement, low certainty/high severity is the optimal combination because it achieves deterrence at the lowest possible cost.

Table VII-1. Combinations of Certainty and Severity with
Identical Expected Penalties; The Risk Neutral Case

Probability of Sanction	Severity of Sanction	Expected Penalty
100%	100	100
50%	200	100
25%	400	100
10%	1000	100

United States v. Gupta

United States District Court for the Southern District of New York
904 F. Supp.2d 349 (2012)

JED S. RAKOFF, District Judge.

The Court is called upon to impose sentence on Rajat K. Gupta, who on June 15, 2012, was found guilty by a jury of one count of conspiracy and three counts of substantive securities fraud, in connection with providing material non-public information to Raj Rajaratnam.

* * *

The heart of Mr. Gupta's offenses here, it bears repeating, is his egregious breach of trust. Mr. Rajaratnam's gain, though a product of that breach, is not even part of the legal theory under which the Government here proceeded, which would have held Gupta guilty even if Rajaratnam had not made a cent. While insider trading may work a huge unfairness on innocent investors, Congress has never treated it as a fraud on investors, the Securities Exchange Commission has explicitly opposed any such legislation, and the Supreme Court has rejected any attempt to extend coverage of the securities fraud laws on such a theory. Prosecution of insider trading therefore proceeds, as in this case, on one or more theories of defrauding the institution (or its shareholders) that owned the information. In the eye of the law, Gupta's crime was to breach his fiduciary duty of confidentiality to Goldman Sachs; or to put it another way, Goldman Sachs, not the marketplace, was the victim of Gupta's crimes as charged.

* * *

In the instant case, however, it is also clear to the Court, both from the jury's split verdict and from the Court's own assessment of the evidence, that the trades in question were those made by Rajaratnam and his Galleon funds on September 23, 2008 and October 24, 2008, directly and immediately as the result of tips from Gupta. In the former case, Gupta, late on the afternoon of September 23, tipped Rajaratnam about Warren Buffett's soon-to-be-announced infusion of $5 billion into Goldman Sachs, whereupon Rajaratnam caused various Galleon funds to purchase large quantities of Goldman stock just before the market closed. When the Buffett investment was announced the following morning, the stock surged, causing Galleon to realize an immediate gain of $1,231,630. In the latter case, Gupta, on October 23, tipped Rajaratnam that Goldman Sachs would soon report third quarter losses, whereas many analysts were predicting a profit. On the next day, Rajaratnam sold 150,000 shares of Goldman. Thereafter, as word began to seep out about Goldman's reduced prospects, the stock began to fall, and when the poor third quarter results were finally made public on December 16, 2008, it fell still further. Based on all the evidence, the Court concludes that it is more likely than not that Rajaratnam, in the absence of Gupta's tip, would not have caused Galleon to sell its valuable Goldman stock until the morning of December 17, 2008. The tip thus enabled Galleon to avoid losses of $3,800,565. Taken together, therefore, the September and October tip-based trades resulted in an illegal "gain" of $5,032,195.

* * *

But when one looks at the nature and circumstances of the offense, the picture darkens considerably. In the Court's view, the evidence at trial established, to a virtual certainty, that Mr. Gupta, well knowing his fiduciary responsibilities to Goldman Sachs, brazenly disclosed material non-public information to Mr. Rajaratnam at the very time, September and October 2008, when our financial institutions were in immense distress and most in need of stability, repose, and trust. Consider, for example, his tip to Rajaratnam on September 23, 2008. With Goldman Sachs in turmoil but on the verge of being rescued from possible ruin by an infusion of $5 billion, Gupta, within minutes of hearing of the transaction, tipped Rajaratnam, so that the latter could trade on this information in the last few minutes before the market closed. This was the functional equivalent of stabbing Goldman in the back.

So why did Mr. Gupta do it? Since motive is not an element of the offenses here in issue, it did not need to be proved at trial, and so one can only speculate. Having finished his spectacular career at McKinsey in 2007, Gupta, for all his charitable endeavors, may have felt frustrated in not finding new business worlds to conquer; and Rajaratnam, a clever cultivator of persons with information, repeatedly held out prospects of exciting new international business opportunities that Rajaratnam would help fund but that Gupta would lead. There is also in some of the information presented to the Court under seal an implicit suggestion that, after so many years of assuming the role of father to all, Gupta may have longed to escape the straightjacket of overwhelming responsibility, and had begun to loosen his self-restraint in ways that clouded his judgment. But whatever was operating in the recesses of his brain, there is no doubt that Gupta, though not immediately profiting from tipping Rajaratnam, viewed it as an avenue to future benefits, opportunities, and even excitement. Thus, by any measure, Gupta's criminal acts represented the very antithesis of the values he had previously embodied.

* * *

As to specific deterrence, it seems obvious that, having suffered such a blow to his reputation, Mr. Gupta is unlikely to repeat his transgressions, and no further punishment is needed to achieve this result. General deterrence, however, suggests a different conclusion. As this Court has repeatedly noted in other cases, insider trading is an easy crime to commit but a difficult crime to catch. Others similarly situated to the defendant must therefore be made to understand that when you get caught, you will go to jail.

* * *

Rajat K. Gupta is therefore sentenced to 24 months' imprisonment, concurrent on all counts, to be followed by one year of supervised release, on the terms stated from the bench and here incorporated by reference. The otherwise mandatory forfeiture has been waived by the Government, but Court imposes a fine in the sum of $5,000,000.

* * *

SO ORDERED.

Notes and Questions

1. Unlikely Detection: In the case, does it make sense for the severity of penalties to be higher because the certainty of punishment is low?

2. Execute the Unlucky: Would the optimal certainty/severity combination be to lower the probability of detection to .001% but execute the convicted?

3. Cheaters: Consider two expected penalties for cheating on exams: (1) cheaters are caught 50 percent chance of the time, and when caught, the cheating student earns an F on the exam or (2) cheaters are caught only 1 percent of the time, but when they are caught, the cheaters are expelled with a permanent mark on their record. Which scenario is closer to reality? Would a low certainty/high severity penalty combination achieve the same deterrence as a high certainty/low severity combination?

4. Certainty and Severity: The majority of empirical studies suggest that the deterrent effect of the certainty of punishment far outweighs the deterrent effect of the severity of punishment. See, e.g., John Donohue, *Assessing the Relative Benefits of Incarceration: The Overall Change Over the Previous Decades and the Benefits on the Margin*, in Do Prisons Make Us Safer? The Benefits and Costs of the Prison Boom (S. Raphael, and M. Stoll eds, 2009). Why might this be the case?

2. Fines versus Imprisonment

Criminal sanctions can be monetary or nonmonetary. As we discussed in the previous section, fines impose little cost on society, and even generate revenue. In contrast, imprisonment imposes substantial enforcement costs on society. Thus, fines are the preferred sanction.

However, a combination of fines and imprisonment is necessary in many situations. If a fine exceeds an individual's wealth level, then the individual's expected penalty will be less than the expected penalty that law enforcement anticipated when selecting the probability and severity of sanctions. For example, in Table 1, a probability of 10% and a fine of $1000 for an individual with a wealth level of only $500 will achieve an expected penalty of only $50 instead of $100 because the fine is effectively capped at $500 by the individual's wealth. When there are wealth constraints, the fine should be set as high as possible, equal to the individual's wealth level. A prison sentence should also be imposed to bring the expected penalty to the desired level.

Tate v. Short

Supreme Court of the United States

401 U.S. 395 (1971)

MR. JUSTICE BRENNAN delivered the opinion of the Court.

Petitioner accumulated fines of $425 on nine convictions in the Corporation Court of Houston, Texas, for traffic offenses. He was unable to pay the fines because of indigency, and the Corporation Court, which otherwise has no jurisdiction to impose prison sentences, committed him to the municipal prison farm according to the provisions of a state statute and municipal ordinance, which required that he remain there a sufficient time to satisfy the fines at the rate of five dollars for each day; this required that he serve 85 days at the prison farm. After 21 days in custody, petitioner was released on bond when he applied to the County Criminal Court of Harris County for a writ of habeas corpus. He alleged that: "Because I am too poor, I am, therefore, unable to pay the accumulated fine of $425." The county court held that "legal cause has been shown for the imprisonment," and denied the application. The Court of Criminal Appeals of Texas affirmed, stating: "We overrule appellant's contention that, because he is too poor to pay the fines, his imprisonment is unconstitutional." We granted certiorari. We reverse on the authority of our decision in Williams v. Illinois.

The Illinois statute involved in Williams authorized both a fine and imprisonment. Williams was given the maximum sentence for petty theft of one year's imprisonment and a $500 fine, plus $5 in court costs. The judgment, as permitted by the Illinois statute, provided that, if, when the one-year sentence expired, Williams did not pay the fine and court costs, he was to remain in jail a sufficient length of time to satisfy the total amount at the rate of $5 per day. We held that the Illinois statute, as applied to Williams, worked an invidious discrimination solely because he was too poor to pay the fine, and therefore violated the Equal Protection Clause.

Although the instant case involves offenses punishable by fines only, petitioner's imprisonment for nonpayment constitutes precisely the same unconstitutional discrimination, since, like Williams, petitioner was subjected to imprisonment solely because of his indigency. In Morris v. Schoonfield, four members of the Court anticipated the problem of this case and stated the view, which we now adopt, that

> "the same constitutional defect condemned in Williams also inheres in jailing an indigent for failing to make immediate payment of any fine, whether or not the fine is accompanied by a jail term and whether or not the jail term of the indigent extends beyond the maximum term that may be imposed on a person willing and able to pay a fine. In each case, the Constitution prohibits the State from imposing a fine as a sentence and then automatically converting it into a jail term solely because the defendant is indigent, and cannot forthwith pay the fine in full."

Our opinion in Williams stated the premise of this conclusion in saying that

> "the Equal Protection Clause of the Fourteenth Amendment requires that the statutory ceiling placed on imprisonment for any substantive offense be the same for all defendants irrespective of their economic status."

Since Texas has legislated a "fines only" policy for traffic offenses, that statutory ceiling cannot, consistently with the Equal Protection Clause, limit the punishment to payment of the fine if one is able to pay it, yet convert the fine into a prison term for an indigent defendant without the means to pay his fine. Imprisonment in such a case is not imposed to further any penal objective of the State. It is imposed to augment the State's revenues, but obviously does not serve that purpose; the defendant cannot pay, because he is indigent, and his imprisonment, rather than aiding collection of the revenue, saddles the State with the cost of feeding and housing him for the period of his imprisonment.

There are, however, other alternatives to which the State may constitutionally resort to serve its concededly valid interest in enforcing payment of fines. We repeat our observation in Williams in that regard:

> "The State is not powerless to enforce judgments against those financially unable to pay a fine; indeed, a different result would amount to inverse discrimination, since it would enable an indigent to avoid both the fine and imprisonment for nonpayment, whereas other defendants must always suffer one or the other conviction."

> "It is unnecessary for us to canvass the numerous alternatives to which the State by legislative enactment — or judges within the scope of their authority — may resort in order to avoid imprisoning an indigent beyond the statutory maximum for involuntary nonpayment of a fine or court costs. Appellant has suggested several plans, some of which are already utilized in some States, while others resemble those proposed by various studies. The State is free to choose from among the variety of solutions already proposed and, of course, it may devise new ones."

We emphasize that our holding today does not suggest any constitutional infirmity in imprisonment of a defendant with the means to pay a fine who refuses or neglects to do so. Nor is our decision to be understood as precluding imprisonment as an enforcement method when alternative means are unsuccessful despite the defendant's reasonable efforts to satisfy the fines by those means; the determination of the constitutionality of imprisonment in that circumstance must await the presentation of a concrete case.

The judgment of the Court of Criminal Appeals of Texas is reversed, and the case is remanded for further proceedings not inconsistent with this opinion.

Notes and Questions

1. Fines versus Imprisonment: According to the economic model of criminal behavior, does deterrence depend on whether a criminal satisfies a penalty by paying a fine or serving a prison sentence?

2. The Economic Model: Is the court's decision in *Tate v. Short* consistent with the economic model of law enforcement?

3. Fines, Prison, and Wealth: Empirical studies indicate that there is a tendency to impose larger fines and shorter prison sentences on wealthy defendants. Joel Waldfogel, *Are Fines and Prison Terms Used Efficiently? Evidence on Federal Fraud Offenders*, 38 Journal of Law and Economics 107 (1995). Would it be ideal to allow wealthy defendants to satisfy their penalty by paying a fine and poorer defendants to satisfy their penalty by serving time in prison?

4. Bill Gates in Prison: For a wealthy individual such as Bill Gates, what level of fine would be equivalent to a 6 month prison term?

3. Extensions of the Basic Model

According to the basic economic model of law enforcement, sanctions should be as high as possible and probabilities should be as low as possible to achieve a given level of deterrence. However, this low certainty/high severity combination is not always optimal.

An Economic Theory of the Criminal Law
Richard A. Posner
85 Columbia Law Review 1193 (1985)

* * *

Once the expected punishment cost for the crime has been set, it becomes necessary to choose a combination of probability and severity of punishment that will bring that cost home to the would-be offender. Let us begin with fines. An expected punishment cost of $1000 can be imposed by combining a fine of $1000 with a probability of apprehension and conviction of one, a fine of $10,000 with a probability of .1, a fine of one million dollars with a probability of .001, etc. If the costs of collecting fines are assumed to be zero regardless of the size of the fine, the most efficient combination is a probability arbitrarily close to zero and a fine arbitrarily close to infinity. For while the costs of apprehending and convicting criminals rise with the probability of apprehension—higher probabilities imply more police, prosecutors, judges, defense attorneys, and so forth because more criminals are being apprehended and tried, than when the probability of apprehension is very low—the costs of collecting fines are by assumption zero regardless of their size. Thus, every increase in the size of the fine is costless, and every corresponding decrease in the probability of apprehension and conviction, designed to offset the increase in the fine and so maintain a constant expected punishment cost, reduces the costs of enforcement.

There are, however, many objections to assuming that the cost of collecting a fine is unrelated to its size:

(1) For criminals who are risk averse, an increase in the fine will not be a costless transfer payment. In Becker's model, the only cost of a fine is the cost of collecting it, because either the fine is not paid—the crime is deterred—or, if paid, it simply transfers an equal dollar amount from the criminal to the taxpayer. But for a risk-averse criminal, every reduction in the probability of apprehension and conviction, and corresponding increase in the fines imposed on those criminals who are apprehended and convicted, imposes a disutility not translated into extra revenue of the state. Thus, the real social cost of fines increases for risk-averse criminals as the fine increases. Nor is this effect offset by the effect on risk-preferring criminals, even if there are as many of them as there are risk-averse criminals. To the extent that a higher fine with lower probability of apprehension and conviction increases the utility of the risk preferrer, the fine has to be put up another notch to make sure that it deters—which makes it even more painful for the risk averse.

(2) The stigma effect of a fine (as of any criminal penalty), noted earlier, is not transferred either.

(3) The model implies punishment of different crimes by the same, severe fine. This uniformity, however, eliminates marginal deterrence—the incentive to substitute less for more serious crimes. If robbery is punished as severely as murder, the robber might as well kill his victim to eliminate a witness. Thus, one cost of making the punishment of a crime more severe is that it reduces the criminal's incentive to substitute that crime for a more serious one. To put this differently, reducing the penalty for a lesser crime may reduce the incidence of a greater crime. If it were not for considerations of marginal deterrence, more serious crimes might not always be punishable by more severe penalties than less serious ones.

* * *

(4) Limitations of solvency cause the cost of collecting fines to rise with the size of the fine—and for most criminal offenders to become prohibitive rather quickly. The solvency problem is so acute that the costs of collecting fines would often be prohibitive even if the probability of punishment were one and fines correspondingly much smaller than in the model. This explains the heavy reliance on nonpecuniary sanctions, of which imprisonment is the most common today. Imprisonment both reduces the criminal's future wealth, by impairing his lawful job prospects, and imposes disutility on people who cannot be made miserable enough by having their liquid wealth, or even their future wealth, confiscated.

(5) The solvency limitation is made all the more acute because a fine generally is considered uncollectable unless the criminal has liquid assets to pay it. The liquidity problem may seem superficial and easily solved by requiring payment on the installment plan or by making the fine proportional to future earnings. But these are more costly forms of punishment than they seem, because by reducing the offender's net income from lawful activity, they increase his incentive to return to a life of crime.

(6) Very low probabilities are difficult to estimate accurately. Criminals might underestimate them or overestimate them, resulting in too little or too much deterrence.

* * *

Imprisonment.—If society must continue to rely heavily on imprisonment as a criminal sanction, there is an argument—subject to caveats that should be familiar to the reader by now, based on risk aversion, overinclusion, avoidance and error costs, and (less clearly) marginal deterrence—for combining heavy prison terms for convicted criminals with low probabilities of apprehension and conviction. Consider the choice between combining a .1 probability of apprehension and conviction with a ten-year prison term and a .2 probability of apprehension and conviction with a five-year term. Under the second approach twice as many individuals are imprisoned but for only half as long, so the total costs of imprisonment to the government will be the same under the two approaches. But the costs of police, court officials, and the like will probably be lower under the first approach. The probability of apprehension and conviction, and hence the number of prosecutions, is only half as great. Although more resources will be devoted to a trial where the possible punishment is greater, these resources will be incurred in fewer trials because fewer people will be punished, and even if the total litigation resources are no lower, police and prosecution costs will clearly be much lower. And notice that this variant of our earlier model of high fines and trivial probabilities of apprehension and conviction corrects the most serious problem with that model— that is, solvency.

But isn't a system under which probabilities of punishment are low "unfair," because it creates ex post inequality among offenders? Many go scot-free; others serve longer prison sentences than they would if more offenders were caught. However, to object to this result is like saying that all lotteries are unfair because, ex post, they create wealth differences among the players. In an equally significant sense both the criminal justice system that creates low probabilities of apprehension and conviction and the lottery are fair so long as the ex ante costs and benefits are equalized among the participants. Nor is it correct that while real lotteries are voluntary the criminal justice "lottery" is not. The criminal justice is voluntary: you keep out of it by not committing crimes. Maybe, though, such a system of punishment is not sustainable in practice, because judges and jurors underestimate the benefits of what would seem, viewed in isolation, savagely cruel sentences. The prisoner who is to receive the sentence will be there in the dock, in person; the victims of the crimes for which he has not been prosecuted (because the fraction of crimes prosecuted is very low) will not be present—they will be statistics. I hesitate, though, to call this an economic argument; it could be stated in economic terms by reference to costs of information, but more analysis would be needed before this could be regarded as anything better than relabeling.

There is, however, another and more clearly economic problem with combining very long prison sentences with very low probabilities of apprehension and conviction. A prison term is lengthened, of course, by adding time on to the end of it. If the criminal has a significant discount rate, the added years may not create a substantial added disutility. At a discount rate of ten percent, a ten-year prison term imposes a disutility only 6.1 times the disutility of a one-year sentence, and a twenty-year sentence increases this figure to only 8.5 times; the corresponding figures for a five percent discount rate are 7.7 and 12.5 times.

Discount rates may seem out of place in a discussion of nonmonetary utilities and disutilities, though imprisonment has a monetary dimension, because a prisoner will have a lower income in prison than on the outside. But the reason that interest (discount) rates are positive even when there is no risk of default and the expected rate of inflation is zero is that people prefer present to future consumption and so must be paid to defer consumption. A criminal, too, will value his future consumption, which imprisonment will reduce, less than his present consumption.

The discounting problem could be ameliorated by preventive detention, whereby the defendant in effect begins to serve his sentence before he is convicted, or sometimes before his appeal rights are exhausted. The pros and cons of preventive detention involve issues of criminal procedure that would carry us beyond the scope of this Article, and here I merely note that the argument for preventive detention is stronger the graver the defendant's crime (and hence the longer the optimal length of imprisonment), regardless of whether the defendant is likely to commit a crime if he is released on bail pending trial.

The major lesson to be drawn from this part of the Article is that criminal sanctions are costly. A tort sanction is close to a costless transfer payment. A criminal sanction, even when it takes the form of a fine, and patently when it takes the form of imprisonment or death, is not. And yet it appears to be the optimal method of deterring most pure coercive transfers—which are therefore the central concern of the criminal law....

* * *

a. Risk Preferences

When criminals are either risk averse or risk seeking, the low certainty/high severity combination may no longer be optimal.

First, consider the case where individuals are risk averse in sentences so that their disutility of the expected penalty rises more than in proportion to the expected penalty. In the case of prison sentences, this could result from an increasing desire for freedom or growing distaste for the prison environment as the time in prison increases. Risk averse individuals prefer a certain penalty, f, to an uncertain penalty with a mean of f.

Table VII-2 shows several combinations of certainty and severity (presented as either a fine or the cost of imprisonment) that produce the same disutility, but have different expected penalties. In contrast to the risk neutral case where combinations with equal expected penalties produce equal deterrence, when severity increases for a risk averse individual, combinations with lower expected penalties produce equal deterrence.

If Table VII-2 referred to fines, it is not clear that a low certainty/high severity combination, such as a 1% probability of a $1000 fine, is more optimal than the other combinations in Table VII-2. Although enforcement costs are low, the expected fine, and therefore fine revenue is also low. If the decrease in fine revenue is greater than the savings in enforcement cost, the high fine combination could be a more expensive combination from society's perspective. For a discussion, see e.g. A. Mitchell Polinsky & Steven Shavell, *The Optimal Tradeoff Between the Probability and Magnitude of Fines*, 69 American Economic Review 880 (1979).

In contrast, if the sanctions in Table VII-2 were prison sentences instead of fines, then low expected sentences would not be costly. That is, the 1% probability of a 1000 day sentence has both low enforcement costs and low imprisonment costs. Thus, when

Table VII-2. Combinations of Certainty and Severity with Identical Disutility; The Risk Averse Case

Probability of Sanction	Severity of Sanction	Disutility of Expected Penalty	Expected Penalty
100%	100	100	100
40%	200	100	80
10%	400	100	40
1%	1000	100	10

Table VII-3. Combinations of Certainty and Severity with Identical Disutility;
The Risk-Seeking Case

Probability of Sanction	Severity of Sanction	Disutility of Expected Penalty	Expected Penalty
100%	100	100	100
60%	200	100	120
40%	400	100	160
30%	1000	100	300

offenders are risk averse, the high sentence/low probability combination is unambiguously the optimal combination.

Next, consider the case when offenders are risk seeking in sanctions; their disutility of the expected penalty rises less than in proportion to the expected penalty. In the case of prison sentences, this could occur for several reasons: if the disutility from the stigma of prison does not increase with the length of imprisonment, if more brutalization of prisoners occurs at the beginning of a sentence, or if discounting of future disutility makes earlier years in prison seem worse than later years. Risk-seeking individuals prefer an uncertain penalty with a mean of f to a certain penalty, f.

Table VII-3 shows several combinations of certainty and severity (presented as either a fine or the cost of imprisonment) that produce the same disutility, but have different expected penalties. In the risk-seeking case, as severity increases, combinations with higher expected penalties produce equal deterrence.

If Table VII-3 referred to fines, then the optimal combination of certainty and severity would be high fine and low probability. This combination would achieve the same deterrence as other combinations, and the expected fine, or fine revenue, would be high and enforcement costs would be low.

If Table VII-3 referred to prison sentences, then the optimal combination may not be the long sentence/low probability combination. Because the increase in prison sentences is proportionally larger than the decrease in the probability, the expected penalty, or expected prison term rises. If the cost of longer imprisonment exceeds the savings in enforcement costs, then the long sentence/low probability combination would not be the cheapest way to achieve deterrence. For a discussion, see e.g. A. Mitchell Polinsky & Steven Shavell, *On the Disutility and Discounting of Imprisonment and the Theory of Deterrence*, 28 Journal of Legal Studies 1 (1999).

b. Marginal Deterrence

The low certainty/high severity combination may also not be optimal if the goal is marginal deterrence. If penalties for all offenses are set at their maximal level, there is no reason to not commit a more serious offense. If an individual decides to mug someone, he might as well shoot the victim and other potential witnesses; murder carries no additional penalty and killing witnesses reduces the probability of being caught. Instead, the severity of sanctions should increase with the seriousness of the crime. Thus, the penalty for mugging should not be set at its maximal level; it should be set sufficiently below the penalty for murder so that the higher penalty for murder will provide an additional deterrent. Although the lower expected penalties will increase lesser crimes, the reduction in harm from the decrease in more serious crimes will more than offset the increase in harm from the lesser crimes, increasing social welfare.

c. Repeat Offenders

The low certainty/high severity combination may also not be optimal for first-time offenders so that there is room to increase the sanction if those offenders become repeat offenders. There are several reasons why it may be optimal to increase sanctions for repeat offenders. First, a prior criminal record signals that an individual has a higher propensity to commit criminal acts because either the costs of crime are lower for her or the benefits of crime are higher. Thus, higher sanctions are necessary to deter these high-risk offenders. Second, imposing higher sanctions on subsequent crimes increases the cost of committing first offenses; not only does a first offense carry an immediate penalty, it also increases future penalties. Thus, higher sanctions for subsequent crimes may deter first crimes. Third, a repeat offender has already suffered the social stigma of conviction from the first offense. The cost of committing subsequent crimes is less because they do not carry the potential cost of social stigma. Thus, other costs of subsequent crimes, like the expected sanction, must be increased to maintain deterrence. Finally, repeat offenders may be better able to avoid detection and apprehension of subsequent crimes because they understand the system and have a larger criminal network. If the probability of punishment is lower for repeat offenders, the magnitude of punishment must be higher to maintain deterrence. See, e.g. A. Mitchell Polinsky & Daniel L. Rubinfeld, *A Model of Optimal Fines for Repeat Offenders*, 46 Journal of Public Economics 291 (1991); T. J. Miceli & C. Bucci, *A Simple Theory of Increasing Penalties for Repeat Offenders*, 1 Review of Law and Economics 71 (2005).

Ewing v. California

Supreme Court of the United States

538 U. S. 11 (2003)

JUSTICE O'CONNOR announced the judgment of the Court and delivered an opinion, in which THE CHIEF JUSTICE and JUSTICE KENNEDY join.

* * *

California's current three strikes law consists of two virtually identical statutory schemes "designed to increase the prison terms of repeat felons." When a defendant is convicted of a felony, and he has previously been convicted of one or more prior felonies defined as "serious" or "violent" in Cal. Penal Code Ann., sentencing is conducted pursuant to the three strikes law. Prior convictions must be alleged in the charging document, and the defendant has a right to a jury determination that the prosecution has proved the prior convictions beyond a reasonable doubt.

If the defendant has one prior "serious" or "violent" felony conviction, he must be sentenced to "twice the term otherwise provided as punishment for the current felony conviction." If the defendant has two or more prior "serious" or "violent" felony convictions, he must receive "an indeterminate term of life imprisonment." Defendants sentenced to life under the three strikes law become eligible for parole on a date calculated by reference to a "minimum term," which is the greater of (a) three times the term otherwise provided for the current conviction, (b) 25 years, or (c) the term determined by the court pursuant to § 1170 for the underlying conviction, including any enhancements.

* * *

On parole from a 9-year prison term, petitioner Gary Ewing walked into the pro shop of the El Segundo Golf Course in Los Angeles County on March 12, 2000. He walked out with three golf clubs, priced at $399 apiece, concealed in his pants leg. A shop employee, whose suspicions were aroused when he observed Ewing limp out of the pro shop, telephoned the police. The police apprehended Ewing in the parking lot.

Ewing is no stranger to the criminal justice system. In 1984, at the age of 22, he pleaded guilty to theft. The court sentenced him to six months in jail (suspended), three years' probation, and a $300 fine. In 1988, he was convicted of felony grand theft auto and sentenced to one year in jail and three years' probation. After Ewing completed probation, however, the sentencing court reduced the crime to a misdemeanor, permitted Ewing to withdraw his guilty plea, and dismissed the case. In 1990, he was convicted of petty theft with a prior and sentenced to 60 days in the county jail and three years' probation. In 1992, Ewing was convicted of battery and sentenced to 30 days in the county jail and two years' summary probation. One month later, he was convicted of theft and sentenced to 10 days in the county jail and 12 months' probation. In January 1993, Ewing was convicted of burglary and sentenced to 60 days in the county jail and one year's summary probation. In February 1993, he was convicted of possessing drug paraphernalia and sentenced to six months in the county jail and three years' probation. In July 1993, he was convicted of appropriating lost property and sentenced to 10 days in the county jail and two years' summary probation. In September 1993, he was convicted of unlawfully possessing a firearm and trespassing and sentenced to 30 days in the county jail and one year's probation.

In October and November 1993, Ewing committed three burglaries and one robbery at a Long Beach, California, apartment complex over a 5-week period. He awakened one of his victims, asleep on her living room sofa, as he tried to disconnect her video cassette recorder from the television in that room. When she screamed, Ewing ran out the front door. On another occasion, Ewing accosted a victim in the mailroom of the apartment complex. Ewing claimed to have a gun and ordered the victim to hand over his wallet. When the victim resisted, Ewing produced a knife and forced the victim back to the apartment itself. While Ewing rifled through the bedroom, the victim fled the apartment screaming for help. Ewing absconded with the victim's money and credit cards.

On December 9, 1993, Ewing was arrested on the premises of the apartment complex for trespassing and lying to a police officer. The knife used in the robbery and a glass cocaine pipe were later found in the back seat of the patrol car used to transport Ewing to the police station. A jury convicted Ewing of first-degree robbery and three counts of residential burglary. Sentenced to nine years and eight months in prison, Ewing was paroled in 1999.

Only 10 months later, Ewing stole the golf clubs at issue in this case. He was charged with, and ultimately convicted of, one count of felony grand theft of personal property in excess of $400. As required by the three strikes law, the prosecutor formally alleged, and the trial court later found, that Ewing had been convicted previously of four serious or violent felonies for the three burglaries and the robbery in the Long Beach apartment complex.

* * *

As a newly convicted felon with two or more "serious" or "violent" felony convictions in his past, Ewing was sentenced under the three strikes law to 25 years to life.

* * *

When the California Legislature enacted the three strikes law, it made a judgment that protecting the public safety requires incapacitating criminals who have already been convicted of at least one serious or violent crime. Nothing in the Eighth Amendment prohibits California from making that choice. To the contrary, our cases establish that States have a valid interest in deterring and segregating habitual criminals.

* * *

The State's interest in deterring crime also lends some support to the three strikes law. We have long viewed both incapacitation and deterrence as rationales for recidivism statutes: "[A] recidivist statute['s] ... primary goals are to deter repeat offenders and, at some point in the life of one who repeatedly commits criminal offenses serious enough to be punished as felonies, to segregate that person from the rest of society for an extended period of time." Four years after the passage of California's three strikes law, the recidivism rate of parolees returned to prison for the commission of a new crime dropped by nearly 25 percent.

* * *

Against this backdrop, we consider Ewing's claim that his three strikes sentence of 25 years to life is unconstitutionally disproportionate to his offense of "shoplifting three golf clubs." We first address the gravity of the offense compared to the harshness of the penalty. At the threshold, we note that Ewing incorrectly frames the issue. The gravity of his offense was not merely "shoplifting three golf clubs." Rather, Ewing was convicted of felony grand theft for stealing nearly $1,200 worth of merchandise after previously having been convicted of at least two "violent" or "serious" felonies. Even standing alone, Ewing's theft should not be taken lightly. His crime was certainly not "one of the most passive felonies a person could commit." To the contrary, the Supreme Court of California has noted the "seriousness" of grand theft in the context of proportionality review. Theft of $1,200 in property is a felony under federal law, 18 U.S.C. § 641 and in the vast majority of States.

* * *

In weighing the gravity of Ewing's offense, we must place on the scales not only his current felony, but also his long history of felony recidivism. Any other approach would fail to accord proper deference to the policy judgments that find expression in the legislature's choice of sanctions. In imposing a three strikes sentence, the State's interest is not merely punishing the offense of conviction, or the "triggering" offense: "[I]t is in addition the interest ... in dealing in a harsher manner with those who by repeated criminal acts have shown that they are simply incapable of conforming to the norms of society as established by its criminal law." To give full effect to the State's choice of this legitimate penological goal, our proportionality review of Ewing's sentence must take that goal into account.

Ewing's sentence is justified by the State's public-safety interest in incapacitating and deterring recidivist felons, and amply supported by his own long, serious criminal record. Ewing has been convicted of numerous misdemeanor and felony offenses, served nine separate terms of incarceration, and committed most of his crimes while on probation or parole. His prior "strikes" were serious felonies including robbery and three residential burglaries. To be sure, Ewing's sentence is a long one. But it reflects a rational legislative judgment, entitled to deference, that offenders who have committed serious or violent felonies and who continue to commit felonies must be incapacitated. The State of California "was entitled to place upon [Ewing] the onus of one who is simply unable to bring his conduct within the social norms prescribed by the criminal law of the State." Ewing's is not "the rare case in which a threshold comparison of the crime committed and the sentence imposed leads to an inference of gross disproportionality."

We hold that Ewing's sentence of 25 years to life in prison, imposed for the offense of felony grand theft under the three strikes law, is not grossly disproportionate and therefore does not violate the Eighth Amendment's prohibition on cruel and unusual punishments.

Notes and Questions

1. Get Tough on Repeat Offenders: What arguments does the court give to explain why repeat offenders should be punished more severely than first-time offenders for the same offense?

2. Go Easy on Repeat Offenders: Some scholars have presented theories where it may be optimal to lower sanctions for repeat offenders. See, e.g., D.A. Dana, *Rethinking the Puzzle of Escalating Penalties for Repeat Offenders,* 110 Yale Law Journal 733 (2001); W. Emons, *A Note on the Optimal Punishment for Repeat Offenders,* 23 International Review of Law and Economics 253 (2003). What arguments can you think of for why repeat offenders should be punished less severely than first-time offenders?

d. Discount Rates

If the penalty is a prison sentence, a low certainty/high severity combination may not achieve adequate deterrence if potential offenders have very high discount rates. Because individuals with high discount rates value their future significantly less than their present welfare, adding additional years to a prison sentence several years into the future increases their perceived costs of crime only slightly.

United States v. Craig

United States Court of Appeals for the Seventh Circuit
703 F.3d 1001 (2012)

PER CURIAM

The defendant pleaded guilty to four counts of producing child pornography.

* * *

[T]he statutory maximum sentence for each count of conviction was 30 years. (It would have been longer had the defendant had previous convictions, but he didn't.) The judge sentenced him to the 30-year maximum on one count and to concurrent sentences of 20 years on each of the remaining three counts, but he ordered that the set of 20-year sentences be served consecutively to the 30-year sentence, making the total sentence 50 years. The judge was entitled to do this ...

* * *

POSNER, Circuit Judge, concurring.

I write separately merely to remind the district judges of this circuit of the importance of careful consideration of the wisdom of imposing de facto life sentences. If the defendant in this case does not die in the next 50 years he will be 96 years old when released (though "only" 89 or 90 if he receives the maximum good-time credits that he would earn if his behavior in prison proves to be exemplary).... [I]n all likelihood the defendant will be dead before his prison term expires.

Federal imprisonment is expensive to the government; the average expense of maintaining a federal prisoner for a year is between $25,000 and $30,000, and the expense rises steeply with the prisoner's age because the medical component of a prisoner's expense will rise with his age, especially if he is still alive in his 70s (not to mention his 80s or 90s). It has been estimated that an elderly prisoner costs the prison system between $60,000 and $70,000 a year.

That is not a net social cost, because if free these elderly prisoners would in all likelihood receive Medicare and maybe Medicaid benefits to cover their medical expenses. But if freed before they became elderly, and employed, they would have contributed to the Medicare and Medicaid programs through payroll taxes—which is a reminder of an additional social cost of imprisonment: the loss of whatever income the prisoner might lawfully have earned had he been free, income reflecting his contribution to society through lawful employment.

The social costs of imprisonment should in principle be compared with the benefits of imprisonment to the society, consisting mainly of deterrence and incapacitation. A sentencing judge should therefore consider the incremental deterrent and incapacitative effects of a very long sentence compared to a somewhat shorter one. An impressive body of economic research … finds for example that forgoing imprisonment as punishment of criminals whose crimes inflict little harm may save more in costs of imprisonment than the cost in increased crime that it creates. Ours is not a "little crime" case, and not even the defendant suggests that probation would be an appropriate punishment. But it is a lifetime imprisonment case, and the implications for cost, incapacitation, and deterrence create grounds for questioning that length of sentence.

For suppose the defendant had been sentenced not to 50 years in prison but to 30 years. He would then be 76 years old when released (slightly younger if he had earned the maximum good-time credits). How likely would he be to commit further crimes at that age? … [A]lthough persons 65 and older are 13 percent of the population, they accounted for only seven-tenths of one percent of arrests in 2010. Last year 1,451 men ages 65 and older were arrested for sex offenses (excluding forcible rape and prostitution), which was less than 3 percent of the total number arrests of male sex offenders that year. Only 1.1 percent of perpetrators of all forms of crimes against children are between 70 and 75 years old and 1.3 percent between 60 and 69. How many can there be who are older than 75?

It is true that sex offenders are more likely to recidivate than other criminals, Virginia M. Kendall and T. Markus Funk, Child Exploitation and Trafficking: Examining the Global Challenges and U.S. Responses 310 (2012), because their criminal behavior is for the most part compulsive rather than opportunistic. But capacity and desire to engage in sexual activity diminish in old age. Moreover, when released, a sexual criminal is subject to registration and notification requirements that reduce access to potential victims.

As for the benefits of a lifetime sentence in deterring other sex criminals, how likely is it that if told that if apprehended and convicted he would be sentenced to 50 years in prison the defendant would not have committed the crimes for which he's been convicted, but if told he faced a sentence of "only" 30 years he would have gone ahead and committed them? …

Sentencing judges are not required to engage in cost-benefit analyses of optimal sentencing severity with discounting to present value. Such analyses would involve enormous guesswork because of the difficulty of assessing key variables, including one variable that I haven't even mentioned, because I can't imagine how it could be quantified in even the roughest way—the retributive value of criminal punishment. By that I mean the effect of punishment in assuaging the indignation that serious crime arouses and in providing a form of nonfinancial compensation to the victims.

But virtually all sentencing, within the usually broad statutory ranges—the minimum sentence that the judge could have imposed in this case, by making the sentences on all four counts run concurrently, as he could have done, would have been 15 years, and the maximum sentence, by making them all run consecutively, as he could also have done, would have been 120 years—involves guesswork. I am merely suggesting that the cost of imprisonment of very elderly prisoners, the likelihood of recidivism by them, and the modest incremental deterrent effect of substituting a superlong sentence for a merely very long sentence, should figure in the judge's sentencing decision.

Notes and Questions

1. Incapacitation versus Deterrence: How does Judge Posner differentiate between the incapacitative effects and deterrent effects of a lengthy prison sentence?

2. Age and Imprisonment: Empirical evidence shows that the highest rates of commission of violent crimes occur when offenders are in their late teens and early twenties, and the highest commission rates of property crimes occur when offenders are in their late teens. Alfred Blumstein, *Prisons*, in Crime 387 (J. Q. Wilson and J. Petersilia, eds; 1995). People begin to desist from violent crimes after age 22 and from property crimes after age 17. Michael Tonry, Sentencing Matters (1996). Thus, incapacitating people beyond these ages may have little incapacitative effect. Would it make sense to release prisoners when they turn 30? Why or why not?

D. Crime in the U.S.

In 2011, both violent crime and property crime in the United States was at its lowest rate in 40 years. Over the 20 year period from 1991 to 2011, violent crime rates fell by 49 percent and property crime rates declined by 43 percent. This drop in crime was felt in all areas of the United States—both urban and rural—and it affected all demographic categories—male and female, young and old, and across all racial categories. Moreover, the drop in crime was significantly greater than that experienced by other countries for which comparable crime data is available.

Understanding Why Crime Fell in the 1990s: Four Factors That Explain the Decline and Six That Do Not

Steven D. Levitt

18 The Journal of Economic Perspectives 163 (2004)

* * *

Six Factors that Played Little or No Role in the Crime Decline

The list of explanations offered as to why crime has fallen is a lengthy one. Here, I begin with six commonly suggested and plausible theories that in practice do not appear important in explaining the decline of crime rates.

1) The Strong Economy of the 1990s

The decade of the 1990s saw sustained economic growth. Real GDP per capita grew by almost 30 percent between 1991 and 2001. The annual unemployment rate fell from 6.8 in 1991 to 4.8 percent in 2001. If macroeconomic performance is an important determinant of crime rates, then the economy could explain falling crime.

* * *

Controlling for other factors, almost all of these studies report a statistically significant but substantively small relationship between unemployment rates and property crime.

* * *

Based on these estimates, the observed 2 percentage point decline in the U.S unemployment rate between 1991 and 2001 can explain an estimated 2 percent decline in property crime (out of an observed drop of almost 30 percent), but no change in violent crime or homicide.

* * *

2) Changing Demographics

The aging of the baby boomers represents a profound demographic shift. The elderly have extremely low rates of both offending and criminal victimization. In 2001, people over the age of 65 had per capita arrest rates approximately one-fiftieth the level of 15–19 year-olds. Perkins (1997), using NCVS data, reports that those over the age of 65 experience victimization rates for serious violent crime that are less than one-tenth of those of teenagers. Given that the share of the elderly population increased during the 1990s, a purely demographically driven decline in crime might be expected.

Two other concurrent demographic changes, however, counterbalance the crime-related benefits of an aging population. First, between 1990 and 2000, the black population rose from 12.1 percent to 12.9 percent. For reasons that are only partly understood, blacks have elevated victimization and offending rates relative to other Americans, particularly for homicide, where the differences across races are almost an order of magnitude. Second, in spite of the overall aging of the population, the echo of the baby boom is leading to a temporary increase in the number of teenagers and young adults. Between 1995 and 2010, the number of 15–24 year-olds is projected to increase by roughly 20 percent, and the share of the population between the ages of 15 and 24 will increase from 13.7 percent to 14.6 percent. (In comparison, 15–24 year-olds represented 18.7 percent of the population in 1980.) This age group has a greatly elevated involvement in crime. Indeed, many of the dire predictions for increased crime rates in the 1990s were based in part on the increasing number of adolescents.

Overall, these various demographic shifts probably had a slight ameliorating effect on crime.

* * *

Thus, demographic shifts may account for a little more than one-sixth of the observed decline in property crime in the 1990s, but are not an important factor in the drop in violent crime.

3) Better Policing Strategies

An enormous amount of media attention has focused on the policing strategies instituted in New York City under the leadership of Police Commissioner William Bratton and Mayor Rudy Guiliani. Their crime-fighting approach involved increased enforcement of nuisance activities like aggressive panhandling and better use of technology in identifying crime "hot spots." Other changes in policing strategy such as "community policing," in which the police attempt to work more closely as allies with communities rather than simply responding to emergency calls, were widely adopted in many other cities in the 1990s. In Boston, an innovative multiagency collaboration targeted gang violence.

* * *

In my opinion, there are reasons for skepticism regarding the claim that New York City's policing strategy is the key to its decline in crime. First, the drop in crime in New

York began in 1990. Crime declines of roughly 10 percent across a wide range of offenses occurred in 1991 and 1992. Guiliani, however, did not take office until 1993, at which point Bratton was moved from the New York City Transit Police, where he had been using the same approaches, and appointed police commissioner. With the exception of homicide, which does decline sharply in 1993, the trend in crime shows no obvious break after Bratton is appointed.

* * *

[Moreover], given that few other cities ... instituted New York City–type policing approaches, and certainly none with the enthusiasm of New York City itself, it is difficult to attribute the widespread declines in crime to policing strategy. Even Los Angeles and Washington, D.C., two cities notorious for the problems they have experienced with their police forces achieved declines in crime on par with New York City once the growth in the size of New York City's police force is accounted for.

* * *

Thus, while the impact of policing strategies on crime is an issue on which reasonable people might disagree given the lack of hard evidence, my reading of the limited data that are available leads me to the conclusion that the impact of policing strategies on New York City crime are exaggerated, and that the impact on national crime is likely to be minor.

4) Gun Control Laws

There are more than 200 million firearms in private hands in the United States—more than the number of adults. Almost two-thirds of homicides in the United States involve a firearm, a fraction far greater than other industrialized countries. Combining those two facts, one might conjecture that easy access to guns in the U.S. may be part of the explanation for our unusually high homicide rates. Indeed, the most careful study on the subject finds that higher rates of handgun ownership, which represent about one-third of all firearms, may be a causal factor in violent crime rates.

There is, however, little or no evidence that changes in gun control laws in the 1990s can account for falling crime.

* * *

Given the realities of an active black market in guns, the apparent ineffectiveness of gun control laws should not come as a great surprise to economists. Even in the late 1980s, prior to the Brady Act, only about one-fifth of prisoners reported obtaining their guns through licensed gun dealers.

Gun buy-back programs are another form of public policy instituted in the 1990s that is largely ineffective in reducing crime. First, the guns that are typically surrendered in gun buy-backs are those guns that are least likely to be used in criminal activities. The guns turned in will be, by definition, those for which the owners derive little value from the possession of the guns. In contrast, those who are using guns in crimes are unlikely to participate in such programs. Second, because replacement guns are relatively easily obtained, the decline in the number of guns on the street may be smaller than the number of guns that are turned in. Third, the likelihood that any particular gun will be used in a crime in a given year is low. In 1999, approximately 6,500 homicides were committed with handguns. There are approximately 65 million handguns in the United States. Thus, if a different handgun were used in each homicide, the likelihood that a particular handgun would be used to kill an individual in a particular year is one in 10,000. The typical gun buy-back program yields fewer than 1,000 guns. Thus, it is not surprising that research evaluations have consistently failed to document any link between gun buy-back programs and reductions in gun violence.

More stringent gun-control policies such as bans on handgun acquisition passed in Washington, D.C., in 1976 and the ban on handgun ownership in Chicago in 1982 do not seem to have reduced crime, either. While initial research suggested a beneficial impact of the D.C. gun ban, when the city of Baltimore is used as a control group, rather than the affluent Washington suburbs, the apparent benefits of the gun ban disappear. Although no careful analysis of Chicago's gun ban has been carried out, the fact that Chicago has been a laggard in the nationwide homicide decline argues against any large impact of the law. From a theoretical perspective, policies that raise the costs of using guns in the commission of actual crimes, as opposed to targeting ownership, would appear to be a more effective approach to reducing gun crime.

* * *

5) Laws Allowing the Carrying of Concealed Weapons

The highly publicized work of Lott and Mustard (1997) claimed enormous reductions in violent crime due to concealed weapons laws. The theory behind this claim is straightforward: armed victims raise the costs faced by a potential offender.

The empirical work in support of this hypothesis, however, has proven to be fragile along a number of dimensions.

* * *

Ultimately, there appears to be little basis for believing that concealed weapons laws have had an appreciable impact on crime.

6) Increased Use of Capital Punishment

In the 1980s, a total of 117 prisoners were put to death in the United States. That number more than quadrupled to 478 in the 1990s. The debate over the effectiveness of the death penalty as a deterrent has been ongoing for three decades.

* * *

Largely lost in this debate, however, are two important facts. First, given the rarity with which executions are carried out in this country and the long delays in doing so, a rational criminal should not be deterred by the threat of execution.

* * *

Second, even taking as given very large empirical estimates of the seven murders deterred per execution or Mocan and Gittings (2003) estimate of six murders deterred per execution—the observed increase in the death penalty from 14 executions in 1991 to 66 in 2001 would eliminate between 300 and 400 homicides, for a reduction of 1.5 percent in the homicide rate, or less than one-twenty-fifth of the observed decline in the homicide rate over this time period. Moreover, any deterrent effect from such executions cannot explain the decline in other crimes. Given the way the death penalty is currently practiced in the United States, it is extremely unlikely that it exerts significant influence on crime rates.

Four Factors That Explain the Decline in Crime

Having argued that many common explanations for the decline in crime are unlikely to hold the true answers, I now turn to four factors that did, in my reading of the evidence, play a critical role in the crime reduction of the 1990s: the increasing number of police, the skyrocketing number of prisoners, the ebbing of the crack epidemic and legalization of abortion in the 1970s.

1) Increases in the Number of Police

Police are the first line of defense against crime. More than $60 billion is spent each year on policing.

* * *

A number of recent studies have ... reached the conclusion that more police are associated with reductions in crime.

* * *

The number of police officers per capita, which is tracked by the FBI and reported annually in the Uniform Crime Reports, increased by 50,000–60,000 officers, or roughly 14 percent, in the 1990s. Although this increase was greater than in previous decades, it was smaller than might have been expected given the 1994 omnibus crime bill, which, by itself, had promised an extra 100,000 new police officers on the streets. Using an elasticity of crime with respect to the number of police of −0.40, the increase in police between 1991 and 2001 can account for a crime reduction of 5–6 percent across the board. The increase in police can thus explain somewhere between one-fifth and one-tenth of the overall decline in crime.

* * *

2) The Rising Prison Population

The 1990s was a period of enormous growth in the number of people behind bars .... After many decades of relatively stable imprisonment rates, the prison population began to expand in the mid-1970s. By 2000, more than two million individuals were incarcerated at any point in time, roughly four times the number locked up in 1972. Of that prison population growth, more than half took place in the 1990s. The increase in prisoners can be attributed to a number of factors, the most important of which were the sharp rise in incarceration for drug-related offenses, increased parole revocation and longer sentences for those convicted of crimes

* * *

Using an estimate of the elasticity of crime with respect to punishment of −.30 for homicide and violent crime and −.20 for property crime, the increase in incarceration over the 1990s can account for a reduction in crime of approximately 12 percent for the first two categories and 8 percent for property crime, or about one-third of the observed decline in crime.

* * *

3) The Receding Crack Epidemic

Beginning in 1985, the market for crack cocaine grew rapidly. Crack cocaine is produced by heating a mix of powder cocaine and baking soda. The resulting precipitate takes the form of airy nuggets. Extremely small quantities of this compound, when smoked, produce an intense, short-lived high. The emergence of crack cocaine represented an important development both because it facilitated the sale of cocaine by the dose for a retail price of $5–$10 and because the extreme high associated with crack proved to be popular among consumers. Crack frequently sold in open-air markets with youth gangs controlling the retail distribution. The crack cocaine trade proved highly lucrative for gangs, leading to violence as rival gangs competed to sell the drug.

* * *

Beginning in 1985, homicide rates for black males under the age of 25 began a steep ascent, more than tripling in less than a decade, before once again falling dramatically to levels slightly above those of the pre-crack era. In stark contrast, the homicide rates of older black males continued on a long-term secular decline. Young white males also experienced a short-run increase in homicide in the late 1980s, but both the base rates and the increases for whites are much lower. The concentration and timing of the homicide spike among the young black males, which coincides with the rise and fall of the crack market, is suggestive of crack cocaine playing a critical role.

* * *

As crack ebbed from 1991 to 2001, young black males experienced a homicide decline of 48 percent, compared with 30 percent for older black males, 42 percent for young white males and 30 percent for older white males. Depending on which control group one views as most reasonable, the estimated impact of crack on homicides committed by young black males ranges from 6 to 18 percent. Given that young black males commit about one-third of homicides, this translates into a reduction of 2–6 percent in overall homicides in the 1990s due to crack receding.

* * *

4) The Legalization of Abortion

The U.S. Supreme Court's *Roe v. Wade* decision in 1973 may seem like an unlikely source of the decline in crime in the 1990s, but a growing body of evidence suggests an important role for legalized abortion in explaining falling crime rates two decades later. The underlying theory rests on two premises: 1) unwanted children are at greater risk for crime, and 2) legalized abortion leads to a reduction in the number of unwanted births.

Donohue and Levitt (2001) report a number of pieces of evidence consistent with a causal link between legalized abortion and crime, a hypothesis that to my knowledge was first articulated in Bouza (1990). The five states that allowed abortion in 1970 (three years before *Roe v. Wade*) experienced declines in crime rates earlier than the rest of the nation. States with high and low abortion rates in the 1970s experienced similar crime trends for decades until the first cohorts exposed to legalized abortion reached the high-crime ages around 1990. At that point, the high-abortion states saw dramatic declines in crime relative to the low-abortion states over the next decade. The magnitude of the differences in the crime decline between high- and low-abortion states was over 25 percent for homicide, violent crime and property crime. For instance, homicide fell 25.9 percent in high-abortion states between 1985 and 1997 compared to an *increase* of 4.1 percent in low-abortion states. Panel data estimates confirm the strong negative relationship between lagged abortion and crime. An analysis of arrest rates by age reveal that only arrests of those born after abortion legalization are affected by the law change.

* * *

Extrapolating the conservative estimates of Donohue and Levitt (2001) to cover the period 1991–2000, legalized abortion is associated with a 10 percent reduction in homicide, violent crime and property crime rates, which would account for 25–30 percent of the observed crime decline in the 1990s.

Notes and Questions

1. Abortion in Romania: In 1966, dictator Nicolae Ceausescu declared abortion and family planning illegal in Romania. What impact would you expect this change to have on crime in Romania? When would you expect the changes to occur?

2. Abortion, Lead Paint, and Fetal Alcohol Syndrome: According to Levitt, the legalization of abortion in 1973 accounts for an amazing 25–30 percent of the crime decline in the 1990s. Are there any other significant changes in the mid-1970s that could explain part of this decline? Hint: The federal government banned the use of lead paint in 1978 and researchers established a link between maternal alcohol abuse and a specific pattern of birth defects that results in weakened impulse control (fetal alcohol syndrome) in the early 1970s.

3. Bullet Control, not Gun Control: Levitt states that "[f]rom a theoretical perspective, policies that raise the costs of using guns in the commission of actual crimes, as opposed to targeting ownership, would appear to be a more effective approach to reducing gun crime." What kinds of policies might be effective?

4. Drugs and Crime: The relationship between illegal drugs and crime is a complicated one. At first glance, one might think that law enforcement efforts to reduce the supply of drugs will decrease crime because drug addicts often commit crime. However, basic economics tells us that any restriction in supply will increase the price of illegal drugs. The increased price will cause consumers whose demand for drugs is elastic to purchase fewer drugs. However, many drug users are addicts whose demand for drugs is inelastic; many of these addicts will turn to crime in an effort to pay the higher prices for drugs. Moreover, as drug prices increase, drug markets become more lucrative, increasing incentives for sellers to engage in crime to increase their market share. Prohibition increased the price of alcohol and made it worthwhile for Al Capone and others to resort to violence to control alcohol markets. Jeffrey Miron, *Violence and the U.S. Prohibitions of Drugs and Alcohol*, 1 American Law and Economics Review 78 (1999). Similarly, current efforts to combat drug use increase incentives for those involved in the drug trade to commit more crime as they fight over control of more lucrative drug markets. See, e.g. Gary S. Becker, Kevin M. Murphy, & Michael Grossman, *The Market for Illegal Goods: The Case of Drugs*, 114 Journal of Political Economy 38 (2006); Jeffrey Miron, *Do Prohibitions Raise Prices? Evidence from the Market for Cocaine*, 85 Review of Economics and Statistics 522 (2003).

Chapter VIII

Labor Markets

Our study of labor markets begins with the familiar supply-and-demand model. On the demand side of the labor market are employers whose decisions about the hiring of labor are influenced by conditions in product and capital markets. On the supply side of the labor market are workers and potential workers whose decisions about where and whether to work must take into account alternative uses of their time.

This chapter presents the basic economic model of labor markets. Section A is an overview of the interaction of labor market supply and demand, with applications to the minimum wage, payroll taxes, and fringe benefits. Section B examines employers' behavior, including the demand for labor, investments in employees, discrimination, and employment at will. Section C considers employees' behavior, including human capital investments and occupational choices. Section D explains the economic role of unions and the collective bargaining process.

A. Supply and Demand Analysis: An Overview

The basic supply-and-demand model for labor is depicted in Figure VIII-1. Employers' demand for workers is downward sloping (due to productivity reasons discussed in Section B). Employees' supply of labor is upward sloping because higher wages attract more workers into the market. The interaction of supply and demand yields a market wage rate, W_M, where Q_M workers are employed. W_M is the market-clearing price.

This model provides insights about many aspects of labor markets. We first consider this model's usefulness by considering the effects of the minimum wage, payroll taxes, and fringe benefits. We then turn to the underpinnings of the market supply and demand curves.

1. The Minimum Wage

The minimum wage is a government-imposed price control, or price floor as noted in Chapter II, that makes it illegal for employers to pay workers less than the minimum wage and makes it illegal for employees to work for less than the minimum wage. Thus, the minimum wage restricts the freedom and employment opportunities of both employers and employees.

The minimum wage must be above the market wage in order to be effective. The market impact of the minimum wage is illustrated in Figure VIII-2. Here, the market

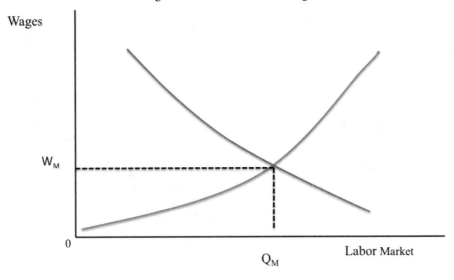

Figure VIII-1. Minimum Wage

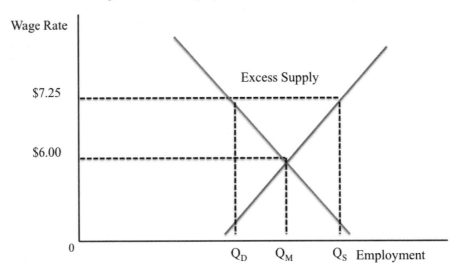

Figure VIII-2. Employment and Minimum Wage

hourly wage, $6.00, is below the minimum wage, $7.25. At $6.00 per hour, the market would clear at Q_M. At $7.25 per hour, the quantity of workers who are willing and able to work increases to Q_S. However, at the minimum wage, employers decrease the number of workers they are willing to hire to Q_D. Thus, the quantity demanded, Q_D, is less than the quantity supplied, Q_S. The minimum wage—a price floor—prevents the market wage from adjusting downward and the market does not clear.

The minimum wage causes unemployment because some workers who want to work at a wage between $6.00 and $7.25 are unable to find jobs. Unemployment—a surplus or excess supply of workers—is illustrated by the difference between Q_S and Q_D in Figure

VIII-2. The minimum wage increases the earnings of workers who are able to find jobs at the higher wage, but it results in some workers losing their jobs and other workers being disappointed when they can't find work at the above market wage, $7.25. The distance from Q_D to Q_M illustrates the number of jobs lost. Q_M to Q_S illustrates the number of disappointed job seekers. The number of workers who receive the higher wage is O to Q_D. However, the workers who receive the higher wage are not necessarily the same workers, O to Q_M, who were working at $6.00. New entrants, Q_M to Q_S, might displace the incumbent workers. Moreover, the excess supply created by the minimum wage gives the employer relatively more discretion in choosing among job applicants. If all workers are equally productive, employers can indulge their personal preferences based on gender, race, physical appearance, political beliefs, age, and so forth, without incurring any costs in terms of lost productivity.

In the absence of governmental restrictions, markets for labor services would clear at the market-determined wage for workers of similar skill and qualifications. The market wages of the great majority of workers in the United States are well above the legal minimum wage. Workers that have the skills and qualifications to compete in those markets are not protected by the minimum wage because they command wages higher than the minimum wage. In effect, they are protected by the rivalry among employers competing for their services.

On the other hand, the market demand for some workers' services, especially those with little skill, training, or experience, is so weak that the market would normally clear at a wage below the legal minimum. Employers would be willing to hire inexperienced or low-skilled workers at a wage below the legal minimum, but they are prohibited from doing so. As a result, many inexperienced or low-skilled workers remain without work. Teenagers, who are typically inexperienced and low skilled, may not be attractive employees at the minimum wage. In fact, considerable empirical evidence indicates that the adverse employment effects of the minimum wage are often borne most heavily by teenagers.

The adverse employment consequences of the minimum wage do not, by themselves, dictate an absolute condemnation of the minimum wage. This is because the employees who manage to keep their jobs earn more money. Somewhat surprisingly, very little research has addressed the question of whether minimum wage legislation is reaching its intended goal of reducing the incidence of poverty. The few studies that have considered this issue have found that minimum wage legislation has only a minor effect on the aggregate distribution of income. This finding is not surprising because not all low wage workers are members of low income families. Many low wage workers, especially teenagers, are second earners in middle or upper income families. Put another way, minimum wage legislation directly affects low wage workers, not necessarily low income families. *See* Ronald Mincy, *Raising the Minimum Wage: Effects on Family Poverty*, 113(7) Monthly Labor Review 18–25 (July 1990). Minimum wage legislation, however, does appear to have a larger effect on the income distribution of African Americans because they are more likely to be members of low income families than are white low wage workers.

The current minimum wage in the United States is $7.25 per hour, last raised in 2009. As mentioned above, many states impose minimum wages higher than this minimum. For example, Connecticut passed legislation in March 2014 raising its minimum wage to $10.10 as of 2017. Some cities and localities also have minimum wages: Seattle has adopted a city minimum wage of $15 per hour. In 2014, President Obama called for both a raise to the national minimum wage and for states to raise their respective minimum wages.

Consider the potential effects of differing national, state, and local minimum wages. What effects on population, employee movement, and immigration do you expect would occur if a city increased its minimum wage? A state? A nation? Do your answers depend on the overall strength of the economy? Overall poverty levels? The presence of social safety programs, such as unemployment insurance?

2. Payroll Taxes

In the United States, several social insurance programs are financed by payroll taxes. Employers, and in some cases, employees, make mandatory contributions to the taxable social insurance trust fund of a fraction of the employee's salary. For example, the Social Security program is financed by a payroll tax paid by both employers and employees. In most states, unemployment insurance and workers compensation insurance programs are financed solely by payroll tax payments made by employers. However, supply-and-demand analysis reveals that the employers and employees share the burden of payroll taxes even though the employer pays the tax to the government.

Assume that an employer must pay a payroll tax equal to 10% of total payments to employees. The tax increases the employers' cost of hiring workers. As a result, the demand for workers decreases. In Figure VIII-3, this decrease in demand is illustrated by a shift from D_1 to D_2. At W_1, employers are willing to hire only Q_2 workers instead of the Q_1 they were willing to hire in the absence of the payroll tax. A new equilibrium wage, W_2, emerges after the market adjusts to the change in demand. At this point, the employment level has fallen from Q_1 to Q_3. Thus, employees bear part of the burden of payroll tax in the form of lower wage rates and lower employment levels. The lesson is clear. The party legally liable for the contribution, the employer, is not necessarily the one who bears the full burden of the actual cost as with the excise tax analyzed in Chapter II.

In general, the extent to which the labor supply curve is sensitive to wages—its elasticity—determines the proportion of the employer payroll tax that gets shifted to employees' wages. The less responsive labor supply is to changes in wages, the lower the number of

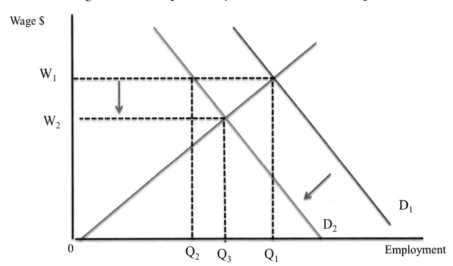

Figure VIII-3. Impact of Payroll Taxes on Market Wages

employees who withdraw from the market, and the higher the proportion of the tax that gets shifted to workers in the form of a wage decrease.

3. Fringe Benefits

The preceding supply-and-demand analysis has limited employee compensation to money wages. Employee compensation also often includes non-wage components called fringe benefits. These benefits include health-care insurance, dental insurance, life insurance, disability income insurance, pension benefits, paid vacation and personal leave, education benefits, on-the-job-training, low-cost on-the-premises child-care services, and so forth. Fringe benefits are an important component of employee compensation.

Employers provide benefits to attract and retain good employees who, on the margin, prefer additional benefits to money wages. The employer considers the total cost of an employee's compensation package in making employment decisions. Typically, employers spend an additional one-third of their payroll on benefits. Employers recognize that different employees have different preferences and thus offer different trade-offs between wages and benefits. For example, employees who do not have children do not receive any benefit from on-premises child care centers. Similarly, an employee whose spouse's employer provides health-care insurance receives little benefit from health-care insurance provided by his or her own employer. As a consequence, some employers provide their employees with the opportunity to choose from a menu of available benefits within a budget provided by the employer. These "cafeteria" plans allow employers to lower total compensation costs by assuring that the fringe benefits actually benefit those employees who opt for them.

The government often requires that employers provide specific benefits. For example, concern that many low wage workers are not covered by health insurance led to the passage of the Patient Protection and Affordable Care Act, which requires most employers to provide their employees with at least a minimal level of insurance coverage. Similarly, concern for the welfare of children has led to requirements that employers provide their employees with unpaid parental leave so that they can care for newborn or ill children without the fear of losing their jobs. While the benefit to employees of each proposal for mandated benefits seems clear, these laws also impose a cost on employers that might ultimately fall on these same employees. In the case of mandated health insurance, the cost to employers is in providing coverage for currently uncovered primarily low wage workers. One study suggested that a mandated insurance plan would increase employers' cost for low wage workers by 15–20%. In the case of mandated parental leave, the employers' costs include any loss of output suffered when workers are on leave and the cost of hiring and training temporary replacements. As with payroll taxes, these costs to employers may be partially or completely passed on to workers in the form of lower wages and unemployment. For example, some employers are reported to be reducing the hours of employees so that they will not be subject to coverage under the Affordable Care Act, a predictable but unintended consequence of the Act.

B. Employers' Behavior

Employers purchase in the labor market. They must determine how much labor to hire, how much to invest in hiring and training employees, how to deal with workforce diversity, and how to terminate employees.

1. The Demand for Labor

The demand for labor, or any factor of production, is a **derived demand**. The demand for the factors of production is derived from the demand for the products that the factors produce. Thus, the demand for labor is directly related to the demand for goods and services that the labor is used to produce. If the demand for lawyers increases (or decreases), then the derived demand for law professors increases (or decreases). If the demand for "law and order" increases, the derived demand for police officers increases. Derived demand also obeys the law of demand. All things being equal, if the price of an input increases, then firms will use less of it.

Firms combine various factors of production, mainly capital and labor, to produce goods or services that are sold in a product market. Their total output, and the way in which they combine labor and capital, depends on product demand, the amount of labor and capital they can acquire at given prices, and the choice of technologies available to them. The study of the demand for labor focuses on finding out how the number of workers employed by a firm, or set of firms, is affected by changes in one or more of these three forces. To simplify the discussion, it is assumed that all other forces, except for the one being studied, are held constant.

A fundamental question is how the number of employees demanded varies when wages change. Suppose that the wages facing a certain industry vary over a long period of time, but the technology available, the conditions under which the capital is supplied, and the relationship between product prices and product demand are unchanged. An increase in the wage rate impacts the quantity of labor demanded in two ways. First, higher wages imply higher costs and usually higher product prices. Because consumers respond to higher prices by buying less, employers tend to reduce their level of output. Lower output levels, of course, imply lower employment levels, other things being equal. This decline of employment is called a **scale effect**—the effect on desired employment of a smaller scale of production. Second, as wages increase, assuming the price of capital does not change, at least initially, employers have incentives to cut costs by adopting a technology that relies more on capital and less on labor. Thus, if wages rise, desired employment falls because of the shift towards a more capital-intensive mode of production. This second effect is called a **substitution effect**, because as wages rise, capital is substituted for labor in the production process.

These two insights yield a demand curve for labor. It shows how the desired level of employment (measured in either labor hours or number of employees) varies with changes in the price of labor when the other forces affecting demand are held constant. These other forces are the product demand schedule, the conditions under which capital can be obtained, and the set of technologies available. If wages change and these other factors do not, one can determine the change in quantity demanded by moving either up or down along the demand curve.

The interaction of supply and demand for labor results in an equilibrium wage. Once this wage is established, the individual buyers of labor—employers—are price takers. Since the equilibrium wage is established, the point of interest becomes the quantity of labor that an individual firm chooses to hire. Assume that the firm has many inputs, one of which is labor. Also, let the quantities of all inputs except labor be fixed. Labor, in other words, is the only variable input in the short run. So, in order to produce more output, the firm must hire more labor. Suppose the firm in this instance is a lawyer who must decide whether to hire a paralegal to help with legal research. Hiring the paralegal will increase output, which is sold to clients to obtain revenue. The increase in revenue as a result of hiring the paralegal is the marginal revenue. At the same time, hiring a paralegal will increase the cost of production because the paralegal must be paid. The increase in cost as a result of hiring the paralegal is the marginal cost. The lawyer makes a profit maximizing decision at the margin. If hiring the paralegal increases total revenue more than it increases total cost, then hiring the paralegal will increase profits. The lawyer will always hire a paralegal if doing so increases profits—that is, if the marginal revenue is greater than the marginal cost. Suppose the lawyer is thinking about hiring a second paralegal. The same decision process is repeated. If the marginal revenue of the additional paralegal is greater than the marginal cost of the additional paralegal, then he or she will be hired. This process continues with every prospective paralegal.

The law of diminishing marginal returns (discussed in more detail in Chapter IX) states that as more and more of a variable input is added to a production process in which there is a fixed input the marginal product of the variable input eventually declines. Here, the focus is on the role of workers as a variable input. As more paralegals are hired, the extra output of each paralegal eventually falls. Since each additional paralegal adds less and less to total output, the additional revenue that each paralegal produces eventually falls below the additional cost of hiring. At some point, the lawyer will stop hiring additional paralegals. In short, the profit maximizing lawyer should hire all paralegals that add more to revenue than to costs, but stop hiring at the point when the addition to revenue is just equal to the addition to cost.

The example of the lawyer's decision to hire paralegals can also be expressed in equation form with economic terminology. The extra output that each additional unit of labor adds to total output is called the **marginal product of labor**, MP_L.

$$MP_L = \Delta TP \div \Delta L$$

Where ΔTP is the change in total product and ΔL is the one unit increase in labor. Adding more of the variable input to other fixed inputs will eventually lead to a decrease in the marginal product of the variable input in the short run. Table VIII-1 shows a marginal product of labor schedule and summarizes the hypothetical choices available to the lawyer. The first column shows the number of paralegals. The second column shows the marginal product of the paralegal, the amount by which total output increases as one more unit

Table VIII-1. Marginal Product of Labor

Number of Paralegals	Marginal Product of Labor MP_L	Revenue $MR_C = P$	Marginal Revenue Product $MRP_L = MR_C \times MP_L$	Marginal Costs $MFC_L = $ Wage
1	14	$2	$28	$7
2	12	2	24	7
3	10	2	20	7
4	8	2	16	7
5	6	2	12	7
6	4	2	8	7
7	2	2	4	7
8	0	2	0	7

of labor is added to the production process. The first paralegal adds 14 units of output, the second adds 12 units of output, and so forth. MP_L decreases as the amount of labor increases, according to the law of diminishing marginal returns.

When the extra legal services produced by each additional paralegal are sold, the resulting increase of total revenue is called the **marginal revenue product of labor**, MRP_L.

$$MRP_L = \Delta TR \div \Delta L$$

Where ΔTR is the change in total revenue and ΔL is the change in the amount of the labor hired. Another method of expressing MRP_L is

$$MRP_L = MR_C \times MP_L$$

Where MR_C is the marginal revenue under competitive conditions (that is, MR_C is the increase in total revenue resulting from selling one more unit of output) and MP_L is the marginal product of labor. For the firm that sells its product in a perfectly competitive market, marginal revenue is equal to the price of the product. Thus, the marginal revenue product is simply the price of the final product times the marginal product of each unit of labor. As shown in Table VIII-1, the marginal revenue product of the firm's first unit of labor is found by multiplying the marginal product by the price of the product. Marginal revenue product, MRP_L, declines as more paralegals are hired because MP_L declines.

Regardless of the economic shorthand used, the profit maximizing firm will continue adding units of labor as long as the additional revenues that labor produces are greater than the additional costs of labor. The firm will stop hiring when the additional revenues are less than the additional costs of hiring. The extra cost of hiring one more unit of labor is called the **marginal factor cost of labor** (MFC_L).

$$MFC_L = \Delta TC \div \Delta L$$

Where ΔTC is the change in total cost and ΔL is the one unit change in labor. Under competitive conditions, the firm may purchase all of the labor it wants at the prevailing wage rate. Each additional paralegal in Table VIII-1 has a marginal factor cost equal to the wage rate ($MFC_L = W$).

The profit maximizing lawyer will hire additional paralegals to the point where $MRP_L = MFC_L$ — or, in the alternative, $MRP_L = W$. The numbers in Table VIII-1 indicate that the lawyer should hire 6 paralegals. Each unit of labor from the first to the sixth adds more to the revenue than to cost. By hiring 6 units the lawyer adds as much as possible to profit. However, the seventh paralegal adds more to cost than to revenue and, therefore, will not be hired.

This process is derived from the manner in which the competitive firm determines its profit maximizing output. The firm follows the same process to equate its marginal cost to marginal revenue in hiring inputs as it does in selling its product. In fact, when the firm hires the profit maximizing quantity of labor, that amount of labor produces the profit maximizing level of output. The numbers used in Table VIII-1 are presented in graphical form in Figure VIII-4. The MP_L curve is drawn by plotting the points from columns 1 and 2. The demand curve for the lawyer's services as shown in panel (b) where price equals $2.00. The MRP_L is shown in panel (c). The competitive wage is $7.00, stated as MFC_L. The profit maximizing quantity of labor is the point where the MFC_L curve crosses the MRP_L curve. At this point, the marginal revenue product of labor equals the marginal factor cost of labor.

Figure VIII-4. The Profit-Maximizing Quantity of Labor

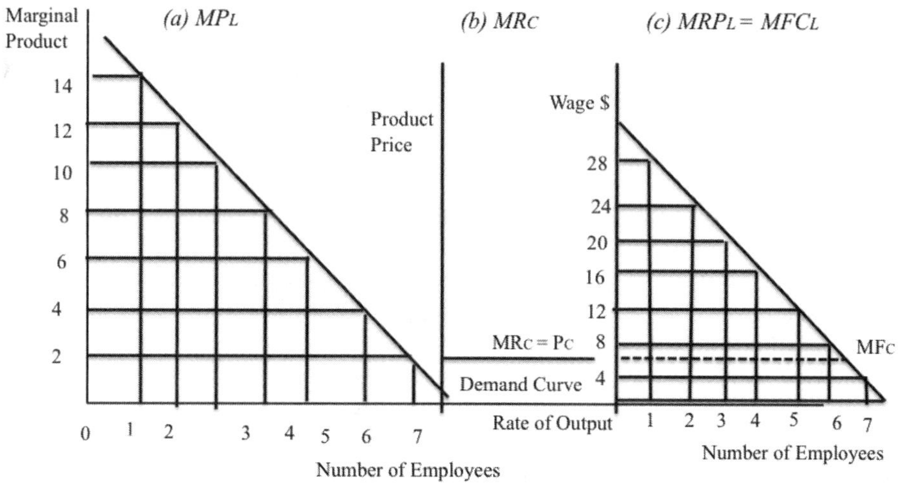

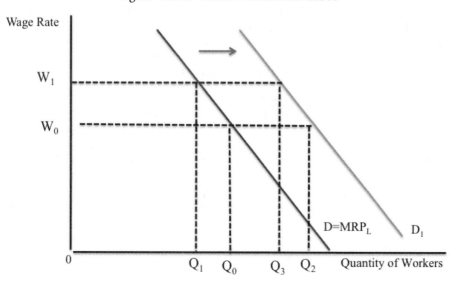

Marginal productivity theory gives insight into the purchasing behavior of firms. Obviously, firms employ many inputs other than labor. The profit-maximizing rule for the level of employment is the same for each resource. In the short run, when labor is the only variable input, the firm is willing to purchase or hire additional units up to the point where $MRP_L = W$. Thus, MRP_L traces the relation between the price of labor, the wage rate, and the amount of labor a firm is willing to purchase. In other words, the marginal revenue product curve is also the firm's short run demand curve for labor. Figure VIII-5 illustrates this. At wage rate, W_0, the firm chooses Q_0 units of labor. At a higher wage, such as W_1, less labor is hired. For each wage, the firm adjusts the level of employment to maintain the equation $MRP_L = W$.

Figure VIII-5. Firm's Demand for Labor

The demand for labor also changes when the factors that we normally hold constant change. For example, suppose the demand for the product of a particular industry increases so that, at any price, more of the goods or services in question can be sold. If the technology and the conditions in which capital and labor are made available to industry do not change, then output levels will rise as firms in the industry seek to maximize profits. This scale, or output effect, would increase the demand for labor at any given wage rate. As long as the relative prices of capital and labor remained unchanged, there is no substitution effect. As a result, the entire demand curve shifts to the right. This rightward shift from D to D_1 in Figure VIII-5 indicates that at every possible wage rate, employers demand more workers.

Consider what would happen if the product demand schedule, technology, and labor supply conditions remain the same, but the supply of capital changes so that the price of capital falls to fifty percent of its prior level. We can divide the effect on labor demanded by this price change into two parts — scale effects and substitution effects. First, when capital prices decline, the cost of producing tends to decline. Lower producer costs stimulate increases in production which tends to raise the level of desired employment at any given wage. The scale effect of a fall in capital rates thus tends to increase the demand for labor at each wage level. The second effect of a fall in capital prices is a substitution effect, whereby firms adopt more capital intensive technologies in response to cheaper capital. Such firms would substitute capital for labor and use less labor to produce a given amount of output than before. With less labor being desired at each wage rate, the labor demand curve tends to shift to the left. The fall in capital prices thus generates two opposite effects on the demand for labor. The scale effect will push the labor demand curve rightward, while the substitution effect will push it to the left. Either effect could dominate; thus economic theory does not yield a clear-cut prediction regarding how a fall in capital prices will affect the demand for labor. A rise is capital prices would generate the same overall ambiguity of effect on the demand for labor.

The hypothesized changes due to changes in product demand and changes in capital prices tend to shift the demand curve for labor. It is important to distinguish between a shift in a demand curve and a movement along the curve. A labor demand curve graphically shows the labor desired as a function of the wage rate. When the wage changes and other forces are held constant, one moves along the curve. However, when one of the other forces changes, the labor demand curve shifts. Unlike wages, these forces are not directly shown when the demand curve for labor is drawn. Thus, when they change, a different relationship between wages and desired employment prevails and this shows up as a shift of the demand curve. If more labor is desired at any given wage rate, then the curve has shifted to the right. If less labor is demanded, then demand curve has shifted left.

The demand for labor can be analyzed on three levels: (1) to analyze the demand for labor by a particular firm, one would examine how an increase in the wage of, say, a paralegal, would affect his employment by a particular law firm; (2) to analyze the effect of this wage increase on the employment of paralegals in the entire law firm industry, one would use an industry demand curve; (3) finally, to see how the wage increase would affect the entire labor market for paralegals in all industries in which they are used, one would use a market demand curve. For example, paralegals are also used in government agencies such as the Securities Exchange Commission. Firm, industry, and market labor demand curves vary in shape, to some extent because scale and substitution effects have different strengths at each level. However, it is important to remember that the scale and substitution effects on wage changes work in the same direction at each level so that firm, industry, and market demand curves all slope downward. One can also distinguish between long run and short run labor demand curves. Over very short periods of time, employers find it difficult to substitute capital for labor, or vice versa. The customers may not alter their product demand very much in response to a price increase. It takes time to fully adjust consumption and production pay. Over long periods of time, of course, responses to changes in wages and other factors affecting the demand for labor are larger and more complete.

A typical objection that is sometimes raised to the theory of labor demand introduced here is that the theory assumes a degree of sophistication on the part of real world employers that is just not there. It is hard to imagine an employer uttering the words "marginal revenue product of labor." Employers, it is argued, are both unfamiliar with the textbook rules of profit maximization and unable in many situations accurately to measure or value the output of individual units of labor. The typical reply to this objection is that regardless of whether employers can verbalize the profit maximizing conditions or explicitly measure the marginal revenue product of labor, they must at least intuit them to survive in a competitive market. This is true because competition weeds out employers who are not good at generating profits in much the same manner as competition weeds out pinball players who do not understand the intricacies of how speed, angles, and spin affect the motion of bodies through space. Yet it would be surprising if the best pinball players in America could verbalize Newton's laws of motion. Employers can know concepts without being able to verbalize them: employers that cannot maximize profits do not last long in competitive markets. Employers that survive in competitive markets know how to maximize profits—whether they articulate the general concepts or not.

2. Employer Investments

Employers attempt to maximize profits by selecting the optimal combination of inputs. The selection and development of employees is an extremely important part of most firms' decision making. Since people vary in their skills and working habits, it often behooves firms to invest time and resources in selecting the right individuals at the lowest possible cost as well as to invest in training some individuals once they have been hired.

a. Hiring

Firms often incur significant costs in selecting employees. Since firms often bear the cost of hiring and training workers, they prefer to obtain a work force of a given quality at the least possible cost. Similarly, they prefer to hire workers who are fast learners, because those workers can be trained at less cost. Unfortunately, it may prove expensive for firms to investigate extensively the background of every possible individual who applies for a job in order to ascertain his or her skill level and aptitude for training. One way to reduce these search costs is to rely on credentials or signals in a hiring process, rather than intensely investigating the qualities of individual applicants. For example, if, on average, college graduates are more productive than high school graduates, an employer might specify that a college degree is a requirement for the job. Rather than interviewing and testing all applicants to try to ascertain the productivity of each, the firm may simply select its new employees from the pool of applicants who meet the educational standard. Similarly, if employees believe that married men are less likely to quit their jobs than single men, or that 25-year-olds are less likely to quit than teenagers, then they may want to give preferential treatment to married men and 25-year-olds over single men and teenagers in the hiring process.

Judging individuals based on group characteristics is one type of statistical discrimination. This discrimination can carry some obvious costs. On the one hand, for example, some high school graduates may be fully qualified to work for a firm that insists on college graduates. Excluding them from the pool of potential applicants imposes costs on them, in the sense that they do not get the job. It also imposes costs on the employer if other qualified applicants cannot be readily found. On the other hand, there may be some unproductive workers among the group of college graduates, and the employer who hires them may well suffer losses while they are employed. However, if the reduction in hiring costs that arises when signals such as educational credentials, marital status, or age are used is large, then it may prove profitable for an employer to use them even if an occasional unsatisfactory worker sneaks through. In other words, the total costs of hiring, training, and employing workers may well be lower for some firms when hiring standards are used than when such firms rely on more intensive investigations of applicant characteristics. The Supreme Court has prohibited at least two obvious proxies for worker ability—possession of a high school diploma and the administration of a generalized intelligence test—as a condition of employment absent a legitimate "business necessity." *Griggs v. Duke Power Co.*, 401 U.S. 424, 431–32, 436 (1971). What effect do you think this prohibition has on employers' costs in finding workers? On labor costs generally? Are these additional costs offset by any other beneficial social policies—including potentially efficient arrangements? (For one, though not the only, possible answer, see our section below on discrimination in labor markets.)

But proxies such as age, degrees, and background are not the only method to find and screen potential employees. Firms may delegate this task to specialized agencies with expertise in evaluating and placing workers. These employment agencies can reduce firms' search costs, but introduce additional economic and legal issues. Consider the information costs involved in interviewing and hiring potential workers while you read the next case.

Columbus Medical Services, LLC v. Thomas

Court of Appeals of Tennessee
308 S.W.3d 368 (2009)

HOLLY M. KIRBY, J.

BACKGROUND

The Arlington Developmental Center ("Arlington") is a residential facility in Arlington, Tennessee, serving persons with disabilities, both physical and mental, ranging from speech impairments to physical incapacity and varying degrees of mental retardation.

* * *

The therapists utilized by Arlington are highly educated and specialized, all with college degrees and some with master's degrees, and staffing a particular therapist position can entail a wide-ranging search. To do so, Arlington engaged the services of Plaintiff/Appellee Columbus Medical Services, LLC ("Columbus"), a staffing agency that provides services to state-run mental health care and mental retardation facilities throughout the United States. Columbus seeks out candidates to fill positions, prescreens the candidates, checks their references, background and credentialing, and brings the candidates to the location to meet with the facility's management. Beginning in 1994, pursuant to a series of exclusive contracts with the State of Tennessee ("State"), Columbus provided Arlington with a staff of physical, occupational, and speech language therapists.

* * *

FACTS AND PROCEDURAL HISTORY

Columbus's exclusive contract with the State to staff Arlington was scheduled to expire by its own terms on June 30, 2003. In the early spring of 2003, in anticipation of the expiration of the Columbus/Arlington contract, the State issued requests for proposals ("RFPs") to staff the successor contract. Under State procedures, the State would accept bids from a variety of vendors and evaluate them in light of the needs of the facility. While cost was a significant component of the bidding process, the State also considered the technical requirements and the qualifications of the entity submitting the bid, and it ultimately would award the contract to the overall "best" bid.

Former Columbus employee Thomas, by then an independent consultant, considered bidding on the Arlington contract but decided that it was "a little big" for his newly formed disabilities consulting firm. Thomas contacted Defendant/Appellant Liberty Healthcare Corporation ("Liberty"), a staffing agency similar to Columbus and a competitor of Columbus. Thomas suggested to Liberty that they collaborate to submit a proposal to the State for Liberty to take over the contract to staff Arlington's therapists.

* * *

On March 14, 2003, the State sent Liberty and Columbus letters notifying them that the State intended to award the Arlington contract to Liberty effective July 1, 2003.

* * *

At the time Liberty won the bid to staff Arlington, Columbus employed twenty-two therapists at Arlington, including the nine therapists at issue in this appeal (hereinafter referred to as the "Therapist Defendants").

* * *

Each of these Therapist Defendants had signed an employment agreement with Columbus that contained the following non-compete provision:

> During the period of employment and for a period of one (1) year after termination for any reason whatsoever, EMPLOYEE shall not directly or indirectly solicit business from, or agree to provide services to FACILITY. EMPLOYEE shall not seek to induce any person who provides services for EMPLOYER to breach, in whole or in part, a contract or agreement with the EMPLOYER, or to terminate same, or fail or refuse to renew same.

> The parties hereto recognize and agree that EMPLOYEE's services pursuant to this Agreement are unique and extraordinary, and that damages incurred by EMPLOYER as a result of EMPLOYEE's breach of previous paragraph would be difficult to ascertain or measure. Accordingly, the parties agree that in the event of a breach of restrictive covenant clause by EMPLOYEE, EMPLOYER will incur minimum liquidated damages of $10,000 if a breach of this Agreement by EMPLOYEE causes actual damages to EMPLOYER in excess of the minimum liquidated damages of $10,000. The parties hereto agree that the sum of $10,000 constitutes a reasonable approximation of the minimum actual damages that would be incurred by EMPLOYER as a result of EMPLOYEE's breach, and that the provisions of this paragraph do not constitute a penalty.

Thus, the non-compete provision states that the employee "shall not directly or indirectly ... agree to provide services to" Arlington for one year after the termination of his employment with Columbus. It provided for liquidated damages in the event of a breach, stating that

$10,000 was "a reasonable approximation of the minimum actual damages" to Columbus resulting from the therapist's breach of the non-compete provision.

After receiving the State's notification of its intent to award the Arlington contract to Liberty, Columbus sent Liberty a letter dated March 19, 2003, informing Liberty that Columbus's therapists at Arlington were subject to the restrictive covenants, and warning that Columbus intended to enforce the covenants. Columbus wrote Liberty that it "expects that, in the event Liberty is ultimately awarded a contract to render services at Arlington, Liberty will continue to respect Columbus' contract rights and refrain from offering employment opportunities to Columbus' employees that violate Columbus' rights." Liberty did not respond to this letter.

In the meantime, Liberty had consulted with independent counsel regarding the non-compete covenants in the Therapist Defendants' contracts and received advice that the covenants were unenforceable. After receiving this opinion, Liberty began to recruit the Therapist Defendants to continue to work at Arlington through Liberty under the new contract. Arlington superintendent Johnson had an interest in maintaining continuity of care for the Arlington residents, was pleased with the therapists' work, and had been in contact with former Columbus executive Thomas, so he encouraged Liberty to recruit incumbent therapists to work at Arlington under the new Liberty contract.

* * *

In a letter dated June 4, 2003, Columbus notified the incumbent Arlington employees that their employment contracts would be terminated as of June 30, 2003. The letter warned the employees that Columbus would take legal action against them if they worked for Liberty at Arlington in violation of their contracts. Columbus representatives also met with some of the Therapist Defendants about Columbus's loss of the Arlington contract, implying that while Columbus might "overlook" the therapists working for the State, Columbus would not "make [it] easy for Liberty" to employ the therapists at Arlington. While Columbus was able to offer alternative employment to some of the therapists who had non-compete agreements, Columbus offered no comparable alternative employment to the nine Therapist Defendants. The Therapist Defendants looked for comparable employment in the same geographic area and beyond, with no success. Finally, despite the warnings from Columbus, on July 1, 2003, the nine Therapist Defendants, among others, began working at Arlington under employment agreements with Liberty.

On December 12, 2003, as promised, Columbus filed a lawsuit against the Therapist Defendants in the trial court below, alleging that the therapists breached their covenants not to compete by providing services at Arlington through Liberty's staffing services.

* * *

On October 26, 2007, the trial court issued a comprehensive memorandum opinion concluding that the non-compete covenants were enforceable, that the Therapist Defendants had breached their employment agreements, and that Liberty had induced those defendants to do so.

* * *

ISSUES ON APPEAL

On appeal, Appellants argue that the trial court erred in several respects. Their main contention is that the non-compete covenant in the Therapist Defendants' employment agreements is not enforceable, because Columbus had no legitimate business interest to protect, particularly after its contract with Arlington expired on June 30, 2003.

* * *

Enforceability of Restrictive Covenant

The trial court correctly observed that Columbus's claims "hinge [ ] upon the existence of a legal and binding contract between Columbus and the [Therapist] Defendants." Thus, we first address the Appellants' argument that the non-compete covenant in the Therapist Defendants' employment agreements is not enforceable.

* * *

... [I]n the instant case, we must ascertain whether Columbus has a legitimate business interest that is protectable by the non-compete covenant at issue. If the employer has such a legitimate business interest, we must then determine whether the non-compete provision is reasonable and enforceable under the circumstances of this case. If the court finds that the employer does not have a legitimate protectable business interest, then the non-compete covenant is unenforceable under Tennessee law.

Legitimate Business Interest

In determining whether Columbus in this case has a legitimate protectable business interest, we are guided by the Supreme Court's analysis in *Hasty v. Rent–A–Driver, Inc.*, in which the Court observed:

> Of course, any competition by a former employee may well injure the business of the employer. An employer, however, cannot by contract restrain ordinary competition. In order for an employer to be entitled to protection, there must be special facts present over and above ordinary competition. These special facts must be such that without the covenant not to compete the employee would gain an unfair advantage in future competition with the employer.

Therefore, Columbus must show special facts beyond protection from ordinary competition that would give *the employee* an unfair advantage in competing with the employer. This Court elaborated on this requirement in *Vantage Tech.*, [*LLC v. Cross*]:

> Considerations in determining whether an employee would have such an unfair advantage include (1) whether the employer provided the employee with specialized training; (2) whether the employee is given access to trade or business secrets or other confidential information; and (3) whether the employer's customers tend to associate the employer's business with the employee due to the employee's repeated contacts with the customers on behalf of the employer. These considerations may operate individually or in tandem to give rise to a properly protectable business interest.

Thus, with due consideration to the three *Vantage* factors, "the employer must show 'special facts present over and above ordinary competition' such that the employee would have an unfair advantage over the employer absent the noncompetition agreement after his employment has ended."

* * *

The trial court in this case determined that Columbus had a legitimate protectable business interest in light of its recruitment and relocation costs for the Therapist Defendants, the specialized training provided by Columbus, and the unique relationships formed between the Therapist Defendants and the patients at Arlington. The specialized training, the court found, "was an integral part of compliance with the Federal Court Order."

On appeal, the Appellants argue that the trial court erred in reaching this conclusion because recruitment costs and goodwill do not fall into any of the legally cognizable business interests recognized in Tennessee as outlined in *Vantage*. In addition, the specialized training to which the trial court referred was provided by the State, not by Columbus. The investment in training, therefore, is not a legitimate business interest of Columbus. Furthermore, the Appellants argue, any investment by Columbus in these Therapist Defendants would be lost regardless, because Columbus's contract with the State to staff Arlington expired by its own terms on June 30, 2003. Consequently, Columbus had no legitimate business interest in enforcing the non-compete covenants after that date.

In response, Columbus argues that the universe of legitimate business interests is not limited to the three enumerated in *Vantage;* the *Vantage* court simply held that an employer seeking to enforce a non-competition covenant must show the existence of "special facts over and above ordinary competition." In any event, Columbus argues, ample evidence supported the trial court's finding that the non-compete covenant in this case protected Columbus's investment in specialized training and its customer relationships. Columbus concedes that the State paid for the Therapist Defendants' specialized training, but claims that the training was made possible by their employment with Columbus and notes that the Therapist Defendants were paid by Columbus during the training. Columbus also relies on cases from other jurisdictions that have recognized a staffing agency's legitimate protectable business interest in preventing "opportunistic disintermediation," that is, either the improper elimination of the staffing agency as the "middle man" or the appropriation of the staffing agency's services without proper compensation. Based on the facts of this case, Columbus argues, it had a legitimate business interest in restricting the Therapist Defendants' employment as prescribed in their non-compete agreements.

The question of whether "opportunistic disintermediation" is recognizable as a legitimate business interest protectable by a restrictive covenant has not been addressed by a Tennessee appellate court. An explanation of the concept is helpful to an understanding of the Appellants' argument on appeal.

The seminal case on this issue appears to be *Consultants & Designers, Inc. v. Butler Serv. Group, Inc. ("C&D")*. In *C&D*, Butler Services Group ("Butler"), an employment agency for technical service employees, contracted to supply technical employees to the Tennessee Valley Authority ("TVA"). The TVA contract was set to expire on May 3, 1980. Butler's contract with its employees contained a non-compete provision similar to the one in the instant case, restricting the employees from accepting employment with the TVA directly or indirectly for ninety days following the completion of their assignments. Sometime in 1979, the TVA requested proposals from several technical service employment agencies, including plaintiff Butler and defendant C & D, to supply employees upon the expiration of Butler's contract. C & D was awarded the TVA staffing contract. Subsequently, C & D began soliciting Butler's employees at TVA to staff the new contract. Butler put C & D on notice that it would seek to enforce the non-compete provision in the employees' contracts.

Butler filed a lawsuit against C & D in federal court for tortious interference with its contract with its employees. Applying the "reasonableness" standard utilized in Tennessee and other states, the federal district court held that the non-compete covenants were unenforceable. The Eleventh Circuit reversed, finding that Butler had a legitimate protectable business interest in preventing its employees and others from appropriating Butler's services as "the much maligned but time-honored middleman" without compensation. The appellate court explained that an employment agency, as the middleman, provides costly and valuable information to both individuals seeking employment and to the businesses seeking skilled employees:

> While in a technical sense the relationship between Butler and its job shoppers was employer-employee, this characterization of the relationship does more to obscure the relevant issues than to enlighten them. It is more revealing to recognize Butler's role as that of the much maligned but time-honored middleman. Butler served as an intermediary in the market for highly-skilled, technically-trained workers. There were individuals seeking such employment and firms seeking to employ them. In a pristine world in which information is costless, there would be no need for the essential service that Butler performs. The client firms and the prospective employees would each know what the other has to offer and could negotiate a contract instantaneously and costlessly. That, however, is not the nature of the world in which we live. Butler and C & D, and the fifteen other firms that applied for the contract with TVA, as well as a myriad of other firms in the technical service and related industries, exist and flourish because information is a costly and valuable commodity.

> Whatever ancillary services Butler supplied to TVA, it was as a provider of information that Butler performed its essential function. Butler's role was to gather, distill, and provide to TVA information on available and suitable people for TVA's positions and simultaneously to provide to prospective job shoppers information about TVA and the positions it was offering. Thus, in this sense, Butler was serving as a form of an employment agency. In the market for the information in which Butler dealt, it had to compete with: (1) all other technical service firms; (2) conventional employment agencies; and (3) disintermediation by firms and workers. Disintermediation is the actualization of the ever-present cry to eliminate the middleman, i.e., direct solicitation, negotiation and contracting between the firm and the worker. Eliminating the middleman is at first blush a facile and attractive alternative. However, middlemen exist because they provide a useful and highly-valued service. If Butler's covenant with its job shoppers is to have any justification, that justification must be to protect Butler's role as a middleman in the market for information between job shoppers and client firms.

Thus, the *C&D* court found that Butler's role as middleman between the employee and the employer had value that warranted protection.

The *C&D* court explained that, once an employee has been placed with a client business, absent some contractual obstacle, the employee and the client business would be free to sever their relationship with the employment agency and "cut out the middleman." The non-compete restriction in the employees' contracts, the *C&D* court reasoned, was crafted to prevent such "opportunistic disintermediation":

> The covenant between Butler and TVA not to hire one another's employees and the restrictive covenants in Butler's contracts with its job shoppers were clearly crafted to prevent such disintermediation. But for these contractual constraints the job shoppers and the TVA could get the benefit of Butler's services without paying the full price of those services. The application of Butler's restrictive covenant after the termination of its contract with TVA was designed to protect against TVA terminating Butler and then hiring either directly, or indirectly through another technical service firm, the Butler job shoppers. TVA had the power and the right to terminate Butler, but not to abrogate Butler's property interest in its job shoppers. Butler's rights under its

employment contracts need not have been enforced. They could have been sold. Regardless of whether Butler would have struck a deal with the job shoppers, TVA, or the successor TSF, Butler was nonetheless protected by the covenant from opportunistic termination of the relationship by TVA. Therefore we conclude that Butler had a legitimate interest in protecting from opportunistic appropriation its investment in acquiring the information necessary to carry on its business, and that the covenant was reasonably well crafted to carry out that task.

Thus, the Eleventh Circuit found that Butler had a legitimate enforceable business interest in preventing opportunistic appropriation of Butler's investment in its employees and in procuring the information necessary to carry on its business. After weighing Butler's business interest against the effect of the non-compete covenant on the general public, the *C&D* court determined that the non-compete covenant was reasonable and enforceable.

*   *   *

We are persuaded by these authorities that the avoidance of such an opportunistic disintermediation should be recognized as a legitimate business interest protectable by a non-compete covenant. As the *C&D* court recognized, the nature of an employment agency's business is unique in that its main service is to provide the "costly and valuable commodity" of time, effort, and expense in finding and putting together prospective employees and employers and negotiating contracts related to their employment. Non-compete provisions may be included in the employees' contracts to protect the agency's investment by preventing unfair disintermediation, i.e., usurpation of the agency's role by the client hiring the employees directly or through another employment agency. Thus, to the extent that an employment agency has invested resources with respect to a particular employee, the agency may have a legitimate business interest in protecting itself against unfair disintermediation.

We now turn to Columbus's business interest with the Therapist Defendants. Here, Columbus had little investment of its resources into the specialized training of the Therapist Defendants. Columbus did pay the employees while they received the training, albeit with the normal reimbursement by the State. However, the training was required by and paid for by the State, not by Columbus. The training was not just for Columbus employees; all employees at Arlington underwent training so that they could serve the unique patient population at Arlington in a manner consistent with the federal court order governing Arlington.

The factor of whether the Therapist Defendants are the "face" of Columbus is complicated somewhat by the unique role of an employment agency. Columbus's customer here is Arlington and the State, not the individual patients with whom the Therapist Defendants developed relationships. Arlington was, of course, always mindful that the Therapist Defendants were staffed through Columbus. In fact, Arlington remained a client of Columbus for purposes of staffing behavioral and psychology positions. However, the Therapist Defendants' relationships with the Arlington patients obviously motivated Arlington to try to keep the Therapist Defendants working at the Arlington Center. The Therapist Defendants were not traditional employees; rather, because Columbus is an employment agency, they were part of the "product" or service sold by Columbus. Thus, the Therapist Defendants' relationship with the patients were part of their value to Columbus. This could constitute a "special fact" that, under *Hasty v. Rent–A–Driver,* could give "the employee … an unfair advantage in future competition with" Columbus in the absence of a non-compete agreement.

The Appellants argue that, because Columbus lost the bid for the Arlington contract, Columbus would have lost its investment in the Therapist Defendants regardless of whether they were later hired by Liberty. This is true and could in the final analysis affect the weight given to Columbus's business interest. However, in evaluating whether Columbus has a legitimate protectable business interest, we must consider the circumstances at the time the parties entered into the employment agreement. If Columbus does its job well and places capable employees with its client, the non-compete covenant provides powerful motivation for the client to keep Columbus as its staffing agency. The fact that the non-compete did not, in this instance, sufficiently motivate the State to award the bid to Columbus does not mean that Columbus had no legitimate protectable business interest.

Without using the "twenty-dollar" term, the trial court in effect found that Columbus had a legitimate business interest in preventing unfair disintermediation by Liberty through its recognition that Columbus had incurred recruitment and relocation costs with respect to the Therapist Defendants. This finding is supported by evidence showing that Columbus, as the employment agency, provided the typical employment agency services of recruiting the employees and negotiating their employment conditions with the client, Arlington. Overall, we find that the preponderance of the evidence supports the trial court's conclusion that Columbus had a legitimate business interest and that Columbus could, under appropriate circumstances, protect its investment through the use of non-compete covenants.

* * *

Notes and Questions

1. Restrictive Covenants and the Middleman: A restrictive covenant is a contract between an employer and employee that restricts the employee from competing against the employer for a certain amount of time after termination. As the court points out, this allowed Columbus to invest in the resources necessary to find jobs for its job-shoppers. Columbus is a middleman whose service is to help the market function by matching buyers and sellers of services. The restrictive covenant allows Columbus to earn a profit on the investment of time and resources in getting the buyers and sellers together. Columbus is compensated by, in effect, marking up the job-shoppers' salary. The mark-up is a tempting target for both Arlington and the job shoppers because it should be possible for them to agree on a new contract with a salary between the salary paid by Columbus to the job seekers and the fees received by Columbus from Arlington. Columbus is vulnerable because its investment in finding workers jobs at Arlington is both firm-specific to Arlington as well as specific to each employee. The restrictive covenant protects Columbus from opportunistic behavior by either the ultimate employer or the job-shoppers. From this viewpoint, the restrictive covenant is necessary for Columbus to stay in business. Is enforcement of the restrictive covenant beneficial to the job shoppers? Is it beneficial to the employers?

2. Wages: How does a restrictive covenant affect wages? Does it allow for higher wages— or does it depress wages? Or both?

b. Training

There are two types of training: **General training**, which increases an individual's productivity to many employers equally, and **specific training**, which increases an individual's productivity only to the firm in which he or she is currently employed. General training might include teaching an applicant basic reading skills, or teaching an aspiring paralegal how to conduct legal research. Specific training might include teaching a secretary how to use a law firm's unique filing system. Employees, in the absence of some type of contractual restraint, will tend to bear the costs of general training because the employees are generally free to take it with them to another employer. Employees often bear these general training costs in the form of lower wages during a training period or an apprenticeship. This perspective partially explains both lower salaries for judicial clerks and why many sophisticated law firms reward judicial clerks with seniority and bonuses in light of their portable experience. On the other hand, the employer is expected to pay for specific training, since the employer will receive higher productivity from the employee from that training, yet the employee will be unable to receive any benefits in the form of higher wages from that training by moving to another job. One major implication of the provision of specific training is that firms who invest in specific training are reluctant to lay off workers in whom they have invested.

One significant implication of the distinction between general and specific training has to do with the effects of the minimum wage on training. Since firms will offer general training only if the employees fully pay for it, the employees must receive an initial period wage that is below actual marginal productivity by an amount equal to the direct costs of training. If the minimum wage is set so that receiving such a low wage is precluded, the employers will not offer them training. They may be willing to hire workers if the minimum wage is not above the marginal productivity. However, any training would have to take place off the job. This is merely one secondary consequence on labor markets that a price floor imposes.

3. Discrimination

Managers, like many other people, have prejudices that are reflected, consciously or unconsciously, in hiring decisions. When one group controls the hiring for most jobs, their prejudices can, and often do, affect their hiring decisions. Whether prejudices should be allowed to affect the hiring decision is a normative question decided through the political process. Virtually every level of government in the U.S. has passed laws making it illegal for employers to discrimination on the basis of race, religion, sex, age, disability, or national origin. Economists cannot provide answers to the normative question of whether society should allow discrimination. Economists can, however, provide insights into how discrimination, and society's attempts to eliminate it, affect the economy.

For whatever reason, some people do not like members of other groups of people. Historically, members of majority groups have discriminated against minorities. If people with those preferences are in positions that control hiring decisions, then the market demand for minorities will be below the market demand for members of the decision making group. As illustrated in Figure VIII-6, the demand for minorities is to the left of the demand for the majority. The result is lower wages (W_M) and fewer job opportunities (Q_M) for minorities. Conceptually, there is a dual labor market—one for the majority and one for minorities. Favored groups are preferred, but the lower wage for minorities makes it expensive for employers to discriminate by substituting expensive majority workers for equally productive (yet less expensive) minority workers. In other words, discrimination can be expensive to employers.

Implicit in the preceding analysis is the assumption that all workers are equally productive—that is, there is no economic justification for the employer's distinction between workers. The following case deals with compensation differences when there is an economic justification for the distinction.

Figure VIII-6. Impact of Direct Wage Discrimination

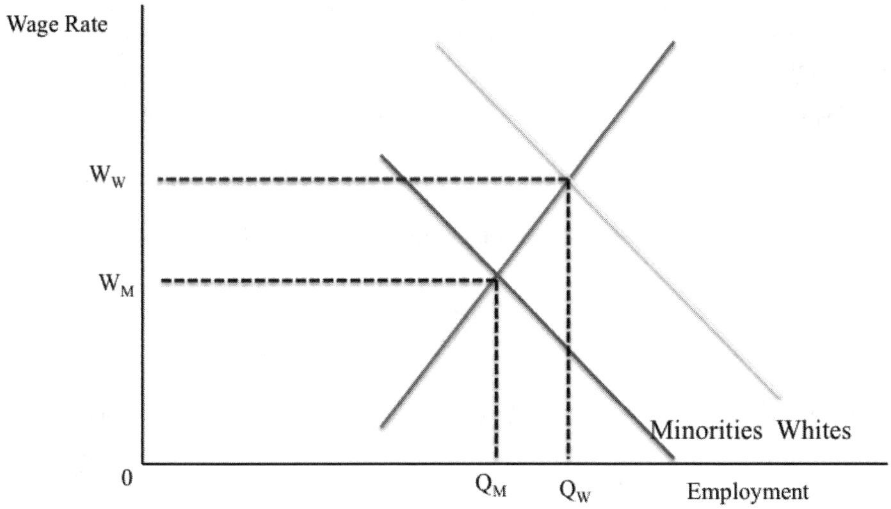

Wood v. City of San Diego

United States Court of Appeals for the Ninth Circuit
678 F.3d 1075 (2012)

B. FLETCHER, Circuit Judge:

Janet Wood ("Wood") brought suit under Title VII of the Civil Rights Act of 1964, alleging that the surviving spouse benefit provided by the City of San Diego ("the City") to its retired employees discriminates on the basis of sex. The district court dismissed Wood's disparate treatment and disparate impact claims and entered judgment in favor of the City. We affirm.

I.

Wood retired in 2005 after over thirty-two years as an employee of the City. Like all City employees, Wood participated in the City's defined benefit pension plan, which is administered by the San Diego City Employee Retirement System ("SDCERS"). City employees are required to contribute a percentage of their salary to their pensions, and the City is required to make "substantially equal" contributions. City employees are also required to contribute a percentage of their salary to fund survivor benefits as well as their pensions. Pension contributions and benefits are calculated by ordinance and are neutral with respect to sex (the characteristic relevant to this case).

When a City employee retires, she must choose among several options for allocating the pension benefit and the survivor benefit. We will refer to the option at issue in this case ... as the "surviving spouse benefit." If a City employee is married (or has a registered domestic partner) at the time of retirement and chooses the surviving spouse benefit, the employee will receive her full monthly pension benefit until her death. At that time, if the employee's spouse or registered domestic partner survives her, the spouse or partner will receive a monthly allowance equal to half of the employee's monthly pension benefit.

If a City employee is single at the time of retirement and has chosen the surviving spouse benefit, the City either refunds the employee her contributions to the survivor benefit (plus interest) as a lump sum, or treats the employee's survivor contributions as voluntary additional contributions made to provide a larger monthly pension benefit. Wood was single when she retired and had chosen the surviving spouse benefit. She elected to have her survivor contributions treated as additional voluntary contributions, adding to her monthly benefit.

On September 24, 2003, Wood filed this class action against the City alleging that the surviving spouse benefit violates Title VII of the Civil Rights Act of 1964 ("Title VII")... Wood's theory of liability is that because, in the aggregate, the City pays a larger amount of money to the married retirees who select the surviving spouse benefits than it does to single retirees who do the same, and male retirees are more likely to be married, the surviving spouse benefit has an unlawful disparate impact on female retirees. The City does not dispute that, in the aggregate, it costs more to fund surviving spouse benefits for married retirees than it does to refund the survivor contributions made by single retirees.

* * *

The City filed a motion to dismiss Wood's amended complaint. The City's sole argument with respect to the disparate impact claim was that the surviving spouse benefit is part of a bona fide seniority system, which is permitted as a matter of law under Title VII. The City also argued that Wood failed to state a claim for disparate treatment because she had not alleged discriminatory intent.

The district court denied the motion to dismiss with respect to the disparate impact claim. The district court found that while SDCERS as a whole is a bona fide seniority system, the surviving spouse benefit is a "component of the system [that] is not based on longevity of service." Although the amount of an employee's monthly pension (and thus the surviving spouse benefit) is based on seniority, the ability to receive the surviving spouse benefit is based only on marital status at the time of retirement.

The district court granted, however, the motion to dismiss the disparate treatment claim. The district court observed that Wood had alleged only that the City was aware of the disparate impact of the surviving spouse benefit at the time it adopted the policy and failed "to allege any facts establishing that the City *deliberately* adopted an employment practice ... in order to discriminate based on gender." Citing Supreme Court and Ninth Circuit case law, the district court ruled that "[a] plaintiff alleging disparate treatment must allege facts showing intentional discrimination.... The fact that an employer was aware of, or totally indifferent to the discriminatory impact of, its policy is not sufficient to state a claim for relief." * * *

On August 2, 2010, the parties filed cross-motions for summary judgment ... and the City filed a motion to dismiss the Title VII claim.... On November 22, 2010, the district court granted the motion to dismiss ... explain[ing] that Wood's allegation that she received a less valuable retirement benefit as a single employee "rests upon a series of contingencies," observing that "[i]f Wood had retired married, the value of her [surviving spouse] benefit ... would have been unknown on the date of retirement because that value was contingent upon a series of events: pre-deceasing her spouse, her spouse surviving her for a period of years, and her spouse's eligibility for the benefit at the time of her death."

The district court also addressed Wood's contention that she suffered economic injury "by receiving a refund of only her employee contributions ... whereas married retirees receive a benefit funded also by 'substantially equal' matching employer contributions." First, after reviewing the applicable City ordinances, the district court determined that there was no evidence that the City was required to make additional matching contributions to the survivor benefit. Second, the district court determined that Wood had no entitlement to any portion of the City's normal contributions that might fund the surviving spouse benefit, because those benefits technically belong to surviving spouses and not retirees.

The district court thus dismissed Wood's disparate impact claim ... Wood timely appealed the dismissal of her Title VII disparate treatment and disparate impact claims.

III.

Before the Supreme Court's decisions in *City of Los Angeles, Department of Water & Power v. Manhart,* and *Arizona Governing Committee for Tax Deferred Annuity & Deferred Compensation Plans v. Norris,* pension plans often openly discriminated on the basis of sex, in order to account for the fact that women as a class live longer than men. The pension plan at issue in *Manhart* required female employees to make larger contributions than male employees. The Supreme Court held that these contribution requirements constituted discrimination and were thus unlawful under Title VII. Five years later, the Court considered the pension plan at issue in *Norris,* which — rather than discriminating with respect to contribution requirements — paid female retirees smaller monthly benefits than male retirees who had made the same contributions. The Court held that this too violated Title VII, and reaffirmed that classification on the basis of sex is not permissible at either the "pay-out stage of a retirement plan" or the "pay-in stage." Retirement contributions and benefits must be facially neutral with respect to sex and other classifications protected under Title VII.

Prior to *Manhart,* the City of San Diego's retirement plan required male employees to make larger contributions to the surviving spouse benefit, based on the assumption that because women live longer, male employees were more likely to still be married when they retired and more likely to die before their spouses. After *Manhart,* the contribution amounts were equalized. The current plan is facially neutral: similarly situated male and female employees make the same contributions and receive the same benefits.

But according to Wood, the surviving spouse benefit continues to violate Title VII in two ways. First, because on average the City pays more in benefits to married retirees who select the surviving spouse benefit than it does to single retirees who do the same, and male retirees are more likely to be married, Wood claims that the surviving spouse benefit has an unlawful disparate impact on women. Second, because the City knew that male employees stood to gain more from the surviving spouse benefit — as evidenced by the original policy requiring men to make larger contributions — Wood claims that the City violated Title VII's disparate treatment provision when it equalized the contribution requirements without otherwise changing the program. We address Wood's disparate treatment claim first.

A.

* * *

Disparate treatment occurs "where an employer has treated a particular person less favorably than others because of a protected trait." "A disparate-treatment plaintiff must establish that the defendant had a discriminatory intent or motive for taking a job-related action." A discriminatory motive may be established by the employer's informal decision-making or "a formal, facially discriminatory policy," but "liability depends on whether the protected trait ... actually motivated the employer's decision." "It is insufficient for a plaintiff alleging discrimination under the disparate treatment theory to show the employer was merely aware of the adverse consequences the policy would have on a protected group."

Wood's disparate treatment claim ... alleges that the surviving spouse benefit "discriminates against women intentionally, within the meaning of Title VII, because it was adopted in 1971 with knowledge of its discriminatory effects." We agree with the district court that this does not adequately allege disparate treatment ... Wood does not claim that the City adopted the surviving spouse benefit *because* it would benefit men more often than women. Her only allegation is that, when the contribution requirements were equalized to comply with *Manhart,* the City was aware that male employees would disproportionately benefit from the change.

* * *

... Wood still does not suggest that she can allege any facts to show that the City had a discriminatory intent. We affirm the district court's dismissal of Wood's disparate treatment claim without granting leave to amend.

* * *

Throughout this litigation, Wood has alleged that ... she has suffered a pecuniary injury—namely, that "if married on the day of retirement, a retiring City employee receives a retirement benefit [the surviving spouse benefit] worth far more than the substitute benefit available to an unmarried employee." * * *

To support her allegation, Wood presented declarations stating (1) that in the aggregate, married retirees who choose the surviving spouse benefit receive a larger amount of money than unmarried retirees; (2) that, in the private market, an annuity providing the benefit that married retirees receive would cost more than an annuity providing the benefit that unmarried retirees receive; and (3) that the City makes matching contributions to fund the surviving spouse benefit but does not contribute to the benefit that unmarried retirees receive. * * *

The district court's analysis centered on the obvious fact that the value of a pension is tied to the length of a retiree's life. Like every other retired City employee, Wood cannot predict what the ultimate value of her pension will be, or whether she and her hypothetical spouse would have received more money had she been married. As the district court observed, these values are based on the "unknown variables of whether she would have pre-deceased her spouse, whether her spouse would have lived long enough to receive benefits, and whether the benefits received by her spouse would have had a value greater than that which she received [as a single employee] on the date of her retirement."

In other words, when Wood retired as a single employee, she received her monthly pension benefits plus a *guaranteed* refund of her survivor contributions (or at least the option to receive a guaranteed refund by taking them as a lump sum). She has no way of knowing whether this benefit is greater or less than what her hypothetical spouse would have received had she retired married and predeceased her spouse. Some married employees will have spouses who outlive them by many years and end up receiving a pension benefit greater than Wood's; other married employees will outlive their spouses, or they will die simultaneously, and thus receive no benefit from their survivor contributions at all. Similarly, Wood's evidence about the value of her retirement benefit as a private annuity was based on assumptions about the age of her hypothetical spouse and how long they both would have lived. Wood simply cannot show that, because she was single, she received a less valuable retirement benefit. * * *

On appeal, Wood ... continues to emphasize her argument that the private, actuarial value of her retirement benefit (if purchased on the private market) is less than the actuarial value of the benefit a similarly-situated married employee would receive.

We note that, in the Title VII context, the Supreme Court has made clear that its focus is on the compensation actually paid as a retirement benefit rather than the actuarial value of the policy. * * * Even if we accept Wood's argument, and review the decision below as a judgment on the merits for the City, we must affirm the decision of the district court, because Wood's claim is foreclosed by the Supreme Court's opinion in *Manhart.* In that case, the Supreme Court expressly recognized that facially neutral pension plans will inevitably have a disparate impact on some protected groups and concluded that such claims are not actionable under Title VII. Thus, even if the district court had considered Wood's disparate impact claim on the merits, it should have dismissed the claim.

As discussed previously, in *Manhart* the Court considered a pension plan that required female employees to make larger contributions than male employees in order to receive the same benefits, on the basis that women live longer than men and their pensions cost more. Recognizing that "the parties accept as unquestionably true" the generalization that women live longer than men, the Court framed its inquiry as "whether the existence or nonexistence of 'discrimination' is to be determined by comparison of class characteristics or individual characteristics."

After examining the text of Title VII, the Court held that "[t]he statute's focus on the individual is unambiguous. It precludes treatment of individuals as simply components of a racial, religious, sexual, or national class." Therefore, the Court concluded that, in order to comply with Title VII, pension plan contributions must be facially neutral with respect to sex (and presumably any other class protected by Title VII). In *Norris,* the Court confirmed that pension plan *benefits* must be facially neutral as well.

As part of the *Manhart* decision, the Court recognized that facially neutral pension plans would necessarily have a disparate impact on certain groups, and it expressly considered the very situation that Wood challenges here. The Court acknowledged, for example, that "unless women as a class are assessed an extra charge, they will be subsidized, to some extent, by the class of male employees." But, the Court noted, this type of subsidy is offset somewhat by survivor benefits: "Since female spouses of male employees are likely to have greater life expectancies than the male spouses of female employees, whatever benefits men lose in 'primary' coverage for themselves, they may regain in 'secondary' coverage for their wives." As a general matter, the Court explained:

> Individual risks, like individual performance, may not be predicted by resort to classifications proscribed by Title VII.... [W]hen insurance risks are grouped, the better risks always subsidize the poorer risks. Healthy persons subsidize medical benefits for the less healthy; *unmarried workers subsidize the pensions of married workers;* persons who eat, drink, or smoke to excess may subsidize pension benefits for persons whose habits are more temperate. Treating different classes of risks as though they were the same for purposes of group insurance is a common practice that has never been considered inherently unfair.

The Court also specifically addressed a disparate impact challenge based on these sorts of subsidies:

> A variation on the Department's fairness theme is the suggestion that a gender-neutral pension plan would itself violate Title VII because of its disproportionately heavy impact on male employees. This suggestion has no force in the sex discrimination context because each retiree's total pension benefits are ultimately determined by his *actual life span;* any differential in benefits paid to men and women in the aggregate is thus "based on [a] factor other than sex," and consequently immune from challenge under the Equal Pay Act. Even under Title VII itself—assuming disparate impact analysis applies to fringe benefits—the male employees would not prevail. Even a completely neutral practice will

inevitably have *some* disproportionate impact on one group or another. *Griggs* does not imply, and this Court has never held, that discrimination must always be inferred from such consequences.

This last paragraph speaks directly to Wood's claim. Her argument is that a gender-neutral survivor benefit "itself violate[s] Title VII because of its disproportionately heavy impact on [female] employees." *Id.* But this suggestion has been firmly rejected by the Supreme Court, based both on its own interpretation of disparate impact liability and on the Bennett Amendment to Title VII, which provides that a compensation differential based on sex is not unlawful if it is authorized by the Equal Pay Act. The Equal Pay Act authorizes differentials "based on any other factor other than sex." While this broad language has been subject to much interpretation ... *Manhart* clearly interprets it to cover the variations in pension benefits challenged here. Thus, even if the district court had considered Wood's disparate impact claim on its merits, it should have dismissed it as a matter of law.

* * *

We AFFIRM the judgment of the district court.

Notes and Questions

1. Ex Ante Bonus: Women, as a class, live longer than men. Under defined pension plans that predominated with employers in the middle of the 20th century, and which still exist for many public employees today, women, as a class, received more pension benefits than men. But, as *Wood* notes, benefits packages including spousal or survivors' benefits will benefit men disproportionately as well. Do these benefits offset? Should they? Are these reasons sufficient to require both sexes to pay equally into benefits plans? Note that the Patient Protection and Affordable Care Act similarly prohibits insurance companies from charging men and women different rates for insurance. In a competitive market, insurers charge women higher rates than men for multiple reasons. First, women tend to consume more medical services. Second, medical services distinct to women as a sex are quite expensive, such as childbirth and maternity care. Aren't these prohibitions on discrimination between the sexes really a form of bonus for women? Pension rules like the ones in *Manhart*, and, arguably, *Wood* raise the costs to the employer of hiring (or promoting) women. Thus, an employer has an incentive not to hire (or promote) women. Did the Supreme Court envision this response?

2. Individualism: Cases like *Wood* stress the tension between treating workers individually and acknowledging statistical facts about groups (such as women's lifespan relative to men's). From the employer's perspective, *ex ante*, how do you know which individual will be close to the statistical median? Is it in the employer's interest to create a pension plan that selects people on a defined set of very strict criteria that achieves the same goal? For example, the pension contracts could be based on factors such as weight, height, hair length, etc., to select women. Employers have, for these and other reasons, moved from defined-benefit retirement plans to defined-contribution retirement plans. These plans allow a individual to place a certain portion of their wages into a pension plan. Generally, the employer matches a percentage of whatever the employee puts in. Would this solution be better for the employer? How about the employee? Does it eliminate the perverse incentive of not hiring (or promoting) women?

3. What About the Market?: Why not let the market govern the types of situations discussed in *Wood*? The plaintiff in *Wood* relied heavily on market information to attempt to prove her discrimination case. If a company went to the open market to purchase an annuity for each of its employees, differences in such costs could be passed on to individual employees. Insurance companies make distinctions between males and females for the purpose of determining premiums. Why shouldn't employers be allowed to do the same? That is, this ruling seems to force companies to use a third party to administer their pension plan, thereby raising the costs of the plan. This hurts all employees. Does the Court consider this? If not, how might the Court respond?

4. Different Types of Discrimination: There are differences in economic productivity between some groups. In this regard, it is helpful to distinguish three types of discrimination: (1) discrimination based on individual characteristics that affect job performance; (2) discrimination based on correctly perceived statistical characteristics of the group; and (3) discrimination based on individual characteristics that don't affect job performance. An example of the first type is that restaurants might discriminate against applicants with sourpuss personalities, or banks might try to hire young loan officers because the bank's clients like to borrow from younger rather than older employees. An example of the second type of discrimination is that a firm may correctly perceive that young people in general have a lower probability of staying on a job than do older people, and therefore discriminate against younger people. An example of the third type of discrimination is a firm might not hire people over 50 because the supervisor doesn't like working with older people, even though older people may be just as productive as, or even more productive than, younger people. This third type of discrimination should be the easiest to eliminate because it doesn't have an economic motivation. Explain why discrimination based on individual characteristics that don't affect job performance is costly to a firm? Should market forces work toward eliminating this type of discrimination?

Discrimination of the first two types is based on characteristics that do affect job performance, either directly or statistically and thus, the discrimination will be harder to eliminate. In some cases, not discriminating can be costly to the firm, so political forces that eliminate sources of discrimination will be working against market forces. Whenever discrimination saves the employer money, it has an economic incentive to attempt to avoid the anti-discrimination laws. Where does the discrimination alleged in *Wood* or *Manhart* fit into this economic classification of types of discrimination?

5. Discrimination and Disabilities: Judge Richard Posner recognized the distinctions between types of discrimination in his discussion of the types of discrimination covered by the Americans with Disabilities Act:

> In 1990, Congress passed the Americans with Disabilities Act. The stated purpose is "to provide a clear and comprehensive national mandate for the elimination of discrimination against individuals with disabilities," said by Congress to be 43 million in number and growing. "Disability" is broadly defined. It includes not only "a physical or mental impairment that substantially limits one or more of the major life activities of [the disabled] individual," but also the state of "being regarded as having such an impairment." The latter definition, although at first glance peculiar, actually makes a better fit with the elaborate preamble to the Act, in which people who have physical or mental impairments are compared to victims of racial and other invidious discrimination. Many such impairments are not in fact disabling but are believed to be so, and the people having them may be denied employment or otherwise shunned as a consequence. Such people, objectively capable of performing as well as the unimpaired, are analogous to capable workers discriminated against because of their skin color or some other vocationally irrelevant characteristic.

The more problematic case is that of an individual who has a vocationally relevant disability—an impairment such as blindness or paralysis that limits a major human capability, such as seeing or walking. In the common case in which such an impairment interferes with the individual's ability to perform up to the standards of the workplace, or increases the cost of employing him, hiring and firing decisions based on the impairment are not "discriminatory" in a sense closely analogous to employment discrimination on racial grounds. The draftsmen of the Act knew this. But they were unwilling to confine the concept of disability discrimination to cases in which the disability is irrelevant to the performance of the disabled person's job. Instead, they defined "discrimination" to include an employer's "not making reasonable accommodations to the known physical or mental limitations of an otherwise qualified individual with a disability who is an applicant or employee, unless … [the employer] can demonstrate that the accommodation would impose an undue hardship on the operation of the … [employer's] business."

Vande Zande v. State of Wisconsin Department of Administration, 44 F.3rd 538, 541–42 (7th Cir. 1995).

6. Equal Pay for Equal Work: The Equal Pay Act of 1963 applies to discrimination based on sex that results in unequal pay for equal work. Equal work is defined as work on jobs the performance of which requires equal effort, skill, and responsibility, where the jobs are performed under similar working conditions. The act allows for pay differentials among employees of the opposite sex when the differential is based on a seniority system, merit system, system which determines wages by the quantity or quality of production, or where the wage differential is based on any fact other than sex.

The Equal Pay Act is a governmental effort to change the status quo of employment practices. It is important, however, to first recognize that an initial understanding of the status quo will facilitate an economic analysis of the applicable federal laws. For example, it is possible to generate a long list of explanations for why women are typically paid less than men in similar occupations. Only one of the explanations is that employers are sexist. Other explanations look to the employment histories of women relative to men and find that women's careers tend to be interrupted much more often than men's. One obvious explanation for the interruptions is that women leave work to have children. From the employer's perspective, such interruptions tend to lower productivity and raise costs, thus making women less desirable employees relative to men. Thus, the employer's decision to pay lower wages to women may be based on the economics of the situation, not necessarily on sexist preferences.

Although valid (i.e., non-discriminatory) productivity reasons may explain why the market wages for women are often less than the market wages for men in similar jobs, assume (for analytical convenience) that the difference in wages is due exclusively to employers' sexist preferences. If men and women are equal in terms of productivity, and women can be hired at a lower wage, then it is costly for employers to hire men instead of women. When employers are required to pay women the same as men, women are no longer a bargain, relative to men. This has several adverse effects on women, as illustrated in Figure VIII-7. Figure VIII-7 is a two-sector market where otherwise equally productive women are paid less, W_W, than men, W_M, because of employers' sexist preferences. The equal pay requirement raises the women's wage to W_M in panel b. As a result of the higher wage, more women enter the job market and employers simultaneously hire fewer women. The resulting surplus of women at the higher wage allows employers to pick and choose among qualified women applicants using discriminatory criteria other than sex (for example, age, appearance, race, etc.). Of course, the women who manage to keep their

Figure VIII-7. Equal Pay for Equal Work

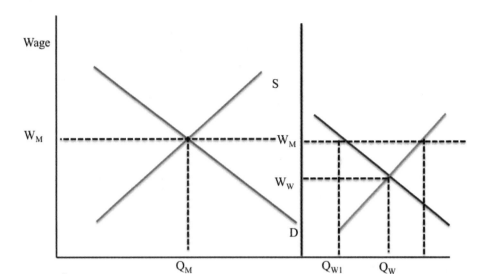

jobs or get hired at the higher wage are made better off. But, as the graphical analysis clearly indicates, the increased well-being of some is purchased at the expense of others.

The individuals most likely to need assistance in the job market are the ones most likely to be displaced. Moreover, a policy designed to decrease discrimination has actually made discrimination more likely to occur. Most observers would agree that such results are perverse. On the other hand, if women generally are paid lower wages for reasons solely due to differences in productivity, a higher wage rate will result in more women entering the job market and employers hiring fewer women. This again results in a surplus of women workers (however, employers are not discriminating on the basis of sex, but on the basis of productivity). The most productive women will be hired (or keep their jobs) and are better off. Those who cannot justify the higher wages on productivity grounds will lose their jobs (or not be hired). Thus, it appears the result (surplus of women workers) is the same regardless of whether lower wages for women is due to sexism or for productivity reasons.

One doctrine advanced largely in the 1970s and 1980s proposed mandating pay based on "comparable worth." Under comparable worth, Title VII would be used to prohibit pay differences between men and women even when the work performed was *not* substantially equal. The theory justifying this apparent subsidy is that employees should be compensated for the value of relative inputs, including training, skill, effort, responsibility, and opportunity costs (such as foregone child care). In economic terms, comparable worth is a supply-side regulation that would require employers to justify differences in prices for labor where the supply showed a substantial sex imbalance. A few states passed laws predicated on comparable worth. What problems in administration can you imagine with such a regime? Who is best positioned to ascertain whether two positions actually demonstrate "comparable worth" to one another? Do the previous two questions presuppose divergent preferences, whether innate or socialized, between the sexes in employment? If so, how could we demonstrate this hypothesis? If not, is "comparable worth" a justified remedy for this imbalance?

7. Institutional Discrimination. Another type of discrimination is institutional demand-based discrimination in which the structure of the job makes it difficult or impossible for certain groups of individuals to succeed. Consider the policies of colleges and universities. To succeed as a professor, university administrator, or other professional in the academic market, one must devote an enormous amount of effort during one's twenties and thirties, while these years are precisely the years when given genetics and culture, many women have major family responsibilities that make it difficult to succeed in the academic market. Thus, one can argue that women face institutional demand-based discrimination in universities. Academic institutions could change their job settings by increasing the number of positions at universities that are designed for high-level part-time work, thus making it easier for women to advance. Of course, one might also argue that it is the supply side institutions where the discrimination occurs, because in relationships, women get more child rearing responsibilities than men. For instance, when parents have a sick child, someone must stay home and in the majority of relationships, the woman, not the man, stays home and jeopardizes her advancement. In general, it is important to recognize that discrimination can be deeply embedded in institutions and that the lack of direct discriminatory actions does not necessarily mean that discrimination does not exist.

4. Employment At Will

Traditionally, employment contracts in the United States are negotiated between individual employers and employees. Third parties, such as governments or unions, were not involved in these contractual relationships. The growth of an industrialized economy and the welfare state has altered these traditional individualistic values. These alterations, especially striking in the areas of unionization and employment discrimination, are also evident in even the simplest employment relationships. Although many areas of the employment relationship have become inundated with federal and state regulations, the duration of the contract between the parties has, until recently, avoided alteration by either the judicial decree or legislation. That is, contract law typically governs employment contracts.

The freedom of contract philosophy underlying the common law of contracts applies to employment contracts. With respect to the duration of a contract, the *laissez-faire* approach means that the common law will enforce any contract length that is reasonable. Moreover, the Thirteenth Amendment of the Constitution prohibits involuntary servitude and thus prevents the enforcement by employers of contracts that amount to slavery. This effectively means that employees are always free to quit a job. The other side of this approach is that contracts that fail to specify a duration for the relationship are deemed to be at the will of either party. That is, employees are free to quit at anytime; and employers are free to fire at anytime. It does not matter whether the employer's motives in the firing are justified or not. This is the essence of the employment-at-will doctrine.

Garcia v. Kankakee County Housing Authority

United States Court of Appeals for the Seventh Circuit
279 F.3d 532 (2002)

EASTERBROOK, Circuit Judge.

Larry Garcia worked his way up from warehouse clerk to Director of Technical Services at the Kankakee County Housing Authority. During 1998 the Authority was in turmoil; its Executive Director and all members of its governing Board quit or were dismissed. The new Board asked Garcia to serve as Interim Executive Director, and he assumed that position on December 4, 1998. Soon Garcia began to make changes in the Authority's operations, and he challenged the authority of Charles Ruch, the Board's new Chairman. Within a week of his appointment, Garcia started writing memos to the Board complaining about Chairman Ruch's conduct and asking other members to rein in their leader. For forgetting who was in charge, Garcia paid a penalty: he lasted exactly 18 days as Interim Executive Director, and he lost his job as Director of Technical Services as well when a majority of the Board deemed him insubordinate and showed him the door.

In this suit under 42 U.S.C. § 1983, Garcia contends that his discharge violated ... the due process clause of the fourteenth [amendment].... [His] theory is that he had a property interest in his job, which the Board could not affect without notice and an opportunity for a hearing. Garcia actually received an elaborate post-discharge hearing but contends that the outcome was a foregone conclusion. The district court was not persuaded by [the] theory and granted summary judgment to the defendants.

* * *

... Garcia's contention [is] that he had a property interest in his job, an interest that under the due process clause he could keep until the Authority provided notice and an opportunity for a hearing. It is hard to see where this gets Garcia, because he *had* a hearing before his discharge became final. True, he was removed from office about a month before the hearing, but he was paid for that period and thus has no complaint about the delay. The hearing also offered him an opportunity to clear his name, squelching any contention that the discharge unconstitutionally besmirched his reputation. What Garcia really wants from this litigation is not another hearing but his job. Yet the Constitution does not require states to keep all promises made in their contracts and regulations. To put this otherwise, a unit of state or local government does not violate the federal Constitution just because it violates a state or local law, including the law of contracts.

For what it may be worth, we add that Garcia lacked any "property" interest in his position, and the due process clause therefore did not require a hearing. No statute, regulation, or individually negotiated contract gave him tenure or the right to stay unless the Authority demonstrated cause for his removal. Garcia sees the necessary legitimate claim of entitlement in a combination of the Authority's personnel manual and an oral promise that he could return to his position as Director of Technical Services once the Authority hired a new permanent Executive Director. Whether such a promise was made is a subject of dispute, but we may assume that it was. Still, Garcia was an employee at will in that position too, unless the personnel manual gave him some protection. So the oral promise is irrelevant; only the manual matters.

Illinois treats employment handbooks as having the potential to form contracts between employers and workers. A clear promise in a handbook therefore creates legal entitlements. Like the parties to other contracts, however, the parties to an employment handbook may elect to keep their affairs out of court. Page 2 of the handbook exercises this option:

> This Manual creates no rights, contractual or otherwise, between the Authority, any prospective or current employee, or any other person. Statements of policy contained in this Manual are not made for the purpose of inducing any person to become or remain an employee of the Authority, and should not be considered "promises" or granting "property" rights. Nothing contained in this Manual impairs the right of an employee or the Authority, to terminate the employment relationship at will....

> The following policies and procedures state current policy and are not themselves to be considered or interpreted as terms of an implied or express contract. The

Authority reserves the right to amend, modify and/or revoke any of its policies, practices, procedures and standards summarized in this handbook.

Disclaimers of this kind are enough in Illinois to show that the handbook does not create legal rights.

According to Garcia, the Housing Authority took back the disclaimer (or at least created an internal contradiction) several pages later, when the handbook said that employees could expect to keep their jobs as long as they performed well, and that an employee could have a hearing before a discharge became final. Garcia's predecessor as Executive Director filed an affidavit stating that the Housing Authority *never* fired anyone without a good reason. That may be true as a factual proposition but the affidavit and the assurances do not contradict the handbook's statement that all employment is at will. To say that employment is "at will" does not mean that the employer randomly or maliciously discharges good workers; that would serve no one's interests. Employment is "at will" when the term of the arrangement is open-ended, and there are no *legal* remedies for bringing the arrangement to a close. See *Richard A. Epstein, In Defense of the Contract at Will*, 51 U. Chi. L.Rev. 947 (1984). Employer and employee have an equal right to end the relation at any time, for any lawful reason. Both employer and employee will want to continue a satisfactory arrangement; thus an employer rarely fires anyone without thinking that it has a good reason. All it means to say that the arrangement is "at will" is that courts do not inquire into the sufficiency of that belief. Judges and juries are not guaranteed to do better than supervisors at determining whether an employee had worked out in the position; and as the legal process is expensive (including the expense of error), both employer and employee may gain from saving those costs. Perhaps the Housing Authority made a mistake in not returning Garcia to his former post as Director of Technical Services, but under the handbook the penalty for any mistake will be paid in the market (because the Authority will have a harder time recruiting a quality replacement, or will need to pay more to make up for the greater uncertainty) rather than in the courts.

AFFIRMED.

Notes and Questions

1. Employer's Reputation: A substantial portion of the modern American workforce is employed "at-will," including many high-skilled jobs, such as most attorneys. Though the doctrine suggests a great deal of employment instability, most at-will employees are fired infrequently, if ever, and typically then either due to economic necessity or for some defensible reason. In many instances, employers are prevented from abusing the discretion of the employment-at-will doctrine because market forces constrain arbitrary behavior. Consider the following proposition. An employer who develops a reputation for unjustly firing her employees will have a difficult time attracting good employees. Employees who take the risk of working for such an employer are usually being compensated in the form of higher wages. This proposition may not be immediately obvious. The initial reaction is that such an employer would be unlikely to offer higher wages to her employees. Those employees who have their choice of where they want to work will not choose to work for this employer; instead, they will work for other employers who are not as prone to fire employees without cause. This will leave our "firing" employer with a choice of employees who are unable to find jobs with other employers at a comparable wage. Accordingly, the lower quality employees are paid higher wages to work in the job where they have a greater likelihood of being fired. Thus, our hypothetical employer pays higher wages not out of choice, but through the natural selection process from the available pool of employees choosing where they want to work. Of course, this analysis does not apply to all employment situations, but it does serve to point out that businesses do not exercise their right to fire at will lightly.

2. Human Capital: The discussion below addresses investment in human capital. In the employment-at-will context, there are two types of human capital. One type is general human capital that can be used by most firms; the other type is firm specific human capital. Firm specific human capital is often obtained through on-the-job training, which is costly. If the employer pays for the on-the-job training, the employee may threaten to quit unless he is paid more because quitting would cause the employer to lose its investment in the training. If the employee pays for the on-the-job training—by accepting a lower salary—the employer may threaten to fire the employee unless he accepts a lower salary, in which case the employee would lose the investment. If both the employer and employee contribute to the cost and risk of creating firm specific human capital the incentive to make these threats is minimized. As such, this gives the employee greater job security. How might the regulation of employment-at-will contracts create inefficiencies?

3. Employees' Incentives: Just as the market creates a barrier to an employer firing employees at will, the market consequences of employment-at-will limits the ability of employees quitting at will. A worker whose employment record indicates that the individual cannot hold a job will have a difficult time finding employment. That is, exercising your right to quit is not free. In summary, the free contracting philosophy underlying the employment-at-will doctrine does not mean that labor markets are characterized by random behavior or very short-term contracts.

4. Decline of Employment at Will: In recent years, especially as the percentage of "at-will" employees has risen, state courts have been moving away from a "strict" application of the employment-at-will doctrine. Recent opinions have limited the "at will" doctrine through an extension of contract law doctrine and an implied "good faith" contract term that prevents termination without cause. This approach limits the discharge of employees for malicious purposes such as resisting sexual advances or to avoid paying an employee commissions earned, but not vested. Other cases alter the doctrine on the grounds that the employee's firing violated some "public policy," such as discharge for serving jury duty or filing a complaint with a regulatory agency. Almost one-half of the states have modified the doctrine in some manner. The typical justification for judicial or statutory modification of the employment-at-will doctrine is that society is more complex and thus complex legal rules are necessary to deal with complicated interdependencies. Such a conclusion, however, does not necessarily follow. For example, it seems just as plausible that simple rules are more appropriate for dealing with complex fact patterns. In general, the more complicated the facts and the more "sophisticated" the legal rule, then the less likely that contracting parties will understand the legal consequences of their actions and the less likely that the bargain will encompass all foreseeable consequences. The abandonment of a simple rule like the employment-at-will doctrine is as likely to frustrate peoples' expectations as it is to facilitate their realization.

C. Employees' Behavior: The Supply of Labor

An individual's decision to enter the job market reflects his or her tradeoff of the benefits of work against the opportunity costs of work. Costs of work include opportunity costs and direct costs. The opportunity costs of work might include foregone leisure or educational opportunities, time away from young children, or lost welfare payments. Direct costs include commuting expenses, additional clothes, child care expenses, etc. Individuals choose to work when their personal evaluation determines that the benefits are greater than the costs.

Once the decision to work has been made, the employee must decide how much work to engage in. Conceptually, at higher wages, individuals are willing to supply more labor. The market supply of labor is obtained by horizontally summing the supply curves of individual workers. As the wage rate rises, a larger quantity of labor is supplied. Supply of labor to any particular occupation thus follows the familiar law of supply.

1. Human Capital Investments

Much of the supply and demand analysis of labor markets emphasizes the effects of current wages, employee benefits, and psychic income on worker decisions. Many labor supply choices, however, require substantial initial investment on the part of the worker. These investments, by definition, entail an initial cost that one hopes to recover over some period of time. Thus, for many labor supply decisions, current wages and working conditions are not the only decision variables. Understanding these decisions requires developing a framework that incorporates investment behavior.

Workers undertake three major kinds of labor market investments: education and training, migration, and search for new jobs. All three investments involve an initial cost, and all three are made in the hope and expectation that the investment will pay off well into the future. To emphasize the essential similarity of these investments to other kinds of investments, economists refer to them as investments in **human capital**. The knowledge and skills a worker has, which come from education and training, including the training that experience yields, generate a stock of productive capital. However, the value of this amount of productive capital is derived from how much these skills can earn in the labor market. Job search and migration are activities that increase the value of one's human capital by increasing the price or wage received from a given stock of skills. Expected returns on human capital investments are a higher level of earnings, greater job satisfaction over one's lifetime, and a greater appreciation of leisure activities and interests.

Generally speaking, human capital investment expenditures can be divided into three categories: (1) out-of-pocket, or direct expenses, including tuition and books, moving expenses and gasoline (education, migration, and job search, respectively); (2) foregone earnings are another source of cost because during the investment period it is usually impossible to work, at least not full time; and (3) psychic losses are incurred because education is difficult, because job search is tedious and nerve-racking, and because migration means saying goodbye to old friends.

Gaining human capital requires an investment period, such as three years in law school. This investment involves a large opportunity cost. A law student loses the next best alternative when attending law school. For many law students, the lost opportunity is the income they would have earned if they had been working in a job commensurate with their college education. Figure VIII-8 portrays a simplified version of two alternative lifetime income streams for an individual. After graduating from college at age 22, individuals have a choice—they may enter the labor market immediately and earn Earnings Stream A from that time until retirement at age 65. This income stream should rise through the years as the individual acquires job related skills. On the other hand, some individuals may decide to go to law school. From age 22 to 25, they do not earn steady

Figure VIII-8. Investing in Human Capital: Alternative Earning Streams

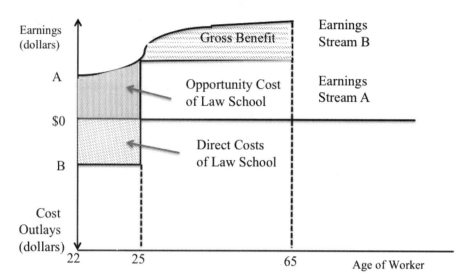

full-time income. The opportunity cost of going to law school—that is, the income that individuals forego by choosing not to work—is represented by the shaded area above the horizontal axis between ages 22 and 25. In addition, they must pay the direct costs of college, tuition, books, and so on. The shaded area below the horizontal axis, between ages 22 and 25, represents the direct costs of law school, conceptually a negative income. The total cost of going to law school is the sum of both the opportunity cost and the direct costs of college. After graduation, these individuals enter the labor market at Earnings Stream B. The shaded area between the earnings streams indicates the gross benefits of their human capital investment—their starting pay at age 25, after completing law school, is higher than it would have been had they not gone to law school. Yet, in order for the human capital investment to make financial sense, Earnings Stream B must offset the three years of negative income. If the deciding factor is money, then the individual determines the relative values of the two income streams and chooses the higher one. One method of doing so is to compare areas c_o and c_d, the investment period, with area b. Areas c_o and c_d represents the total cost of going to law school, the direct cost plus the lost income. Area b represents the benefits of going to law school. It is the income earned with a law degree. If area b is greater than areas c_o and c_d, then it pays to go to college. Of course, the values of c_o, c_d and b must be discounted to present value as is the case for any investment.

For an attempt to estimate the lifetime returns to investment in a legal education, see Michael Simkovic & Frank McIntyre, *The Economic Value of a Law Degree* (Apr. 13, 2013).

O'Brien v. O'Brien

Court of Appeals of New York
498 N.Y.S.2d 743 (1985)

SIMONS, Judge.

In this divorce action, the parties' only asset of any consequence is the husband's newly acquired license to practice medicine. The principal issue presented is whether that license, acquired during their marriage, is marital property subject to equitable distribution under Domestic Relations Law § 236(B)(5). Supreme Court held that it was and accordingly made a distributive award in defendant's favor. It also granted defendant maintenance arrears, expert witness fees and attorneys' fees. On appeal to the Appellate Division, a majority of that court held that plaintiff's medical license is not marital property and that defendant was not entitled to an award for the expert witness fees. It modified the judgment and remitted the case to Supreme Court for further proceedings, specifically for a determination of maintenance and a rehabilitative award. The matter is before us by leave of the Appellate Division.

We now hold that plaintiff's medical license constitutes "marital property" within the meaning of Domestic Relations Law § 236(B)(1)(c) and that it is therefore subject to equitable distribution pursuant to subdivision 5 of that part....

I

Plaintiff and defendant married on April 3, 1971. At the time both were employed as teachers at the same private school. Defendant had a bachelor's degree and a temporary teaching certificate but required 18 months of postgraduate classes at an approximate cost of $3,000, excluding living expenses, to obtain permanent certification in New York. She claimed, and the trial court found, that she had relinquished the opportunity to obtain permanent certification while plaintiff pursued his education. At the time of the marriage, plaintiff had completed only three and one-half years of college but shortly afterward he returned to school at night to earn his bachelor's degree and to complete sufficient premedical courses to enter medical school. In September 1973 the parties moved to Guadalajara, Mexico, where plaintiff became a full-time medical student. While he pursued his studies defendant held several teaching and tutorial positions and contributed her earnings to their joint expenses. The parties returned to New York in December 1976 so that plaintiff could complete the last two semesters of medical school and internship training here. After they returned, defendant resumed her former teaching position and she remained in it at the time this action was commenced. Plaintiff was licensed to practice medicine in October 1980. He commenced this action for divorce two months later. At the time of trial, he was a resident in general surgery.

During the marriage both parties contributed to paying the living and educational expenses and they received additional help from both of their families. They disagreed on the amounts of their respective contributions but it is undisputed that in addition to performing household work and managing the family finances defendant was gainfully employed throughout the marriage, that she contributed all of her earnings to their living and educational expenses and that her financial contributions exceeded those of plaintiff. The trial court found that she had contributed 76% of the parties' income exclusive of a $10,000 student loan obtained by defendant. Finding that plaintiff's medical degree and license are marital property, the court received evidence of its value and ordered a distributive award to defendant.

Defendant presented expert testimony that the present value of plaintiff's medical license was $472,000. Her expert testified that he arrived at this figure by comparing the average income of a college graduate and that of a general surgeon between 1985, when plaintiff's residency would end, and 2012, when he would reach age 65. After considering Federal income taxes, an inflation rate of 10% and a real interest rate of 3% he capitalized the difference in average earnings and reduced the amount to present value. He also gave his opinion that the present value of defendant's contribution to plaintiff's medical education was $103,390. Plaintiff offered no expert testimony on the subject.

The court, after considering the life-style that plaintiff would enjoy from the enhanced earning potential his medical license would bring and defendant's contributions and efforts toward attainment of it, made a distributive award to her of $188,800, representing 40% of the value of the license, and ordered it paid in 11 annual installments of various amounts beginning November 1, 1982 and ending November 1, 1992. The court also directed plaintiff to maintain a life insurance policy on his life for defendant's benefit for the unpaid balance of the award.... It did not award defendant maintenance.

* * *

II

The Equitable Distribution Law contemplates only two classes of property: marital property and separate property. The former, which is subject to equitable distribution, is defined broadly as "all property acquired by either or both spouses during the marriage and before the execution of a separation agreement or the commencement of a matrimonial action, regardless of the form in which title is held. Plaintiff does not contend that his license is excluded from distribution because it is separate property; rather, he claims that it is not property at all but represents a personal attainment in acquiring knowledge. He rests his argument on decisions in similar cases from other jurisdictions and on his view that a license does not satisfy common-law concepts of property. Neither contention is controlling because decisions in other States rely principally on their own statutes, and the legislative history underlying them, and because the New York Legislature deliberately went beyond traditional property concepts when it formulated the Equitable Distribution Law. Instead, our statute recognizes that spouses have an equitable claim to things of value arising out of the marital relationship and classifies them as subject to distribution by focusing on the marital status of the parties at the time of acquisition. Those things acquired during marriage and subject to distribution have been classified as "marital property" although, as one commentator has observed, they hardly fall within the traditional property concepts because there is no common-law property interest remotely resembling marital property. "It is a statutory creature, is of no meaning whatsoever during the normal course of a marriage and arises full-grown, like Athena, upon the signing of a separation agreement or the commencement of a matrimonial action. [Thus] [i]t is hardly surprising, and not at all relevant, that traditional common law property concepts do not fit in parsing the meaning of 'marital property'" (Florescue, "Market Value", Professional Licenses and Marital Property: A Dilemma in Search of a Horn, 1982 N.Y.St.Bar Assn.Fam.L.Rev. 13 [Dec.]). Having classified the "property" subject to distribution, the Legislature did not attempt to go further and define it but left it to the courts to determine what interests come within the terms of section 236(B)(1)(c).

* * *

Section 236 provides that in making an equitable distribution of marital property, "the court shall consider: * * * (6) any equitable claim to, interest in, or direct or indirect contribution made to the acquisition of such marital property by the party not having title, including joint efforts or expenditures and contributions and services as a spouse, parent, wage earner and homemaker, and to the career or career potential of the other party [and] * * * (9) the impossibility or difficulty of evaluating any component asset or any interest in a business, corporation or profession. Where equitable distribution of marital property is appropriate but "the distribution of an interest in a business, corporation or profession would be contrary to law" the court shall make a distributive award in lieu of an actual distribution of the property. The words mean exactly what they say: that an interest in a profession or professional career potentially is marital property which may be represented by direct or indirect contributions of the non-title-holding spouse, including financial contributions and nonfinancial contributions made by caring for the home and family.

The history which preceded enactment of the statute confirms this interpretation. Reform of section 236 was advocated because experience had proven that application of the traditional common-law title theory of property had caused inequities upon dissolution of a marriage. The Legislature replaced the existing system with equitable distribution of marital property, an entirely new theory which considered all the circumstances of the case and of the respective parties to the marriage. Equitable distribution was based on the premise that a marriage is, among other things, an economic partnership to which both parties contribute as spouse, parent, wage earner or homemaker. Consistent with this purpose, and implicit in the statutory scheme as a whole, is the view that upon dissolution of the marriage there should be a winding up of the parties' economic affairs and a severance of their economic ties by an equitable distribution of the marital assets. Thus, the concept of alimony, which often served as a means of lifetime support and dependence for one spouse upon the other long after the marriage was over, was replaced with the concept of maintenance which seeks to allow "the recipient spouse an opportunity to achieve [economic] independence."

The determination that a professional license is marital property is also consistent with the conceptual base upon which the statute rests. As this case demonstrates, few undertakings during a marriage better qualify as the type of joint effort that the statute's economic partnership theory is intended to address than contributions toward one spouse's acquisition of a professional license. Working spouses are often required to contribute substantial income as wage earners, sacrifice their own educational or career goals and opportunities for child rearing, perform the bulk of household duties and responsibilities and forego the acquisition of marital assets that could have been accumulated if the professional spouse had been employed rather than occupied with the study and training necessary to acquire a professional license. In this case, nearly all of the parties' nine-year marriage was devoted to the acquisition of plaintiff's medical license and defendant played a major role in that project. She worked continuously during the marriage and contributed all of her earnings to their joint effort, she sacrificed her own educational and career opportunities, and she traveled with plaintiff to Mexico for three and one-half years while he attended medical school there. The Legislature has decided, by its explicit reference in the statute to the contributions of one spouse to the other's profession or career, that these contributions represent investments in the economic partnership of the marriage and that the product of the parties' joint efforts, the professional license, should be considered marital property.

The majority at the Appellate Division held that the cited statutory provisions do not refer to the license held by a professional who has yet to establish a practice but only to a going professional practice. There is no reason in law or logic to restrict the plain language of the statute to existing practices, however, for it is of little consequence in making an award of marital property, except for the purpose of evaluation, whether the professional spouse has already established a practice or whether he or she has yet to do so. An established practice merely represents the exercise of the privileges conferred upon the professional spouse by the license and the income flowing from that practice represents the receipt of the enhanced earning capacity that licensure allows. That being so, it would be unfair not to consider the license a marital asset.

Plaintiff's principal argument, adopted by the majority below, is that a professional license is not marital property because it does not fit within the traditional view of property as something which has an exchange value on the open market and is capable of sale, assignment or transfer. The position does not withstand analysis for at least two reasons. First, as we have observed, it ignores the fact that whether a professional license constitutes marital property is to be judged by the language of the statute which created this new species of property previously unknown at common law or under prior statutes. Thus, whether the license fits within traditional property concepts is of no consequence. Second, it is an overstatement to assert that a professional license could not be considered property even outside the context of section 236(B). A professional license is a valuable property right, reflected in the money, effort and lost opportunity for employment expended in its acquisition, and also in the enhanced earning capacity it affords its holder, which may not be revoked without due process of law. That a professional license has no market value is irrelevant. Obviously, a license may not be alienated as may other property and for that reason the working spouse's interest in it is limited. The Legislature has recognized that limitation, however, and has provided for an award in lieu of its actual distribution.

* * *

… Limiting a working spouse to a maintenance award, either general or rehabilitative, not only is contrary to the economic partnership concept underlying the statute but also retains the uncertain and inequitable economic ties of dependence that the Legislature sought to extinguish by equitable distribution. Maintenance is subject to termination upon the recipient's remarriage and a working spouse may never receive adequate consideration for his or her contribution and may even be penalized for the decision to remarry if that is the only method of compensating the contribution. As one court said so well, "[t]he function of equitable distribution is to recognize that when a marriage ends, each of the spouses, based on the totality of the contributions made to it, has a stake in and right to a share of the marital assets accumulated while it endured, not because that share is needed, but because those assets represent the capital product of what was essentially a partnership entity." The Legislature stated its intention to eliminate such inequities by providing that a supporting spouse's "direct or indirect contribution" be recognized, considered and rewarded.

Turning to the question of valuation, it has been suggested that even if a professional license is considered marital property, the working spouse is entitled only to reimbursement of his or her direct financial contributions.… Such a result is completely at odds with the statute's requirement that the court give full consideration to both direct and indirect contributions "made to the acquisition of such marital property by the party not having title, including joint efforts or expenditures and contributions and services as a spouse, parent, wage earner and homemaker." If the license is marital property, then the working spouse is entitled to an equitable portion of it, not a return of funds advanced. Its value is the enhanced earning capacity it affords the holder and although fixing the present value of that enhanced earning capacity may present problems, the problems are not insurmountable. Certainly they are no more difficult than computing tort damages for wrongful death or diminished earning capacity resulting from injury and they differ only in degree from the problems presented when valuing a professional practice for purposes of a distributive award, something the courts have not hesitated to do. The trial court retains the flexibility and discretion to structure the distributive award equitably, taking into consideration factors such as the working spouse's need for immediate payment, the licensed spouse's current ability to pay and the income tax consequences of prolonging the period of payment and, once it has received evidence of the present value of the license and the working spouse's contributions toward its acquisition and considered the remaining factors mandated by the statute, it may then make an appropriate distribution of the marital property including a distributive award for the professional license if such an award is warranted. When other marital assets are of sufficient value to provide for the supporting spouse's equitable portion of the marital property, including his or her contributions to the acquisition of the professional license, however, the court retains the discretion to distribute these other marital assets or to make a distributive award in lieu of an actual distribution of the value of the professional spouse's license.

* * *

MEYER, Judge (concurring).

I concur in Judge Simons' opinion but write separately to point up for consideration by the Legislature the potential for unfairness involved in distributive awards based upon a license of a professional still in training.

An equity court normally has power to "change its decrees where there has been a change of circumstances." The implication of Domestic Relations Law § 236(B)(9)(b), which deals with modification of an order or decree as to maintenance or child support, is, however, that a distributive award pursuant to section 236(B)(5)(e), once made, is not subject to change. Yet a professional in training who is not finally committed to a career choice when the distributive award is made may be locked into a particular kind of practice simply because the monetary obligations imposed by the distributive award made on the basis of the trial judge's conclusion (prophecy may be a better word) as to what the career choice will be leaves him or her no alternative.

The present case points up the problem. A medical license is but a step toward the practice ultimately engaged in by its holder, which follows after internship, residency and, for particular specialties, board certification. Here it is undisputed that plaintiff was in a residency for general surgery at the time of the trial, but had the previous year done a residency in internal medicine. Defendant's expert based his opinion on the difference between the average income of a general surgeon and that of a college graduate of plaintiff's age and life expectancy, which the trial judge utilized, impliedly finding that plaintiff would engage in a surgical practice despite plaintiff's testimony that he was dissatisfied with the general surgery program he was in and was attempting to return to the internal medicine training he had been in the previous year. The trial judge had the right, of course, to discredit that testimony, but the point is that equitable distribution was not intended to permit a judge to make a career decision for a licensed spouse still in training. Yet the degree of speculation involved in the award made is emphasized by the testimony of the expert on which it was based. Asked whether his assumptions and calculations were in any way speculative, he replied: "Yes. They're speculative to the extent of, will Dr. O'Brien practice medicine? Will Dr. O'Brien earn more or less than the average surgeon earns? Will Dr. O'Brien live to age sixty-five? Will Dr. O'Brien have a heart attack or will he be injured in an automobile accident? Will he be disabled? I mean, there is a degree of speculation. That speculative aspect is no more to be taken into account, cannot be taken into account, and it's a question, again, Mr. Emanuelli, not for the expert but for the courts to decide. It's not my function nor could it be."

The equitable distribution provisions of the Domestic Relations Law were intended to provide flexibility so that equity could be done. But if the assumption as to career choice on which a distributive award payable over a number of years is based turns out not to be the fact (as, for example, should a general surgery trainee accidentally lose the use of his hand), it should be possible for the court to revise the distributive award to conform to the fact. And there will be no unfairness in so doing if either spouse can seek reconsideration, for the licensed spouse is more likely to seek reconsideration based on real, rather than imagined, cause if he or she knows that the nonlicensed spouse can seek not only reinstatement of the original award, but counsel fees in addition, should the purported circumstance on which a change is made turn out to have been feigned or to be illusory.

* * *

Notes and Questions

1. The License as Marital Property: The *O'Brien* court decides that the husband's medical license is marital property subject to a distributive award. Is this consistent with the discussion of property rights as developed throughout this casebook? If so, is there a solution to the marital assets problem that is consistent with the Coase Theorem? Why does the court consider an award to Mrs. O'Brien equal to the dollar amount of her contributions during the marriage to be an inadequate form of compensation? Is such a conclusion consistent with economic theory? How does the *O'Brien* decision impact the incentives of married couples to invest in human capital? Couples considering marriage? Couples considering divorce? Are these "side effects" justifiable on-balance? The concurring opinion expressing concern that decisions such as the one made in *O'Brien* may in effect force Dr. O'Brien to practice a particular type of medicine for the sole purpose of being able to pay the award to Mrs. O'Brien. Is this a justifiable concern? How does it balance with the need for judicial efficiency?

2. Valuing the Homemaker's Services: The services performed by homemakers are not sold in the market place, but this does not imply they are not valuable. For purposes of settling claims involving the wrongful death of a homemaker and often in cases in which property must be divided upon divorce, it is important to place a value on homemakers' services. For a discussion of approaches that can be taken in evaluating these services, see Haugan v. Haugan, infra Chapter X.

3. Severance Pay: An important economic function of alimony is to provide the spouse who remains at home with a form of severance pay or unemployment benefits. Where one of the marriage partners specializes in household production, any market skills that they developed prior to the decision to stay at home depreciate. As a result, the stay-at-home spouse loses prime employment possibilities should the present marriage dissolve. The next best alternative at this point may be to remarry and form a new household. Although some other kind of work could always be found in the marketplace, the skilled household producer forced to work as a waitress or file clerk is like the lawyer who, unable to find a legal job, becomes a process server. Thus, alimony pays the stay-at-home spouse unemployment rather than force them to find inefficient work in the marketplace.

4. The Definition of Marriage? The *O'Brien* court and the preceding discussion presuppose marriage as a relationship between a man and a woman. As discussed above, various forces, both market and social, result in differing employment outcomes and interests between men and women. Alimony, or an unequal distribution of marital property, can be viewed as one potential form of unemployment insurance in part predicated on these differing outcomes between the sexes. But an increasing number of states have given legal protections and recognition to same-sex couples through marriage, which will inevitably, in some cases, lead to same-sex divorce. To what extent do you think alimony as an institution is predicated on sexual differences in employment outcomes? Same-sex couples should, all else equal, face comparable market conditions for employment based on their sex. Do the rationales for alimony discussed above apply with equal force to a same-sex couple's divorce?

2. The Cobweb Model: Earnings Differences and the Demand for Education

The demand for education is influenced by the differences in earnings made possible by an educational investment in human capital. However, the returns to education are themselves affected by the number of people who attend school. To obtain an overall picture of how enrollments and returns are interrelated, it is necessary to return briefly to our simple model of the labor market.

Figure VIII-9 shows the labor market demand for, and supply of, law school graduates. The reason the supply curve for law school graduates slopes upward is that expected wages need to increase to attract applicants with progressively higher opportunity costs. If the earnings of law school graduates were to rise, more individuals would want to attend law school. If they were to rise even more, even more students would enroll in law school. If the demand for law school graduates were to shift outward, more graduates would be demanded at any given wage, as illustrated by a shift in the demand curve from D_1 to D_2. Because it takes time to produce law school graduates, the number of lawyers available in the short run does not shift dramatically from N_0. As a result, the wages of law school graduates would rise from W_0 to W_1. This increase in wages of law school graduates would serve as an incentive for more people to attend law school and the number of law school graduates would rise. This increase in quantity supplied will drive down wages to W^*.

The adjustment of law school enrollments to changes in the returns to education is not always smooth or rapid. The problem is that if lawyers' wages were to go up suddenly in 2014, the supply of law school graduates would not be affected for three years, owing to the time that it takes to complete school and be admitted to the bar. Likewise, if lawyers' wages fall, many students enrolled in law school would understandably be reluctant to leave the field immediately. They have already invested a lot of time and effort, and they prefer to take their chances in law, rather than devote more time and money to learning a new field. The inability to respond immediately to changed market conditions can cause boom and bust cycles in the market for highly technical workers such as lawyers and

Figure VIII-9. The Labor Market for Lawyers

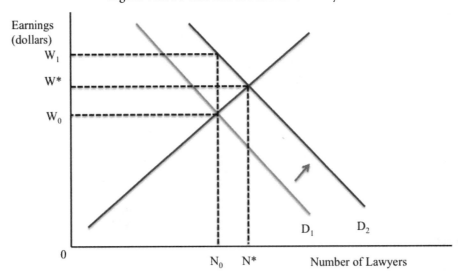

engineers. Suppose the market for lawyers is in equilibrium, where the wage is W_0 and the number of lawyers is N_0, as shown in Figure VIII-10. Now assume that the demand curve for lawyers shifts from D_0 to D_1. Initially, this increase in the demand for lawyers does not induce the supply of lawyers to increase beyond N_0, because it takes a long time to become a lawyer once one has decided to do so. Thus, while the increased demand for lawyers causes more people to decide to enter the field, the number available for employment at the moment is still N_0. These N_0 lawyers, therefore, can currently obtain a wage of W_1. In effect, there is a vertical supply curve at N_0 for a few years, until the supply of law school graduates increases.

Now, W_1, the current lawyers wage, is above W^*, the new long run equilibrium wage, caused by the intersection of D_1 and S_1. Market participants, however, are unaware of W^*, observing only W_1. If people assume that W_1 is the new equilibrium wage, N_1 number of people will enter the legal profession. When these N_1 graduate, there will be a surplus of lawyers. Remember that W_1 is above long run equilibrium. With the number of lawyers now temporarily fixed at N_1, the wage falls to W_2. This causes students and workers to shift out of law, but that effect will not be fully felt for a few years. In the meantime, note that W_2 is below long run equilibrium, still at W^*. Thus, when supply does adjust, it will adjust "too much" — all the way to N_2.

Then, there will be another shortage of lawyers, because after supply adjusts to N_2, quantity demanded (N_1) exceeds quantity supplied (N_2) at a wage W_2. This causes wages to rise to W_3, and the cycle repeats itself. Over time, the swings become smaller and, eventually, equilibrium is reached. Because the adjustment path in Figure VIII-10 looks somewhat like a cobweb, the adjustment process described above is sometimes called a Cobweb Model. Critical to cobweb models is the assumption that workers form myopic expectations about the future behavior of wages. In the preceding example, they first assume that W_1 will prevail in the future, and ignore the possibility that the occupational choice decisions of others will, in three years, drive the wage below W_1. Just how workers and other economic actors, such as investors and taxpayers, form expectations about future wages or price levels is very important to the understanding of many key issues affecting the labor market. The simplest and most naive way to predict future wage levels

Figure VIII-10. The Labor Market for Lawyers: A Cobweb Model

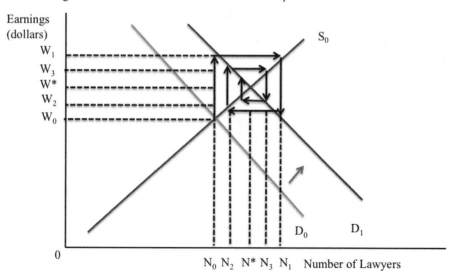

is to assume that what is observed today will occur in the future. This naive assumption underlies the cobweb model. A more sophisticated way to form predictions about the future is with an adaptive expectations approach. Adaptive expectations form by setting future expected wages equal to a weighted average of current and past wages. While more weight may be given to current wages than past wages in forecasting future wage levels, changes in those levels, prior to the current period, are not ignored. Thus, it is likely that wage expectations formed adaptively do not alternatively overshoot and undershoot the equilibrium wage as much as those formed using the naive approach. If adaptive expectations, however, also lead workers to first overpredict, and then underpredict the equilibrium wage, cobweb-like behavior of wages and labor supply will still be observed, although the fluctuations will be of a smaller magnitude if the predictions are closer to the mark than if they are made naively.

Clearly, how people form expectations is an important and unsettled issue. In the case of lawyers, doctors, and engineers, periodic fluctuations that characterize the cobweb model have been found. Whether these fluctuations are the result of naive expectations or not, the lesson to be learned from cobweb models should not be lost on government policy makers. When government policy makers attempt to take an active role in dealing with labor shortages and surpluses, they must be aware that because supply adjustments are slow in highly technical markets, wages in those markets tend to overadjust. In other words, to the extent possible, governmental predictions and market interventions should be based on rational expectations. For example, at the initial stages of a shortage, when wages are rising towards W_1, the government should be pointing out that W_1 is likely to be above the long run equilibrium. Instead, if it attempts to meet the current shortage by subsidizing people already in that field, it will be encouraging an even greater surplus later on. The moral of the story is that a complete knowledge of how markets work is necessary before one can be sure that government intervention will do more good than harm.

3. Occupational Choice and Compensating Wage Differentials

One of the major functions of the labor market is to provide the signals and the mechanisms by which workers seeking to maximize their utility can be matched to employers trying to maximize profits. Matching is a formidable task because workers have varying skills and preferences and because employers offer jobs that differ in skill content and working environment. The process of finding the worker-employer pairings that are best for each is truly one of trial and error, and whether the process is woefully deficient or reasonably satisfactory is a question implicitly underlying this analysis. The assumption that workers are attempting to maximize utility implies that they are interested in both the pecuniary and nonpecuniary aspect of their jobs. On the one hand, high compensation levels in an occupation, holding job tasks constant, attracts more workers to that occupation. Different occupations have different tasks and workers have different preferences concerning these duties. At a given level of pay, only a certain numbers of workers will be interested in a particular occupation. If the level of pay rises, others will become attracted to it. On the other hand, it is clear that pay is not all that matters. Occupational tasks and how workers' preferences mesh with those tasks are critical elements in the matching process.

If all jobs were exactly alike and located in the same place, an individual's decision about where to seek work would be relatively simple. He or she would attempt to obtain a job where the compensation was highest. Any difference in compensation would cause workers to seek work with the highest paying employers and avoid applying for work with the low paying ones. The high paying employers, having an abundance of applicants, might decide they were paying more than they had to in order to fill vacancies. The low paying employers would have to raise their wage offers in order to compete for workers. Ultimately, if the market worked without hindrance, the compensation paid to all employees would equalize.

However, all jobs are not the same. Some jobs require much more education or training than others, some jobs are in clean modern offices, while others are in noisy, dusty and dangerous factories. Some permit the employee discretion over the hours or pace of work, while others allow less flexibility. Some employers offer more generous employee benefit packages than others, and different places of employment involve different commuting distances and neighborhood environments. The desire of workers to avoid unpleasantness or risk should force employers offering unpleasant or risky jobs to pay higher wages than they would otherwise have to pay. In other words, in order to attract a work force, these employers will have to pay higher wages to their workers—called a compensating wage differential—than firms that offer pleasant and safe jobs to comparable workers. This compensating wage differential serves two related socially desirable goals. First, it serves a social need by giving people an incentive to voluntarily do dirty, dangerous or unpleasant work. Likewise, the existence of a compensating wage differential imposes a financial penalty on employers who have unfavorable working conditions. Second, at an individual level, it serves as a reward to workers who accept unpleasant jobs by paying them more than comparable workers in more pleasant jobs.

Any society has a number of jobs that are unavoidably nasty or would be very costly to make safe and pleasant. Coal mining, deep sea diving, police work, and garbage collection are examples. There are essentially two ways to recruit the necessary labor for such jobs. One is to compel people to do these jobs. The military draft is the most obvious American example of forced labor. The second way is to induce people to do the jobs voluntarily. Most modern societies rely mainly on incentives or compensating wage differentials to recruit labor to do unpleasant jobs voluntarily. Workers who mine coal, bolt steel beams together 50 stories off the ground, or agree to work at night do so because compared to alternative jobs for which they could qualify, these jobs pay better. Night work, for example, could be stressful because it disrupts normal patterns of sleep and family interactions. However, employers often find it efficient to keep their plants and machines in operation around the clock. Results indicate that manufacturing production employees that work at night are paid about three percent more than if they worked during the day.

Compensating wage differentials also serve as individual rewards by paying those who accept bad or arduous working conditions more than they would otherwise receive. Analogously, those who opt for more pleasant conditions have to buy them by accepting lower pay. For example, if a person makes $8.00 an hour with firm X, he or she is giving up the $8.50 per hour with the less pleasant conditions in firm Y. The better conditions are being bought in a very real sense for $0.50 per hour. Professors who claim that they are underpaid because they could earn more money in the private business sector are mischaracterizing the reality of their job situation. In effect, they are giving up that pay in order to consume the many perks that go along with being a university professor. Thus, compensating wage differentials become the prices at which good working conditions can be purchased or bad ones sold to workers. Contrary to what is commonly asserted, a monetary value can be attached to events or conditions with effects that are primarily psychological in nature. Compensating wage differentials provide the key to the valuation of these nonpecuniary aspects of employment.

The predicted outcome of this theory of job choice is not that employees working under bad conditions receive more than those working under good conditions. The prediction is that holding worker characteristics constant, employees working under poor conditions receive higher wages than those working under more pleasant conditions. The characteristics that must be held constant include all the other things that influence wages: skill level, age, race, gender, union status, region of the country, and so forth. The basic point is that observed wage differences across occupations may reflect differences in non-monetary aspects of employment. There are many reasons for wage differences other than those caused by human capital investments. In addition to the observation that wages will vary directly with the disagreeableness of the job, several more reasons for wage differences have been identified: the more seasonable or irregular the job, the higher the pay will be; jobs that require trustworthiness will carry a higher wage; jobs with greater risk to health will have higher pay; jobs that carry the possibility of tremendous success will have a lower wage; jobs will vary by region.

For more discussion of compensating wage differentials, see supra Chapter VI.

4. Occupational Licensing

The public interest explanation for occupational licensing is that protection of consumers from unlicensed competitors may be justified in order to allow a profession to upgrade the quality of services offered for sale in the marketplace. This upgrading is thought to occur from the imposition of higher educational standards on potential practitioners who wish to offer their services for sale. It is argued that licensing is the most effective way to protect the public from low quality professional services.

An alternative, interest-group explanation is that professional associations seek licensing to restrict entry into the profession, thereby decreasing competition and increasing earnings. Indeed, regulation may not be necessary to achieve the public interest goals because advertising and other market mechanisms—such as developing a reputation as an "honest lawyer"—could provide information to consumers about the quality of unlicensed professionals. Moreover, the existence of the licensing requirement might give consumers a false sense of protection when, in fact, the licensing is designed to restrict entry, not control quality.

States license many professions—from morticians and barbers to doctors and lawyers. In addition, professional associations impose state-approved restrictions on entry and conduct. Failure to conform to these requirements can result in legal action being instituted to stop an individual from engaging in the unauthorized practice.

In re Doering

Supreme Court of Nebraska
751 N.W.2d 123 (2008)

GERRARD, J.

* * *

FACTS

Doering received a bachelor of science degree in criminal justice from the University of Nebraska–Lincoln in 1977. In 1979, Doering enrolled at Western State. After successfully completing 3 years of coursework, Doering earned a juris doctor degree from Western State in 1982.

Doering's transcript shows that his first-year law school curriculum consisted of two terms of civil procedure, two terms of contracts, two terms of property, two terms of torts, and one term of criminal law. During his second and third years, Doering took courses in family law, constitutional law, media law, law office management, space law, wills and trusts, community property, education law, legal research and writing, evidence, investigative technique, remedies, the Uniform Commercial Code, agency and partnerships, corporations, criminal procedure, clinical education, and professional responsibility. The record indicates that at some point while attending Western State, Doering took the Multistate Professional Responsibility Examination (MPRE) and received a score that satisfies Nebraska's MPRE requirement.

At all times relevant to this case, Western State was accredited by the Committee of Bar Examiners of the State of California and accredited by the Western Association of Schools and Colleges. However, during the time that Doering attended and eventually graduated from Western State, the law school was not accredited by the ABA.

After graduation, Doering took, but failed, bar examinations in Montana and California. In 1992, Doering sat for and passed the Georgia bar examination, and was admitted to the Georgia bar in 1992. Beginning in March 1995 and continuing until February 1996, Doering worked as a volunteer for the Georgia Indigent Defense Council. In February 1996, the felony trial division of the Georgia Indigent Defense Council made the decision to start its own office and separated from the Georgia Indigent Defense Council. The director of the felony trial division offered Doering a position with the felony trial division as a staff attorney, which Doering accepted. Doering worked as a staff attorney and was eventually promoted to senior attorney, where he remained until he moved to Nebraska in 2006.

The record reflects that Doering is currently a lawyer in good standing with the Georgia bar. Doering testified that he moved to Nebraska in 2006 in order to be closer to his parents, who were in poor health.

On April 12, 2007, Doering submitted a Class I–A application to the Commission seeking admission to the Nebraska bar without examination. In a letter dated June 18, 2007, the Commission denied Doering's application because he had not received his law degree from an ABA-approved law school. Doering appealed the Commission's denial, and a hearing was held.

Doering testified and presented evidence at the hearing. Included in the evidence offered by Doering were two affidavits by Richard E. Jenkins, an associate dean and professor of law at Western State. In his affidavits, Jenkins testified to, among other things, Western State's curriculum and its accreditations. Jenkins, who graduated from Western State in 1974 and later joined the teaching faculty at Western State in 1976, testified that he is familiar with the accreditation standards of the bar examiners of the State of California and the ABA and that both accreditation standards "are equal or substantially equivalent."

Attached to one of Jenkins' affidavits was an exhibit which set forth various ABA accreditation requirements as they existed in 1982. These requirements included standards relating to the law school library, the number of full-time faculty members, and faculty workload and compensation. Given these ABA standards, Jenkins opined that "[r]elative to the number of full-time faculty ... and other requirements relative to faculty teaching loads, study and law library requirements, ... Western State ... offered a program substantially similar to ABA-approved law schools."

* * *

On October 23, 2007, the Commission again denied Doering's application on the basis that he lacked a first professional degree from an ABA-approved law school. Doering now appeals to this court.

* * *

ANALYSIS

The Nebraska Supreme Court is vested with the sole power to admit persons to the practice of law in this state and to fix qualifications for admission to the Nebraska bar. Rule 5A(1)(b) requires a Class I–A applicant, such as Doering, to have attained "educational qualifications at least equal to those required" of Class II applicants (i.e., those required to take the written examination). And Class II applicants, pursuant to rule 5C, must possess their first professional degree from an ABA-approved law school. Thus, Doering must meet the ABA-approved law school requirement or, in the absence of such degree, seek a waiver of rule 5C.

Doering concedes that Western State was not accredited by the ABA at the time he graduated in 1982. Nevertheless, Doering requests that we waive the application of the educational qualifications in rule 5C as they apply to him. This court has the power, under appropriate circumstances, to waive the application of its own rules regarding the admission of attorneys to the Nebraska bar. In determining whether a waiver of the educational qualifications requirement is appropriate, we are guided by certain principles. We have explained that our "admission rules [are] intended to 'weed' out unqualified applicants, not to prevent qualified applicants from taking the bar." We have also noted that "exceptions should be recognized and waivers granted '"whenever it can be demonstrated that the rules operate in such a manner as to deny admission to a petitioner arbitrarily and for a reason unrelated to the essential purpose of the rule."'"

Doering notes that under certain circumstances, we have waived rule 5C where a foreign-educated applicant proves that the education he or she received was equivalent to that for a juris doctor degree available at an ABA-approved law school. Doering argues that given his circumstances — in particular, his allegation that Western State would have been ABA-accredited at the time of his graduation but for its proprietary status — we should extend to him, a graduate of an unaccredited United States law school, the same waiver opportunity afforded to foreign-educated applicants. This we decline to do.

While we have, on occasion, granted waivers to graduates of foreign law schools, there is a critical distinction between graduates of foreign law schools and graduates of nonaccredited U.S. law schools. The ABA does not evaluate foreign law schools for accreditation; thus, there is no way for citizens of foreign countries to attend an ABA-accredited school in their own country. Accordingly, we reaffirm what we said [previously]: While a strict application of rule 5C may not always be appropriate for those who attended law school outside the United States, a strict application of rule 5C is appropriate for graduates of nonaccredited U.S. law schools.

For applicants who graduate from U.S. law schools, we have chosen, as reflected in rule 5C, to rely upon the ABA accreditation process as an objective determination of the educational environment for prospective attorneys. The ABA's process for evaluating law schools is extensive and involves many detailed standards for law school organization and administration, the educational programs offered, the faculty, admissions, the library, and the law schools' actual physical facilities. The ABA's standards are an appropriate, effective, and objective means of measuring the quality of a law school and "provide assurance that applicants to the bar 'have experienced a generally uniform level of appropriate legal education.'"

In the present case, Doering would have us evaluate nonaccredited U.S. law schools on a case-by-case basis to determine whether a particular school, at a certain point in time, provided a legal education that was substantially equivalent to that from an ABA-accredited law school. But such a case-by-case approach into the individual qualifications and standards of every nonaccredited U.S. law school, whenever a graduate from that school applies to the bar, would impose upon this court an unreasonable and unnecessary burden. The resources of this court are neither sufficient nor suited to the task of conducting such individualized waiver determinations. Furthermore, we believe that for us to evaluate U.S. law schools on a case-by-case approach would yield results far less reliable than those of the ABA, and would invite challenges as to the quality of such determinations. Simply stated, the ABA is best equipped to perform the function of accrediting law schools, and we will continue to rely on its determinations.

* * *

The ABA has the resources to conduct an examination that is far more credible than any that could be performed by this court or an applicant for admission to our bar. And to evaluate law schools case by case, based on the limited evidence adduced by a particular applicant, would risk inconsistency and unfairness to students who were otherwise identically situated. As we [have] stated[:] "[i]f we do not apply rule 5 uniformly rather than on a case-by-case basis, it will cease to operate as a rule at all."

It is for precisely these reasons that we have chosen, in rule 5C, to rely on the ABA's well-founded, consistent, and definitive conclusions. Therefore, we continue to hold that waiver of rule 5C is not available to graduates of nonaccredited U.S. law schools. Because Western State was not ABA-accredited at the time Doering graduated, we affirm the decision of the Commission to deny his application for admission.

* * *

DENIAL OF APPLICATION AFFIRMED.

Notes and Questions

1. Public Interest Restriction on Entry?: Many state bar associations require that applicants graduate from an ABA accredited law school. Thus, lawyers must be accepted and graduate from an acceptable law school and pass the bar exam. The Court in *Hansen* advances several justifications for such requirements. Are these public interest arguments valid? Are they consistent with economic theory? Is the market capable of protecting the consumers of legal services or is some form of intervention necessary? If intervention is necessary, what does economic theory suggest regarding the nature of such regulation? What are the impacts of professional licensing requirements on incentives to invest in human capital?

2. The Deadweight Loss of Licensing: The licensing system used by the legal profession can be considered a barrier to entry that restricts the supply of lawyers relative to what would be forthcoming in an unrestricted market. This barrier raises the prices that lawyers can charge and society is forced to pay more for legal services than would be the case under unrestricted entry. Because of the higher prices, some legal services that would have been sought in the absence of licensing are not purchased. Like any other monopoly or cartel restriction of output, the licensing of the legal profession results in a deadweight loss. See Chapter IX. Which members of society are harmed the most by professional licensing? Does the legal profession take other steps to alleviate such disparate impacts?

3. Antitrust and Occupational Licensing: Occupational licensing, because of its potentially anticompetitive side effects, may be subject to legal constraints under the antitrust laws. The courts tend to grant immunity from the antitrust laws to occupational self-regulation involving members of a "learned profession," but only if the licensing does not involve price fixing. In *Goldfarb v. Virginia State Bar*, 421 U.S. 773 (1975), the Supreme Court held that a fee schedule adopted by a county bar association and adhered to by virtually all members was a violation of the antitrust laws. Thus, while it is permissible to regulate quality of service, it is impermissible to regulate the price of the service.

More recently, however, states have occasionally conferred regulatory power on licensees to regulate directly not only themselves, but the entire market. In 2011, Mississippi transferred regulatory power over pharmacists and pharmacy-related entities from its Insurance Commissioner to its Board of Pharmacy, which consists generally of privately practicing pharmacists. In response, the Board moved to exclude market rivals whose practices generally save consumers money from working in Mississippi. Similarly, the United States Supreme Court is going to examine whether a group of dentists may, consistent with the antitrust laws, prohibit non-dentists from performing certain dental procedures, including teeth whitening. That case, *North Carolina Board of Dental Examiners v. Federal Trade Commission*, is expected to be decided in the Court's 2014–15 term. Each of these regulations is effectively a constraint on not just its profession's labor markets (pharmacists, dentists), but on related markets. Prices rise for consumers at large. These private regulators are often justified on expertise grounds, or because the "learned professions" are best situated to regulate themselves. Is there a way to distinguish between regulations of these labor markets for the professions' interest versus the public's? Can the regulation of one labor market by another labor market's participants ever be economically efficient? Otherwise socially justified?

4. The Constitution and Occupational Licensing. In addition to the antitrust laws, in a handful of cases courts have invalidated occupational licensing regimes on constitutional grounds. See Chapter III.

D. Labor Unions and Collective Bargaining

The preceding section on the employment contract examined the relationship between an employee and an employer. Although government regulations limit the flexibility of some of the terms of that contractual relation, the predominant aspect of those labor contracts was the interaction of *individual* employees with an employer. In this section, the emphasis changes dramatically as the role of unions in representing *groups* of individual employees is examined.

The primary appeal of unions to the U.S. worker is economic. Workers organize a union in order to get higher wages, better benefits, and improvements in other conditions of employment. Economists point out, however, that such improvements are not free to the employer, workers as a group, or society in general.

Economic welfare is maximized when resources are allocated to their highest valued uses through the operation of unconstrained competitive forces. Unions interfere with the market's role in allocating resources to their highest valued use by raising wages above the competitive level. To the economist, unions are legalized cartels attempting to monopolize labor markets in much the same manner that business firms attempt to monopolize a product market. Monopolies, or monopoly behavior by cartels, misallocate

Figure VIII-11. Supply Restrictions, Bargaining Power, and Wage Rates

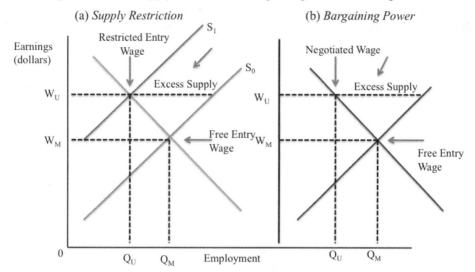

resources relative to the way that they would be allocated in a competitive market. The economic analysis of unions is similar.

Unions increase wages above market wages by either (a) restricting entry of non-union workers into union controlled jobs and allowing the market to clear at a higher price or (b) negotiating higher wages with employers. These two strategies are demonstrated in panels (a) and (b), respectively, of Figure VIII-11. Both panels reflect an initial market clearing wage of W_M. In panel (a), the supply restriction, in effect, shifts the supply curve back to the left and the market clears at W_U. In panel (b), the negotiated wage of W_U results in an excess supply of workers willing and able to work. The union allocates the limited number of jobs, Q_U, among its members. The supply restriction strategy is discussed in the following case.

American Steel Erectors, Inc. v. Local Union No. 7, International Association of Bridge, Structural, Ornamental & Reinforcing Iron Workers

United States Court of Appeals for the First Circuit
536 F.3d 68 (2008)

STAHL, Circuit Judge.

Five non-union New England-based steel erectors—Aerial Services, Inc.; D.F.M. Industries, Inc.; American Steel Erectors, Inc.; Bedford Ironworks, Inc.; and Ajax Construction, Inc. ("Plaintiffs" or "non-union contractors")—brought suit against Local Union No. 7 of the International Association of Bridge, Structural, Ornamental & Reinforcing Iron Workers ("Local 7" or "the Union"), an iron workers union that has a collective bargaining agreement ("CBA") with the Building Trades Employers' Association of Boston and Eastern Massachusetts ("BTEA"). Plaintiffs' complaint alleged that Local 7 conspired with the BTEA and assorted named and unnamed union contractors to shut non-union contractors out of the structural steel industry in the greater Boston area, in violation of federal antitrust and labor laws.... The district court dismissed the state law claims as pre-empted by federal labor law, and, in a subsequent order, granted Local 7's motion for summary judgment on the federal claims. Plaintiffs now appeal. We ... reverse the district court's grant of summary judgment on the federal labor and antitrust claims, and remand for further proceedings consistent with this opinion.

I. Background

... To understand the context from which Plaintiffs' allegations arise, some explication of the relevant industry is warranted. The structural steel industry is comprised of steel fabricators, who manufacture steel products to meet design specifications, and steel erectors, who assemble the fabricated steel. General contractors requiring structural steel work typically solicit bids for "fab and erect" packages. The packages are submitted by fabricators, who solicit bids for the erection work from steel erectors. In New England there are relatively few fabricators (around twenty) and many erectors (over 200). As a result, the competition for erection subcontracts in the Boston area is fierce, and the general rule is that the lowest bidder will be awarded the erection contract. That fierce competition gave rise to the instant dispute.

Local 7 negotiates collective bargaining agreements with contractors that employ iron workers in eastern Massachusetts, such as steel erection contractors. Among other things, employers who sign a CBA ("signatory contractors" or "union employers") agree to pay Local 7 workers a union scale wage. Plaintiffs have not entered into a CBA with Local 7.

Because of the labor-intensive nature of steel erection work, labor expenditures account for about half of the cost. Signatory contractors are obligated to pay laborers the minimum wage set by the CBA. Non-union contractors, such as Plaintiffs, are not bound to the CBA minimum wage and can negotiate their labor costs. As a result, non-union erectors are often able to submit lower bids for erection contracts.

The gravamen of Plaintiffs' complaint relates to a job targeting program, the Market Recovery Program ("MRP"), which Local 7 created to mitigate the disadvantage imposed on signatory contractors by union wages. Under the MRP, Local 7 "targets" certain construction projects and offers a subsidy to signatory contractors bidding on the project. The subsidy is intended to offset the higher cost of union labor, thus enabling union employers to bid competitively against non-union contractors. When a signatory contractor is awarded the target project contract, Local 7 executes an agreement with the contractor detailing the terms and amount of the subsidy. The subsidy is taken from the target fund (the "Fund"), which is financed with sums withheld by union employers from Local 7 member paychecks. The job targeting program was first established by member vote, and it was incorporated into the Union by-laws in 1992.

The plaintiff steel erection contractors bid on many of the projects that Local 7 targeted. Plaintiffs allege a conspiracy between the Union and union employers to monopolize the structural steel industry in the Boston area and push non-union employers like Plaintiffs out of the market. To this end, Plaintiffs claim that Local 7 used Fund subsidies and other tactics to ensure that contracts were awarded to signatory contractors, rather than Plaintiffs. Specifically, Plaintiffs assert that Local 7 used Fund subsidies to assist signatory employers in underbidding Plaintiffs on erection jobs. Plaintiffs also claim that Local 7 used subsidies, threats, and picketing to pressure fabricators, developers, owners, and general contractors (none of which directly employ Local 7 workers) into breaching contracts with Plaintiffs and replacing them with signatory contractors.

As a result of Local 7's efforts, Plaintiffs argue that they were excluded from a large portion of the structural steel market in the greater Boston area. * * * John J. Paulding, the president of fabricator C & I Steel, Inc., ("C & I") submitted an affidavit averring that

Local 7 agents had offered him Fund money if he agreed to "work" with them and that, on a number of projects, Local 7 threatened "problems" on the job if he did not hire a signatory contractor. Paulding contended that "problems" is well-known industry shorthand for project delays, increased financial costs, and property destruction.

On December 2, 2004, Plaintiffs filed a complaint against Local 7, its agent, Charles Wright, and the Steel Erection and Ornamental Iron Industry Advancement Fund, alleging violations of the Sherman Act and the Labor Management Relations Act ("LMRA").... In particular, Plaintiffs alleged a conspiracy between Local 7 and its signatory contractors to pressure fabricators to hire only union employers, through a combination of threats, disruptive behavior, and MRP subsides. Additionally, Plaintiffs argued that the MRP constituted an unlawful restraint on trade because the Fund was the recipient of deductions from paychecks of Local 7 members working on public projects, and subsidies were paid to signatory contractors working on public projects.... Plaintiffs also alleged that Local 7's conduct violated a provision of LMRA, which prohibits unions from engaging in any unfair labor practices as defined by § 8(b)(4) of the National Labor Relations Act ("NLRA"). * * *

Local 7 filed an Amended Motion for Summary Judgment on the remaining claims on August 1, 2006. The district court issued a Memorandum and Order on March 30, 2007, finding that (1) the conduct of Local 7 in administering the MRP was sheltered from antitrust liability by the statutory labor exemption, and (2) the conduct of Local 7 in using Fund subsidies to encourage the use of signatory contractors was not coercive conduct prohibited by the LMRA.

Plaintiffs now appeal. * * *

II. Discussion
A. Antitrust Liability

* * *

We turn first to the district court's finding that Local 7's conduct is protected from antitrust liability by virtue of the statutory labor exemption.

"[T]here is an inherent tension between national antitrust policy, which seeks to maximize competition, and national labor policy, which encourages cooperation among workers to improve the conditions of employment." In an effort to balance these competing interests, Congress passed the Clayton Act and the Norris–LaGuardia Act, which immunize certain organized labor conduct from antitrust liability. A review of Supreme Court jurisprudence on the dichotomy between federal labor and federal antitrust law renders it pellucid that antitrust laws must not be applied to vitiate congressional intent to permit organized labor activity; the Court has noted that "the [Sherman] Act is aimed primarily at combinations having commercial objectives and is applied only to a very limited extent to organizations, like labor unions, which normally have other objectives."

Nonetheless, unions, particularly when acting in concert with non-labor groups, are not given carte blanche to engage in anticompetitive activities. As the Supreme Court has explained, "[i]t would be a surprising thing if Congress, in order to prevent a misapplication of [antitrust] legislation to labor unions, had bestowed upon such unions complete and unreviewable authority to aid business groups to frustrate its primary objective."

To balance the competing federal policies supporting organized labor on one hand and business competition on the other, two labor exemptions from the antitrust laws have been developed, one statutory and one nonstatutory. The Supreme Court articulated the statutory exemption in *United States v. Hutcheson,* 312 U.S. 219, 231 (1941), determining that the Sherman, Clayton, and Norris–LaGuardia Acts must be read in harmony to effectuate Congress's intent to free organized labor from certain constraints imposed by the antitrust laws. Reading the three statutes together, the Supreme Court held that union activity is exempt from antitrust liability "so long as [the] union acts in its self-interest and does not combine with non-labor groups." Regarding the first prong of this "two-prong test," our court has stated that "activities are in the self-interest of a labor organization if they bear a reasonable relationship to a legitimate union interest."

It soon became apparent, however, that much legitimate collective bargaining activity, which Congress did not intend to be quelled by the lumbering behemoth of antitrust liability, nevertheless fell outside the purview of the statutory exemption. Such activity was vulnerable to antitrust attack because it constituted a combination between labor unions and non-labor employers. Accordingly, the Supreme Court recognized "that a proper accommodation between the congressional policy favoring collective bargaining under the NLRA and the congressional policy favoring free competition in business markets requires that some union-employer agreements be accorded a limited nonstatutory exemption from antitrust sanctions." The nonstatutory exemption shields some restraints on competition imposed through the bargaining process, where the alleged anticompetitive conduct is anchored in the collective-bargaining process, concerns only the parties to the collective bargaining relationship, and relates to wages, hours, conditions of employment, or other mandatory subjects of collective bargaining.

The district court entered judgment for Local 7 on Plaintiffs' antitrust claims on the grounds that the Union's job-targeting program was protected by the statutory labor exemption. In reviewing this determination, we focus first on the second part of the *Hutcheson* test: whether, in administering the MRP, Local 7 was acting in combination with a non-labor group.

There is no serious dispute that Local 7, as an iron workers union, is a "labor group," and that the signatory contractors, as employers of the members of Local 7, are a "non-labor group." The only question remaining, then, in determining whether the disputed activity here fails the second prong of *Hutcheson*, is whether the MRP constitutes a "combination" between Local 7 and the signatory contractors.

Local 7 argues that the MRP is the brainchild of the Union alone, and was established and incorporated into the Union's by-laws over a year before the wage deduction provision was added to its CBA with the BTEA. According to Local 7, only the Union determines which jobs to target, and sets the amount of the wage deductions and subsidies. Plaintiffs concede that the MRP was established and administered unilaterally by the Union, but argue that it was funded by deductions from member paychecks pursuant to a CBA between the Union and signatory contractors. Additionally, Plaintiffs contend that Local 7 and signatory contractors collaborated in identifying target projects, and that Fund subsidies were doled out pursuant to ad-hoc agreements between the Union and the signatory contractor successful in its bid on a targeted project.

Upon examination of how the MRP operates, it is a thin fiction to pretend that the program does not represent a combination between labor and non-labor groups. The MRP may have been initially conceived by Local 7 alone, but the method and amount of wage deductions that entirely finance the Fund are written into the CBA between Local 7 and the BTEA; the agreement that $0.85/hr would be deducted from each employee's wages and earmarked for the "Market Recovery Program" is codified within the text of a negotiated CBA between the Union and a non-labor employers' group. A collective bargaining agreement is by definition a combination between a labor group and a non-labor group. Additionally, funds were distributed to signatory contractors working on targeted projects pursuant to separate agreements between Local 7 and those contractors on a project-by-project basis. Thus with regard to both the input and output of its funds, the MRP could not operate except in tandem with signatory contractors. Furthermore, although Local 7 disputes this, there is evidence in the record from which a rational fact-finder could reasonably infer that the Union and signatory contractors worked together to identify and "win" targeted projects away from non-union employers. Accordingly, because the MRP was codified by and operated through agreements between a labor group and a non-labor group, the statutory exemption cannot apply.

The fact of that combination takes the MRP out of the purview of the statutory exemption but does not necessarily render it vulnerable to antitrust liability. The nonstatutory exemption was created for this express purpose; through it, courts recognized that in order "to give effect to federal labor laws and policies and to allow meaningful collective bargaining to take place, some restraints on competition imposed through the bargaining process must be shielded from antitrust sanctions." Because the district court chose not to make a finding as to the applicability of the nonstatutory exemption to this case, it is left to us to determine whether Local 7 adduced sufficient evidence to prove its entitlement to that exemption or whether we must remand the question for further development of the record.

The case for the applicability of the nonstatutory exemption is strongest where the alleged restraint operates primarily in the labor market and has only tangential effects on the business market. Conversely, the Supreme Court has generally refused to exempt union-employer agreements "that were alleged to have injured or eliminated a competitor in the employer's business or product market ... in spite of any resulting detriment to the labor policies favoring collective bargaining." (providing overview of Supreme Court's nonstatutory exemption jurisprudence). As the Court has explained,

> [t]he nonstatutory exemption has its source in the strong labor policy favoring the association of employees to eliminate competition over wages and working conditions.... Labor policy clearly does not require, however, that a union have freedom to impose direct restraints on competition among those who employ its members. Thus, while the statutory exemption allows unions to accomplish some restraints by acting unilaterally ... the nonstatutory exemption offers no similar protection when a union and a nonlabor party agree to restrain competition in a business market.

Connell Constr. Co. v. Plumbers & Steamfitters Local Union No. 100, 421 U.S. 616, 622–23 (1975). The Court most recently found the nonstatutory exemption applicable where the disputed "conduct took place during and immediately after a collective-bargaining negotiation. It grew out of, and was directly related to, the lawful operation of the bargaining process. It involved a matter that the parties were required to negotiate collectively. And it concerned only the parties to the collective-bargaining relationship."

Other circuits have found that job targeting programs, similar in structure and implementation to the program at issue here, do fall within the bailiwick of the nonstatutory exemption. But Plaintiffs' allegations do not relate only to the MRP; rather, they paint the MRP as only one part—if the central part—of a wider conspiracy between Local 7, its signatory contractors, and the general contractors and steel fabricators from which they solicit steel erection work, to shut open-shop outfits such as Plaintiffs out of the steel erection market in the greater Boston area. * * *

Plaintiffs have alleged concerted union-employer action that extended beyond merely the wage deduction provided for in the CBA and the job-by-job subsidy agreements, to collaboration in the identification and acquisition of target projects. Local 7 has steadfastly maintained, however, that target projects are identified solely by the Union and then announced to signatory contractors simultaneously ... Plaintiffs have argued that signatory contractors and the fabricators or general contractors who employ them are complicit in the union's efforts to shut non-union employers out of the market, pointing to evidence that fabricators broke contracts with non-union employers and replaced them with union employers in response to threats and/or monetary inducements by Local 7. * * * Accordingly, we reverse the district court's grant of summary judgment to defendant Local 7 on Plaintiffs' antitrust claims. We remand for further fact-finding with regard to the extent of the collaboration between Local 7, signatory contractors, and the construction companies that hire them, to determine whether Local 7 is protected from antitrust liability by the non-statutory exemption. * * * Nevertheless, it may be that it is not within the interest of federal labor policy to protect the unlawful provision of subsidies to signatory contractors on prevailing wage jobs.

B. LMRA Claim

In addition to their antitrust claims, Plaintiffs allege a violation of § 303 of the LMRA. "Section 303(a) [of the LMRA] makes it unlawful for a labor organization to engage in conduct defined as an unfair labor practice under § 8(b)(4)of the NLRA.". Under § 8(b)(4)(ii), it is an unfair labor practice for a union to threaten, coerce, or restrain an employer with an object of forcing the employer (A) to join any labor or employer organization or enter into an agreement prohibited by § 8(e) of the NLRA, or (B) to cease doing business with another party.

The district court refused to read Plaintiffs' complaint to allege a § 8(b)(4)(ii)(B) "cease doing business" violation. It seems to us that the complaint clearly does allege such a violation; Paragraph 177 of the complaint states:

> Since on or about July 1999 Local 7 has violated § 8(b)(4)(ii)(A) and (B) of the Labor Act, 29 U.S.C. §§ 158(b)(4)(ii)(A) & (B), by engaging in threats of picketing and other restraint and coercion against Plaintiffs and other contractors to obtain agreements prohibited by § 8(e) ... and where an object is to cause Non–Labor businesses to ... cease doing business with Plaintiffs.

We ... turn our attention to whether summary judgment was warranted on Plaintiffs' § 8(b)(4)(ii)(A) claim, regarding Local 7's alleged use of coercive tactics to pressure neutral employers into unlawful § 8(e) agreements. The Supreme Court has held that

> [T]he relevant inquiry under ... 8(e) is whether a union's activity is primary or secondary—that is, whether the union's efforts are directed at its own employer on a topic affecting employees' wages, hours, or working conditions that the employer can control, or, instead, are directed at affecting the business relations of neutral employers and are 'tactically calculated' to achieve union objectives outside the primary employer-employee relationship.

However, an agreement between an employer and a union representing that employer's employees is not prohibited by § 8(e), even if it may impact the business of a secondary party, as long as the union's objective is the preservation of work for those employees.

Plaintiffs contend Local 7 used coercive tactics—including picketing, threats, and the lure of lucre—to pressure fabricators and general contractors (i.e., "neutral employers" who do not themselves hire Local 7 members or have a collective bargaining relationship with Local 7) into agreements to hire only union erectors. As evidence, Plaintiffs point to substantially the same factual allegations underlying their antitrust claims, discussed above. Therefore, the same factual disputes remain. For example, Local 7 argues that there is no evidence the Union entered into generalized agreements with fabricators for across-the-board exclusion of all non-union employers from jobs in the relevant market. This argument both mischaracterizes Plaintiffs' factual allegations and misapprehends the law. There is no requirement that an agreement need be of a generalized exclusionary nature to fall afoul of § 8(e); rather, the use of coercive measures by a union to pressure a single neutral employer into a single agreement to cease doing business with a single non-union employer, or the application of such measures on a project-by-project basis (both of which Plaintiffs have alleged), would suffice.

In evaluating Plaintiffs' § 8(b)(4)(ii)(A) claim, the district court again focused only on the MRP and did not address Plaintiffs' other allegations. Viewing the facts in the light most favorable to Plaintiffs, as we must, we find that there are genuine issues of material fact with regard to the nature and extent of Local 7's allegedly coercive tactics, and whether Local 7 through use of those tactics pressured neutral employers into agreements to refrain from using non-union contractors in violation of § 8(e). We therefore reverse the district court's grant of summary judgment to defendant Local 7 on Plaintiffs' LMRA claim, and remand for further proceedings. * * *

III. Conclusion

For the reasons stated above, we … reverse the district court's summary judgment order and remand for further proceedings consistent with this opinion.

Notes and Questions

1. "Displaced" Workers: Employers respond to the higher wages associated with unionization by reducing the number of employees. Of course, the workers that keep their jobs experience an increase in wealth, but this is of little value to the displaced employees. Moreover, the workers that keep their jobs tend to be the highest skilled workers, so unions increase the wages of higher skilled workers at the expense of lower skilled workers. This disparity is magnified even further when it is realized that the "displaced" workers from the union jobs increase the supply of workers in nonunion jobs, which drives down nonunion wages. This effect is illustrated in Figure VIII-12, which shows a two-sector, union and non-union, labor market where the workers are substitutes for each other. In the absence of the union wage, the market wage, W_M would prevail and Q_M employees would have jobs in each sector. The union wage, W_U, would attract more workers, Q_S in panel (a), but employers would reduce their quantity demanded to Q_U. The displaced workers are represented by the reduced employment in the union sector from Q_M to Q_U. The displaced workers are added to the supply curve in the non-union sector, resulting in a shift to the right of the supply curve. The influx of displaced workers forces the non-union wage down to W_{N-U}. Does the union exemption discussed in *American Steel* and *Connell* address such concerns? In light of this economic analysis, should Congress revamp its policy towards labor unions? Can you articulate a justification for the trade-offs involved in the current policy towards labor unions?

2. Labor Economics, Industrial Relations, and the Role of Unions: There has been widespread disagreement over the role of unions in a capitalistic economy since small trade unions were first organized in the eighteenth century. In this century, economists have debated the merits of unionization. Until recently, economists were split in their evaluations, with some stressing the positive effects of unions and others focusing on the adverse effects of unions on productivity. In recent years, the economics profession appears to have become united in its condemnation of unions. Other academics, particularly in

Figure VIII-12. Two-Sector Model with "Displaced" Workers

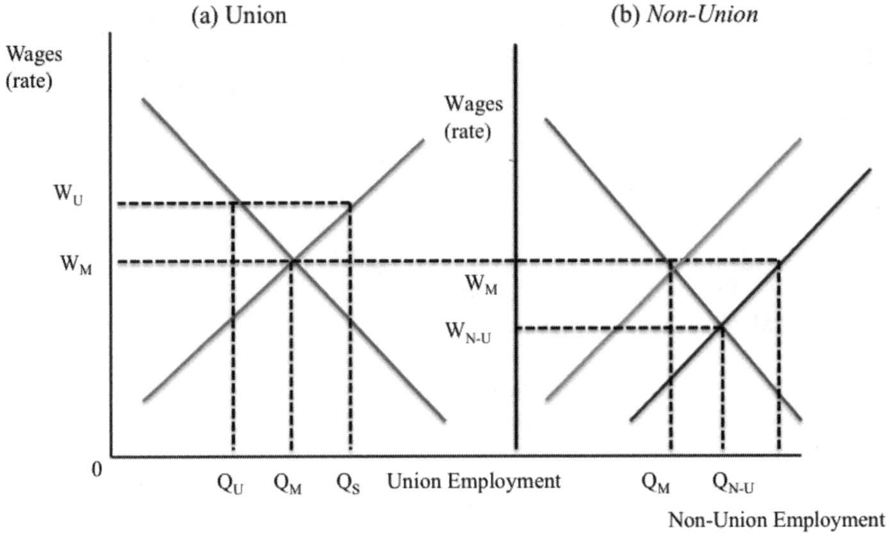

(a) Union   (b) *Non-Union*

the field known as industrial relations, continue to defend unions on the basis of their positive impacts on productivity.

3. The Industrial Relations View of Unions: In contrast to the economic view of unions, the industrial relations view of unions portrays unions as productive organizations that not only protect the interests of their members but also represent the political interest of all workers. *See* Richard B. Freeman & James L. Medoff, *The Two Faces of Unionism,* 57 The Public Interest 69–93 (Fall 1979). Industrial relations specialists point to several impacts of unionization that may actually lead to greater productivity and enhance economic efficiency. The general theme of their assertions is that unions promote industrial harmony, which in turn increases productivity. By providing for means through which disputes may be resolved, unions reduce the number of firings and employees who quit. This resulting reduction in turnover reduces the costs of hiring and training new employees. With fewer disruptions in the daily operations, productivity is maintained. Conflict among workers is reduced through specified seniority programs that tie wages and benefits to length of service. Employees are thus encouraged to devote their energies to performing their jobs through cooperation, since competition among workers is senseless in a seniority system. However, it is also well recognized that seniority programs may adversely affect productivity by promoting employees to positions for which they are not qualified. Unionism is also alleged to raise efficiency by increasing the awareness of employees that their wages may be tied to the profitability of the employer. Employees often have an informational advantage over employers in daily operations of the company, and because of this they often have good ideas about how to improve productivity. It is alleged that union employees have a greater incentive to pass on such ideas to management than do nonunion employees. However, it must be pointed out that many nonunion employers implement incentives programs designed to tap their employees' knowledge and expertise.

The major economic criticism of these allegedly productive attributes of unionization may be summed up in the following question: If unions are so efficient and productive, why do profit maximizing employers invariably oppose unionization? In fact, it would appear that employers would have a comparative advantage at helping unions organize as employers can act as the agent who overcomes the free-riding problem that often plagues union organizing efforts. Further, if unions enhance productivity, then why is the unionized sector declining?

4. The Distribution of Income and Higher Union Wages: In addition to the "displaced worker" effect, unions can also cause wage differentials between workers of comparable skills. This will result if the pool of skilled workers is sufficiently large to fill all union jobs with workers left over. In general; extreme inequities of pay among workers of the same skill (horizontal inequities) and among workers of differing skills (vertical inequities) may be counterproductive. Given these observations, labor economists have wondered whether unions really have the best interests of their fellow workers at heart. In direct contrast to the economist's view of union impact on the distribution of income, the industrial relations view suggests that the unions must attempt to reduce inequality in order to have the support of the majority of its members. This political argument is misleading in two respects. First, majority support can always be gained by transferring wealth from 49 percent of the workers to the 51 percent covered by the union contract. Second, and most importantly, it compares wages within a union, rather than between different unions or between the union and nonunion sector. The economic analysis is based on union versus nonunion wages. Any examples that illustrate union efforts at equality of wages by appealing to union policies without comparing them to nonunion practices is misleading. For example, union seniority provisions and standard wage rates may increase equality within the union, but is says nothing about the impact of the above market union wage on the nonunion labor markets.

5. Unions and Discrimination: A major economic criticism of unions was that they lower the cost to employers of discriminating against minorities, thus, in effect, encouraging discrimination. It is axiomatic that when unions raise wages above competitive rates, the number of workers willing and able to perform the job increases while the number of jobs available decreases. These changes in the quantity demanded (jobs available) and the quantity supplied (workers available) result in a surplus of workers. This surplus puts both unions and employers in stronger positions with respect to their ability to discriminate against workers (fellow workers, in the case of unions) on whatever basis they see fit, including race, sex, national origin, and religion. The shortage of jobs (another way of saying "surplus of workers") must be rationed in some manner, and it is very easy (that is, inexpensive) for union leaders and employers to indulge their preferences for discrimination in rationing jobs.

The history of unionization in the United States indicates that unions often have been as guilty of discrimination in their membership practices as have employers in their hiring practices. Supporters of unions counter this analysis with several observations—two of which are based on empirical studies. First, unionization reduces discrimination within firms by having wages determined by standard rate and seniority promotion policies. Of course, this does not relate to the discrimination argument, which is based on discrimination in hiring. A second observation tends to refute the discrimination in hiring argument: a larger percentage of African American workers are organized than are white workers. Third, although organized white workers tend to be paid more than organized African American workers, the divergence between the two groups is smaller than it is when they are unorganized. On the basis of this evidence, union supporters conclude that unions increase the status of African American workers.

6. Political Activity of Unions: Union political activity is often controversial (as is corporate political activity). Unions may exert political clout in several ways. See generally Chapter 14, *Labor in National and State Politics*, in Derek C. Bok and John T. Dunlop,

Labor and the American Community (1970). Unions can lobby, endorse candidates, contribute money to campaigns, and have their members become active in political campaigns by engaging in voter registration drives, handing out campaign literature before and on election day, addressing envelopes, providing rides to the polls for sympathetic voters, etc. Traditionally, the sheer number of members in unions has dictated that they engage in the more labor-intensive types of campaigning. Moreover, almost all unions lobby extensively: unions representing over one-half of the union members have lobbying offices in Washington, D.C. It is clear that union political activity is largely motivated by economic considerations affecting the union. Union political activity, in addition to being concerned with the unionization of workers, is also concerned with maintaining the demand for goods and services produced by unionized employers because such goods and services typically cost more due to higher wages. Consider the following statement:

> Much of the political activism of unions can be understood as attempts to protect or increase the demand of union labor. Examples are the union label ("Always look to the union label ..."), tariffs and quotas on foreign goods competing with union-made products (Japanese cars), law requiring "Made in Korea" labels, building codes that require installation of union-supplied material or labor, reduced class sizes to expand the demand for school teachers, federal subsidies to unionized industries like the merchant marine or mass transit, or opposition to contracting out work to outside bidders. Other political measures promoted by unions — restrictions on foreign immigration, compulsory apprenticeship requirements, child labor laws, minimum wage rates, and occupational licensing — restrict trade by hampering the ability of other suppliers to serve the market, so that union labor is relatively more attractive.

Morgan O. Reynolds, The History and Economics of Labor Unions 9 (1985). Unions often claim to represent the political interests of not only all workers, including minorities, but also the interests of all disadvantaged and lower income persons. In this regard, unions were a vital part of the liberal political coalition that engineered the adoption of much of the welfare state legislation. The good intention of advocates of those types of programs is not to be disputed here, but there is overwhelming evidence that many of those programs have not worked and indeed may have been counterproductive. Theoretical and empirical evidence has demonstrated that programs like affirmative action, equal pay for equal work, social security, and the minimum wage all create incentives that may end up injuring the intended beneficiaries. Either unions must change union politics that lead to these inefficient results, or the unions' motives in supporting such policies must be examined more carefully. In general, economic analysis suggests that union political activities benefit the union at the expense of other workers.

7. Capital and Labor: In a competitive market, firms respond to prices and wages to find the optimal, or most efficient, mix of capital and labor in their production processes. When unions raise wages, the firm's optimal mix of capital and labor shifts in favor of employing more capital. That is, at higher wages the firm will substitute capital for labor because of the higher price of labor. The inefficiency of this adjustment results because the additional capital must be released from some other presumably higher valued use in the free market and the released workers go to other areas of the economy. The market prior to higher union wages had already indicated the efficient means of production in its mix of capital and labor. The allocative inefficiency is that the firm uses more capital and less labor than the efficient allocation in the market. Unions may also cause inefficiencies by imposing work rules that decrease productivity and lower society's output through strikes and other disruptive practices.

Chapter IX

Market Structure and Antitrust

This chapter introduces industrial organization economics—the study of firm behavior under various market conditions ranging from perfect competition to monopoly. Earlier chapters have provided the foundation for the material covered here. Chapter II showed how the basic supply-and-demand model can provide valuable insights regarding market reactions to changes in legal rules and regulations. Chapter I introduced standard assumptions regarding individual utility maximization and firm profit maximization. In particular, the underlying assumptions of consumer choice were examined. This chapter examines in detail some of the factors that determine an individual firm's response to changes in market conditions as well as changes in legal rules and regulations.

Section A examines firm production decisions, with an emphasis on the underlying relationships that determine costs of production. Section B examines how firms behave under various competitive market conditions, first considering the benchmark cases of perfect competition and monopoly, and later more realistic models of competition that involve product differentiation and oligopolistic interdependence.

A. Costs & Production

Producers of any good or service are faced with the constant task of adjusting their output in response to changes in market conditions. The effectiveness of a firm in responding to changes in market demand is in part determined by its ability to alter the quantity and mix of inputs used in its production process. In analyzing the ability of firms to alter their input use, economists distinguish between the short-run and the long-run. We discuss each of the scenarios below.

1. Short-Run Production

In the **short-run**, at least one input used in the production process cannot be altered. Inputs that can be altered within the short-run are called **variable resources**. Inputs that cannot be altered within the short-run are called **fixed resources**. Thus, in the short-run, firm output can be adjusted by changing the variable resources used, but some of the necessary resources are fixed and cannot be altered in response to changes in the desired output level. Traditionally, this distinction has led to a separation of the costs of production into two components: fixed and variable costs. **Fixed costs** are those that do not vary with the amount of output produced and must be paid even if output is zero. **Variable costs** are those that change based upon the amount of output produced and are equal to zero if output is zero.

A factory—and the costs associated with owning or renting a factory—is a traditional example of a fixed resource or fixed cost. In the short-run, a firm cannot build, expand, sell, or purchase a factory to meet changes in market demand. Furthermore, a firm cannot stop paying rent or loan payments in the short-run without breaching contracts. Fixed costs also include inputs purchased on a long-term supply contracts.

Suppose GM uses four factories to manufacture one million Chevrolet Volts, an electric car. In the first year, GM sells one million Volts. In January of the second year, Tesla drops the price of its electric sedan by 50 percent and the demand for the Volt drops by 90 percent. In the short run, GM must incur the costs of owning all four factories even though they are not being used. Suppose instead that fuel prices quadruple causing demand for the Volt to increase to four million cars. GM instantly begins using all four of the factories, but it still needs many more factories to meet the increased demand. However, in the short-run, GM cannot expand its existing factories, or build new factories quickly enough to meet the demand.

Firms, however, can adjust their use of workers and materials in the short run. A factory worker with a terminable at-will employment contract, for example, is a traditional example of a variable resource or variable cost. When Tesla decreases the price of its sedan by 50 percent and demand for the Volt decreases, GM immediately terminates enough employment contracts so that it does not pay unneeded employees. Once the fuel prices quadruple and the demand for the Volt increases, GM immediately hires enough factory workers for all four factories to operate at capacity.

a. The Law of Diminishing Marginal Returns

Consider the hypothetical home construction company Sam's Shacks, owned and operated by Sam. In its production of new homes, Sam's Shacks uses several different fixed resources. Examples of Sam's fixed resources include heavy equipment (trucks and tractors), an office, and tools. For Sam, the most important variable input—and focus of this example—is labor, though other variable resources include lumber, wire, and nails. In the short-run, as the market demand for new homes changes, Sam is able to alter his firm's output—as in the GM example above—by increasing or decreasing the number of workers he employs. The most important decision that Sam must make is how many workers he should hire with his given level of fixed inputs.

When the construction season starts, Sam approaches the hiring of workers conservatively—he always starts by hiring one worker. As demand for new homes picks up, Sam realizes that this one worker cannot complete all of the necessary work. As a result, he hires a second worker. After Sam hires the second worker, he always notices something unusual about the company's total level of output. When only one worker was employed, Sam's output was 100 square feet per week. However, by hiring a second worker, the total output of the company jumps to 210 square feet per week. In other words, the addition of a second worker more than doubles the total output of his company. Yet, Sam knows this increase in production has nothing to do with the inherent abilities of the second worker—both are equally skilled and efficient. Having taken an economics course in college, Sam wisely attributes this result to the division of labor and specialization (recall Leonard E. Read's story *I, Pencil, supra* Chapter 2). No longer does the single worker have to perform all of the tasks necessary to build a new home. Now, one worker spends the

Table IX-1

Number of Workers	Total Product	Marginal Product
0	0	
1	100	100
2	210	110
3	330	120
4	460	130
5	570	110
6	650	80
7	690	40
8	680	−10

day doing carpentry while the other does electrical work. With each worker focused only on a single task, they become better and faster at what they do because they no longer have to take a break between each project to work on something else.

As the building season progresses, Sam continues to notice unusual output results as he hires additional workers. When Sam hires a third and fourth worker, the company's output increases to 330 and then 460 square feet per week—continuing the trend of each worker increasing total output by more than the previous worker. This is summarized in Table IX-1. The increases in output for the third and fourth workers can also be attributed to continued specialization. Now two workers do the carpentry work and two workers do the electrical work, each specializing more within each field. One carpenter measures and cuts all of the lumber while the other puts it together. Furthermore, one worker drills the holes and runs the wire through the walls while the other wires the individual outlets and fixtures.

When total output increases by greater amounts for each additional variable input added to the firm's fixed resources, the firm is said to be experiencing **increasing marginal returns**. This is what Sam witnesses with the first four workers—each of these workers increased the total number of square feet constructed by more than the previous worker. Increasing marginal returns are, as Sam noted, caused by the division of labor and specialization.

However, Sam always seems to hit a point where each additional worker hired adds less to the company's total output than when the previous worker was hired. As summarized in Table IX-1, total output is 570, 650, 690, and 680 for the fifth through eighth worker, respectively. Once again, all the workers are equally skilled and efficient. Sam is very confused by this. It seems as if he hits a point where the division of labor and specialization just does not add as much to the company's output.

The phenomenon that Sam witnesses as he hires these additional workers is known as the law of diminishing marginal returns. The **law of diminishing marginal returns** states that, as additional quantities of a variable resource are added to a given amount of fixed resources, a point is eventually reached where each additional variable resource will add smaller and smaller amounts to total output. For workers five through eight, Sam experiences the law of diminishing marginal returns. This occurs because after the fourth worker, the jobsite becomes too crowded and limits the ability of each worker to complete as much work as she could have if there were fewer workers. Aside from generally bumping into each other, once there are more workers, the carpenters will have to take turns using saws and other equipment instead of just being able to use tools when they are needed.

Figure IX-1. The Law of Diminishing Marginal Returns Product Curves for Sam's Shack

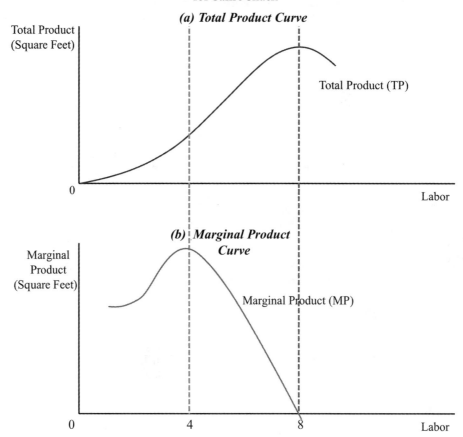

For the workers doing electrical work, adding workers means that one will have to wait for another to finish drilling before he can use the drill to run wires through a wall.

The law of diminishing marginal returns is shown graphically in Figure IX-1. **Total product** (TP) is the total output of goods or services produced by a firm. For Sam's Shacks, TP is measured in square feet of construction (column two in Table IX-1). **Marginal product** (MP) is the change in TP that results from a one unit change in variable re-sources—in this case each additional worker hired (column three in Table IX-1). Figure IX-1 displays these two curves for Sam's Shacks. The MP curve is graphed in panel (b). Each of the first four workers that Sam hires adds more to the TP than the worker hired previously. Thus, Sam's MP of labor increases for the first four units hired. This is reflected in panel (b) with an MP curve that increases over the first four units of labor. For each of the next four workers that Sam hires, MP becomes progressively smaller because of the law of diminishing marginal returns—each additional worker hired adds a smaller— and eventually negative—amount to the TP. As a result, the MP curve declines over this range. When Sam hires the eighth worker, TP actually decreases and the MP curve drops below zero, indicating that MP is negative.

The TP curve is graphed in panel (a). Note that when MP is increasing, TP grows at an increasing rate. However, as MP begins to decline because of the law of diminishing marginal returns, the TP curve begins to grow at a decreasing rate. Finally, as MP becomes negative with the eighth worker, the TP curve begins to decline.

b. Short-Run Costs

As will be discussed later in this chapter, variable costs of production affect production decisions. Variable costs are determined by the price of the variable resource *and its marginal product* (MP). Let us return to the example of Sam's Shacks in order to examine the relationship between costs and marginal productivity. For Sam, MC first decreases and then increases. This pattern is a function of the law of diminishing marginal returns. Remember that for each of the first four workers hired, MP increases. Thus, fewer and fewer units of labor are required to produce an additional unit of output. This greater productivity causes MC to decrease as these four workers are employed. Furthermore, remember that marginal product decreases as Sam hires workers five through eight. In this range, more and more workers are required to produce an additional unit of output. This drop in marginal productivity causes the MC of production to start increasing. In other words, when diminishing marginal returns set in, the MC of production begins to increase. The relationship between marginal productivity and MC for Sam's Shacks is included in Table IX-2 and can be seen in Figure IX-2(b). Notice that the MC curve is U-shaped. MC decreases because of increasing marginal returns and then increases because of diminishing marginal returns.

Short-run cost curves describe the relationship between costs and output when there is at least one fixed input. Seven different measures of short-run costs are of interest.

1. **Marginal cost** (MC) is the cost of producing each additional unit of output.

2. **Fixed cost** (FC) is the price paid for inputs that cannot be varied in the short-run.

3. **Variable cost** (VC) is equal to the price of the variable input multiplied by the quantity of the variable input used.

4. **Total cost** (TC) is equal to the sum of fixed and variable costs: TC = FC + VC.

5. **Average fixed cost** (AFC) is fixed cost divided by the firm's total output (Q): AFC = FC ÷ Q.

6. **Average variable cost** (AVC) is equal to variable costs divided by the firm's total output: AVC = VC ÷ Q.

7. **Average total cost** (ATC) is the total cost of production divided by the firm's total output: ATC = TC ÷ Q.

Table IX-2 provides example values for all of these cost curves for Sam's Shacks where Q is the total construction conducted in square feet per week. It is assumed that Sam's fixed costs are $50 and that he pays each worker he hires $20.

It is important to recognize that the cost curves reflect both the explicit and implicit costs of production. Thus, fixed costs, such as the cost of a building or factory (Sam's heavy equipment and tools in this example), include the rent or return that the building could earn in its next best alternative use. When all costs are covered, the firm is receiving a normal return on the fixed assets, or zero economic profits. Of course, the goal of most firms is to achieve more than a normal return. An above normal return is an economic profit.

Figure IX-2(a) shows the FC curve for Sam's Shacks based on the values in Table IX-2. Note that FC is represented by a horizontal line at the $50 level, demonstrating that FC does not vary with changes in output. VC is also graphed in Figure IX-2(a). For Sam, this is the cost of the workers, who Sam pays $20 each, per quantity produced. This curve

Figure IX-2. Total and Marginal Cost Curves

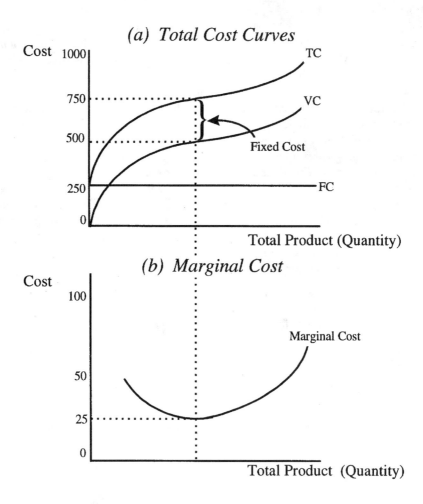

indicates that VC equals zero when output is zero. VC initially increases at a decreasing rate as the firm realizes increasing marginal returns, and then begins to increase at an increasing rate at the point where diminishing marginal returns sets in. The TC curve for Sam's is also shown in Figure IX-2(a). The TC curve is simply the vertical summation of the fixed and variable cost curves (or FC + VC in Table IX-2). Thus, the TC curve is the VC curve shifted upwards by the amount of FC.

Average cost data for Sam's Shacks graphed in Figure IX-3 also reflect the law of diminishing marginal returns. The shape of the AVC curve is determined by the shape

Table IX-2. Cost Measures for Sam's Shacks

Q	FC	VC	TC	MC	AFC	AVC	ATC
0	50		50				
100	50	20	70	20	0.5	0.2	0.7
200	50	37	87	17	0.25	0.185	0.435
300	50	52	102	15	0.167	0.173	0.34
400	50	66	116	14	0.125	0.165	0.29
500	50	81	131	15	0.1	0.162	0.262
600	50	98	148	17	0.083	0.163	0.247
700	50	118	168	20	0.071	0.169	0.24
800	50	142	192	24	0.063	0.178	0.24

of the MC curve. When MC is below AVC, AVC declines. When MC is above AVC, AVC begins to rise. The MC curve intersects the AVC curve at its minimum point — indicated by point A. This basic relationship is known as the **average-marginal rule**. The MC curve has the same relationship with the ATC curve as it did with the AVC curve — the MC curve will intersect the ATC curve at its minimum point — indicated by point B. AFC declines over the entire range of output. This reflects the fact that FC is spread over a larger total output as production expands.

Gregory Mankiw compares the average-marginal rule and why the marginal cost curve intersects the AVC and AFC curves at the minimum to a student's GPA. N. Gregory Mankiw, Principles of Microeconomics 279 (3d ed. 2004). He likens MC to the student's grade in one class and AVC or ATC to the overall GPA. If the grade in the class is less than the student's GPA, the GPA will decline; if the grade is higher than the GPA, the GPA will increase. So it is with MC and AVC or ATC. If the MC is less than AVC, AVC is falling; if it is higher, then AVC is rising. This means the intersection will be the minimum. For Sam's Shacks, MC is less than AVC when Sam is producing 0 to 500

Figure IX-3. Average & Marginal Cost Curves

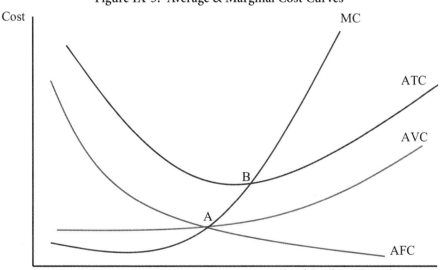

square feet, then MC is greater than AVC. Thus, somewhere between 500 and 600 square feet, MC intersects AVC.

c. Changes in Costs of Production

Changes in the cost of producing any good or service cause the cost curves to shift by an amount reflecting the change in cost. In general, there are two important sources that change the costs of production: (1) changes in the cost of inputs and (2) changes in production technology. Taxes on output also affect costs as do government regulations that impact technology or input costs. When variable costs of production increase, the MC curve shifts to the left; when these costs of production decrease, the MC curve shifts to the right. When either fixed or variable costs of production increase, the ATC curve shifts up and when either of these costs of production decrease, the ATC curve shifts down.

Consider Figure IX-4, which shows two sets of MC and ATC curves for a firm—MC_1 and ATC_1, and MC_2 and ATC_2. If the cost of an input used in the production of this firm's goods or services increases, the MC curve shifts to the left. This can be seen in Figure IX-4 as a shift from MC_1 to MC_2. Furthermore, increased input costs shift the ATC curve up from ATC_1 to ATC_2. An increase in the excise tax shifts the MC and ATC curves in the same way. Changes in regulation that increase the costs of compliance similarly cause the costs of production to increase. Technological improvements cause the MC curve to shift to the right, indicating a decrease in the costs of production—movement from MC_2 to MC_1 in Figure IX-4. Likewise, the ATC curve shifts down from ATC_2 to ATC_1.

d. Economies of Scale

The short run ATC curve is U-shaped, reflecting two competing forces. First, ATC declines as output expands because the reductions in ATC from spreading fixed costs over an increasingly large number of units of output are larger than the increase in ATC from

Figure IX-4. The Effect of an Increase in Resource Prices on Costs

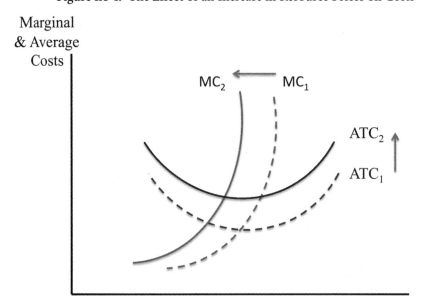

diminishing marginal returns. The firm is said to enjoy **economies of scale** over this range of declining ATC. At some point however, the increase in variable costs due to diminishing marginal returns swamp the reductions in fixed costs, causing ATC to increase. Firms suffer **diseconomies of scale** over the range of increasing ATC. **Constant returns to scale** occur when long-run average cost does not change as output expands over some range. For example, there may be a long range of output over which ATC is at its minimum.

Economies of scope exist when the joint production of multiple outputs is more cost efficient than producing each output separately. For example, the provision of both savings and checking accounts by the same bank is more cost efficient than having bank A provide checking and bank B provide savings. Imagine the amount of duplication that is avoided by having one bank provide both savings and checking accounts. When such economies arise, one firm would produce both outputs rather than two firms each producing only one. Moreover, it would be a better use of resources for a single firm to produce both outputs because to do so would minimize the total opportunity cost of the resources used in production.

2. Long-Run Production

In the **long-run**, all inputs used in the production process are variable. Thus, in the long-run, there are no fixed resources—all inputs can be varied in response to a change in the desired level of output. Unlike in the short-run, firms can build, expand, or shut down factories. From the GM example above, in the long run GM is able to sell unused factories or build new ones as demand changes in the long-run—making even the number of factories variable. Thus, one of the most important long-run decisions that the firm must make is the selection of the optimal plant size—the plant size that will minimize the long-run costs of producing the profit maximizing output.

Assume that a particular manufacturer has five choices regarding plant size, and that the ATC curve for each of these plants is depicted in Figure IX-5. The plant size that is best for a particular manufacturer depends on the level of output to be produced. For example, if output less than Q_1 needs to be produced, then the plant size that corresponds to ATC_1 is the optimal choice. For output choices between Q_1 and Q_2, ATC_2 is optimal. Likewise, for output between Q_2 and Q_3, ATC_3 is optimal. Thus, the optimal plant size for any given output can be found along the continuous portion of the five ATC curves in Figure IX-5. The continuous portions of the five ATC curves in Figure IX-5 are the basis for a new curve—the long-run average cost curve.

Long-run average cost (LRAC) is the lowest per unit cost of producing any level of output when the firm can choose from all possible plant sizes. For the firm in Figure IX-5, the continuous portion of the ATC curves represent the LRAC curve where only five possible plant sizes are available. Figure IX-6 shows a smooth LRAC curve. This curve represents the lowest per unit cost of producing any level of output when a firm can choose from an infinite number of possible plant sizes. Notice that this smooth LRAC curve is tangent to an infinite number of short-run ATC curves. As the LRAC curve slopes downward, it is tangent to the short-run ATC curves before the point of minimum cost for each plant size; as the LRAC curve slopes upward, it is tangent to the short-run ATC curves past the point of minimum cost. At the lowest point on the LRAC curve, the LRAC curve is tangent to the minimum point on a short-run ATC curve. Figure IX-6 also depicts the long-run marginal cost curve. **Long-run marginal cost** (LRMC) is the change in *total cost* that results from a one unit increase in production. This reflects the fact that, in the long-run, all resources are variable. Thus, everything from labor to plant size is incorporated

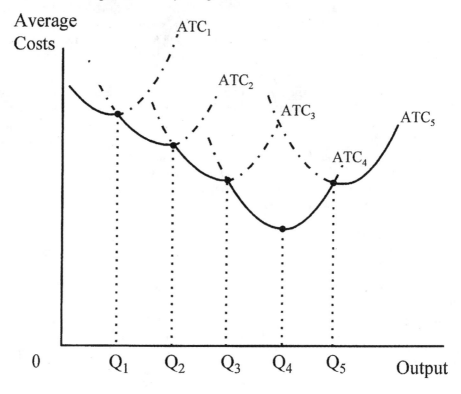

Figure IX-5. Adjusting Plant Size to Minimize Costs

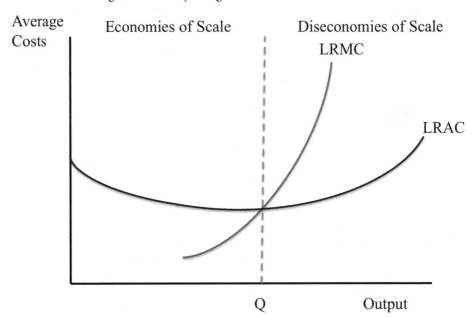

Figure IX-6. Adjusting Plant Size to Minimize Costs

into the LRMC number. As with short-run average costs curves, LRMC intersects long-run average curves at their minimum point. Thus, as long as LRMC is below LRAC, LRAC will decrease. When LRMC is greater than LRAC, LRAC will increase.

Like the short run ATC curve, the LRAC curve is also U-shaped over the full range of possible levels of output. First, the firm enjoys economies of scale as output increases because the opportunities for specialization and division of labor increase. Second, firms often learn how to reduce the costs of production after gaining some experience in actually producing the product. In other words, as the firm's output grows, managers and employees gain more and more experience with the production process and hence learn more efficient production techniques. Third, as output expands, firms can begin to take advantage of mass production technology. The combination of these factors helps to explain why LRAC decreases as output approaches Q from the left in Figure IX-6.

The Sam's Shack example elaborates on economies of scale. In the long run, when all factors of production are variable, Sam can vary his output by purchasing more heavy equipment and more tools. As he increases equipment, he is able to keep more workers busy and change the point where he experiences diminishing marginal returns. He is even able to buy enough heavy equipment and tools to have his company building many homes at the same time. Sam enjoys economies of scale because of all three potential sources listed in the previous paragraph. First, as he expands the company so that it builds many homes at once, his workers can very narrowly specialize and still keep busy by moving from one home to the next. For example, he can have workers that dig one foundation each day and then move to the next home, workers that only put shingles on, and workers that only pour concrete sidewalks around the home. Because these projects cannot be done simultaneously with other projects (workers cannot put shingles on before the foundation is poured and the home is built), workers could not have specialized on such narrow areas without Sam's Shacks dramatically increasing its size. Second, as the Sam's Shacks workers build many homes a year, they will learn new tricks that speed up the process. Third, once Sam's Shacks is large enough, it becomes worthwhile for Sam to purchase expensive machinery that prefabricates the walls to a home and then delivers them to the construction site—something that could not have been profitable without substantial expansion. These three things allow Sam's Shacks to benefit from economies of scale.

Diseconomies of scale begin to set in as the firm's output grows larger. Diseconomies of scale arise primarily as a result of the fact that, at some point, the firm grows too large for its managers to control. As firm output expands, more employees and managers are hired, which increases the firm's bureaucracy. As this bureaucracy grows, communication becomes difficult and decision making can grind to a halt. Eventually, the diseconomies outweigh the economies of scale. Thus, in Figure IX-6, LRAC increases as output expands to the right of Q.

The output level that minimizes LRAC is called the **minimum efficient scale**. Minimum efficient scale can have a large impact on the number of firms that compete in a particular industry. When minimum efficient scale can be achieved at low levels of output relative to industry demand, many firms will be able to enter and survive in the industry. On the other hand, if minimum efficient scale can be reached only at levels of output that constitute a large portion of the entire market demand, then only a few firms will be able to survive in the industry.

In Figure IX-6, LRAC comes to a unique minimum point at Q. This implies that there is one specific plant size—output level—that minimizes the costs of production in the

Figure IX-7. Alternative LRAC Curves

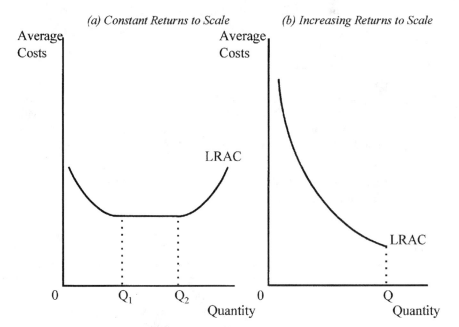

long-run. The LRAC curve does not have to decrease to a unique minimum point, however. Two other types of LRAC curves can be observed. First, Figure IX-7(a) depicts a LRAC curve that is exhibiting constant returns to scale. **Constant returns to scale** occur when long-run average cost does not change as output expands over some range. In Figure IX-7(a), economies of scale exist to the left of Q_1, constant returns to scale exist between Q_1 and Q_2, and diseconomies of scale exist to the right of Q_2. Constant returns to scale indicate that firms can produce at output levels between Q_1 and Q_2 without a difference in per unit costs.

Another LRAC cost curve of interest is one that exhibits increasing returns to scale, as depicted in Figure IX-7(b). **Increasing returns to scale** occur when LRAC decreases continually as output expands, indicating that economies of scale persist over all levels of output. This LRAC curve would indicate that the larger the firm, the better. In fact, such a curve suggests that a single firm would supply the entire industry output at the lowest average cost in the long-run. Public utilities such as electricity, natural gas, and water are often assumed to exhibit LRAC curves with increasing returns to scale.

B. Market Structures

1. Perfect Competition

Competition occupies a central role in the economic analysis of firm activity. In general, the effects of competition are seen as highly desirous and beneficial to overall social welfare. As the Supreme Court has said, "competition will produce not only lower prices, but also better goods and services. 'The heart of our national economic policy long has been faith in the value of competition.'... [C]ompetition is the best method of allocating resources in a free market ... [A]ll elements of a bargain—quality, service, safety, and durability—and not just the immediate cost, are favorably affected by the free opportunity to select among alternative offers."[1] This section examines the structural characteristics of competitive markets. These structural characteristics are enumerated in the model of perfect competition. A perfectly competitive market is a hypothetical model used to demonstrate the benefits of intense competition. In a perfectly competitive market both consumers and sellers complete all transactions that increase their welfare. This model is often used as a benchmark for analyzing real world markets.

To demonstrate this model, imagine a market where there are 1,000 sellers who are all selling exactly the same product. Each of these sellers is fully accessible to you. They are selling a product that you and everyone you know wants to buy. Despite this product's popularity, there are never any shortages or wait times to get your hands on it. The resources necessary to manufacture this product are readily available and cheap. And although some of the sellers may close down there is always another seller ready and able to take its place. Finally, you can readily find out everything you need to know about each seller, including its price, availability, location, and production capability. What would competition be like in this scenario?

First, no firm has an incentive to invest in improving technology because such innovations can be immediately imitated. Second, no firm has an incentive to advertise because all products and prices are alike. Third, no individual firm will have meaningful control over the price it can charge. Intuitively, this makes sense. The firm's output is so small relative to the market that its individual transactions do not affect the market price. Fourth, because all products are identical and market participants have complete information, no individual firm can raise its price without losing all of its sales. If firm A tries to raise its price, consumers already know about firm B that sells an identical product at the lower price. Because individual firms in a perfectly competitive market have no control over price, they are said to be **price takers**. Firms in a perfectly competitive market must offer their goods and services for sale at whatever price is established by the interaction of market demand and supply.

a. Short-Run Individual Firm Behavior: Profit Maximization

The perfectly competitive firm as a price taker is illustrated graphically in Figure IX-8. Market demand and supply appear in panel (b), and the demand curve for the output of a single firm is shown in panel (a). In panel (b), market demand and supply intersect at a price of $4.00 per unit. This market price is the price that the perfectly competitive firm must accept. Thus, the demand curve for a single competitive firm is a horizontal line drawn at the level of the market price—$4.00. Recall from the discussion of demand elasticity in Chapter II that a horizontal demand curve signifies totally elastic demand. If the firm were to try to raise its price above $4.00, its output would drop to zero. At the market price, the firm can sell as much as it can produce. A profit maximizing firm would never sell below the market price because it can already sell as much as it wants at the market price. Firms that face totally elastic demand have no power over price—no market power. In this situation, price is set by the market and individual firms have no ability to affect that price.

Firms in a perfectly competitive market attempt to maximize economic profit. Although a firm in a perfectly competitive industry has no control over price, it does control its level of output. Thus, the perfectly competitive firm must find the level of output that

---

1. Nat'l Soc. of Prof'l Engineers v. U. S., 435 U.S. 679, 695 (1978) (quoting Standard Oil Co. v. FTC, 340 U.S. 231, 248 (1951)).

**Figure IX-8. The Firm's Demand Curve and Market Equilibrium
in Perfect Competition**

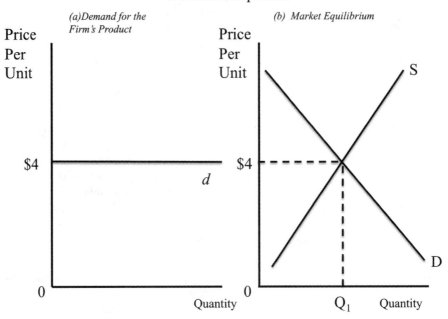

maximizes its profits. **Profit maximization** occurs at the level of output where the difference between total revenue (TR) and total costs (TC) is maximized. **Total revenue** is equal to the market price multiplied by the quantity of output sold.

A firm always maximizes its profits by producing that the point where MC equals **marginal revenue,** which is the additional revenue earned from a one unit increase in output. In a perfectly competitive market, the marginal revenue will always equal to the price because, as a price taker, the firm will always be able to sell at the market price (P). Therefore, the market price will always represent the marginal revenue gained by the firm when it sells an additional unit of output. Thus, for firms in a perfectly competitive industry, marginal revenue equals price — MR = P.

A firm should continue to produce additional units of output as long as the gain in TR exceeds the increase in TC, or stated differently, as long as MR is greater than MC. Every firm should ask itself if manufacturing and selling an additional unit of output will bring in more money in revenue than it will cost to produce. In other words, a firm will continue to produce additional units as long as the MR from producing those units exceeds the MC. This method for determining the profit maximizing level of output is illustrated in Figure IX-9(b), which shows the MR and MC curves for a firm in a perfectly competitive market. The MR curve is a horizontal line at $4.00 reflecting the fact that the firm is a price taker and will earn $4.00 in MR for each additional unit sold.

Consider the output decisions available to the profit maximizing firm faced with these MR and MC curves. At output levels from 0 to 10, MR > MC. Thus, the firm can increase profits by producing additional units. At any output level greater than 11, MC > MR and profits are increased by cutting back output. When the firm produces 11 units of output, MR = MC. At this level of output, the firm incurs an economic loss if it expands production and sacrifices profits if it reduces output — the firm can do no better than producing 11

Figure IX-9. Profit-Maximizing Output for a Purely Competitive Firm

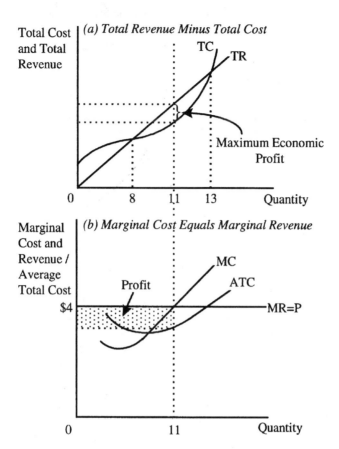

units. More generally, the profit maximizing level of output for all firms occurs where MR = MC. The amount of profit that the firm will earn at this level of production can be determined by multiplying the vertical difference between P and ATC by total output. Profit is shown by the shaded area in Figure IX-9(b).

Figure IX-9(a) can be used to illustrate the profit maximizing decision making process. As each additional unit is sold, the firm earns additional revenue equal to $4.00. Thus, the TR curve is a straight line which increases $4.00 for every additional unit of output sold. The TC curve first increases at a decreasing rate—a result of increasing marginal returns—and then increases at an increasing rate—caused by the inevitable diminishing marginal returns. Figure IX-9(a) shows that TC exceeds TR at output levels below 8 and above 13. Thus, if the firm were to produce less than 8 or more than 13 units of output, it would incur an economic loss. Figure IX-9(a) also shows that TR exceeds TC at output levels between 8 and 13. It follows then that an economic profit can be earned by the firm when it produces at any level between 8 and 13 units of output. However, economic profits are maximized when the vertical distance between the TR curve and the TC curve is maximized. This profit maximizing result occurs at an output of 11 units in Figure IX-9(a). Another way to think about this result is that firms want to maximize the difference between TR and TC because that is the point at which they earn the largest possible profit.

b. Loss Minimization: The Shut-Down Decision

Whenever market price falls below a firm's ATC, the firm will incur an economic loss. This loss will be equal to the difference between ATC and price multiplied by output—$(P - ATC)\, Q$. In the short-run, the firm has two options: it can continue to operate and attempt to minimize losses; or, it can shut down, thereby reducing its variable costs to zero, and suffer losses equal to its fixed costs.

Because the firm has both fixed and variable costs in the short-run, it is possible to incur smaller losses by operating than by shutting down. When a firm shuts down, it will suffer an economic loss equal to its FC. The shut-down solution may not always be the best, however. The profit maximizing firm will make its decision on whether to operate in the face of economic losses based upon the relationship between market price and AVC. If price exceeds AVC, then the revenue generated by the firm will cover all VC and some revenue will be left over. This residual revenue is offsets some of the FC. By continuing to operate, the firm's economic loss is less than its FC.

It might be useful to consider an example. Imagine a factory that is operating at a point where its price exceeds AVC, but where its MC are greater than its MR. It is easy to think that the owner of the factory should shut it down because it is losing money. But the factory will, in the short-run, continue to incur the costs of owning the property (paying the mortgage), and it has already incurred the costs of buying machinery, training employees, and purchasing the inputs for its production. Even if the factory shuts down, those costs cannot be avoided in the short-run—the fixed costs are considered sunk. The important thing for the factory owner to consider is whether the factory is covering its variable costs, which only include the price of paying its employees and operating its machinery. The FC will be its losses if it shuts down. So long as the factory's TR is higher than its VC, then it is preferable to operate in the short-run because operation will reduce the firm's costs below its unavoidable FC.

Figure IX-10(a) demonstrates how to derive the loss minimizing result via marginal analysis. The figure shows the MC, ATC, AVC, and MR curves for a perfectly competitive

Figure IX-10. Loss Minimization: The Shutdown Decision

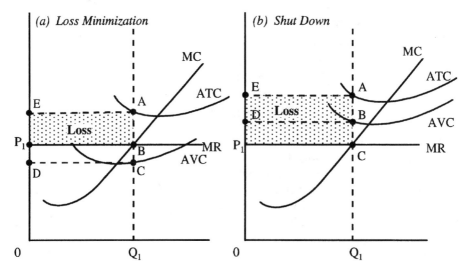

firm. The loss minimizing level of output is found by increasing production as long as MR > MC. This MR = MC rule is subject to one limitation. Namely, the MR and MC curves must intersect—be equal—at a point above the AVC curve. Recall that the vertical distance between the ATC and AVC curves is equal to AFC and that FC = AFC(Q). Thus, when price moves above AVC, revenue cuts into some portion of the AFC that lies between ATC and AVC. In Figure IX-10(a), the loss minimizing strategy is indeed met where MR = MC at Q_1 units of output. Total revenue generated at this level of output is equal to the area in the rectangle framed by (P_1BQ_10). Because the firm is able to cover all of its VC and a portion of its FC it is better off not shutting down. The economic loss is equal to (ATC – P) Q.

The case for shutting down is considered in Figure IX-10(b). Notice that at Q_1, (P_1 < AVC), (AFC > (ATC – AVC)), total revenue ($0P_1CQ_1$) earned by the firm does not cover variable costs ($0DBQ_1$), and losses (P_1EAC) are greater than fixed costs (ABDE). The rational firm will minimize losses by shutting down and incurring losses only equal to FC. Another way to consider this situation is to realize that different prices result in substantially different business decisions for a single firm. In other words, the prevailing exogenous market price can determine whether or not a factory will operate or shut down in the short-run, which is dependent on whether the factory is able to cover its VC.

c. The Short-Run Supply Curve

The perfectly competitive firm considers three factors in determining its profit maximizing level of output: (1) price (where P = MR); (2) marginal cost (MC); and (3) average variable cost (AVC). As P changes, the firm will produce the quantity where P = MC as long as P is above AVC. This relationship can be seen in Figure IX-11, which demonstrates that at different market prices, firms make different choices about their

Figure IX-11. Summary of Short-Run Decisions

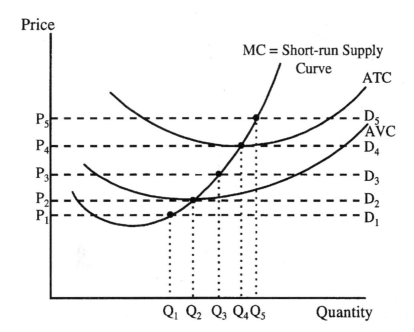

short-run operations. At P_5, P > ATC and the firm earns positive economic profits. At P_4, P = ATC of production and the firm earns a normal economic profit. At P_3, AVC < P < ATC, the firm seeks to minimize its economic loss by continuing to operate. At P_2, P = AVC, the firm is indifferent between shutting down with a loss equal to its FC or producing an output just sufficient to cover VC. Regardless of whether the firm produces or shuts down at this price level, the economic loss is equal to FC. Finally, P_1 < AVC and, thus, the firm will produce zero output in order to minimize economic losses. The above analysis leads us to an important conclusion regarding the perfectly competitive firm's MC curve in the short-run. For the perfectly competitive firm, the portion of the MC curve that lies above the AVC curve is the firm's short-run supply curve. Thus, in the short-run, firms minimize losses or maximize profits by adjusting their output subject to their MC curve.

d. Long-Run Firm Behavior: Industry Supply

Firms have substantially more options in the long-run. In the long-run, all resources can be varied—there are no fixed inputs or fixed costs—and firms are capable of making any number of structural changes to the way they do business. Firms can expand or contract their plant size as well as enter or exit an industry. In the short-run, firms are capable of earning economic profits because it takes time for new firms to construct plants and enter the market, and existing firms cannot immediately expand production beyond the capacity of current plants. In the long-run, economic profits attract new firms to the market and encourage existing firms to expand their plant and output. As firms move into industries earning positive economic profits, industry supply expands. The result of this increase in supply is to force the market price down. As the market price drops, so do economic profits. In the long-run, the entry of firms into industries earning positive economic profits eliminates those profits. This is the long-run process of industry competition.

A short-run economic loss will have a similar impact on the industry in the long-run. Firms suffering from an economic loss will observe other industries that are either making a normal return or a positive economic return. The rational response for these firms is to transfer their resources to a more profitable use. In the long-run, profit maximizing firms exit industries with short-run economic losses. As firms leave the industry, industry supply decreases. This decrease in supply causes the price for the good or service in that industry to increase. This process continues until supply contracts to the point that a normal profit is earned by the remaining firms.

The tendency for perfectly competitive firms to earn only a normal profit in the long-run is at the core of understanding long-run production decisions. As firms enter or exit a market, they impact industry supply and market price. The process of entry or exit will continue, in the long-run, until the market supply curve intersects the market demand curve at a price that is equal to the lowest point on each firm's LRAC curve. At any price that does not meet this condition, further adjustments to market supply will occur. A price above the minimum point on the LRAC curve will result in economic profits, attracting more firms or expanded output to the industry. On the other hand, a price below the minimum point on the LRAC curve would indicate that economic losses were being incurred. This would encourage additional firms to exit or cut back on production. This process makes a lot of intuitive sense. When one firm is making a lot of money producing a good or offering a service, other firms are going to want to enter that industry and try to gain some of those profits. When an industry is, instead, losing money, firms will drop out of that industry and seek another venture that will make them economic profit.

Figure IX-12. Long-Run Equilibrium for the Firm and the Industry

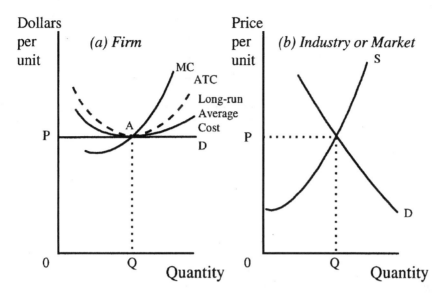

In this quest to maximize economic profits in the long-run, firms vary their scale of production until their average costs of production are minimized. Figure IX-12 demonstrates the equilibrium position at which the firm will earn a normal profit. At point A, the firm's MC, short-run average total cost (ATC), and LRAC are all equal. At this point, no firm in the industry has a reason to alter its output, and no firm outside of the industry has an incentive to enter the market. Thus, the market is in a stable equilibrium as shown in Figure IX-12(b).

Further insight into the long-run adjustment process can be gained by considering a specific example that shows short-run profits and a long-run shift in the market. For purposes of this example, assume that the costs of production do not change based on the number of firms in the industry. Figure IX-13(b) shows a perfectly competitive market in equilibrium at point A. Here, S_1 intersects D_1 and equilibrium price and quantity are P_1 and Q_1 respectively. Consider what occurs as a result of an increase in demand for the industry product in the short-run. In Figure IX-13(b) this is represented by movement to point B as demand shifts from D_1 to D_2. In the short-run, equilibrium price is P_2. Figure IX-13(a) demonstrates the reaction of individual firms to this increase in demand. At P_2, MR > MC at the original level of production, q_1. Thus, the profit maximizing firms will increase output along their short-run supply curve, up to the point where MR = MC. For this particular firm, MR = MC after the demand shift at an output of q_2. As all firms in the industry respond in this way to the price increase, industry supply will increase to Q_2 in panel (b). Note that in the short-run, each firm is earning an economic profit equal to the area P_2EFG. This indicates that an increase in demand can generate profits for firms because in the short-run, before more competitors enter the market, firms are able to sell more quantity at a higher price without substantial increases to their costs.

In the long-run, the firms' economic profits disappear because of the entry of new firms into the industry. Firms that are in industries earning a normal profit or an economic loss have an incentive to switch their productive resources to industries in which positive economic profits are being earned. The entry of these new firms causes the supply of the industry product to increase. New firms will continue to enter and industry supply will

Figure IX-13. Long-Run Adjustment to an Increase in Demand

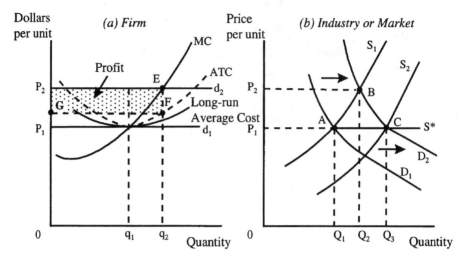

increase as long as individual firms in the industry are capable of earning economic profits. Thus, in the long-run, equilibrium moves from point B to point C as supply shifts from S_1 to S_2. At this point, equilibrium quantity has increased to Q_3 and equilibrium price is once again P_1. This example also demonstrates the difference between a move along the supply curve and a shift in the supply curve. In the short-run the firm is able to supply more and gain economic profits whereas in the long-run the entire industry will produce more and those profits will reduce to 0.

The effect on the individual firm of the decrease in price that results from new firms entering the industry can be seen in Figure IX-13(a). The fall in the market price causes the demand curve faced by the individual firm to decline from d_2 to d_1. As a result, the firm reduces output from q_2 to q_1. At this equilibrium price and quantity combination, the firm earns only a normal profit. In other words, the individual firm's marginal cost, price (marginal revenue), and long-run average cost are equal and the long-run average cost curve is at a minimum—MC = MR = P = LRAC. In the long-run, the price of a good or service is determined by the minimum point on the firm's long-run average cost curve. Despite the fact that industry output increases from Q_1 to Q_3, individual firm output remains at q_1 in the long-run. Thus, the increase in industry output is supplied by the entry of new firms.

A decrease in demand has an opposite effect on both the industry and the individual firm. Figure IX-14(b), shows the industry in equilibrium at point A, with demand curve, D_1, supply curve, S_1, market price, P_1, and quantity, Q_1. Point A represents the current long-run equilibrium, where MC = MR = ATC = LRAC. The equilibrium condition for the firm is shown in Figure IX-14(a).

Let us suppose that demand in this industry suddenly decreases. This decrease is seen as a shift in demand from D_1 to D_2. This decline in demand causes the market price to decrease to P_2—the market is now in equilibrium at point B in the short-run. Because of the decrease in market price, the demand curve facing the individual firm declines. This event can be seen in Figure IX-14(a) as movement from d_1 to d_2. Again, the firm will determine the level of output to produce by identifying the point at which MR = P = MC. This causes individual firms to cut production from q_1 to q_2. As a result of each

Figure IX-14. Long-Run Adjustments to a Decrease in Demand

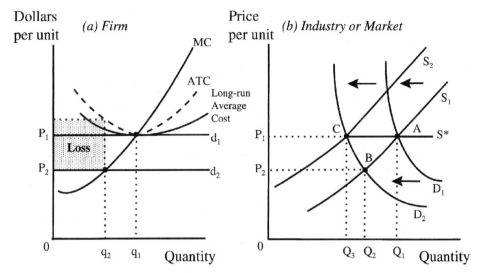

individual firm cutting back output in the short-run, industry-wide output declines from Q_1 to Q_2. This is a change in the quantity supplied which is indicated by movement along the supply curve from point A to point B. Thus, the market is now in equilibrium at point B, with an output of Q_2 and a price P_2.

At this lower price, the firm is selling q_2 units at a price below the average total cost of production. In other words, the firm operates at a loss equal to the vertical difference between the ATC curve and the demand curve at q_2 multiplied by total output, q_2. This is the shaded portion of Figure IX-14(a). In the long-run, these losses force some firms to exit the industry. As these firms leave, market supply decreases. Firms will continue to exit the market until the supply curve has shifted from S_1 to S_2. In the long-run, the market will be in equilibrium at point C, where S_2 and D_2 intersect. As a result of these changes, industry output has declined to Q_3 and market price has returned to P_1. At this new equilibrium position, marginal cost, price (marginal revenue), short-run average total cost, and long-run average cost are equal—$P = MC = ATC = LRAC$. In other words, individual firms in the industry are once again earning a normal profit. As was the case with an increase in demand, after long-run adjustments, individual firms again produce an output of q_1— the same output as before the change in demand. However, market output has declined from Q_1 to Q_3. The decline in industry output came as the result of firms exiting the market and not as a result of cuts in the remaining firms' production. As you might have expected this result was quite predictable. In the short-run, when there is a sudden decline in demand, industry output and price will drop and firms will lose money. In the long-run, some firms will drop out of the market reducing supply which will bring price back up to a stable equilibrium. Because demand is often out of control of the firms selling goods, markets constantly see this give and take of fluctuating prices and adjustments to supply.

The above analysis considered the response of an industry and its individual firms to a change in demand. In the short-run, firms responded by changing the quantity supplied to the market—movement along their marginal cost curve. In the long-run, however, firms entered or exited the industry until a new short-run supply curve was established that returned individual firms to a normal profit. The long-run supply curve for any particular industry can be identified by connecting the points of long-run equilibrium.

This can be seen in Figures IX-13(b) and IX-14(b) as the horizontal line marked S*. This long-run supply curve is horizontal and, thus, totally elastic. This implies that as output expands, the costs of production do not increase because in the long-run, firms do not need a price increase to supply the additional output. This type of industry is known as a **constant cost industry** because it can expand without affecting the prices of the resources it employs.

A constant cost industry is usually one in which the industry consumes only a small portion of the total amount of a particular productive resource available in the market. The producers of golf tees are an example of a constant cost industry. A large increase in the demand for golf tees is not likely to cause the market price of timber to increase. The production of golf tees utilizes only a small portion of all wood that is available as a production input.

Increasing cost industries are industries where increasing output in the long-run leads to an increase in the costs of production. Because the costs of some resources increase as output expands in these industries, individual firms' cost curves shift upward. Thus, long-run supply curves for increasing cost industries have a positive slope. The oil industry is an example of an increasing cost industry. As production of oil goes up, the obvious and convenient places to drill for oil run out and it becomes increasingly costly and difficult to find and reach new sources of oil. **Decreasing cost industries** experience lower production costs as output increases in the long-run. This decrease in the cost of production causes a downward shift in the individual firms' cost curves. Thus, such firms experience downward sloping supply curves in the long-run. An example of a decreasing cost industry would be many manufacturing industries because the marginal costs of manufacturing often decline as output expands because of economies of scale. Regardless of the effect of expanding output on the costs of production, the long-run conclusion is always the same. Individual firms in perfectly competitive markets can earn economic profits in the short-run, but the entry or exit of firms in the long-run results in a normal economic profit.

e. The Economic Benefits of Competition

When firms produce exactly the goods that consumers desire most at the lowest possible price, they are said to be achieving **allocative efficiency**. Perfect competition results in allocative efficiency. The market demand curve reflects the consumers' value for each additional unit of consumption, and the value attached to the last unit of output purchased by consumers is equal to the market price. In the perfectly competitive model, market price equals the marginal cost of the last unit producers are willing to supply. Furthermore, marginal cost is defined as a measure of the opportunity cost of the resources used in the production of each additional unit. By assumption the marginal benefit consumers attach to the last unit consumed is equal to the marginal opportunity cost of the resources used to produce that same unit, and thus the last unit produced is valued as much or more than any other good or service that could have been produced using those same resources. In other words, resources could not be reallocated, in any way, in order to increase the value of output to society. That is, allocative efficiency is achieved—and social welfare is maximized—in perfectly competitive industries. This is also a condition that economists refer to as Pareto efficiency. It represents a point where no one can be made any better off by reallocating resources.

The perfect competition model provides a **competitive benchmark** for the economic analysis of other industry structures. In general, industry production at the quantity where P = MC provides a benchmark for comparing an industry's performance with the allocative efficiency of the ideal perfectly competitive market.

In the perfect competition model, market price reflects the value of the resources that are used in the production of a product. This is important because prices are the most important signal in guiding the allocation of resources. If prices are distorted by a lack of competition, then the allocation of resources that results is less than efficient. Consider the following example.

Suppose, in the beginning, everyone in a small town bakes his or her own bread. One day a baker moves into town and decides that there is a profit to be made by baking bread for others. The baker adds all the expenses for a loaf of bread, including labor time, plus a premium for risk bearing, and determines that this cost should be the price to charge customers. Many people in town decide that it is cheaper to buy bread than to bake it themselves, and use their increased time to produce other products. Those people who do not produce other products or services with their time continue to bake their own bread. After a while, the baker determines that she could make more profit by exerting her market power and raising her price. Although some customers would return to baking their own bread, the baker would still make more revenue from the loaves sold than she would lose from the reduced volume.

Although it may appear that the increase in profits to the baker is simply a transfer of wealth from her customers and that there is no net effect on society, there is a hidden efficiency loss that makes society worse off. The customers who return to baking their own bread because of the artificially higher price must now reduce the time they spend producing other products in order to bake bread for themselves. Hence, society loses other valuable products because the price of bread has increased.

If baking bread were a relatively easy industry to enter, new competitors would enter the market and charge a lower price. The original baker, finding that she is losing her customers, would have to match her new competitor's price or perhaps charge less in order to get all of her customers back. The price war would continue until neither baker could lower prices any more without losing money. At this point, the price of bread accurately reflects the value of the resources used in manufacture. That is, competition has generated a market price that equals the marginal cost of production. Customers who returned to baking their own bread can buy their bread again and return to producing other products.

2. Monopoly

A monopoly exists when there is only one producer of a particular good or service in a market with no competition. Often these markets are characterized by a lack of close substitutes and the producer is protected from competition by impenetrable barriers to entry. Barriers to entry allow monopolies to earn higher than normal profits by reducing their output and raising prices above competitive levels. Monopolies are a form of market failure that results in a misallocation of resources. Yet, the very existence of monopolies poses a difficult problem for policy makers—in a market economy, monopoly profits encourage innovation and efficiency. Public policies designed to restrain monopolistic practices must be carefully designed to avoid dampening competitive incentives.

a. Profit Maximizing Price and Quantity

A monopolist is the only producer of a particular good or service and, therefore, by its actions alone, determines the market price. In contrast to the perfectly competitive model where the demand curve faced by price taking firms is horizontal and equal to a market price established by the interaction of industry supply and demand, the monopolist is the only firm in the industry and its demand curve is the same as the industry demand curve. Thus, the monopolist faces a downward sloping demand curve—the monopolist must lower price in order to sell additional units. This has important implications for the monopolist's production decisions because, unlike the price taker, the monopolist's marginal revenue does not equal price.

For the monopolist, marginal revenue is less than price except for the very first unit sold. The divergence of marginal revenue and price occurs because the demand curve faced by the monopolist is downward sloping. When demand is downward sloping, and a uniform price is charged for all units sold, marginal revenue will always be less than market price. This result is illustrated in Figure IX-15. A price cut from P_1 to P_2 increases the quantity sold from Q_1 to Q_2. So, total revenue at point A on the demand curve is equal to P_1AQ_10; at point B, it is equal to P_2BQ_20. The change in total revenue in moving from A to B is the result of two offsetting influences. First, revenue is increased as a result of the sale of additional units of output from Q_1 to Q_2. This increase in revenue is the area CBQ_2Q_1. Second, revenue is lost due to a lower price on units 0 to Q_1 that could have been sold at the higher price P_1 instead of P_2. This reduction is represented by the area P_1ACP_2. The marginal revenue derived from the sale of an additional unit is the difference between these two offsetting effects. That is, marginal revenue is the difference between the total revenue at A and the total revenue at B. Because the marginal revenue for any output charged is less than the corresponding price for that level of output, the marginal revenue (MR) curve will always lie below the demand curve—with the one exception being the first unit sold. For the first unit sold, marginal revenue is equal to market price. Beyond that the general rule always holds—P > MR. When a monopolist lowers prices it must ask whether the new revenue from increased sales will offset the lost revenue from lower prices. The answer to that question depends heavily on understanding the effect of demand elasticity.

Figure IX-16, which shows a standard demand curve with MR below price at every level of output, demonstrates the relationship between total revenue, marginal revenue,

Figure IX-15. The Dual Effects of a Price Reduction on Total Revenues

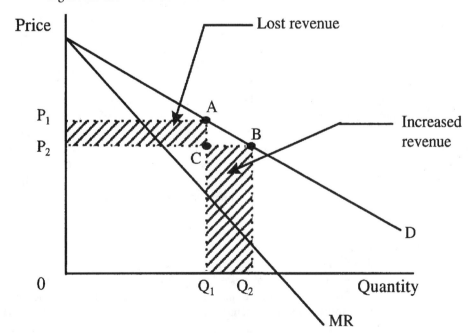

Figure IX-16. Changes in Elasticity of Demand and Total Revenue as Price Changes

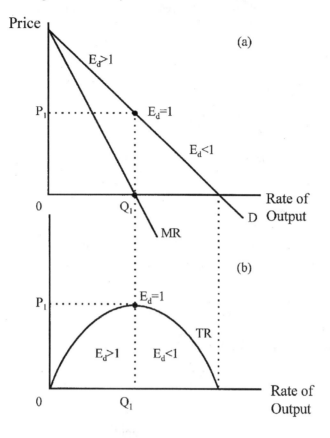

demand, and elasticity. Recall from Chapter II that when price reductions cause total revenue to rise, demand is elastic. If MR > 0, then TR increases with increases in output. The only way to sell the increased output is to lower the price. If the lower price is more than offset by increased output, then TR increases and demand is elastic. Thus, if MR > 0, then demand is elastic. In Figure IX-16, $E_d > 1$ to the left of Q_1 and $E_d < 1$ to the right of Q_1. A minute change in price around P_1 will not change total revenue, so $E_d = 1$ at output Q_1.

The relationship between total revenue, marginal revenue, and demand elasticity is the starting point for analyzing the profit maximizing output and pricing decisions of a monopolist. Common sense tells us that no rational profit maximizer will produce output in the range where marginal revenue is negative. Thus, the profit maximizing monopolist will always operate along the elastic or unit elastic portion of the demand curve—at a quantity below Q_1 in Figure IX-16. If a firm were to find itself at an output level in the inelastic range, it could increase profits by simply reducing output (and costs) while increasing revenue.

Of course, in determining the profit maximizing level of output for the monopolist, the costs of production must be considered. Generally speaking, the monopolist has no special power in the resource or input market. In other words, when it comes to buying factors of production, the monopolist is just like any perfectly competitive firm. Thus, the cost curves for the monopolist have the same characteristics as those of the perfectly competitive firm. Moreover, profit maximizing monopolists follow the same general rule as firms in a perfectly competitive industry—expand production until marginal revenue (MR) equals marginal cost (MC). The monopolist follows this rule for exactly the same reasons as the perfect competitor—it will only produce the next unit of production if it earns more money selling the unit than it costs to produce that unit. This is the only way to grow profits.

The profit maximizing decision of the monopolist is demonstrated in Figure IX-17. The profit maximizing output is Q*, where MR = MC. To the left of Q*, MR > MC and the firm can increase profits by expanding production. To the right of Q*, MC > MR and the firm can increase profits by reducing production. At Q*, the firm cannot increase profits by changing the level of production—profits are maximized at Q*. The demand curve shows that Q* units can be sold at P*. In Figure IX-17, this corresponds with point A on the demand curve. Thus, P* is the profit maximizing price.

The level of monopoly profits is calculated in the same manner as profits for the perfectly competitive firm. Specifically, profit is equal to Q*(P* − ATC), for ATC at the output level where MR = MC. In Figure IX-17, monopoly profits are equal to the area P*ABC.

When the monopolist earns a profit, it means that the firm has earned a return in excess of the opportunity cost of the resources used to produce its output. In a perfectly competitive industry, above normal profits attract the entry of new firms. However, entry is not possible for a pure monopoly industry because, by definition, new entry is precluded. Thus, unlike the competitive industry, which is restored to a normal return in the long-run, economic profits can continue to exist in the long-run for the monopolist.

An important note of caution is in order here. Not all monopolies are profitable. Consider the cost and revenue information for the monopolist graphed in Figure IX-18.

Figure IX-17. Monopoly Profits

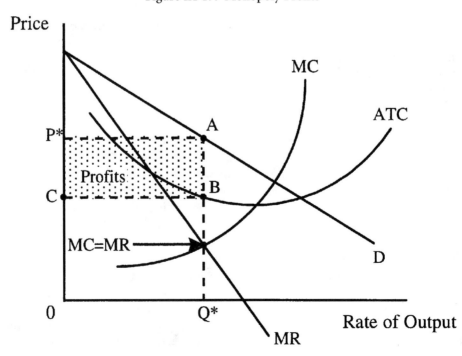

Figure IX-18. An Unprofitable Monopoly

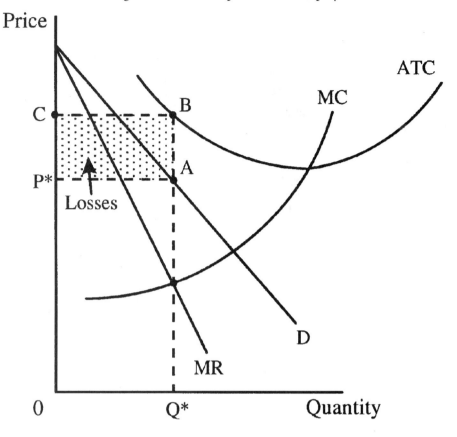

MR = MC at Q* which yields a profit maximizing price of P*. Q* corresponds to point A on the demand curve and point B on the ATC curve. Thus, at Q*, ATC > P*, and losses equal to Q*(P* − ATC) are shown by the rectangle ABCP*. When a monopolist suffers a loss, the firm is earning a return on the resources it uses that is less than their opportunity cost. As under perfect competition, in the face of a short-run economic loss, the monopolist has a choice between continuing production or shutting down. The same shutdown rule applies here as well. That is, as long as revenue exceeds variable cost, the monopolist firm will continue to produce in the short-run. If these loss conditions persist in the long-run, however, the firm will exit the industry and transfer its resources to an industry in which it can earn a normal return.

One final point must be made regarding the profit maximizing price and quantity decision of a monopolist. A supply curve is evidence of a unique relationship between market price and the quantity that the firm is willing and able to supply. In a perfectly competitive market, the price taking firm's marginal cost curve is the same as its supply curve. The monopolist, however, does not set price equal to marginal cost. In order to determine the profit maximizing output, the monopolist needs to know the marginal revenue and marginal cost curves. After determining the profit maximizing quantity, the monopolist finds the corresponding price on the demand curve. Thus, for the monopolist, there is no unique relationship between quantity supplied and price. In other words, because the monopolist is the only seller in the market, it does not have a supply curve.

b. Barriers to Entry

But for barriers to entry, long-run profits would not exist in a pure monopoly. Monopoly profits would dissipate as a result of competition from new entrants. Thus, the fundamental source of monopoly power is the fact that barriers to entry persist even in the long-run.

Economic barriers to entry can result from very large economies of scale or the total control of an essential resource. Previously, we introduced the notion of a long-run average cost curve that decreases continually as output expands. This suggests that one firm could supply the entire industry output at the lowest possible cost. When such conditions arise, the process of competition guarantees that only one firm will survive. Again, firms that gain monopoly power because of these pronounced economies of scale are called **natural monopolies**. The early development of railroads is a good example of a natural monopoly because building a railroad requires huge fixed costs and massive construction capabilities. These costs represent a substantial barrier to entry to competitors, and railroad companies benefit from economies of scale in production.

Another economic barrier to entry is the control of the entire supply of an essential resource. In this case, entry by new firms is blocked because they cannot gain access to the particular resource. A common example is De Beers Diamond Jewellers, which controls a large portion of the world's diamond mines. You might be surprised to discover that diamonds are not a particularly rare gem but that this company's control has artificially created scarcity and raised prices. Absolute control over a resource will be reflected in the value of the firm. Thus, individuals who purchase a firm that controls an essential resource will not earn a monopoly profit.

Legal barriers to entry are restrictions placed upon the entry of new firms into an industry by the government. A familiar example of a government granted monopoly is the right to be the sole provider of basic public utilities. Other examples include patents and licenses. **Patents** give the inventor of a product or process a monopoly over the use of that invention for 20 years from the filing date. **Licenses** are required to participate in many professions—e.g., medical and legal—and to operate many types of businesses— e.g., radio stations, cable, and airlines. The rent-seeking costs of monopoly discussed below (and more generally in Chapter III) often result from attempts by businesses to obtain legal barriers to entry. Firms sometimes attempt to erect entry barriers through the use of private contracts or even technological hurdles. Consider the case below.

United States v. Microsoft Corp.

United States Court of Appeals for the District of Columbia Circuit
253 F.3d 34 (2001)

Microsoft Corporation appeals from judgments of the District Court finding the company in violation of §§1 and 2 of the Sherman Act and ordering various remedies.

The action against Microsoft arose pursuant to a complaint filed by the United States and separate complaints filed by individual States. The District Court determined that Microsoft had maintained a monopoly in the market for Intel-compatible PC operating systems in violation of §2; attempted to gain a monopoly in the market for internet browsers in violation of §2; and illegally tied two purportedly separate products, Windows and Internet Explorer ("IE"), in violation of §1. *United States v. Microsoft Corp.*, 87 F. Supp. 2d 30 (D.D.C. 2000).

* * *

II. MONOPOLIZATION

Section 2 of the Sherman Act makes it unlawful for a firm to "monopolize." The offense of monopolization has two elements: "(1) the possession of monopoly power in the relevant market and (2) the willful acquisition or maintenance of that power as distinguished from growth or development as a consequence of a superior product, business acumen, or historic accident." *United States v. Grinnell Corp.*, 384 U.S. 563, 570–71 (1966). The District Court applied this test and found that Microsoft possesses monopoly power in the market for Intel-compatible PC operating systems. Focusing primarily on Microsoft's efforts to suppress Netscape Navigator's threat to its operating system monopoly, the court also found that Microsoft maintained its power not through competition on the merits, but through unlawful means. Microsoft challenges both conclusions. We defer to the District Court's findings of fact, setting them aside only if clearly erroneous. We review legal questions *de novo*.

We begin by considering whether Microsoft possesses monopoly power ... and finding that it does, we turn to the question whether it maintained this power through anticompetitive means. Agreeing with the District Court that the company behaved anticompetitively, and that these actions contributed to the maintenance of its monopoly power, we affirm the court's finding of liability for monopolization.

A. *Monopoly Power*

While merely possessing monopoly power is not itself an antitrust violation, *see* Northeastern Tel. Co. v. AT & T, 651 F.2d 76, 84–85 (2d Cir.1981), it is a necessary element of a monopolization charge, The Supreme Court defines monopoly power as "the power to control prices or exclude competition." United States v. E.I. du Pont de Nemours & Co., 351 U.S. 377, 391 (1956). More precisely, a firm is a monopolist if it can profitably raise prices substantially above the competitive level. Where evidence indicates that a firm has in fact profitably done so, the existence of monopoly power is clear. FTC v. Indiana Fed'n of Dentists, 476 U.S. 447, 460–61 (1986) (using direct proof to show market power in Sherman Act § 1 unreasonable restraint of trade action). Because such direct proof is only rarely available, courts more typically examine market structure in search of circumstantial evidence of monopoly power. 2A Areeda et al., Antitrust Law ¶ 531a, at 156. Under this structural approach, monopoly power may be inferred from a firm's possession of a dominant share of a relevant market that is protected by entry barriers. "Entry barriers" are factors (such as certain regulatory requirements) that prevent new rivals from timely responding to an increase in price above the competitive level.

The District Court considered these structural factors and concluded that Microsoft possesses monopoly power in a relevant market. Defining the market as Intel-compatible PC operating systems, the District Court found that Microsoft has a greater than 95% share. It also found the company's market position protected by a substantial entry barrier.

Microsoft argues that the District Court incorrectly defined the relevant market. It also claims that there is no barrier to entry in that market. Alternatively, Microsoft argues that because the software industry is uniquely dynamic, direct proof, rather than circumstantial evidence, more appropriately indicates whether it possesses monopoly power. Rejecting each argument, we uphold the District Court's finding of monopoly power in its entirety.

1. Market Structure
a. Market definition

"Because the ability of consumers to turn to other suppliers restrains a firm from raising prices above the competitive level," Rothery Storage & Van Co. v. Atlas Van Lines,

Inc., 792 F.2d 210, 218 (D.C.Cir.1986), the relevant market must include all products "reasonably interchangeable by consumers for the same purposes." *du Pont*, 351 U.S. at 395. In this case, the District Court defined the market as "the licensing of all Intel-compatible PC operating systems worldwide," finding that there are "currently no products—and … there are not likely to be any in the near future—that a significant percentage of computer users worldwide could substitute for [these operating systems] without incurring substantial costs." Calling this market definition "far too narrow," Microsoft argues that the District Court improperly excluded three types of products: non-Intel compatible operating systems (primarily Apple's Macintosh operating system, Mac OS), operating systems for non-PC devices (such as handheld computers and portal websites), and "middleware" products, which are not operating systems at all.

* * *

b. Market power

Having thus properly defined the relevant market, the District Court found that Windows accounts for a greater than 95% share. The court also found that even if Mac OS were included, Microsoft's share would exceed 80%. Microsoft challenges neither finding, nor does it argue that such a market share is not predominant. [The court cited three Supreme Court decisions that found market shares of 87%, 80%, and 75% predominant.]

Instead, Microsoft claims that even a predominant market share does not by itself indicate monopoly power. Although the "existence of [monopoly] power ordinarily may be inferred from the predominant share of the market," *Grinnell*, 384 U.S. at 571, we agree with Microsoft that because of the possibility of competition from new entrants, looking to current market share alone can be "misleading." Hunt-Wesson Foods, Inc. v. Ragu Foods, Inc., 627 F.2d 919, 924 (9th Cir.1980). In this case, however, the District Court was not misled. Considering the possibility of new rivals, the court focused not only on Microsoft's present market share, but also on the structural barrier that protects the company's future position. That barrier—the "applications barrier to entry"—stems from two characteristics of the software market: (1) most consumers prefer operating systems for which a large number of applications have already been written; and (2) most developers prefer to write for operating systems that already have a substantial consumer base. This "chicken-and-egg" situation ensures that applications will continue to be written for the already dominant Windows, which in turn ensures that consumers will continue to prefer it over other operating systems.

Challenging the existence of the applications barrier to entry, Microsoft observes that software developers do write applications for other operating systems, pointing out that at its peak IBM's OS/2 supported approximately 2,500 applications. This misses the point. That some developers write applications for other operating systems is not at all inconsistent with the finding that the applications barrier to entry discourages many from writing for these less popular platforms. Indeed, the District Court found that IBM's difficulty in attracting a larger number of software developers to write for its platform seriously impeded OS/2's success.

Microsoft does not dispute that Windows supports many more applications than any other operating system. It argues instead that "[i]t defies common sense" to suggest that an operating system must support as many applications as Windows does (more than 70,000, according to the District Court) to be competitive. Consumers, Microsoft points out, can only use a very small percentage of these applications. As the District Court explained, however, the applications barrier to entry gives consumers reason to prefer the dominant operating system even if they have no need to use all applications written for it:

The consumer wants an operating system that runs not only types of applications that he knows he will want to use, but also those types in which he might develop an interest later. Also, the consumer knows that if he chooses an operating system with enough demand to support multiple applications in each product category, he will be less likely to find himself straitened later by having to use an application whose features disappoint him. Finally, the average user knows that, generally speaking, applications improve through successive versions. He thus wants an operating system for which successive generations of his favorite applications will be released — promptly at that. The fact that a vastly larger number of applications are written for Windows than for other PC operating systems attracts consumers to Windows, because it reassures them that their interests will be met as long as they use Microsoft's product.

Findings of Fact ¶ 37. Thus, despite the limited success of its rivals, Microsoft benefits from the applications barrier to entry.

Of course, were middleware to succeed, it would erode the applications barrier to entry. Because applications written for multiple operating systems could run on any operating system on which the middleware product was present with little, if any, porting, the operating system market would become competitive. But as the District Court found, middleware will not expose a sufficient number of APIs [Application Programming Interfaces] to erode the applications barrier to entry in the foreseeable future.

Microsoft next argues that the applications barrier to entry is not an entry barrier at all, but a reflection of Windows' popularity. It is certainly true that Windows may have gained its initial dominance in the operating system market competitively — through superior foresight or quality. But this case is not about Microsoft's initial acquisition of monopoly power. It is about Microsoft's efforts to maintain this position through means other than competition on the merits. Because the applications barrier to entry protects a dominant operating system irrespective of quality, it gives Microsoft power to stave off even superior new rivals. The barrier is thus a characteristic of the operating system market, not of Microsoft's popularity, or, as asserted by a Microsoft witness, the company's efficiency.

Finally, Microsoft argues that the District Court should not have considered the applications barrier to entry because it reflects not a cost borne disproportionately by new entrants, but one borne by all participants in the operating system market. According to Microsoft, it had to make major investments to convince software developers to write for its new operating system, and it continues to "evangelize" the Windows platform today. Whether costs borne by all market participants should be considered entry barriers is the subject of much debate. *Compare* 2A Areeda & Hovenkamp, Antitrust Law § 420c, at 61 (arguing that these costs are entry barriers), *and* Joe S. Bain, Barriers to New Competition: Their Character and Consequences in Manufacturing Industries 6–7 (1956) (considering these costs entry barriers). We need not resolve this issue, however, for even under the more narrow definition it is clear that there are barriers. When Microsoft entered the operating system market with MS-DOS and the first version of Windows, it did not confront a dominant rival operating system with as massive an installed base and as vast an existing array of applications as the Windows operating systems have since enjoyed. Moreover, when Microsoft introduced Windows 95 and 98, it was able to bypass the applications barrier to entry that protected the incumbent Windows by including APIs from the earlier version in the new operating systems. This made porting existing Windows applications to the new version of Windows much less costly than porting them to the operating systems of other entrants who could not freely include APIs from the incumbent Windows with their own.

* * *

Notes and Questions

1. Market Shares and Monopolies: The court finds that Microsoft's 95 percent market share is persuasive evidence of monopoly power. Are market shares always a good proxy for monopoly power? What is the difference between market power and monopoly power? Is there a clear cut-off between a firm with monopoly power and one without it, or is it more of a spectrum of influence and control? Although a rough rule, Judge Learned Hand in the case United States v. Aluminum Co. of Am., 148 F.2d 416, 424 (2d Cir. 1945), articulated a rule of thumb for market shares and monopolists whereby "it is doubtful whether sixty or sixty-four percent would be enough; and certainly thirty-three per cent is not." However, he concluded that the Aluminum Company of America was a monopolist with around ninety percent of the market. Think about some of the biggest and most dominant brand names in today's American economy. Can you think of any monopolies?

2. Market Power and Emerging Technologies: The government's case for Microsoft's market power was much more complex than just market shares. The government pointed to and relied on multiple kinds of proof, including market shares, barriers to entry, network effects, pricing data, profit margins, and more. Considering the rise of competing technology giants such as Apple, Google, and Facebook, does the court's opinion seem wrong or overly cautious by today's standards? Doesn't the subsequent existence of competing technology giants disprove the anticompetitive nature of emerging technology markets? This was a concern that the D.C. Circuit certainly wrestled with in its opinion but ultimately rejected. The court considered that:

> Rapid technological change leads to markets in which "firms compete through innovation for temporary market dominance, from which they may be displaced by the next wave of product advancements." [A. Shelanski & J. Gregory Sidak, Antitrust Divestiture in Network Industries, 68 U. Chi. L. Rev. 1, 11–12 (2001)] (discussing Schumpeterian competition, which proceeds "sequentially over time rather than simultaneously across a market"). Microsoft argues that the operating system market is just such a market.

> Whether or not Microsoft's characterization of the operating system market is correct does not appreciably alter our mission in assessing the alleged antitrust violations in the present case.

United States v. Microsoft Corp., 253 F.3d 34, 49–50 (D.C. Cir. 2001).

3. How Can Monopolies Compete?: The allegation in the Microsoft case was that Microsoft had impeded the growth and entry of potential rivals Java and Netscape into competing markets. How much of a threat do those rivals have to be to raise antitrust claims? If Microsoft could prove that these companies were going to fail anyway, would it change the analysis? Is Microsoft unable to compete vigorously with potential competitors solely because it is a monopolist? If so, what limitations are there to Microsoft's ability to compete?

4. Drastic Measures: The district court sought a remedy to break up Microsoft into two smaller companies to prevent it from causing anticompetitive harm to the market. The decision sought to separate the hardware and operating system of Microsoft from its related products and software. This drastic remedy was related to a claim in the case that Microsoft was unlawfully using its monopoly in the operating system market to gain market share in the web browser market—a cause of action referred to as tying in antitrust law. This severe remedy was never realized because it was vacated and remanded by the D.C. Circuit, and the case settled before that remand was issued. The D.C. Circuit explained that:

> [J]ust over six years have passed since Microsoft engaged in the first conduct plaintiffs allege to be anticompetitive. As the record in this case indicates, six years seems like an eternity in the computer industry. By the time a court can assess liability, firms, products, and the marketplace are likely to have changed dramatically. This, in turn, threatens enormous practical difficulties for courts considering the appropriate measure of relief in equitable enforcement actions, both in crafting injunctive remedies in the first instance and reviewing those remedies in the second. Conduct remedies may be unavailing in such cases, because innovation to a large degree has already rendered the anticompetitive conduct obsolete (although by no means harmless). And broader structural remedies present their own set of problems, including how a court goes about restoring competition to a dramatically changed, and constantly changing, marketplace. That is just one reason why we find the District Court's refusal in the present case to hold an evidentiary hearing on remedies—to update and flesh out the available information before seriously entertaining the possibility of dramatic structural relief—so problematic.

United States v. Microsoft Corp., 253 F.3d 34, 49 (D.C. Cir. 2001). This remedy, however, was used against AT&T in the government's earlier case in the 1980s. AT&T was segmented into a number of smaller "Baby Bells" that have subsequently re-merged into a similarly powerful telecommunications conglomerate. Is this remedy a feasible means of deterring anticompetitive conduct or preventing future harmful conduct? Should courts have this power to forcibly divide and split up companies? Can you think of an alternative, less strict remedy that would accomplish the same goal?

c. Price Discrimination

The practice of selling the same product to different customers at different prices is known as **price discrimination**. If three conditions are met, firms can increase their economic profits by engaging in price discrimination. First, the firm must face a downward sloping demand curve—the firm must be a price searcher. Recall that perfectly competitive firms are price takers. These firms have no control over price and therefore, cannot charge different customers different prices. On the other hand, a pure monopolist has a great deal of control over market price. Second, the firm must have some way of identifying separate groups of customers with differing demands for its product. In general, the price discriminating seller will charge a higher price to those customers with a relatively inelastic demand. Third, the firm must be able to prevent **arbitrage**—resale by low-price purchasers to the higher price purchasers.

Commonly observed forms of price discrimination satisfy these criteria. Take the example of "senior citizen discounts" at restaurants. Senior citizens typically have more elastic demand curves, they are easily identified, and the goods and services (like meals) sold to them at a discount are difficult to resell. Judge Frank Easterbrook recently described an innovative manner by which software developers can price discriminate between consumer and commercial users of software:

> ProCD, the plaintiff, has compiled information from more than 3,000 telephone directories into a computer database.... ProCD sells a version of the database, called SelectPhone (trademark), on CD-ROM discs.... The database in

SelectPhone (trademark) cost more than $10 million to compile and is expensive to keep current. It is much more valuable to some users than to others. The combination of names, addresses, and SIC codes enables manufacturers to compile lists of potential customers. Manufacturers and retailers pay high prices to specialized information intermediaries for such mailing lists; ProCD offers a potentially cheaper alternative. People with nothing to sell could use the database as a substitute for calling long distance information, or as a way to look up old friends who have moved to unknown towns, or just as an electronic substitute for the local phone book. ProCD decided to engage in price discrimination, selling its database to the general public for personal use at a low price (approximately $150 for the set of five discs) while selling information to the trade for a higher price....

If ProCD had to recover all of its costs and make a profit by charging a single price—that is, if it could not charge more to commercial users than to the general public—it would have to raise the price substantially over $150. The ensuing reduction in sales would harm consumers who value the information at, say, $200. They get consumer surplus of $50 under the current arrangement but would cease to buy if the price rose substantially. If because of high elasticity of demand in the consumer segment of the market the only way to make a profit turned out to be a price attractive to commercial users alone, then all consumers would lose out—and so would the commercial clients, who would have to pay more for the listings because ProCD could not obtain any contribution toward costs from the consumer market.

To make price discrimination work, however, the seller must be able to control arbitrage. An air carrier sells tickets for less to vacationers than to business travelers, using advance purchase and Saturday-night-stay requirements to distinguish the categories. A producer of movies segments the market by time, releasing first to theaters, then to pay-per-view services, next to the videotape and laserdisc market, and finally to cable and commercial TV. Vendors of computer software have a harder task. Anyone can walk into a retail store and buy a box. Customers do not wear tags saying "commercial user" or "consumer user." Anyway, even a commercial-user-detector at the door would not work, because a consumer could buy the software and resell to a commercial user. That arbitrage would break down the price discrimination and drive up the minimum price at which ProCD would sell to anyone.

Instead of tinkering with the product and letting users sort themselves—for example, furnishing current data at a high price that would be attractive only to commercial customers, and two-year-old data at a low price—ProCD turned to the institution of contract. Every box containing its consumer product declares that the software comes with restrictions stated in an enclosed license. This license, which is encoded on the CD-ROM disks as well as printed in the manual, and which appears on a user's screen every time the software runs, limits use of the application program and listings to non-commercial purposes.

ProCD, Inc. v. Zeidenberg, 86 F.3d 1447, 1449–1450 (7th Cir. 1996).

Figure IX-19 illustrates the advantages of price discrimination to a monopolist. The monopolist is able to divide the market into two segments of buyers. The demand for each of these segments is depicted in the two panels of Figure IX-19. The demand for the monopolist's product is relatively more elastic in panel (a) than in panel (b). Because one

Figure IX-19. Price Discrimination

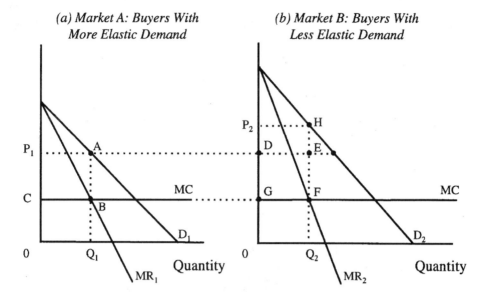

(a) Market A: Buyers With More Elastic Demand

(b) Market B: Buyers With Less Elastic Demand

firm supplies both of these "markets," the marginal cost of supplying the product is the same in both markets.

The monopolist desires to maximize profit in each of these "markets." To maximize profits, the monopolist will set $MR_1 = MC$ in panel (a) and $MR_2 = MC$ in panel (b). In panel (a), the market with the more elastic demand, the monopolist charges P_1. However, in panel (b), the market with the relatively inelastic demand, the monopolist charges a higher price of P_2. In this case, individuals with relatively inelastic demand are charged a high price and those with a relative elastic demand are charged a low price.

Price discrimination can increase total welfare by expanding sales to consumers who would not purchase at the single profit-maximizing price. Further price discrimination can lead to more intense competition if firms lure consumers, who prefer rival brands, with special offers as compensation for purchasing a less-preferred brand. See James C. Cooper et al, *Does Price Discrimination Intensify Competition? Implications for Antitrust*, 72 Antitrust Law Journal 327 (2005).

d. Predatory Pricing

Predatory Pricing is a strategy by which a firm reduces its price below its costs of production in order to drive its rivals out of the market in and then to raise prices to capture monopoly profits once it has the market to itself. In practice it is difficult to distinguish predatory behavior from normal rivalrous competition. Because it is rational for a profit maximizing firm to continue to operate in the short-run even if P < ATC, as long as P > AVC, setting price below ATC is not considered evidence of predatory pricing—price must be less than AVC in order to establish something other than normal competitive behavior. By setting price below its average variable cost, the predator firm operates in a range where most firms shut down in the short-run. Thus, the theory of predatory pricing states that the predator attempts to earn monopoly profits in the long run by incurring economic losses in the short-run. It is alleged that such behavior can increase the value of the firm. For this to occur, the present value of the long-run monopoly profits must be greater than the short-run losses.

A major difficulty for predatory pricing theory is explaining why new firms do not attempt to enter the market once the successful predator begins charging monopoly prices. Remember that the key to reaping monopoly profits in the long-run is barriers to entry. It is not at all clear where the predator gains such a barrier. A common response to this criticism is to trust that the predator's past price reductions discourage potential entrants from entering the market.

Predatory pricing may be attacked under Section 2 of the Sherman Act as an attempt to monopolize. However, the following case raises doubts about the future of predatory pricing as an antitrust violation.

Matsushita Elec. Indus. Co. v. Zenith Radio Corp.

Supreme Court of the United States
475 U.S. 574 (1986)
and accompanying Notes and Questions
Read *supra,* Chapter I

1. Predatory Pricing: The Probability of Success: The Court observes that the success of any predatory pricing scheme depends on the ability of the predator to charge monopoly profits after its rivals have exited the market. Moreover, to be economically rational, the present value of the monopoly profits must exceed the losses incurred in driving rivals out of the market. Zenith and NUE allege that the Japanese firms have been pricing below cost for over twenty years—thereby incurring substantial losses in a not yet successful effort to drive the American firms out of the CEP industry. How long will it take to recoup these losses? Does it seem likely that Japanese firms will be able to charge monopoly prices for a period long enough to break even? How about making an economic profit?

2. Predatory Pricing by a Cartel: The Probability of Success?: For any single firm, predatory pricing is a risky strategy. The risk arises because of the need to maintain barriers to entry after the extinction of rivals for a period long enough to recapture losses and make an economic profit. Zenith and NUE do not accuse a single firm of predatory pricing. Rather, they claim that over twenty-one Japanese firms engaged in this predatory pricing scheme. In other words, Zenith and NUE have accused a cartel of predatory pricing. What about the inherent difficulties of organizing and maintaining a cartel? If the probability of a single firm engaging in predatory pricing is remote, what would happen to that probability if the accusation were against a cartel? The payoff for a successful predatory pricing scheme is the monopoly profits earned after all rivals have been eliminated. Thus, post elimination, a monopoly price and output must be set. For a cartel to engage in predatory pricing, all firms in the cartel must agree on price and output. Not only would coming to such an agreement be difficult, but there is a huge incentive to cheat. After sustaining losses in order to drive rivals out of the market, each individual firm in the cartel will be eager to earn monopoly profits. Each individual firm will believe that by increasing its output by only a small amount over the agreed upon level, no other firm in the cartel will notice and the cheating firm will be able to earn even greater monopoly profits. The greater the number of firms in the cartel, the greater the incentive to cheat. Moreover, the longer the time period involved, the less likely the cartel will succeed. What do these facts say about the alleged Japanese cartel's chance for success? If all of these factors are combined, what can be said about the probability that a predatory pricing scheme was in fact under way in the CEP market?

3. An Alternative Story: Price Discrimination: Recall the prerequisites for a firm to engage in price discrimination. First, the seller must have some way of identifying separate groups of customers with differing demands for the seller's product. Second, the seller must be able to prevent the resale of its good or service from the low-price purchasers to the high-price purchasers. For the Japanese firms, there are clearly two markets for CEPs — one in the United States and one in Japan. Japanese consumers are faced with a well-organized cartel that is protected by government restrictions on foreign competition. Therefore, Japanese consumers face monopoly prices and output. On the other hand, the American CEP market is much more competitive and prices are lower. Thus, Japanese firms face two markets with differing elasticities of demand for the seller's product, and resale between these two markets is prohibited by the Japanese government. What is the effect on American consumers of Japanese price discrimination?

e. The Social Costs of Monopoly

Recall that perfect competition provides a benchmark, P = MC, for evaluating the allocative efficiency of a market. A monopolist operates at a quantity where P > MC and, thus, the monopolist falls short of the competitive benchmark for allocative efficiency. Monopoly is a form of market failure. This section explores the social costs of this market failure.

i. Deadweight Costs

The most widely accepted criticism of monopolies is that monopolists distort the allocation of resources by restricting output when buyers are willing to pay a price greater than the marginal costs of producing additional output. Consider the cost and demand curves for a hypothetical industry presented in Figure IX-20. For simplicity, assume that the average total cost of production is the same at all levels of production — that is, this is a constant cost industry and MC = ATC at all levels of output.

If this were a perfectly competitive industry, the firms would produce Q_C where PC = MC. At Q_C, the sum of producer and consumer surplus (ABP_C) is maximized. All potential gains from trade are realized, and the last unit produced is valued by customers at an amount equal to the opportunity cost of the resources used in its production.

The monopolist's profit maximizing quantity occurs at Q_M where MR = MC. Q_M is less than the competitive level, Q_C. As a consequence of the restriction of output, consumer surplus is reduced to the area ADP_M, which is considerably less than the consumer surplus (ABP_C) in the competitive industry. Some of the lost consumer surplus goes to the monopolist in the form of profits, $P_M DEP_C$. By reducing output and increasing price above a competitive level, monopolists are able to capture a portion of the consumer surplus that would exist in a competitive market. There can be a reasonable debate about whether society benefits more from those profits going to consumers or monopolists. Such distributional issues (i.e., how the economic pie is divided) are usually not addressed by economists because it is difficult to develop and test hypotheses that deal with interpersonal comparisons of utility from wealth.

Economists are concerned, however, with another portion of consumer surplus that disappears when monopolists restrict output — the triangle DBE in Figure IX-20. The monopolist's decision to not produce beyond QM means that buyers located between points D and B on the demand curve are unable to purchase the product even though they are willing to pay a price greater than the marginal costs of producing those additional units. The triangle DBE represents unrealized potential gains from trade. Those

Figure IX-20. Social Costs of Monopoly

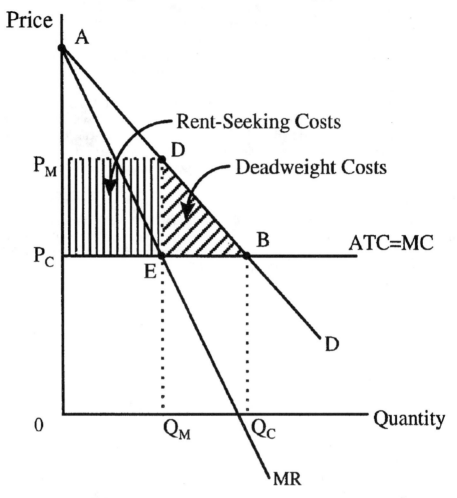

opportunities are lost. The triangle DBE represents a reduction in social welfare, which is referred to as the **deadweight costs of monopoly.**

The impact of this deadweight cost on society can be illustrated by the example of a baker. Suppose that the total cost of making a loaf of bread (assuming constant marginal cost) is $1.00, including a normal return to the baker for labor time and entrepreneurship. Suppose, further, that it takes a particular individual, who paints houses competitively for $1.50 an hour, a total of one hour to bake a loaf of bread. When the baker opens the bakery selling bread for $1.00, the painter can buy his bread instead of baking it himself because the value of his time is better spent painting a house for $1.50 than baking bread. Instead of using an hour to bake bread, the painter spends the time painting houses. Not only is the painter better off by $0.50, but society is also better off because it has gained $1.50 of painted houses at a cost of only $1.00. Now imagine that the baker has no competition (that is, she is a monopolist), and she discovers that she can increase profits by increasing the price of her bread to $2.00. As a result, the painter would return to baking his own bread. Society loses $1.50 of output and gains only $1.00 (not $2.00) because the true value of baking bread is only $1.00 — this is the point where P > MC. The deadweight cost equals $0.50. This lost production can never be regained — bygones are bygones.

The size of the deadweight costs has been estimated in several empirical studies by economists.[2] Although the results of the studies are controversial because of their methodology and assumptions, it is worth noting that the studies indicate that the deadweight costs of monopoly are less than one percent of gross national product (GNP). These results sent industrial organization economists scurrying to come up with explanations for why the estimates were so low. After all, it is difficult to justify any government antitrust policy if the potential gains from an effective policy are less than one percent of GNP—and the repeal of the antitrust laws would eliminate a major source of consulting income for economists. Of course, one explanation for the low estimates of deadweight costs is that they prove that antitrust policy was effectively preventing monopolistic practices.

One general criticism of the deadweight cost estimates is that they use above-normal profits as one of the proxies for the presence of monopoly power. Thus, the explanations for the relatively low estimates are, at least in part, really concerned with explaining why monopoly profits are not very high. In that regard, one of the most persuasive explanations for the low deadweight cost estimates is that political competition for the right to earn monopoly profits (economists refer to monopoly profits as **rents**) may have increased the monopolist's costs to the point that the monopoly return was simply a normal profit. This explanation is investigated in the following subsection.

ii. Rent-Seeking Costs

The potential of earning monopoly profits (rents) leads firms to use resources to capture those rents. Such **rent-seeking** expenditures represent an additional social cost of monopoly. Rent-seeking expenditures attempt to use the power of the state to transfer wealth from one group to another. See Chapter III. This use of scarce resources represents a social loss, because those resources could have been used for more productive purposes. That is, rent-seeking expenditures are concerned with merely dividing up the economic pie, rather than increasing the size of the pie.

Firms invest resources in the pursuit of monopoly profits up to the point where the marginal opportunity cost of the last dollar invested is equal to its expected return in increased profits. For example, if the sole domestic producer of a certain product expects a proposed import restriction or tariff (designed to solidify its monopoly) to increase the value of the firm by $1 million (the present value of future monopoly profits), then the domestic producer would be willing to spend up to $1 million on lobbying and campaign contributions in order to secure the favorable regulation. Moreover, those who expect to be injured by the change in the law would be willing to make similar investments to prevent the adoption of the import restriction or tariff. Consequently, rent-seeking expenditures can equal, or even exceed, the total amount of potential monopoly profits.[3] That is, the rectangle representing monopoly profits, $P_M DEP_C$, will be consumed by rent-seeking expenditures. Thus, in Figure IX-19, the social costs of monopoly include the deadweight costs, DBE, plus the rent-seeking costs, $P_M DEP_C$. In an ironic twist of fate,

---

2. The most famous of these studies is Arnold C. Harberger, *Monopoly and Resource Allocation*, 54 American Economic Review 77 (1954).

3. It also can be the case that those who expect to be injured might not have the resources to fight the rent-seeking, they may not even be aware that the rent-seeking is occurring, or there can be a collective action problem—that is, the cumulative injury is spread among many individuals and the transaction costs of cooperating are higher than the resulting benefit of fighting the regulation. In these cases, the monopolist may not need to expend substantial resources on rent-seeking.

American antitrust laws have an exception for private firms that seek to influence the political process and pass laws that might have anticompetitive effects.[4]

iii. Other Criticisms of Monopoly

Some economists have argued that monopolies should be attacked because the lack of product market competition makes the managers lazy and allows them to deviate from technically efficient decisions concerning cost minimization and innovation. As Sir John Hicks, a famous English economist, once put it: "The best of all monopoly profits is a quiet life."[5] There are, however, theoretical reasons for doubting the validity of this hypothesis.

Competition in the product market is not the only constraint on managerial behavior. Managers are forced to attempt to maximize profits by a number of competitive mechanisms other than product market competition. For example, from the typical shareholder's perspective, profits that are sacrificed due to managerial laziness are an opportunity cost that is reflected in a lower stock price. Competition in the stock market will lead to the identification of the poorly performing firm as an attractive takeover target, and managers may lose their jobs in the event of a takeover. Thus, even in monopoly firms, managers have the incentive to maximize profits through cost minimization. Further, the quest to become a monopolist can drive innovation through dynamic competition. This type of competition is present in high-tech markets where disruptive technologies can take over the field only to be replaced by the next big thing. Such jockeying for market dominance is the force behind much of innovation.

Verizon Communications Inc. v. Law Offices of Curtis V. Trinko, LLP

Supreme Court of the United States
540 U.S. 398 (2004)

* * *

III

The complaint alleges that Verizon denied interconnection services to rivals in order to limit entry. If that allegation states an antitrust claim at all, it does so under §2 of the Sherman Act, which declares that a firm shall not "monopolize" or "attempt to monopolize." It is settled law that this offense requires, in addition to the possession of monopoly power in the relevant market, "the willful acquisition or maintenance of that power as distinguished from growth or development as a consequence of a superior product, business acumen, or historic accident." *United States v. Grinnell Corp.*, 384 U.S. 563 (1966). The mere possession of monopoly power, and the concomitant charging of monopoly prices, is not only not unlawful; it is an important element of the free-market system. The opportunity to charge monopoly prices — at least for a short period — is what attracts "business acumen" in the first place; it induces risk taking that produces innovation and economic growth. To safeguard the incentive to innovate, the possession of monopoly power will not be found unlawful unless it is accompanied by an element of anticompetitive *conduct*.

---

4. If you are interested in learning how this doctrine works in practice, take a look at *Enforcement Perspectives on the* Noerr-Pennington *Doctrine,* Fed. Trade Comm'n (2006), *available at* http://www.ftc.gov/reports/P013518enfperspectNoerr-Penningtondoctrine.pdf.

5. *See* J.R. Hicks, *Annual Survey of Economic Theory: The Theory of Monopoly*, 3 Econometrica 1, 8 (1935).

Firms may acquire monopoly power by establishing an infrastructure that renders them uniquely suited to serve their customers. Compelling such firms to share the source of their advantage is in some tension with the underlying purpose of antitrust law, since it may lessen the incentive for the monopolist, the rival, or both to invest in those economically beneficial facilities. Enforced sharing also requires antitrust courts to act as central planners, identifying the proper price, quantity, and other terms of dealing—a role for which they are ill suited. Moreover, compelling negotiation between competitors may facilitate the supreme evil of antitrust: collusion. Thus, as a general matter, the Sherman Act "does not restrict the long recognized right of [a] trader or manufacturer engaged in an entirely private business, freely to exercise his own independent discretion as to parties with whom he will deal." *United States v. Colgate & Co.*, 250 U.S. 300, 307 (1919).

* * *

Against the slight benefits of antitrust intervention here, we must weigh a realistic assessment of its costs. Under the best of circumstances, applying the requirements of § 2 "can be difficult" because "the means of illicit exclusion, like the means of legitimate competition, are myriad." United States v. Microsoft Corp., 253 F.3d 34, 58 (C.A.D.C.2001) (en banc) *(per curiam)*. Mistaken inferences and the resulting false condemnations "are especially costly, because they chill the very conduct the antitrust laws are designed to protect." Matsushita Elec. Industrial Co. v. Zenith Radio Corp., 475 U.S. 574, 594 (1986). The cost of false positives counsels against an undue expansion of § 2 liability.

* * *

The 1996 Act is, in an important respect, much more ambitious than the antitrust laws. It attempts "*to eliminate the monopolies* enjoyed by the inheritors of AT&T's local franchises." *Verizon Communications Inc. v. FCC*, 535 U.S. [467,] 476 (2002) (emphasis added). Section 2 of the Sherman Act, by contrast, seeks merely to prevent *unlawful monopolization*. It would be a serious mistake to conflate the two goals. The Sherman Act is indeed the "Magna Carta of free enterprise," *United States v. Topco Associates, Inc.*, 405 U.S. 596, 610 (1972), but it does not give judges *carte blanche* to insist that a monopolist alter its way of doing business whenever some other approach might yield greater competition. We conclude that respondent's complaint fails to state a claim under the Sherman Act.

Notes and Questions

1. The Benefits of Monopolies: As noted in the case, monopolies are not illegal in the United States. Section 2 of the Sherman Antitrust Act makes illegal the acquisition or maintenance of monopoly power through anticompetitive means. Often it is difficult to distinguish between aggressive market competition and anticompetitive behavior. Monopolies are allowed in the United States because it is important to provide a carrot to encourage businesses to innovate by finding more efficient ways of operating and developing better products. When these better methods or processes are developed, companies should benefit from the ability to charge monopoly prices and earn higher profits. Accordingly, the quest for monopoly profits drives innovation and technological development.

2. Error Costs from Aggressive Antitrust Enforcement: One major concern noted by the court in *Trinko* is that in heavily regulated industries, the goals of Congressional statutory schemes may diverge from the antitrust laws. The Telecommunications Act, in that case, sought to end an artificially created government monopoly in favor of more robust competition. The Act forced Verizon to allow its competitors to use its infrastructure in order to facilitate new competitors. The court concluded that although Congress imposed this burden on Verizon, the antitrust laws do not impose such an obligation to deal with rivals. The court was concerned that the costs of imposing a bad antitrust rule would outweigh the benefits. This approach has been summarized by Judge Frank Easterbrook in his seminal article on error costs. He writes that:

> A fundamental difficulty facing the court is the incommensurability of the stakes. If the court errs by condemning a beneficial practice, the benefits may be lost for good. Any other firm that uses the condemned practice faces sanctions in the name of stare decisis, no matter the benefits. If the court errs by permitting a deleterious practice, though, the welfare loss decreases over time. Monopoly is self-destructive. Monopoly prices eventually attract entry. True, this long run may be a long time coming, with loss to society in the interim. The central purpose of antitrust is to speed up the arrival of the long run. But this should not obscure the point: judicial errors that tolerate baleful practices are self-correcting while erroneous condemnations are not.

Frank H. Easterbrook, *The Limits of Antitrust*, 63 Tex. L. Rev. 1, 2–3 (1984)

3. *Sociopolitical Arguments Against Monopoly:* In addition to the economic criticisms of monopoly, there are several sociopolitical arguments against monopoly. The following excerpt from Professor (now Judge) Richard Posner's *Antitrust Law: An Economic Perspective* summarizes many of these criticisms and their validity.

> Having considered the economic objections to monopoly, I want to discuss now three broadly political arguments against it. The first is that monopoly transfers wealth from consumers to the stockholders of monopolistic firms, a redistribution that goes from the less to the more wealthy. This appealing argument is undermined by the point made earlier that competition to become a monopolist will tend to transform the expected gains from monopoly into social costs. To the extent that this occurs, consumers' wealth will not be transferred to the shareholders of monopoly firms but will instead be dissipated in the purchase of inputs into the activity of becoming a monopolist.
>
> A second argument is that monopoly, or more broadly any condition (such as concentration) that fosters cooperation among competing firms, will facilitate an industry's manipulation of the political process to obtain protective legislation aimed at increasing the industry's profits. Often such protection takes the form of controls over entry and price competition, coupled with exemption from the antitrust laws, that result in cartelizing the industry much more effectively than could be done by private agreement. This is not the place to pursue the intricacies of the nascent economic analysis of the determinants of political power. It is enough to note that, while concentration may reduce the costs of organizing effectively to manipulate the political process, it may also reduce the demand for public assistance in suppressing competition, since ... a concentrated industry, other things being equal, is in a better position to suppress competition through private agreement, express or tacit, than an unconcentrated industry. It is therefore unclear whether on balance concentrated, or monopolistic, industries will obtain greater help from the political process than unconcentrated, or competitive, industries. This theoretical indeterminacy is mirrored in the empirical world, where we observe many unconcentrated industries—agriculture, trucking, local broadcasting, banking, medicine, to name a few—enjoying governmental protection against competition.

In any event, however, this political objection to monopoly and concentration is not sharply different from the economic objection. The legislation sought by an industry—a tariff, a tax on substitute products, control of entry—will usually have economic effects similar or even identical to those of a private cartel agreement. The political argument—which is simply that concentration facilitates monopoly pricing indirectly through the legislative process, as well as directly through cartelization—thus implies no change in the character of an antitrust policy deduced from economic considerations. (This is also true, incidentally, of the wealth-redistribution argument: the implications for public policy are not sharply different whether one objects to monopoly pricing because it wastes resources or because it brings about undesirable changes in the redistribution of wealth.)

The last political argument that I shall discuss has, in contrast, implications for antitrust policy that diverge sharply from those of economic analysis. The popular (or Populist) alternative to an antitrust policy designed to promote economic efficiency by limiting monopoly is a policy of restricting the freedom of action of large business firms in order to promote small business. (It may be possible to conceive of a different alternative to an efficiency-based antitrust policy, but this is the only one suggested with any frequency.) The idea that there is some special virtue in small business compared to large is a persistent one. I am not prepared to argue that it has no merit whatever. I am, however, confident that antitrust enforcement is an inappropriate method of trying to promote the interests of small business as a whole. The best overall antitrust policy from the standpoint of small business is *no* antitrust policy, since monopoly, by driving a wedge between the prices and the costs of the larger firms in the market (it is presumably they who take the lead in forming cartels), enable the smaller firms in the market to survive even if their costs are higher than those of the large firms. The only kind of antitrust policy that would benefit small business would be one whose principal objective was to limit the attempts of large firms to underprice less efficient small firms by sharing their lower costs with consumers in the form of lower prices. Apart from raising in acute form the question of whether it is socially desirable to promote small business at the expense of the consumer, such a policy would be unworkable because it would require comprehensive and continuing supervision of the prices of large firms.... The tools of antitrust enforcement are poorly designed for effective discrimination in favor of small firms, compared, for example, to the effectiveness of taxing larger firms at higher rates. We shall have frequent occasion in this book to remark how difficult it is to press the antitrust laws into the service of small business. The realistic choice is between shaping antitrust policy in accordance with the economic (and congruent political) objections to monopoly and—if we think that limiting big business and promoting small is more important than efficiency—abandoning it.

Richard A. Posner, Antitrust Law: An Economic Perspective 18–20 (1976).

3. More Realistic Models of Competition: Differentiated Products Markets & Oligopoly

The perfect competition model is an interesting and important tool in economic analysis. Competition in the real world, however, is characterized by a wide variety of **rivalrous**

behavior. Competitors engage in advertising, price-cutting, and quality improvement programs. Consider the following observation by Professor McNulty regarding the dangers of confusing the model of perfect competition with the meaning of competition:

> [T]he most general tendency concerning the meaning of competition in economic theory is to regard it as the opposite of monopoly. An unfortunate result of this way of thinking has been no little confusion concerning the relationship between economic efficiency and business behavior. There is a striking contrast in economic literature between the analytical rigor and precision of competition when it is described as a market structure, and the ambiguity surrounding the ideas of competition whenever it is discussed in behavioral terms. Since, as Hayek has rightly noted, "the law cannot effectively prohibit states of affairs but only kinds of action," a concept of economic competition, if it is to be significant for economic policy, ought to relate to patterns of business behavior such as might reasonably be associated with the verb "to compete." That was the case with the competition which Adam Smith made the central organizing principle of economic society in the *Wealth of Nations*.... Whether it was seen as price undercutting by sellers, the bidding up of prices by buyers, or the entry of new firms into profitable industries, the fact is that competition entered economics as a concept which had empirical relevance and operational meaning in terms of contemporary business behavior. Yet on the question of whether such common current practices as advertising, product variation, price undercutting, or other forms of business activity do or do not constitute competition, modern economic theory offers the clarification that they are "monopolistically" competitive. While this is a useful way of illustrating the truth that most markets are in some degree both controlled and controlling, it is less useful as a guide in implementing a policy, such as our antitrust policy, which seeks at once to restrain monopoly and promote competition.

McNulty, *Economic Theory and the Meaning of Competition*, 82 Quarterly Journal of Economics 639, 639–40 (1968). Thus, in reality, perfect competition rarely, if ever, exists. Instead, most firms participate in markets that lie on the spectrum somewhere between perfect competition and monopoly. The following sections discuss two such markets: differentiated products markets and oligopoly.

a. Competition with Differentiated Products

The perfect competition model assumes homogenous consumers and firms. In reality, however, consumers have different tastes and preferences and some firms enjoy lower costs structures than others or are more innovative. **Differentiated products** have distinguishing features relative to the goods or services they are in competition with, like McDonalds and the other fast food restaurants. Differentiation can occur across different dimensions. Product quality can be an important source of product differentiation. Quality differences can be measured in objective dimensions—for example, first class vs. coach air travel—or in subjective dimensions—for example, Coca-Cola vs. Pepsi. Another common source of product differentiation is customer service.

Another important distinction between the real world and the perfectly competitive market involves information. The perfect competition model assumes perfect information is available at zero cost. But, in reality, information is scarce and costly to obtain. The market process approach stresses that economic decision making in the real world is a "discovery process." The discovery process takes place under conditions of ignorance far removed from the perfect knowledge assumption in the model of perfect competition.

In the model of perfect competition, it was assumed that all firms produced an identical product. Thus, perfectly competitive firms face a totally-elastic, or horizontal demand curve, making them price takers. Relaxing the assumptions of perfect information and homogeneity, means that firms face downward sloping demand curve. That is, the firm with a differentiated product has some degree of price control. In general, the more (less) elastic the demand curve, the more (less) similar are competitor's products, and the less (more) control competitors have over price. As always, a firm maximizes it profits by setting price where its marginal cost equals marginal revenue. Because a firm's demand curve slopes downward, however, the price charged will be greater than marginal cost. The gap between marginal cost and price is largely dependent upon the availability of substitutes.

Just because price is greater than marginal cost, however, does not mean that firms earn economic profits in the long run. As in the model of perfect competition, entry and exit are relatively easy in differentiated products market, which means that new firms will be attracted to profitable product spaces. Consider the following example. Suppose Henry lives in a community that had always been exclusively zoned residential. Then, the town council changes the zoning to commercial and Henry decides to open a new fast food restaurant, Henry's Hamburgers. The restaurant is immediately successful and Henry is able to charge high enough prices to make significantly more money than he would using his resources in other ways; in economic parlance, Henry earns economic profits. National chains observe Henry's success and open six new fast food restaurants—KFC, McDonalds, Five Guys, Chipotle, Taco Bell, and Panda Express. These restaurants provide slightly distinguished services and different food, but are certainly close substitutes to Henry's Hamburgers. As each restaurant opens, Henry realizes that demand decreases for his hamburger and he must decrease his prices to keep selling hamburgers. Soon enough, Henry's restaurant makes the same amount as he could if he allocated his resources in other ways—he and the others experience zero economic profits.

Three additional entrepreneurs mistakenly think that Henry's Hamburgers and the other restaurants are still earning positive economic profits. Consequently they each build new fast food restaurants in Henry's community. This mistake is possible and unfortunately frequent in the dynamic process because firms do not have perfect information as assumed in perfectly competitive markets. As these firms enter the market, demand continues to fall for Henry's Hamburgers and the others and they begin to operate at a loss. This means that these firms could increase their profits by using their resources in other ways. Consequently, firms begin to exit the fast food industry in Henry's community. As each firm exits, demand for the remaining firms increases because there are fewer substitutes available. Firms will exit until economic profits are back to zero again.

One characteristic of firms that produce differentiated products is the use of **advertising**. Advertising is a means of communicating both the existence of alternate sellers as well as the distinguishing features of a product. Advertising is a critical and necessary condition for dynamic competitive markets. For example, new firms need to make consumers aware of their products' existence, location, and characteristics. Without advertising, it would be very difficult for new entrants to challenge an established firm. The greater consumer awareness of product alternatives, availability, prices, and other characteristics, the less the consumer is bound to any one seller. Economists have argued that the provision of product information contained in advertising lowers the total search costs to consumers. Moreover, empirical studies have shown that continued advertising improves product quality, maximizes firm profitability, and decreases price. Thus, it seems clear that consumers are the prime beneficiaries of advertising.

Production and sale of goods and services is a complicated and competitive process. Specialization creates economic efficiencies derived from dividing the manufacturing, distribution, and retail sales functions among separate firms. **Vertical relationships** are arrangements down the chain of distribution—from input suppliers to manufacturers to wholesale distributors to retailers. A typical vertical relationship is organized in the following way. A bicycle manufacturer recognizes that certain efficiencies can be gained by selling its product to wholesale distributors (who, in turn, sell the bikes to local retailers) rather than performing all of these functions itself.

For the manufacturer, however, there is a fundamental danger in this type of vertical relationship. Specifically, the bicycle manufacturer wants to sell the profit maximizing quantity of bikes; however, it does not control the retail sales function. The manufacturer wants its retailers to engage in aggressive competitive behavior geared (no pun intended) toward selling its bikes. Retailers can take several actions that affect the sales of the manufacturer's bikes. Obviously, the price set by the retailer will affect sales. Further, the retailer can promote the manufacturer's bikes on its web site, it can place the bikes prominently in the store, and train employees to provide information about the bikes or to promote the bikes over other brands.

Because retailers and producers are different entities, however, they have different objectives; retailers do not necessarily have the same incentive—a desire to maximize the sale of the manufacturer's product. As a result, manufacturers have resorted to numerous contractual devices to encourage their retailers to promote their products, for example, limiting retail pricing discretion or requiring certain types of point-of-sale service. The case below involves an antitrust challenge to once such contractual limitation—**resale price maintenance**.

Leegin Creative Leather Products, Inc. v. PSKS, Inc.

Supreme Court of the United States
551 U.S. 877 (2007)

JUSTICE KENNEDY delivered the opinion of the Court

In Dr. Miles Medical Co. v. John D. Park & Sons Co., 220 U.S. 373 (1911), the Court established the rule that it is *per se* illegal under § 1 of the Sherman Act for a manufacturer to agree with its distributor to set the minimum price the distributor can charge for the manufacturer's goods. The question presented by the instant case is whether the Court should overrule the *per se* rule and allow resale price maintenance agreements to be judged by the rule of reason, the usual standard applied to determine if there is a violation of § 1. The Court has abandoned the rule of *per se* illegality for other vertical restraints a manufacturer imposes on its distributors. Respected economic analysts, furthermore, conclude that vertical price restraints can have procompetitive effects. We now hold that *Dr. Miles* should be overruled and that vertical price restraints are to be judged by the rule of reason.

I

Petitioner, Leegin Creative Leather Products, Inc. (Leegin), designs, manufactures, and distributes leather goods and accessories. In 1991, Leegin began to sell belts under the brand name "Brighton." The Brighton brand has now expanded into a variety of women's fashion accessories. It is sold across the United States in over 5,000 retail establishments, for the most part independent, small boutiques and specialty stores. Leegin's president, Jerry Kohl, also has an interest in about 70 stores that sell Brighton products. Leegin asserts that, at least for its products, small retailers treat customers better, provide customers more services, and make their shopping experience more satisfactory than do larger, often impersonal retailers. Kohl explained: "[W]e want the consumers to get a different experience than they get in Sam's Club or in Wal-Mart. And you can't get that kind of experience or support or customer service from a store like Wal-Mart."

Respondent, PSKS, Inc. (PSKS), operates Kay's Kloset, a women's apparel store in Lewisville, Texas. Kay's Kloset buys from about 75 different manufacturers and at one time sold the Brighton brand. It first started purchasing Brighton goods from Leegin in 1995. Once it began selling the brand, the store promoted Brighton. For example, it ran Brighton advertisements and had Brighton days in the store. Kay's Kloset became the destination retailer in the area to buy Brighton products. Brighton was the store's most important brand and once accounted for 40 to 50 percent of its profits.

In 1997, Leegin instituted the "Brighton Retail Pricing and Promotion Policy." Following the policy, Leegin refused to sell to retailers that discounted Brighton goods below suggested prices.

* * *

Leegin adopted the policy to give its retailers sufficient margins to provide customers the service central to its distribution strategy. It also expressed concern that discounting harmed Brighton's brand image and reputation.

* * *

In December 2002, Leegin discovered Kay's Kloset had been marking down Brighton's entire line by 20 percent. Kay's Kloset contended it placed Brighton products on sale to compete with nearby retailers who also were undercutting Leegin's suggested prices. Leegin, nonetheless, requested that Kay's Kloset cease discounting. Its request refused, Leegin stopped selling to the store. The loss of the Brighton brand had a considerable negative impact on the store's revenue from sales.

PSKS sued Leegin in the United States District Court for the Eastern District of Texas. It alleged, among other claims, that Leegin had violated the antitrust laws by "enter[ing] into agreements with retailers to charge only those prices fixed by Leegin." Leegin planned to introduce expert testimony describing the procompetitive effects of its pricing policy. The District Court excluded the testimony, relying on the *per se* rule established by *Dr. Miles*.

* * *

The jury agreed with PSKS and awarded it $1.2 million. Pursuant to 15 U.S.C. § 15(a), the District Court trebled the damages and reimbursed PSKS for its attorney's fees and costs. It entered judgment against Leegin in the amount of $3,975,000.80.

The Court of Appeals for the Fifth Circuit affirmed. On appeal Leegin did not dispute that it had entered into vertical price-fixing agreements with its retailers. Rather, it contended that the rule of reason should have applied to those agreements.

* * *

We granted certiorari to determine whether vertical minimum resale price maintenance agreements should continue to be treated as *per se* unlawful.

* * *

A

Though each side of the debate can find sources to support its position, it suffices to say here that economics literature is replete with procompetitive justifications for a manufacturer's use of resale price maintenance. See, *e.g.,* Brief for Economists as *Amici Curiae* 16 ("In the theoretical literature, it is essentially undisputed that minimum [resale price maintenance] can have procompetitive effects and that under a variety of market conditions it is unlikely to have anticompetitive effects"); Brief for United States as *Amicus Curiae* 9 ("[T]here is a widespread consensus that permitting a manufacturer to control the price at which its goods are sold may promote *inter*brand competition and consumer welfare in a variety of ways"); ABA Section of Antitrust Law, Antitrust Law and Economics of Product Distribution 76 (2006) ("[T]he bulk of the economic literature on [resale price maintenance] suggests that [it] is more likely to be used to enhance efficiency than for anticompetitive purposes"); *see also* H. Hovenkamp, The Antitrust Enterprise: Principle and Execution 184–191 (2005) (hereinafter Hovenkamp); R. Bork, The Antitrust Paradox 288–291 (1978) (hereinafter Bork). Even those more skeptical of resale price maintenance acknowledge it can have procompetitive effects. See, *e.g.,* Brief for William S. Comanor et al. as *Amici Curiae* 3 ("[G]iven [the] diversity of effects [of resale price maintenance], one could reasonably take the position that a *rule of reason* rather than a *per se* approach is warranted"); F. Scherer & D. Ross, Industrial Market Structure and Economic Performance 558 (3d ed.1990) (hereinafter Scherer & Ross) ("The overall balance between benefits and costs [of resale price maintenance] is probably close").

* * *

The justifications for vertical price restraints are similar to those for other vertical restraints. Minimum resale price maintenance can stimulate interbrand competition — the competition among manufacturers selling different brands of the same type of product — by reducing intrabrand competition — the competition among retailers selling the same brand. The promotion of interbrand competition is important because "the primary purpose of the antitrust laws is to protect [this type of] competition." [*State Oil Co. v.*] *Khan,* 522 U.S. [3,] 15 [(1997)]. A single manufacturer's use of vertical price restraints tends to eliminate intrabrand price competition; this in turn encourages retailers to invest in tangible or intangible services or promotional efforts that aid the manufacturer's position as against rival manufacturers. Resale price maintenance also has the potential to give consumers more options so that they can choose among low-price, low-service brands; high-price, high-service brands; and brands that fall in between.

Absent vertical price restraints, the retail services that enhance interbrand competition might be underprovided. This is because discounting retailers can free ride on retailers who furnish services and then capture some of the increased demand those services generate. Consumers might learn, for example, about the benefits of a manufacturer's product from a retailer that invests in fine showrooms, offers product demonstrations, or hires and trains knowledgeable employees. R. Posner, Antitrust Law 172–173 (2d ed.2001) (hereinafter Posner). Or consumers might decide to buy the product because they see it in a retail establishment that has a reputation for selling high-quality merchandise. Marvel & McCafferty, *Resale Price Maintenance and Quality Certification*, 15 Rand J. Econ. 346, 347–349 (1984). If the consumer can then buy the product from a retailer that discounts because it has not spent capital providing services or developing a quality reputation, the high-service retailer will lose sales to the discounter, forcing it to cut back its services to a level lower than consumers would otherwise prefer. Minimum resale price maintenance alleviates the problem because it prevents the discounter from undercutting the service provider. With price competition decreased, the manufacturer's retailers compete among themselves over services.

* * *

Resale price maintenance can also increase interbrand competition by encouraging retailer services that would not be provided even absent free riding. It may be difficult and inefficient for a manufacturer to make and enforce a contract with a retailer specifying the different services the retailer must perform. Offering the retailer a guaranteed margin and threatening termination if it does not live up to expectations may be the most efficient way to expand the manufacturer's market share by inducing the retailer's performance and allowing it to use its own initiative and experience in providing valuable services. See Mathewson & Winter, *The Law and Economics of Resale Price Maintenance*, 13 Rev. Indus. Org. 57, 74–75 (1998); Klein & Murphy, *Vertical Restraints as Contract Enforcement Mechanisms*, 31 J. Law & Econ. 265, 295 (1988); see also Deneckere, Marvel, & Peck, *Demand Uncertainty, Inventories, and Resale Price Maintenance*, 111 Q.J. Econ. 885, 911 (1996) (noting that resale price maintenance may be beneficial to motivate retailers to stock adequate inventories of a manufacturer's goods in the face of uncertain consumer demand).

* * *

While vertical agreements setting minimum resale prices can have procompetitive justifications, they may have anticompetitive effects in other cases; and unlawful price fixing, designed solely to obtain monopoly profits, is an ever–present temptation. Resale price maintenance may, for example, facilitate a manufacturer cartel. An unlawful cartel will seek to discover if some manufacturers are undercutting the cartel's fixed prices. Resale price maintenance could assist the cartel in identifying price-cutting manufacturers who benefit from the lower prices they offer. Resale price maintenance, furthermore, could discourage a manufacturer from cutting prices to retailers with the concomitant benefit of cheaper prices to consumers.

Vertical price restraints also "might be used to organize cartels at the retailer level." *Business Electronics* [*Corp. v. Sharp Electronics Corp.*, 485 U.S. 717,], 725–726 [(1988)]..A group of retailers might collude to fix prices to consumers and then compel a manufacturer to aid the unlawful arrangement with resale price maintenance. In that instance the manufacturer does not establish the practice to stimulate services or to promote its brand but to give inefficient retailers higher profits. Retailers with better distribution systems and lower cost structures would be prevented from charging lower prices by the agreement. Historical examples suggest this possibility is a legitimate concern. See, *e.g.,* Marvel & McCafferty, *The Welfare Effects of Resale Price Maintenance*, 28 J. Law & Econ. 363, 373 (1985) (providing an example of the power of the National Association of Retail Druggists to compel manufacturers to use resale price maintenance); Hovenkamp 186 (suggesting that the retail druggists in *Dr. Miles* formed a cartel and used manufacturers to enforce it).

* * *

Resale price maintenance, it is true, does have economic dangers. If the rule of reason were to apply to vertical price restraints, courts would have to be diligent in eliminating their anticompetitive uses from the market. This is a realistic objective, and certain factors are relevant to the inquiry. For example, the number of manufacturers that make use of the practice in a given industry can provide important instruction. When only a few manufacturers lacking market power adopt the practice, there is little likelihood it is facilitating a manufacturer cartel, for a cartel then can be undercut by rival manufacturers. Likewise, a retailer cartel is unlikely when only a single manufacturer in a competitive market uses resale price maintenance. Interbrand competition would divert consumers to lower priced substitutes and eliminate any gains to retailers from their price-fixing agreement over a single brand. See Posner 172; Bork 292. Resale price maintenance should be subject to more careful scrutiny, by contrast, if many competing manufacturers adopt the practice. Cf. Scherer & Ross 558 (noting that "except when [resale price maintenance] spreads to cover the bulk of an industry's output, depriving consumers of a meaningful choice between high-service and low-price outlets, most [resale price maintenance arrangements] are probably innocuous"); Easterbrook 162 (suggesting that "every one of the potentially-anticompetitive outcomes of vertical arrangements depends on the uniformity of the practice").

The source of the restraint may also be an important consideration. If there is evidence retailers were the impetus for a vertical price restraint, there is a greater likelihood that the restraint facilitates a retailer cartel or supports a dominant, inefficient retailer. See Brief for William S. Comanor et al. as *Amici Curiae* 7–8. If, by contrast, a manufacturer adopted the policy independent of retailer pressure, the restraint is less likely to promote anticompetitive conduct. Cf. Posner 177 ("It makes all the difference whether minimum retail prices are imposed by the manufacturer in order to evoke point-of-sale services or by the dealers in order to obtain monopoly profits"). A manufacturer also has an incentive to protest inefficient retailer-induced price restraints because they can harm its competitive position.

As a final matter, that a dominant manufacturer or retailer can abuse resale price maintenance for anticompetitive purposes may not be a serious concern unless the relevant entity has market power. If a retailer lacks market power, manufacturers likely can sell their goods through rival retailers. See also *Business Electronics, supra,* at 727, n. 2 (noting "[r]etail market power is rare, because of the usual presence of interbrand competition and other dealers"). And if a manufacturer lacks market power, there is less likelihood it can use the practice to keep competitors away from distribution outlets.

* * *

The manufacturer has a number of legitimate options to achieve benefits similar to those provided by vertical price restraints. A manufacturer can exercise its *Colgate* right to refuse to deal with retailers that do not follow its suggested prices. The economic effects of unilateral and concerted price setting are in general the same. The problem for the manufacturer is that a jury might conclude its unilateral policy was really a vertical agreement, subjecting it to treble damages and potential criminal liability. Even with the stringent standards in *Monsanto* and *Business Electronics,* this danger can lead, and has led, rational manufacturers to take wasteful measures. A manufacturer might refuse to discuss its pricing policy with its distributors except through counsel knowledgeable of the subtle intricacies of the law. Or it might terminate longstanding distributors for minor violations without seeking an explanation. The increased costs these burdensome measures generate flow to consumers in the form of higher prices.

Furthermore, depending on the type of product it sells, a manufacturer might be able to achieve the procompetitive benefits of resale price maintenance by integrating downstream and selling its products directly to consumers. *Dr. Miles* tilts the relative costs of vertical integration and vertical agreement by making the former more attractive based on the *per se* rule, not on real market conditions. [S]ee generally Coase, The Nature of the Firm, 4 Economica, New Series 386 (1937). This distortion might lead to inefficient integration that would not otherwise take place, so that consumers must again suffer the consequences of the suboptimal distribution strategy. And integration, unlike vertical price restraints, eliminates all intrabrand competition.

There is yet another consideration. A manufacturer can impose territorial restrictions on distributors and allow only one distributor to sell its goods in a given region. Our cases have recognized, and the economics literature confirms, that these vertical nonprice restraints have impacts similar to those of vertical price restraints; both reduce intrabrand competition and can stimulate retailer services.... The same legal standard (*per se* unlawfulness) applies to horizontal market division and horizontal price fixing because both have similar economic effect. There is likewise little economic justification for the current differential treatment of vertical price and nonprice restraints. Furthermore, vertical nonprice restraints may prove less efficient for inducing desired services, and they reduce intrabrand competition more than vertical price restraints by eliminating both price and service competition. See Brief for Economists as *Amici Curiae* 17–18.

* * *

For these reasons the Court's decision in Dr. Miles Medical Co. v. John D. Park & Sons Co., 220 U.S. 373 (1911), is now overruled. Vertical price restraints are to be judged according to the rule of reason.

V

* * *

The judgment of the Court of Appeals is reversed, and the case is remanded for proceedings consistent with this opinion.

Notes and Questions

1. Resale Price Maintenance and the Leegin Factors: The business conduct at issue in this case was minimum resale price maintenance (RPM). RPM occurs where a manufacturer demands that retailers only sell the manufacturer's product above an established price floor. As evidenced in the opinion, the Court gave substantial weight to academic literature claiming that this practice carries with it both a possibility for anticompetitive harm to markets and procompetitive benefits. The Court rejected the previously standing 100-year rule of *per se* condemnation of RPM and replaced it with the rule of reason. The Court placed the onus of further development of the rule of reason on the district courts and advised them to be "diligent in eliminating their anticompetitive uses from the market." Justice Kennedy points to three factors as guidance for when to be concerned about the anticompetitive harms of minimum RPM. Those three factors include: (1) when RPM covers the bulk of an industry's goods, (2) when a single dominant retailer, rather than manufacturers, implements or encourages RPM, and (3) when RPM is instituted by firms with discernible market power. Do these three factors, purportedly increasing the dangers of RPM, make economic sense? How should a court go about weighing the magnitude of economic harm and procompetitive benefit? Is evidence of what the court calls free-riding by low-cost retailers on the customer service of higher cost retailers, such as showrooms, product demonstrations, and knowledgeable employees, dispositive evidence of economic harm?

2. Intrabrand v. Interbrand Rivalry: The Court recognizes a distinction between intrabrand and interbrand competition. Should these two different types of competition be analyzed in the same manner for purposes of antitrust regulation? The Court observes that some vertical nonprice restraints on intrabrand competition may actually improve interbrand competition. How does this work? Does this also mean that the losses in efficiency resulting from restraints in intrabrand competition are made up for by improved interbrand competition? At least one prominent commentator is quite skeptical of the balancing the court seems to support. Judge Frank Easterbrook has written that:

> No one can sensibly weigh inter- and intrabrand competition against one another; they are not commensurable. The reduction in "intrabrand competition" is the *source* of the competitive benefit that helps one product compete against another. Intrabrand competition as such is worthless; one might as well complain when a corporation does not have internal competition to make the product most cheaply. Vertical integration eliminates this form of "competition," but in so doing it may enable the manufacturer to reduce its delivered price. No manufacturer wants to have less competition among its dealers for the sake of less competition. The reduction in dealers' rivalry in the price dimension is just the tool the manufacturer uses to induce greater competition in the service dimension. As I spelled out above, restricted dealing alters the product's attributes. There is no "less" in one column to "balance against a gain" in the other, any more than the manufacturer's sole prerogative to decide what physical product to make creates a "reduction in intrabrand competition."

Frank H. Easterbrook, *Vertical Arrangements and the Rule of Reason*, 53 Antitrust L.J. 135 (1984).

3. Development of the Rule of Reason in Vertical Restraint: Justice Kennedy's opinion recognized that the Court had slowly but surely been moving in the direction of handling most business conduct under the rule of reason rather than condemning the same conduct under a rule of *per se* illegality. *Leegin* was foretold by a major shift in the court's approach to nearly all vertical restraints. The Court cited *GTE Sylvania* for the proposition that non-price vertical restraints should be evaluated under a rule of reason. In that case, a manufacturer of television sets used vertical restraints in the form of location-specific exclusive contracts. The agreements only allowed the retailer to sell the product at specific stores specified in the agreement. One retailer, despite agreeing to this term and having notable success with the sale of Sylvania TVs, sued under the antitrust laws because it wanted to sell this product in other geographical regions disallowed under the contract. The Supreme Court, in an argument similar to the one adopted in *Leegin*, highlighted the possibility for vertical restrictions on goods to increase interbrand competition and allow smaller manufacturers to compete. It reasoned that:

> Vertical restrictions reduce intrabrand competition by limiting the number of sellers of a particular product competing for the business of a given group of buyers. Location restrictions have this effect because of practical constraints on the effective marketing area of retail outlets. Although intrabrand competition may be reduced, the ability of retailers to exploit the resulting market may be limited both by the ability of consumers to travel to other franchised locations and, perhaps more importantly, to purchase the competing products of other manufacturers. None of these key variables, however, is affected by the form of the transaction by which a manufacturer conveys his products to the retailers.
>
> Vertical restrictions promote interbrand competition by allowing the manufacturer to achieve certain efficiencies in the distribution of his products. These "redeeming virtues" are implicit in every decision sustaining vertical restrictions under the rule of reason. Economists have identified a number of ways in which manufacturers can use such restrictions to compete more effectively against other manufacturers. See, e. g., Preston, *Restrictive Distribution Arrangements: Economic Analysis and Public Policy Standards*, 30 Law & Contemp. Prob. 506, 511 (1965).

For example, new manufacturers and manufacturers entering new markets can use the restrictions in order to induce competent and aggressive retailers to make the kind of investment of capital and labor that is often required in the distribution of products unknown to the consumer. Established manufacturers can use them to induce retailers to engage in promotional activities or to provide service and repair facilities necessary to the efficient marketing of their products. Service and repair are vital for many products, such as automobiles and major household appliances. The availability and quality of such services affect a manufacturer's goodwill and the competitiveness of his product. Because of market imperfections such as the so-called "free rider" effect, these services might not be provided by retailers in a purely competitive situation, despite the fact that each retailer's benefit would be greater if all provided the services than if none did.

Economists also have argued that manufacturers have an economic interest in maintaining as much intrabrand competition as is consistent with the efficient distribution of their products. Bork, *The Rule of Reason and the Per Se Concept: Price Fixing and the Market Division (II)*, 75 Yale L.J. 373, 403 (1966). Although the view that the manufacturer's interest necessarily corresponds with that of the public is not universally shared, even the leading critic of vertical restrictions concedes that *Schwinn*'s distinction between sale and nonsale transactions is essentially unrelated to any relevant economic impact. Comanor, *Vertical Territorial and Customer Restrictions:* White Motor *and Its Aftermath*, 81 Harv. L. Rev. 1419, 1422 (1968).25 Indeed, to the extent that the form of the transaction is related to interbrand benefits, the Court's distinction is inconsistent with its articulated concern for the ability of smaller firms to compete effectively with larger ones. Capital requirements and administrative expenses may prevent smaller firms from using the exception for nonsale transactions. See, e. g., Phillips, Schwinn *Rules and the "New Economics" of Vertical Relation*, 44 Antitrust L.J. 573, 576 (1975).

* * *

In sum, we conclude that the appropriate decision is to return to the rule of reason that governed vertical restrictions prior to Schwinn. When anticompetitive effects are shown to result from particular vertical restrictions they can be adequately policed under the rule of reason, the standard traditionally applied for the majority of anticompetitive practices challenged under § 1 of the Act. Accordingly, the decision of the Court of Appeals is Affirmed.

Cont'l T. V., Inc. v. GTE Sylvania Inc., 433 U.S. 36, 54–59 (1977).

Another shift in the court's approach to vertical restraints came in *State Oil v. Khan*. There, a gasoline supplier terminated an agreement with an owner of a gas station who promptly sued alleging that State Oil's policies mandated a maximum resale price that should be condemned as a per se violation of the antitrust laws. The agreement provided the gas station owner with a 3.25 cent margin on the purchase price of every gallon of gasoline. If the gas station charged any price higher than the supplier's suggested retail price the extra money had to be rebated back to State Oil. In dismissing the application of the *per se* rule, a unanimous Court affirmed the reasoning, although not the decision, of Judge Posner in the Seventh Circuit. There, Judge Posner applied the *per se* rule in accordance with *stare decisis* but not without analyzing the answer to the question:

Why might competitors fix a maximum resale price? The difference between what a supplier charges his dealer and what the dealer charges the ultimate customer is, functionally, compensation to the dealer for performing the resale service; so by agreeing on the resale prices of their goods competing sellers can reduce their dealers' margin below the competitive price for the dealers' service. This is a form of monopsony pricing, which is analytically the same as monopoly or cartel pricing and so treated by the law. E.g., Mandeville Island Farms, Inc. v. American Crystal Sugar Co., 334 U.S. 219 (1948).

The questionable next step (logically, not chronologically, next) in the evolution of antitrust law was to affix the per se label to contracts in which a single supplier, not acting in concert with any of its competitors, fixed its dealers' retail prices. Dr. Miles Medical Co. v. John D. Park & Sons Co., 220 U.S. 373 (1911). Here the economic difference between fixing a minimum resale price and fixing a maximum resale price becomes more pronounced, although most economists believe that neither form of price fixing is pernicious when the supplier is neither the cat's paw of colluding distributors nor acting in concert with his competitors. A supplier acting unilaterally might fix a minimum resale price in order to induce his dealers to furnish valuable point-of-sale services (trained salesmen, clean restrooms — whatever) to customers, which they could not afford to do without a guaranteed margin to cover the costs of the services, because the customers would use the services provided by the full-service dealers but then purchase the product from a competing dealer who could sell the product at a discount because he had not borne the expense of providing the services. Lester G. Telser, *Why Should Manufacturers Want Fair Trade?*, 3 J. Law & Econ. 86 (1962).

As for maximum resale price fixing, unless the supplier is a monopsonist he cannot squeeze his dealers' margins below a competitive level; the attempt to do so would just drive the dealers into the arms of a competing supplier. A supplier might, however, fix a maximum resale price in order to prevent his dealers from exploiting a monopoly position. We do not know anything about the competitive environment in which Khan and State Oil operate — which is why the district judge was right to conclude that if the rule of reason is applicable, Khan loses. But suppose that State Oil, perhaps to encourage the dealer services that we mentioned, has spaced its dealers sufficiently far apart to limit competition among them (or even given each of them an exclusive territory); and suppose further that Union 76 is a sufficiently distinctive and popular brand to give the dealers in it at least a modicum of monopoly power. Then State Oil might want to place a ceiling on the dealers' resale prices in order to prevent them from exploiting that monopoly power fully. It would do this not out of disinterested malice, but in its commercial self-interest. The higher the price at which gasoline is resold, the smaller the volume sold, and so the lower the profit to the supplier if the higher profit per gallon at the higher price is being snared by the dealer.

Khan v. State Oil Co., 93 F.3d 1358, 1361–62 (7th Cir. 1996) *vacated*, 522 U.S. 3 (1997).

4. A Spirited Dissent: There was a four-Justice dissent in the *Leegin* opinion written by Justice Breyer that stressed the value of *stare decisis* and the limited authority of the court to overrule well-established decisions. Arguing that antitrust policy required stable and predictable rules he contended that "the fact that a rule of law has become 'embedded' in our 'national culture' argues strongly against overruling. The *per se* rule forbidding minimum resale price maintenance agreements has long been 'embedded' in the law of antitrust. It involves price, the economy's 'central nervous system.' It reflects a basic antitrust assumption (that consumers often prefer lower prices to more service). It embodies a basic antitrust objective (providing consumers with a free choice about such matters). And it creates an easily administered and enforceable bright line, 'Do not agree about price,' that businesses as well as lawyers have long understood." Leegin Creative Leather Products, Inc. v. PSKS, Inc., 551 U.S. 877, 926–27 (2007) (citations omitted).

Is predictability a good reason to keep old precedent? What do you think happens in the business world when the Supreme Court changes a long-established rule that substantially affects the way that corporations compete? The Supreme Court frequently overrules itself. Why should this opinion be any different?

5. Manufacturers' Interest in Retailer Service and Prices: For minimum resale price maintenance, a manufacturer conditions a retailer's right to sell the manufacturer's products on the retailer's agreement not to sell the product below a certain price. This seems counterintuitive for the manufacturer because a retailer's margin over cost does not impact the manufacturer's profit. Put another way, a manufacturer sets its price regardless of what the retailer does so why does he care about the retailer's price? Some insight may be provided by a statement made by Leegin's president: "[W]e want the consumers to get a different experience than they get in Sam's Club or in Wal-Mart. And you can't get that kind of experience or support or customer service from a store like Wal-Mart." 551 U.S. at 882. Why does the president care how much service retailers provide? Are you convinced that high quality service benefits Leegin, as the manufacturer? If so, what is the logic?

6. Rule of Reason's Structure: The majority recognizes that there is a valid concern that minimum resale price maintenance is nothing but a ruse among retailers to cartelize the market. This valid concern, as elaborated by the dissent, is why most scholars promulgate a rule or reason for minimum resale price maintenance instead of a standard of per se legality. *But see* Richard A. Posner, *The Next Step in the Antitrust Treatment of Restricted Distribution: Per Se Legality*, 48 U. Chi. L. Rev. 6 (1981). *Leegin's* actual impact will not be fully established until courts determine how the rule of reason should apply. If the factfinder finds that the minimum resale price maintenance was imposed by the retailers, what does this say about the likely anticompetitive effect of the agreement? Is the analysis different if the factfinder finds that the manufacturer initiated the minimum resale price agreement? How should the answers to this question impact how courts should apply the rule of reason to these agreements? For more information on the potential structure for the rule of reason, see Thomas A. Lambert, Dr. Miles *Is Dead. Now What?: Structuring A Rule of Reason for Evaluating Minimum Resale Price Maintenance*, 50 Wm. & Mary L. Rev. 1937 (2009).

7. The Intersection of State and Federal Antitrust Law: Leegin's impact on firms' actual pricing practices is very difficult to predict given the complicated overlap of state and federal law in this area. Some state antitrust laws are identical to the Sherman Act, and precedent or statutes require the state court to follow federal precedent interpreting the Sherman Act. Those states presumably will follow *Leegin.* Other states, however, have codified the per se illegal standard for minimum resale price maintenance. In these states, a firm implementing resale price maintenance may not be liable under federal law but still will be liable under state law. See Michael A. Lindsay, *An Update on State RPM Laws Since* Leegin, Antitrust Source, Dec. 2010 (providing a table of all the states and how each treats minimum resale price maintenance). With this structure of laws, is it likely that national firms will even bother with resale price maintenance because they will essentially have a complicated patchwork of pricing schemes depending on state boundaries and statutes? If a national firm proceeds and implements a patchwork of pricing strategy even though it is very complicated and costly to implement, does this lend support to the majority's view that minimum resale price maintenance is procompetitive?

8. *Who Is the Loser:* The majority argues that minimum resale price maintenance can alleviate the market of the free-rider problem:

> If the consumer can ... buy the product from a retailer that discounts because it has not spent capital providing services or developing a quality reputation, the high-service retailer will lose sales to the discounter, forcing it to cut back its services to a level lower than consumers would otherwise prefer. Minimum resale price maintenance alleviates the problem because it prevents the discounter from undercutting the service provider. With price competition decreased, the manufacturer's retailers compete among themselves over services.

551 U.S. at 891. This argument is criticized because preventing the free-rider problem converts consumer welfare into producer welfare—certainly not the goal of antitrust. Critics argue it is better to know that consumers are getting lower prices than to hope that pricing schemes that increase prices somehow result in higher demand and increased total welfare. Does the knowledge that rational consumers will choose more consumer welfare over less resolve this concern since rational profit maximizing firms will choose a strategy that benefits consumers?

The most likely loser under the rule of reason is an individual that does not want point of service sales and is satisfied with little or no service and lower prices. Is the Court right to ignore this consumer in its analysis? Is this resolved by the difference in a per se illegal standard, the rule of reason standard, and a per se legal standard?

9. *RPM and Increased Prices:* Justice Breyer stated that "[m]ost economists today agree that, in the words of a prominent antitrust treatise, 'resale price maintenance tends to produce higher consumer prices than would otherwise be the case.'" 551 U.S. at 912. At least one empirical study attempted to measure *Leegin*'s impact on prices and found some evidence that prices did increase after *Leegin* was decided. Nathaniel J. Harris, Leegin's *Effect on Prices: An Empirical Analysis*, 9 J.L. Econ. & Pol'y 251 (2013). Is this price increase evidence dispositive and mean *Leegin* was incorrectly decided? If price increases, does consumer welfare—the ultimate standard for antitrust—necessarily have to decrease? If minimum resale price maintenance shifted the demand curve outward, would price increase? Would this shift necessarily increase consumer welfare?

10. *Vertical Restraints and Evidence:* Economists have continued to seek ways to use data, empirical methods, and quantitative approaches to test and confirm economic theories. Reviews of empirical literature seem to suggest that vertical restraints are associated with higher levels of output. For example, economists Francine Lafontaine and Margaret Slade concluded from their review that:

> Specifically, it appears that when manufacturers choose to impose such restraints, not only do they make themselves better off, but they also typically allow consumers to benefit from higher quality products and better service provision.... The evidence thus supports the conclusion that in these markets, manufacturer and consumer interests are apt to be aligned, while interference in the market is accomplished at the expense of consumers (and of course manufacturers).

For the details of their quantitative results, read Francine Lafontaine & Margaret Slade, *Exclusive Contracts and Vertical Restraints: Empirical Evidence and Public Policy*, 45 J. Econ

Lit. 629 (2005). A group of economists from the FTC reached a similar conclusion from their review of the empirical literature. *See* James C. Cooper, Luke M. Froeb, Dan O'Brien, & Michael G. Vita, *Vertical Antitrust Policy as a Problem of Inference*, 23 INT'L J. INDUS. ORG. 639 (2005).

b. Oligopoly

A market that consists of a few firms is called an oligopoly. Common oligopoly markets include wireless service providers (AT&T, Verizon, T-Mobile, and Sprint), commercial airline manufacturers (Boeing and Airbus), tennis ball manufacturers (Wilson, Penn, Dunlop, and Spalding), and accounting service providers (PWC, Deloitte, KPMG, and Ernst & Young). There are only a few firms in these markets because the optimal size of firm in these industry is very large (i.e., minimum ATC is only achieved when the firms are large) and the demand is not sufficient to support many large firms. The costs required for a firm to get to the point where minimum ATC is achieved and the fact that oligopoly markets can only sustain a limited number of firms serve as natural barriers to entry. Entry can also be limited by the strategic behavior of incumbent firms that do not want to be replaced by another firm.

Firms in an oligopolistic market can influence price and have the potential to earn monopoly profits. Each firm in an oligopoly controls such a large portion of the market that if it suddenly increases or decreases its quantity, the price will change drastically. This is unlike perfect competition and monopolistic competition, because individual firms in those markets are unable to substantially impact market price. An oligopoly firm's decision making process also varies from that of a monopolist because an oligopolist's decisions must be conditioned on what the other firms in the market—which also have the ability to impact the price—will do. Below, we examine how interdependence can lead firms to engage in parallel conduct. We also explore the extent to which oligopolies can coordinate their actions through explicit collusion.

i. Interdependence

One of the distinguishing characteristics of oligopolistic markets is interdependence; each firm's profitability depends on the decisions of the other firms in the market. As discussed earlier in this chapter, the profit-maximizing level of output is where its marginal cost equals marginal revenue. Marginal cost does not depend on the action of other firms, but marginal revenue does. Revenue is price multiplied by quantity sold, and price in the market will depend on all the firms' decisions because each of the firms in an oligopoly market can impact price depending on the quantity they sell. Thus, a firm's profit maximizing decision depends on pricing and output decisions of other firms.

Not surprisingly, in oligopoly industries, firms can arrive at similar prices and output levels due solely to rational independent responses to other firms' decisions. The U.S. antitrust laws recognize the interdependent nature of oligopoly markets, which is why similar pricing patterns or other tandem behavior alone do not violate the antitrust laws.

Bell Atlantic Corporation v. Twombly

Supreme Court of the United States
550 U.S. 544 (2007)

SOUTER, J.

I

The upshot of the 1984 divestiture of the American Telephone & Telegraph Company's (AT&T) local telephone business was a system of regional service monopolies (variously called "Regional Bell Operating Companies," "Baby Bells," or "Incumbent Local Exchange Carriers" (ILECs)), and a separate, competitive market for long-distance service from which the ILECs were excluded. More than a decade later, Congress withdrew approval of the ILECs' monopolies by enacting the Telecommunications Act of 1996 (1996 Act), which "fundamentally restructure[d] local telephone markets" and "subject[ed] [ILECs] to a host of duties intended to facilitate market entry."

* * *

"Central to the [new] scheme [was each ILEC's] obligation ... to share its network with competitors," which came to be known as "competitive local exchange carriers" (CLECs). A CLEC could make use of an ILEC's network in any of three ways: by (1) "purchas[ing] local telephone services at wholesale rates for resale to end users," (2) "leas[ing] elements of the [ILEC's] network 'on an unbundled basis,' " or (3) "interconnect[ing] its own facilities with the [ILEC's] network."

* * *

Respondents William Twombly and Lawrence Marcus (hereinafter plaintiffs) represent a putative class consisting of all "subscribers of local telephone and/or high speed internet services ... from February 8, 1996 to present."

* * *

The complaint alleges that the ILECs conspired to restrain trade in two ways, each supposedly inflating charges for local telephone and high-speed Internet services. Plaintiffs say, first, that the ILECs "engaged in parallel conduct" in their respective service areas to inhibit the growth of upstart CLECs. Their actions allegedly included making unfair agreements with the CLECs for access to ILEC networks, providing inferior connections to the networks, overcharging, and billing in ways designed to sabotage the CLECs' relations with their own customers. According to the complaint, the ILECs' "compelling common motivatio[n]" to thwart the CLECs' competitive efforts naturally led them to form a conspiracy; "[h]ad any one [ILEC] not sought to prevent CLECs ... from competing effectively..., the resulting greater competitive inroads into that [ILEC's] territory would have revealed the degree to which competitive entry by CLECs would have been successful in the other territories in the absence of such conduct."

Second, the complaint charges agreements by the ILECs to refrain from competing against one another. These are to be inferred from the ILECs' common failure "meaningfully [to] pursu[e]" "attractive business opportunit[ies]" in contiguous markets where they possessed "substantial competitive advantages," and from a statement of Richard Notebaert, chief executive officer (CEO) of the ILEC Qwest, that competing in the territory of another ILEC " 'might be a good way to turn a quick dollar but that doesn't make it right[.]' "

* * *

II

A

Because § 1 of the Sherman Act "does not prohibit [all] unreasonable restraints of trade ... but only restraints effected by a contract, combination, or conspiracy," *Copperweld Corp. v. Independence Tube Corp.,* 467 U.S. 752, 775 (1984), "[t]he crucial question" is whether the challenged anticompetitive conduct "stem[s] from independent decision or from an agreement, tacit or express," *Theatre Enterprises,[Inc. v. Paramount Film Distr. Corp.,]* 346 U.S. [537,] 540 [(1954)]. While a showing of parallel "business behavior is admissible circumstantial evidence from which the fact finder may infer agreement," it falls short of "conclusively establish[ing] agreement or ... itself constitut[ing] a Sherman Act offense." *Id.,* at 540–541. Even "conscious parallelism," a common reaction of "firms in a concentrated market [that] recogniz[e] their shared economic interests and their interdependence with respect to price and output decisions" is "not in itself unlawful." *Brooke Group Ltd. v. Brown & Williamson Tobacco Corp.,* 509 U.S. 209, 227 (1993); see 6 P. Areeda & H. Hovenkamp, Antitrust Law ¶ 1433a, p. 236 (2d ed.2003) ("The courts are nearly unanimous in saying that mere interdependent parallelism does not establish the contract, combination, or conspiracy required by Sherman Act § 1")[.]

The inadequacy of showing parallel conduct or interdependence, without more, mirrors the ambiguity of the behavior: consistent with conspiracy, but just as much in line with a wide swath of rational and competitive business strategy unilaterally prompted by common perceptions of the market. Accordingly, we have previously hedged against false inferences from identical behavior at a number of points in the trial sequence. An antitrust conspiracy plaintiff with evidence showing nothing beyond parallel conduct is not entitled to a directed verdict; proof of a § 1 conspiracy must include evidence tending to exclude the possibility of independent action; and at the summary judgment stage a § 1 plaintiff's offer of conspiracy evidence must tend to rule out the possibility that the defendants were acting independently.

B

This case presents the antecedent question of what a plaintiff must plead in order to state a claim under § 1 of the Sherman Act. Federal Rule of Civil Procedure 8(a)(2) requires only "a short and plain statement of the claim showing that the pleader is entitled to relief," in order to "give the defendant fair notice of what the ... claim is and the grounds upon which it rests," *Conley v. Gibson,* 355 U.S. 41, 47 (1957). While a complaint attacked by a Rule 12(b)(6) motion to dismiss does not need detailed factual allegations, a plaintiff's obligation to provide the "grounds" of his "entitle[ment] to relief" requires more than labels and conclusions, and a formulaic recitation of the elements of a cause of action will not do.

* * *

In applying these general standards to a § 1 claim, we hold that stating such a claim requires a complaint with enough factual matter (taken as true) to suggest that an agreement was made. Asking for plausible grounds to infer an agreement does not impose a probability requirement at the pleading stage; it simply calls for enough fact to raise a reasonable expectation that discovery will reveal evidence of illegal agreement. And, of course, a well-pleaded complaint may proceed even if it strikes a savvy judge that actual proof of those facts is improbable, and "that a recovery is very remote and unlikely." In identifying facts that are suggestive enough to render a § 1 conspiracy plausible, we have the benefit of the prior rulings and considered views of leading commentators, already quoted, that lawful parallel conduct fails to bespeak unlawful agreement. It makes sense to say, therefore, that an allegation of parallel conduct and a bare assertion of conspiracy will not suffice. Without more, parallel conduct does not suggest conspiracy, and a conclusory allegation of agreement at some unidentified point does not supply facts adequate to show illegality. Hence, when allegations of parallel conduct are set out in order to make a § 1 claim, they must be placed in a context that raises a suggestion of a preceding agreement, not merely parallel conduct that could just as well be independent action.

The need at the pleading stage for allegations plausibly suggesting (not merely consistent with) agreement reflects the threshold requirement of Rule 8(a)(2) that the "plain statement" possess enough heft to "sho[w] that the pleader is entitled to relief." A statement of parallel conduct, even conduct consciously undertaken, needs some setting suggesting the agreement necessary to make out a § 1 claim; without that further circumstance pointing toward a meeting of the minds, an account of a defendant's commercial efforts stays in neutral territory. An allegation of parallel conduct is thus much like a naked assertion of conspiracy in a § 1 complaint: it gets the complaint close to stating a claim, but without some further factual enhancement it stops short of the line between possibility and plausibility of "entitle[ment] to relief." Cf. *DM Research, Inc. v. College of Am. Pathologists*, 170 F.3d 53, 56 (C.A.1 1999) ("[T]erms like 'conspiracy,' or even 'agreement,' are border-line: they might well be sufficient in conjunction with a more specific allegation—for example, identifying a written agreement or even a basis for inferring a tacit agreement, ... but a court is not required to accept such terms as a sufficient basis for a complaint").

---

ii. Collusion

A **cartel** is a combination of independent producers attempting to limit competition among themselves by acting together to fix prices, divide markets, or restrict entry into a market. A cartel exists when individual firms collude to act as one firm—as a monopoly—and make price and output decisions that maximize the profits to the industry. Such **collusive behavior** is a major focus of antitrust law because, if successful, it can result in a misallocation of resources similar to that generated by single-firm monopoly behavior.

Palmer v. BRG of Georgia

Supreme Court of the United States
498 U.S. 46 (1990)

PER CURIAM.

In preparation for the 1985 Georgia Bar Examination, petitioners contracted to take a bar review course offered by respondent BRG of Georgia, Inc. (BRG). In this litigation they contend that the price of BRG's course was enhanced by reason of an unlawful agreement between BRG and respondent Harcourt Brace Jovanovich Legal and Professional Publications (HBJ), the Nation's largest provider of bar review materials and lecture services. The central issue is whether the 1980 agreement between respondents violated § 1 of the Sherman Act.[6]

---

6. Section 1 of the Sherman Act, 26 Stat. 209, as amended and set forth in 15 U.S.C. § 1, provides in relevant part:

"Every contract, combination in the form of trust or otherwise, or conspiracy, in restraint of trade or commerce among the several States, or with foreign nations, is declared to be illegal."

HBJ began offering a Georgia bar review course on a limited basis in 1976, and was in direct, and often intense, competition with BRG during the period from 1977 to 1979. BRG and HBJ were the two main providers of bar review courses in Georgia during this time period. In early 1980, they entered into an agreement that gave BRG an exclusive license to market HBJ's material in Georgia and to use its trade name "Bar/Bri." The parties agreed that HBJ would not compete with BRG in Georgia and that BRG would not compete with HBJ outside of Georgia.[7] Under the agreement, HBJ received $100 per student enrolled by BRG and 40% of all revenues over $350. Immediately after the 1980 agreement, the price of BRG's course was increased from $150 to over $400.

On petitioners' motion for partial summary judgment as to the § 1 counts in the complaint and respondents' motion for summary judgment, the District Court held that the agreement was lawful. The United States Court of Appeals for the Eleventh Circuit, with one judge dissenting, agreed with the District Court that *per se* unlawful horizontal price fixing required an explicit agreement on prices to be charged or that one party have the right to be consulted about the other's prices. The Court of Appeals also agreed with the District Court that to prove a *per se* violation under a geographic market allocation theory, petitioners had to show that respondents had subdivided some relevant market in which they had previously competed. The Court of Appeals denied a petition for rehearing en banc that had been supported by the United States.

In *United States v. Socony-Vacuum Oil Co.,* 310 U.S. 150 (1940), we held that an agreement among competitors to engage in a program of buying surplus gasoline on the spot market in order to prevent prices from falling sharply was unlawful, even though there was no direct agreement on the actual prices to be maintained. We explained that "[u]nder the Sherman Act a combination formed for the purpose and with the effect of raising, depressing, fixing, pegging, or stabilizing the price of a commodity in interstate or foreign commerce is illegal *per se.*" *Id.* at 223.

The revenue-sharing formula in the 1980 agreement between BRG and HBJ, coupled with the price increase that took place immediately after the parties agreed to cease competing with each other in 1980, indicates that this agreement was "formed for the purpose and with the effect of raising" the price of the bar review course. It was, therefore, plainly incorrect for the District Court to enter summary judgment in respondents' favor. Moreover, it is equally clear that the District Court and the Court of Appeals erred when they assumed that an allocation of markets or submarkets by competitors is not unlawful unless the market in which the two previously competed is divided between them.

In *United States v. Topco Associates, Inc.,* 405 U.S. 596 (1972), we held that agreements between competitors to allocate territories to minimize competition are illegal:

> One of the classic examples of a *per se* violation of § 1 is an agreement between competitors at the same level of the market structure to allocate territories in order to minimize competition.... This Court has reiterated time and time again

---

We do not reach the other claims alleged in petitioners' nine-count complaint, including violations of § 2 of the Sherman Act, 15 U.S.C. § 2.

7. The 1980 agreement contained two provisions, one called a "Covenant Not to Compete" and the other called "Other Ventures." The former required HBJ not to "directly or indirectly own, manage, operate, join, invest, control, or participate in or be connected as an officer, employee, partner, director, independent contractor or otherwise with any business which is operating or participating in the preparation of candidates for the Georgia State Bar Examination." Plaintiffs' Motion for Partial Summary Judgment, Attachment E, p. 10. The latter required BRG not to compete against HBJ in States in which HBJ currently operated outside the State of Georgia. *Id.* at 15.

that "[h]orizontal territorial limitations ... are naked restraints of trade with no purpose except stifling of competition." Such limitations are *per se* violations of the Sherman Act.

Id. at 608 (citations omitted).

The defendants in *Topco* had never competed in the same market, but had simply agreed to allocate markets. Here, HBJ and BRG had previously competed in the Georgia market; under their allocation agreement, BRG received that market, while HBJ received the remainder of the United States. Each agreed not to compete in the other's territories. Such agreements are anticompetitive regardless of whether the parties split a market within which both do business or whether they merely reserve one market for one and another for the other.[6] Thus, the 1980 agreement between HBJ and BRG was unlawful on its face.

The petition for a writ of certiorari is granted, the judgment of the Court of Appeals is reversed, and the case is remanded for further proceedings consistent with this opinion.

Notes and Questions

1. Agreements on Price: In *Palmer*, BRG argues that their arrangement with HBJ never involved an actual agreement on price. Antitrust law requires violations of the Sherman Act to result from an unlawful agreement. Do you see why their arrangement was still price fixing? Direct competition in the Georgia market for bar review services should bring down prices for law students, something the readers of this textbook would certainly be sympathetic to. By agreeing to clearly divide the markets and avoid competition, these two companies unlawfully created a small monopoly where BRG can raise the price of bar review services. The economic effect is as simple as an artificial reduction in supply that will reduce output and raise prices.

2. Application of the Per Se Rule: In *BRG*, the Supreme Court remands for further proceedings consistent with its opinion. This case will be dealt with on remand under a rule of *per se* illegality. That is, the conduct is inherently harmful and the mere existence of the agreement on price will be enough to find a violation of the antitrust laws. This can be contrasted with the rule of reason, where the plaintiff will have to fulfill a much heavier burden of proving actual harm to consumers through evidence of higher prices or reduced output. Why draw a distinction between the burdens of proof in antitrust cases? The rule of reason is applied to other circumstances in which competitors work together and cooperate through arrangements such as joint ventures, partnerships, and other forms of corporate integration.

The typical cartel is faced with three major problems: (1) agreeing on a common price, (2) dividing the market share among members, (3) discouraging entry, and (4) monitoring the agreement. Looking at the first problem, consider that when a pure monopolist sets price, it only needs to compare its own cost and revenue data. When a cartel attempts to set price, it must aggregate all of the members' cost curves in order to select the profit-maximizing price and output combination. In order for the cartel to be profitable, it requires a restriction in output relative to the quantity the firms were producing when they were competing with one another. The restricted output will lead to a higher price, and the price will be greater than the marginal cost of producing the last unit sold by each firm.

The second problem facing the cartel is the division of the market, because each firm desires to increase its output at the cartel price and thus maximize its own profits. For example, suppose the cartel has agreed to restrict total output by 20%. The most straight-forward solution to this would be for every firm to agree to restrict its output by exactly 20%. However, the firms with the lowest costs of production may argue that they shouldn't have to reduce their output as much because they are more profitable. In other words, it would cost them more to reduce output by 20%. Alternatively, the firms with the highest costs of production might argue that the other firms should absorb most of the restrictions in output because the higher-cost firms need to sell more in order to earn as much from the cartel as do the other firms. There is no way to predict how this conflict will be resolved, but it seems clear that haggling over the division of the market can threaten the formation of a cartel.

Third, cartels must prevent entry by firms that will erode the cartel's monopoly profits. Suppose that firm A wants to enter the automobile market. Firm A's cars are higher quality and lower priced than two of the three firms in an existing cartel of automobile manufacturers and firm A wants to steal business from the incumbent firms and enjoy monopoly profits. The incumbent firms do not want firm A to enter the market so they agree to flood the market with cars or engage in a price war as soon as firm A enters in order to prevent firm A from obtaining enough revenue to offset its costs. Other potential entrants observe how the cartel reacted to firm A's attempted entry and may be deterred from even attempting to enter the market. Of course, there is a limit to how many times the cartel can decrease its prices to ward off entrants before it is unable to recoup enough profits to offset the losses from the price war.

The fourth problem faced by the cartel involves the enforcement of the cartel agreement because there is much to be gained from a member of the cartel cheating on the agreement. Assume that the cartel is formed and that its members have agreed upon a price and the division of the restricted output. The cartel must now deal with the incentive that each member has to cheat on the cartel. In Figure IX-21, the cartel and each firm has agreed to restrict output by 20%—from Q_C to Q_M for the industry and from q^* to q_M for each firm. Restricting output causes price to increase from P_C to P_M. If the cartel agreement works as planned, then each firm earns monopoly profits of abP_CP_M. However, each cartel

Figure IX-21. Individual Firm's Incentive to Cheat Under a Cartel

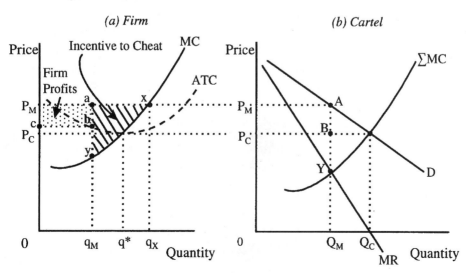

member is aware that the sale of a few additional units at the cartel price, which is well above the marginal cost of producing those additional units, will yield a substantial profit in addition to its cartel (monopoly) profits. That is, on the margin, each individual firm observes that P_M is greater than its marginal cost of producing each unit of output from q_M to q_X. Each firm has the incentive to increase its output to q_X and earn additional profits equal to the area axy. Because the cartelized industry has numerous competitors, each cartel member thinks that its increased output is so small that it will not have an adverse impact on the cartel price and thus will not be detected. For example, suppose that 100 firms form a cartel; a firm with 1 percent of the cartel's market share would not expect to have a significant impact on the total output of the cartel, so the firm has the impression that it can cheat — and earn even higher profits — by increasing its output and still have little chance of detection. The problem for the cartel and its members is that each firm feels that it can get away with the cheating, so everyone cheats and the cartel collapses.

Because of these incentives, economists argue that all cartels are unstable in the long-run. This, however, is not a justification for an antitrust policy that ignores the existence of cartels, because the cartels may impose considerable costs on society before they collapse. Cartels will also attempt to lengthen the life of the cartel through different enforcement mechanisms. In some scenarios where law enforcement is underdeveloped, cartels may be enforced through violence. However, this is not common. Cartels can also be enforced by internally imposed penalties — the agreement could be that if a firm cheats on the cartel, the next year that firm's output is restricted as punishment. The question arises though, what will keep C from cheating again and ignoring the penalty? Firms recognize the benefits of a cartel in the long run and a cheating firm would prefer monopoly profits on a smaller percentage for a short time period as a penalty with a potential of more monopoly profits after the fact instead of operating in a crumbled cartel where each firm is likely earning zero economic profits. This analysis is better understood through the lens of game theory, as discussed in Chapter I.

An understanding of the incentives to cheat on a cartel can also provide some guidance to antitrust authorities about conditions conducive to cartelization and, thus, where to look for collusion. For example, firms in highly concentrated industries are more prone to cartelization because agreements can be more easily formed and policed between a small number of firms. Conversely, as the number of firms in an industry increase, successful cartelization is less likely because it is more difficult to reach agreement, it is more difficult to detect cheating, and there is more incentive to cheat because each firm feels that it will have an inconsequential impact on total output.

Another factor conducive to cartelization is the presence of highly standardized products across firms. Standardized products permit easier monitoring of the cartel agreement. Price differences between firms are not due to differences in quality because of the standardized product, but instead most likely reflect cheating on the cartel arrangement. Firms are not able to raise prices above the cartel price because consumers will switch to other producers. However, if one firm lowers its price, consumers will switch to that producer. The other producers will observe shifts by consumers and, in all likelihood, learn of the lower price and the cheating. Because all producers know they will be detected if they cheat, cheating is less likely. It is interesting to note that the most famous attempt to form a cartel in recent decades, the Organization of Petroleum Exporting Countries (OPEC), has not been successful in setting a uniform price. Saudi Arabia, in particular, consistently undercuts the cartel price.

For more information on what makes a market conducive to coordination, see George J. Stigler, *The Theory of Oligopoly*, 72 J. Pol. Econ. 44 (1964); and Hospital Corporation of America v. FTC, 807 F.2d 1381 (1986) (Posner, J.).

Finally, the existence of a uniform price in an industry is not definitive evidence of the presence of a cartel. The perfectly competitive model of economic theory—the model that is often used as the example of the optimum allocation of resources—also predicts that all firms in an industry will sell at the same price. A major challenge in the application of the antitrust laws is determining whether a certain observed practice is indicative of competition or collusion.

Global Cartels Redux: The Amino Acid Lysine Antitrust Litigation
John M. Connor (1996)

In the evening of June 27, 1995, more than 70 FBI agents simultaneously raided the world headquarters of Archer-Daniels-Midland Company (ADM) in Decatur, Illinois and interviewed a number of ADM officers in their homes. Serving subpoenas authorized by a federal grand jury sitting in Chicago, the agents collected documents related to ADM's lysine, citric acid, and corn sweeteners businesses. Within a day or two, investigators had also raided the offices of four other companies that manufactured or imported lysine. These subpoenaed documents, together with hundreds of secret tape recordings of the conspirators' meetings and conversations, built a strong case that five companies had been illegally colluding on lysine prices around the world for three years.

The FBI raids were widely reported in the mass media and unleashed a torrent of legal actions, some of which were still unresolved seven years later. The three major federal antitrust actions were the result of an undercover investigation by the U.S. Department of Justice (DOJ) that had begun in November 1992 with the cooperation of the ADM lysine-division president. The first suit was a treble-damages class action settled in the summer of 1996. A few months later, the DOJ sought and obtained convictions for criminal price fixing by the five corporate lysine sellers. Although all the corporate members of the cartel pleaded guilty and paid historic fines, not all of the executives who managed the conspiracy were willing to plead guilty. Therefore, the DOJ prosecuted four lysine executives in a highly publicized jury trial held in Chicago in the summer of 1998; three of the four were found guilty and heavily sentenced. The five corporate conspirators were later investigated and fined by the antitrust authorities of Canada, Mexico, Brazil, and the European Union.

Within a year of the FBI raids, more than 40 civil antitrust suits were filed in federal district courts by direct buyers of lysine, each suit incorporating multiple plaintiffs. In early 1996, approximately 400 plaintiffs were certified as a single federal class, and the case called *Amino Acid Lysine Antitrust Litigation* was assigned to a judge of the U.S. District Court of Northern Illinois. In April 1996, the three largest defendants offered the class $45 million to settle the damages allegedly caused by their price fixing. Final approval of the settlement occurred in July 1996. Additional follow-up suits include about 15 actions filed by farmers, consumers and other indirect buyers of lysine in the courts of six states and two Canadian provinces. ADM was further distracted by derivative shareholders' suits charging mismanagement by the company's managers and board of directors.

The three federal lysine cases were important for at least four reasons. First, it was the U.S. Government's first completely successful conviction of a global cartel in more than four decades.

* * *

Second, the conviction of the lysine cartel was the first public manifestation of a sea change in enforcement priorities by U.S. and overseas antitrust officials. Prior to 1995, less than 1 percent of the price-fixing indictments by the DOJ involved at least one non-U.S.-based corporation or non-U.S. resident. By contrast, beginning during 1998–2000 more than half of all criminal price-fixing indictments were brought against international conspirators. The investigation of the lysine cartel led directly to the discovery and successful prosecution of 30 multinational corporations that participated in global price fixing in the markets for lysine, citric acid, sodium gluconate, and ten bulk vitamins. Since 1996, more than a score of global cartels have been uncovered and prosecuted by the DOJ, the Competition Policy Directorate of the European Commission (DG-IV), and other antitrust agencies around the world. Cartel enforcement remains a high priority for the Antitrust Division of the DOJ, which is devoting 30 percent of its resources to criminal price-fixing prosecution.

* * *

Finally, the lysine cases and those that followed soon thereafter showed that the sanctions for criminal price-fixing had escalated enormously in the 1990s. Not only has Congress steadily raised the statutory fine for Sherman Act violations (up to $10 million for corporations), it also in 1994 made criminal antitrust violations felonies instead of misdemeanors. Combined with the U.S. Sentencing Guidelines first promulgated in 1987, corporate price fixers are now liable for criminal penalties as high as "double the harm" caused by a cartel. That is, corporations can be fined by the government up to twice the monopoly overcharge generated by a cartel, an amount that can easily exceed the $10-million statutory cap when market sales are large. ADM, the leader of the lysine cartel, was fined $100 million for its role in two criminal price-fixing schemes — a record amount that was twice eclipsed in the late 1990s by leaders of highly injurious global cartels. In fiscal years 1998–2001, the Antitrust Division collected more than $2 billion in fines for criminal price fixing, of which more than three-fourths was from members of international cartels. The EU's DG-IV, which operates on a somewhat delayed schedule, imposed record fines of 1.84 billion euros on hard-core cartels in 2001 alone; these fines are loosely based on the cartels' overcharges to customers in the European Economic Space. Both U.S. and EU authorities are empowered to base their fines on worldwide overcharges rather than their jurisdictional injuries, and the U.S. DOJ has done so at least twice.

U.S. Government fines are mere paper cuts compared to the financial wounds that may be inflicted by plaintiffs in civil actions. Direct buyers suing in federal courts, the principal focus of this chapter, are entitled to seek treble damages. In some cases, direct buyers abroad are permitted to seek treble damage in U.S. courts. However, antitrust liability does not stop there. Nearly 20 states allow their residents who are *indirect* purchasers to sue in state courts, most of which permit treble damages. In addition, state attorneys general increasingly have banded together to pursue antitrust claims in federal courts (*parens patriae* suits) to recover treble damages for their state governments and for corporate and individual indirect buyers residing in their states. For example, in October 2000, the attorneys general of more than 40 states announced a settlement totaling $340 million to be paid by the six largest members of the vitamins cartels. Not counting the losses associated with derivative shareholders' suits, legal fees, and reputational effects, corporations accused of criminal price fixing now face maximum antitrust liabilities that range from *eight to twelve times* the cartel's U.S. overcharges. The fines and prison terms meted out to cartel managers have also risen.

The major role played by economic analysis in horizontal price-fixing cases is the calculation of the *overcharge* on buyers in markets affected by a cartel. The overcharge is the value of purchases of a cartelized product actually made minus what the sales would have been for the same volume of product absent the cartel. Accurate estimates of conspiracy-induced overcharges are important not only because of recovery of civil damages, but also because overcharges are the basis for the calculation of government fines.

Notes and Questions

1. The Informant: The investigation of the lysine cartel was successful much to the credit of one Mark Whitacre. Whitacre was the president of ADM's bioproducts division and came forward as an informant whose aid to the government was invaluable. The story is more complicated than that and Whitacre's actions are well-documented in Kurt Eichenwald, The Informant: A True Story (2001). These actions have also been chronicled in a popular NPR radio show (see This American Life: The Fix is In, Chicago Public Radio (Sept. 15, 2000)) and a Hollywood big screen adaptation starring Matt Damon. To give you just a taste of the twists and turns of the case read the following description from the Seventh Circuit Court of Appeals:

The Investigation:

Mark E. Whitacre joined ADM in 1989 as president of its bioproducts division. That year, ADM announced that it would enter the lysine market dominated by Asian producers. Whitacre, who held a Ph.D. in biochemistry from Cornell University and degrees in agricultural science, answered directly to Mick Andreas. Just 32 years old when he joined the company, Whitacre's star clearly was rising fast at ADM, and some industry analysts thought he could be the next president of ADM.

In 1992, Whitacre began working with Wilson, and the two attended the first meetings of the lysine producers in Mexico City. Also in 1992, Whitacre began embezzling large sums of money from ADM and eventually stole at least $9 million from the company by submitting to ADM phony invoices for work done by outside companies, who would then funnel the money to Whitacre's personal offshore and Swiss bank accounts. To cover up the embezzlement, Whitacre hatched a scheme in the summer of 1992 to accuse Ajinomoto of planting a saboteur in ADM's Decatur plant. Whitacre would accuse the saboteur of contaminating the delicate bacterial environment needed for the production of lysine, a story made believable because of the many early difficulties the ADM lysine plant encountered.

In accordance with the plot, Whitacre told Mick Andreas that an engineer at Ajinomoto named Fujiwara had contacted him at his home and offered to sell ADM the name of the saboteur in exchange for $10 million. The story was a lie. However, Dwayne Andreas believed it and feared it could jeopardize relations between the United States and Japan. He called the CIA, but the CIA, considering the matter one of federal law enforcement rather than national security, directed the call to the FBI, which sent agents out to ADM to interview Whitacre and other officials about the extortion. Whitacre apparently had not expected this and realized quickly that his lie would be discovered by the FBI, particularly after Special Agent Brian Shepard asked Whitacre if he could tap Whitacre's home telephone to record the next extortion demand. Whitacre knew that when the extortionist failed to call, Shepard would know Whitacre had invented the story. Whitacre confessed the scheme to Shepard, but to save himself, he agreed to become an undercover informant to help the FBI investigate price fixing at ADM. He did not come totally clean with the FBI, however; he failed to mention the millions he embezzled and in fact continued to embezzle after he began working for the government. For the next two-and-a-half years, Whitacre acted as an undercover cooperating witness — legally a government agent — and secretly taped hundreds of hours of conversations and meetings with Wilson, Mick Andreas and the other conspirators. In addition, the FBI secretly videotaped meetings of the lysine producers.

Whitacre made between 120 and 130 tapes for the FBI during the investigation, beginning with a November 9, 1992, conversation with Yamamoto, by using recording equipment, tapes and instruction provided by the government. FBI agents met with Whitacre more than 150 times during the investigation. The tapes were collected and reviewed usually within a day or two of the FBI receiving them, and Department of Justice (DOJ) attorneys regularly participated in reviewing the tapes and monitoring the supervision of Whitacre. However, the FBI's supervision of Whitacre was not flawless. Whitacre was, to say the least, a difficult cooperating witness to handle. Whitacre lied to the FBI during the probe, failed polygraph tests, bragged to his gardener about his role as an FBI mole, all while continuing to embezzle millions of dollars from the company. He even envisioned himself ascending to the ADM presidency as a hero once Andreas, Wilson and Randall were taken down in the FBI sting. In short, he was out of control, and the FBI struggled to keep him on track. Nonetheless, the FBI and the DOJ considered him the best opportunity to stop a massive price-fixing scheme.

Whitacre exercised much discretion in deciding which conversations to record. He was given a tape recorder that could be hidden in his coat breast pocket and another that could be stowed in his briefcase. Agent Shepard showed him how to use the devices and sometimes affixed a recording device to Whitacre's body. Another recording device was used to tap one of Whitacre's home telephones, but not his cellular telephone. All recordings were done with Whitacre's express, signed consent, and all but one were done after Whitacre confessed that his story about a saboteur was a hoax and he began cooperating.

Whitacre was told to record conversations relevant to the conspiracy, but not to record anything about ADM's legitimate business. In direct contravention of the FBI's recording policy, Whitacre did not record many conversations he had with the alleged conspirators. The record shows Whitacre telephoned Ajinomoto and Kyowa 114 times, but 80 were never recorded or documented by the FBI as required. In addition, many conversations with co-defendants Wilson and Andreas were never recorded or documented.

Whitacre once claimed that Shepard ordered him to destroy tapes bearing exculpatory conversations, but Shepard denied this charge and Whitacre later recanted it in a sworn affidavit. Both Whitacre and a friend he entrusted with some of the tapes testified that no tapes were destroyed at Shepard's command. A tape expert testified for the government that none of the tapes exhibited evidence of splicing or alteration and that only a few showed evidence of "bulk erasure" or over-recording. Although that meant that some recordings may have been taped over, the expert expressed an opinion that none of the final recordings had been altered.

Andreas and Wilson moved to suppress the inculpatory tapes before trial and to allow them to introduce evidence that exculpatory tapes had been destroyed.

For reasons explained below, the motion was denied although the trial court found that the FBI's supervision of Whitacre and its blatant inability to follow its own internal policies "border on gross negligence."

United States v. Andreas, 216 F.3d 645, 654–56 (7th Cir. 2000).

2. Other Global Cartels, Vitamins and DRAM: The discovery of such a massive price fixing scheme highlighted the general failure of the government's ability to adequately enforce the antitrust laws. Even the lysine cartel was stumbled onto basically by accident. In an effort to increase the likelihood of discovery the government changed its leniency program to be more effective by making both the individual and the corporation immune from criminal and civil prosecution if an investigation had not already been opened. As the Justice Department describes it, the program "is its most important investigative tool for detecting cartel activity. Corporations and individuals who report their cartel activity and cooperate in the Division's investigation of the cartel reported can avoid criminal conviction, fines, and prison sentences if they meet the requirements of the program." *See* The Antitrust Division's Leniency Program, U.S. Dep't of Justice, available online at http://www.justice.gov/atr/public/criminal/leniency.html.

This change has been credited with helping to increase successful detection of cartels. A small list of cartels that have been uncovered with cooperation through the program include the Vitamins Cartel (garnering over $700 million in U.S. fines), the Dynamic Random Access Memory Cartel (over $600 million in U.S. fines from microchip manufacturing companies), the Graphite Electrodes Cartel (over $350 million in U.S. fines), and the Fine Arts Auctions Cartel (with $45 million in U.S. fines). This strategy has been defined as a carrot and a stick approach, offering harsh fines and jail times for participants and leniency for those who come forward and cooperate.

3. The Rise of Criminal Antitrust: Adam Smith wrote in the Wealth of Nations, his groundbreaking treatise on capitalism, that "people of the same trade seldom meet together, even for merriment and diversion, but the conversation ends in a conspiracy against the public, or in some contrivance to raise prices." The antitrust laws have strived to deter this behavior and have increasingly sought out more strict punishments as a means of enforcement. Recent results have been substantial. Corporate fines increased from $1.6 billion in the 1990s to $4.2 billion in the 2000s. Criminal fines have seen a similar increase. Jail time, representing individual criminal accountability for cartel behavior, has also seen a nearly five-fold increase with the DOJ seeking jail time for more participants and higher profile corporate executives. There has also been a strong expansion of antitrust laws worldwide and greater cooperation between governments to help investigate and bring cartels to justice. For more information, see Scott D. Hammond, The Evolution of Criminal Antitrust Enforcement Over the Last Two Decades, U.S. Dep't of Justice (Feb. 25, 2010), available at http://www.justice.gov/atr/public/speeches/255515.pdf.

4. Apple, eBooks, and Price-Fixing. Consider the recent case of United States v. Apple Inc., 12 CIV. 2826 DLC, 2013 WL 3454986 (S.D.N.Y. July 10, 2013). In this case, Apple Inc. (Apple), a massive U.S. technology company renowned for its personal computers, smart phones (iPhones), personal music players (iPods), electronic tablets (iPads), and other computerized electronic devices, organized a new bookstore for ebooks, which could be read on Apple's new iPad device—an electronic tablet capable of serving as a multi-functional handheld computer and ebook reader. The bookstore offered books from five of the six largest ebook publishers in the U.S. The marker had previously been dominated by Amazon.com Inc. (Amazon).

Amazon offered the Kindle, a handheld ebook reader, and had controlled around 90 percent of ebook sales in the U.S. Amazon priced its books based on the wholesale model, where Amazon purchased the right to sell and determine the final sales price of ebooks. Amazon offered most of its ebooks for the very low price of $9.99 and substantial anecdotal evidence indicated that the ebook publishers believed this price was shockingly low and jeopardized their ability to continue to profitably operate in the market.

The Department of Justice alleged that Apple had organized a price-fixing conspiracy between the five ebook publishers that led to a change from the wholesale model to an agency model where the publishers retained control and conspired to raise the final sales price of ebooks. Having already settled this case with each of the five publishers, the DOJ proceeded to trial against Apple alone and alleged that Apple directly organized a horizontal conspiracy between the publishers.

The DOJ also alleged that Apple negotiated maximum pricing tiers on all ebooks and then imposed a most-favored-nations clause (MFN) that promised that Apple would charge the lowest price that any ebook retailer offered on the market. The effect of the MFN was that if the publishers wanted to raise prices, they had to institute their new and higher pricing scheme on all the other ebook retailers including Amazon, something that happened briefly after the formation of the Apple bookstore. Despite Apple's defense that it did not force the publishers to raise prices and was unaware of the effect the agreement would have on the market, comments from its then-CEO Steve Jobs seemed to indicate that Apple knew exactly what it was doing. The court recounted Jobs' interaction with a reporter after announcing the iBookstore when he was asked:

> [W]hy people would pay $14.99 in the iBookstore to purchase an e-book that was selling at Amazon for $9.99, Jobs told a reporter, "Well, that won't be the case." When the reporter sought to clarify, "You mean you won't be 14.99 or they won't be 9.99?" Jobs paused, and with a knowing nod responded, "The price will be the same," and explained that "Publishers are actually withholding their books from Amazon because they are not happy."

The court then concluded that Apple violated Section 1 of the Sherman Antitrust Act. Consider Apple's arguments that it 1) was vertically related to the publishers, 2) was opening a bookstore that required the participation of multiple competitors, 3) lacked any market power or even a presence in this market prior to the opening of the bookstore, and 4) did not directly set or determine the final prices of ebooks. Is it fair to find Apple liable for an antitrust violation? Many of the publishers argued that Amazon sold ebooks at a loss and that the $9.99 price was too low to operate their business. Accordingly, they contended that any higher prices in the market were reasonable, still very low, and a return to a market clearing equilibrium. If this fact is true does it change the approach to a price-fixing conspiracy? Should it? The DOJ's case drew criticism from commentators who believed that the shift from the wholesale model to the agency model was not one motivated by price but by an industry's desire to retain control over its own final products. Is this kind of pricing model any different from the resale price maintenance in the *Leegin* case? Are there any procompetitive business justifications for using the agency model over the wholesale model? Currently, Apple intends to appeal the decision, if you were the appellate court judge how would you rule? For a more nuanced analysis of this case, see David Bosco, et al., *e-Books and the Boundaries of Antitrust*, 3-2012 Concurrences (Sept. 3, 2012), *available at* http://papers.ssrn.com/sol3/papers.cfm?abstract_id= 2140778.

5. Using Government to Enforce a Cartel. Price fixing is an agreement between individual firms that are competitors for the purpose of setting a specific price, a range of prices, or otherwise raising, depressing or stabilizing the market price. One of the greatest difficulties that cartels face in earning monopoly profits is enforcing the cartel price. Given the difficulty of enforcing the cartel agreement, it is not surprising that many cartels seek government assistance in policing the agreement. In lobbying for the government to help enforce the cartel agreement, cartels often attempt to invoke a public interest rationale.

Consider the case Goldfarb v. Virginia State Bar, 421 U.S. 773 (2004). The Fairfax County State Bar published a minimum fee schedule for all attorney services. Although the Virginia State Bar had never formally punished anyone for violations of the fee schedule they enforced it by publicizing support for the fee schedule and had twice issued ethical opinions making clear that attorneys are not free to ignore the suggested prices. One such opinion stated that "an attorney [who] habitually charges less than the suggested minimum fee schedule adopted by his local bar Association, raises a presumption that such lawyer is guilty of misconduct."

The plaintiffs in the case were a husband and wife who were contracting to buy a house in Fairfax, Virginia. In order to secure financing they were required to secure title insurance and have a title examination done on the property. Only a registered Virginia attorney could legally perform the service. The attorney in question always set his fees in line with the minimum fee schedule. The couple sent letters to 36 other Fairfax County lawyers and found that none that responded offered price lower than the suggested minimum prices of the fee schedule. The couple then brought a class action against the State and County Bar Associations alleging violations of § 1 of the Sherman Act, claiming that the minimum fee schedule was a price-fixing scheme and an agreement between competitors in restraint of trade. The Supreme Court agreed, finding that:

> The County Bar argues that because the fee schedule is merely advisory, the schedule and its enforcement mechanism do not constitute price fixing. Its purpose, the argument continues, is only to provide legitimate information to aid member lawyers in complying with Virginia professional regulations. Moreover, the County Bar contends that in practice the schedule has not had the effect of producing fixed fees. The facts found by the trier belie these contentions, and nothing in the record suggests these findings lack support.
>
> A purely advisory fee schedule issued to provide guidelines, or an exchange of price information without a showing of an actual restraint on trade, would present us with a different question. The record here, however, reveals a situation quite different from what would occur under a purely advisory fee schedule. Here a fixed, rigid price floor arose from respondents' activities: every lawyer who responded to petitioners' inquiries adhered to the fee schedule, and no lawyer asked for additional information in order to set an individualized fee. The price information disseminated did not concern past standards, but rather minimum fees to be charged in future transactions, and those minimum rates were increased over time. The fee schedule was enforced through the prospective professional discipline from the State Bar, and the desire of attorneys to comply with announced professional norms; the motivation to conform was reinforced by the assurance that other lawyers would not compete by underbidding. This is not merely a case of an agreement that may be inferred from an exchange of price information, for here a naked agreement was clearly shown, and the effect on prices is plain.

Moreover, in terms of restraining competition and harming consumers like petitioners the price-fixing activities found here are unusually damaging. A title examination is indispensable in the process of financing a real estate purchase, and since only an attorney licensed to practice in Virginia may legally examine a title, consumers could not turn to alternative sources for the necessary service. All attorneys of course, were practicing under the constraint of the fee schedule. The County Bar makes much of the fact that it is a voluntary organization; however, the ethical opinions issued by the State Bar provide that any lawyer, whether or not a member of his county bar association, may be disciplined for "habitually charg[ing] less than the suggested minimum fee schedule adopted by his local bar Association...." These factors coalesced to create a pricing system that consumers could not realistically escape. On this record respondents' activities constitute a classic illustration of price fixing.

Why does the State Bar Association publish a schedule of suggested minimum fees? In light of the costs imposed upon society by these fees, the answer to this question is very important. The State Bar's Committee on Legal Ethics seems to play a large role in the justification for the minimum fee schedule. What is the ethical justification for the minimum fee schedule? Consider what the Court observes in footnote 16: "The reason for adopting the fee schedule does not appear to have been wholly altruistic. The first sentence in respondent State Bar's 1962 Minimum Fee Schedule Report states: 'The lawyers have slowly, but surely, been committing economic suicide as a profession.'"

How would you characterize the industry structure in *Goldfarb*? The market for legal services is limited to those who have gone to law school and passed a state bar examination. Thus, the number of sellers in the market is limited. Moreover, the State Bar Association could be used as a tool by which attorneys could engage in collusion. For example, the State Bar could help the legal profession act in concert for restriction of output and increased prices. This is one reason that the U.S. Government has kept a close eye on centrally organized professional organizations. The regulation of these organizations is both necessary and beneficial for consumers by maintaining standards and quality yet they also represent a danger of collusion, cartel-behavior, and price-fixing. If you are interested in learning more about these kinds of cases take a look at National Society of Professional Engineers v. United States, 435 U.S. 679 (1978); Federal Trade Commission v. Superior Court Trial Lawyers Association, 493 U.S. 411 (1990); and California Dental Association v. Federal Trade Commission, 526 U.S. 756 (1999).

6. Policing the Cartel: A cartel for legal services would face the same fundamental problem that all cartels face. Each individual attorney has an incentive to cheat by setting his price just below the minimum imposed by the cartel. In this way he can increase the quantity of his services provided and earn a greater portion of the monopoly profits. If enough cheating were to occur, the cartel would fall apart and the attorneys would earn only a normal profit for their services. The challenge to the Bar Association is how to stop individual attorneys from cheating on the cartel. Footnote 4 of the Court's opinion contains a quote from the State Bar Committee on Legal Ethics suggesting that any attorney who lowers his price below the "customary charges" risks violation of ethical canons forbidding solicitation and encroachment. In addition, professional sanctions were available to enforce these "ethical" considerations against those who would cut prices. Moreover, the State Bar's second fee schedule stated that "lawyers should feel free to charge more than the recommended fees; and to avoid condemnation of higher fees charged by some lawyers." What if, hypothetically, the fees on the schedule actually represented the competitive market price for lawyers' services? If the Bar Association could prove that fact would it still be price-fixing? In other words, is price fixing only illegal under the Sherman Act when prices are unreasonable or is the coordination of rivals sufficient to constitute a violation?

iii. Other Horizontal Arrangements and the Rule of Reason

Many agreements among competitors have nothing to do with price fixing or market allocation, but instead are attempts to increase efficiency. For example, the vast majority of mergers—which are agreements among competitors to merge their businesses—are not challenged because they are unlikely to pose a competitive threat and often generate efficiencies that the parties could not achieve absent the merger.

By law, parties to mergers involving assets above a certain threshold must inform the antitrust agencies—the FTC and DOJ—prior to the consummation of the merger. This filing, under the Hart-Scott-Rodino Act,[8] allows the agencies to review these transactions before they occur—thereby providing them an opportunity to prevent any competitive harm that is likely to result. Broadly, the agencies apply a cost benefit test to mergers, weighing likely competitive harms from combining rivals' economic decision-making against efficiencies generated from the transaction. U.S. Dep't of Justice & Fed. Trade Comm'n, Horizontal Merger Guidelines (2010). In 2012, 1,429 transactions were filed with the federal government. This is slightly less than in 2011. Of those mergers, 44 were challenged by either the DOJ or the FTC. The FTC brought 25 actions; 15 led to consent orders for public comment, seven mergers were abandoned or restructured, and 3 resulted in FTC-initiated administrative litigation. The DOJ Antitrust Division challenged 19 mergers; in eight the Antitrust Division filed a complaint in federal district court, of which seven mergers settled and one was abandoned. In the other eleven cases, six mergers were abandoned, two mergers were restructured, and in three the companies altered their conduct to avoid anticompetitive concerns. A full report reviewing these actions is filed annually by the agencies and can be found at U.S. Dep't Justice & Fed. Trade Comm'n, Hart-Scott-Rodino Annual Report: Section 7A of the Clayton Act, Antitrust Improvements Act of 1976 (2012), *available at* http://www.ftc.gov/os/2013/04/130430hsrreport.pdf.

Other types of horizontal agreements fall short of mergers, but are also necessary to create efficiencies. The creation of new information plays an important part in improving our societal standard of living. New medicines lead to healthier and more productive lives. New technologies improve efficiency, reducing the amount of resources consumed in production and, therefore, increasing the scope of activities that can be pursued. However, information is intangible and thus open to easy duplication. The rewards for discovering new information may then be short lived. In other words, despite the costs that one may incur in order to develop new information, the rewards may be easily confiscated by competitors. This fact may serve as a disincentive towards investment in discovering new information. In response to this disincentive, Congress has created statutory patent and copyright laws.

Patents and copyrights provide their holder with a time-constrained monopoly. This time constraint is just as economically important as the original monopoly grant. As discussed in Chapter I, the monopoly grant creates an incentive to invest time and other resources in the production of new information. Limiting the time that the monopoly is "good for" ensures that at some point this information will be handed over to a competitive market. This presents a delicate balancing act. On the one hand, it is desirable to encourage the innovation of new information; on the other hand, enormous benefits emerge from competitive markets.

---

8. 15 USC § 18a.

Broadcast Music, Inc. v. Columbia Broadcasting System, Inc.

Supreme Court of the United States

441 U.S. 1 (1979)

Mr. Justice WHITE delivered the opinion of the Court.

This case involves an action under the antitrust and copyright laws brought by respondent Columbia Broadcasting System, Inc. (CBS), against petitioners, American Society of Composers, Authors and Publishers (ASCAP) and Broadcast Music, Inc. (BMI), and their members and affiliates. The basic question presented is whether the issuance by ASCAP and BMI to CBS of blanket licenses to copyrighted musical compositions at fees negotiated by them is price fixing *per se* unlawful under the antitrust laws.

I

CBS operates one of three national commercial television networks, supplying programs to approximately 200 affiliated stations and telecasting approximately 7,500 network programs per year. Many, but not all, of these programs make use of copyrighted music recorded on the soundtrack. CBS also owns television and radio stations in various cities....

Since 1897, the copyright laws have vested in the owner of a copyrighted musical composition the exclusive right to perform the work publicly for profit, but the legal right is not self-enforcing. In 1914, Victor Herbert and a handful of other composers organized ASCAP because those who performed copyrighted music for profit were so numerous and widespread, and most performances so fleeting, that as a practical matter it was impossible for the many individual copyright owners to negotiate with and license the users and to detect unauthorized uses. "ASCAP was organized as a 'clearing-house' for copyright owners and users to solve these problems" associated with the licensing of music. As ASCAP operates today, its 22,000 members grant it nonexclusive rights to license nondramatic performances of their works, and ASCAP issues licenses and distributes royalties to copyright owners in accordance with a schedule reflecting the nature and amount of the use of their music and other factors.

BMI, a nonprofit corporation owned by members of the broadcasting industry, was organized in 1939, is affiliated with or represents some 10,000 publishing companies and 20,000 authors and composers, and operates in much the same manner as ASCAP. Almost every domestic copyrighted composition is in the repertory either of ASCAP, with a total of three million compositions, or of BMI, with one million.

Both organizations operate primarily through blanket licenses, which give the licensees the right to perform any and all of the compositions owned by the members or affiliates as often as the licensees desire for a stated term. Fees for blanket licenses are ordinarily a percentage of total revenues or a flat dollar amount, and do not directly depend on the amount or type of music used. Radio and television broadcasters are the largest users of music, and almost all of them hold blanket licenses from both ASCAP and BMI. Until this litigation, CBS held blanket licenses from both organizations for its television network on a continuous basis since the late 1940's and had never attempted to secure any other form of license from either ASCAP[9] or any of its members.

The complaint filed by CBS charged various violations of the Sherman Act and the copyright laws. CBS argued that ASCAP and BMI are unlawful monopolies and that the

---

9. Unless the context indicates otherwise, references to ASCAP alone in this opinion usually apply to BMI as well.

blanket license is illegal price fixing, an unlawful tying arrangement, a concerted refusal to deal, and a misuse of copyrights. The District Court, though denying summary judgment to certain defendants, ruled that the practice did not fall within the *per se* rule. After an 8-week trial, limited to the issue of liability, the court dismissed the complaint, rejecting again the claim that the blanket license was price fixing and a *per se* violation of § 1 of the Sherman Act, and holding that since direct negotiation with individual copyright owners is available and feasible there is no undue restraint of trade, illegal tying, misuse of copyrights, or monopolization.

Though agreeing with the District Court's factfinding and not disturbing its legal conclusions on the other antitrust theories of liability, the Court of Appeals held that the blanket license issued to television networks was a form of price fixing illegal *per se* under the Sherman Act. This conclusion, without more, settled the issue of liability under the Sherman Act ... and required reversal of the District Court's judgment, as well as a remand to consider the appropriate remedy.[10]

ASCAP and BMI petitioned for certiorari, presenting the question[] of the applicability of the *per se* rule. ... CBS did not cross petition to challenge the failure to sustain its other antitrust claims. We granted certiorari because of the importance of the issues to the antitrust and copyright laws. Because we disagree with the Court of Appeals' conclusions with respect to the *per se* illegality of the blanket license, we reverse its judgment and remand the cause for further appropriate proceedings.

II

In construing and applying the Sherman Act's ban against contracts, conspiracies, and combinations in restraint of trade, the Court has held that certain agreements or practices are so "plainly anticompetitive," and so often "lack ... any redeeming virtue," that they are conclusively presumed illegal without further examination under the rule of reason generally applied in Sherman Act cases. This *per se* rule is a valid and useful tool of antitrust policy and enforcement. And agreements among competitors to fix prices on their individual goods or services are among those concerted activities that the Court has held to be within the *per se* category. But easy labels do not always supply ready answers.

A

To the Court of Appeals and CBS, the blanket license involves "price fixing" in the literal sense: the composers and publishing houses have joined together into an organization that sets its price for the blanket license it sells. But this is not a question simply of determining whether two or more potential competitors have literally "fixed" a "price." As generally used in the antitrust field, "price fixing" is a shorthand way of describing

---

10. The Court of Appeals went on to suggest some guidelines as to remedy, indicating that despite its conclusion on liability the blanket license was not totally forbidden. The Court of Appeals said: "Normally, after a finding of price-fixing, the remedy is an injunction against the price-fixing—in this case, the blanket license. We think, however, that if on remand a remedy can be fashioned which will ensure that the blanket license will not affect the price or negotiations for direct licenses, the blanket license need not be prohibited in all circumstances. The blanket license is not simply a 'naked restraint' ineluctably doomed to extinction. There is not enough evidence in the present record to compel a finding that the blanket license does not serve a market need for those who wish full protection against infringement suits or who, for some other business reason, deem the blanket license desirable. ... Our objection to the blanket license is that it reduces price competition among the members and provides a disinclination to compete. We think that these objections may be removed if ASCAP itself is required to provide some form of per use licensing which will ensure competition among the individual members with respect to those networks which wish to engage in per use licensing."

certain categories of business behavior to which the *per se* rule has been held applicable. The Court of Appeals' literal approach does not alone establish that this particular practice is one of those types or that it is "plainly anticompetitive" and very likely without "redeeming virtue." Literalness is overly simplistic and often overbroad. When two partners set the price of their goods or services they are literally "price fixing," but they are not *per se* in violation of the Sherman Act. Thus, it is necessary to characterize the challenged conduct as falling within or without that category of behavior to which we apply the label "*per se* price fixing." That will often, but not always, be a simple matter.

Consequently, as we recognized in *United States v. Topco Associates, Inc.,*"[i]t is only after considerable experience with certain business relationships that courts classify them as *per se* violations...." We have never examined a practice like this one before; indeed, the Court of Appeals recognized that "[i]n dealing with performing rights in the music industry we confront conditions both in copyright law and in antitrust law which are *sui generis*." And though there has been rather intensive antitrust scrutiny of ASCAP and its blanket licenses, that experience hardly counsels that we should outlaw the blanket license as a *per se* restraint of trade.

B

* * *

The Department of Justice first investigated allegations of anticompetitive conduct by ASCAP over 50 years ago. A criminal complaint was filed in 1934, but the Government was granted a midtrial continuance and never returned to the courtroom. In separate complaints in 1941, the United States charged that the blanket license, which was then the only license offered by ASCAP and BMI, was an illegal restraint of trade and that arbitrary prices were being charged as the result of an illegal copyright pool. The Government sought to enjoin ASCAP's exclusive licensing powers and to require a different form of licensing by that organization. The case was settled by a consent decree that imposed tight restrictions on ASCAP's operations. Following complaints relating to the television industry, successful private litigation against ASCAP by movie theaters, and a Government challenge to ASCAP's arrangements with similar foreign organizations, the 1941 decree was reopened and extensively amended in 1950.

Under the amended decree, which still substantially controls the activities of ASCAP, members may grant ASCAP only nonexclusive rights to license their works for public performance. Members, therefore, retain the rights individually to license public performances, along with the rights to license the use of their compositions for other purposes. ASCAP itself is forbidden to grant any license to perform one or more specified compositions in the ASCAP repertory unless both the user and the owner have requested it in writing to do so. ASCAP is required to grant to any user making written application a nonexclusive license to perform all ASCAP compositions either for a period of time or on a per-program basis. ASCAP may not insist on the blanket license, and the fee for the per-program license, which is to be based on the revenues for the program on which ASCAP music is played, must offer the applicant a genuine economic choice between the per-program license and the more common blanket license. If ASCAP and a putative licensee are unable to agree on a fee within 60 days, the applicant may apply to the District Court for a determination of a reasonable fee, with ASCAP having the burden of proving reasonableness.

The 1950 decree, as amended from time to time, continues in effect, and the blanket license continues to be the primary instrument through which ASCAP conducts its business under the decree. The courts have twice construed the decree not to require ASCAP to issue licenses for selected portions of its repertory. It also remains true that the decree guarantees the legal availability of direct licensing of performance rights by ASCAP members; and the District Court found, and in this respect the Court of Appeals agreed, that there are no practical impediments preventing direct dealing by the television networks if they so desire. Historically, they have not done so. Since 1946, CBS and other television networks have taken blanket licenses from ASCAP and BMI. It was not until this suit arose that the CBS network demanded any other kind of license.

Of course, a consent judgment, even one entered at the behest of the Antitrust Division, does not immunize the defendant from liability for actions, including those contemplated by the decree, that violate the rights of nonparties. But it cannot be ignored that the Federal Executive and Judiciary have carefully scrutinized ASCAP and the challenged conduct, have imposed restrictions on various of ASCAP's practices, and, by the terms of the decree, stand ready to provide further consideration, supervision, and perhaps invalidation of asserted anticompetitive practices. In these circumstances, we have a unique indicator that the challenged practice may have redeeming competitive virtues and that the search for those values is not almost sure to be in vain. Thus, although CBS is not bound by the Antitrust Division's actions, the decree is a fact of economic and legal life in this industry, and the Court of Appeals should not have ignored it completely in analyzing the practice....

* * *

III

Of course, we are no more bound than is CBS by the views of the Department of Justice, the results in the prior lower court cases, or the opinions of various experts about the merits of the blanket license. But while we must independently examine this practice, all those factors should caution us against too easily finding blanket licensing subject to *per se* invalidation.

A

As a preliminary matter, we are mindful that the Court of Appeals' holding would appear to be quite difficult to contain....

Although the Court of Appeals apparently thought the blanket license could be saved in some or even many applications, it seems to us that the *per se* rule does not accommodate itself to such flexibility and that the observations of the Court of Appeals with respect to remedy tend to impeach the *per se* basis for the holding of liability.

CBS would prefer that ASCAP be authorized, indeed directed, to make all its compositions available at standard per-use rates within negotiated categories of use. But if this in itself or in conjunction with blanket licensing constitutes illegal price fixing by copyright owners, CBS urges that an injunction issue forbidding ASCAP to issue any blanket license or to negotiate any fee except on behalf of an individual member for the use of his own copyrighted work or works. Thus, we are called upon to determine that blanket licensing is unlawful across the board. We are quite sure, however, that the *per se* rule does not require any such holding.

B

In the first place, the line of commerce allegedly being restrained, the performing rights to copyrighted music, exists at all only because of the copyright laws.... Although the copyright laws confer no rights on copyright owners to fix prices among themselves or otherwise to violate the antitrust laws, we would not expect that any market arrangements reasonably necessary to effectuate the rights that are granted would be deemed a *per se* violation of the Sherman Act. Otherwise, the commerce anticipated by the Copyright

Act and protected against restraint by the Sherman Act would not exist at all or would exist only as a pale reminder of what Congress envisioned.

C

More generally, in characterizing this conduct under the *per se* rule, our inquiry must focus on whether the effect and, here because it tends to show effect, the purpose of the practice are to threaten the proper operation of our predominantly free-market economy — that is, whether the practice facially appears to be one that would always or almost always tend to restrict competition and decrease output, and in what portion of the market, or instead one designed to "increase economic efficiency and render markets more, rather than less, competitive."

The blanket license, as we see it, is not a "naked restrain[t] of trade with no purpose except stifling of competition," *White Motor Co. v. United States*, 372 U.S. 253, 263 (1963), but rather accompanies the integration of sales, monitoring, and enforcement against unauthorized copyright use. As we have already indicated, ASCAP and the blanket license developed together out of the practical situation in the marketplace: thousands of users, thousands of copyright owners, and millions of compositions. Most users want unplanned, rapid, and indemnified access to any and all of the repertory of compositions, and the owners want a reliable method of collecting for the use of their copyrights. Individual sales transactions in this industry are quite expensive, as would be individual monitoring and enforcement, especially in light of the resources of single composers. Indeed, as both the Court of Appeals and CBS recognize, the costs are prohibitive for licenses with individual radio stations, nightclubs, and restaurants, and it was in that milieu that the blanket license arose.

A middleman with a blanket license was an obvious necessity if the thousands of individual negotiations, a virtual impossibility, were to be avoided. Also, individual fees for the use of individual compositions would presuppose an intricate schedule of fees and uses, as well as a difficult and expensive reporting problem for the user and policing task for the copyright owner. Historically, the market for public-performance rights organized itself largely around the single-fee blanket license, which gave unlimited access to the repertory and reliable protection against infringement. When ASCAP's major and user-created competitor, BMI, came on the scene, it also turned to the blanket license.

With the advent of radio and television networks, market conditions changed, and the necessity for and advantages of a blanket license for those users may be far less obvious than is the case when the potential users are individual television or radio stations, or the thousands of other individuals and organizations performing copyrighted compositions in public. But even for television network licenses, ASCAP reduces costs absolutely by creating a blanket license that is sold only a few, instead of thousands, of times, and that obviates the need for closely monitoring the networks to see that they do not use more than they pay for. ASCAP also provides the necessary resources for blanket sales and enforcement, resources unavailable to the vast majority of composers and publishing houses. Moreover, a bulk license of some type is a necessary consequence of the integration necessary to achieve these efficiencies, and a necessary consequence of an aggregate license is that its price must be established.

D

This substantial lowering of costs, which is of course potentially beneficial to both sellers and buyers, differentiates the blanket license from individual use licenses. The blanket license is composed of the individual compositions plus the aggregating service.

Here, the whole is truly greater than the sum of its parts; it is, to some extent, a different product. The blanket license has certain unique characteristics: It allows the licensee immediate use of covered compositions, without the delay of prior individual negotiations and great flexibility in the choice of musical material. Many consumers clearly prefer the characteristics and cost advantages of this marketable package, and even small-performing rights societies that have occasionally arisen to compete with ASCAP and BMI have offered blanket licenses. Thus, to the extent the blanket license is a different product, ASCAP is not really a joint sales agency offering the individual goods of many sellers, but is a separate seller offering its blanket license, of which the individual compositions are raw material.[11] ASCAP, in short, made a market in which individual composers are inherently unable to compete fully effectively.

E

Finally, we have some doubt—enough to counsel against application of the *per se* rule—about the extent to which this practice threatens the "central nervous system of the economy," *United States v. Socony-Vacuum Oil Co.*, 310 U.S. 150, 226 n.59 (1940), that is, competitive pricing as the free market's means of allocating resources. Not all arrangements among actual or potential competitors that have an impact on price are *per se* violations of the Sherman Act or even unreasonable restraints. Mergers among competitors eliminate competition, including price competition, but they are not *per se* illegal, and many of them withstand attack under any existing antitrust standard. Joint ventures and other cooperative arrangements are also not usually unlawful, at least not as price-fixing schemes, where the agreement on price is necessary to market the product at all.

Here, the blanket-license fee is not set by competition among individual copyright owners, and it is a fee for the use of any of the compositions covered by the license. But the blanket license cannot be wholly equated with a simple horizontal arrangement among competitors. ASCAP does set the price for its blanket license, but that license is quite different from anything any individual owner could issue. The individual composers and authors have neither agreed not to sell individually in any other market nor use the blanket license to mask price fixing in such other markets. Moreover, the substantial restraints placed on ASCAP and its members by the consent decree must not be ignored. The District Court found that there was no legal, practical, or conspiratorial impediment to CBS's obtaining individual licenses; CBS, in short, had a real choice.

With this background in mind, which plainly enough indicates that over the years, and in the face of available alternatives, the blanket license has provided an acceptable mechanism for at least a large part of the market for the performing rights to copyrighted musical compositions, we cannot agree that it should automatically be declared illegal in all of its many manifestations. Rather, when attacked, it should be subjected to a more discriminating examination under the rule of reason. It may not ultimately survive that attack, but that is not the issue before us today.

IV

As we have noted, the enigmatic remarks of the Court of Appeals with respect to remedy appear to have departed from the court's strict, *per se* approach and to have invited

---

11. Moreover, because of the nature of the product—a composition can be simultaneously "consumed" by many users—composers have numerous markets and numerous incentives to produce, so the blanket license is unlikely to cause a decreased output, one of the normal undesirable effects of a cartel. And since popular songs get an increased share of ASCAP's revenue distributions, composers compete even within the blanket license in terms of productivity and consumer satisfaction.

a more careful analysis. But this left the general import of its judgment that the licensing practices of ASCAP and BMI under the consent decree are *per se* violations of the Sherman Act. We reverse that judgment, ... and remand for further proceedings to consider any unresolved issues that CBS may have properly brought to the Court of Appeals. Of course, this will include an assessment under the rule of reason of the blanket license as employed in the television industry, if that issue was preserved by CBS in the Court of Appeals.

The judgment of the Court of Appeals is reversed, and the cases are remanded to that court for further proceedings consistent with this opinion.

It is so ordered.

Mr. Justice STEVENS, dissenting.

The Court holds that ASCAP's blanket license is not a species of price fixing categorically forbidden by the Sherman Act. I agree with that holding. The Court remands the cases to the Court of Appeals, leaving open the question whether the blanket license as employed by ASCAP and BMI is unlawful under a rule-of-reason inquiry. I think that question is properly before us now and should be answered affirmatively.

* * *

I

* * *

[I]t cannot seriously be questioned ... that ASCAP and BMI have steadfastly adhered to the policy of only offering overall blanket or per-program licenses, notwithstanding requests for more limited authorizations.... It is the refusal to license anything less than the entire repertoire—rather than the decision to offer blanket licenses themselves— that raises the serious antitrust questions in this case.

* * *

Under our prior cases, there would be no question about the illegality of the blanket-only licensing policy if ASCAP and BMI were the exclusive sources of all licenses....

* * *

... But ... ASCAP does not have exclusive control of the copyrights in its portfolio, and it is perfectly possible—at least as a legal matter—for a user of music to negotiate directly with composers and publishers for whatever rights he may desire. The availability of a practical alternative alters the competitive effect of a ... blanket-licensing policy....

[Whether such a policy is unlawful] depends on an evaluation of the effect of the practice on competition in the relevant market. And, of course, it is well settled that a sales practice that is permissible for a small vendor, at least when no coercion is present, may be unreasonable when employed by a company that dominates the market. We therefore must consider what the record tells us about the competitive character of this market.

III

The market for music at issue here is wholly dominated by ASCAP-issued blanket licenses.[12] Virtually every domestic copyrighted composition is in the repertoire of either ASCAP or BMI. And again, virtually without exception, the only means that has been used to secure authority to perform such compositions is the blanket license.

The blanket all-or-nothing license is patently discriminatory. The user purchases full access to ASCAP's entire repertoire, even though his needs could be satisfied by a far more

---

12. As in the majority opinion, my references to ASCAP generally encompass BMI as well.

limited selection. The price he pays for this access is unrelated either to the quantity or the quality of the music he actually uses, or, indeed, to what he would probably use in a competitive system. Rather, in this unique all-or-nothing system, the price is based on a percentage of the user's advertising revenues, a measure that reflects the customer's ability to pay but is totally unrelated to factors—such as the cost, quality, or quantity of the product—that normally affect price in a competitive market. The ASCAP system requires users to buy more music than they want at a price which, while not beyond their ability to pay and perhaps not even beyond what is "reasonable" for the access they are getting, may well be far higher than what they would choose to spend for music in a competitive system. It is a classic example of economic discrimination.

The record plainly establishes that there is no price competition between separate musical compositions. Under a blanket license, it is no more expensive for a network to play the most popular current hit in prime time than it is to use an unknown composition as background music in a soap opera. Because the cost to the user is unaffected by the amount used on any program or on all programs, the user has no incentive to economize by, for example, substituting what would otherwise be less expensive songs for established favorites or by reducing the quantity of music used on a program. The blanket license thereby tends to encourage the use of more music, and also of a larger share of what is really more valuable music, than would be expected in a competitive system characterized by separate licenses. And since revenues are passed on to composers on a basis reflecting the character and frequency of the use of their music, the tendency is to increase the rewards of the established composers at the expense of those less well known. Perhaps the prospect is in any event unlikely, but the blanket license does not present a new songwriter with any opportunity to try to break into the market by offering his product for sale at an unusually low price. The absence of that opportunity, however unlikely it may be, is characteristic of a cartelized rather than a competitive market.

The current state of the market cannot be explained on the ground that it could not operate competitively, or that issuance of more limited—and thus less restrictive—licenses by ASCAP is not feasible. The District Court's findings disclose no reason why music-performing rights could not be negotiated on a per-composition or per-use basis, either with the composer or publisher directly or with an agent such as ASCAP. In fact, ASCAP now compensates composers and publishers on precisely those bases. If distributions of royalties can be calculated on a per-use and per-composition basis, it is difficult to see why royalties could not also be collected in the same way. Moreover, the record also shows that where ASCAP's blanket-license scheme does not govern, competitive markets do. A competitive market for "synch" rights exists,[13] and after the use of blanket licenses in the motion picture industry was discontinued, such a market promptly developed in that industry. In sum, the record demonstrates that the market at issue here is one that could be highly competitive, but is not competitive at all.

IV

Since the record describes a market that could be competitive and is not, and since that market is dominated by two firms engaged in a single, blanket method of dealing, it surely seems logical to conclude that trade has been restrained unreasonably. ASCAP argues, however, that at least as to CBS, there has been no restraint at all since the network is free to deal directly with copyright holders.

---

13. The "synch" right is the right to record a copyrighted song in synchronization with the film or videotape, and is obtained separately from the right to perform the music. It is the latter which is controlled by ASCAP and BMI.

The District Court found that CBS had failed to establish that it was compelled to take a blanket license from ASCAP. While CBS introduced evidence suggesting that a significant number of composers and publishers, satisfied as they are with the ASCAP system, would be "disinclined" to deal directly with the network, the court found such evidence unpersuasive in light of CBS's substantial market power in the music industry and the importance to copyright holders of network television exposure. Moreover, it is arguable that CBS could go further and, along with the other television networks, use its economic resources to exploit destructive competition among purveyors of music by driving the price of performance rights down to a far lower level. But none of this demonstrates that ASCAP's practices are lawful, or that ASCAP cannot be held liable for injunctive relief at CBS's request.

* * *

Far from establishing ASCAP's immunity from liability, these District Court findings, in my judgment, confirm the illegality of its conduct. Neither CBS nor any other user has been willing to assume the costs and risks associated with an attempt to purchase music on a competitive basis. The fact that an attempt by CBS to break down the ASCAP monopoly might well succeed does not preclude the conclusion that smaller and less powerful buyers are totally foreclosed from a competitive market. Despite its size, CBS itself may not obtain music on a competitive basis without incurring unprecedented costs and risks. The fear of unpredictable consequences, coupled with the certain and predictable costs and delays associated with a change in its method of purchasing music, unquestionably inhibits any CBS management decision to embark on a competitive crusade. Even if ASCAP offered CBS a special bargain to forestall any such crusade, that special arrangement would not cure the marketwide restraint.

Whatever management decision CBS should or might have made, it is perfectly clear that the question whether competition in the market has been unduly restrained is not one that any single company's management is authorized to answer.... Even without judicial intervention, the ASCAP monopoly might eventually be broken by CBS, if the benefits of doing so outweigh the significant costs and risks involved in commencing direct dealing. But that hardly means that the blanket-licensing policy at issue here is lawful. An arrangement that produces marketwide price discrimination and significant barriers to entry unreasonably restrains trade even if the discrimination and the barriers have only a limited life expectancy. History suggests, however, that these restraints have an enduring character.

Antitrust policy requires that great aggregations of economic power be closely scrutinized. That duty is especially important when the aggregation is composed of statutory monopoly privileges. Our cases have repeatedly stressed the need to limit the privileges conferred by patent and copyright strictly to the scope of the statutory grant. The record in this case plainly discloses that the limits have been exceeded and that ASCAP and BMI exercise monopoly powers that far exceed the sum of the privileges of the individual copyright holders. Indeed, ASCAP itself argues that its blanket license constitutes a product that is significantly different from the sum of its component parts. I agree with that premise, but I conclude that the aggregate is a monopolistic restraint of trade proscribed by the Sherman Act.

Notes and Questions

1. The Competitive Virtues of Blanket Licensing: Have no doubt that blanket licensing, where a single price is set on access to millions of songs, represents a price fixing agreement between, not one or two competitors, but as the Court put it "some 10,000 publishing companies and 20,000 authors and composers." However the Court, instead of condemning this behavior as one of the largest price fixing schemes in history, endorsed the behavior as beneficial to consumers. In deciding whether to find blanket licenses *per se* unlawful, the Court takes note of the following quote from *United States v. Topco Associates Inc*: "[i]t is only after considerable experience with certain business relationships that courts classify them as *per se* violations." The Court concludes that it has never dealt with practices like those of ASCAP and BMI. However, it finds that the fact that the Antitrust Division of the Department of Justice has issued a consent decree governing the now-challenged practices "[is] a unique indicator that the challenged practice may have some redeeming competitive virtues." What are the redeeming virtues of ASCAP and BMI's challenged practices? The free market is suppressed in favor of some other structural method for making price and output decisions. The blanket licensing agreement in BMI provided an alternative to free market transactions between each individual copyright holder and each firm that wanted to use the copyrighted material. It is possible and in fact likely that ASCAP and BMI were developed and are maintainable because their method for making price and output decisions for copyrighted material is superior to a free market. How can this be?

2. *A New Product Created with the Least Restrictive Means:* The Court notes that in this scheme "the whole is truly greater than the sum of its parts; it is, to some extent, a different product." Why should this matter? The Court draws a line between fixing the price of pre-existing products and creating an entirely new one. So long as the pricing agreement creates something new then the application of the antitrust laws is less strict and uses the more liberal rule of reason. Why should this be so?

The Court also finds it important that "there was no legal, practical, or conspiratorial impediment to CBS's obtaining individual licenses" directly from the artists or publishing companies. If the blanket license had restricted the ability of the artists to sell licenses to their copyrights individually would this case have come out differently?

3. *Transaction Costs Economics:* The field of **transaction costs economics** studies the costs of carrying out certain transactions based upon the type of transaction and the way such transactions are organized. **Transaction costs** are the costs of time, information, contracting and monitoring that are required to execute an exchange. If the goal is to maximize the efficiency by which transactions are made, then it makes sense to utilize the structure that minimizes transaction costs. In this light, when transaction costs are minimized by allocation through a free market, then that structure will be used. However, when transaction costs are minimized by using some other formal structure, then a free market may no longer be superior. The Court finds that a blanket fee lowers transaction costs because the costs of negotiating with thousands of different artists would be prohibitive. What are the transaction costs involved in buying the right to use copyrighted material? Would market exchange or ASCAP's current method minimize these transaction costs? Can you think of an even more efficient method for the copyright use market?

4. *Developing the Rights of Copyright Holders:* The benefits of intellectual property rights were discussed just prior to the *BMI* case. As a result of these benefits, Congress has enacted patent and copyright laws. These laws are supposed to encourage the development of new creations and information by granting a time constrained monopoly. Moreover, these laws also protect the rights of the creators to their monopoly. Part of the Court's decision in *BMI* relied on the fact that, absent ASCAP and BMI's blanket licensing agreement, copyright holders would have a difficult time marketing their products and enforcing their rights against infringement. That is, individual negotiation and enforcement

would be very costly both to the copyright holders and users. Thus, the blanket licensing agreement seems to encourage the sale and use of copyrighted material in conjunction with a cost effective method for enforcing the copyrights. Moreover, those copyright holders or potential users who found individual negotiation to be more cost efficient were not foreclosed from using market mechanisms. In other words, the Court found the blanket licensing price restraint to be a necessary component in further developing the goals of copyright laws. Can you think of an alternative for marketing individual copyrights that is more in line with the model of pure competition? Will technology have an effect on the necessity of the blanket licensing agreement in supporting trade? Is there any other way for individual copyright holders to enforce their monopoly rights?

5. "Inherently Suspect" Restraints and the Rule of Reason: Some arrangements among competitors fall short of the naked price fixing or market allocations subject to per se condemnation, but nonetheless pose serious competitive consequences. In these circumstances, courts require defendants to explain the efficiency justifications for the agreement before the court proceeds to a rule of reason balancing. If the defendant cannot carry its burden of persuasion, the practice is condemned. Courts have employed this analysis in restraints involving advertising. See Polygram Holding, Inc. v. F.T.C., 416 F.3d 29 (D.C. Cir. 2005) and Realcomp II, Ltd. v. F.T.C., 635 F.3d 815 (6th Cir. 2011). Does this approach make sense?

Chapter X

Principles of Valuation

Market prices are often viewed as the best measure of the value of a good or service. Because market prices can be determined objectively and generally cannot be manipulated, they are often relied upon to generate unbiased, independent measures of value. Obviously, market prices are important in many legal contexts, whether they are used for filling gaps in contracts or determining the appropriate compensation for governmental takings of property. However, in many legal situations, adequate market indicators are not available and surrogates for market value must be calculated. This chapter focuses on the concept of **the time value of money**—that cash flows received at earlier points in time are worth more than cash flows received at later points in time. Among these concepts are prejudgment interest calculations—the methodology for determining the value today of money lost in the past—and present value calculations—the methodology for determining the value today of payments to be received in the future.

Section A considers prejudgment interest calculations and explains what the interest rate in the calculations represents. Section B discusses discounting of future payments into present values and demonstrates how those general principles are applied in lawsuits by focusing on the determination of the relevant future stream of dollars and the selection of the proper discount rate. Section C considers two methodologies that courts apply in determining the value of life. Finally, Section D demonstrates how to value close corporations using two different approaches.

A. Prejudgment Interest

Prejudgment interest is interest accruing on the amount of a legal award from the time of the injury or damage to the time the judgment is entered by the court. It compensates a plaintiff for the loss of the use of funds and the effects of inflation after she suffered a cognizable economic harm caused by the defendant. Prejudgment interest is necessary to fully compensate plaintiffs because of the time value of money. If the plaintiff had never suffered economic damages, she could have instead invested that money and earned income or interest.

Prejudgment interest is calculated as a small percentage tacked onto the principal award. For example, if only one year has elapsed between injury and judgment, the economic damages are $1,000,000 and the relevant interest rate is 4%, then the prejudgment interest would be $1,000,000 × .04 = $40,000. Thus, the plaintiff's total award would be $1,040,000.

What if four years elapsed between injury and judgment? Courts are split on whether they use simple or compound interest to compute prejudgment interest. Simple interest is interest paid on the original principal award only. Thus, if the prejudgment interest was $40,000 a year and four years elapsed between injury and judgment, the total prejudgment interest award would be $160,000, and the total damage award would be $1,160,000. Compound interest is interest earned not only on the original principal, but also on all interest amounts earned previously. If we assume that interest compounds once per year, then we can use a simple formula for future value calculations to compute the total damage award to the plaintiff:

$$FV = P \times (1+I)^n$$

where

P = the principal award

I = the relevant interest rate in the economy (assumed constant)

n = the number of years elapsed

FV = the future value or total damage award

In our example, the plaintiff's total award would be $1,169,859 ($1,000,000 × 1.04^4).

As the amount of damages and length of time between injury and judgment increases, the amount of prejudgment interest increases. Similarly, slight changes in the interest rate can have significant impacts on the prejudgment interest award. If the interest rate in the above calculation had been 8% instead of 4%, the plaintiff's award would have been $1,360,489 ($1,000,000 × 1.08^4), a difference of over $190,000!

Yet despite the importance of prejudgment interest, there is no uniform method for determining it. Many jurisdictions have strict statutory or common law prescriptions on both when prejudgment interest is awarded and the interest rate used in the calculations. Other jurisdictions give courts discretion on whether to award it and how to calculate it. In these jurisdictions, courts have grappled with what the interest rate should represent. Should it reflect the interest that the plaintiff could have earned on her money, or the risk of the defendant's default?

Gorenstein Enterprises, Inc. v. Quality Care-USA, Inc.

United States Court of Appeals for the Seventh Circuit
874 F. 2d 431 (1989)

POSNER, Circuit Judge.

This protracted litigation over a franchise resulted in a resounding defeat for the franchisee and its principals — the Gorenstein brothers. Substantial and experienced businessmen who own and operate several nursing homes in the Chicago area, they had obtained a franchise in 1978 from Quality Care-USA to provide home health care services in the Chicago area under Quality Care's registered trademark. Home health care services involve the provision of nursing and other medical care in the home rather than in an institution. Licensed home health care providers can provide some services that unlicensed ones cannot; the parties disagree over whether Quality Care undertook as part of its deal with the Gorensteins to obtain a license for the franchised operation.

Shortly after obtaining the franchise from Quality Care the Gorensteins defaulted on their royalty obligations, and in 1980 Quality Care terminated the Gorensteins' franchise and demanded that they cease using the Quality Care trademark forthwith. Ignoring the demand, the Gorensteins instead sued Quality Care in an Illinois state court, seeking rescission of the franchise agreement....

* * *

Quality Care's case then went to the jury, which found in its favor and awarded damages. The judge trebled the jury's award of damages for trademark infringement, and also awarded Quality Care attorney's fees on the entire judgment, plus prejudgment interest, at 9 percent per annum, on the award of trademark damages (untrebled), making a grand total that with postjudgment interest is now approaching $900,000.

* * *

There is no federal statutory interest rate on prejudgment interest. But as the 9 percent figure used by the district judge was well below the average interest rate for "securities" comparable in riskiness to Quality Care's cause of action for trademark infringement against the Gorensteins, he can hardly be criticized for setting too high a rate. Surely the rate was too low; there were times while this suit was pending when the prime rate exceeded 20 percent. For the future, we suggest that district judges use the prime rate for fixing prejudgment interest where there is no statutory interest rate. That is a readily ascertainable figure which provides a reasonable although rough estimate of the interest rate necessary to compensate plaintiffs not only for the loss of the use of their money but also for the risk of default. The defendant who has violated the plaintiff's rights is in effect a debtor of the plaintiff until the judgment is entered and paid or otherwise collected. At any time before actual payment or collection of the judgment the defendant may default and the plaintiff come up empty-handed. The plaintiff is an unsecured, uninsured creditor, and the risk of default must be considered in deciding what a compensatory rate of interest would be.

A federal statute, 28 U.S.C. Sec. 1961, fixes the post judgment interest rate for federal cases (including diversity cases) as the rate on 52-week Treasury bills at the last auction of those bills before the judgment was entered. This rate is too low, because there is no default risk with Treasury bills. Of course the courts are bound by that rate so far as post-judgment interest is concerned. But prejudgment interest is governed by federal common law, and the courts are free to adopt a more discriminating approach. We have chosen the prime rate for convenience; a more precise estimate would be the interest rate paid by the defendant for unsecured loans. We do not want to straitjacket the district judges but we do want to caution them against the danger of setting prejudgment interest rates too low by neglecting the risk, often nontrivial, of default.

* * *

Notes and Questions

1. Posner and Interest Rates: Why does Posner believe the interest rate paid by the defendant for unsecured loans is the precise rate to use? Consider our discussion of risk and market prices in Chapter VI.

2. Back-Door Prejudgment Interest: Suppose a plaintiff had to take out a loan as a result of suffering economic harm caused by the defendant. If the court awards the interest paid on the loan as part of the plaintiff's damage award, is that different from an award of prejudgment interest? Consider the following opinion:

United Telecommunications, Inc. v. American Television and Communications Corp.

United States Court of Appeals for the Tenth Circuit
536 F.2d 1310 (1976)

William E. Doyle, Circuit Judge.

Involved here is the exchange of an interest in Jefferson-Carolina Corp., a cable television company, by United Telecommunications, Inc. ("United") for 175,000 shares of American Television & Communications Corp. ("ATC").

... The purchase agreement between United and ATC ... outlined the basic terms, that is, that United would receive 175,000 unregistered shares of ATC. The agreement also gave United the right to demand registration of these shares any time after the transaction was closed. Upon the making of such a call by United, ATC undertook to use its "best efforts" to obtain registration by preparing and filing a registration statement and by causing the statement to become and remain effective....

* * *

The essence of this action by United is that ATC failed to use its best efforts to register United's ATC shares.... The claim was for $9.6 million in damages. However, the jury awarded a lesser amount, $2,021,500.

ATC's appeal is based on the ... contention[] [t]hat it was error for the court to charge the jury that United was entitled to recover interest costs or borrowing costs or expenses which allegedly it paid as a result of failure of ATC to use its best efforts to bring about the registration....

WHETHER UNITED WAS ENTITLED TO RECOVER INTEREST AS DAMAGES

At the trial United presented testimony which showed the amount of its borrowing costs and the nexus between these costs and the breach of ATC. United also presented testimony showing that ATC was aware before entering into the agreement that United had planned to convert the ATC stock to cash and would use that cash to reduce its short-term debts. Evidence was also offered to show that parties were aware that registration was necessary in order to have a successful public sale of the stock and that they also were aware that a private sale could be obtained only at a significant discount. For this element of damage United claimed the sum of $1.6 million.

The trial court explained to the jury that the plaintiff was claiming that it suffered an additional direct loss "by being unable to reduce its short-term debt by the amount of money which it would have received on the sale to the public of the registered shares of ATC stock." The trial court also explained that the claim was that the cost of continued borrowing was a part of actual damages from the breach....

ATC maintains that this instruction was erroneous. Its argument is that the instruction allowed United to recover prejudgment interest, and that applicable Colorado law bars such interest. United responds that this is not prejudgment interest in that it is not the kind of interest contemplated by the Colorado statutes and, instead, it is, according to United, borrowing costs which are recoverable like any other element of contract damage.

In general, we agree with the United argument and with the position taken by the trial court that interest as an item of damage or loss related to the substantive claim differs from interest measured by a percentage of the judgment. In our view the kind of interest that was here awarded is not barred or limited by the Colorado interest statute and the Colorado cases. Here our concern is with United's borrowing costs and expenses. The

Colorado statute does not deal with interest charges which arise from an independent debt owed by the plaintiff to a third party....

Had United claimed damages of $8 million for lost market value stemming from the stock not being registered together with interest measured by a percentage of that loss, the claim would have been one for prejudgment interest subject to the limitations of Colorado law. When United claims, however, that it is entitled to recover from ATC expenses which resulted from interest which it was obligated to pay on money which it was required to borrow as a result of ATC's unwarranted delays and manipulations, a wholly different theory is presented. This latter type of interest is not regulated by the Colorado interest statute.

B. Discounted Present Value

Discounting is a method of translating a flow of future dollars into its current worth. For example, suppose a smooth-talking, high-pressure defense attorney has offered your client a settlement in a personal injury case of $20,000 a year for the rest of your client's life and the rest of her children's lives. The defense attorney claims that the payments could easily last 50 years. The $20,000 can thus be considered an annuity—a constant payment for a fixed period of time. Your client is 45, but she has two children in their twenties. The defense attorney exclaims that the settlement could result in "payments totaling more than $1 million!" Prior to this offer, you advised your client that she should accept any settlement worth more than $250,000. In fact, on your advice, she has already rejected a $200,000 settlement. Is the new offer acceptable? What do you advise your client to do?

To decide how much the offered annuity is worth, you need some way of valuing the $20,000 per year. It is incorrect to calculate the total value of the payments by simply adding up the $20,000 fifty times. In fact, to do so could result in a terrible injustice for your client and could even be considered malpractice. The reason is that such a calculation ignores the time value of money. The $20,000 your client receives this year will be worth more than the $20,000 she receives next year. And next year's $20,000 will be worth more than the following year's $20,000, and so on. How much less depends on several factors that we will discuss in this chapter. So instead of just adding up the $20,000 fifty times, you must discount all future dollars by the appropriate discount rate. Discounting is required because a dollar in the future is worth less than a dollar now.

Present value calculations are used to determine the difference in present value versus future value. The reasons for this difference in value are best explained by considering your personal preferences when given the choice between receiving a dollar today or a dollar exactly one year from today. First, a dollar is worth less in the future than today because of opportunity costs. During the interim period between today and when you expect to receive the dollar in the future you are not able to enjoy the consumption benefits of whatever the dollar could have purchased today. Even if you do not spend the dollar in the interim period, you had the choice to spend, save, or invest, and generally, more choices or opportunities are preferred to fewer. Second, inflation may erode the value of money in that the dollar today has greater purchasing power. Third, a dollar today may earn interest in a savings account, or other investment, and thus total more than one dollar a year from now. Alternatively, if you wish to borrow money today in exchange for a promise to pay one dollar a year from now, the amount lenders would be willing to lend is less than one dollar. The difference between the dollar you wish to repay and the amount investors are willing to give you today for the dollar in the future can also be viewed in terms of opportunity costs. If investors or lenders give you an amount of money today they are no longer able to invest or lend that money to anyone else. Finally, there may be some risk of loss, in other words, that some unforeseen contingency will occur and prevent the payment of a dollar a year from now. As the saying goes: "A bird in the hand is worth two in the bush."

If you have $1 now, you can take that dollar, put it in the bank, and in a year you will have that dollar plus interest. For example, if the interest rate you can get from the bank is 5 percent, then the dollar will grow to $1.05 a year from now. That also means that if the interest rate in the economy is 5 percent, if you have 95 cents now, in a year it will be worth $.9975 (5% × $0.95 = $0.0475). Reversing the reasoning, $1 one year in the future is worth approximately 95 cents today. So the present value of $1 one year in the future at 5 percent interest is approximately 95 cents.

A dollar two years from now is worth even less today. Carry out that same reasoning and you'll see that if the interest rate is 5 percent, $1 two years from now is worth approximately 90 cents today. You could put 90 cents in the bank now at 5 percent interest, and in two years have $1.

1. The Present Value Formula

Carrying out such reasoning for every case would be very time consuming. Fortunately, there is a simple formula that can be used to determine the present value (PV) of future income. The formula is:

$$PV = A_1/(1+I) + A_2/(1+I)^2 + A_3/(1+I)^3 + \ldots + A_n/(1+I)^n$$

where

A_n = the amount of money received in period n in the future

I = the interest rate in the economy (assumed constant)

Still, solving this formula for any time period longer than two or three years can be very tedious. The easiest way to solve the formula is to use a spreadsheet, a multifunction financial calculator, or a present-value table like that in Table X-1.

Table X-1 gives the present value of a single dollar at some time in the future at various interest rates. The table reveals two important relationships that should become an intuitive part of your understanding of present value. First, the further into the future one goes, the lower the present value. Second, the higher the interest rate, the lower the present value.

Table X-2 shows the impact of compound interest over time. Compound interest accrues when interest is earned on the interest earned from a prior period. For example, at a 10 percent interest rate, $1 earns $0.10 per year. If the $0.10 is compounded at the end of the first year, interest for the second year is earned on $1.10. So, the interest earned for the second year is $0.11. As indicated in Table X-2, the value of $1 after earning 10 percent interest for 2 years is $1 + $0.10 + $0.11 = $1.21.

Table X-3 is an annuity table; it tells us how much a constant stream of payments for a specific number of years is worth. Notice that as the interest rate rises, the value of an annuity falls. At a 10 percent interest rate, $1 per year for 50 years has a present value of $9.91, while at a 15 percent interest rate, $1 per year for 50 years has a present value of $6.60. To get the value of amounts other than $1, you simply multiply the entry in the table by the amount of the annuity. For example, using the information from the settlement offer discussed at the start of this section, and assuming a 15 percent interest rate, $20,000

Table X-1. Present Value of a Future $1: What a Dollar at End of Future Year Is Worth Today

Year	3%	4%	5%	6%	7%	8%	10%	12%	15%	20%
1	0.971	0.962	0.952	0.943	0.935	0.926	0.909	0.893	0.870	0.833
2	0.943	0.925	0.907	0.890	0.873	0.857	0.826	0.797	0.756	0.694
3	0.915	0.889	0.864	0.840	0.816	0.794	0.751	0.712	0.658	0.579
4	0.888	0.855	0.823	0.792	0.763	0.735	0.683	0.636	0.572	0.482
5	0.863	0.822	0.784	0.747	0.713	0.681	0.621	0.567	0.497	0.402
6	0.837	0.790	0.746	0.705	0.666	0.630	0.564	0.507	0.432	0.335
7	0.813	0.760	0.711	0.665	0.623	0.583	0.513	0.452	0.376	0.279
8	0.789	0.731	0.677	0.627	0.582	0.540	0.467	0.404	0.327	0.233
9	0.766	0.703	0.645	0.592	0.544	0.500	0.424	0.361	0.284	0.194
10	0.744	0.676	0.614	0.558	0.508	0.463	0.386	0.322	0.247	0.162
11	0.722	0.650	0.585	0.527	0.475	0.429	0.350	0.287	0.215	0.135
12	0.701	0.625	0.557	0.497	0.444	0.397	0.319	0.257	0.187	0.112
13	0.681	0.601	0.530	0.469	0.415	0.368	0.290	0.229	0.163	0.0935
14	0.661	0.577	0.505	0.442	0.388	0.340	0.263	0.205	0.141	0.0779
15	0.642	0.555	0.481	0.417	0.362	0.315	0.239	0.183	0.123	0.0649
16	0.623	0.534	0.458	0.394	0.339	0.292	0.218	0.163	0.107	0.0541
17	0.605	0.513	0.436	0.371	0.317	0.270	0.198	0.146	0.0929	0.0451
18	0.587	0.494	0.416	0.350	0.296	0.250	0.180	0.130	0.0808	0.0376
19	0.570	0.475	0.396	0.331	0.277	0.232	0.164	0.116	0.0703	0.0313
20	0.554	0.456	0.377	0.312	0.258	0.215	0.149	0.104	0.0611	0.0261
25	0.478	0.375	0.295	0.233	0.184	0.146	0.0923	0.0588	0.0304	0.0105
30	0.412	0.308	0.231	0.174	0.131	0.0994	0.0573	0.0334	0.0151	0.0042
40	0.307	0.208	0.142	0.0972	0.067	0.0460	0.0221	0.0107	0.00373	0.00068
50	0.228	0.141	0.087	0.0543	0.034	0.0213	0.00852	0.00346	0.000923	0.000110

per year for 50 years has a present value of $132,000. If you had told your client to accept the offer, you might be guilty of malpractice. The interest rate would have to be below eight percent in order for the present value to rise to $250,000.

2. Rules of Thumb for Determining Present Value

Most lawyers don't carry financial calculators or present value tables with them. Fortunately, a few simple rules of thumb can serve as initial guides to present value calculations. The two most useful rules are the Perpetuity Rule and the Rule of 72.

a. The Perpetuity Rule

A perpetuity is an annuity that pays the same amount every year forever. To find the present value of an annuity that will pay $1 per year for an infinite number of years in the future when the interest rate is 5 percent, simply divide $1 by 5 percent (0.05), which yields a present value of $20. The general perpetuity rule for an annuity of any amount is:

$$PV = X \div I$$

That is, the present value of an infinite flow of income, X, is that income divided by the interest rate, I.

Table X-2. Impact of Compound Interest Over Time

Year	3%	4%	5%	6%	7%	8%	10%	12%	15%	20%
1	1.03	1.04	1.05	1.06	1.07	1.08	1.10	1.12	1.15	1.20
2	1.06	1.08	1.10	1.12	1.14	1.17	1.21	1.25	1.32	1.44
3	1.09	1.12	1.16	1.19	1.23	1.26	1.33	1.40	1.52	1.73
4	1.13	1.17	1.22	1.26	1.31	1.36	1.46	1.57	1.75	2.07
5	1.16	1.22	1.28	1.34	1.40	1.47	1.61	1.76	2.01	2.49
6	1.19	1.27	1.34	1.42	1.50	1.59	1.77	1.97	2.31	2.99
7	1.23	1.32	1.41	1.50	1.61	1.71	1.95	2.21	2.66	3.58
8	1.27	1.37	1.48	1.59	1.72	1.85	2.14	2.48	3.06	4.30
9	1.30	1.42	1.55	1.69	1.84	2.00	2.36	2.77	3.52	5.16
10	1.34	1.48	1.63	1.79	1.97	2.16	2.59	3.11	4.05	6.19
11	1.38	1.54	1.71	1.90	2.10	2.33	2.85	3.48	4.65	7.43
12	1.43	1.60	1.80	2.01	2.25	2.52	3.14	3.90	5.35	8.92
13	1.47	1.67	1.89	2.13	2.41	2.72	3.45	4.36	6.15	10.70
14	1.51	1.73	1.98	2.26	2.58	2.94	3.80	4.89	7.08	12.84
15	1.56	1.80	2.08	2.40	2.76	3.17	4.18	5.47	8.14	15.41
16	1.60	1.87	2.18	2.54	2.95	3.43	4.59	6.13	9.36	18.49
17	1.65	1.95	2.29	2.69	3.16	3.70	5.05	6.87	10.76	22.19
18	1.70	2.03	2.41	2.85	3.38	4.00	5.56	7.69	12.38	26.62
19	1.75	2.11	2.53	3.03	3.62	4.32	6.12	8.61	14.23	31.95
20	1.81	2.19	2.65	3.21	3.87	4.66	6.73	9.65	16.37	38.34
25	2.09	2.67	3.39	4.29	5.43	6.85	10.83	17.00	32.92	95.40
30	2.43	3.24	4.32	5.74	7.61	10.06	17.45	29.96	66.21	237.38
40	3.26	4.80	7.04	10.29	14.97	21.72	45.26	93.05	267.86	1,469.77
50	4.38	7.11	11.47	18.42	29.46	46.90	117.39	289.00	1,083.66	9,100.44

Most of the time, people don't offer to sell annuities for the infinite future. A typical annuity runs for 30, 40, or 50 years. However, the perpetuity rule is still useful because it serves as a reality check on other present value calculations. We can use the perpetuity rule as an approximation of long-lasting, but less than infinite, flows of future income because the longer the time period, the closer the perpetuity rule is to the actual present value. Dollars way off in the future are not worth much — as you can see from Table X-1, in 30 years at a 10 percent interest rate, the present value of $1 is only 5.73 cents. Returning to the example at the start of this section, and assuming that the interest rate is 10 percent, then the present value of the $20,000 per year for fifty years must be less than $200,000 (= $20,000 ÷ 0.10), the present value of $20,000 in perpetuity. In fact, according to Table X-3 the present value is $198,200 (= $20,000 × 9.91).

b. The Rule of 72

A rule of thumb for determining present value across shorter time periods is the rule of 72, which states:

> The number of years it takes for a certain amount to double in value is equal to 72 divided by the rate of interest.

If the interest rate is 4 percent, how long will it take for your $100 to become worth $200? Dividing 72 by 4 yields 18. So, the present value of $200 at a 4 percent interest rate 18

Table X-3. Present Value of Annuity of $1, Received at End of Each Year

Year	3%	4%	5%	6%	7%	8%	10%	12%	15%	20%
1	0.97	0.96	0.95	0.94	0.93	0.93	0.91	0.89	0.87	0.83
2	1.91	1.89	1.86	1.83	1.81	1.78	1.74	1.69	1.63	1.53
3	2.83	2.78	2.72	2.67	2.62	2.58	2.49	2.40	2.28	2.11
4	3.72	3.63	3.55	3.47	3.39	3.31	3.17	3.04	2.85	2.59
5	4.58	4.45	4.33	4.21	4.10	3.99	3.79	3.60	3.35	2.99
6	5.42	5.24	5.08	4.92	4.77	4.62	4.36	4.11	3.78	3.33
7	6.23	6.00	5.79	5.58	5.39	5.21	4.87	4.56	4.16	3.60
8	7.02	6.73	6.46	6.21	5.97	5.75	5.33	4.97	4.49	3.84
9	7.79	7.44	7.11	6.80	6.52	6.25	5.76	5.33	4.77	4.03
10	8.53	8.11	7.72	7.36	7.02	6.71	6.14	5.65	5.02	4.19
11	9.25	8.76	8.31	7.89	7.50	7.14	6.50	5.94	5.23	4.33
12	9.95	9.39	8.86	8.38	7.94	7.54	6.81	6.19	5.42	4.44
13	10.63	9.99	9.39	8.85	8.36	7.90	7.10	6.42	5.58	4.53
14	11.30	10.56	9.90	9.29	8.75	8.24	7.37	6.63	5.72	4.61
15	11.94	11.12	10.38	9.71	9.11	8.56	7.61	6.81	5.85	4.68
16	12.56	11.65	10.84	10.11	9.45	8.85	7.82	6.97	5.95	4.73
17	13.17	12.17	11.27	10.48	9.76	9.12	8.02	7.12	6.05	4.77
18	13.75	12.66	11.69	10.83	10.06	9.37	8.20	7.25	6.13	4.81
19	14.32	13.13	12.09	11.16	10.34	9.60	8.36	7.37	6.20	4.84
20	14.88	13.59	12.46	11.47	10.59	9.82	8.51	7.47	6.26	4.87
25	17.41	15.62	14.09	12.78	11.65	10.67	9.08	7.84	6.46	4.95
30	19.60	17.29	15.37	13.76	12.41	11.26	9.43	8.06	6.57	4.98
40	23.11	19.79	17.16	15.05	13.33	11.92	9.78	8.24	6.64	5.00
50	25.73	21.48	18.26	15.76	13.80	12.23	9.91	8.30	6.66	5.00

years in the future is about $100. Actually, according to Table X-1, it's $98.80 (0.494 × $200). Thus, the Rule of 72 gets you pretty close to the correct answer.

Alternatively, say that you will receive $1,000 in 10 years. Would you accept $500 for that amount now if the interest rate is 8 percent? Using the rule of 72, we know that at an 8 percent interest rate it will take about nine years (72 ÷ 8 = 9) for $500 to double. Thus, the future value of $500 today is more than the $1,000 in ten years. In fact, using Table X-2, we know that the $500 dollars today will be worth $1,080 (2.16 × $500) in ten years. You should therefore accept the $500.

3. Discounting and Litigation

There are two major components to present value calculations, the future dollars (future economic benefits) and the interest rate. Both of these are extremely important to lawyers. Much litigation deals with determining the present value of lost earnings, future profits, and structured settlements. This section focuses on how courts determine the relevant future stream of income or damages, as well as which interest rate should be used in the present value calculation of some identified stream of dollars.

a. Determining the Relevant Future Stream of Economic Benefits

Haugan v. Haugan

Supreme Court of Wisconsin

343 N.W.2d 796 (1984)

Abrahamson, J.

This is a review of an unpublished decision of the court of appeals filed April 26, 1983, ... affirming a division of property in a judgment of divorce of the circuit court for Brown County, Charles E. Kuehn, Circuit Judge. The issue on review is whether the circuit court abused its discretion by failing to compensate the wife adequately for her contribution to her husband's medical education and training when the circuit court divided the marital property and denied an award for maintenance upon dissolution of the marriage. Because we conclude that the circuit court abused its discretion, we reverse the decision of the court of appeals; we vacate that part of the circuit court's judgment relating to the division of the property and denial of an award for maintenance; and we remand the matter to the circuit court.

The couple, Patricia and Gordon Haugan, were married on August 4, 1973. About a month later the husband entered medical school and the wife began gainful employment. Each already had a bachelor's degree. For the first four years of their marriage the wife taught elementary school while the husband attended medical school in South Dakota and then in Minnesota. The wife's total earnings of between $26,187 and $28,974 supported the couple during these four years. The husband received a stipend of $2,200 and borrowed money to pay education expenses.

The wife continued to teach school for the next three years of their marriage while the husband, having graduated from medical school, was in a medical residency in Chicago. The husband's aggregate earnings for that three-year period were between $49,254 and $49,548, and the wife's were between $43,339 and $45,056. In addition to working full time outside the home, the wife performed virtually all of the household duties over the seven years.

In 1980, in anticipation of the husband's completing his medical training and beginning his practice of medicine, the couple bought a house in Green Bay, Wisconsin, and the wife resigned from her teaching job. On May 13, 1980, however, about two months before the husband completed his medical residency, the couple separated. In August 1980 the husband began practicing pediatric medicine in Green Bay at an annual salary of $48,000 ($4,000 a month) plus bonuses, for a total annual compensation of $55,498. The wife was unemployed until February 1981, when she began a job with IBM in Green Bay at an annual salary of $19,680 ($1,640 a month). Between August 1980 and August 1981 the husband voluntarily paid the wife a total of $10,150 ($817 a month in temporary maintenance plus half of a joint income tax refund of $693).

* * *

The trial court divided the parties' assets as follows: It treated the $20,000 equity in the house as an asset subject to property division and awarded the wife $10,000, payable by the husband in four equal annual installments, with interest at 10 percent. The husband was awarded the other $10,000 equity by being awarded the house subject to the land contract liability.

The trial court divided the tangible personal property ... [so that the wife] received assets valued at $11,908 plus the $10,000 payable in installments that represented one half of the equity in the house; [the husband] received assets valued at $10,225, plus one half of the equity in the house valued at $10,000.

All of the debts of the parties—the debts the husband incurred before marriage, the debts the parties incurred during marriage, and the debts the husband incurred for medical education—were assigned to the husband.

* * *

The trial court denied the wife's request for maintenance payments on the grounds that her post-divorce income would exceed her pre-divorce income and she would not be in financial need after the divorce.

* * *

The problem this case poses is not uncommon. University degree—divorce decree cases are frequent. In many marriages, while one spouse pursues an undergraduate, graduate, or professional degree or license, the other works to support the couple and foregoes his or her own education or career and the immediate benefits of a second income which the student spouse might have provided. The couple typically expects that the degree will afford them a higher shared standard of living in the future. That standard of living is never realized by the supporting spouse when the marriage breaks up just as the newly educated spouse is beginning the long-awaited career. In addition, little marital property has accumulated, because the couple's income was used for education and living expenses.

In a marriage of significant duration, the marital partners in sharing life together—with all its joys, sorrows, debts, and assets—share the return on their investment in the marriage. When the marriage ends in divorce the accumulated property is divided according to law and maintenance may be awarded.

But in a marital partnership where both parties work toward the education of one of the partners and the marriage ends before the economic benefit is realized and property is accumulated, it is unfair under these circumstances to deny the supporting spouse a share in the anticipated enhanced earnings while the student spouse keeps the degree and all the financial rewards it promises.... A compensatory award to the supporting spouse can ensure that both marital partners, and not only the one who has received the education, participate in the financial rewards attributable to the enhanced earnings of the student spouse.

* * *

In exercising its broad discretion in rendering a fundamentally fair and equitable decision in each case, the trial court has the difficult task of quantifying the value of the supporting spouse's and student spouse's contributions to the marriage and determining the rights and responsibilities of the parties on divorce. Because circumstances vary so much from case to case, this court cannot set down a formula for the trial court to apply in assigning a dollar value to each partner's contribution. We can, however, suggest several approaches for the trial court to consider in reaching its decision as to a maintenance award, property division, or both for the supporting spouse. These approaches are illustrative only; there are other approaches.

One approach the trial court may consider is the cost value approach whereby it calculates the value of the supporting spouse's contributions, not only in terms of money for education and living expenses but also in terms of services rendered during the marriage. In this case, for example, the wife worked full-time outside the home and also performed the household duties, and the fair market value of those homemaking services might be considered along with her financial input. Furthermore, the trial court should consider adjusting the value of the supporting spouse's contributions by a fair rate of return or for inflation. Such an award is restitutionary in nature; it does not account for a return on the supporting spouse's investment in terms of a share in the future enhanced earnings of the student spouse.

On review the wife in this case urges that the trial court should have calculated the contributions she made to the support of her student husband by using the cost value approach set forth in DeLa Rosa v. DeLa Rosa, 309 N.W.2d 755 (Minn. 1981).... In *DeLa Rosa*, the Minnesota court developed the following formula for awarding such compensation to the working wife:

> "We subtract from ... [the working spouse's] ... earnings her own living expenses. This has the effect of imputing one-half of the living expenses and all the educational expenses to the student spouse. The formula subtracts from ... [the working spouse's] ... contributions one-half of the couple's living expenses, that amount being the contributions of the two parties which were not used for direct educational costs; working spouse's financial contributions to joint living expenses and educational costs of student spouse *less* 1/2 (working spouse's financial contributions *plus* student spouse's financial contributions less cost of education) *equals* equitable award to working spouse."

Using this formula, the wife in this case asserts that she contributed $69,526 to $74,030 in earnings to the marriage; that her husband contributed earnings and stipends of $51,454 to $51,748; that the direct costs of his medical education were $18,220; and that he contributed medical school loans of $13,457 (valued as of the trial date). Applying these figures to the *DeLa Rosa* formula, the wife calculates her contribution as $13,000, without including interest, adjustments for inflation, or her non-financial contributions. The wife introduced evidence at trial that the value of the $13,000 contribution indexed for inflation is $28,560.

A second approach is looking at opportunity costs. The trial court may in determining the award to the supporting spouse consider the income the family sacrificed because the student spouse attended school rather than accepting employment. In this case the wife introduced evidence that the husband's increased earnings during the seven-year marriage had he not pursued medical education and training would have been $45,700 after taxes, or $69,800 indexed for inflation.

A third approach enables the trial court to consider compensating the supporting spouse according to the present value of the student spouse's enhanced earning capacity. This approach recognizes the spouse's lost expectation of sharing in the enhanced earning capacity; it gives the supporting spouse a return on his or her "investment" in the student spouse measured by the student spouse's enhanced earning capacity. In this case an economist, called as a witness by the wife, estimated the value of the husband's enhanced earning capacity to be $266,000. The economist's figure was the product of multiplying the husband's after-tax annual enhanced earnings of $13,000 (the difference between the husband's annual salary as a physician and the 1979 mean salary for white college-educated males in his age group) by 32.3 (estimated years remaining in the husband's expected working life) discounted to its present value. Using this calculation the wife asserts she would be entitled to one half of the present value of the husband's enhanced earning capacity, or $133,000.

Because many unforeseen events may affect future earnings, this third approach has been subject to criticism. Calculations of the expected stream of income may not take into account such variables as market opportunities, individual career choices and abilities, and premature death. Other approaches are, however, subject to criticism for giving the student spouse a windfall and for failing to recognize the supporting spouse's lost expectations.

Another approach is a variation of the labor theory of value suggested by wife's counsel at oral argument. Under this approach the trial court considers the value of the supporting spouse's contribution to the marriage at one half of the student spouse's enhanced yearly earning power for as many years as the supporting spouse worked to support the student. Under this theory the wife's contribution might be valued at $45,500 (one half of $13,000 [times] 7), which perhaps should be discounted to present value.

As stated before, no mathematical formula or theory of valuation settles the case. Each case must be decided on its own facts. The guiding principles for the trial court are fairness and justice.... Accordingly the trial court may in each case use one or more of the above described approaches, as well as any other approach suitable for that case.

The trial court's discretion must, of course, be exercised within the guidelines set forth in the statutes and cases. And whatever factors the trial court takes into account in determining the award to the supporting spouse, it must also take into account the student spouse's contributions and efforts in supporting the family and attaining the degree and the efforts that will be expended in earning the enhanced income. The student spouse has worked hard to obtain the degree, will have to work hard to earn the future stream of income, and should not be penalized. Granting equity to the supporting spouse should not result in inequity to the student spouse.

* * *

Where the marriage terminates before the parties benefited economically from the university degree or license acquired during the marriage and before substantial assets are accumulated, an award of 50 percent or even more of the marital assets is unlikely to compensate the supporting spouse fully. The wife would have received 50 percent of the assets even if she had not supported her husband while he was in school.... The award in this case which denied maintenance, divided the assets equally, and relieved the wife of approximately $14,000 in debts seems insufficient compensation for her significant financial and non-financial contributions to this marriage over a seven-year period, her lost expectation of sharing in his enhanced earning capacity, and the valuations of her contribution.

Because the trial court did not articulate its reasoning and did not specifically address the guidelines set forth in the statutes and the cases and because the award on its face appears inadequate, we conclude that the trial court abused its discretion. We therefore vacate the award and remand the cause to the trial court to reconsider all the evidence and provide for fair and equitable compensation to the wife for her contribution to the enhanced earning capacity of the husband, whether it be by further award of property or award of maintenance or both.

* * *

Notes and Questions

1. Income Versus Wealth: Income is a flow of economic benefits (for individuals it is usually in the form of cash) received in a specified period of time, usually a calendar year. Wealth is the capitalized value of future income. Students often experience low incomes while their wealth is increasing.

2. Investments in Human Capital: Some occupations, such as medicine and law, require many years of training. The fact that the wages in these skilled professions are higher than the wages of unskilled labor is not coincidental. Before people are willing to endure the years of training to become highly skilled professionals, they must be reasonably sure that their investment of time and other resources will pay off in the long run. People frequently choose to invest in some form of training to make themselves more productive and to enhance their income earning potential. While a person is going to college, attending trade school, or gaining on-the-job training, he or she is building human capital. Gaining human capital requires an investment, such as three years of law school. This investment involves a large opportunity cost—a law student loses the next-best alternative when attending law school. For most law students, the lost opportunity is the income that they would have earned if working. The expected return on the investment is higher wages.

3. The Haugans' Human Capital Investment: The court stated: "In a marriage of significant duration, the marital partners in sharing life together—with all its joys, sorrows, debts, and assets—share the return on their investment in the marriage." It could be argued that both spouses made a substantial investment in Dr. Haugan's education: they both endured periods of significantly lower income because of their devotion to their common goal. Clearly the supporting spouse expected to reap some of the benefits of the investment. The question for the court to determine, of course, was what is the proper compensation?

4. Opportunity Cost Is the Next-Best Alternative to the Human Capital Investment: It is reasonable to assume that the supporting wife chose to invest in her husband's education because she expected to be better off than if she did not invest. Thus, compensation for past opportunities foregone would be less than the return expected from the investment. Instead of looking to the past, the proper approach is to consider the future—the enhanced earning capacity of Dr. Haugan.

Diocese of Buffalo v. State of New York

Court of Appeals of New York
248 N.E.2d 155 (1969)

FULD, C. J.

In each of these three condemnation proceedings, we are primarily called upon to decide the method to be employed in computing a claimant's damages where there has been a partial taking of cemetery lands....

It is settled that, as a general proposition, the measure of damages in partial taking cases is the difference between the value of the whole *before* the taking and the value of the remainder *after* the taking.... Consequently, the decision on each of these appeals turns on whether that rule should have been applied in these cemetery cases.

Our decision in St. Agnes Cemetery v. State of New York (3 N.Y.2d 37) pointed the method of valuing cemetery lands in condemnation proceedings. After first observing that these lands were to be appraised on the basis of their value for their highest and best use—in that case, for continued cemetery use—the court went on to hold that such value is to be ascertained by first arriving at a probable sale price of the land as cemetery plots or graves, based on the "average" price which the cemetery obtained for the sale of burial plots located in adjoining sections.... After the cost of making such future sales is deducted, an estimate is made of the number of years it would take to sell off all the plots in the cemetery as it existed prior to the condemnation. The amount of net income expected annually over the projected number of years is treated as if it were an annuity whose present value, determined by reference to annuity tables, is regarded as the fair market value of the cemetery's undeveloped grave sites. In other words, the value of the land is equivalent to the present worth of future net income to be derived from the steady sale of a continuously diminishing inventory of cemetery plots, year by year, until the supply of land is depleted.

On the appeals before us, the claimants as well as the State accept the formula adopted in *St. Agnes* as the method to be followed in determining the valuation of a cemetery. More, the State acknowledges that the courts below correctly applied that formula to find the value of the entire area of unsold plots or graves *before* the taking. However, contends the State, the courts below erred in failing to use the formula in order to ascertain the value of the property retained by the claimants *after* such taking; indeed, they made no attempt whatsoever to find that vitally significant figure, the value of the land retained *after* the taking. Instead of employing the "before and after" measure of damages rule, the trial court averaged the value of all the unsold graves before the taking—according to the *St. Agnes* formula—and, then, simply multiplied the average unit plot value by the number of unsold plots which had been taken in condemnation.

The departure from the "before and after" rule resulted in error. The court's decision in the *St. Agnes* case was premised on the dual assumption that cemetery land is valuable as an inventory of individual grave sites which may properly be treated as fungible and that sales will continue at a constant rate until they are all sold. On this premise, any particular undeveloped cemetery plot could be substituted for any other, and the only direct effect of a partial taking is to reduce the economic life of a cemetery. In other words, since the sales will presumably continue at the same rate, the condemnation taking will merely decrease the period of time during which the supply will be available. This economic assumption—that the only effect of a partial taking is to reduce the economic life of the cemetery—underlies the "before and after" approach urged by the State, a contention which relates to the measure of damages in these cases. This particular question, critical to decision herein, was not raised by the parties nor considered by the court in *St. Agnes*. In that case and in the others which followed it, we were concerned only with the method of valuation, not with the measure of damages.

No reason exists for not applying the "before and after" rule in cases involving a partial taking of cemetery lands. What the owner has lost is, after all, the ultimate measure of damages.... In the main, uncomplicated by any claim or issue of consequential damages or benefits to the retained property ... the only effect of the taking has been to reduce the size of each cemetery, just as would a street widening, if the cemeteries had fronted on city streets. The remaining property still retains its essential characteristics *after* the taking, is still just as useful for cemetery purposes, as it was *before* the taking.

This being so, there is no reason why the *St. Agnes* method of valuation should not be used to determine the value of the retained land *after* the taking in precisely the same way as it was used by the courts below to determine the value of the entire cemetery *before* the taking....

* * *

In this case, the Court of Claims found that it would have taken 55 years to sell off the grave sites as the cemetery stood before the taking. The claimant owned 65,450 grave sites which would have been sold at the rate of 1,190 a year. And, since the parcel taken involved 3,500 graves, the effect of the appropriation was simply to reduce the life of the annuity by three years, the length of time during which they would have been sold. The court found the "before" value—i.e., the value of the income from the sale of 1,190 plots a year over a 55-year period—to be $1,870,462.33 but made no finding as to the "after" value—i.e., the value of the income from the annual sale of those 1,190 plots over a period of 52 years—and there must, therefore, be a new trial.[1]

The court made an award of $100,030; it arrived at this figure by (1) taking the "before" value of the entire property—$1,870,462 for the 65,450 graves—(2) finding the average value of each grave to be $28.58 and, then, (3) multiplying that figure by the total number of graves appropriated, 3,500. Quite obviously, if, as the State maintains, the value of the property retained after the appropriation is $1,855,354.77, an award of $100,030 for the land taken would leave the claimant with property worth their combined sum—$1,955,384—an amount far in excess of $1,870,462 which the trial court found to be the value of its property before the taking. Simply put, the "averaging" procedure adopted below resulted in a windfall to the claimant.

There was a flaw in the reasoning of the courts below which led to such a result. The present value of a grave site depends, to a great extent, on the time when it will be sold. Thus, in this particular case, plots which were to be sold immediately were found to be worth over $130 each, while those which would not yield any income for 55 years were only worth about $5. The figure used by the Court of Claims—$28.58 per grave—represented an "average value" which would apply only to those graves sold toward the middle of the cemetery's life. However, as we have already stated, the claimant's sales will presumably continue at an undiminished rate of 1,190 a year throughout its life, in consequence of which the claimant will experience no loss until 52 years have elapsed and it is forced to terminate its sales three years earlier than had there been no condemnation. It is only the value of the sales lost during the period at the very end of the cemetery's existence, rather than an "average" figure, which properly reflects the damage resulting from the taking.

* * *

In sum, then, there must be a reversal and a new trial in each of these cases. The Court of Claims failed to consider the value of the land which remained in the ownership of the claimant after the taking and, in so doing, rendered awards which were far in excess of the claimants' actual loss. Upon the new trials, it will be incumbent on the court to make awards solely on the basis of the difference between the value of the claimants' property before and after the taking plus such special damages as may be shown to be appropriate in the individual case.

The order appealed from … should be reversed, and the matter remanded to the Court of Claims for further proceedings in accordance with this opinion.

BURKE, J. (dissenting).

In this case, here by permission of this court, the claimants … have been denied just compensation…. [The majority discards the *St. Agnes* approach] without any discussion of the uncertainties which the discarded approach at least attempted to meet and deal

---

1. According to the State, reliance on the same actuarial tables used to obtain the "before" value would have yielded an "after" value of $1,855,354.77. The State argues that the difference between those figures—$15,107.56—would represent the damages to the claimant. It will be for the trial court to take evidence on this issue and determine the exact amount of the claimant's damages.

with, and it does so by use of a method which, if used as the case relied upon by the majority used it, would result in an award in excess of $100,000 instead of the award of some $15,000 which results from the majority's approach. For instance, the majority states that, because the burial plot units are fungible, there is no way of telling when any particular area would be used and that, therefore, the average discounted price used below would reflect the expected earnings from sales in the middle years of the cemetery's life. The implication is that this results in an excessive award to the claimant. What the majority does not recognize is that, by its approach, it decides that the taken plots would *necessarily be the last ones to be sold* and, therefore, awards only the discounted value of the expected income flow for the last years of the cemetery's life lost due to the taking. The approach heretofore followed recognized that it could not be determined whether the taken plots would have been sold first, last or somewhere in between and, therefore, in fairness both to the State and to the claimant, chose the *via media* which, in effect, "split the difference" between the two extremes. Thus, at the same time that the majority deplores the idea of a "windfall" to the claimant by use of this average, it summarily and incongruously endorses a "windfall" for the State by use of its arbitrary determination that the taken plots should be considered as those which would necessarily be sold last.

* * *

Notes and Questions

1. Reasonable Expectations About the Future: An old adage from the real estate business — "Location, location, location!" — could be applicable here. If every plot has the same price, and if some plots are in more desirable locations than others (a reasonable assumption), then the condemned plots would have to be in the least desirable locations in order to be the last ones sold. Did the court need more information before making its assumptions about the order of sale? What information could lead to a more accurate estimate of the timing of the sales revenue?

2. Expected Value: People (and courts) often guess at numbers they don't know, such as the score of tomorrow's ball game, their income after ten years, their salary upon graduation from law school, or in this case the order in which condemned burial plots would have been sold. Under certain conditions, a rational guess is the expected value — an average of the sum of every possible number, weighted by the probabilities (chances) that they will occur. An expected value is calculated in three steps:

(1) List the number (e.g., the score or the income) in each possible situation.

(2) Multiply each number by its probability or chance of occurring.

(3) Add the results from Step 2.

For example, suppose that you have a 9/10 chance of earning $50,000 per year ten years from now and a 1/10 chance of earning $300,000. Then your expected salary is:

$$(9/10) (\$50,000) + (1/10) (\$300,000) = \$45,000 + \$30,000 = \$75,000$$

3. Expectations About the Timing of the Sale of the Burial Plots: Suppose that plots sold immediately were worth $130 and plots sold in 55 years had a present value of $5. Assume there was a 50 percent chance that all of the lots would be sold immediately and a 50 percent chance that all of them would be sold in 55 years. The expected value of each condemned burial plot, if it had not been condemned, would be:

$$EV = 0.5 (\$130) + 0.5 (\$5) = \$65 + \$2.50 = \$67.50$$

b. Determining the Proper Interest Rate

An important determinant in evaluating the value of money over time is the interest rate. The higher the current (and assumed constant) interest rate, the more a given amount of money invested today will be worth in the future. Alternatively, the higher the current interest rate, the less a given amount of money in the future will be worth in the present. Thus, after the future flow of dollars has been determined, the key issue is to select the proper interest rate for discounting.

The earlier discussion of present value calculations did not distinguish between what economists call the **nominal** or **market rate** of interest and the **real** or **pure rate**. The nominal rate differs from the real rate because the nominal rate includes a premium reflecting the fact that the promised dollar payments will be affected by changes in the purchasing power of those payments (inflation), as well as the risk of the asset. The following case illustrates how inflation affects the selection of a discount rate and the calculation of damages.

Trevino v. United States

United States Court of Appeals for the Ninth Circuit
804 F.2d 1512 (1986)

SNEED, J.

Sophia Trevino and her parents sued the United States for medical malpractice, pursuant to the Federal Torts Claims Act (FTCA), 28 U.S.C. §§ 1346(b), 2674, arising from the negligent treatment given to Sophia's mother during Sophia's birth. The government concedes liability but appeals the award of over $6.3 million in damages. We modify in part, reverse in part, and remand.

I. FACTS AND PROCEEDINGS BELOW

On November 3, 1981, Rachael Trevino gave birth to Sophia at Madigan Army Medical Center in Tacoma, Washington (Madigan). During labor, Rachael suffered from a condition known as abruptio placentae, meaning that her placenta was partially detached from the uterine wall. The medical care that she received during labor did not take this condition into account. As a result, Sophia was born severely disabled. She has permanent brain damage, a form of cerebral palsy that involves all four extremities, and a seizure disorder....

Sophia and her parents filed a FTCA action against the United States, alleging that Sophia's injuries had been caused by the negligent treatment provided by Madigan. After a five-day bench trial, the district court entered a judgment for the plaintiffs. It awarded Sophia $2,000,000 in nonpecuniary damages and $3,932,504 in pecuniary damages, and it awarded her parents as a unit $200,000 for loss of love and companionship and $200,000 for injury to the parent-child relationship. The United States moved for a new trial or, in the alternative, for an amended judgment. The court denied the motion, and the United States appeals.

II. DISCUSSION

A. *Standard of Review*

We review damage awards in FTCA cases for clear error. The award is clearly erroneous if, after a review of the record, we are "'left with the definite and firm conviction that a mistake has been committed.'" ... The choice of a discount rate, used to adjust to present value an award based on an income stream spread over time and, at the same time, to adjust for the effects of inflation, should be reviewed for an abuse of discretion.

* * *

E. The Pecuniary Award to Sophia

1. *Choice of a Discount Rate*

The district court applied a –2% discount rate to the pecuniary component of the damage award. It explained its reason for this choice as follows:

> The –2% discount rate was determined by the application of a set formula which assumes as [sic] constant relationship between inflation and discount rates. The differential between the growth rates and the tax-free rate of return has been stable and has averaged more than two percentage points during the 30-year period 1954–1984. To obtain the present value of economic loss using tax-free short-term interest as the appropriate discount rate, a net discount rate of –2% was applied (wage and cost increases exceed tax-free interest rates by 2%) and calculated [with] the amounts testified to by the economic expert, Dr. Lowell Bassett.

We hold that the district court abused its discretion in applying a negative discount rate to the estimated pecuniary losses. Such a rate relies on assumptions not generally accepted by the courts or economists.

The Supreme Court addressed the discount rate issue in its opinion in *Jones & Laughlin Steel Corp. v. Pfeifer*, 462 U.S. 523 (1983). Its analysis of the methods of computing damage awards, including the choice of the proper discount rate, need not be repeated except to the extent necessary to reveal our thinking....

We begin by recognizing that awards based on income streams spread over time are usually discounted to present value to account for the fact that a plaintiff, by receiving the money in a lump sum, "up front," will invest the sum and earn additional income from the investment.[2] Were it not for inflation, that simple calculation would end the matter. With inflation, however, dollars received in the future will buy less than would those same dollars if received today. A net positive discount rate implies that the gains from safe investments exceed the losses induced by inflation—in other words, that the rate chosen to reflect the interest rate on the safest investments over a fixed period of time will be a larger number than the rate chosen to reflect the rate of inflation over the same period of time....

Obviously it is possible for the true rate of inflation to outstrip the return on the safest investments for some period of time. This would justify for that period of time a negative discount rate. The district court's use of a negative discount rate is based on this possibility.

The district court's choice is flawed, however. First, it relied on an unrepresentative timespan. That period was from 1954 to 1984. This span includes the aberrational years 1974–82: years in which oil prices tripled from 1974 to 1979, inflation reached double-digit proportions, and "[r]ecessions in 1974, 1975, 1980, and 1982 mark[ed] the 1974–82 period as the most recession-plagued nine years since the Great Depression."...

We cannot deny history, nor can history provide an always reliable basis for predicting the future. However, we can base our estimates on long time periods that will diminish the effect of shorter aberrational periods. Fluctuations that are great for a short time span

---

2. The reason that risk-free investments are preferred to more remunerative but riskier investments is that the plaintiff should not be faced with the burden of becoming a full-time broker merely to safeguard his award.

are less dramatic, and skew results less, when they are seen as part of a longer period. We have no confidence in the ability of experts, the district court, or this court, to predict inflation or interest rates over the period of Sophia's life other than by extrapolating from the past.

The district court must also select an accurate measure of historical inflation as the basis for its prediction of future inflation. Here, the district court used the historical increase in wages and medical costs. But this gives the illusion of greater inflation, because some portion of wage increases is not due to inflation....

Pfeifer's discussion of discount rates technically is only an interpretation of section 5(b) of the Longshoremen's and Harbor Workers' Compensation Act (LHWCA). But the general discussion of alternative methods of calculating discount rates is extensive. The Court mentions several options:

> 1. Calculate the lost income stream by excluding the effects of inflation and the "real" interest rate by fixing the difference between the market rate of interest and the anticipated rate of inflation;

> 2. Calculate the size of the lost income stream by including the effects of inflation and discounting by the market interest rate; and,

> 3. Calculate the value of pecuniary damages by employing a zero discount rate (the total offset approach).

The last option (the total offset approach) was considered unacceptable as a uniform method to calculate damages, although it could be stipulated to by the parties, or applied by the trial court in an appropriate case. After examining a plethora of economic studies, the Court concluded as to the "real" interest rate option that: "Although we find the economic evidence distinctly inconclusive regarding an essential premise of those approaches, we do not believe a trial court ... should be reversed if it adopts a rate between 1 and 3% and explains its choice." Obviously a decision interpreting section 5(b) of the LHWCA is not binding in an FTCA case; however, the Court's guidance on the issue of economic predictions and discount rates cannot be disregarded. We accept this guidance and choose to regard it as controlling in this case. In reliance on *Pfeifer*, and in the absence of Washington state law to the contrary, we decline to embrace a negative discount rate on the basis of this record.

We do not hold, however, that any discount rate above 3% or below 1% is impermissible. Supported by credible expert testimony, a court could certainly adopt a different rate. We do hold, however, that it is impermissible to select a time period over which to compare inflation and interest rates that provides a decidedly aberrational result. We also point out that it is impermissible either (1) *to exclude* the effects of inflation in determining the size of the lost income stream and employ a discount rate equal to the market rate of interest, or (2) *to include* the effects of inflation in determining the size of the lost income stream and employ a discount rate measured by the difference between the market rate of interest and the rate of inflation. The former denies the injured party any adjustment for inflation while making available such adjustment to the party deemed responsible for the injury. The latter, on the other hand, provides to the injured party an adjustment for inflation in determining the size of the lost income stream and denies to the party deemed responsible for the injury any benefit of that adjustment in determining the proper discount rate. Put more succinctly, the former accords the party deemed responsible for the injury a "double benefit," while in the latter the "double benefit" passes to the injured party. Neither party is entitled to a "double benefit."

Finally, we point out that the choice of an interest rate yield on Sophia's lump sum award, or for other purposes in fixing the final amount of the award for the loss of earning capacity, is not dictated by the manner in which taxes are treated. The yield of tax-free securities enjoys no special status. That yield merely indicates what a yield would be to an investor who is strongly averse to both risk and taxes. No sensible investment counselor would advise Sophia to invest the entire lump sum in tax-free securities. Nor is it probable that she will do so. For these reasons the use of the yield of tax-free securities to arrive at the "real rate" of interest is suspect. The tax-free rate of interest is substantially below that yielded by securities not enjoying that privilege. Its use, when coupled with a period of unrepresentative high inflation, as was done in this case, yields an unnaturally low discount rate. This should be avoided on remand.

* * *

We remand for the recalculation of Sophia's pecuniary loss in accordance with [this Part] of this opinion.

Notes and Questions

1. The Real Rate of Return: The real rate of return on an investment, r, is defined as the nominal rate of return (the return stated on the face of the financial instrument or the percent change in stock price), R, minus the rate of inflation, i , over the same time period:

$$r = R - i.$$

Alternatively,

$$R = r + i$$

Thus, the nominal rate must be greater than inflation for money to grow in real terms. As the court points out, it is doubtful that the plaintiffs will put all of Sophia's money into a tax-free bond, which typically grows at a slower rate than inflation. Thus, since the nominal rate of return should be above inflation (usually 2–3%), the lower court erred in its negative discount value. The court is correct in assuming that Sophia's family will invest in financial instruments with a positive expected real rate of return.

2. Inflation Expectations and Interest Rates: The court states that the inflationary period that the lower court used is unrealistic because it included the oil embargo and a period of stagflation. Predicting the future is perilous, but it must be done in order to make present value calculations. The bond market reflects inflation because it must provide an interest rate greater than inflation to attract investors. Thus, the long term and short term bond market gives interest rates that are greater than projected long term and short term inflation.

3. Risk Aversion and Discounting: In each of these cases, the court had to address the question of the appropriate discount rate to be applied in the present value calculation. However, in considering this issue, courts appear to ignore an important assumption about economic behavior—the concept of **risk aversion**. Risk aversion implies the existence of a positive relationship between risk and return; or stated differently, the greater the perceived risk, the greater the expected return. An example should make this clear. Suppose a rich relative sends you a check for $1,000. Your roommate offers you the following bet: if you flip a fair coin and get a head, you will double your money, but if you get a tail you lose the entire $1,000. The expected value of the bet is zero [i.e., (0.5)($1,000) +

(0.5)(–$1,000) = 0]. However, most people would refuse this gamble because the value placed on the one thousand dollars lost is greater than the additional value that would be obtained if you won an additional thousand dollars. In other words, because of risk aversion, most people would demand additional compensation for taking such a bet. For example, you might refuse to play unless the payoff is increased to compensate you for taking the risk—e.g., you could demand that the payoff be $1,500 instead of $1,000 if you win. Then the expected value would be positive—[i.e. (0.5)($1,500) + (0.5)(–$1,000) = ($750 – $500) = $250].

That most people are risk averse is demonstrated by: (1) the widespread purchase of insurance, which is nothing more than a substitution of a certain small loss—the insurance premium—for the probability of a large loss; (2) and the observation of securities markets where riskier investments have higher returns than less risky investments.

How does this insight affect the choice of a discount rate? As we saw in *Trevino*, the rule appears to be that the court should apply a riskless interest rate in discounting lost future earnings to present value. In other words, the use of a riskless discount rate will result in the award of a present value sum that can be invested at a riskless rate of return to yield a guaranteed stream of earnings equal to what was lost. Note, however, that what a plaintiff loses in a wrongful injury case is not a riskless stream, i.e., a guaranteed amount in each particular year, but a risky stream of future income. Moreover, if the plaintiff is risk averse, he or she will *prefer* the sum certain to its expected value equivalent, i.e., its actuarial value, since he could not have diversified away all of the risk in his earnings stream.

4. Risk, Diversification, and Human Capital: Assuming (for now) this positive relationship between risk and return, the next insight (often ignored by courts) is that not every risk will be compensated. Modern portfolio theory teaches that risks that can be diversified away command no increased return. In other words, the market will pay no premium to bear fully diversifiable risk. The primary source of income to an individual is what economists refer to as **human capital**. Human capital is the acquired skills and knowledge from which an individual generates an earning stream. (Recall that this was the asset being valued in *Haugan*. Was it riskless?) It is asserted that the risk implicit in human capital cannot be diversified away since an individual cannot hold a portfolio of occupations. (Is this literally true?) Thus, if a court uses a riskless discount rate to calculate the present value of lost earnings, the plaintiff will be overcompensated in the sense that the plaintiff will value the sum certain received by a lump sum payment more than the stream of income he or she would have earned absent the tort.[3]

c. Pulling It All Together

There are two fundamental components to any present value calculation. First, the relevant future stream of economic benefits (typically cash flows) must be identified. Second, an appropriate interest rate needs to be selected. The cases in the preceding subsections dealt with each of these components independently. As the following case

---

3. It is important here to note that the risk we speak about in the text is not the physical risk of a profession, but economic risk. Economists have long recognized that the market compensates workers in jobs that require a greater risk of physical injury or death, e.g., a roughneck in the North Sea oil fields. This market risk premium will be included in wage estimates used to calculate the lost earnings.

demonstrates, however, the correct method for calculating either one of these components depends upon how the other component is calculated.

O'Shea v. Riverway Towing Co.
United States Court of Appeals for the Seventh Circuit
677 F.2d 1194 (1982)

POSNER, Circuit Judge

This is a tort case under the federal admiralty jurisdiction. We are called upon to decide questions of contributory negligence and damage assessment, in particular the question—one of first impression in this circuit—whether, and if so how, to account for inflation in computing lost future wages.

On the day of the accident, Margaret O'Shea was coming off duty as a cook on a towboat plying the Mississippi River. A harbor boat operated by the defendant, Riverway Towing Company, carried Mrs. O'Shea to shore and while getting off the boat she fell and sustained the injury complained of. The district judge found Riverway negligent and Mrs. O'Shea free from contributory negligence, and assessed damages in excess of $150,000. Riverway appeals only from the finding that there was no contributory negligence and from the part of the damage award that was intended to compensate Mrs. O'Shea for her lost future wages.

* * *

[The district judge's finding that Mrs. O'Shea was not contributorily negligent is not clearly erroneous on these facts....]

The more substantial issues in this appeal relate to the computation of lost wages. Mrs. O'Shea's job as a cook paid her $40 a day, and since the custom was to work 30 days consecutively and then have the next 30 days off, this comes to $7200 a year although, as we shall see, she never had earned that much in a single year. She testified that when the accident occurred she had been about to get another cook's job on a Mississippi towboat that would have paid her $60 a day ($10,800 a year). She also testified that she had been intending to work as a boat's cook until she was 70—longer if she was able. An economist who testified on Mrs. O'Shea's behalf used the foregoing testimony as the basis for estimating the wages that she lost because of the accident. He first subtracted federal income tax from yearly wage estimates based on alternative assumptions about her wage rate (that it would be either $40 or $60 a day); assumed that this wage would have grown by between six and eight percent a year; assumed that she would have worked either to age 65 or to age 70; and then discounted the resulting lost-wage estimates to present value, using a discount rate of 8.5 percent a year. These calculations, being based on alternative assumptions concerning starting wage rate, annual wage increases, and length of employment, yielded a range of values rather than a single value. The bottom of the range was $50,000. This is the present value, computed at an 8.5 percent discount rate, of Mrs. O'Shea's lost future wages on the assumption that her starting wage is $40 a day and that it would have grown by six percent a year until she retired at the age of 65. The top of the range was $114,000, which is the present value (again discounted at 8.5 percent) of her lost future wages assuming she would have worked till she was 70 at a wage that would have started at $60 a day and increased by eight percent a year. The judge awarded a figure—$86,033—near the midpoint of this range. He did not explain in his written opinion how he had arrived at this figure, but in a preceding oral opinion he stated that he was "not certain that she would work until age 70 at this type of work," "although she certainly was entitled to" do so and "could have earned something"; and that he had not "felt bound by (the economist's) figure of eight percent increase in wages" and had "not found the wages based on necessarily a 60 dollar a day job." If this can be taken to mean that he thought Mrs. O'Shea would probably have worked till she was 70, starting at $40 a day but moving up from there at six rather than eight percent a year, the economist's estimate of the present value of her lost future wages would be $75,000.

* * *

... [S]ince Riverway neither challenges the district judge's (apparent) finding that Mrs. O'Shea would have worked till she was 70 nor contends that the lost wages for each year until then should be discounted by the probability that she would in fact have been alive and working as a boat's cook throughout the damage period, we may also assume that her wages would have been at least $7200 a year for the 12 years between the date of the accident and her seventieth birthday. But Riverway does argue that we cannot assume she might have earned $10,800 a year rather than $7200, despite her testimony that at the time of the accident she was about to take another job as a boat's cook where she would have been paid at the rate of $60 rather than $40 a day. The point is not terribly important since the trial judge gave little weight to this testimony, but we shall discuss it briefly. Mrs. O'Shea was asked on direct examination what "pay you would have worked" for in the new job. Riverway's counsel objected on the ground of hearsay, the judge overruled his objection, and she answered $60 a day. The objection was not well taken. Riverway argues that only her prospective employer knew what her wage was, and hence when she said it was $60 she was testifying to what he had told her. But an employee's wage is as much in the personal knowledge of the employee as of the employer. If Mrs. O'Shea's prospective employer had testified that he would have paid her $60, Riverway's counsel could have made the converse hearsay objection that the employer was really testifying to what Mrs. O'Shea had told him she was willing to work for. Riverway's counsel could on cross-examination have probed the basis for Mrs. O'Shea's belief that she was going to get $60 a day in a new job, but he did not do so and cannot complain now that the judge may have given her testimony some (though little) weight.

We come at last to the most important issue in the case, which is the proper treatment of inflation in calculating lost future wages. Mrs. O'Shea's economist based the six to eight percent range which he used to estimate future increases in the wages of a boat's cook on the general pattern of wage increases in service occupations over the past 25 years. During the second half of this period the rate of inflation has been substantial and has accounted for much of the increase in nominal wages in this period; and to use that increase to project future wage increases is therefore to assume that inflation will continue, and continue to push up wages. Riverway argues that it is improper as a matter of law to take inflation into account in projecting lost future wages. Yet Riverway itself wants to take inflation into account—one-sidedly, to reduce the amount of the damages computed. For Riverway does not object to the economist's choice of an 8.5 percent discount rate for reducing Mrs. O'Shea's lost future wages to present value, although the rate includes an allowance—a very large allowance—for inflation.

To explain, the object of discounting lost future wages to present value is to give the plaintiff an amount of money which, invested safely, will grow to a sum equal to those wages. So if we thought that but for the accident Mrs. O'Shea would have earned $7200 in 1990, and we were computing in 1980 (when this case was tried) her damages based on those lost earnings, we would need to determine the sum of money that, invested safely for a period of ten years, would grow to $7200. Suppose that in 1980 the rate of interest on ultra-safe (i.e., federal government) bonds or notes maturing in 10 years was

12 percent. Then we would consult a table of present values to see what sum of money invested at 12 percent for 10 years would at the end of that time have grown to $7200. The answer is $2318. But a moment's reflection will show that to give Mrs. O'Shea $2318 to compensate her for lost wages in 1990 would grossly undercompensate her. People demand 12 percent to lend money risklessly for 10 years because they expect their principal to have much less purchasing power when they get it back at the end of the time. In other words, when long-term interest rates are high, they are high in order to compensate lenders for the fact that they will be repaid in cheaper dollars. In periods when no inflation is anticipated, the risk-free interest rate is between one and three percent.... Additional percentage points above that level reflect inflation anticipated over the life of the loan. But if there is inflation it will affect wages as well as prices. Therefore to give Mrs. O'Shea $2318 today because that is the present value of $7200 10 years hence, computed at a discount rate—12 percent—that consists mainly of an allowance for anticipated inflation, is in fact to give her less than she would have been earning then if she was earning $7200 on the date of the accident, even if the only wage increases she would have received would have been those necessary to keep pace with inflation.

There are (at least) two ways to deal with inflation in computing the present value of lost future wages. One is to take it out of both the wages and the discount rate—to say to Mrs. O'Shea, "we are going to calculate your probable wage in 1990 on the assumption, unrealistic as it is, that there will be zero inflation between now and then; and, to be consistent, we are going to discount the amount thus calculated by the interest rate that would be charged under the same assumption of zero inflation." ...

An alternative approach, which yields the same result, is to use a (higher) discount rate based on the current risk-free 10-year interest rate, but apply that rate to an estimate of lost future wages that includes expected inflation. Contrary to Riverway's argument, this projection would not require gazing into a crystal ball. The expected rate of inflation can, as just suggested, be read off from the current long-term interest rate. If that rate is 12 percent, and if as suggested earlier the real or inflation-free interest rate is only one to three percent, this implies that the market is anticipating 9–11 percent inflation over the next 10 years, for a long-term interest rate is simply the sum of the real interest rate and the anticipated rate of inflation during the term.

* * *

Applying our analysis to the present case, we cannot pronounce the approach taken by the plaintiff's economist unreasonable. He chose a discount rate—8.5 percent—well above the real rate of interest, and therefore containing an allowance for inflation. Consistency required him to inflate Mrs. O'Shea's starting wage as a boat's cook in calculating her lost future wages, and he did so at a rate of six to eight percent a year. If this rate had been intended as a forecast of purely inflationary wage changes, his approach would be open to question, especially at the upper end of his range. For if the estimated rate of inflation were eight percent, the use of a discount rate of 8.5 percent would imply that the real rate of interest was only .5 percent, which is lower than most economists believe it to be for any substantial period of time. But wages do not rise just because of inflation. Mrs. O'Shea could expect her real wages as a boat's cook to rise as she became more experienced and as average real wage rates throughout the economy rose, as they usually do over a decade or more. It would not be outlandish to assume that even if there were no inflation, Mrs. O'Shea's wages would have risen by three percent a year. If we subtract that from the economist's six to eight percent range, the inflation allowance built into his estimated future wage increases is only three to five percent; and when we subtract these figures from 8.5 percent we see that his implicit estimate of the real rate of interest was very high (3.5–5.5 percent). This means he was conservative, because the higher the discount rate used the lower the damages calculated.

If conservative in one sense, the economist was most liberal in another. He made no allowance for the fact that Mrs. O'Shea, whose health history quite apart from the accident is not outstanding, might very well not have survived and been working as a boat's cook full time or in an equivalent job — until the age of 70. The damage award is a sum certain, but the lost future wages to which that award is equated by means of the discount rate are mere probabilities. If the probability of her being employed as a boat's cook full time in 1990 was only 75 percent, for example, then her estimated wages in that year should have been multiplied by .75 to determine the value of the expectation that she lost as a result of the accident; and so with each of the other future years.... The economist did not do this, and by failing to do this he overstated the loss due to the accident.

But Riverway does not make an issue of this aspect of the economist's analysis....

Although we are not entirely satisfied with the economic analysis on which the judge, in the absence of any other evidence of the present value of Mrs. O'Shea's lost future wages, must have relied heavily, we recognize that the exactness which economic analysis rigorously pursued appears to offer is, at least in the litigation setting, somewhat delusive. Therefore, we will not reverse an award of damages for lost wages because of questionable assumptions unless it yields an unreasonable result — especially when, as in the present case, the defendant does not offer any economic evidence himself and does not object to the questionable steps in the plaintiff's economic analysis. We cannot say the result here was unreasonable. If the economist's method of estimating damages was too generous to Mrs. O'Shea in one important respect it was, as we have seen, niggardly in another. Another error against Mrs. O'Shea should be noted: the economist should not have deducted her *entire* income tax liability in estimating her future lost wages.... While it is true that the damage award is not taxable, the interest she earns on it will be (a point the economist may have ignored because of his erroneous assumption that she would invest the award in tax-exempt bonds), so that his method involved an element of double taxation.

If we assume that Mrs. O'Shea could have expected a three percent annual increase in her real wages from a base of $7200, that the real risk-free rate of interest (and therefore the appropriate discount rate if we are considering only real wage increases) is two percent, and that she would have worked till she was 70, the present value of her lost future wages would be $91,310. This figure ignores the fact that she did not have a 100 percent probability of actually working till age 70 as a boat's cook, and fails to make the appropriate (though probably, in her bracket, very small) net income tax adjustment; but it also ignores the possibility, small but not totally negligible, that the proper base is really $10,800 rather than $7200.

So we cannot say that the figure arrived at by the judge, $86,033, was unreasonably high. But we are distressed that he made no attempt to explain how he had arrived at that figure, since it was not one contained in the economist's testimony though it must in some way have been derived from that testimony. Unlike many other damage items in a personal injury case, notably pain and suffering, the calculation of damages for lost earnings can and should be an analytical rather than an intuitive undertaking. Therefore, compliance with Rule 52(a) of the Federal Rules of Civil Procedure requires that in a bench trial the district judge set out the steps by which he arrived at his award for lost future earnings, in order to assist the appellate court in reviewing the award.... The district judge failed to do that here. We do not consider this reversible error, because our own analysis convinces us that the award of damages for lost future wages was reasonable.

But for the future we ask the district judges in this circuit to indicate the steps by which they arrive at damage awards for lost future earnings.

JUDGMENT AFFIRMED.

Notes and Questions

1. Consistency in Accounting for Inflation: The defendant in *Riverway* argues "that it is improper as a matter of law to take inflation into account in projecting lost future wages." However, Judge Posner is quick to draw attention to a very important conceptual error made by the defendant. Specifically, the defendant objected to incorporating inflation into the future cash flow component, but continued to utilize an interest rate component that accounted for inflation. As Judge Posner noted, the defendant's method would result in the plaintiff being undercompensated. Can you make an intuitive explanation for why this is so? The defendant's conceptual error clearly demonstrates that the correct method for estimating one of the present value components depends upon the manner in which the other was estimated. In other words, consistency is an important element of sound present value calculations.

2. The Probability of Future Income: Judge Posner questions the validity of the assumption that Mrs. O'Shea would continue to work until the age of 70. In Posner's opinion the failure to account for the chance that Mrs. O'Shea would not work that long results in an overstatement of the loss. To account for this uncertainty, Posner suggests that estimates of future income should be multiplied by the probability that she would actually be working in that year. For example, assume that the expert projects that Mrs. O'Shea would have earned $12,000 in the tenth year. However, there is only a 75% chance that Mrs. O'Shea will be working in 10 years. Thus, Posner suggests that Mrs. O'Shea's expected future income for the tenth year be calculated as 0.75 × $12,000 = $9,000. What do you think of this suggestion? Can you think of an alternative way to account for this uncertainty?

3. Tax Considerations: Section 104(a)(2) of the Internal Revenue Code excludes from income any damages received, whether by suit or agreement, lump-sum or periodic payment, on account of personal injury or sickness. Thus, Mrs. O'Shea's award for the present value of lost future wages will not be taxed. However, any interest or other income that Mrs. O'Shea receives as a result of investing her award will be taxed. As a result, Judge Posner observes that by accounting for taxes in the estimate of future income the plaintiff has been subjected to double taxation. Do you agree with Posner's assessment? Are there alternative methods for avoiding double taxation? How would a structured settlement fit into this analysis?

C. The Value of Life

People often claim that life is priceless—that there is no amount of money that they would accept for their own life or the life of a family member or a close friend. Yet, as illustrated by the *Competitive Enterprise Institute* case in Chapter II, it is common for people knowingly to accept life-threatening risks. Sometimes a court must determine the value of a deceased person's life when calculating monetary damages. In this section, we explore two methodologies for determining the value of life.

1. Economic Value of Life

Traditionally, most courts have focused on the economic value of life—that is, the amount of money a person would have earned over his lifetime discounted to a present value. This includes a valuation of all wages and other sources of income minus living expenses, such as food and rent. Figuring the exact amount of economic value that a person has been deprived of can be an emotional and somewhat speculative process.

Cappello v. Duncan Aircraft Sales of Florida

United States Court of Appeals for the Sixth Circuit

79 F.3d 1465 (1996)

MERRITT, C.J.

This diversity case for wrongful death arises from an airplane crash. The parties agreed that the substantive questions in the case are governed by Tennessee law.

At 1:42 in the early morning of March 16, 1991, in fair weather, the pilot of a small "Hawker" jet chartered from the defendant flew into the side of a 3,500 [foot high] mountain two minutes after taking off from a closed airport in San Diego. All nine people on board were killed. The pilot, Donald Holmes, had chosen to take off at night in a mountainous area under the visual flight rules ("VFR") of the Federal Aviation Administration, rather than the instrument flight rules ("IFR").... He was therefore not under the direction or control of an FAA controller, and consequently, he had received no radio instructions or clearances before the crash. Under these circumstances of VFR flight ... the pilot in command had the sole responsibility to maintain eye contact with the ground and to avoid obstructions.... The defendant corporation, Duncan Aviation, had chartered the plane and provided the pilot in order to carry a band for country music singer, Reba McEntire, to her next concert engagement. The plaintiffs' decedent in this wrongful death action was the band leader, Kirk Cappello. Able counsel for the defendant declined to admit that pilot negligence was the cause of the accident and sought successfully at the jury trial below to shift responsibility to two nonparty FAA employees on the basis of comparative negligence.... The jury found the pilot who flew into the mountain only 45% responsible, attributing 55% of the responsibility for the crash to the FAA employees. After the deduction for FAA negligence, the jury awarded plaintiffs $329,773 in damages against defendant for their son's death.

* * *

This leaves as the last question a serious issue concerning the propriety of the jury's award of total damages of $732,829 prior to making its 55% deduction for comparative fault.

The parties concede that the jury accepted in its entirety the view of defendant's expert, John Sartain, that the economic value of the deceased band leader was $732,829. The jury accepted this testimony instead of the testimony of four other experts, including another for the defendant who testified that the decedent's income would have been substantially higher than Sartain assumed. In addition, the jury made obvious errors by refusing to include in the award the decedent's substantial funeral expenses and by refusing to bring forward to the date of trial the discounted economic value of the life in question.

The worst mistake made by Sartain, and hence by the jury, however, was in relying upon an assumption that the economic value of decedent's life should be based on an average income for the last five years before his death of $59,920. The unreasonableness of this assumption is demonstrated by the fact that decedent was only 28 years old when he died and had earned as a musician an average of $98,171 for the last two years. He earned over $100,000 in income during the last year before his death. Sartain could only reach his rock bottom figures by averaging the decedent's very low earnings for the preceding five years when he was in music school and then when he was just getting started in his profession. Those early low income years reduced by almost a half the income used in the calculation of a portion of the stream of income, the discounted present value of which represents the economic evaluation of the decedent's projected earnings. If Sartain had based his evaluation on the $98,171 figure the result would have exceeded $1.2 million. Sartain assumed that the decedent's income would have been much less for each of the next seven years than it had been for the last two years of his life. We believe that there is no justification for such an approach in the evaluation of this decedent's life. As pointed out in detail in plaintiff's briefs, Sartain's assumption is entirely inconsistent with his own chart based on empirical studies projecting the average lifetime earnings profile of college educated males.[4]

Unfortunately, the jury in this case went far astray on both liability and damages. Thus, in accordance with this opinion, the judgment of the court below must be vacated and the case remanded to the district court with instructions that (1) the liability of the defendant has been established, and (2) the damages issue must be retried.

Accordingly, it is so ordered.

Notes and Questions

1. The Earnings Projection: The judge says that the damages were understated because Cappello's earnings had begun an upward trend in the two years before his death. Does a straight line extrapolation of his earnings along the more recent trend make sense? Does it overestimate or underestimate his worth?

2. Economic Loss: Why should Cappello's family be allowed to sue for an economic loss to an adult son? Is there any economic rationalization for allowing the family of the deceased to sue the airline for the actions of the deceased pilot?

3. Regulations, Cost-Benefit Analysis, and the Value of Life: Government health and safety regulations are intended to reduce injuries and save lives. Compliance with those regulations is costly. In attempting to determine whether a certain regulation should be adopted, regulators often need to compare the costs of the regulation with the benefits

---

4. Plaintiff's reply brief at page 24 accurately explains the situation: He [Sartain] introduced as Exhibit 101 a chart showing the average age earnings profile of male full-time workers with four years of college. The curve on this chart shows that the average worker had 40% higher earnings at age 28 than at 23 and that for every year after age 28, the income increases until age 54 and the income at age 36 is 30% higher than the income at 28. Although Sartain testified that he relied on that age earnings profile "to show how earnings change at different ages for men with college education, like with Cappello's," his conclusion that Kirk P. Cappello's 1991 income at age 28 would have been only $59,920, the average of his previous five years is in direct conflict with the earnings profile. If Sartain had relied on the earnings curve on the profile, he could not have concluded that Kirk P. Cappello's 1991 income would have reduced to his average income for the previous five years or that he would not again have equaled his 1990 income until he reached the age of 36. If he had relied on the profile, he would have concluded that Kirk P. Cappello's 1991 income would have been more than his 1990 income of $100,000 and would have increased every year until he reached 54. This would have resulted in a pecuniary value of far more than $732,829. Sartain's own testimony established that there was absolutely no justification for using $59,920 as the 1991 income of Kirk P. Cappello.

of the lives that the regulation is intended to save. Choices, preferably informed choices, must be made. Judge Stephen Williams of the District of Columbia Circuit has observed:

> Cost-benefit analysis requires identifying values for lost years of human life and for suffering and other losses from non-fatal injuries. Nothing we say here should be taken as confining the discretion of OSHA to choose among reasonable evaluation methods. While critics of cost-benefit analysis argue that any such valuation is impossible, that is so only in the sense that pin-point figures are necessarily arbitrary, so that the decisionmaker is effectively limited to considering some range of values. In fact, we make implicit life and safety valuations each day when we decide, for example, whether to travel by train or car, the former being more costly (at least if several family member are traveling together) but safer per passenger-mile. Where government makes decisions for others, it may reasonably be expected to make the trade-offs somewhat more explicitly than individuals choosing for themselves. The difficulty of securing agreement even on a range of values hardly justifies making decisions on the basis of a pretense that resources are not scarce.

UAW v. Occupational Safety and Health Administration, 938 F.2d. 1310, 1320–21 (D.C. Cir. 1991) (Williams, J., concurring).

4. A Rational Upper Limit on the Value of Life?: Indeed, the contention that regulators should not put a value on human life is not only mistaken, but it may result in lost lives. Judge Williams explains:

> [E]ven where the application of cost-benefit analysis would result in less stringent regulation, the reduced stringency is not necessarily adverse to health or safety. More regulation means some combination of reduced value of firms, higher product prices, fewer jobs in the regulated industry, and lower cash wages. All the latter three stretch workers' budgets tighter (as does the first to the extent that the firms' stock is held in worker's pension trusts). And larger incomes enable people to lead safer lives. One study finds a 1 percent increase in income associated with a mortality reduction of about 0.05 percent. Jack Hadley & Anthony Osei, "Does Income Affect Mortality?," 20 Medical Care 901, 913 (September 1982). Another suggests that each $7.5 million of costs generated by regulation may, under certain assumptions, induce one fatality. Ralph L. Keeney, "Mortality Risks Induced by Economic Expenditures," 10 Risk Analysis 147, 155 (1990) (relying on E.M. Kitagawa & P.M. Hauser, Differential Mortality in the United States of America: A Study of Socioeconomic Epidemiology (1973)). Larger incomes can produce health by enlarging a person's access to better diet, preventative medical care, safer cars, greater leisure, etc.
>
> Of course, other causal relations may be at work too. Healthier people may be able to earn higher income, and characteristics and advantages that facilitate high earnings (e.g., work ethic, education) may also lead to better health. Nonetheless, higher income can secure better health, and there is no basis for a casual assumption that more stringent regulation will always save lives.
>
> It follows that while officials involved in health or safety regulation may naturally be hesitant to set any kind of numerical value on human life,[5] undue

---

5. Preference-based techniques are a commonly used approach, but are subject to such pitfalls as wealth bias, age bias and inconsistency. See, e.g., Lewis A. Kornhauser, "The Value of Life," 38 *Clev. St. L. Rev.* 209 (1990). For example, if estimates of the benefit of reducing risks are based on the affected workers' willingness to pay for risk reduction, low-paid workers will receive less protection

squeamishness may be deadly. Incremental safety regulation reduces incomes and thus may exact a cost in human lives. For example, if analysis showed that "an individual life was lost for every $12 million taken from individuals [as a result of regulation], this would be a guide to a reasonable value trade-off for many programs designed to save lives." Keeney, 10 Risk Analysis at 158. Such a figure could serve as a ceiling for value-of-life calculated by other means, since regulation causing greater expenditures per life expected to be saved would, everything else being equal, result in a net loss of life.

Id. at 1326–27 (Williams, J., concurring).

5. Risk and the Statistical Value of Life: By applying actual wage-risk labor decisions, economics can be used to determine how individuals value their own life. For instance, if your job is riskier you demand a higher wage to compensate for that risk.

The Value of Life

Kip Viscusi,
2 The New Palgrave Dictionary of Economics
(Steven N. Durlauf and Lawrence E. Blume, eds., 2008)

* * *

Valuing Risks to Life

Although economics has devoted substantial attention to issues generally termed the 'value of life,' this designation is in many respects a misnomer. What is at issue is usually not the value of life itself but rather the value of small risks to life. As Schelling (1968) observed, the key question is how much are people willing to pay to prevent a small risk of death? For small changes in risk, this amount will be approximately the same as the amount of money that they should be compensated to incur such a small risk. This risk-money tradeoff provides an appropriate measure of deterrence in that it indicates the individual's private valuation of small changes in the risk. It thus serves as a measure of the deterrence amount for the value to the individual at risk of preventing accidents and as a reference point for the amount the government should spend to prevent small statistical risks. Because the concern is with statistical lives, not identified lives, analyses of government regulations now use these [value of statistical life] levels to monetize risk reduction benefits.

Suppose that the amount people are willing to pay to eliminate a risk of death of 1/10,000 is $700. This amount can be converted into a value of statistical life estimate in one of two ways. First, consider a group of ten thousand individuals facing that risk level. If each of them were willing to contribute $700 to eliminate the risk, then one could raise a total amount to prevent the statistical death equal to ten thousand people multiplied by $700 per person, or $7 million. An alternative approach to conceptualizing the risk is to think of the amount that is being paid per unit risk. If we divide the willingness to pay amount of $700 by the risk probability of one in ten thousand, then one obtains the value per unit risk. The value per statistical life is $7 million using this approach as well.

Posing hypothetical interview questions to ascertain the willingness to pay amount has been a frequent survey technique in the literature on the value of life. Such studies are often classified as contingent valuation surveys or stated preference surveys, in that they

---

than better paid ones. There are, however, solutions. The wealth bias problem, for example, could be avoided by estimating the willingness to pay by persons of median or mean wealth.

seek information regarding respondents' decisions given hypothetical scenarios. Survey evidence is most useful in addressing issues that cannot be assessed using market data. How, for example, do people value death from cancer compared with acute accidental fatalities? Would people be interested in purchasing pain and suffering compensation, and does such an interest vary with the nature of the accident? Potentially, survey methods can yield insights into these issues.

Evidence from actual decisions that people make is potentially more informative than tradeoffs based on hypothetical situations if suitable market data exists. Actual decision-makers are either paying money to reduce a risk or receiving actual compensation to face a risk, which may be a quite different enterprise than dealing with hypothetical interview money. In addition, the risks to them are real so that they do not have to engage in the thought experiment of imagining that they face a risk. It is also important, however, that individuals accurately perceive the risks they face. Surveys can present respondents with information that is accurate. Biased risk perceptions may bias estimates of the money-risk tradeoff in the market.

* * *

2. The Hedonic Value of Life

Plaintiffs in personal injury or wrongful death actions will assert claims to a variety of other losses in addition to damages for lost earnings. One of the most controversial types of loss claimed by plaintiffs in such actions are hedonic damages. **Hedonic damages** compensate parties who are condemned to watch life's amenities pass them by and suffer from an inability to enjoy life's pleasures. For example, a plaintiff who suffers from complete paralysis due to defendant's negligence and no longer has the ability play a pickup basketball game has suffered a hedonic loss. However, for a variety of reasons, courts have denied or constrained plaintiffs' access to awards for hedonic damages.

Indeed, claims for hedonic damages in wrongful death actions have had little success. Almost all of the courts that have considered the issue have not awarded hedonic damages in such actions for three reasons. First, wrongful death actions are brought for the benefit of surviving relatives for *the damages that they have suffered*. Hedonic damages contemplate a loss suffered by the decedent. Thus, such an award would be an inappropriate element of damages to a surviving relative. Second, hedonic damages are supposed to compensate a party for the suffering they must endure while standing on the sideline and watching life's pleasures pass them by. A decedent, however, does not stand on the sideline and watch life's pleasures pass them by. In short, a dead person cannot suffer the type of harm which hedonic damages are intended to cover. Third, most wrongful death statutes do not provide for the recovery of hedonic damages. In this regard, it is important to remember that actions for wrongful death did not exist at common law. Because wrongful death is a purely statutory creation, the damages available under such provisions are limited to those clearly provided for by the legislature.

Claims for hedonic damages in personal injury cases have also met resistance for two fundamental reasons. First, awards for pain and suffering have traditionally included compensation for the types of harms claimed as hedonic damages. In a sense, pain and suffering is simply the "flip side" of hedonic damages. For example, consider a person who suffers brain damage as a result of defendant's negligence and no longer has the ability to participate fully in advising and raising his children. Watching his children develop without his advice causes the plaintiff a great deal of mental anguish, commonly the ground for an award of pain and suffering. These same facts can be reinterpreted, however, as a restriction on the plaintiff's ability to enjoy participating in raising his children with all of the pleasures and heartbreaks that such a pursuit can provide. By instructing a jury to make an award for pain and suffering and hedonic damages, courts have felt that they run the risk of providing plaintiffs with a double recovery. A second source of resistance to hedonic damage awards stems from limitations on the type of expert testimony that courts will entertain to place a dollar amount on the damages. The following case illustrates the difficulties courts have in allowing expert testimony as to the hedonic value of life.

Mercado v. Ahmed

United States Court of Appeals for the Seventh Circuit
974 F.2d 863 (1992)

COFFEY, Circuit Judge.

In this diversity suit, plaintiff Lucy Mercado ("Mercado"), individually and as next friend of her minor son, Brian, filed a complaint in the district court against defendants Salim Ahmed ("Ahmed") and his former employer, the Checker Taxi Company, Inc. ("Checker"), alleging that due to Ahmed's negligence his taxi struck and injured Brian. The plaintiff further alleged that Checker was negligent in employing Ahmed because he was not qualified to operate the taxi....

* * *

Trial testimony established that Brian, 11 years old, suffered from a wide range of problems prior to the accident. His ability to process visual and auditory information is substantially impaired, making reading, writing, and arithmetic very difficult for him. The boy has been diagnosed as suffering from severe emotional problems and as suicidal. He is unable to perform such rudimentary tasks as dressing properly or managing his personal hygiene. Both the plaintiff's and defendants' witnesses testified that Brian will require some form of institutionalization or structured environment for the remainder of his life. At the time of trial, Brian was a patient in the children's unit of Hartgrove Hospital. His employment prospects are limited to those positions which require the performance of only the most menial tasks.

Mercado argued at trial that Brian's many problems were caused by a closed head injury he suffered when he was struck by the taxi in [a] museum parking lot, an injury which she claims went undetected the day of the accident. The defendants countered that Brian's myriad problems stem from a condition which predated the taxi accident and are not related to the injuries he suffered when he was struck by Ahmed's taxi. The jury found against both Ahmed and Checker on the plaintiff's complaint, and awarded $29,000 for medical expenses and $50,000 for pain and suffering. The jury awarded no damages for disability from the injury, or for future medical expenses, much less anything for future lost earnings.

* * *

III.

The plaintiff also argues that the trial judge committed four evidentiary errors, each of which require a reversal of the damages verdict and a new trial on damages....

A.

The first alleged evidentiary error centers on the district court's refusal to allow the receipt in evidence of the testimony of Stanley Smith. Smith was offered by the plaintiff as an expert on the disability damages owed Brian Mercado because of the "pleasure of living" the boy will be denied as a result of the injuries he received in the taxi accident. Smith, a professional economist who holds a Masters degree in Business Administration from the University of Chicago, would have testified as to the monetary value of "the reduction of Brian's ability to engage in and experience the ordinary value of life that he was experiencing prior to the injury." These damages are sometimes referred to as "hedonic damages."[6]

The district court conducted an extensive voir dire to determine the method Smith employs in calculating the monetary value of the "lost pleasure of living" an individual such as Brian suffers due to an injury. Smith testified that in his computation he first assumes a "percentage range" representing the degree an injured individual's capacity to experience life has been diminished. This method measures an individual's impairment in four areas: occupational, practical functioning, emotional, and social functioning. Smith does not compute this figure himself, but instead consults with a medical expert to arrive at the appropriate range. In this case the expert was Dr. Kathleen Pueschel, a clinical neuropsychologist. According to the plaintiff, Dr. Pueschel concluded that Brian's disabilities were "severe," and that the boy's capacity to experience life was diminished 66% to 83%.

Smith then applies his own analysis to the diminished capacity figure. As the district court noted, the method attempts to get at the value of life by indirection; no one is ever asked "what is the monetary value of living?," because most people would probably respond that life is priceless, scuttling the endeavor. Instead, Smith focuses on how much Americans are willing to pay for reductions in health and safety risks, and how much they are compensated for assuming extra risk. This method, according to Smith's economic theory, reveals the value we actually place on living, and avoids the astronomical answers people would give in response to a hypothetical question. He relies on three types of willingness-to-pay studies: studies of how much consumers, through the purchase of devices such as smoke detectors and seat belts, pay for increased personal safety; studies of how much more people who assume extra risk (e.g., policemen) are paid because their jobs are dangerous; and studies of cost-benefit analyses conducted in the evaluation of government safety regulation. Smith testified that he relied on some 75 such studies in his valuation.

Through this analysis, Smith concluded that the value of the enjoyment of a statistically average person's life was $2.3 million in 1988 dollars. (The statistically average person is 31 years old with a 45 year additional life expectancy.) This averages out to approximately a $60,000-per-year value on the enjoyment of life. Smith took this figure and multiplied it by the percentage range of Brian's loss of the full experience of life, 66% to 83% (drawn from Dr. Pueschel's calculations). Adjusting for Brian's young age, the plaintiff informs us that Smith concluded the value of Brian's lost pleasure of living due to the injuries he suffered in the taxi accident was $2,207,827 to $2,762,227.

The district judge, after listening to Smith out of the presence of the jury, ruled, pursuant to Fed. R. Evid. 702, that Smith's proposed testimony on the value of Brian Mercado's lost pleasure of living would not be allowed.... The opinion sets out two basic doubts about Smith's testimony. First, the court was troubled by the lack of any "basic agreement among economists as to what elements ought to go into" or "which studies

---

6. Defendants do not argue that damages for the lost pleasure of living are unavailable under Illinois law. Thus, we, like the district court, will assume their availability in our consideration of the admissibility of Smith's testimony.

ought to be considered" in life valuation. In order to allow a witness to testify as an expert, the court must be convinced that the witness will rely only upon evidence a reasonable expert in the field would rely. The court determined that no consensus existed among economists as to what was proper evidence of the value of living.

The district court's second and more significant concern centered on Smith's methodology. The court reasoned that Smith's valuation, based as it was on studies meant to determine how much Americans pay to reduce risks or charge for assuming them, did not qualify as the sort of "scientific, technical or other specialized" knowledge contemplated in Fed. R. Evid. 702. Referring to Smith's method of valuing life, the district court observed:

> "Survey of attitudes and views of others as a basis for concluding something is true is not necessarily wrong. Some science as it comes into court is the result of consensus by practitioners of some area of expertise that a certain law of nature is correct. What is wrong here is not that the evidence is founded on consensus or agreement, it is that the consensus is that of persons who are no more expert than are jurors on the value of life. Even if reliable and valid, the evidence may fail to 'assist the trier of fact to understand the evidence or determine a fact in issue' [quoting Fed. R. Evid. 702] in a way more meaningful than would occur if the jury asked a group of wise courtroom bystanders for their opinions."

A witness who knows no more than the average person is not an expert. The "theory upon which expert testimony is ... [admitted] is that such testimony serves to inform the court about affairs not within the full understanding of the average man." As the Supreme Court has noted, "expert testimony not only is unnecessary but indeed may properly be excluded in the discretion of the trial judge—if all the primary facts can be accurately and intelligibly described to the jury, and if they, as men of common understanding, are as capable of comprehending the primary facts and of drawing correct conclusions from them as are witnesses possessed of special or peculiar training, experience, or observation in respect of the subject under investigation.'" Salem v. United States Lines Co., 370 U.S. 31, 35 (1962) (citation omitted).

The district court, confronting this novel legal problem, was not persuaded that Smith's technique for valuing the lost pleasure of living provided expert assistance to the jury. On appeal, the plaintiff attacks the reasoning of the trial judge directly, asserting that Smith should have been given the "opportunity to supplant the jurors' own knowledge as to the value of life...." This frames the issue precisely: does Stanley Smith, supported by his extensive willingness-to-pay research, know better than the average juror how much life is worth?

As we noted above, the district judge did not believe that Smith offered the jury any "expertise" because (1) no consensus among experts supported Smith's method of valuing life and (2) Smith's research was no more than a compilation of the opinions, expressed through spending decisions, of a large number of Americans as to the value of life. The first criticism is irrefutable: the plaintiff could point to no expert consensus supporting Smith's methodology. The second criticism is also on the mark, since Smith concedes that his method relies on arriving at a valuation of life based on analyzing the behavior of non-experts.

However, even accepting Smith's premise that his method of determining the value of life is different in an important way from submitting the question to a jury because it focuses on observable behavior and not opinion, we have serious doubts about his assertion that the studies he relies upon actually measure how much Americans value life. For example, spending on items like air bags and smoke detectors is probably influenced as much by advertising and marketing decisions made by profit-seeking manufacturers and by government-mandated safety requirements as it is by any consideration by consumers of how much life is worth. Also, many people may be interested in a whole range of safety devices and believe they are worth-while, but are unable to afford them. More fundamentally, spending on safety items reflects a consumer's willingness to pay to reduce risk, perhaps more a measure of how cautious a person is than how much he or she values life. Few of us, when confronted with the threat, "Your money or your life!" would, like Jack Benny, pause and respond, "I'm thinking, I'm thinking." Most of us would empty our wallets. Why that decision reflects less the value we place on life than whether we buy an airbag is not immediately obvious.

The two other kinds of studies Smith relies upon are open to valid and logical criticism as well. To say that the salary paid to those who hold risky jobs tells us something significant about how much we value life ignores the fact that humans are moved by more than monetary incentives. For example, someone who believes police officers working in an extremely dangerous city are grossly undercompensated for the risks they assume might nevertheless take up the badge out of a sense of civic duty to their hometown. Finally, government calculations about how much to spend (or force others to spend) on health and safety regulations are motivated by a host of considerations other than the value of life: is it an election year? how large is the budget deficit? on which constituents will the burden of the regulations fall? what influence and pressure have lobbyists brought to bear? what is the view of interested constituents? And so on.

All this is not to imply that we can state conclusively that Smith's approach is devoid of any merit. But given that "we review a district court's decision to exclude expert testimony under an abuse of discretion standard," and that the trial court's "determination will be affirmed unless it is 'manifestly erroneous,'" we can say with confidence that the district court's decision to bar Smith's testimony was not reversible error. Smith has taken up a daunting task: to develop a methodology capable of producing specialized knowledge to assist jurors in determining the monetary value of being alive. The district court ruled that, despite Smith's training, extensive research and countless calculations, his testimony would not aid the jury in evaluating the evidence and arriving at its verdict (the true test of expert testimony under Fed. R. Evid. 702) because Smith was no more expert in valuing life than the average person. This conclusion may be less a reflection of the flaws in Smith's methodology than on the impossibility of any person achieving unique knowledge of the value of life.

[The court's discussion of the other three alleged evidentiary errors is omitted.]

* * *

IV.

The verdict of the jury is AFFIRMED.

Notes and Questions

1. Mutually Beneficial Exchange and the Value of Life: The methodology the plaintiff's expert used attempts to develop a value for life based upon society's revealed preferences. For example, by using the prices paid for air bags or smoke detectors, the plaintiff's expert claims to have developed a value of life calculation based on objectively determined market values (as introduced in the Viscusi excerpt above). However, as the court properly observes, to the extent that market participants are required by regulation to make such purchases, the prices paid are not determined by a voluntary mutually beneficial exchange. Thus, the expert's value of life calculations are not truly based on objectively determined market prices. Due to this fact, can we rely on the expert's numbers as revealing the value that society places on life? In which way would the expert's value of life number be biased as a result of this error? How does the economic reasoning developed thus far in the casebook square with the court's analysis of the expert's wage differential analysis?

2. Evidentiary Hurdles to Hedonic Damage Awards: Federal Rule of Evidence 702 contemplates that courts will play a "gate keeping" function with respect to the types of expert testimony which will be allowed into evidence. In *Mercado*, the court felt that the jurors were in as good a position to place a value on life as the plaintiff's expert. In other words, there is no need for expert testimony as to the value of life. The fear is that, by allowing the plaintiff's expert to testify, jurors will develop the impression that they do not have the requisite knowledge or skill to determine the value of life. The result of allowing such testimony would be to prejudice the jury's factual determination of value. In a sense, Rule 702 is an attempt to prevent "junk science" from misleading the fact finder. In *Daubert v. Merrill Dow Pharmaceuticals, Inc.*, 509 U.S. 579 (1993), the Supreme Court provided a non-exclusive list of considerations to assist courts in their gate keeping function. The considerations introduced by the *Daubert* court are: 1) Is the evidence capable of being tested?; 2) Has the evidence been subject to peer review?; 3) What is the potential rate of error for the evidence?; and 4) What is the acceptance level of the methodology in the relevant scientific community? How would the plaintiff's expert in *Mercado* fare under the considerations introduced in *Daubert*? If the court is in a position where it must determine a subjective value for purposes of a damages award, who should make the calculation?

3. The Break-Up Value of Human Life: In discussing the value of a business, investors often refer to a firm's break-up value. That is, the value of the firm if all of its components were divided up and sold separately. Would it make sense to value a human life in the same manner? Why not place the value of life at the amount of money that can be received for each of the parts that make up a human body? For example, hearts sell at $500, blood at $350, kidneys at $610, etc. How much would a person with terminal heart disease pay for the heart of a recently deceased donor? Wouldn't this be a voluntary mutually beneficial exchange — that is, an objective measure for the value of life? This is obviously an extreme example, but when compared to the method used by the plaintiff's expert in *Mercado*, is it any less reasonable?

4. Property Law — The Case of Takings: The Fifth Amendment of the Constitution of the United States provides that individuals are entitled to just compensation for property taken by the government. Courts have interpreted just compensation to be the objectively determined market value for the property in question. Why not allow someone to testify as to the subjective enjoyment they receive as a result of owning the property in question? Would it be reasonable to allow expert testimony as to the loss of enjoyment due to a taking? Couldn't one formulate a methodology similar to that used by the plaintiff's expert in *Mercado* to make such estimates?

5. Pain and Suffering v. Hedonic Damages: Pain and suffering describes the physical discomfort and emotional trauma which are recoverable as an element of damages in a tort claim. How do the type of losses that hedonic damages contemplate differ from the losses that pain and suffering damages contemplate?

D. Valuation of Close Corporations

A **close corporation,** or **closely held corporation,** is characterized by a concentrated group of shareholders who are often involved in setting corporate policy—typically as active managers—and whose shares are infrequently traded. Another name for this type of corporation is a privately held corporation because the company's stock is not traded on public exchange. Legal questions regarding the value of such shares arise in a variety of circumstances, ranging from bankruptcy reorganizations, to estate and gift taxes, to mergers and acquisitions. Difficulties in the valuation of close corporations stem from the fact that there is no organized market on which such shares are actively traded. Thus, the determination of value is not simply a matter of looking to an efficiently determined stock market price.

In general, the valuation of close corporations is no different from the valuation questions that have been discussed in previous sections of this chapter or from the valuation of public corporations. Namely, the value of a closely held share depends on the present value of future economic benefits attributable to ownership of the share. The value of such shares is calculated by projecting some stream of future benefits, usually cash flow, and choosing an appropriate discount rate to get to a value in today's terms. The purpose of any business is to earn a profit or make money for the owners over and above the amount they invested. A productive and efficient enterprise will make money, or earn a "return on investment," for many years into the future. By estimating those returns on a yearly basis and then discounting them into a present value, the "worth" of a company can be determined. The fundamental difficulty behind a discounted future returns methodology is the estimation of future economic benefits and the selection of an appropriate discount rate. This difficulty is compounded in the courtroom because of evidentiary requirements. Unlike the entrepreneur or business manager, judges and juries are often not willing to rely on a "hunch" or "educated guess" regarding projected financial performance. They are often reluctant to rely on data that is "too speculative." Despite these potential difficulties, the discounted future benefits method, with its reliance on projected financial data, remains the generally accepted theoretical model for valuing close corporations.

Because of the "proof problems" that often arise when using projected financial data, historical financial data often become a significant factor in calculating the value of shares in a closely held corporation. However, regardless of whether one is using projected or historical financial data, the goal is still to develop a present value for future economic benefits attributable to the company's shares of stock. Thus, in theory, present value calculations using projected financial data and methodologies should approximate present value calculations based on historical data and methodologies. In practice, it is wise to use these alternative sources of data and methods as a means for checking the accuracy and strength of one's results. Moreover, it is important to recognize that although the use of historical and projected financial data are being discussed as alternatives here, they are not mutually exclusive. For example, in making earnings projections, a financial analyst will surely consider the corporation's historic earnings trend. Alternatively, when using historic earnings numbers, the financial analyst will consider whether historic performance is likely to be representative of future performance.

An important lesson regarding the valuation of closely held shares is that the decision about whether to place emphasis on projected data and methodologies or historical data and methodologies depends on the particular purpose for the valuation. Different areas of the law have developed different legal standards based upon varying statutory and decisional backgrounds. For example, gift and estate tax questions tend to be resolved by an analysis which uses historical data to project the present value of closely held shares. On the other hand, it would be quite contradictory for courts to rely on historical data for projecting the future benefits stream of firms involved in bankruptcy reorganizations. Thus, valuation analysis in the bankruptcy reorganization context tends to rely much more on projected data. Thus, prudence lies in checking statutory and decisional authority when choosing the specific method and standards for purposes of business valuation.

A critical factor when determining the value for closely held shares is the assumption that must be made regarding the future status of the business. In general, an appraiser makes one of two assumptions regarding the future status of the business—either it will continue to operate or it will shut down. This assumption will have a specific effect on the manner in which a business is valued. **Going-concern value** assumes that the business will continue to operate for an indefinite period of time and represents the present value of the future economic benefits to be derived from the operation of the business. On the other hand, **liquidation value** assumes that business operations will be terminated and represents the net amount that can be realized by breaking up the company and selling the individual assets.

Another factor that has a significant impact on the valuation of a business is the perspective from which value will be determined. Because of the perceived benefits of using a market price, the goal in many legal contexts is to attempt to replicate a market determination of price. Thus, the most common standard of value invoked in legal proceedings is fair market value. **Fair market value** is the price at which property would change hands in an **arm's length transaction**—a transaction between a hypothetical willing buyer and a hypothetical willing seller, neither of whom are under any compulsion or ulterior motive to buy or sell, and both of whom have reasonable knowledge of the relevant facts. Thus, fair market value attempts to establish an objective measure of current value. This differs from another factor of valuation known as book value. **Book value** is simply the amount of equity a company has, or the value of a company's assets after subtracting its liabilities. Book value is regarded as the most objective way to value a company because it is a function of the price originally paid for all of a company's assets less any debt obligations used to help pay for those assets. Book value is also considered the most conservative approach to valuation because it does not reflect any current fluctuations in demand and therefore corresponding changes in value. Also in opposition to the objective nature of fair market value, the concept of investment value represents a very subjective notion of value. **Investment value** represents the value of a business in a particular investor's hands. Investment value helps to explain why some individuals are willing to pay a premium in order to acquire a business. For example, XYZ manufacturing may be willing to pay a higher price than any other bidder to acquire ABC distributors because of specific synergies between the operations of XYZ and ABC. In most instances, courts attempt to eliminate the idiosyncratic value that particular parties attach to closely held shares.

1. Discounted Future Returns Approach

An important tool in determining the value of close corporation stock is the discounted future returns approach to present value. Much of the discussion throughout this chapter has focused on the two primary hurdles in the use of such present value analysis—determination of the relevant stream of economic benefits and selection of the appropriate discount rate. Estimating the stream of benefits and the relevant discount rate continue to be the challenging factors in valuing close corporations using discounted future returns. In fact, much of the litigation that arises in the valuation of closely held shares involves disputes among expert witnesses as to the appropriate stream of future benefits and the discount rate.

Of primary importance in selecting the appropriate benefits stream is to choose a measure of benefits that accurately reflects the economic value of holding the shares. In this regard, five important proxies for economic value are widely used in the valuation of close corporations—earnings, cash flow, dividends, revenue, and assets. Despite the common usage of these measures, a great deal of litigation revolves around two important issues. First, how does one define earnings, cash flow, dividend capacity, revenue, or assets? Variations in the manner in which each of these financial variables is defined can explain to a large degree differences in the present value numbers generated by different experts valuing the same business. Second, if different measures lead to different present value calculations, which calculation should be relied on by the judge or jury? The following case demonstrates both of these issues and the manner in which such differences are often resolved.

Kleinwort Benson, Ltd. v. Silgan Corp.

Court of Chancery of Delaware
1995 Del. Ch. LEXIS 75

CHANDLER, Vice Chancellor

Petitioners, holders of 400,000 shares of Class B common stock of Silgan Corporation ("Silgan" or "Respondent"), seek an appraisal ... to assess the fair value of their shares.... For the reasons set forth below, I find the fair value of Silgan on the date of the merger to be $5.94 per share....

I. BACKGROUND

Silgan, a Delaware corporation, was organized in August 1987 under the name MS/S&H Holdings, Inc. Silgan had three classes of common stock, Classes A, B and C. Classes A and B are identical, except that each class votes separately to elect two directors. Class C stock is non-voting. R. Philip Silver ("Silver") and D. Greg Horrigan ("Horrigan") beneficially owned all of the Class A stock. The Morgan Stanley Group, and the Morgan Stanley Leveraged Equity Fund, L.P. (MSLEF I), owned more than two thirds of the Class B stock....

* * *

On April 28, 1989, Silgan entered into a merger agreement with Silgan Holdings, whereby Silgan was to combine with Silgan Holdings' wholly owned subsidiary, Silgan Acquisition Inc. Under the terms of the merger agreement, Class B stockholders were to receive $6.50 per share, and Class A stockholders were to receive $12.2 million in cash and shares of Class A common stock of Silgan Holdings equal to 50% of Silgan Holdings's voting stock. Silgan retained William Blair & Co. to render a fairness opinion on the price offered to Silgan stockholders. Silgan distributed the fairness opinion, as well as management's financial projections for Silgan, along with its Solicitation of Stockholders Consents. The merger was approved by a majority of Silgan stockholders, with Morgan Stanley and MSLEF I consenting to the merger. The merger was completed on June 30, 1989, making Silgan a wholly owned subsidiary of Silgan Holdings.

Petitioners dissented to the merger and validly exercised their appraisal rights.... During the trial, Petitioners and Respondent presented expert testimony as to the value of Silgan. Petitioners' expert, Louis Paone ("Paone"), ... valued Silgan at $12.65 per share. Respondent's expert, James Kovacs ("Kovacs"), ... valued Silgan at $4.88 per share. In addition to the parties' experts, the Court appointed a neutral expert, Joel Lawson ("Lawson").... Lawson critiqued the opinions of the parties' expert witnesses, but the Court instructed him not to provide an independent valuation of Silgan.

II. THE EXPERTS' VALUATION METHODS

Paone and Kovacs used fairly similar methods to appraise Silgan. Paone conducted a reconstructed market analysis, which looked at market prices of comparable publicly traded corporations and at the price paid in comparable mergers. He also conducted a discounted cash flow ("DCF") analysis to establish a present value for Silgan's projected returns. Like Paone, Kovacs conducted a market analysis and a DCF analysis. However, he did not look at comparable mergers in his market analysis. I will weigh the reliability of each method employed by the experts, then adopt the methods that most reliably measure Silgan's fair value as of June 30, 1989.

* * *

III. MARKET ANALYSIS

Both experts used a comparative market analysis as part of their evaluations. Kovacs analyzed five similar publicly traded companies in order to estimate the market value of Silgan's stock. Paone considered the same five companies plus Kerr Glass in his analysis. The most dramatic difference in the approaches taken by the experts is Paone's inclusion of an 86% premium over market price to adjust for an inherent minority discount in the price of publicly traded shares....

Respondent contends that Paone's market analysis is improper as a matter of law, citing several decisions of this Court for the proposition that the appraisal value of a corporation does not include a "control premium." Petitioners respond that Paone did not include a "control premium," but merely adjusted the price for minority interests available in publicly traded markets to reflect the enterprise value of the entire corporation.

* * *

Paone testified that the market price reflects the value of a minority interest in a corporation because only small lots of stock are available at the market price. Kovacs, the Respondent's expert, and Lawson, the Court's neutral expert, also expressed a belief that publicly traded shares trade below the proportionate enterprise value of the stock. Respondent's expert stated at trial that "the preponderance of opinion is that there is some minority interest that's implicit in a publicly traded company's price." Upon the record presented, I conclude that both experts should have adjusted market value to compensate for an inherent minority discount.

* * *

Although Kovacs erred in not attempting to account for an implicit minority discount in the market data, I find his market analysis much more reliable than Paone's market analysis. Paone purportedly adjusted the available market data to remove the imbedded minority discount, but his methods do not discriminate between a minority discount and a premium that includes post-merger value.... Kovacs and Lawson testified that the premium over market price paid by an acquiror includes more than an adjustment for a minority discount. The acquiror may value the target corporation above its going concern value because of potential synergies or because the acquiror believes it will manage the target better. This portion of a control premium cannot be included in the appraisal value of a corporation because it reflects value arising from the accomplishment or expectation of the merger.... Paone applied a premium in his market analysis that explicitly includes value arising from the expectation of a merger.

* * *

Kovacs did not attempt to account for a minority discount in the price of publicly traded stock because Respondent's counsel instructed him that it was improper as a matter of law. Had Kovacs attempted to present such evidence, he probably would have been stymied anyway. Lawson states in his report that setting an exact figure for the minority discount comes down to an arbitrary determination. Respondent asserts that the Court should not adjust the market data to remove the minority discount because no reliable proof has been presented on the issue. It seems to me that acknowledging the existence of the minority discount, but setting it at zero, is more arbitrary than endeavoring to find its true value. At trial, Kovacs stated that a reasonable estimate of the minority discount is around 10–15%. Based on that testimony, I will adjust Kovacs' market analysis by 12.5% to account for the minority discount inherent in publicly traded shares.

* * *

IV. DISCOUNTED CASH FLOW ANALYSIS

Kovacs and Paone each valued Silgan by using a DCF analysis. Kovacs labels his study an Income Approach, while Paone refers to his study as a Discounted Future Returns Analysis, but they used nearly identical methods. They estimated Silgan's revenues from 1989–1995 on a debt free basis, set a terminal value for the company at the end of the period, and then discounted those future values to reach a present value for Silgan's market value of invested capital ("MVIC"). Because they valued Silgan's revenues on a debt free basis, they subtracted the market value of Silgan's debt from its MVIC to reach a value for Silgan's common equity....

* * *

A. Management's Projections

As this Court has noted before, the outcome of a DCF analysis depends heavily on the projections used in the model.... Prior to the merger, Silgan's management projected Silgan's costs and revenues for the period from 1989–1995 for use by Silgan's lenders. Silgan distributed these projections with its Solicitation of Stockholder Consents. Both experts relied heavily on these projections in their DCF analyses, but Kovacs revised some of the estimates. Kovacs testified that he needed to revise some of management's original projections because they were not generated for use in an appraisal proceeding. He altered some of the projections based on Silgan's books and records, discussions with Silgan's management, and general trends in the industry. Petitioners criticize Kovacs for revising management's contemporaneous projections to reach a lower value for Silgan's stock. Paone worked exclusively from the original projections, adjusting them only for the purposes of a debt free analysis. Petitioners contend that by conducting interviews with Silgan's managers Kovacs improperly considered evidence that was unavailable as of the merger date. Petitioners request that I prevent Respondent from revising its optimistic pre-merger forecast to suit its purposes in this lawsuit.

The Court will not bar Respondent from presenting evidence relevant to the fair value of Silgan, ... but Respondent's revisions of its original projections merit close inspection....

B. June 30, 1989–1995 Cash Flows

In both DCF models, the experts used management's projections to estimate Silgan's cash flows from June 30, 1989 through the end of 1995. In his estimates of cash flows, Kovacs revised management's original projections in several respects.... [After reviewing each of Kovacs' revisions, the court concluded that the revisions were proper.]

C. Terminal Value

In addition to estimating cash flows for the projection period, the DCF model requires the experts to set a value for Silgan at the end of the period, which is labeled a terminal value. The two experts' extremely divergent estimates of Silgan's terminal value account for much of the difference in the outcomes of the two experts' DCF analyses....

Kovacs' terminal value differs drastically from Paone's because he did not use management's projections for 1989–1995 to create a terminal value. Paone extrapolated a value in perpetuity from Silgan's expected performance from 1989 through 1995. Kovacs believes that management's projections for the specific time period, 1989 through 1995, cannot be used to value Silgan in perpetuity. During the projection period, Silgan's depreciation exceeds its investment, which Kovacs believes cannot be sustained in the long run. Kovacs believes Paone's extrapolation of the current data ignores Silgan's need to make new capital investments to sustain its growth.... I find that Kovacs' has presented the more reliable terminal value calculation. Paone's model unrealistically extrapolates Silgan's short run circumstances into perpetuity. Kovacs correctly recognized the need for an adjustment in the data so that capital investment relates to growth and depreciation in a sustainable manner. Kovacs projected Silgan's future capital expenditures from the historical trends of the company and comparable industry data. Kovacs testified that capital investment should slightly exceed depreciation to sustain perpetual growth.... I will not alter Kovacs' terminal value calculation.

* * *

D. Respondent Has Presented The More Reliable DCF Analysis

In every respect, Respondent has provided more reliable valuations of Silgan's cash flows and terminal value. I carefully scrutinized Respondent's revision of the original projections, but each revision is supported by well-reasoned analysis. In contrast, Petitioners' steadfast refusal to reassess any of the original figures damages their expert witness' credibility. I conclude that Kovacs' DCF analysis is a better indicator of Silgan's fair value than Paone's DCF analysis. Yet, many aspects of Kovacs analysis reflect an overly adversarial approach.... By contrasting the methods used by Kovacs and Paone, and employing Lawson's very helpful critique of both experts' opinions, I will make [the necessary] adjustments.

E. Discounting Future Returns To Present Value

In a DCF analysis, the future returns must be discounted to their present value. The parties' experts used similar discount rates: Kovacs, 12.8%, Paone, 12.5%. Kovacs rounded the 12.8% rate to 13% for his calculations. Kovacs offered no justification for rounding the figure, and I believe it was done to create as low a final result as possible. I will remove the effect of this rounding from Kovacs' DCF analysis.

Kovacs also timed Silgan's cash flows in a manner that unreasonably lowers Silgan's value. Kovacs assumed that Silgan receives all of its cash at the end of the year. Paone assumed a mid-year receipt of cash flows as a surrogate for receipts occurring over the course of the year. Respondent submitted some evidence that Silgan, a company with a seasonal business, receives most of its cash at the end of the year. Other evidence in the record indicates that Silgan received cash throughout the year. I find the mid-year point to be the better estimate for receipt of Silgan's cash flows....

* * *

V. FAIR VALUE

I have decided that Kovacs' market study and DCF analysis, with some adjustments, provide reliable methods for valuing Silgan. In reaching a final conclusion as to fair value, I do not give the two approaches equal weight. I give greater weight to the DCF model because it actually values Silgan as a going concern, rather than comparing Silgan to other businesses. I apply 2/3 weight to the DCF analysis and 1/3 weight to the market study to reach a value of Silgan's common equity of $79,429, unadjusted for stock options. For the purposes of this appraisal, all of the experts agree that the stock options should be treated as fully outstanding and the proceeds from the exercise of these options included in the equity value. Kovacs subtracted a market value for the options in his original report, so I add back that $9,100. Finally, I add $1,646 to reflect the exercise price of the options to reach a fair value of Silgan's common equity of $90,177. Dividing $90,177 by 15,179,000 shares, I find the fair value for Silgan's stock as of the merger date to be $5.94 per share.

* * *

Notes and Questions

1. Controlling Versus Minority Interests: One of the primary issues that arose in *Kleinwort Benson* was whether a premium for control should be applied to the estimated share values. Control can take on a variety of forms. For example, one might have the ability to control the board of directors, the selection of management, the direction of the business in general, compensation policy, capital expenditures and liquidations, dividend policy, capital structure, or the decision to go public. Moreover, the extent to which any individual shareholder has control over particular decisions is a matter of varying degrees. An individual shareholder of a widely traded public corporation may have very little control over the decisions of the corporation, whereas a corporation wholly owned by a single individual places these control rights with that one individual. In between these two extremes are innumerable levels of control.

It makes sense to assume that purchases of widely traded public shares do not carry any sort of a premium for control rights. However, does the absence of public trading necessarily imply that shareholders have control? The best approach is to consider the various control rights that might exist and the extent to which the shareholders actually possess such power—a willing buyer would certainly conduct such analysis. Reconsider the share classifications in *Kleinwort Benson*. Does it appear clear that the holders of Class B shares had any control rights? Moreover, an important source of constraint on control rights would be restrictive covenants included in the debt contracts. The facts of the case indicate that Silgan was highly leveraged. In short, does the Chancery Court sufficiently consider the issue of control?

2. Capital Base Must Support Projected Growth: Capital base refers to those assets that are expected to create future returns more than a year into the future, such as manufacturing plants and equipment. As a business continues to grow it eventually reaches a point where it is constrained by the existing capital base. Thus, if such a firm intends to continue to grow, it must spend money to expand its capital base. Funding for such investments can come from two different sources—the earnings retained from profitable operations or outside financing. Where an assumption of earnings growth is made in present value calculations, it may be necessary to investigate whether such growth can be achieved with the current capital base. The answer is typically no when the business is valued as an ongoing concern ("it takes money to make money"), so a reduction in the estimated future economic benefits must be accounted for. If expenditures for an expanded capital base—capital expenditures—are necessary to achieve the projected growth rates, then present value would be overestimated by not deducting such expenditures from the flow of future benefits.

3. Appraisal Rights and the Delaware Block Rule: The issue in *Kleinwort Benson* revolved around the legal concept of appraisal rights. **Appraisal rights** are essentially a statutory remedy for shareholders who object to certain extraordinary actions taken by a corporation.

The effect of appraisal rights is to allow dissenting shareholders to exit the corporate form by requiring the corporation to purchase the dissenters' shares for a price equal to the share value immediately prior to the objectionable action. For years, the primary method of appraisal valuation was the Delaware Block Rule. Under the Delaware Block Rule, share values were determined by the weighted average of four "measures of value"—earnings, dividends, assets, and market price. Earnings, dividends, and asset values were determined primarily through the use of historical data under the Delaware Block Rule. Market values under the Delaware Block Rule were determined by studying the trading prices for stocks of comparable public corporations. In general, projected financial data were not utilized under the Delaware Block Rule and, thus, discounted future returns methodologies did not factor heavily in appraisal rights litigation.

However, in *Weinberger v. UOP, Inc.*, 457 A.2d 701 (Del. 1983), the Delaware Supreme Court held that the four factors considered under the Delaware Block Rule were not exclusive in the determination of appraised values. Rather, the court indicated that all relevant factors should be considered in determining share values including methods which utilized projections of future earnings. In *Kleinwort Benson*, a Delaware Chancery Court placed primary emphasis on values determined through the use of projected financial data. Given the historical preeminence of Delaware corporate law, it would appear that present value and discounted future returns methodologies may come to play a greater role in valuations for appraisal rights.

4. Investment Value Versus Fair Value: The Chancery Court rejects the use of data from mergers which involved companies similar to Silgan. In the context of the control premium, the Chancery Court notes that the premiums paid in mergers usually include more than just a premium for control: "The acquiror may value the target corporation above its going concern value because of potential synergies or because the acquiror believes it will manage the target better." It is important in estimating the value of close corporations to determine and follow the relevant standard of value. Here, the petitioners' expert used comparison values that were characteristic of idiosyncratic transactions (investment value) not hypothetical bargainers (fair market value). The use of such data harmed the expert's credibility in the eyes of the Chancery Court. Not only did this error result in the share value being miscalculated, but the loss of credibility suffered by the petitioners' expert probably affected the Chancery Court's decisions regarding other aspects of the expert's analysis.

5. The Timing of Future Returns: In working with discounted future benefits problems, the timing of future returns is critical. This fact should be intuitively obvious from our general discussion of the time value of money. Specifically, the longer one has to wait for a future return, the more such a return will be discounted, all else being equal. Thus, a party who has to wait until the end of the year to receive cash will have a lower present value than some other individual who receives cash at mid-year, all else being equal. Even small differences in the timing of future benefits can matter greatly, especially when such values are extrapolated over several years because the sooner the future benefits are received, the sooner those benefits can compound and earn a return themselves.

6. Use of a Terminal Value: In general, the discounted future returns model contemplates that all future benefits will be estimated. The assumption behind the corporate form of organization is that the life of the firm is perpetual. Combining these two factors suggests that the future benefits from owning closely held shares must be calculated for each year in perpetuity. Obviously, this is an impossible task. A common method for resolving this difficulty is to divide the future into two periods. During the first period, called the near-term, a financial analyst will attempt to estimate the future benefits attributable to each specific year. This period is usually based on the expected real growth of the company. In *Kleinwort Benson*, both expert witnesses estimated specific values for future benefits six years into the future. Because any company whose real growth is indefinite will eventually become the entire economy, the general assumption is that most companies' growth will eventually slow to keep pace with inflation and capital expenditures. It is from the end of the real growth period forward that most financial practitioners calculate the terminal value. The period beyond which the analyst feels comfortable estimating future benefits for specific years can be called the distant period. For the distant period, the financial analyst will estimate a terminal value to represent an infinite stream of future benefits. The most common method for calculating a terminal value is to make some assumption regarding the slowing of the growth rate of future benefits to keep pace with capital expenditures and inflation and then utilize the perpetuity or a growth perpetuity model of present value.

2. Approaches Using Current or Historical Data

Due to the difficulty of estimating the stream of future economic benefits attributable to closely held shares and courts' general reluctance to rely on financial data that is "too speculative," a number of valuation approaches based on current or historical data have become widely used. As is the case with projected financial data, historical data is used to make projections regarding the future economic benefits from share ownership. In this sense, the use of historical data is simply another means from which the present value of future benefits can be estimated. There are a variety of methods from which current or historical data can be used to calculate the value of closely held shares. The choice of methods in any given case will depend upon the facts of the situation and legal precedent, but usually the process involves comparing relevant financial data from the close corporation to the same financial data from comparable publicly traded corporations.

The most common way in which current or historical data can be used in the estimation of share value is through the process of capitalization. **Capitalization** refers to the simple mathematical process of taking some measure of historical or current benefits known as the **base value** and either dividing by a capitalization rate or multiplying by a capitalization multiple, which is based on a comparative rate or multiple from a similar company that is publicly traded. Such calculations result in a measure for the share value. For example, the general form for valuations using a capitalization rate is:

$$\text{Share Value} = \text{Base Value} \div \text{Capitalization Rate}$$

The general form for the capitalization multiple method of valuation is:

$$\text{Share Value} = \text{Base Value} \times \text{Capitalization Multiple}$$

However, as is the case with the discounted future benefits method, despite the relative simplicity of the formulas, a great deal of controversy can arise regarding the proper application of capitalization methods. Three primary difficulties encountered when using such valuation methods are: choosing an appropriate proxy for current or historical economic benefit (choosing the base value); the measurement of the selected proxy (measuring the base value); and the estimation of the capitalization rate or multiple. In general, the process of capitalization for the valuation of closely held shares using current or historical data can be characterized by the following steps:

1. Selecting of the relevant base value.

2. Selecting the appropriate historical time frame from which to estimate the base value.

3. Accounting for historical trends in the estimation of the base value.

4. Adjusting base values across firms for comparison purposes.

5. Estimating the appropriate capitalization rate or multiple based on a comparable publicly traded corporation.

6. Calculating share values.

The first step in the process of using a capitalization method for the valuation of closely held shares is to select an appropriate economic variable to serve as the base value. A wide variety of proxies for historical or current economic benefits have been used as base values when determining the value of closely held corporations. Such proxies include earnings, revenue, dividends, asset value, and output or capacity. Selection of the best base value for a particular valuation will depend on a number of factors. First, the goal is to value the economic benefits of share ownership, and the best measure of economic benefits will often vary as a result of the line of business in which the corporation is involved. For example, the primary economic benefit to the shareholders of an ongoing manufacturing concern comes from the firm's ability to generate net income and cash flow. Thus, some measure of earnings will be the relevant measure of economic benefit to those shareholders and should be used as the base value. On the other hand, the economic benefit from owning shares in a holding company is derived from the financial value of the assets. Capitalization on the basis of asset values would then be appropriate. Second, capitalization rates and multiples are calculated by studying such rates and multiples for comparable publicly traded corporations. As a result, the measure of economic benefit selected as a base value must be one that is measurable for both the closely held corporation and the comparable publicly traded corporations.

The second step in the capitalization method of valuation is to select the appropriate historical time frame from which to estimate the base value. Selection of the appropriate historical time frame involves a balancing between two confounding considerations. First, data used in calculating the base value must go back far enough to develop a range of performance possibilities that are likely to reflect probable future outcomes. Second, the collection of data must not go so far back as to include information that will no longer have relevance in predicting future financial performance. For example, it would be highly unlikely if the cash flows generated from the preceding year alone were the best estimate of future performance. In fact, the most recent year may represent either a high or a low for the cash flow performance variable. Moreover, any particular variable such as cash flow is likely to vary to some degree simply as a matter of general fluctuations in the economy. Thus, it is probably best to include more than one year of data when estimating the base value. On the other hand, the level of cash flow generated by a firm ten years ago may have no relevance to the firm's ability to generate cash in the future. For instance, a firm may have doubled its production capacity in the past four years and, thus, measures of cash flow before this period are likely to severely understate cash flow potential.

The third step in the process of valuing closely held shares using a capitalization method is to account for historical trends in the estimation of the base value. This is basically a question of how much weight should be assigned to the data from each of the past years used in the calculation of the base value. Consider, for example, an estimation of cash flows based on the last three years of data. If these cash flow numbers demonstrate an identifiable trend, then it might be appropriate to assign greater weights to the cash flow numbers generated in the most recent years. However, if the cash flow number displays a high degree of variability, then it is perhaps best to assign equal weight to each of the past three years. Alternatively consideration must be given to events that are not likely to regularly occur year to year. For example, it may be the case that the most recent years' cash flows were highly unusual and not likely to occur again. Under such circumstances, the financial analyst may choose to give a great deal of weight to the cash flow numbers generated several years ago and give very little weight to the most recent years' cash flow.

The fourth step in the capitalization process is to adjust the financial statements of the relevant comparison firms so that the base values can be fairly compared. It is unlikely that the financial statements for the closely held corporation and publicly traded comparison corporations as they currently exist will be ready for accurate comparison. Accounting terms such as earnings or cash flows are not universally defined. In fact, firms often have wide latitude in terms of how such financial variables are calculated. Thus, for example, one would expect to find that the exact components of the term "cash flow" will vary across firms. In order to fairly compare the performance of the closely held corporation with that of publicly traded corporations, the financial analyst must adjust such numbers so that they approximate the same economic benefit (base value) across comparison firms. A failure to do so would result in distorted estimations of share value.

The fifth step in the capitalization process is to determine the appropriate capitalization rate or multiple. Two important considerations dominate litigation issues involving capitalization rates or multiples. First, these variables are estimated by looking at the financial data of publicly traded corporations that are sufficiently comparable to the closely held firm for which we are estimating a value. The issue of sufficient comparability is highly contested among the experts in such litigation. Second, as a general matter, these capitalization variables are an attempt to establish a relationship between the base value and price in terms of an amount buyers would be willing to pay per unit of the base variable. One of the most popular variables, for example, is the price-to-earnings ratio, which is a measure of the market price of a share in terms of a particular firm's earnings. After determining that earnings is the relevant base value, a financial analyst would identify a set of publicly traded corporations comparable to the close corporation which is being appraised. After identifying a good set of comparison firms, the analyst would calculate the average price to earnings ratio for the group of comparison firms. The price-to-earnings ratio is found by dividing the average market price by the average earnings of comparable firms and thus establishes the appropriate earnings multiple to apply to the earnings base of our close corporation. In this regard, questions may arise concerning the correct variable for capitalizing a particular base value.

The variety of potential capitalization rates or multiples that exist are as varying as the number of different base values that might be calculated. Unfortunately, the actual calculation of capitalization rates or multiples is not sufficiently generic to lend itself to easy exposition in this book. The following case demonstrates a great variety in the methodologies used to construct a value for a closely held corporation. Moreover, all of the analysis in this case is based on current or historic data, not on a projection of future benefits.

Central Trust Co. v. United States

United States Court of Claims
305 F.2d 393 (1962)

OPINION OF THE COMMISSIONER

These suits are for the refund of federal gift taxes. They involve the common question of the value of shares of stock of the same company. A joint trial was therefore conducted.

On August 3, 1954, Albert E. Heekin made gifts totaling 30,000 shares of stock of The Heekin Can Company.... Following his death on March 10, 1955, the executors of his estate filed a gift tax return in which the value of the stock was fixed at $10 a share. On October 28, 1957, however, they filed an amended gift tax return and a claim for refund, contending that the correct value of the Heekin Company stock on August 3, 1954 was $7.50 a share.

On October 25, 1954, James J. Heekin made gifts totaling 40,002 shares of Heekin Can Company stock.... Separate gift tax returns with respect to these (and other) gifts were filed by both James J. Heekin and his wife, Alma (who joined in the stock gifts), in which the value of the stock was similarly declared to be $10 a share. However, on January 21, 1958, James filed an amended gift tax return and a claim for refund, also contending that the correct value of the stock on October 25, 1954, was $7.50 a share, and on the same day, the executor of Alma's estate (she having died on November 9, 1955) filed a similar amended return and claim for refund.

On February 5, 1958, the District Director of Internal Revenue sent to James J. Heekin and the executors of the estates of Alma and Albert E. Heekin notices of deficiency of the 1954 gift taxes. Each of the three deficiencies was based on a determination by the Commissioner of Internal Revenue that the value of the Heekin Company stock on the gift dates was $24 a share.

Consistent with his deficiency notices, the District Director, on May 15, 1958, disallowed the three refund claims that had been filed, and in July 1958 payment was made of the amounts assessed pursuant to the deficiency notices. After the filing in August and September 1958 of claims for refund concerning these payments, the claims again being based on a valuation of $7.50, and the rejection thereof by the District Director, these three refund suits were instituted....

The Heekin Can Company is a well-established metal container manufacturer in Cincinnati, Ohio. In 1954, the year involved in these proceedings, its principal business consisted of manufacturing two kinds of containers, its total production being equally divided between them. One is known as packer's cans, which are generally the type seen on the shelves of food markets in which canned food products are contained. The other is referred to as general line cans, which consist of large institutional size frozen fruit cans, lard pails, dairy cans, chemical cans, and drums. This line also includes such housewares as canisters, bread boxes, lunch boxes, waste baskets, and a type of picnic container familiarly known by the trade names of Skotch Kooler and Skotch Grill. On the gift dates its annual sales, the production of five plants, were approximately $17,000,000.

* * *

On the gift dates, the Company had 254,125 shares of common stock outstanding, there being no restrictions on their transferability or sale. There was no other class of stock. Including the 70,002 shares involved in these cases, a total of 180,510 shares were owned by 79 persons who were related to James Heekin, the founder. Thus, the Heekin family owned approximately 71 percent of all of the outstanding stock. The remaining 73,615 shares were owned by 54 unrelated persons, most of whom were employees of the Company and friends of the family.

* * *

The Heekin stock was not listed on any stock exchange, and trading in it was infrequent. There was some such activity in 1951 and 1952 resulting from the desire of certain minority stockholders (the descendants of a partner of James Heekin, the founder) to liquidate their holdings, consisting of 13,359 shares. One individual alone had 10,709 shares.

Arrangements were privately made in early 1951 by these stockholders with Albert E. Heekin and his son, Albert E. Heekin, Jr., to sell these holdings at the prearranged price of $7.50 a share. These shares were all sold, commencing March 22, 1951, and ending April 16, 1952, in 44 separate transactions, 35 of which took place in 1951 and 9 in 1952. No attempt was made to sell the shares to the general public on the open market. All sales were made to Heekin employees and friends of the Heekin family at such $7.50 price. Other than these 1951 and 1952 sales, the only sales of stock made prior to the gift dates consisted of one sale of 100 shares in 1953 by one Heekin employee to another, and one sale in 1954 of 200 shares, again by one Heekin employee to another, both sales also being made for $7.50 a share.

Against these background facts, the valuation question in dispute may be approached. Section 1000 of the Internal Revenue Code of 1939, ... the applicable statute, imposed a tax upon transfers of property by gift, whether in trust or otherwise. Section 1005 provided that "If the gift is made in property, the value thereof at the date of the gift shall be considered the amount of the gift."

Section 86.19(a) of the Regulations issued with respect thereto ... defines such property value as the price at which the property "would change hands between a willing buyer and a willing seller, neither being under any compulsion to buy or to sell.... Such value is to be determined by ascertaining as a basis the fair market value at the time of the gift of each unit of the property...."

* * *

[To summarize, Heekin's stock has been valued as of August 3 and October 25, 1954, in blocks of 30,000 and 40,002 shares respectively, as follows: $10, originally, by two donors and the executor of the third; $7.50, in amended returns; $7.88 by one expert of plaintiffs (upon which valuation plaintiffs now stand); $9.50 and $9.65 respectively by plaintiffs' second expert; $11.76 and $9.47 respectively by plaintiffs' third expert; $16 and $15.25 respectively by defendant's expert; $21.85 and $21.35 respectively by defendant in these proceedings; and $24 by the Commissioner of Internal Revenue.]

Various major criticisms can fairly be made of these three appraisals offered by plaintiffs. First, they all give undue weight as a factor to the $7.50 price of the prior stock sales. Almost all of these sales occurred in the relatively remote period of 1951 and early 1952. Only one small transaction occurred in each of the more recent years of 1953 and 1954. Such isolated sales of closely held corporations in a restricted market offer little guide to true value.... Furthermore, the $7.50 price of the 1951 and 1952 sales evolved in early 1951 during a period when the Company was experiencing rather severe financial difficulties due to an unfortunate experience with a subsidiary which caused a loss of around $1,000,000, and when, consequently, the Company found itself in a depleted working capital position and was paying no dividends. Further, there is no indication that the $7.50 sales price evolved as a result of the usual factors taken into consideration by informed sellers and buyers dealing at arm's length. Fair market value presupposes not only hypothetical willing buyers and sellers, but buyers and sellers who are informed and have "adequate knowledge of the material facts affecting the value...." The sales were all made at a prearranged price to Heekin employees and family friends. The artificiality of the price is indicated by its being the same in 1951, 1952, 1953 and 1954, despite the varying fortunes of the Company during these years and with the price failing to reflect, as would normally be expected, such differences in any way.

Secondly, in using the Company's full 1954 financial data, and then working back from December 31, 1954, to the respective gift dates, data were being used which would not have been available to a prospective purchaser as of the gift dates.... Furthermore, in the working-back procedure, general market data were used although it is evident that the stocks of a particular industry may at times run counter to the general trend. This was actually the situation here. Although the market generally advanced after August 3, 1954, container industry stocks did not.

Thirdly, the converse situation applies with respect to the data used by the third expert. His financial data only went to December 31, 1953, since the Company's last annual report prior to the gift dates was issued for the year 1953. But the Company also issued quarterly interim financial statements, and by the second gift date, the results of three-quarters of 1954 operations were available. In evaluating a stock, it is essential to obtain as recent data as is possible....

Fourth, it is accepted valuation practice, in ascertaining a company's past earnings, to attempt to detect abnormal or nonrecurring items and to make appropriate eliminations or adjustments. As shown, only the plaintiffs' expert who came out with the highest August 3 valuation attempted to do this by adjusting the excessive Korean war earnings and by eliminating the unusual losses suffered in 1950, 1951 and 1952 arising from the operations of a financing subsidiary ... that had been liquidated in 1952. The reason this is important is that past earnings are significant only insofar as they reasonably forecast future earnings. The only sound basis upon which to ground such a forecast is the company's normal operation, which requires the elimination or adjustment of abnormal items which will not recur....

Fifth, in deriving a past earnings figure which could be used as a reasonable basis of forecasting future earnings, none of plaintiffs' experts gave any consideration to the trend of such past earnings. They simply used the earnings of prior years and averaged them. But such averages may be deceiving. Two corporations with 5-year earnings going from the past to the present represented by the figures in one case of 5, 4, 3, 2, and 1, and in the other by the same figures of 1, 2, 3, 4, and 5, will have the same 5-year averages, but investors will quite naturally prefer the stock of the latter whose earnings are consistently moving upward....

* * *

Sixth, it is generally conceded that ... in evaluating stocks of manufacturing corporations such as Heekin, earnings are the most important factor to be considered.... Yet only one of plaintiffs' experts, who assigned double value to this factor, gave it such weight. As shown, the other two assigned the dividend factor equal weight. Some investors may indeed depend upon dividends. In their own investment programs, they may therefore stress yield and even compare common stocks with bonds or other forms of investment to obtain the greatest yields. However others, for various reasons, may care little about dividends and may invest in common stocks for the primary purpose of seeking capital appreciation. All investors, however, are primarily concerned with earnings, which are normally a prerequisite to dividends. In addition, the declaration of dividends is sometimes simply a matter of the policy of a particular company. It may bear no relationship to dividend-paying capacity. Many investors actually prefer companies paying little or no dividends and which reinvest their earnings, for that may be the key to future growth and capital appreciation.

And further, in capitalizing the dividend at 6 and 7 percent, as did two of the experts, rates of return were used which well exceeded those being paid at the time by comparable container company stocks. And still further, one of the experts used a 35-cent dividend rate as the basis for his capitalization because that was the average paid for the 5 years ended December 31, 1954. However, it seems clear that an annual dividend rate of 50 cents a share would be the proper rate to capitalize since that was the dividend paid by Heekin every year since 1945 except for the year 1950 and the first half of 1951 when, as shown, dividends were temporarily suspended. By the end of 1951 the Company had recovered from the situation causing the suspension and the normal dividend (quarterly payments of 12 1/2 cents per share) was then resumed. By August and October 1954, Heekin's demonstrated earning capability and financial position were such that there was little doubt it would at least continue its 50-cent annual dividend, which represented only about 25 percent of its current earnings per share. To dip back into this 1950–51 a typical period to compute an "average" of dividends paid for the past 5 years is unrealistic.

Finally, the record indicates that all three experts took too great a discount for lack of marketability. Defendant disputes the propriety of taking this factor into consideration at all. It seems clear, however, that an unlisted closely held stock of a corporation such as Heekin, in which trading is infrequent and which therefore lacks marketability, is less attractive than a similar stock which is listed on an exchange and has ready access to the investing public. This factor would naturally affect the market value of the stock. This is not to say that the market value of any unlisted stock in which trading is infrequent would automatically be reduced by a lack of marketability factor. The stock of a well-known leader in its field with a preeminent reputation might not be at all affected by such a consideration, as was the situation with Ford Motor Company stock before it was listed.... But the stock of a less well-known company like Heekin which is a comparatively small factor in its industry is obviously in a different position. In such a situation, a consideration of this factor is appropriate, especially where, as here, only a minority interest is involved....

Defendant concedes that if such a factor is appropriate in these cases, a reasonable method of determining the diminution in value attributable to lack of marketability is to determine how much it would cost to create marketability for the block of stock in question.... The record shows that for a company of Heekin's size, and for blocks of 30,000 and 40,000 shares, which would appear to be the appropriate considerations, flotation costs would amount to about 12.17 percent of the gross sales prices. However, as shown, the discounts taken by plaintiffs' experts for this factor ranged from 15 to 25 percent

For all the above reasons, the opinions of plaintiffs' experts are not wholly acceptable.

Defendant produced one expert, an employee of a recognized appraisal company.... His opinion was that the value of the Heekin stock in question on August 3 and October 25, 1954, was $16 and $15.25 per share, respectively.

* * *

This witness' study has certain meritorious features. It is based on justifiable adjustments in Heekin's earnings records to eliminate abnormal and nonrecurring items.... It considers earnings trend. It disregards the prior $7.50 sales prices as a major factor. And in employing the Company's financial data going up to June 30 and September 30, 1954, it is based on its most recent performance. However, it has certain weaknesses too, the principal one being the limitation of the comparative companies to two, one of which, Crown Cork & Seal, leaves much to be desired as a comparative because its principal business is the manufacture of bottle caps and bottling machinery, an entirely different business. Only 40 percent of its business is in can production. On the basis of size too there are great differences. At that time, Crown, including its foreign subsidiaries, was doing about $115,000,000 worth of business as against Heekin's $17,000,000. And the other comparative, United Can and Glass, presents the complication that it declared periodic stock dividends to which the witness gave no consideration, although it seems that some element of value should fairly be attributed to them. Although no two companies are ever exactly alike, ... so that absolute comparative perfection can seldom be achieved, nevertheless the comparative appraisal method is a sound and well-accepted technique. In employing it, however, every effort should be made to select as broad a base of comparative companies as is reasonably possible, as well as to give full consideration to every possible factor in order to make the comparison more meaningful.

* * *

Defendant, considering its own expert's valuations to be unduly conservative, and disagreeing as a matter of law with any deduction for lack of marketability (and in any event with the amount deducted by its expert for such factor), now offers valuations on what it claims to be a more realistic basis.

* * *

... [D]efendant arrives at a fair market value figure of $21.85 as of August 3, 1954. Since there was a slight drop in the market price of can manufacturing stocks between August 3 and October 25, 1954, defendant concludes the fair market value on the latter date would be about 50 cents less per share, or $21.35.

Thus, defendant now seeks a fair market value determination as of the gift dates of $21.85 and $21.35 respectively, in lieu of the $24 value fixed by the Commissioner of Internal Revenue.

In its selection of the three basic factors to be considered in determining fair market value [earnings, dividend yield, and book value], the weights to be assigned to these factors, the earnings adjustments, and the use of 50 cents per annum as the proper dividend basis, this estimate has merit. However, the selection of such companies as American Can and Continental Can as comparatives — companies held in esteem in the investment world — will obviously give an unduly high result. It simply is not fair to compare Heekin with such companies and to adopt their market ratios for application to Heekin's stock.... And the refusal to make any allowance for lack of marketability contributes further to the unrealistic nature of defendant's fair market value estimate.

* * *

The proper use of the comparative appraisal method, applying the principles already indicated, should provide a reasonably satisfactory valuation guide in these cases. In its application, it would under all the circumstances herein involved appear appropriate to select the three factors of (1) earnings, (2) dividends and dividend-paying capacity, and (3) book value, as being the important and significant ones to apply....

As to earnings, an examination of them for the periods from 1950 to June 30 and September 30, 1954, which are the most recent periods in relation to the gift dates, would be most representative. For this purpose, the annual profit and loss statements, plus the Company's interim balance sheets, from which can be derived with reasonable accuracy the Company's earnings for the 12-month periods ending June 30 and September 30, 1954 (thus eliminating distortions due to seasonal factors), are the starting points.... [I]t would then be proper to make such adjustments therein as would be necessary to eliminate abnormal and nonrecurring items and to redistribute items of expense to their proper periods....

As indicated, it would then be appropriate to give due consideration and weight to the trend of such earnings. Greater weight should fairly be given to the most recent years and periods. The method adopted ... of assigning greater weight to the later periods is a reasonably accurate one, and indicates that as of June 30 and September 30, 1954, Heekin's reasonably expected annual earnings per share would be $1.93 and $1.79, based on average annual earnings of $491,460.86 and $454,492.82, respectively.

As to dividends and dividend-paying capacity, it has already been indicated that as of the gift dates, it could reasonably be expected that Heekin would continue to pay in the foreseeable future its usual 50-cent annual dividend....

As to book value, the Company's balance sheets showed the book value per share to be, conservatively, $33.15 and $33.54 as of June 30 and September 30, 1954, respectively....

With the above basic data applicable to Heekin, it is then appropriate to select as closely comparable companies as is possible whose stocks are actively traded on an exchange, and to ascertain what ratios their market prices bear to their earnings, dividends, and book values. The application of such ratios to Heekin would then give a reasonable approximation of what Heekin's stock would sell for if it too were actively traded on an exchange.

A study of all the numerous companies considered by the experts as proper comparatives indicates that five of them, i.e., Pacific Can Company, United Can and Glass Company, National Can Corporation, Brockway Glass Co., Inc., and Thatcher Glass Manufacturing Co., Inc., are, while by no means perfect comparables, certainly at least reasonably satisfactory for the purpose in question.... In size they all fall generally into Heekin's class, and the nature of their operations is also comparable. In addition, five companies give a sufficiently broad base....

After similarly computing the earnings, as adjusted, of the comparatives for the same periods as for Heekin, and similarly weighting them to give effect to the trend factor, the average ratio of their market prices to their adjusted earnings as of August 3 and October 25, 1954 (the "price-earnings" ratio), was 9.45 and 9.84 to 1, respectively. Thus, on the basis only of earnings, Heekin's stock would similarly sell for $18.24 and $17.61 per share on such dates.

Similarly, the comparatives' dividend payments for the 12 months ending June 30 and September 30, 1954, after making some allowance for United's stock dividend, show an average percent yield of 3.50 and 3.56 respectively. Thus, on the basis only of dividend yield, Heekin's stock would similarly sell for $14.29 and $14.05 per share on August 3 and October 25, 1954, respectively.

As to book value, the average market prices of the comparatives were 83.96 and 86.39 percent, respectively, of the book values of their common stocks on said dates. Thus, on the sole basis of the average relationship between such book values and market prices, Heekin's comparable market prices on said dates would be $27.83 and $28.98.

However, since the three factors of earnings, dividends, and book value are not entitled to equal weight, it becomes necessary to consider their relative importance in the case of a company such as Heekin....

Considering all the circumstances, it would appear appropriate to accept defendant's proposals in this respect and to consider earnings as entitled to 50 percent of the contribution to total value, and to give dividend yield (which in this case would appear to be substantially equivalent to dividend-paying capacity) 30 percent, and book value 20 percent, thereof....

On the above percentage bases, the fair market value of Heekin's stock on August 3 and October 25, 1954, would be $18.98 and $18.83 respectively.

These prices, however, assume active trading for Heekin's stock on an exchange, as was the situation with the comparatives. As shown, the closely held nature of, and the infrequent trading in, Heekin's stock resulted in a lack of marketability which would affect its market value. Equating the proper discount to be taken for this factor with the costs that would be involved in creating a market for the stock, a method which defendant concedes is reasonable, results in a deduction of approximately 12.17 percent for a company of Heekin's size and for blocks of 30,000 and 40,000 shares. On this basis, the fair market values of the Heekin stock as of August 3 and October 25, 1954, would be $16.67 and $16.54 respectively.

These are the values resulting largely from strictly formula and statistical applications. While such use of figures and formulas produces, of course, results which are of important significance, and may in certain instances be given conclusive weight, it is nevertheless recognized that determinations of fair market value can not be reduced to formula alone, but depend "upon all the relevant facts," including "the elements of common sense, informed judgment and reasonableness." The question of fair market value of a stock "is ever one of fact and not of formula" and evidence which gives "life to [the] figures" is essential. . . . The selection of comparatives has been a particularly troublesome problem in these cases. National Can's erratic earnings record, even though adjustments are attempted to normalize its situation, and its nonpayment of dividends, certainly weaken its position as a comparative, and suggest the desirability of an adjustment in the final market value figures set forth above. Pacific Can's sharp rise in price after August 3, 1954, justifies a similar adjustment for the October 25, 1954, valuation. While the inclusion of the glass container manufacturers with their higher dividend yields tends to neutralize somewhat the National Can situation, an adjustment downward would, in fairness to plaintiffs, nevertheless guard against their being prejudiced by the aforementioned selections of comparatives. Furthermore, while the sales of Heekin stock at $7.50 warrant, as hereinabove pointed out, only minimal consideration, the figures derived from the above formula give them no cognizance whatsoever.

Giving important weight to the figure of $16.67 produced by the application of the comparative appraisal method as applied herein, but viewing it in light of all the facts and circumstances involved in these cases, it is concluded that the fair market value of the 30,000 shares given on August 3, 1954, was $15.50 per share.

The market for stocks of the can and glass container manufacturing companies fell somewhat between August 3 and October 25, 1954, so that ordinarily on that basis as well as on the basis of Heekin's own financial and operating positions on October 25 as compared with August 3, a slightly lower value would be justified as of October 25. . . . It seems clear, however, that the brightened prospects for increased business and profits resulting from the Company's decision in August 1954 to embark upon the beer can business and to satisfy further the demands of its largest customer for new products would, in Heekin's instance, tend to neutralize the market decline and to make its stock at least as valuable on October 25 as it had been on August 3. Accordingly, it is concluded that the fair market value of the 40,002 shares given on October 25, 1954, was also $15.50 per share.

A $15.50 valuation represents a price to adjusted earnings ratio on the gift dates of between 8 and 9 percent (somewhat less than the 9–10 percent average of the comparatives), a dividend yield of 3.23 percent (slightly less than the 3.5 percent average of the comparatives), and only 46 percent of book value (considerably less than the approximately 85 percent of the comparatives). On these bases, it is a figure that is fair to both sides.

* * *

On this valuation basis, plaintiffs are entitled to recover, the amount of the recovery to be determined in accordance with Rule 38(c).

* * *

Notes and Questions

1. Prior Market Transactions and the Fair Market Value Standard: In *Central Trust*, several transactions involving the shares of Heekin Can Co. were executed. The court suggests that the plaintiff's experts relied too much on the share price established in these transactions. Why was the price established in these transactions not acceptable to the court? Were these not market prices? Consider how the fair market value standard relates to the court's decision regarding these transactions.

2. Calculating the Base Value: Several different financial variables were introduced as potential base values by the experts in *Central Trust*. The court criticized several aspects of these base values including their estimation and relative merits as proxies for future economic benefits. Return to the steps for estimating a capitalized value given in the section preceding the *Central Trust* case. In what ways did the experts fail to follow this procedure? What things did the experts do right? Which of the court's criticisms are valid?

3. Discounts for the Lack of Marketability: Marketability relates to the relative ease by which one can conduct transactions in the shares of a particular corporation. If shares of a particular corporation are traded on a widely recognized stock exchange, then it is probably fairly easy to buy and sell such shares. The ability to find a willing buyer with ease can be of great value to the holder of a company's shares because it makes his investments relatively more liquid. Individuals who purchase the shares of closely held corporations, on the other hand, tend to be relatively locked-in to their purchase decision. In general, it is safe to assume that most shareholders value liquidity and are willing to pay a premium for it. Why? Alternatively, purchasers of closely held shares desire to be compensated for sacrificing liquidity by paying a lower purchase price relative to a comparable publicly traded share, all else being equal. Thus, it seems relatively clear that some discount for the lack of marketability is valid. But how should the court measure marketability? Does marketability exist at varying degrees? Does the court's analysis contemplate such a continuum?

4. Qualitative Factors Affecting Value: What was the value to Heekin Can Co. of the human capital possessed by the Heekin Family? If this trial were about the Heekin family selling the company to the Smith family, would it be correct to arrive at the same value for share prices? What other qualitative factors might factor into the value of a company? In general, there are many potential factors affecting the value of a close corporation, which are very difficult to quantify in any meaningful sense. Nonetheless, these factors clearly affect future economic benefit and, accordingly, some adjustment should be made.

Glossary

Ability-to-pay principle The equity concept that people with larger incomes (or more consumption or more wealth) should be taxed at a higher rate because their ability to pay is presumably greater. The concept is subjective and fails to reveal how much higher the rate of taxation should be as income increases.

Absolute advantage The ability of a nation or a trading partner to produce a product with fewer resources than some other trading partner.

Absolute liability Liability for an act that causes harm even though the actor was not at fault.

Accounting profits The sales revenues minus the expenses of a firm over a designated time period, usually one year. Accounting profits typically make allowances for changes in the firm's inventories and depreciation of its assets. No allowance is made, however, for the opportunity cost of the equity capital of the firm's owners, or other implicit costs.

Adverse selection A situation in which two people might trade with each other and one person has relevant information about some aspect of the product's quality that the other person lacks.

Advertising Any communication that firms offer customers in an effort to increase demand for their product.

Agency The relationship that exists between a person identified as a principal and another by virtue of which the latter may make contracts with third persons on behalf of the principal.

Agent One who is authorized by the principal or by operation of law to make contracts with third persons on behalf of the principal.

Allocative efficiency The allocation of resources to the production of goods and services most desired by consumers. The allocation is "balanced" in such a way that reallocation of resources could not benefit anyone without hurting someone else.

Allocative inefficiency The use of an uneconomical combination of resources to produce goods and services, or the use of resources to produce goods that are not intensely desired relative to their opportunity cost.

Annuity A level stream of cash flow for a fixed period of time.

Antitrust law A law that prohibits monopolies and cartels or monopoly-like behaviors.

Antitrust policy The laws and agencies created by legislation in an effort to preserve competition.

Arbitration Hiring private judges (arbitrators) to issue a binding decision that resolves the parties' dispute.

Assumption of risk The common-law rule that an employee could not sue the employer for injuries caused by the ordinary risks of employment on the theory that the employee had assumed such risks by undertaking the work. The rule has been abolished in those areas governed by worker's compensation laws and most employers' liability statutes.

Asymmetric-information problem A problem arising when either buyers or sellers have important information about the product that is not possessed by the other side in potential transactions.

Average cost Total cost divided by the quantity produced.

Average fixed cost Fixed cost divided by the number of units produced. It always declines as output increases.

Average product The total product (output) divided by the number of units of the variable input required to produce that output level.

Average revenue Total revenue divided by the quantity produced.

Average tax rate A person's tax payment as a fraction of income.

Average total cost Total cost divided by the number of units produced. It is sometimes call per unit cost.

Average variable cost The total variable cost divided by the number of units produced.

Bankruptcy A procedure by which one unable to pay debts may be declared a bankrupt, after which all assets in excess of any exemption claim are surrendered to the court for administration and distribution to creditors, and the debtor is given a discharge that releases the unpaid balance due on most debts.

Barriers to entry Obstacles that limit the freedom of potential rivals to enter an industry.

Behavioral law and economics Economic analysis of the legal system that departs to some degree from the standard assumption that individuals behave rationally, based on psychological studies identifying various cognitive biases and heuristics in individual decision making.

Benefit principle The notion that people who receive the benefits of publicly provided goods should pay for their production.

Black market An illegal market.

Capital Resources that enhance our ability to produce output in the future. Also, the net assets of a corporation.

Capital good An input that a firm can use repeatedly to produce other goods.

Capital market The financial market in which long-term securities such as stocks and long-term bonds are traded.

Capital structure The mixture of debt and equity maintained by a firm.

Capitalism An economic system based on private ownership of productive resources and allocation of goods according to the price signals provided by free markets.

Capitalist economy An economic system in which the means of production are privately owned.

Capture view of regulation The view that regulatory agencies originally established to serve the general public interest end up serving the special interests of the industries they were intended to regulate.

Cartel An organization of sellers designed to coordinate supply decisions so that the joint profits of the members will be maximized. A cartel will seek to create a monopoly in the market.

Cartel enforcement An effort by the administrators of a cartel to prevent its members from secretly cutting price below the cartel price.

Case selection bias Bias in empirical studies of court decisions that results from parties' settlement of cases.

Caveat emptor Let the buyer beware. This maxim has been nearly abolished by warranty and strict tort liability concepts.

Change in demand A change in the numbers in the demand schedule and a shift in the demand curve. An increase in demand shifts the demand curve to the right; a decrease shifts it to the left.

Change in supply A change in the numbers in the supply schedule and a shift in the supply curve. An increase in supply shifts the supply curve to the right; a decrease shifts it to the left.

Choice The act of selecting among alternatives.

Choices at the margin Decisions made by examining the benefits and costs of small, or one-unit, changes in a particular activity.

Class action Lawsuit brought on behalf of many individual claimants by a class representative or class representatives.

Classical economists Economists from Adam Smith to the time of Keynes who focused their analysis on economic efficiency and production. With regard to business instability, they thought market prices and wages would decline during a recession quickly enough to bring the economy back to full employment within a short period of time.

Coase theorem Externalities will adjust to the same level when ownership rights are assigned and when the costs of negotiation are nonexistent or trivial, regardless of which party receives the rights.

Cognitive biases Biases identified by psychologists that affect individual decision making in a predictable manner.

Collective decision making The method of organization that relies on public-sector decision making (voting, political bargaining, lobbying, and so on). It can be used to resolve the basic economic problems of an economy.

Collusion Agreement among firms to avoid various competitive practices, particularly price reductions. It may involve either formal agreements or merely tacit recognition that competitive practices will be self-defeating in the long run. Tacit collusion is difficult to detect. The Sherman Act prohibits collusion and conspiracies to restrain interstate trade.

Command economy An authoritarian socialist economy characterized by centralized planning and detailed directives to productive units. Individual enterprises have little discretionary decision-making power.

Common-property resource A resource for which rights are held in common by a group of individuals, none of whom has a transferable ownership interest. Access to the resource may be open (unrestricted), or may be controlled politically.

Common resource A resource that belongs to no one or to society as a whole.

Common stock Equity without priority for dividends or in bankruptcy.

Comparative advantage The ability to produce a good at a lower opportunity cost than others can produce it. Relative costs determine comparative advantage.

Compensating wage differentials Wage differences that compensate workers for risk, unpleasant working conditions, and other undesirable nonpecuniary aspects of a job.

Competition The process by which people attempt to acquire scarce goods for themselves.

Competition as a dynamic process A term that denotes rivalry or competitiveness between or among parties (for example, producers or input suppliers), each of which seeks to deliver a better deal to buyers when quality, price, and product information are all considered. Competition implies a lack of collusion among sellers.

Complement inputs Two inputs for which an increase in the price of one raises demand for the other.

Complements Products that are usually consumed jointly (for example, coffee and nondairy creamer). An increase in the price of one will cause the demand for the other to fall.

Compound interest Interest earned on both the initial principal and the interest reinvested from prior periods.

Concentrated interest A benefit to a small group of people or firms.

Constant cost Long-run marginal cost and long-run average cost that do not change with the level of output.

Constant cost industry An industry for which factor prices and costs of production remain constant as market output is expanded. Thus, the long-run market supply curve is horizontal.

Constant returns to scale Unit costs are constant as the scale of the firm is altered. Neither economies nor diseconomies of scale are present.

Consumer surplus The difference between the maximum amount a consumer would be willing to pay for a unit of a good and the payment that is actually made.

Consumption of a good The amount of a good people use for their current benefit (wearing, eating, driving, or watching the good, for example).

Contingent fee contract A contract between a lawyer and his or her client under which the lawyer agrees to provide legal services in exchange for a percentage share of any recovery obtained.

Corporation A business firm owned by shareholders who possess ownership rights to the firm's profits, but whose liability is limited to the amount of their investment in the firm.

Correlation A measure of how closely two variables are related.

Cost-benefit analysis The process of finding and comparing the costs and benefits of a regulation, tax, or other policy.

Cost of capital The minimum required return on a new investment.

Cross-price elasticity of demand (or supply) The percentage change in the quantity demanded (or supplied) of one good when the price of another good rises by 1 percent.

Damages A sum of money recovered to redress or make amends for the legal wrong or injury done.

Deadweight loss A net loss associated with the forgoing of an economic action. The loss does not lead to an offsetting gain for other participants. It thus reflects economic inefficiency.

Deadweight social loss The amount that people would be willing to pay to eliminate an inefficiency.

Demand schedule A table that shows various possible prices and a person's quantity demanded at each price.

Depreciation The fall in the value of a good over time.

Deregulation A situation in which government ceases to regulate a previously regulated industry in an effort to improve the performance of that industry.

Differentiated products A product that buyers consider to be a good, but not perfect, substitute for another.

Diffuse interest A benefit that is spread across many people.

Discount rate The rate used to calculate the present value of future cash flows.

Discounted cash flow (DCF) valuation The process of valuing an investment by discounting its future cash flows.

Discounted present value (of a future amount of money) The money you would need to save and invest now to end up with that specific amount of money in the future.

Discovery Process by which information is exchanged between parties in court.

Disequilibrium A situation in which the quantity demanded and the quantity supplied are not equal at the current price.

Distribution of prices A situation in which some sellers charge higher prices than others.

Diversification A method of decreasing risk by spreading investments among different asset categories, such as stocks and bonds, and different companies in different industries within the stocks and bonds, and different companies in different industries within the stock category.

Dividend Payment made out of a firm's earnings to its owners, either in the form of cash or stock.

Durable input An input that a firm buys for future use or one that the firm can use repeatedly.

Economic costs All of a firm's costs, explicit and implicit.

Economic efficiency Proper allocation of resources from the firm's perspective.

Economic goods Scarce goods.

Economic model A description of logical thinking about an economic issue stated in words, graphs, or mathematics.

Economic profit Total revenue minus total economic costs.

Economic rent The price of an input minus the economy's opportunity cost of using that input.

Economic system A means of determining what, how, and for whom goods and services are produced.

Economic welfare The situation in which products and services are offered to consumers at the minimum long-run average total cost of production.

Economically efficient A situation that cannot be changed so that someone gains unless someone else loses.

Economically efficient method of production The technically efficient method with the lowest cost.

Economically efficient (or Pareto efficient) situation A situation that allows no potentially Pareto-improving change.

Economically inefficient A situation that can be changed so that at least one person gains while no one else loses.

Economically inefficient (or Pareto inefficient) situation A situation that is not economically efficient, so a potentially Pareto-improving change could be made.

Economics The study of how a society uses its limited resources to produce, trade, and consume goods and services; also the study of people's incentives and choices and what happens to coordinate their decisions and activities.

Economies of scale The relation between long-run average total cost and plant size that suggests that as plant size increases, the average cost of production decreases.

Egalitarianism The view that fairness requires equal results.

Elastic demand (or supply) Elasticity with an absolute value greater than 1.

Elasticity of demand (or supply) The percentage change in the quantity demanded (or supplied) divided by the percentage change in price.

Eminent domain The power of a government and certain kinds of corporations to take private property against the objection of the owner, provided the taking is for a public purpose and just compensation is made therefor.

Entrepreneur A person who conceives and acts on a new business idea and takes the risk of its success or failure.

Entry When a firm begins producing and selling a product.

Equilibrium A balance of forces permitting the simultaneous fulfillment of plans by buyers and sellers. A state of balance between conflicting forces, such as supply and demand.

Equilibrium price The price at which quantity supplied equals quantity demanded.

Equilibrium quantity The quantity at which quantity supplied equals quantity demanded.

Evidence Any set of facts that helps to convince people that a positive statement is true or false.

Excess burden of taxation A burden of taxation over and above the burden associated with the transfer of revenues to the government. An excess burden usually reflects losses that occur when beneficial activities are forgone because they are taxed.

Excess capacity The opportunity for a firm to reduce its average cost by raising its output.

Excess demand (shortage) A situation in which the quantity demanded exceeds the quantity supplied.

Excess supply (surplus) A situation in which the quantity supplied exceeds the quantity demanded.

Exchange rate The price of one country's currency expressed in terms of another country's currency.

Exclusive contract An agreement between manufacturer and retailer that prohibits the retailer from carrying the product lines of firms that are rivals of the manufacturer. Such contracts are illegal under the Clayton Act when they "lessen competition."

Exit When a firm stops selling a product.

Expected return Return on a risky asset expected in the future.

Expected value An average of numbers weighted by the probabilities (chances) that they will occur.

Expected value model Economic model of court litigation under which plaintiffs decide whether to file suit based on the expected value of the outcome—i.e., whether the expected benefits of the lawsuit exceed the expected costs.

Explicit costs Payments by a firm to purchase the services of productive resources.

External benefits Beneficial effects of a group or individual action on the welfare of non-paying secondary parties.

External costs Harmful effects of an individual's or a group's action on the welfare of nonconsenting secondary parties, not accounted for in market prices. Litterbugs, drunk drivers, and polluters, for example, create external costs.

Externalities The side effects, or spillover effects, of an action that influence the well-being of nonconsenting parties. The nonconsenting parties may be either helped (by external benefits) or harmed (by external costs).

Firm An organization that coordinates the activities of workers, managers, owners, lenders, and other participants to produce and sell a good or service.

Fixed costs Costs that do not vary with output. They will be incurred as long as the firm continues in business and the assets have alternative uses.

Fixed input An input whose quantity a firm cannot change in the short run.

Franchise (a) A privilege or authorization, generally exclusive, to engage in a particular activity within a particular geographic area, as a government franchise to operate a taxi company within a specified city, or a private franchise as the grant by a manufacturer of a right to sell products within a particular territory or for a particular number of years; (b) the right to vote.

Free enterprise Economic freedom to produce and sell or purchase and consume goods without government intervention.

Free entry or exit Entry or exit opportunities with no legal barriers.

Free rider One who receives the benefit of a good without contributing to its costs. Public goods and commodities that generate external benefits offer people the opportunity to become free riders.

Future value The estimated value at a future date of a present sum of money, based on appropriate interest rates.

Gains from trade The net benefits to people (as consumers and producers) from trading.

Game theory Analyzes the strategic choices made by competitors in a conflict situation, such as decisions made by members of an oligopoly.

Goods All tangible things that satisfy people's wants and desires.

Government failure Failure of government action to meet the criteria of ideal economic efficiency.

Government regulation A limit or restriction on the actions of people or firms, or a required action.

Health and safety regulation Legislation designed to improve the health, safety, and environmental conditions available to workers and/or consumers. The legislation usually mandates production procedures, minimum standards, and/or product characteristics to be met by producers and employers.

Heuristics "Rules of thumb" or shortcuts individuals use in making decisions.

Historical cost A price paid for something in the past.

Homogeneous product A product of one firm that is identical to the product of every other firm in the industry. Consumers see no difference in units of the product offered by alternative sellers.

Horizontal equity A tax structure under which people with equal incomes pay equal amounts of taxes.

Horizontal merger The combining of the assets of two of more firms engaged in the production of similar products into a single firm.

Imperfect competition A market model in which there is more than one firm but the necessary conditions for a purely competitive solution (homogeneous product, large number of firms, free entry) do not exist.

Implicit costs The opportunity costs associated with a firm's use of resources that it owns. These costs do not involve a direct money payment. Examples include wage income and interest foregone by the owner of a firm who also provides labor services and equity capital to the firm.

Implicit labor contract An informal agreement or understanding about the terms of employment.

Implicit rental price The cost of owning and using a capital good over some period of time.

Import quota A specific quantity (or value) of a good permitted to be imported into a country during a given year.

Incentive The expected benefit of a decision minus its opportunity cost.

Income The value of money and goods that a person receives over some time period.

Income effect The part of an increase (decrease) in amount consumed that is the result of the consumer's real income (the consumption possibilities available to the consumer) being expanded (contracted) by a reduction (rise) in the price of a good.

Income elasticity The percent change in the quantity of a product demanded divided by the percent change in consumer income causing the change in quantity demanded. It measures the responsiveness of the demand for a good to a change in income.

Increase in economic efficiency A change that is a potential Pareto improvement.

Increasing cost Long-run marginal cost and long-run average cost that rise with increase in output.

Increasing cost industry An industry for which costs of production rise as the industry output is expanded. Thus, the long-run quantity supplied to the market is directly related to price.

Increasing returns to scale A situation in which average cost of production decreases with higher output.

Indemnity The right of a person secondarily liable to require that a person primarily liable pay for loss sustained when the secondary party discharges the obligation which the primary party should have discharged; the right of an agent to be paid the amount of any loss or damage sustained without fault because of obedience to the principal's instructions; an undertaking by one person for a consideration to pay another person a sum of money to indemnify that person when a specified loss is incurred.

Indifference curve A curve, convex from below, that separates the consumption bundles that are more preferred by an individual from those that are less preferred. The points on the curve represent combinations of goods that are equally preferred by the individual.

Indirect business taxes Taxes that increase the business firm's costs of production and therefore the prices charged to consumers. Examples would be sales, excise, and property taxes.

Inelastic demand (or supply) Elasticity with an absolute value less than 1.

Inferior goods Goods for which the income elasticity is negative. An increase in consumer income causes the demand for such a good to decline.

Inflation A continuing rise in the general level of prices of goods and services. The purchasing power of the monetary unit, such as the dollar, declines when inflation is present.

Innovation The successful introduction and adoption of a new product or process; the economic application of inventions and marketing techniques.

Interest The price a borrower pays for a loan or a lender receives for saving, measured as a percentage of the amount; the price of not consuming now but waiting to consume in the future.

Interest rate The price of a loan, expressed as a percentage of the loaned amount per year.

Intermediate goods Goods purchased for resale or for use in producing another good or service.

Internalizing an externality Changing the private costs or benefits so that they equal social costs or benefits; making people responsible for all the costs to other people of their own actions.

Intertemporal substitution (substitution over time) A change in the current demand or supply of a good caused by a change in its expected future price.

Invention The creation or discovery of a new product or process, often facilitated by the knowledge of engineering and scientific relationships.

Inventories Goods that a firm owns, including raw materials or other inputs, partially finished goods (goods in process), or finished goods that the firm has not yet sold.

Investment The flow of expenditures on durable assets (fixed investment) plus the addition to inventories (inventory investment) during a period. These expenditures enhance our ability to provide consumer benefits in the future. The purchase, construction, or development of capital resources, including both human and nonhuman capital. Investments increase the supply of capital.

Investment in human capital Expenditures on training, education, skill development, and health designed to increase the productivity of an individual.

Invisible hand principle The tendency of market prices to direct individuals pursuing their own interest into productive activities that also promote the economic well-being of society.

Joint and several contract A contract in which two or more persons are jointly and severally obligated or are jointly and severally entitled to recover.

Laissez-faire A government policy of not interfering with market activities.

Laissez-faire economy A market economy that is allowed to operate according to competitive forces with little or no government intervention.

Law of comparative advantage A principle that states that individuals, firms, regions, or nations can gain by specializing in the production of goods that they produce cheaply (that is, at a low opportunity cost) and exchanging those goods for other desired goods for which they are a high-opportunity-cost producer.

Law of demand A principle that states there is an inverse relationship between the price of a good and the amount of its buyers are willing to purchase.

Law of diminishing marginal utility The basic economic principle that as the consumption of a commodity increases, the marginal utility derived from consuming more of the commodity (per unit of time) will eventually decline. Marginal utility may decline even though total utility continues to increase, albeit at a reduced rate.

Law of diminishing returns The postulate that as more and more units of a variable resource are combined with a fixed amount of other resources, employment of additional units of the variable resource will eventually increase output only at a decreasing rate. Once diminishing returns are reached, it will take successively larger amounts of the variable factor to expand output by one unit.

Law of supply A principle that states there is a direct relationship between the price of a good and the amount of it offered for sale.

Legal barriers to entry A legal franchise, license, or patent granted by government that prohibits other firms or individuals from producing particular products or entering particular occupations or industries.

Liability Anything that is owed as a debt by a firm and therefore takes away from the net worth of the firm.

Liability rule A legal statement of who is responsible under what conditions for injuries or other harms in a tort; a rule that requires the payment of damages.

License A personal privilege to do some act or series of acts upon the land of another, as the placing of a sign thereon, not amounting to an easement or a right of possession.

Limited liability Loss of contributed capital or investment as maximum liability of investors.

Limited partnership A partnership in which at least one partner has a liability limited to the loss of the capital contribution made to the partnership, and such a partner neither takes part in the management of the partnership nor appears to the public to be a partner.

Liquid asset An asset that can be easily and quickly converted to purchasing power without loss of value.

Liquidated damages A provision stipulating the amount of damages to be paid in event of default or breach of contract.

Logrolling The exchange between politicians of political support on one issue for political support on another.

Long run (in production) A time period long enough to allow the firm to vary all factors of production.

Long-run demand (or supply) curve A curve that shows prices and quantities demanded (or supplied) at each price after buyers (or sellers) have adjusted completely to a price change.

Long-run equilibrium An equilibrium over a time long enough to allow firms to enter or exit the industry; a situation in which entry or exit has adjusted the market until each firm earns zero economic profit.

Loss Deficit of sale revenue relative to the cost of production, once all the resources used have received their opportunity cost. Losses are a penalty imposed on those who use resources in lower, rather than higher, valued uses as judged by buyers in the market.

Macroeconomics The branch of economics that focuses on how human behavior affects outcomes in highly aggregated markets, such as the nationwide markets for labor or consumer products.

Margin The difference in costs or benefits between the existing situation and a proposed change.

Marginal Term used to describe the effects of a change in the current situation. For example, the marginal cost is the cost of producing an additional unit of a product, given the producer's current facility and production rate.

Marginal analysis Study of the difference in costs and benefits between the status quo and the production or consumption of an additional unit of a specific good or service. This, not the average cost of all goods produced or consumed, is the actual basis for rational economic choices.

Marginal benefit The increase in total benefit from doing something once more.

Marginal costs The extra costs of producing one more unit of output; the change in total costs divided by the change in output.

Marginal factor cost (MFC) The cost of employing an additional unit of a resource. When the employer is small relative to the total market, the marginal factor cost in simply the price of the resource. In contrast, under monopsony, marginal factor cost will exceed the price of the resource, since the monopsonist faces an upward-sloping supply curve for the resource because wages must be raised for all workers.

Marginal opportunity costs The extra costs associated with the production of an additional unit of a product; these costs are the lost amounts of an alternative product.

Marginal private costs The increase in a firm's total costs resulting from producing one more unit.

Marginal product (MP) The change in total output that results from the employment of one additional unit of a factor of production—one workday of skilled labor, for example. The increase in the total product resulting from a unit increase in the employment of a variable input. Mathematically, it is the ratio of the change in total product to the change in the quantity of the variable input.

Marginal rate of substitution The change in the consumption level of one good that is just sufficient to offset a unit change in the consumption of another good without causing a shift to another indifference curve. At any point on an indifference curve, it will be equal to the slope of the curve at that point.

Marginal revenue The incremental change in total revenue derived from the sale of one additional unit of a product; the change in total revenue divided by the change in amount sold.

Marginal revenue product (MRP) The change in the total revenue of a firm that results from the employment of one additional unit of a factor of production. The marginal-revenue product of an input is equal to its marginal product multiplied by the marginal revenue (price) of the good or service produced.

Marginal social costs The increase in total costs to society (the firm plus everyone else) resulting from producing one more unit.

Marginal tax rate (MTR) Additional tax liability divided by additional income. Thus, if $100 of additional earnings increases one's tax liability by $30, the marginal tax rate would be 30 percent. Since it establishes the fraction of an additional dollar earned that an individual is permitted to keep, it is an important determinant of the incentive to work.

Marginal utility The additional utility received by a person from the consumption of an additional unit of a good within a given time period.

Market An arrangement that brings together buyers and sellers of products and resources; any area in which prices of products or services tend toward equality through the continuous negotiations of buyers and sellers.

Market coordination The process that directs the flow of resources into the production of desired goods and services through the forces of price mechanism.

Market demand Demand for a good by all buyers, including the private sector and the government.

Market demand curve A graph of the market demand schedule.

Market demand schedule A table of many hypothetical prices of a good and the quantity demanded by all buyers at each price.

Market equilibrium A situation, described by a combination of price and quantity traded, in which the quantity supplied equals the quantity demanded.

Market failure The failure of the market system to attain hypothetically ideal allocative efficiency. This means that potential gain exists that has not been captured. However, the cost of establishing a mechanism that could potentially capture the gain may exceed the benefits. Therefore, it is not always possible to improve the situation.

Market power A situation characterized by barriers to entry of rival firms, giving an established firm control over price and, therefore, profit levels.

Market process The coordination of people's economic activities through voluntary trades.

Market quantity demanded The total amount of a good that all buyers in the economy would buy during a time period if they could buy as much as they wanted at a given price.

Market quantity supplied At a given price, the total amount of a good that all sellers in the economy would sell during a time period if they could sell as much of the good as they wanted.

Market structure The classification of a market with regard to key characteristics, including the number of sellers, entry barriers into the market, the control of firms over price, and type of products (homogeneous or differentiated) in the market.

Market supply curve A curve graphing the market supply schedule.

Market supply schedule A table showing many hypothetical prices of a good and the quantity supplied at each price.

Markup (or profit margin) Price minus average cost.

Maximum legal price (or price ceiling) The highest price at which the government allows people to buy or sell a good.

Microeconomics The branch of economics that focuses on the behavior of individual decision-making units within an economic system, from individuals to specific households to specific business firms.

Middleman A person who buys and sells, or who arranges trades. A middleman reduces transaction costs, usually for a fee or a markup in price.

Minimum legal price (or price floor) The lowest price at which the government allows people to buy or sell a good.

Minimum wage legislation Legislation requiring that all workers in specified industries be paid at least the stated minimum hourly rate of pay.

Mixed capitalism An economy in which both market forces and government forces determine the allocation of resources.

Monitoring Obtaining information about an agent's actions (perhaps by watching).

Monopolistic competition A situation in which there are a large number of independent sellers, each producing a differentiated product in a market with low barriers to entry. Construction, retail sales, and service stations are good examples of monopolistically competitive industries.

Monopoly A market structure characterized by a (a) single seller of a well-defined product for which there are no good substitutes and (b) high barriers to the entry of other firms into the market for the product.

Monopsony A market in which there is only one buyer. The monopsonist confronts the market supply curve for the resource (or product) bought.

Moral hazard A situation in which a principal cannot observe the actions of an agent who lacks an incentive to act in the best interests of the principal.

Nash equilibrium A situation in which each firm makes its best response, that is maximizes its profit, given the actions of rival firms.

Nationalized firm A firm that the government owns.

Natural monopoly A monopoly that occurs because of a particular relation between industry demand and the firm's average total costs that makes it possible for only one firm to survive in the industry.

Negative correlation A relationship between variables that tend to move in opposite directions (inversely).

Negative expected value claim Claim where the expected costs of the bringing the claim exceed the expected benefits.

Negative externality A cost of producing or consuming a good that is not paid entirely by the sellers or buyers but is imposed on a larger segment of society; a situation in which the social costs of producing or consuming a good are greater than the private costs.

Negative slope The shape of a curve that runs downward and to the right.

Net benefit (or profit) Total benefit minus total cost.

Net present value (NPV) The difference between the present value of an income stream and the present value of an expenditure stream.

Net present value of a durable input The discounted present value of the future value of the input's marginal product minus the discounted present value of its cost.

Neutral tax A tax that does not (1) distort consumer buying patterns or producer production methods or (2) induce individuals to engage in tax-avoidance activities. There will be no excess burden if a tax is neutral.

Nominal price The money price of a good.

Nominal return Return on an investment not adjusted for inflation.

Nominal values Values expressed in current dollars.

Nondurable input An input that a firm uses soon after acquiring it and can use only once to produce a product.

Nonexcludable good A good that is prohibitively costly to provide only to people who pay for it while excluding other people from obtaining it.

Nonprice competition Any means that individual firms use to attract customers other than price cuts, such as better-quality products or product characteristics designed to match the preferences of specific groups of consumers.

Nonprice rationing A system for choosing who gets how many goods in a shortage.

Nonrival good A good for which the quantity available to other people does not fall when someone consumes it.

Normal (accounting) profit The level of accounting profit required for a zero economic profit.

Normal good A good whose demand increases if income rises.

Normative economics Value judgments about how markets should operate, based on certain moral principles or preferences.

Oligopoly A market situation in which a small number of sellers comprise the entire industry. Oligopoly is competition among the few.

Open-access resource A resource to which access is unrestricted. No one has the right to exclude others from using the resource. Overuse and abuse of such a resource is typical.

Opportunity cost The highest valued alternative that must be sacrificed as a result of choosing among alternatives. The value placed on opportunities forgone in choosing to produce or consume scarce goods.

Opportunity cost of equity capital The implicit rate of return that must be earned by investors to induce them to continue to supply financial capital to the firm.

Optimal contract An agreement that maximizes the principal's profit while providing an incentive for the agent to participate in the agreement.

Optimal taxation A system of tax rates that minimizes the total deadweight social loss from taxes while raising a certain amount of revenue for the government.

Option The right to buy (call) or the right to sell (put) an asset at a specified price within a fixed period of time.

Ownership The rights to make decisions about a good, including the use, exclusion, and sale of the good.

Pareto improvement A change that helps at least one person without hurting anyone.

Partnership A business firm owned by two or more individuals who possess ownership rights to the firm's profits and are personally liable for the debts of the firm.

Patent The grant of an exclusive right to use a specific process or produce a specific product for a period of time (17 years in the United States).

Payoff The amount that a player wins or loses in a particular situation in a game.

Percentage change 100 times the change in a number divided by the average (or midpoint) of the original number and the new number.

Perfect competition Competition among price-taking sellers.

Perfect information A condition in which information about prices and products is free to market participants; combined with conditions for pure competition, perfect information leads to perfect competition.

Perfect market A market in which there are enough buyers and sellers to that no single buyer or seller can influence price.

Perfect price discrimination Charging each customer the highest price that the customer is willing to pay.

Perfectly elastic demand (supply) Infinite elasticity illustrated by a demand (or supply) curve that is a horizontal line.

Perfectly inelastic demand (or supply) Elasticity equal to zero, illustrated by a demand (or supply) curve that is a vertical line.

Perpetuity An annuity in which the cash flows continue forever.

Political equilibrium A situation, characterized by peoples' votes and campaign contributions, the positions and strategies of candidates for office, and the decisions and actions of government officials, that shows no tendency for a change unless some underlying condition changes.

Political good Any good (or policy), whether a public good or a private good, supplied through the political process.

Pork-barrel legislation A package of spending projects benefiting local areas at federal expense. The projects typically have costs that exceed benefits, but are intensely desired by the residents of the district getting the benefits without having to pay much of the costs.

Positive correlation A relationship between variables that tend to rise or fall together.

Positive economics Observations or predictions of the facts of economic life.

Positive externality A benefit of producing or consuming a good that does not accrue to the sellers or buyers but can be realized by a larger segment of society; a situation in which the social benefits of producing or consuming a good are greater than the private benefits.

Positive slope The shape of a curve that runs upward and to the right.

Positive statement A statement of fact, of what is or what would be if something else were to happen; such a statement is either true or false.

Positive-sum game Environment in which everyone can gain at the same time.

Post-hoc fallacy False reasoning that because one event happened before another, the first event must have caused the second event.

Potential Pareto improvement A change that could allow the winners to compensate the losers to make the change a Pareto improvement.

Predatory pricing The practice in which a dominant firm in an industry temporarily reduces price to damage or eliminate weaker rivals, so that prices can be raised above the level of costs at a later time.

Prediction markets Markets designed to generate predictions of the likelihood of events occurring, based on the buying and selling decisions of participants in the market.

Present value (PV) The current worth of future income after it is discounted to reflect the fact that revenues in the future are valued less highly than revenues now; the estimated value today of a future sum of money, discounted at an appropriate interest rate.

Price The amount of something that a buyer trades away (pays) per unit of the good he receives.

Price ceiling A legally established maximum price that sellers may charge.

Price control Government intervention in the natural functioning of supply and demand.

Price differential A difference between the prices of identical goods in two different locations.

Price discrimination A practice whereby a seller charges different consumers or groups of consumers different prices for the same product or service. The difference in price is not the result of differences in the costs of supplying the two groups.

Price elasticity of demand The percent change in the quantity of a product demanded divided by the percent change in the price causing the change in quantity. Price elasticity of demand indicates the degree of consumer response to variation in price.

Price floor A legally established minimum price that buyers must pay for a good or resource.

Price rigidity Slow adjustments of prices to changes in costs or demand.

Price searcher A firm that must choose a price from a range of prices rather than have a single price imposed on it; such a firm has a downward-sloping demand curve for its product.

Price takers Sellers who must take the market price in order to sell their product. Because each price taker's output is small relative to the total market, price takers can sell all of their output at the market price, but are unable to sell any of their output at a price higher than the market price. Thus, they face a horizontal demand curve.

Price taker in an input market A firm that faces a perfectly elastic supply of an input.

Prices The opportunity costs established in markets for scarce goods, services, and resources.

Principal One who employs an agent; the person who, with respect to a surety, is primarily liable to the third person or creditor. The capital or face amount of a debt or other obligation upon which interest accrues.

Principal-agent problem The incentive problem arising when the purchaser of services (the principal) lacks full information about the circumstances faced by the seller (the agent) and thus cannot know how well the agent performs the purchased services. The agent may to some extent work toward objectives other than those sought by the principal paying for the service.

Principle of diversification Spreading an investment across a number of assets will eliminate some, but not all, of the risk.

Private benefit The benefit to people who buy and consume a good.

Private cost The cost paid by a firm to produce and sell a good.

Private ownership A property right held by one person or a small group of people.

Private-property rights A set of usage and exchange rights held exclusively by the owner(s) and that can be transferred to others at the owner's discretion.

Privatization Creation of private property rights in a nationalized firm so that it becomes privately owned.

Producer surplus The benefit to a producer from being able to sell goods at the equilibrium price, rather than being unable to sell them at all.

Profit An excess of sales revenue relative to the cost of production. The cost component includes the opportunity cost of all resources, including those owned by the firm. Therefore, profit accrues only when the value of the good produced is greater than the sum of the values of the individual resources utilized.

Property The rights and interests one has in anything subject to ownership.

Property rights The right to use, control, and obtain the benefits from a good or service.

Proprietorship A business firm owned by an individual who possesses the ownership right to the firm's profits and is personally liable for the firm's debts.

Public choice analysis The study of decision making as it affects the formation and operation of collective organizations, such as governments. The discipline bridges the gap between economics and political science. In general, the principles and methodology of economics are applied to political science topics.

Public goods Jointly consumed goods. A good that no individual can be excluded from consuming, once it has been provided to another. National defense, poetry, and scientific theories are all public goods.

Punitive damages Damages in excess of those required to compensate the plaintiff for the wrong done, which are imposed in order to punish the defendant because of the particularly wanton or willful character of wrongdoing.

Pure competition A model of industrial structure characterized by a large number of small firms producing a homogeneous product in a industry (market area) that permits complete freedom of entry and exit.

Pure discount bond A bond, such as a Treasury bill, that pays no coupon but sells for a discount from par value.

Put An option by which one investor acquires the right, but not the obligation, to sell an underlying asset to another investor for a specified price during a specified period of time.

Rational ignorance Voter ignorance resulting from the fact that people perceive their individual votes as unlikely to be decisive. Therefore, they rationally have little incentive to seek the information needed to cast a informed vote.

Rationing An allocation of a limited supply of a good or resource to users who would like to have more of it. Various criteria, including charging a price, can be utilized to allocate the limited supply. When price performs the rationing function, the good or resource is allocated to those willing to give up the most "other things" in order to obtain ownership rights.

Real options model Economic model of court litigation under which plaintiff's decisions whether to proceed at various steps of the lawsuit are viewed as decisions whether to exercise "option."

Real return Return adjusted for the effects of inflation.

Real values Values that have been adjusted for the effects of inflation.

Relative price The price of a product related in terms of other goods that could be purchased rather than in money terms.

Rent seeking The activity of individuals who spend resources in the pursuit of monopoly rights granted by government; the process of spending resources in an effort to obtain an economic transfer.

Repeat-purchase item An item purchased often by the same buyer.

Residual claimant(s) Individuals who personally receive the excess, if any, of revenues over contractual fixed claims (costs).

Resource An input used to produce economic goods. Land, labor, skills, natural resources, and capital are examples.

Resource market A highly aggregate market encompassing all resources (labor, physical capital, land, and entrepreneurship) that contribute to the production of current output. The labor market forms the largest component of this market.

Resource mobility A term that refers to the ease with which factors of production are able to move among alternative uses. Resources that can easily be transferred to a different use or location are said to be highly mobile. In contrast, when a resource has few alternative uses, it is immobile. For example, the skills of a trained rodeo rider would be highly immobile, since they cannot be easily transferred to other lines of work.

Scarcity Fundamental concept of economics which indicates a limitation of the amount of resources available to individuals and societies relative to their desires for the products that resources produce.

Scientific thinking Development of theory from basic postulates and the testing of the implications of that theory as to their consistency with events in the real world. Good theories are consistent with and help explain real-world events. Theories that are inconsistent with the real world are invalid and must be rejected.

Secondary effects Economic consequences of an economic change that are not immediately identifiable but are felt only with the passage of time.

Securities and Exchange Commission The federal agency responsible for regulating the securities and options markets.

Shareholder A person who owns shares of stock (equity) in a corporation.

Shirking Working at less than a normal rate of productivity, thus reducing output. Shirking is more likely when workers are not monitored, so that the cost of lower output falls on others than themselves.

Short run (in production) A time period so short that firm is unable to vary some of its factors of production. The firm's plant size typically cannot be altered in the short run.

Shortage A condition in which the amount of a good offered by sellers is less than the amount demanded by buyers at the existing price. An increase in price would eliminate the shortage.

Shortsightedness Misallocation of resources that results because public-sector action is biased (1) in favor of proposals yielding clearly defined current benefits in exchange for difficult-to-identify future costs and (2) against proposals with clearly identifiable current costs but yielding less concrete and less obvious future benefits.

Shut down A temporary halt in the operation of a business in which the firm anticipates a return to operation in the future and therefore does not sell its assets. The firm's variable cost is eliminated for the duration of the shutdown, but its fixed costs continue.

Simple interest Interest earned only on the original principal amount invested.

Social costs The sum of (1) the private costs incurred by a decision maker and (2) any external costs imposed on nonconsenting secondary parties. If there are no external costs, private and social costs will be equal.

Spot price The current cash price for immediate delivery of goods.

Standard deviation The positive square root of the variance.

Stock An instrument that provides the holder an equity, or ownership, interest in a corporation.

Strict tort liability A product liability theory which imposes liability on the manufacturer, seller, or distributor of goods for harm caused by defective goods.

Subsidy A government cash grant to a favored industry.

Substitutes Products that are related such that an increase in the price of one will cause an increase in demand for the other (for example, butter and margarine, Chevrolets and Fords).

Substitution effect That part of an increase (decrease) in amount consumed that is the result of a good being cheaper (more expensive) in relation to other goods because of a reduction (increase) in price.

Sunk costs Costs that have already been incurred as a result of past decisions. They are sometimes referred to as historical costs.

Surplus A condition in which the amount of a good that sellers are willing to offer is greater than the amount that buyers will purchase at the existing price. A decline in price would eliminate the surplus.

Tariff A tax levied on a good imported into a country.

Tax incidence The manner in which the burden of the tax is distributed among economic units (consumers, employees, employers, and so on). The tax burden does not always fall on those who pay the tax.

Tax rate The per unit or percentage rate at which an economic activity is taxed.

Team production A process of production wherein employees work together under the supervision of the owner or the owner's representative.

Technological advancement The introduction of new techniques or methods of production that enable a greater output per unit of input.

Technology The body of skills and technological knowledge available at any given time. The level of technology establishes the relationship between inputs and the maximum output they can generate.

Tort A private injury or wrong arising from a breach of a duty created by law.

Total cost The costs, both explicit and implicit, of all the resources used by the firm. Total cost includes an imputed normal rate of return for the firm's equity capital.

Total product The total output of a good that is associated with alternative utilization rates of a variable input.

Transaction costs The time, effort, and other resources needed to search out, negotiate, and consummate an exchange.

Tying arrangement The requirement imposed by the seller that the buyer of particular goods or equipment also purchase certain other goods from the original property desired.

Unlimited liability A legal term that indicates that the owner or owners of a firm are personally responsible for the debts of a firm up to the total value of their wealth.

User charge A payment that users (consumers) are required to make if they want to receive certain services provided by the government.

Usury The lending of money at greater than the maximum rate of interest allowed by law.

Utility The benefit or satisfaction expected from a choice or course of action.

Variable costs Costs that vary with the rate of output. Examples include wages paid to workers and payments for raw materials.

Welfare loss due to monopoly The lost consumer surplus resulting from the restricted output of a monopoly.

Worker's compensation A system providing payments to workers because they have been injured from a risk arising out of the course of their employment while they were employed at their employment or have contracted an occupational disease in that manner, payment being made without consideration of the negligence or lack of negligence of any party.

Index